DICTIONARY OF
AMERICAN BIOGRAPHY

American Council of Learned Societies

American Philosophical Society, Philadelphia, Pennsylvania

American Academy of Arts and Sciences, Cambridge, Massachusetts

American Antiquarian Society, Worcester, Massachusetts

American Oriental Society, New Haven, Connecticut

American Numismatic Society, New York, New York

American Philological Association, Swarthmore, Pennsylvania

Archeological Institute of America, New York, New York

Society of Biblical Literature and Exegesis, Haverford, Pennsylvania

Modern Language Association of America, New York, New York

American Historical Association, Washington, District of Columbia

American Economic Association, Evanston, Illinois

American Philosophical Association, Middletown, Connecticut

American Anthropological Association, Chicago, Illinois

American Political Science Association, Evanston, Illinois

Bibliographical Society of America, Albany, New York

Association of American Geographers, Minneapolis, Minnesota

American Sociological Society, Washington, District of Columbia

American Society of International Law, Washington, District of Columbia

College Art Association of America, New York, New York

History of Science, South Hadley, Massachusetts

Linguistic Society of America, Washington, District of Columbia

Mediaeval Academy of America, Cambridge, Massachusetts

Population Association of America, Washington, District of Columbia

~ Dictionary of ~

American Biography

PUBLISHED UNDER THE AUSPICES OF

American Council of Learned Societies

EDITED BY

Allen Johnson

Barsotti — Brazer

VOLUME II

NEW YORK

Charles Scribner's Sons

MCMXLIII

Prompted solely by a desire for public service the New York Times Company and its President, Mr. Adolph S. Ochs, have made possible the preparation of the manuscript of the Dictionary of American Biography through a subvention of more than $500,000 and with the understanding that the entire responsibility for the contents of the volumes rests with the American Council of Learned Societies.

The Dictionary of American Biography is published under the auspices of the American Council of Learned Societies and under the direction of a Committee of Management which consists of J. Franklin Jameson, *Chairman*, John H. Finley, Allen Johnson, Frederic L. Paxson, Iphigene Ochs Sulzberger, Carl Van Doren, Charles Warren.

The editorial staff consists of Allen Johnson, Harris E. Starr, Ernest S. Bates, George H. Genzmer, H. W. Howard Knott, Frank Monaghan.

The American Council of Learned Societies consists of the following societies:

American Philosophical Society
American Academy of Arts and Sciences
American Antiquarian Society
American Oriental Society
American Philological Association
Archaeological Institute of America
Modern Language Association of America

American Historical Association
American Economic Association
American Philosophical Association
American Political Science Association
American Sociological Society
Linguistic Society of America
History of Science Society

Mediaeval Academy of America

CONTRIBUTORS TO VOLUME II

Adeline Adams	A. A—s.	Harry J. Carman	H. J. C.
James Truslow Adams	J. T. A.	Clarence Edwin Carter	C. E. C.
Robert G. Albion	R. G. A.	Hope S. Chamberlain	H. S. C.
Edmund Kimball Alden	E. K. A.	Frank H. Chase	F. H. C.
Albert Allemann	A. A—n.	Wayland J. Chase	W. J. C.
Charles Henry Ambler	C. H. A.	Francis Albert Christie	F. A. C.
Katharine H. Amend	K. H. A.	Allen L. Churchill	A. L. C.
John Clark Archer	J. C. A.	Dora Mae Clark	D. M. C.
Raymond Clare Archibald	R. C. A.	Robert Glass Cleland	R. G. C—d.
Benjamin Wisner Bacon	B. W. B.	Oral S. Coad	O. S. C.
Theodore D. Bacon	T. D. B.	Frederick W. Coburn	F. W. C.
John Bakeless	J. B.	James Fairbanks Colby	J. F. C.
Ray Palmer Baker	R. P. Ba—r.	Fannie L. Gwinner Cole	F. L. G. C.
Hayes Baker-Crothers	H. B–C.	Kenneth Colegrove	K. C.
James Curtis Ballagh	J. C. B.	Henry C. Conrad	H. C. C.
Thomas S. Barclay	T. S. B.	Lane Cooper	L. C.
Charles Russell Bardeen	C. R. B.	Edward S. Corwin	E. S. C.
Viola Florence Barnes	V. F. B.	R. S. Cotterill	R. S. C.
Ernest Sutherland Bates	E. S. B.	Ellis Merton Coulter	E. M. C.
William A. Beardsley	W. A. B.	Isaac Joslin Cox	I. J. C.
Charles F. D. Belden	C. F. D. B.	John Cox, Jr.	J. C.
Wells Bennett	W. B—t.	Verner W. Crane	V. W. C.
John M. Berdan	J. M. B.	Avery O. Craven	A. O. C.
Francis S. Betten	F. S. B.	Henry Crew	H. C.
Ralph Paul Bieber	R. P. Bi—r.	Walter Hill Crockett	W. H. C.
Theodore C. Blegen	T. C. B.	Merle E. Curti	M. E. C.
G. Alder Blumer	G. A. B.	Harrison Clifford Dale	H. C. D.
George Blumer	G. B.	Elizabeth Thompson Davison	E. T. D.
Theodore Bolton	T. B.	Ralph Davol	R. D.
Milledge Louis Bonham	M. L. B.	Charles De Kay	C. De K.
Stephen Bonsal	S. B.	Charles Allen Dinsmore	C. A. D.
Witt Bowden	W. B—n.	Eleanor Robinette Dobson	E. R. D.
Sarah G. Bowerman	S. G. B.	Augustus Waldo Drury	A. W. D.
Charles N. Boyd	C. N. B.	Raymond Smith Dugan	R. S. D.
William Kenneth Boyd	W. K. B.	J. H. Easterby	J. H. E—y.
Benjamin Brawley	B. B.	Walter Prichard Eaton	W. P. E.
Edward Breck	E. B.	Edwin Francis Edgett	E. F. E.
Clarence Saunders Brigham	C. S. B.	John H. Edmonds	J. H. E—s.
Herbert O. Brigham	H. O. B.	Samuel Atkins Eliot	S. A. E.
Albert Britt	A. B.	Forest Chester Ensign	F. C. E.
Robert Preston Brooks	R. P. B—s.	Charles R. Erdman, Jr.	C. R. E.
John S. Brubacher	J. S. B.	Logan Esarey	L. E.
Kathleen Bruce	K. B.	Harold Underwood Faulkner	H. U. F.
Philip Alexander Bruce	P. A. B.	John Alfred Faulkner	J. A. F.
George Sands Bryan	G. S. B.	Albert Bernhardt Faust	A. B. F.
Oscar MacMillan Buck	O. M. B.	Carl Russell Fish	C. R. F.
Guy H. Burnham	G. H. B.	Morris Fishbein	M. F.
Walter Lincoln Burrage	W. L. B.	Walter Lynwood Fleming	W. L. F.
Pierce Butler	P. B.	Alexander Clarence Flick	A. C. F.
William B. Cairns	W. B. C.	Blanton Fortson	B. F.
Charles F. Carey	C. F. C.	Harold North Fowler	H. N. F.

Contributors to Volume II

EARLY LEE FOX	E. L. F.	CHARLES RAMSDELL LINGLEY.	C. R. L.
CLAUDE MOORE FUESS	C. M. F.	HENRY MILLER LYDENBERG	H. M. L.
KEMPER FULLERTON	K. F.	THOMAS DENTON McCORMICK	T. D. M.
JOHN F. FULTON	J. F. F.	ROSWELL CHENEY McCREA	R. C. M.
CLARENCE M. GALLUP.	C. M. G.	PHILIP B. McDONALD	P. B. M.
FIELDING H. GARRISON	F. H. G.	WILLIAM MacDONALD	W. M.
SAMUEL W. GEISER	S. W. G.	GEORGE TREMAINE McDOWELL	G. T. M.
GEORGE H. GENZMER	G. H. G.	JOHN H. T. McPHERSON	J. H. T. M
BEATRICE CHANDLER GESELL.	B. C. G.	HARRY A. MARMER	H. A. M.
W. J. GHENT	W. J. G.	THOMAS M. MARSHALL	T. M. M.
COLIN B. GOODYKOONTZ	C. B. G.	FREDERICK HERMAN MARTENS	F. H. M.
GLADYS GRAHAM	G. G—m.	LAWRENCE SHAW MAYO	L. S. M.
WALTER S. GRANT	W. S. G.	LEILA MECHLIN	L. M.
LOUIS H. GRAY	L. H. G.	GEORGE PERKINS MERRILL	G. P. M.
GILBERT GROSVENOR	G. G—r.	ROGER B. MERRIMAN	R. B. M.
PETER GUILDAY	P. G.	EDWIN MIMS	E. M.
AMELIA MOTT GUMMERE.	A. M. G.	MARY HEWITT MITCHELL	M. H. M.
MARY C. HAM	M. C. H.	CARL W. MITMAN.	C. W. M.
PHILIP M. HAMER	P. M. H.	FRANK MONAGHAN	F. M.
J. G. DE ROULHAC HAMILTON.	J. G. de R. H.	CHARLES MOORE	C. M.
TALBOT F. HAMLIN	T. F. H.	THOMAS F. MORAN	T. F. M.
FAIRFAX HARRISON	F. H.	SAMUEL ELIOT MORISON	S. E. M.
BENJAMIN HARROW	B. H.	RICHARD L. MORTON	R. L. M.
EDWARD HART	E. H.	MONTROSE J. MOSES	M. J. M.
LOUIS C. HATCH	L. C. H.	GEORGE FULMER MULL	G. F. M.
THOMAS ROBSON HAY	T. R. H.	EDWIN G. NASH	E. G. N.
STELLA HERRON	S. H.	ALLAN NEVINS	A. N.
RUSSELL HICKMAN	R. H.	LYMAN C. NEWELL	L. C. N.
JOHN DONALD HICKS	J. D. H.	CLAUDE M. NEWLIN	C. M. N.
FRANK L. HISE	F. L. H.	ROY F. NICHOLS	R. F. N.
ALBERT A. HOPKINS.	A. A. H.	A. B. NOBLE	A. B. N.
ARTHUR HORNBLOW	A. H.	CHARLES NOBLE	C. N.
WALTER HOUGH	W. H.	FRANK M. O'BRIEN	F. M. O.
HAROLD HOWLAND	H. H.	JOHN W. OLIVER	J. W. O.
HANNAH CLOTHIER HULL	H. C. H.	ROBERT B. OSGOOD	R. B. O.
WILLIAM JACKSON HUMPHREYS	W. J. H.	MARIE B. OWEN	M. B. O.
EDITH J. R. ISAACS	E. J. R. I.	FRANCIS RANDOLPH PACKARD	F. R. P.
A. V. WILLIAMS JACKSON	A. V. W. J.	VICTOR H. PALTSITS	V. H. P.
JAMES ALTON JAMES	J. A. J.	STANLEY M. PARGELLIS	S. M. P.
W. L. G. JOERG	W. L. G. J.	FREDERIC LOGAN PAXSON	F. L. P.
ALFONSO JOHNSON	A—o J.	C. C. PEARSON	C. C. P.
ALLEN JOHNSON	A—n J.	HENRY G. PEARSON	H. G. P.
HOPE FRANCES KANE	H. F. K.	DONALD CULROSS PEATTIE	D. C. P.
MARIE A. KASTEN	M. A. K.	FREDERICK TORREL PERSONS	F. T. P.
LYMAN F. KEBLER	L. F. K.	A. EVERETT PETERSON	A. E. P.
HERBERT A. KELLAR	H. A. K.	JAMES M. PHALEN	J. M. P.
LOUISE PHELPS KELLOGG	L. P. K.	FRANCIS S. PHILBRICK	F. S. P.
ISOLINE RODD KENDALL	I. R. K.	DAVID PHILIPSON	D. P.
WILLIAM JOSEPH KERBY	W. J. K.	PAUL CHRISLER PHILLIPS	P. C. P.
GRANT C. KNIGHT	G. C. K.	WILLIAM WHATLEY PIERSON, JR.	W. W. P.
H. W. HOWARD KNOTT	H. W. H. K.	HENRY AUGUSTUS PILSBRY	H. A. P.
ALOIS F. KOVARIK	A. F. K.	FRANK W. PITMAN	F. W. P.
WILLIAM CHAUNCY LANGDON	W. C. L.	JOHN A. POLLARD.	J. A. P.
CONRAD H. LANZA	C. H. L—a.	HERBERT INGRAM PRIESTLEY	H. I. P.
JAMES MELVIN LEE	J. M. L.	RICHARD J. PURCELL	R. J. P.
PAUL S. LEINBACH	P. S. L.	ARTHUR HOBSON QUINN	A. H. Q.
ORIN G. LIBBY	O. G. L.	CHARLES HENRY RAMMELKAMP	C. H. R.
CHARLES H. LINCOLN	C. H. L—n.	CHARLES WILLIAM RAMSDELL	C. W. R.

Contributors to Volume II

Belle Rankin	B. R.
Charles Dudley Rhodes	C. D. R.
Lyon N. Richardson	L. N. R.
Irving Berdine Richman	I. B. R.
William Alexander Robinson	W. A. R.
Lindsay Rogers	L. R.
John J. Rolbiecki	J. J. R.
George Rose III	G. R.
A. S. W. Rosenbach	A. S. W. R.
Frank Edward Ross	F. E. R.
Henry Kalloch Rowe	H. K. R.
Robert R. Rowe	R. R. R.
Dunbar Rowland	D. R.
Ralph L. Rusk	R. L. R.
Sumner Salter	S. S.
Joseph Schafer	J. S.
Robert Livingston Schuyler	R. L. S.
Louis M. Sears	L. M. S.
Benjamin F. Shambaugh	B. F. S.
Muriel Shaver	M. S.
William Bristol Shaw	W. B. S.
Hiram H. Shenk	H. H. S.
Clarence A. Skinner	C. A. S.
David Eugene Smith	D. E. S.
Edgar Fahs Smith	E. F. S.
W. E. Smith	W. E. S.
James A. Spalding	J. A. S.
Thomas Marshall Spaulding	T. M. S.
Charles W. Spencer	C. W. S.
Harris Elwood Starr	H. E. S.
Henry P. Stearns	H. P. S.
Nathaniel Wright Stephenson	N. W. S.
Earl Gregg Swem	E. G. S.
Edwin Platt Tanner	E. P. T.
Frank A. Taylor	F. A. T—r.
David Y. Thomas	D. Y. T.
Wilbur Fisk Tillett	W. F. T.
Ezra Squier Tipple	E. S. T.
Francis A. Tondorf	F. A. T—f.
Alfred M. Tozzer	A. M. T.
Alfred Charles True	A. C. T.
William Treat Upton	W. T. U.
Arnold J. F. Van Laer	A. J. F. V–L.
Victor C. Vaughan	V. C. V.
Henry R. Viets	H. R. V.
Jonas Viles	J. V.
Eugene M. Violette	E. M. V.
Dayton Voorhees	D. V.
John Donald Wade	J. D. W.
James Elliott Walmsley	J. E. W—y.
Frank Weitenkampf	F. W.
Raynor G. Wellington	R. G. W.
Allan Westcott	A. W.
Arthur P. Whitaker	A. P. W.
Walter Lincoln Whittlesey	W. L. W—y.
Robert J. Wickenden	R. J. W.
Jeanne Elizabeth Wier	J. E. W—r.
Walter F. Willcox	W. F. W.
Clarence Russell Williams	C. R. W—s.
Stanley Thomas Williams	S. T. W.
H. Parker Willis	H. P. W.
James A. Woodburn	J. A. W.
Clinton Rogers Woodruff	C. R. W—r.
Carter Godwin Woodson	C. G. W.
Thomas Woody	T. W.
Ernest H. Wright	E. H. W.
Helen Wright	H. W.
Herbert F. Wright	H. F. W.
Walter L. Wright, Jr.	W. L. W—t.
Mary A. Wyman	M. A. W.
Julien C. Yonge	J. C. Y.
Edna Yost	E. Y.
Andrew C. Zenos	A. C. Z.

DICTIONARY OF

AMERICAN·BIOGRAPHY

—

Barsotti — Brazer

BARSOTTI, CHARLES (Jan 4, 1850–Mar. 30, 1927), editor, publisher, philanthropist, born in Bagni di San Giuliano, near Pisa, doubtless inherited from his father, Giulio, who had achieved success as a country landowner, that executive and managerial ability which enabled him to be successful in his business enterprises. From his mother, Rosa Pannocchia, a native of Santa Maria del Giudice, near Lucca, came his love of music and sculpture. He came to America in 1872, settled in New York City, and in 1880 established, in the old Herald Building, *Il Progresso,* the first Italian daily in the United States. Its success was so remarkable that new quarters had to be secured at 42 Duane St. Continued success made another change necessary, this time to a building owned by the paper itself at 42 Elm St. Subscribers were in a way partners of Barsotti in that they aided him in erecting statues to famous Italians: Giovanni da Verrazano in Battery Park, Giuseppe Garibaldi in Washington Square, Christopher Columbus occupying the pivotal position in Columbus Circle at Fifty-ninth St. and Eighth Avenue, Dante at Broadway and Sixty-third St., and Giuseppe Verdi at Broadway and Seventy-third St. His subscribers also aided him in contributing to the relief of suffering in Italy. In recognition of service in this field Barsotti was decorated by the King of Italy with the Cross of Grand Officer of the Crown of Italy. In his later years he contributed $250,000 toward a tunnel through that mountain, separating Pisa from Lucca, which has been famous ever since Dante's line—*"Per che i Pisan veder Lucca non ponno."* The woman who shared in these enterprises as a life partner was Margaret Heist of Frankfort, Germany, whom Barsotti married in 1875. His last years were spent, not in New York City, but in the little New Jersey town of Coytesville, on the Palisades across the Hudson.

[Long obituary in the *N.Y. Times,* Mar. 31, 1927. In J. Sanford Saltus and Walter E. Tisney, *Statues of New York* (1923), may be found details about the statues erected through Barsotti's efforts.]
J.M.L.

BARSTOW, WILLIAM AUGUSTUS (Sept. 13, 1813–Dec. 14, 1865), governor of Wisconsin, was the son of William A. Barstow, one of seven brothers who served in the Revolutionary War. He was born in Connecticut, but settled in Wisconsin in 1839. In April 1844 he married Maria Quarles of Southport, now Kenosha, Wis. He became secretary of state in 1850, and his name never escaped the unkind implication of a phrase used in that year by a Madison editor who was determined to get the contract for state printing even if he had to "buy up Barstow and the balance" of the members of the printing board. He was elected governor, on the Democratic ticket, in 1853. Declared reëlected in 1855, by a slender plurality of 157 votes, he took office for his second term in January 1856; but on the same day his Republican rival in the election, Coles Bashford [*q.v.*], also took the oath of office, and there were two pretending governors in the state. By tacit agreement of the contenders and the legislature, Barstow was left *de facto* governor, pending an examination of the claims of Bashford by the supreme court. The leaders of the Wisconsin bar for the next generation were paraded in this litigation. Barstow denied the right of the court to take jurisdiction over a coördinate branch of the government. He refused to plead when the court assumed jurisdiction, and resigned after testimony had been heard indicating that fraudulent returns had been manufactured in Madison and counted as from precincts which proved to be nonexistent. Bashford was awarded the office by the supreme court, Mar. 24, 1856. Barstow became interested in railroads and their development and in 1855 became president of the St. Croix & Lake Superior Railroad Company. He was also a miller and a banker. During the Civil War he was commissioned colonel on Nov. 9, 1861, raised his own regiment, and in the spring of 1862 was sent as provost-marshal-general to Kansas, where he was defeated and narrowly avoided capture. He served in Arkansas and Missouri (1862–63), after which, because of ill health, most of his military duty was upon courts martial.

[Brief sketches of his life are in *Wis. Hist. Soc. Colls.*, VI, 93–122; see also *The Trial in the Supreme Court . . . of Coles Bashford vs. Wm. A. Barstow* (Madison, 1856).]
                                                        F.L.P.

BARTHOLOMEW, EDWARD SHEF-FIELD (July 8, 1822–May 1858), sculptor, after spending the first fourteen years of his life at Colchester, Conn., where he attended the Bacon Academy, moved with his parents, Abial Lord and Sarah Gustin, to Hartford. The change made him shy; even in after life he found it difficult to meet strangers. He worked as assistant, first to a bookbinder, then to a dentist, but was dissatisfied and was regarded somewhat as a vagabond by the thrifty people among whom he lived. To escape the uncongenial atmosphere he went to New York, and for a year studied in the "Antique and Life School" of the Academy of Design. On his return to Hartford he became curator of the Wadsworth Gallery and at the same time continued his art work. He soon discovered, however, that he was color-blind. Bitterly disappointed, he turned to sculpture, for even as a boy he had been fond of modeling in clay. He first attempted, with inadequate tools, a medallion of Mrs. Sigourney; then, with better implements, a bust of "Flora." In 1848 he went again to New York to attend a series of anatomical lectures. While there he contracted smallpox, followed by a hip affection which crippled him. Hitherto he had been strong and vigorous, and of prepossessing appearance—tall and dark, but after this calamity he was lame and unwell for the rest of his brief life. Shortly after this an opportunity to go to Italy came and he departed in 1850. Thereafter he made but two visits to America, on one of which he superintended the erection of his monument to Charles Carroll. In Rome he began, with a bas-relief of "Homer led by the Genius of Poetry," the productive period of his life. He studied under Ferrero, working particularly at bas-relief. His first year in Rome was an uphill struggle, but after a four months'

journey to Athens and the Near East, he began to win recognition. His most admired work was a statue of "Eve Repentant." Though frequently using biblical subjects ("Paradise Lost"; "Hagar and Ishmael"; "Ruth, Naomi and Orpah"), he more generally resorted to classical themes ("Sappho"; "Calypso"; "Ganymede"; "Diana"; "Belisarius"). He likewise did numerous portraits, such as those of the Colts and their children. True to contemporary American taste and to Italian teaching he was thoroughly neo-classic in the treatment of subject, though fonder of introducing superfluous and picturesque accessories than was Canova or Thorwaldsen. His execution was not always adequate, but this fault he was overcoming when, shortly after his return from his second American trip, he was taken ill. On the advice of his physician he went to Naples, but only to die.

[G. W. Bartholomew, *Record of the Bartholomew Family* (1885); Susan Crane in *Conn. Quart.*, vol. II, no. 3; *Art and Artists in Conn.*, by H. W. French (1879). Articles and notices on Bartholomew are frequently in disagreement as to minor details, *e.g.*, the date of his death which is variously given as the 1st, 2nd, or 3rd of May. A number of his works, either originals or casts, are in the Morgan Memorial Museum at Hartford.]
                                                        E.G.N.

BARTHOLOW, ROBERTS (Nov. 28, 1831–May 10, 1904), physician and author, was born at New Windsor, Md. He attended Calvert College (B.A. 1848, M.A. 1854), and in 1852 he graduated from the Medical Department of the University of Maryland. In 1855, he was commissioned assistant surgeon in the United States Army and during the next four or five years saw considerable active service in the West in the troubles with the Mormons and Indians. During the Civil War he was on duty in various military hospitals; wrote *A Manual of Instruction for Enlisting and Discharging Soldiers* (1863), which was the standard authority for many years; and also wrote a book entitled *Qualifications for the Medical Service*. In 1864 he resigned from the army and began the practise of medicine in Cincinnati, receiving the appointment of professor of medical chemistry in the Medical College of Ohio. He soon acquired a large practise but nevertheless found time to establish and edit a medical journal, the *Clinic*. In 1867, he was transferred from the chair of chemistry to that of materia medica. In 1874, he aroused a great sensation by publishing in the *American Journal of the Medical Sciences* the report of a case of malignant tumor of the scalp and skull in which the brain had been exposed by the progress of the disease. With the full consent of the patient, who realized that he was fatally ill, Bartholow applied electric stimulation to various areas of the exposed brain in order to corroborate the results obtained by Hitzig and Ferrier in lower animals. Although his experiments confirmed the observations of these investigators, they resulted in serious damage to the patient, who succumbed a few days later from an extension of the cancer producing a thrombus of the longitudinal sinus. This was candidly admitted by Bartholow in his very full report of the affair ("Experimental Investigations into the Functions of the Human Brain," *American Journal of the Medical Sciences,* April 1874, pp. 305–13). His paper raised a perfect storm of disapprobation and protest, but the consensus of opinion finally turned in his favor. He was appointed professor of the practise of medicine in the Medical College of Ohio, but in 1879 resigned to go to Philadelphia as professor of materia medica and therapeutics in Jefferson Medical College. He resigned this position in 1893 because of failing health and eleven years later died at his home in Philadelphia at the age of seventy-two. Bartholow was a voluminous contributor to periodical medical literature. He wrote no less than four essays which received prizes and after giving up the editorship of the *Clinic* on his removal to Philadelphia he became one of the editors of the *Medical News.* His *Practical Treatise on Materia Medica and Therapeutics* (1876) went through eleven editions, and eight editions were published of his *Treatise on the Practise of Medicine* (1880).

[James W. Holland, "Memoir of Roberts Bartholow," *Trans. Coll. Physicians of Phila.,* ser. 3, vol. XXVI (1904), pp. 43–52; Davina Waterson, sketch in *Am. Medic. Biogs.* (1920), ed. by Kelly and Burrage; *Phila. Pub. Ledger,* May 11, 1904.]   F.R.P.

BARTLET, WILLIAM (Jan. 31, 1748 N.S.–Feb. 8, 1841), merchant, philanthropist, was born in Newburyport, Mass., the son of Edmund and Hannah (Hall) Bartlet and a direct descendant of Richard Bartlet, who settled in Newbury in 1635. At an early age he left school to learn shoemaking. Naturally shrewd and enterprising, he was soon actively engaged in commerce and acquired a considerable fortune. At the close of the Revolution he became the owner of a large fleet of merchant vessels and numerous wharves and warehouses, and was one of the first in New England to undertake textile manufacturing. He served three terms as representative in the Massachusetts General Court, from 1800 to 1802. In 1774 he married Betty (Coombs) Lascomb, widow of Robert Lascomb. As he became increasingly prosperous, he erected in 1798 a large three-story brick mansion on Federal St., in Newburyport, where he lived until his death.

An inscription on his monument describes him as "a distinguished merchant and a liberal patron of theological learning." The money which Bartlet accumulated through thrift and wise investments he devoted largely to philanthropic projects, especially to Andover Theological Seminary, opened in 1808. Although he attended public worship regularly, he was not a church member; but Dr. Samuel Spring, a Newburyport clergyman, persuaded him to join with Moses Brown, a fellow townsman, and John Norris of Salem, in supplying the necessary funds for a school in which Calvinistic divinity students could be trained for the ministry. At about the same period a similar plan was formed by Dr. Eliphalet Pearson and a group of his friends living in Andover, Mass., twenty miles from Newburyport, with whom they formed a coalition. To Andover Theological Seminary, Bartlet gave originally $20,000. He later added $15,000 for the endowment of a Bartlet professorship of sacred rhetoric and built two houses for the accommodation of members of the faculty. He provided the money for the erection of Bartlet Chapel (1818) and of Bartlet Hall (1821) for the growing seminary. These structures, when Andover Theological Seminary was transferred to Cambridge in 1908, were purchased by Phillips Academy, Andover, and are to-day occupied by that preparatory school. At his death Bartlet left a bequest of $50,000 to the seminary, and his benefactions to it aggregated more than $160,000. Physically Bartlet was large and powerful, imposing in his bearing, and kept his bodily vigor to extreme old age. His tastes were simple, even crude; he cared nothing for the graces of polite society. In his business dealings he was scrupulously just, paying his debts promptly and insisting that others do the same. He combined frugality in small matters with lavish generosity when his emotions were aroused. Unassuming and modest in his benefactions, he did not wish his name to be mentioned in connection with them and looked upon himself as "the mere steward of a merciful Providence."

[The best account of Bartlet's career is found in the *Hist. of Newburyport, Mass.* (1909), by John J. Currier. *A Memorial of the Semi-Centennial Celebration of the Founding of the Theological Seminary at Andover* (1859) and the *Hist. of the Andover Theological Seminary* (1885), by Leonard Woods, contain additional information. The story of the founding of Andover Theological Seminary is told in *An Old New England School* (1917), by Claude M. Fuess.]   C.M.F.

BARTLETT, ELISHA (Oct. 6, 1804–July 19, 1855), physician, teacher, and author, was born at Smithfield, R. I., the son of Otis and Waite Buffum Bartlett, who were Quakers. His preliminary education was had at a Friends' institution in New York, the details being lacking. We know that he studied medicine with Dr. George Willard of Uxbridge, Dr. John Green and Dr. B. F. Heywood of Worcester, and Dr. Levi Wheaton of Providence; he attended medical lectures in Boston and Providence, entered the medical department of Brown University, and took his degree in 1826, two years before the closing of this branch of the University. In June of that year he sailed for Europe, where he attended the Jardin des Plantes to hear the lectures of Cloquet and Cuvier. In 1827, he settled in Lowell, where he lived for nearly twenty of his remaining twenty-eight years of medical activity. In 1829 he married Elizabeth Slater of Smithfield, R. I. When he had been a citizen for nine years he was elected the first mayor of the new city (1836). From this will be seen that he had an interest in public service. He held his first teaching position in 1832, when not yet twenty-eight years old, as professor of pathological anatomy and materia medica in the Berkshire Medical Institution at Pittsfield, Mass., then a strong school which turned out more graduates in medicine than the Harvard Medical School. A list of Bartlett's teaching positions in the succeeding years is a long one: professor of theory and practise of medicine at Transylvania University, Lexington, Ky., 1841, also 1846; professor of the theory and practise of medicine at the University of Maryland, Baltimore, 1844–46; the same position at the University of Louisville, Ky., 1849–50; professor of the institutes and practise of medicine in New York University, 1850–52; and finally professor of materia medica and medical jurisprudence in the College of Physicians and Surgeons, New York, 1852–55. He had also lectured on the topics of materia medica and obstetrics at the Vermont Medical College in the spring and summer months from 1843 to 1852. It was said of him that he could make the dryest and most barren subject interesting.

Bartlett began his career as a medical writer in the *Monthly Journal of Medical Literature and American Medical Students' Gazette,* only three numbers of which were issued. Then in July 1832 he was associated with Dr. A. L. Pierson and Dr. J. B. Flint in the *Medical Magazine,* which was published monthly in Boston for the succeeding three years. Independently he printed in 1831 a small book entitled *Sketches of the Character and Writings of Eminent Living Surgeons and Physicians of Paris,* translated from the French of J. L. H. Peisse. It contained the lives of nine French physicians and gave an attractive insight into the history of medicine in Paris at the beginning of the nineteenth century. Bartlett's chief work was his treatise on *The Fevers in the United States* (1842), reprinted in 1847, 1852, and 1857, the last after his death. In it he gave a remarkably accurate description of typhoid fever, which in its main outlines cannot be improved to-day. It was one of the most noteworthy contributions to medicine of the first half of the nineteenth century. In his *Essay on the Philosophy of Medicine* (1844), he shows himself to be an acute and thoughtful observer; he applies deductive reasoning to medical problems. It is called by William Osler "a classic in American medical literature" (*American Medical Biographies,* edited by H. A. Kelly and W. L. Burrage, 1920, p. 65). Four years later appeared *An Inquiry into the Degree of Certainty of Medicine, and into the Nature and Extent of Its Power over Disease.* It was a small pamphlet of eighty-four pages that expounded views that were in advance of the times, shocking some of the conservative members of the profession, who preferred to be governed in their ideas by tradition and not by what they saw. Bartlett published, in 1849, *A Discourse on the Life and Labors of Dr. H. Charles Wells, the Discoverer of the Philosophy of Dew,* and the next year a brochure entitled *History, Diagnosis and Treatment of Edematous Laryngitis.* Among his occasional addresses, in which he was at his best, a lecture delivered in 1843, on *The Sense of the Beautiful,* was a plea for the education of the faculty of medicine, and another, *The Head and the Heart, or the Relative Importance of Intellectual and Moral Education,* was an exhortation for a higher tone in social and political morality. One of his last publications was *A Discourse on the Times, Character, and Writings of Hippocrates,* delivered as an introductory address before the trustees, faculty, and students of the College of Physicians and Surgeons, at the opening of the session of 1852–53. This was considered a masterpiece of medical biography, depicting the founder of medicine in the different phases of his life with the utmost clearness and interest.

At the close of the session of the College of Physicians and Surgeons in New York, of 1853–54, a nervous malady from which Bartlett had been suffering, the exact nature of which is not known, became worse. He retired to his birthplace, Smithfield, and after a protracted illness, during which he became paralyzed without impairment of his mental faculties, he died at the comparatively early age of fifty. Bartlett was in his mental outlook and his power of expression far in advance of most of the men of his time.

Most instructors were then everyday practitioners who were content to impart to their students the facts they had gathered, without comment or general application. Bartlett was a man of vision, of wide interests, who saw the relation of medicine to the affairs of the community, and could forecast the trend of doctrines and evaluate them.

[Samuel Henry Dickson, "Memoir of Elisha Bartlett" in S. D. Gross, *Lives of Eminent Am. Physicians and Surgeons* (1861); William Osler, *Elisha Bartlett, a Rhode Island Philosopher* (1900); Elisha Huntington, *An Address on the Life of Elisha Bartlett* (Lowell, 1855).]

W. L. B.

BARTLETT, HOMER NEWTON (Dec. 28, 1845–Apr. 3, 1920), musical composer, was born at Olive, Ulster County, N. Y., and died at Hoboken, N. J. His father, Henry B. Bartlett, claimed descent from Josiah Bartlett [*q.v.*], a signer of the Declaration of Independence, and his mother, Hannah C. Hall, from John Rogers, eighteenth signer of the Mayflower Compact. In his early childhood the family removed to Ellenville, N. Y., where the father kept a general store. At the age of five Bartlett gave signs of musical precocity by playing the violin, holding the instrument cello-fashion between his knees. He played in public at the age of nine and at ten began to compose. His general education, begun at the Ellenville Academy, from which he graduated in 1861, was then continued under private tutors in New York, where he studied piano under Emil Guyon (pupil of Thalberg) and S. B. Mills, organ under Max Braun, and harmony and counterpoint under O. F. Jacobsen. He at once became organist at "Old Spring Street" Church, soon after going to the Marble Collegiate Church, where he remained twelve years, and later to the Madison Avenue Baptist Church, which he served for a period of thirty-one years, when he was retired as organist emeritus in 1912. A man of modest but friendly disposition, he was sympathetic to all progressive tendencies in music and contributed much to the success of the Manuscript Society, the American Guild of Organists, the National Association of Organists, of which he was at one time president, and the Musicians Club of New York. He was an indefatigable worker in his art, one for whom composition was not merely an absorbing interest but virtually a dominant passion. Even when opus numbers had mounted to 269 in the publisher's catalogue and he was near his end, he craved length of days to compose, saying that he had "just begun to know how to write." His music was in general tinged by the suavity which characterized the man. Incapable of giving offense,

he gave no intimation of radical tendencies. As he was largely self-taught and a diligent student of the works of his more immediate predecessors, it is not surprising to find in his music numerous instances of imitation. His youthful study of the violin, as also his piano training in the school of Thalberg, somewhat predetermined the marked melodic trend in his compositions, which, while often rich in primary harmonic color and often embellished in florid figuration, show less resource in the use of chromatic tints both in choice and treatment of themes and in infrequent resort to the polyphonic idiom. His Opus 1, "Grand Polka de Concert" (1867), written as a birthday present to the young lady who became his wife, perhaps the most deservedly popular and successful of any Opus 1 by an American composer, is outstanding for its enduring vitality. The list of his published compositions includes about seventy songs, an equal number of piano pieces, and about as many part songs and pieces of church music, besides music for organ and violin.

[For lists of published compositions, see catalogues of G. Schirmer, Inc., and Oliver Ditson Co. Biog. information and critical comment in R. Hughes and A. Elson, *Am. Composers* (revised ed. 1914), pp. 317-23; A. Farwell and W. D. Darby, *The Art of Music* (1915), IV, 383; *Grove's Dict., Am. Supp.* (1920); obituary in *N. Y. Times*, Apr. 4, 1920.]

S. S.

BARTLETT, ICHABOD (July 24, 1786–Oct. 19, 1853), lawyer, politician, was born at Salisbury, N. H., the son of Dr. Joseph and Hannah (Colcord) Bartlett. His father was a trusted and skilful physician with a large practise, and active in the affairs of the community. Ichabod attended the local academy and after graduation at Dartmouth in 1808 studied law. He was admitted to the bar in 1811 and after practising for several years at Durham moved to Portsmouth in 1818, where he resided until his death. He was never married. He began his political career as a Jeffersonian Republican, was clerk of the state Senate in 1817–18, and in the latter year was appointed by Gov. Plumer to study the subject of internal improvements in New Hampshire, preparing an elaborate report on the improvement of roads and waterways which was laid before the legislature of 1819. He represented Portsmouth in the legislature 1819–21, being speaker in the latter year, and again in 1830, 1838, 1851, and 1852 (*New Hampshire Register*). In 1852 he was unsuccessfully supported for the speakership by the Whigs. During his first term in the legislature he supported the Toleration Act in an unusually forceful and eloquent address, one of the few of his speeches which has been preserved (*New Hampshire Patriot*, July 20, 27, 1819). His success at the bar came early, as is evidenced by the fact that in 1817 he appeared before the superior court as counsel for Woodward in the Dartmouth College Case, with which the most eminent lawyers in the state were associated (Timothy Farrar, *Report of the Case of the Trustees of Dartmouth College against William H. Woodward*, Portsmouth, 1819. Bartlett's argument is printed on pp. 116–206). He was solicitor for Rockingham County, 1818–21 (*New Hampshire Register, 1819–21*), and throughout his life appeared in noted civil and criminal cases. In 1822 he was elected to Congress and served three successive terms. He was not prominent in the House, but his sympathies with National Republicanism appear in the few speeches he made in that body. His longest address was a vigorous defense of the administration of President John Quincy Adams, Feb. 6, 1828 (*Register of Debates*, 20 Cong., 1 Sess., 1402–17). He continued more or less active in politics after his retirement from Congress in 1829. In 1831 and 1832 he was National Republican candidate for governor, but was defeated. In 1850 he was a member of the constitutional convention, serving as chairman of the committee on the Bill of Rights. One of the last of his recorded public services occurred in 1852 when, as a member of the judiciary committee of the House, he successfully advocated a bill repealing the "personal liberty law" which had been adopted July 10, 1846. He was recognized as one of the leaders of the bar at a time when New Hampshire possessed a group of lawyers of unusual ability. A contemporary described him as "the Randolph of the North, the brilliant flashes of whose wit, keen sarcasm, and pungent irony, gave life and spirit to the dry juridical discussions, whose logical congruity they were allowed to relieve, but not to impair" (*Eulogy on Levi Woodbury* by Robert Rantoul, Jr., Oct. 16, 1851). He was one of the founders of the New Hampshire Historical Society and its president, 1826–30.

[Sketch by Chas. H. Bell in *The Bench and Bar of N. H.* (1894); another by Henry P. Rolfe, with portrait in John J. Dearborn, the *Hist. of Salisbury, N.H.* (1890). The *Portsmouth Jour.*, Oct. 22, 1853, contains an obituary notice of some length and the issue of Oct. 29 gives, in full, the memorial resolutions of the Rockingham County Bar and addresses by several of Bartlett's associates. Cf. also *Biog. Cong. Dir.* (1913) and L. Bartlett, *Geneal. and Biog. Sketches of the Bartlett Family in England and America* (1876).]

W.A.R.

BARTLETT, JOHN (June 14, 1820–Dec. 3, 1905), editor, publisher, son of William and Susan (Thacher) Bartlett, was born at Plymouth, Mass. His paternal grandfather and his father were both sea-captains, and his maternal grandfather was Dr. James Thacher, a surgeon and his-torian of the Revolutionary period. His education was that of the Plymouth public schools, and at sixteen he was employed in the University Book Store of Cambridge. This proved for him a college, as he there became a book lover and student. In 1849 he was owner of the store, which grew to be the meeting place for Harvard professors and students who cared for books. "Ask John Bartlett" was the customary advice when any one had difficulty in finding a book or a quotation, and Bartlett was so anxious to deserve his reputation that he began keeping a commonplace-book, which was the embryo of his famous *Familiar Quotations*. During the Civil War he was for a few months a volunteer paymaster in the United States Navy. In 1863 he joined the publishing firm of Little, Brown & Company and in 1878 became senior partner. His work here included personal dealings with authors and he made many warm friends among them, especially those of the Cambridge and Concord group.

In addition to his *Familiar Quotations* (1855), Bartlett was the author of a *New Method of Chess Notation* (1857), *The Shakespeare Phrase Book* (1882), a *Catalogue of Books on Angling, including Ichthyology, Pisciculture, Etc.* (1882), which he presented to Harvard College Library, and a *Complete Concordance to Shakespeare's Dramatic Works and Poems* (1894). He was an ardent fisherman, and his friend James Russell Lowell commemorated a present from him in the poem "To John Bartlett, Who Had Sent Me a Seven Pound Trout." His other favorite recreation was whist; for a quarter of a century he belonged to a whist club of which the other members were Lowell, Charles Choate, and John Holmes, brother of O. W. Holmes; the club was broken up by Lowell's death. In 1851 Bartlett married Hannah Staniford Willard, granddaughter of Joseph Willard, a president of Harvard. They had no children. After her death, a year before his own, he seldom left his home in Brattle St., Cambridge. Before that, in spite of feebleness, he had frequently driven about the streets of Cambridge and the surrounding country, and his face, with its large white mustache, and kindly eyes behind big spectacles, was well known to old residents. He died at the age of eighty-five at his Cambridge home. *Familiar Quotations*, John Bartlett's chief accomplishment, went through nine editions during his life and a tenth edition was revised and enlarged by Nathan Haskell Dole. It contains selections from British and American authors and translations, including the Old and New Testaments. With little formal education, Bartlett yet achieved a measure of scholarship, which was recognized by the conferring upon him of an honorary A.M. degree by Harvard University and by his election to the American Academy of Arts and Sciences.

[The chief source of information is a manuscript book which Bartlett gave to Harvard Coll. Lib. A biographical article based on this appeared in the *Proc. Am. Acad. Arts and Sci.*, vol. XLI. Obituaries in the *Boston Herald*, Dec. 4, 1905, and the *Boston Transcript*, Dec. 4, 1905. Sketch in *Who's Who in America*, 1903–05.]

S. G. B.

BARTLETT, JOHN RUSSELL (Oct. 23, 1805–May 28, 1886), antiquarian, bibliographer, descended from a long line of Rhode Island ancestors, was born at Providence, R. I., the son of Smith and Nancy (Russell) Bartlett. While he was an infant his family moved to Kingston, Ontario, Canada, where he lived until he was eighteen. In the Kingston schools, and later at Lowville Academy in New York and at Montreal, he received his education. In 1824 he returned to Providence, where he became a clerk in the dry-goods store of his uncle William Russell, then took a position as bookkeeper in a bank, and finally in 1831 was chosen cashier of the Globe Bank. During this period his early love of literature and history manifested itself. He became a member of the Franklin Society, which was founded to study the natural sciences, was elected to the Rhode Island Historical Society in 1831, and in the same year was instrumental in the founding of the Providence Athenæum. It was through his connection with the Historical Society that his first antiquarian research was performed. In 1834 Prof. C. C. Rafn, of the Royal Society of Northern Antiquaries of Copenhagen, addressed to the Society certain queries regarding the inscriptions on Dighton Rock, which he hoped to prove were Norse. Bartlett was appointed on a committee to investigate the subject and drew two views of the Rock, with its inscriptions, which are now among the most valuable contributions to this much discussed problem. (*Transactions of the Colonial Society of Massachusetts*, XX, 296).

In 1836 Bartlett moved to New York, where he engaged in mercantile life, but soon became associated with Charles Welford, a bookseller, under the firm name of Bartlett & Welford. Their business consisted largely of the importing of foreign books, and their rooms became a resort for the leading literary and historical scholars of the city. Bartlett was elected corresponding secretary of the New York Historical Society, which brought him into close touch with its president, Albert Gallatin [*q.v.*], with whom he helped to form the American Ethnological Society. He prepared papers to be read before the two societies, aided many scholars, such as E. G. Squier and John L. Stephens, in their historical researches, and began to publish works of his own. His *Progress of Ethnology,* an account of recent researches throughout the world, appeared in 1847, his *Dictionary of Americanisms* in 1848, and the *Reminiscences of Albert Gallatin* in 1849. Of these the *Dictionary* became the best known, passing through four editions, the last in 1878, and being translated into Dutch and German.

In 1850 Bartlett retired from business life and was appointed by President Taylor United States commissioner to run the boundary line between the United States and Mexico, under the Treaty of Guadalupe Hidalgo, in which duty he was employed nearly three years, until February 1853. While on this service he made extensive explorations in Texas, New Mexico, Chihuahua, Sonora, California, and the country now known as Arizona, the particulars of which were published in 1854 in two volumes under the title of *Personal Narrative of Explorations and Incidents Connected with the United States and Mexican Boundary Commission.* He then returned to Rhode Island, where he was elected secretary of state in 1855, which office he continued to hold by annual election for seventeen years. During this period he not only conducted his office efficiently, especially during the troublesome years of the Civil War, but also arranged and classified the great mass of public papers which had accumulated for two hundred years, and had them bound in ninety-two volumes and twenty-eight portfolios. Under authority of the General Assembly, he published in ten volumes the *Records of the Colony of Rhode Island, 1636–1792,* printing in addition to the records many valuable documents from private and institutional collections. He also aided the cause of history in his state by publishing an *Index to the Acts, Resolves and Reports of Rhode Island, from 1758 to 1862,* in twelve volumes (1856–63); *Bibliography of Rhode Island* (1864); *The Literature of the Rebellion* (1866); and *Memoirs of Rhode Island Officers in the Rebellion* (1867).

For the last thirty years of his life Bartlett was closely associated with John Carter Brown in the acquisition and care of the noted collection of books which that scholar had formed at Providence. From 1865 to 1882 he published the *John Carter Brown Catalogue,* a monumental work in four volumes which marked a great advance over all previous attempts to provide a bibliography of early Americana. Its bibliographical descriptions, historical notes, critical valuations, and reproductions of titles and illustrations made this one of the most indispensable works, even to-day, for the student of early American discovery and history.

Bartlett died in Providence on May 28, 1886. He was twice married, first on May 15, 1831, to Eliza Allen Rhodes, by whom he had seven children, and who died Nov. 11, 1853; and second, on Nov. 12, 1863, to Ellen Eddy, who survived him.

[The best biographical sketch is the *Life and Services of John Russell Bartlett,* read before the R. I. Hist. Soc. by Wm. Gammell, 1886. See also long obituary in *Providence Jour.,* May 29, 1886; and sketch by Charles Deane in *Proc. Am. Antiquarian Soc.,* Oct. 1886, p. 179. Bartlett's correspondence and a lengthy autobiography are preserved in the John Carter Brown Lib. at Providence.]
                                          C. S. B.

BARTLETT, JOHN SHERREN (1790–Aug. 23, 1863), physician, journalist, was born in Dorsetshire, England, son of Thomas, a descendant of the Stropham family of Bartletts. He pursued medical studies in London under the direction of Sir Astley Cooper, and was appointed an assistant surgeon in the British navy in 1812. Assigned to the packet *Swallow* bound for Jamaica, he became an American prisoner when that ship was captured by Commodore Rodgers cruising with the frigates *President* and *Congress* in search of the enemy's vessels. Although held as a prisoner in Boston for several months before being exchanged, he experienced much kindness and hospitality there. In turn his was the pleasure, combined with duty, in the latter part of the war, to attend to the wounds of American naval prisoners, including the officers and crew of the *Chesapeake,* at Halifax. The war over, he was satisfied to remain on American soil and set up his physician's sign in friendly Boston. It was as a journalist, however, that Bartlett was to gain his reputation. He conceived the idea of establishing an English newspaper in the United States, a journal which should give to British residents on this continent a true exposition of public affairs, and a general view of the news, politics, and literature of the United Kingdom, and which would aim "to preserve the peace and good understanding between the United States and Great Britain." He thought New York the best center for such a publication and the first issue of the *Albion* appeared there, June 22, 1822. For over a quarter of a century he continued its publication, always contending successfully that "a love for England was not incompatible with respect and regard for this country" (*Albion,* May 6, 1848). At the time when England was claiming her exclusive right to the Oregon territory and the Democrats of the United States were shouting "Fifty-four forty or fight," Bart-

lett insisted that both parties had rights, and that nothing but a calm and dispassionate examination of them, with a determination mutually to admit these rights, was necessary to a happy issue of the affair. The paper resembled the modern tabloid in its convenient size but in no other respect. It appealed to the reading public because of its reports of naval intelligence from Portsmouth, of police news from Bow St., of the new plays at the London theatres, of the proceedings of Parliament, and of the high literary quality of the contributed articles. To Bartlett must be given credit for introducing Indian corn into England. Besides pointing out in the *Albion* the excellence of the maize as a cheap and wholesome article of diet for the poor, he circulated several pamphlets emphasizing its value and giving directions for preparing and cooking it.

Another publication, the *European,* was begun by Bartlett with the opening of the Cunard Line, in 1840. The paper was printed in Liverpool, containing the latest news from Europe, and forwarded to America at each sailing. The editor's ill health forced him to abandon this enterprise at the end of eighteen months, but it was continued as Willmer's *European Times.* Another breakdown in health caused him to retire from the editorship of the *Albion,* May 6, 1848. In 1847, he was president of the St. George's Society of New York and, ten years later, on the death of the British consul in Baltimore, he was put in charge of the consulate for a time. During his last years he was a resident of New York City and Middletown Point, N. J.

[The best sources of information are the obituary notice in the *Albion,* Aug. 29, 1863, and an article contributed by Bartlett May 6, 1848, on his retirement from the paper. See also editorials in *N. Y. Evening Post,* May 9, 1848, and *N. Y. Jour. of Commerce,* Mar. 25, 1848. The account in *Sketches of the Bartlett Family in England and America* (1876) is faulty in several particulars.]
                                          A. E. P.

BARTLETT, JOSEPH (June 10, 1762–Oct. 20, 1827), adventurer, lawyer, politician, and author, had a spectacular career in New England in the days immediately following the Revolution, and became widely known for his eccentricities, his wit, and his writings. He was born in Plymouth, Mass., the son of Sylvanus and Martha (Wait) Bartlett; graduated at Harvard in 1782, where his scholarship was such that he was one of the three charter members of the Phi Beta Kappa chapter; and then went to Salem to study law. Here he also conducted a school, in connection with which his interest in dramatics appeared, for in *The Holyoke Diaries,* under date of Jan. 21, 1783, is recorded, "We were at a play at the Brick Store." Note: *"The Distracted*

Mother, presented by Mr. Bartlett's school. Music, two fiddles and a drum." An entry of Apr. 29, 1783, mentions another play by "Mr. Bartlett's scholars." With no motive, apparently, but love of adventure, he went to London, where at a play in which American soldiers were ridiculed he arose and shouted, "Hurrah, Great Britain beaten by barbers, tailors, and tinkers." This audacity won him favor with the bloods of the day, and for a time he lived a gay life which ended in the debtors' prison. From this he secured funds for release by writing a play, which he claimed was the first American play presented on the English stage. Unfortunately, the title has not been preserved. Going to Edinburgh, he acted under the stage name of "Mr. Maitland," appearing as Belcour in *The West Indian.* Tiring of this life, he bought a ship-load of merchandise with borrowed money and sailed with it for America. The ship was wrecked on Cape Cod, and Bartlett is said to have shown unseemly haste in saving himself. He resumed the study of law in Boston, and at the time of Shays's Rebellion started for Worcester at the head of a company of volunteers, but news that the insurrection had been put down halted the expedition.

Bartlett was admitted to the bar, and began his legal and political career in Woburn, Mass., where, to attract attention, seemingly, he painted his house black and called it "The Coffin." "As odd as Joe Bartlett" soon became a common expression. His wife, Anna May, daughter of Thomas and Ann Wetherell, whom he married Nov. 15, 1795, was not able long to live with him. He was interested in educational matters and in 1792 was one of a committee of seven "to examine into the government of the schools and recommend some uniform system of instruction." His fellow lawyer, Samuel Lorenzo Knapp, who was too prejudiced to be entirely trustworthy, said that Bartlett's clients were chiefly "harlots, rogues, and knaves of every size and grade." As a political speaker he had the power of setting his audience in a roar, and even sober, thinking men found him irresistible. His political writings had a pungency and satire that made them very effective.

From Woburn, Bartlett removed to Cambridge, without changing his manner of life. He was sufficiently respected, however, to be selected as poet for the Harvard Phi Beta Kappa celebration of 1799. His poem on that occasion, *Physiognomy,* published in 1810, attracted much notice, and even Knapp reluctantly acknowledges that it has "taste and no little splendor, however unjust and satirical it may be." At several sessions, also, Bartlett represented Cambridge in the

General Court. By 1803, however, he had moved to Saco, in the present state of Maine, and in 1804 was chosen senator in the Massachusetts legislature from the County of York. He missed an election to Congress by about six votes. In 1805 he was editor of the Saco *Freeman's Friend.* Later he lived in Portsmouth, N. H. A book of more than 400 aphorisms was issued by him in 1810, among which are such sayings as "Conceit more than knowledge influences men to write"; "There never was a party man who acted as cool reason would approve"; and "Men had rather be censured for want of morals than for want of understanding." On the downward road financially and otherwise, he returned to Boston, where he delivered a Fourth-of-July address at the Exchange Coffee-House Hall in 1823, which was published the same year in a pamphlet entitled *The Fourth of July Anticipated,* which also included "The New Vicar of Bray," probably his best known work. He spent his last days in poverty, supported by his friends.

Bartlett is described as "fat, jolly, and infinitely amusing." He was an ardent democrat and a disciple of Thomas Paine. Possessed of exceptional gifts, he lacked sufficient mental and moral balance to use them to the highest advantage. Shortly before his death he wrote his own epitaph:

"'Tis done! The fatal stroke is given,
And Bartlett's fled to Hell or Heaven;
His friends approve it, and his foes applaud,—
Yet he will have the verdict of his God."

[The dates of Bartlett's birth, graduation from college, and death are variously given. The authorities for those stated are Jas. S. Loring, *The Hundred Boston Orators* (1852); *Harvard Quinquennial Cat.* (1915); and the *Columbian Centinel,* Boston, Oct. 24, 1827. See also Ignatius L. Robertson (Samuel L. Knapp), *Sketches of Public Characters* (1830); Samuel Sewall, *Hist. of Woburn* (1868); Geo. F. Dow, *The Holyoke Diaries* (1911); *The Saco Register,* 1906; W. T. Davis, *Bench and Bar of the Commonwealth of Mass.* (1895), I, 189.]

H.E.S.

BARTLETT, JOSIAH (Nov. 21, 1729–May 19, 1795), physician, Revolutionary patriot, chief justice and governor of New Hampshire, was a son of Stephen and Mary (Webster) Bartlett, and was born in Amesbury, Essex County, Mass. He was educated in the common schools, and after acquiring under private tuition some knowledge of the Greek and Latin languages began, when sixteen years of age, the study of medicine, in his native town, in the office of Dr. Ordway, a distant relative. The large clinical advantages of this office, supplemented by the diligent use of several medical libraries and one large general library, in neighboring towns, qualified him, according to the custom of the times, five years later to enter upon the practise of his profession, which he did in 1750 in the town of Kingston in southern New Hampshire. In this place, which proved to be his permanent home, Bartlett rapidly acquired a large practise as an all-round country physician and early in his career became widely known through his diagnosis of an obscure, malignant, and prevalent disease of the throat and through its successful treatment by the use of Peruvian bark. His experience gradually led him to reject the then accepted pathology and treatment of several other diseases, and relying more and more upon observation of particular cases and experiment in their treatment he introduced many medical reforms. He was married on Jan. 15, 1754, to his cousin, Mary Bartlett of Newton, N. H. They had twelve children, and three of his sons and seven of his grandsons became physicians.

Bartlett's wide intelligence, integrity, and active interest in public affairs led his fellow citizens to choose him as the representative from Kingston to the Provincial Assembly in 1765 and regularly to reëlect him till the outbreak of the Revolution. In 1767 he was appointed by the royal governor, John Wentworth, a justice of the peace and soon after a colonel of a regiment of militia, but when, during the progress of the controversy between Great Britain and the Colonies, he took the side of the people and maintained it with vigor and unfaltering courage, he was summarily dismissed from these offices, in February 1775. Previously, during the critical year 1774 he was recognized as an active patriot by his appointment on the important Committee of Correspondence of the Provincial Assembly and by his election to that Assembly's Revolutionary successor, the first Provincial Congress, which chose him as one of two delegates from New Hampshire to the first Continental Congress. Although he was unable to accept this election, because of the recent destruction of his house by fire, believed to have been set because of his activity in the popular cause, in 1775–76 he was again chosen as a delegate to the Continental Congress, and in the latter year was the first to give his vote in favor of the adoption of the Declaration of Independence, to which his name was duly affixed. Although reëlected to the Continental Congress for 1777 he was unable to serve, because he was worn out by his arduous duties in that body during the previous year, but while at home he was still busy with public affairs.

In 1778–79 he was once more a member of the Continental Congress, and, as the states were called, had the honor of being the first to vote for the proposed Articles of Confederation and Perpetual Union which took effect Mar. 1, 1781. The records of the proceedings of these two Congresses in which he served, as well as his private correspondence, show that he was a member of the most important standing committees in each of these bodies, those of Safety and Secrecy, Munitions, Marines and Privateering, as well as of numerous special committees, such as that on civil government for the United States in 1775 and also on the committee to draft Articles of Confederation in 1778. His constant, painstaking, and arduous service upon these committees made him one of the most influential members of these Congresses in shaping legislation, though he took relatively small part in the debates, of whose too frequent prolixity and futility he was a caustic critic. Physically exhausted by his labors at Philadelphia and New York during 1777–78 and by the difficulties of travel in following the Continental Congress, he declined reëlection and sought a chance to recruit his strength at home, but in 1779 New Hampshire appointed him chief justice of its court of common pleas. In thus elevating a layman to the bench, the State was following an occasional practise due to its social and political conditions in the last quarter of the eighteenth century, but in this case it ran scant risk, since the appointee not only had large knowledge of practical affairs but also was prepared by previous reading of law books, experience as justice of the peace, and fifteen years of almost constant association with lawyers engaged in legislative work.

In 1782 he was promoted to be associate justice of the superior court, and having become chief justice in 1788, ended his service on the bench in 1790. Tradition and his own reported statement make it probable that his decisions, like those of other lay judges of that period, were based upon equity. Some of the ablest lawyers of that time declared that justice was never better administered in New Hampshire than when the judges knew very little law. In 1788, while still upon the bench, Bartlett was a member and temporary chairman of the state convention called to ratify the proposed Constitution of the United States. In this body he was one of the most skilful and resourceful advocates of ratification, and it is doubtful whether, without his personal efforts to allay the opposition of the smaller towns during the three months' interval between the two sessions of the convention, New Hampshire would have had the honor, on June 21, 1788, of being the ninth State to ratify the Constitution, and so establish the Union. In 1790 and each of the two following years he was elected to the highest office in the gift of the State, that of chief executive, then styled president. His popularity appears by the election returns in that year which show that out of a total of 9,854 votes he received 7,385. In June 1793, the newly amended Constitution having changed the title of the chief executive, he was chosen as the first governor of the state. The policy of Bartlett, steadily pursued during the four years of his administration, was expressed in his successive recommendations to the legislature in which he urged: any changes in the laws of the state which might be found necessary to enable it to fulfil its obligations to the recently organized Federal Government; provision for the early payment of the state debt; strict adherence to all engagements, both public and private; economy in public expenditures; the early compilation and revision of all the laws and statutes deemed to be in force, and a better method of selecting certain judicial officers; the promotion of agriculture and manufactures; improvement of roads and possibly the building of canals in some parts of the state, in order to unite the people in a common interest; and the encouragement in every possible way of the rising generation in virtue, morality, and patriotism. At the close of his term of office in 1794, because of ill health he withdrew from politics.

In 1790 Dartmouth College had conferred upon Bartlett, whose keen interest in his profession had not abated during the long period when his preoccupation with public affairs had interrupted his regular practise, the honorary degree of Doctor of Medicine, and in the following year he rendered what was perhaps his greatest service to his profession by securing from the legislature a charter for the New Hampshire Medical Society which, when organized with a constitution and by-laws drafted by his own hand, fittingly elected him as its first president. But he did not long survive his retirement from public life, for he died at his home in Kingston on May 19, 1795. He is described by his contemporaries as a tall man of fine figure, affable but dignified in his manner, and very particular in his dress. He wore his auburn hair in a queue, a white stock at his throat, ruffles at his wrists, short clothes, silk hose, low shoes with silver buckles. His bronze statue, unveiled in 1888, stands in the public square of his native town, Amesbury. His portrait, an oil painting, a copy from the original by Jonathan Trumbull, hangs in the State House in Concord, N. H.

[Levi Bartlett, *Sketches of the Bartlett Family in England and America* (1875–76); Robt. Waln, Jr., *Biog. of the Signers to the Declaration of Independence* (2nd ed., 1828), III, 123; E. C. Burnett, *Letters of Members of the Continental Cong.* (1921–23); J. Farmer and J. B. Moore, "Collections, Hist. and Biog. relating to N. H.,"
in *N. H. State Papers,* vol. XXII, index; J. B. Walker, *Hist. of N. H. Convention for Ratif. of Fed. Constitution, 1788* (1888), "Presidential Address and Sketch of Josiah Bartlett," by Thomas Luce in *N. H. Medic. Soc. Proc.,* 1926.]

J.F.C.

BARTLETT, PAUL WAYLAND (Jan. 24, 1865–Sept. 20, 1925), sculptor, son of Truman Howe Bartlett and Mary Ann White Bartlett, was born in New Haven, Conn. His father, a sculptor and critic remembered to-day chiefly through his Wells and Clark monuments in Hartford, and his *Art Life of William Rimmer* (1882), was for twenty-three years instructor in modeling at the Massachusetts Institute of Technology, where his vivid and reputedly difficult personality is said to have had a "quickening influence on the artistic life of Boston." The sculptor Herbert Adams, for a brief period a pupil in Truman Bartlett's studio, recalls an emphatic remark: "I would never have a son of mine get his art education in this country!" Paul Bartlett was then already established with his mother in Paris. They had made their home in France since the boy was nine years old. During his most impressionable years he lived in Paris as schoolboy and art student, alert, aggressive, yet thoughtful and sensitive to beauty. Entering the École des Beaux Arts at fifteen, he studied under the sculptor Cavelier, and at about the same time followed the deservedly popular courses in animal sculpture given by Frémiet at the Jardin des Plantes. His animal studies proved immediately rewarding. Early thrown on his own resources, he was able to earn something as "animal specialist" in the studios of sculptors versed merely in the human form and its trappings. Bits of his youthful work are to be found to-day in important sculptural groups abroad. Gardet, the well-known *animaliste,* often employed him as assistant. His skill in the various handicrafts connected with sculpture was not unlike that displayed in youth by Rodin, a master whose influence he later felt.

This early and entire consecration to art gives the key to Bartlett's career. The transplantation from the sober light-and-shade of the New England elms into the gayer arabesques of the Luxembourg Garden, with statues gleaming and fountains playing, had opened his young eyes all the wider to the marvels of art around him. Thanks to his New England inheritance of a persevering spirit and an industrious mind, to say nothing of that desire for expression which was an immediate gift from his father, his education in art was a natural process, liberating and creative from its beginning. At fourteen, he exhibited in the Salon a bust of his grandmother. A few years later his "Bear Tamer," a man standing over two cubs, now a favorite bronze of young visitors at the Metropolitan Museum, received *mention honorable* at the Salon of 1887. With the "Bear Tamer" may be classed the "Dying Lion," as well as the "Ghost Dancer," a lithe savage performing a tribal rite, a figure admired for its anatomy in the Chicago Exposition of 1893, and now in the Pennsylvania Academy of the Fine Arts.

At the Paris Exposition of 1895 was a collection of small bronzes, cast by Bartlett himself, *à la cire perdue*. The subjects were ethnographic whimseys of fishes and serpents, of batrachians, crustaceans, and the like. To the artists who hung over this display, its radiant gemlike colors were even more alluring than its forms. Sculptors who had experimented arduously in alloys and *patines* were the first to acclaim Bartlett's success. His name still brings to many minds a vision of rainbow hues such as they had never before dreamed of associating with the dark stuff they knew as bronze. Jean Carriès declared that Bartlett's *patines* vied with those of the classic Japanese school. These "essays," as the author called them, express his delight in craftsmanship. Even during the last summer of his life, he was eagerly working with pottery and glazes.

In 1895, he received from France the ribbon of the Legion of Honor. But between his native and adoptive countries, his allegiance was never divided. As his position in art became more secure, he visited America more frequently, called home by commissions enthusiastically offered. The Rotunda of the Library of Congress holds twelve heroic bronze statues, two of which, the Columbus and the Michelangelo, are by Bartlett. The architect had naturally given all the sculptors a definite scale for their models. Bartlett remarked, after the placing of his two heroes, "Yes, I made my figures larger than the others. I wanted them to dominate" (personal recollection). A highly unsound principle! His figures not only dominate in spirit, they domineer in size. Aside from this fault, these two romantic portrait-statues are among the best of their kind. The world-map of the great seeker and the leather apron of the great interpreter play their proud parts in dramatic light-and-dark. The Columbus and Michelangelo stand at the portal of Bartlett's great period in his art. He had already acquired the grand style. It now remained for him not to subdue this, but to enhance it by bringing it into noble relationship with architecture.

Later, a more harmonious visualization of sculpture as an element in an architectural ensemble reveals itself in his six decorative figures in marble, for the attic story of the New York Public Library, designed by Carrère and Hastings. The first studies were accepted in 1910. Male figures of "History" and "Philosophy" occupy the end spaces, while between these, and in pairs, are female figures of "Romance" and "Religion," "Poetry" and "Drama." Save only "Drama," with her mask, all might have had other names, since the sculptor has not perturbed them with too much symbolism. They are a happy family of beings from a timeless Golden Age, ample enough to hold something both of Greek beauty and Gothic earnestness. The men are stately, the women gracious, and all their vestments are of that noble nondescript dear to poets but disconcerting to modistes. The marble draperies of the four women suggest music, dancing, flowers.

During one of Bartlett's many visits to his native land, he collaborated (1908–09) with the veteran sculptor Ward in the sculpture for the pediment of the New York Stock Exchange building. The design of the gigantic sculpture, a high relief centering about the "Genius of Integrity," is from the elder master, but we are assured by Lorado Taft that the modeling was Bartlett's. Shortly afterward, this initial experience in pedimental sculpture became of value to Bartlett in his own now untrammeled creation of the sculpture for the pediment of the House wing of the national Capitol. In Roosevelt's administration, the joint committee of the Senate and the House having such matters in charge wrote to the National Sculpture Society asking for ten names of sculptors best fitted to decorate this long-vacant space. As Bartlett's name headed the list, the commission was awarded to him (1909). The plaster models were finished in 1914. The work was carved in marble, in place; it was unveiled in 1916. The problem was to enrich, without disturbing architectural lines, a huge triangle generally seen from below and sidewise. Bartlett's first vision of the work took shape as "Peace Protecting the Arts," with expressive groups leading up to the central figure. His gradually evolved revision created something finer. The central figure, nine feet high, became "Democracy Protecting the Arts of Peace," which are shown on the left by foundryman, printer, textile worker, fisherman; on the right by a Lincoln-like reaper, the husbandman with his ox, the woman in her home, and an idyllic episode of a cherub with a ram. All these groups, each with its special appeal to human sympathy, are bound together in rhythmic unity. The theme is somewhat less magnificent than that chosen by Crawford for the Senate pediment, but it naturally received an ampler treatment than the earlier sculptor could command, out of the meager resources of his time. The two pediments, taken together, are an object lesson in artistic progress during two generations.

Another instance of Bartlett's mature conception of his art as related to the architect's was his so-called "Quadriga of Victory" brilliantly executed to rise above New York's Victory Arch, designed by Thomas Hastings in 1919 to honor Gen. Pershing's troops on their return from the World War. Bartlett's enthusiasm summoned to his Chariot of Victory six horses instead of the customary four. But all who were working for the arch were too busy in that hour of exaltation to be pedantic about the name of this group. It was a work of immense vigor and style, but was not made permanent, the arch itself having been destroyed. At this time Bartlett was chairman of New York's committee on war memorials. As president of the National Sculpture Society (1918), he protested to some purpose against the government's poor designs for military medals and insignia. Throughout the war, he used his gift of literary expression in both French and English, for the comfort and support of France. His war-time messages to that country are models of vigorous prose. Equally fine in literary form is his essay on *American Sculpture and French Influence upon Its Development*, an address which he delivered in Paris under the auspices of the Comité France-Amérique, expounding his theme with brilliant acumen, and with appreciation of his American fellow sculptors. This paper was translated into English, and published in the *New York Times*, Feb. 9, 1913. To academic circles in France, he already spoke with authority. He had been promoted to the grade of Officer in the Legion of Honor in 1908, and elected corresponding member of the Institute of France in 1911, the same year in which he became a member of the American Academy of Arts and Letters. Because he loved America, and desired her progress in the arts, he was always eloquent in pointing out to American students the advantage, indeed, the necessity, of study abroad. Worthy art movements here received his stanch support, while "freak schools," both here and abroad, "studios where they draw with closed eyes" and "cultivate mental aberration" had his vehemently expressed abhorrence. "One has no idea," he writes, "of the swiftness in propagation and the penetrating power of artistic sophisms, when they flatter human fatuity."

Chronologically and artistically, the central work of Bartlett's career is the bronze equestrian statue of Lafayette, in the court of the Louvre. This position in itself would have been a mark of honor to a sculptor of France, a Dubois or a Frémiet. At the turn of the century, a citizen of Chicago had conceived a plan of having American school children contribute a cent or a nickel or a dime each toward an American salute to France in the form of an equestrian statue of Lafayette, to be made by an American sculptor. Karl Bitter was approached; and Bitter, rightly feeling that such an offering ought to be the handiwork of a sculptor with French affiliations, successfully urged the obvious fitness of Bartlett. The opportunity moved Bartlett deeply, and held him long. His first sketches were approved by the architect of the Louvre, in New York, July 4, 1899, the plan being to set up the full size plaster model just a year later, in Paris, in honor of the French Exposition. Bartlett retired to the little French village of St. Leu, where, with a beautiful horse at his command, he worked in solitude and at white heat, returning to Paris to mobilize the various skilled artisans necessary to the conclusion of what was an extraordinary feat. The model when seen in the court of the Louvre was voted a success (1900), but the artist himself was not satisfied. Many months it remained in place, under his criticism. Experience had taught him the value of serene contemplation as well as fierce concentration. Starting anew, he devoted to the work every resource of his art. He made frequent changes, which, as not always happens, were of ultimate advantage. The three-cornered hat of the first study was doffed, the gay coat was exchanged for a severer habit, the action of the hand holding aloft the sword was made more decisive. A different type of horse was used, less flamboyant in movement and in caparison. Every alteration in detail was an improvement in ensemble. With head and sword and spirit uplifted, the young Marquis rides to a victory that will change the world. There is austerity and splendor in the sculpture as in the thought. In 1908, the completed bronze was set up, a signal honor to the soldier, the sculptor, and the two countries they loved. Long studied by the artist, the monument makes an instant appeal to the spectator, whether he views it from the court, or from the Louvre windows. When signing his masterpiece, Bartlett added a tortoise in playful comment. In 1920, the American Knights of Columbus presented to France a bronze replica, which was placed in the city of Metz, where Lafayette was stationed when he dedicated himself to the American cause.

Bartlett's own phrase, "as a fact and as a symbol," used by him to describe his Lafayette, applies fitly to all his statues; to his marble "Puritans" for the Capitol at Hartford, to his Robert

Morris in Philadelphia, his Benjamin Franklin in Waterbury, Conn. As facts and as symbols the citizens of Boston look upon their statues of Alexander Agassiz and of Gen. Joseph Warren. Bartlett's penetrating studies of each subject's psychology were not snap judgments. They resulted from that wise reading which implies constant sifting and choosing. On the whole, he was at his best quite as much in showing real beings whose lives were poetic, or philosophic, or patriotic, as in presenting such abstractions as Poetry, Philosophy, Patriotism. As a fact and as a symbol, therefore, the seated bronze Franklin at Waterbury, completed in 1921, suggests both by its handsome pyramidal composition and its keen characterization the firm basis of common sense from which this apostle of American liberty took his flights into the regions of science and political philosophy. As a fact and as a symbol, Robert Morris, patriot financier of the Revolution, paces his pedestal in front of the Custom House in Philadelphia, studying as of yore the fiscal weather, for which he needs his three-cornered hat, his greatcoat, and his staff. This was the last of Bartlett's statues to be placed in this country (1924).

Reviewing these works, we note that the sculptor was very lucky in one thing, namely, that he was not called upon to celebrate contemporary frock coat and trousers. He appreciated this immunity. His romanticism abhorred the prosaic, and refused to come to grips with it. Yet the poetry of man at his work appealed to him deeply, as his Capitol pediment shows. Aside from a number of portrait busts such as the Elizabeth Cady Stanton of 1887, the Walter Shirlaw owned by the National Academy of Design, and the Walter Griffin of recent date, contemporary subjects did not greatly engage him. His vein led toward the historic. His realm was heroic portraiture, imaginatively conceived, historically documented, and monumentally presented. Yet Taft devotes a page of appreciation to the "logical decorative syntheses" of fishes, sea-horses, and the like, shown in Bartlett's fountain, "The Genius of Man," a feature of the Pan-American Exposition of 1901, at which he received a gold medal. Later, in the Capitol pediment, the ox, ram, lamb, and fish, used in perfect harmony with the draped and partly draped human figures, added much to the appeal of the whole.

Honors too numerous to note followed his path. Wherever his workshop was, there was his home, whether in Washington, New York, or Paris. At the time of his death, he had a beautifully appointed studio in Washington, as well as that celebrated Paris studio and garden where in

an earlier generation the French sculptor Bartholdi had created the enormous symbolic "Liberty" now in New York harbor. Bartlett's purchase from France of this studio, and his bequest of it back to France, were in line with his ardor for French-American amity. Welcomed in Belgium, he was made an associate of the Royal Academy, and at the Liège Exposition of 1905, he received first medal. In 1913, he was chosen director of sculpture at the Glasgow School of Art, a position more honorary than arduous. His last important work was the statue of Blackstone, presented by the American Bar Association to the British Bar Association, to be placed in the Royal Law Courts, London. Never had the sculptor developed his teeming ideas with greater zest than in this tribute to British jurisprudence. A successful statue, yet a difficult one, since in less capable hands the subject's greatness might have been smothered under circumstantial wig and robe. Bartlett had also in hand at this time portrait busts of Washington and Franklin for St. Paul's Church in New York. He had just finished his Independence Pilgrimage medal, to be given to those young Americans who having worked best toward making Monticello, Jefferson's home, a shrine, had earned a trip abroad. In the spring of 1925, he came to New York, bringing a copy of the medal. With his customary friendliness, he planned in both countries for the reception, diversion, and enlightenment of those youthful summer pilgrims to France.

In the full tide of a creative power unusual at sixty years, his life was ended by an accident of the everyday kind, in appearance trivial. A misstep in the dark on a steep terrace near a friend's house in the Ardennes, a wrist slightly cut by a jagged rock, that was all. Care was taken in treating the wound, yet within a month, he died of septicæmia, in Paris. He was twice married, each time to an American woman of charm and social prominence. His first marriage took place in Paris. It proved unhappy, and was legally dissolved. In 1913, he was married in Washington to Mrs. Samuel F. Emmons. He had no children.

Fellow artists have well interpreted his personality, Charles Noel Flagg in an oil painting, Charles Grafly in a bronze bust, John Flanagan in a bas-relief. Bartlett's figure was well-knit. He carried himself gallantly, and his years lay lightly on him. His head was striking. He had abundant bright hair, scarcely touched by time; a broad, full brow; brilliant, wide-set blue eyes, with uncommonly large pupils; a ruddy, expressive countenance, the traditional Vandyke mustache and beard, and a strong aquiline nose, a harmonious variant of the type Nature often supplies to her children of genius—witness Saint-Gaudens, Rodin, Anatole France. It was the head of a dreamer, a doer, an enthusiast, a diplomat; a head with a Nordic beginning and a Gallic finish, each noble after its own kind. In short, Paul Bartlett looked what he was, an American citizen whose artistic achievement honors two republics, and is in turn honored by both. The Yankee was born, but the Commandeur was made. Frenchmen speak of him as formed by the *"solide Frémiet,"* the *"illustre Rodin,"* but what he had from these and other masters was fused and transfigured by his own spirit.

[Lorado Taft, *Am. Sculpture* (1903) and *Modern Tendencies in Sculpture* (1917); C. H. Caffin, *Am. Masters of Sculpture* (1903); *Am. Art Annual,* vol. XIV, 1917; Archives Am. Acad. Arts and Letters; Wm. Walton, *Scribner's,* July 1910, and Oct. 1913, C. N. Flagg, *Scribner's,* Mar. 1909; C. V. Wheeler, *Am. Mag. of Art,* Nov. 1925; leading article in *La Peinture,* Paris, Oct. 1923; article in *La Peinture,* 1925. Obituaries and editorials, French and American papers, notably *Le Matin* (Paris), *N. Y. Times, N. Y. Herald Tribune,* on the day following his death.]   A. A—s.

BARTLETT, SAMUEL COLCORD (Nov. 25, 1817–Nov. 16, 1898), Congregational clergyman, college president, was born in Salisbury, N. H. His father was also Samuel Colcord Bartlett, a name frequently repeated in the family, whose first American ancestor was Richard Bartlett, who came from England to Newbury, Mass., in 1635; his mother was Eleanor (Pettingill) Bartlett, also of English Puritan stock, her ancestors having come from Yorkshire in 1640. Bartlett's early education was all in the New Hampshire atmosphere. Salisbury Academy, Pinkerton Academy at Derry, and an unnamed private tutor were his teachers. He graduated with high honors at Dartmouth in 1836, and spent the next two years as principal of the Caledonia County Grammar School at Peacham, Vt. After a year as tutor in mathematics at Dartmouth, he entered Andover Theological Seminary. This was the period when Andover was the chief champion of New England Calvinism against Unitarianism; and Bartlett always acknowledged the influence on his thought of Professors Park and Stuart, who were among the most distinguished conservative scholars and theologians of that day. Licensed to preach, Apr. 12, 1843, by the Andover Congregational Association, he was ordained Aug. 2, at Monson, Mass. On Aug. 16, 1843, he was married to Laura Bradlee, of Peacham, Vt., who died Dec. 1 of that year. On May 12, 1846, he married Mary Bacon Learned, daughter of Rev. Erastus Learned and Sophia Bacon Learned, of Canterbury, Conn. In the latter year he became professor of philosophy and rhetoric at Western Re-

serve College, Hudson, Ohio, an institution which years later, as Adelbert College, became a part of the Western Reserve University, at Cleveland. He continued for five years in this position, and then returned to New England as pastor of the Franklin Street Church in Manchester, N. H. The attraction to the new fields in the West led him in 1857 to accept a call to the New England Congregational Church in Chicago, Ill. When he reached this new field, however, he was at once drafted into the work of establishing a theological institution. In 1858 he was installed as professor of biblical literature and sacred theology in the infant Chicago Theological Seminary. For nineteen years he built his life into the institution, organizing and arranging its first classes, and making his influence strongly felt in all its policies, and generally in educational and religious movements throughout the Middle West.

In 1877, when he was sixty years old, he began the work by which he will be most distinctly remembered. He was elected president of Dartmouth College; and he remained actively connected with the institution for twenty-one years, fifteen as president, and after his resignation at the age of seventy-five, for six years more, as lecturer on "The Bible and its Relations to Science and Religion." His active service as president was a period of continuous growth and progress, but not an untroubled experience. He had decided opinions and policies, and maintained them firmly and persistently. There was much discussion in faculty meetings and with trustees; but never any break. The period of great donations by multi-millionaires had not arrived; but Bartlett's administration saw an addition of $700,000 to the endowments, an increase in the faculty from twenty-one to thirty-four, of endowed chairs from one to six, numerous buildings on the campus, and the development and firm establishment of the scientific department.

Besides numerous sermons, addresses, etc., the list of Bartlett's published volumes includes the following: *The Study of God's Word in the Original Languages* (1858); *Life and Death Eternal* (1866); *Sketches of the Missions of the American Board* (1866); *Historical Sketch of the Hawaiian Mission* (1869); *Future Punishment* (1875); *From Egypt to Palestine through Sinai* (1879); *Sources of History in the Pentateuch* (1883); *Veracity of the Hexateuch* (1897); *Anniversary Addresses* (1893); and *Lectures on Universalism* (undated).

[Gabriel Campbell, "President Bartlett, Reminiscent and Otherwise," *Dartmouth Lit. Mo.,* Mar. 1899; E. J.

Bartlett, *Genealogy of the Descendants of S. C. Bartlett and Eleanor Pettingill* (1915) ; S. C. Bartlett, "How
I was Educated," *Forum,* II, 18–26 ; J. J. Dearborn,
Hist. of Salisbury, N. H. (1890) ; Levi Bartlett, *Genealogy and Biog. Sketches of the Bartlett Family* (1876) ;
obituaries in *People and Patriot* (Concord, N. H.),
Concord Evening Monitor, and *Manchester Union,* Nov.
17, 1898.]

C. N.

BARTLEY, MORDECAI (Dec. 16, 1783–
Oct. 10, 1870), governor of Ohio, was of English
descent on both sides of the family. Emigrating
from Northumberland County in 1724, his paternal grandfather settled in Loudon County, Va.
His father, Elijah Bartley, born in Virginia,
married Rachel Pearshall, an English woman,
and commenced his family life in Fayette County,
Pa. It was in this new home that Mordecai was
born. He spent his early years in hard work on
his father's farm, obtaining his schooling after
the usual fashion of country boys at that time—
in the nearest district school during the intervals
of farm labor. In 1804 he was married to Miss
Welles of Pennsylvania. He was early attracted
by the possibilities of the newer country farther
west and at the age of twenty-six went to Jefferson County, Ohio, where he settled as a farmer.
At the outbreak of the war with Great Britain
he raised a company of volunteers, of which he
was captain, subsequently serving as adjutant of
a regiment under Gen. Harrison. At the close of
the war he removed to the almost unbroken wilderness of Richland County, in the interior of the
state (1814). Mansfield, then a small settlement,
was near-by, but there were no settlers west of the
site chosen by Bartley for his new home. Opening a clearing in the forest for his dwelling and
first crops, he soon obtained a competence far
beyond that of others who followed him. He continued here for twenty years, in the meantime
establishing a mercantile house in the town of
Mansfield.

Bartley's success as farmer and merchant,
coupled with a character that won the confidence
of the community, led to his election to the Ohio
state Senate (1817). Henceforth he was to spend
many years in public life. During his term in the
Senate he was appointed by the legislature to the
position of register of the Land Office—a position which placed him in charge of the Virginia
military district school lands. His keen interest
in the advance of public education in Ohio dates
from this time. In 1823 he was elected to Congress and was reëlected for three successive
terms. At the end of his fourth term he declined
again to become a candidate. In Congress he was
affiliated with the National Republicans and became a strong supporter of President John

Quincy Adams and a warm friend of Henry
Clay. One of his few speeches in Congress was
in defense of Clay and Adams against the cor-
rupt-bargain charge. Bartley was the first to propose in Congress the conversion of the land
grants of Ohio into a permanent fund for the
support of the common schools. He secured the
earliest Federal appropriations for the improvement of the harbors of Cleveland and other
towns on the shore of Lake Erie.

Upon his retirement from Congress (1831) he
devoted his entire time to agricultural and mercantile pursuits until his election as governor of
Ohio (1844). He was elected by a small majority
over David Tod, his Democratic opponent. The
gubernatorial succession at this time was a remarkable one : Bartley, elected as a Whig, succeeded his son, Gov. Thomas Bartley, who was
a Democrat. The latter had been a candidate for
the nomination in the Democratic convention
and had lost by one vote. The elder Bartley was
sixty-one years old and the younger thirty-two.
The Mexican War occurred during Bartley's
term as governor, and he was confronted by the
difficult task of reconciling his duty as the chief
executive of the State with his own personal
opposition to the war—an opposition which was
shared by almost all the members of the Whig
party in the state. When President Polk issued
his call for troops Bartley's friends and associates strongly urged him against taking steps to
fill Ohio's quota. But he took the high ground
that the State was constitutionally bound to respect the requisitions of the national government. His message to the legislature on this point
is an able state paper. He therefore adopted
prompt measures to raise the necessary volunteers, who were organized under his personal
supervision and delivered to the United States
authorities. He declined a second nomination, although strongly urged to permit it. After his retirement he abstained entirely from public life.
But he remained a stanch and active Whig until
the disruption of that party, subsequently joining
the Republican party which he supported until
his death.

Bartley was a quiet, retiring, undemonstrative
man, who enjoyed the respect of his neighbors
and constituents, though never arousing their
enthusiasm. He was a product of the frontier,
but he did not share that section's narrow, provincial outlook. His messages as governor reveal
a broad, liberal grasp of affairs. He was unambi-
tious for political power and refused to seek
higher honors which were often within his grasp.
In his last years he was severely afflicted with
paralysis. He died at his home in Mansfield.

[The chief sources are *Register of Debates in Congress*, 1824–33; *Messages, Reports, and other Communications made to the . . . General Assembly of the State of Ohio*, 1845, 1846; and *Documents, including Messages and other Communications made to the Forty-fifth General Assembly of the State of Ohio*, 1847. There are no private letters or memoirs. A short sketch of Bartley's life appears in John S. C. Abbott, *Hist. of the State of Ohio* (1875). An account of the legislative history of Ohio during his administration as governor is found in C. B. Galbreath, *Hist. of Ohio* (1925), vol. II. An obituary appears in the *Dayton Jour.*, Oct. 13, 1870.]
C. E. C.

BARTOL, CYRUS AUGUSTUS (Apr. 30, 1813–Dec. 16, 1900), Unitarian clergyman, was a leader of religious thought and life in the city of Boston in the last half of the nineteenth century. He was born in Freeport, Me., and was educated in the schools of Portland and then at Bowdoin College, where he graduated in 1832. He studied at the Harvard Divinity School, graduating in 1835; preached for a year in Cincinnati and elsewhere; and was then called to the West Church of Boston as associate of the venerable Dr. Charles Lowell, the father of James Russell Lowell. On Mar. 1, 1837, he was ordained as Lowell's successor, and continued as the active pastor until 1889 and as pastor emeritus until his death. On Feb. 7, 1838, he was married to Elizabeth Howard.

The West Church, organized in 1737, had always been the center of liberal religious influences and patriotic enthusiasms. One of its earlier ministers, Jonathan Mayhew, had been a leader among the Revolutionary patriots, and the church had always represented a certain independency in thought and allegiance. It found its fellowship chiefly among the Unitarians, but its free pulpit offered an opportunity for the unhampered development of Bartol's talents. He was neither a controversialist nor a partisan, but he was an inspiring interpreter of life. It was said of him that "his mind was like a mint continually striking off bright coins of thought and speech" (Ames, *post*, pp. 1–2). He was a man of faith and hope and love who worshipped neither antiquity nor novelty but found the presence of God in nature, in history, and in humanity. He was one of the noteworthy circle of self-reliant and independent men and women who more or less identified themselves with the ideas and ideals of Ralph Waldo Emerson, and the Bartol home at 17 Chestnut St., Boston, was for many years the meeting place of the group of transcendental thinkers and writers who in large measure made the fame of literary Boston in the middle of the nineteenth century.

Bartol was a man of slight physique, and his delicate frame, long white hair, and searching eyes gave him a kind of elfish appearance which lent fascination to his personality. His sermons were original and radical in thought and epigrammatic in expression. He sought everywhere the evidences of enlarging truth and enfolding love. With childlike simplicity he saw the best in every man, and the world was to him a temple of the living God in which it was good to dwell. He loved the mystic aspects of religion and indulged in many an airy flight of imagination. There was, too, an unexpectedly practical side to his nature, and in his later years he proved that he could be a shrewd and successful man of business, for he made a comfortable fortune by selling land for summer residences at Manchester-by-the-Sea. He was the author of many articles, addresses, and books, of which the most important were: *Discourses on the Christian Spirit and Life* (1850); *Pictures of Europe Framed in Ideas* (1855); *Radical Problems* (1873); *The Rising Faith* (1874).

[Sketch by C. G. Ames in *Heralds of a Liberal Faith*, ed. by S. A. Eliot, III (1910), 17–22, containing complete bibliography of Bartol's publications; *West Church, Boston, Commemorative Services* (1887); *Harv. Grad. Mag.*, Mar. 1901, p. 421.]
S. A. E.

BARTON, BENJAMIN SMITH (Feb. 10, 1766–Dec. 19, 1815), physician and naturalist, was born in 1766 at Lancaster, Pa., the son of the Episcopalian rector, Thomas Barton, whose avocation was the study of botany and mineralogy. His mother, Esther (Rittenhouse) Barton, was a sister of David Rittenhouse, the astronomer. Both parents died before he was fifteen, leaving him well provided for. As a lad he attended the York Academy, a well-known classical institution, spending his spare time in the woods collecting birds, plants, and insects. After the death of his parents he moved to Philadelphia to live with an older brother, and studied literature, the sciences, and medicine at the College of Philadelphia. As a young man he was one of the survey party which defined the western boundary of Pennsylvania. At this time he met with and became interested in the American Indian and began his collection of native simples. In 1786 he went to Great Britain and studied medicine at Edinburgh and London. He became a member of the Royal Medical Society and won a Harveian prize. In London he came under the influence of the well-known physician, John Coakley Lettsom, and of Sir Joseph Banks, the naturalist. Leaving London, he went to Göttingen where he received his M.D. degree in 1789. Returning immediately to the United States, he settled in Philadelphia, where he practised medicine and taught in the College of Philadelphia, which in 1791 was incorporated with the University. In 1790 he was appointed professor of natural history and botany, later he was transferred to materia medica, and on the death of Benjamin Rush in 1813 he succeeded that worthy in the chair of theory and practise of medicine.

He was never robust and his naturally delicate constitution was impaired by his habits of work. He realized this himself, for he wrote of "the pernicious consequences of his midnight and injurious toils." As an adult he suffered from gout and he finally succumbed to pulmonary tuberculosis in 1815, aged forty-nine. He had married, in 1797, a daughter of Edward Pennington, of Philadelphia, and had two children, one of whom, Thomas Pennant Barton, was a collector of Shakespeariana. There is an excellent picture of Barton in an article by G. F. Butler in the *American Journal of Clinical Medicine,* XVIII, 43. It is a profile and shows clear-cut features said to resemble those of Goethe, with a rather long nose of the Roman type, a well-shaped head, and a firm chin. Barton's chief medical work is his *Collections for an Essay Towards a Materia Medica of the United States* (pt. I, 1798, pt. II, 1804), a systematic treatise on the medicinal plants of the country. It contains lists and descriptions of the various plants, much of the material being based on original investigation. The wide scope of Barton's interests is shown in his non-medical writings, namely, in his *Memoir concerning the Fascinating Faculty which has been ascribed to the Rattlesnake and other American Serpents* (1796), his *New Views of the Origin of the Tribes and Nations of America* (1797), his *Fragments of the Natural History of Pennsylvania* (1799), and his *Elements of Botany* (1803), the first elementary botany written by an American, and in his contributions to the *Transactions of the American Philosophical Society* and to the *Philadelphia Medical and Physical Journal,* which he founded in 1805 and edited until it was abandoned three years later. One finds in this journal articles by him on such diverse subjects as the earthquakes of North America, the anthropology of the Indians, the food of the humming bird, the torpid state of the North American alligator, etc. His writings show that he was more interested in matter than in manner. His style was casual and careless, and it is stated that he was not particularly impressive as a lecturer. He was enthusiastic and perhaps a little over-credulous, particularly as regards the virtues of vegetable remedies. In his articles on natural history, however, he exhibited a proper degree of scientific caution.

[Wm. P. C. Barton, *A Biog. Sketch of Prof. Barton* (1816), containing full bibliography of his writings, and "An Account of the Life of B. S. Barton" in the *Port Folio,* Apr. 1816; Howard A. Kelly, *Some Am. Medic. Botanists* (1914); John W. Harshberger, *The Botanists of Phila. and Their Work* (1899); J. Thacher, *Am. Medic. Biog.,* vol. I (1828); Alex. Harris, *Biog. Hist. of Lancaster County* (1872).]   G. B.

BARTON, CLARA (Dec. 25, 1821–Apr. 12, 1912), philanthropist, was named by her parents Clarissa Harlowe. Her father, Stephen, a descendant of Edward Barton who came to Salem, Mass., from England in 1640, was a typical New England farmer, upright and intelligent, hard-working, devoted to his family, able and willing to take his turn as selectman and representative in the legislature. His wife, Sarah Stone, thirteen years younger, and married at seventeen, was the faithful New England housewife and mother, endowed with practical common sense, a strong will, and a quick temper. Their home was in Oxford, Mass., and here their children were born. During the first seven years of their union they had two boys and two girls. No other children came to them until ten years later when Clara was born.

Among the circumstances of her early days which affected her subsequent career was the fact that, owing to her late arrival, she was the only child in the home. Having no playmates, she was left much to her own devices. Her brothers and sisters took her education in hand, and perhaps spoiled her a little. She grew up to be a rather wilful woman, unable to act as a subordinate gracefully or to coöperate easily. Had she received more of the discipline playmates give each other, she might have been saved trouble and humiliation. Her father, who had served in the Indian wars under Mad Anthony Wayne, gave her instruction in army lore, so that when she was thrust into war conditions she was, she declared, far less a stranger there than most women, or even men. For two years her brother David was an invalid. Day and night she was his nurse, leaving him but one half day during that period. Afterward he gave her instruction in handling tools, tying knots, and similar practical accomplishments, which, together with the skill in nursing she had acquired, were of much use to her later. Although supersensitive, shy, and easily thrown into a panic of fear, she had plenty of courage for such adventuresome undertakings as crossing a river on teetering logs, and riding partly broken colts. Her sensitiveness and shyness so troubled her mother that she consulted Lorenzo N. Fowler, the phrenologist, who was lecturing in Oxford and staying at the Bartons'. "Throw responsibility upon her," was his advice. "As soon as her age will permit, give her a school to teach." This counsel was followed, and at fifteen she began an eighteen-year period of teaching.

In spite of her youth and inexperience, she was successful from the start. Furthermore, she acquired self-confidence and initiative. After conducting several district schools, she went to North Oxford where her brothers had a mill, planned a schoolhouse there, and for ten years superintended the education of the children and operatives. Feeling the need of more education herself, in 1851 she went to Clinton, N. Y., for a course in the Liberal Institute, at the completion of which she accepted an invitation to teach at Bordentown, N. J. Here she did a piece of work in connection with which she displayed the characteristics which determined her whole career—quick and practical response to an immediate need, delight in directing a difficult enterprise, aggressive independence, persistence, courage, and intense nervous energy. Free public schools were rare in New Jersey at that time. In Bordentown the pupils paid fees which constituted the teacher's salary. Disturbed by the large number of children running the streets, Miss Barton offered to serve three months without pay if the town would make the school free to all. In the face of the strongest opposition, she persuaded the committee to try the experiment. It was so successful that soon a more commodious schoolhouse had to be built, and an assistant teacher employed. Presently opposition to a woman's being in charge of so large a school arose, and a male principal was appointed. To be second in command was never to Clara Barton's taste. She resigned, and her career as a teacher closed.

There followed a period of nervous exhaustion and in 1854 she went to Washington to recuperate. Through the influence of the representative from her home district, Col. Alexander De Witt, employment was soon secured for her in the Patent Office, and she made Washington her permanent home. Her war service began in April 1861, with the arrival at the Capital of the Sixth Massachusetts Regiment. It had had to fight its way through Baltimore and many of the men had lost their baggage. Clara Barton was most energetic in supplying their needs. After the battle of Bull Run, she was greatly impressed by the stories she heard regarding the suffering on the field, due in part to lack of supplies. With characteristic independence, she advertised in the *Worcester Spy* for provisions for the wounded. They came pouring in, and she established a distributing agency. Realizing that it was during battles that supplies and ministration were most needed, in July 1862 she succeeded in getting

Surgeon-General Hammond's permission "to go upon the sick transports in any direction, for the purpose of distributing comforts for the sick and wounded, and nursing them," and orders from Generals Wadsworth and Pope affording her transportation for supplies and passage through the lines (see copies of official records in W. E. Barton's *Life of Clara Barton*, I, 164–66). During the remainder of the year, with Washington as her base, she rendered heroic service in getting her supplies to the front, distributing them, and ministering personally to the wounded during action. In 1863 she carried on her particular form of work in the operations about Charleston, S. C. The next year after the battle of the Wilderness she was at Fredericksburg, and later with the Army of the James where, under the authority of Surgeon McCormack and Gen. Butler, she acted as superintendent of nurses.

As a war-worker Clara Barton was never associated with the Sanitary Commission, or any other organization. Except possibly for a short time when she was with Gen. Butler's command, she never had any official connection with the army. At the opening of the war she recognized a need, devised a plan for meeting it, and carried it out on her own lines; but it never became anything but her own personal enterprise. Then, as later, she preferred to direct things herself, disliked being under any one's authority, and was by nature incapable of functioning as a related member of a great body. She showed courage, endurance, and resourcefulness on the battlefield, and gave sympathetic aid to many, but in no higher degree probably than did others less known. She was not primarily a hospital nurse. Her particular service was that of securing supplies for the relief of suffering, and getting to a place of great need with them promptly.

For four years after the war, under the authority of the government, Miss Barton superintended a search for missing soldiers. She also delivered lectures on her war experiences. Her health failing, in September 1869 she went abroad for rest. Soon she was in the midst of war again. With the outbreak of the Franco-Prussian conflict, she became associated with the International Red Cross of Geneva, and distributed relief in Strassburg, Paris, Lyons, Belfort, and Montpellier. Characteristically enough, while at Strassburg she devised a plan of her own for aiding destitute women, by which they were to work and be paid for what they did, wrote to Count Bismarck about it, and obtained official recognition of that type of relief. Later, she introduced it at Lyons, and established a workroom, similar to one she had established in Strassburg. In 1873 she returned home, with the Iron Cross of Merit, presented by the Emperor and Empress of Germany, and the Gold Cross of Remembrance, presented by the Grand Duke and Duchess of Baden.

From her experiences abroad resulted the great and chief service of her career, the establishment of the American Red Cross. Due principally to its traditional policy to hold aloof from European alliances, the United States had not been a party to the Geneva Convention, which made the Red Cross possible, when it was drawn up and signed in 1864, although the Government was informally represented at the congress. In 1866, however, Rev. Henry W. Bellows, with others who had been active in the Sanitary Commission, founded the American Association for the Relief of Misery on the Battlefields. It was the first Red Cross organization in this country and its object was to secure the Government's approval of the Geneva treaty, but it was unable to arouse public interest and went out of existence in 1871. It remained for Miss Barton to accomplish what it had failed to do. She had heard of the Red Cross, apparently for the first time in Geneva, where certain of its officials called upon her to inquire why the United States did not enter the compact. This interview led her to study the history of the organization, and later she saw its workings practically exemplified. Upon her return to this country, she was for a long time a nervous invalid, and in 1876 in search of health she went to Dansville, N. Y., which place she made her residence for some years, living first at a sanatorium, and subsequently in a home of her own which she purchased. All the while the need of the Red Cross in this country was on her mind, and in 1877 she wrote to Dr. Louis Appia, one of the Swiss representatives of the society who had called upon her in Geneva, asking if any effort on her part to establish the Red Cross in the United States would be acceptable, and saying that while she was far from desiring the position, if he had no one else in mind, she would be willing to head the enterprise (see correspondence with Dr. Appia printed in Barton's *Life*, II, 121–39). In his reply he said, "I do not see any inconvenience that you should be for America the *head of the Order, the active working head*," and gave her instructions how to proceed. Monsieur Moynier, president of the International Red Cross Committee, sent her a letter to President Hayes, informing him of Miss Barton's appointment, and requesting that the United States come into the international agreement. As had been her way in previous undertakings, she attempted and carried through this enterprise practically single-handed. She began a campaign of education, personally visiting heads of the State and War Departments, members of the bar, and influential congressmen. In 1878 she published a pamphlet addressed to the people of the United States and the members of Congress on *The Red Cross of the Geneva Convention, What It Is*. She presented Monsieur Moynier's letter to President Hayes, who referred her to the State Department, which took the position that the original decision regarding entering the alliance made in Secretary Seward's day was final. Her efforts with the next administration were more successful, however, and May 20, 1881, Secretary Blaine wrote her a letter, stating that President Garfield would undoubtedly recommend the adoption of the treaty. The following day a meeting was held at which a National Society of the Red Cross was organized, and it was later incorporated. At a subsequent meeting Miss Barton was elected president, though she had tried to get President Garfield to accept that office. The latter was assassinated before he could recommend the adoption of the Geneva Convention, but President Arthur and Secretary Blaine secured its confirmation by the Senate in March 1882. After a four years' struggle an American Red Cross had been established, and it was largely Miss Barton's personal achievement.

For the next twenty-three years she was engaged in directing the activities of the organization, though for a few months in 1883, at the solicitation of Gov. Benjamin Butler who had observed her work in the war, she acted as superintendent of the Woman's Reformatory Prison at Sherborn, Mass. The relief work which the Red Cross carried on during the numerous calamities of this period, she supervised, in most instances personally visiting the fields, even going to Turkey after the Armenian massacres in 1896, and though more than seventy years old, sailing for Cuba with a cargo of supplies for the *reconcentrados* in 1898. At the time of the Galveston flood, when she was seventy-nine, she spent six weeks on the scene. She represented the United States at International Conferences at Geneva in 1884, Carlsruhe (1887), Vienna (1897), and St. Petersburg (1902). At the first of these she caused the introduction of the "American Amendment," which stipulated that when extraordinary calamities occur in times of peace the Red Cross engage in humanitarian work analogous to the duties devolving upon it in periods of war.

While Miss Barton had the abilities which fitted her to bring about the establishment of the Red Cross in this country, she was not so well qualified to direct and develop such an institution.

Her tendency to keep things in her own hands instead of delegating responsibility, her arbitrariness, and her disinclination to seek the best advice available, were not conducive to the most satisfactory management, or to the building up of a great national society. As a result, down to 1905, it had few members and little organization. Furthermore, she seems to have lacked an adequate sense of the society's accountability to the general public, and she failed to devise such a system of accounting as would safeguard herself and preclude the possibility of embarrassing questions. Public confidence in the society therefore weakened, as is evinced by the fact that at the time of the Galveston disaster, only $17,341 of the $1,300,000 contributed for relief was intrusted to the Red Cross. The demand that there should be a reorganization of the financial and business management became insistent, and in 1900 the American Red Cross was reincorporated by act of Congress, the charter requiring that a financial report should be made annually. Dissensions soon arose in the society over Miss Barton's habit of acting in important matters without consulting the executive committee, the fact that in times of disaster a large part of the contributions went to her instead of passing through the hands of the treasurer, and the methods she employed in meetings of the society to achieve her purposes. Finally a minority of the members presented a memorial to Congress, setting forth the unsatisfactory conditions existing in the Red Cross. Miss Barton proceeded to fight to retain her control, and had the "Remonstrants" suspended from the society, though later, for the "harmonizing of existing conditions" she offered to reinstate them. They replied that the real cause of the division in the organization "lay in the method of administration and the personal character of its business management," and suggested a full and thorough investigation. At the annual meeting of the society in 1904, Mr. Richard Olney was asked to appoint a committee to investigate "all matters and differences between the minority and majority members of this corporation," and a committee of three, of which Senator Redfield Proctor was chairman, was named. It held hearings Apr. 12, Apr. 16, and May 2, 1904, and a Treasury expert was employed to audit the books. After the third meeting the investigation was abruptly dropped. The committee never presented a report, and the stenographic records of the testimony introduced by the "Remonstrants" establish nothing more than poor business methods on Miss Barton's part. On June 16, 1904, she resigned, making possible the complete reorganization of the society. She was much embittered by what she considered her ill-treatment, and for a time entertained a wild idea of going to Mexico to organize the Red Cross there, but was dissuaded by her friends from undertaking the enterprise, although she already had packed her things. The remaining years of her life she spent at Glen Echo, just outside of Washington. Here she died in her ninety-first year, and her body was taken back to Oxford for burial.

Clara Barton was a little woman, five feet tall, of slight build, erect carriage, and an air of resolution and strength. She had an expressive face, with prominent nose and large mouth, brown eyes and abundant hair of the same color. Capable of great endurance and hard work under excitement, she was subject during the first half of her life to periods of nervous prostration. She had the New Englander's religious proclivities, and was brought up in the Universalist Church, but was never a church member. For a time she was interested in Christian Science, but she did not adopt it. She had a good mind, kept herself well informed on current affairs, wrote in a clear and interesting style, and was successful as a public speaker. Her early self-consciousness she never wholly overcame, and she was always sensitive to criticism. Unquestionably she enjoyed prominence and leadership. Sincerely patriotic and philanthropic, she was not a reformer in the common acceptance of the term. She did not try to bring conditions into accord with preconceived ideals, but when she saw a practical need, she gave every ounce of her strength to remedying it. Her initiative, inflexible will, tenacity of purpose, and devotion to human welfare, lifted her out of the obscurity of a country farm where she had had few advantages and enabled her to do a great work which gave her a world-wide reputation.

Besides numerous pamphlets she published *History of the Red Cross* (1882); *Report: America's Relief Expedition to Asia Minor under the Red Cross* (1896); *The Red Cross: a History of This Remarkable International Movement in the Interest of Humanity* (1898), subsequently republished as *The Red Cross in Peace and War*; *A Story of the Red Cross* (1904); *Story of My Childhood* (1907).

[This biography is based on documentary material furnished by the American Red Cross including the stenographic records of the 1904 investigation; Miss Barton's *Story of My Childhood;* Wm. E. Barton, *Life of Clara Barton* (1922); P. H. Epler, *Life of Clara Barton* (1915); and Mabel T. Boardman, *Under the Red Cross Flag* (1915).]
H. E. S.

BARTON, JOHN RHEA (April 1794–Jan. 1, 1871), surgeon, was born at Lancaster, Pa., son of Judge William and Elizabeth (Rhea) Barton, nephew of Dr. Benjamin Smith Barton [*q.v.*], and younger brother of Dr. W. P. C. Barton [*q.v.*]. After serving as an apprentice at the Pennsylvania Hospital while attending the Medical School of the University of Pennsylvania, he received his M.D. degree in 1818 at the age of twenty-four. From 1820 to 1822 he acted as surgeon to the Philadelphia Hospital, and in 1823 he was appointed on the surgical staff of the Pennsylvania Hospital. Here he was probably greatly stimulated in his work by the then senior member of the surgical staff, Philip Syng Physick. On Nov. 22, 1826, Barton performed a very remarkable and pioneer operation at this hospital on a case of anchylosis of the hip-joint. By a wedge-shaped incision into the femur he was not only able to straighten a badly placed bone, but also to make an artificial joint at the point of incision which remained useful and in good position for over five years. The operation was done, it is recorded, in seven minutes and "not one blood vessel had to be secured." Barton was assisted by Drs. Hewson and Parrish. In 1837, he reported a similar case, although in his second operation he did not attempt to make an artificial joint. In addition to these two important orthopædic procedures, Barton is also remembered on account of his description of fracture of the lower end of the radius, his bran dressings for fractures of the leg, and for "Barton's bandage," to immobilize fractured jaws. He wired a fractured patella as early as 1834. Only two important papers were published by him: "On the Treatment of Anchylosis, by the Formation of Artificial Joints," *North American Medical and Surgical Journal*, 1827, III, 279–92, and "A New Treatment in a Case of Anchylosis," *American Journal of Medical Science*, 1837, XXI, 332. He retired from practise in 1840 and died in Philadelphia on New Year's Day, 1871, in his seventy-seventh year. His widow, Susan (Ridgway) Barton, as a memorial to her distinguished husband gave $50,000 to the University of Pennsylvania to establish a chair in the principles and practise of surgery in the Medical School.

[*Medical Times*, 1870–71, I, 163; Arthur Keith, *Menders of the Maimed* (1919), p. 173; Alexander Harris, *Biog. Hist. of Lancaster County* (1872), p. 38; *Phila. Pub. Ledger*, Jan. 4, 1871.]

H. R. V.

BARTON, ROBERT THOMAS (Nov. 24, 1842–Jan. 17, 1917), lawyer, author, was descended from English ancestors who had settled in Ireland in the seventeenth century. The Rev. Thomas Barton of Monaghan, a Church of England minister and graduate of Trinity College, Dublin, emigrated in 1751 and became rector of St. James's Church, Lancaster, Pa. His grandson, David W. Barton, a lawyer and scholar, married Fannie L. Jones and resided in Winchester, Va., where their son, Robert Thomas Barton, was born. He received a good education, attending Winchester and Bloomfield Academies in Albemarle County, Va., and commenced the study of law, but on the outbreak of the Civil War, he joined the Confederate army, enlisting as a private in Company F, 2nd Virginia Infantry. Five of his brothers also served, three of whom were killed. On the termination of the war he resumed his legal studies and was admitted to the bar in 1865. He opened an office in his home town, Winchester, and practised there for more than fifty years. Inheriting from his father a keen legal instinct, which he fortified with wide study, he soon acquired a substantial practise. He became known as an authority on the practise of the courts, more particularly on the Chancery side, and wrote two manuals, *Law Practice* (1877) and *Chancery Practice* (1881), both of which were received with favor by the profession. In 1883 he was elected a member of the House of Delegates for one term. Although he was more interested in his profession than in politics, he was always to the fore in local and municipal affairs, serving at one time as mayor of Winchester. In 1893 he became president of the Virginia State Bar Association. In 1894 he was nominated for the position of judge of the supreme court of Virginia, but was not elected. His later years were occupied in extensive explorations of the unpublished public papers and records of the colony, as a result of which he prepared *Virginia Colonial Decisions: The Reports by Sir John Randolph and by Edward Barradall of Decisions of the General Court of Virginia 1728–1741*, which was published in two volumes in 1909. These reports of decisions of the highest court of the chief English colony had been preserved only in manuscript form inaccessible to the profession and the public alike. He prefaced the reports with an erudite Introduction, giving a "perspective sketch of the contemporaneous conditions during the times of the decisions, with some account of the writers of them and of the lawyers who practised at the Bar of the General Court of that day." He was also the author of a number of articles and addresses, mostly on historical subjects. He was twice married: on Feb. 19, 1868, to Katie K. Knight of Cecil County, Md.; and on June 10, 1890, to Gertrude W. Baker of Winchester.

[An appreciative sketch of Barton's life will be found in *Va. State Bar Ass. Report*, 1917–18, p. 91. Interesting details appear also in *The Story of Winchester in Va.* (1925), by Oren Frederic Morton.]

H. W. H. K.

BARTON, SETH MAXWELL (Sept. 8, 1829–Apr. 11, 1900), Confederate soldier, the son of Thomas Bowerbank Barton, was born at Fredericksburg, Va. Although he was less than sixteen years old when he was admitted as a cadet at West Point, he was more mature mentally than most of his classmates. As often happens, however, his superiority in this respect did not manifest itself in high scholastic standing. As a classmate (Gen. Holabird) tactfully phrases it, "he was fond of reading and gave more attention to the pursuit of general knowledge than to the specific requirements of the course"; and he graduated, in 1849, somewhat below the middle of the class. He was commissioned in the infantry and first assigned to duty at Governors Island, New York Harbor, but went to New Mexico the next year and was at frontier stations during the remainder of his service in the army. In 1853 he was promoted to first liutenant, and in 1857 to captain. He was in action against hostile Comanches in 1857. On June 11, 1861, he resigned his commission, and went from Fort Leavenworth, Kan., to offer his services to his native state. He was appointed a captain of infantry in the regular army of the Confederate States, but in July 1861 was made lieutenant-colonel of the 3rd Arkansas, and joined his regiment. For the next few months he served in West Virginia and the Shenandoah Valley. He was present at the engagements at Cheat Mountain and the Greenbrier River. In the absence of an engineer officer, he designed the defensive works on the Greenbrier, and acted as Jackson's chief engineer in the valley district through the winter. His nomination as brigadier-general was sent to the Confederate Senate in January 1862, withdrawn a few days later, and renewed in March. His brigade was a part of Kirby Smith's command in East Tennessee until December, when he joined the forces at Vicksburg. He took part in the fighting at Chickasaw Bayou, Chickasaw Bluffs, and Champion's Hill, and in the siege of Vicksburg. He was paroled with the other prisoners taken when the city was surrendered, July 4, 1863, and was exchanged a few days later. Assigned to Pickett's division, to command the brigade which had been Armistead's until his death at Gettysburg, Barton joined it in North Carolina, where the division was recruiting and reorganizing. In its operations against Newbern, in January 1864, Pickett alleged want of coöperation on Barton's part. His handling of his brigade was again severely criticized, during the operations south of Richmond in May, and he was summarily relieved from command by his immediate superior, Gen. Ransom. In spite of his earnest request for a court of inquiry, and strong expressions of confidence presented by his regimental commanders in writing, he remained unemployed until the autumn of 1864, when he was assigned to a brigade in the defenses of Richmond. In January 1865 his brigade became a part of G. W. C. Lee's division, with which he served until captured at Sailor's Creek (Apr. 6). A few days later, while confined at Fort Warren, he joined with other eminent prisoners there in indorsement of Gen. Ewell's letter to Gen. Grant, expressing their "feelings of unqualified abhorrence and indignation" at the assassination of President Lincoln (*Official Records*, XLVI, pt. 3, p. 787). With his release from Fort Warren in July 1865, he disappears from history. He died at Washington, and was buried in Arlington Cemetery.

[G. W. Cullum, *Biog. Reg.* (3rd ed. 1891), II, 391; *Confed. Mil. Hist.* (1899), III, 579–81; S. B. Holabird, in *Bull. Ass. Grads. U. S. Mil. Acad.*, 1900, pp. 138–40; *Official Records*, ser. 1, vols. X (pts. 1, 2), XVI (pt. 2), XVII (pt. 1), XXIV (pts. 1, 2, 3), XXIX (pt. 2), XXXIII, XXXVI (pts. 2, 3), XLVI (pt. 2), LI (pt. 2); unpublished Confederate records in the War Department.]

T. M. S.

BARTON, THOMAS PENNANT (1803–Apr. 5, 1869), diplomat, bibliophile, was born in Philadelphia, the only son of Dr. Benjamin Smith Barton [*q.v.*] and Mary Pennington, a daughter of Edward Pennington, of Quaker stock. He was named for the Welsh naturalist, Thomas Pennant, a correspondent of his father, was educated in Philadelphia, and, after the death of his father in 1815, went to France, where he remained for a considerable period. In April 1833 he married Cora Livingston, daughter of the Hon. Edward Livingston [*q.v.*]. When Livingston was sent as minister to France for the purpose of securing a settlement in 1833 of the French Spoliation Claims, Barton accompanied him as secretary of legation. His knowledge of French, and the charm of Mrs. Barton made his life in Paris socially brilliant. Political conditions caused the path of negotiations to be thorny, and in May 1835 Livingston demanded his passports, leaving Barton behind as chargé d'affaires. The Chamber of Deputies finally voted to pay the claims, but attached such conditions, that, acting under instructions, Barton in turn asked for his passports and sailed for home, landing in New York early in January 1836. His duty completed by rendering a report to the government, he retired with his father-in-law to the beautiful family estate, Montgomery Place, near Barrytown on the Hudson.

He devoted himself to forming an arboretum and to collecting the great library which still bears his name and which was his controlling interest for more than thirty years. Most of it was left in his winter house, 8 West Twenty-second St., New York City. He had collected books when a young man, and while in Paris was already devoting special attention to the English drama. He formed close relations with scholarly booksellers in Europe, and became a connoisseur of fine bindings. By 1860 his library already contained 16,000 volumes, and was widely known as one of the great private libraries of the country. Barton was the first important American collector of Shakespeare, of whose works he possessed all the folio editions, and eighteen quartos published before 1623; but his library was also rich in other departments, especially in original editions of Elizabethan authors and in all branches of French literature. Barton was an exact bibliographer, and left elaborate catalogues in his own handwriting, showing the most minute pains in preparation. He loved his books, and no one else was ever permitted to dust them even in his later days when he was a sufferer from gout. He directed that on his death the collection should be kept intact until its sale to some public institution. His widow disposed of the whole to the Public Library of the City of Boston for $34,000; her death occurred two days after the delivery of the books was completed. A catalogue of them was published in 1888. Barton was a man of great refinement, high character, and fastidious taste. A miniature of him, painted in Paris in 1835 by Étienne Bouchardy, shows a young man of marked elegance, mild in expression, with a face framed in handsome brown hair and beard.

[Louise L. Hunt, *Memoir of Mrs. Edward Livingston* (1886); Chas. H. Hunt, *Life of Edward Livingston* (1864); Jas. Wynne, *Private Libraries of N. Y.* (1860), pp. 59–96; *Bull. Boston Pub. Lib.*, July–Sept. 1921 (with portr.); *Ibid.*, Dec. 1927; letters from Miss Julia Barton Hunt, Summit, N.J.]
F. H. C.

BARTON, WILLIAM (May 26, 1748–Oct. 22, 1831), Revolutionary soldier, the son of Benjamin and Lydia Barton, was born at Warren, R. I. When twenty-two years of age he married Rhoda Carver, daughter of Joseph Carver of Bridgewater, Mass. He was a hatter by trade. At the beginning of the Revolutionary War he enlisted, was soon a captain, and on Aug. 19, 1776 became major of Rhode Island troops.

The circumstances under which he sprang into national fame were these: the English commander, Brig.-Gen. Prescott, occupied the island of Rhode Island in December 1776. He held arbitrary rule at Newport, quartered his force largely in farmhouses, laid waste the neighborhood,

and exacted contributions. Personally he was ill-tempered, insolent, and contemptuous of Americans. In a previous campaign he had ill-treated Ethan Allen, had been taken prisoner and exchanged for Gen. Sullivan. It occurred to Barton that the recapture of Prescott would serve to procure the release of Gen. Charles Lee, something which seemed very desirable, since Barton shared the prevailing delusion of Lee's loyalty and military importance. Admitting few into his confidence, Barton planned his route and the details of the capture. The men, forty-one in all, were carefully selected, though the entire regiment had volunteered. The force started in boats from Tiverton, on the night of July 4, touched at Bristol, and proceeded thence to Warwick Neck on the mainland. From there, with muffled oars it crossed Narragansett Bay, skirting Prudence Island, and on the night of July 9 landed on the western shore of Rhode Island itself. The house which Prescott occupied with a small body of troops was a mile inland. Barton's party silenced the sentinel, broke into the house, and captured the English general. He was conducted safely to Warwick, sent to the state authorities in Providence, treated apparently with courtesy, and in due time exchanged. He was soon promoted to major-general, but did not escape lampoons and criticisms in the English press, due to the humiliating features of his capture.

Barton returned to Tiverton, and was promoted on Nov. 10, 1777, to the rank of lieutenant-colonel. His achievement, regarded as a most gallant act, had greatly helped morale in a time of especial need. He received a vote of thanks from the Rhode Island General Assembly, and from Congress a resolution of thanks and the gift of a sword. He served through the war, and was wounded in the British retreat from Warren in 1778. In 1787 when his state declined to send delegates to the Federal convention, Barton joined with others in a letter to the convention, pledging support (I. B. Richman, *Rhode Island,* 1905, pp. 250–51). Naturally therefore, he was a member of the state convention in 1790 which adopted the Federal Constitution. In later life he was unfortunate. Having bought (or obtained by grant from Congress) a tract of land in Vermont, he refused to pay a judgment upon it, and was detained as a prisoner for fourteen years, kept in a kind of honorable captivity in the inn at Danville, Vt. On the occasion of Lafayette's famous semi-centennial visit to America in 1824–25 he learned of Barton's plight and paid the claim, thus setting Barton free. The old soldier returned to Rhode Island, and died in Providence.

[Barton's account of his exploit, in MS., is in possession of the R. I. Hist. Soc. See "Life" by Catharine R. Williams in *Biog. of Rev. Heroes* (1839), and especially J. Lewis Diman, *The Capture of Gen. Rich. Prescott by Lt.-Col. Wm. Barton* (1877).]　　　　E. K. A.

BARTON, WILLIAM PAUL CRILLON (Nov. 17, 1786–Feb. 29, 1856), botanist, teacher, and naval surgeon, came of a distinguished scientific and professional family. His father, Judge William Barton, was a well-known Pennsylvania lawyer; his mother was Elizabeth (Rhea) Barton, and his uncle was the botanist and physician, Benjamin Smith Barton [*q.v.*], while his grandfather, the Rev. Thomas Barton, had married Esther Rittenhouse, sister of David Rittenhouse [*q.v.*], the celebrated pioneer mathematician and astronomer. W. P. C. Barton grew up in the scholastic atmosphere of what was then the nation's intellectual capital. He received a classical education at Princeton, and his lectures and writings bear the stamp of training in the humanities. Graduating in 1805 with distinction, he studied medicine under his uncle, Dr. B. S. Barton, at the University of Pennsylvania, and upon the recommendation of the celebrated Drs. Physick and Rush, he was in 1809 appointed surgeon in the navy, serving on active duty with the frigates *United States, Essex, Brandywine* and in the naval hospitals, then called marine hospitals, at Philadelphia, Norfolk, and Pensacola. He acquitted himself of his medical duties with unusual distinction; although he was severely criticized for declining sea-duty in wartime (1813), it was Commodore Decatur who urged Barton, then in bad health, not to go on active duty. In 1815 Barton was chosen professor of botany at the University of Pennsylvania, charming many by his light-hearted herborizing expeditions along the Schuykill and by his lectures which were, contrary to the bookish times, demonstrated in his well-stocked conservatories. A court martial faced him in 1818, instigated by rival surgeons of the navy, on charges of conduct unbecoming an officer and a gentleman. Specifically, he was charged with having criticized the marine hospital organization and having intrigued for preferment in his post. The first charge was undeniable, but apparently the court felt that grounds for criticism of the unsanitary hospitals of the day were justified; the second charge was also true in a sense; Barton's correspondence evidences continual remonstrances and petitions to be changed to this or that place or to be excused from this or that duty. President Monroe was cited as a witness for the defense. The court dismissed the case with a mild reproof to Barton.

For three years he was instructor in materia medica at the Jefferson Medical School, an organization which arose from the ashes of an earlier institution which Barton had largely instigated as an insurgent movement against the conservative medical spirit of the day. In 1842 he was ordered by the Navy Department to Washington and became the first of the chiefs of the Bureau of Medicine and Surgery. His tenure of this office was marked by rigid economy and an attempt at radical reforms in the sanitation and temperance of the navy. This won the enmity of many regular navy men and gave rival surgeons an opportunity to attack him, so that in 1844 he resigned the post in the belief that jealousy and intrigue were leagued against him. He was succeeded by his former friend and chief rival, Surgeon Thomas Harris. Barton was retained upon the navy's inactive list, so that in 1852 he was president of the Board of Medical Examiners, and at the time of his death was buried in Philadelphia with full military honors.

As a botanist, Barton was systematic and accurate; for the most part he contented himself with works of limited scope: *Flora Philadelphicæ Prodromus* (1815); *Compendium Floræ Philadelphicæ* (1824); *Syllabus of Lectures . . . on Vegetable Materia Medica* (1819)—all essentially catalogues and compilations. But his *Vegetable Materia Medica of the United States* (1817–19) is an excellent account of our medicinal plants, while his *Flora of North America* (1821–23), magnificently illustrated by his wife, is, if not as complete as its title might imply, at least a fine piece of popularization of the work of earlier systematists.

Barton's political diatribes, the outgrowth of his controversies in the navy, are marked by a style that appears now as merely quaint classical ornamentation, but was then considered rhetorical grandeur. In 1828 he issued his fruitless *Polemical Remonstrance against the Project of Creating the New Office of Surgeon General to the Navy,* wherein it chiefly appears that Barton was jealous of the new office. His *Hints for Naval Officers Cruising in the West Indies* (1830) contains many literary references and moral admonitions, with remarks on gambling and temperance. Nevertheless, this book and his report on marine hospitals were, according to Pleadwell, the first signs of a modern medical view of sanitation and provision for the sick in the history of the navy. Barton in early life (September 1814) married Esther Sergeant, a granddaughter of his distinguished grand-uncle, David Rittenhouse. He was noted for witty conversation, caustic comment, and a love of the classics and music.

[*William Paul Crillon Barton—A Pioneer in American Naval Medicine*, an extended monograph by Capt. Frank Pleadwell, appeared in the *Mil. Surgeon*, XLVI, 241–81; it is primarily an account of Barton's medical and official work, with extended quotations from his letters and from an unpublished memoir in the possession of the family. For an account of his botanical career see J. W. Harshberger, *Botanists of Philadelphia* (1899).]

                                    D. C. P.

BARTRAM, JOHN (Mar. 23, 1699–Sept. 22, 1777), first native American botanist, was, in the opinion of Linnæus, the greatest contemporary "natural botanist" in the world. His great-grandfather, Richard Bartram, who traced his family to the Norman invaders, lived in Derbyshire, England; his grandfather, John Bartram, left England in 1682 and settled near Darby in Delaware County, Pa., where Bartram's father, William, and his mother, Elizabeth Hunt, continued to live. Bartram's ancestors for three generations belonged to the Society of Friends, and the stamp of the Quaker was evident in his life and character. It is true that toward the latter part of his life his co-religionists "read him out of meeting." The reason for this action was probably merely that as Bartram had learned more of the world and science he had found it difficult to remain as orthodox as his brethren.

He was born at Marple, near Darby, and from the first, in his hardy life as a farm boy, he was struck by the soft charm of the low country south of Philadelphia. There is a pretty story of him, related in a letter from an imaginary Iwan Alexiowitz (*Letters from an American Farmer*, 1782, by St. Jean de Crèvecœur) in which Bartram is made to say that his attention was first attracted to botany when he overturned a daisy with his plow and fell to musing upon the symmetry of its structure. Desirous of learning more about plants, he went, so the story goes, to Philadelphia and purchased such books as he needed, and in this way, despite the persuasions of his wife, who thought he was wasting time, he taught himself the gentle science. The story has been quoted by J. W. Harshberger and by William Darlington. Bartram's son, William, in his sketch of his father says that his father stated that from the age of ten he had had a passion for botany (which is borne out by John Bartram's letters to Collinson), and that being interested also in medicine, his attention turned naturally to healing plants. His systematic study of them was probably first encouraged by James Logan, founder of the Loganian Library, who got him Parkinson's *Herbal,* and it is fairly certain that Bartram went to a tutor in order to acquire the Latin necessary to read Linnæus. He brought to his favorite subject a mind keen to learn yet essentially untutored and never given to bookishness. He had no desire to amass an herbarium or describe new species in formal systematic style. From the outset he was a lover of living plants, a gatherer and distributer of them.

Perhaps to improve his prospects as a husbandman, perhaps in order to found a Botanic Garden, Bartram in 1728 purchased a plot of land at Kingsessing, three miles from Philadelphia, on the banks of the Schuylkill. Here he laid out his Garden and began what were probably the first experiments in hybridizing in America. Here too he erected one of the four stone houses which he built with his own hands, carving over its door a pious inscription in faulty Greek.

Bartram's celebrated correspondence with Peter Collinson, the English plantsman, began at an uncertain date, probably about 1733 (Youmans, p. 27), and forms a delightful chapter in the history of American horticulture. The two Quaker botanists never met, but their letters are marked by an informality and a racy loquacity; the success and failure of every bulb and cutting is discussed, and as the letters were accompanied by a constant interchange of American plants from Bartram and English plants from Collinson, the epistles constitute a very fair historical source book of the first introductions of many plants now famous as exotics in the two countries (for a list of the American plants which England owes to Bartram, see R. H. Fox, *Dr. John Fothergill and His Friends*, 1919, pp. 163–65). Bartram's plants found their way, through Collinson, into the celebrated greenhouses of Dr. Fothergill and Lord Petre, and soon Bartram was illustrious in Europe, corresponding with Linnæus and his patron the Queen of Sweden, with Dillenius of Oxford, Gronovius of Holland, who had published John Clayton's *Flora Virginica* (1762), and with Philip Miller, the great herbalist and gardener of Chelsea. In America, Bartram soon became the admiration of Linnæus's friends and correspondents, John Clayton and John Mitchill of Virginia, Gov. Cadwallader Colden of New York, and Dr. Alexander Garden of Charleston. Benjamin Franklin and George Washington came often to Bartram's garden to rest and philosophize. The fictitious letter from a Russian gentleman, previously alluded to, has value in giving a picturesque thumbnail sketch of the simple farmer who entertained these great men, and others like André Michaux and Peter Kalm, one of Linnæus's favorite students, who made a pilgrimage to his door. Each one he received with the utmost cordiality and simplicity and with no embarrassment either at high estate or learning.

In search of wider and fresher fields, Bartram made many journeys, at his own expense, to the frontiers, traveling generally alone, for he complains that few Americans showed any interest in science or in nature for itself. He traveled usually in autumn in order to gather ripe seeds and roots and bulbs in proper condition for transplanting. His first trip was a brief five weeks' journey to Williamsburg, Va. (1738), and thence up the James and across the Blue Ridge, 1,100 miles in all. In 1751 he published his best journal, *Observations on the Inhabitants, Climate, Soil, etc.... made by John Bartram in his travels from Pensilvania to ... Lake Ontario*. He explored the Catskills with his son, William, in 1755, and in 1760 visited the Carolinas. During his journey to Pittsburgh, then a frontier fort, in 1761 he met with Indians, one of whom snatched the hat from Bartram's head "in a great passion, and chawed it all round . . .," which Bartram took to be a cannibalistic threat, so that in the French and Indian wars of the next years, Friend though he was, he said that the only way to deal with Indians was to "bang them stoutly" (Youmans, p. 34). In 1765, through Collinson's intervention, Bartram was appointed to the post of Botanist to the King (George III), with a stipend of fifty pounds a year. In royal service, then, he immediately set sail for Charleston, whence he journeyed by land through Georgia to St. Augustine and traveled on foot to Picatola, where he obtained a canoe for the exploration of the San Juan (St. John's) River. Nothing missed Bartram's eye—tree, flower, fruit, bird, fish, or mineral, and as he went he prepared a map of the river's course and depths, shoals, and currents. As an example of the value of Bartram's narrative as a source book (*Description of East Florida, with a Journal by John Bartram,* William Stork, London, 1769), there is his description of the royal palm, not known to him by account or by name. Bartram, characteristically, did not publish his discovery as a new species, but contented himself with a delineation of this great tree so unmistakable that no botanist has failed to recognize it. Bartram's discovery of the royal palm where he found it is illustrative of his intuition for unusual discoveries, for that species is not now known except at the extreme southern tip of Florida, the famous outlying colony found by Bartram having been destroyed by a great cold wave in the 1830's.

Bartram gave his attention to other matters besides botany, collecting shells, birds, insects, fishes, and turtles for his English friends, and setting his son to draw them. But a certain tender-heartedness and piety always inhibited his zoological activities.

Geology, too, and the science of the soil fired his imagination, and contrary to the beliefs of his time, he conceived limestones and marbles to have been formed as geologists now believe they were. In a letter to Garden he proposed that extensive borings be made in order to construct a map of the underlying rocks of the country—the first hint of the task later undertaken by the Geological Survey. He seems to have been the first to propose a great western survey trip and suggested this idea to Franklin, who in turn interested Thomas Jefferson in it. Jefferson's instructions to Lewis and Clark bear a strong resemblance to Bartram's suggestions to Franklin.

Bartram's stand against slavery was forthright in an age when abolition was unpopular. He freed his slaves, who remained his paid servants; and like a Saxon lord of old surrounded by his vassals, Bartram always had his negroes at his table, whether alone or entertaining his most distinguished guests.

Bartram was twice married: in January 1723, to Mary Morris, who bore him two sons, and, after her death in 1727, to Ann Mendenhall in September 1729, who gave birth to five boys and four girls. One, William, became in his turn a distinguished botanist. In appearance John Bartram is described by his son as "rather above the middle size, and upright. His visage was long and his countenance expressive of a degree of dignity with a happy mixture of animation and sensibility." No portrait of him exists, the one published in the *Gardener's Monthly* in 1860 being fictitious.

Bartram's Garden was studied by André Michaux, Nuttall, and other celebrated naturalists during its tenancy by his sons John and William. When, much enlarged by William's additions, it passed through mortgage into the Eastwick family it still remained in interested hands, and for a time the well-known editor and botanist, Thomas Meehan, was its caretaker. A period of neglect followed, but it was saved by the efforts of C. S. Sargent of the Arnold Arboretum, and others, and now forms part of Philadelphia's small park system and remains the oldest shrine to botanists in America. Many giant trees known to have been planted by Bartram's hand are still to be seen there.

Bartram's name in science is commemorated by *Bartramia,* a genus of mosses.

[Bartram's life has never been written in detail, despite rich materials; only brief articles have been devoted to him, the best authority being that of his son William, in *Phila. Med. and Phys. Jour.,* Nov. 13, 1804.

The sketch in Wm. Darlington's *Memorials of John Bartram and Humphrey Marshall* (1849) is not wholly accurate, but has immense value as a collection of Bartram's celebrated correspondence with Collinson. Bartram's correspondence with other naturalists might still be assembled but has not yet been. W. J. Youmans's chapter on the two Bartrams in his *Pioneers of Science in America* (1896, pp. 24–39) is more trustworthy than J. W. Harshberger's account of him in *Botanists of Phila. and Their Work* (1899), though the latter contains much of interest about Bartram's houses, gardens, and horticultural remains. A detailed study could best be made from Bartram's own letters and from his various journals and itineraries. Howard Pyle wrote and illustrated a charming article on Bartram's Garden in *Harper's Mag.*, LX, 321–30.]

D. C. P.

BARTRAM, WILLIAM (Feb. 9, 1739–July 22, 1823), traveler and naturalist, was a son of the noted botanist, John Bartram, and his second wife Ann Mendenhall (for ancestry see John Bartram). "Billy," the "Flower-hunter" (Puc-puggy) of the Seminole Indians, was born and reared in the house of stone erected by John with his own hands in his Botanic Garden (the first in North America) at Kingsessing, on the Schuylkill River, now a part of Philadelphia. The boy early displayed great talent for drawing natural objects. Benjamin Franklin offered to teach him printing, and then suggested for him the trade of engraver; but at eighteen William was placed with a Philadelphia merchant named Child. After four years he tried to settle as an independent trader at Cape Fear, N. C. In 1765–66 he accompanied his father in exploring the St. John's River, which they ascended for almost 400 miles (see the father's *Journal,* appended to Wm. Stork's *Description of East Florida,* 3rd ed., 1769). Nothing will now do with "Billy" (1766), "but he will be a planter upon St. John's River"; yet the next year he is again near his birthplace, merely working on a farm. His father's friend, the English naturalist Peter Collinson, had before his death in 1768 shown drawings by William—"elegant performances" —to the Duchess of Portland, and to Dr. John Fothergill, a botanist and a Friend, who soon extended his patronage to the young American. At Fothergill's expense, Bartram spent the years 1773–77 in exploring the southeastern part of the United States. In return, Fothergill was to have seeds, specimens, and drawings; journals and exquisite drawings, some colored, ultimately reached England, but, in that time of war, probably few parcels of seeds or specimens. Bartram made his way back to Pennsylvania in January 1778. In 1782 he was elected professor of botany in the University of Pennsylvania, but declined the position for reasons of health. In 1786 he became a member of the American Philosophical Society, which Franklin had organized as early

as 1743, with John Bartram as an original member.

In 1791 Bartram published at Philadelphia his fascinating *Travels through North and South Carolina, Georgia, East and West Florida, the Cherokee Country, the Extensive Territories of the Muscogulges, or Creek Confederacy, and the Country of the Chactaws*. This work was the chief cause of his fame, being republished in London, Philadelphia, and Dublin, and translated into German by Zimmermann, 1793, into Dutch by Pasteur, 1797, and into French by Benoist, 1799. The literary influence of Bartram's *Travels* would furnish meat for a dissertation. The volume fell into the hands of Chateaubriand, Coleridge, Wordsworth, and many another, with happy results to be seen in *Atala, Kubla Khan,* and *Ruth.* Bartram's varied knowledge was at the service of all who applied to him; he corresponded with naturalists abroad, and was honored with membership in foreign learned societies. To B. S. Barton he probably gave the *Observations on the Creek and Cherokee Indians* (1789) which were brought to light by Squier in 1853 (in *Transactions of the American Ethnological Society,* III, 81). His manuscript *Pharmacopœia* of 89 pages (see below) may well have been useful to the same Barton, who repeatedly cites Bartram in *Collections for an Essay towards a Materia Medica of the United States* (part I, 1798, reprinted, 1900). Most of the plates in Barton's *Elements of Botany* (1803) were engraved from drawings by Bartram, and this work is otherwise indebted to his investigations. Barton "loved him for the happiest union of moral integrity with original genius and unaspiring science." William Bartram contributed a biographical sketch of his father to the first volume of Barton's *Philadelphia Medical and Physical Journal,* as well as two articles on birds, "Anecdotes of an American Crow" (in part I, 1805, pp. 89–95; excerpted in William Nicholson's *Journal of Natural Philosophy,* XIII, 1805, pp. 194–98), and "Description of an American Species of Certhia, or Creeper" (in part II, 1805, pp. 103–6). Another of his fugitive writings was an "Account of the Species, Hybrids, and other Varieties of the Vine of North America" (*New York Medical Repository,* I, 1804, 19–24). His list of 215 native species of birds (in the *Travels,* 1791) was the most complete one before that of Alexander Wilson, whom he inspired to the production of the *American Ornithology* (1808–14). "Bartram's Sandpiper" (the upland plover) was so named by Wilson for his benefactor. Portions of a diary he kept at intervals from 1802 to 1822 have been published by

Witmer Stone ("Bird Migration Records of William Bartram," in the *Auk*, XXX, 325–58). He doubtless had a hand in the periodical *Catalogue* of the Botanic Garden, of which an extant copy is dated 1807, but which is said to have been issued annually from 1801 (or earlier).

Bartram was short in stature; his health, never robust, was even; he girt himself from neck to foot in leather when he worked. He was shy but affectionate, his countenance refined and intellectual. He shared his father's enthusiastic Deism, but, unlike him, did not leave the Society of Friends.

His father had died in 1777, and the Botanic Garden passed to William's brother, John, who subsequently took William into partnership with him. After John died in 1812, the Garden belonged to John's daughter, Mrs. Ann Carr, with whom the unmarried William continued to reside until the end. Death came suddenly and kindly to the aged botanist, from a ruptured blood-vessel in the lungs; he had just finished writing the description of a plant, and was stepping out for a stroll in his beloved Garden.

[No adequate biography of William Bartram exists. The chief printed sources of information concerning him are his *Travels*, and Wm. Darlington's *Memorials of John Bartram and Humphrey Marshall* (1849). Research is needed in the Bartram Memorial Lib. at the Univ. of Pa.; in the collection of the Hist. Soc. of Pa., where there are four large manuscript volumes of Bartram papers (see the first volume in particular), two smaller manuscript volumes of portions of his *Travels*, one volume of his letters and papers, 1761–62, his manuscript *Pharmacopœia*, and answers in his handwriting to queries about Indians in J. H. Paine's *Commonplacebook*; in the lib. of the Acad. of Natural Sciences, Phila., where Bartram's manuscript Diary ("Calendar of Natural Hist., Memorable Events, etc.") reposes; and in the archives of the Am. Philosophical Soc., of which at least four of the Bartram family were members before 1787. For the Diary, see W. Stone, as above, and J. H. L. in the *Gardener's Monthly*, May 1869. Two small volumes of Bartram's Journals, in his handwriting, are in the Lib. of the British Museum Herbarium; on this and other points, see R. Hingston Fox, *Dr. John Fothergill and His Friends* (1919), pp. 185–91. Some of his drawings, including several colored ones, are in the botanical collections of the South Kensington Museum, London. There is a good sketch of Bartram's life (with portr.) by G. S. Morris in *Cassinia, Proc. Del. Valley Ornithological Club*, No. 10 (Phila., 1906–7, pp. 1–9). The sketch in J. W. Harshberger's *Botanists of Phila. and Their Work* (1899) is negligible. On the Botanic Garden, see E. O. Abbot, *Bartram's Garden* (illus.), issued by the John Bartram Ass. (1904, reissued 1907, 1915); and John M. Macfarlane in *Univ. Lectures*, by the Univ. of Pa. Faculty, VII, 263–85. For Bartram's relations with Wilson, see *Supp. to the Am. Ornithology*, by Alexander Wilson (1825), containing a life of Wilson by George Ord. For the literary position and influence of Bartram, see E. H. Coleridge in *Trans. Royal Soc. of Lit.*, XXVII (1906), 69–92; Lane Cooper, in *Methods and Aims in the Study of Lit.* (1915), pp. 110–25, and in the *Cambridge Hist. of Am. Lit.*, I (1917), 194–98; J. Bédier, *Études Critiques* (1903), pp. 196–294; G. Chinard, *L'Exotisme Américain dans l'Œuvre de Chateaubriand* (1918) and in *Univ. of Cal. Publications in Modern Philology*, VII, 201–64.]   L. C.

BARUCH, SIMON (July 29, 1840–June 3, 1921), physician, the son of Bernard and Teresa (Green) Baruch, was born in Schwersen, which up to 1918 was included in the German Empire and is now part of Poland. His early education was received in the Gymnasium of his native town; but he emigrated to America before completing his studies and continued his professional training in Charleston, S. C., and at the Medical College of Virginia. At the age of twenty-two he received his M.D. degree and immediately joined the Confederate Army with the rank of assistant surgeon. During the next three years he saw much active service. At the close of the war, he settled in Camden, S. C., and there practised medicine until 1881, when he moved to New York. He came prominently before the profession and the public in 1888, when he insisted upon an immediate operation in a case which he had diagnosed as appendicitis. The successful outcome of this operation—said to have been the first of its kind in America—led to a treatment of appendicitis which has saved innumerable lives. Baruch was, however, perhaps best known as the leading exponent of hydrotherapy, a subject largely developed by Winternitz in Vienna. Two of Baruch's books, *The Uses of Water in Modern Medicine* (1892), and *The Principles and Practice of Hydrotherapy* (1898) as well as his introduction into this country of the Brand treatment of typhoid fever by means of full baths, attest his deep interest in and extensive knowledge of the subject. Official recognition of his services to medicine came when he was appointed professor of hydrotherapy at the College of Physicians and Surgeons, Columbia University.

The transition from a physician to a public-spirited citizen and philanthropist was in his case a very natural one; for, being interested in the uses of water in medicine, he turned his attention to the importance of free cleansing baths; and largely through his efforts what is claimed to have been the first public bath in America was opened in Rivington St., New York City, in 1901. Since then more than 100 free municipal bath-houses have been established throughout the country. It was this interest in hydrotherapy which led to Baruch's appointment as a member of the Saratoga Commission, when New York State purchased and restored the Saratoga Mineral Springs. The value of his services may be gauged by the report of the chairman of the Commission, George Foster Peabody: "Without compensation, Dr. Baruch devoted months of his time in making observations at the European Spas and brought to the Commission a complete guide to the building up of Saratoga as a cure."

Baruch was deeply attached to the United States. Even as late as 1917, when this country entered the World War, he wrote: "If I did not stand ready to consecrate heart and soul and all that I possessed to the defense of my adopted country, I would despise myself as a scoundrel and a perjurer and regard myself as an ingrate to the Government that has, for sixty years, enhanced and protected my life, honor and happiness." On Nov. 27, 1867, he married Isabel Wolfe, of Winnsboro, S. C., a descendant of an old American family.

[Irving A. Watson, *Physicians and Surgeons of America* (1896), pp. 534–35 ; Wm. B. Atkinson, *Physicians and Surgeons of the U. S.* (1878), p. 164 ; *N.Y. Times,* June 4, 1921 ; personal information from H. B. Baruch, M.D.]

B.H.

BARZYŃSKI, VINCENT (Sept. 20, 1838–May 2, 1899), Catholic priest, born at Sulisławice near Sandomierz, Poland, was the son of Joseph Barzyński and Mary Sroczyńska. His earlier education was private. He began his studies for the priesthood at the diocesan seminary of Lublin in 1856. He was ordained in 1861. He was engaged in active ministry at Tómaszów when the Polish insurrection broke out in 1863. Owing to his aiding the revolutionists he was obliged to flee after the collapse of the uprising. After a sojourn of more than a year in Austria he went to Paris in 1865. There he met Fathers Semenenko and Kajsiewicz, the founders of the new Congregation of the Resurrection, who invited him to join them. He became a member in Rome. About this time the bishop of Galveston, Tex., was in search of priests for the recent Polish settlements in his diocese. The superior of the Congregation agreed to send him a few priests. Thus Barzyński, in the company of Fathers Bakanowski and Zwiardowski came to Texas in 1866.

Here he labored strenuously, attending the religious needs of the poor Polish farmers, until he was called to Chicago in 1874. He became pastor of the church of St. Stanislaus Kostka, the first Polish congregation in Chicago. He now began the busiest and most constructive period of his career. His work among the ever increasing Polish immigrants in Chicago was beset with many difficulties. He was obliged to contend with the liberal and irreligious elements among the laity as well as with the ill will of many of the Polish clergy. The clergy opposed to him effected his recall by his superiors in Europe. He expressed his willingness to leave, but pleaded to be permitted to extricate his parish from its financial straits. Hence he was allowed to continue his work in Chicago. During his in-

cumbency the large St. Stanislaus Church was erected, and also the largest parochial school in the city. His activities increased with the growing population. It became imperative repeatedly to divide his parish and to organize new ones. He organized more large parishes among the Poles than any other priest in the United States. Despite the founding of new congregations his own grew by leaps and bounds, so that during his lifetime its membership exceeded 50,000.

The labors of Barzyński were not confined to his own parish. He was instrumental in founding an orphanage, establishing Polish newspapers, and introducing and organizing the teaching sisterhoods. He was very active in establishing religious confraternities in his congregation as well as mutual benefit societies. He became the recognized spiritual guide and leader of the Poles in the city of Chicago. Owing to his indomitable energy a writer in a German paper (*Illinois Staatszeitung,* Jan. 20, 1879) compared him to Gregory VII. In January 1899 he suffered an attack of pneumonia. He recovered, but his forces were spent; he fell ill again and died in the Alexian Brothers Hospital. He was buried in St. Adalbert's Polish Cemetery in Chicago.

[Wacław Kruszka, *Historya Polska w Ameryce* (1905) ; Sanisław Siatka, *Krótkie Wspomnienie o Życiu i Działalności Ks. M. Wincentego Barzyńskiego* (1901), portr. ; *Cath. Encyc.,* XVI, 7–8. A brief notice of his death appeared in the *Daily Inter-Ocean,* Chicago, May 4, 1899.]

J.J.R.

BASCOM, HENRY BIDLEMAN (May 27, 1796–Sept. 8, 1850), college president and Methodist bishop, was born at Hancock, N. Y., the son of Alpheus Bascom of French Huguenot stock and Hannah (Houk) Bascom of German ancestry. His parents were very poor, and it was only by the assistance of his mother's brother, after whom he was named, that he was enabled to attend school from his sixth to his twelfth year, at which time his education ended, so far as schools and teachers were concerned. His father moved to Little Valley in western New York in 1808, and it was while residing here that young Henry was converted and joined the Methodist Church at fifteen years of age. In 1812 the family moved to Maysville, Ky., on the southern bank of the Ohio River, but after only a short residence there they moved to the north side of the river and settled permanently in Brown County, Ohio. At an early age Bascom manifested unusual gifts for public speaking and leadership. He was given license to preach when he was only seventeen and the presiding elder immediately appointed him assistant to the pastor of the Brush Creek Circuit in bounds of which the country home of the Bascoms was located. When the Ohio Annual Conference met on Sept. 1, 1813, Bascom was one of the ten young ministers "admitted on trial." The Methodist Circuits of those days embraced as a rule from twenty to thirty preaching places, each of which had preaching once a month. After spending three years on circuits in the Ohio Conference he was transferred to the Tennessee Conference (which at that time had within its bounds a considerable portion of Kentucky) and was appointed two years in succession to Danville, Ky., followed by two years at Louisville. When the Kentucky Annual Conference was organized in 1820, and took over the Kentucky territory then held by the Tennessee Conference, he became a member of the newly established conference, but after preaching for two years on large circuits, he was transferred back to the Ohio Conference and was put in charge for that year of the Brush Creek Circuit where he had begun his ministry nine years before. While pastor at Steubenville, Ohio, in 1823, he was, on the nomination of Henry Clay, elected chaplain to the Congress of the United States. During and following his residence in Washington, 1824–26, he traveled extensively and preached in Maryland, Virginia, and Pennsylvania, making a profound impression by his oratory and drawing vast crowds wherever he went. He was next stationed for a short time at Pittsburgh and later at Uniontown, Pa.; the seat of a newly organized Methodist school called Madison College, of which he was president from 1827 to 1829. He was agent for the American Colonization Society, 1829–31, during which time he traveled far and wide, pleading eloquently for the objects to be accomplished by that society. In 1832 he was elected professor of moral science in Augusta College, Ky., and was thereupon transferred from the Pittsburgh to the Kentucky Conference. Ten years later he was selected for the presidency of Transylvania University at Lexington, Ky., which office he filled from 1842 until 1849, dividing his time after 1846, between duties in this university and his work on the new *Southern Methodist Quarterly Review* to the editorship of which he was elected by the General Conference of 1846.

In the meantime, he had taken an active part in the trying struggle between the Northern and Southern delegates in the General Conference of 1844 over slavery, the outcome of which was the division of the Church. It was he who wrote, at the request of his fellow delegates from the South, the "Protest" of the southern representatives against the action of that Conference with reference to Bishop Andrew of Georgia, exclud-

ing him from the exercise of his episcopal office because his wife was a slaveholder. In the "Convention" that met at Louisville, in 1845, to consider and perfect the method and plans for the organization of the Southern Church he wrote the able report of the committee to whom this important matter was referred. These and other state papers showed that he was not only American Methodism's foremost pulpit orator, but one of her greatest ecclesiastical statesmen. In addition to his election as editor of the *Quarterly Review,* the General Conference of 1846 had made him chairman of the commission charged with arranging and settling with representatives of the Methodist Episcopal [Northern] Church all matters relating to, and growing out of, the division of the church. At the meeting of the second General Conference of the Methodist Episcopal Church, South, held in St. Louis in May 1850, when it was decided that only one new bishop was needed, he was elected on the second ballot by a large majority. He lived to preside over only one Annual Conference, the St. Louis, which met at Independence, Mo., on July 10, only six weeks after his ordination as bishop. Returning to his home at Lexington, Ky., he was taken ill in Louisville, where he died.

All his life Bascom was hampered and embarrassed by poverty, having early gone in debt to help support his father and family, who were always in financial straits. During one of the early years of his ministry he traveled 5,000 miles, preached 400 times, and received for the year's service only $12.10! His salary at the institutions which he served as professor or president was inadequate to his necessities. This in part accounts for his postponement of all thought of matrimony until late in life. On Mar. 7, 1839, when he was nearly forty-three years of age, he was married to Miss Van Antwerp of New York City, by whom he had two children.

Bascom possessed the elements that go to make a great orator. Whenever and wherever he preached, he easily and powerfully swayed vast audiences, but his type of oratory, though well suited to impress the typical American of seventy-five or a hundred years ago, would doubtless be accounted too florid, rhetorical, and emotional to impress in an equal degree an audience of the present day. His published works were: *Methodism and Slavery* (1847); two volumes of *Sermons* (1849), of which 20,000 copies were sold; *Works* in four volumes, published posthumously (1855).

[M. M. Henkle, *Life of Bascom* (1856); H. H. Kavanaugh, "Memoir" in Vol. I of the bound copies of *Gen. Minutes of M. E. Ch., South,* pp. 811–15; H. N. Mc-

Tyeire, *Hist. of Methodism* (1884), pp. 655–58; Gross Alexander, *Hist. of the M. E. Ch., South* (1894), pp. 60–61; W. B. Sprague, *Annals of the Am. Pulpit* (1857–69), VII, 534–40; *Southern Meth. Quart. Rev.* for 1850 and 1852.]
                                                    W.F.T.

BASCOM, JOHN (May 1, 1827–Oct. 2, 1911), philosopher, college president, was born at Genoa, N. Y., under three unlucky omens. He was "the son of a minister, the youngest child, the only son" (Bascom, *Things Learned by Living*, p. 18). While he was still an infant, his father, the Rev. John Bascom, died; his mother, Laura (Woodbridge) Bascom, was left in straitened circumstances. Both parents were of New England descent and strict Puritanical principles. The shadow of genteel poverty which hung over Bascom's early life was further darkened by what he later called the "perverse theory" of Calvinism, whose intensity of moral idealism nevertheless remained the most striking note of his own character. The energy of an older sister provided for his education as well as that of herself and two other sisters. He attended Williams College, where he distinguished himself in mathematics and not at all in the languages. After graduation in 1849, he taught for a year in Hoosick Falls, N. Y., and then studied law for eight months in a lawyer's office. He was repelled by the conventionality, moral compromises, and personal interests involved in legalism. "My nature called me to crucifixion, but the law would have been to me crucifixion by a rabble of bad boys" (*Ibid.*, p. 52). In search of crucifixion, he entered Auburn Theological Seminary in 1851. There he was profoundly influenced by Laurens Hickok [*q.v.*], professor of theology, and one of the ablest philosophers of his time.

In 1852 he accepted a position as tutor in rhetoric and oratory at Williams, where, according to the custom of the college, the young instructor was badgered by the students and made as unhappy as possible. In the same year he married Abbie Burt, who died two years later. In 1854 he attended Andover Theological Seminary but returned to Williams in 1855 as professor of rhetoric and oratory. In 1856 he married Emma Curtiss. Bascom's vacillation between the careers of clergyman and educator was now over. Yet for the nineteen years during which he remained at Williams his college work was largely distasteful to him. He was not particularly interested in either oratory or rhetoric. He lessened to some extent the drudgery of composition courses, however, by the introduction of æsthetics and English literature, subjects which were then rarely taught. He also solaced himself by the publication of numerous magazine articles and four text-books: *Political Economy* (1859), written before Bascom's faith in technical political economy had been weakened by knowledge of the broader field of sociology; *Æsthetics or the Science of Beauty* (1862), founded on Kames and Campbell; *Philosophy of Rhetoric* (1866), an endeavor to base the rules of rhetoric upon laws of thought; *Principles of Psychology* (1869), revised as *The Science of Mind* (1881), a strict exposition of rational psychology, founded mainly upon Hickok. He also delivered two courses of Lowell Lectures, published as *Science, Philosophy, and Religion* (1871) and *Philosophy of English Literature* (1874).

In 1874 Bascom was offered the presidency of the University of Wisconsin. "As I despaired," he writes, "of a favorable change of work at Williams, and found that my growing freedom of religious thought was making my presence less agreeable to the college, I accepted the invitation" (*Ibid.*, p. 60). The University of Wisconsin was then hardly more than a large academy. There were only 407 students and but eighteen faculty members; there was only one recitation building, with a solitary laboratory stowed away in the basement. Worst of all, there was no definite educational program or subordination of departments. Yet the institution was already on a good foundation; the establishment of a millage tax in 1876 soon assured it a small but steadily increasing income; the faculty was above the average in ability; the students, though rough and undisciplined, were eager. Bascom's incumbency, like that of Angell at Michigan, was notable for internal rather than external improvement. Only a few more buildings were added, the enrolment was increased by only one hundred, but the entire spirit of the place was changed. Bascom left it, at the end of his thirteen years of office, an effective educational institution, organized about the college of liberal arts as its center.

At first he was far from popular. His sharp New England features, challenging eyes, and reserved manner accorded ill with the indiscriminating cordiality of the West. Gradually, however, his underlying kindliness came to be appreciated, while his firmness won him general respect. He assumed direct supervision of disciplinary matters and by a union of reasonableness and determination succeeded in imparting a sense of discipline to the students themselves. All the members of the senior class came under his immediate instruction in philosophy, and for Bascom philosophy was essentially the vision of a rational life. Resisting the vocational appeals of the day, he made the campus a home of liberal culture. He impressed his personality upon both students and faculty, few of whom failed to acknowledge educational indebtedness to him. In his relations with the regents he was less fortunate. In American state universities, then as now, "Rarely, indeed, was any man granted the position of Regent who had any special knowledge of the methods of education, or interest in them" (*Things Learned by Living*, p. 70). The most important figure among the regents at Wisconsin toward the end of Bascom's term was Edwin W. Keyes, the Republican political boss of the state. The friction between this gentleman and Bascom, due to entire difference of outlook, was accentuated by Bascom's advocacy of prohibition which was at that time an unpopular measure in Wisconsin. By 1887, Bascom writes, "I felt it wise to resign rather than to expose myself to those accidents which might make resignation compulsory" (*Ibid.*, p. 74). He returned to Williamstown, and soon was in a condition of poverty, owing to unfortunate financial investments. Hence he accepted a subordinate position as lecturer on sociology at Williams College, where in 1891 he became professor of political science. In 1903 he resigned in order to devote his entire time to writing and public service. He became president of the Williamstown Improvement Society and was active in the establishment of a state reservation and park on Mount Greylock. He died in 1911.

Bascom was a facile and copious writer. The partial bibliography in his *Things Learned by Living* (1913) lists 178 titles, of which twenty refer to books. Of these the most important were *Philosophy of Religion* (1876), *Ethics or Science of Duty* (1879), *Natural Theology* (1880), *Problems in Philosophy* (1885), *The New Theology* (1891), *Historical Interpretation of Philosophy* (1893), *Evolution and Religion* (1897). In these philosophical works he remained to the end essentially a disciple of Laurens Hickok. He adopted the epistemological dualism of Hickok's "Conservative Realism," and like his master he stressed the *a priori* principles of the mind so far as to be on the verge of idealism. At the same time he made more concessions to empirical fact, particularly in the realm of ethics, than Hickok's dogmatic rationalism permitted. He was much interested in harmonizing theology with evolutionary science, and in its main conclusions his philosophy belonged to the most liberal form of Christian apologetics. His writing possessed unusual clarity and stylistic charm. It exercised little influence, however, upon the development of American philosophic thought.

[Bascom's spiritual autobiography, *Things Learned by Living* (1913), is the primary source. For his career at the Univ. of Wis., see *Memorial Service in Honor of John Bascom* (1911), containing addresses by Van Hise, Birge, et al.; J. F. A. Pyre, *Wisconsin* (1920); and R. G. Thwaites, *Hist. of the Univ. of Wis.* (1900). His philosophy is eulogistically expounded by Sanford Robinson, *John Bascom, Prophet* (1922).]

E.S.B.

BASHFORD, COLES (Jan. 24, 1816–Apr. 25, 1878), first Republican governor of Wisconsin, was born of native stock in eastern New York, and emigrated up-state, where he established himself in law and became district attorney of Wayne County in 1847. He moved to Oshkosh shortly after the admission of Wisconsin, entered politics as a Whig, and deserted the Whigs to assist in organizing the Republican party. Nominated for governor in 1855, and apparently defeated by his Democratic opponent, William A. Barstow [*q.v.*], he succeeded, after the latter had assumed office, in proving fraudulent election returns, and was himself awarded the office by the supreme court of the state, Mar. 24, 1856 (*The Trial in the Supreme Court . . . of Coles Bashford vs. Wm. A. Barstow*, 1856). The railroad land grant offered by Congress to Wisconsin in 1856 made necessary a special session of the legislature for its disposition, and occasioned the most spectacular jobbery in the history of the state. The promoters of the La Crosse and Milwaukee Railroad, who lobbied for and won the grant, donated their securities to a majority of the legislature, and rewarded Gov. Bashford with $50,000 (nominal value) of their bonds. In the administration of his successor, a storm of exposure, made more intense by the financial depression of 1857, broke upon the state. Ex-Gov. Bashford removed to Washington, whence he soon departed to the new territory of Arizona, which was created in 1863. Here he filled the offices of attorney-general, councillor and president of the legislative council, territorial delegate, and secretary. He died in Prescott in 1878, survived by his wife, Frances (Foreman) Bashford.

[Material upon the critical point of Bashford's career exists in *Report of the Joint Select Committee, Appointed to Investigate into Alleged Frauds and Corruption in the Disposition of the Land Grant by the Legislature of 1856* (Madison, 1858). P. V. Lawson has a sketch of his life in *Oshkosh Northwestern*, Feb. 8, 1908.]

F.L.P.

BASHFORD, JAMES WHITFORD (May 29, 1849–Mar. 18, 1919), college president, Methodist bishop and missionary, was the son of Samuel Morris Bashford, a physician and Methodist preacher, and Mary Ann McKee, of a distinguished Virginia, Illinois, and Kentucky family. Born at Fayette, Wis., Bashford was prepared for college in a school opened at Fayette by

Parkinson, later professor of mathematics in the University of Wisconsin. He received the degrees of A.B. from that university in 1873, B.D. from the School of Theology of Boston University in 1876, and Ph.D. from the same university in 1881. He was much influenced by the personality and sermons of Phillips Brooks. In 1878 he married Jane M., daughter of W. W. Field of Madison, Wis. His churches were: Harrison Square, Boston, 1875, First, Jamaica Plain, 1878, Auburndale, 1881, Chestnut Street, Portland, Me., 1884, and Delaware Avenue, Buffalo, N. Y., 1887. He was offered the presidency of eleven colleges while pastor at Buffalo and accepted the last, that of Ohio Wesleyan University, where he remained from 1889 to 1904. In May 1904 he was elected a bishop with designation of his field or "area" (not diocese in the usual sense) as China. Here the main work of Bashford's life was done. He brought to it enthusiasm, intelligence, unselfish devotion, and common sense. He became a master in things Chinese; he cultivated friendship with missionaries of other churches, with foreign diplomats, with Chinese statesmen and leaders. He interested himself in China's political development. He personally urged President Taft in 1912 to recognize the Chinese Republic. He was opposed to the adoption of Christianity as a state religion, or even to the official setting apart of Sunday as a day of rest. When Japan presented secretly and with request for immediate acceptance her Twenty-one Demands on China in January 1915, Bashford secured a copy, studied it carefully, and in March wrote two letters, one to Secretary Bryan, the other to President Wilson, in which he sought to arouse the American government to the gravity of the situation (for full text see Grose, *Bashford,* pp. 142–54). In that same spring he was asked by the Board of Missions to return to America. He went immediately to see the Secretary and the President. While his dealings with the Japanese had been always frank, kind, and statesmanlike, Bashford was opposed to the Japanese militaristic policy, as to all militarism. Besides numerous articles in periodicals (see "Prophecy" in the *Methodist Review,* May 1902, and especially "Wesley's Conversion" in the same, September 1903), Bashford published *Wesley and Goethe* (1903), *China and Methodism* (1906), *Christian Missions* (1906), *God's Missionary Plan for the World* (1907), *China: an Interpretation* (1916), *The Oregon Missions* (1918). The last two or three years were spent in much suffering though he worked on with indomitable will. He died in Pasadena, Cal., Mar. 18, 1919.

[In spite of G. R. Grose's admirable brief biog., *James W. Bashford* (1922), the fifty-four volumes of Bashford's notes are still unexplored. For important estimates see the *Christian Advocate* (N.Y.), Mar. 27, 1919, pp. 387 ff.]   J. A. F.

BASKERVILLE, CHARLES (June 18, 1870–Jan. 28, 1922), chemist, was born in Deer Brook, Miss., the son of Charles and Augusta (Johnston) Baskerville. He studied successively at the University of Mississippi, the University of Virginia, Vanderbilt University, and the University of North Carolina (B.S., 1892; Ph.D., 1894). In 1891 he was appointed instructor of chemistry at the University of North Carolina. From then on his promotion at this institution was rapid; and in 1900 he became professor of chemistry in succession to Dr. F. P. Venable, who had been elected to the presidency. In 1904 Baskerville accepted the directorship of the chemical laboratories of the College of the City of New York, in succession to Dr. R. O. Doremus, and here he remained until his death. On Apr. 24, 1895, he had married Mary B. Snow, by whom he had two children.

Baskerville was the author of nearly 200 educational, scientific, and technological papers, in addition to being the author or co-author of a number of books, such as *Qualitative Analysis,* with L. J. Curtman (1910); *Municipal Chemistry,* with other experts (1911); and *Anæsthesia,* with J. T. Gwathmey (1914). His earlier researches dealt with the rare earths (thorium, lanthanum, praseodymium and neodymium) and rare metals (titanium and zirconium). Later, in New York, he turned his attention more to industrial problems: the manufacture and use of several anesthetics employed in surgery; the methods of treating and refining edible vegetable oils; the development of the oil-shale industry; and the recovery of used stock in the pulp and paper industry. Valuable as these contributions may be, Baskerville's name is more particularly memorable for his effectiveness as a teacher of chemistry, and for his activities in connection with the development of the American Chemical Society and its New York branch.

[Obit. notices by W. A. Hamor in *Science,* LV, 693–94 and R. H. Moody in *City Coll. Quart.,* XVIII, 3; additional information furnished by W. H. Pierce, of the Coll. of the City of N. Y.]   B. H.

BASS, EDWARD (Nov. 23, 1726–Sept. 10, 1803), Episcopal bishop, was the great-grandson of Ruth, daughter of John and Priscilla Alden, who married John Bass, the son of Samuel Bass, the first of that family in this country. Edward Bass was born in Dorchester, Mass., and was one of a family of eleven children. His parents were Joseph and Elizabeth (Breck) Bass.

He gained admission to Harvard College at the age of thirteen, graduated in the class of 1744, and for the next three years remained in the college, studying for the M.A. degree, which he received in 1747. He still continued to reside in the college and to carry on his theological studies, but transferred his allegiance from the Congregationalism of his fathers to Episcopacy. This necessitated a trip to England to receive that which he regarded as essential to a valid ministry, but which could not be obtained in this country, ordination at the hands of a bishop. On May 17, 1752, he was made deacon by the Bishop of London, Thomas Sherlock, and a week later was ordained to the priesthood by the same bishop. Upon his return to America, he took charge in the fall of 1752, of St. Paul's Church, in that part of Newbury, Mass., which later became Newburyport.

During the Revolution Bass lukewarmly supported the colonial cause but did not escape altogether from patriot persecutions. At the close of the Revolution the Episcopal Church in America was in a deplorable state, badly shattered, and regarded with disfavor because of its connection with the Church of England. To rehabilitate it and adapt it to the new conditions was a difficult and delicate task. Bishops were chosen in Connecticut, Pennsylvania, New York, Virginia, Maryland, and South Carolina. When Massachusetts was ready to choose its bishop, it turned to Bass, who had been so long in charge of the parish at Newburyport. He was elected June 4, 1789, but his consecration was delayed, and then was indefinitely postponed. His first wife, Sarah Beck, whom he married in 1754, had died May 5, 1789, and within six months he married Mercy Phillips. Such celerity was considered unseemly in a prospective bishop and occasioned much criticism. But on May 24, 1796, he was again elected, and on May 7, 1797, in Christ Church, Philadelphia, he was consecrated the first Bishop of Massachusetts.

The fact that he was now a bishop did not alter his relation to the parish at Newburyport. He continued in charge of that as before. The Episcopal Church in Rhode Island had been under the supervision of Bishop Seabury of Connecticut, but he had died in 1796, and it now placed itself under the charge of Bishop Bass, as did also the Church in New Hampshire. The years covered by the episcopate of Bass were only six, but they were tense years both in church and state. He steered his course through them with honor, aiding by his kindliness and forbearance to put a rein upon bitter party spirit, and to make friends for his church. Not a man of scholarly

attainment, he left nothing in print, save one or two sermons in pamphlet form.

[John N. Norton, *Life of Bishop Bass* (1859) ; Daniel Dulany Addison, *Life and Times of Edward Bass* (1897) ; *Churchman's Mo. Mag.*, Oct. 1805 ; *Evergreen*, July 1845, in which is an engraved likeness ; Jas. S. Morss, *Brief Hist. of the Episc. Ch. in Newburyport and Vicinity, Being the Substance of Two Discourses Preached in St. Paul's Ch.*, Dec. 31, 1837 ; W. B. Sprague, *Annals Am. Pulpit*, V (1859) ; sketch by Wm. S. Bartlett, in appendix to his life of Rev. Jacob Bailey, *Colls. P. E. Hist. Soc.*, II (1853).]

W. A. B.

BASS, SAM (July 21, 1851–July 21, 1878), desperado, was born near Mitchell, Lawrence County, Ind., one of the ten children of Daniel and Elizabeth (Sheeks) Bass. The parents, who were highly respected by their neighbors, were the owners of a small but well-stocked farm. The mother died when the boy was ten. The father, who had married again, died in 1864, whereupon the younger children were placed under the guardianship of a maternal uncle. Sam had no liking for school and it is said did not even learn to read. In the fall of 1869 he left home for St. Louis, going then to Rosedale, Miss., where for nearly a year he worked in a mill. He then went to Denton, Denton County, Tex., and for eighteen months was in the employ of a Mrs. Lacy, who kept a hotel. Later he worked as a cowboy for Col. W. F. Egan, and on the latter's election as sheriff served for a time as one of his deputies. Up to about his eighteenth year he was a well-behaved boy. Before he left home he had become unruly, and had begun to associate with some of the rougher characters of the community. All accounts agree, however, that for his first four years in Texas he was industrious, sober, and honest. The break came in 1875. One of his biographers, moralizing on the transformation, attributes it to his purchase of a racing mare. A period of dissipation, gambling, and dare-deviltry followed, culminating in a horse-stealing raid on the herds of the Choctaws and the Cherokees in the Indian Territory. A desire for new scenes next possessed him, and with Joel Collins, a local cattleman, he assisted in driving a herd of beeves to Kansas, where it was sold. The proceeds, however, most of which belonged to Collins's friends in Texas, were soon squandered. Bass and Collins, with four others, then went to the new town of Deadwood, in the Black Hills, where they shortly began to recoup their losses by robbing stage coaches. Later they moved into Nebraska, and on Sept. 19, 1877, at Big Springs, they held up a Union Pacific train, getting $60,000 in gold from the express car and some $5,000 from the passengers. They fled southward, closely pursued. Collins and a companion were overtaken in Kansas and killed, and a third was killed in Missouri. Bass, however, returned safely to Denton County. Here he organized a new gang, and in the late winter and spring of 1878 held up and robbed four trains in the Dallas-Fort Worth region. Texas Rangers pursued and killed one of the bandits and captured three others. One of the prisoners, Jim Murphy, consented to rejoin Bass and his two remaining companions and give information of their movements. Though suspected by Bass, he was permitted to accompany the gang in a foray southward. An attempt to rob the bank at Round Rock, in the southern part of Williamson County, was frustrated on July 19, through a warning sent by Murphy to the Rangers, and in the ensuing fight Bass was mortally wounded. He died two days later, on his birthday, and was buried at old Round Rock.

Bass was about five feet eight inches tall, somewhat stoop-shouldered, and weighed about 140 pounds. "He would be taken for a good-looking man anywhere," said the *Denton Monitor*. On his tombstone was placed the inscription: "A brave man reposes in death here. Why was he not true?"

[Charles L. Martin, *A Sketch of Sam Bass, the Bandit* (1880); James B. Gillett, *Six Years with the Texas Rangers*, with intro. by M. M. Quaife (1925); Ed. F. Bates, *Hist. and Reminiscences of Denton County* (1918); Owen P. White, *Trigger Fingers* (1926).]

           W.J.G.

BASS, WILLIAM CAPERS (Jan. 13, 1831– Nov. 15, 1894), college president, youngest of the six children of Henry and Amelia M. (Love) Bass, was born in Augusta and died in Macon, Ga. His father was born in Connecticut, but removed as a child to North Carolina, and later to South Carolina, where he became a Methodist minister. William was sent to the Cokesbury School in South Carolina, and later to Emory College in Georgia, both Methodist institutions. He abandoned his plans to become a lawyer in order to enter the ministry, but as he had borrowed money to maintain himself in school, he determined to teach until he could accumulate enough to pay his debt. He was a pedagogue until he died. His first position was in Greensboro, Ga., where he formed his intimate and enduring friendship with Cosby W. Smith, and where in 1854 he married Octavia Nickelson, daughter of James Blake and Ann Maria (Willy) Nickelson. After one year, Smith left Greensboro to teach at the Methodist Wesleyan Female College in Macon, but Bass continued at Greensboro for two years longer before he became professor of natural science at the Female College in Madison, Ga. A year later he was invited to teach the same subject at Wesleyan, but loyalty

to the Madisonians made him decline. The invitation was renewed in 1859, and he accepted. For virtually the remainder of his life he was at Wesleyan—till 1874, as professor of natural science, and afterward as president until his resignation in April 1894. He was not officially connected with the Methodist Conference till 1867, but upon the license of that body he had preached with fair regularity from the beginning of his residence in Greensboro. When his connection at last did become official, his practical activities were not affected—he was merely "appointed" year after year to carry on the work he was already doing. His term of office as executive at Wesleyan covered years of the heaviest financial depression, but he was under the responsibility not only of providing funds for the conduct of the college, but of teaching mental and moral philosophy and of preaching before the young ladies once and sometimes twice every Sunday. He personally attended even to such small matters as purchasing groceries and keeping books for 250 people. And in addition he preached once a month at each of three country churches in the vicinity of his home. He once had as many as sixty students in a senior class, and during the twenty years of his presidency the college graduated far more than half the number of persons it had graduated in the fifty-five years of its existence. From a practical standpoint, the greatest event of his administration was the bestowal upon the college of $125,000 by the philanthropist, George I. Seney. For all his capability in business, he was devout, generous, and affectionate. An estimate of him written when he was an old man said that he was "universally recognized not only as one of the best educators in the South, but as an eloquent preacher and a finished gentleman" (*Biographical Souvenir*, p. 52).

[Sources: *Biog. Souvenir of the States of Ga. and Fla.* (1889); C. E. Jones, *Education in Ga.* (1889); W. J. Scott, *Biog. Etchings of Ministers and Laymen of the Ga. Conferences* (1895); W. J. Northen, ed., *Men of Mark in Ga.* (1911), III, 30–34.]

           J.D.W.

BASSE, JEREMIAH (d. 1725), colonial governor, was actively connected with the troubles which caused the overthrow of proprietary rule in New Jersey and disturbed the earlier period of royal government. Of his earlier life nothing is known save that he was an Anabaptist minister. In 1692 he was appointed agent of the West Jersey Society, an influential group of Non-Quaker English capitalists who had secured a part of the interest in West Jersey formerly held by the Friend, Edward Byllinge (*New Jersey Archives*, II, 91). In 1697 he was commissioned governor of both East and West Jersey, it being customary for the proprietors of both provinces to name the same person (*Ibid.*, II, 143, 209). But apparently his appointment had been brought about by an active minority. Basse was coolly received by the Friends of West Jersey and his authority denied by Lewis Morris [*q.v.*] and other prominent proprietors of East Jersey on the ground that his commission was not signed by the requisite number of proprietors (*Ibid.*, II, 217). Thus opposed, Basse adopted a policy favorable to the anti-proprietary elements in East Jersey which desired escape from the hated quit-rent. The party strife became in consequence so keen that a revolt led by Morris against Basse was threatened. By showing activity against the pirates, for whom the Jersey shore was a favorite refuge, Basse endeavored to win favor from the Crown. At the same time he tried to show collusion between the pirates and the powerful group of Scotch proprietors at Perth Amboy. But he came into conflict with the royal authorities at New York over the right of East Jersey to have a port of entry (*Ibid.*, II, 157, 218), and was superseded as governor in 1699. But the opposition to the proprietors in East Jersey had gathered such force that the tumultuous "East Jersey Revolution" soon nullified proprietary government.

When royal government was established in New Jersey, Basse secured a royal patent as secretary. Consequently he shared in the ill fame of the corrupt administration of Lord Cornbury [*q.v.*]. He was violently accused of perversions of power (*Ibid.*, III, 127, 152, 253, 254, 325, 429; IV, 71–74, 88, 97). Continuing to act with the anti-proprietary party, he became the ally of Col. Daniel Coxe who was at variance with the Friends in West Jersey (*Ibid.*, IV, 237). Secure in his patent, Basse remained as secretary till the death of Queen Anne. After the opponents of the proprietors had been routed by Gov. Robert Hunter [*q.v.*], Basse made his peace with that crafty Scot. He served with credit in the assembly, being apparently regarded as an authority in finance. In 1719 he was named attorney-general by Hunter himself. Meanwhile he had come under the influence of the Rev. John Talbot [*q.v.*], and joined the group of militant Anglicans at St. Mary's Church in Burlington. Here he officiated as warden and lay reader. From his pen is an interesting history of St. Mary's. From his activities as a whole one gets the impression of an adroit and rather shifty politician of some ability and literary skill. He was denounced in scathing terms by opponents, but allowance must be made for partisanship.

[G. M. Hills, *Hist. of the Ch. in Burlington, N. J.* (1876), gives valuable material, including Basse's will and his own account of St. Mary's; a personal notice is found in Wm. A. Whitehead, *East Jersey under the Proprietary Governments,* pub. in 1846 as *N.J. Hist. Soc. Colls.,* I, and separately in 1875.]
E. P. T.

BASSETT, JAMES (Jan. 31, 1834–Mar. 10, 1906), Presbyterian missionary, was born at Mundus, near Hamilton, Ontario, Canada. He graduated in 1856, at the age of twenty-two, from Wabash College, Indiana, the third of three brothers who took their degrees from this institution. In 1859 he finished his seminary course at Lane. Thereafter he served successively at Yellow Springs, Ohio, and Knoxville, Ill., as pastor of the Presbyterian Church. During 1862–63 he served as chaplain in the Federal army. In 1863 he became pastor of the Presbyterian Church at Neenah, Wis., and during 1869–71 was pastor at Englewood, Ill. On June 19, 1871, he was appointed a missionary of the Presbyterian Church for service in its Persia Mission. Sailing from New York City on Aug. 9, 1871, he arrived in Urumiah, Persia, on Oct. 18. During this year the Urumiah station along with all the Persian work of the American Board was turned over to the care of the Presbyterian Church, and in January 1872 the Urumiah Presbytery was organized for the general administration of the field. Toward the close of the same year Bassett and Mrs. Bassett opened for the Mission a new station at Teheran, the Persian capital. They were welcomed by both Moslems and Armenians who, it may be said, little understood the real nature of this missionary venture. Two French Lazarists and one Gregorian priest were already there. Not long after Bassett's arrival he baptized a "Mohammedan priest" (*i.e.,* a mullah), the first Moslem convert of the Mission.

At Teheran Bassett took up the study of Turkish and Persian, and opened shortly two day schools, one for boys and one for girls. In 1873 he prepared a translation of Christian hymns into Persian. In 1874 he opened a boarding-school for girls. By this time he was preaching regularly in Persian in a school on the east side of town, and in a chapel on the west side. In 1875 he organized a training-school for young men, from which helpers were sent out to work in Hamadan and Resht. Until 1876 the work of the station had been mainly among Armenians, but early in that year a Friday meeting was begun for Moslems. During the year (Mar. 26) the Teheran Presbyterian Church was organized with twelve members, including one former Moslem. In 1878 the membership had grown to twenty-three. At the time there was "considerable activity in the work of distributing the Scriptures."

During 1879–81 the Bassetts were in America on furlough. He wrote for *Leisure Hour* (London) an article, "Out Among the Turcomans" (vol. XXIX, 1880), and prepared a translation of the Gospel of Matthew into Jaghatai Turki (published in London, 1880). In the summer of 1881 he and his wife returned to Persia, where he took charge of all the boys' schools of the Mission, making his home in Teheran. In the next year the Persia Mission was divided, and thereafter Bassett was senior missionary and head of the Eastern Mission. On Christmas Day, 1882, he began in his house services in English for the many English-speaking residents of the capital city. Friction with the government arose over the attendance of Moslems upon mission meetings, and the government prohibited the Mission from allowing Moslem attendance. Bassett, however, persuaded the authorities to place the responsibility upon the Moslems and not upon the Mission, and was enabled to open again the regular chapel services. In 1883 a new chapel building with a seating capacity of 300 was erected on the mission compound, and services were held weekly therein on Sundays and Fridays. The same year saw the appointment of the first United States minister to Persia, effected partly through Bassett's efforts. During 1884 he published from native presses a revised and enlarged edition of the Persian hymnal and his translation of the Westminster Shorter Catechism, and in the *Journal* of the American Oriental Society an article on "The Simnuni Dialects." In the summer of 1884 he resigned from the Mission and returned to America with his family, arriving in October. The rest of his life was spent in pastoral work and in the preparation of two books, *Persia, the Land of the Imams* (1886), frequently cited by later writers on Persia, and *Persia, Eastern Mission* (1890). Relinquishing his last charge in 1905 at Wading River, L. I., he moved to Los Angeles, Cal., where he died. His widow, one son, and four daughters survived him.

[Wabash Coll. Records; contemporary *Annual Reports* of the Board of Foreign Missions of the Presbyt. Ch. in the U. S. A.; data on file in the Board offices.]

J.C.A.

BASSETT, JOHN SPENCER (Sept. 10, 1867–Jan. 27, 1928), historian, was born at Tarboro, N. C., being the second child of Richard Baxter Bassett and Mary Jane (Wilson) Bassett. The Bassett family was of Matthews County, Va., but Richard Bassett, father of Richard Baxter Bassett, located in Williamsburg, where he and his son after him became contractors and

architects. Both were strongly opposed to the institution of slavery, but took no part in the anti-slavery agitation. Indeed, Richard Bassett purchased a slave woman at her request, and Richard Baxter Bassett from necessity of his business rather than from choice purchased some negro mechanics. Just prior to the Civil War, Richard Baxter Bassett removed from Virginia to eastern North Carolina, where he became prominent in the construction enterprises of the region. When the war opened he joined Company A (Edgecombe Guards), 1st North Carolina Regiment; but soon after the battle of Big Bethel, he was transferred to the Commissary Department and assigned the duty of manufacturing army supplies.

After preparatory training in the Graded School of Goldsboro, where his father located after the Civil War, and also at the Davis Military School at LaGrange, N. C., John Spencer Bassett in 1886 entered Trinity College (now Duke University), then located in Randolph County, and graduated in 1888. After teaching two years in the Durham Graded School, he returned to Trinity as an instructor, and in February 1890 he organized the 9019, the first scholarship society in the institution. In 1891 he entered the Johns Hopkins University, receiving the doctorate in 1894. He then returned to Trinity, which had been removed to Durham in 1892, as professor of history. The following twelve years marked him as a teacher of ability and resourcefulness. The historical section of the college library was small, but Bassett persuaded the members of a local history club and others to contribute rare books, pamphlets, and manuscripts; such was the beginning of an excellent collection of Southern Americana. Many of the papers read before the club were worthy of publication, and in 1897, through Bassett's initiative, there was established the first publication of the College strictly devoted to scholarship, the *Historical Papers of the Trinity College Historical Society*. His own productivity was notable. *The Constitutional Beginnings of North Carolina* (Johns Hopkins Studies, 1894), his doctoral thesis, was followed by the *Regulators of North Carolina* (American Historical Association, 1895), *Slavery and Servitude in the Colony of North Carolina* (Johns Hopkins Studies, 1896), *Anti-Slavery Leaders in North Carolina* (*Ibid.*, 1898), *Slavery in the State of North Carolina* (*Ibid.*, 1899), *The Writings of Colonel William Byrd* (New York, 1901), *The Federalist System* (New York, 1906), and numerous periodical articles. Yet his interests were not entirely with matters recondite; he was also a social critic, interested in the contemporary cultural and political transformation in the Southern states. As a medium for criticism he persuaded the 9019 to establish the *South Atlantic Quarterly* (1902) of which he was the first editor. In 1903 an editorial article entitled "Stirring up the Fires of Race Antipathy" (vol. II, no. 4), in which a comparison was made of the rise of submerged classes in past ages and the progress of the American negro, so antagonized certain elements of public opinion in North Carolina as to lead to a demand for Bassett's resignation from Trinity. The trustees of the institution, however, refused to yield to this demand and issued a statement in defense of academic liberty ("Trinity College and Academic Liberty," *South Atlantic Quarterly,* vol. III, no. 1). This episode was the last agitation of the race question in North Carolina from that time until the present writing.

In 1906 Bassett was called to Smith College. There he instituted the *Smith College Studies in History,* the first learned publication of that college. His *Life of Andrew Jackson* (2 vols., 1911) was the first well-balanced biography of President Jackson, based to a large degree on manuscript sources. It was followed in 1913 by a *Short History of the United States*; *The Plain Story of American History* (1916); *The Middle Group of American Historians* (1917); *The Lost Fruits of Waterloo* (1918); *Our War with Germany* (1919); *Expansion and Reform* (1926); *The League of Nations, a Chapter in World Politics* (1928); and *Makers of a New Nation* (1928). He was also interested in the collection of the letters of eminent historians and records illustrative of plantation life in the ante-bellum South; hence the *Correspondence of George Bancroft and Jared Sparks* (1917), *The Westover Journal of John Selden, Esq.* (1921), *Major Howell Tatum's Journal* (1922); "Letters of Francis Parkman to Pierre Margry" (1925), which appeared in the *Smith College Studies,* and the *Plantation Overseer as Revealed in His Letters* (Smith College Anniversary Publications, 1925). He was also editor of the *Correspondence of Andrew Jackson,* published by the Carnegie Institution, of which three volumes had appeared at the time of his death, and *Selections from the Federalist* (1921). He contributed an essay on "The Present State of History-Writing" to a symposium, *The Writing of History* (1926), which he also edited, the other contributors being J. J. Jusserand, W. C. Abbott, and C. W. Colby. In 1919 he was elected secretary of the American Historical Association. In the duties of that office he took a peculiar interest, and was one of those responsible for the movement under-

taken in 1925 to endow the Association. His death, in Washington, D. C., resulted from an accident which occurred while he was on his way to a meeting of the Council of Learned Societies to represent the American Historical Association. He was married on Aug. 19, 1892, to Jessie Lewellin. Geniality, a certain ruggedness of mind, and an instinct for the practical were his dominating traits. Ever friendly, he was unyielding in matters of principle or conviction. Persistently busy with his pursuits, he always found time to give counsel to others; and he had the faculty of utilizing limited resources for large purposes.

[This sketch is based on a short manuscript memoir by Prof. Bassett and on the writer's personal recollection. His bibliography in *Who's Who in America,* 1926–27, should be supplemented by that in *Herbert B. Adams, Tribute of Friends with a Bibliography* (Johns Hopkins Studies, 1902).]   W. K. B.

BASSETT, RICHARD (Apr. 2, 1745–Sept. 15, 1815), Revolutionary statesman, jurist, was born in Cecil County, Md., the son of Michael and Judith Bassett. His father, who was a tavern-keeper at Bohemia Ferry, Md., deserted his wife, and Richard was adopted by a relative named Peter Lawson, from whom he ultimately inherited Bohemia Manor. The active years of Bassett's life were passed in Delaware. In the Revolutionary War he was captain of a troop of Dover Light Horse, and thenceforth for a quarter of a century his career was passed in the politics of his adopted state. Between 1776 and 1786 he was a member of the council of safety and of the state constitutional convention, and served in both branches of the legislature. He was a delegate to the Annapolis Convention, and with the same fellow members from his state represented Delaware in the Federal Convention. Here he was comparatively silent, a far less notable figure than his colleague Bedford. Delaware was the first state to accept the Constitution, and Bassett was a leading member in its ratifying convention. He was one of the first senators from the state, serving in the years 1789–93; on the noteworthy question whether the president should have the power of removal, the vote of Bassett was recorded in the affirmative; on the question of the assumption of state debts, he was recorded in the negative. In the succeeding years, 1793–99, he was chief justice of the court of common pleas; in 1797 as a Federalist presidential elector he voted for Adams. His term as governor, 1799–1801, seems to have been honorable, if not especially important. When President Adams, on Mar. 3, 1801, just prior to his retirement from office, made the famous appointment of "midnight judges" that excited Jefferson's wrath, Gov. Bassett was one of the offending appointees; he was nominated and confirmed judge of the United States circuit court, but his office was soon legislated out of existence. Bassett impressed his contemporaries as a statesman of common sense; in the language of J. T. Scharf, "Few men have served the State in more capacities or with greater efficiency." He had considerable wealth, owned homes in Dover, Wilmington, and Maryland, and, as an enthusiastic Methodist and life-long friend of Bishop Asbury, paid one-half the cost of the First Methodist Church in Dover. He died at his home in Bohemia Manor. His wives were Ann Ennals of Dorchester County, Md., and a Miss Bruff of Talbot County. His daughter Ann married James A. Bayard [q.v.], Feb. 11, 1795, and his adopted daughter, Rachel, married Gov. Joshua Clayton [q.v.].

[R. E. Pattison, "Life and Character of Richard Bassett" (1900) in *Papers of the Del. Hist. Soc.*, No. 29; H. C. Conrad, *Hist. of Del.* (1908); J. T. Scharf, *Hist. of Del.* (1880); C. P. Mallery, "Ancient Families of Bohemia Manor" (1888) in *Papers of the Del. Hist. Soc.*, No. VII; G. Johnston, *Hist. of Cecil County, Md.*(1881), pp. 170–85; *Biog. Dir. of the Am. Cong. 1774–1927* (in MS.).]

E. K. A.

BATCHELDER, JOHN PUTNAM (Aug. 6, 1784–Apr. 8, 1868), physician and surgeon, was born in Wilton, N. H., the only son of Archelaus and Betty (Putnam) Batchelor. He studied medicine with Dr. Fitch and Dr. Matthias Spalding of Greenfield, nearby, and in 1807 obtained a license to practise from the State Medical Society, at the subsequent meetings of which he was prominent as a speaker. He practised first in Charlestown, N. H., but soon wearied of practise in a small village and moved to Pittsfield, Mass., thence to Utica, N. Y., and finally to New York City. During these wandering years he obtained a medical degree at Harvard, with a thesis on *The Disease of the Heart Styled Aneurism*.

Once settled in New York, he became noted as a surgeon and was elected lecturer on anatomy and surgery at Castleton, Vt., and at the Berkshire Institute in Massachusetts. He wrote distinguished medical papers on cholera and paralysis and surgical papers on tracheotomy and fractures. He was a first-rate operator, cutting for stone, and removing cataracts by extraction rather than by couching. In 1825 he gained a wide reputation through ligation of the carotid and subsequent removal of an enormous sarcoma of the lower jaw. He was said to be the first American surgeon to remove the head of the femur; he performed many rhinoplastic operations, and was a specialist in facial surgery. He was clever as an inventor and improver of surgical instruments and his last gift to the profession was a one-handed craniotome in place of the former clumsy instruments used with two. He died in New York City at the age of eighty-three.

[*Med. and Surg. Biogs.* (Phila. 1865), XI, 587–590; H. A. Kelly and W. L. Burrage, *Am. Med. Biogs.* (1920); S. W. Francis, *Biog. Sketches of Distinguished Living N. Y. Surgeons* (1866); F. C. Pierce, *Batchelder, Batcheller Genealogy* (1898).]

J. A. S.

BATCHELDER, SAMUEL (June 8, 1784–Feb. 5, 1879), manufacturer, inventor, son of Samuel and Elisabeth (Woodberry) Batchelder, was born at Jaffrey, N. H. He was reared and educated at New Ipswich, where his father was first postmaster of the town and conducted a tavern and general store. Before his sixteenth year he became manager of his father's store but in 1804 engaged in business for himself at Peterboro, N. H., and in 1806 at Exeter. On his return to New Ipswich, in 1808, he purchased an interest in one of the town's two cotton-mills, which produced 300 pounds of yarn weekly, and gave employment to about 100 home weavers, and before 1812 was its principal owner and manager. As a leading citizen, he filled such offices as selectman, town clerk, postmaster, and, eventually, representative in the legislature, where he was a member of the committee first proposing Daniel Webster for nomination to Congress. In 1810 he married Mary Montgomery, by whom he had six children. His active career, continuing to the advanced age of eighty-six years, included connections with various prominent concerns, notably the Hamilton Manufacturing Company, of which he was manager (1824–31), president (1859–70), and treasurer (1869–71); the Exeter Manufacturing Company, of which he was manager (1855–72); the Everett Mills, of which he was treasurer (1859–70); and the Essex Company, of which he was president (1867–70). He removed, in 1825, to East Chelmsford, Mass., where he was a member of its first board of selectmen; and in 1846, to Cambridge, where he resided until his death, serving on the first board of aldermen, under the new city charter, and as representative in the Massachusetts legislature (1847).

Batchelder invented and introduced many new devices for cotton manufacture, although generally neglecting to seek patent protection. One of his earliest inventions was a machine for winding "cotton balls" for darning and fancy work. Later he produced a loom to weave pillow cases without a seam, providing a hand-controlled movement to close the bottom. In 1832, he invented a stop-motion for the drawing frame, a valuable innovation, since, before its introduction, the slender fleeces of cotton, without twist, had not been strong enough to stand the operation of drawing. A device for dressing yarn for weaving substituted brass steam-cylinders for the usual wood rolls, but was little used because of the small number of power mills then existing. His best known invention is his dynamometer, or "force-measurer," perfected in 1837, for weighing the power of belt-driven machinery, which afforded improved means for determining the power required for driving by water or steam (Julius Weisbach, *Manual of the Mechanics of Engineering*, II, 53–55). He was a constant writer for newspapers and the author of *Responsibility of the North in Relation to Slavery* (1856); *Young Men of America* (1860); *Free Trade and the Tariff* (1861); *Introduction and Early Progress of Cotton Manufacture in the United States* (1836).

[W. R. Bagnall in *Contributions of Old Residents' Hist. Ass. Lowell, Mass.*, III (1887), 187–211; *Samuel Batchelder* (Morning Mail Press, 1885); U. S. Patent Office Records; F. Kidder, *Hist. of New Ipswich* (1852); D. B. Cutter, *Hist. of the Town of Jaffrey, N.H.* (1881).]

BATCHELLER, GEORGE SHERMAN (July 25, 1837–July 2, 1908), Union soldier, statesman, son of Sherman and Mary (Noyes) Batcheller, was a native of Batchellerville, Saratoga County, N. Y. His father was well-known in the county as a citizen and politician, and the family was related to Roger Sherman and to Daniel Webster. He took the degree of LL.B. at the Harvard Law School in 1857, was admitted to the bar the following year, and began at once the practise of law in Saratoga Springs. At the unusually early age of twenty-one he was elected to the Assembly, and in the session of 1859 he was assigned to the important judiciary committee. On Oct. 8, 1860, he was married to Catherine Phillips Cook. Enlisting in the war in the 115th New York Regiment, he rose to the rank of its lieutenant-colonel, having served in several engagements, having been taken prisoner at Harper's Ferry in 1862 and, after his exchange, having been present at the siege of Charleston. During 1863–64 he was deputy provost-marshal-general in the South. After the war he held the office of inspector-general of the New York militia in 1865–68, and in that capacity he reorganized the National Guard of the state. One of his military duties was acting as escort to the funeral cortège as the body of Lincoln was conducted across the state of New York on the way to Illinois. He resumed the practise of law, and also his political activities, being a presidential elector for Grant in 1868, and a member of the Assembly in 1873 and 1874. In the former year he was chairman of the committee on canals and a member of the committee on militia. In the following

year he retained his membership on the militia committee, and received the chairmanship of the all-important committee on ways and means. It was undoubtedly his prominence as a politician and lawyer which led President Grant to appoint him as United States judge in the newly created International Tribunal for the legal administration of Egypt. These "Mixed Tribunals," composed of both foreigners and natives, had jurisdiction in cases between foreigners of different nationalities (in certain contingencies also, when foreigners of the same nationality were involved), and in cases between foreigners and natives. They commenced to function in 1876, and Batcheller was soon chosen by his colleagues as the presiding justice. He resigned the position in 1885 and in the year following was again a member of the New York Assembly, serving on the important committees of ways and means, general laws, and military affairs. President Harrison appointed him assistant secretary of the treasury in 1889 and minister to Portugal in 1891. From 1893 he acted as manager of the European interests of various American companies, and in 1897 he was called to preside over the Universal Postal Congress. He was returned to the International Tribunal (his last office) in 1898, at the request of the Egyptian government. President Roosevelt promoted him in 1902 to the Tribunal's court of appeals, and ultimately he became president of that body. His acquaintance with Mohammedan law was evinced in two articles on the subject which he contributed to the *North American Review* for July 1906 and August 1907. The regard in which he was held in Egypt was shown at the time of Mrs. Batcheller's death by unusual courtesies on the part of the Khedive. He was Grand Officer of the Order of The Medjidie, and was decorated with the cross and insignia of the Order of the Crown of Italy. His death occurred in Paris.

[*Albany Evening Jour.*, July 3, 1908; *N. Y. Evening Post, Tribune*, and *Times* of the same date; *Who's Who in America*, 1908–09; F. C. Pierce, *Batchelder, Batcheller Genealogy* (1898). Some of the authorities give the year of his birth as 1836.]

E. K. A.

BATCHELOR, GEORGE (July 3, 1836–June 21, 1923), Unitarian clergyman, was born in Southbury, Conn., the son of George and Mary (Axford) Batchelor. His father, a Baptist minister, while not actually identified with the "Millerite" movement which at that time was active in New England, was among the believers in the speedy end of the world, and Batchelor was reared in an atmosphere of fervent evangelical piety. It was in reaction from the ardors of the Millerites that he became a pronounced liberal, while at the same time retaining a keen interest in religious ideas and principles. He believed it possible to unite an essentially evangelical spirit with progressive and liberal thinking. With this purpose in mind he attended the theological school at Meadville, Pa., graduating in 1863. He was assistant superintendent of the United States Sanitary Commission, 1864–65. On Sept. 18, 1866, he was married to Priscilla Stearns of Cambridge, Mass. He received the degree of A.B. at Harvard in 1866 and that of A.M. in 1870. Meanwhile he became pastor of the Barton Square Church in Salem, Mass., where he had a happy and fruitful ministry. In 1882 he was called to the pastorate of Unity Church, Chicago, and in 1889 he became minister of the First Unitarian Church in Lowell, Mass. Meanwhile he had served as the executive secretary of the National Conference of the Unitarian Churches with such efficiency that in 1893 he was chosen secretary of the American Unitarian Association, the missionary organization of his denomination. He resigned this office in January 1898 to become editor of the *Christian Register* and held that position until his retirement July 3, 1911.

Batchelor was a man of slender frame and slight bodily power but distinguished for sound judgment, thorough thinking, and good administrative capacity. He was a preacher of more than average ability and the author of *Social Equilibrium* (1887), which had a considerable circulation. His influence as editor of the *Christian Register* was wide-spread. As a writer he possessed a lucid and attractive style fortified by a large fund of historical knowledge. While always self-reliant and vigorous in the expression of his own ideas, he was fair and just to those of opposing views. His gifts of mind and heart made him in his generation one of the conspicuous leaders of liberal Christian thought and life in America.

[*Who's Who in America,* 1920–21 ; *Unitarian Yr. Bk.,* 1924–25 ; *Boston Transcript,* June 21, 1923.]

S. A. E.

BATE, WILLIAM BRIMAGE (Oct. 7, 1826– Mar. 9, 1905), Confederate soldier, governor of Tennessee, was a descendant of a pioneer family which came to Tennessee in the early days of the Cumberland settlement. He was born at Bledsoe's Lick, one of the Middle Tennessee pioneer settlements, now known as Castalian Springs, in Sumner County. His father, James Henry Bate, the grandson of a Revolutionary soldier, was a farmer. His mother, Amanda (Weathered) Bate, was related to the families of Gen. Sumter of South Carolina and Gen. Coffee of Tennessee. The little formal education he had was gained at

a log schoolhouse, later known as the Rural Academy. When he was sixteen years of age, upon his father's death, he left school to become second clerk on the steamboat *Saladin* running on the Cumberland and Mississippi rivers between Nashville and New Orleans. At the outbreak of the war with Mexico, Bate, who was of an ardent temperament, enlisted in New Orleans as a private in a Louisiana company, and is said to have been the first Tennessean to reach Mexican soil. Later he became first lieutenant in Company I of the 3rd Tennessee Volunteer Infantry.

After the Mexican War, Bate established in Gallatin, Tenn., an intensely democratic newspaper called the *Tenth Legion,* and in 1849 he was elected to the state legislature where he served one term. He then decided for the profession of law and studied at the Law School in Lebanon, Tenn., now a part of Cumberland University, where he was graduated after a year's study, in 1852. After a brief practise, he was elected in 1854 as attorney-general of Nashville District, embracing three counties. Notwithstanding his meager knowledge of the law, he appears to have made an efficient attorney-general. In politics he was a strong state-sovereignty man and a supporter of secession, and by 1860 had attained sufficient prominence to be made a presidential elector on the Breckinridge-Lane ticket. In 1856 he was married to Julia Peete of Huntsville, Ala.

Bate went into the Civil War in 1861 as a private in his home company from Gallatin and came out four years later as a major-general. With his command he was distinguished in the fighting at Shiloh, Murfreesboro, Chattanooga, Missionary Ridge, in the Atlanta campaign, and in the fatal Tennessee campaign, which ended in the battles of Franklin and Nashville. His military career closed under Joseph E. Johnston in North Carolina. Bate was a noted fighting general, was wounded three times, and had six horses killed under him in battle. At the end of the battle of Shiloh there were five members of the Bate family lying on the field, dead or wounded. Next to Forrest, he had the most spectacular career of any of the Tennessee generals. In June 1863 he was tendered the nomination for governor of Tennessee, an offer which reached him on the battle-field. His answer became historic, but has reached us in half a dozen different forms. It was probably about as follows : "While an armed foe treads our soil and I can fire a shot or draw a blade, I will take no civic honor. I had rather, amid her misfortunes, be the defender than the Governor of Tennessee" (for another version, see Marshall, *post,* pp. 64–65).

When he came back to his home near Nashville, he found himself disfranchised by the Brownlow régime, and remained so for several years until a more moderate administration came into power in the state. While still disfranchised, he was a delegate to the National Democratic Convention in 1868, and thereafter was for ten years a member of both state and national Democratic executive committees. Gov. Brownlow's hostility to the ex-Confederates was so strong that there was danger of civil war within the state, and on Aug. 1, 1868, Bate, with ten other Confederate generals, among them Gen. Forrest, united in a memorial to the legislature protesting against the hostile policies of the administration. But not until Brownlow left the state, in 1869, were the Confederates restored to political rights. Bate was a presidential elector in 1876 on the Tilden and Hendricks ticket, and in 1882 was elected governor, and later reëlected for a second term. His chief accomplishment while governor was the settlement of the state debt, a problem which had been upsetting the finances of Tennessee since 1865. Bate secured the passing of a plan by the legislature in 1883, which provided that all the old debts about which there was no question should be paid in full, and that those made since the War, particularly those under the Brownlow administration which were tainted with fraud, should be scaled and paid only in part. Bate also secured the passage of an act which established a commission for the regulation of railroads within the state. Notwithstanding strong opposition even within his own party, he became more popular each year and three times came near election as United States senator. Finally in 1886 he was elected by the legislature on the sixty-eighth ballot to succeed Senator Whitthorne. Joining the strong delegation of ex-Confederate leaders who were now, after Reconstruction, coming to Washington to represent the Southern states, he became a useful and influential senator. In 1893 he was the author of the act which repealed all laws then on the statute-book providing for the supervision of local elections by Federal officials, thus removing the last vestige of the Reconstruction legislation. By continued reëlection he was retained in the Senate until his death.

[Park Marshall, *William B. Bate* (1908), a non-critical biography ; brief sketches by John Allison in *Notable Men of Tenn.* (1905), and by J. G. Cisco in *Historic Sumner County, Tenn.* (1909) ; obituaries in the *Nashville Banner*, Mar. 9, 1905, *Chattanooga Daily Times*, Mar. 10, 1905, *Memphis Commercial Appeal*, Mar. 10, 1905. In the Tenn. State Lib. is a collection of undated newspaper clippings, evidently printed about the time of Bate's death. His speeches can be found in the *Cong. Record*, 1887–1905.]
                                        W. L. F.

BATEMAN, KATE JOSEPHINE (Oct. 7, 1843–Apr. 8, 1917), actress, was the eldest daughter of Sidney Frances Cowell Bateman [*q.v.*] and Hezekiah Linthicum Bateman (see *Dictionary of National Biography*), and the granddaughter of Joseph Leathley Cowell (see *Dictionary of National Biography*). With her sister Ellen she made her first appearance at Louisville, Ky., Dec. 11, 1846, in *Children of the Wood*. For several years thereafter the two, known as The Bateman Children, were regarded as prodigies. In 1849, in the New York Broadway Theatre, Kate played Richmond to Ellen's Richard III, Portia to Ellen's Shylock, and Artixaminous to Ellen's Bombasta. Thence they went to the Walnut Street Theatre, Philadelphia, in an engagement beginning on Jan. 7, 1850. Barnum, quick to sense the value of such youthful work, took the girls to London. In 1851 they appeared under the great showman's management at the St. James's Theatre and at the Surrey Theatre. Returning to America in 1852, they toured the United States, going as far west as San Francisco, where they were seen on Apr. 10, 1854.

Kate's father, in 1855, was manager of a St. Louis theatre. Interest in his children's education prompted him to come to New York in 1859, and his daughter temporarily retired from the stage (1856–60). Then she made a second début in her mother's play, *Evangeline*. On Jan. 19, 1863, she appeared at Niblo's Garden, New York, and later on Oct. 1 at the London Adelphi Theatre in *Leah the Forsaken,* a version of Mosenthal's *Deborah,* made for Bateman by young Augustin Daly, then at the outset of his career (J. F. Daly, *Life of Augustin Daly,* 1917 ; G. W. Curtis, *Harper's Weekly,* Mar. 7, 1863). It was in London during 1865 that she was seen to great advantage as Julia in *The Hunchback,* Bianca in *Fazio,* and Juliet in *Romeo and Juliet* (for critical comment, see Pascoe's *Dramatic List,* 1879). In 1866 she reappeared at Niblo's Garden in such rôles as Pauline and Parthenia. During the year, however, she was married to George Crowe, M.D., one-time editor of the *News* (London), and again retiring from the stage set sail for England. But in 1868, she played at the London Haymarket in a revival of *Leah,* and assumed the new rôle of Pietra in a tragedy by Mosenthal. In June 1869 she was Mary Warner in Tom Taylor's play of that name. Her father became the manager of the London Lyceum Theatre on Sept. 11, 1871. He struggled to make it a success, and it was a young man in his company, Henry Irving, who, by his acting of Mathias in *The Bells* (Nov. 25, 1871), helped him gain financial security. Inasmuch as there was no Ellen Terry at the Lyceum in those days, it was natural that the Bateman daughters should become identified with the early career of Irving. Several years passed, however, before Kate acted with him. She appeared in New York in October 1869 as Leah and Mary Warner, and in 1871 was seen for the first time in the rôle of Beatrice in *Much Ado About Nothing*. In 1872, at the London Lyceum, she once more essayed her favorite part of Leah, and won acclaim as Medea in Wills's adaptation of Legouvé's tragedy, *Medea in Corinth*. It was after Bateman's death, and while Mrs. Bateman was in charge of the Lyceum that Kate was seen with Irving in a revival of *Macbeth* on Sept. 18, 1875. The papers suggested that Irving's Thane was a medieval Mathias and that Miss Bateman's Lady Macbeth displayed too amply the grand manner of acting. Thereafter, with Irving, she was seen on Apr. 18, 1876, as Queen Mary in Tennyson's poetic drama of that name, and on Jan. 29, 1877, as Queen Margaret in *Richard III*. The critics recognized in her work sound judgment, keen intelligence, and power. Irving's prestige was making him ambitious and restless; and he soon announced that he intended leaving the Lyceum. This was the death-knell of Mrs. Bateman. She transferred her energies to Sadler's Wells Theatre, and there she was again aided by her daughters. Kate had been obliged to retire from the stage because of an accident that had marred her personal appearance, but, under her mother's direction, she acted the rôle of Helen Macgregor in *Rob Roy* in October 1879. From this time on, her appearances on the stage were occasional, and added nothing to her fame. Of her acting it was said (London *Times*, Apr. 10, 1917) that she showed "a certain staginess of gait and gesture, and excessive love of the merely picturesque, and the monotony of utterance so often to be found in players whose voices have been exercised in the theatre at an early age." But the general agreement was that she possessed passion and emotion, even though there was a tendency to overaccentuate these.

[T. Allston Brown, *Hist. of the Am. Stage* (1870); Tompkins and Kilby, *Hist. of the Boston Theatre* (1908); Geneal. Table of the Bateman Family in J. Parker, *Who's Who in the Theatre* (1925); Clement Scott and Cecil Howard, *Life and Reminiscences of E. L. Blanchard* (1891); Laurence Hutton, *Curiosities of the Am. Stage* (1891); Wm. Winter, *Brief Chronicles,* Dunlap Society Pubs., 7, 8, 10 (1889–91); Austin Brereton, *Life of Henry Irving* (1908); Bram Stoker, *Personal Reminiscences of Henry Irving* (1906); Percy Fitzgerald, *Sir Henry Irving* (1906); H. B. Baker, *Hist. of the London Stage* (1904); W. D. Adams, *Dict. of the Drama* (1904); J.F. Daly, *Life of Augustin Daly* (1917).]
M.J.M.

BATEMAN, NEWTON (July 27, 1822–Oct. 21, 1897), educator, was born at Fairton, Cumberland County, N. J., the son of Bergen and Ruth (Bower) Bateman. He was of Scotch and English ancestry. When he was eleven years old the family migrated to Illinois. The toilsome, leisureless, moneyless life of the frontier could not cool the boy's eagerness for an education. With $2.50 in cash and only four months of preparation behind him he entered Illinois College, of which the Rev. Edward Beecher, a son of Lyman Beecher, was president. Plain living and high thinking characterized the five professors and rather less than forty students, but young Bateman, in order to stay in college, boarded himself for four years on so narrow a margin that he permanently injured his health. Upon his graduation in 1843 he went to Lane Theological Seminary for one year, but left on account of illness and traveled the country for another year as an agent for a historical chart. After various teaching experiences in St. Louis and in St. Charles, Mo., he became in 1851 principal of the main public school in Jacksonville, Ill. To this position he later added that of county superintendent of schools and in 1857 the principalship of the Jacksonville Female Academy. In 1850 he married Sarah Dayton of Jacksonville. She died in 1857 and in October 1859 he married Annie N. Tyler, who had come to Jacksonville from Massachusetts. She died May 28, 1878. In 1858 the Republican state convention nominated him for state superintendent of public instruction. He was elected and served, 1859–63 and 1865–75, being defeated in the election of 1862. With others he began in 1858 the movement that established the state Normal University. He helped found and for a time edited the *Illinois Teacher*. During his tenure of office the common school system of the state was developed and brought to a high degree of efficiency. His practical sagacity as an administrator and his statesmanlike view of the major aspects of public education are exemplified in seven biennial reports, which were studied with interest all over the United States and even abroad. The moral conviction underlying his work is expressed in the sentence with which he closed the first and the last of these documents: "In the name of the living God it must be proclaimed, that licentiousness shall be the liberty—violence and chicanery shall be the law—superstition and craft shall be the religion—and the self-destructive indulgence of all sensual and unhallowed passions shall be the only happiness of that people who neglect the education of their children." Bateman's head projected only a little above the elbows of his friend Lincoln, who was wont to introduce him as "my little friend, the big schoolmaster of Illinois." He was a member of the committee of three that drafted the bill creating the United States Bureau of Education. He was a member of the state board of health 1877–91, was appointed an assay commissioner by President Hayes in 1878, was president of Knox College 1874–92 and president emeritus from his retirement until his death. His last undertaking was the editing of the *Historical Encyclopedia of Illinois.* He died in Galesburg of angina pectoris.

[N. Bateman and P. Selby, eds., *Hist. Encyc. of Ill.* (Biog. and Mem. ed., 1915) with portr.; *Cat. of Ill. Coll.* (1841, 1855); *Chicago Inter-Ocean,* Oct. 22, 1897; Carl Sandburg, *Abraham Lincoln, the Prairie Years* (1926); information from President C. H. Rammelkamp of Ill. Coll., Apr. 9, 1928.]
                                                    G.H.G.

BATEMAN, SIDNEY FRANCES COWELL (Mar. 29, 1823–Jan. 13, 1881), playwright, actress, manager, was the daughter of Joseph Cowell, the English actor, whose real name was Witchett. According to his *Thirty Years Passed Among the Players in England and America* (1844), Cowell was in New York City in 1823, but he states that his family was in New Jersey on account of the yellow fever, and the place of Sidney's birth is uncertain. Her mother, Frances Sheppard, died soon after Sidney's birth and the latter's early years were spent in various places as her father's engagements permitted. His association with the theatre brought her upon the stage in New Orleans about 1837. She married, Nov. 10, 1839, Hezekiah Linthicum Bateman, an actor and manager in St. Louis, Mo. Mrs. Bateman was not a great actress, but was a guiding force in the careers of her husband and children, three of whom, Kate, Ellen, and Isabella, became actresses. The Batemans made their first appearance in New York City in 1849 when Kate and Ellen played Richard III and Richmond, at the ages of four and six years.

Mrs. Bateman's comedy, *Self,* was first produced anonymously at Bateman's St. Louis Theatre, June 18, 1856, and was published in the same year. The play is a satire upon social and business life in New York City, and nearly all the characters are conventional stage types. The part of John Unit, a retired banker, the lovable godfather of the heroine, redeemed the play, however, and secured for it a long life. This part was first played by Mark Smith, but when *Self* was repeated at the People's Theatre in St. Louis in April 1857 H. L. Bateman played Unit, and the creation of the part has been incorrectly ascribed to him. In 1859 the Batemans were in New York, where Mrs. Bateman's romantic play, *Geraldine, or Love's Victory,* was produced at Wallack's Theatre on Aug. 22, and ran nightly

until Sept. 14, showing unusual vitality for that period. On Mar. 19, 1860, Kate Bateman appeared at the Winter Garden, New York, in a dramatization by her mother of Longfellow's poem *Evangeline,* and at the same theatre on May 21, 1862, in the title rôle of *Rosa Gregorio, or the Corsican Vendetta.* The success of Kate Bateman in Augustin Daly's *Leah the Forsaken,* when her father took her to England in 1863, led to the permanent removal of the family to that country. On June 12, 1865, H. L. Bateman appeared in Mrs. Bateman's play, with the title altered to *Geraldine; or The Master Passion,* at the Adelphi Theatre, London. In 1871, Mr. and Mrs. Bateman undertook the management of the Lyceum Theatre. Here, on Sept. 11, 1871, was produced her adaptation from *Die Grille,* under the title of *Fanchette; or The Will o'-the Wisp,* it having been already tried out at the Edinburgh Theatre Royal on Mar. 6. The great success of the Lyceum, which was partly due to the presence of Henry Irving in the company, led Mrs. Bateman to continue its management after her husband's death in 1875. In 1878 she transferred the lease to Irving and soon after took the Sadler's Wells Theatre, rebuilt it, and during her brief management, restored it to the high position it had held under Samuel Phelps. One of her enterprises was the presentation on Apr. 2, 1880, of the McKee Rankin Company in Joaquin Miller's *The Danites,* claimed by Rankin to be the first instance of a complete American company playing an American play in England. Her death, caused by pneumonia, was the occasion for cordial tributes from the English press. Especial stress was laid upon her extraordinary attention to detail, her versatility, her energy, her courage, and the delicacy and discernment of her taste in theatrical matters.

[Scattered references to Mrs. Bateman's plays are found in J. N. Ireland, *Records of the N. Y. Stage* (1866–67), II, 661, 689, 701. Accurate reports of the first production and of the revival of *Self,* correcting the usual printed statements, are in the *Missouri Republican,* of St. Louis, June 18, 19, 1856, and Apr. 6, 7, 1857. See also London *Times,* Jan. 14, 17, 18, 1881; *Academy,* No. 455, pp. 70–71, which gives an appreciation of her character; and, for collateral items, Laurence Hutton's *Curiosities of the Am. Stage* (1891), pp. 79–80; J. F. Daly's *Life of Augustin Daly* (1917), pp. 48–53. For English performances of her plays, see *"The Stage" Cyclopedia* (1909), ed. by R. Clarence.]
                                                    A.H.Q.

BATES, ARLO (Dec. 16, 1850–Aug. 24, 1918), author, educator, was born in East Machias, Me., the son of Susan (Thaxter) Bates and Niran Bates, a physician of strong literary tastes. His formal education began with the schools of East Machias, where he graduated from the Washington Academy in 1870. His class in Bowdoin was that of 1876 and it was during his college course that his literary career began. His first payment for writing was a check for three dollars from the *Portland Transcript*. In 1876 he went to Boston, lived in an attic, and wrote copiously; but the greater part of his manuscript was returned, and for a year he had to support himself by teaching and by painting china. In 1878 he was made secretary of a Republican organization and edited a fortnightly political journal called *The Broadside*, and served also as a clerk in the office of "a firm dealing in metals." His work on *The Broadside* may very probably have led to his appointment as editor of the *Boston Sunday Courier*, in 1880, a position which he held till 1893. During this period he produced the larger part of his purely literary work, including nine novels and four volumes of verse. In 1893 he became professor of English in the Massachusetts Institute of Technology. His marriage in 1882 to Harriet L. Vose, daughter of Prof. George L. Vose and Abby Thompson Vose, was a singularly happy union, but was cut short by her untimely death in 1886. She had written for publication under the pseudonym of "Eleanor Putnam"; and the young couple together wrote a fantastic fairy tale, called *Prince Vance*, which had the unusual distinction of being translated and published in Esperanto. His volumes of poetry were all dedicated to her memory. The one entitled *Sonnets in Shadow* is a threnody upon her death. That he carried on his work as teacher of English with enthusiasm and success is clear from the number and quality of his published writings related to that service; particularly, *Talks on Writing English* (1896–1901), *Talks on Teaching Literature* (1906), and *Talks on the Study of Literature* (1895), the last being the Lowell Lectures for 1895. In 1894, at the centennial celebration of the incorporation of Bowdoin College, he read a poem called *The Torch Bearers*, afterward published separately. In 1911, at a meeting of the Phi Beta Kappa Society at Tufts College, he delivered a poem, *The Supreme Gift*, which also was separately published. The later years of his life were spent in Otis Place, Boston, where his life work had been done, and where, after a long illness, he died.

The list of his published writings includes the following: novels—*Patty's Perversities* (1881); "Ties of Blood," serial in the *Boston Courier*, never appearing in book form (1882); *Mr. Jacobs* (1883); *The Pagans* (1884); *A Wheel of Fire* (1885); *A Lad's Love* (1887); *Prince Vance* (1888); *The Philistines* (1889); *The Puritans* (1898); *Albrecht* (1890); *Love in a Cloud* (1900); *The Diary of a Saint* (1902); volumes of short stories—*A Book o' Nine Tales*

(1891); *In the Bundle of Time* (1893); *The Intoxicated Ghost* (1908); volumes of poetry— *Sonnets in Shadow* (1887); *Berries of the Brier* (1886); *The Poet and His Self* (1891); *Told in the Gate* (1892); *Under the Beech Tree* (1899); single poems, or odes—*The Torch Bearers* (1894); *The Supreme Gift* (1911); dramatic works—*A Mother's Meeting* (1909); *A Business Meeting, A Gentle Jury, Her Deaf Ear, An Interrupted Proposal*—undated, one-act plays.

[*Who's Who in America*, 1918–19; "Maine in Lit.," *New Eng. Mag.*, Aug. 1900; Interview with Bates, by E. F. Harkins, *Lit. World*, June 1904; *Obit. Record of the Grads. of Bowdoin Coll. for the Year Ending June 1919* (1920).]

C.N.

BATES, BARNABAS (1785–Oct. 11, 1853), pioneer in postal reform, was born in Edmonton, England. His parents brought him to America when he was a child and settled in Rhode Island. He was educated for the ministry, and in May 1814 was chosen pastor of the Baptist church in Bristol. A decided change in his views leading toward Unitarianism brought about, in 1818, a schism in his church, but though he is said to have been deposed from the ministry his faction retained the church edifice. He served a term as collector of the port of Bristol, continuing, however, to preach. On the completion of his term he was again nominated, but according to his statement, through the antagonism of a pro-slavery senator from his state the nomination was rejected by the Senate. He is said to have become, about this time, a zealous Freemason. Sectarian, anti-Masonic and pro-slavery agitators brought on a riot, in which his life seems to have been endangered and he suffered some loss of property. Because of the schism in his church in Bristol and because of his growing doubt that preaching should be a gainful occupation, he declined, during nearly the whole of the last five years of his pastorate, to accept pay, while out of his own funds he advanced to the church $2,000, only a small part of which was ever returned to him. He left Bristol, probably about the end of 1824, and went to New York, where he opened a bookstore. In January of the following year he started a small weekly journal, *The Christian Inquirer*, "devoted to the support of Free Inquiry, Religious Liberty and Rational Christianity." It was carried on at considerable expense, for though it reached a total of 800 subscribers not many of them, it appears, felt called upon to pay for it. The issue for July 1, 1827, though partly set up, did not appear until Apr. 2, 1828, when notice was given that the paper had been turned over to the *Olive Branch*. Bates had preached in some of the independent pulpits of the city, but in the final issue of his paper announced his retirement from the ministry.

For a time under the Jackson administration he was assistant postmaster of New York. Sir Rowland Hill's famous pamphlet on cheap postage, which appeared in 1837, influenced him greatly, and by 1839 he had become an active advocate of postal reform. His article, "Post-Office Reform—Cheap Postage," in *Hunt's Merchants' Magazine* for March 1840, may well have been, as he asserts, the first argument published in America in behalf of the change. He also arranged the first public meeting in America to advance the cause. This meeting, held in New York, Nov. 24, 1843, petitioned Congress for a flat rate of five cents an ounce, irrespective of distance, and an abolition of the franking privilege. Against great opposition, particularly from the postal authorities, the movement was carried on. A law reducing letter postage to five cents an ounce on distances not exceeding 300 miles, but charging ten cents on greater distances and greatly increasing the already burdensome rates on ocean postage, was signed by President Tyler on the day before he left office, Mar. 3, 1845. It was unsatisfactory to the friends of postal reform, but the results of even the partial reduction of rates were encouraging, and at a meeting in New York on July 1, 1846, demands were made for a uniform rate of two cents an ounce. The New York Cheap Postage Association, with Bates as corresponding secretary, was organized May 26, 1848, following the formation of a similar body in Boston, and renewed efforts were made to bring about further reductions. Bates had lived to see the first authorized issue of postage stamps, Mar. 3, 1847; he was to see (Mar. 3, 1851) the compulsory prepayment of postage and the reduction of rates to three cents a half-ounce for distances under 3,000 miles, but not to see any material reduction in the rates of ocean postage. He died on a visit to Boston, probably in connection with the work of his society.

[Wilfred H. Munro, *The Hist. of Bristol, R. I.: The Story of the Mount Hope Lands* (1880); *Christian Inquirer*, n.s., Jan. 1826–Apr. 1828; Barnabas Bates, *A Brief Statement of the Exertions of the Friends of Cheap Postage in the City of N.Y.* (1848); *N.Y. Tribune*, Oct. 12, 1853.]
W. J. G.

BATES, DANIEL MOORE (Jan. 28, 1821– Mar. 28, 1879), jurist, the son of Jacob and Mary (Jones) Moore and grandson of Elzey Moore, both Methodist clergymen, was born at Laurel, Del. Members of the Moore family had been among the earliest settlers of the state. His parents both died when he was a child and he was adopted by Martin Waltham Bates, a leading Democratic politician, United States senator and lawyer of Dover, Del., who procured an act of the legislature changing the child's name to Daniel Moore Bates. His early education was received at a private school, and he entered Dickinson College in 1835, graduating in 1839. He studied law in Martin W. Bates's office, was admitted to the bar in 1842, and entered into partnership with his adopted father. The firm enjoyed an extensive practise and he soon became generally known as possessing qualities of industry and reliability which marked him out for public employment. In 1847 he was made secretary of state of Delaware, a position which he occupied for four years. In 1849 he removed to Wilmington, and in the same year was by resolution of the General Assembly appointed a commissioner to revise and codify the state statutes, a work which took ultimate shape as the Revised Code of 1852. He was in 1852 appointed United States district attorney for Delaware by President Pierce and held this office till 1861, being reappointed by President Buchanan. In 1861, as one of the five Delaware commissioners, he attended the abortive Peace Conference at Washington, serving on the committee which drafted the scheme of adjustment subsequently submitted to Congress. On Dec. 12, 1865, he was, with the indorsement of the entire state bar, appointed chancellor of Delaware. On his accession to the bench, he addressed himself with great energy to increasing the efficiency of the court, revising the rules and reforming the old practise. In addition, he prepared a manual of Chancery practise and forms for the use of the profession. The General Assembly held in 1871 passed a resolution directing the Chancellor to collect and publish such equity cases as in his judgment should be proper for public information, and he accordingly commenced to assemble the unreported decisions of his predecessors in office. Failing health compelled him, however, to relinquish all work and he resigned Oct. 15, 1873. As a judge he enjoyed the confidence of both the profession and the public. Possessing great patience, an infinite capacity for taking pains, and a logical precision of thought, his decisions carried great weight and always bore evidence of anxious deliberation. Immediately after his resignation, he undertook a long visit to Europe with his family, returning in September 1875 much benefited by the change. He resumed his work on the chancery records and as a result published *Reports of Cases Adjudged and Determined in the Court of Chancery of the State of Delaware*, Volumes I and II, which incorporated all the decisions of utility from 1814 to 1865 (1876, 1878). At the same time he commenced to practise in a small way at Wilmington, but did not attempt any heavy responsibilities. He died rather suddenly at Richmond, Va., while on a business visit. He had married in November 1844 Margaret Handy, daughter of Isaac P. Smith of Snow Hill, Md., an adopted daughter of George Handy of Philadelphia, who predeceased him.

[J. T. Scharf, *Hist. of Del.* (1888), I, 551; *Hist. and Biog. Encyc. of Del.* (1882); *Am. Law Rev.*, XIII, 749; *Daily Republican* (Wilmington), Mar. 29, 1879.]

H.W.H.K.

BATES, EDWARD (Sept. 4, 1793–Mar. 25, 1869), statesman, was the son of Thomas Fleming Bates, a Virginia planter and merchant, who on Aug. 8, 1771, had married Caroline Matilda Woodson. The young couple first lived in Henrico County and there three children were born. About 1776 the family moved to Goochland County, where a home called "Belmont" was established, and where nine more children were born, of whom Edward was the youngest. Thomas F. Bates fought as a volunteer soldier under Lafayette at the siege of Yorktown, but, as a Quaker, paid the price of this patriotic service by being read out of meeting. He also suffered heavy financial losses during the Revolutionary War and died leaving his family in straitened circumstances. Edward was taught to read and write by his father and at the age of ten was placed under the instruction of a cousin, Benjamin Bates of Hanover, Va., and by him was prepared to enter Charlotte Hall Academy in St. Mary's County, Md. He had hoped to attend Princeton, but a serious injury cut short his course at the academy and caused him to give up the idea of a college education. Through the influence of a relative, James Pleasants, a member of Congress, he was then appointed a midshipman in the navy; but because of his mother's objections he declined the appointment. In February 1813 he joined a volunteer militia company which was raised in Goochland County to assist in repelling a threatened attack on Norfolk; and he remained in the army until October, serving successively as private, corporal, and sergeant.

At the suggestion of his brother, Frederick Bates [*q.v.*], then secretary of Missouri Territory, Edward went out to St. Louis in 1814 and began the study of law under Rufus Easton, the foremost lawyer of the territory. In November 1816 he took out a license to practise law, and two years later formed a partnership with Joshua Barton, the brother of David Barton, one of the first United States senators from Missouri. The partnership continued until June 30, 1823, when Barton was killed in a duel. On May 29,

1823, Bates married Julia Davenport Coalter, the daughter of David Coalter, a South Carolinian who had moved to Missouri in 1817. She bore him seventeen children, eight of whom survived him.

Until he was elected to Congress in 1826, Bates held only minor public offices, though he had served acceptably as a member of the state constitutional convention of 1820, as attorney-general, and as a member of the state legislature. In the Twentieth Congress he was the sole representative of Missouri in the lower house, and already the choice of the Whig party for the United States Senate. The followers of Thomas H. Benton, however, had a majority in the state legislature, and Bates was defeated by a few votes. So strong was Jacksonian democracy in Missouri, indeed, that Bates was defeated for reëlection to Congress in 1828. He was still regarded as the leader of his party but he led a forlorn hope. About this time he moved to St. Charles County and located on a farm on Dardenne Prairie. He continued the practise of law, his services being in demand in all of the neighboring counties. There he remained until 1842 when he resumed practise in St. Louis. In 1830 he was elected to the state Senate, where he served for four years, and in 1834 was again elected to the Missouri House of Representatives. The door to more important offices seemed closed to him, but in 1847 his opportunity came. As president of the River and Harbor Improvement Convention which met at Chicago, he made an eloquent speech which attracted the attention of the public and made him a national figure (*Niles' Register*, LXXII, 366–67). In 1850 President Fillmore appointed him secretary of war, but for personal and domestic reasons he declined the appointment.

From this time on his views on social and constitutional questions and on national politics were sought and frequently expressed in speeches and newspaper articles. He opposed the repeal of the Missouri Compromise, a stand which aligned him with the "free labor" party in Missouri, though he still considered himself a Whig and in 1856 acted as president of the Whig national convention which sat at Baltimore. He drew closer to the Republican party when he opposed the admission of Kansas under the Lecompton constitution. His upright and clear-headed course attracted nation-wide attention, and in 1858 Harvard University conferred upon him the honorary degree of LL.D., an unusual honor for a Missourian of that day. Early in 1860 a Bates-for-president movement was launched in Missouri. His supporters contended that a Free-Soil Whig from a border state, if elected on the Republican ticket, would avert secession. The movement received the support of many leaders, particularly in the border states. But the decision of the national Republican committee to hold the convention at Chicago instead of at St. Louis was a serious setback to the Bates supporters and added strength to the candidacy of Lincoln. On the first ballot Bates received only 48 votes; on the second ballot 35; and on the third and deciding ballot only 22.

Soon after the Chicago convention Lincoln decided to offer Bates a cabinet position. Some of Bates's friends had urged, indeed, that he should be appointed secretary of state, but the President felt that the first place in the cabinet should go to Seward. He gave Bates his choice of any other cabinet position and the latter wisely chose that of attorney-general. He was the first cabinet officer to be chosen from the region west of the Mississippi River. For a time he had much influence in the cabinet. It was at his suggestion that the Navy Department began the equipment of a fleet on the Mississippi River. In the *Trent* affair, he urged that the question of legal rights be waived and that every effort be made to avert a war with Great Britain. He differed with Lincoln on the question of the admission of West Virginia to the Union. As attorney-general he filed an elaborate opinion in which he contended that the West Virginia Government represented and governed but a portion of the state of Virginia and that the movement for separate statehood was "a mere abuse, nothing less than attempted secession, hardly veiled under the flimsy forms of law."

From this time Bates's influence in the cabinet gradually waned. He disagreed with many of the military policies. He felt that as the war progressed constitutional rights were giving way before the encroachments of the military authorities. He resented the interference of Seward in matters which belonged to the attorney-general's office. He had little confidence in Stanton, Seward, or Chase, and he felt that Lincoln lacked the will-power to end what Bates considered abuses. In Missouri, moreover, the radical Republicans got control of the state government in 1864, and this meant the end of law in his home state. Weary of a cabinet position in which his views had little weight, and in the belief that he could best serve his country and his state as a private citizen, he tendered his resignation as attorney-general on Nov. 24, 1864.

On Jan. 6, 1865, a radical state constitutional convention assembled in St. Louis and drew up a new state constitution. It also passed an ordinance emancipating the slaves and an ouster ordinance, the intention of which was to place the state judiciary in the hands of the radicals. It also adopted a stringent test oath for voters. Bates fought the radicals by publishing a series of newspaper articles in which he pleaded for a government of law instead of a government of force. By many letters to prominent men all over the North he attempted to arouse them to the dangers of radical rule, insisting that the extreme radicals were nothing less than revolutionists who had seized upon the general zeal for putting down the rebellion and had perverted it into a means of destroying all government by law. This struggle against the Missouri radicals was his last great contest. A few months after his return to Missouri his health began to break. It steadily declined and on Mar. 25, 1869, he died.

In person Edward Bates was small. His early portraits show a strong countenance with clean-cut features, piercing eyes, and a well-formed chin. Until middle life he was clean-shaven, but in his later years he wore a full beard. He was modest and unpretending, but a courageous fighter for law and justice.

[The largest collection of Bates papers, including letters and diary (June 3, 1846–Dec. 25, 1852), is deposited with the Mo. Hist. Soc. in St. Louis. His diary (Apr. 20, 1859–July 30, 1866) is deposited in the MS. Div. of the Lib. of Cong. See Charles Gibson, "Edward Bates," in *Mo. Hist. Soc. Colls.*, II, 52–56 (1900); F. W. Lehman, "Edward Bates and the Test Oath," *Ibid.*, IV, 389–401 (1923); "Letters of Edward Bates and the Blairs," *Mo. Hist. Rev.*, XI, 123–46 (1917); Nicolay and Hay, *Lincoln* (1890); Gideon Welles, *Diary* (1911); Onward Bates, *Bates, et al. of Va. and Mo.* (1914).]

T.M.M.

BATES, FREDERICK (June 23, 1777–Aug. 4, 1825), governor of Missouri, was the eldest son of Thomas Fleming Bates and Caroline Matilda Woodson, and brother of Edward Bates [*q.v.*]. The early death of the father left the family in straitened circumstances and made impossible anything more than a common schooling for the first of the sons. Frederick seems to have supplied the lack of formal instruction by constant reading, for his more famous brother afterward said of him that he was "well-versed in the English classics, not ignorant of French literature and a good historian of all times." At the age of seventeen or eighteen he began the study of law while he served as postmaster and as deputy clerk of the court of Goochland County, Va. Removing to Detroit in 1797, he served in the quartermaster's department of the Army of the Northwest, resigning three years later to become a merchant. He appears to have prospered until June 11, 1805, when his store was burned in the conflagration which destroyed Detroit. Upon the creation of Michigan Territory, he was made an associate judge, and assisted Gov. William Hull and the other judges in drawing up the first territorial code. In November 1806 he was appointed secretary of Louisiana Territory, as well as member of the board of land commissioners and recorder of land titles. His appointment as secretary was due to the fact that the Burr Conspiracy was then developing and Jefferson wanted an official in the trans-Mississippi region on whom he could rely. As secretary Bates succeeded Dr. Joseph Browne, a brother-in-law of Aaron Burr. Until Meriwether Lewis, the new governor, arrived, Bates was acting governor, exhibiting no little initiative and energy. He removed from office dishonest officials, won the support of the French inhabitants, and did much to offset the influence of British traders among the Indians. He was mainly responsible for the revision of the territorial code, and in 1808 published a compilation of the laws of Louisiana Territory, the first book to be printed in what is now the state of Missouri. Three times thereafter he served as acting governor because of the enforced absence or resignation of his chief. He acted as secretary of Louisiana Territory until 1812, and was secretary of Missouri Territory until Missouri was admitted into the Union as a state. Finally in 1824 he became governor in his own right, having defeated no less an opponent than William Henry Ashley. It was during his incumbency that Lafayette visited St. Louis and was lavishly entertained, but the Governor, characteristically, refused to attend the official reception because the legislature had made no appropriation for the occasion. On Mar. 4, 1819, he had married Nancy Opie Ball, daughter of Col. John S. Ball of St. Louis County. After the marriage he and his bride made their home at "Thornhill," an estate of a thousand acres in Bonhomme Township near modern Chesterfield, Mo. There four children were born, and there he died of pleurisy on Aug. 4, 1825. Edward Bates said of his brother, "F[rederick] B[ates] was a man naturally of good parts, far above mediocrity, and by life long practise, methodical and exact in business. . . . He was no public speaker, having never practised, but his powers of conversation were somewhat remarkable—fluent always, sometimes brilliant, and generally, at once, attractive and instructive. He was a very ready writer, using some diversity of style, but generally clear, terse and pungent. His habits were very retired . . . his friends few, but strong and abiding." His portrait shows a refined countenance, a wealth of curly hair, kind but brilliant eyes, a well-formed nose, and firm lips. It is the coun-

tenance of a scholarly gentleman of the old school.

[*The Life and Papers of Frederick Bates* (2 vols., 1926), ed. by T. M. Marshall. For the geneal. of the Bates family, see Onward Bates, *Bates, et al. of Va. and Mo.* (printed for private distribution, 1914).]

T.M.M.

BATES, GEORGE HANDY (Nov. 19, 1845–Oct. 31, 1916), lawyer, publicist, son of Judge Daniel Moore Bates [*q.v.*], was born at Dover, Del., and received his primary education in the Wilmington, Del., schools. In 1862 he entered the University of Pennsylvania, but after prosecuting his studies there for two years went West and engaged in business in Michigan. His health, however, became impaired and in 1866 he returned to the East and read law in his father's office at Wilmington. He also attended the Harvard Law School and was admitted to the Kent County (Del.) bar in April 1869. Commencing practise in Wilmington he identified himself actively with the Democratic party and was appointed deputy attorney-general, in this capacity engaging in a number of notable criminal prosecutions, among which was that of the Delaware Bank robbers. Resuming private practise in 1874 he devoted much time to the study of constitutional and international law, and took a prominent part in local politics, being a delegate to the National Democratic Conventions of 1880, 1884, and 1888. He represented New Castle County in the Delaware legislature 1882–83; and was speaker of the House in the latter year. In 1883 he was also appointed a member of the Board of Park Commissioners for the City of Wilmington, an office which he retained till 1894. His political affiliations had brought him into close association with Senator Thomas F. Bayard, and, though never a "practical" politician, he occupied for some years an influential position in the councils of the Democratic party in the state. Retained in much important litigation, his work as special counsel for Delaware in the Delaware-New Jersey boundary dispute was of a high order and exhibited great ability. In 1886 he was, at the instance of Bayard—then secretary of state—appointed by President Cleveland special agent to investigate the condition of affairs in Samoa, concurrently with but independent of similar representatives of Great Britain and Germany. He spent some months in the Islands and his able and exhaustive report, Dec. 10, 1886, reviewed in detail the causes of the difficulties under which the Samoan Government labored and suggested as a solution the formation of a native government but with the real executive power exercised by whites nominated by the three powers, who should mutually guarantee the neutrality and autonomy of the new Government (*House Executive Document No. 238,* 50 Cong., 1 Sess., Appendix A, p. 137). In the futile negotiations which followed he took no part, but he was appointed by President Harrison one of the United States commissioners to the joint conference with Great Britain and Germany on Samoan affairs which met at Berlin April 29, 1889, his colleagues being W. W. Phelps and J. A. Kasson. The treaty which was there concluded between the three powers was a signal triumph for him since its major provisions followed the recommendations embodied in his report to Secretary Bayard. After his return from Berlin he took little part in public affairs, but continued to practise law in Wilmington till 1896, when he removed to Philadelphia. He edited *Delaware Chancery Reports,* Volumes III and IV, and during his later years was associated with Francis Rawle in the second and third revisions of Bouvier's *Law Dictionary.*

He married May 26, 1870, Elizabeth B. Russell, daughter of C. T. Russell, a Boston lawyer, and sister of William E. Russell [*q.v.*], governor of Massachusetts.

[Details of Bates's early career appeared in *Hist. & Biog. Encyc. of Del.* (1882), p. 408. His connection with the Samoan controversy is dealt with in J. M. Callahan, *Am. Relations in the Pacific and the Far East 1784–1900* (1901), pp. 141–43, and Hugh M. Herrick, *Wm. Walter Phelps* (1904), pp. 210–18, which contains a reference to Bates's article "Some Aspects of the Samoan Question," in the *Century Mag.,* Apr. 1889, p. 945. Obituaries in the *N.Y. Times* and *Pub. Ledger* (Phila.), Nov. 1, 1916.]

H. W. H. K.

BATES, JAMES (Sept. 24, 1789–Feb. 25, 1882), physician, congressman, was the eldest son of Solomon and Mary (Macomber) Bates. He was born in Greene, Me., but when he was only seven years of age his father moved to Fayette, Me. There James Bates obtained such education as was possible in the local schools. At twenty-one he entered on the study of medicine with a Fayette physician and with Dr. Ariel Mann of Hallowell. He then took the course given by the Harvard Medical School. In 1813 he joined the medical department of the army and remained there till May 1815, prolonging his service that he might bring the 700 patients under his charge to a condition in which they could make the journey home with safety. After resigning, he was married on July 27, 1815, to Mary Jones of Fayette. For four years he practised at Hallowell, Me., and for twenty-six at Norridgewock, Me. In 1830 he was elected to Congress on the Democratic ticket and served one term. His chief activities were in relation to the tariff and nullification controversy. Bates was a vigorous supporter of the compromise, he moved a post-

ponement of the "force bill," and announced that both he and his constituents were opposed to protection, knowing that it did them more harm as consumers than it did good to them as producers. In 1845 he was made superintendent of the insane asylum at Augusta, Me. In December 1850, part of the asylum was burned with a loss of twenty-eight lives. A coroner's jury found that the fire was due to the faulty construction of an air-chamber planned by Bates. In January 1851, the Governor of Maine appointed him a commissioner to examine the methods of heating and ventilating used in public institutions of other states. He accepted the position and resigned his office of superintendent. His investigations were fruitful and the commissioners for rebuilding the hospital adopted many suggestions made by him (James W. North, *History of Augusta,* 1870, pp. 551 ff.). He then resumed private practise chiefly in Fairfield and North Yarmouth. When about eighty he withdrew from practise but lived twelve years longer, dying in full possession of his faculties at the age of ninety-two. He won great success in his profession and at his death was said on good authority to have been one of the best all-round men in surgery that Maine had produced.

[Sketch in *Trans. Maine Medic. Ass.,* VII, 514; Wm. B. Atkinson, *Physicians and Surgeons of the United States* (1878); Howard A. Kelly, *Cyc. Am. Medic. Biog.,* vol. I (1912).]

L. C. H.

BATES, JOHN COALTER (Aug. 26, 1842–Feb. 4, 1919), soldier, was born in St. Charles County, Mo. His father, Edward Bates [*q.v.*], was attorney-general in Lincoln's cabinet, his mother was Julia Davenport (Coalter) Bates. He was educated at Washington University, St. Louis, and in the opening year of the Civil War he enlisted, and was at the age of nineteen a first lieutenant. He served in the Army of the Potomac until the end, and participated in nearly all its great battles, Antietam, Fredericksburg, Chancellorsville, and Gettysburg. During the last two years he was on the staff of Gen. Meade. He reached the rank of captain in 1863, and was brevetted major and lieutenant-colonel. Continuing in the regular army after the war, he passed about thirty years in the West, largely in northwestern posts and along the Mexican border. In the Spanish-American War of 1898, when the decision was made to invade Cuba, Bates was put at the head of an independent brigade of the 5th Corps. Directly after the landing he was placed in command at Siboney, June 25, and on July 1 he joined Gen. Lawton. He was prominent in the assault on El Caney, and marching to headquarters was active in the fighting of July 2 and

3; his brigade had a record of almost continuous marching and warfare. In the course of the year he was commissioned brigadier-general of volunteers and major-general of volunteers. Like many others among the higher officers he signed the "Round Robin" letter. His Cuban experience has been characterized in these words: "To him as to all of his comrades of rank in Cuba, the Santiago campaign was more of an adventure, with a touch of the romantic in it, than the ordeal of war" (*New York Times,* editorial, Feb. 9, 1919). In 1899 he was ordered to the Philippines, where the insurrection under Aguinaldo had just broken out. In August of that year he negotiated with the Sultan of Sulu a treaty (often called the "Bates Treaty"), by which the Sultan received a monthly subsidy, and acknowledged the sovereignty of the United States. As the treaty recognized the existence of slavery, it did not escape criticism, unwarranted though the criticism may have been. The following year Bates attacked the insurgents in Cavité, and established garrisons on the island of Mindanao. He was commissioned brigadier-general of the United States Army in 1901 and major-general in 1902. At the beginning of 1906 when Gen. Chaffee retired, Bates succeeded as chief of staff and was commissioned lieutenant-general, being one of a comparatively small number in the army to hold this last rank. He retained the office of chief of staff for a few months only, retiring in April 1906. The remainder of his career was uneventful, down to his death at San Diego in 1919.

[F. E. Chadwick, *Relations of the U. S. with Spain* (1911), II; J. H. Latané, *America as a World Power* (1907); H. H. Sargent, *Campaign of Santiago de Cuba* (1907); F. B. Heitman, *Hist. Reg.* (1903); *Who's Who in America,* 1918–19.]

E.K.A.

BATES, JOSHUA (Oct. 10, 1788–Sept. 24, 1864), financier and philanthropist, was born in Weymouth, Mass., the youngest of the three children of Col. Joshua and Tirzah (Pratt) Bates. His ancestors on both sides of the family were among the earliest settlers in New England, their names appearing in the colonial records previous to 1640; his father had been an officer in the Revolution and was a man of some prominence in the community. A boy of delicate health, Joshua received his education partly in the public schools and partly under the tuition of Rev. Jacob Norton, minister of the First Church of Weymouth. A weakness of the eyes, however, which troubled him for many years, prevented a college education. His business career started at the early age of fifteen when he entered the counting house of William R. Gray, eldest son of William Gray,

the leading shipping merchant of New England. Here the young man served his apprenticeship, after which he formed a partnership with a Capt. Beckford of Charleston, a former employee of William Gray, but the firm of Beckford & Bates, like hundreds of other concerns, went to smash as a result of the critical commercial years of the War of 1812.

This failure was probably a blessing in disguise. Young Bates during his apprenticeship had so impressed William Gray with his industry, integrity, and ability that the great merchant offered in 1816 to send him to Europe as his general agent. Gray at that time was the largest ship-owner in America, having between thirty and forty square-rigged vessels afloat. Although Bates asserted later that for the first twenty years of his residence abroad he felt like a man with his back to the wall, those were years in which he not only handled with marked success Gray's multitudinous European interests but laid the foundation of a brilliant career as an international banker. A chance acquaintanceship with M. Peter Cæsar Labouchère, related to the Baring family and senior member of the great house of Hope & Company of Amsterdam, resulted in the formation in 1826 of a partnership between John Baring (son of Sir Thomas Baring) and Joshua Bates. This concern, financed by M. Labouchère, specialized in American accounts, and was so successful that it was absorbed two years later by Baring Brothers & Company in which John Baring and Joshua Bates were admitted as partners. This connection Bates maintained until his death, becoming eventually senior partner and building up a large fortune.

During his later years Bates was probably the most influential foreigner in private life in the British Isles. As chief of Baring Brothers & Company, which, ~~with the exception of a short period under Jackson and Van Buren,~~ had been the fiscal agents in England of the United States since the organization of our government, Bates was tied to his native land by economic as well as patriotic interests, and his powerful influence was ever exerted to promote amicable relations between the two nations. In 1854 he acted as umpire (under the convention of 1853) between the British and American commissioners in the disputes over outstanding claims upon which the commissioners could not agree. These claims which ran into several millions had been a matter of controversy between the two nations for nearly thirty years. They were now reduced by the awards to approximately $600,000, and the skill with which Bates, although not a lawyer, decided the delicate questions of international law involved was a matter of satisfaction to both governments.

In 1852 the City of Boston in negotiating with the house of Baring for a water loan submitted numerous city documents, one of which spoke of the project of a public library. The interest of Bates was aroused, and in October of that year he offered $50,000 to the city for the purchase of books if a building be provided and care taken of them, the only conditions being "that the building shall be such as to be an ornament to the city —that there shall be room for 100 to 250 persons to sit at reading-tables—that it shall be perfectly free to all" (*Twelfth Annual Report of the Trustees of the Public Library*, p. 16). The offer was accepted and three years later he announced his intention, in addition to his former donation, "to purchase and present to the city a considerable number of books in trust," a donation which also amounted to $50,000. Upon his death the trustees of the Library "cheerfully" accorded "to him, as its largest benefactor . . . the name and honors of the Founder of the Boston Public Library" and resolved that the large hall of the Library be henceforth known and designated as Bates Hall (*Ibid.*, p. 39).

Joshua Bates is portrayed as a man with round head, broad forehead, prominent nose, firm mouth but small chin—the whole giving an impression of intelligence and kindliness. He was married to Lucretia Augusta Sturgis, by whom he had one son and one daughter.

[Geneal. information can be found in George W. Chamberlain, "Geneal. of Weymouth Families," vol. III of *Hist. of Weymouth, Mass.* (4 vols., 1923). The best account of his life is the *Twelfth Annual Report of the Boston Pub. Lib.* (1864). This is reprinted in *A Memorial of Joshua Bates from the City of Boston* (1865), which likewise contains all of the correspondence relative to the founding of the lib. The story of his benefactions is also told in Horace J. Wadlin, *The Pub. Lib. of the City of Boston* (1911), p. 44 ff. The Boston Pub. Lib. contains a marble bust copied by Noble from one by Wm. Behnes, a portr. in oil by E. U. Eddis, and a daguerreotype.]

H.U.F.

BATES, SAMUEL PENNIMAN (Jan. 29, 1827–July 14, 1902), educator, the son of Laban and Mary (Thayer) Bates, was born at Mendon, Mass. He received his education in the common schools of Massachusetts, at Worcester Academy, and at Brown University. He graduated from the last-named institution in 1851. His intellectual interests were diversified. While in college he was proficient in mathematics and philosophy. The year after his graduation he devoted part of his time to a study of Milton and Shakespeare and for the five years following taught ancient languages in the academy at Meadville, Pa. While at Meadville he gained a local

reputation as a lecturer on educational topics at teachers' institutes and served as principal of the academy from 1851 to 1857. He then served as superintendent of the Crawford County schools until his appointment as deputy state-superintendent of public instruction in 1860. He was an active member of the National Teachers' Association and strongly influenced the agitation on the subject of founding a great national university, where professors for colleges and universities might be trained in the science of teaching. His lecture on "Liberal Education" was published in Barnard's *American Journal of Education,* March 1865, pp. 155–76. He was designated by Gov. Curtin to visit the colleges of the state and report upon their condition, and was employed by Edward James of West Chester to prepare a brief exposition of the school laws of Pennsylvania for use in James's volume of *Township and Local Laws.* His thorough acquaintance with the details of the routine of teaching made it possible for him to organize efficiently the details of the work of the Department of Public Instruction. He prepared a series of articles on the subject of physical culture, for the *Pennsylvania School Journal,* after pursuing a thorough course on the subject at the Boston School of Physical Culture. Maj. William C. Armor, feeling that Bates was eminently capable, employed him to write *Lives of the Governors of Pennsylvania* (1873). In 1866 Gov. Curtin appointed him state historian, a position created by the state legislature for the purpose of gathering material and forming complete accounts of the organizations from Pennsylvania that engaged in the Civil War. The results of his efforts were published in the *History of Pennsylvania Volunteers,* in five volumes (1869–70). In 1877 Bates toured Europe and upon his return prepared a series of lectures on "Art Centers of Italy, Naples, Rome, Venice and Florence," which are in the possession of the Meadville Public Library. He married Miss Sarah Josephine Bates of Massachusetts in August 1856, and they were the parents of seven children all of whom were active in the life of the community and state.

[*Meadville Gazette,* 16th year, No. 30; *Meadville Daily Tribune Republican,* XXXVII, No. 5532; Paul Monroe, *Cyc. of Ed.,* I (1911), 332; *Barnard's Am. Jour. of Ed.,* Dec. 1865, p. 682.]

H.H.S.

BATES, WALTER (Mar. 14, 1760–Feb. 11, 1842), Loyalist, the son of John and Sarah (Bostwick) Bates, was born in the eastern part of Stamford, now Darien, Conn. The family was devoted to the Anglican Church, was strongly Loyalist, and at the outbreak of the Revolution was suspected, unjustly, of being in communication with the British. Walter, then a lad of fifteen, was seized and confined in the guard house. What followed may be told in his own words: "I was taken out by an armed mob, conveyed through the field gate one mile from the town to back Creek, then having been stripped my body was exposed to the mosquitoes, my hands and feet being confined to a tree near the Salt Marsh. . . . Twenty stripes was then executed with severity, after which they sent me again to the Guard House" (*Kingston and the Loyalists,* p. 8). Eventually he was released and fled to the mountains; later he joined the Tories in Long Island. In 1783 he made one of the party of 100 New England Loyalists who sailed with their families on the *Union* to Nova Scotia, where each was granted 200 acres of land. He was the first man to be married in the new colony, and rose to a position of some importance, acting for many years as sheriff of King's County. His book, *Kingston and the Loyalists of the "Spring Fleet" of 1783,* left in manuscript and unpublished until 1889, is an important source book on the Connecticut Loyalists. More interesting, extraordinarily readable in fact, is the work which he published in 1816 (second ed. 1817) entitled *The Mysterious Stranger; or Memoirs of Henry More Smith; alias Henry Frederick Moon; alias William Newman: Who Is Now Confined in Simsbury Mines, in Connecticut, for the Crime of Burglary; Containing an Account of His Extraordinary Conduct During His Confinement in the Gaol of King's County, Province of New Brunswick, Where He Was under Sentence of Death: with a Statement of His Succeeding Conduct, Before and Since His Confinement in Newgate.* This apparently authentic tale of the sheriff's experiences with a man who, in addition to other unusual accomplishments, could escape from all chains and who while handcuffed in a dark cell constructed and operated an elaborate marionette show of straw figures, is written with no little literary skill, holding the reader's interest by its command of suspense and its appearance of absolute veracity. If the story is true, Henry More Smith, alias Henry Frederick Moon, etc., was certainly one of the most remarkable criminals on record; if it was fabricated, Walter Bates as a writer of fiction belongs in the class with Daniel Defoe.

[The only known sources are Bates's two volumes and a brief sketch by E. B. Huntington in *Hist. of Stamford, Conn.* (1865). There is a résumé of *The Mysterious Stranger,* by Ernest Sutherland Bates, in "Nor Iron Bars a Cage," *Dalhousie Rev.,* Jan. 1928.]   E. S. B.

BATTERSON, JAMES GOODWIN (Feb. 23, 1823–Sept. 18, 1901), business man, the son of Simeon Seeley and Melissa (Roberts) Batterson, was born in Wintonbury, later Bloomfield, Hartford County, Conn. His early years were passed in New Preston, Conn. He attended a country school and an old-time academy. Having made his way, partly afoot, to Ithaca, N. Y., he there served a three-year apprenticeship in a printing-shop, and after that was associated in business with the elder Batterson, who had set up in Litchfield as a tombstone-cutter. For a year he read law in the office of Origen S. Seymour, afterward chief justice of the state supreme court of errors. In 1851 he was married to Eunice Elizabeth Goodwin. Having removed his business to Hartford, he widened its scope to include contract-work for residences, office buildings, and public structures. By 1875 it had so grown that it was organized into a joint stock company, the New England Granite Works. Batterson introduced labor-saving apparatus and himself invented a turning-lathe for cutting and polishing stone columns. In 1860 he established in New York City large works for supplying interior marbles. One of the numerous important memorials constructed by him is the Soldiers' Monument at Gettysburg. His notable buildings include the State Capitol of Connecticut, which he completed for $13,000 less than the $2,000,000 appropriation. He also furnished the gray Concord granite for the Library of Congress at Washington. Deriving his basic idea from English methods of insurance against railway accidents, he founded the Travelers Insurance Company in 1863 and thus became the pioneer of accident insurance in the United States. The first premium received by the new company was two cents for insuring a Hartford banker from the post office to his house. At first Batterson's venture was opposed and ridiculed; then within two years no less than seventy other companies arose for but a brief existence. The Travelers charter soon was amended to permit business in general accident and life insurance, and subsequently to take in liability insurance also. A lifetime of directed study and wide reading made Batterson uncommonly versatile and well-informed. His researches in geology and mineralogy comprised field-work with James G. Percival in the first geological survey of Connecticut (see Percival's report, 1842), and with Isambard K. Brunel in the Nile Valley during the winter of 1858–59. Deeply interested in sociology and economics, he subsidized the publication of the first complete edition of Walter Bagehot's writings (edited by Forrest Morgan, 5 vols., Hartford, 1889) and wrote *Gold and Silver as Currency in the Light of Experience, Historical,*

Economical, and Practical (Hartford, 1896), a brochure employed as a campaign document. He was a devoted student of the classical languages, and was acquainted with several modern tongues; contributed articles on insurance matters and current topics to the *Travelers Record,* house-organ of the Travelers company; made a number of renderings from the Greek and Latin; and "produced considerable poetry, none of which is so bad as John Quincy Adams's" (New York *Sun,* Sept. 22, 1901).

[*The Travelers Record,* Oct. 1901, pp. 4–5; an article signed "E. D. C." in the *Commemorative Biog. Record of Hartford County* (1901), pp. 23–28; *Jas. G. Batterson,* an address by Wm. F. Henny, delivered at a public memorial service held at Hartford, Sept. 18, 1904, and printed in booklet form; and a biog. in the *Geneal. and Family Hist. of Conn.,* ed. by W. R. Cutter and others (1911), III, 1240–43; *Hartford Times, Hartford Courant,* Sept. 18, 1901.]

G. S. B.

BATTEY, ROBERT (Nov. 26, 1828–Nov. 8, 1895), physician and surgeon, came from English Quaker stock, the American branch of the family having settled in Providence, R. I. His father, Cephas Battey, was born in New York, while his mother, Mary (Magruder) Battey, was a native of Georgia. Born in Augusta, Ga., Robert was educated at the Richmond Academy there and at Phillips Academy, Andover, Mass. (1838–44). He then gave up school and worked in Detroit and in Marshall, Mich., later returning to Rome, Ga., where he became a clerk in a drugstore. By 1849, when he was twenty-one years of age, he had become owner of a drugstore there, which he continued to run until 1855. In 1849 he married Martha B. Smith, by whom he had fourteen children. He studied medicine in Rome under his brother's guidance, and in 1855 entered Prof. James C. Booth's School of Analytical Chemistry, Philadelphia. He also studied at the Philadelphia College of Pharmacy, and subsequently attended two courses of lectures at the Jefferson Medical College and the University of Pennsylvania, receiving his medical degree from the former, Mar. 7, 1857. He then returned to Rome to practise, where his brother was well established. In 1858 an early successful operation for vesico-vaginal fistula brought him local renown; in 1859 he described a simple treatment for congenital club-foot. As a result of this work he was invited to London. Before going abroad, he attended the American Pharmaceutical Association convention in Boston (1859) and presided as vice-president. In Europe, he spoke on vesico-vaginal fistula before the Obstetrical Society of London, on Nov. 2, 1859 (*Transactions of the Obstetrical Society, London, I, 1860*). He performed his operation for fistula successfully at the Dublin Hospital on a case that had been operated five times before. He also visited Scotland, Paris, and Brussels, and was everywhere well received.

He returned home the next year and resumed his practise in Rome, but the Civil War soon interfered. He served throughout the war, first as medical officer in a battalion of artillery, and later as surgeon in the 19th Georgia Volunteers. He saw active service with the Army of Virginia and later under Stonewall Jackson, when he was surgeon to Hampton's and Archer's brigades. After 1862, he was put in charge of various hospitals, first at Atlanta and later at Rome. When he was driven out of Rome by the Northern forces, he took charge of hospitals elsewhere in Georgia and in Mississippi. In 1864 he established a successful hospital in Macon especially for the treatment of soldiers with hernias and fistulas. In April 1865 he was discharged from the army, after a very honorable service. He again returned to Rome, where he resided the rest of his life, except for a few years in Atlanta as professor of obstetrics at the Atlanta Medical College and editor of the *Atlanta Medical and Surgical Journal* (1872–75). He established the Martha Battey Hospital in Rome in honor of his wife, who assisted him at many operations. He was an ardent member of numerous medical societies.

Battey's reputation rests largely on what is known as "Battey's Operation," first performed by him Aug. 17, 1872. He described it as "an operation for the removal of the normal human ovaries, with a view to establish at once the 'change of life,' for the effectual remedy of certain otherwise incurable maladies" (*Atlanta Medical and Surgical Journal,* X, 321). By 1891 he was able to report 300 consecutive cases with a mortality of nine. The reasoning on which his operation was based has long since been recognized as unsound, but his method of procedure by abdominal, and later by vaginal, section opened up an important field of surgery. He also performed other operations, radical in nature for the times, such as perineal cystotomy. In 1877 he introduced iodized phenol as a drug of value in gynecological work. All his work, especially in pelvic surgery, was carefully described in a manner which led even the more conservative members of the profession to study and if necessary operate upon the female reproductive organs. The experience gained by these procedures, plus the advent of asepsis, led to the high standard of abdominal surgery as we know it to-day.

Battey's operative skill, combined with his personal magnetism, drew patients to Rome from a large area. He was in broken health for some years before his death. His son, Dr. Henry H. Battey, continued his practise.

[*Atlanta Medic. and Surgic. Jour.*, ser. 3, I, 496–503; obituaries in *Trans. Am. Gynecologic. Soc.*, XXI, 467–72; *Codex Medicus*, II, 62–63; *Trans. Southern Surgic. and Gynecologic. Ass.*, XV, 415–17; *Atlanta Medic. and Surgic. Jour.*, ser. 3, XII, 489, 613. Battey's principal papers will be found in *Trans. Am. Gynecologic. Soc.*, vols. I to XIII; *Atlanta Medic. and Surgic. Jour.*, vol. X, ff.; and in *A System of Gynecology* (1888), ed. by M. D. Mann, II, 837–49.]

H. R. V.

BATTLE, BURRELL BUNN (July 24, 1838–Dec. 21, 1917), jurist, son of Joseph J. and Nancy (Stricklin) Battle, was born in Hinds County, Miss. He was descended in the sixth generation from John Battle, who came from Yorkshire, England, and settled in 1654 on the Nansemond River in Virginia. His father moved from North Carolina to Mississippi and later to Arkansas, where he settled in Lafayette County and became county judge (J. H. Wheeler, *Historical Sketches of North Carolina*, II, 146). Battle received the A.B. degree at Arkansas College, Fayetteville, in 1856 and the LL.B. at Cumberland University in 1858. He entered upon the practise of law at Lewisville, Ark. In 1861 he enlisted in the Confederate army as a private in the artillery and served until the end of the war. When peace was declared he took up law again at Lewisville, but in 1869 moved to Washington, Ark. He represented Hempstead County in the legislature of 1871 and was one of the leaders in the opposition to Gov. Powell Clayton [*q.v.*] and his successor, O. A. Hadley. When the House voted to impeach Clayton, Battle was appointed a member of the House managers, but the Senate was favorable to the Governor and they could do nothing (J. M. Harrell, *Brooks and Baxter War*, 1893, pp. 98–100; *House Journal*, 1871). In 1879 he moved to Little Rock and there continued the practise of law until his election to the supreme court in 1885. His service on the bench was continuous until 1911, when he declined to stand for reëlection, largely on account of increasing deafness brought about by an injury received in the war. His length of service on the supreme bench, twenty-five years, was the longest in the history of the state up to that time. Battle was considered a remarkable jurist. In the memorial service held at the time of his death Judge W. E. Hemingway said: "His temper was essentially judicial. . . . He deferred a decision until everything that should influence it had been heard." He recognized the established law as "the absolute master of his judicial work" and had no patience with bench-made law. This means that he was conservative. His associates recognized that a bench made up entirely of

men of his type would have been wanting in the progressive spirit which is essential to accommodate the law to the changing conditions of society, but considered the presence of one man of his type "a sheet anchor of safety" (*136 Arkansas Reports,* 612–15). During his tenure the laws affecting railroads, carriers, master and servant, and other subjects developed, and "in many instances his opinion constitutes the leading case" (*136 Arkansas Reports,* 618). After retirement he continued to reside in Little Rock until his death. In the opinion of the Little Rock Bar Association "he was a consistent member of the Baptist Church and an ideal Christian gentleman." In 1871 he married Mrs. Josephine A. Witherspoon (*née* Cannon), who died in 1899 without issue.

[The bare facts of Battle's life are found in *Who's Who in America*, IX; his judicial opinions in *Ark. Reports*, XLV–XCVI. The memorial addresses in *136 Ark. Reports* are strong on character, but need to be checked on facts; obit. in *Ark. Democrat* (Little Rock), Dec. 21, 1917.]

D. Y. T.

BATTLE, CULLEN ANDREWS (June 1, 1829–Apr. 8, 1905), politician and soldier, was born at Powelton, Hancock County, Ga., the son of Dr. Cullen Battle, a man of some local prominence, and Jane A. (Lamon) Battle. His brother, Rev. A. J. Battle, was for seventeen years president of Mercer University, Macon, Ga. In 1836 the family removed to Alabama and settled at Eufaula (then called Irwinton). Cullen Battle studied at the University of Alabama, and then read law in the office of John G. Shorter, afterward governor of the state. In 1851 he was married to Georgia F. Williams. He was admitted to the bar in 1852, and soon afterward formed a partnership with William P. Chilton. He acquired considerable reputation as an orator, and began to take some part in politics as an ardent and uncompromising secessionist. In the presidential campaign of 1860 he made, with Senator Yancey, an extensive speaking tour, which not only covered the state but extended to several northern cities, including Boston, New York and Philadelphia. Battle himself was chosen a presidential elector, casting his vote for Breckinridge. After the John Brown raid, he had organized a military company and offered it to Gov. Wise of Virginia, for the defense of that state. The offer was of course declined, but the company was not disbanded, being incorporated with an Alabama regiment of which Battle was appointed lieutenant-colonel. At the beginning of hostilities in 1861 the regiment was called into service to take part in the operations about Pensacola. His state commission being terminated, Battle was appointed major of the 3rd Alabama, a regiment newly organized for Confederate service, and was almost immediately promoted to be its lieutenant-colonel. He served through the Peninsular campaign with it, and when the Colonel (Lomax) was killed at Seven Pines, was promoted to fill his place. He commanded the regiment in the Maryland campaign in 1862, and at Fredericksburg. A few days before the battle of Chancellorsville, he was hurt by his horse's rearing and falling into a ditch. He returned to duty the day before the battle, but wrenched his injured back so severely, in riding, that he was unable to resume command for seven weeks. Rejoining after the army had entered Pennsylvania, he was present at the battle of Gettysburg. In the confusion of the first day's fighting the brigade was broken up, and Battle found his regiment separated from the rest of the command, but adjacent to Gen. Ramseur's brigade. "Attaching his regiment to my command on his own responsibility," wrote Ramseur, "he came in at the right place, at the right time, and in the right way" (*Official Records*, XXVII, pt. 2, p. 587). The brigade was not engaged on the second day. On the third, it was attached to Johnson's division for the attack delivered and repulsed on the Union right, early in the morning. Next month, Battle was appointed brigadier-general, his brigade forming part of Rodes's division of Ewell's corps. He received a vote of thanks from the Confederate Congress (Feb. 6, 1864) when his brigade reënlisted for the war (*Ibid.*, XLIII, 1149). He was present in command through the fighting in the Wilderness and at Spotsylvania, where the brigade lost heavily. At one time when it was driven back in disorder, but rallied, Battle makes the bald report: "I took the colors of the 3rd Alabama in my hand, went forward and asked the men to follow" (*Ibid.*, XXXVI, pt. 1, p. 1084). Later in 1864, while with Early in his Shenandoah Valley campaign, a severe wound received at Cedar Creek ended his active service. He was appointed major-general, and assigned to a division, but the war ended before he had recovered sufficiently to take command. He returned to the practise of law at Tuskegee, Ala., and once more became prominent in politics. Chosen for Congress in 1868, his inability to take the "iron-clad oath" prevented his admission. He was a strong candidate for the Democratic nomination for senator in 1870, but the probability that he could not take his seat if elected caused his name to be eliminated. In 1874 he was a delegate to the Alabama constitutional convention. He removed to Newbern, N. C., in 1880, became editor of the *Newbern Journal*, and was mayor of the city for a time. He died at Greensboro, N. C., and was buried at Petersburg, Va.

[*Confed. Mil. Hist.*, VII (1899), 388–93; unpublished Confed. records in the War Dept.; W. Brewer, *Alabama . . . 1540 to 1872* (1872), pp. 341–42; obituary in the *News and Observer* (Raleigh, N. C.), Apr. 9, 1905.]
T.M.S.

BATTLE, KEMP PLUMMER (Dec. 19, 1831–Feb. 4, 1919), college president, was born in Franklin County, N. C., the third son of William Horn Battle [*q.v.*] and Lucy (Plummer) Battle. Upon his father's coming to live at Raleigh, N. C., in 1839, he was sent to the Raleigh Male Academy. After the removal of his parents to Chapel Hill, he was prepared at the village school for the University of North Carolina, which he entered at the early age of thirteen. At seventeen he graduated, sharing first honor with two others and giving the valedictory. After graduation Battle became tutor, first of Latin, then of mathematics, remaining at the University for four years, during which time he also took his master's degree and a law course. He was then admitted to the bar and practised law in Raleigh with his brother, Richard H. Battle. He also became a director of the State Bank of North Carolina and engaged in various financial and agricultural enterprises. In politics he was, like his father, a Whig. When the Civil War came on he was outspoken as a Union man; but after Lincoln's call for troops he cast his fortune with his state and approved the secession ordinance of 1861. He was active in electing Z. B. Vance governor of North Carolina, and advised and assisted him in withstanding the too great encroachments of the Confederate Government. He was elected state treasurer in 1866, but the Act of Congress of March 1867 deprived him of office. In 1875 he was a leader, as chairman of the reorganized board of trustees, in working for reopening the University of North Carolina, closed since 1868, and in 1876 he was elected president of the revived institution. Battle set to work to raise funds from outside sources because all the endowment of the University had been sunk in Confederate securities. He was successful in collecting enough money for a beginning, and in inducing the legislature to appropriate the first state money ever set apart for the University. His unerring tact, human sympathy, kindly ways, and firm integrity, made him capable of steering the reopened institution to safety through the rocks and shallows of that difficult time. For fifteen years he remained president, was made president emeritus in 1891, accepted the chair of history, and was made professor emeritus in 1907.

During his whole life Battle wrote historical articles for publication, made addresses, and recorded facts such as provide the raw material for history. His short papers have never been collected, but many of them are listed in the Pamphlet Collections of the State Library of North Carolina, and in various periodicals. He wrote a "History of the Supreme Court of North Carolina," published in volume CIII of *North Carolina Reports*. His great work, undertaken in the years of his retirement, was the *History of the University of North Carolina*, in two large volumes (I, 1907; II, 1912), the repository of a mass of facts extending over more than a century of educational development. Battle was a genial man, humorous and humane. He maintained good discipline but by persuasion rather than command. Like his father he was a lifelong Episcopalian and like him a member of the councils of his church. On Nov. 28, 1855, he had married Martha Ann Battle, of Edgecombe County, a distant kinswoman. Their family life was most happy. He survived his wife many years, and lived to a great age, respected and beloved.

[*Biog. Hist. of N. C.*, ed. by S. A. Ashe, VI (1907); letter to Mrs. C. P. Spencer from Battle, giving story of his life, Spencer Papers, II, N. C. State Lib.; *Who's Who in America*, 1899–1919.]   H. S. C.

BATTLE, WILLIAM HORN (Oct. 17, 1802–Mar. 14, 1879), lawyer, jurist, was born in Edgecombe County, N. C., the son of Joel Battle of North Carolina and grandson of Elisha Battle of Virginia. Joel Battle built and operated one of the first cotton-mills in the South. He married Mary P. Johnson of Edgecombe. William H. Battle was the eldest of a large family including six sons. He entered the sophomore class of the University of North Carolina and graduated in two years, as valedictorian, at the age of eighteen. He immediately began the study of law with Chief Justice Henderson of North Carolina, and continued for three years, acting as the amanuensis of his teacher. He was admitted to the bar in 1825, examination being waived by recommendation of Justice Henderson. In this same year he married Lucy M. Plummer of Warrenton, N. C., and settled to practise law in Louisburg, N. C. He was not an orator or impressive as a criminal lawyer, and his success at his profession came slowly. He employed his leisure in intensive study of law, and in editing the *North Carolina Reports from 1789 to 1798*. The older edition of these was exhausted, and the confusion due to new laws conflicting with ancient English statutes was reconciled by Battle's comment in this edition.

In 1833–34, after two previous defeats, he represented his county in the North Carolina House of Commons, although he was in politics a "Henry Clay Whig" and his county was overwhelmingly Democrat. He moved to Raleigh and was a supreme court reporter, 1834–39 inclusive. In 1833 he was appointed with two others to revise the statutes of North Carolina; the revision was published in 1837. In 1839 he was a delegate to the Whig national convention which nominated Harrison. The next year he was appointed judge of the superior court of North Carolina by the Governor. In 1843 he decided to remove to Chapel Hill, N. C., the seat of the University, to educate his sons, and in 1845 he became trustee-professor of law there, serving continuously without compensation until the closing of the institution in 1868. In 1852 he was elected associate justice of the supreme court of North Carolina, which office he filled until 1868 when the state government was overthrown under Act of Congress, March 1867. He left Chapel Hill to return to Raleigh in 1868, where he practised law with two of his sons. The legislature of 1872–73 chose him to revise the statutes of North Carolina a second time. He did this unaided and hurriedly—a great task for any one man. He said that this work was not so well done as he could wish. At this period he was president of the Raleigh National Bank for several years. His wife died in 1874, and returning to Chapel Hill in 1876, he latterly made his home with his son Kemp P. Battle [*q.v.*], then president of the reopened University of North Carolina. He died in 1879 and was buried in Raleigh, N. C.

Battle was a small man in stature, a cheerful and friendly person in disposition. Very modest, laborious, and learned in the law, he was not in any way spectacular, but highly esteemed and respected. He was a life-long Episcopalian, a leading layman of his church, attending its conventions for twenty-five consecutive years. Beside his legal writings, he published in the *University of North Carolina Magazine* before the war short memoirs of early justices of the supreme court of North Carolina—Taylor, Haywood, Gaston, and Henderson—also reminiscences of early days at the University.

[*Raleigh Observer*, Mar. 15, 1879; Mrs. C. P. Spencer, *Churchman*, Apr. 12, 1879; *Obituaries, Funeral and Proc. of Bar in Memory of W. H. Battle* (1879); Proc. in supreme court, *80 N. C. Reports*, 455–64; *Address at Univ. of N. C. Commencement 1879*, by Hon. S. F. Phillips; *Address at Presentation of Portrait to Supreme Court of N. C.*, by Jos. B. Bachelor, in *90 N. C. Reports*, App., Mar. 15, 1892. See also Kemp P. Battle, *Hist. of the Univ. of N. C.*, 2 vols. (1907–12).]   H. S. C.

BAUGHER, HENRY LOUIS (July 18, 1804–Apr. 14, 1868), Lutheran clergyman, college president, was born at Abbottstown in Adams County, Pa., the son of Christian Frederick and Ann Catharine Baugher. His paternal grandfather, John George Bager, who migrated to Lebanon County, Pa., from the Palatinate in 1752, was one of the pioneer German Lutheran clergymen in America. Henry gained his preparatory training at Gettysburg from the Rev. David McConaughty and graduated in 1826 as Latin salutatorian from Dickinson College at Carlisle, Pa. His inclination had been toward the law, and he had already arranged to study under Francis Scott Key, the author of the "Star Spangled Banner," at Georgetown, D. C., but the death of his mother changed the direction of his thoughts, and he decided to enter the ministry. He attended the Princeton Theological Seminary, later transferring to the Lutheran seminary recently established at Gettysburg. In 1828 he was licensed to preach by the West Pennsylvania Synod of the Lutheran Church; in 1829 he became pastor at Boonsboro in Washington County, Md., and on October 29 of that year married Clara Mary Brooks of Carlisle, Pa. In April 1831 he returned to Gettysburg to succeed the late Rev. David Jacobs as a teacher in the gymnasium that had been opened in 1827 as an adjunct to the theological seminary.

The gymnasium prospered and was chartered in 1832 as the Pennsylvania College of Gettysburg. Baugher taught Greek and rhetoric until he succeeded the Rev. Charles Philip Krauth as president in 1850. During Baugher's professorship and presidency, the college remained small, never graduating more than twenty-one students in a single year. Although its resources were meager, the standard of scholarship was high for the time, and the institution exercised an influence wholly beneficial over a great part of the American Lutheran Church. Much of the success of the college was due to the energy, skill, and devotion of its second president, who served it for thirty-six years, performing his duties as teacher and executive until within eight days of his death.

Baugher was of middle height, somewhat stout, with a firm, straight mouth, a delicate, aquiline nose, and remarkably clear eyes. In character he was a slightly irascible saint, but the irascibility softened as age crept upon him, while the saintliness was undiminished. Homer and the Greek Testament were his favorite reading. In theology he was decidedly conservative, finding his masters in the German Lutheran divines of the sixteenth and seventeenth centuries. He was an efficient teacher and administrator, a strict disciplinarian, and the master of a plain, succinct, yet moving pulpit style.

[Pa. Coll. Bk., 1832–82 (1882), ed. by E. S. Breidenbaugh; Decennial Report Alumni Ass. Pa. Coll., June 30, 1870 (1871); H. E. Jacobs: Hist. of the Evangelical Luth. Ch. in the U. S. (1893), pp. 293, 373, 416, 434; Am. Luth. Biogs. (1890), ed. by J. C. Jensson, pp. 63–65; and Baugher's printed baccalaureate sermons for 1855, 1856, 1857, 1858, and 1861; A. R. Wentz, ed., Hist. of the Gettysburg Theol. Sem. (1927).]

G.H.G.

BAUM, LYMAN FRANK (May 15, 1856–May 6, 1919), writer, playwright, was born in Chittenango, N. Y., the son of Benjamin Ward and Cynthia (Stanton) Baum. His childhood and early manhood were uneventful. The latter part of his education was received at an academy in Syracuse, N. Y. At twenty-four he began newspaper reporting and 1888–90 was editor of the *Dakota Pioneer,* at Aberdeen, S. D. In 1882 he married Maude Gage of Fayetteville, N. Y. In 1897 he became editor of the *Chicago Show Window,* a periodical for window decorators which he edited until 1902. He had dallied with poetry and prose for some years, and had published a little. In 1899, in collaboration with an artist, W. W. Denslow, he prepared the draft of a book called *Father Goose: His Book.* It was an instant success, selling 90,000 copies in ninety days. This was a great stimulus to Baum, who had been laboring to support a large family on a small income. F. K. Reilly, the publisher, became Baum's friend and adviser; and when Baum read to him the first draft of his *Wizard of Oz,* Reilly immediately suggested that he had the basis of a stage production. The *Wonderful Wizard of Oz* was published in 1900, and in 1901 the play was produced in Chicago, raising Fred Stone and Dave Montgomery, two obscure vaudeville performers, to stardom over night. After the success of the play Baum went abroad for several months, doing much writing in Italy and Sicily. Upon his return he moved to Pasadena, Cal., where he built a home to his liking. One of its interesting features was an enormous birdcage in the flower garden. The cage contained scores of song birds. He liked to write in his garden. He became a grower of dahlias, his varieties taking many prizes in California. Besides several miscellaneous items he published two novels, *The Fate of a Clown* (1905) and *Daughters of Destiny* (1906), issued over the *nom de plume* of "Schuyler Staunton," six books for boys under the pen name of "Floyd Akers," and twenty-four books for girls under the name of "Edith Van Dyne." These books are of no literary value, but were popular for a time, and brought Baum considerable money. The fourteen Wizard of Oz stories will perhaps have a permanent place among children's books. The most typical are *The Wonderful Wizard of Oz, The Woggle-Bug Book,* and *The Tik-Tok Man of Oz.* Eight of Baum's stories were dramatized and produced. He died at his home in Hollywood, Cal.

[Most of the information concerning Baum was obtained from his publisher, Mr. F. K. Reilly of Chicago, who was his close friend; see also *Who's Who in America*, 1912–13; *Chicago Tribune*, May 18, 1919.]

M. S.

BAUSMAN, BENJAMIN (Jan. 28, 1824–May 8, 1909), clergyman of the German Reformed Church, editor, writer, the son of John and Elizabeth (Peters) Bausman, was born on his father's farm near Lancaster, Pa., the youngest of nine children. His ancestry was German, of the Lower Palatinate. What is probably the oldest house now standing in Lancaster bears the inscription, "William Bowsman and Elisabeth Built this House, 1762." Life on the farm was serious. The hard work inured the boy to that habit of tireless industry which was so marked a characteristic of his versatile career. He was six feet in height, lean and lank, of the Lincoln type, with a long, spare countenance and sad brown eyes. He was graduated from Marshall College, Mercersburg, Pa., in 1851, and took one year of professional study in the Theological Seminary at the same place, under the distinguished professors, John W. Nevin and Philip Schaff. In 1853 he was ordained a minister of the German Reformed Church and immediately began the practise of his profession. His most abundant pastoral work was done in Reading, Pa. (1863–1909), where it was virtually concentrated in one congregation, that of St. Paul's, of which he was the founder. He greatly extended the power and influence of his denomination by establishing, at a dozen strategic missionary points in the city, Sunday-schools which afterward developed into flourishing churches. Gifted with a deep and understanding sympathy with the common people he exerted a profound spiritual influence upon the entire community. Bethany Orphans' Home is the most significant memorial of his power of achievement in the field of organized philanthropic endeavor. In the wider sphere of ecclesiastical government he played a large part. He was at one time or another a member of every executive board of the church. He was editor of the *Guardian* (1867–81), a religious and literary magazine for young people. He founded and edited *Der Reformirte Hausfreund* (1866–1903), a bi-weekly paper which, as a moulding force in the religious and social life of the Pennsylvania Germans, was regarded as the most unique of his many undertakings. Appointed delegate to the Evangelical Church Diet at Lübeck, Germany, he seized the opportunity to spend a year of study and leisurely travel in Europe and the Holy Land (1856–57). His observations and impressions are recorded in two books: *Sinai and Zion* (1861), which ran through eleven editions; and *Wayside Gleanings in Europe* (1875). He also edited and published *Harbaugh's Harfe* (1902), a small volume of poems in Pennsylvania-German by Henry Harbaugh, the "poet-preacher" of the Reformed Church—a contribution of distinct value to the study of this peculiar and philologically interesting type of local vernacular. Late in life, Apr. 6, 1875, he was married to Amelia B. Bingaman of Reading, Pa., who survived him. In his theology he was conservative. He accepted the tenets of the Mercersburg school, but no controversial word seems to have come from his lips or pen to feed the flame of theological discontent. "Let us put such theology as we have into harness—get it to work in acts of beneficence, in extending Christ's kingdom," he wrote to a friend. "Witness-bearing for Jesus Christ" was the subject of his last sermon, written four days before his death.

[*Life of Benjamin Bausman,* by H. H. Ranck (1912); *Franklin and Marshall Coll. Obit. Record,* II; *Proc. Alliance of Reformed Churches, Belfast, Ireland, 1884;* "Civil War Reminiscences" in the *Guardian,* 1874; obituaries in the *Ref. Ch. Messenger,* May 13 (portr.), July 15, Aug. 26, 1909.]

G. F. M.

BAXLEY, HENRY WILLIS (June 1803– Mar. 13, 1876), physician and surgeon, son of George and Mary (Merryman) Baxley, was born in Baltimore, where he spent most of his life. He received his collegiate education at St. Mary's College and graduated in medicine at the University of Maryland in 1824. His first public position was that of attending physician to the Baltimore General Dispensary, 1826–29. He subsequently was appointed physician to the Maryland Penitentiary, 1831–32. In the latter year when cholera made its appearance he was sent by the president and directors of that institution to New York to investigate the history and pathology of the disease. His elaborate report was subsequently published in the Baltimore newspapers.

In 1837 Baxley became the occasion, if not the cause, of the temporary disruption of the University of Maryland Medical School. The board of regents of that institution had been abolished by the Maryland legislature in 1825, and a board of trustees created, with the new power of appointing professors regardless of the nomination of the faculty. These trustees were charged by the older professors with extravagance, inefficiency, and financial corruption. Baxley was appointed demonstrator of anatomy in the school in 1834 and allied himself with the trustees. He was unpopular with both students and faculty. Three years later the head of his department, Professor Geddings, resigned, owing, it was thought, to pressure from the trustees. The faculty nominated Dr. William N. Baker to succeed Geddings, but the trustees appointed Baxley. The faculty thereupon resigned in a body and led by Professors Potter and Hall, who had been appointed by the old board of regents, they proceeded to call these regents together, to take possession of some of the buildings, in which they continued their instruction, and to enter suit for the recovery of the other buildings. Meanwhile the trustees, retaining Baxley, appointed new professors to the vacated chairs, and these in their turn gave instruction in the buildings which remained to them. The anomalous situation was ended in 1839 by the court of appeals which declared the act of 1825 unconstitutional and reinstated the regents in control (E. G. Cordell, *Historical Sketch of the University of Maryland School of Medicine,* 1891).

Baxley then joined with Dr. Horace H. Hayden, a pioneer teacher of dentistry, and Dr. Thomas E. Bond, Jr., in the establishment, in 1839, of the first dental college to be formally organized either in this country or abroad, the Baltimore College of Dental Surgery. He became its first professor of anatomy. In 1839 he reported a case of removal of the entire lower jaw of a patient suffering from osteosarcoma. In 1846 he was appointed professor of surgery in the Washington Medical College of Baltimore but resigned in 1847. He was physician to the Baltimore Alms House 1849–50. He is said by Dr. Judson Gilman (*post*) to have been one of the first on record to operate for strabismus. In 1850 he was called to the chair of anatomy in the Medical College of Ohio at Cincinnati and in 1852 was transferred to that of surgery, but remained for only two sessions. During President Buchanan's administration, Baxley visited the west coast of South America and California and the Pacific Islands on a mission to reform hospital work under consular supervision. This mission extended through eighteen months. On his return to America he published a pamphlet entitled *Republican Imperialism, Not American Liberty* and somewhat later his first book, under the title, *What I Saw on the West Coast of South and North America and at the Hawaiian Islands* (1865). He was appointed Government Inspector of Hospitals in 1865. In 1866 failing health caused him to go to Europe where he spent the next nine years mainly in Italy and Spain. During this time he wrote a two-volume book entitled *Spain, Art Remains and Art Realities, Painters, Priests and Princes* (London, 1875).

Baxley was tall, well built, very neat and ac-

curate in all matters, dress included, and in later years had a snow-white beard which reached almost to his waist.

His name is perpetuated in the Baxley Medical Professorship of the Johns Hopkins Medical School. By his will a sum of money amounting to $23,836.52 was received by the trustees of the University to endow any medical professorship that they might think proper. This fund, the first substantial gift received by the University outside of the original endowment, was kept intact and allowed to accumulate until 1901 when it was set apart to endow the professorship of pathology.

[Obituary by Dr. Judson Gilman, *Trans. Medic. and Chirurgical Faculty of Md.,* Apr. 1876; brief biog. by E. F. Cordell in *Am. Med. Biogs.* (1920); additional information from Dr. Henry M. Baxley of Baltimore.]

C.R.B.

BAXTER, ELISHA (Sept. 1, 1827–May 31, 1899), jurist, prominent in Arkansas politics in the Reconstruction period, was born in Rutherford County, N. C., the son of William Baxter, an Irishman, and his second wife, Catherine (Lee) Baxter (*Biographical and Historical Memoirs of North East Arkansas,* 1889, p. 640). In 1849 Elisha Baxter married Harriet Patton of Rutherford County, by whom he had six children. In 1852 he moved to Arkansas where in 1853 he opened a general store at Batesville with his brother Taylor. Two years later they went into bankruptcy, but ultimately paid all their debts. Elisha then worked in a printing office and studied law. He was elected to the legislature in 1854 and 1858, was a Whig and opposed secession, but for a time held the office of prosecuting attorney under the Confederate state government. When Gen. S. R. Curtis entered Batesville, Baxter cast in his lot with the Union but refused to fight against friends (F. Hempstead, *A Pictorial History of Arkansas,* 1890). Forced to leave Batesville, he took his family to Missouri, but was captured and brought to trial at Little Rock on a charge of treason. Escaping from prison, possibly with connivance, he raised the 4th Arkansas Mounted Infantry (Union) and was placed in command at Batesville. Upon the organization of the loyal Murphy state government in 1864, he was elected to the supreme court, but soon resigned on election to the United States Senate. By this time Congress had become wary of Lincoln's plan of reconstruction, and the Wade-Davis Bill was passed in opposition. Several efforts were made to secure the admission of Baxter to the Senate, but all attempts failed, the most favorable vote being 18 to 27. The case was important as setting a precedent for the other Southern states.

In 1868 Baxter became judge of the third circuit under the Reconstruction government. Four years later, in an effort to stem the tide of adverse public sentiment due to the misgovernment of the carpet bag régime, the regular Republicans ("Minstrels"), headed by Powell Clayton [q.v.], nominated Baxter for governor on a reform platform. But the "Brindletail" faction refused to accept him and nominated Joseph Brooks on a platform calling a little more forcefully for the removal of political disabilities from the whites. The Democrats endorsed Brooks. The campaign was a heated one, but Baxter was elected by a majority of 2,919. Brooks at once contested the result; the legislature, however, supported Baxter, who was inaugurated Jan. 6, 1873. In his inaugural Baxter promised to carry out reforms, and in a few days the legislature submitted an amendment reënfranchising the whites. Satisfied with this, the Democrats began to lose interest in Brooks, but he did not give up the contest. He tried both the supreme court and a local court, but his case hung fire and many of his Republican friends deserted him. As Baxter continued his program of reform some of the regular Republicans became alarmed and left him for Brooks, but Senators Clayton and Dorsey, the former being the Republican boss, stood by him for another year. Baxter had opposed a bill for the issuance of more bonds for aid to railroads; when in March 1874 he refused to issue any more of those already authorized, because convinced of crookedness in the affair, even Clayton and Dorsey deserted him for Brooks. By a clever move the latter now secured a decision from the supreme court in his favor and seized the executive office. Baxter refused to yield, and both called out the militia. In proportion as the Republicans abandoned Baxter the Democrats rallied to his side. Both parties appealed to Washington. At first President Grant was inclined toward Brooks, but after investigation left the decision to the legislature. The amendment to reënfranchise the whites had been adopted, and special elections to fill vacancies had given the Democrats a majority in the legislature. This body again decided for Baxter, and Brooks was forced to retire. The legislature then called a convention to draw up a constitution, which was adopted by a very large majority. The Democratic nomination was open to Baxter for reëlection, but he declined and retired to his home in Batesville, where he resumed his law practise and engaged in farming until he died.

[John M. Harrell, *The Brooks and Baxter War* (1893) is the best source of information about the chief event in Baxter's life. The text itself, written by an eye-witness, is source material and it gives extensive quotations from the testimony taken by the Poland Committee, *House Report, No. 771*, 43 Cong., 1 Sess. *Appleton's Ann. Cyc.*, 1873, 1874, contains useful information. T. S. Staples, *Reconstruction in Ark.* (1923) is the most recent and scholarly account. The press of the country, especially the *N.Y. Herald, N.Y. World*, and *St. Louis Dispatch* (April–May, 1874), gave considerable space to the contest between Baxter and Brooks. There are good obituaries of Baxter in the *Ark. Democrat*, June 1, 1899, and *Ark. Gazette*, June 2, 1899.] D.Y.T.

BAXTER, HENRY (Sept. 8, 1821–Dec. 30, 1873), Union soldier, was a native of Sidney Plains, Delaware County, N. Y. His parents were Levi and Lois (Johnson) Baxter. Both grandfathers were veterans of the Revolution. In early life he was associated with his father in the keeping of a store and mill. He made a journey to California at the time of the gold fever. Before the Civil War he organized at his home in Michigan the Jonesville "Light Guards." He entered the war as a captain, was commissioned colonel in 1862 and brigadier-general of volunteers in 1863, and was mustered out of the army in 1865 with the brevet of major-general of volunteers. References to his activities are numerous in the annals of the Army of the Potomac. (Longstreet, *Manassas to Appomattox,* 1896, speaks of Baxter's command composed of volunteers for that act, as crossing the Rappahannock River under fire, shortly before the battle of Fredericksburg, an action which has been characterized as a "brilliant exploit.") At Gettysburg he commanded a brigade in Gen. Robinson's division, belonging to the 1st Corps, then temporarily under Gen. Abner Doubleday. (Doubleday, *Chancellorsville and Gettysburg*, 1882, describes Baxter's brigade as being in the "thickest of the fighting.") In the first day of the battle he captured nearly all of the Confederate brigade commanded by Iverson (*Battles and Leaders of the Civil War*, 1887–88, III, 285). In the final campaigns of 1864–65 under Grant, his brigade formed part of the 5th Army Corps under Gen. Warren. He was desperately wounded at Antietam and again at Fredericksburg, and a third time at the Wilderness, where two horses were shot under him, but recovered in time to serve in the closing battle of Five Forks. His brevet cited his gallantry and services at the Wilderness, Dabney's Mill, and Five Forks. After the war he was register of deeds, and later United States minister to Honduras for three years from 1869 to 1872. His death occurred in his home at Jonesville, Mich. He was married in 1854 to Elvira E. George of Hillsdale County, Mich.

[*Hist. of Hillsdale County* (1879); *Portr. and Biog. Album of Hillsdale County* (1888), pp. 990–91; F. B. Heitman, *Hist. Reg.* (1903).] E.K.A.

BAXTER, JOHN (Mar. 5, 1819–Apr. 2, 1886), Southern Unionist, was a son of Catherine (Lee) Baxter and William Baxter, an Irish immigrant, who came to Rutherford County in western North Carolina, where he accumulated a modest competence. The only formal education John Baxter received was in the "old field schools." To the last he had little taste for general reading and was markedly a man of slender education except in law. He was first a merchant in a country town, and then after a brief study of law, rose to some prominence at the North Carolina bar. He was several times a member of the North Carolina legislature, and once speaker of the lower house. On June 26, 1842, he married Orra Alexander. In 1844 he was district elector on the Henry Clay presidential ticket. In May 1857 he removed to Knoxville, Tenn., where he soon attained leadership in the law. A Whig in politics, he was a slaveholder with strong sympathies for the Southern position, but was not a secessionist. When the Civil War was drawing near, he advocated in vain a convention of delegates from the Southern states for the purpose of considering means of saving the Union. Against secession he took the stump and made many bitter speeches, but later became more moderate. At a Union convention, held in Greeneville, East Tennessee, on June 17, 1861, it was proposed that a new state be formed which would raise an independent army with Baxter as general, a movement which was not successful on account of the encircling of the region by Confederate forces. For a time it seemed that Baxter might follow the state into the Confederacy, but in 1862 he was publishing a Union newspaper in East Tennessee. The same year he was arrested in Memphis and held in prison for several days as an enemy of the South. When he went back to Knoxville, he openly joined the Unionist sympathizers and was a thorn in the side of the Confederate cause. After the Confederacy failed, Baxter tried in vain, with Thomas A. R. Nelson, to organize a new party, to occupy a middle ground between the Democrats and the Republicans. In the state constitutional convention of 1870 he was one of the few ex-Unionist delegates but in recognition of his learning in the law, he was made chairman of the important judiciary committee, and had much to do in framing the new constitution. At some time between 1872 and 1875 he became a political follower of William G. Brownlow [*q.v.*]. He was now not only a leader of the East Tennessee bar, but was generally considered one of the best lawyers in the state and was engaged in most of the well-known cases which developed in the ten years following the Civil War. He was appointed United States circuit judge by President Hayes in 1877. As judge he made no notable decisions and wrote no notable opinions, but managed to simplify procedure in his court and used drastic measures to clear cases before him of technicalities. He was a man of great native ability, assertive, self-reliant, and of marked individuality. He was fairly learned in the law and based his arguments, even in the more important cases, upon general principles. He was a good speaker with a rather harsh manner, who made bitter enemies and devoted friends.

[W. M. Garrett and A. V. Goodpasture, *Hist. of Tenn.* (1900), pp. 205, 268; W. T. Hale and D. L. Merritt, *Hist. of Tenn. and Tennesseeans* (1913), pp. 1471–72; J. W. Caldwell, *Sketches of the Bench and Bar of Tenn.* (1898); Oliver P. Temple, *Notable Men of Tenn.* (1912); William Rule, *Standard Hist. of Knoxville* (1900); obituaries in *Knoxville Daily Chronicle, Memphis Appeal, Memphis Avalanche, Nashville Daily American,* Apr. 3, 1886.]

W. L. F.

BAXTER, WILLIAM (July 6, 1820–Feb. 11, 1880), clergyman, educator, son of Henry and Mary Baxter, was born in Leeds, Yorkshire, England. In 1828 he came with his parents to Allegheny City, Pa., where he learned the tinner's trade; and also prepared for college. In early life he was a member of the Methodist Protestant Church, but when eighteen years old he joined the "Christian Church," or "Disciples of Christ," with whom he was actively associated for the rest of his life. In 1845 he graduated at Bethany College. After a pastorate in Pittsburgh, Pa., he went south in 1848, serving as pastor at Port Gibson, Miss., and at Baton Rouge, La., conducting evangelistic services in various places, and for three years holding a professorship of belles-lettres at Newton College, Miss. On Mar. 7, 1854, he was married to Mrs. Fidelia (Pico) Vail, widow of a Mississippi planter but born in Massachusetts. In 1860 he became president of Arkansas College, in Fayetteville, Ark. His situation in the little college town was one of peculiar difficulty. Although he had now lived for twelve years in Mississippi and Louisiana, and had, part of the time, held slaves and managed a plantation, his convictions as to Union and anti-slavery were those of the North. He tried to live in peace with his neighbors, while making no secret of his convictions, and to keep his college in operation. It was an effort to do what was impossible; and it ended in 1863, when the college building was burned to the ground, the students were scattered, and he, with his family, was forced to leave the state. His book, *Pea Ridge and Prairie Grove, or Scenes and Incidents of the War in Arkansas* (1864), is important as an authentic record of the experience of a Union man in one of the seceding states, and incidentally reveals its author as a person of character and independence.

For two years after the war Baxter lived in Cincinnati, Ohio, preaching in various places, and active in journalistic and social work. From 1865 to 1875 he was pastor of the Christian Church in Lisbon, Ohio. He died at New Castle, Pa., Feb. 11, 1880. Besides *Pea Ridge and Prairie Grove* he was the author of poems, temperance addresses, and a *Life of Elder Walter Scott* (1874) which is valuable as a record of the early history of the Disciples.

[Alanson Wilcox, *Hist. of the Disciples of Christ in Ohio* (1918); Records of Bethany Coll., 1841–45; Memorabilia of Christian Church, Lisbon, O., through Rev. R. J. Bennett, 1927; letters from sons, William Baxter of Los Angeles, Cal., and R. G. Baxter of E. Baton Rouge, La.]

C. N.

BAYARD, JAMES ASH(E)TON (July 28, 1767–Aug. 6, 1815), statesman, diplomat, was a leader among the Federalists of the United States during the first quarter-century. Of old Huguenot stock, he was descended from Petrus Bayard whose mother Anna, widow of Samuel Bayard and sister of Peter Stuyvesant, came with three children on *The Princess* to New Amsterdam May 11, 1647. Petrus obtained land in New York, Pennsylvania, and Maryland, and his son Samuel in 1698 chose Bohemia Manor, Md., for his home. Here James, of the third generation, brought Mary Ashton, his wife, and here on Aug. 11, 1738, the first James Ashton Bayard was born. He was a surgeon in Philadelphia until his death in Charleston, S. C., Jan. 8, 1770. In 1760 he married Agnes Hodge, who on July 28, 1767, gave him a second son, James Ashton (as the name was originally spelled, although custom has fixed the modern spelling as Asheton).

At the death of his father, James Ashton Bayard was placed under the guardianship of his father's twin brother, John Bayard [q.v.] of Philadelphia, which continued until James's graduation from Princeton College, Sept. 29, 1784. During these fourteen years, and especially after the death of his mother in 1774, his immediate surroundings did much to determine the young man's future. His education was essentially conservative, whether at Piqua in Lancaster County from his uncle, at Princeton, or in the circle of Pennsylvania society in which he moved. Upon the completion of his college work he studied law with Joseph Reed and after 1785 with Jared Ingersoll, each of whom strengthened the conservative tone of his earlier training. When, therefore, he was admitted to the New Castle bar in August 1787, and at Philadelphia in September, and began the practise of his profession at Wil-

mington the same year, he was welcomed as a useful member of the Federalist party. And when on Feb. 11, 1795, he married Ann, daughter of Chief Justice Richard Bassett [q.v.] of Delaware, he acquired an important political and social position among the Federalist leaders.

The election of 1796 demonstrated Bayard's vote-getting ability in Delaware, sending him to the House of Representatives, which he entered May 15, 1797. An excellent opportunity to demonstrate his strength came soon after he had taken his seat. On July 3, 1797, Adams sent Congress a message and papers disclosing a plan of certain United States citizens to aid Britain in seizing Spanish territory in Louisiana. Earlier fears of a British attack in this section had been brought to the notice of Timothy Pickering, secretary of state since Dec. 10, 1795, by the Spanish, but such intentions had been denied by the British minister. Now a letter of William Blount [q.v.], senator from Tennessee, to James Carey, interpreter to the Cherokee Indians, dated Apr. 21, 1797, had come to light involving the British minister and Blount himself in the plan. The manuscripts were laid before Congress and Blount's guilt seemed plain. No one claimed his innocence, but Gallatin and other Republicans declared that as a senator he was exempt from impeachment. The real criminal, continued Gallatin, was Robert Liston, the British minister, or President Adams, who had had "improper understandings" with him. In this crisis Bayard managed the case against Blount so ably that the latter was expelled from the Senate in July 1797.

Bayard played a decisive part in the disputed presidential election of 1800 when the decision between Jefferson and Burr, both Republicans, was thrown into the House of Representatives. The Federalists, on the principle that any one was preferable to Jefferson, supported Burr for thirty-five inconclusive ballots. Then their leaders decided to shift to Jefferson if they could obtain from him certain assurances as to the future. Bayard's position as the most important Federalist in a border state, as well as his work for Federalist financial measures, 1798–1800, made him the most fitting negotiator for that impartial treatment desired by business interests as well as by office-holders in the National Government. His first approach was through John Nicholas, representative from Virginia and a particular friend of Jefferson. To him Bayard stated that "if certain points of the future administration could be understood and arranged with Mr. Jefferson . . . three states would withdraw from any opposition to his election." They sought only assurance of support for the public credit, the maintenance of the naval system, and security for minor office-holders in their government positions. "I explained," continued Bayard, "that I considered it not only reasonable but necessary, that offices of high discretion and confidence should be filled by men of Mr. Jefferson's choice." In the latter group he placed cabinet officers, and as examples of the former he mentioned collectors at ports of entry. He was assured by Nicholas that the points seemed reasonable, and that Jefferson with the men about him would undoubtedly be of the same opinion. Bayard replied that he "wanted an engagement," and if this were conceded by Jefferson, "the election should be ended." He was unable to obtain a direct promise from Nicholas, but in his deposition of Apr. 3, 1806 (*Bayard Papers,* pp. 128–29), he states that Gen. Samuel Smith took the same three points to the Virginian and was authorized by Jefferson "to say that they corresponded with his views and intentions and that we might confide in him accordingly." Although no Federalist voted for Jefferson, by absence or refusing to vote "the opposition of Vermont, Maryland, South Carolina and Delaware was immediately withdrawn and Mr. Jefferson was made President by the votes of ten states," on the thirty-sixth ballot (Bayard's letter of Feb. 17, 1801, pub. in *Niles' Weekly Register,* Nov. 16, 1822). Shortly afterward, Bayard wrote to President Adams declining the proffered ministry to France as he would have to hold it during Jefferson's term to make it worth while, and if he did so he would be accused of having made an agreement with him.

In the discussions of "the judiciary reform measure" of 1801 and its repeal, Bayard ably defended the Federalist position. The fact that his father-in-law, Richard Bassett, was one of the new judges involved, was unnecessarily invoked to explain his stand. The personal factor may have added vigor to his words, but Bayard's belief in the need for the law and in the increased importance it gave to Delaware (Bayard to Bassett, Jan. 25, 1800) as well as his conviction that the repeal was "a most flagrant violation of the Constitution" and "prostrated the independence of the judicial power," were in all probability quite genuine.

Bayard's work in the Senate began Jan. 15, 1805, and continued until May 3, 1813. Much of his time was occupied with legal business, for while he disagreed thoroughly with the administration which "distinguishes itself only by its weakness and hypocrisy," he was equally certain that "no Federal prescription" would ever be taken to end the "political malady" of the

period (to Andrew Bayard Apr. 2, 1805; Jan. 30, 1806; *Bayard Papers,* pp. 164–65). Sane and moderate in his views, Bayard strove to uphold the dignity of his country against Britain or France as readily as he opposed the fitting out of the Miranda Expedition against Spain in 1806. A stanch believer in the superior abilities of an educated leadership, he was willing to subordinate himself if he could thereby be useful. An excellent illustration of Bayard's position was his national service under a hostile administration before and during the War of 1812. In 1808 he was willing to give Gallatin the credit of securing the renewal of the charter of the United States Bank expiring in 1811, or to join in obtaining a charter for a new one. The former was his preference, but during 1810–11 when renewal seemed impossible Bayard willingly served as chairman of the committee to secure a charter for a new institution. Defeated at this time by the vote of Vice-President Clinton, Bayard sought to keep the nation from the war into which she seemed to be drifting. He had little confidence in Napoleon's promises and saw clearly that Britain could not be coerced by commercial regulations (Bayard to Andrew Bayard July 3, 1809; Mar. 5, 1810; to Wells Jan. 12, 1812; *Bayard Papers,* pp. 177, 179, 188). He therefore joined Adams in urging that United States vessels be allowed to defend themselves and was pleased when our war-ships did so in the skirmishes with the Barbary States. He advised Federalist agreement in defensive measures and earnest support for all acts strengthening the army and navy. As late as May 2, 1812, he hoped the fear of additional free states from conquered Canada might induce the South to favor a naval war with Britain rather than land campaigns, a hope which had an unexpected measure of fulfilment in the war which followed. During this war Bayard is said to have "helped with his own hands to build a fort almost on the site of Fort Christina," the old Swedish fortress of 1638. Meanwhile necessity compelled the Republican leaders to abandon many of the methods used by Jefferson to obtain popularity. This brought Bayard and the President more in harmony as to the means of carrying on the war. A careful and judicious man devoted to his nation as well as to family and friends, Bayard was regarded as representing at this time both Federalist and Republican sentiment. The death of his sister Jane, Sept. 30, 1809, after serious mental derangement requiring much care from Bayard, allowed him more time for national service in those trying years, while his wife, who survived him until 1854, helped her husband during the war period by assuming many of the family cares.

With the European crisis of 1813 and the ability of the United States to maintain her rights upon the sea demonstrated, both Britain and the United States wished peace. Adams, Bayard, and Albert Gallatin, from different sections of the country, were appointed by President Madison to represent the United States. Bayard sailed from New Castle, Del., on May 9, 1813. By August 1814 when the representatives of the two nations met at Ghent, Napoleon had been captured, three armies had been sent to America, and Castlereagh, British foreign secretary, was willing to show the contempt he felt for the United States. A description of the negotiations is out of place here. Suffice it to say that eventually a treaty resulted, giving to neither party what it proposed but securing for the United States the control of the Mississippi River, eliminating from discussion certain questions which time alone could settle and others which the war itself had decided. In Bayard's opinion no power in Europe would soon disturb America again (*Papers,* pp. 366–67). On Feb. 27, 1815, Bayard was nominated minister to Russia, but he declined the position as he considered his services at that court unnecessary. His diplomatic ability was recognized in 1814–15, when he was chosen to continue with Adams, Clay, and Gallatin in negotiations for a treaty of commerce with Great Britain. Ill health prevented the completion of this mission, and on June 18, 1815, Bayard sailed from England for Wilmington, where he died six days after his arrival.

[The papers of James A. Bayard, *Am. Hist. Ass. Reports, 1913,* II (1915), ed. by Elizabeth Donnan, and referred to as *Bayard Papers;* Bayard's letters to Cæsar A. Rodney in *Del. Hist. Soc. Papers for 1901* (XXXI); *Mass. Hist. Soc. Proc., Dec. 1914;* J. T. Scharf, *Hist. of Del.* (1888); J. G. Wilson, *Col. John Bayard and the Bayard Family* (1885); *Annals of Cong., 1795–1815; Aurora Gen. Advertiser,* and *Aurora* (Phila., 1795–1815); the more gen. histories of the United States, especially those by Adams, Hildreth, McMaster, and Schouler; *Writings of John Quincy Adams; Works of John Adams; Complete Works of Benjamin Franklin; Works of Alexander Hamilton; Writings of Thomas Jefferson; Writings of James Madison.*]

C. H. L—n.

BAYARD, JAMES ASHETON (Nov. 15, 1799–June 13, 1880), lawyer, senator, was born at Wilmington, Del. He was the younger son of James A. Bayard [*q.v.*] and Ann (Bassett) Bayard, and brother of Richard Henry Bayard [*q.v.*]. He was educated at Princeton and Union Colleges, graduating at the latter school at the age of nineteen. Although intended for a mercantile career, he turned to the study of law and

in the spring of 1822 was admitted to the Delaware bar. A year later on July 8, 1823, he married Ann, daughter of Thomas and Dorothy Willing Francis of Philadelphia, thereby uniting important Pennsylvania families. He won success in his profession, being counsel in many important cases, among them one in which the Chesapeake & Ohio Canal Company was a party, involving about $250,000, and establishing Bayard's reputation. In 1843 he removed to New York City but returned to Wilmington three years later where he assisted in the legal training of his son Thomas Francis Bayard [*q.v.*].

During his early life Bayard had some political experiences, although few victories fell to his share. In the formation of parties 1820–28 he had enlisted with the Democrats and his popularity in Delaware was not increased by Jackson's nomination of him in December 1833 as one of five government directors of the United States Bank for 1834. He was defeated as candidate for the House of Representatives from Delaware in 1828 and 1832, and when the four other nominees of the President had been rejected by a Whig Senate, Bayard refused to serve in the position offered him in 1833. In the Congressional elections of 1834 he was again defeated by John J. Milligan, Whig candidate for reëlection, by 155 votes. In a close contest for the senatorship in 1838 Bayard's campaign failed owing to the refusal of the Whig state Senate to sit in joint session with the Democratic House, preferring that the state should have but one senator rather than lose the opportunity of electing a Whig the following year. Twelve years later, following the agreement of both parties in the state to support the Wilmot proviso, Bayard was elected United States senator (1851–57) upon the sixteenth ballot, being again returned in 1857 and in 1863. Meanwhile as a delegate to the Delaware constitutional convention of 1852–53 he considered his county of Newcastle unfairly treated in the constitutional changes agreed upon. He therefore opposed the work of the convention and helped to defeat it in 1853. The Native Americans carried the state in 1854 so that as a result Delaware waited until 1882 for her new constitution.

Bayard's position in the Senate was not an easy one. From 1851 to 1864, if ever in American history, statesmen were needed. The deaths of Calhoun (1850), Clay and Webster (1852) had deprived the nation of her prominent leaders. Bayard, a friend of the Union as governed by Andrew Jackson, and from a border state as was Jackson, saw his party split by the Dred Scott decision of March 1857. He could join neither Breckinridge nor Douglas, while the personalities of Frémont and Lincoln appealed to him; he, therefore, entered the new Republican party but with his faith in the ideals of Jackson unchanged. The election of 1860 precipitated the crisis, and Bayard supported the new President. His position during the war was bound to prove embarrassing at the best. With Charles Sumner shouting that "nothing against slavery can be unconstitutional" and a growing tendency everywhere to accept the maxim that *inter arma silent leges* as the basis of policy, Senator Bayard adhered to his conservative tradition. He opposed most of the anti-slavery measures enacted between 1861 and 1864. He made a notable speech on Apr. 3, 1862, in opposition to emancipation in the District of Columbia, declaring that it was an outrageous invasion of property rights. It was furthermore, he declared, exceedingly impolitic and likely to cause disloyalty in the border states. If his emphasis on the property aspects of slavery seems anomalous at the present time, his presentation of the race problem which would inevitably accompany emancipation shows that he had a far better appreciation of its magnitude than his Senate contemporaries, and subsequent history has justified many of his predictions. His financial training compelled him to oppose the Legal Tender Act of Feb. 25, 1862, in the Senate and to urge more conciliation and compromise in the Reconstruction policies adopted by the Republicans. On the death of Lincoln the aggressive nature of Thaddeus Stevens repelled him, and he was not at home in the party with which he acted. He opposed the test oath for officeholders, and when the Senate passed the measure, Bayard, although subscribing to it, expressed his dissent by resigning his seat (Jan. 30, 1864). He was succeeded by George Read Riddle, but upon the death of the latter, Mar. 29, 1867, Gov. Gove Saulsbury appointed and the legislature elected Bayard for the remainder of his original term. Like his brother Richard, Senator Bayard gradually returned to the Democratic party and upon the expiration of his term, Mar. 4, 1869, gladly saw his place taken by his son, Thomas Francis Bayard, a Democrat. With this event Bayard's active career ceased, and he passed the remainder of his life in retirement at Wilmington. A conservative in political opinion, Bayard was unfortunate in living in an era which demanded constructive statesmen.

[A few MSS. of James A. Bayard, Jr., are in the Lib. of Cong. and others—originals or copies—are in the Bayard Family collection referred to in *Am. Hist. Ass. Reports, 1913*, II (1915). J. G. Wilson, *Col. John Bayard and the Bayard Family* (1885); J. T. Scharf, *Hist. of Del.* (1888); *Cong. Globe*, 1833–69; *Jour. of the U. S. Senate*, 1851–69; J. B. McMaster, *Hist. of the People of the U. S.*, IV–VII (1895); J. F. Rhodes, *Hist. of the U.S. from the Compromise of 1850*, I–III (1893); Woodrow Wilson, *Hist. of the Am. People* (1918); *Del. Hist. Soc. Papers* (1879), I, No. 7.]

C. H. L—n.

BAYARD, JOHN BUBENHEIM (Aug. 11, 1738–Jan. 7, 1807), merchant and statesman, son of James and Mary (Ashton) Bayard, was born at Bohemia Manor, Md. [for ancestry see James Ashton Bayard]. Educated at Nottingham Institution and by George Duffield, Bayard went to Philadelphia in 1756 and entered the business house of John Rhea. The close of the French War found him a commercial and social leader in the city, a vigorous upholder of provincial rights and a logical signer of the Non-Importation Agreement of 1765. He was no advocate of extreme measures, however, lest they result in a premature break with Great Britain. A member of the Sons of Liberty organized in 1766 and of the Provincial Convention of 1774, Bayard in 1775 urged the appointment of Washington as commander-in-chief of the Continental forces, and by May 1776, when chairman of the Committee of Inspection, he was ready, "at the request of a number of persons," to call a general town-meeting to consider proposals for a convention. This gathering declared "the present government of the province not competent to the exigencies of its affairs." On Oct. 21 Bayard presided over another popular meeting summoned to discuss the new state constitution as announced on Sept. 28. In March 1777 and November 1778, he was chosen speaker of the Assembly to which body he was elected several times, becoming also a member of the Board of War. Bayard's military activities were important. He was major of the second battalion of Philadelphia gentlemen "Associators" which volunteered for service with the Continental forces, and was complimented by Washington for gallantry at Princeton. He became colonel of his battalion in 1777, and later, as a member of the Council of Safety, he visited Washington at Valley Forge. He served one year also on the Supreme Executive Council of the state.

Bayard's principal influence in American affairs resulted from his business and social prestige. In Philadelphia and in New Brunswick, N. J., whither he removed in 1788, his residence was a rallying point for Pennsylvania leaders and for Federalist statesmen throughout the nation. Work for Princeton College and as Whitefield's friend in the Presbyterian Church increased his reputation, as did a good knowledge of the French language. In 1785 he was elected to the Continental Congress from Pennsylvania and was chosen later for various civil and political positions in New Jersey, among them justice of the court of common pleas. Bayard was married three times: his first wife was Margaret Hodge; his second, Mrs. Mary Hodgden or Hodgson; his third, Johannah White, sister or daughter of Gen. Anthony W. White.

[A few manuscripts in the Hist. Soc. of Pa., and others, including those of Bayard's daughter Margaret Bayard Smith, in the Lib. of Cong.; the *Pa. Gazette* and the *Packet*; Thompson Westcott, *Hist. of Phila.* (as published in the *Dispatch* or in the three vol. ed. by Scharf and Westcott, 1884); J. G. Wilson, *Col. John Bayard and the Bayard Family*, with portr. (1885); *N. J. Hist. Soc. Proc.*, ser. 2, vol. V, 139–160; ser. III, vol. II, 100–15.]

C.H.L—n.

BAYARD, NICHOLAS (1644–1707), secretary of the province of New York, was of French descent although born in Alphen, Holland. His grandfather, Balthazar, was at one time pastor of a French church in Antwerp and prior to 1599 was a college professor. Samuel, the father of Nicholas, was a wealthy merchant. Upon his death, he left a family of three sons, a daughter, and his widow Anna, who was a sister of Peter Stuyvesant. She is described as imposing in appearance, highly educated, of good business capacity, and of somewhat imperious temper. When Nicholas was three years of age the family fortunes were transferred to the New World and the little family established itself in New Amsterdam. They were accompanied by a tutor, but he was discharged soon after their arrival and the education of the children was conducted by their mother. This included the teaching of the French, English, and Dutch languages. Association with his uncle, Peter Stuyvesant, director general of the province of New Netherland, and the touch which this gave him with people and affairs of the colony presumably shaped to a considerable extent the life of Nicholas Bayard. At an early age, he began his career as English clerk in the office of the secretary of the province, a position which, after three years of experience, yielded him the equivalent of $5.60 a month. His knowledge of the English language was naturally to his advantage when, in 1664, the English forces secured control of the colony. With the organization of the government, Bayard was assigned to assist the Dutch clerk in translating minutes and other records, and soon succeeded him. He was later appointed surveyor of customs. Under the second short Dutch occupation, he continued as provincial secretary, was commissioned receiver general, was made lieutenant of a newly formed company of militia, and was given power of attorney to collect debts for the Dutch Government.

With the reëstablishment of English control, troubles began for Bayard. With others he presented a petition to Gov. Andros requesting freedom in religion and exemption from bearing arms against the Dutch in case occasion demanded. This was made cause for judgment against him, his "goods and chattels" were forfeited, and he was made a prisoner in the "Hole" in the fort. While awaiting trial, release was obtained only upon giving heavy bonds. But four years later under Gov. Dongan, his star was again in the ascendant. He became a city alderman and a member of the governor's council. In 1685 he was commissioned mayor of New York for two years, continuing to serve at the same time as a member of the governor's council. When Jacob Leisler usurped governmental control, Bayard was one of the especial targets of his attacks. "I was obliged to obscund myselfe upwards the space of five months," he wrote (*New York Colonial Documents*, III, 635). He went to Albany where he was sought in vain by Leisler's forces until his whereabouts were discovered through captured letters and he was seized and imprisoned. Broken in health and spirit, he now petitioned for pardon; Leisler not only refused but, as if to gloat over his downfall, had him carried triumphantly through the fort in a chair in chains. His imprisonment lasted over a year.

At last the long-expected Gov. Sloughter arrived from England and demanded the release of Bayard, who was to be one of his councillors. Leisler in his turn was imprisoned and Bayard's chain was "put on Leisler's legg." In fact, Bayard is said to have been influential in securing the signature of Sloughter (who lodged at the Bayard home) to Leisler's death warrant. In 1697, he was still on the council, but the new governor, Bellomont, soon after his arrival accused his predecessor, Fletcher, of having encouraged and protected pirates with Bayard acting as his broker. Extravagant grants of land made by Fletcher to Bayard and others were declared illegal and finally Bayard was removed from the council. He was later accused of being a leader of sedition and mutiny and of being a Jacobite. A charge of high treason was made against him and he was sentenced to death. While he was in prison awaiting execution of this judgment, Gov. Cornbury arrived. Upon investigation of Bayard's case, the new Governor appealed in his behalf to Queen Anne and after many delays Bayard was ordered reinstated in his honors and property. Aside from his political activities, he was influential in church affairs, holding offices of deacon and elder. He served on a committee to plan the new Dutch church. The clergy of New York testified to his devotion to the "true faith" and that he was a "pious, candid, and modest man." On May 23, 1666, he married Judith Varlet (Varlith) who had in 1662 been imprisoned as a witch by the settlers at Hartford, Conn. They had one son, Samuel Bayard.

[*N. Y. Col. Docs.*, III, IV; *Calendar of N. Y. Hist. MSS., Dutch*; *Records of New Amsterdam*, V; *N. Y. Documentary Hist.*, XI; *N. Y. Hist. Soc. Colls.* (1868). I. N. Phelps Stokes, *Iconography of Manhattan Island* (1922), IV, collates much of the above material in chronological order. J. R. Brodhead, *Hist. of the State of N. Y.* (1853), and Mrs. Schuyler van Rensselaer, *Hist. of the City of N. Y.* (1909), are secondary authorities which adhere closely to the original sources. J. G. Wilson, *Col. John Bayard and the Bayard Family* (1885), furnished geneal. data.]   A. E. P.

BAYARD, RICHARD HENRY (Sept. 26, 1796–Mar. 4, 1868), lawyer, senator, son of James A. and Ann Bassett Bayard, was born at Wilmington, Del., shortly before his father entered the national House of Representatives [for ancestry see James Ashton Bayard]. Richard was named for his grandfather Richard Bassett [*q.v.*]. He was educated under Rev. Louis Guillaume Valentin Dubourg of the College of Saint Mary in Baltimore, 1805–10, following which he went to Princeton College, N. J. Upon his graduation he began the study of law. This was temporarily interrupted by military service during the closing period of the War of 1812 in a position secured for him by his mother while his father was absent in Europe. Upon the conclusion of the war he returned to his law studies. On Feb. 28, 1815, he married Mary Sophia, daughter of Charles and Harriet (Chew) Carroll and grand-daughter of Charles Carroll of Carrollton. This connection with the Carroll and Chew families reënforced Bayard's predilection for the law so that he continued heartily in the work after his father's death and was admitted to the New Castle bar in December 1818. For the next decade he pursued his practise seriously and with success. Many of the clients of his late father came to him, and he soon became prominent in the professional and social life of Delaware. His purchase of the John Dickinson mansion at Ninth and Market Sts., Wilmington, which he occupied for years and made a center of social entertainment, increased his popularity in that city. On Oct. 6, 1824, at the time of Delaware's greeting to Lafayette, Bayard was on the committee which extended hospitality to the visitor, and in 1829 he represented one group in the state at the dinner to Louis McLane upon the latter's appointment by President Jackson as minister to Great Britain.

Bayard's participation in politics had begun in 1828 when he was defeated for the national House of Representatives by Kensey Johns, Jr. In January 1830 he was at Washington at the time of the famous Webster-Hayne debate, with manuscripts and other material to aid Senator John M. Clayton in his defense of Bayard's father from the accusations of Jefferson in his memoirs. Returning to Wilmington, he was elected first mayor of the city under the charter of 1832, holding the office for three years. On June 17, 1836, he was chosen to the Senate following the resignation of Arnold Naudain, and served from June 1836 until September 1839. During this period he was among the most resolute opponents of Benton's resolution to expunge from the Senate records the censure of Mar. 28, 1834, passed upon Jackson for his removal of the national deposits in the United States Bank, as Bayard considered such action a "mutilation of the Senate Journal." When the elections of November 1838 gave the newly formed Whig party control of the Delaware Senate, Bayard resigned his national senatorship to become chief justice of his own state. In 1840 he was once more elected to the United States Senate and served until Mar. 3, 1845. He then resumed his law practise until he was appointed chargé d'affaires to Belgium, from Dec. 10, 1850, to Sept. 12, 1853. Upon his return from Europe, he maintained his legal position in Delaware and Pennsylvania for fifteen years but took no active part in politics. After his removal to Philadelphia he lived in retirement until his death.

[The papers of James A. Bayard, *Am. Hist. Ass. Reports, 1913*, II (1915), referred to as *Bayard Papers*; J. G. Wilson, *Col. John Bayard and the Bayard Family* (1885); J. T. Scharf, *Hist. of Del.* (1888); *Cong. Globe*, 1836–45; *Jour. of the U. S. Sen.*, 1836–45; *Jour. of the Executive Proc. of the U. S. Sen.*, 1836–45; J. B. McMaster, *Hist. of the People of the U. S.*, V–VII (1906); J. F. Rhodes, *Hist. of the U. S. from the Compromise of 1850*, I–III (1893); *Del. Gazette*, 1824–36; *Niles' Reg.*, 1836–45; T. H. Benton, *Thirty Years' View* (1854–56).]   C. H. L.—n.

BAYARD, SAMUEL (Jan. 11, 1767–May 11, 1840), jurist, was born in Philadelphia, fourth son of John Bayard [*q.v.*] and Margaret Hodge [for ancestry see James Ashton Bayard]. He was one of a large family of children brought up in a hospitable home where leading men of the period were entertained. At the time of the Revolutionary War, his father early allied himself with the American cause, and Philadelphia consequently was no longer a safe home for his family. For a few years it was a roving life for the boy Samuel; now at the old manor house in Maryland where aged family slaves were still cared for, now in Philadelphia, and now back again to the farm on the Schuylkill where a cottage was fitted up as a school-room and a teacher secured for the Bayard children and those of a few neighbors. A much interrupted education must have been his but it proved sufficient to permit his graduation from Princeton as valedictorian of his class at the age of seventeen. He studied law with William Bradford and became his law partner, practising law in Philadelphia for seven years. In August 1790 he married Martha Pintard of New Rochelle, N. Y., daughter of Lewis Pintard and Susan (Stockton) Pintard. The following year he was appointed clerk of the United States Supreme Court. When a man was wanted to prosecute United States claims before the British admiralty courts, following the ratification of Jay's treaty with Great Britain, Nov. 19, 1794, Washington chose Bayard to act as the agent of the United States. For four years he with his family was in London in this capacity. The results of his official endeavors indicate the success of his efforts. He with his associates obtained from the British Government, for losses sustained by citizens from illegal and unauthorized captures. of their ships on the high seas by English cruisers, the sum of $10,345,000.

When Bayard returned to the United States, he spent several years in New Rochelle and served as presiding judge of Westchester County under appointment of Gov. Jay. In 1803 he removed to New York City and resumed his law practise there. The following year, the New York Historical Society was founded, and Bayard was "a hearty coöperator in establishing this Association." He presented to the society "that remarkable series of MSS., the Journals of the House of Commons during the Protectorate of Cromwell." In 1806 he purchased an estate in Princeton where he lived for nearly forty years. During this time he was widely identified with affairs of community, county, and state. He was a trustee of Princeton College and its treasurer for many years and was one of the founders of Princeton Theological Seminary. For a considerable period he was a presiding judge of the court of common pleas of Somerset County, and he served for several years in the legislature of New Jersey. In 1814 he suffered defeat as a Federalist candidate for Congress. For many years he was a delegate to the General Assembly of the Presbyterian Church; he aided with generous hand St. Clement's Episcopal Church in New York City, of which his eldest son, Rev. Lewis Pintard Bayard, was pastor; and for thirty years he contributed to various religious periodicals. He published a funeral oration on Gen. Washington (1800); *A Digest of American Cases on the Law of Evi-*

dence, Intended as Notes to Peake's Compendium (1810); *An Abstract of the Laws of the United States which Relate to the Duties and Authority of Judges of Inferior State Courts and Justices of the Peace* (1834); *Letters on the Sacrament of the Lord's Supper* (1825).

[J. G. Wilson, *Col. John Bayard and the Bayard Family* (1885); *Judge Bayard of N. J. and His London Diary of 1795–96*, ed. by J. G. Wilson; F. B. Lee, *Geneal. and Memorial Hist. of the State of N. Y.*, IV (1910), 1543.]

A. E. P.

BAYARD, THOMAS FRANCIS (Oct. 29, 1828–Sept. 28, 1898), statesman, diplomat, was the son of James Asheton Bayard, Jr. [*q.v.*] and Ann (Francis) Bayard, and was born in Wilmington, Del., where the family had for several generations been prominent in politics and business. He was educated at a private school in Flushing, N. Y., and never attended college. His father temporarily moved to New York in 1843, where Thomas entered the employ of a mercantile house, and later that of another firm in Philadelphia. When about twenty, however, he began the study of law in Wilmington, was admitted to the bar in 1851, and for the next eighteen years, with the exception of a few years in Philadelphia, practised with great success in that city, becoming a permanent resident in 1858. He had a lucrative practise, serving, in a confidential capacity, in the administration of many estates. In October 1856 he married Louise, daughter of Josiah Lee, a wealthy Baltimore banker. She died Jan. 31, 1886, and on Nov. 7, 1889, he married Mary W., daughter of Dr. George Clymer of the Navy.

In 1869 he was elected as a Democrat to the United States Senate. His only previous experience in public office had been less than a year's service as United States attorney for Delaware in 1853–54. His friends considered his election as a tribute to his professional standing and high reputation for integrity and ability; his opponents, as evidence that the state was a pocket borough of the Bayard family. His service in the Senate, 1869–85, covered a period when the fortunes of his party were, in general, at a low ebb. Throughout most of his congressional career it was in the minority, and had relatively few men of outstanding ability in either house. Bayard acquired a recognized position almost from the start, but being a minority leader, he is naturally remembered rather for his opposition to Republican policies, for his exposure of abuses, for the energy with which he defended unpopular minorities and hopeless causes, than for constructive legislation or the successful solution of great problems. He was to the last a Democrat of the older school, although he lived to see a new generation abandon many of its historic principles for miscellaneous political and economic vagaries. He began by fighting the Reconstruction policies of the Radicals both because he considered them harsh and impolitic, and because they involved an undue centralization of federal power with a corresponding aggrandizement of the Executive branch of that Government. The currency, he declared, could not be "lawfully or safely anything else than a currency of value— The gold and silver coin directed by the Constitution" (*Congressional Record,* 43 Cong., 2 Sess., App., 971 ff.). He hated class legislation of every sort, whether it took the form of ship subsidies, railroad land grants, or tariff protection. Militarism and socialism he considered equally inimical to freedom. Law making, he declared again and again, should be restricted to measures universally accepted as necessary, and administration should above all else be honest and frugal. Admirable as many of these doctrines appear in the abstract, it is hard to believe that he ever grasped the full significance of the changes wrought by the Civil War and the nationalization of economic and social life which followed it.

He was a candidate for the presidential nomination in 1880, and again in 1884, receiving considerable support. The exigencies of party politics, however, made his nomination impossible. He became secretary of state, Mar. 6, 1885, relinquishing his place in the Senate, it was believed, with some reluctance, and largely out of a desire to render President Cleveland any assistance in his power. As secretary, he was confronted with troublesome problems from the beginning of his term. A believer in civil service reforms, and on the whole successful in putting his beliefs into practise (*Nation,* Mar. 7, 1889), he found himself confronted with the demands of party workers whose hunger for patronage had been unsatisfied for twenty-five years. In spite of the fact that foreign governments "had schooled themselves against surprise" at the character of our diplomatic service, wrote one of his critics, some of Bayard's appointments "succeeded in startling more than one of them out of the composure which befits great kings and commonwealths" (Arthur Richmond, in *North American Review,* CXLVIII, 23). Thus Italy and Austria emphatically rejected A. M. Keily as *persona non grata* when appointed successively as minister to those countries, the correspondence thereon achieving the immortality which belongs to "classic cases" in text-books of diplomacy and international law (documen-

tary history of these incidents is found in *Foreign Relations of the United States,* 1885, pp. 28–57, and pp. 549–52). Toward the close of his administration Bayard had the equally unpleasant and famous task of dismissing the British minister for his unfortunate indiscretions during the presidential campaign of 1888 (*Ibid.,* 1888, II, 1667–1729). The three major diplomatic issues of his term he was obliged to pass on unsettled to his successors. The North Atlantic Fisheries question, that perennial source of friction, had suddenly become acute with the expiration of the "fisheries clauses" of the Washington Treaty, July 1, 1885. Complicated by the Canadian desire for tariff concessions, the subject caused a serious clash. Seizure of United States vessels in 1886–87 led to jingoistic talk of reprisals, and even war. The Secretary was apparently better acquainted than many of his critics with certain legal defects in the claims of the United States, and pursued a conciliatory policy which resulted in the Bayard-Chamberlain Treaty of Feb. 15, 1888. Assailed in many quarters as a surrender of United States rights, and considered in the Senate while the presidential campaign was in progress, it was rejected six months later. Fortunately a *modus vivendi* had been arranged to meet such a contingency. The other two issues arose in the Pacific. British protests at the seizure of Canadian sealing vessels in Bering Sea led Bayard to confer with interested Powers regarding the protection of the seal herds by international agreement, but any such agreement was frustrated by Canadian objections, May 16, 1888, apparently in anticipation of the expected defeat of the Fisheries Treaty. Through June and July 1887, another conference with representatives of Germany and Great Britain wrestled unsuccessfully with the problem of adjusting conflicting interests in Samoa. It is also worth noting in view of subsequent developments that Bayard tendered the good offices of the United States (1886) to bring about a settlement of the boundaries dispute between Great Britain and Venezuela. If unsuccessful, his policies were at least consistently on the side of peace and arbitration and the subsequent outcome of the North Atlantic and Bering Sea disputes disproved some of the contentions put forward by opponents who charged him with failure to uphold United States "rights."

Following Cleveland's second inauguration, 1893, he was appointed ambassador to Great Britain, the first time such diplomatic rank had been conferred by the United States. He was in many respects a successful representative, but was probably better appreciated in London than at home. When the Venezuelan flurry of 1895–96 took place, he refused to be stampeded into unfriendly speech or action, and a letter to the President shows that he was perturbed at the prospect of allowing "the interests and welfare of our country to be imperiled or complicated by such a government and people as those of Venezuela" (R. M. McElroy, *Grover Cleveland*, II, 191). He worked quietly, but steadily in the interests of Anglo-American friendship. "He did much to cement cordial relations," says Sir Willoughby Maycock, who had first met him when discussing the Fisheries Treaty some years before. "He entertained on a liberal scale, and was in addition a good sportsman, a keen deer-stalker in the Highlands, while his face was not unfamiliar at Epsom, Ascot and Newmarket Heath" (*With Mr. Chamberlain in the United States and Canada*, 1887–88, p. 37). He was frequently invited to deliver public addresses, a mark of British appreciation which eventually caused him some trouble with his own government. In 1895 several speeches caused unfavorable comment, and when on Nov. 7 in an address on "Individual Freedom," before the Edinburgh Philosophical Institution, he took advantage of the occasion to assail the protective tariff as a form of state socialism responsible for a host of moral, political, and economic evils, the House of Representatives began to rumble with indignation. Threats of impeachment were made, but the offended representatives finally contented themselves with a resolution of censure Mar. 20, 1896 (*Congressional Record,* 54 Cong., 1 Sess., p. 3034. See also *House Document 152,* 54 Cong., 1 Sess.). Bayard's health began to fail while he was abroad and after his return in 1897 he took no part in affairs and seldom appeared in public. He died at Dedham, Mass.

Bayard was a strikingly handsome man, over six feet in height, and of a powerful physique. His contemporaries agree that he had an unusually fine presence, and manners which Maycock describes as "dignified, courteous and prepossessing." He had, however, the convictions of an earlier day as to the responsibilities of political leadership and was never inclined, either politically or socially, to seek popularity with the country at large. He was, therefore, occasionally regarded as austere and even snobbish. As to his integrity there was no difference of opinion. He came unsmirched through a period of legislative service when ethical standards in Congress were at their nadir. John W. Foster, an opponent who severely criticized his conduct of the State Department, declares, "No man of higher ideals or of more exalted patriotism ever

occupied the chair of Secretary of State" (*Diplomatic Memoirs,* 1909, II, 265. See also the *Nation,* June 17, 1897).

[The chief sources of information regarding Bayard are speeches made during his career in the Senate, his diplomatic papers found in the *Foreign Relations of the United States* and other pub. records, and a considerable number of political, commemorative, and scholarly addresses, reprinted from time to time and available in larger libraries. Edward Spencer, *An Outline of the Pub. Life and Services of Thomas F. Bayard* (1880), has the common defects of campaign biographies. R. M. McElroy, *Grover Cleveland* (1923), and M. M. Gresham, *Life of Walter Gresham 1832–95* (1919), include interesting references. Files of current journals, especially the *Nation* (N. Y.), contain valuable comments and criticisms on his later career. There is a considerable literature on the Fisheries question, the Bering Sea dispute, Samoa, the Venezuelan boundary, and similar issues which throws light on Bayard's diplomatic activities. An appreciative obituary by G. F. Parker appears in the *Contemp. Rev.,* LXXIV, 675 ff. The *Morning News,* Wilmington, Del., Sept. 29, 30, Oct. 1, has a large amount of obit. material, anecdotes, memorial resolutions, personal reminiscences, etc.]

W. A. R.

BAYARD, WILLIAM (1761–Sept. 18, 1826), merchant, son of Col. William and Catherine (McEvers) Bayard, and descendant of Balthazar Bayard, the Huguenot ancestor of the American family, was born in the village of Greenwich outside New York City. His father, a colonial merchant, extensive landowner, and outspoken Tory, raised a Loyalist regiment and lost his property by confiscation. He sailed for England in 1783, taking all his family except young William, who had just married Elizabeth, the daughter of Samuel Cornell. On Dec. 1, 1786, young Bayard formed a partnership with Herman Le Roy, each investing £2,000. A venture to Teneriffe for liquor was the first step in the development of this firm, which became the leading commercial house of New York during the next forty years. James McEvers, Bayard's cousin, was later taken into partnership, but he and the reserved Le Roy were overshadowed by the personality of Bayard. The commerce of New York was at its lowest ebb when the firm started, but the long wars between England and France brought increased opportunities. Several of their ships were condemned by the belligerents, but the remainder brought in good profits. During the War of 1812, they owned a number of successful privateers. The close of the war found Le Roy, Bayard & McEvers in a commanding position in New York, trading extensively with Europe and the East and West Indies. They had the confidence of the wary Dutch bankers and their London drafts could be used in the place of coin in the East Indian trade. By 1822, they had several ships trading along the South American coast, taking advantage of the revolutions. During the interruption of trade caused by the Embargo the partners had turned to land speculation and the town of Le Roy is still a reminder of their activity in developing Genesee County. Bayard had many other interests. In 1817, he was sounding out the Amsterdam bankers for a loan to finance the Erie Canal. He served as president of the Bank of America, the Chamber of Commerce of the State of New York, the Morris Canal Company, and various other organizations. When merchants assembled at Philadelphia from all the northern states in 1824 to protest against the tariff increase, Bayard was made chairman of the gathering. By that time, his former partners had died and their places were filled by his sons, William, Jr., and Robert. They, rather than their father, were responsible in part for the apparently shameless profiteering of the Bayards and Howlands in building two frigates for the Greeks in 1825. The notoriety caused by this affair undoubtedly hastened the death of the elder Bayard at Greenwich on Sept. 18, 1826, after a long illness. His portrait, by William Dunlap, reveals the face of a statesman rather than a merchant (*Catalogue of Portraits in the Chamber of Commerce*, p. 13). He had a reputation for mildness of temper and charm of manner in addition to the unusual business acumen which made him one of the wealthiest men in the country.

[The principal sources of information are Bayard's extensive commercial and private correspondence in the Bayard, Campbell, Pearsall Papers in the N.Y. Pub. Lib., and his father's lengthy depositions in the Loyalist Transcripts in the same lib. The episode of the Greek frigates is described in his son Wm. Bayard's *Exposition of the Conduct of the Two Houses of G. G. & S. Howland and Le Roy, Bayard & Company in Relation to the Frigates Liberator and Hope* (1826). Notices of Bayard's death appeared in the *Evening Post* and the *Commercial Advertiser* of Sept. 19, 1826.]   R.G.A.

BAYLES, JAMES COPPER (July 3, 1845–May 7, 1913), editor, engineer, was born in New York, son of James and Julia Halsey (Day) Bayles. His education in the public schools was terminated by enlistment in the Union army. In 1862, at the age of seventeen, he entered the 22nd Regiment of New York and was soon commissioned an artillery lieutenant. He served eighteen months when his health became impaired. After a year's illness he did some work for the Delamater Iron Works of New York and later was on the engineering staff of the Raritan & Delaware Bay Railroad. In 1865 he formed a connection with Gen. Charles G. Halpin, proprietor of the *New York Citizen*, and during the illness of Halpin he acted as editor of the paper. From 1868 to 1869, Bayles was editor of the *Commercial Bulletin*, from which he resigned to accept the editorship of the *Iron Age*. In 1870 he was married to Ianthe Green, daughter of a

New York lumber merchant. For twenty years he remained editor of the *Iron Age;* the position gave him a standing among engineers and business men. In 1874 he assisted the publisher of the *Iron Age*, David Williams, to found another trade-paper called the *Metal Worker* (later changed to the *Sheet Metal Worker*), and he acted as its first editor. He was president of the American Institute of Mining Engineers in 1884 and 1885, although he was not strictly a mining engineer; his actual work in that profession was confined to editorial writings on metals and iron ore and a little research in electro-metallurgy and the microscopic analysis of metals. When the American Society of Mechanical Engineers was founded in 1880 he was a prominent charter member. His sincerest interest in engineering, however, was in sanitation and water supply. He lectured eloquently on these subjects and wrote a text-book on *House Drainage and Water Service* (1878) that passed through several editions. In 1884 he became president of the New Jersey State Sanitary Association. During 1887–88, he was president of the Board of Health of New York City, having been appointed by Mayor Hewitt although he was not a politician. In 1886 he wrote *The Shop Council* to reconcile employers and wage-earners; his advice to workers urged moderation and reason. During the same year he served as non-resident lecturer on labor problems at Sibley Engineering College of Cornell University. Upon his resignation from the *Iron Age* in 1889 when he was forty-four, he engaged in manufacturing ventures but was unsuccessful. He became a member of the editorial staff of the *New York Times* and subsequently engaged in consulting engineering practise in connection with city departments and public utilities. He was a brilliant and versatile editor of the old school, an accomplished speaker, and a refined gentleman. He was not a specialist in the modern industrial sense. In appearance he had the distinguished look of a professional man, with a small pointed beard and mustache. He was an amateur painter. His death, which occurred eight years after that of his wife, was due to pneumonia.

[*Bull. Am. Inst. Mining Engineers*, June 1913; *Iron Age*, May 15, 1913; *N.Y. Times*, May 9, 1913; *Who's Who in America*, 1910–11; *Who's Who in N.Y.*, 1911.]

P.B.M.

BAYLEY, JAMES ROOSEVELT (Aug. 23, 1814–Oct. 3, 1877), Roman Catholic bishop, historian, son of Guy Carleton and Grace (Roosevelt) Bayley, was born at Rye, N. Y. On the maternal side, he was the grandson of James Roosevelt, a prominent New York merchant. His paternal grandfather was Dr. Richard Bayley [*q.v.*], professor of anatomy and surgery at Columbia College, New York (1792–1801). He was the nephew of Elizabeth Ann Bayley Seton [*q.v.*], who founded the Daughters of Charity in the United States (1809). Owing to the high position in medical science held by his father and grandfather, he first thought of becoming a physician; but after finishing his secondary studies at Amherst College, he entered Trinity College, Hartford, Conn., to prepare for the Episcopal ministry. After his ordination (1835), he was made rector of St. Peter's Church, Harlem, N. Y. Theological controversy in the Anglican communion over the Tractarian Movement was then reaching a climax; and when Newman's *Tract 90* appeared (February 1841), Bayley decided to give up the ministry in order to go abroad for the purpose of studying the claims of Catholicism. He became a Catholic in Rome on Apr. 28, 1842. He then entered the Seminary of St. Sulpice, Paris, to study for the priesthood. He was recalled by Bishop Hughes of New York and ordained on Mar. 2, 1844. His first post was that of vice-president of St. John's College, Fordham, then the diocesan seminary. Four years later, he became secretary to Bishop Hughes, and on Oct. 30, 1853, was consecrated bishop of the newly created Diocese of Newark, N. J., by Archbishop Bedini, Papal nuncio to Brazil. During his years as secretary to Bishop Hughes (1848–53), he became interested in American Church history. In 1847, Dr. De la Hailandière, who succeeded Bishop Bruté of Vincennes (1834), gave to Bishop Hughes of New York a large collection of original letters and documents on early American Catholic history. These Bayley used for his first volume, *A Brief Sketch of the Early History of the Catholic Church on the Island of New York* (1853, 1874). Out of this valuable material he also published *Memoirs of the Rt. Rev. Simon William Gabriel Bruté, First Bishop of Vincennes* (1855, 1876). At the death of Archbishop Spalding of Baltimore, he was promoted to that archepiscopal see (July 30, 1872). Owing to increasing ill-health, he asked for a coadjutor and Bishop James Gibbons of Richmond was appointed (May 20, 1877).

Bayley's English and Dutch colonial ancestry and his New England training produced in him one of the charming personalities of his day. His bearing was princely, his manner most courteous, but what attracted most in him was a frankness of speech that accentuated his influence far beyond his own communion. He was not a profound scholar, though he read widely, especially in the field of Church history. His busy life of administration left him little leisure for prolonged study. A thorough New Yorker, quick, alert, resourceful and a born leader, he went to Baltimore after thirty years of an uncommonly active life in the North, unfortunately at a time when his energies began to wane. The Roosevelt in him found his Southern flock, priests and people, of a nature different from that of the North and less responsive to his enthusiasm for efficient Church government. Once he had secured the coadjutorship of the future Cardinal Gibbons (1877), his heart naturally turned to his old home in Newark, and here death overtook him. He was buried by his own request at the side of his aunt, Mother Seton, at St. Joseph's Convent, Emmitsburg, Md.

[There is no biog. of Archbishop Bayley, except the sketch in Clark's *Lives of the Deceased Bishops* (1888). His life in New York is treated in J. R. G. Hassard, *Life of Archbishop Hughes* (1866). The years spent as first Bishop of Newark are described in J. M. Flynn, *The Cath. Ch. in N. J.* (1902). James Cardinal Gibbons speaks of him in his *Retrospect of Fifty Years* (1916). See also *The Am. Convent Movement* (1923), by E. I. Mannix and *Cath. Builders of the Nation* (1923), ed. by C. E. McGuire.]

P. G.

BAYLEY, RICHARD (1745–Aug. 17, 1801), physician, came from English and French stock. His mother's family were undoubtedly Huguenots, who settled at New Rochelle, N. Y., about 1688. He was born in Fairfield, Conn., and it is said that he had a good knowledge of French and the Latin classics. About 1766, he went to New York to study with a fashionable English physician, John Charlton, and later he married Charlton's sister. In 1769, Charlton sent him to London, where he remained two years, working under the famous anatomist, William Hunter. On returning to New York, he renewed his connections with Charlton. About this time (1774) his attention was drawn to an epidemic of fatal croup. He carefully examined his patients, making pathological studies of the fatal cases, and clearly differentiated diphtheria from other forms of sore throat. By basing his treatment on his sound knowledge of the pathological process, it is said that he cut the mortality rate of this malignant disease nearly in half. His findings were embodied in a letter to William Hunter (1781).

During the winter of 1775–76 Bayley was again in England, working with Hunter. Returning to America as a surgeon in the English army under Howe, he was stationed at Newport, R. I., where he met Michaelis, the Hessian military surgeon. In 1777, he resigned his army position and returned to New York, where he found his wife in a dying condition. Once again he established himself in New York. In spite of his excellent reputation among physicians, reports soon began to be circulated by the public, no doubt due to Bayley's ardent desire to investigate the pathology of disease, that he had performed cruel experiments upon soldiers in Newport and that he was in the habit of "cutting up" his patients. In 1787, he delivered anatomical lectures in an unoccupied building, using his specimens for demonstration purposes. In this work he was assisted by his son-in-law, Wright Post. Public feeling against him increased; a mob broke into his anatomy room and destroyed all his valuable anatomical and pathological preparations (1788).

In spite of his adversities, Bayley persevered with his studies. In 1792 he was made professor of anatomy, and later of surgery, in the Columbia College medical faculty. His surgery was based upon actual experience and observation. He was the first in this country to amputate an arm at the shoulder-joint. He also was an early promoter of the New York Dispensary. His last contribution to medicine was concerned with yellow fever. This dreaded disease appeared in epidemic form in New York soon after the Revolutionary War. Many fled from the city, but Bayley remained, personally attending his cases and making extensive observations. His views were embodied in a book, published in New York in 1796, entitled, *An Account of the Epidemic Fever Which Prevailed in the City of New York during Part of the Summer and Fall of 1795*. In this volume the disease was clearly described, its seasonal prevalence emphasized, and stress put upon its contagious rather than its infectious nature. About this time Bayley was made health physician to the port of New York and his noteworthy *Letters from the Health Office Submitted to the New York Common Council* dealt with the epidemiology of yellow fever. He assisted in the early formulation of both the federal and the New York state quarantine laws. But he himself died from yellow fever on Aug. 17, 1801.

[The first mention of Bayley's treatment of croup appears in a letter by H. D. Michaelis, published in Richter's *Chirurgische Bibliothek* (1779), V, 734–46. Bayley's letter to Wm. Hunter on the same subject was published by Hugh Gaine, N. Y., 1781. It was reprinted in the *Medic. Repository*, 1809, XII, 331–39, and 1811, XIV, 345–50. Practically all of our knowledge of Bayley is derived from James Thacher, *Am. Medic. Biog.* (1828).]

H. R. V.

BAYLIES, FRANCIS (Oct. 16, 1783–Oct. 28, 1852), scholar, statesman, was descended from the pioneer, Thomas Baylies, who came to Boston from London in 1737. He was a Quaker ironmaster of such uncompromising pacifism that he resigned his position rather than manufacture cannon balls for the Louisburg Expedition (1745). His descendants in the third generation, still making iron from bog ore, overcame their scruples and served with distinction during the American Revolution. Francis, son of Dr. William Baylies, was educated at Bristol Academy, Taunton, Mass.; studied law at Bridgewater with his elder brother William, a member of Congress, and in 1820 was himself elected to Congress, continuing three terms. When the presidential election (1824) was thrown into the House of Representatives, Baylies was the only member from New England to vote against John Quincy Adams, alleging the latter's "moral unfitness." Defeat for reëlection naturally followed. After Jackson became president, friends of Baylies endeavored, unsuccessfully, to secure for him a cabinet portfolio. Later Jackson appointed him acting minister to Buenos Aires with full power to negotiate a treaty. In 1829 the *de facto* governor of the Falkland Islands had issued a proclamation forbidding pelagic fishing thereabout. Fishermen from New England, acting upon long usage, defied the proclamation of a *mare clausum* with the result that four Yankee vessels were seized and held for condemnation. President Jackson sent the sloop of war *Lexington* to disperse the pirates and protect American fishermen's alleged prescriptive rights. The acting governor and his associates were forcibly deported for trial. When Baylies arrived (June 8, 1832) he denied the right of Argentina to prohibit fishing around the Falklands. The government at Buenos Aires declined to negotiate with the United States until apologies and reparations were made for kidnapping Falkland officials. Baylies was unyielding. After suffering personal indignities he requested his passports and sailed (Sept. 8, 1832) with the United States Consul and took with him all archives of the legation in anticipation that war would eventuate. Diplomatic relations were not renewed until 1844. A comprehensive report by Baylies discussing rights of fishermen and titles to subpolar regions was published (1833) in Spanish and English.

Baylies was an indefatigable student and painstaking writer. *An Historical Memoir of the Colony of New Plymouth* (1830), published in four parts, brought literary recognition. Being written before the recovery (1855) of the lost Bradford chronicles, the original edition contains misleading statements based upon hearsay tradition not in harmony with Bradford's contemporaneous record. A second edition (1866), edited by S. G. Drake, contains important corrections. Baylies's other published writings include several pamphlets and fugitive political pasquinades contributed to various newspapers. He prepared a number of lectures for popular lyceums and was occasional orator at Masonic, military, political, and agricultural gatherings. He was married, in his fortieth year, to Mrs. Elizabeth Moulton Deming of Troy, N. Y.

[Private papers in possession of Old Colony Hist. Soc., Taunton, Mass., including Baylies's MSS. for unpublished books on hist., biog. and literary subjects; *Annals of Cong.* and *Reg. of Debates,* 1820–26; archives of State Dept.; biog. sketch by S. G. Drake (who knew Baylies personally) in second edition of *An Hist. Memoir of the Colony of New Plymouth* (1866).]

R. D.

BAYLOR, FRANCES COURTENAY (Jan. 20, 1848–Oct. 19, 1920), author, was born at Fort Smith, Ark., and died in Winchester, Va. Her parents, James L. and Sophie (Baylor) Dawson, maintained only the shifting residence to be expected in the family of an army officer. They lived for a while in San Antonio and New Orleans, but the child's education was conducted by her mother. Toward the close of the Civil War, Mrs. Dawson, having resumed her maiden name both for herself and daughter, came to Virginia, where along with Frances, she took up residence with another daughter, Sophie, married to Gen. J. G. Walker (C. S. A.). Virginia was home to them. There Mrs. Baylor had lived as a girl, a member of an intensely family-conscious group, of a distinguished tradition in colonies as well as state. Soon the entire Walker household went for a long visit in England. Their association here with people of considerable literary importance probably emphasized the habitual bookishness of their surroundings. Frances responded to these surroundings faithfully. Returning to America, she began writing in earnest; first, she gave to the world an anonymous play, *Petruchio Tamed,* and later a series of newspaper articles published in papers from New Orleans to London, and signed with the name of one of her male relatives. In 1885 she published *On Both Sides,* a British-American novel, which had first appeared as two stories in *Lippincott's Magazine.* These stories the author states in her preface, "are now bound together, as I earnestly trust that John Bull and his Cousin Jonathan may be in the future." Other writings followed. Of the novels, *Behind the Blue Ridge* (1887) confined itself to American characters, but all the others—*Juan and Juanita* (1888), *Claudia Hyde* (1894), *Miss Nina Barrow* (1897), *The Ladder of Fortune* (1899) and *A Georgian Bungalow* (1900)—derive much of their interest from the contrast of character between persons of different nationalities. The story-interest of these books is slight, and the character-delineation, while pleasant, is not searching enough to

confer permanence. Only one of them, *Juan and Juanita,* a child's book, as were also *Miss Nina Barrow* and *A Georgian Bungalow,* retains its vitality. Dealing with the capture and escape of two Mexican children, it draws too deeply upon the standard devices of suspense to perish readily. It was republished in an elaborate edition in 1926. *A Shocking Example,* a volume of stories collected from the *Atlantic Monthly* and elsewhere, was published in 1889. Her poems were not numerous, but some of them —especially the patriotic ones—were widely popular. In 1896, Miss Baylor was married to George Sherman Barnum of Savannah, Ga. Left a widow after a short time, she took up a brief residence in Lexington, Va., before returning permanently to her old home in Winchester. There, with her mother and her sister and her sister's daughters, she lived placidly, occupied chiefly with projects for a new novel, "The Matrimonial Coolie" (never published), but diverting herself from time to time, after her custom, with music and with pleasant visitors. She died while reading in a public library.

[The chief sources of this article are a letter from Miss Frances A. Walker, the subject's niece; E. A. Alderman and J. C. Harris, *Lib. Southern Lit.* (1908), I; *Book Buyer,* Jan. 1888; *Critic,* Apr. 7, 1888; O. W. and H. B. Baylor, *Baylor's Hist. of the Baylors* (1914); A. C. Gordon, Jr., *Virginian Writers of Fugitive Verse* (1923).]

J. D. W.

BAYLOR, GEORGE (Jan. 12, 1752–March 1784), Revolutionary soldier, was born at ~~Newmarket in the Shenandoah Valley of Virginia,~~ the son of Col. John and Fanny (Walker) Baylor. His wife was named Lucy Page. Early in the Revolutionary War he became one of the military aides of the commander-in-chief, an appointment possibly due to Washington's personal acquaintance with Baylor's father. He served at the battle of Trenton, and directly afterward was sent by Washington to Congress, bearing the news of the victory, and carrying also a captured Hessian standard. In a letter dated Dec. 27, 1776, written by Washington to the president of Congress, Baylor was highly commended. He received the thanks of Congress; John Hancock, its president, wrote to Washington recommending that Baylor be promoted to the rank of colonel and receive the gift of a horse, and these recommendations were promptly carried into effect. When Baylor requested the command of a regiment of cavalry, Washington consented, and wrote to him a letter of advice regarding his selection of officers.

The event with which Baylor's name is chiefly associated occurred in 1778, and is still a matter of debate. After the battle of Monmouth, there

the country seat "Newmarket" in Caroline County, Virginia

were no general engagements by the northern armies, but there were various isolated affairs on a smaller scale. One of these was a British attack on the American forces below the Hudson Highlands, in order to cover operations elsewhere. Part of their force under the Hessian Knyphausen planned to surprise one of the American detachments at New Tappan, but this attempt was detected and failed. The other force under Gen. Grey—"No Flint Grey" of Paoli notoriety in the previous campaign—was directed against Baylor's detachment. This regiment of light horse, the so-called "Mrs. George Washington's Guards," was cantoned at Old Tappan or Harrington near the Hackensack River, about two and a half miles from the main body. It has been stated that Baylor encamped at a distance "to be free, as is supposed, from the control of Wayne" (Washington Irving, *Washington,* 1856–59, III, 472). It is also asserted that there were few precautions against a surprise. Gen. Grey, guided by Tories, on the night of Sept. 27–28 attacked the dragoons who were asleep in barns. The bayonet was freely used. Many were killed or taken prisoners, among the latter being Baylor, who had been bayoneted through the lungs. Out of 104 privates, the loss was sixty-seven (William Gordon, *History of the Rise, Progress, and Establishment of the United States,* 1788, III, 194). Grey was accused of inhumanity, as on the previous occasion at Paoli. His epithet "No Flint Grey" was derived from his order to remove the flints from the soldiers' muskets, in order to preserve silence; the charge was made that his men were commanded to refuse quarter. Baylor on Oct. 19, 1778, wrote a letter to Washington in justification of his action, asserting that his patrols had been cut off, and his communications thereby severed. It does not appear that he was reprimanded by the commander-in-chief. Four years later he was in charge of light troops in the South, and was referred to in a communication by Laurens as a trustworthy officer. He died at Bridgetown, Barbados.

[See Jared Sparks, *Corres. of the Am. Rev.* (1853); Chas. Campbell, *Hist. of Va.* (1860); Wm. Meade, *Old Churches, Ministers and Families of Va.* (1857); O. W. and H. B. Baylor, *Baylor's Hist. of the Baylors* (1914). The older accounts of Tappan in Ramsay, Lossing and Washington Irving emphasize the cruelty of the British. There is a favorable notice of Gen. Grey in the *Dict. of Nat. Biog.*]
E.K.A.

BAYLOR, ROBERT EMMET BLEDSOE (May 10, 1793?–Dec. 30, 1873), jurist, Baptist preacher, was the son of Jane (Bledsoe) Baylor and of Walker Baylor, a soldier in Washington's army, and nephew of George Baylor [*q.v.*],

aide-de-camp to Washington. His maternal grandfather, Aaron Bledsoe, was a Baptist preacher in Virginia. R. E. B. Baylor was born in Kentucky, according to one account in Bourbon County, on May 10, 1791, according to another in Lincoln County, May 10, 1793. After being educated in the local schools, he served in the War of 1812, first under Col. Boswell in the fighting at Fort Meigs, later under Gen. Harrison in the campaign against Proctor (autobiographical letter in *Dallas Daily Herald,* Jan. 8, 1874). After the war he studied law in the office of his uncle, Judge Jesse Bledsoe, a noted Kentucky lawyer. In 1819 he was elected to the Kentucky legislature and served one term. In 1820 he moved to Tuscaloosa County, Ala. Here he was elected to the legislature for one term, 1824; and in 1829 he was elected as one of Alabama's three representatives to the Twenty-first Congress. His work in Congress seems to have been undistinguished, and he was defeated for reëlection. In 1833 he moved to Dallas County where he formed a law partnership with G. W. Gayle. He commanded a battalion of volunteers during the Creek Indian troubles in 1836. In the same year he moved again, this time to Mobile. In 1839 he emigrated to the Republic of Texas, settling first in Fayette County and later in Washington, where he resided until his death. Just before leaving Alabama he had joined the Baptist Church and had become a preacher. Though his chief vocation was that of a lawyer, or judge, he continued also as a preacher "without a charge"; and he was from the first a zealous leader in all the affairs of his Church in Texas. He soon achieved prominence in his new home. Within a year after his arrival he took part in the important battle of Plum Creek against the Comanche Indians. On Jan. 7, 1841, he was appointed by the Texas congress judge of the third district of Texas. As the judicial system of the Republic was organized this made him also an associate justice of the supreme court. He held this position until Texas entered the Union; he was then appointed one of the first district judges under the constitution of 1845 and remained on the bench continuously until the Civil War. Although the statement is frequently made that he was a member of the Texas congress, his name does not appear on the rolls of that body. He was a delegate from Fayette County to the constitutional convention of 1845 and served on the committee to report an ordinance accepting the terms of annexation offered by the United States, on the judiciary committee, and on the committee on general provisions of the constitution. He seems to have been highly respected by the other members of the convention. His speeches were few in number, but were always short, clear, and pointed. He favored the exemption of homesteads from forced sale, annual elections, the exclusion of the clergy from the legislature; he opposed the grant of any veto power to the governor (*Journal of Texas Constitutional Convention, 1845,* pp. 8, 15, 136-38, 163, 425-26, 510). Rigidly honest, yet kindly in manner and given to tempering justice with mercy, he enjoyed popularity and even veneration as a judge. Wherever he held court—so great was his religious zeal—he usually followed his work on the bench during the day by preaching or holding other religious services at night. He was always interested in education, and in 1843 was made president of the first Baptist education society in Texas. In 1845 he and W. M. Tryon projected the first Baptist college in Texas. He drew the charter and was chiefly instrumental in procuring its passage through the congress, and despite his protests the college was named for him. Baylor University was first established at Independence, Washington County; in 1886 it was moved to its present site at Waco, and "the female department," Baylor College, was moved to Belton. Judge Baylor made the largest cash contribution to its initial endowment and was for many years chairman of the board of trustees. From 1857 to the Civil War he served as professor of law without pay. For a long time he was moderator of the Texas Baptist Union Association and president of the Baptist State Convention. The last years of his life were spent quietly at his home at Gay Hill. He was never married. He is said to have been a man of impressive appearance, over six feet two inches in height, and of great dignity of face and bearing.

[It is generally stated that Judge Baylor's father was Robert Baylor and that he was an aide-de-camp to Gen. Washington. In the autobiographical letter above referred to, Baylor himself said that his father was Walker Baylor and that the aide-de-camp was his uncle Robert. But in W. C. Ford's *Writings of George Washington,* this man's name is always given as George Baylor. There are four different dates given for Baylor's death, but that adopted is best sustained by contemporary evidence. Apparently Baylor County, Tex., was not named for Judge Baylor, but for a relative, Dr. Henry W. Baylor. In addition to the sources mentioned above, data on the life of Judge Baylor may be found in J. M. Carroll, *Hist. of Tex. Baptists* (1923); Mrs. Georgiana J. Burleson, *Life and Writings of Rufus C. Burleson* (1901); C. W. Raines, *Year Book for Tex.* (1901); Jas. D. Lynch, *The Bench and Bar of Tex.* (1885), and O. W. and H. B. Baylor, *Baylor's Hist. of the Baylors* (1914).]

C. W. R.

BAYLY, THOMAS HENRY (Dec. 11, 1810–June 22, 1856), jurist, congressman, son of Thomas M. and Margaret (Cropper) Bayly, was born at Mount Custis, his father's 675-acre estate about three miles north of Accomac, Va. His father was a graduate of Princeton, a well-to-do and public-spirited planter, who served his state in public office for about forty years, as member of the Virginia Assembly, representative in Congress, colonel of militia during the War of 1812, member of the Virginia convention of 1829-30. Thomas H. Bayly inherited his father's country estate, his political talents, and the good will of his constituency. He went from private schools to the University of Virginia, where he was trained as a lawyer. When only twenty-six years of age, he was elected to the Virginia House of Delegates in which he served from 1836 to 1842. The Assembly appointed him brigadier-general of militia. In 1840, he was chairman of a very important select committee to investigate a controversy between Gov. Gilmer of Virginia and Gov. Seward of New York (*Virginia House Journal and Documents,* 1839-40, Document 57). Sixteen years later, Seward declared in Congress, "I felt his ability and power, while I was compelled also to acknowledge his manliness and dignified bearing" (obituary remarks in Congress, June 27, 1856, in *Congressional Globe,* 34 Cong., 1 Sess., p. 1501). When Judge Upshur entered Tyler's cabinet in 1842, Bayly was appointed in his place as judge of the circuit court of his district. He was elected two years later to the federal House of Representatives to succeed Henry A. Wise (appointed minister to Brazil). In spite of the fact that his party was continually in the minority in his district during the period, Bayly was so well-liked and trusted that he was always reëlected, serving from 1844 until his death in 1856. Though not eloquent, he was a forceful and well-informed speaker. He was a Democrat, a champion of state's rights, but strongly attached to the Union. He was independent, sane, and unusually temperate and free from partisanship during a trying period in national politics (debates in *Congressional Globe;* letters of contemporaries in *Annual Reports of the American Historical Association,* 1899, II, 1032, 1171; 1911, II, 138). A warm friend of Thomas Ritchie, the influential editor of the *Washington Union,* Bayly was sought by the friends of both Calhoun and Clay to enlist Ritchie's influence in their favor. He was instrumental in bringing Ritchie and Clay together; and thus aided materially in carrying through the compromises of 1850 (*Ibid.,* 1899, II, 955-56; C. H. Ambler, *Thomas Ritchie,* 1913, pp. 279 ff). Bayly was an affectionate husband and parent, and a kind master. He was an enthusiastic hunter, and kept a fine pack of foxhounds. He was over six feet tall, fair, and well proportioned. He was married to Evelyn H. May of Petersburg, Va.

[A few printed speeches and reports of Bayly's made in the Virginia Assembly are in the *Bull. Va. State Lib.*, 1917, X. Conway Robinson's *Va. Reports*, I, II (1843–44), contain his judicial decisions. Obituary remarks delivered in Cong. on June 27, 1856, are often inaccurate in details. References in *Ann. Reports, Am. Hist. Ass.* (note Index volume, 1914). Obit. notice in *Richmond Dispatch*, June 27, 1856. L. G. Tyler, *Letters and Times of the Tylers* (1885), I, 589; II, 284. Letter from his daughter, Mrs. Tiffany. Will at Accomac Court House dated July 7, 1853, probated July 28, 1856. The tombs of Judge and Mrs. Bayly are at Mount Custis.]

R. L. M.

BAYMA, JOSEPH (Nov. 9, 1816–Feb. 7, 1892), Jesuit priest, mathematician, physicist, was born at Ciriè, a township twelve miles north-west of Turin. During his childhood his residence was changed by his parents to Turin to insure for him a better education. Having completed his undergraduate studies at the Jesuit College of this city, he matriculated at the Royal Academy of Turin apparently intent on specializing in medicine, the profession of his father. Very shortly, however, he abandoned this project to enter the Jesuit novitiate at Chieti in February 1832. With an unusual combination of scientific and literary talents, at about this time he wrote an epic on Columbus in *ottava rima*, as well as poems in Latin. When his two years of probation, his biennium in philosophy, the prescribed years of professorship in the Jesuit colleges, and his course in theology had been finished, he was ordained to the priesthood in 1847. Thereupon he spent one year in missionary work in Algiers, ministering to the bodily and spiritual welfare of the sick in the Military Hospital. Recalled to Rome by his superiors, for a short period he acted as assistant to the noted astronomer, Fr. Angelo Secchi, then the director of the Osservatorio del Collegio Romano. This position he relinquished to collaborate with Fr. Enrico Vasco in editing the monumental work, *Il Ratio Studiorum adattato ai tempi presenti.* In 1852 he was designated as rector of the Episcopal Seminary of Bertinoro in the Romagna. During the same year he published *De studio religiosæ perfectionis excitando* in three volumes. Transferred to England in 1858, because of the religious intolerance then at its height in Italy, he filled the chair of philosophy at Stonyhurst College for eleven years.

In 1861 he printed for private circulation three volumes entitled *Philosophia Realis.* Until within a few years of his death he persisted in supplementing this work with additions and corrections. The revised copy never reached beyond the manuscript form. His chief work, *Elements of Molecular Mechanics,* appeared in 1866. Prof. Morgan, the mathematican, adjudged this treatise as "being a century before its time" and declared "that not seven of England's scientists were equal to understanding it." Bayma followed the main principles of Ruggiero Boscovich, the parent of modern dynamism, holding that physical matter is reducible to unextended points, materially and mathematically non-continuous. These point-like structures, some attractive, some repulsive, act on each other, and that at a distance, for contact there is none, and so are bound into molecules, and these in turn into bodies. But whereas Boscovich taught that if the distance between these points is infinitesimal, they are repulsive, while, if the distance, remaining always small, is nevertheless slightly increased, the repulsive force is initially decreased, then nullified, then at still greater distances transformed into a force of attraction, Bayma, on the other hand, contended that simple elements cannot be at once attractive at greater and repulsive at lesser distances. If a given element is attractive at any distance, he urged, it will be so at all distances; and if repulsive at any distance, it will be repulsive at all distances. Hence some of the points, he held, must be inherently attractive or repulsive. Objecting to this system of Bayma, metaphysicians urge that he fails to account for the extension and inertia of matter.

In 1869 Bayma was ordered to California to aid with his talents and counsel the newly established mission of California. On his arrival in San Francisco he was installed as president of St. Ignatius College. This position he held for three years, thereafter to become professor of higher mathematics at this same institution of learning. Impaired health forced him to seek rest in the Santa Clara Valley in 1880 and here he launched out, by way of diversion, on a new work on "Cycloidal Functions." Unable to complete these computations, he entrusted them to the Smithsonian Institution at Washington and thereafter they were reconsigned to the then director of Georgetown University Observatory. Apparently they still await publication. At about this same time Bayma brought out several elementary text-books in mathematics. He was taken ill about the middle of January 1892, and his recovery was early despaired of; he died at Santa Clara College on Feb. 7. He was a man of majestic frame and magnificent physique, a profound thinker, but in his personality as simple and guileless as a child.

[*Woodstock Letters,* XXI (privately printed); *De Claris Sodalibus Provinciæ Taurinensis* (Turin 1906);

Cath. Encyc. (1907), articles on "Bayma" and "Dynamism"; documents in archives of Georgetown University.]   F. A. T—f.

BAYNHAM, WILLIAM (Dec. 7, 1749–Dec. 8, 1814), physician and surgeon, was the son of Dr. John Baynham of Carolina. After five years of study under Dr. Walker, considered one of the ablest surgeons in America, he went, at the age of twenty, to London. Here he entered St. Thomas's Hospital as a student and so distinguished himself that he soon gained the attention and later the close friendship of Else, the professor of anatomy. In 1772 he was employed, on Else's recommendation, by Charles Collignon, professor of anatomy at Cambridge, to dissect and prepare the subjects for his lectures. He continued in this employment for several winters and in the remaining part of each year was a partner with a surgeon of Margate, named Slater. In 1776 he accepted an offer from Else on the following terms: "He was to superintend the anatomical theatre and dissecting room, prepare bodies for his public demonstrations, make preparations for the museum and to instruct his pupils in the arts of dissecting, injecting, making anatomical preparations, etc., at a salary of eighty and ninety pounds the first two years and one hundred pounds a year for five succeeding years—at the expiration of which (having qualified himself in the interim for the office) Mr. Else was to relinquish to him the professor's chair or to take him as joint professor on equal terms as he might choose." Before the end of this period, however, Else died suddenly, in 1781. Baynham missed by a narrow margin election by the governors of the Hospital to the professorship thus left vacant. Disappointed in his expectations, he became a member of the "Company of Surgeons" and practised surgery for a few years in London and then returned to America, after an absence of sixteen years, and settled in Essex, Va. Here he built up a large practise, becoming especially distinguished in surgery. He performed several operations for stone, cataract, and extra-uterine conception. A detailed account of a case of the latter may be seen by reference to the *New York Medical and Surgical Journal,* I. He is credited with having performed the first successful operation for extra-uterine pregnancy. An alleged discovery by Baynham of a fine vascular membrane on the surface of the cutis immediately under the *rete mucosum* was incorrectly reported by Cruikshank and copied into Wistar's *Anatomy.* Baynham is said to have been slow and not very distinct in the enunciation of his ideas. He generally, on first acquaintance, disappointed those whose expectations had been raised and whose opinions of him had been formed from his reputation. But if not "a ready man," he was a "full and accurate one." He died at the age of sixty-six.

[The chief source of information is the anonymous biographical sketch which appeared in the *Phila. Jour. Medic. and Physic. Sci.,* IV, 1822, pp. 186–203. This sketch is composed of information from three sources and contains in addition a brief paragraph by the editor of the *Journal,* Dr. N. Chapman, who evidently desired to make the account as accurate as possible. The main part of the sketch is by a Virginian who the editor's note states was a friend of Baynham but "not in the profession." This friend supplements his account by extracts from "a Gentleman of high medical reputation both in Europe and America to whom we had applied for information on the subject" and who had been a fellow student of Baynham in London. The editor of the *Journal* in turn supplements the article by extracts from a statement furnished by a "near relative" of Baynham.]   C. R. B.

BEACH, ALFRED ELY (Sept. 1, 1826–Jan. 1, 1896), inventor, editor, was born at Springfield, Mass., the son of Nancy (Day) and Moses Yale Beach [*q.v.*], cabinet-maker and inventor. He was six years old when his uncle, Benjamin H. Day [*q.v.*], established *The Sun* (New York), which was eventually purchased by Moses Yale Beach from his brother-in-law. Alfred E. Beach obtained an excellent idea of journalism while working for his father. The *Scientific American* had been founded by Rufus Porter in 1845. Young Beach desired to secure the property, which was unique, and for this purpose formed a partnership (1846) with Orson D. Munn and Salem H. Wales, under the title of Munn & Company—a partnership continued for almost fifty years. The young men purchased the paper, and in time the editorial chair was occupied by Beach. His great service was the technical and legal advice given to inventors. He was prolific in ideas and patented the following: typewriter, 1847; typewriter for the blind, 1857; cable railways, 1864; pneumatic tubes for mail and passengers, 1865; and a tunneling shield. His typewriter had considerable merit and some of its ideas are still used; such as the basket or pot arrangement of the type rods. In his last model the tape was embossed with a male and female die, such as is used in notarial presses. In 1856 the American Institute awarded him a gold medal for this device. He cannot be called the basic inventor of the typewriter, but his contribution was substantial. Though his cable traction system was probably never used, he lived to see the general plan adopted. He likewise invented a pneumatic carrier system. He gave demonstrations of this system in 1867 at the Fair of the American Institute and people rode 107 feet in a tube like those in London and the Hudson Tubes in New York, except that air instead of electricity was used as the motive power. To-day the same principle is utilized in mail-tubes and cash-carriers. In 1869 he obtained a charter for a tube to carry mail from Liberty Street, New York, to the Harlem River, with the proviso that the street must not be disturbed. This clause led him to perfect the tunneling shield, which had already been used by Brunel for the Thames Tunnel in 1843. He built a section of an underground road a block long between Warren Street and Murray Street. A 100-horse-power blower was used to propel the car. No profit could be derived under the charter and the idea was finally abandoned, but all may pass through the actual remains of the tunnel which now forms the City Hall station of the Brooklyn-Manhattan Subway. On June 30, 1847, he married Harriet Eliza, daughter of John F. and Harriet (Converse) Holbrook, at Boston, Mass.

[Biog. accounts may be found in H. Ely, *Records of the Descendants of Nathaniel Ely* (1885), p. 386; in *Sci. American,* Jan. 11, 18, 1896; and in *N. Y. Evening Sun,* Sept. 1, 1926. For pneumatic tunnel, see *Sci. American Suppl.,* no. 764, Aug. 23, 1890; for tunneling shield, *Suppl.* no. 574, Jan. 1, 1887; for typewriter, W. Kaempffert, *Pop. Hist. of Am. Invention* (1924), I, 264, 282, 452; II, 366, 372; and E. W. Byrn, *Progress of Invention in the Nineteenth Century* (1900), pp. 174–75, 347.]
            A. A. H.

BEACH, FREDERICK CONVERSE (Mar. 27, 1848–June 18, 1918), patent solicitor, publisher, was born on Columbia Heights, Brooklyn, N. Y. His heritage was that of journalism handed down from his grandfather, Moses Yale Beach [*q.v.*]. When he was quite young, his parents, Alfred Ely Beach [*q.v.*] and Harriet Eliza (Holbrook) Beach, moved to Stratford, Conn. A college education was apparently fixed upon for the youth and he received his preparatory education at the public schools in Bridgeport. At the age of seventeen he entered Yale University, graduating in 1868 from Sheffield Scientific School. Two undertakings of his father probably directed young Beach toward invention and the patent business. One of these was his father's typewriter invention and the other his construction of a section of passenger subway, operated by compressed air, beneath Broadway in New York City between Warren and Murray Streets. While still in college Beach, who had become interested in photography, brought to the attention of the United States commissioner of patents the utility and practicability of the photo-lithographic process for patent specifications and suggested a plan of use that was subsequently adopted. Immediately

after his graduation from college he represented his father's company, which had started a patent business besides publishing a technical journal, in Washington, D. C. Within a few years he returned to New York for the company and continued in business there. Upon the death of his father in 1896, Beach succeeded him as a director of the Scientific American Company, which office he held to the day of his death. His interest in this business was intense, particularly in those phases pertaining to invention and patents, and in these he showed an unflagging devotion that made him a most valuable business associate. In addition to these several interests he engaged for a time in the manufacture of electrical instruments. He was also vice-president of the Union Waxed and Parchment Paper Company, and was for many years president of the Postal Progress League, which was largely instrumental in bringing about the establishment of the parcel-post system in the United States. Beach's hobby was photography. He was one of the first amateur photographers of note in the United States, his interest leading him to help found the New York Society of Amateur Photographers, now the Camera Club of New York, in 1884. Later, in 1889, with the assistance of several other amateurs, he started a magazine called the *American Amateur Photographer,* later changed to *American Photography,* of which he was editor for many years. In 1902 he became editor-in-chief of the *Encyclopedia Americana.* In 1875 he married Margaret A. Gilbert, of Stratford, Conn.

[*Scientific American,* vol. CXVIII, No. 25; *Am. Photography,* vol. XII, No. 8; *Who's Who in America,* 1916–17.]
            C. W. M.

BEACH, MOSES SPERRY (Oct. 5, 1822–July 25, 1892), journalist, inventor, was the second of the eight children of Moses Yale Beach [*q.v.*] and his wife, Nancy Day. He was born at Springfield, Mass., at a time when his father, then only twenty-two years old, was at work on a variety of inventions. When he was twelve years old, his father began his connection with the New York *Sun,* and the boy was well taught by him the craft of the composing and pressrooms. In 1845 Moses Sperry Beach became joint owner, with George Roberts, of the *Boston Daily Times* but in a few months he returned to New York and, on Oct. 2, 1845, with his brother, Alfred Ely Beach [*q.v.*], entered the new firm of Moses Y. Beach & Sons, owners of the *Sun.* During the same year he was married to Chloe Buckingham of Waterbury, Conn. In December 1848 the elder Beach retired, leaving the property to the sons. On Apr. 6, 1852, Alfred Ely Beach withdrew from the *Sun,* and Moses Sperry Beach, then only thirty years old, became sole proprietor of the newspaper. His administration was characterized by the same enterprise and liberality that marked his father's. The *Sun* supported Buchanan in 1856, but was not pro-slavery. It denounced the Dred Scott decision and declared that John Brown belonged in a madhouse rather than on the gallows. Early in 1860, swayed perhaps by his chief editorial writer, John Vance, Beach supported Douglas against Lincoln, although the *Sun* had advised the Democratic party to nominate Sam Houston for president. Before the election, however, Beach turned over the *Sun* (Aug. 6, 1860) to a group of men, headed by the wealthy Archibald M. Morrison, whose intent was to transform this popular daily into a semi-religious newspaper. The price was $100,000 for good will, with a rental to be paid for the building and machinery, Beach retaining all physical ownership. As the new control not only urged the Union generals not to attack on Sunday (*Sun,* July 23, 1861) but refused to accept advertisements on the day of rest, the enterprise failed. On Jan. 1, 1862, Beach announced: "Once more I write myself Editor and sole proprietor of the New York *Sun.* My day dream of rural enjoyment is broken." He set out energetically to recoup the paper's loss of popularity and advertising income. He was able to lower expenses by adopting the stereotyping process and by reducing the number of columns from seven to five. The *Sun* had sold for one cent a copy since its foundation in 1833, but the Civil War sent the price of news-print to twenty-four cents a pound and Beach in 1863 announced with regret, mixed with humor, that thereafter the price of the paper would be "one cent in gold, or two cents in currency." The price remained two cents thereafter for fifty-three years. Beach never pretended to give to the *Sun's* public a news service such as Bennett offered in the *Herald,* profound editorial articles such as Greeley printed in the *Tribune,* or the thorough political news that marked the *Times* under Raymond. The *Sun* was a working man's newspaper and Beach catered to his readers by offering five or six columns of condensed news, one column of editorial, one of jokes and miscellany, one or two of fiction, and nine or ten of advertising. Fiction was one of his specialities and he bought liberally from the authors of the best-sellers of the time, Mary Jane Holmes, Horatio Alger, Jr., H. Warren Trowbridge, and Ann S. Stephens. On the physical side of newspaper production Beach made important contributions, inheriting

as he did his father's talent for mechanics. He invented a device for feeding paper to presses from a roll, thus doing away with the use of flat sheets; apparatus for wetting the paper before printing and for cutting after printing; and he is credited with being the first to print both sides of the sheet at once.

His desire for "rural enjoyment" was so deepseated that in January 1868, when he was only forty-five years old, he sold the *Sun* to a syndicate headed by Charles A. Dana, retaining a small portion of the stock. The price was $175,-000. With this and the accumulated profits of previous years he was able to find the leisure he wished. In 1873 he made an extended tour through Norway, Sweden, and Russia. The rest of his life was passed at his large estate at Peekskill, N. Y., where he died at the age of seventy. Beach was a man of dignity, possessor of a pleasing manner and an even temper that reflected itself in his strong, handsome face. He passed almost unruffled through a stormy period of American journalism, perhaps because he was more deeply interested in publishing than in politics. The kindness of his nature is reflected in an incident set down by Mark Twain in *The Innocents Abroad.* Beach was one of the tourists on the immortal voyage of the steamer *Quaker City* in 1867. At Jaffa the Americans were hailed by forty destitute New Englanders—men, women, and children—who had been lured to Palestine by "Prophet" Adams. They begged to be taken at least as far as Alexandria, Egypt—anywhere to get away from Adams and his misguided colony. On reaching Alexandria Beach inquired how much it would cost to send the penniless forty back to Maine by way of Liverpool and, on learning that $1,500 would cover the expense, paid it out of his own pocket—"an unselfish act of benevolence," as Mark Twain called it. Beach, who was a warm admirer and friend of Henry Ward Beecher, brought back from that voyage an olive tree from the Mount of Olives. The wood was made into a pulpit-stand for Plymouth Church, Brooklyn, and still is there.

[Most of the material of this sketch is taken from *The Story of the Sun* by Frank M. O'Brien (1918); cf. also H. Ely, *Records of the Descendants of Nathaniel Ely* (1885), p. 385.]

F. M. O.

BEACH, MOSES YALE (Jan. 15, 1800–July 19, 1868), journalist, inventor, was a descendant of John Beach who came from England about 1635 and settled in the New Haven colony. The father, grandfather, and great-grandfather of Moses Yale Beach all bore the name Moses, the first of them being the son of Thomas, son of John. Each Moses Beach was born on and worked in succession a farm at Wallingford, Conn. (C. H. S. Davis, *History of Wallingford,* 1870). Moses Yale Beach was the son of Moses Sperry Beach and Lucretia Yale, daughter of Capt. Elihu and Lucretia (Stanley) Yale. His mother died when he was four months old and his early years were directed by his stepmother. At the age of ten, according to Dr. Davis, the boy "took charge of considerable of the outdoor work on the farm, besides going a long distance to school" and "from 4 o'clock in the morning until 11 o'clock at night he was generally up and doing, yet found leisure to exercise his mechanical ingenuity in the manufacture of playthings for himself and others." When he was fourteen years old he was bound as an apprentice to Daniel Dewey, a cabinet-maker of Hartford, Conn. The lad's industry was so great that he soon won from his master a contract by which he received two cents an hour for overtime work—a concession which Beach used to describe, in his years of affluence, as the happiest incident of his whole business career. He later bargained with Dewey to buy his freedom at the age of eighteen years for $400; and so diligent was he in extra work at two cents an hour that in 1818 he not only released himself from his apprenticeship but had $100 of business capital. He worked a short time as a journeyman at Northampton and then formed a partnership with another cabinet-maker named Loveland. Their work received a prize from the Franklin Institute. On Nov. 19, 1819, he married Nancy Day of West Springfield, Mass. His next ten years were a struggle for success in the field of mechanics. He invented an engine, the power of which came from explosions of gunpowder. When this failed he turned to steam, then in its early stages, as the motive power for a boat which he intended to run on the Connecticut River from Springfield to Hartford, but his pecuniary resources were too limited to let him make a success of this enterprise. His next invention was a rag-cutting machine for use in paper mills. This would have meant a fortune for him if he had taken out a patent in time, as the process is still used. As it was, his device enabled him to obtain an interest in a paper-mill at Saugerties, N. Y., whither he removed in 1829. This, like his previous ventures, was not a financial success. Five years later Beach went to New York City to join his wife's brother, Benjamin H. Day [*q.v.*], the owner of the *Sun,* as manager of the mechanical department of that newspaper. Day had started the *Sun* on Sept. 3, 1833, and in January 1834 took in his principal reporter, George W. Wisner, as a partner. In 1835 Beach bought Wisner's share for $5,200,

and in 1838 Day's interest for $40,000. The *Sun* was then popular, having a circulation of 30,000 copies daily, but its profits, which at one time under Day had reached $20,000 a year, were small. It appeared for a time as if Beach would record another failure. "The first six months after he became entire owner of the paper," says Dr. Davis, "it did not prove as profitable as he had expected and he was ready to sell it out; and he offered it and all the property he then possessed if anyone would take it off his hands and pay his obligations (about $20,000) to Mr. Day; but, not succeeding in effecting a sale he went to work with renewed ardor and before two years had passed the last dollar was paid off." At the age of thirty-eight Beach's unflagging industry was at last rewarded by the beginning of real success.

The following ten years were as busy as any preceding decade of his life. The *Sun,* although first in the field of "penny papers," had to face the competition of the *New York Herald,* which James Gordon Bennett started in 1835. Though enterprising, Beach lacked Bennett's audacity. He established a ship news-service, the *Sun's* own sailing vessels meeting incoming steamships down the bay and there obtaining the freshest news from Europe. Beach used horse expresses to bring important news from Albany "with unparalleled expedition, in spite of wind, hail and rain," as the *Sun* said on Jan. 6, 1841, when it was able to print Gov. Seward's message twenty hours after the Governor presented it to the legislature. Beach ran special trains from Baltimore to New York with the news of the National Democratic Convention of 1844, beating the United States mail train by an hour or more. When Beach bought for the *Sun,* in 1842, the building at the southwest corner of Nassau and Fulton Sts., he built a huge pigeon house which stood for half a century on the roof. There lived the birds that brought to the *Sun* news from the ships at Sandy Hook, from Albany, and even from Washington (*Sun,* Dec. 14, 1843). The craze for speed manifested by Beach and Bennett is supposed to have inspired Edgar Allan Poe to write the "Balloon-Hoax," which he sold to Beach and which appeared in the *Sun* on Apr. 13, 1844. In this fabrication Poe made it appear that the aeronauts Monck Mason and Robert Holland, the novelist Harrison Ainsworth, and five other Englishmen had crossed the Atlantic in a dirigible balloon in three days, landing near Charleston, S. C. The hoax caused as great a sensation as the "Moon Hoax," which the *Sun* had printed eight years before; but in this case Beach made no effort to prolong the delusion, admitting two days after the first publication that Poe had merely tried to satirize the passion for speed.

Most of Beach's energies were directed toward the collection of legitimate news. He had a London correspondent who ran a special horse-express with the news-letters from London to the ships at Bristol. He sent a reporter to cover Webster's speech at the unveiling of the Bunker Hill monument. In the Mexican War, when news was delayed between Mobile, where Mexican tidings arrived by steamer, and Montgomery, he established a special railroad news-service between those Alabama cities. The war showed Beach how the New York newspapers, each acting for itself, were wasting much money. At a conference in his office the *Sun,* the *Herald,* the *Tribune,* the *Courier and Enquirer,* the *Express,* and the *Journal of Commerce* founded the New York Associated Press, designed to coöperate in the gathering of news in Washington, Albany, Boston, Philadelphia, New Orleans, and other news-centers. This conference also formed the Harbor Association, a syndicate through which the New York newspapers were able, with one fleet of news-boats, to do the work in which half a dozen fleets had been employed. Beach is also credited with inventing the syndicated newspaper article, for in 1841, when the *Sun* received by special messenger President Tyler's message to Congress, Beach printed in his office a special message-edition (all alike except the title heads) for twenty other newspapers, which were thus saved the delay and cost of setting up the message. He was the first American publisher to issue a "European edition." This was the *American Sun,* a weekly, issued in 1848, and sold abroad at twelve shillings a year. He also established the *Weekly Sun,* printed every Saturday and circulated among farmers at one dollar a year. Another venture was the *Illustrated Sun and Monthly Literary Journal,* a sixteen-page magazine lavishly illustrated with woodcuts. He personally wrote a brochure entitled *The Wealth of New York: a Table of the Wealth of the Wealthy Citizens of New York City Who Are Estimated to be Worth One Hundred Thousand Dollars or Over, with Brief Biographical Notices.* Several editions of this were published between 1841 and 1856. The price of this early "Who's Who" was twenty-five cents. Copies of it are in the New York Public Library.

Beach devoted himself more to the success of his newspapers than to the political quarrels which marked most journals of his day. His principal adversary was Horace Greeley, who founded the *New York Tribune* in 1841, three years after Beach became owner of the *Sun.* The newsboys of these rival journals fought in the streets, and Greeley's *Tribune* denounced Beach's *Sun* as "the slimy and venomous instrument of Locofocoism, Jesuitical and deadly in politics and grovelling in morals." But the truth was that Beach was an honorable man of business, bent on keeping his *Sun* in its enviable place as the most popular newspaper in the world. On its tenth birthday, Sept. 3, 1843, he was employing eight editors and reporters, twenty compositors, sixteen pressmen and one hundred carriers. The *Sun's* circulation was 38,000. Beach was compelled to buy a new dress of type every three months, for stereotyping had not arrived. In 1848, when Beach turned the newspaper over to his sons, Moses Sperry Beach [*q.v.*] and Alfred Ely Beach [*q.v.*], he anounced that the penny paper, then only fifteen years old, had a circulation of 50,000, "together with the largest cash advertising patronage on this continent." Beach had brought the *Sun* from a tiny three-column paper to one of eight columns, although he never increased the number of pages beyond the original four. Charles A. Dana [*q.v.*], who bought the *Sun* from the Beach family in 1868, wrote of Moses Yale Beach that he was "a business man and a newspaper manager rather than what we now understand as a journalist," but added that "under the stimulus of Mr. Beach's energetic intellect, aided by the cheapness of its price, the *Sun* became in his hands an important and profitable establishment."

In 1846 President Polk commissioned Beach to go to Mexico with a view to arranging terms of peace. The errand was halted by a false report that announced the defeat of Gen. Taylor by Santa Anna. Beach retired from business life in December 1848 because of ill health, and spent his remaining years in his native town of Wallingford, where he died at the age of sixty-eight. He left five sons and three daughters.

[Most of the information not otherwise credited is taken from *The Story of the Sun,* by Frank M. O'Brien (1918); cf. also H. Ely, *Records of the Descendants of Nathaniel Ely* (1885), and *N. Y. Tribune,* July 20, 1868.]

F. M. O.

BEACH, WILLIAM AUGUSTUS (Dec. 9, 1809–June 21, 1884), lawyer, was a descendant of Thomas Beach, the youngest of three brothers who came to New Haven from England in the ship *Elizabeth and Anna* in June 1638 and settled at Milford, Conn. He was the son of Miles and Cynthia (Warren) Beach, and was born at Saratoga Springs, N. Y., where his father had established a mercantile business. His education was received there and at Partridge's Military Institute, Norwich, Vt., after which he entered the office of his uncle, Judge Warren, studying law under the direct supervision of the latter. He was admitted to the bar in August 1833 and opened an office at Saratoga Springs. His father was influential, and the son soon acquired a good connection in the community. Saratoga Springs was then one of the legal centers of the state and Beach became known as a successful advocate and a tireless worker. He was appointed district attorney for Saratoga County, Sept. 11, 1843, and held this office till June 1847, acquiring an intimate knowledge of criminal law and a wide reputation for impressive oratory. In 1851 he moved to Troy, where he obtained a large practise, being particularly effective in jury cases. His fame extended beyond his own county and in 1865 he was retained to defend Col. North before a military commission in Washington on a charge of tampering with the soldiers' votes at the 1864 presidential election. Contrary to all expectations he persuaded the commission that they had no jurisdiction. This was probably the greatest purely forensic feat of his career. He also became associated with the Vanderbilt interests and appeared with C. A. Rapallo on behalf of Commodore Vanderbilt in the Erie Railroad litigation—"the Five Million Dollar Suit"—so impressing his client that, on the elevation of Rapallo to the bench in 1870, Beach was given a general retainer by the Commodore and removed to New York City. For the next fourteen years he appeared as counsel in almost all the *causes célèbres* of the period. In 1872 he was leading counsel for Judge G. G. Barnard, impeached on charges of judicial corruption by the state Assembly before the Senate and court of appeals sitting at Saratoga Springs as a court of impeachment, and though Barnard was convicted, the ability of the defense was universally recognized. One of his few conspicuous failures was in the Tilton-Beecher case, where he was leading counsel for the plaintiff. His final speech here occupied thirteen days whereas "he could have said all that should have been said in a day and with much better effect." He appeared for the defense in most of the notorious murder cases of his period in New York, his particular genius being perhaps more happily exhibited in this class of contest than on the civil side of the courts. Beach excelled as a mere orator. His command of language was wonderful, his sentences exquisitely modeled, his gestures graceful, and his voice musical. He had, however, grave defects, chief of which was a complete lack of humor. Irving Browne said of him that "his side of the case was always a funereal function, conducted with an oppressive and appalling grav-

ity!" His efforts were often marred by outbursts of invective and aggressive displays, symptomatic of his want of tact and control. His intellectual horizon was not extensive, he was a very weak cross-examiner, and his knowledge of the law, though varied, was never profound. He had no interests outside his profession. His own remark that he had always been a wide reader of worthless literature probably accurately expressed the depth of his general culture. In physical appearance he was tall, athletic, and handsome. "He had one of the coldest, most impassive and sphinx-like countenances that I ever beheld. . . . His bearing and dress were impressive. There was a gravity about him, a kind of *noli me tangere* characteristic that forbade anything like familiarity. . . . He invariably wore a double-breasted coat tightly buttoned and there was a sort of military erectness and precision about him which attracted attention and rendered him conspicuous" (Theron G. Strong, p. 285).

[The newspapers of the period are perhaps the best source of information as to Beach's legal achievements. An excellent but somewhat eulogistic review of his life appeared in the *Green Bag,* II, 509, and Irving Browne contributed a very good character sketch to the *Albany Law Jour.*, XLII, 468. Theron G. Strong, in *Landmarks of a Lawyer's Lifetime* (1914), pp. 285–88, has some valuable criticism of his legal career based on personal knowledge. See also E. R. Mann, *The Bench and Bar of Saratoga County* (1876), p. 310; *Central Law Jour.*, III, 36; *Hist. of the Bench and Bar of N. Y.* (1897), ed. by D. McAdam *et al.*, I, 256.]

H. W. H. K.

BEACH, WOOSTER (1794–Jan. 28, 1868), medical agitator, born in Trumbull, Conn., received the usual scanty education of those who then attended the rural schools. Late in his teens he was apprenticed to Dr. Jacob Tidd, a German herb collector and physician of Hunterdon County, N. J., with whom he remained until Tidd's death in 1825. He then moved to New York and matriculated at the College of Physicians and Surgeons, and later, Mar. 7, 1832, was elected member of the New York County Medical Society (*List of Members,* 1806–61, Albany). At the age of thirty-one Beach began to write prolifically in many fields of medical thought, and though not always original he was unusual in his defiance of authority and in the relentless energy with which he urged his views. He opposed blood-letting and purging with mercurials, and preached that most diseases would respond more readily to nature's remedies, such as herbs and roots. In 1833 he published a three-volume work, *The American Practice of Medicine,* which was, as expressed in the subtitle, "A Treatise on the Character, Causes, Symptoms, Morbid Appearances, and Treatment of the Diseases of Men, Women and Children of All Climates, on Vegetable or Botanical Principles; Containing Also a Treatise on Materia Medica and Pharmacy, with an Appendix on Cholera, etc." This text-book had a large circulation and is noteworthy for being the first systematic compendium of medical practise published in America in which pathological changes were correlated with disease processes. Copies of the work were sent to many crowned heads of Europe, and the author received much regal praise, all of which was duly printed in the second edition. There was an abridgment of the treatise in 1846, which passed through at least fourteen editions. The last edition of *The American Practice* (1852) brought heavy losses on the author because of the large number of colored plates illustrating pathological conditions. One may also mention Beach's *Treatise on Pulmonary Consumption, Phthisis Pulmonalis, with Remarks on Bronchitis* (1840), and *An Improved System of Midwifery* (1851). At least a dozen other less important medical works also came from his pen. In addition to Beach's medical activities he for many years published two broadsheets, the *Telescope* and the *Ishmaelite,* and through these channels he had an outlet for many of his novel views and speculations on religion, sociology, and medicine. In the heat of argument a friend once referred to Beach as an "eclectic." He replied quickly, "You have given me the term which I have wanted; I am an Eclectic." So enamoured was he of the epithet that in 1836 he founded an *Eclectic Medical Journal,* and in 1855 became president of the National Eclectic Medical Association. The *Journal* and the Society have had a long record and both are still in existence (1927), but the *Journal* is not recognized by the American Medical Association. Unfortunately Beach's followers attempted to extol him as a prophet and in this way did much to injure his reputation. Beach emphasized early the value of hospital practise for those who would keep abreast of medical progress. In 1828 he opened the United States Infirmary on Eldredge St., New York, where he had a large out-patient clinic. He was the founder of the New York Medical Academy which later became the Reformed Medical Society of the United States. In 1830 he helped to establish a medical department in the new university at Worthington, Ohio. Beach was not unlike Paracelsus: he had brilliant flashes but even his best contributions were marred by a vain boasting and exaggeration. His protests against over-dosing with mercury, though they served a useful purpose, were untruthful in grossly exaggerating the harmful effects of that metal, and this unfortunate tendency is to be found in many of his controversial writings. His logic was often

faulty and he allowed himself to be carried away by absurd prejudices. To the end of his life he refused to use a stethoscope (*American Practice,* 1852 ed., I, 529), but he employed direct ear-to-chest auscultation. Though his faults were many he worked unremittingly and wrote with admirable devotion to his subject. Had he possessed a broader cultural background he would undoubtedly have reached greater heights. In 1823 Beach married Eliza de Grove, and had two sons. The drowning of his second son led to a physical and mental break-down and he died shortly thereafter. His oldest son, Wooster Beach, Jr., practised medicine.

[Beach has left biog. material in the introductions to his various works. He frequently gives dates of important events in his life (see esp. *The Family Physician,* 4th ed., 1844, pp. 5–11), and in the 1852 edition of the *Am. Practice* he devotes fifty closely printed pages to a description of his trip to Europe in 1848–49. A. Wilder, follower of the Eclectic school, has written extensively of Beach in his *Hist. of Medicine* (1901), and also in the *Eclectic Medic. Jour.,* 1893, LIII, 113–21, and *Medic. Advocate,* II, 235–37, but these are all injudicious estimates of the man, with fulsome praise; obituary in *N.Y. Herald,* Jan. 30, 1868.]

J.F.F.

BEADLE, WILLIAM HENRY HARRISON (Jan. 1, 1838–Nov. 13, 1915), educator, was born in a log cabin, built by his father, close to the Wabash River in Parke County, Ind. His parents, James Ward Beadle and Elizabeth Bright, had moved after their marriage from Kentucky to the frontier in western Indiana. His early life was typical of the frontier. He learned to use the axe, plow, and rifle, got his education in a log schoolhouse and later in the graded school at the county seat, and enjoyed reading books in the township public library and others which his father brought back from his river trips to New Orleans. His father offered him a farm, but he chose to take instead a thousand dollars for a college education. Entering the University of Michigan in the fall of 1857, he specialized in civil engineering. After his graduation in June 1861 he entered the Union army as first lieutenant of Company A, 31st Indiana Volunteer Infantry. He was repeatedly promoted, and was given the rank of brevet brigadier-general when he was discharged, Mar. 26, 1866. During the war, on May 18, 1863, he had married Ellen S. Chapman at Albion, Mich. Beadle attended the University of Michigan Law School for a year after his discharge and received his LL.B. in March 1867. After practising law in Evansville, Ind., and Boscobel, Wis., he was appointed, March 1869, surveyor general of Dakota territory. As he rode up the broad Missouri Valley to Yankton, the territorial capital, he talked with his predecessor about the natural resources of the state that was to be. "On that journey the school lands were mentioned and I then opened to my companion the theory that these were the great trust of the future commonwealth and should be absolutely secured from waste and cheap sales" ("Memoirs," p. 90). All of Beadle's public services in Dakota territory assisted in the accomplishment of this purpose. In the next four years he became acquainted with the country and early settlers. As secretary of the commission which drew up the code of 1877, he gained valuable experience in clear exposition of complicated ideas. The responsibility for passing the code through the legislature fell largely on Beadle through his chairmanship of the judiciary committee in the House. He accepted the superintendency of public instruction in 1879 with the condition that he "should stand strongly for the principle that no school lands should ever be sold for less than their appraised value, and never for less than ten dollars an acre" (*Ibid.*, p. 169), when statehood was attained. For the next six years Beadle was busily engaged in organizing new schools necessitated by the rapid expansion of settlement, in introducing the township unit of administration, and in holding teachers' institutes. On every occasion, in conversation or on the platform he talked about the protection of the school lands. Many opposed the ten-dollar minimum, as only one state, Colorado, in 1875, had placed a limit as high as $2.50 per acre, and land could be bought in Iowa in the early 80's for $2.50 to $4.00 an acre. But Rev. Joseph Ward, missionary pastor in Yankton since 1868 and founder of Yankton College, gave his whole-hearted support to the movement from the beginning and proved a valuable advocate in the constitutional convention of 1885, where the real test came. To win in the convention it was necessary to get the unanimous indorsement of the committee on school lands. Beadle was not a member of the convention, but was commandeered by the committee to sit with them and give advice. Taking the initiative he drafted an article embodying his main ideas. "It was that formal and complete document, not oral discussions and misunderstandings, that won the case" (*Ibid.*, p. 214). Beadle's careful explanation and Ward's persuasion converted a hostile majority, and the report of the committee was accepted by the convention shortly before adjournment. Thus the matter was settled, as this constitution in 1889 became the state constitution. So strongly was Congress impressed by this movement for the ten-dollar minimum that it required a similar provision for the admission of North Dakota, Montana, and Washington in 1889 and of Idaho and Wyoming in

1890. Beadle continued his educational service by his able and inspiring presidency of the Madison State Normal School from 1889 to 1905 and as professor of history until his retirement in 1912. He died in San Francisco, while on a visit to his daughter. A statue of Beadle, paid for by the contributions of the school children of the state, stands to-day in the capitol building at Pierre with the inscription, "Wm. H. H. Beadle, educator. He saved the school lands."

[The chief source is "Personal Memoirs of Wm. H. H. Beadle," *S. Dak. Hist. Colls.* (1906), III, 85–265; see O. W. Coursey, *A Complete Biog. Sketch of Gen. Wm. Henry Harrison Beadle* (1913); obituary in *Sioux Falls* (S. D.) *Daily Argus Leader*, Nov. 15, 1915. For Beadle's Civil War service, see *Official Records*, ser. I, vol. XXXVII, pt. 2 (1891), and ser. III, vol. V (1900).]

R. G. W.

BEAL, WILLIAM JAMES (Mar. 11, 1833– May 12, 1924), botanist, teacher, was born at Adrian, Mich., the son of a Quaker, William Beal, and of Rachel Comstock. Beal's was the day of homespun clothes, log houses, wooden plows, and this early environment made him through later life economical of time, equipment and energy, and tirelessly industrious. The waste of forests seen in his boyhood made him a conservationist, while his knowledge of the farm boy was invaluable to him in his teaching. He entered the University of Michigan with the class of 1859, and acquired a smattering of zoölogy and botany taught entirely from books. With the degree of A.B. he went to Union Springs, N. Y., in 1859, teaching till 1868. During vacations he studied at Harvard, where Agassiz took him in hand and made a thoroughgoing naturalist of him. Then Beal went to Asa Gray, who led him through systematic botany and what little was then known of the physiology and morphology of plants, converting him easily to the Darwinian theory of evolution. In 1865 he received his S.B. from Harvard, and in 1875 his M.S. from the old University of Chicago, where he went to teach botany in 1868. In 1871 he began teaching at the Michigan Agricultural College, where he continued until his retirement in 1910. Beal is usually considered one of the three pioneers who grew up in the "old botany" and by their efforts helped to usher in the "new botany." He probably did not produce so many botanists as did Bessey and Burrill, but his influence on the raw farm boy was on the side of science. He would drill his students for hours in the Latin names of plants, because he felt that they stood in need of formal training. But he was one with them in his homely use of proverbs and wise saws, the most characteristic of which was his "Keep on squintin'," which he gave to beginning students exasperated with microscopic scrutiny. His publications are said to have numbered more than 1,200; of these, *The New Botany* (1881) had the greatest pedagogic influence. The *Grasses of North America* (2 vols., 1887) in its first edition had to be published at the author's expense, but so great was its popularity among amateurs that it readily found a publisher for subsequent editions. Unfortunately for systematic botany, the book was full of inaccuracies and has thrown much confusion into the tangled nomenclature of the grasses. *Seed Dispersal* (1898) was also immensely popular, and scientifically sound. In *The History of Michigan Agricultural College* (1915), "Pioneer Life in Southern Michigan in the Thirties," chapter IV of *An American Pioneer of Science,* and "Studying the Sciences Fifty Years Ago," in *Michigan Alumnus,* February 1917, he gave historically valuable glimpses of the times. In 1887 he procured legislation creating the Forestry Commission. He founded the college forest preserve in 1875 and in 1906 planted its "Pinetum." To him the college owes its well-stocked botanical garden. He had, it is said, but three antipathies: for alcohol, tobacco, and quack-grass. One might add, as a fourth, hatred of idleness, for after his retirement, when too feeble to walk alone, he would sit and saw up firewood. He died in his sleep, after a paralytic stroke, at the home of his son-in-law, Ray Stannard Baker, at Amherst. His wife was a childhood friend, Hannah Proud, whom he married Sept. 2, 1863.

[R. S. and J. B. Baker, *An Am. Pioneer of Sci.* (privately printed, 1925); *Mich. Alumnus,* May 22, 1924, pp. 946–47; E. A. Bessey, "W. J. Beal" (with portr.) in *Bot. Gazette,* Mar. 1925, pp. 103–06; C. W. McKibbin, "W. J. Beal, Michigan's Pioneer Forester," *Am. Forests and Forest Life,* Apr. 1924, pp. 216–17.]   D.C.P.

BEALE, EDWARD FITZGERALD (Feb. 4, 1822–Apr. 22, 1893), "pioneer in the path of empire," as Bayard Taylor termed him, was born in the District of Columbia. His father was George Beale, a paymaster in the navy, who had won a Congressional Medal for gallantry in the battle on Lake Champlain, Sept. 11, 1814; and his mother was Emily Truxtun, youngest daughter of the famous Commodore. He was a student at Georgetown College when, at the solicitation of his widowed mother, he was appointed by President Jackson to the Naval School, from which, in 1842, he graduated. Early in October 1845, he sailed on the frigate *Congress,* under Commodore Stockton, for California, but twenty days later was sent back with important dispatches. After a long and roundabout voyage, the first of many government missions that were to carry

him tens of thousands of miles, he reached Washington in the middle of March 1846. Promoted to the grade of master, he sailed for Panama and overtook the *Congress* at Callao, Peru, in May. Hostilities with Mexico had already begun when the vessel reached Monterey on July 20, and he was at once detached to serve with the land forces. He was with the small body under Lieut. Gillespie that left San Diego and joined Kearny's column just before the disastrous battle of San Pasqual (Dec. 6), and was one of the three men (his Delaware Indian servant and Kit Carson being the other two) who, after the battle, performed the desperately heroic act of creeping through the Mexican lines and carrying the news of Kearny's plight to Stockton.

Two months later (Feb. 9, 1847), still suffering greatly from the effects of that adventure, he was sent east, in the company of Carson and a small guard, with dispatches. He reached Washington about the first of June, and in October was a witness for Frémont in the court martial of "the Pathfinder" instituted by Kearny. As a bearer of dispatches he was now to make, within the short space of two years, six journeys from ocean to ocean. On the second of these (July–September 1848), when he crossed Mexico at imminent danger of his life, he brought the first authentic news of the gold discoveries and a bag of the precious metal. After the fourth journey he was married, June 27, 1849, to Mary, the daughter of Representative Samuel Edwards, of Chester, Pa., but immediately started west again. In December he was back in Washington, where for a time he rested. On Aug. 3, 1850, he was made a lieutenant. In the following May he resigned from the navy and returned to California as a manager for W. H. Aspinwall and Commodore Stockton, who had acquired large properties there. By November 1852 he was again in Washington. President Fillmore appointed him superintendent of Indian affairs for California and Nevada, and Congress, on Mar. 3, 1853, appropriated $250,000 for making effective a project of his for improving the condition of his wards. With his kinsman, Gwinn Harris Heap, and a party of twelve others he left Westport May 6, making on the way a preliminary survey for a railroad, and, traversing southern Colorado and southern Utah, reached Los Angeles on Aug. 22. He held this office until 1856, receiving from the governor of the state the appointment of brigadier-general of militia. In the following year, by appointment of President Buchanan, he commanded an expedition to survey a wagon road from Fort Defiance, N. Mex., to the Colorado River, using for transport a part of the camel herd he had persuaded the Government to import from Tunis. In 1858–59 he surveyed another road to the Colorado River, this time from Fort Smith, Ark. He was appointed, shortly after Lincoln's inauguration, surveyor general of California and Nevada, and, though he asked instead for service in the army, was induced to retain this post until the end of the war. He then retired to the Rancho Tejon, an immense tract that he had bought near the present Bakersfield. Later he bought the Decatur house in Washington, and from about 1870 usually spent half the year in each home. In 1876 President Grant appointed him minister to Austria-Hungary, a post that he held for a year. A Republican, somewhat active in politics, he was strongly but unsuccessfully supported by Grant and others for appointment by President Arthur as secretary of the navy. He died at his Washington home. "A sparkling combination of scholar, gentleman and Indian fighter," Charles Nordhoff described him after a visit to his ranch in 1872 (*California*, 1872, pp. 229–30). Between Carson and himself, each of whom had saved the other's life, existed a bond of the tenderest fellowship. He was the faithful ally of Frémont, and the intimate friend of Bayard Taylor, U. S. Grant, and J. G. Blaine.

[Sources for a study of Beale's life are scattered over a wide field of government documents, Cong. speeches, and chronicles of the frontier. A biog., *Edward Fitzgerald Beale*, by Stephen Bonsal, was published in 1912. Gwinn Harris Heap's jour. of the expedition from Westport to Los Angeles in the summer of 1853 was published in 1854, under the title *Central Route to the Pacific*. The report of the survey from Fort Defiance to the Colorado was published as *House Ex. Doc. 124, 35 Cong., 1 Sess.*, and that of the survey from Fort Smith to the Colorado as *House Ex. Doc. 42, 36 Cong., 1 Sess.*]

W.J.G.

BEALE, RICHARD LEE TURBERVILLE (May 22, 1819–Apr. 21, 1893), politician, Confederate soldier, was born at Hickory Hill, Westmoreland County, Va., a descendant of Thomas Beale, who came from England to York County in 1645 and served as a member of Gov. Berkeley's council. His son removed to Westmoreland County, where the family was prominent for the next two hundred years. The Hickory Hill estate was settled by the Turbervilles about 1700, and came into the possession of Robert Beale on his marriage with Martha Felicia, the daughter of George Lee Turberville, an officer in the Revolutionary army and an early member of Phi Beta Kappa. Richard Beale, their son, was educated at Dickinson College and at the University of Virginia, was admitted to the bar in 1839, and took up the practise of law near his birthplace. He was a member of Congress from 1847 to 1849, a delegate to the state constitutional convention in 1851, and a state senator from 1858 to 1860. In May 1861 he was mustered into the Confederate service as a first lieutenant of "Lee's Legion," or "Lee's Light Horse." A month later he saw his first fighting when he commanded a small force which put out in two flatboats from Mathias Point to capture a vessel aground in the Potomac. Lee's Legion was sent to join the army at Bull Run, but arrived the day after the battle, and soon returned to patrol duty along the Potomac. Beale was promoted to captain in July and major in October. Next spring the legion was merged in the 9th Virginia Cavalry, of which Beale was appointed lieutenant-colonel in April and colonel in October. He served with the regiment in all the campaigns of the Army of Northern Virginia, with credit but not with satisfaction. For some reason, which does not appear, he offered his resignation three times, at decent intervals—Nov. 22, 1862, Feb. 8, 1863, and Aug. 25, 1863—but it was not accepted. In his last letter of resignation, he pleaded to be allowed to organize a company of rangers or to enlist as a private. Severely wounded in a skirmish in September 1863, he was unable to resume command for more than three months. Late in 1864 he was given command of a brigade, and his appointment as brigadier-general was recommended. Just at that time, however, a large draft was made upon the adjutant-general's force of clerks, for service in the field, and in the confusion Beale's papers were misplaced. It was not until Feb. 6, 1865, that the appointment was made. After the general surrender he again took up the practise of law at Hague, in his native county, where he lived the rest of his life. He was again a member of Congress from 1879 to 1881.

[R. L. T. Beale, *Hist. of the Ninth Va. Cavalry in the War between the States* (1899); *Confed. Mil. Hist.* (1899), III, 581; *Official Records*, ser. I, vols. XXI, XXV (pt. I), XXXIII.]

T. M. S.

BEALL, JOHN YATES (Jan. 1, 1835–Feb. 24, 1865), Confederate soldier, was born in Jefferson County, Va., in the upper part of the Shenandoah Valley. He came of good family. His mother, a Yates, claimed descent from those English Howards whose ancestor was the "Belted Will" of Scott's poem. His father, George Beall, was the owner of a large farm. John Yates Beall attended the University of Virginia and studied law, but did not take a degree. His intimate friends described him as an earnest and serious young man, of exemplary habits and a marked religious nature. At the beginning of the Civil War he was a private in the "Stonewall

Brigade," but was soon severely wounded and compelled to leave the army. Traveling to relatives in Iowa, he from there proceeded to Canada, and formed schemes for operations against the Federals on inland waters. Returning to the Confederacy, he was appointed by Secretary Mallory acting master in the navy, and was soon at work in Chesapeake Bay. With a band limited in numbers he captured the *Alliance* and other small vessels, cut cables, and performed various exploits until his own capture. Held at first as a pirate, he was released upon threats of retaliation on certain Federals held as hostages. He fought for a short time in front of Richmond, but soon disappeared, and making his way to Canada entered upon the last and noted part of his career. He formed a plan in September 1864 to seize the Federal war-vessel *Michigan* on Lake Erie; and with the aid of helpers on the land, under one Cole, to set free the Confederate prisoners interned on Johnson's Island (entrance to Sandusky Bay). Associated with him was one Burley—known later as a famous English war-correspondent under the name "Bennet Burleigh." The conspirators seized the steamers *Philo Parsons* and *Island Queen* and scuttled the latter. But the plot failed through a "mutiny" of Beall's men and a break-down on Cole's part. The *Parsons* was beached and abandoned, and Beall returned to Canada. On Dec. 16, 1864, he was arrested on the New York side of the frontier at Suspension Bridge, after making several futile attempts to derail trains near Buffalo. His motives are not clear (Shepard, p. 41); perhaps he designed to liberate Confederate prisoners. He was taken to New York, where Gen. Dix was in command, and imprisoned in Fort Lafayette. He was brought to trial on the charges of being a spy, and of "violation of the laws of war." In defense he attempted to show that he was regularly engaged in the Confederate service, but was found guilty and condemned to death. Strenuous efforts were made for a commutation of the sentence by prominent Baltimoreans, by Gen. Roger Pryor, a fellow prisoner, and by such noted men as Thaddeus Stevens and Gov. Andrew of Massachusetts. A petition signed by many congressmen was presented to Lincoln through a personal friend, Orville Browning, but the President declined to interfere, and Beall was executed by hanging on Governors Island. Afterward there appeared a "weird and lurid story" (Markens, p. 10)—thoroughly exploded—that Wilkes Booth, reputed to have been Beall's intimate friend, had a midnight interview with Lincoln; that the President, moved to tears, promised a pardon for Beall but was overruled by Secretary Seward; whereupon Booth, in revenge, formed his plot of assassination.

[F. J. Shepard, "The Johnson's Island Plot" in *Pubs. Buffalo Hist. Soc.* (1906), IX; Daniel B. Lucas (Beall's college room-mate), *Memoir of John Yates Beall* (1865) including Beall's Diary; Isaac Markens, *President Lincoln and the Case of John Yates Beall* (1911); Rev. Jas. H. McNeilley in *Confederate Veteran* (1899), pp. 66–69; W. W. Baker, *Memoirs of Service with John Yates Beall, C. S. N.* (1910); G. A. Foote, *Old Watering Places in Warren County* (1899); and J. H. Crawford in *Southern Hist. Soc. Papers* (1905), XXXIII, 71–78; *Official Records,* ser. I, II, and IV; *Trial of John Y. Beall as a Spy and Guerrillero by Military Commission* (1865).]

E. K. A.

BEALL, SAMUEL WOOTTON (Sept. 26, 1807–Sept 26, 1868), public official, politician, son of Lewis and Eliza Beall, was descended from Ninian Beall, a member of a well-known Scottish family of royalist stock, who came to Maryland and settled in Calvert County shortly after 1650. Samuel was born in Montgomery County, received his education at Union College, Schenectady, and when only a student married Elizabeth Fenimore, daughter of Isaac Cooper of Cooperstown, N. Y., and niece of J. Fenimore Cooper, the novelist. On his graduation in 1827, he was, through the influence of Chief Justice Taney, appointed receiver for the sale of public lands in the northwest, whither he proceeded, establishing the first land office at Green Bay, Wis., and taking an active part in opening up the sparsely settled territory immediately west of Lake Michigan. In 1834 he returned to the East and took up his residence in the vicinity of his wife's relatives at Cooperstown, where his house became the center of a brilliant group of literary notables, including Washington Irving. In 1840 the lure of the wild again drew him to Wisconsin. He first located at Tychora, Marquette County, shortly afterward removing to Taycheedah in Fond du Lac County, where he engaged in farming, and for a short time was Indian agent with the Stockbridge tribe. In 1836 Wisconsin had been detached from Michigan and made a separate territory, and the advisability or otherwise of forming a state government became a subject of much controversy. Beall threw himself with ardor into the fight on behalf of statehood. He was a delegate from Marquette County to the constitutional convention held at Madison, Oct. 5, 1846, was chairman of the committee for the organization of state government, and took a prominent part in the proceedings. When the constitution as then drafted was submitted to the people, Apr. 6, 1847, it was rejected. A second convention was thereupon summoned for Dec. 15 at Madison, which Beall attended as a delegate from Taycheedah, being a member of the committee on general provisions. The constitution then prepared was ratified by the people, Mar. 13, 1848. Beall's activities at these conventions had brought him into considerable prominence, and on Wisconsin's being admitted as a state he was recognized as one of its leading figures. In 1850 he was elected lieutenant-governor, serving in this position for two years, following which he again became Indian agent, in this capacity escorting the tribal chiefs within his district to Washington. Always enamoured of frontier life, in 1859 he was leader of an exploration party to Pike's Peak, Colo., and assisted at the location and founding of Denver. The growth of the new city was such that he was sent specially to Washington to procure the grant of a charter. He returned to Wisconsin in 1861 at the outbreak of the Civil War, and in 1862 was appointed lieutenant-colonel of the 18th Wisconsin Regiment, with which body he took part in much severe fighting. Wounded at both Shiloh and Vicksburg, he was incapacitated for active service during the last stages of the conflict. At the conclusion of the war he returned to Wisconsin for a short time and then moved to Helena, Mont. He was shot and killed in the office of the *Montana Post,* at Helena, Sept. 25, 1868, by George M. Pinney, manager of the *Post,* in the course of an altercation relative to certain articles reflecting on Beall's character which Pinney had published.

Beall was a curious compound of strength and instability. His intellectual endowment was of a high order and his general culture wide. As a man of affairs, he was respected for his invariable courtesy and undoubted integrity. He was a fluent speaker, and the embodiment of dignity when the occasion demanded. Unfortunately he always seemed to act on the impulse of the moment. Of an intensely restless nature, during the last twenty years of his life he was unable to live anywhere but on the fringe of civilization. Many tales are told of his warm-heartedness and generosity. One most characteristic action was on the occasion of the death of his mother who had bequeathed him a small patrimony in Maryland and some thirty slaves: though Beall was not in very good financial circumstances he at once gave the slaves their freedom, at the same time selling the property and devoting the proceeds to their support until they could find employment.

[Beall's forebears are discussed in *Historic Sketches of the Beall and Edwards Families* (1910), by A. S. Edwards. A competent sympathetic sketch of his life appeared in *Memorial Records of the Fathers of Wisconsin* (1880), by H. H. Tenney and D. Atwood. The circumstances of his marriage are narrated in *The Story of Cooperstown,* by R. Birdsall (1917), pp. 191, 195–96. Details of his death, together with extracts from the *Helena Herald* and *Montana Post,* appeared in the *N. Y. Times,* Oct. 13, 1868.]

H. W. H. K.

BEAMAN, CHARLES COTESWORTH (May 7, 1840–Dec. 15, 1900), lawyer, traced his descent from Gamaliel Beaman, probably a native of Bridgnorth, Shropshire, who, emigrating at the age of twelve in 1635, settled in Massachusetts. Sixth in direct line of descent from Gamaliel was Charles Cotesworth Beaman, a New England Congregational minister, who married Mary Ann Stacey of Wiscasset, Me., their eldest son, Charles Cotesworth Beaman, Jr., being born in Houlton, Me. His early education was received at Smithtown Seminary, North Scituate, R. I., whence he proceeded in 1857 to Harvard, graduating in 1861. For the next two years he was principal of the academy at Marblehead, Mass., and then studied law at the Harvard Law School. His Harvard prize essay, "Rights and Duties of Neutrals in Respect to the Armed Vessels of Belligerents," published under a shorter title in the *North American Review,* was read by Senator Sumner, chairman of the Senate Committee on Foreign Relations who thereupon engaged Beaman as private secretary, and after his call to the bar in November 1865, procured his appointment as clerk of the Committee. Beaman occupied this position for three years, during which he laid the foundation for an intimate knowledge of international law. In 1868 he resigned and, going to New York, commenced practise. At this period the controversy between the United States and Great Britain respecting the depredations committed by Confederate cruisers was becoming acute and he made an exhaustive study of the subject. As a result he wrote *The National and Private "Alabama Claims" and their "Final and Amicable Settlement,"* which was published in March 1871. Two months later, by the Treaty of Washington, the Geneva Tribunal of Arbitration was constituted to adjudicate the dispute, and Beaman was appointed solicitor for the United States in the arbitration proceedings. At Geneva his intimate knowledge of all the details proved of inestimable value. He assisted J. C. Bancroft Davis, the United States agent, by arranging the evidence presented with the American case, representing both national and individual claims, and "did his work with admirable fidelity" (Report of Davis, Sept. 21, 1872, *House Executive Document, No. 1, pt. 1,* 42 Cong., 3 Sess.) On his return to New York in 1872 he resumed practise. Following the arbitration award, a Court of Commissioners of Alabama Claims was established at Washington, and he was retained as counsel by a number of the more important claimants. One remarkable case was that of the *Texan Star,* where he successfully maintained a claim for the destruction of that ship by a Confederate cruiser, although it had acquired a British registry in order to avoid capture. In connection with this work he wrote *The Rights of Insurance Companies under the Geneva Award* (1876). During the Geneva proceedings he had come into close contact with W. M. Evarts, whose daughter, Hettie Sherman, he married Aug. 19, 1874, and in 1879 he was offered and accepted a partnership in the firm of Evarts, Southmayd & Choate. He was endowed with exceptionally sound judgment, which, combined with a thorough grasp of legal principles and a wide experience of international matters, gave him unusual prestige professionally. Personally he was much liked, possessing a genial temperament which attracted old and young, and a perfect sincerity of language and demeanor which never left any room for doubt as to his attitude toward any subject under discussion. He was much interested in politics, though the only occasion upon which he aspired for office was in 1894, when he was the unsuccessful Republican and Independent Democratic candidate for the office of judge of the New York supreme court. In 1899 he was appointed a member of the Commission for the Revision of the Charter of the City of New York. He died in New York in December of the following year.

[Details of his ancestry will be found in *The Beaman and Clark Genealogy* by Emily Beaman Wooden (1909). An authoritative review of his life and career, "Memorial of Charles C. Beaman," prepared by Edmund Wetmore, appeared in *Bar of the City of N. Y. Report,* 1901, p. 96. See also *Hist. of the Bench and Bar of N. Y.,* ed. by D. McAdam *et al.* (1897), II, 30, and *Hist. and Digest of the International Arbitrations to which the United States has been a party,* by John Bassett Moore, (1898), I, 495–678; obituary, *N. Y. Times,* Dec. 16, 1900.]

H. W. H. K.

BEAN, TARLETON HOFFMAN (Oct. 8, 1846–Dec. 28, 1916), ichthyologist, the son of George and Mary (Smith) Bean, was born at Bainbridge, Pa., and received his early education at the State Normal School, Millersville, Pa. He obtained a medical degree in 1876 from the Columbian (now the George Washington) University, but, being little disposed to take up the practise of medicine, permitted himself to follow his early zoölogical interests and within a few years became a foremost authority on the fresh-water fish of America and of the northern salt waters. From 1880 to 1895 he was curator of the Department of Fisheries in the United States National Museum, and from 1895 to 1898 director of the New York Aquarium. He acted also as a member of the United States Fish Commission, and from 1906 until his death he was

head fish culturist of New York state. Owing to Bean's activities New York became the first state to attempt the preservation of its fish through "green-house" methods of propagation. He was in fact largely responsible for initiating the national movement for preservation of native fish in this country. A profound student of nature, Bean was also a prolific writer, and the bibliography of his books and scientific papers contains 322 titles. His most important contribution was *Oceanic Ichthyology* (1895) written in conjunction with Goode (529 pp., 124 colored plates). His other books were: *Fishes of Pennsylvania* (1893); *Fishes of Long Island* (1901); *Fishes of New York* (1903); *Fishes of Bermuda* (1906). With W. C. Harris he published an important monograph on *The Basses, Fresh-water and Marine* (1905). Bean's scientific attainments were recognized abroad, for he was made Chevalier de la Légion d'Honneur and Officier du Mérite Agricole of France; Knight of the Imperial Order of the Red Eagle, Germany, and of the Order of the Rising Sun, Japan; and honorary member of the Society of Danish Fisheries. In 1908–09 he was president of the American Fisheries Society. His discoveries were noteworthy scientifically, and his studies of the periodic migration of fish proved of great commercial value. For twenty years before his death he was by common consent the most distinguished fish culturist in America, and he had no peers among American ichthyologists. On Jan. 1, 1878, he married Laurette H. van Hook. While in Albany in October 1916 he was injured in an automobile accident, and he died two months later as a result of his injuries.

[Pubs. of the U. S. Fish Commission; *Proc. of U. S. Nat. Museum;* biog. by E. W. Gudger in Kelly and Burrage, *Dict. of Am. Medic. Biog.* (1928); *Jour. Am. Medic. Ass.,* LXVIII, 211; obituary in *Albany Evening Jour.,* Dec. 29, 1916.]

J. F. F.

BEARD, GEORGE MILLER (May 8, 1839– Jan. 23, 1883), physician, son of the Rev. Spencer F. Beard, a Congregational minister, and of Lucy A. Leonard, was born at Montville, Conn. He prepared for college at Phillips Academy, Andover, Mass., and graduated from Yale College in 1862, and from the College of Physicians and Surgeons of New York in 1866. While still a medical student he served as acting assistant surgeon in the West Gulf squadron of the United States Navy. His initial essay in medical literature, to which he soon became a ceaseless contributor, was a paper on "Electricity as a Tonic" (1866). In that year he associated himself with Dr. A. D. Rockwell of New York, with whom, as with a kindred spirit, he conducted researches in electro-therapeutics for a series of years, the results of which were embodied in articles on the *Medical Use of Electricity* and later, in 1871, in *The Medical and Surgical Uses of Electricity.* This latter work was translated into German, had a wide vogue in Europe, and at once gave Beard an international reputation as an investigator. He introduced and popularized the terms "central galvanization" and "general faradization" and gained for them universal acceptance. To the public he early became known by his *Our Home Physician* (1869), *Eating and Drinking* (1871) and *Stimulants and Narcotics* (1871). His literary output, which was continuous and enormous, included: *The Legal Responsibility in Old Age, based on Researches into the Relations of Old Age to Work* (1874); *The Longevity of Brain Workers* (1867); *Hay Fever* (1876); *The Scientific Basis of Delusions* (1877); *Nervous Exhaustion* (1880); *Sea-Sickness* (1880); *American Nervousness* (1881); *Trance and Muscle Reading* (1882); *Psychology of the Salem Witchcraft Excitement of 1692* (1882); *Medical Education and the Medical Profession in Europe and America* (1883); *How to Use the Bromides* (1881); *Current Delusions Relating to Hypnotism* (1882). He founded the *Archives of Electrology and Neurology* (1874–75). In 1868 he became a lecturer on nervous diseases in New York University and later physician to the Demilt Dispensary in the department of electro-therapeutics and nervous diseases. He was several times a delegate to foreign scientific associations, and in 1881 a delegate to the International Medical Congress in London. In neurology he was an American pioneer and made a notable contribution to the study of "neurasthenia," being the first to show clearly and positively that Americans possess a peculiar nervous organization. He maintained that the cause of the greater prevalence of nervous diseases in the United States is dryness of the air and extremes of heat and cold. To him science likewise owes the conception of sea-sickness as a functional neurosis induced mechanically by concussion, and he, too, introduced to the profession and to the public the treatment of sea-sickness by bromides. In psychiatry he was an early champion of reforms, many of which, through his initiative and zeal, became incorporated in subsequent practise, and he was one of the originators of the "National Association for the Protection of the Insane and the Prevention of Insanity." He took strong ground, on the unpopular side, in his published opinions on the trial of Guiteau, the assassin of President Garfield, declaring him insane and irresponsible. Undaunted by the clamor of the

people and of many respectable members of his own profession for the death penalty, he prepared a petition to prevent what he regarded as the judicial hanging of a man whose innocence was implicit in his mental disease. His passion for investigation and analysis persisted till the day of his death when, in almost his last words, he said to bystanders at his bed, "Tell the doctors it is impossible for me to record the thoughts of a dying man. It would be interesting to do so, but I cannot. My time has come. I hope others will carry on my work." Dr. A. D. Rockwell, in offering resolutions on Beard's death at a meeting of the Medical Society of the County of New York, on Mar. 26, 1883, said of his associate: "As an investigator he was original and conscientious. As a friend he was generous and steadfast. Exposed by his restless activity to many peculiar attacks, he ever manifested the utmost charity and good humor. Of his worst enemies, he seldom spoke a harsh, and never a vindictive, word." Beard married Dec. 25, 1866, Elizabeth Ann Alden, of Westville, Conn., who survived her husband's death but a few days.

[Kelly and Burrage, *Dict. of Am. Medic. Biog.* (1928); *Jour. of Nervous and Mental Diseases,* X, 130–34 (portr.); *Medic. Record,* Jan. 27, Mar. 3, 1883; *Trans. Medic. Soc. of the State of N. Y.* (1883); R. S. Tracy in *Twenty Years' Record of the Yale Class of 1862* (1884); *Obit. Record Grads. Yale Coll., 1883* (1883).]

G. A. B.

BEARD, JAMES CARTER (June 6, 1837– Nov. 15, 1913), illustrator, author, the son of James Henry Beard [*q.v.*] and Mary Caroline (Carter) Beard, was born at Cincinnati, Ohio. Privately educated, he read law with Rutherford B. Hayes, afterward president of the United States. He was admitted to the bar in 1861, practising long enough to win one case. His brother, Daniel C. Beard, says, "When he got his sheepskin as an attorney and counselor at law, handing it to his father he said, 'I did this for you. I am now going into art for myself.'" During the Civil War he served with the Hundred Days' Men. On Dec. 25, 1862, he married Martha J. Bray of Terre Haute, Ind., the ceremony being performed by Lyman Abbott. For many years he held an editorial position with D. Appleton & Company. He also did a mass of special work for the newspapers, but it is as a writer of illustrated articles on plant and animal life that he is chiefly known. *Harper's Magazine, Saint Nicholas, Century, Outing, Country Life,* and the *Scientific American* were some of the periodicals for which he wrote and drew. He illustrated *Hunting Trip of a Ranchman* (1886), by Theodore Roosevelt, and was the author of *The Adventures of Little Fantasy among the Water*

Devils (published anonymously, 1871) ; *Little Workers* (1871) ; *Painting on China* (1882) ; *Curious Homes and their Tenants* (1897) ; and *Billy Possum* (1909). For many years he lived in Brooklyn. He moved to New Orleans about the year 1910 and died there Nov. 15, 1913.

[*Who's Who in America,* 1899–1913 ; information from brother, Daniel C. Beard.]　　　　T.B.

BEARD, JAMES HENRY (May 20, 1812–Apr. 4, 1893), artist, was born in Buffalo, N. Y., the son of Capt. James and Harriet (Wolcott) Beard. He was descended on his father's side from Sir James Beard and on his mother's side from Sir Lochlan Maclean. He was the brother of William Holbrook Beard [*q.v.*], who was likewise an artist. Capt. Beard moved his family to a farm near Painesville, Ohio, and died when James was eleven years old. An itinerant portrait painter gave the boy his first thoughts of becoming an artist and when the traveler left town young James started painting portraits on his own account, charging five dollars for a head and fifteen for a portrait including the hand holding a book. At the age of seventeen he ran away from home and worked his way to Pittsburgh. He then worked on the Ohio River, acting as a shipping clerk on a river boat. He lived in Cincinnati about the year 1835. Shortly after that date he made a second visit to Pittsburgh. He now decided to try his fortunes in the South, visiting first Louisville, and then making his way down to New Orleans. He finally returned to Cincinnati, where he married on Aug. 28, 1833, Mary Caroline Carter, the daughter of Col. Thomas Carter, and where he lived for several years. There he made the acquaintance and won the friendship of many prominent men from both North and South who had him paint their portraits. Among the sitters to his brush were Henry Clay, John Quincy Adams, Gen. Harrison, and Gen. Taylor. Harriet Martineau expressed her admiration for Beard in her book of travels in America. In 1846 he went to New York City, where he exhibited his picture entitled "North Carolina Emigrants," for which he received $750. He was a charter member of the Century Club. In 1848 he was made an honorary member of the National Academy. During the Civil War he served in the Union army on the staff of Gen. Lew Wallace, with the rank of captain. In 1870 he returned to New York and in 1872 was elected a National Academician. In 1887 he painted a portrait of Gen. Sherman. During his later years he relinquished portrait painting almost entirely and devoted his attention to painting animals. Whereas his brother, W. H.

Beard, showed a fondness for the painting of wild animal life, he himself preferred to paint domestic animals. "The Streets of New York," "The Window," and "There's Many a Slip" are the titles of some of his compositions. He died Apr. 4, 1893, at Flushing, L. I. His four sons, James Carter Beard [*q.v.*], Harry Beard (1841–89), Thomas Francis Beard [*q.v.*], and Daniel Carter Beard (born 1850) all became well-known as artists.

[H. T. Tuckerman, *Book of the Artists* (6th ed., 1882) ; L. Mead, "Apprenticeship of an Academician," *Am. Mag.*, IX, 192 ; Ruth Beard, *Geneal. of the Descendants of Widow Martha Beard of Milford, Conn.* (1915) ; *N.Y. Tribune,* and *N.Y. Herald,* Apr. 6, 1893.]
　　　　　　　　　　　　　　　　T.B.

BEARD, RICHARD (Nov. 27, 1799–Dec. 2, 1880), Cumberland Presbyterian clergyman, educator, the son of John and Mary (Bartley) Beard, was born in Sumner County, Tenn., and was licensed to preach at the age of twenty-one. After some years of circuit-riding, school-teaching, and study, he entered Cumberland College in Princeton, Ky. Upon graduation he was appointed to the faculty of the college and shortly thereafter, Jan. 21, 1834, married Cynthia Ewing Castleman. In 1838 he took charge of Sharon Academy in Mississippi, but within a few years returned to Cumberland College to become in 1843 its president. Believing in the desirability of a better-educated clergy, he aided in the establishment by his Church of a theological department in Cumberland University, Lebanon, Tenn. To this department, as its first professor of systematic theology, Beard went in 1854, and there he spent the most fruitful years of his life. In the earlier years of this service, inadequately paid, overworked, at times in despair because of the little encouragement given him, he was the only professor in the department and taught almost the whole theological course, including Hebrew, the Greek Testament, evidences of Christianity, and systematic theology. Nevertheless, shortly before the Civil War, he was able to begin putting into printed form his lectures on theology, the "crystallization of Cumberland Presbyterian thought and faith." After the war, in addition to his work in the theological department, he taught for some years as professor of Latin and Greek in the college department. Moreover, he continued publication of his theological lectures and other products of his pen. He served on several occasions as church moderator, and was prominent in committee work, particularly in support of education and of reunion with the Presbyterian Church. His published writings are as follows: *Lectures on Theology* (three volumes, 1860, 1864, 1870) ; *Why Am I a Cumber-*

land Presbyterian? (1870); *Brief Biographical Sketches of Some of the Early Ministers of the Cumberland Presbyterian Church,* two volumes (1867, 1874); and *Miscellaneous Sermons, Reviews and Essays* (1875).

[*Hist. of the Cumberland Presbyt. Ch.* (1888), by B. W. McDonnold, for many years Beard's colleague in Cumberland Univ.; *Theological Medium,* Oct. 1876; F. B. Catchings, *Baird and Beard Families* (1918); obituary in *Pub. Ledger* (Memphis), Dec. 4, 1880.]

P.M.H.

BEARD, THOMAS FRANCIS (Feb. 6, 1842–Sept. 28, 1905), illustrator, the son of James H. Beard [*q.v.*] and Mary Caroline (Carter) Beard, came of a talented and well-known Cincinnati family. He was educated in the Cincinnati and Painesville, Ohio, schools. His father, his uncle, William H. Beard [*q.v.*], and his brother James Carter Beard [*q.v.*] were painters, and another brother, Dan Beard, a writer, lecturer, and inventor, is still popular for his Boys' Handybooks of Camp-lore, and boys' stories. Known always as Frank Beard, the illustrator started his career early. Before he was twelve he was sending sketches to all the important periodicals, including *Yankee Notions,* one of the earliest American illustrated papers. At the outbreak of the Civil War, though only a boy of eighteen, he was commissioned by *Leslie's Weekly* and *Harper's Weekly* to act as cartoonist for the Army of the Potomac. He served at the same time in the 7th Ohio Regiment. After the war he began lecturing, and at this time originated his "Chalk Talks," popular lectures with rapid chalk illustrating. He was married in 1867 to Helen Augusta Goodwin. From 1881 to 1884 he held the chair of æsthetics and painting at Syracuse University and in 1884, during the Blaine campaign, was editor of *Judge.* A. B. Paine in *Thomas Nast, His Period and His Pictures* (1904) has described the remarkable bitterness of the Cleveland-Blaine campaign. George William Curtis and Thomas Nast were almost equally victims of newspaper attacks. In *Judge,* Frank Beard "never missed an opportunity of presenting him (Curtis) as a saint, a circus performer, or a 'Miss Nancy' . . . usually grinding an organ, while Nast, as a monkey, performed at his command" (Paine, p. 501). Nast's own ideas and illustrations were used against him. As early as 1877, Beard had published *The Blackboard in the Sunday School, A Practical Guide for Superintendents and Teachers,* and he now became more interested in religious publications and in Chautauqua lectures than in social and political reform by means of cartoons. Most of his best-known work was done in connection with Sunday-schools and the Chautauqua movement. About twenty years before his death he began illustrating for the *Ram's Horn,* a religious weekly published in Chicago. In 1890 he became one of the editors and thereafter devoted all of his time to it. The *American Art Annual,* 1905–06, in an obituary notice, states that his cartoons directed against the liquor evil were often extremely effective. He also illustrated a few religious and other books.

[*Who's Who in America,* 1903–05; A. B. Maurice and F. T. Cooper, *Hist. of the Nineteenth Century in Caricature* (1904); *Publisher's Weekly,* Oct. 7, 1905; *Chicago Tribune,* Sept. 29, 1905.]

M.A.K.

BEARD, WILLIAM HOLBROOK (Apr. 13, 1824–Feb. 20, 1900), artist, brother of James Henry Beard [*q.v.*], was born in Painesville, Ohio, the son of James and Harriet (Wolcott) Beard. His mother, left a widow while the boy was still an infant, made every effort to give him an education, for which he showed little inclination. At an early age he became interested in plants and wild life, and showed also great aptitude for swimming, hunting, and wrestling. Following an unsuccessful attempt to earn his living at Painesville, as a portrait painter, he started on a tour of the state as a peripatetic portrait painter. This affording little more than a bare livelihood, he went to New York about 1845, where his brother, James Henry Beard, had established himself. He again specialized in portraits, and then, after several years of travel, moved to Buffalo in 1850 and opened a studio. After a struggle of six years he secured orders sufficient to keep him busy and sailed for Europe in 1856. In Rome he met Gifford, Whittredge, and other American artists, who were later to distinguish themselves. Within two years he was back in Buffalo, where in 1859 he married Flora Johnson, who died a few months after the wedding. On July 7, 1863, he married Carrie, daughter of Thomas Le Clear, the portrait painter. In 1860 he settled in New York. He brought with him a few compositions, humorous story-pictures of animals with such titles as "Grimalkin's Dream" and "Bears and a Bender" and became so popular at this branch of painting that he was condemned to paint animals acting like human beings almost all the rest of his life. He was a member of the National Academy, the Century Club, the Artists' Fund Society, and the Artists' Aid Society. The following are the titles of some of his pictures: "Kittens and Guinea Pig"; "Power of Death"; "Deer in a Wood"; "Spreading the Alarm"; "Flaw in the Title"; "Swan and Owls." He died in New York City.

[H. T. Tuckerman, *Book of the Artists* (1867); L. G. Sellstedt, *Art in Buffalo* (1895), pp. 104–10, and *From*

Forecastle to Academy (1904), p. 282; G. W. Sheldon, *Am. Painters* (1879); obituary in *N.Y. Tribune,* Feb. 21, 1900.]

T. B.

BEARDSHEAR, WILLIAM MILLER (Nov. 7, 1850–Aug. 5, 1902), United Brethren minister, college president, was of Scotch and Welsh descent; his forebears emigrated from Pennsylvania to Dayton, Ohio, about 1796. His parents, John and Elizabeth (Coleman) Beardshear, were pious, industrious farmers of the hardy, pioneer type. Large of frame, the boy at fourteen enlisted in the 184th Ohio Infantry and served till the end of the Civil War. In 1873, when the death of his father interrupted his course at Otterbein University, he married Josephine Mundhenk, also a student there. Returning a year later, he received the B.A. degree in 1876. In 1878 he entered Yale Divinity School, but in the second year broke down from overwork and did not complete the course. He held two pastorates—at Arcanum, Ohio (1876–78), and at the Summit Street Church in Dayton, Ohio (October 1880–July 1881). At thirty his success as a preacher, his striking personality, and the confidence he inspired resulted in a unanimous call to the presidency of Western College, at Toledo, Ia., a position he held for eight years (1881–89). In 1889 he was elected superintendent of the city schools of West Des Moines. In February 1891 he became president of the Iowa State College of Agriculture and Mechanic Arts, a position which he held until his death in 1902. Here he did his chief work (*Proceedings of the National Education Association,* 1903, p. 368). During his presidency the attendance, the number of teachers, and the state appropriation were all more than trebled. New departments were added, new courses organized. To make the work of the college known he gave addresses all over the state—at commencements, teachers' institutes, farmers' clubs. His success was due to a combination of sterling qualities. He had a great-souled enthusiasm, an untiring devotion to his work. "Thank God, I am an enthusiast," he said ("The Geography of Character," in *A Boy Again and Other Prose Poems,* 1904, p. 177). His vision of industrial education was high and exalted, comprehending the harmonious development of the head, the hand, and the heart. He was deeply religious and had the soul of a poet. In his chapel talks he quoted freely from a wide range of authors, mainly the poets and the essayists. "Some books are the livest things in the world," he wrote, "and of such poetry furnishes the largest proportion, for 'poets are the rulers of men's spirits'" ("The Influence of Poetry in

Education," *Proceedings and Addresses N. E. A.,* 1900, p. 57).

[*Proc. and Addresses N. E. A.,* 1902, contains "appreciations" by people who knew Beardshear well. The *Iowa Hist. Record* for Oct. 1902 contains about the same "appreciations" with some additions. *Proc. and Addresses N. E. A.,* 1903, pp. 368–69, contains the memorial tribute by Pres. H. H. Seerley. *A Hist. of Western-Leander Clark Coll.,* by Henry W. Ward (Dayton, Ohio, 1911), gives the record of Western College while Dr. Beardshear was president; obituary in *Des Moines Register and Leader,* Aug. 6, 1902.]

A. B. N.

BEARDSLEY, EBEN EDWARDS (Jan. 8, 1808–Dec. 21, 1891), Episcopal clergyman, the son of Elihu and Ruth (Edwards) Beardsley, was descended from William Beardsley, by occupation a mason, who in April 1635 came to America from London in the ship *Planter.* Born in the village of Stepney, town of Monroe, Fairfield County, Conn., Eben worked on the family farm until he was sixteen years old, attending the village school as he had opportunity. Then for a year he went to the Staples Academy, Weston, Conn., and this was followed by a period of teaching in the district school. But the youth's ambition was for an academic education, and to make his final preparation for admission to college he went to the Episcopal Academy in South Norwalk, Conn. He then entered Washington (now Trinity) College, Hartford, graduating with distinction in the class of 1832. After graduation he took charge for a year of a private classical school in Hartford, and then for the next two years served as tutor in his own college. During this time he was preparing himself for holy orders, and on Aug. 11, 1835, was ordained deacon in the Episcopal Church by Bishop Brownell, and by the same bishop was advanced to the priesthood on Oct. 24, 1836. After his ordination to the diaconate he was placed in charge of St. Peter's Church, Cheshire, Conn., where, in addition to his ministerial duties, he undertook the charge of the Episcopal Academy of Connecticut. In April 1848 he was called to the rectorship of the newly organized parish of St. Thomas's Church, New Haven, Conn., a position which he retained until his death. Always deeply interested in the history of the Episcopal Church in this country, and especially in Connecticut, he found time, in the midst of his parochial duties, to gratify his fondness for historical research, and in 1865 published Volume I of *The History of the Episcopal Church in Connecticut.* This was followed by Volume II in 1868. Then came in rapid succession *The Life and Correspondence of Samuel Johnson, D.D.* (1874); *The Life and Times of William Samuel Johnson* (1876); *The Life and Correspondence of the Right Reverend*

Samuel Seabury, D.D. (1881). An abridged edition of the last-mentioned work was published in London in 1884, the year which marked the centenary of Seabury's consecration. In the course of his ministry he preached numerous historical sermons on parish anniversaries. These he had collected and prepared for publication, and in 1892 shortly after his death, they appeared in a volume bearing the title, *Addresses and Discourses.* For half a century Beardsley was one of the conspicuous leaders of his Church. In the diocese of Connecticut, where he lived all his life and did all his work, every distinction was bestowed upon him. He was sent as a deputy from Connecticut to eight general conventions, and twice was elected president of its House of Deputies, the highest honor conferred upon a presbyter. His interest in educational matters was evidenced by his serving as trustee of the Episcopal Academy of Connecticut, of St. Margaret's School for Girls, and of Trinity College. He was active in the formation of the New Haven Colony Historical Society, of which he was president 1873–74. He was married on Oct. 11, 1842, to Jane Margaret Matthews, daughter of Rev. Edmund Matthews of St. Simon's Island, Ga.

[The chief sources of information are manuscript records in the possession of the author of this article and a *Sketch of Wm. Beardsley* (1867), by E. E. Beardsley. A paper on E. E. Beardsley read before the New Haven Colony Hist. Soc., by Rt. Rev. E. S. Lines, D.D., was published in Vol. VII of the Society's *Papers,* and a memorial sermon preached by Rt. Rev. John Williams, D.D., was published in pamphlet form. This has for a frontispiece an engraved likeness by Ritchie.]

W. A. B.

BEARDSLEY, SAMUEL (Feb. 6, 1790–May 6, 1860), congressman, judge, was born at Hoosick, Rensselaer County, N. Y. His parents, Obadiah and Eunice (Moore) Beardsley, removed to a farm at Monticello, Otsego County, while he was an infant. Attending school in the winter and working on the farm in the summer, the lad manifested a love for books and made sufficient progress in learning to become a schoolteacher. Ambitious for a professional career, he first studied medicine with Dr. Joseph White at Cherry Valley and then at the age of eighteen turned to law, entering the office of Judge Hathaway in Rome, whose daughter he married. During this period he supported himself by clerking in the post office and serving as clerk in the county surrogate's court. After admission to the bar, he practised law in Watertown for a year, and then settled in Rome. In 1813 he joined the militia to defend Sackett's Harbor and in 1815 he was made captain. Three years later he was appointed brigade judge advocate, and in 1820 his name appears as major in the Oneida County militia.

Meanwhile this military duty did not prevent the young lawyer from serving as town clerk in 1817 and county supervisor in 1818–20. He was appointed district attorney of Oneida County in 1821 and by this time had gained the reputation of being a well-informed and able lawyer. Chosen state senator for the 5th district on the Democratic ticket in 1822, he held that office for but one year because of the determination of tenure by lot. In 1823 he removed to Utica and the same year President Monroe appointed him United States attorney for northern New York, a post he retained for seven years, refusing in 1824 appointment as first judge of Oneida County. Well-known and highly respected in 1830, he was elected to Congress as a Democrat and was subsequently reëlected three times. His speech on the currency question in 1834 attracted national attention for both its eloquence and partisanship. An ardent champion of President Jackson, he became one of the President's confidential advisers and the leader of his party in New York. Fearless and outspoken in his convictions on public questions, he was regarded as a progressive leader and defender of free speech and of the right of petition. Jackson and his friends persuaded him when nominated as circuit judge in 1834 by Gov. Marcy, to remain in Washington. In 1836 he accepted the office of attorney-general of New York, which he filled acceptably for three years. In 1844 Gov. Bouck promoted him to an associate judgeship in the New York supreme court and three years later he became chief justice, the last person to hold the honor in the old supreme court. When the new supreme court was put on an elective basis in 1847, not being among the justices chosen, he resumed the practise of law at Utica. For several years important legal business induced him to reside in New York City. Henceforth his time was devoted almost exclusively to important cases in the court of appeals. He was described by those who knew him best as an ideal judge because of his patient and thorough investigation of every case, his wide legal knowledge, his impartial decisions, his quick perceptions, and his uniform courtesy and dignity. As a lawyer he held high rank, and in terse, vigorous, discerning argument he had few equals, although his manner was constrained and his diction not always graceful. A tall, commanding figure with a large, well-formed head, he was an able leader whose antagonism was felt by his opponents. A weakened vision gave his face the appearance of frowning, but his eyes beamed with kindness and his voice was cordial.

[M. M. Bagg, *Pioneers of Utica* (1877), pp. 559–67; D. E. Wager, *The City of Rome* (1896), pp. 196–98, and *Oneida County* (1896), pp. 235–36; Isaac H. Beardsley,

Geneal. Hist. of the Beardsley-lee Family in America (1902); D. McAdam et al., Hist. of the Bench and Bar of N.Y. (1897), I, 258.]   A.C.F.

BEASLEY, FREDERICK (1777–Nov. 1, 1845), Episcopal clergyman, philosopher, was born near Edenton, N. C., the son of John Beasley, a planter, and Mary (Blount) Beasley. His early years were spent at home; in 1793 he entered the College of New Jersey, graduating in 1797 with high honors; for the next two years he was a tutor in the college while he studied philosophy and theology under Dr. Samuel Stanhope Smith, its president. He was ordained deacon in 1801, priest in 1802, and in the latter year became rector of St. John's Church, Elizabethtown, N. J. In June 1803 he accepted a call to St. Peter's Church, Albany, where he remained until 1809 when he assumed charge of St. Paul's Church, Baltimore. In July 1813 he accepted the provostship of the University of Pennsylvania, which carried with it the chair of moral philosophy. He resigned in 1828, and was rector of St. Michael's Church, Trenton, N. J., 1829–36, after which he lived in retirement at Elizabethtown. He was twice married: on Aug. 22, 1803, to Susan Dayton by whom he had one child; and on Nov. 27, 1804, to Maria Williamson by whom he had nine children.

Beasley published numerous sermons, pamphlets, and books, of which the most important are: *A Sermon on Duelling* (1811); *American Dialogues of the Dead* (1815); *A Search of Truth in the Science of the Human Mind* (1822); *A Vindication of the Argument a priori in Proof of the Being and Attributes of God, from the Objections of Dr. Waterland* (1825); *A Vindication of the Fundamental Principles of Truth and Order in the Church of Christ, from the Allegations of the Rev. Wm. E. Channing, D.D.* (1830); *An Examination of No. 90 of the Tracts for the Times* (1842). Although in personal relations gentle and confiding to the point of being often victimized, as soon as he took his theological pen in hand Beasley became a polemicist. Proud of his conservatism in thought and dress—still powdering his hair long after the custom had gone out—he was absolutely convinced of absolute truth and his acquaintance with it. The more abstract a proposition, the more violently it seemed to engage his emotions. Although educated by Dr. Smith in the Scottish philosophical tradition, he became convinced that Scottish Realism had been hopelessly contaminated by the empirical idealism of Hume, while John Locke, he believed, was free from all trace of idealism. Thus his most noted work, *A Search of Truth,* was devoted to an elaborate but none too subtle

defense of Locke's system, which, he asserted, "never has been and never can be overthrown." The "detestable sophistries" of Berkeley, Hume, Reid, Channing, and Newman drew from Beasley attempted refutations mingled with cries of pain. The spectacle of these sophists so tormented him that his own possession of the truth brought little peace.

[Wm. B. Sprague, *Annals of the Am. Pulpit* (1859), V, 477–84; S. A. Clark, *Hist. of St. John's Ch., Elizabethtown, N. J.* (1857); Joseph Hooper, *Hist. of St. Peter's Ch. in the City of Albany* (1900); Isaac Woodbridge Riley, *Am. Philosophy: the Early Schools* (1907), bk. V, ch. VII.]   E.S.B.

BEASLEY, MERCER (Mar. 27, 1815–Feb. 19, 1897), jurist, was born in Philadelphia, the son of Frederick [q.v.] and Maria (Williamson) Beasley. His father, an Episcopal minister, was then serving as provost of the University of Pennsylvania. In 1830 the family moved to Trenton, N. J., where Beasley was destined to spend the greater part of his life. After studying with his father he entered in 1833 the junior class of the College of New Jersey (now Princeton University), but remained only a year. In 1834 he was studying law under Senator Samuel V. L. Southard of Trenton, later continuing his studies under his kinsman, former Chancellor Isaac H. Williamson at Elizabeth. He was admitted to the bar in September 1838, and settled in Trenton. For some years thereafter he was more noted as a billiard player and wing shot than for legal acumen. Gradually, the law, especially trial work, absorbed more and more of his interest, and his personal charm and real ability brought him success. His name first appears in the records of the higher state courts in 1849 in a case which he won against the Delaware and Raritan Canal Company (*2 Zabriskie*, 243). Thereafter he acted with increasing frequency as counsel in important cases before the appellate courts. Perhaps his marriage at this period to Frances Higbee of Trenton stimulated his ambition. He interested himself in local politics as a Whig, served on the Common Council of Trenton, and was defeated as a candidate for mayor in 1850. When the Whig Party expired he became a Democrat (*New Jersey Law Journal*, XX). On the death of Chief Justice Whelpley, Gov. Joel Parker appointed Beasley chief justice of New Jersey, Mar. 8, 1864. The term of office was seven years, but he was reappointed four successive times by different governors, some of them of the opposite political party from his own, and thus served continuously until his death, a period just short of thirty-three years. To review his work on the bench would be to outline the development of law in New Jersey for a generation. His decisions in three political cases show his impartiality and courage. In 1866 the Republicans in the legislature passed a bill which put the police of Jersey City under control of a state commission. The city authorities, being Democrats, refused to recognize the act and two mutually hostile police forces preserved disorder in the city. The Chief Justice settled the strife by sustaining the Republican contention in an opinion since followed by the courts of other states because of its clear legal reasoning (Pangbourn *vs.* Young, *32 New Jersey Law Reports,* 29). A few years later he upheld the State's claim to its riparian lands against strong pressure from railroads and land speculators (Stevens *vs.* P. & N. Railroad Company, *34 New Jersey,* 532). In 1890 New Jersey was afflicted with two Senates. A quorum of Democratic "hold overs" had organized against the newly elected Republican senators, who thereupon went into separate session. Violence was imminent when the aged Chief Justice, again deciding against his own party, restored the reign of law. In appearance he was strikingly handsome with bold, clear-cut features and a mobile mouth. His second wife, whom he married Oct. 16, 1854, was Catherine Ann, daughter of Charles Haven of Trenton. He remained in office with his mental powers unimpaired until his death from pneumonia, Feb. 19, 1897.

[J. W. McGeehan, "Mercer Beasley" in *N. J. Law Review,* I (1915–16), 71–85; J. Whitehead, "The Supreme Court of N. J.," in the *Green Bag,* Nov. 1891, p. 457; W. S. Sackett, *Modern Battles of Trenton* (1895); M. D. Ogden, ed., *Memorial Cyc. of N. J.* (1917), p. 231; *Newark Daily Advertiser,* Feb. 19, 1897; *Daily True American* (Trenton), Feb. 20, 24, 1897.]

D. V.

BEATTIE, FRANCIS ROBERT (Mar. 31, 1848–Sept. 3, 1906), Presbyterian clergyman, was born at Guelph, Ont., Canada, the son of a Scotch emigrant, Robert Beattie, and of Janet McKinley. He was reared in the Presbyterian faith, although apparently with no thought of his later ministry. From his father's farm he went to the University of Toronto where he graduated in 1875, receiving the M.A. degree one year later. In 1878 he graduated from Knox Theological College and entered immediately on a ministry which ended only with his death. For ten years he served as pastor in Canadian churches, five of the ten being spent in Brantford, Ont. During this Canadian pastorate he wrote and published two books which attracted attention among clergymen—*The Utilitarian Theory of Morals* (1884) and *Methods of Theism* (1887). Because of the first-mentioned book, Illinois Wesleyan College conferred on him the Ph.D. degree

in 1884, and the Columbia Seminary (South Carolina) elected him to the chair of apologetics in succession to Dr. Woodrow. Five years at Columbia gave him a reputation as educator and minister that resulted in his election in 1893 to the professorship of apologetics and systematic theology in the newly founded Presbyterian Theological Seminary at Louisville, Ky. In this position he remained until his death. At Louisville Dr. Beattie continued to add to his reputation. *Radical Criticism* appeared in 1896, *Presbyterian Standards* in 1898, *Apologetics* in 1903, and *Christianity and Modern Revolution* in 1906. The *Apologetics* was his most ambitious work, being designed for three volumes. Only one volume was completed and this has been widely used as a text in theological schools. Dr. Beattie was associate editor of the *Christian Observer* after 1893, and associate editor of the *Presbyterian Quarterly Review* after 1895.

He was twice married. His first wife, Jean G. Galbraith of Toronto, whom he married in 1879, died in 1897; his second wife was Lily R. Satterwhite, who survived him. He was by all accounts a vigorous and inspiring teacher, but his work in this field necessarily brought little recognition. He was an outstanding figure among the Louisville ministers and was well-known throughout the South for his work as a harmonizer. His chief claim to distinction lay in his writings. His books were scholarly and not without interest, though their appeal was limited.

[*Who's Who in America,* 1906–07; files of the *Louisville Courier–Jour.* and of the *Christian Observer;* information from Dean C. R. Hemphill of the Presbyt. Theological Seminary at Louisville. There are obituaries in the *Louisville Herald, Courier–Jour.,* and *Evening Post* of Sept. 4, the *Globe* (Toronto) of Sept. 5, and the *Christian Observer* of Sept. 12, 1906.]

R. S. C.

BEATTY, ADAM (May 10, 1777–June 9, 1858), lawyer, agricultural writer, the son of an Englishman, William Beatty, and of Mary Grosh, daughter of a New York family of German extraction, was born at Hagerstown, Md., and in 1800 moved to Lexington, Ky. He studied law there with James Brown, brother-in-law of Henry Clay. In 1802 he began the practise of law at Washington, Mason County, Ky., in 1804 married Sally Green, daughter of Capt. John Green of Mason County, and in 1811 was appointed circuit judge by Gov. Charles Scott, serving in that office until November 1823. He became a member of the Kentucky legislature in 1809 and was reëlected several times. From 1836 to 1839 he was a state senator. In 1840 he served as a presidential elector, voting for Harrison. He was an unsuccessful candidate for Congress in 1829 and in 1831. From 1823 on he made farming his principal business, and after the organization of the Kentucky State Agricultural Society in 1838 he was active in its affairs and became vice-president. He was greatly interested in the improvement of agriculture, studied the available American and foreign literature on the subject, and imported purebred live stock. He was early a contributor to the agricultural press and for many years wrote often for the *Kentucky Farmer* and other papers. He was the author of many essays and letters on agricultural subjects, and for some of them received prizes from the Kentucky Society. A considerable number of these essays and letters were assembled in a book first published in 1843 as *Southern Agriculture,* and in a revised edition as *Essays on Practical Agriculture* in 1844. This work includes a general article on the agriculture of Kentucky and special articles on corn, hemp, tobacco, a system of agriculture best adapted to Kentucky, rotation of crops, advantages of manufactures to agriculture, breeding horses for agricultural purposes, grass in woodlots, feeding cattle and sheep, wheat in rich vegetable soils, etc. It also contains letters to Thomas B. Stephenson on soils and grasses, and to Edmund Ruffin on soils. Beatty died at the age of eighty-one on his farm in Mason County.

[H. Levin, *The Lawyers and Lawmakers of Ky.* (1897); L. Collins, *Hist. of Ky.* (rev. and enlarged by R. H. Collins, 1874), vol. II; J. L. Coulter in *Cyc. of Am. Ag.,* ed. by L. H. Bailey (1909), vol. IV; Vital Statistic Records in possession of Ky. State Hist. Soc.]

A. C. T.

BEATTY, CHARLES CLINTON (*c.* 1715–Aug. 13, 1772), Presbyterian clergyman, was born in County Antrim, Ireland, the son of John Beatty, an officer in the British army, and of Christiana Clinton, who was an aunt of George Clinton [*q.v.*]. The father died while Charles was young, and his mother came to America in 1729 with her brother Charles, father of George Clinton. Beatty had received a classical and religious education in Ireland but on reaching America, because of his poverty, he became a pedler. He stopped at the Log College, Neshaminy, Pa., where William Tennent, the head master, persuaded him to enroll as a student and prepare for the ministry. In 1742 he was licensed to preach at Nottingham. The next year he was assigned to William Tennent's church at Neshaminy and upon Tennent's retirement succeeded him in the pastorate, being formally ordained and installed in December 1743. The church was disrupted by discordant factions, but Beatty met the situation with prudence and dignity. He was interested in all missionary experiments and sympathized with David Brainerd in his efforts to convert the Indians. Brainerd visited Beatty's house and took part in a communion service at his church, which he mentions in his journal. In 1764 Beatty was chosen moderator of the synod. He was married, June 24, 1746, to Anne Reading, whose father was president of the Council of New Jersey and later governor of the province. He was appointed to take a missionary trip to Virginia and North Carolina in 1754. In the next year he became chaplain to the Pennsylvania troops who were sent under William Franklin to defend the northwestern borders of the state after the massacre of the Moravian missionaries near Lehighton. In 1758 the two synods of New Brunswick which had differed on matters of doctrine were united, and Beatty was appointed on a committee to establish a fund for the relief of poor Presbyterian ministers, ministers' widows, and their children. Two years later he was sent to England by the synod to solicit funds for the committee. He was successful and received a donation from George III. ~~Three years later~~ he was sent with Duffield to investigate the condition of the Indian tribes. In the next year Beatty went again to England because of his wife's health, but she died shortly after their arrival. Since 1763 he had been a trustee of the College of New Jersey, and in 1772 because it was greatly in need of funds he agreed to visit the West Indies and solicit money. He died of yellow fever, soon after reaching the island of Barbados. One of the most popular preachers of his day, he published only one sermon, *Double Honour Due to the Laborious Gospel Minister* (1756), preached at the ordination of the Rev. William Ramsay. His other publications include the *Journal of a Two Months' Tour Among the Frontier Inhabitants of Pennsylvania* (1768), a *Letter to the Rev. John Erskine,* in which the hypothesis that the Indians are the descendants of the Ten Tribes is maintained by a variety of arguments, and *Further Remarks Respecting Indian Affairs,* an account of what had been done for the Indians in America.

[W. B. Sprague, *Annals Am. Pulpit,* III (1858), 119; A. Alexander, *The Log College* (1851); *Presbyt. Mag.* (1852), pp. 412–19; J. Smith, *Old Redstone, Hist. Sketches of Western Presbyterianism* (1854), pp. 119–27; T. Murphy, *The Presbytery of the Log College* (1889), pp. 113–17.]

M. A. K.

BEATTY, JOHN (Dec. 19, 1749–Apr. 30, 1826), Revolutionary soldier and politician of New Jersey, was born in Neshaminy, Pa., the eldest son of the Rev. Charles Clinton Beatty [*q.v.*] and Anne (Reading) Beatty. There were ten children in the family; all four of the brothers who volunteered in 1776 became Continental officers. Graduating at Princeton in 1769, Beatty studied medicine with Benjamin Rush, and in 1772 began to practise at Hartsville, Bucks County, Pa. He married Mary, daughter of Richard Longstreet of Princeton, Mar. 22, 1774. Enlisting in the war, he was commissioned captain in the Pennsylvania Battalion on Jan. 5, 1776, and major of the 6th Pennsylvania the same year. In the disastrous battle and surrender of Fort Washington, Nov. 16, 1776, Beatty was one of the captives. He was severely treated and was not exchanged until May 8, 1778. Perhaps in consequence of this experience, he was appointed in 1778 commissary general of prisoners with the rank of colonel. In this capacity he received from Washington explicit instructions, in 1779, with regard to prisoners on parole, and with reference to exchanges. Arrested and tried on the charge of trading with the enemy, he resigned from the army on Mar. 10, 1780, after receiving a severe reprimand in general orders from headquarters. He passed the remainder of his life in New Jersey, at his home near Princeton, occupied with the practise of medicine, with state politics, business, and church affairs. He was a member of the New Jersey legislature, a delegate to the Continental Congress 1784–85, a member of the state convention that in 1787 ratified the Federal Constitution, and a member of the Third Congress, 1793–95. On the expiration of his term in Congress he became secretary of state of New Jersey, and held that office until 1805. His first wife dying in 1815, in 1818 he married Mrs. Kitty Lalor of Trenton. In his later years he was president of the Trenton Banking Company and of the Delaware Bridge Company.

[*Biog. Encyc. of N. J.* (1877), p. 271; *Biog. Cong. Dir. 1774–1911* (1913); *Pa. Archives*, ser. 2, vol. X, pp. 142–43; F. B. Lee, *Geneal. and Personal Memorial of Mercer County, N. J.* (1807); J. M. Beatty, "Letters of the Four Beatty Brothers of the Continental Army, 1774–94" in *Pa. Mag. of Hist. and Biog.*, XLIV, 193.]

E. K. A.

BEATTY, JOHN (Dec. 16, 1828–Dec. 21, 1914), soldier, legislator, banker, writer, was born near Sandusky, Ohio, the son of James and Elizabeth (Williams) Beatty. His grandfather, John Beatty, born in Ireland, located in Norwich, Conn., in 1796, later moving to New London. In 1815 he led a group from Connecticut into the Western Reserve, settling near the present site of Sandusky, Ohio. Young John received a fair education in the common schools and then engaged in the banking business. Shortly after his marriage to Lucy Tupper of Cleveland, in 1854, he moved to Cardington, where he and his brother William opened Beatty Brothers' Bank, conducting the business under that name until 1863, when

it was incorporated as the First National Bank. Beatty took an active interest in public affairs, but though more or less identified with local politics, did not hold office until 1860. From his grandfather, who was an Ohio leader of the ante bellum schism in the Methodist Church and a staunch anti-slavery man of the James G. Birney school, young Beatty acquired his first political tenets and adhered to them through life. In 1852 he supported John P. Hale for the presidency; in 1856 he cast his vote for John C. Frémont. In 1860 he was the Republican presidential elector for the 13th (Ohio) congressional district.

In April 1861 he organized a company, led it to Camp Dennison at Columbus, and when it was incorporated in the 3rd Ohio Volunteer Infantry became its captain. On Apr. 27, 1861, he was appointed lieutenant-colonel of the regiment. After a short period of training he accompanied his command to western Virginia where he served in the forces under Gen. McClellan. In November 1861, Beatty, with his regiment, was transferred to Kentucky and on Feb. 12, 1862, was made colonel. In the spring of 1862 the regiment became a part of the command of Gen. O. M. Mitchell and participated in an extended raid into Tennessee and northern Alabama. When Bragg began his movement through Kentucky in the summer of 1862, Beatty's regiment marched with Buell's pursuing army and in October participated in the bloody battle of Perryville. On Dec. 26, 1862, Beatty was assigned to a brigade command and was engaged in the four-day battle at Murfreesboro, Dec. 29, 1862–Jan. 2, 1863, during which he had two horses shot under him. On Mar. 12, 1863, he was promoted to brigadier-general, to rank from Nov. 29, 1862, in recognition of his gallant conduct at Murfreesboro. Leading his brigade during the Tullahoma, Chickamauga, and Chattanooga campaigns, he commanded the first of Thomas's corps to cross Lookout Mountain. Following Grant's defeat of Bragg at Missionary Ridge, Beatty's command accompanied Sherman on his march to Knoxville, Tenn., for the relief of Burnside's besieged command (Whitelaw Reid, *Ohio in the War*, 1868, I, 924–25; J. W. Keifer, *Slavery and Four Years of War*, 1900, I, 180 ff., 211 ff., 233, 241, 264 ff., 279, 300 ff.; *Memorial, Military Order of the Loyal Legion*, Feb. 3, 1915, pp. 3–4).

On Jan. 28, 1864, Beatty resigned from the army and returned to his banking business in Cardington so as to allow his brother William to enter the army. He continued in the banking business and in the management of his large farm until in 1868 he was elected to the Fortieth Congress from the 8th Ohio district in place of Cornelius S. Hamilton, deceased. He took his seat on Feb. 5, 1868; was reëlected to the Forty-first and Forty-second Congresses; and served until Mar. 13, 1873. He was first a member of the committee on invalid pensions, then chairman of the committee on public buildings and grounds, and finally chairman of the committee on public printing. At the close of his second full term, though strongly solicited to be again a candidate for reëlection, he declined. Some of his army friends in Columbus had urged him to come there and open a bank. This he did, organizing the Citizens' Saving Bank, which opened for business July 1, 1873. Beatty was elected president and served until July 1, 1903, when his bank was consolidated with the Citizens' Trust and Savings Bank. He retired from active business to devote his time to writing, but did not lose contact with public affairs. In 1884 he was an unsuccessful Republican candidate for the nomination for governor against J. B. Foraker (Foraker, *Notes of a Busy Life*, 1916, I, 175–90) and later was one of the Republican presidential electors-at-large for Ohio; in 1886–87 he served as Republican member of the state board of charities; and from 1891 to 1895 was president of the Ohio Chickamauga and Chattanooga Military Park Commission (W. H. Perrin and J. H. Battle, *History of Morrow County, Ohio*, 1880; *Biographical Congressional Directory*, 1911; letter from F. R. Shinn of Columbus, Ohio, Feb. 23, 1927).

During his war service Beatty had kept a diary which he published in 1879 under the title *The Citizen Soldier*. Emboldened by its success, and following a natural inclination, he wrote *The Belle o' Becket's Lane* (1883), the scene of which is laid near his birthplace, and *McLean, A Romance of the War* (1904), both of them historical novels. In 1902 appeared *The Acolhuans*, a prehistoric novel dealing with the mound builders of Ohio. In 1894 *High or Low Tariff, Which?* was printed and in 1896, during the silver controversy, Beatty published his *Answer to "Coin's Financial School."* He was also the author of a number of miscellaneous papers (Randall and Ryan, *History of Ohio*, 1912, V, 64; *Ohio Archæological and Historical Publications*, XII, 104 ff.).

[In addition to references above, see O. C. Hooper, *Hist. of the City of Columbus, Ohio*; Chas. Robson, *Biog. Encyc. of Ohio* (1876), p. 641; A. J. Bauchman and R. F. Bartlett, *Hist. of Morrow County, Ohio* (1911); H. L. Peeke, *Centennial Hist. of Erie County, Ohio* (1925); obituary in the *Ohio State Jour.* (Columbus), Dec. 22, 1914; *Who's Who in America*, 1914–15.]

T. R. H.

BEATTY, WILLIAM HENRY (Feb. 18, 1838–Aug. 4, 1914), jurist, was born at Mon-

clova, Lucas County, Ohio. His parents (Henry Oscar and Margaret Boone Beatty) were Kentuckians and soon after William Henry's birth went back to Kentucky where they remained until the boy was fifteen. They then joined the movement to California and, journeying by way of the Isthmus, reached Sacramento in 1853. Some years later Beatty returned to the East to enter a preparatory school and afterward matriculated at the University of Virginia. In 1858 he returned to California to join his father, whose career had been his source of inspiration, in his practise of law. In 1863, the silver excitement drew him to Nevada, where he was appointed the first city attorney of Austin. Less than a year later, upon the admission of Nevada, he became judge of the district court of Lander County. This office he held in Lander and White Pine Counties until 1875, when he became associate justice of the supreme court of Nevada. Three years later he was made chief justice and served in this capacity for two years. He then returned to Sacramento to resume his private practise. In 1888, because of his recognized ability and experience, he was called upon to assume the position of chief justice of the State of California, left vacant by the death of Chief Justice Morrison. At the close of this term, in 1890, he was elected chief justice for the full term of twelve years and in 1902 was reëlected for a second term but did not live to serve out the entire time. He died at his home in San Francisco on Aug. 4, 1914. During his long years of service as chief justice he had won for himself an outstanding place in the development of California jurisprudence, not only because of the clarity and soundness of his decisions, but also because of his high ideals of justice and his unswerving loyalty to the best traditions of his office. "For more than a quarter of a century he presided over the Supreme Court of California with dignity and rare ability. . . . Throughout his long life he knew but one fear, and that was the fear of doing an injustice to his fellow man" (Memorial of the California State Bar Association, *168 California Reports*, 802–03). The more personal records of his life show him to have been a man of extremely lovable disposition and irreproachable character. He was married in 1874 to Elizabeth M., daughter of Robert Carter Love of Salisbury, N. C.

[A memorial prepared by the Cal. State Bar Ass. in *168 Cal. Reports*, 799–803, gives the most complete account of Beatty's life. Additional material is given in O. T. Schuck, *Hist. of the Bench and Bar of Cal.*(1901). Beatty's decisions as chief justice of Cal. are found in *77–166 Cal. Reports*.]

R. G. C—d.

BEAUCHAMP, WILLIAM (Apr. 26, 1772–Oct. 7, 1824), Methodist clergyman, was born in

Kent County, Del., the son of a Methodist clergyman, William Beauchamp. He was sent to a good school where he was taught English grammar and Latin. At sixteen he joined the Methodist Episcopal church. At eighteen he taught in a neighborhood school at Monongahela, Pa. It was his desire, however, to enter the ministry and he gave his time to systematic and regular classical reading and study and became proficient in Latin, Greek, and mathematics, and later in Hebrew. At nineteen he began to preach, two years later he left home to travel with the presiding elder, and in 1794 became an itinerant preacher on trial on the Alleghany Circuit. In 1796 he was admitted into full connection on the Pittsburgh Circuit and at twenty-five was an elder. The next years saw him in Pittsburgh, New York, Boston, and Provincetown, Mass., and in 1800 he was on Nantucket Island. Because of ill health he asked to be allowed to remain there and was not transferred for seven years. He married Mrs. Frances (Rand) Russell, June 7, 1801. From 1807 until 1815 he lived in his father's neighborhood in Wood County, Va., as local preacher and here he did his first writing, *Essays on the Truth of the Christian Religion* (1811) which established his reputation. He edited the *Western Christian Monitor,* the only paper of its kind in the Methodist Church in 1816, in Chillicothe, Ohio. While he lived in this region there was a great revival of religion, which was attributed to his eloquence as a preacher. In 1817 with Thomas S. Hinde and William McDowell, both Methodist preachers, he established the town of Mount Carmel, Ill. He surveyed the town, helped draw up a rigid code of puritanical laws, and built up a congregation. In 1821 because of ill health he lived quietly for some time on his farm near Mount Carmel, but the next year saw him a member of the Missouri Conference stationed at St. Louis. In 1823 when he was a delegate to the Methodist General Conference in Baltimore he was nominated for bishop, but lost the election by a few votes. The next year, which was his last, he was appointed presiding elder of the Indiana District. He was considered one of the ablest men of his profession. Though he had not had great advantages in formal education, he was a formidable opponent in controversy and his attainments were varied and extensive. In addition to his classical knowledge, he was acquainted with medicine and often made use of it in his pioneer surroundings. His reputation as a writer was considerable. Besides his work as editor of the *Western Christian Monitor* and his early *Essays on the Truth of the Christian Religion,* he published in 1849 *Letters on the Call*

and Qualifications of Ministers and *Letters on the Eternal Sonship of Christ.* He died in Paoli, Orange County, Ind.

[W. B. Sprague, *Annals of the Am. Pulpit,* VII (1865) ; *Minutes of the Ann. Conferences of the M. E. Ch. for 1733–1828,* I, 1840 ; Theophilus Arminius, "Memoir of the Rev. W. Beauchamp" in the *Meth. Mag.,* Jan., Feb., Mar., 1825.]

M. A. K.

BEAUCHAMP, WILLIAM MARTIN (Mar. 25, 1830–Dec. 13, 1925), archeologist, historian, was born in Coldenham, Orange County, N. Y., the son of William Millett Beauchamp and Mary (Jay) Beauchamp. His father had come from Somerset, England, in 1829, and in 1831, taking his family and possessions in two white-covered wagons, removed to Skaneateles, Onondaga County, where in 1840 he founded the *Skaneateles Democrat.* In his father's printing office William learned to love printing and writing. He decided, however, to enter the Episcopal ministry. Educated at the Skaneateles Academy and the Delancey Divinity School at Geneva, N. Y., he was ordained priest in 1863. As rector of Grace Church, Baldwinsville, N. Y., he served from July 1, 1865, to Oct. 1, 1900, when he retired from the active ministry. After 1900 he resided at Syracuse and, though often preaching, devoted himself mainly to research and writing (*Syracuse Post-Standard,* Dec. 14, 1925). Though deeply versed in local history, his dominating interest was in the past of the Six Nations and other aborigines. He became, among white men, the greatest authority on the history and institutions of the Iroquois. In a sense he was the successor of Lewis Morgan in this field. His interest in the Indians began in childhood, and was increased by his friendship with Albert Cusick, an Onondaga in orders in the Episcopal Church. From him he received much valuable information. In 1904 he was himself adopted into the Eel Clan of the Onondagas as Wah-Kat-yu-ten, the "Beautiful Rainbow." He was the author of many books and papers, among them: *The Iroquois Trail* (1892) ; *Indian Names in New York* (1893) ; *History of the New York Iroquois* (1905) ; *Past and Present of Syracuse and Onondaga County* (1908) ; *Revolutionary Soldiers Resident or Dying in Onondaga County, N. Y.* (1913) ; *Moravian Journals Relating to Central New York, 1745–66* (1916) ; *Iroquois Folk-lore* (1922) ; and *The Life of Conrad Weiser* (1925). Especially noteworthy was his work as archeologist of the New York State Museum. Preparing thirteen bulletins for the Museum, he threw much new light on the past of the aborigines. He possessed unusual skill in sketching Indian relics. From these sketches his bulletins were often illustrated. He was one of the first (1897–1902) to discover Eskimo influence and culture in New York State dating from a very early period (*Bulletin of the New York State Museum, no. 16*, p. 11, *no. 22*, p. 75, *no. 50*, pp. 328–30). He was active in promoting the Onondaga Historical Association of Syracuse and was a member of many learned societies. He was very short of stature, but deep in chest and powerful. "His ruddy cheeks, snow-white beard, and twinkling eyes made him beloved by all who knew him" (*Syracuse Journal,* Dec. 14, 1925). Of genial disposition, he was possessed of a quaint and whimsical humor. Always an out-door man, he roamed with keen eye the hills and woods of central New York and knew their flora and geology as well as their archeology. He became notable for extreme age and as a nonogenarian retained in a remarkable degree his strength and mental power. His best work was done after three score and ten. He was married to Sarah Carter of Ravenna, Ohio, Nov. 26, 1857.

[Beauchamp left ten large manuscript volumes entitled "Antiquities of Onondaga," and numerous notebooks. These are in possession of his family. A brief memoir by R. D. Burns appears in *Researches and Trans. of the N. Y. State Archæol. Ass.,* vol. III, no. 1. A similar sketch is prefixed to W. M. Beauchamp's "Notes of Other Days in Skaneateles" in *Ann. Vol. of the Onondaga Hist. Ass. for 1914* (1915).]

E. P. T.

BEAUMONT, JOHN COLT (Aug. 27, 1821–Aug. 2, 1882), naval officer, was born at Wilkes-Barre, Pa., of New England stock, third of the ten children of Andrew and Julia (Colt) Beaumont. Through the influence of his father, who was a member of Congress (1833–37) and a friend of President Jackson, he secured an appointment as midshipman, Mar. 1, 1838. Two years later he sailed in the *Constellation* on a long cruise to the East Indies and around the world. In the Mexican War he served on the *Ohio* at the fall of Vera Cruz, and later in the Pacific. Sea service was varied by tours of duty at the Naval Observatory, Washington, in 1848 and 1852–54. As a passed midshipman (promoted May 20, 1844) he visited Mediterranean ports on the *Independence,* 1849–52; and as a lieutenant (promoted Aug. 29, 1852) he was in the *Hartford* in the East Indies at the opening of the Civil War. His war service was entirely as a ship commander on the Virginia rivers and Atlantic coast. He was in the gunboat *Aroostook* in attacks on Confederate batteries in the James River and at Fort Darling in May 1862, and in the *Sebago,* in the South Atlantic Blockading Squadron, 1862–63. Transferred to the monitor *Nantucket,* he took a leading part in the capture of Fort Wagner in July 1863, and was

engaged in other attacks on the defenses of Charleston. In the first bombardment of Fort Fisher, Dec. 24–25, 1864, he declined to withdraw, though the boiler of his ship, the *Mackinaw,* was pierced by a shell and ten of his crew were wounded. In the *Mackinaw* he was also in the second attack on Fort Fisher, and in subsequent operations on the Cape Fear River. Of a jovial, social disposition, with a host of friends, and with a reputation as a skilful officer experienced in ironclads, he was selected to command the new monitor *Miantonomoh,* in the squadron which took Assistant Secretary of the Navy Fox to Russia in the summer of 1866 to express American appreciation of Russia's friendly attitude during the war. The first monitor to cross the Atlantic, the *Miantonomoh* was a "show ship," visited by thousands during her tour of the chief ports from Kronstadt to Lisbon. In July 1867, Beaumont was promoted to captain, but complaints of no very serious nature regarding the reception of visitors on the *Miantonomoh* led to his temporary retirement. He was restored to the active list by Act of Congress, June 10, 1872; was chief signal officer, 1874–79; and was commandant of the Portsmouth Navy Yard at the time of his retirement as rear admiral, Feb. 3, 1882. He died of heart disease at Durham, N. H., and was buried in the National Cemetery at Arlington. He was twice married: on Oct. 27, 1852, to Fanny Dorrance, who died in 1855; and again, in 1874 to Fannie S. King of Washington, D. C.

[Numerous letters, reports, etc., relating to Beaumont appear in the *Official Records* (see index, esp. of vols. VII–XIV). His service record is available in *Navy Registers, Reports of the Secretary of the Navy,* and in T. H. S. Hamersly's *Gen. Reg. of the U. S. Navy*(1882). Information regarding his personal life has been drawn from the *Hist. of Luzerne County, Pa.* (1893) and from papers in the possession of his son, Lieut.-Col. John C. Beaumont, U. S. Marine Corps.]

A. W.

BEAUMONT, WILLIAM (Nov. 21, 1785–Apr. 25, 1853), surgeon, was descended from William Beaumont, who in 1635 sailed on the *Eliza de Lond* for Massachusetts, where he tarried long enough to marry Lydia Danforth at Cambridge, and then sought a more permanent residence in Connecticut. In the sixth American generation, William Beaumont, the son of Samuel and Lucretia (Abel) Beaumont, was born. He was the third child and the second son in a family of nine, four brothers and five sisters. The father, following the English custom, bequeathed all his land to his oldest son, Samuel. The War of Independence, in which William's father and uncles had served, had recently closed, and the financial condition of the Connecticut farmer required the closest economy in family expenses. There was much bitterness along party lines between neighbors, Jeffersonian democrats and Hamiltonian federalists, the Beaumonts adhering to the former. Even religious discourses took second place at town meetings and other assemblies. The family attended the Congregational Church but feeling as to creed seems to have been devoid of extravagant expression. William Beaumont never affiliated with any church. In his maturity, replying to a letter from one of his sisters, he wrote: "Though I am not a professor or even a convert to any particular religious sect, yet I am a strict believer in the great good effects of moral and virtuous examples."

There is no evidence that young Beaumont had more than a common school education, but that he attained proficiency in the English language and some knowledge of Latin is shown by his subsequent writings. In early manhood he began a diary which he continued through life and this was fortunately preserved by one of his daughters and later was turned over to Dr. Jesse S. Myer, who wisely used these records in his *Life and Letters of Dr. William Beaumont* (1912). This diary contains not only records of his professional experiences but his observations and comments in his extensive travels, and notes on the books he read. He early showed the possession of three essential qualifications to success: intelligence, industry, and integrity. In 1806 with a horse and cutter and $100 of hard-earned money he drove to Champlain, a village in New York, near the Canadian border. Here he taught school and read medicine for three years. Dr. Pomeroy of Burlington, Vt., supplied him with books and directed his reading. In 1810 Beaumont became an apprentice to Dr. Benjamin Chandler of St. Albans, Vt. In this capacity he swept the office, kept up the fires, learned to fill prescriptions, rode with his preceptor long distances through the forests, studied the symptoms of patients, assisted in surgical operations, and made autopsies in fatal cases. Of all these the student made notes which even now are well worth reading. Between preceptor and apprentice there appears to have been only one rift. The doctor was a violent Federalist and when his apprentice differed from him, he would threaten to turn him out of doors and have nothing more to do with him. In this connection there are interesting points in the letters. Beaumont's father heard that Dr. Chandler had converted the young man to Federalism and wrote a chiding letter. The son replied as follows: "Yes, dear Sir, erase and let any impression be obliterated from every mind of my ever being

made a convert to the present system of Federalism. Sooner might they remove the everlasting hills than bribe my integrity, make my faith waver, shake my belief or break my course from the pole star of Republicanism while reason holds her empire over the province of my intellect."

When the lad had finished his apprenticeship the doctor gave him a most hearty indorsement and on the second Tuesday in June 1812 Beaumont was licensed by the Third Medical Society of Vermont to practise medicine. On Sept. 13, 1812, the young doctor was commissioned by President Madison as surgeon's mate to the 6th Infantry at Plattsburg, N. Y. Beaumont has left a graphic description of the battle of York (Toronto) where the retreating English exploded a magazine of 300 barrels of powder under the feet of the advancing Americans. Three hundred were wounded and sixty killed. "A most distressing scene ensues in the hospital—nothing but the groans of the wounded and the agonies of the dying are to be heard." The young surgeon operated for forty-eight consecutive hours and it may be mentioned that this was done without anesthetics. At the close of the war (1815) the strength of the army was reduced to 10,000 and the officers carefully culled. In this process Beaumont was retained while many older men were discharged. Seeing no career in the army in peace, however, he resigned and began private practise in Plattsburg. During his army service his work came under the observation and won the admiration of Joseph Lovell, who, in 1818, became the first surgeon-general. He offered Beaumont a position in his office which was first accepted and then declined. But private practise in Plattsburg did not prove lucrative or stimulating, and in 1820 Beaumont again enlisted, was given the rank of post surgeon, and was ordered to Fort Mackinac. In the travel journal from Plattsburg to Mackinac may be found much of the young man's philosophy. At that time the Fort was occupied by five or six companies, while the village had a population of about 500, swelled in summer-time to about 5,000 by the incoming of the employees of the fur company, consisting largely of drunken Indians and halfbreeds. Among these were many brawls and broken heads. Beaumont was the only doctor within a radius of 300 miles and had abundant surgical material. In 1821 he married Mrs. Deborah Platt of Plattsburg, who proved in every way a fit companion for the army surgeon. Although a Quaker, she was devoted to Shakespeare and devised amateur theatricals in various posts to which her husband was assigned. Many officers both of the line and of the staff testified in their letters to the wholesome hospitality and good cheer found in her home. Immediately after the marriage she accompanied her husband to Fort Mackinac where their first child, a daughter, was born.

On June 6, 1822, occurred the accident to Alexis St. Martin, which was to make him and his surgeon immortal. Beaumont records the case in his diary as follows: "St. Martin, a Canadian lad, about nineteen years old, hardy, robust and healthy, was accidentally shot by the unlucky discharge of a gun on the 6th of June, 1822. The whole charge, consisting of powder and duck shot, was received in the left side at not more than two or three feet distance from the muzzle of the piece, in a posterior direction, obliquely forward and outward, carrying away by its force the integuments more than the size of the palm of a man's hand; blowing off and fracturing the sixth rib from about the middle anteriorly, fracturing the fifth, rupturing the lower portion of the left lobe of the lung and lacerating the stomach by a spicule of the rib that was blown through its coat; landing the charge, wadding, fire in among the fractured ribs and lacerated muscles and integuments and burning the clothing and flesh to a crisp. I was called to him immediately after the accident. Found a portion of the lung as large as a turkey's egg protruding through the external wound, lacerated and burnt, and below this another protrusion resembling a portion of the stomach, what at first view I could not believe possible to be that organ in that situation with the subject surviving, but on closer observation, I found it to be actually the stomach with a puncture in the protruding portion large enough to receive my forefinger, and through which a portion of the food he had taken for breakfast had come out and lodged among his apparel. In this dilemma I considered any attempt to save his life entirely useless. But as I had ever considered it a duty to use every means in my power to preserve life when called to administer relief, I proceeded to cleanse the wound, give it a superficial dressing, not believing it possible for him to survive twenty minutes. On attempting to reduce the protruding portions, I found that the lung was prevented from returning by the sharp point of the fractured rib, over which its membrane had caught fast, but by raising up the lung with the forefinger of my left hand I clipped off, with my penknife in my right hand, the sharp point of the rib, which enabled me to return the lung into the cavity of the thorax, but could not retain it there on the least effort of the patient to cough, which was frequent."

The patient was placed in the military hospital where Beaumont dressed the wound once and often twice a day for quite a year. Fortunately the stomach adhered to the intercostal muscles and did not drop back into the abdominal cavity. For a long time food could be kept in the stomach only by the daily application of a pad of lint held in place by adhesive straps. Ultimately a flap of the inner coat of the stomach formed a valve closing the orifice, but easily pushed back exposing the interior of the organ. Beaumont made every possible effort to close the orifice but fortunately for science was unable to do so. About the end of the first year, St. Martin was adjudged a pauper and was ordered to be transported to Lower Canada, a distance of nearly 2,000 miles as one had to go at that time, in an open boat. Beaumont, seeing that this could only end in great suffering and death, made an earnest plea in which he indulged in sarcastic words about "Charity." The authorities were deaf to appeals and the doctor took his patient to his own home, continued to dress his wounds, and clothed and fed the injured man. How he did this when his salary was only $40 a month, with himself and family to support, is a question which only the charitable can solve. The idea of making scientific studies in digestion on his patient apparently did not occur until early in 1825. By this time St. Martin had become quite a lusty man, capable of doing heavy service, such as chopping wood and keeping the house fires going. Late in 1824 Beaumont reported the case to the surgeon-general, but by a strange irony of fate, the report appeared in the *Medical Recorder* as "A Case of Wounded Stomach, by Joseph Lovell, S.G., U.S.A." This mistake was not intentional on the part of Lovell and was soon corrected. In March 1825 the Medical Society of Michigan Territory at a meeting in Detroit made Beaumont an honorary member. This was the first recognition he received from the profession.

With his experiments only fairly begun, Beaumont was ordered to Fort Niagara with two months leave of absence. He took St. Martin to Plattsburg via Burlington and settled down quite satisfied with the prospect of a few weeks of uninterrupted study, when he awoke one morning to find that his patient had stolen away and had probably gone to his home in Lower Canada. Beaumont put his experiments in shape and the article appeared in the *Medical Recorder*. In this series he had studied the temperature of the stomach in digestion, the movements of the walls, the relative digestibility of certain foods, and had shown that the gastric juice, when removed from the stomach and placed in bottles, digests food in the same way but more slowly than under natural conditions. These findings were sufficient to overthrow many of the prevalent theories as to stomachic digestion. Some had held that the stomach is only a reservoir for food and has no digestive action; others, that it is only a grinding or triturating organ; others still, that the stomach is only a fermentation vat.

An incident occurred at Fort Niagara which illuminates the character of Beaumont. A Lieut. Griswold presented himself at sick report. Beaumont admitted him to the hospital and after making a thorough study of the case came to the conclusion that he was a malingerer. The doctor prepared a potion containing some twenty grains of calomel and five or six of tartar emetic. After informing the lieutenant of the composition of this powder he told him that he could take it or report for duty. The lieutenant chose duty. The result was a court martial in which Beaumont was the chief witness, and the lieutenant was pronounced guilty and it was recommended that he be dismissed from the service. The President of the United States reversed this finding and in doing so criticized the doctor severely, whereupon Beaumont issued a circular containing the following passage: "Whether the plan adopted, either in a moral or professional point of view, be justifiable or not I leave for medical men and candid judges to decide; it was salutary and had the intended effect of returning Lieut. Griswold to his duty without prejudice to his health or constitution; neither is it of very great moment with me whether a successful experiment be of *less* or *more* than doubtful propriety, that speedily returns a soldier from *sick report* to the effective service of the government, be he *private, non-commissioned* or *commissioned officer;* neither do I think it of very great consequence whether it be done *secundum artem, secundum naturam* or *terrorem,* provided it be *well done.*" The circular runs through many pages in like tone. It is to the credit of President John Quincy Adams that there is no record of a second court martial. It is to the further credit of President Adams that he commissioned Beaumont surgeon on Nov. 28, 1826.

In May 1826 Beaumont was transferred to Fort Howard on Green Bay and in 1828 to Fort Crawford on the upper Mississippi. During these years he kept up a correspondence with the officers of the fur company in his search for St. Martin. Finally the truant was located in Lower Canada, where he had married and become the father of two children. At Beaumont's expense the whole family was transferred to the far-distant post and in August 1829, after an interruption of four years, the experiments were again begun and continued until the spring of 1831, when St. Martin and his family, increased by two, were allowed to go home with the promise to return when requested. It is worthy of note that this journey was made in a canoe down the Mississippi, up the Ohio, across to Lake Erie and thence to Montreal. Beaumont had long been desirous of enlisting the interest of some competent chemist in the study of the gastric juice. With this in view he asked for a year's leave of absence with permission to carry St. Martin to Europe. This was granted in May 1831 but was subsequently withdrawn. The reason for this change on the part of the Secretary of War was the outbreak of the Black Hawk War and the simultaneous appearance of Asiatic cholera for the first time in this country. One of the early cases developed in a soldier on a transport on Lake Erie. At Detroit, and a few days later at Chicago, a panic ensued; soldiers deserted and the disease was carried to remote posts. Beaumont saw more of this disease than he did of battle and has left a fanciful theory of its nature. As it turned out, it is just as well that he did not get to Europe, as will be seen later.

On Aug. 22, 1832, Col. Zachary Taylor, commanding officer at Fort Crawford, issued an order granting Beaumont six months' furlough, and on the next day the latter left with the intention of taking St. Martin to Europe. The Canadian kept his promise, reported to the doctor in October at Plattsburg, and signed a document binding himself to serve for one year. A like contract has probably never been written. Alexis pledged himself to submit to all experiments and William agreed to pay all expenses, furnish Alexis with good sustenance, suitable housing, wearing apparel, washing, and $150. Beaumont wisely concluded that his furlough of six months was not sufficient to justify the journey to Europe. Both took residence in Washington and the experiments were continued from November 1832 to March 1834. In December 1832, Alexis was enlisted as sergeant at $12 a month, $2.50 a month for clothing, and 10 cents a day for subsistence. In his enlistment papers his age is given as twenty-eight; his birthplace as Berthier, Lower Canada; and his occupation as a laborer.

These were the golden days of the experimentation, and the facilities enjoyed by the investigator were largely due to the intelligent appreciation of the work by Surgeon-General Lovell, supported by the Secretary of War, Lewis Cass. Foreign books were secured and the literature on gastric digestion was thoroughly studied. Giving up hope of taking Alexis to Europe, Beaumont sought aid in this country. He was fortunate in securing the interest of Prof. Robley Dunglison of the University of Virginia, recently established along scientific lines through the efforts of Thomas Jefferson. Dunglison had written a voluminous compend on physiology, in which he discussed the multitudinous theories of digestion. He wrote to Beaumont, suggested lines of experimentation, and made a visit to Washington to see for himself. Beaumont supplied Dunglison with samples of the juice, and the latter, with the aid of his colleague, Prof. Emmet, made an analysis and pronounced the acid to be free hydrochloric. Prout, in 1824, had come to the same conclusion, but his evidence was not altogether convincing and the scientific world was slow to believe that a mineral acid could be formed in the body. Even after Beaumont's publication, Lehmann in Germany wrote a paper showing, to his own satisfaction at least, that it could not be true.

On the expiration of his furlough Beaumont was assigned to duty in New York City, but after six weeks, he wrote the Surgeon-General: "I expect to leave the city in a few days to visit my family at the North . . . I doubt not this measure will meet your approbation. I have not been able to complete the series I had on hand when I left Washington, but I am determined to do it soon even if I have to shut myself up with Alexis in a convent, or retire to some seclusion in the country. My official duties are very light and would not interfere at all with my experiments could I avoid the vexatious social intercourse to which I am perpetually exposed in this city. It is an unfavorable place for the pursuit of physiological inquiries and experiments." While in New York, Beaumont, with bottles of the gastric juice, visited Prof. Silliman of Yale, but this distinguished chemist, although deeply interested and inclined to be helpful, could only advise Beaumont to send the fluid to Prof. Berzelius of Stockholm. This was done, but the great chemist of his time acknowledged his inability to make the analysis. Indeed, the only help Beaumont received from any chemist was the information given by Dunglison, who determined the nature of the free acid and suggested the presence of a second digestive factor which later research proved to be pepsin.

Beaumont wished to publish his studies in book form, but found that he could do so only at his own expense. The first edition of 1,000 copies, bearing the title: *Experiments and Observations on the Gastric Juice and the Physiology of Digestion,* was published at Plattsburg in 1833. The paper was poor; the illustrations were crude;

typographical errors were many; but the contents constituted the greatest contribution ever made to the knowledge of gastric digestion. Beaumont had made such an exact study of the physical and chemical properties of the gastric juice that with the exception of the discovery of pepsin, the closest research of modern times has added but little to the work done by him. Both the medical and lay press gave most complimentary reviews, some of which would prove amusing to present-day readers. Prominent members of Congress and other public men to whom complimentary copies were sent thanked the author most profusely, but when a bill was presented to Congress to appropriate $10,000 for further prosecution of the work it failed by a vote of 56 to 129. Financially the publication was a failure. Lilly, Wait & Company, booksellers of Boston, took 500 copies, but in Beaumont's papers he instructs a cousin to sue the company for unpaid dues, and there is no record that any part was collected. A German translation and an English edition appeared within a few years, and since that time no writer on gastric digestion has failed to utilize Beaumont's work. In 1847 Chauncey Goodrich of Burlington published a second edition of 1,500 copies. The agreement was that the author was to receive 200 copies and should have the exclusive sale in Missouri and in all states south and west thereof. Beaumont did receive a few copies but otherwise the agreement was not observed.

The book detailed 238 experiments. These were followed by a table showing the relative digestibility of many articles of diet and the results stated have been but little modified by subsequent studies. There are fifty-one conclusions, most of which are still accepted. The presence of a second digestive factor in the gastric juice (which the discovery of pepsin has since proved) was surmised. Our knowledge of alimentary digestion has been greatly widened since Beaumont's time. The peptic glands, their innervation, the *modus operandi* by which free acid is formed, pancreatic and intestinal digestion, were unknown to him. Nevertheless, no other man, with the possible exception of Claude Bernard, has made so important a contribution to the physiology of digestion. An American physician studying in Paris wrote Beaumont in 1850: "The publication of your observations exposing so clearly and analytically the physiology of the stomach was the commencement of a new era in the study of this important organ and those associated with it. Your experiments are constantly imitated here upon animals by a large number of investigating physiologists among whom M. Bernard probably stands first. His discoveries, of which you have doubtless heard, have rendered the functions of the pancreas, liver, etc., as clear as yours do those of the stomach, but his observations have necessarily been limited to animals, and in the absence of yours upon man, would lose much of their value, since no other evidence exists of the identity of the process of digestion in man and the lower animals. . . . He feels some interest in knowing the subsequent history of Martin and requested me to write you inquiring whether you have kept sight of him, what is the nature of his occupation, his health, etc., if he is still living, with such other information concerning him not contained in your publication as you may think fit to communicate."

Early in 1834, the patient "with a lid on his stomach" returned to Canada and although Beaumont succeeded in locating him and made many attempts to have him returned, once sending his son for him, he failed. St. Martin lived twenty years longer than his doctor and died at St. Thomas de Jolliette, at the age of eighty-three. His family refused an autopsy and buried him eight feet below the surface in order to make difficult attempts at resurrection.

In 1834 Beaumont was ordered to Jefferson Barracks, twelve miles below St. Louis, and later was transferred to the St. Louis Arsenal where he was permitted to live in the city and engage in private practise, which soon became large and lucrative. In 1836 Beaumont's good angel, Surgeon-General Lovell, died and was succeeded by Thomas Lawson, who continued in this position until 1861. No more favors could be obtained and Beaumont's first request was granted only under unjust conditions and in derogatory terms. It was soon rumored that Beaumont was to be transferred to Jefferson Barracks where it would be impossible for him to do private practise. But he had many stanch friends among the line officers stationed in the central west, among whom were Maj. Ethan Allen Hitchcock and Robert E. Lee and, besides, his work was highly appreciated by the Missouri senators, Thomas H. Benton and Lewis F. Linn, the latter having previously served with Beaumont as an army surgeon. Through the intercession of these and other friends the blow was delayed. It must be admitted that Beaumont's letter to the Surgeon-General on receipt of the denial of his request for a furlough was not tactful. Indeed, he was never tactful. He possessed an excess of *fortiter in re* and was deficient in *suaviter in modo*. He did not hesitate to use forceful language even when addressing the President of the United States or the Surgeon-General. It is evident, however, from the Washington letters to Beaumont from

Hitchcock and Lee that Lawson was seeking an opportunity to humiliate his subordinate. It came in General Order 48, dated Sept. 18, 1839. This assigned Beaumont to a board to convene at Fort Brook, Fla., on Nov. 15 following. It was met by Beaumont's resignation, conditional on the withdrawal of the order. Lawson attempted further humiliation by declining to accept the resignation until the order had been complied with. The resignation was accepted, however, on Jan. 20, 1840, to take effect as of date of Dec. 31, 1839. Thus the second Surgeon-General drove from the corps the man who, up to that time, had most highly honored it and to whose work under adverse conditions every member of the corps now points with pride. But Beaumont at this point committed a great indiscretion. He sought reinstatement, memorialized President Van Buren and characterized the Surgeon-General as one whose capacity was at zero. His friends, Hitchcock and Lee, did the best they could for him, but the request was undignified and the language vitriolic.

The subsequent history of Beaumont is that of a private physician in St. Louis. He had all the professional work he could do, acquired ample means, bought a forty-acre tract, then in the country, now bounded by Jefferson Avenue and Beaumont St. In the profession he had his warm friends and bitter enemies and was involved in two malpractise suits in both of which his reputation was sustained by the courts. In one of these he had trephined a broken skull and there were colleagues who testified that death was due to the operation and that Beaumont wanted to see what was going on within the brain as he had done with St. Martin's stomach. In the cholera epidemic of 1849 he rendered heroic service to both poor and rich. In March 1853 he fell upon ice-covered stone steps and developed a carbuncle on his neck; he died on Apr. 25. He and his wife, who lived until Jan. 23, 1870, now lie in Bellefontaine Cemetery. They left one son and two daughters.

St. Martin was not the first man with a gastric fistula. The record of a round dozen or more may be found in medical literature. Some of these were housed for long periods in great hospitals and seen by the most eminent physicians of the time, but nothing came from these opportunities. In this instance the man met the opportunity. "Every physician who prescribes for digestive disorders and every patient who is benefited by such a prescription owes gratitude to the memory of William Beaumont for the benefit of mankind."

[Jesse S. Myer, *Life and Letters of Dr. Wm. Beaumont* (1912); Wm. Osler, "Wm. Beaumont; A Pioneer

Am. Physiologist," *Physician and Surgeon,* Dec. 1902; Thos. Reyburn, "Memoirs of the Late Dr. Beaumont," *St. Louis Medic. and Surgic. Jour.,* 1854; John Goltra, "Wm. Beaumont as a Scientist," *Physician and Surgeon,* Dec. 1902; Victor C. Vaughan, "Wm. Beaumont and His Work," *Trans. Mich. State Medic. Soc.,* 1896; *Physician and Surgeon,* Dec. 1902.]　　　　　V.C.V.

BEAUPRÉ, ARTHUR MATTHIAS (July 29, 1853–Sept. 13, 1919), diplomat, was born in Oswego township, Kendall County, Ill., his father, Matthias Beaupré, a French Canadian, having migrated in 1838 from Canada to Joliet, Ill., where he married Sarah J. Patrick, a native of Ontario, subsequently moving to Oswego. Arthur's youth was spent in Kendall County and his education was procured in the public schools at Oswego and De Kalb, to which latter place the family moved in 1865. On leaving school in 1869 he entered the office of the *De Kalb County News,* learning the printing business and supplementing his education by individual study. A Republican, he became interested in politics at an early age, and on his removal to Aurora in 1874 was elected city clerk and commenced to study law. Shortly afterward he was appointed deputy clerk of Kane County and having been admitted to the Illinois bar commenced practise in Aurora. He was married, on Oct. 20, 1880, to Mary F., daughter of C. W. Marsh of De Kalb, the inventor of the "Marsh harvester." In 1886 he received the Republican nomination for clerk of Kane County and, being elected by a large majority, retained the position for eight years. Both as lawyer and official he showed marked ability and his prominence in local and state politics induced President McKinley to appoint him consul general and secretary of the United States legation to Guatemala and Honduras, Oct. 7, 1897. In this position he met with unqualified success, his urbane, dignified manners and courtly demeanor making a deep impression on the temperamental Guatemalans. He also attracted the confidence of his foreign colleagues to such an extent that in March 1899 he was invited by Great Britain and Honduras to act as sole arbitrator in the dispute respecting the detention of the British schooner *Lottie May* and the arrest and imprisonment of her captain by the government of Honduras in 1892 (*Foreign Relations of the United States,* 1899, pp. 371–72). Beaupré was transferred to Bogota as consul general and secretary of the legation to Colombia, Oct. 27, 1899. At that period the question of a trans-isthmian canal was being vehemently debated, and the conclusion of the Hay-Pauncefote Treaty in 1901 left the United States free to negotiate with Colombia relative to the cession of rights over territory in Panama. Though Beaupré was only in a subordinate position at Bogota, he enjoyed the confidence of President Roosevelt, and on Feb. 12, 1903, three weeks after the signing of the Hay-Herren Treaty the President appointed him minister to Colombia and entrusted to him the delicate task of inspiring the ratification of the treaty by the Colombian Congress. His promotion from consul to minister was almost unprecedented, the records of the State Department affording but one other instance of such an appointment. Deceived at first as to the good faith of the Colombian government, he later realized its intention to extort better financial terms, and in striking dispatches he kept Secretary Hay *au fait* with the tortuous policy pursued by President Marroquin, which ultimately resulted in the rejection of the treaty. The revolution which immediately followed in Panama, and the prompt recognition by President Roosevelt of the new government produced intense excitement in Bogota. Enraged mobs menaced the United States legation, and Beaupré was threatened with personal violence. His position had been a difficult one and this was accentuated by the cutting of the cables, thus severing his communications with Washington. His conduct throughout, however, met with the cordial approval of the President and Secretary of State (*Foreign Relations of the United States,* 1903, pp. 132–230). In 1904 he was appointed minister to the Argentine Republic, remaining at Buenos Aires four years, and becoming minister to the Netherlands and Luxemburg in 1908. While at The Hague President Taft appointed him a member of the administrative council of the Permanent Court of Arbitration and he was also a delegate to the International Exchange Conference. In August 1911 he was appointed minister to the Republic of Cuba and held this position till June 1913. The last months of his residence in Havana were signalized by scurrilous attacks upon him and Hugh S. Gibson, secretary of legation, in the newspaper *Cuba,* wherein they were accused of enriching themselves by blackmail and graft. The author of the libels was ultimately forced to make a complete retraction (*Foreign Relations of the United States,* 1913, p. 412). Beaupré's last diplomatic appointment was as chief of the special mission to represent President Wilson at the inauguration of Menocal as President of Cuba, May 14, 1913. Six weeks later he retired from the service, his diplomatic career having extended over a period of sixteen years. On returning to the United States he took up his residence in Chicago. Stricken with paralysis in June 1915, he was a confirmed invalid during the last four years of his life.

[Details of his family and early life appeared in *Commemorative Portr. and Biog. Record of Kane and Kendall Counties, Ill.* (1888), p. 657. See also R. W. Joslyn and Frank W. Joslyn, *Hist. of Kane County, Ill.* (1908), II, 75; *Who's Who in America*, 1918–19; obit. notices in Chicago *Herald and Examiner* and *Chicago Daily Tribune*, Sept. 15, 1919.]

H. W. H. K.

BEAUREGARD, PIERRE GUSTAVE TOUTANT (May 28, 1818–Feb. 20, 1893), Confederate soldier, was of French ancestry. About the year 1600 the Chevalier de Beauregard, scion of an ancient and honorable family, married the daughter of one Toutant, a French gentleman of Welsh ancestry, and their son assumed the surname of Toutant de Beauregard. Later generations contracted this to Toutant-Beauregard, and eventually the hyphen was dropped. Jacques Toutant-Beauregard, after visiting the colony of Louisiana in the service of Louis XIV, finally settled there. His grandson, also named Jacques, married Hélène Judith de Reggio, of a family which traced descent from the house of Este. Their son Gustave (he did not use the name of Pierre) was born in the parish of St. Bernard, near New Orleans, and received his early education in that city and in New York. He graduated at West Point in 1838, second in a class of which Irvin McDowell, his opponent at Bull Run twenty-three years later, was also a member. As second lieutenant and first lieutenant of engineers he was employed on fortification work chiefly in Louisiana, until 1846, when he went to Mexico as an engineer on the staff of Gen. Scott. He was present at the siege of Vera Cruz and the battles of Cerro Gordo and Contreras, and received a brevet Aug. 20, 1847, for gallant conduct in the latter engagement. Whether or not he originally suggested attacking the City of Mexico by way of Chapultepec, it is certain that he advocated it in opposition to nearly all the general officers and engineers, and that his views finally prevailed (Justin H. Smith, *War with Mexico*, 1919, II, 149). He was twice wounded at the taking of the city and received another brevet on Sept. 13, 1847. After the war he was engaged in engineering in his native state almost continuously until the Civil War, being chief engineer in charge of draining the site of New Orleans, 1858–61. He was promoted captain Mar. 3, 1853. In 1860 he was selected as superintendent of West Point, but his openly expressed intention of going with his state if it should pass an ordinance of secession made the expediency of his appointment more than doubtful, and he had hardly arrived at West Point, in January 1861, when the Secretary of War directed his transfer. He was superintendent of the Academy for just five days. On Feb. 20 his resignation from the army was accepted.

He was at once appointed brigadier-general in the Confederate army and was sent to take command of the forces around Charleston. Acting on instructions from the Confederate government, he demanded the surrender of Fort Sumter, and upon Maj. Anderson's refusal ordered the bombardment that compelled the evacuation of the fort and began four years of civil war. His high reputation as a soldier and his popularity on account of the taking of Sumter dictated his assignment to an important field command. On June 1, near Manassas, Va., he took charge of one of the two Confederate armies which were being assembled near the Potomac, and which were later merged to form the historic Army of Northern Virginia. Gen. Joseph E. Johnston, with the other, was in the Shenandoah Valley, but when Gen. McDowell advanced toward Manassas, he evaded the forces which had been directed to detain him, and joined his army with Beauregard's on the eve of the battle of Bull Run. Johnston, being the senior, commanded the combined force, but as he was unfamiliar with the ground and the disposition of the troops, the preliminary orders for the battle were drawn up by Beauregard. The disastrous defeat of the Union army of July 21, however, was not due to any control of the action by general headquarters. During the day Beauregard was in personal charge of the Confederate left, bore himself bravely, and had a horse killed under him. His popular reputation was greater than ever, and his government recognized his services by promotion to the full rank of general. In the spring of 1862 he was sent to the western theatre of operations, and was second in command, under Gen. A. S. Johnston, of the army which attacked Grant at Shiloh on Apr. 6. Beauregard succeeded to the command when Johnston was killed, pressed the attack, and ended the day with an apparent victory; but the arrival of Buell's army turned the scale against him and he was forced to retreat after the second day's fighting. He fell back to Corinth, Miss., fortified it for a siege, and delayed the advance of the Union army as long as possible, finally evacuating the town. In June sickness compelled him to turn his command over to Gen. Bragg. Upon his recovery he was charged with the defense of the South Carolina and Georgia coasts, particularly of Charleston, which the United States government made vigorous efforts to capture. Although repeated attacks were made in 1863 by land and water, and Fort Sumter reduced to ruins, the city remained in Confederate possession. In the spring of 1864

Beauregard was again in the field. Grant's plan of operations contemplated an advance toward Richmond from the southeast by Butler's Army of the James, while Meade's Army of the Potomac, which Grant himself accompanied, engaged Lee in front. Beauregard, however, defeated Butler at Drewry's Bluff, "bottled him up" at Bermuda Hundred, and removed him from the board for all practical purposes. When the Army of the Potomac shifted to the south of Richmond and began the siege of Petersburg, June 15, it fell to Beauregard to hold back the enemy until Lee could come to his assistance. His command was now merged with Lee's. In September he returned to the west in administrative command. The closing months of the war found him once more second in command, as at Bull Run, to Gen. J. E. Johnston, with whom he served through the campaign of the Carolinas until the surrender. After the war, he was for five years president of the New Orleans, Jackson & Mississippi Railway, declining offers of the command of the army of Roumania in 1866 and of that of Egypt in 1869 and again in 1870. He then became manager of the Louisiana lottery, a lucrative position, but one in which he was naturally subjected to much criticism. In 1888 he became commissioner of public works of the City of New Orleans. He was for many years adjutant-general of Louisiana. He wrote *Principles and Maxims of the Art of War* (1863), *Report of the Defense of Charleston* (1864), *A Commentary on the Campaign and Battle of Manassas* (1891), and numerous papers on Civil War subjects. He is described as a small man, of typically French appearance, soldierly in bearing, animated and agreeable in manner. "As a general, Beauregard was strong in fortification, and of unquenchable courage, but weak in strategy and wanting in coolness, insight, and method on the battlefield. His dispatches lack clearness, and at times candor; while rhetoric is a pitfall he rarely resists" (Johnston, p. 35). In September 1841 he married Laure, daughter of Jules Villère, a sugar planter of Plaquemines Parish. In 1860 he married Caroline, daughter of André Deslonde, a sugar planter of St. James's Parish. She died in the spring of 1864.

[Alfred Roman's *Mil. Operations of Gen. Beauregard* (1884) covers its subject in great detail, quotes many documents in full, and was personally approved by Beauregard, but its tone is one of uncritical admiration throughout. Articles (including several by himself) in vols. I (1887) and IV (1888) of *Battles and Leaders of the Civil War* give a full hist. of his campaigns. For Bull Run, see also R. M. Johnston's *Bull Run—Its Strategy and Tactics* (1913); for Drewry's Bluff and Petersburg, an article by Johnson Hagood in vol. XXVIII (1900) of the *Southern Hist. Soc. Papers,* pp. 318–36. Other references are G. W. Cullum, *Biog. Reg.* (3rd ed.,

1891), I, 697–98 and *Official Records,* ser. 1, vols. I, II, X (pts. 1, 2), XXV (pts. 1, 2), XXXVI (pts. 2, 3).]

T.M.S.

BEAVER, JAMES ADDAMS (Oct. 21, 1837– Jan. 31, 1914), Union soldier, governor of Pennsylvania, traced his ancestry to George Beaver, an Alsatian Huguenot, who came from Rotterdam on the *Friendship,* reached Philadelphia, Nov. 2, 1744, and settled in Chester County, Pa. From George Beaver was descended Jacob, a country storekeeper who married Ann Eliza, daughter of Abraham Addams. James Addams Beaver, born in Millerstown, Perry County, was the third of their four children. The early death of his father and Beaver's poor health left the education of this son until 1852 to his grandfathers and his stepfather, Rev. S. H. McDonald. When James was thirteen years old his mother moved to Belleville in Mifflin County. Two years later he entered Pine Grove Academy (in Center County) and in 1854 became a junior at Jefferson College, Canonsburg, receiving his A.B. in 1856 at the age of nineteen. Upon leaving college he began the study of law under Hugh Nelson McAllister at Bellefonte, and was admitted to the Center County bar in January 1859. The Lincoln campaign of 1860 made Beaver expect war, and he joined the Bellefonte Fencibles, a military company under Andrew G. Curtin, the later war governor. The next year he tendered the services of this company to Gov. Curtin and became its first lieutenant on Apr. 21, 1861, when it enlisted for three months as Company H of the 2nd Pennsylvania Volunteer Infantry. The company saw service in the Shenandoah Valley under Sheridan. At the expiration of three months Beaver was honorably mustered out, only to become lieutenant-colonel of the 45th Pennsylvania Infantry, stationed in South Carolina. He remained in the South until Sept. 4, 1862, when he resigned to accept the colonelcy of the 148th Pennsylvania Regiment, recruited near his home for three years. With these men he joined the Army of the Potomac after Fredericksburg (Dec. 13, 1862), was wounded at Chancellorsville (May 3, 1863) and was taken to a Washington hospital. Before complete recovery he took charge (June 18, 1863) of Camp Curtin, a recruiting station in Pennsylvania under Major-General Darius N. Crouch. Here, by June 30, he had organized three emergency regiments which fought at Gettysburg. Relieved from duty at Camp Curtin on July 15, 1863, Beaver rejoined the main army July 31 with little active service before the Wilderness campaign (May 5–7, 1864) and the march against Petersburg. His gallant work at Cold Harbor (June 3) and distinguished conduct until his leg was shot through at Ream's Station (Aug. 25) justified his appointment as brevet brigadier-general of volunteers Nov. 10, to rank from Aug. 1, 1864.

Incapacitated for active service, Beaver was honorably discharged from the Union forces Dec. 22, 1864, and resumed the responsibilities of civil life. On Dec. 26, 1865, he was married to Mary Allison McAllister, the daughter of his former partner, at Bellefonte. He acquired a lucrative practise at the Center County bar. Defeated for governor by Robert E. Pattison in 1882 (by 40,-202 votes) he established the Bellefonte Nail Works in 1883, and three years later was elected governor (by a plurality of 42,651 votes) over Chauncey F. Black for the four years beginning Jan. 18, 1887. As governor he won advances for temperance, industrial education, good roads, and waterways throughout the state. He presided at the Forestry Congress in Atlanta, Dec. 7, 1888, and in 1889 he urged adequate forest reserves in his own state to prevent the recurrence of such distress as was caused by the Johnstown flood in the Conemaugh Valley. Retiring from office in 1891, he resumed his law practise and was also president of the Blubacker Coal Company of Cambria County. On July 1, 1895, his appointment of June 28 as judge of the Pennsylvania superior court became effective. This commission was renewed by election for ten years on Dec. 19, 1895, and again for an equal period Dec. 19, 1905, his work as a jurist ending only with his death.

[A campaign life of Beaver by Frank A. Burr was published at Phila. in 1882. Short biog. sketches are in John B. Linn's *Hist. of Centre and Clinton Counties* (1883), and in the Pennsylvania press at the time of Beaver's death, *e.g.* the *Pub. Ledger*, Feb. 1, 1914. Certain family items are in the *U.S. Census of 1790* (1908). The best records of Beaver's military life during the Civil War are in the *Official Records*; ser. 1, vol. XIV, covers his service in S.C.; vol. XXV, pts. 1 and 2 relate to the Chancellorsville campaign; vol. XXVII, pts. 2 and 3, and vol. XXXVI, pts. 1, 2, and 3 cover the period of his later service in the Army of the Potomac.]

C. H. L—a.

BECK, CARL (Apr. 4, 1856–June 9, 1911), surgeon, son of Wilhelm and Sophia (Hoehler) Beck, was born at Neckargemünd, near Heidelberg, Germany. He was a grandson of Carl Hoehler, a surgeon in the army of Napoleon I. He was educated at the home of his grand-uncle, August Hoehler, a Lutheran minister of Freiburg, and at the universities of Heidelberg, Berlin, and Jena, obtaining the degree of M.D. at the latter university in 1879. In 1881 he was married to Hedwig Loeser, youngest daughter of Heinrich Loeser, president of the supreme court of Saxony. During the same year he came to America and settled in New York where he soon attracted attention as a bold and skilful surgeon. He was appointed professor of surgery at the New York Postgraduate School and was president of St. Mark's Hospital for twenty-five years. He devised a new method for extensive excision of ribs, a method of operating in hypospadias, and a new suture in hare-lip operations. When Roentgen, in 1895, discovered the X-ray, Beck was one of the first to study its application to medicine and surgery and to develop its diagnostic and therapeutic possibilities.

He was a very active man and a prolific writer. Among his medical works may be mentioned: *Fractures, with an Appendix on the Practical Use of the Roentgen Ray* (1899); *Principles of Surgical Pathology* (1905); *Surgical Diseases of the Chest* (1907); *Roentgen Ray Diagnosis and Therapy* (1909). He was also a frequent contributor to American and German medical journals. Being a man of an idealistic turn of mind, he did not lose himself in his professional work, but amid the cares of his professional life found time to devote himself also to literature. In his *Heidelberg und Studententhum* he described the gay and carefree life of his student days, while in his novel *Der Schwabenkonrad* he related the adventures of one of his forebears in the Thirty Years' War. During the last years of his life the heavy work began to tell on him. He died in Pelham, near New York.

[*Boston Med. and Surgic. Jour.*, 1911, CLXIV, 869; *Deutsche Med. Presse* (Berlin), 1911, XV, 112; *Med. Wochenschrift* (München), 1911, LVIII, 1105; *Surgery, Gynecology, and Obstetrics* (Chicago), V, 683 (portr.).]

A. A—n.

BECK, CHARLES (Aug. 19, 1798–Mar. 19, 1866), classical scholar, was born at Heidelberg, in Baden. His father, a merchant, died when Charles was a boy, and his mother married Dr. De Wette, a well-known theologian, Biblical critic and interpreter, who was at that time professor at Heidelberg and later at Berlin. He was a gentle, kind, learned, and wise step-father, and Charles had excellent advantages. As a student in the University of Berlin he devoted himself chiefly to the classics, then he studied theology and was ordained at Heidelberg, July 7, 1822. He obtained the degree of Ph.D. at Tübingen in 1823, and expected to enter the ministry, but was prevented by the political conditions of the time. In 1819 a young German fanatic, named Sand, had murdered the poet and dramatist Kotzebue as a traitor, spy, and mercenary tool of Russia. De Wette wrote a letter to the mother of Sand after her son's execution, and this was construed against him, as implying, in one passage, extenuation of the crime. De Wette was removed from his professorship and went with his family to Basel, where he was given a professorship in the university. Here Beck, after finishing his theological studies, was employed as docent in the university. Meanwhile Dr. Follen, an older friend of Beck, became an object of political suspicion, was compelled to leave Germany, and went to Switzerland, where he taught first in a school at Chur, then at the university of Basel, until, in 1824, the government at Basel yielded to the pressure exerted by the Allied Sovereigns and exiled him. He went to America, and Beck, feeling that there was no hope for the friends of freedom in Germany, or even personal safety in Switzerland, went with him. They sailed from Havre Nov. 5, 1824, and reached New York Dec. 19.

Beck soon became connected with the Round Hill School at Northampton, Mass. (at that time under J. G. Cogswell), and then, in 1830, with two others, opened a school at Philipstown on the Hudson, opposite West Point. In 1832 he was elected professor of Latin at Harvard College. After serving in that capacity for eighteen years with eminent success, he retired in 1850. As professor he was distinguished for his unvarying fidelity to his work, for the conscientious strictness and fulness of his instruction, and for his gentlemanly courtesy and dignity. He became a member of the American Oriental Society in 1843, and a member of the American Academy of Arts and Sciences in 1845. In 1865 he was appointed by the governor and council of Massachusetts a trustee of the Massachusetts School for Idiotic and Feeble-minded Youth. He was for two years a representative of Cambridge in the state legislature. He married in 1827 Louisa A. Henshaw, of Northampton, Mass., who died in 1830; in the following year he married her sister, Mrs. Teresa H. Phillips, who died in 1863. Beck was a man of large views, high public spirit, and consistent moral and religious principle. He had a deep sense of his civic and political duties, and was a loyal and patriotic citizen of his adopted country. As a scholar he was careful, conscientious, and independent, though he lacked something of the constructive imagination which the truly great scholar must possess. He was one of those who introduced into the United States the scholarship of Germany, which made the teaching of the classics more alive and worth while, and he must be included among those whose influence led the ambitious young American scholars of the two following generations to study in German universities.

Beck's published works include, in addition to articles in American and foreign periodicals, a Latin monograph entitled *Statius: Ad Calpurnium Pisonem Poemation auctori vindicavit et adnotatione instruxit Carolus Beck* (1835); an *Introduction to the Metres of Horace* (1835); a *Latin Syntax,* chiefly from the German of Zumpt (1838); a translation of Munk's treatise on metres (1844); editions of Cicero's *Brutus* (1837), Seneca's *Medea* (1834), and Seneca's *Hercules Furens* (1845); and a collation and description of the manuscripts of the *Satyricon* of Petronius Arbiter (1863). This last is perhaps his most important work. A monograph *On the Consolidation of the Worcester and Western Railroads* (1864) shows his interest in the affairs of his own time.

[*The Christian Citizen: A Discourse Occasioned by the Death of Chas. Beck,* delivered Mar. 25, 1866, before the First Parish Church in Cambridge, by Wm. Newell (1866); Andrew P. Peabody, *Harvard Reminiscences* (1888); J. L. Chamberlain, *Harvard Univ.* (1900).]

H.N.F.

BECK, JOHANN HEINRICH (Sept. 12, 1856–May 25, 1924), conductor, composer, violinist, teacher, was the son of Charles and Rebecca Butler Beck of Cleveland. On June 19, 1890, he married Blandina Fellar of Tiffin, Ohio. Beck was born in Cleveland and except for the period of his study abroad, spent his whole life there. He was educated in the Cleveland schools; at the age of twenty-three he went to Leipzig where he studied for three years, specializing in stringed instruments and composition. His teachers in the latter were Richter, Reinecke, and Jadassohn, while his violin study was under Schradieck and Herman. He also studied the history of music with Oscar Paul. He made his début as both violinist and composer in the Gewandhaus, Leipzig, May 17, 1882, appearing in his own "String Quartette in C Minor." In referring to this quartette, the *Leipziger Tageblatt* called attention to the originality of the themes, and the natural and unconstrained flow of the different parts. The first *allegro* and the *scherzo* were particularly praised (Mathews, *A Hundred Years of Music in America,* p. 666). Soon afterward he returned to Cleveland. Shortly after his return he organized the Schubert String Quartette, which did valuable pioneer work in making known the best class of chamber music. Some years later he undertook a long and arduous term as orchestral conductor, spending one season as director of the Detroit Symphony Orchestra (1889–90) and the period from 1901 to 1912 as director of the Cleveland "Pop" Orchestra, the immediate predecessor of the present Cleveland Symphony Orchestra. In these semi-popular programs the fine discrimination and high ideals of the conductor were always in evidence.

Along with this regular work, he conducted the Pilgrim Orchestral Club (1904–10) and the Elyria Orchestra (1905–07). During these busy years of directing and teaching he found time also for composition; but little or none of it has been published. He appeared as guest-conductor frequently in the presentation of his own works, as for instance, the Overtures, "Romeo and Juliet" and "Lara," Boston Symphony Orchestra, Chicago, 1886; "Skirnismal," 1887; "Moorish Serenade," Philadelphia, 1889; "Scherzo in A Major," Thomas Orchestra in Detroit, 1890; "Der Freudekuss," Cleveland Orchestra, 1900, and at the request of the music committee, St. Louis Exposition, 1904; a "Scherzo in F," Thomas Orchestra, Cleveland; also a string sextette, Indianapolis, 1888. He also wrote a tone poem for orchestra, "Aus meinem Leben"; "The Sea at Evening" and "Wie schön bist Du" for voice and orchestra; a cantata, "Deukalion" (Bayard Taylor). There is also a string quartette in D Minor beside songs and violin pieces. The "Scherzo in A," mentioned above, was later taken to Europe by F. X. Arens and played in Vienna, Dresden, Leipzig, and Hamburg. The "Sextette in D Minor" has been played in New York, Boston, Cincinnati, Philadelphia, Detroit, Indianapolis, and other cities.

On the occasion of Beck's sixty-seventh birthday, the Cleveland Public Library paid notable tribute to the respect in which he was held by his fellow townsmen, by placing on exhibition original manuscripts of his compositions, programs from the days when he directed Cleveland's first "Pop" orchestra, and books containing allusions to his reputation as a scholar and composer. Death came suddenly to him as he was returning with some friends from an orchestral concert, and just as he had been remarking the death of his good friend, Victor Herbert, which had occurred that afternoon.

His influence on the musical life about him was always wholesome. As a composer, primarily for the orchestra, he showed that he had not spent his formative years in Leipzig for nothing; he was sincerely fearful of anything savoring of the decadent in his art; yet he was not unduly conservative, and observed with real sympathy the ever increasing richness and power of modern orchestral technique and did not hesitate to take his own share in it.

[The most detailed study of Beck's work is found in Rupert Hughes and Arthur Elson, *Am. Composers* (new revised ed., 1914), pp. 406–11. Other sources of information are the *Times* (Cleveland), and *Topics* (Cleveland), May 31, 1924; *Who's Who in America,* 1924–25; C. Saerchinger, *Who's Who in Music* (1918); *Grove's Dict. of Music and Musicians, Am. Supp.* (1920).]

W. T. U.

BECK, JOHN BRODHEAD (Sept. 18, 1794–Apr. 9, 1851), physician, expert in medical jurisprudence, was born in Schenectady, N. Y. He was the third son of Caleb Beck, who had married Catherine, only daughter of the Rev. Derick Romeyn, a founder of Union College. Dr. Theodric Romeyn Beck [*q.v.*], distinguished in American medical jurisprudence, was an older brother. A younger brother was Lewis Caleb Beck [*q.v.*], naturalist and sometime professor of chemistry at Albany Medical College. Early left fatherless, John went to live at Rhinebeck, N. Y., with his uncle, the Rev. John B. Romeyn, who guided the boy's education. In 1804 Dr. Romeyn took his nephew to New York. Beck entered Columbia College at the age of fifteen, and four years later graduated with highest honors. Immediately thereafter he went abroad with his uncle and patron, applying himself assiduously, while in London, to the study of Hebrew. On his return to America he took up the study of medicine with Dr. David Hosack of New York. In 1817 he graduated at the College of Physicians and Surgeons of New York, having submitted a thesis on Infanticide, which afterward, with additions, was incorporated into the great treatise of his brother, T. Romeyn Beck of Albany, on Medical Jurisprudence, a medical classic in which John Brodhead collaborated. For many years he was looked upon as the standard authority on the medico-legal aspects of infanticide, both in this country and England. In 1820 he made to the New York Board of Health a "Report Concerning the Nature and Origin of Malignant Fever (Yellow Fever) in Middletown, N. Y.," which subsequently was published in the *New York Medical and Physical Journal,* of which (in 1822) he was one of the founders and editors. To that publication he also contributed, among other articles, one entitled, "An Examination of the Medico-legal Question whether in cases of Infanticide the floating of the lungs in water can be depended on as a certain test of the child's having been born alive"—an exhaustive inquiry into the subject which enhanced the author's renown. In 1826 he became professor of materia medica and botany in the College of Physicians and Surgeons of New York, which chair was subsequently exchanged for that of medical jurisprudence. He was married in 1831 to Anne, daughter of Fanning C. Tucker. In 1835 he was appointed one of the physicians of the New York Hospital, in which position he developed marked skill in the clinical investigation of disease. In 1843 he published *Medical Essays;* in 1849 his work on *Infantile Therapeutics* appeared, and in the following year he wrote a *Historical Sketch of the State* *of Medicine in the Colonies,* being his inaugural address as president of the State Medical Society.

Although for many years Beck was an invalid and a martyr to pain, he had untiring energy as practitioner, teacher, and writer. He was an able controversialist, for he possessed a logical mind, with clearness of apprehension and scholarly diction. In the moral sphere of conduct he never sacrificed principle to expediency. He died of malignant disease of the bowel, after long suffering. His chief biographer, Dr. C. R. Gilman, relates that his friend told him, some months before his death, that for five years he had not been free from pain for one single half-hour.

[*N. Y. Jour. of Med.,* Sept. 1851 ; H. A. Kelly and W. L. Burrage, *Am. Medic. Biogs.* (1920) ; S. D. Gross, *Lives of Eminent Am. Physicians and Surgeons of the 19th Cent.* (1861), pp. 605 ff.]

G. A. B.

BECK, LEWIS CALEB (Oct. 4, 1798–Apr. 20, 1853), physician, chemist, son of Caleb and Catherine (Romeyn) Beck, and brother of John Brodhead Beck [*q.v.*] and Theodric Romeyn Beck [*q.v.*], was born at Schenectady, N. Y., a few months after the death of his father. His early education was acquired in the grammar schools of his native city. In 1817 he received the A.B. degree from Union College. He immediately began the study of medicine with Dr. Thomas Dunlop; studied in the College of Physicians and Surgeons, New York, 1816; and was licensed to practise medicine in February 1818. In the autumn of 1819 he entered into active practise in his home city. On the solicitation of his brother Abram, an attorney, he went to St. Louis to establish a practise, but found no opening to his liking. Instead, he conceived the idea of collecting information for a gazetteer. A year later found him back in New York State. The death of his brother again took him to St. Louis but after a brief sojourn he returned to Albany, N. Y., where he began the practise of medicine. These journeys, mostly on horseback, proved of great value to the young observer. During his travels he made notes on botany, geology, mineralogy, climate, and the habits of the people; these, having already served him for articles in St. Louis and Albany newspapers, 1820–21, formed the basis of the *Gazetteer of the States of Illinois and Missouri* (1823), completed in 1822. The same year he published some observations on milk sickness, a serious disease, the cause of which is still unknown ("Facts Relative to a Disease, generally known by the name of Sick Stomach, or Milk Sickness," in the *New York Medical and Physical Journal,* 1822).

Notwithstanding the fact that he engaged in the practise of his profession early in life and

gained eminence therein, Beck's energies were directed mainly along educational and investigational lines. He began his public life in 1824 as teacher of botany in Berkshire Medical Institution and during the same year became junior professor of botany, mineralogy, and zoölogy in Rensselaer Polytechnic Institute in Troy, N. Y. On Oct. 17, 1825, he was married to Hannah Maria, daughter of Maj. Israel Smith. In 1826 he accepted the chair of botany and chemistry in the Vermont Academy of Medicine. Four years later he was professor of chemistry and natural history in Rutgers. He was professor in New York University in 1836 and accepted the professorship of chemistry and pharmacy in the Albany Medical College in 1840. He held his Albany and Rutgers positions simultaneously for many years. His lectures were continued at Albany up to the time of his death. He made numerous contributions to medicine, chemistry, botany, mineralogy, and the purity of foods and drugs. In 1831 there appeared his *Manual of Chemistry Containing a Condensed View of the Present State of the Science.* Two years later the *Botany of the Northern and Middle States* was published. His manual, *Adulterations of Various Substances Used in Medicine and the Arts, with the Means of Detecting Them* was made available in 1846. A committee of the New York state legislature selected him to make an investigation of the purity, character, and manufacture of potash. The results were published as a state document in 1836. The same year the New York state officials decided to make a geological survey. Beck was employed as mineralogist, and published a *Mineralogy of New York* in 1842. The United States Congress in 1848 made the first appropriation for chemical examinations of foodstuffs. Beck was selected for the task and the results of his investigations, dealing primarily with breadstuffs, were published in Appendix I to the "Report of the Commissioner of Patents for the Year 1848" (*House Executive Document 59,* 30 Cong., 2 Sess.) and in Part II of the "Report of the Commissioner of Patents for the Year 1849" (*House Executive Document 20,* and *Senate Executive Document 15,* 31 Cong., 1 Sess.).

[J. V. P. Quackenbush, sketch of Beck in *Trans. N. Y. Medic. Soc.,* 1854, p. 63 ; A. March, "Lewis C. Beck," in S. D. Gross, *Lives of Eminent Am. Physicians and Surgeons of the 19th Century* (1861) ; sketch by Mrs. C. E. Van Cortlandt in *Annals Medic. Soc., County of Albany* (1864) ; L. F. Kebler, "A Pioneer in Pure Foods and Drugs : Lewis C. Beck," in *Industrial and Engineering Chemistry,* Sept. 1, 1924.]

L. F. K.

BECK, THEODRIC ROMEYN (Aug. 11, 1791–Nov. 19, 1855), physician, was the eldest of five brothers, three of whom, John Brodhead Beck [*q.v.*], Lewis C. Beck [*q.v.*], and himself, attained distinction in medicine. Of mixed English and Dutch descent, he was born in Schenectady, N. Y. His father, Caleb Beck, a lawyer, dying while Theodric was quite young, his early training fell to his mother, Catherine Theresa Romeyn, a well-educated, well-balanced woman. She instilled into her sons the importance of system. Her father, the Rev. Derick Romeyn, a professor of theology in the Dutch Reformed Church and a founder of Union College, doubtless counseled her. Beck received his formal education in the Schenectady Grammar School and in Union College, from which he graduated at sixteen. Soon thereafter he entered on the study of medicine under Doctors Low and McClelland of Albany, the former a man of talent, a classical scholar and a lover of books, the latter a practical Scot. A year later Beck moved to New York City and studied at the College of Physicians and Surgeons under David Hosack's preceptorship. He graduated in 1811, aged twenty. In the same year he began practise in Albany and continued until 1817. While well fitted for the work, he probably did not enjoy the arduous life of a general practitioner. His strength was unequal to the task, and the inevitable scenes of suffering wore on him. No doubt, too, his literary trend was a factor in his decision to abandon practise. An unsolicited appointment as principal of the Albany Academy came to him in 1817. He held this position until 1853. Under his administration the Academy attained and held high rank. In 1815 he had been appointed professor of the institutes of medicine and lecturer on medical jurisprudence in the Western College of Physicians and Surgeons in Fairfield, Herkimer County, N. Y. The title of his chair was changed in 1826 to professor of medical jurisprudence and in 1836 to professor of materia medica. In 1840 the school was given up. From 1840 to 1843 Beck was professor of materia medica in the Albany Medical College. He was president of the State Medical Society for three successive terms, was secretary of the New York State Board of Regents from 1841 almost to the time of his death, and had much to do with the foundation and policy of the New York State Library and the State Cabinet of Natural History. On the establishment of the State Lunatic Asylum at Utica in 1842, he was made a member of the board of managers, and was president of the board in 1854. His interest in this work was very great, and, on the death of the first superintendent, Amariah Brigham, he undertook the editorship of the *American Journal of Insanity*

which he continued for four years. The philanthropic side of his character is shown by his interest in the deaf and dumb. He was a friend of Gallaudet and collected statistics of the deaf and dumb in New York State to call attention to their needs. He was also interested in all aspects of natural science. In 1813, as a counselor of the Society for the Promotion of Useful Arts, he delivered an address urging a survey and development of the mineral resources of the United States. His biographer, Frank Hamilton, says: "To that elaborate and timely paper, the American manufacturer is, to-day, in no small degree indebted for his wealth and prosperity" (*Lives of Eminent American Physicians and Surgeons of the Nineteenth Century,* edited by S. D. Gross, 1861, pp. 776–95). Beck's fame as a writer mainly rests, however, upon his *Elements of Medical Jurisprudence*. The first edition was published in 1823, after ten years' preparation; numerous American and foreign editions followed. It was the first authoritative book on medical jurisprudence published in the United States and was extensive in scope, well planned, clearly and logically written.

Beck always had excellent health except for a brief period in his early professional career when he became apprehensive and perhaps a trifle neurasthenic. His portrait shows regular, strongly marked features, a broad brow, rather widely set eyes with somewhat puffy lower lids, heavy eyebrows, a large Roman nose, a long upper lip, a firm, well-shaped mouth, and a good chin with a slight median cleft. He had a mane of dark, shaggy hair in artistic confusion. He was married, in 1814 at Caldwell, Warren County, N. Y., to Harriet, the daughter of James Caldwell. She died in 1823, at the age of thirty-one, leaving two daughters.

[E. H. Van Deusen, *Am. Jour. of Insanity,* 1855, XII, 105; *N. Y. Jour. of Medicine,* Jan. 1856, p. 2; *Albany Evening Jour.,* Nov. 19, 1855; *Albany Evening Atlas,* Nov. 19, 20, 1855.]

G. B.

BECKER, GEORGE FERDINAND (Jan. 5, 1847–Apr. 20, 1919), geologist, mathematician, and physicist, was born in New York City. His father was Alexander Christian Becker of a Danish family settled in Archangel, Russia, where Samuel Becker, the head of the house, held for a time the office of Danish consul. He was a man of wealth and given to lavish entertainment, but lost his property through his absorption in science, particularly chemistry. Because of financial troubles Alexander Becker emigrated, and settled in New York. His first venture was in mercantile life. Finding this distasteful, he studied medicine and entered upon the practise of his profession, but died when his son George was only two years of age. The latter's mother was Sarah Cary Tuckerman, a daughter of the Rev. Joseph Tuckerman [*q.v.*] known in Boston as a philanthropist and the first "Minister at Large." He was a graduate of Harvard and an overseer and intimate friend of William Channing, Joseph Story, and other prominent men of his day. With a view to the education of the two children, Alexander Rudolph and George F., it was natural therefore that the family should move to Cambridge where the mother's circle of friends and acquaintances included such men as Benjamin Gould, Louis Agassiz, Benjamin Pierce, Jeffries Wyman, Asa Gray, H. W. Longfellow, and J. R. Lowell. It was a stimulating atmosphere for a young, studious, and growing boy, and one by which George profited, particularly through the friendly interest of Agassiz, Pierce, and Wyman. There is abundant evidence of a strong attachment between mother and son, and it is told that when he was four years old he quietly listened the evening through while she read the history of the Commonwealth of Massachusetts. After he had been put to bed and sleep had come to him, his lonely mother, overcome with memories, kneeled at his bedside and as he turned to her, said, "O my child, whom do you love?" and the little fellow sleepily responded, "Any one who will do good to the Commonwealth of Massachusetts."

Becker showed early a leaning toward the natural sciences. Games and sports interested him but little. He preferred roaming the fields and woods, collecting and studying plant and animal life, and came to know all the New England birds and many of the batrachians and other reptilia. In this work he received direct encouragement from men like Wyman and Pierce. He was fitted for college in Latin and Greek under the tutelage of Prof. William B. Atkinson and entered Harvard in 1864. He wrote that he had no difficulty in keeping up with his class and had plenty of leisure for his field studies. Along toward the middle of his college course his interest in natural history became secondary to that in mathematics and chemistry. Immediately after graduation, he went to Germany where he received the degree of Ph.D. (*summa cum laude*) from the University of Heidelberg in 1869. At the outbreak of the Franco-Prussian War he obtained a position on the Crown Prince's staff as a reporter for the *New York Herald.* He was at the battle of Werth, Aug. 6, 1870, and was under fire at Strasbourg, but soon after the fall of that city on Sept. 28, 1870, he went to Berlin to resume his studies. He was graduated with high honors

from the Royal Academy of Mines in 1871. Determination to master certain of the problems in the metallurgy of iron and steel caused him to undertake, while in Germany, the somewhat unusual task of a puddler in the Royal Iron Works. His success was such as to win him a certificate as practical worker. Returning to America, he was employed during 1872–73 as a construction engineer in steel works at Joliet, Ill., and while here he is stated to have invented, but not to have patented, an improved puddling process which was in use in both Joliet and Youngstown for many years. Shortly after this, he went to California, partly it is stated on account of his health, though it seems probable that the field was the most promising to one of his profession. Here he remained during 1874–79 as lecturer and instructor in mining and metallurgy in the state university at Berkeley. While here he came under the influence of Clarence King who was then engaged with the 40th Parallel survey. In 1879, when King became director of the consolidated geological surveys, Becker was among the first to receive an appointment, and it was here that his career as a geologist and physicist may well be said to have begun.

Soon after his appointment, Becker made a reconnaissance survey of the San Francisco, Utah, Eureka, Nev., and Bodin, Cal., mining districts, with a view of planning future work rather than of making exhaustive studies in any single district. Owing to a change in plans by the director this work was never carried out in detail. Early in 1880 Becker was instructed by the director of the Survey to undertake, in addition to his Survey duties, those of a special agent of the 10th Census and to assist in the compilation of statistics and technical information relative to the precious-metal industries of the country. The work was carried on in collaboration with S. F. Emmons [*q.v.*], and the results were published in Volume XIII of the Census Reports, entitled *Statistics and Technology of the Precious Metals* (1885). It contained chapters on the geology of the western states and territories, statistics of production, and information on most of the important features of hydraulic mining. In March of 1880, Becker had been also instructed on the part of the Survey to make a reëxamination of the Comstock Lode. This work, which was carried on at the same time with the Census investigation, was completed in two years, the report, *Geology of the Comstock Lode and the Washoe District,* forming Monograph III (1882) of the Survey series. While many of the ideas which Becker put forward in this report have been the subject of controversy, it may safely be said to mark a new era in geological investigations in America. No previous investigations, by any survey, had been undertaken on so broad a basis. No known and available means of discovery were left untried. The appearance of this monograph placed Becker in the front rank among American geological investigators.

His next field of work comprised, under the administration of J. W. Powell, a study of the quicksilver deposits of the Pacific Coast. This proved a somewhat prolonged investigation and for its satisfactory completion necessitated a study of deposits of similar nature in Italy and Spain. Though under government authority he was obliged to carry on this portion of the work at his own expense. The results of these studies appeared in 1888, as Monograph XIII of the Survey series, under the caption, *Geology of the Quicksilver Deposits of the Pacific Slope*. In 1896, under the auspices of an English company and at the instance of John Hays Hammond, he visited the Witwatersrand of South Africa, for the purpose of studying the gold fields. It was while employed in this work that he became conversant in some detail with matters relating to the Jameson raid and the Boer War, and prepared an article on "The Witwatersrand and the Revolt of the Uitlanders," published in the *National Geographic Magazine,* November 1896. In this he set forth in a dispassionate and impartial way the prevailing conditions as they appeared to an outsider. In accordance with an arrangement made with the War Department, Becker, under orders of July 8, 1898, visited the Philippines for the purpose of investigating and reporting on the mineral resources of these islands. He here became involved in a number of military reconnaissances and engagements, and even exposure to gun fire; and was twice cited for bravery. Later he was one of a committee of five called by President Roosevelt to report upon a plan for a scientific survey of the islands. He was also a member of the committee of the National Academy of Sciences appointed in 1915 by President Wilson to report upon the possibility of controlling the slides in the Panama Canal, which then seriously threatened to interfere with its usefulness, but he was prevented by ill health from visiting the Canal in person.

The most original, outstanding, and valuable of Becker's work was not along the lines of descriptive geology. His interests lay largely in the more abstruse chemico-physical problems concerning which he had almost from the start taken advanced grounds, not merely in relation to the problems to be solved, but as well in re-

gard to the methods of their solution. Along these lines he was a pioneer and it is not too much to claim that the present Carnegie Geophysical Laboratory is the outgrowth of his work more than of that of any other one man. With all his close attention to detail in matters of science, he was by no means oblivious of his duties as a citizen. Convinced of the soundness of his own views on any subject, he did not hesitate to make them known wherever he felt it necessary or advisable. A striking feature of his career was his versatility which he seems to have cultivated rather than restrained. This is illustrated in a lecture prepared by him in 1904 entitled: *How Small an Army We Need,* which was favorably reviewed even by military authorities. He enjoyed a wide range of acquaintances both among the scientific fraternity in America and abroad and in what is commonly spoken of as "society," particularly that of the higher circles of political life. Around his hospitable table there gathered members not only of the congressional delegations but of the cabinet, Supreme Court, and foreign legations as well. He was an original fellow of the Geological Society of America and was president of the same in 1914. He was a member of the National Academy of Sciences, the Washington Academy of Sciences, the Geological Society of Washington, the American Institute of Mining Engineers, and an honorary member of the Geological Society of South Africa. He was married first to Sarah M. Barnes from whom he was legally separated in 1879, and on June 17 of the same year to Alice Theodora Watson who died early in the year following; then on Feb. 11, 1902, he was married to Florence Serpell Deakins. During the later years of his life, he suffered severely from asthma and its complications, but retained active interest in his work until the last. He died at his home in Washington at the age of seventy-two years.

[Geo. P. Merrill, "Biog. Memoir of Geo. Ferdinand Becker," *Memoirs Nat. Acad. Sci.,* XXI, to which is appended a full bibliography of Becker's publications; *Harvard College Class of 1868, Fortieth Anniversary, Secretary's Report No. 8, 1868–1908*.]
G. P. M.

BECKNELL, WILLIAM (*c.* 1790–*c.* 1832), [handwritten: *b–Apr 30, 1865*] explorer and trader, ~~was possibly a native of Kentucky but was early domiciled in Missouri.~~ His claim to recognition rests on his pioneer achievements in the Santa Fé trade. Until the arrival of Pike's expedition, which entered the country without authorization, the Spanish government of New Mexico seems not to have been hostile toward the occasional Americans who settled within its jurisdiction. After 1810, however, a number of Americans ventured into New Mexico, many of whom were either imprisoned or deported. The overthrow of Spanish power in 1821 seemed again to open up possibilities for better relations, and a number of expeditions, including one under Becknell, left immediately. Setting out with a pack outfit, like the others he followed the old route to the upper waters of the Arkansas and thence south to Taos and Santa Fé where he sold at a distinct profit the supply of goods he had transported from the states. The entire expedition consumed only five months. Encouraged by his first success, Becknell set out again in 1822, this time with wagons and a larger company who apparently had answered his alluring advertisement in the *Missouri Intelligencer* for men "to go westward for the purpose of trading for horses and mules and catching wild animals of every description." It is this expedition that gives Becknell his fame as the founder of the Santa Fé trail, for instead of crossing from the Missouri to the Arkansas and following the latter to its upper waters, he left the Arkansas near Dodge City, crossed to the Cimarron which, according to Gregg, he reached after great suffering from heat and thirst, followed up the South Fork and over the divide to the forks of the Canadian and across the mountain pass to San Miguel. Thus was traced the famous Santa Fé trail soon to be the accepted route for the substantial commerce of the prairies. Caravan followed caravan in the next decade, and hundreds of thousands of dollars worth of Yankee merchandise was conveyed over this famous trail and profitably disposed of in Santa Fé and the other settlements of the southwest. Becknell made at least one more journey to New Mexico whence he proceeded on a trapping expedition to Green River (Colorado) in 1824. ~~His later life is quite obscured though it is possible that he died in 1832.~~

[The best account of Becknell's historic expedition to Santa Fé is his jour. of the expedition published in the *Missouri Intelligencer*, Apr. 22, 1823, and reprinted in *Mo. Hist. Soc. Colls.*, July 1906. He published an account of his 1824 trip in the same jour., June 25, 1825. See also Letter of Alphonso Wetmore to John Scott, Aug. 19, 1824, in *House Doc. No. 79*, 18 Cong., 2 Sess., and *The Jour. of Jacob Fowler* (1898), ed. by Elliott Coues, pp. 167–68. The principal secondary materials are Josiah Gregg, *Commerce of the Prairies* (1884), and Hiram M. Chittenden, *The Am. Fur Trade of the Far West* (1902).]

H. C. D.

BECKWITH, JAMES CARROLL (Sept. 23, 1852–Oct. 24, 1917), painter, was the son of Charles and Martha (Owen) Beckwith, who had moved from the Eastern States to Hannibal, Mo., where James Carroll was born. His father later became a prominent wholesale grocer in Chicago, and James's boyhood was spent in that city. His tendencies toward art manifested themselves early

and were encouraged by his mother who possessed much personal taste and charm. He began his studies at the Chicago Academy of Design in 1868 under Walter Shirlaw, but these were cut short by the great Chicago fire of 1871. This event altered the family fortunes. His father, who up to this time had frowned upon an artistic career, now gave his consent, and Beckwith went to New York. Entering the classes of the National Academy of Design under Prof. L. E. Wilmarth, he worked there for two years. In October 1873 he sailed for Paris. Here he entered the National School of Fine Arts, studying in its various classes and especially in the *Cours Yvon*. Adolphe Yvon had been a favorite artist under the Second Empire, having painted the Prince Imperial's and other portraits, and especially battle scenes from the Crimean and Italian campaigns, to be seen at Versailles. As a master of drawing he was unrivaled. At this time in the Paris art world also appeared the painter Carolus Duran (whose real name was Charles Durand), who opened a studio where a chosen group of the younger men sought his instruction. Among them were John Singer Sargent and Beckwith, who became fast friends. Taking a studio at 73 rue Notre Dame des Champs, they lived and worked together during the four succeeding years. Carolus Duran associated them with himself in the decoration of a ceiling at the Luxembourg Palace, of which the subject was "The Glory of Marie de Medicis," introducing their portraits, with his own, in the work. Beckwith exhibited at the Salon of 1877 the "Head of an Old Man," and to the Paris Universal Exhibition of 1878 sent "The Falconer," afterward exhibited in America.

Returning to Chicago in 1878, he set up his easel in that city, so as to be near his family, and began to paint portraits. After the intense art life of Paris, Chicago had a most depressing effect on the enthusiastic young painter and as he wrote in 1882, "I determined to come on to New York, sink or swim, survive or perish, rather than rot in the miserable mediocrity of a Western Studio" (letter to the writer). He came to New York in 1879, and, his uncle Mr. Sherwood having erected the Sherwood Studios at the corner of Sixth Ave. and West Fifty-seventh St., he took a studio and worked there during the thirty succeeding years. At this time, a number of the younger artists had returned from foreign schools, and, meeting with a rather cool welcome from the conservative elements of the old Academy of Design, formed the Society of American Artists, a rallying point for the advanced elements. Beckwith was one of its most active members. A corresponding means of education, the Art Student's League of New York, was organized, the most efficient of the younger men becoming instructors. Beckwith at first had charge of the antique classes and later of the life classes. The effect of his teaching was evidenced in the success of many who worked there under his instruction during the last two decades of the century. It gave nothing to be unlearned, whether students proceeded to European art centers or remained to develop their art in this country. At the same time Beckwith became one of New York's most efficient and popular portrait painters. At the National Academy Exhibition of 1879, he had shown a portrait of Mrs. R. H. Mc-Curdy which was much remarked, as were succeeding contributions to the Academy and to the Society of American Artists' Exhibitions. Several summers were spent in Europe studying and making some remarkable copies of Velasquez, Van Dyck, Rubens, and the Venetians. Among prominent New Yorkers whom he painted was LeGrand B. Canon, who had been useful in financial crises of the Government during the Civil War (1861–65). This portrait is now at the Century Association and a replica is at the Union League Club. A series of the captains of Company K, 7th Regiment, included the portrait of Capt. Joseph Lentilhon, in service uniform, with drawn sword passed under his folded left arm. That of John Murray Mitchell in crimson tunic and white gauntlet was painted for the New York Fencing Club, of which Beckwith was president for some time. Another is that of William Walton, the artist and writer, exhibited in New York, Paris, and other cities and now at the Century Association. Other sitters were Theodore Roosevelt, Mark Twain, Thomas P. Janvier, Paul du Chaillu the African explorer, and William M. Chase the painter. In "Mr. Isaacson," the portrait of a man of many languages who had been translator for the Hirsch Fund, the subject stands smiling benignly with hands clasped in front, full of Hebrew good humor. Beckwith used the same model in "The Diamond Broker." His portraits of women showed a delicate perception and sympathetic appreciation of feminine beauty and character, whether in the flush of youth or in the gentler phases of later years. He was married on June 1, 1887, to Bertha Hall, daughter of a prominent New York merchant, and her full-length portrait was shown in the Paris Exposition of 1900. Another of Luisita Leland, exhibited at Knoedler's in 1909, is of the utmost brilliance in light, color, and refined design. Pictorial quality was united to careful likeness in "The Authoress." Genre was united

to portraiture in "A Baptism at Onteora." In the mess hall at West Point is "1806," an old soldier with quizzical expression, wearing the high shako and close-buttoned tunic of the date indicated. Beckwith's skill in decorative design was exemplified in a number of paintings and pastels for which the draped and undraped figure furnished motives. Such was "La Cigale" from La Fontaine's fable, a blonde girlish type shivering under the first snowflakes. "The Awakening," "Danse Antique," and "The Nautilus" gave opportunities for expressing an almost Greek sense of beauty. At the Chicago Exhibition of 1893, Beckwith decorated one of the domes of the Liberal Arts Building, typifying Electricity as a sprightly genius at the apex, throwing forked flashes to female figures in the pendentives, representing the Dynamo, the Arc-light, the Telegraph, and the Telephone. The wrecker's axe destroyed the originals with other similar works after the Exhibition, though the preparatory studies may remain. At the village of Onteora in the Catskills, where Beckwith had a summer home and studio, he painted "The Blacksmith," purchased for the National Gallery in Washington.

In all that could advance the interests of art and artists in New York and throughout the country, Beckwith's activity was unbounded. He was among the earliest promoters of the Art Guild of New York and president of the Free Art League, as a result of whose efforts examples of original works from abroad now come and go without restraint for the better education of artists and public. In the Artist's Fund Society of New York, he worked for the benefit of needy artists and their families, leaving a generous bequest for this purpose. He was an active member of the Century Association of New York, and of the National Institute of Arts and Letters. He was elected a National Academician in 1894, and was a member of the American Water Color Society and of a number of other art clubs throughout the country. In 1910, he and his wife went to Europe, visiting France, Belgium, and Italy, and bringing back a series of fresh figure and landscape subjects. Historic monuments and the Châteaux fountains and statues, especially of Versailles, were portrayed with a freshness which vividly recalled their ancient splendors. By taste, education, and practise Beckwith believed in precise design and had no sympathy with careless, bizarre, or slovenly work that invoked originality as its excuse. As a member of the New York Metropolitan Museum of Art and as chairman of the Ways and Means Committee of the National Academy of Design, he sought to increase their educational usefulness. After 1911 he lived and had his studio at the Hotel Schuyler, 59 West Forty-fifth St., New York. Slight in figure, he was quick and elegant in his movements. His features were finely modeled, with a broad brow and ample coronal development. Deep-set gray eyes looked out with penetrating kindliness. A small mustache and a touch of pointed beard aided a certain resemblance to De Champaigne's portrait of Richelieu, while Van Dyck's portrait of Van der Gheest, sometimes called Gevartius, in the National Gallery at London, looks strangely like him. His diction was precise, clear, and musically resonant; with the distinction of manner characteristic of a seventeenth-century cavalier, he was more genially occupied with the activities and life of his own day. At the time of his association with John Sargent under Carolus Duran, there was little room for choice between the brilliancy of their studies. As Samuel Isham remarks (*History of American Painting*, 1905, p. 526), "Beckwith has kept the quality of his master's handling better than almost any other of his pupils. It does not change his personality; it does not make him a copyist, but it enables him to say what he has to say easily and rather sumptuously with heavy impasto, rich shadows and broad strong handling." Sargent remained in Europe amid more helpful conditions to achieve unequaled success as a portraitist. Beckwith returned to America and sacrificed a large part of his time and talent for its art education and general advancement. The honors he received were scarcely commensurate with his merits or the benefits he bestowed: awards at the Paris Salon, and at the Paris Expositions of 1889 and 1900, medals at the Atlanta and St. Louis Expositions, and a gold medal at Charleston in 1902. He exhibited in the Royal Academy at London in 1892, at the Chicago World's Fair, and at other American and European Expositions. He worked unceasingly, though his health was never robust. Less than three months before he died, he published a letter, "Right Art Training," in the *New York Times* (Aug. 5, 1917), deploring the extravagancies encouraged in various schools. These were its closing words: "Do not imagine that there is any short road to mastery of this most difficult profession, but look at the methods and example of our ally France, from whom the American people are just beginning to realize how much they can learn." He died from a sudden heart attack in New York, Oct. 24, 1917, and his funeral at St. Thomas's Church was attended by the leaders in New York's art, literary, and social life, with which he had so actively associated for nearly forty years. "A Romance in the Life of Van Dyck," by Carroll and Bertha Beckwith, was published in *Scribner's Magazine*, July 1, 1918.

[*Who's Who in America*, 1916–17; "The Portraits of Carroll Beckwith" by Robt. J. Wickenden, *Scribner's Mag.*, Apr. 1910; obituaries in the *N. Y. Times*, Oct. 25 and Oct. 29, 1917.]

R. J. W.

BECKWOURTH, JAMES P. (Apr. 26, 1798–*c.* 1867), hunter, squaw-man, raconteur, was born in Virginia, the son of a mulatto mother and a white father, and closely resembled an Indian in figure and physique. Having removed with his father to St. Louis, he joined the fur-trading expedition organized by William H. Ashley and Andrew Henry in 1823, apparently as a groom. He appears to have performed his duties with sufficient faithfulness to have warranted Ashley in taking him along as a sort of body-servant and horse-wrangler on his expedition to the Rocky Mountains in the winter of 1824–25. He continued in the employ of Ashley's successors, married a series of Blackfoot, Snake, and Crow maidens, finally abandoning the whites for about six years to live among the Crows upon whom, if we are to believe his account, he made as great an impression for strength and skill as he had upon the whites. By 1833 he had abandoned his Indian associates and resumed civilized life. In 1844 he was in California where he joined Kearny's force, but following the Mexican War returned to California. Removing to Missouri he joined the stampede to Colorado in 1859, took part in the Cheyenne War of 1864, and settled near Denver, where he died about 1867. There is little to differentiate Beckwourth's exploits from those of a number of his contemporaries save that he was fortunate in finding a biographical editor, T. D. Bonner, whose *Life and Adventures of James P. Beckwourth, Mountaineer, Scout, and Pioneer and Chief of the Crow Nation of Indians*, "written from his own dictation," appeared in 1856. In 1892, Charles G. Leland ("Hans Breitmann") reëdited the *Life* with a brief introduction. The inflated style and high-sounding phrases of the biography, whether they be Beckwourth's own words or Bonner's, reflect the bombast and egotism of the narrator.

[Ashley's narrative of his expedition (H. C. Dale, *Ashley-Smith Explorations*, 1918) furnishes practically the only test by which to gauge the truth of any considerable portion of Beckwourth's self-glorifying autobiography. For the main incidents in which he participated Beckwourth is shown to be, aside from his patent egotism, singularly reliable. His last years are covered in L. R. Hafen, "The Last Years of Jas. P. Beckwourth" in the *Colo. Mag.*, Aug. 1928.]

H. C. D.

BEDFORD, GUNNING (Apr. 7, 1742–September 1797), Revolutionary soldier and politician, has been constantly confused by historians with his namesake and cousin, the delegate to the Federal Convention, who styled himself Gunning Bedford, Jr. [q.v.]. The confusion is heightened by the fact that their careers were almost precisely contemporary and that both held high office in Delaware and in the nation. The subject of this article is often alluded to as Col. Bedford, or Gov. Bedford; in the records he is sometimes mentioned as Gunning Bedford, Sr. The family came from New Jersey or Pennsylvania and settled in New Castle Hundred, Del. Gunning's father, William Bedford, was a farmer. He himself first appears in history as a major in the Revolutionary War. He was deputy quartermaster-general, lieutenant-colonel of a Delaware regiment Jan. 19, 1776, and muster-master-general June 18, 1776. His regiment took part in the battle of Long Island, but he was detained that day in New York, serving on a court martial. Soon after, he fought at the battle of White Plains and was wounded. The list of political offices which he held is an extended one. He became a prothonotary in 1779; was a representative in the Delaware legislature 1784–86, and a member of the state Senate 1788; he was elected to the privy council in 1783 and 1790. In 1788 he was appointed register of wills, and in the following year a justice of the peace. Meanwhile he was a delegate to the Continental Congress 1783–85, and to the state convention which met in 1787 to ratify the Federal Constitution. As presidential elector he voted for Washington in the first election. The culmination of his political career was his term as governor of the state, an office which he held from January 1796 until his death. His wife, Mary, was the sister of the Delaware statesman George Read, a signer of the Declaration of Independence.

[H. C. Conrad, *Papers of the Del. Hist. Soc.*, vol. III, no. 26 (1900); and the same writer in his *Hist. of Del.* (1908).]

E. K. A.

BEDFORD, GUNNING (1747–Mar. 30, 1812),

Revolutionary statesman, came from a family that settled originally in Jamestown, Va. His parents were Gunning and Susannah (Jacquett) Bedford. He was born in Philadelphia, and graduated at Princeton in 1771 in the class with James Madison. He styled himself Gunning Bedford, Jr., and is frequently confused with his cousin Gov. Gunning Bedford (called also Col. Gunning Bedford in military allusions). In Philadelphia he studied law with Joseph Read, and was admitted to the bar. At about this time he was married to Jane Ballareau Parker. He soon settled in Dover, Del., removing thence to Wilmington,

Del., and—much later—to a farm called "Lombardy" on the Brandywine. That he served in the war as aide to Washington cannot be confirmed in the records, though it is so stated by his daughter in her will. His active life was closely associated with the history of his adopted state. He was a member of the legislature, of the state council, delegate to the Continental Congress, 1785–86, to the Annapolis Convention, 1786, to the Federal Convention, 1787, and to the Delaware Convention which ratified the United States Constitution in December of that year. During part of this period he was attorney-general of the state, having been appointed in 1784, and serving until 1789. He played a considerable part in the Federal Convention. Delaware, in commissioning its delegates, restrained them from assenting to any change in the "rule of suffrage"—that is, one vote for each state—and Bedford was a champion of the small states in general and of Delaware in particular. He was a fluent speaker, debated often and with emphasis, and was "impetuous" and "irrepressible." At first he supported the project of amending the Articles. Later, he favored equal representation of the states, and removal of the president on request of the state legislatures; he favored a short term of three years for the president, who was to be reëligible only after nine years. He opposed a strong central government and opposed every check upon the legislative branch. When the debates reached their most dangerous point, he made the "most intemperate speech uttered in the Convention"; he "challenged the large States to do their worst," and hinted that the small states might seek foreign alliances. He was a member of the grand committee to consider representation. On July 17, he moved to confer on Congress the power "to legislate in all cases for the general interests of the Union, and also in those in which the States are severally incompetent . . ." (*Madison Papers*, II). After this he apparently took little part in the Convention. In his last year as attorney-general, the draft of the new judiciary bill was sent to him for criticism. Washington appointed him a judge for the Delaware district in 1789, and he held this office until his death. He was a presidential elector in 1789 and in 1793, and president of the trustees of Wilmington Academy and of the college which developed from the Academy. Personally he has been described as tall and stout, handsome, and sociable.

[Henry C. Conrad, in *Papers of Del. Hist. Soc.*, vol. III, no. 26 (1900); John P. Nields, *Paper, Nov. 18, 1897, on presentation of a portr. of Bedford to the U. S. Courts at Wilmington*; *Records of the Federal Convention*, ed. by M. Farrand (1911); W. T. Read, *Life and Correspondence of Geo. Read* (1870).]

E. K. A.

BEDINGER, GEORGE MICHAEL (Dec. 10, 1756–Dec. 8, 1843), soldier, pioneer, congressman, was born in York County, Pa., the third child of Henry and Magdalene (von Schlegel) Bedinger, but soon afterward was taken to Shepherdstown, Va. (now West Va.). His grandfather, Adam Büdinger, was a German emigrant from Alsace. As a boy George attracted attention as a ballad singer, and on the outbreak of the Revolution joined Washington's command at Cambridge. He reënlisted at various times for short terms until the spring of 1779, when he made a trip to Boonesborough, Ky. At this time the Kentucky settlements were hard-pressed by the Indians from the north of the Ohio. Col. John Bowman organized an expedition against the Indian villages around Chillicothe and selected Bedinger as his adjutant and quartermaster, who rendered valuable aid. On their retreat they were followed by the Indians and attacked in the most distressing circumstances. Bedinger was one of the leaders in a counter charge by a cavalry detachment that prevented any further pursuit. After seven months in Kentucky Bedinger returned to eastern Virginia and in 1780 went with a wagon train to South Carolina. The next year he rejoined Washington's army and was present at the siege of Yorktown, leaving, however, before Cornwallis surrendered. About the time hostilities with England ended he formed a partnership in the milling business with James Rumsey [q.v.]. In 1784 he journeyed down the Ohio again to Louisville. For the next few years he visited back and forth a number of times between Shepherdstown and the Kentucky country. His love of adventure and excitement led him to join the St. Clair expedition against the Indians in 1791. Although taking no part in the contentions and turmoils preceding Kentucky's admission into the Union, he immediately thereafter entered politics and was honored with both state and national offices. In 1792 and 1794 he represented Bourbon County in the legislature and from 1803 to 1807 served in the lower house of Congress. One of the earliest and most bitter opponents of slavery in Kentucky, he tried while a congressman to circumscribe the institution as much as possible. He also opposed paying the claims arising out of the Georgia Yazoo Fund. Bedinger was married twice: first to Nancy Keene, who died at the birth of her first child in 1787, and then to Henrietta Clay, who bore him nine children. One son, Henry, became a congressman from Virginia and later served as minister to Denmark. Bedinger died on his farm near Blue Licks and was buried in the family cemetery on the banks of the Licking River.

[The Bedinger MSS., consisting mostly of reminiscences of contemporaries concerning him, are in the Draper Collection, in the Wis. His. Soc. Lib. Other sources are, Mrs. Danske, *Geo. Michael Bedinger* (1909); Lewis and Richard H. Collins, *Hist. of Ky.* (1882); *Louisville Weekly Jour.*, Jan. 19, 1844; W. H. Perrin, et al., *Kentucky: a Hist. of the State* (1886), pp. 167 ff.; L. F. Bittinger, *Bittinger and Bedinger Families: Descendants of Adam Büdinger* (1904).]
E. M. C.

BEE, BARNARD ELLIOTT (February or March 1824–July 22, 1861), Confederate soldier, was born at Charleston, S. C., the son of Barnard E. Bee, who in 1835 removed to Texas, and later became secretary of state of the short-lived Republic. Although the father had thus expatriated himself, the son was appointed a cadet "at large" at West Point, entered in 1841, and graduated in 1845. He was commissioned in the 3rd Infantry and at once returned to his adopted state with Gen. Taylor's army of occupation. He served with this army in the early part of the Mexican War, being engaged in the battles of Palo Alto and Resaca de la Palma. After a brief period of recruiting duty, he returned to the front with Gen. Scott's army, went through the entire campaign against the City of Mexico, was wounded at Cerro Gordo, and received brevets for gallant and meritorious conduct there and at Chapultepec. In 1854 his native state presented him with a sword of honor for "patriotic and meritorious conduct" in the war. The rest of his service in the army was on the frontier. He was promoted to first lieutenant in 1851, and upon the organization of the 10th Infantry in 1855 was appointed captain in the new regiment. Resigning on Mar. 3, 1861, he was commissioned a major of infantry in the Confederate army, and on June 17, 1861, was appointed brigadier-general and assigned to a brigade in Gen. Johnston's army. His brigade was one of those that bore the brunt of the first attack at Bull Run on July 21. It suffered heavily, and finally broke up, but had held back the Union advance long enough for the defense to be organized in the rear. Pointing to Jackson's brigade, "standing like a stone wall," he reformed the remnant of his command in line with it, and held his ground. To hold the raw and undisciplined troops up to their work required desperate exertions and reckless exposure on the part of the officers. Having lost nearly all of his field officers, Bee himself at last fell mortally wounded. He died the next day. As a general officer who lost his life in a heroic and successful fight, he naturally became a popular hero in the South. He is chiefly remembered now as the man who gave Stonewall Jackson the name by which he is known in history. These accidental titles to fame have rather obscured his real merit. He showed a capacity for command that was not usual in the early days of the war, and it is fair to suppose that he would have risen high if he had lived.

[G. W. Cullum, *Biog. Reg.* (3rd ed., 1891); *Confed. Mil. Hist.*, vol. V (1899), pp. 375–77; *Official Records*, ser. I, vol. II; R. M. Johnston, *Bull Run, Its Strategy and Tactics* (1913), pp. 202–03.]   T. M. S.

BEE, HAMILTON PRIOLEAU (July 22, 1822–Oct. 2, 1897), Confederate soldier, was born in Charleston, S. C. His grandfather, Thomas Bee, had been a federal judge. His father, Barnard E. Bee the elder, removed to Texas in 1835, took a leading part in the establishment of the Republic, and was its secretary of state under President Lamar. His family joined him in 1837. Hamilton Bee was secretary of the commission for determining the boundary between the United States and Texas in 1839, and secretary of the senate of Texas in 1846. Enlisting as a private in the Mexican War, he became a lieutenant in the Texas Rangers and afterward in Bell's regiment of Texas Volunteers, seeing service under Taylor in northern Mexico. After the war he was a member of the legislature, serving a term as speaker of the House of Representatives. In 1861, he was elected brigadier-general of militia, but did not long remain satisfied with an inactive position. The blockade was shutting off commerce through southern ports and stimulating traffic through Mexico, and Bee applied for command at Brownsville. "I am not much of a military man," he wrote, Dec. 12, 1861, "but was under fire at Monterey and did not run"; and pointed out that the commander on the border should be one "who speaks the language and understands the Mexican people." He was appointed brigadier-general in the Confederate army in March 1862 and was assigned to the post he desired. His most important duties were to facilitate the importation of munitions from Europe through Mexico and the exportation of the cotton which paid for them. Military operations in his district were on a small scale. His services to the Confederacy in this administrative position were great, but he had no opportunity to acquire the military experience which he lacked, and which other volunteer generals, no better qualified than he, were slowly and painfully gaining. Accordingly, when called into the field in command of a cavalry brigade to resist Banks's advance up the Red River in the spring of 1864, his handling of troops was severely criticized. It was alleged that the Confederate victory at Sabine Cross Roads (or Mansfield) might have been decisive if he had acted more aggressively, and Gen. Taylor censured his defense at Monett's Ferry, though Kirby Smith declared

that in this engagement his "defense of the position was that of a brave and gallant soldier." Gen. J. G. Walker wrote: "His courage, honor, and integrity are universally conceded,—but I would regard it as a public calamity to know of his being assigned to an important command." Bee continued on duty in the field, but there were no further operations of importance west of the Mississippi. In February 1865 he was assigned to command a division in Wharton's cavalry corps, and later he had a brigade in Maxey's infantry division. He surrendered along with the rest of the trans-Mississippi troops, and was paroled at Columbus, Tex., June 26, 1865, being then designated as a major-general. He had never been legally appointed to this rank, but Kirby Smith, cut off from his government as he was, assumed the right to make promotions in his army on his own authority. Bee withdrew to Mexico, but returned to Texas in 1876, and spent the rest of his life in San Antonio. In 1854 he married Mildred Tarver of Alabama.

[F. B. Heitman: *Hist. Reg.* (1903), II, 44; *Confed. Mil. Hist.* (1899), XI (Tex.), 225–26; *Official Records*, ser. I, vols. IV, IX, XV, XXVI (pts. 1, 2), XXXIV (pts. 1, 2), XLI (pt. 2), XLVIII (pts. 1, 2), LIII; unpublished Confederate records in the War Department.]   T. M. S.

BEECHER, CATHARINE ESTHER (Sept. 6, 1800–May 12, 1878), educator, reformer, was the eldest of the nine children of Rev. Lyman and Roxana (Foote) Beecher; she was born at East Hampton, Long Island, where her father was pastor of the Congregational Church. Henry Ward Beecher [*q.v.*] and Edward Beecher [*q.v.*] were her brothers and Harriet Beecher Stowe [*q.v.*] her sister. The large family was brought up in great measure under her care. Trained to industry by her mother, who, as her daughter wrote, "was remarkable not only for intelligence and culture, but for a natural taste and skill in domestic handicraft," she obtained her early education principally at home. When she was ten years of age her father removed to Litchfield, Conn. There she attended a private school at which what was taught was typical of the educational opportunity for girls of that period—the primary branches and drawing, painting, and music. When she was sixteen her mother died and for two years thereafter, till her father married again, she shared with her aunt the care of the home. At nearly twenty she again took up the study of the piano and of drawing, and about a year and a half later began teaching in a private school for young ladies in New London, Conn. Largely by independent study she had gained a knowledge of mathematics, Latin, and philosophy. In 1823 by the sudden death of her affianced lover, Prof. Alexander Metcalf Fisher of Yale College, both her plans for married life were shattered and her religious faith deeply shaken. Eventually determining, as she said, "to find happiness in living to do good," she began in 1824 at Hartford, Conn., a small private school for young ladies. Success at once attended this venture which came to be a school of more than 150 pupils, famous for its advanced curriculum and its excellence of teaching in a day when school opportunities for women in the higher branches of learning were very few. In 1832 when her father accepted the presidency of Lane Theological Seminary in Cincinnati, Ohio, she disposed of her interests in the Hartford school and went west with him. In Cincinnati she organized "The Western Female Institute" on the model of her Hartford school. This enterprise flourished till 1837, when because of failing health and the financial stringency of that period of panic, she gave it up.

Having secured some restoration to vigor through rest and travel, she directed her energies to the promotion of several enterprises she had originated. One of these was, as she said, "the securing professional advantages of education for my sex equal to those bestowed on men." And another, the finding in the East capable and devoted women teachers for the new and isolated communities of the South and West. In the interest of these movements she helped to organize in Boston "The Ladies' Society for Promoting Education at the West," and secured the founding of "female colleges" at Burlington, Ia., Quincy, Ill., and Milwaukee, Wis. Having had experience of the almost insuperable task of promoting higher education without endowment, she sought to develop a public opinion that would provide for "American women a liberal education . . . by means of endowed institutions on the college plan of organization . . . to include all that is gained by normal schools, and also to train women to be healthful, intelligent, and successful wives, mothers and housekeepers" (*Educational Reminiscences,* pp. 154–55). Thus she was one of the early forces which created in this country the opportunity for the higher education of women, promoting it by her career as a teacher, by her writings and her lectures and by the schools she helped to establish. Her works on domestic science, also, and her public advocacy of this branch of knowledge helped to create a public opinion favorable to its entrance into the curriculum of the schools. With both voice and pen she was a determined opponent of woman suffrage and came to be one of the leaders of the early anti-suffragists. In appearance she strongly resembled her brother, Henry Ward Beecher, as the portrait of her that has come down to us shows: endowed with great force of character and of personality, she possessed both charm and sparkling wit. She did not marry. The following are her chief writings: *A Treatise on Domestic Economy for the Use of Young Ladies at Home and at School* (1841); *Miss Beecher's Domestic Receipt Book* (1846); *Physiology and Calisthenics for Schools and Families* (1856); *The Duty of American Women to their Country* (1845); *An Essay on Slavery and Abolitionism, with Reference to the Duty of American Females* (1837); *The Evils Suffered by American Women and American Children: the Causes and the Remedy* (1846); *Woman Suffrage and Woman's Profession* (1871).

[The chief source of information about Miss Beecher is her *Educational Reminiscences and Suggestions* (1874), reprinted in abbreviated form in Henry Barnard, *Am. Jour. of Education,* XXVIII, 65–94. See also Lyman Beecher's *Autobiography* (1864) and Charles E. Stowe's *Life of Harriet Beecher Stowe* (1889).]

W. J. C.

BEECHER, CHARLES (Oct. 7, 1815–Apr. 21, 1900), Congregational clergyman, was born in Litchfield, Conn., the last of the nine children of Lyman Beecher by his first wife, Roxana Foote. Almost forty years later he prefaced his *Redeemer and Redeemed* with the words: "To her who gave me birth; consecrated me to the ministry; died before I knew her; whom, next to my Redeemer, I most desire to meet in the Resurrection, to Roxana Beecher, I dedicate this work, for the execution of which I am chiefly glad to have lived; in the hope that she will not, on account of it, be sorry for having borne me." For some years it seemed as if the mother's hope for her last-born would not be fulfilled, for after being prepared for college at the Boston Latin School, and Lawrence Academy, Groton, Mass., graduating from Bowdoin College (1834), and studying theology under his father at Lane Seminary, he lost practically all faith in the Christian doctrines in which he had been schooled. He taught music, for which he had much aptitude, in Cincinnati, and later was a shipping clerk in New Orleans. Settling in Indianapolis while his brother, Henry Ward, was pastor there, he took charge of the music in the latter's church, and finally, Nov. 9, 1844, having become more settled in his views, he was ordained pastor of the Second Presbyterian Church, Fort Wayne, Ind. Two sermons preached there he published in 1846 under the title, *The Bible a Sufficient Creed.* On July 23, 1840, he had been married to Sarah, daughter of Nathaniel and Mary (Porter) Coffin of Jacksonville, Ill.

His career was a varied one. In 1851 he became pastor of the Free Presbyterian, later the First Congregational Church, Newark, N. J., where his anti-slavery views separated him and his church from the fellowship of the other churches of the city. Here he published in 1851 *The Duty of Disobedience to Wicked Laws, a Sermon on the Fugitive Slave Law.* For a short time he was professor of rhetoric in Knox College, Ill. From Nov. 19, 1857, to May 4, 1881, he was pastor of the First Congregational Church, Georgetown, Mass. In 1863 he was convicted of heresy by the Essex North Conference because of his belief in the preëxistence of souls, but his church sustained its pastor, and later the Conference rescinded its action. In 1864 he represented the town in the Massachusetts legislature. He made his home in Florida from 1870 to 1877, and was superintendent of public instruction in that state (1871–73). From 1885 to 1893 he was acting pastor of the church in Wysox, Pa., and he spent his closing years in Georgetown, Mass.

He was a man of wide learning and of musical as well as literary ability. In 1851 he published in collaboration with John Zundel, organist of his brother Henry's church in Brooklyn, *The Metronome or Music Teacher's Assistant, a New Manual of Sacred Song.* He also wrote several hymns, and selected the music for the *Plymouth Collection* (1855). In 1849 he published *The Incarnation, or Pictures of the Virgin and Her Son,* which portrays Gospel narratives in the aspects which they present to an imaginative mind, with the appliances of geographical, historical, and critical knowledge. He wrote two books on spiritualism, *A Review of the "Spiritual Manifestations"* (1853), and *Spiritual Manifestations* (1879), in which he states his view of the spirit world, and expounds a kind of "Christian spiritualism." Based in part on ingenious and sometimes fantastic symbolic interpretations of portions of the Bible, he evolved a theology, or cosmology, which is presented in the last mentioned work and in *Redeemer and Redeemed* (1864), *The Eden Tableau* (1880), and *Patmos, or the Unveiling* (1896). He also edited the *Autobiography, Correspondence, etc., of Lyman Beecher, D.D.* (1864).

[*Congreg. Yr. Bk.,* 1901; *Obit. Record Grads. Bowdoin Coll.* (1911); *Outlook,* LXIV, 943.] H. E. S.

BEECHER, CHARLES EMERSON (Oct. 9, 1856–Feb. 14, 1904), paleontologist, the son of Moses and Emily (Downer) Beecher, was born in Dunkirk, N. Y. He was fitted for college at the high school in Warren, Pa., whither his parents moved shortly after his birth, and was graduated from the University of Michigan with the degree of B.S. in 1878. For the first ten years immediately succeeding his graduation he served as an assistant to the eminent paleontologist, James Hall [*q.v.*], in Albany, N. Y. In 1888, having been given charge of invertebrate fossils in the Peabody Museum, he removed to New Haven where he remained the rest of his life. In 1891–92 he took charge of Prof. J. D. Dana's classes in Yale University, and showed such capacity for teaching that in the last named year he was appointed assistant professor of historical geology in the Sheffield School. In 1897 he was appointed to full professorship and became a member of the governing board of the School. Two years later (1899) he succeeded Prof. O. C. Marsh as curator of the geological collections and became a member of and secretary to the board of trustees of the Museum. In 1902 his title was again changed, this time to that of University Professor of paleontology.

Beecher was a born naturalist with leanings toward paleontology, and was, moreover, skilful in the manipulation of tools and materials. Some of his most interesting discoveries, as for instance that in 1893 of limbs and antennæ on trilobites, were rendered possible by his skill in cleaning and uncovering these most delicate portions of the fossil remains. It is stated that he began collecting shells and fossils when not more than twelve years of age, and at twenty, while a student in college, he published his first paper—a list of the fresh-water shells in the region of Ann Arbor, Mich. His first paleontological paper, dealing with new genera and species of Devonian fossils, was published by the Geological Survey of Pennsylvania in 1884. As a collector he was unexcelled and on his appointment to the position of curator of the geological collections at Yale he presented without restrictions his entire personal collection of upward of 100,000 specimens to the Museum.

Of a kindly and enthusiastic disposition, he was eminently successful as a teacher in both graduate and undergraduate schools. As an investigator he was of a philosophic turn of mind, caring little for the mere description of species, his most monumental writings dealing with the ontogenetic stages in fossil species and their genetic sequence through the geological formations. His writings on the origin and significance of species may also be mentioned in this connection. In 1899 he was elected to the National Academy of Sciences. He was also a fellow of the Geological Society of America, the Geological Society of Washington, the Boston Society of Natural History, the American Association of Conchologists, the Connecticut Academy of Arts and Sciences, and the Malacological Society of London. Personally he was of a quiet and unassuming nature, industrious in the extreme, loyal and trustworthy. He was married on Sept. 12, 1894, to Mary Salome Galligan of Warren, Pa., by whom he had two daughters. His death through heart failure was sudden and wholly unexpected. He was "one whom science could ill afford to lose, and to whom, humanly speaking, there should have remained many years of industry and fruitful research" (W. H. Dall, *Science*, Mar. 18, 1904).

[C. Schuchert, in *Am. Jour. Sci.*, June 1904, gives a full bibliography of Beecher's publications, pp. 421–22. W. H. Dall, in *Biog. Memoirs, Nat. Acad. Sci.*, vol. VI (1909).]				G. P. M.

BEECHER, EDWARD (Aug. 27, 1803–July 28, 1895), Congregational clergyman, college president, the third child of Rev. Lyman and Roxana (Foote) Beecher, was born at East Hampton, Long Island. He was the brother of Catharine Beecher [*q.v.*], Henry Ward Beecher [*q.v.*], and Harriet Beecher Stowe [*q.v.*]. After graduating from Yale in the class of 1822, teaching at Hartford, Conn., for a year, studying for a short time at Andover Seminary and tutoring at Yale for another year, he became in 1826 pastor of the Park Street Church, Boston. Four years later, on the recommendation of President Day of Yale, he became the first president of Illinois College at Jacksonville. (See Theron Baldwin, and J. M. Sturtevant.) That he should have been willing to give up the pastorate of a prominent church on Boston Common to become president of a college that could boast only one small brick building, located on the outskirts of a little log-cabin village on the western prairies, showed that he had in him the qualities of a true pioneer missionary. He served as president of Illinois College for nearly fourteen years, gathering about him a faculty of able young men who in time won real distinction for this western college. A new and commodious dormitory for students and faculty was added to the college plant in less than two years after he came to his post. He was frequently in the East trying to raise additional funds for the enterprise and met with a measure of success, but the panic of 1837 gave the college a financial blow from which it never recovered during his administration.

It was hardly to be expected that a member of the Beecher family could remain passive when the clouds of the slavery controversy cast their shadow over the community. A large majority of the settlers in that part of the state were from the South and the president, realizing that the fortunes of the college might be seriously jeopardized by radical utterances, hesitated at first to take a determined stand, but when, as he himself remarked, the principles of free speech and a free press became involved in the issue, he could remain "silent no longer." He fearlessly stood by Elijah P. Lovejoy, helping him to guard his press in the warehouse at Alton the night before Lovejoy was shot. He took an active part in helping to organize the first state anti-slavery society of Illinois. Some of his students were indicted by a local grand jury for harboring runaway slaves, and personal violence was threatened against some of his colleagues on the faculty. Religious controversies also disturbed the peace of the campus, but Beecher and his colleagues courageously stood their ground against local bigotry.

In 1842, when college finances were at a low ebb, he again went East to see if he could retrieve the failing fortunes of the institution. Begging for money, however, was a task which he did not enjoy, for he was primarily a preacher and a scholar. He never returned to his post as president, resigning in 1844 to accept the pastorate of the Salem Street Church in Boston. He became one of the founders of the *Congregationalist* and served as its editor-in-chief from 1849 to 1853. In 1855, he returned to the West as first pastor of the First Congregational Church of Galesburg, Ill., where he served until 1871, when he removed to Brooklyn, apparently to be with his distinguished brother. He remained henceforth without any regular pastoral charge except for a few years when he served a small Congregational church at Parkville, near Brooklyn. He died at the ripe age of nearly ninety-two years. His wife, Isabella P. Jones of Wiscasset, Me., who had borne him eleven children, survived him a few months.

He was a somewhat prolific writer on theological subjects, among his more important books being: *Baptism, Imports and Modes* (1841); *The Conflict of Ages* (1853); *The Papal Conspiracy Exposed* (1855); *The Concord of Ages* (1860). He also wrote a *Narrative of the Alton Riots*—an important contemporary account of that episode in the slavery controversy.

[Material on Edward Beecher is scant. See his *Alton Riots* (1838); Bateman and Selby's *Hist. Encyc. Ill.* (1906); *Congreg. Yr. Bk.* for 1896; J. M. Sturtevant, *Autobiography* (1896); *Summary of the Record of the Class of 1822, Yale College, to the Close of 1879* (1879); *Record of the Meetings of the Class of 1822, Yale College, etc.* (1869).]				C. H. R.

BEECHER, HENRY WARD (June 24, 1813–Mar. 8, 1887), clergyman, one of the most conspicuous figures in the public life of his time, was born in Litchfield, Conn., and lived there until he was thirteen years old. Outdoor life in this New England hill town, where, he once said, "it almost required medical help to get sick," developed the physical robustness he inherited through his father, and the love of nature and appreciation of beauty which he derived from his mother. The Beecher line, English with a slight admixture of Scotch and Welsh, went back to the company of Puritans who came over to Boston with John Davenport in 1637, and the next year founded New Haven. It was a succession of hardy Connecticut farmers and blacksmiths, noted for their Samson-like feats of strength. They were much given to marrying; Henry's grandfather had five wives and twelve children, and his father Lyman [*q.v.*], three wives and thirteen children. The latter, pastor of the church in Litchfield, was one of the leaders of New England Congregationalism, a man of keen mind, quick wit, and fertile imagination, but averse to hard study. Revivals and doctrinal combat afforded him his keenest delights. He was restless, impulsive, and of unstable nervous organization, bursting into tears at the slightest provocation. Preaching excited him to a high degree, and a thunderstorm stirred him almost to frenzy. Moods of hilarious cheerfulness took possession of him, in which he was capable of horseplay and rather crude practical jokes. He was erratic, disorderly in his habits, and a careless spender. On the other hand, Henry's mother, Roxana Foote, was a shy, sensitive, self-abnegating woman, who loved flowers and all beautiful things, sang, played the guitar, did fine embroidery, and painted on ivory. With all her artistic temperament, however, she had far more poise and sound judgment than her husband. Her ancestry went back to Nathaniel Foote, one of the original settlers of Wethersfield, Conn., and still farther, to James Foote, a cavalier who, according to tradition, helped King Charles II conceal himself in the royal oak. Her father and mother, Eli and Roxana (Ward) Foote, were Episcopalians and Loyalists. After bearing Lyman Beecher nine children she died of consumption when Henry was about three years old. Not long after her death, her place was taken by Harriet Porter, a beautiful, aristocratic person of elegant manners and exquisite sense of rectitude and propriety, who awakened in the Beecher children awe rather than warm affection.

For a boy of Henry Ward's nature and needs, life in the Litchfield parsonage was both favorable and unfavorable. There was an atmosphere of intellectual virility there, but an unwholesome amount of theological discussion, and as he became older he had agonizing periods of concern over the unsaved condition of his soul. A spirit of cheerfulness and even hilarity pervaded the household, however. Lyman Beecher romped with the children and went fishing with them. Strict discipline was enforced and independence and resourcefulness were developed. "I was brought up to put my hand to anything," Henry once declared, and boasted that he could go into an abandoned blacksmith's shop, start a fire and put a shoe on his horse. He also learned to knit mittens and suspenders, an accomplishment for which he professed to be thankful. Nevertheless the Beecher household was too busy and crowded for a younger child to receive much personal attention and affection, and Henry needed both. In spite of the fact that he was robust, fun-loving, and full of animal spirits, he was a shy, backward lad, so thick of speech that he could hardly be understood. Undreamed of emotional possibilities were stored up within him. In the fields and woods where he loved to be by himself, these were stirred, but not at home. Unquestionably, as a youth, he was lonely, self-centered, and suppressed.

It was his "misfortune," he said in after years, "to go to a district school." "I have not a single pleasant recollection of my schoolboy days." Diffidence and a defect in verbal memory, which he never overcame, caused him to be regarded as unusually stupid. So backward was he that when he was ten years old, his father sent him to a school in Bethlehem, Conn., conducted by a Rev. Mr. Langdon. Here he was home-sick and studied little, spending as much time as he could in the woods. He was next sent to the school which his sister Catharine was teaching in Hartford, where he was the only boy among some forty girls. When in 1826 Lyman Beecher became pastor of Hanover Church, Boston, Henry was at the age of inner turbulence and longing for romantic adventure. He wanted to go to sea. His shrewd old father told him that if he was to follow the sea he ought to learn navigation. Henry swallowed the bait and was landed in the Mount Pleasant Classical Institute, Amherst, Mass. Here for the first time he had the advantage of contact with boys of varying types from different parts of the country. He became popular with them and a leader in their sports. William P. N. Fitzgerald, an ex-cadet at West Point, instructor in mathematics, taught him how to study; and John E. Lovell, with persistent, interested coöperation on Beecher's part, made something of an orator out of him. Here, too, for the first time, his fervid emotional nature had some expression and human response, partly through his practise in declamation, but more particularly through one or two intimate friendships.

In 1830 he entered Amherst College, graduating four years later. He stood low in his classes, for he had his father's averseness to hard study, and was never disposed to subject himself to a fixed régime. As his moods dictated, however, he read widely in the English classics. He also acquired a considerable knowledge of phrenology, which he always felt was a great help to him in appraising men's powers and tendencies. In public speaking he attracted some attention, and he made frequent contributions to the *Shrine,* one of the college papers. During the long winter vacations he taught school, and on occasions lectured or preached. He was a lusty youth, active in such athletics as were then common, popular with his fellows, noted for his skill in storytelling and mimicry, his quickness in repartee, his hilarity, and practical jokes.

Thus far young Beecher had had no satisfying religious experience. During a revival at Mount Pleasant Academy he had gone through a brief period of religious excitation which he hoped was conversion, and his father had hustled him into the church. He had no firm ground to stand upon, however, and in college suffered much from uncertainty and doubt. He knew that his mother on her death-bed had dedicated him to the ministry, and that his father expected all his sons to become preachers. Upon graduating from college, therefore, following the course of least resistance possibly, he entered Lane Theological Seminary, Cincinnati, of which his father had become the head. Here his exuberant vitality and his interest in what was going on about him, led him to give as much time to extra-curriculum activities as to his studies. He continued his general reading, lectured, preached, wrote articles for the *Daily Evening Post* of Cincinnati, and for a few months, acted as editor of the *Cincinnati Journal,* a Presbyterian weekly. During the excitement which followed the destruction of James G. Birney's printing office by a pro-slavery mob, he was sworn in as special constable. His doubts about entering the ministry continued. For systematic theology he had no appetite then or thereafter, and scant intellectual capacity for dealing with its problems. Calvinism, which had overshadowed him from infancy, with its emphasis upon the sovereignty of God, its rigidity and sternness, was repellent to a nature like his, rebellious to all restraint, ex-

traordinarily sensitive to the beauty and joyousness of life, and craving love and companionship. He was determined to preach the Gospel, if at all, as it was revealed to him and not as it was taught in the schools. Religious certitude finally came to him through an ecstatic personal experience. One beautiful May morning in the Ohio woods there entered his soul an intoxicating sense of God as one who loves "a man in his sins for the sake of helping him out of them," not "out of compliment to Christ, or to a law, or to a plan of salvation, but from the fulness of His great heart"; and of Christ as one whose nature it is to lift man "out of everything that is low and debasing to superiority." Later there came a realization of Christ as ever near him, a companion and friend to uphold and sustain him. Here was a conception opening up possibilities of a highly emotional religious life, and a field for preaching exactly suited to Beecher's temperament and gifts.

After this May morning experience he had no more doubts as to his life work. In 1837 he was licensed to preach by the Cincinnati Presbytery, and accepted a call to a church of twenty members in Lawrenceburg, Ind. He went back East in the summer of that year and, on Aug. 3, married Eunice White Bullard of West Sutton, Mass., to whom he had become engaged while he was a student at Amherst. The young couple had no capital and began housekeeping in two rooms over a warehouse, the scanty furnishings being provided through the sale of some of their personal belongings, and gifts from their parishioners. The salary was meager and Beecher was not too proud to wear the cast-off clothing of others. It did not always fit, but he was never particular about his personal appearance. A child was soon born to them, the first of ten. Beecher applied for ordination to the Miami Presbytery, a decidedly Old School body, the Scotch-Irish members of which suspected his orthodoxy because he was Lyman Beecher's son. With more cleverness than candor apparently, he answered their questions satisfactorily. A resolution was passed, however, to the effect that the Presbytery would ordain only those who would give adhesion to the Old School Presbyterian General Assembly. With this condition Beecher refused to comply, and he returned to Lawrenceburg unordained. His church supported him and became an independent Presbyterian body. Later, Nov. 9, 1838, he was ordained by the New School Presbytery of Cincinnati. Beecher remained in Lawrenceburg until July 1839, when he became pastor of the Second Presbyterian Church of Indianapolis, a New School congregation which had withdrawn from the First Church. Here he remained eight years.

During the first decade of his ministry, Beecher was feeling his way, getting command of himself and learning how to use his endowment. He began his career with a considerable fund of varied information derived from wide reading; a passionate fondness for outdoor life; a liking for people whatever their station which sometimes made him dangerously careless in his choice of associates; an ambition to be an effective preacher; and beneath all, a powerful and sincere moral earnestness. He was disposed to be a law unto himself, not only theologically, but in all things. In a lesser degree he had his father's emotional instability, and the latter's zest for action, disorderly habits, strain of coarseness, and financial ineptitude. Neither in the pulpit nor out of it did he pay much attention to the conventionalities. There was little in his dress or his demeanor to suggest his profession. He went hunting and fishing, romped with the young, played copenhagen at Sunday-school picnics, painted his house, pushed a wheelbarrow through the streets, went to fires and held the hose, with the same indifference to appearances with which in after years he would walk the streets of New York munching peanuts, and leaving a trail of shucks behind him. His high spirits, genial disposition, interest in all aspects of human life, and his freedom from any ostentatious piety made him popular generally. For a long time his preaching did not satisfy him. Finally through a study of Jonathan Edwards and the methods employed by the apostles as revealed in the book of Acts, he grasped the idea that the secret of successful preaching lies in its singleness of aim—that of effecting a moral change in the hearers; and that a sermon is good only as it has power on the heart. Upon this principle, therefore, he shaped all his preaching. People flocked to hear him; he assisted in revival services about the state; and with increasing frequency was called to give lectures and addresses for special occasions.

He also began that association with periodicals through which his influence was to have a reach which the pulpit alone could never have afforded. The *Indiana Journal* introduced into its columns an agricultural department, the contents of which were published every month in magazine form under the title, *Indiana Farmer and Gardener,* later changed to *Western Farmer and Gardener,* and of this Beecher was made the editor. His knowledge of agriculture was not extensive, although he was an enthusiastic experimental gardener; but with the remarkable capacity for assimilating and putting to prac-

tical use the results of other people's labors, which was a life-long characteristic, he perused Loudon's encyclopedias of horticulture and agriculture, together with works on botany, and wrote for the *Farmer,* according to an associate, "all the articles in it that were good for anything." Many of them were later published under the title *Plain and Pleasant Talk About Fruits, Flowers and Farming* (1859). They are written in a direct, pithy style, with touches of humor and imagination, contain a goodly amount of worldly wisdom, and besides imparting agricultural information, advocate cleanliness, temperance, better public schools, more education for farmers, and attention to beauty as well as to utility.

A Beecher could hardly help being a reformer. Henry Ward's early efforts to improve social conditions were directed chiefly against the vices which commonly exist in a frontier community. While in Indianapolis he delivered a series of addresses which included such subjects as "Industry and Idleness," "Twelve Causes of Dishonesty," "Gamblers and Gambling," "The Strange Woman," "Popular Amusements." They attracted much attention at the time, and, published in 1844 under the title *Seven Lectures to Young Men,* were widely read in this country and abroad. They are remarkable for their shrewd analysis of human motives, their graphic descriptions, and picturesqueness of language, their realism, and their trenchant style. He was criticized at the time, and has been condemned since, for seeming to side-step the slavery question in a community where abolitionists were not popular. His comparative silence on this subject could not have been due to lack of courage, for Beecher always displayed a boldness, not to say rashness, in doing what he wanted to do. The Beechers were all opposed to slavery, but Henry shared his father's antipathy to the extreme abolitionists, "he-goat men," the latter called them, "who think they do God service by butting everything in their line of march which does not fall in or get out of their way." Not only did he distrust their methods, but their anger, malice, and evil-speaking were foreign to his genial, kindly disposition. The probability is that he was unwilling to do anything which might interfere with the main purpose of his life—preaching the Gospel with power to all sorts and conditions of men. Running through his intensely emotional nature, there was a strain of hard, practical common sense, exhibited in the advice he gave to his brother Charles: "Preach little doctrine, except what is of mouldy orthodoxy, keep all your improved breeds, your short-horned Durhams, your Berkshires, etc., way off to pasture. They will get fatter, and nobody will be scared. . . . I do not ask you to change yourself; but, for a time, while captious critics are lurking, adapt your mode so as to insure that you shall be rightly understood." In line with this advice, with respect to slavery, in his early days he permitted himself to be governed by expediency rather than by a heroism of questionable wisdom. In his later years he affirmed that he had often touched upon this subject indirectly, but it was not until his Presbytery recommended that all Presbyterians preach upon it at least once annually that he made it the theme of a sermon.

By 1847 Beecher's fame had gone abroad. That year he received calls to the Park Street Church, Boston, and to the Old South Church of the same city. These he declined. He liked the West, and wanted to stay there; but his wife did not, and her health was poor. Accordingly when invited to take charge of the newly organized Plymouth Church of Brooklyn, Congregational in polity, he accepted. Here, Oct. 10, 1847, he began a public career which for conspicuousness and influence has probably not been equaled by that of any other American clergyman. People came to hear him in increasing numbers. His unconventionality, his audacity, wit and humor, his theological latitude, his dramatic ability and picturesqueness of language, his friendly intimacy and naturalness, fascinated them. At first they came out of curiosity, but they kept coming, and from other motives. His sympathetic understanding of the human heart, and his appreciation and varied application of fundamental spiritual truths met their religious needs. In January 1849 the church building which the society had acquired burned, and a larger one, with a semi-circular auditorium, especially designed to give the audience opportunity to see and hear Beecher, and Beecher freedom to exercise his powers, was erected. Thereafter his weekly congregation averaged about 2,500 persons. Visitors to New York from all over the country and from abroad made it a point to hear him. His sermons, taken down stenographically, for they were never written out, were printed each week in pamphlet form and widely circulated. Entering the lecture field, he was soon one of the most popular of public speakers. He early became a regular contributor to the *Independent*, and his connection with it did much to make it widely read. From 1861 to 1864 he was editor, and from 1870 to 1881, editor of the *Christian Union*. For these papers he wrote some of the "strongest editorials in the American press" (*Cambridge History of American Literature*, 1921, III, 325). He was also for a time a contributor to the *New York Ledger*. The effect of his personality and gifts was extraordinary. "He has had the misfortune of a popularity which is perfectly phenomenal," his sister, Harriet Beecher Stowe, wrote to George Eliot. . . . "I remember being in his house one evening in the time of early flowers, and in that one evening came a box of flowers from Maine, another from New Jersey, another from Connecticut—all from people with whom he had no personal acquaintance, who had read something of his and wanted to send him some token" (Charles E. Stowe, *Life of Harriet Beecher Stowe*, 1889, p. 478).

From the beginning he used his pulpit, or platform, for he would have no pulpit in his church, for the discussion of public questions and the advocacy of reforms. His pronouncements therefrom and through the press made him a recognized leader of the anti-slavery forces. While not always consistent or well advised, on the whole his views and policies stand the test of time. He believed that slavery is fundamentally wrong, but held that under the Constitution there could be no interference with it in the slave states. He insisted, however, that it should be rigidly confined therein, and thus circumscribed, he felt, it would die. He opposed the compromise measures of 1850, on the ground that liberty and slavery are irreconcilable elements in our political system. He counseled disobedience to the Fugitive Slave Law, declaring that the requirements of humanity are above those of the Constitution. He urged Northerners to emigrate to Kansas, and use force to make it free soil. While expressing sympathy for John Brown, he deprecated his raid at Harper's Ferry as the act of a crazy old man, and denied the right of Northerners to attempt to breed discontent among the bondsmen, or to stir up bitterness against the South. He campaigned for Frémont, and in 1860 for Lincoln. After the war broke out, he urged its vigorous prosecution by the North, criticizing Lincoln severely for his delay in issuing an emancipation proclamation. In 1863 he visited England, and in the face of violent opposition supported the North in a number of speeches, which, while their influence in determining English opinion may have been exaggerated, were extraordinary platform accomplishments. After the war, although solicitous for the rights of the freedmen and advocating that they be given the franchise, he was in sympathy with President Johnson in the latter's desire that the seceding states be promptly admitted to the privileges of statehood in the Union, and military government in the South be discontinued as soon as possible. A letter expressing these sentiments written to a convention of soldiers and sailors held in Cleveland, Ohio, known as the "Cleveland Letter," was interpreted as a repudiation of the Republican party, and brought down upon him much criticism and abuse.

Neither in political nor in religious matters did Beecher display any particular originality. He broke no paths into new realms of truth; he started no new movements. He was not an investigator, a close reasoner, or even a student in the common acceptance of the term. He had little capacity for dealing with abstruse subjects, and seldom discerned the subtler elements in matters spiritual or temporal. The more or less obvious and practical were always his forte. Nevertheless, he had unusual intellectual vitality and fertility. He exploited every field of human interest, and was able to grasp fundamental principles, perceive essential facts, and with rare expository ability set them forth clearly and persuasively. Quickness of wit and resourcefulness enabled him always to take command of a situation. His type of mind, however, was preëminently that of the poet. He thought in images and analogies. Never when speaking, he affirmed, was he at a loss for a word or a figure; his embarrassment was in choosing from the number which rose up before him.

The physical and emotional, in fact, were the dominant elements in Beecher's nature. These gave to his career both its strength and its weakness. In personal appearance he is said to have been one of the most striking figures in New York. He was of medium height and large girth, with broad shoulders upon which rested a lionesque head. His hair, gray in his later years, hung down in flowing locks over his coat collar. He was full-blooded, and his face, always clean-shaven, was ruddy in hue. His grayish-blue eyes were full of changing expression. He had a rich, sympathetic, flexible voice, responsive to every shade of emotion. His physical resources seemed inexhaustible. He exuded vitality and with it exuberant good humor. His senses were unusually acute. He had the artist's eye for colors, and took a sensuous delight in them. He deliberately turned to beautiful objects for their intoxicating effect, carrying precious stones in his pocket to be brought forth and gazed at when he felt so disposed. Some of them soothed him; others, he confessed, produced much the same effect as champagne. He craved an emotional atmosphere for his preaching, always had flowers in the church, and insisted upon hearty congregational singing. He displayed great charm and tact in meeting people, and a freedom with his friends, including women, which was unconventional, but so spontaneous and natural as to be inoffensive. There was nothing mean or petty in his constitution, but an overflowing good-will toward all. Free from race or sectarian prejudices, he was a Congregationalist because of the freedom that denomination afforded, but he appreciated the good in other churches, though he opposed all efforts to bring about organic church unity, convinced that the differing beliefs, tastes, and needs of men will forever make it impossible. When all is said, however, he was essentially a man of moods and impulses. He never thoroughly disciplined himself, or held himself to a fixed routine. He did what he felt like doing, and lacking a fine sense of propriety he frequently did and said what was in bad taste and unworthy of him. If he liked a thing he wanted it, an art dealer once commented, and no one could convince him that something else was more beautiful or better. Similarly he gave his approval to men and measures, because something in them appealed to him strongly, often to the chagrin of his friends and to his own later embarrassment.

His attitude on matters great as well as small was likewise determined by his emotional reactions. Just as the theological conceptions which came to him in the Ohio woods were precisely those which satisfied his inner cravings, so, throughout his career, his beliefs and activities were determined, not by critical, intellectual tests, but by the fact that they coincided with his feelings, predispositions, and intuitions. His intense love of freedom was due in no small part to his rebellion against the repressing influences and restraining Calvinism under which he grew up; his hatred of theological controversy and his tolerance, to the same cause. He believed in a personal God, but God had little reality to him except as personified in Christ. It was the latter to whom he prayed, and in whom his passionate nature found that for which it hungered. "Shall I twine about him every affection," he said, . . . "feed upon him as my bread, my wine, my water of life; . . . in his strength vanquish sin, draw from him my hope and inspiration; . . . die in his arms, awake with eager upspring to find him whom my soul loveth, only to be put away with the announcement that he is not the recipient of worship!" (*Sermons*, Harper's ed., 1868, I, 85). "I accept without analysis," he elsewhere says, "the tri-personality of God. I accept the Trinity; perhaps because I was educated in it. No matter why, I accept it" (Theological Statement, given in Lyman Abbott, *Henry Ward Beecher*, 1903, p. 432). He preached the love of God and the joy and glory of the Christian life, but put comparatively little emphasis upon God's righteousness and the importance of self-discipline, sacrifice, and the sterner virtues. Similarly, his activities in behalf of reform were determined by his dominant feelings. The condition of the slaves stirred his sympathies, and slavery itself was opposed to his love of freedom and his religious sentiments. He supported the woman suffrage movement, because he felt that the franchise is a natural right, and rebelled against interference with the exercise of it. He was a free-trader, because he believed protection to be socialistic in principle, and his individualism revolted against the militaristic aspects of that system. In his later years he embraced the theory of evolution gladly, because, as he interpreted it, it fitted in with his optimistic confidence in the possibilities of human nature, and his conviction that man had never fallen, but had ever been ascending. At the same time, he clung to his belief in miracles and special providences.

It is a mooted question whether Beecher's intensely emotional and sensuous nature, his lack of rigorous self-discipline, his rather unstable religious convictions, and his tendency to be a law unto himself, resulted in his being guilty of immoral acts; or whether he was the victim of false accusations. Theodore Tilton, a brilliant literary and newspaper man, and a radical reformer, was in his early years one of Beecher's admirers and protegés. Both Mr. and Mrs. Tilton were members of Plymouth Church and its pastor was a frequent caller at their home. Through Beecher's influence Tilton had been made assistant editor of the *Independent,* and upon the former's retirement from that office had become editor-in-chief. His criticism of the "Cleveland Letter" had caused Beecher to sever all connection with that paper. Tilton's unconventional views on marriage and religion became offensive to many of the subscribers, and that fact, together with the popularity of the *Christian Union* under Beecher's charge, reduced its circulation. Henry C. Bowen, its proprietor, relieved Tilton from the editorship, retaining him as a regular contributor, and made him editor of the *Brooklyn Union.* Late in 1870, partly through his influence, Beecher affirmed, Bowen summarily severed Tilton's connection with both papers. Rumors of gross immoralities on Tilton's part were afloat, and Beecher, on the advice of Mrs. Beecher, had counseled Mrs. Tilton to separate from him.

Scandalous stories affecting Beecher's character seem also to have had a clandestine existence for some years. In an interview on Dec. 30, 1870, Tilton accused Beecher of improper relations with his wife, on the basis of a written con-fession made by her, which, after a call from Beecher, she retracted, saying it had been obtained under duress. A policy of silence was adopted by all concerned, but the story leaked out. On Nov. 2, 1872, Victoria Woodhull published in *Woodhull and Claflin's Weekly* a highly colored account of "the character and conduct of Rev. Henry Ward Beecher in his relation with the family of Theodore Tilton." Not until June 30, 1873, however, did Beecher make public denial of the stories and rumors concerning him. In June 1874, Tilton published a statement in which he charged Beecher with an "offense against him which he forebore to name." Beecher then asked a committee of six from his church and society to investigate. After examining thirty-six witnesses, including Tilton, who made a partial statement and then refused to be questioned further, the committee reported that it "found nothing whatever in the evidence that should impair the perfect confidence of Plymouth Church or the world in the Christian character and integrity of Henry Ward Beecher." On Aug. 20, 1874, Tilton filed a complaint against Beecher, charging him with adultery with Mrs. Tilton, and demanding damages of $100,000. The trial lasted six months, and was discussed all over the country. Public opinion was sharply divided. After nine days' deliberation, the jury failed to agree on a verdict, the final vote being nine to three in favor of the defendant. A year and a half later, a council of Congregational churches, made up of 244 representatives, convened at Plymouth Church, and, after an examination, declared: "We hold the pastor of this church, as we and all others are bound to hold him, innocent of the charges reported against him, until substantiated by proof." A committee of five was appointed to receive any charges and proof that might be offered, but none was forthcoming.

A review of the evidence presented at the trial, by an impartial body of people, would probably result in a difference of opinion such as existed in the jury. One cannot escape the conviction, however, that Beecher spoke truly when, as alleged, he told two of his attorneys who apologized for coming to consult with him on a Sunday afternoon: "We have it on good authority that it is lawful to pull an ass out of the pit on the Sabbath day. Well, there never was a bigger ass, or a deeper pit." Even his friends would probably have admitted a measure of truth in this statement from a newspaper review of the case: "Sensible men throughout the country will in their hearts be compelled to acknowledge that Mr. Beecher's management of his private friendships and affairs has been entirely unworthy of his name, position, and sacred calling" (*New York Times,* July 3, 1875).

The remainder of Beecher's career was somewhat shadowed by this scandal. His popularity, however, was not destroyed. The trial had cost him $118,000, and although for years his income had been large, he was always poor. To rehabilitate himself financially he lectured throughout the country. His voice was still heard on public matters. He attacked the corrupt judges of New York, advocated President Arthur's renomination, opposed Blaine, and actively supported Cleveland for the presidency. He also worked on his *Life of Jesus the Christ,* the first volume of which had appeared in 1871. He did not live to finish the task, but it was completed by his sons and published in 1891. Beecher's purely literary attempts were not particularly successful. In 1867 he had published a novel, *Norwood, or Village Life in New England,* a series of descriptive sketches rather than a story. Just before his trial he had delivered the first three courses of the Lyman Beecher Lectures at Yale (*Yale Lectures on Preaching,* 1872–74). They still rank high among the many given in this series, and contain a wealth of homiletical wisdom. His disbelief in a literal Hell, and his acceptance of the evolutionary hypothesis, subjected him to much criticism, and on Oct. 10, 1882, he withdrew, against its protest, from the Association of Congregational Ministers to which he belonged, that his brethren might not "bear the burden of responsibility of being supposed to tolerate the views" he had held and taught. In 1885 his *Evolution and Religion* appeared. For four months in 1886 he was in England where he preached and lectured. He conducted the services in Plymouth Church with his usual vigor on Feb. 27, 1887, but on the following Sunday was at the point of death from cerebral hemorrhage, the end coming two days later. Forty thousand people viewed his body as it lay in the church before being taken for burial to Greenwood Cemetery.

[Much autobiographical material may be found in Beecher's sermons and addresses. For the former, see *Plymouth Pulpit,* vols. I–X (1868–73), new series, vols. I–VII (1873–84), and *Sermons by Henry Ward Beecher* (2 vols., 1868). *Lecture Room Talks* (1870, 1872) is also illuminating. *Star Papers, or Experiences of Art and Nature* (1855) and *New Star Papers, or Views and Experiences of Religious Subjects* (1859) contain contributions to the *Independent; Eyes and Ears* (1862), contributions to the *N. Y. Ledger. Freedom and War* (1863) is a collection of discourses on topics of the times. See also *Patriotic Addresses* (1887) ed. by John R. Howard, and *Lectures and Orations by Henry Ward Beecher* (1913) ed. by N. D. Hillis. Many compilations of his utterances have been made. There are a number of lives of Beecher, no one of which is altogether satisfactory. The latest, Paxton Hibben's *Henry Ward Beech-*

er, *An American Portrait* (1927), while bringing to light some new material and valuable for the social background it sketches and its list of sources, is decidedly unfriendly and fails to give a well-rounded portrayal. Earlier biographies are for the most part laudatory and uncritical. Among them are Lyman Abbott and S. B. Halliday, *Henry Ward Beecher* (1887); Thos. W. Knox, *Life and Work of Henry Ward Beecher* (1887); Jos. Howard, Jr., *Life of Henry Ward Beecher* (1887); Frank S. Child, *The Boyhood of Henry Ward Beecher* (1887); Wm. C. Beecher and Sam. Scoville, *A Biog. of Rev. Henry Ward Beecher* (1888); John R. Howard, *Henry Ward Beecher, a Study* (1891); J. H. Barrows, *Henry Ward Beecher* (1893). Lyman Abbott, *Henry Ward Beecher* (1903), is an interpretation of Beecher's life and views, which while eulogistic is not without discrimination and contains a bibliography of Beecher publications prepared by W. E. Davenport. An analysis of Beecher's qualities as a preacher may be found in L. O. Brastow, *Representative Modern Preachers* (1904). For report of the Tilton–Beecher Case see, *Theodore Tilton vs. Henry Ward Beecher, Action for Crim. Con. . . . Verbatim Report by the Official Stenographer,* pub. by McDivitt, Campbell & Co., New York (3 vols., 1875), and Austin Abbott, *Official Report of the Trial of Henry Ward Beecher* (2 vols., 1875).]

H. E. S.

BEECHER, LYMAN (Oct. 12, 1775–Jan. 10, 1863), Presbyterian clergyman, was born in New Haven, Conn., the son of David Beecher by his third wife, Esther (Lyman) Beecher. His father and grandfather were blacksmiths. His mother died of consumption two days after he was born, and he was brought up by an uncle and aunt on their farm in Guilford, Conn. Entering Yale when he was eighteen years of age, he was profoundly influenced by Timothy Dwight [*q.v.*], who became president of the college at the end of Beecher's sophomore year. After graduation he remained as a student of divinity under Dwight, who was also the professor of theology. In 1799 he was ordained over the Presbyterian Church at East Hampton, L. I., and on Sept. 19, 1799, he was married to Roxana Foote of Guilford, Conn. In East Hampton he preached with ever increasing power and reputation for ten years. His salary, at first $300 and fire-wood, was raised to $400, but a growing family made a change desirable. A published sermon of his so impressed Judge Reeve, founder of the Litchfield Law School, that he was called to the church in that town. Litchfield was then famous in New England for its distinguished men and for the wealth and culture of its leading families. Hither Beecher removed his household in 1810. Belonging to the new school of Calvinism which laid unremitting stress on the freedom of the human will, he aimed, according to the custom of those days, at a continuous revival. Preaching twice on Sunday, holding services during the week in school-houses and private homes, he soon made a deep impression on the town, and the meeting-house was crowded. At that time enforcement of the liquor laws was lax, and sentiment was apathetic to the evils of excessive drinking, even at the formal meetings of the ministers. Beecher was deeply concerned and preached in 1825 six successive sermons on the evil of intemperance; these had great effect and, when published, passed through many editions in this country and in England and were translated into several foreign languages. Largely through Beecher's efficient leadership the General Association of Connecticut adopted drastic recommendations regarding temperance. Beecher took a prominent part in the formation of a Domestic Missionary Society for the education of young men for the ministry, as well as in establishing the American Bible Society, and he was a founder and constant contributor to the *Connecticut Observer*. In 1826 a wave of reaction against Unitarianism was so evident that the orthodox churches of Boston considered the time ripe for the establishment of a new church, which was organized in Hanover Street with thirty-seven members. Lyman Beecher was called as the minister most capable of expounding and enforcing evangelical doctrines. Astonishing results came from his six and a half years of intense activity. Leonard Bacon in his memorial address declared "that no such religious movement had been known in Boston since the period of the Great Awakening eighty years before." The revival unfortunately also had its less attractive side. In 1831 Beecher delivered a series of fiery and intolerant lectures and sermons against the Catholics and thus became indirectly responsible for the sacking of a convent of Ursuline nuns at Charlestown by the Boston mob (James Truslow Adams, *New England in the Republic 1776–1856*, 1926, pp. 334–36). Meanwhile, for the training of ministers in the West, Lane Theological Seminary had been started in Cincinnati; and Lyman Beecher was chosen as its first president and professor of theology, with a pledged endowment of $60,000 dependent upon his acceptance. This opportunity for influencing the religious life of the West made a strong appeal to Beecher. In 1832 he removed to Cincinnati to be the head of the new seminary and also pastor of the Second Presbyterian Church of that city. Almost immediately he was plunged into a violent theological controversy. The conservative Presbyterians assailed him bitterly with formal charges of heresy, slander, and hypocrisy: of heresy because his interpretation of the Westminster Confession differed from theirs, of slander because he maintained that his views were those of a large body of evangelical Christians, of hypocrisy because he pretended that his doctrines squared with the Scriptures and the Confession.

He was acquitted by the local presbytery and then by the synod. His opponents appealed to the General Assembly, but after three years of litigation were persuaded to withdraw the case. This debate had a disastrous effect on Presbyterianism in the West and was one of the causes which led to the division of 1837–38. Himself a discreet abolitionist, Beecher opposed the rules issued by the trustees in his absence in August 1834, which forbade all discussion of slavery by the students. He obtained a revision of these rules, but the seminary lost most of its students to Oberlin College, where a more liberal attitude prevailed. After eighteen years of service Beecher resigned in 1850, and the last years of his life were spent in the home of his son, Henry Ward Beecher, in Brooklyn, where he died. His first wife bore him five sons and four daughters, and died of consumption Sept. 24, 1816. He married Harriet Porter of Portland, Me., in November 1817; after bearing him three sons and one daughter, she died July 7, 1835; his third wife was Mrs. Lydia (Beals) Jackson of Boston.

[For general characterization of Lyman Beecher see sketch of Henry Ward Beecher. The chief sources for Lyman Beecher's biography are: F. B. Dexter, *Biog. Sketches Grads. Yale Coll.*, vol. V (1911); *Autobiog., Correspondence, etc., of Lyman Beecher* (1864); L. Beecher, *Works* (3 vols., 1852–53); C. E. Beecher, "Sketches and Recollections of Dr. Lyman Beecher" in *Congreg. Quart.*, July 1864; *Obit. Record Grads. Yale Coll.*, 1863; D. H. Allen, *Life and Services of Rev. Lyman Beecher* (1863); J. C. White, *Personal Recollections of Lyman Beecher* (1882); E. T. Hayward, *Lyman Beecher* (1904); C. M. Rourke, *Trumpets of Jubilee* (1927); G. C. Woodruff, *Geneal. Reg. of the Inhabitants of the Town of Litchfield, Conn.* (1900); N. Goodwin, *The Foote Family: or the Descendants of Nathaniel Foote* (1849); Paxton Hibben, *Henry Ward Beecher* (1927).]

C. A. D.

BEECHER, THOMAS KINNICUT (Feb. 10, 1824–Mar. 14, 1900), Congregational clergyman, was born in Litchfield, Conn., the twelfth of Lyman Beecher's thirteen children. His mother was Harriet (Porter) Beecher. He was educated chiefly in the West, where, after a pastorate of some years in Boston, his father went to take charge of Lane Theological Seminary, when Thomas was about eight years old. He graduated from Illinois College, of which his brother Edward was president, in 1843; and later studied theology under his father. Like the rest of the Beecher children he found himself unable to accept the Calvinistic doctrines which had overshadowed his youth, and instead of immediately entering the ministry he turned to teaching. He was principal of the North East Grammar School, Philadelphia, and later of the high school in Hartford, Conn. The urge to preach finally mastered him, however, and he was ordained in September 1851 at Williamsburg, N. Y., where he organized a Congregational church. In June 1854 he became pastor of the Independent Congregational Church, Elmira, N. Y., of which he continued as pastor and pastor emeritus until his death. On Sept. 24, 1851, he married Olivia Day, daughter of President Day of Yale College. She died in August 1853, and on Jan. 21, 1857, he married Julia, daughter of Rev. Henry and Eliza (Webster) Jones, a grand-daughter of Noah Webster. In 1863 he was chosen chaplain of the 141st New York Volunteers and served four months with the Army of the Potomac.

During his long residence in Elmira he became one of its most picturesque and best known citizens. A striking figure with his waving white hair, always shabbily dressed, for he impoverished himself by his generosity, highly unconventional according to ministerial standards of the days, he was popular with all classes. To his parishioners he was affectionately known as "Father Tom." Having a liking for mechanics, he long kept the town clock in order, and on his trips to New York, it is said, frequently ran the locomotive of the train on which he traveled. For years he edited a weekly "Miscellany," first in the *Elmira Advertiser,* and later in the *Gazette,* in which he expressed independent, if not always defensible, views, some of which attracted wide attention. He was the candidate of various parties for political offices, but was never elected. He also became known as a pioneer in the "institutional church" movement. He built a new edifice, one of the first of its kind, equipped with gymnasium, library, lecture rooms, and other provisions for social work, which Mark Twain described under the title "A New Beecher Church" in *A Curious Dream* (1872). He took an advanced position regarding Sunday-school methods, grading his school and requiring serious, systematic work on the part of teachers and pupils. Although essentially orthodox, he was broad in his sympathies and in 1870 published *Our Seven Churches,* in which he set forth the admirable characteristics of the various denominations represented in Elmira, and in the last chapter, his own conception of the "Church of Christ." He also published a considerable number of short pamphlets on various subjects, and after his death appeared *In Tune with the Stars* (1902), stories for children.

[*Congreg. Yr. Bk.,* 1901; *Who's Who in America,* 1899–1900; *N. Y. Times,* Mar. 15, 1900; *Appleton's Ann. Cyc., 1900* (1901); W. S. B. Matthews, "A Remarkable Personality," *Outlook,* LXXXII, 555.]

H. E. S.

BEER, GEORGE LOUIS (July 26, 1872–Mar. 15, 1920), historian, publicist, the second son of Sophia (Walter) and of Julius Beer, a member of the Jewish community of Hamburg who had come to the United States in early life and had established himself in business as an importer of tobacco, was born on Staten Island and received his early education, which was of the best, in New York schools. At the age of sixteen he entered Columbia College, where he came in contact with the group of scholars—Burgess, Osgood, Seligman, and others—who were building the reputation of the Columbia Faculty of Political Science. After graduation in 1892, he returned to Columbia for further study. His master's essay, *The Commercial Policy of England toward the American Colonies* (1893), which was published in the Columbia Studies in History, Economics and Public Law, shows that the youthful author was already possessed of mature judgment and is marked by the same historical-mindedness and freedom from distorting patriotic bias that are evident in his later historical writings. For the next ten years Beer was engaged in the tobacco business, in which he was very successful, but historical scholarship never lost its attraction for him, though as a lecturer at Columbia, 1893–97, he showed no great interest in teaching. In order to devote himself to the more exhaustive study of the subject which he had sketched in his master's essay he retired from business in 1903. Accompanied by his wife, Edith C. Hellman of New York, a niece of Prof. Seligman, he went to London, where he remained for more than a year, spending most of his time in examining unpublished documents in the Public Record Office.

Beer's reputation as an historian rests upon three books that he wrote as instalments of a projected work on the economic aspects of British colonial policy in the seventeenth and eighteenth centuries. The first of these to appear was *British Colonial Policy, 1754–65* (1907). Based largely upon official documents, it did full justice to the British official point of view during a critical period in the history of the empire and served as a much-needed corrective of interpretations of British policy inspired by American patriotism. In *The Origins of the British Colonial System, 1578–1660* (1908), Beer placed the early English colonial movement in its historical setting and described the beginnings of the imperial economic system. Following further research in England, he brought out in two volumes *The Old Colonial System, Part I* (1912), the most thorough and authoritative work that has been writen on English colonial policy and practise with respect to imperial trade and defense during the period 1660–88. Beer had accumulated a great mass of material for the volumes that he had planned on the history of the colonial system from 1689 to 1754, but the outbreak of the World War turned him to enterprises of a different nature. His historical work, though unfinished, ranks as one of the major contributions to knowledge made by American historical scholarship in the present century.

During the war Beer devoted much time and energy to the promotion of sympathetic understanding between the United States and the British Empire. As American correspondent of the *Round Table* he made regular contributions to that journal from 1915 to 1918, in which he surveyed for its readers in England and the British dominions the development of American public opinion concerning the war; and during the same years articles from his pen on the British Empire, American foreign policy, and other subjects relating to the war appeared in American periodicals. In 1917 he published the most widely read of all his books, *The English-Speaking Peoples,* in which he urged the formation of an intimate, coöperative alliance between the United States and the British Empire as the best hope for a better world order in the future. In the autumn of 1917 he became a member of the group of investigators, popularly known as "The Inquiry," formed by Col. House at President Wilson's request, to study questions that were likely to come before the peace conference. As colonial expert Beer prepared a number of reports, the more important of which were published after his death in *African Questions at the Paris Peace Conference* (1923). He believed that the guiding principle of colonial administration should be the welfare of the native peoples, and in a report on Mesopotamia, which he completed in January 1918, occurs what is probably the earliest use of the term "mandate" in its present meaning. He was chief of the colonial division of the American delegation at the Paris Peace Conference and sat on a number of its important commissions. As a member of the Mandates Commission he had much to do with drafting the mandates for the administration of the former German colonies, and there is no doubt that his views counted heavily in the colonial settlement for which the Treaty provided. The extent and accuracy of his knowledge on many subjects that came before the conference and the sanity of his judgment made a deep impression, and his views were often sought on other than colonial questions. When the secretariat of the League of Nations was organized Beer was appointed head of the Mandates Division, but the failure of the United States to join the League

prevented him from entering upon the duties of this office. Until almost the end of his life he cherished the hope of returning to his historical labors, but the progress of a fatal disease, probably hastened by the strain of his work at Paris, made this impossible.

[*George Louis Beer: A Tribute to His Life and Work in the Making of History and the Moulding of Public Opinion* (1924) contains a series of biog. sketches, including an estimate of his work as an historian by Prof. Chas. M. Andrews and an account of his activities at the Peace Conference by Prof. James T. Shotwell, together with a number of shorter appreciations by prominent men who had been brought into personal contact with him; his work on the commissions of the Peace Conference is described by Prof. Louis Herbert Grey in his introduction to Beer's *African Questions at the Paris Peace Conference;* an unsigned appreciation appeared in *Pubs. Am. Jewish Hist. Soc.,* Nov. 28, 1922.]

R. L. S.

BEER, WILLIAM (May 1, 1849–Feb. 1, 1927), librarian, son of Gabriel and Harriet (Ferguson) Beer, was born at Plymouth, England. He early developed an interest in libraries, acting as one of the directors of the Cottonian Library at Plymouth, 1869–71. He was also secretary of the Devon and Cornwall Natural History Society, and, with his friend, J. Burt, discovered a Lake village at Dossmire Pool in Cornwall. From 1871 to 1877 he was in Paris, where he studied medicine, modern languages, and art, and formed associations with the students in the studios of Gerôme and Duran. He returned to England in 1877, and accepted, at Newcastle-on-Tyne, a position in a glass manufacturing company, learning many valuable secrets of the art of stained-glass window making. Here, for two years, at the College of Physical Science, he studied mining engineering under Alexander Herschel. He became a member of the Newcastle Antiquarian Society, and investigated such subjects as the Roman occupation of Britain, and more especially the Roman wall, in which research he was associated with D. Brun and John Clay of the Chesters. He worked also in the public library of Newcastle, and formed an excellent collection of the literature of Northumberland. In 1884 he went to Canada, but soon after settled in the United States and practised mining engineering in Michigan, Montana, and Wyoming. In 1889 he withdrew from this profession to become librarian of the free public library of Topeka, Kan. He also organized here a series of extension lectures. Two years later he was made librarian of the Howard Memorial Library of New Orleans, then newly organized by Miss Annie Howard (Mrs. Parrott). In 1896 he was also appointed librarian of the New Orleans Free Public Library, then newly formed by consolidating the Fisk Free Library and the Lyceum Library.

After organizing this institution, he resigned in 1906 to devote himself exclusively to the Howard Library, which he developed on a broad basis as a reference library, giving particular attention to material connected with Louisiana. At his death, the library contained over 80,000 volumes, and many valuable manuscripts and maps. Beer, who never married, was a prominent figure in the social and literary life of New Orleans for many years. He was an intimate friend of George W. Cable, Ruth McEnery Stuart, and Grace King. Until his death he was a member of the Advisory Board of Editors of the *Louisiana Historical Quarterly,* and contributed frequently to its pages.

[This sketch is based on material furnished by Beer himself and on the recollections of his friends in New Orleans. There is an appreciation of Beer by Henry P. Dart in the *La. Hist. Quart.,* Apr. 1927. See also *Who's Who in America,* 1926–27; *Times-Picayune* (New Orleans), Feb. 2, 1927; J. S. Kendall, *Hist. of New Orleans* (1922), III, 1184; Edward Laroque Tinker, "Wm. Beer, 1849–1927," in *La. Hist. Quart.,* Jan. 1928, containing bibliography of Beer's writings.]   I. R. K.

BEERS, ETHEL LYNN (Jan. 13, 1827–Oct. 11, 1879), poet, was born at Goshen, N. Y., the daughter of Horace William Eliot and Keziah (Westcott) Eliot. On the side of her father, who was a soldier in the War of 1812, druggist, justice of the peace, and postmaster, she was a descendant, in the seventh generation, of John Eliot, the apostle to the Indians. Her mother was a daughter of David N. Westcott, colonel of state militia, member of the state legislature, and member of the state constitutional convention. The girl, baptized Ethelinda, early began to contribute to the magazines under the name of Ethel Lynn. At the age of nineteen she was married, on Mar. 5, 1846, to William H. Beers, son of Cyrenius Beers of New York, and henceforth wrote under the name of Ethel Lynn Beers. On Nov. 30, 1861, there appeared in *Harper's Magazine* her poem "The Picket Guard," better known from its opening words "All Quiet Along the Potomac"—a poem suggested by seeing that oft-repeated caption in a newspaper, followed by the notice "A Picket Shot." The verses pay a tender tribute to the unknown soldier and, while a little sentimental for modern taste, achieve a genuine pathos. Over a year later the poem was reprinted anonymously in a Southern paper with the statement that it had been found on the dead body of a soldier. The authorship was generally ascribed in the South either to Lamar Fontaine or Thaddeus Oliver, both Southerners, and the former repeatedly urged his claim but without being able to support it by any satisfactory evidence. Alone of the three, Mrs. Beers produced

other poems of some merit, the three most popular being entitled "Weighing the Baby," "Baby Looking Out for Me," and "Which Shall It Be?" She was a frequent contributor to the *New York Ledger* and in 1863 she published *General Frankie: a Story for Little Folks.* Although a woman of cheerful personality, she had a premonition that she should die immediately after the appearance of her collected poems. *All Quiet Along the Potomac, and Other Poems* was published on Oct. 10, 1879, and she died on the following day.

[*Geneal. of the Descendants of John Eliot 1598–1905* (1905); *N. Y. Times,* Oct. 13, 1879, p. 5; *N. Y. Evening Post,* Oct. 14, 1879, p. 3; *N. Y. Ledger,* Nov. 8, 15, 1879. On the authorship of "All Quiet Along the Potomac" see James Wood Davidson, *The Living Writers of the South* (1869), pp. 194–201.]   E. S. B.

BEERS, HENRY AUGUSTIN (Jan. 2, 1847– Sept. 7, 1926), author and educator, was born in Buffalo, N. Y., where his parents, Connecticut people, were spending the winter on a visit. On his paternal side he was descended from James Beers, who came from England in 1634 and settled in Fairfield, Conn., in 1659. His grandfather, Seth Preston Beers, was the leading lawyer of Litchfield County, and a prominent member of the Connecticut legislature. His father, George Webster Beers (1816–63; B.A. Trinity College, Hartford, 1839), lived in Litchfield. There Beers gained his intimate knowledge of New England nature and in his grandfather's library his intimate knowledge of New England literature. His mother was Elizabeth Victoria Clerc. On the maternal side his inheritance was entertainingly different. Both grandparents were deaf-mutes. His grandfather, Laurent Clerc, had been one of the favorite pupils of the Abbé Sicard in the national institution for deaf-mute instruction at Paris, and had come to this country to assist Thomas Gallaudet in founding the asylum for deaf-mutes at Hartford, where he taught many years. The family occupied the Lydia Sigourney house, the former home of the "Swan of Hartford" so that in Hartford also his associations were literary.

From the Hartford High School Beers passed his examinations for Yale College in 1864, when he was slightly over seventeen years of age. Partly on account of his youth and partly on account of his health he was kept out of college for a year and entered Yale as a member of the class of '69. The composition of this class was exceptional in that there were enrolled in it a number of men who had fought through the Civil War. They were both older than the normal Yale undergraduate and less amenable to discipline. The resulting humorous situations later found in Beers a chronicler (*The Ways of Yale in the Consulship of Plancus,* 1895). In the class was Maj. Edward Heaton, who married Beers's only sister Charlotte, and whose sister, Mary, Beers himself married in Covington, Ky., July 7, 1873. Beers was an able student. He won first prize in English composition and the prize for an original English poem in his sophomore year; a Philosophical Oration appointment in his junior year; and a High Oration appointment in his senior year. Yet he was far from being merely a student. He participated in the various extracurriculum activities of his day. In the debating society, Brothers in Unity, he won the first prize in its junior debate; he was a member of Kappa Sigma Epsilon, Alpha Delta Phi, and Skull and Bones; a member of the Varuna Boat Club, the Red Letter Literary Club, and a contributor to the *Yale Literary Magazine.* Such diverse interest reflected the breadth of his nature, and his college course was successful in the three directions, study, books, friends.

On leaving college he studied law in the office of Pierrepont, Stanley, Langdell & Brown, and was admitted to the bar in May 1870. His practise was not so lucrative but that he was willing to resign it to accept the position of tutor in Yale College. There his life followed the usual routine of appointment: tutor, 1871–74; assistant professor, 1875–80; professor, 1880–1916; professor emeritus, 1916–26. The only breaks in this succession were in the summer and autumn of 1876 when he studied in Europe, chiefly at Heidelberg with Kuno Fischer, where, with characteristic modesty he remarks, "I attended a few lectures," and some weeks in 1877 when he attended Bronson Alcott's School of Philosophy at Concord, where he had the opportunity of knowing Lowell and Emerson. For forty continuous years he taught at Yale where his slight figure was a familiar and greatly beloved sight on the campus. In spite of his dislike of publicity, his great knowledge of English literature and his keen critical judgment won him admirers, but he refused all honorary degrees; "empty honors" he called them. Two of his students, however, in 1923 founded in Yale College the Henry A. Beers Prize in American Literature as a memorial to him. Toward the end of his life he became a personified Yale tradition, one who embodied the past in himself and stood for the best in old Yale.

Beers's published work may be divided into three classes: his poetry; his creative prose; his scholarly prose. His poetry varied from *vers de société* to dramatic monologue, from burlesque to intimate studies of New England landscape. The sonnet, "The Singer of One Song," and the dramatic monologue, "The Dying Pantheist," are both well known. The preference of the author was, however, for the poems dealing with scenery around New Haven, such as "The Upland," "The Pasture Bars," or "Beaver Pond Meadow." His creative prose consisted for the most part of short stories contributed to various magazines. They show his interest in the subtleties of everyday life. He aimed to present only those moments when the soul is at the cross-roads and a slight impetus may change the course of life. His scholarly work is best represented by his volumes on the history of romanticism in England. Here he was the first to trace the development of this movement in English literature from its slow beginnings in the first quarter of the eighteenth century to its culmination in the age of Walter Scott (*History of English Romanticism in the Eighteenth Century,* 1899) and then to its decline in the Victorian period (*History of English Romanticism in the Nineteenth Century,* 1901).

[Family knowledge and personal reminiscence; Records in the Dean's Office, Yale Coll., Secretary's Office and Treasurer's Office, Yale Univ.; class books of the class of '69; *Men of Mark in Conn.,* ed by N. G. Osborn, I (1906), 120.]

J.M.B.

BEHAN, WILLIAM JAMES (Sept. 25, 1840– May 4, 1928), sugar planter, political leader, was born in New Orleans, the son of John Holland and Katherine (Walker) Behan. He attended the University of Louisiana—now Tulane—and the Western Military Institute in Nashville. At the beginning of the Civil War he enlisted with the New Orleans Washington Artillery, and being soon promoted to commissioned rank, served with the Army of Northern Virginia from Bull Run to Appomattox. After the war he returned to New Orleans and became a wholesale grocer, and there in June 1866 he was married to Katie Walker. A determined opponent of carpet-bag government, he took an important part in organizing the Crescent City White League, and in September 1874 he was one of the two men in command of the League forces in their battle against the Federal forces then in New Orleans —the Battle of the Custom House. In 1874–82 he was major-general of the Louisiana National Guard, in 1882–84 mayor of New Orleans, in 1888–92 a member of the state Senate, in 1889–91 major-general of the state Confederate Veterans Association, and from 1905 for many years Commander of the Washington Artillery Veterans Association. During his administration as mayor he manifested his accustomed great vigor and integrity, and, exerting himself particularly to thwart ring politics, he was on that issue defeated for a second term. The conviction among his followers that his defeat was fraudulent was so intense as to tempt them to protest the election by violence, but plans in that direction were at length abandoned. In the early 1890's he removed from New Orleans to his extensive and efficiently conducted sugar-plantation at White Castle, La., and at about this time, along with a number of other planters, in protest against the Democratic scheme for reducing the tariff on sugar, he went over to the Republican party. From 1896 he was a regular delegate at Republican national conventions, in 1900–12 he was a member of the Republican Executive Committee of Louisiana, and in 1904 he was Republican candidate for governor. In 1902 he returned to live in New Orleans. His wife, herself a person of large public usefulness, died in 1918. During the World War he was one of a commission appointed to visit France. His death occurred suddenly in New Orleans.

[J. S. Kendall, *Hist. of New Orleans* (1922), vols. I and II, esp. the articles on Behan and his wife, II, 784–88, *Who's Who in America,* 1924–25; *New Orleans Item,* May 4, 1928.]

J.D.W.

BEHRENDS, ADOLPHUS JULIUS FREDERICK (Dec. 18, 1839–May 22, 1900), clergyman, was born in Nymwegen, Holland, the son of Martina Everdina (Jacobs) Behrends and Charles Augustus Behrends, a Lutheran minister. When he was but five years old the family emigrated to Ohio. He graduated from Denison University in 1862, and from the Rochester Theological Seminary in 1865. In the latter year he became pastor of the Warburton Avenue Baptist Church at Yonkers, N. Y., and remained in that position till the fall of 1873, when he accepted a call to the First Baptist Church in Cleveland. There his opposition to the Baptist custom of restricted or "close" communion was expressed in a sermon that provoked criticism and led to his resignation in January 1876. This was a turning point in his life. He said, shortly before his death, that when he cut loose from the Baptists he stood ready for an open door and determined to accept the first call that came, whether it was Methodist, Presbyterian, or Congregational. It came from the Union Congregational Church of Providence, R. I.; and here he remained till 1883, when he was invited to the pulpit of the Central Congregational Church of Brooklyn, N. Y. This congregation had not attained the commanding position that it reached under Behrends and his successor, Cadman; but it was already one of the prominent churches of the denomination, and its pastor had to stand comparison with Henry Ward

Beecher, Richard S. Storrs, and T. DeWitt Talmage. How Behrends met the test may be judged from an editorial in the *Outlook,* June 2, 1900, which characterized him as "one of the not large number of truly great preachers." Behrends was popular not only as a preacher; his services were in request for lectures. In 1886 he gave a course on "Socialism and Christianity" at the Hartford Theological Seminary; in 1890 he delivered the Lyman Beecher Lectures on Preaching at Yale University, his topic being "The Philosophy of Preaching"; and in 1896 he gave a series of addresses at Syracuse University on missions. He was twice married: first on Aug. 24, 1865, to Harriet E. Hatch of Rochester, N. Y., who died Jan. 27, 1882, leaving him with six children; and second on June 6, 1885, to Mrs. Frances Rouse Otis of Cleveland, who bore him one child and survived him. His published writings include: *Counting the Cost* (1881), a sermon; *The World for Christ* (1896); *The Old Testament Under Fire* (1897); *Sursum Corda, a Book of Praise* (1898). In 1904 William Herries edited a number of writings by Dr. Behrends, and issued them with a biographical introduction under the title, *The Christ of Nineteen Centuries.*

[*Congreg. Yr. Bk.,* 1901; *Brooklyn Daily Eagle,* May 22, 23, 1900; information from Mrs. Geo. H. Olney, Behrends's daughter.]

C.N.

BEHRENS, HENRY (Dec. 10, 1815–Oct. 17, 1895), priest of the Society of Jesus, was born at Munstadt, Hanover. Nothing is known about his parents and childhood. He entered the Society of Jesus Dec. 27, 1832, at Stäffis (Estavayer), Switzerland, and spent the next ten years in the ascetical and scientific training customary in his order. His first position as educator in the College of Freiburg, which disclosed an uncommon ability, was terminated in 1847 by the political troubles in Switzerland. The city had joined the Sonderbund. It was conquered by the troops of the opposition who were bent on killing the Jesuits. After all the other Jesuits had fled from the college, Behrens alone remained in disguise, and by his courage and presence of mind prevented the destruction of the building and saved much of its property. Later a hasty flight with a number of hairbreadth escapes saved his life. Some forty of the exiled Jesuits were sent to found an institution in America, with Behrens as superior. Among them were Father Anthony Anderleddy, later Superior General of the order, and Father Miege, who eventually became Vicar Apostolic of Kansas. The journey from Antwerp to New York, made in a frail sailing vessel under a rather inexperienced captain and a less experienced crew, lasted forty-two days, and ended in a great

disappointment. At New York the exiles learned
that the institution they intended to found had become impossible by the death of the bishop who
had invited them to America. So Behrens returned home, after providing for his charges as
best he could. The Jesuits, now exiled from
Switzerland, began to work in Germany. Behrens may be said to have been one of the pillars
of the new German province. He always held
responsible positions. Nearly all the time he was
master of novices and local superior. For three
years he governed the province as Provincial.
During the Franco-Prussian War he acted as
superior of the Jesuits who labored in the German army as chaplains and nurses. He soon
brought it about that the Jesuits and other religious, including the Sisters, became the preferred workers in the hospitals, though at first
they had been merely tolerated. In spite of these
unselfish services to the country, the Jesuits,
two years later, were expelled from Germany.
For a second time Behrens was a man without a
country.

The German Jesuits at that time had in America what was called the Buffalo Mission, that is,
several houses which were in many ways independent of the American Jesuit authorities. (It
was dissolved in 1907.) The Buffalo Mission became the field of Behrens's activity for the rest of
his life. He arrived at Buffalo, in 1872, and at
once became superior of the Mission. He held
this office 1872–78, and again 1886–92. His first
care was to learn the language of the country, a
task to which the man of nearly sixty devoted himself with the alacrity of a studious boy. His administration was marked by that vigor combined
with paternal kindness which had always distinguished him. He wanted his men to be earnest
workers, inspired by the noblest motives, and untiring in their various occupations. In 1886 he
established St. Ignatius College (now John Carroll University) at Cleveland. His zeal extended to the Indians of South Dakota, where the mission stations of St. Francis and Holy Rosary
arose through his efforts. While not engaged in
the duties of superior he labored humbly as one
of the rank and file. What perhaps made him
especially popular among the people of Buffalo
was his work in the confessional, to which he
remained attached all the years of his life. He
also acted as chaplain in the hospitals of the city,
and was indefatigable in caring for the inmates
of the Good Shepherd Home. The Golden Jubilee of his priesthood, in 1892, was an almost city-
wide celebration. All who had come within the
radius of his kind, if somewhat stern, influence
were his devoted friends.

[P. Heinrich Behrens, Eine Skizze seines Lebens und
Wirkens (Buffalo, 1896); unprinted documents in the
archives of the houses of the former Buffalo Mission;
recollections gathered from those who knew Behrens
personally.]
                                                F.S.B.

BEISSEL, JOHANN CONRAD (April 1690–
July 6, 1768), hymn-writer and founder of the
Solitary Brethren of the Community of Seventh
Day Baptists at Ephrata, was born in Eberbach,
Germany. A posthumous child, born two months
after the death of his drunken father, who was a
baker, Beissel also lost his mother when he was
only a boy of eight. Early apprenticed to a baker,
who was a musician and taught the boy to play
the violin, he displayed extraordinary natural
gifts, learning much by reflection without any
instruction. He was small and insignificant in
body. His conversion took place in his twenty-
seventh year. He early revealed a pietistic trend,
accepting celibacy as a primary requirement for
a man who intends to devote himself to the service of God. Before his death, he named the
many blessings which he had received and placed
high in the list that God had "preserved him from
the allurements of the female sex." He worked
as a journeyman baker at various places, but because of his views he was soon banished from the
Palatinate. Persuaded by his friends, Stiefel
and Stuntz, he started with them for America
in 1720, arriving that autumn in Boston. He
went first to Germantown, in Pennsylvania,
where for a year he studied the weaver's trade,
under Peter Becker, a Baptist and organizer
of the Church of the Brethren. In 1721 Beissel and Stuntz erected a "Solitary" residence in
Muehlbach (Mill Creek, Lebanon County). Here
Stiefel came, declaring that henceforth he would
work on Sunday, observing Saturday as the Sabbath; but Beissel was too much of an ascetic for
Stiefel, and the latter left for Bethlehem. One
after another who had joined themselves to Beissel forsook him, Stuntz finally selling the dwell-
ing-house to reimburse himself for the traveling
expenses he had loaned to Beissel. After much
fasting and prayer, Beissel came to the decision
to submit to apostolic baptism at the hands of his
friend, Peter Becker. He now assumed the name
"Friedsam Gottrecht." Seven years after his
baptism, he founded the "Economy" at Ephrata,
located in Lancaster County. In 1732 he was
joined by some of the Solitary Brethren (unmarried men), Sisters (devoted to virginity), and
married couples, who on joining the settlement
were pledged to continence, being convinced by
Beissel that "the married state had originated in
sin, and would therefore have to come to an end."
At first the Order of Spiritual Virgins and the
Solitary Brethren were quartered in the same

building. This gave rise to much suspicion and bitter persecution. Nevertheless, some persons of wealth and prominence were attracted by the zeal and strict regimen of the sect, notably Conrad Weiser, an elder of the Lutheran Church, who for a time was regarded as a follower of Beissel. Pastor Peter Miller of Philadelphia, a graduate of Heidelberg and a scholarly theologian, also became a follower of Beissel, and ultimately his successor as head of the Order. The wife of Christopher Sauer, the well-known printer and publisher, deserted her husband to win spiritual regeneration among the mystics of Ephrata, and later became the Prioress. The Community gradually grew, until about the middle of the eighteenth century it contained several hundred members. The men then lived in a large communal dwelling or monastery, and the women in another house of the same sort. The largest chapel in Pennsylvania at that time was provided for their joint use. The meeting-house for divine worship also contained large halls for holding Agapae (Love-Feasts), as well as cells for the Solitary, after the manner of the old Greek churches. The Sisters were veiled, and both sexes were garbed with unattractive hoods with cowls, like the Capuchin, so designed that but little was visible of "that humiliating image revealed by sin." All members of the settlement were required to give Beissel weekly written confessions of their spiritual condition. These confessional papers (called Lectiones) were read by Beissel to the congregation, and several hundred of these were later published. The colony excelled in the printing of books and in the making of illuminated manuscripts. In the year 1747 appeared the *Turtel Taube* ("Turtle Dove"), the hymnal of the Ephrata Kloster (Cloister), with both words and tunes largely from the pen of Beissel. He is said to have composed over 1,000 hymns, of which 441 were printed. Although he had no sense of meter or of rhythm, he evolved a distinctive system of harmony, a unique musical notation, and a series of quaint melodies which exerted considerable influence on American hymnology. He often led the Sisters and Brothers of the cloister on a midnight tour of the grounds, singing hymns. Schism and frequent quarrels marked the brief history of the colony, but despite the rigors of their experience Beissel had no difficulty in holding a considerable part of his band of followers together. The decline of the colony began with his death, although its customs were continued well into the nineteenth century, particularly at Snowhill Monastery in Franklin County, Pa. The influence of the little order, which disbanded long ago,

is still traceable, and perhaps its chief legacy is the "Paradisiacal Wonder Music," which Beissel and his followers composed and which remains as proof of the native genius of this self-instructed baker, who might have gained eminent distinction as a composer, if he had been properly trained in the art of composition.

[*Chronicon Ephratense,* compiled by Brothers Lamech and Agrippa, translated from the original German by Dr. J. Max Hark (1889); *The German Sectarians of Pa. 1708–1800* (1899–1900) by Julius F. Sachse; *Hist. of the Ch. of the Brethren of the Eastern District of Pa.* (1915), pp. 32–43; *Pa. German Soc. Proc. and Addresses,* XXI; *Phila. Bulletin,* Mar. 9, 1927.]

P. S. L.

BELCHER, JONATHAN (Jan. 8, 1681/2– Aug. 31, 1757), merchant and colonial governor, was descended from Andrew Belcher, the first of his family to emigrate from England to Massachusetts, son of Thomas Belcher of London, clothworker, and grandson of Robert Belcher of Kingswood, Wiltshire, weaver. The date of Andrew's arrival in New England is unknown but we find him keeping a tavern in Cambridge from 1654 to 1673. He married a sister of Deputy-Governor Danforth, and his second son by this marriage, another Andrew, lived at various times at Hartford, Cambridge, Charlestown, and Boston. Through his marriage to Sarah Gilbert of Hartford he eventually inherited a large property at Meriden which passed to his son Jonathan, the subject of this sketch (W. H. Whitmore, "Record of the Descendants of Andrew Belcher," in *New England Historical and Genealogical Register,* 1873). The future governor's background was thus intercolonial from his earliest connections, so that Gov. Talcott of Connecticut later wrote to him that "our Assembly look upon you to be at least half a Connecticut man by birth."

Jonathan's father became a prosperous merchant and was a member of the Massachusetts Council from 1702 until his death, Nov. 6, 1717. His second daughter Elizabeth married Daniel Oliver and became the mother of Lieutenant-Governor Andrew Oliver and of Chief Justice Peter Oliver. Her sister Mary married George Vaughan of Portsmouth, afterward lieutenant-governor. With such a setting, the career of Jonathan as merchant and politician was obviously a natural one. He was born at Cambridge and went to Harvard, where he graduated in 1699. He then went to Europe, traveling somewhat extensively on the continent as well as in England, for a number of years. Returning to Boston, he established himself as a merchant and accumulated a considerable fortune. On Jan. 8,

1705, he married Mary, daughter of Lieutenant-Governor William Partridge of Portsmouth, N. H.; she died on Oct. 6, 1736, and on Sept. 9, 1748, he married Mary Louisa Emilia Teal in Burlington, N. J., who survived him.

Belcher's political career began with his election to the Massachusetts Council in 1718. He was reëlected in 1719, 1720, 1722, 1723, 1726, 1727, and 1729, but his last election was negatived by Gov. Burnet. The perennial question of the executive's salary as a dispute between governor and Assembly was in especial evidence during Burnet's term, and in 1728 Belcher was appointed by the House to represent its side of the case in England as a colleague of the colony's regular agent, Francis Wilks. Two months earlier Belcher had also been appointed by the Connecticut Assembly to attempt to secure a reversal in England of the decision in the important case of Winthrop *vs.* Lechmere, which was threatening the validity of all land titles in the colony. He arrived in London early in 1729, and, soon after, word was received of the death of Gov. Burnet. Belcher, with the advantage of being on the spot at the critical moment, secured the post for himself, the government being probably partly influenced by the facts that he was colonial born and at the same time a "prerogative man," and so presumably pleasing to parties on both sides of the water. His commission was dated Jan. 8, 1729/30, and he landed in Boston on Aug. 10 as governor of Massachusetts and New Hampshire.

From the nature of its duties, the position of royal governor in energetic, liberty-loving colonies was one in which it was impossible to please all. The difficulties were rather enhanced than diminished when the governor was a son of the colony. Belcher's term offered no exception. There was the inevitable and interminable quarrel over the salary question, but in Belcher's case there were other factors which led to his eventual downfall. He was fond of office, and as governor tried to compromise by maintaining the royal prerogative sufficiently to retain his post, and by advancing colonial interests, at the expense of the Crown, to maintain his popularity at home. The colonials had by this time thoroughly awakened to the value of their natural resources, and the larger business men were striving to "utilize them through commerce." One sphere of speculation was the eastern territory of Maine, and there Belcher came into conflict with royal authority which was trying to retain control of the timber. Moreover, a rapidly expanding commerce had created currency difficulties, and when an unsound scheme was set on foot to found a "Land Bank" to issue notes, Belcher promptly took sides with the more conservative business elements. The object was good but the methods of reducing the opposition indulged in by the governor and the conservatives were high-handed and drastic. Belcher's temper was irascible and his language vituperative. His words as well as his acts constantly created enemies for him. A boundary dispute between Massachusetts and New Hampshire brought about much ill-feeling. In this case Belcher was accused, unjustly apparently, of accepting a bribe. Finally, a group of enemies brought charges against him in England, some of which were signed with forged names, and he was dismissed from both governorships May 7, 1741.

A few years later, he went to England, rehabilitated himself in the opinion of the English government, and in July 1746 was appointed governor of New Jersey, the commission being dated the following February and he himself arriving in his new province in August. Although serious riots occurred over the land question, his term there was much more tranquil than in New England and, on the whole, satisfactory. He was greatly interested in the founding of the College of New Jersey (Princeton), and on his death bequeathed his library of 374 volumes to that institution. It had been proposed to give to the present Nassau Hall the name "Belcher Hall," but he had declined the honor and suggested the name now in use. His character appears clearly in the large mass of correspondence left by him. With wealth, literary tastes, and unusual advantages in travel, he yet remained an uncultured man of small views. He was sanctimonious yet showered abusive epithets on all who differed from him. Aggressive where he felt he had the power, no one could fawn lower to secure advantages for himself and his family. He was vain and self-seeking but as an official was by no means below the average of the day, and in such matters as his opposition to unsound currency in Massachusetts and in the founding of Princeton he rendered genuine service.

[The chief sources of information are the volumes of his published letters. The most important of these are the "Belcher Papers," *Mass. Hist. Soc. Colls.,* ser. 6, vols. VI, VII. There are also many letters in the "Talcott Papers," *Conn. Hist. Soc. Colls.,* IV, V. The letters relating to his N. J. period are printed in *N. J. Archives,* VII, VIII. The *N. H. Provincial Papers,* IV, contain much documentary material relating to his administration of that colony. There is an almost contemporary, and very fair, account of his term in Massachusetts in Thomas Hutchinson's *Hist. of the Province of Mass. Bay* (1764–1828), vol. II. His commission as governor of Mass. and N. H. may be found in *Col. Soc. of Mass. Pubs.,* II, 119 ff.; see also H. L. Osgood, *Am. Colonies in the Eighteenth Cent.* (1924), vol. III, ch., XVI.]

J. T. A.

BELCOURT, GEORGE ANTOINE (Apr. 22, 1803–May 31, 1874), Catholic missionary, was born at Bay du Febvre, Province of Quebec, Canada. His parents were Antoine Belcourt and Josephte (Lemire) Belcourt. He was educated at the college of Nicolet and was ordained as a priest Mar. 18, 1827. In 1831 he was selected for the mission field of western Canada to work among the Saulteux, or Chippewas. After some months of study of the Algonquin language, he set out for his mission field, arriving at St. Boniface (Winnipeg) on the Red River June 17, 1831, after a canoe voyage of over 2,000 miles. In 1834 he established his permanent mission at Baie St. Paul on the Assiniboine River, thirty-five miles west of the present city of Winnipeg. Here he spent thirteen years of arduous labor, receiving but $500 annually for the support of his work. In 1845 at the request of the leaders, he accompanied the annual buffalo hunt of half-breeds and Indians into what is now North Dakota. They spent six weeks in the region between Devil's Lake and the Missouri River, bringing back their year's supply of meat, hides, and pemmican for the inhabitants of the lower Red River Valley. The priest held a daily religious service, took an active part in the hunting of the buffaloes, and left an interesting and accurate eye-witness account of the entire hunt. As an historical document this narrative is of considerable importance as furnishing a picture of what had come to be a regular frontier institution of over sixty years' standing. The next year he again accompanied the buffalo hunt, but on this occasion his services as a physician were most in demand. He had to combat an epidemic of dysentery and measles that raged among the families on the expedition during the entire hunt. When his supply of medicine was exhausted, he traveled from the camp, west of Dog Den Butte, to the Fort Berthold village of the Mandans and Gros Ventres on the Missouri River where the white traders gave him the much-needed medicine. By request he preached in this Indian village, which numbered 2,000 souls, and after the service he was asked to return and establish a mission there. In 1846 a bitter contest broke out between the half-breeds and merchants of Fort Garry and the officials of the Hudson's Bay Company, the latter being opposed to permitting free trade with Pembina and Fort Snelling on the American side of the line. Father Belcourt, by his great influence with the half-breeds, prevented them from resorting to violence. Later he persuaded them to conform to the English custom and to petition the Crown for redress of their trading grievances. Chief-Factor Christie

and other officers of the Hudson's Bay Company were so angered at the part played by Father Belcourt that he felt obliged, in the interest of harmony, to resign his position in 1847. He was immediately appointed as missionary at Pembina on the Red River, a short distance south of the Canadian line. He traveled to this station from Quebec by way of Chicago and St. Paul, arriving in July 1849. He built himself a bark cabin and spent the winter in traveling on snowshoes over an area 900 miles in breadth, going as far west as Turtle Mountain. For the next two years he had as his assistant a missionary who afterward became well known as Father Lacombe of the Edmonton district. In 1850 he abandoned Pembina on account of the flood that spring and established a new mission at St. Joseph, now Walhalla. In pursuance of the policy of encouraging the Indians to adopt a more settled life, he set up the first saw-mill and grist-mill in this part of the northwest. Gov. Ramsay of Minnesota Territory was a great admirer of Father Belcourt and aided him in his work wherever possible. In 1858 the latter resigned his position and returned to Quebec. He held a pastorate at Rustico, Prince Edward Island, for ten years, and died at Shediac, New Brunswick. He was known throughout the northwest as one of the greatest of the pioneer missionaries of his time. His unflagging zeal for the cause of his mission field was equaled only by his tireless researches in the language of the Saulteux. His *Principes de la Langue des Sauvages appelés Saulteux* was published in Quebec in 1839.

[G. A. Belcourt, "Mon itinéraire du lac des Deux-Montagnes à la Rivière Rouge," *La Revue Canadienne* (1913); *Proc. Royal Soc. of Canada*, 1920, XIV, 23; *Colls. State Hist. Soc. of N. Dak.*, V, 134 ff.; *Minn. Hist. Soc. Colls.*, I, 193 ff.; *House Ex. Doc. No. 51*, 31 Cong., 1 Sess., pp. 44 ff.]

O. G. L.

BELDEN, JOSIAH (May 4, 1815–Apr. 23, 1892), California pioneer, was born in Cromwell, Conn., the son of Josiah and Ruth (McKee) Belden and a descendant of Richard Bayldon, who came to that state from England in 1645. His mother died when he was four years old. He attended the common schools until he was fifteen, when his father died, and he was then apprenticed to a jeweler in Albany. In 1836 he moved to Philadelphia and later to Vicksburg, continuing in the jewelry business. At Independence, Mo., in May 1841, he joined the Bartleson-Bidwell party, which was to make the first emigrant wagon-train journey from the Missouri to the Pacific. With about half of the original company, though without the wagons, which had been abandoned east of the Sierras, Belden arrived at the

Marsh ranch, near Mount Diablo, Nov. 4. At Monterey, Oct. 20, 1842, when Commodore Jones, in the belief that war had been declared, compelled the surrender of the town, Belden raised the American flag. He also, a few days later, after serving in the interim as the town's *alcalde,* pulled the flag down. For two years he ran a branch store at Santa Cruz for Thomas O. Larkin, the American consul. In 1844 he became a Mexican citizen and was awarded a tract of land in the Sacramento Valley. Here he established a ranch, though he gave most of his time to business ventures in Monterey and San Francisco. He seems to have borne only a minor, if any, part in the contest of 1846. At the time of the gold discovery he was in San José in charge of a branch store for Mellus & Howard, the largest firm on the coast. He left for the mines, but soon came back and resumed his business, which now, due to the influx of gold and the eagerness of the Mexicans to buy everything offered for sale, became exceedingly prosperous. In 1849 he married Sarah M. Jones, a pioneer of 1846. In the same year he closed his business and invested heavily in San Francisco real estate. On the incorporation of San José as a city, in 1850, he was elected its first mayor, and he later served on its council. He supported the Union party in the campaigns of 1860–61 and during the Civil War he took a special interest in the Sanitary Fund, to which he made large contributions. In 1876 he was a delegate to the Republican National Convention. About 1881 he moved from San José to New York. In his later years he spent much time in foreign travel. At the time of his death, which occurred in his New York home, he was a member of the Union League Club and a director of the Erie Railroad.

Belden is described as domestic in his tastes, unassuming and democratic in manner, and punctiliously honest in his dealings. Bancroft speaks of him as "clear headed" and praises a chronicle of his California experiences which at the request of the historian he wrote in 1878. The considerable fortune which he built up had its beginnings in the friendship and confidence which he inspired among his Mexican fellow-citizens of San José, who not only bought his goods with great prodigality but entrusted to him, on his mere word of honor, large quantities of gold. From his profits he bought real estate, of which at the time of his death he was a large holder.

[Jessie Perry Van Zile Belden, *Concerning Some of the Ancestors and Descendants of Royal Denison Belden and Olive Caldwell Belden* (1898); H. H. Bancroft, *Hist. of Cal.* (1885), II, 715; T. H. Hittell, *Hist. of Cal.* (1885), II, 331; Zoeth Skinner Eldredge (ed.), *Hist. of Cal.* (1915), III, 362; obituaries in the *N. Y. Tribune,* Apr. 25, 1892, and *N. Y. Sun,* Apr. 26, 1892. An account of the historic journey to the coast is given by Gen. John Bidwell in the *Century Mag.,* Nov. 1890.]

W. J. G.

BELKNAP, GEORGE EUGENE (Jan. 22, 1832–Apr. 7, 1903), naval officer, the son of Sawyer B. and Martha (Aiken) Belknap, was born at Newport, N. H. He was appointed midshipman in 1847 and was promoted to be passed midshipman in 1853, master in 1855, and lieutenant in September of the same year. From 1847 to 1850 he served on the brig *Porpoise* off the coast of Africa, and later (1856–57), serving on the sloop *Portsmouth* of the East India Squadron, he was commended for gallant behavior during the naval attack on the Barrier Forts at Canton, China. In April 1863 he served as executive officer of the *New Ironsides,* flagship of Admiral Du Pont, in the attack on the forts in Charleston Harbor, and was especially commended for the state of efficiency to which he had brought his ship, as well as for his conduct in action. He commanded the monitor *Canonicus* in the attacks on Fort Fisher in December 1864 and January 1865, after which he returned to duty off Charleston, his ship firing the last gun before the surrender of that city. Belknap was promoted to be commander in 1866, commanding the *Hartford* on the Asiatic Station, and directing, among other activities, the expedition against Formosa. In the *Tuscarora,* in 1873 and 1874, he made extensive deep-sea surveys for submarine cable routes, developing the use of piano wire for sounding. He became captain in 1875, and commanded the Navy Yard at Pensacola and then the cruiser *Alaska* in the Pacific. After a tour of service at the Norfolk Navy Yard he served as superintendent of the Naval Observatory, and as commandant of the Mare Island Navy Yard, California. He was promoted to be commodore in 1885. He then became commander-in-chief of the Asiatic Station for three years, and was president of the Board of Inspection and Survey until his retirement in 1894, having been made rear admiral Feb. 12, 1889. After retirement he was appointed chairman of the Board of Commissioners of the Massachusetts Nautical Training School and during the war with Spain was appointed chairman of a board on naval coaling stations. He died at Key West while again on special duty. He was greatly respected as an officer of high character and uncommon ability, his wide experience, especially in foreign relations, giving much weight to his influence and opinion. He was married twice: to Ellen D. Reed in Newport, N. H., in 1861, and to Frances G. Prescott in Calcutta, India, in 1866.

[Navy Registers, 1848–1903; *Report of the Secretary of the Navy*, 1863–65; obituary in *Army and Navy Jour.*, Apr. 11, 1903; *Who's Who in America*, 1901–02.]

E. B.

BELKNAP, JEREMY (June 4, 1744–June 20, 1798), Congregational clergyman, was born in Boston, Mass. He was christened Jeremiah by his parents, Joseph and Sarah (Byles) Belknap, but later adopted the abbreviated form of his first name. His father was a leather-dresser and furrier; his mother was a niece of Rev. Mather Byles. Jeremy prepared for college at Mr. Lovell's school, and entered Harvard before he was fifteen years old. Upon graduating from Harvard in 1762 he taught school at Milton, Mass., for a year or two, and afterward at Portsmouth and Greenland, N. H. While thus engaged, he was studying for the ministry, and in 1766 he went to Dover, N. H., where he was installed as pastor of the Congregational church. In the following year he married Ruth Eliot, daughter of Samuel Eliot, a bookseller in Cornhill, Boston. Although the relations between Belknap and Gov. John Wentworth were distinctly cordial, the former favored the American cause in the approaching Revolution, especially after the passage of the Boston Port Bill. Soon after hostilities began he was appointed chaplain to the New Hampshire troops at Cambridge, but his health and other considerations prevented him from accepting the office (*New Hampshire State Papers*, VII, 562). After the war, in 1786, he resigned from his parish at Dover, and after preaching at various places in New Hampshire and Massachusetts he accepted, early in 1787, a call to the Federal Street Church in Boston. He continued as minister of that society during the remainder of his life.

Belknap's reputation rests chiefly on his *History of New Hampshire*, a work in three volumes which is remarkable for its research, impartiality, and literary merit. The author began it soon after establishing himself at Dover and he completed it more than twenty years later. The first volume appeared in 1784; the others followed in 1791 and 1792. In many ways Belknap's *New Hampshire* is the counterpart of Hutchinson's *History of Massachusetts-Bay*, but it has the additional merit of being a complete study to 1789, including a valuable treatise on the natural history of New Hampshire. About 1787 Belknap amused himself by writing *The Foresters*, a humorous allegory describing the origin and rise of the British colonies in North America. It appeared serially in the *Columbian Magazine*, and later (1792) the chapters were collected and put forth as a small book. Belknap's next production was his *American Biography*, two volumes containing sketches of the lives of the more famous early explorers and colonial leaders. The first volume was published in 1794; the second, just after his death in 1798.

In Boston, Belknap discovered other gentlemen who were interested in the writing of history and in the preservation of historical papers and memorabilia. Conspicuous among these were William Tudor, the Rev. John Eliot, the Rev. Peter Thacher, and James Winthrop. In the summer of 1790 Belknap formulated a plan for an "Antiquarian Society," and in January of the following year he and his four friends mentioned above held their first meeting. This was the beginning of the Massachusetts Historical Society, which was incorporated in 1794. Its first president was James Sullivan, who later became governor of Massachusetts; Belknap was elected corresponding secretary. This society was the first of its kind in the United States, and Belknap endeavored to promote the formation of similar institutions in the other states. Besides his historical works he wrote a biography of Isaac Watts, which appeared anonymously in 1793 in the same volume with a life of Dr. Doddridge by Andrew Kippis. In 1795 he published *Dissertations on the Character, Death, and Resurrection of Jesus Christ, and the Evidence of his Gospel;* in the same year he issued a collection of psalms and hymns, which was widely used by the Congregational churches of New England for many years. Other significant publications were a *Sermon on Military Duty* (1773), a *Discourse intended to Commemorate the Discovery of America by Christopher Columbus* (1792), and a *Sermon delivered before the Convention of the Clergy of Massachusetts* (1796). A portrait of Belknap by Henry Sargent in the possession of the Massachusetts Historical Society shows a thick-set, perhaps corpulent man, with an intelligent and benevolent countenance. His health appears never to have been robust, but he seldom spared himself on that account either in his ministry or in his literary pursuits.

[There is a good brief biography of Belknap by his grand-daughter, Jane Belknap Marcou (1847). Several volumes of his correspondence are preserved in the library of the Mass. Hist. Soc. Many of these papers have been printed in the Society's *Collections*, ser. 5, vols. II, III, and ser. 6, vol. IV. His "Journal of a Tour from Boston to Oneida, June, 1796," is printed in the *Mass. Hist. Soc. Proc.*, XIX, 396–423. A number of interleaved almanacs containing notes made by Belknap are also preserved in the Society's library.]

L. S. M.

BELKNAP, WILLIAM WORTH (Sept. 22, 1829–Oct. 13, 1890), secretary of war, was born in Newburgh, N. Y., the son of Gen. William Goldsmith Belknap, who later gained prominence in the Mexican War, and Ann Clark Belknap. The younger Belknap attended Princeton College, studied law at Georgetown, D. C., was admitted to the bar in 1851, began practise in Keokuk, Ia., and sat in the Iowa legislature as a Douglas Democrat, 1857–58. At the opening of the Civil War Belknap received a commission as major of the 15th Iowa Infantry, and served with distinction at Shiloh. Of this engagement, Col. H. T. Reid reported: "Major Belknap was always in the right place at the right time, directing and encouraging officers and men as coolly as a veteran" (*Official Records*, ser. I, vol. X, p. 289). He was mentioned for "conspicuous gallantry" at Corinth, was in command of the 15th Iowa at the siege of Vicksburg and during the Meridian expedition under Sherman in the early months of 1864. On July 30, 1864, he was commissioned brigadier-general on Sherman's recommendation, and placed in command of the 4th Division of the 17th Corps, of which the 15th Iowa was a part. Until the close of the war, he was in command of the 4th Division through Sherman's campaign in Georgia and northward across the Carolinas. The opinion of Belknap's work which was held by his superiors is typified in the report of Col. William Hall, referring to an engagement before Atlanta on July 22, 1864: Belknap displayed "at all times the highest qualities of a soldier, cheering his men by his voice, and encouraging them by his personal disregard of danger" (*Ibid.*, vol. XXXVIII, pt. 3, p. 595). He was mustered out on July 27, 1865. Upon his return to civil life, Belknap became a collector of internal revenue in Iowa, and in 1869 secretary of war in the cabinet of President Grant. On Mar. 2, 1876, the chairman of the committee on expenditures in the War Department reported to the House of Representatives that he had found "unquestioned evidence of the malfeasance in office by General William W. Belknap." The evidence was read and the Secretary impeached by a unanimous vote. Meanwhile Belknap resigned, and Grant accepted his resignation. The gravamen of the charges was that Belknap had received $24,450 during 1870–76 for appointing a certain John S. Evans to the post-tradership at Fort Sill. In the resulting trial before the Senate, thirty-five voted "guilty" and twenty-five "not guilty," short of the necessary two-thirds for conviction; of the twenty-five, however, twenty-two declared that Belknap's resignation took him outside the jurisdiction of the Senate (cf. Constitution, article II, sec. 4). The fact of the payments by Evans for his immunity from removal seems to have been admitted on both sides of the controversy. It is impossible to be sure, however, whether Belknap was aware of the bargain, or whether his wife made the arrangement and received the money without his knowledge. After his retirement from public office, Belknap lived for a long time in Philadelphia, but later practised law in Washington. Belknap was three times married. His first wife was Cora Le Roy, of Vincennes, Ind., and his second, Carrie Tomlinson of Kentucky, who died in 1870. He then married Mrs. John Bower, the sister of his second wife. His death occurred in Washington.

[Jesse R. Grant, *In the Days of My Father General Grant* (1925); the military record is best followed in the *Official Records;* official records of the impeachment are found in: *Reports of Committees of the House of Representatives*, 44 Cong., 1 Sess., *No. 186*, "Malfeasance of W. W. Belknap, Late Secretary of War," *No. 345*, "Impeachment of William W. Belknap," and *No. 791*, "Report of the House Managers on the Impeachment of W. W. Belknap, Late Secretary of War"; the best account of the trial is in the *Cong. Record*, vol. IV, pt. 7, 44 Cong., 1 Sess., "Trial of W. W. Belknap"; *Iowa Hist. Record*, July 1885; *Ibid.*, Jan. 1891; obituaries in the *Evening Star* (Washington, D. C.), Oct. 13, 1890; *Washington Post*, Oct. 14, 1890; *Hist. of Lee County, Ia.* (1879), p. 683; E. M. Ruttenber, *Hist. of the County of Orange, N. Y.* (1875), pp. 360 ff.; *Hist. of the 15th Reg., Ia. Veteran Volunteer Inf.* (1887), ed. by W. W. Belknap; L. D. Ingersoll, *Hist. of the War Dept. of the U. S.* (1879); H. White, *Life of Lyman Trumbull* (1913).]

C. R. L.

BELL, ALEXANDER GRAHAM (Mar. 3, 1847–Aug. 2, 1922), inventor of the telephone and the outstanding figure of his generation in the education of the deaf, was born in Edinburgh, the second of the three sons of Alexander Melville Bell [*q.v.*], a scientist and author in the field of vocal physiology and elocution, and of Eliza Grace Symonds (1809–97), the daughter of a surgeon in the Royal Navy. His grandfather, Alexander Bell (1790–1865), was a professor of elocution in London. From both sides of the family he inherited a scientific tendency and an instinct for applying knowledge to practise. During his earlier years he was taught at home, by his mother, a woman of admirable character who was also unusually gifted, a musician and painter of ability. From her Bell obtained his accuracy and sensitiveness of hearing and his love for music. When he was ten years old he went to McLauren's Academy in Edinburgh, and then to the Royal High School, from which he graduated at the age of thirteen. A visit to his grandfather in London extended to more than a year, and brought him many educational and cultural advantages. At the age of sixteen he secured a position as a pupil-teacher of elocution and music in Weston House Academy, at Elgin in Morayshire. The next year he spent at the University of Edinburgh, and then returned to Elgin for two years, thereafter spending a year (1866–67) as an instructor in Somersetshire College at Bath in England.

The distinctive achievement of his father, Alexander Melville Bell, was the invention of Visible Speech, a system of symbols by which the position of the vocal organs in speech was indicated. When the grandfather died in 1865, Alexander Melville Bell moved to London to take up his father's work there, and about two years later Alexander Graham Bell became his father's professional assistant in London. At this time he matriculated at University College, London, taking courses in anatomy and physiology for three years, 1868–70. While his father was absent in America on a lecture tour in 1868, Alexander Graham Bell took entire charge of his father's professional duties. The next year Alexander Melville Bell took his son into full partnership with him, an arrangement which continued until the family sailed for America, arriving in Quebec on Aug. 1, 1870.

Alexander Graham Bell early showed an aptness for systematic investigation and promise of inventive ability, which his father encouraged. The former's first piece of original scientific work was set forth in a letter to his father, from Elgin, Nov. 24, 1865, on the resonance pitches of the mouth cavities during the utterance of vowel sounds. His father suggested to him that he send this study to Alexander J. Ellis, an eminent phonetician and friend in London. Ellis called his attention to the work of Helmholtz on vowel sounds. This resulted in Bell's beginning the study of electricity as applied in telegraphy. At this time he conceived his first idea for the electrical transmission of speech. His work for the deaf, also, grew out of his position as his father's assistant. One of his father's pupils, Miss Susanna E. Hull, had a school for deaf children in Kensington. At her request in May 1868, Alexander Melville Bell sent his son, then twenty-one years old, to her school to adapt Visible Speech and its teaching to the work for the deaf, and during the same year in an influential lecture at the Lowell Institute, Boston, he told of the use of Visible Speech in the London School. As a result, in the following year through the efforts of the Rev. Dexter King a special day school for the deaf, the first of its kind anywhere, was started by the Boston School Board with Miss Sarah Fuller as principal. She had heard Alexander Melville Bell's lecture and persuaded the School Board to engage his son to come and train her teachers in the use of Visible Speech. Bell began his work at Miss Fuller's school on Apr. 10, 1871. He added to Visible Speech a system of notation that improved it for use with the deaf. This is still the basis of the method used in teaching the deaf to talk.

After three months of Miss Fuller's school, Bell visited the Clarke Institution for the Deaf at Northampton, Mass., and the American Asylum for the Deaf at Hartford, Conn. As a demand for his services resulted, in October 1872 he opened a private normal class in Boston to which institutions could send teachers for training in the use of Visible Speech. Early in 1873 he was appointed professor of vocal physiology and the mechanics of speech in the School of Oratory of Boston University. There also he started a normal class for the training of teachers of the deaf. Bell's lectures at Boston University attracted wide attention and the University of Oxford invited him to deliver a course there. This he did with notable success in 1878. His normal work became still more extensive through a series of conventions of teachers of speech to the deaf, which he started and led. His work also became more intensive, as he took a number of private pupils. One of these was the five-year-old son of Thomas Sanders of Haverhill, Mass., who was born deaf. Bell had charge of the child's entire education for more than three years, 1873–76, living with him at the home of the grandmother in Salem. Believing that the principle of Froebel's kindergarten method would be useful in the teaching of the deaf, he used both playing and working as direct means of instruction.

Bell's inventive activities were not suspended by these interests, though invention was always subordinate in his own mind to his main purpose to devote his life to the welfare of the deaf. His approach to his inventive work through the science of acoustics and his work for the deaf was particularly favorable to the success later of his telephonic experiments. Further, so remarkable was his teaching of the little Sanders boy that Thomas Sanders in generous gratitude offered to meet all the expenses of his experimenting and of securing patents for his inventions. A little later Gardiner G. Hubbard, a man of notable public spirit and an active friend of the education of the deaf, also became interested in Bell and gave most important and effective assistance in the commercial management of his inventions. During the years 1873–76, Bell was experimenting along three related lines—to invent a phonautograph; a multiple telegraph; and an electric speaking telegraph or telephone. He hoped in his phonautograph to invent an instrument with which he could explain to his deaf pupils how to make their tone-vibrations correctly by comparing visual records of the sounds they made with standard records. For this Dr. Clarence J. Blake, an aurist, suggested that he use an actual human ear in studying the question, and prepared one for him. Bell never brought his phonautograph to such a stage as to be of practical use for his purpose, but it was of value to him in his telephone experiments; from it he took the conception of the membrane element in the telephone.

His experiments in telegraphy Bell had begun at Elgin when only eighteen. At that time telegraphy constituted the whole art of electrical communication. Before leaving London for America in 1870, Bell had secured a copy in French of Helmholtz's book, *The Sensations of Tone*. His study of this book was an important help in gaining a correct knowledge of the physical principles underlying the theory of sound. Thereafter he advanced with a firmer step in all his researches. After coming to America, what time he could spare from his work for the deaf he gave to telegraphy, hoping to invent a device that would send two or more telegraph messages over a wire at the same time. In his multiple harmonic telegraph he utilized the fact that a tuned reed will vibrate when its own note is sounded near it. A number of reed transmitters were attached by leads to the one wire; at the other end of the wire a similar number of leads ran to receivers in which the reeds were attuned accurately to their corresponding transmitters. Each receiver would in operation vibrate in response only to its own transmitter. These experiments resulted in two patents. The first was No. 161,-739, Apr. 6, 1875, for an Improvement in Transmitters and Receivers for Electrical Telegraphs; the other was No. 178,399, June 6, 1876, for Telephonic Telegraph Receivers. From his arduous study and experimentation in telegraphy Bell gained invaluable advantage in the mastery of the principles of electrical wave transmission.

But the speaking telephone was always in Bell's mind the most important invention. In the summer of 1874, following his usual custom, he had gone to his father's home at Brantford, Ontario, to spend his vacation. While there, on July 26, 1874, Bell tells us, he formed clearly in his mind the theory of the telephone that ultimately proved to be correct. How to realize this theory in practise was a problem which presented many difficulties. Bell had learned at the Massachusetts Institute of Technology that some of the points he had discovered concerning the application of acoustics to telegraphy had already been discovered by Joseph Henry [*q.v.*]. In order to learn which of his own discoveries were new and which were old he called upon Prof. Henry at the Smithsonian Institution. The aged scientist treated him with genuine interest and gracious respect,

even asking permission to verify Bell's experiments and publish them through the Smithsonian Institution, giving Bell full credit for them. Much encouraged, Bell told Joseph Henry about his telephone idea and asked Henry whether he ought to publish it at its present stage and allow others to work it out or try to finish it himself. Henry declared it to be the "germ of a great invention" and told him to go ahead himself. Bell then said that he lacked the electrical knowledge that was necessary. Henry emphatically replied, "Get it!" This sympathetic and unhesitating confidence in him by Joseph Henry led Bell to persevere. Whatever observations he made, whatever experiments he was conducting, his mind henceforth was always alert to note anything which might throw light on his telephone problem. At length on June 2, 1875, in the shop at 109 Court St., Boston, while preparing the apparatus used in his harmonic telegraph for an experiment, Bell observed an effect, the significance of which he alone was competent to appreciate. He was tuning the receiver reeds and his assistant, Thomas A. Watson, was plucking the transmitting reeds to give him the pitch over the wire. In one transmitter the contact point was screwed down too far and Bell's sensitively accurate ear heard not only the pitch or tone of the reed but also the overtones. He knew at once that he had found what he had been seeking, that any condition of apparatus that would reproduce the tone and overtones of a steel spring could be made to reproduce the tone and overtones of the human voice. After repeatedly verifying the fact he had observed, Bell gave Watson directions for making the first telephone. When tested the next morning Watson could recognize Bell's voice, and could almost understand some of the words. Experimenting to improve the quality of the transmission followed. On Mar. 10, 1876, the telephone transmitted its first complete intelligible sentence, "Mr. Watson, come here; I want you." Bell's subsequent development of the telephone in quality and distance of transmission was rapid, until in about a year, Apr. 3, 1877, he was able to conduct a telephone conversation between Boston and New York with some degree of success. In September and October 1875, Bell had written the specifications for his application for a patent. The historic first Telephone Patent, No. 174,465, had been allowed on Bell's twenty-ninth birthday, Mar. 3, and had been issued to him on Mar. 7, 1876. On Jan. 30, 1877, another patent was issued to him, No. 186,787, for the substitution of an iron or steel diaphragm for the membrane and armature in the telephone of the first patent. Many claimants now came forward to contest Bell's rights, but after the most prolonged and important litigation in the history of American patent law, including about 600 cases, the United States Supreme Court upheld all of Bell's claims, declaring that he was the discoverer of the only way that speech could be transmitted electrically (*126 United States Reports*). His first announcement and demonstration of the telephone to the scientific world was in an address before the American Academy of Arts and Sciences in Boston on May 10, 1876. On June 25, 1876, at the International Centennial Exhibition at Philadelphia, through the interest of Dom Pedro II, the Emperor of Brazil, who was present as a guest of honor, and to whom a few months before Bell had shown the school for the deaf in Boston, Bell had an opportunity to explain his telephone to the judges, among whom were Sir William Thomson, Joseph Henry, and other prominent scientists. This demonstration was in itself an important introduction of the telephone to the scientific world. Lectures before scientific societies led to a demand for lectures for the general public. At Salem on Feb. 12, 1877, the telephone was used for the first time to send a report to a newspaper. With the spring of 1877 the commercial development of the invention came to the front. The first telephone organization was effected on July 9, 1877, in the form of a trusteeship called the Bell Telephone Company with Gardiner G. Hubbard as trustee and Thomas Sanders as treasurer.

On July 11, 1877, Bell married Mabel G. Hubbard, the daughter of Gardiner G. Hubbard. This girl of eighteen, who was to be an exceptional help-meet for him the rest of his life, was entirely deaf from early childhood. There was, therefore, a keen personal element in his sympathy for the deaf and in his work for them. Early in August he sailed with his bride for Europe to introduce the telephone into England and France. A prospectus which he wrote for a group of capitalists in London contains a remarkable prediction of the development of telephone service, describing in detail its uses fifty years later. While he was in England he also gave considerable attention to the education of the deaf, and took part in the inception of a day school for the deaf at Greenock in Scotland. He returned to America in the fall of 1878, and that winter moved to Washington, D. C. His inventive work now followed related lines rather than the development of the telephone itself. In 1880 the French Government awarded him the Volta Prize of 50,000 francs, for the invention of the electric speaking telephone. He devoted this money to the promotion of research and invention and to the work

for the deaf by financing the Volta Laboratory, in which he associated with him his cousin, Chichester A. Bell, and Sumner Tainter. Each had his own special work, and all three coöperated on some undertaking of common interest and probable profit whereby the laboratory might be maintained. Bell continued in the Volta Laboratory an investigation, which he had started in 1878, into the causes and conditions of congenital deafness in New England. He prepared a memoir on *The Formation of a Deaf Variety of the Human Race* (1884) and a study of the results of the marriage of the deaf. He also initiated a movement for certain fundamental improvements in the taking of the Census of 1890 with respect to the deaf. During these years of the Volta Laboratory he invented the photophone, an apparatus for transmitting speech over a ray of light by means of the variable electric resistance of selenium to light and shade. He also invented the induction balance for locating metallic objects in the human body, first used on President Garfield, and the telephone probe which he developed from the former invention. These he did not patent but gave to the world. He further invented an audiometer, thus bringing his inventive work a step nearer to his service to the deaf.

Bell was interested in Edison's invention for recording sound, the phonograph. But Edison's tinfoil records left much to be desired. Accordingly the members of the Volta Laboratory Association invented an improved recorder, a flat wax record, a wax cylinder record, and an improved reproducer, and jointly received patents for these improvements on May 4, 1886. When these patents were sold to the American Graphophone Company, the Laboratory was converted into a Volta Bureau for the Increase and Diffusion of Knowledge Relating to the Deaf. This Bureau worked in close coöperation with the American Association for the Promotion of the Teaching of Speech to the Deaf, organized in 1890, of which Bell was elected president and to which he gave altogether more than $300,000.

Through his study of marriage among the deaf, Bell was led to give attention to the whole field of longevity and eugenics. An important contribution to this subject was his *Duration of Life and Condition Associated with Longevity* (1918). In this connection he made an excursion into the breeding of multi-nippled and twin-bearing sheep at his summer home on Cape Breton Island. This broad interest in eugenics and his optimistic attitude toward its problems was recognized by his election as honorary president of the Second International Congress of Eugenics.

During the last twenty-five years of Bell's life

aviation was his predominant interest. He was one of the first to consider aerial locomotion practicable, and in 1891 encouraged and financially coöperated with Samuel P. Langley, the secretary of the Smithsonian Institution, in the study of aviation. His own experiments followed the line of kite development and resulted in his invention of the tetrahedral kite and the application of that principle of construction to various uses. In 1907 Bell founded the Aerial Experiment Association, of which he was president and to which he gave $50,000. The first public flight of a heavier-than-air machine was made under the auspices of this organization in 1908. He and his associates also solved the problem of the stability of balance in a flying machine, using rigid instead of flexible supporting surfaces and providing ailerons for the wings and the rudders. During the war Bell invented a motor boat which attained a speed of seventy-one miles an hour. In 1883 with the coöperation of Gardiner G. Hubbard, he established *Science,* now the organ of the American Association for the Advancement of Science, and maintained it for several years. From 1896 to 1904 he was president of the National Geographic Society and did much to forward the development of the society and its magazine. In 1898 he was appointed a regent of the Smithsonian Institution, serving continuously until his death. In 1891 he had started by a generous gift the Astrophysical Observatory of the Smithsonian, and in 1904 he brought the body of James Smithson from Genoa to Washington. The honors, medals, and degrees that were received by him were numerous. In these marks of recognition from Harvard, Oxford, Heidelberg, Edinburgh, and other institutions, Bell's work for the deaf, his inventions for the hearing, and his other services and attainments were alike honored. In 1915 he opened the first transcontinental telephone line from New York to San Francisco. In 1917, at Brantford, Ontario, the Duke of Devonshire, as governor general of Canada, unveiled the Bell Telephone Memorial in honor of the inventor of the electric speaking telephone and dedicated the old home at Tutelo Heights as a public park. In 1920, the home of his childhood, Edinburgh, Scotland, conferred upon him the freedom of the city and elected him a burgess and guild brother of the city. He had taken out his first papers for citizenship in the United States at Lawrence, as early as Oct. 27, 1874, and he received his final papers from the supreme court of the District of Columbia at Washington, Nov. 10, 1882, but he never lost his love for his native Scotland and had a large estate in the new Scotland (Nova Scotia), on the

Bras d'Or Lakes of Cape Breton Island. There he spent his summers, and there he died. He was buried on top of a mountain in a tomb cut in the rock, while every telephone on the continent of North America remained silent.

In appearance, during his earlier years, he was a tall, spare young man, with pale complexion, piercing black eyes and bushy, jet black hair and side whiskers, quick of motion, serious and grave. In his later years he was conspicuous for his majestic presence and his radiant manner. His hair and beard had become pure white but his keen black eyes still dominated the situation. The gravity of his youth had given way to a sympathy and joviality which won both old and young.

[Papers in possession of the Bell family and of the Am. Telephone and Telegraph Company; *The Deposition of Alexander Graham Bell* (1908); Fred De Land, *Dumb No Longer* (1908); Thomas A. Watson, *Exploring Life* (1926).]

W.C.L.

BELL, ALEXANDER MELVILLE (Mar. 1, 1819–Aug. 7, 1905), educator, the younger son of Alexander Bell, professor of elocution in London, was born in Edinburgh and mainly educated at home. Like his elder brother who had already settled in Dublin, he followed the family profession and in 1843 established himself in Edinburgh. The father and two sons were the leading teachers of the science of correct speech at the three capitals of England, Ireland, and Scotland for the ensuing twenty-two years. At that time teachers of elocution, especially those who undertook to cure stammering and other defects of utterance, made a great mystery of their art. Bell, with the candor and truthfulness that were a marked feature of his family, declared that there was no mystery about it except such as arose from the little attention that had been paid to the science of speech. At the outset he published his methods. He early conceived the idea of a physiological alphabet which would furnish to the eye a complete guide to the production of any oral sound. This idea he carefully worked out during the next twenty-three years and gave to the world in his *Visible Speech: the Science of Universal Alphabetics* (1867). In his physiological or pictorial alphabet "each symbol means a definite position of the organs of speech, which, if correctly assumed, produces a definite result. Every sound possible for the human voice can be represented by these symbols. There is, therefore, no language or variation of language in dialect, or even individual idiosyncrasy of utterance, which cannot be represented by Visible Speech and reproduced vocally by any one knowing the system." Some of its more important practical uses are in the recording of unwritten languages and disappearing dialects, the correction of defects of vocal utterance, and the training of oral teachers of the deaf. It is upon this universal alphabet that Alexander Melville Bell's claim to lasting remembrance chiefly rests. Fourteen of his forty-nine published works relate to this subject. His books on elocution remain the standard authority, more than 250 editions of *The Principles of Elocution* and *The Standard Elocutionist* having been printed.

After the death of his father Bell moved to London, where he lived for five years, lecturing on elocution in University College and giving public readings from Shakespeare and Dickens. In 1868 he visited America to give a course of lectures before the Lowell Institute of Boston and in other cities of the United States and Canada. Two years later he returned to deliver a second course of twelve lectures before the Lowell Institute, and the following year had the honor of presenting a third and similar course. He settled in Brantford, Ontario, Canada, in 1870 and later held the professorship of elocution in Queens College, Kingston. When his distinguished son, Alexander Graham Bell [*q.v.*], permanently located in Washington, D. C., the father was persuaded to move to the same city (1881), and at the age of seventy-eight he was admitted to American citizenship, Jan. 12, 1897. He was twice married: to Eliza Grace Symonds in 1844, and to Mrs. Harriet Guess Shibley in 1898.

[S. S. Curry, *Alexander Melville Bell* (1906); John Hitz, "Alexander Melville Bell" in the *Ass. Rev.*, VII, 421 ff.; the *Washington Post*, Aug. 8, 1905. For further information consult the Volta Bureau of the Am. Ass. to Promote the Teaching of Speech to the Deaf, 1601 Thirty-fifth St., Washington, D. C.]   G. G—r.

BELL, CHARLES HENRY (Nov. 18, 1823–Nov. 11, 1893), lawyer, politician, author, son of John and Persis (Thom) Bell, and nephew of Samuel Bell [*q.v.*], was born at Chester, N. H., in a neighborhood where the family had been prominent for a century or more. Both his father and uncle held numerous public offices, including the governorship. Charles Bell enjoyed the best educational opportunities available in the state, attending Pembroke and Phillips Exeter Academies and graduating from Dartmouth in 1844. He entered the legal profession and practised at Chester, Somersworth, and Exeter. He settled at the latter town in 1854 and there resided for the rest of his life. He was twice married: on May 6, 1847, to Sarah Gilman of Exeter, who died Aug. 22, 1850; and on June 3, 1857, to Mary (Gray) Gilman, widow of Joseph Gilman of Exeter. He was a successful lawyer and Chief Justice Charles Doe once remarked of him, "A mind more capable of grasping, mastering, and

presenting legal questions quickly, clearly and thoroughly, I have never known." In 1868, however, he gave up active practise, although still handling occasional cases of special importance. In 1856 he had begun a period of ten years' service as solicitor for Rockingham County. He represented Exeter in the lower house 1858–60, being speaker in the latter year, and again in 1872 and 1873. He was a member of the Senate 1863–64, serving as president in his second term. In 1879 he was appointed to fill a vacancy in the United States Senate, serving for a few months pending the meeting of the legislature. The legality of his appointment was contested in the Senate, but he was finally seated (*Congressional Record*, 46 Cong., 1 Sess., p. 355). He was governor, 1881–83, and in 1889 was president of the seventh constitutional convention.

He is, however, chiefly remembered as a student and writer of New Hampshire history, and a collector of miscellaneous Americana. He was active in the New Hampshire Historical Society, the Prince Society, and similar organizations. His most important works were *John Wheelwright* (1876), a monograph showing research and critical ability, *History of the Town of Exeter, New Hampshire* (1888), and *The Bench and Bar of New Hampshire* (1894), which was in the hands of the printer at the time of Bell's death. The latter is his most important work and contains biographical sketches of 871 New Hampshire jurists and lawyers. It shows laborious research and great skill in presentation. His work throughout is characterized by clearness and simplicity of style. In addition to the above, he was the author of numerous shorter studies, and many of his addresses and commemorative orations were reprinted.

[A brief account of the life and services of Chas. H. Bell, by Jeremiah Smith, is included in the former's *The Bench and Bar of New Hampshire*. This sketch, which pays special attention to Bell's legal career, was privately printed in 1894, together with a character sketch by Mellen Chamberlain. It contains, p. 19, a list of Bell's published works and addresses. In Jan. 1895 there appeared "A Memoir of Chas. H. Bell," by Edmund F. Slafter in the *New Eng. Hist. and Geneal. Reg.*]

W. A. R.

BELL, CLARK (Mar. 12, 1832–Feb. 22, 1918), lawyer, the son of Philander F. and Sylvia (Jones) Bell, was born at Whitesville, Jefferson County, N. Y. He was educated at Franklin Academy, and after leaving school assisted his father in the blacksmith business. He studied law in his leisure hours and was admitted to the bar at Rochester in 1853. Opening an office at Hammondsport, N. Y., he continued in practise there till 1861, when he removed to Bath, and acted as assistant district attorney for Steuben

County, 1861–62. Shortly thereafter he became associated with the promoters of the Union Pacific Railroad and Telegraph Company which, organized under Acts of Congress in 1862, found itself unable to proceed with construction, partly owing to the depression caused by the war. He was appointed attorney to the company, assisted in its reorganization in October 1863, and the same year moved his office to New York City. He drafted the act which was passed by Congress and approved July 2, 1864, radically changing the constitution of the company and the terms under which federal aid was extended, and he continued to act as the company's attorney during the whole period of construction (1864–69). He was later retained by the Pacific Mail Steamship Company and the Rock Island Railroad, and, so long as he remained in active practise, was associated with important corporation and industrial enterprises. In 1870 he was elected a member of the Medico-Legal Society of New York, and two years later became its president, devoting a large part of his time to its business and taking a prominent part in all its discussions. He soon became recognized as a leading New York expert in medical jurisprudence, and contributed valuable papers on that subject to the proceedings of the Medico-Legal Society. In 1872 he was counsel for George Francis Train, against whom lunacy proceedings had been commenced under somewhat extraordinary circumstances. The trial before Chief Justice Daly and a jury was lengthy, lasting from Apr. 9 to May 6, 1873. Bell had for some years prior to this studied the subject of mental diseases extensively and his successful contest with the professional mental experts in this case brought him into great prominence. In 1884 he was active in establishing the *Medico-Legal Journal* and became its editor. Thenceforth he was a constant contributor to its columns on matters of common interest to the legal and medical professions. In 1885 he represented the United States at the Paris Congress of Medical Jurisprudence. His *Judicial History of the Supreme Court of the United States and Provinces of North America* was published in 1895. He founded the American Congress on Tuberculosis in 1900, editing the *Bulletin* of its proceedings in four volumes. He was appointed United States delegate to the International Medical Congresses held in Paris in 1900 and Lisbon in 1906, taking an important part in the discussions. He also wrote *Spiritism, Telepathy and Hypnotism* (1902), which attracted much attention and passed through several editions. The first of his *Medico-Legal Studies* had appeared in 1889, and they had reached eleven volumes

when advancing years compelled him to retire from his activities. In addition to his writings he edited the *Bulletins of the Medico-Legal Congresses,* 1889 and 1895, and *Medico-Legal Papers* in three volumes. He died very suddenly in New York on Feb. 22, 1918. He was married in 1858 to Helene S. Taylor. He had always evinced a love for country life, and much of his leisure was devoted to the study of agricultural problems. He was known in New York quite as much as a breeder of trotting horses as he was in the capacity of medico-legal expert.

[The various volumes of the *Medico-Legal Jour.* contain elaborate notices of his activities in the field of medic. jurisprudence. An article in *The Lawyer and Banker,* V, 336, gives details of his career, but must be used with caution since on several points it is inaccurate. A good appreciative obituary appeared in the *N.Y. Times,* Feb. *23,* 1918. For particulars of the reorganization of the Union Pacific Railway see N. Frohman, *Hist. of the Union Pacific* (1923) and J. P. Davis, *Union Pacific Railway* (1894). Bell's speech to the jury in the Train case was printed verbatim in pamphlet form in 1873 accompanied by an excellent report of the whole case itself.]

H. W. H. K.

BELL, HENRY HAYWOOD (Apr. 13, 1808– Jan. 11, 1868), naval officer, born in North Carolina, was appointed a midshipman in the United States Navy Aug. 4, 1823, and was promoted to be lieutenant Mar. 3, 1831, commander Aug. 12, 1854, and commodore Aug. 21, 1862. In 1828– 29 he was in the *Grampus,* clearing the Cuban coast of pirates, and in 1856 he commanded the *San Jacinto,* flagship of the East India Squadron, taking a prominent part in the capture and destruction of four barrier forts near Canton, China, in November of that year. He was on that occasion in command of one wing of a landing party from the fleet which stormed the first fort, and held it until the following day, when the fleet shelled the remaining forts into submission. At the outbreak of the Civil War, Bell, a Southerner by birth and married to a Virginia lady, was compelled to make the distressing decision between devotion to his native state and loyalty to his flag, under which he had served long and honorably. This decision, however, appears to have caused him little effort, his sense of duty triumphing over all other considerations. His friend, Edward A. Pollard, writes (*Galaxy,* November 1868) that, though he expected him to go with his state, when the subject was broached, shortly after President Lincoln's proclamation of war, Bell cut the conversation short with the emphatic declaration, "I have made up my mind; I shall stand by the flag."

His most conspicuous service in the Civil War was as fleet-captain of the West Gulf Squadron under Farragut, whose chief-of-staff he was during the actions leading to the opening of the Mississippi River in 1862. In the battle between the fleet and Forts Jackson and St. Philip he commanded one of the three naval divisions, consisting of six vessels. When the fleet lay before New Orleans, Bell was chosen by Farragut to carry out the hazardous task of hoisting the flag of the United States over the custom house and hauling down the flag of the State of Louisiana which floated over the city hall, and which the mayor of New Orleans had declined to remove. With a party of sailors and marines, at the risk of his life, he marched through the hostile streets and directed from the roofs of the custom house and the city hall the raising of the one flag and the lowering of the other. The landing party returned to its boats taunted with cries of "Hurrah for Beauregard! Hurrah for Jeff Davis!" (*Official Records*, ser. I, vol. XVIII, p. 698). In 1863 he was for a time in command of the West Gulf Squadron, and in 1865 was ordered to command the East India Squadron, in which capacity he was active in subduing the pirates infesting the China seas. On July 25, 1866, he became rear admiral; he was placed on the retired list in 1867; but, while awaiting his relief, he was drowned by the capsizing of his barge on a bar in the river near the city of Osaka, Japan, as he was about to pay a visit to the United States minister. He was buried at Hiogo, Japan, the American and British squadrons taking part in the funeral ceremonies. Bell was distinguished by high technical skill in his profession, and an almost fanatical devotion to duty, tempered by great kindliness and a quiet sense of humor.

[Navy Registers, 1824–68; *Report of the Secretary of the Navy*, for 1857, 1864, 1866, 1868; *Official Records of the Union and Confederate Navies*, ser. I, vol. XVIII; L. Farragut, *Life of Wm. Glasgow Farragut*.]

E. B.

BELL, ISAAC (Nov. 6, 1846–Jan. 20, 1889), cotton merchant, politician, was the son of Isaac Bell, for many years commissioner of Charities and Corrections of the State of New York. He was educated in private schools in New York City. Starting his business career in a clerkship with Brown Brothers & Company in New York, he became interested in the cotton business which in those years (from 1870 on) was assuming an extraordinary speculative activity. He determined to establish a brokerage house in the cotton region itself and went to Savannah, Ga., where he successfully conducted his own office. An attractive offer from the firm of Arthur Barnwell & Company led him to move to Charleston, S. C., there becoming a member of that firm, and repeating the success already gained in Sa-

vannah. As his knowledge of the cotton business increased, he determined to carry out what appears to have been his original design, that of uniting actual operations in the cotton region with the speculative market of the North, a familiar method to-day, but representing a plan then relatively little known in practise. Accordingly he established two houses of his own, one in New Orleans, the other in New York City, under the firm name of Isaac Bell, Jr., & Company. The venture was profitable, and with the money he had accumulated and inherited he retired from business in 1877 and removed to Newport, R. I. In the year 1878 Bell married Jeannette Gordon Bennett (the sister of James Gordon Bennett [*q.v.*]) and affiliated himself with the social and literary circles in which the Bennett family was conspicuous. Bell now took up politics as an avocation and began to play a considerable part as a Democrat in the local public affairs of Rhode Island. He was, however, rather too much of an aristocrat to catch the popular fancy, besides running counter to the traditional prejudices of the region, and a campaign for election to the United States Senate on the Democratic ticket proved a complete failure. President Cleveland, nevertheless, in his effort to consolidate the Democratic support of the Eastern seaboard communities and especially to recognize the wealthier element among the Democrats of New York and the adjacent states, named him minister to the Netherlands. His career in that position (March 1885–May 1888) was of no special note. Returning from Europe he became a delegate to the St. Louis convention of 1888 and shared actively in the campaign of that year, but the defeat of President Cleveland for a second term naturally resulted in his retirement from politics; and a decline in health shortly set in which developed into the illness (pyæmia) which caused his death.

[The principal sources of information concerning Bell's activities are to be found in current newspaper discussion during the period of his greatest activity in the cotton market, 1870–77, and during his political campaign in R. I. Incomplete and unsatisfactory newspaper biographies were generally published by the N. Y. newspapers at the time of his death. See *N. Y. Herald, Times, Tribune*, Jan. 21, 1889.]

H. P. W.

BELL, JACOB (Dec. 17, 1792–July 21, 1852), ship-builder, the son of John and Deborah Clock Bell, was born at Middlesex (now Darien), Conn., where his ancestor, Francis Bell, had been one of the first settlers in 1641. Jacob Bell entered into partnership with David Brown about 1820 and they took over the shipyard formerly run by Adam and Noah Brown on the East River at the foot of Houston St., New York City. In 1821 they launched their first ships, the *William Tell* and *Orbit*. The firm was known as Brown & Bell until the former's death about 1848, when Bell conducted it in his own name until his death. Their yard held its own with the principal local rivals, William H. Brown and William H. Webb. They seem to have been equally successful in turning out fast sailing vessels and in keeping up with the latest developments in steamships. The firm was in close relation with Edward K. Collins [*q.v.*]. In 1834 they joined with him in starting the New York Marine Dry Dock Company, and, shortly afterward, built the *Garrick, Roscius, Sheridan,* and *Siddons* for his transatlantic Dramatic Line of sailing packets. They are credited with building in 1840 the first ocean steamships launched in New York, the *Lion* and the *Eagle,* which became Spanish war-ships. A year later they built the fast little schooner *Angola* for the opium trade. Their clippers were surpassed only by the products of their former pupil, Donald McKay. The partners built the *Houqua* (1844) and *Samuel Russell* (1847). Among the best clippers built by Bell alone were the *Oriental* (1849), *White Squall* (1850), *Trade Wind* (1851), the largest clipper yet built, and *Messenger,* launched three months before his death. The *Jacob Bell,* named for himself, was completed four months after he died by his son Abraham. Even more conspicuous products of the Bell yard were the steamships *Pacific* and *Baltic* for the Collins Line. Bell was married on May 10, 1821, to Mary Clock of Darien, Conn.

[Frequent references to Bell's shipbuilding will be found in J. H. Morrison, *Hist. of the N. Y. Shipyards* (1909) and A. H. Clark, *The Clipper Ship Era* (1910). Complete details of the principal clippers are given in O. T. Howe and F. C. Matthews, *Am. Clipper Ships* (2 vols., 1926, 1927). Statistics of the output of the various New York yards will be found in contemporary issues of *Hunt's Merchant's Mag.* Genealogical details are given in the *N. Y. Geneal. and Biog. Reg.*, XXVIII, 153, XXIX, 63. Biographical details are given in E. F. Hatfield, *Riches in Death: a Discourse Occasioned by the Decease of Mr. Jacob Bell* (1852); a short obituary appeared in the *N. Y. Jour. of Commerce,* July 22, 1852.]

R. G. A.

BELL, JAMES MADISON (Apr. 3, 1826–1902), negro poet and lecturer, was born at Gallipolis, Ohio. Here he lived until 1842, when he removed to Cincinnati, where he lived with his brother-in-law, George Knight, and learned the plasterer's trade. Meanwhile his radical feeling against slavery was encouraged by the persecution that he saw visited upon some persons of missionary spirit who taught negroes. In his twenty-second year he married Louisiana Sanderline, who became the mother of several children. In August 1854 he removed with his family to Canada, where he lived until 1860. He be-

came a personal friend of John Brown and assisted in getting men to go on the raid of 1859. In 1860 he went to California, where he worked earnestly against the disabilities that the negroes suffered and where he wrote some of his poems. In 1865 he removed to Toledo, Ohio, bringing his family from Canada. After the Civil War he traveled much in the Eastern states, encouraging the freedmen to make the most of their new opportunities and instructing them in their civic duties. In 1868 he was elected delegate from Lucas County to the state convention and then delegate at large from Ohio to the national Republican convention that nominated Grant for a second term, and he later appeared on the public platform in behalf of Grant's candidacy. Bell was an able speaker and was also well known as a reader of his own poems. "The Day and the War" was inscribed to the memory of John Brown, and "The Progress of Liberty" is suggestive of Byron; but in general the verse is without any distinctive literary quality.

[*The Poetical Works of James Madison Bell* (1901) with a biog. sketch by Bishop B. W. Arnett, is practically the sole authority. For year of death see *Ohio Centennial Anniversary Celebration . . . Complete Proceedings* (1903), p. 639.]

B. B.

BELL, JAMES STROUD (June 30, 1847–Apr. 5, 1915), merchant miller, the son of Samuel and Elizabeth (Faust) Bell, was born in Philadelphia. After graduating from the Central High School in that city at the age of sixteen, he began work in his father's milling and flour brokerage establishment. He received a thorough training in every department of the business. Five years later he was admitted to the firm (which now became Samuel Bell & Sons) as a partner, and here he remained for twenty years. The firm was a sales agent for Washburn, Crosby & Company, operating by lease the mills of the C. C. Washburn Flouring Mills Company in Minneapolis, and through the connection Bell came to be well known to the officers of this company. The year 1888 was a critical one for the milling industry. Speculators had forced up the price of flour beyond an export basis, and the millers—particularly the Minneapolis company, which in 1887 had sold forty per cent of its product abroad—faced the necessity of making an intensive cultivation of the home market. Bell was asked to become a partner in the firm, and on his acceptance it was reorganized (September 1888), as Washburn, Martin & Company. He at once took a leading part in its direction, and when, a year later, it was changed to a corporation, under the name of the Washburn-Crosby Company, he was chosen president. He had been a miller and a broker of mill products; he was now to become a merchant miller—perhaps, as the press termed him at the time of his death, "the greatest merchant miller of the world." In methods of reaching the public, both with his product and with the arguments for buying it, he was an originator; he placed on the market a wide range of cereal preparations in attractively labeled cartons, and by effective advertising made them known throughout the country. Under his control the corporation steadily expanded. In 1899 the leased mills were bought and the capital stock was increased to $1,200,000. A branch mill was built at Buffalo in 1903, another in the following year at Louisville, and others later at Great Falls and at Kalispell, Mont. Further increases in the capital stock were made in 1903 and 1907 and again in 1909, when it was placed at $6,000,000. At the time of his death the productive capacity of the mills, which had been 8,000 barrels a day when he joined the company, had risen to 27,700 barrels. He had wide commercial and financial interests; for many years he was vice-president of the Minneapolis Trust Company as well as of three other companies and a director of the Northwestern National Bank.

The obituaries of Bell give him a commanding position in the trade; no other man, said the *Northwestern Miller,* in so short a time made so great an impress on the milling industry. They stress, among his personal qualities, his helpful kindness to young men, many of whom, by his encouragement, he set on the pathway to material success. Though a strict disciplinarian, he was not an autocrat; his democracy and humaneness were shown, said one, by the fact that men could take orders from him and still love him. His business standards were of the highest; his word was his bond, and though hesitant in making promises he was faithful in keeping them. He was twice married—on Jan. 8, 1873, to Sallie Montgomery Ford, who died, and on Sept. 28, 1912, to Mabel Sargent, who survived him.

[*Who's Who in America,* 1914–15; W. C. Edgar, *The Medal of Gold* (1925); obituaries in the *Minneapolis Tribune* and the *St. Paul Pioneer Press,* Apr. 6, 1915, and the *Northwestern Miller,* Apr. 7, 1915.]

W. J. G.

BELL, JOHN (Feb. 15, 1797–Sept. 10, 1869), Southern statesman, was the son of Samuel Bell and Margaret Edmiston Bell, pioneer settlers of Tennessee. He was born on his father's farm near Nashville a few months after Tennessee had come into existence as a state. He was a precocious youth. In 1814, at the age of seventeen, he graduated from Cumberland College, an institution that later became the University of

Nashville. Before he was twenty-one he had been admitted to the bar, had begun practise at Franklin, Tenn., and had served as senator in one session of the state legislature. Declining reëlection, he moved to Nashville where for some years he devoted himself to the practise of his profession and became one of the most eminent of the members of the Nashville bar. He was twice married: first, early in life, to Sally Dickinson, and after her death to Jane Erwin Yeatman, wealthy widow of Thomas Yeatman. In 1827 he began the first of fourteen successive years in the lower house of Congress. In his first campaign he defeated by a considerable majority Felix Grundy, who had the support of the popular idol of his state, Andrew Jackson. Yet Bell was a supporter of "Old Hickory" for the presidency and in his address to the voters in 1826 he had denounced the Henry Clay-John Quincy Adams combination and had urged upon the voters the support of Jackson as the instrument for their destruction. For some years in Congress he was a member of the Jackson party and supported the chief measures of the Jackson administration. He could never be, however, the unquestioning follower of any man, and in time there developed a breach between Jackson and Bell that ultimately made the latter the leader of the Whig party in Tennessee. In Jackson's war against the national bank Bell refused to follow the President despite the latter's threat that if he should "not come out clearly and distinctly against all national banks he" would be "politically destroyed" (Jackson to Van Buren, Aug. 16, 1834, Van Buren Papers, Library of Congress). In 1834 Bell was the opponent of a fellow Tennessean, James K. Polk, for the speakership of the House, and with the support of anti-Jackson members he won this coveted office. For more than a decade these two men were both political and personal enemies, and not until after Polk had become president were they even on speaking terms. Jackson preferred Polk, who was always a loyal follower. A complete break with Jackson occurred when Bell became the leading advocate of the presidential candidacy of Hugh Lawson White in opposition to Jackson's selection, Martin Van Buren. Bell still professed allegiance to the principles of the Democratic party; he declared White to be a better Jackson man than was Van Buren; yet Jackson declared that Bell had "turned a good Whig" (*John Bell; his "Past History connected with the Public Service,"* 1860, p. 7). This Bell finally admitted on the politician's plea that this new party was pledged to support the policies of the original Jackson party. The Whig party now became and continued for two decades to be the dominant party in Tennessee and Bell was its acknowledged leader. Despite Jackson's continued efforts, Bell's constituents returned him to Congress until in 1841 he entered the cabinet of President Harrison as secretary of war. He held this position only a few weeks, however, for after Harrison's death his successor, Tyler, rejected the legislative program of the Whigs, and Bell and other cabinet members resigned.

For the next six years Bell remained in retirement, but in 1847 he was elected to the United States Senate and he continued in this office till 1859. During this period of twelve years, characterized by the development of an increasingly bitter sectional spirit, Bell distinguished himself as one of the most consistently conservative and nationally-minded Southerners. He was a large slave owner; he had no love for the abolitionists; yet he never entered the camp of the apostles of slavery. Temperate in his emotions, judicial always in the formation of his opinions, yet on occasion powerful in attack upon his enemies, he had no sympathy for extremists North or South. As a member of the lower house of Congress he had voted with John Quincy Adams in defense of the right of petition against those who sought to prevent the reception or the consideration of anti-slavery petitions. In the Senate, when the controversy over the question of slavery in the territories that had been acquired from Mexico threatened a dissolution of the Union, Bell affirmed the constitutionality of congressional prohibition of slavery in the territories, though he opposed the use of this power on grounds of policy. He was the outstanding supporter of President Taylor's plan of avoiding the direct issue by admitting the territories to statehood even though the exclusion of slavery should be the result of this. He also offered a plan of compromise. He objected to certain features of Henry Clay's compromise measures of 1850, but after their passage he gave them his support. In 1854 he parted reluctantly from his Southern colleagues and opposed the reopening of the bitter controversy over slavery by the passage of the Kansas-Nebraska Act. The well-known results of this act were as he had predicted. Four years later he defied instructions from the Tennessee legislature to support the admission of Kansas under the Lecompton constitution and spoke and voted against that attempt to force slavery upon an unwilling people. For his attitude in the slavery controversy he was most bitterly denounced by increasing numbers in the South, but gained commendation in the North.

The Whig party was now dead. Bell gave support to the short-lived Americans and even considered the possibility of a uniting of moderate Republicans and former Southern Whigs. To many a Southerner he was "harloting" with the hated Black Republicans. The possibility of such a union passed, however, and secession and civil war drew on apace. In the momentous presidential campaign of 1860 moderate men, most of them former Whigs, nominated John Bell for the presidency and Edward Everett for the vice-presidency. Their party they called the Constitutional Union Party and their platform was "The Constitution of the country, the Union of the states, and the enforcement of the laws." But the time for moderation had passed; the slavery question could not be settled by ignoring it; and Bell secured the electoral votes of only three states, Tennessee, Kentucky, and Virginia. His campaign had been a plea for the preservation of the Union, and for some months after Lincoln's election and while states of the lower South seceded he and his followers opposed secession, and Tennessee remained within the Union. When Lincoln's administration began Bell was in Washington and sought there to promote a compromising spirit and the adoption of a temperate policy that would, he hoped, prevent civil war. But when Maj. Anderson's small garrison at Fort Sumter was fired upon and Lincoln called for troops, Bell was compelled to make what was probably the most momentous decision of his many years in public life. Disapproving secession "both as a constitutional right, and as a remedy for existing evils," he urged that if the federal government should attempt the coercion of the "seceded States," Tennessee should enter into "alliance" with them and resist suppression of the "Revolution" "at all hazards, at any cost, *and by arms . . .*" (*Nashville Patriot,* Apr. 19, May 10, 1861). Tennessee did as Bell advised. His own career was ended. When the state was invaded by troops of the United States he left for the lower South. Family tradition tells of an old man, heartbroken, who paced the floor lamenting the war and what war brought to the South and to the nation. When the war ended he returned to Tennessee; his health failed; and in Stewart County, near Bear Spring Furnace, he died.

[A small but valuable group of Bell's letters was edited by St. George L. Sioussat in *Tenn. Hist. Mag.,* III, 196–227. Information regarding his life can be secured from the newspapers and the congressional debates. See also brief campaign document, *The Public Record and Past History of John Bell* (1860); A. V. Goodpasture, "John Bell's Political Revolt and his Vauxhall Garden Speech," *Tenn. Hist. Mag.,* II, 254–63; article by O. Z. Bond in the *Nashville Banner,* Mar. 19, 1910. The most satisfactory sketch of Bell's life is by Joshua W. Caldwell in *Am. Hist. Rev.,* IV, 652–64. The best discussion of his break with Jackson and Polk is in Eugene I. McCormac, *Jas. K. Polk* (1922), *passim*.]

P. M. H.

BELL, LOUIS (Dec. 5, 1864–June 14, 1923), physicist, engineer, was descended from John Bell, a staunch Scotch-Irishman who in 1719 left County Antrim, Ireland, to join, in 1720, the small colony of his countrymen already settled at Londonderry in the southeastern corner of New Hampshire. Here the family prospered and became prominent in the public affairs of county and state. The grandfather of Louis Bell was Samuel Bell [*q.v.*], twice elected senator from New Hampshire and Daniel Webster's intimate friend, while his father was Col. Louis Bell, educated at Brown University, a man of commanding physique, clear head, and scientific tastes. In the final charge by which the Union troops captured Fort Fisher, N. C., on Jan. 15, 1865, Col. Bell took part, and died of wounds received in action on that day. It is little wonder that the son, then only six weeks old, always regarded his father as a hero. His broken-hearted mother, Mary Ann Persis (Bouton) Bell, died a few months later; the boy Louis and his sister, four years older, grew up in the home of their grandmother, the widow of Gov. Samuel Bell, at Chester, N. H. Twelve years in this quiet, remote village where he was in close contact with nature and enjoyed the privileges of a well-stocked library, breathing the atmosphere of a family acquainted with men of large affairs, turned the child into a lad with a mind which was as clear and alert as his body was strong and vigorous.

At Phillips Exeter Academy he prepared for Dartmouth College, where he matriculated in 1880 and graduated in 1884. It is easy to see that Bell's later life and qualities were foreshadowed in his college career. Here we find him exhibiting that keen literary taste which never deserted him and a remarkable accuracy in the bending of words to give precisely the meaning which he intended. Poet at the freshman class dinner, associate editor of the *Dartmouth,* he won honorable mention in English, and final honors in physics. An innate sense of humor led him to take the initiative in certain gibes and pranks; for one of these he was rusticated during a period of three months, a time of exile spent mostly at the Astor Library in New York City where he lived with an uncle. A year of graduate work at Dartmouth preceded three years of residence at Johns Hopkins University. In Baltimore, he began serious work in physics and chemistry, taking an active part in the Journal Club, investigating the absorption spectrum of nitrogen peroxide (*American Journal of Chem-*

istry, 1885–86), the ultra-violet spectrum of cadmium (*American Journal of Science,* 1886), and other similar problems. His most important work at Baltimore was his determination of the wave-length of the D_1 line in the spectrum of sodium. Rowland had just completed (1887) his atlas of the solar spectrum and had spent several of the best years of his life in measuring relative wave-lengths throughout this spectrum. It was clear that the value of this work would be greatly enhanced if these relative wave-lengths were all referred to one standard line whose length was known with high precision. Bell spent two years of skilful and careful work, with four of Rowland's finest gratings, in an attempt to arrive at just such a value for the D_1 line. To his result, Rowland gave a weight equivalent to that of all four of the best previous observers and used this mean as the base of his justly celebrated Preliminary Table of Solar Spectrum Wavelengths. The accuracy of Bell's value at the time of its publication (1888) was estimated to be of the order of one part in 100,000. Within three or four years, however, the interferometer method was employed by Michelson—also by Perot and Fabry—for the same purpose. The fact then emerged that the grating method used by Bell was inevitably, if not inherently, affected with an error of at least one part in 30,000.

On leaving Johns Hopkins University in 1888, Bell spent two years in finding himself, one of these at Purdue University in charge of the recently initiated course in electrical engineering. Two years later he accepted the editorship of the *Electrical World.* In 1893, he was married to Sarah G. Hemenway of Somerville, Mass. In the same year he was appointed chief engineer in the Power Transmission department of the General Electric Company. Polyphase transmission which at this time was just coming into practise challenged and fascinated Bell's admiration; he made himself an authority on the subject and installed at Redlands, Cal., the earliest three-phase transmission plant for general service. After 1895, however, he maintained a private office, as consulting engineer, in Boston. Here, as he once remarked, a large part of his business was "to diagnose sick electric railways." Along with his engineering practise he found time to join O. T. Crosby in the authorship of *The Electric Railway* (1892). In 1896, appeared his *Power Transmission for Electric Railroads,* which was almost immediately followed by his *Electric Power Transmission.* His text-book on *The Art of Illumination* first appeared in 1902. The two articles contributed to the eleventh edition of the *Encyclopædia Britannica,* "Motors,

Electric" and "Power Transmission, Electric," illustrate Bell's scientific style at its best; excellent analysis, clarity, and precision of language, together with emphasis, not on defunct apparatus, but upon general principles. Within the last year of his life Bell published *The Telescope* (1922), giving the history of the instrument and the principles which underlie its numerous and diverse modern forms. This volume is the work of an amateur in the high and literal sense of that word.

Bell's first love and his ruling passion was the subject of light. Naturally therefore he was an active member of the Illuminating Engineering Society (which came into existence in the same year with the tungsten lamp) and of the American Academy of Arts and Sciences, and was a frequent contributor to the proceedings of each. The former of these societies elected him to its presidency. A large number of patents—more than forty—bear witness to his originality. In any group he was a striking figure; a tall blond, with a rather high-pitched voice, socially inclined, seeing a humorous side to every question, penetrating in his judgments, tenacious in his beliefs, but not to the point of allowing prejudice to produce blindness. His fascinating mastery of English and his sense of fairness made him the best of company.

[J. P. Houston, *Hist. of the Class of 1884, Dartmouth*; Louis Bell, *John Bell of Londonderry and his Scottish Ancestry*, a privately printed pamphlet of twenty pages; A. E. Kennelly, *Proc. Am. Acad. Arts and Sciences*, 1925, LIX, 633–39; Edward S. King, *Popular Astronomy*, 1923, XXXI, 635–40; editorial in *Electrical World*, June 1923.]   H. C.

BELL, LUTHER VOSE (Dec. 20, 1806–Feb. 11, 1862), physician, politician, was descended from Robert Le Bel, a Norman, who migrated to Scotland in the eleventh century. A descendant, Matthew Bell, born about 1650, moved to Londonderry, Ireland. His son, John, emigrated to Londonderry (now Derry), N. H., in 1720. The latter's son, John Bell, senator, and his grandson, Samuel [*q.v.*], chief justice, governor, and senator, were both New Hampshire products. Luther Vose, fifth child of Samuel's first wife, Mehitable (Dana) Bell, was born in Francestown, N. H. He went to school at local institutions, and entered Bowdoin College at twelve. Graduating in 1823 he immediately began the study of medicine in New York City under his elder brother, Dr. John Bell. Soon he moved to Hanover and in 1826 he received his M.D. from Dartmouth. Too young to practise, he spent a year in a "Commercial Emporium," where he doubtless picked up some knowledge of men and affairs. Starting practise in Chester, N. H., he

led the strenuous life of a country doctor and became deeply interested in the needs of the insane. In 1835 and 1836 he was elected representative and persuaded the state legislature to establish an institution for their proper care. He was called in 1836 to be physician and superintendent of the McLean Hospital for the Insane at Charlestown, Mass. Here he took a lively interest in medical and administrative problems. His annual reports are models, and in them he discusses and illuminates various psychiatric subjects. He resigned on account of ill health after twenty years of admirable service.

Bell early showed literary aptitude. In 1835 he wrote a Boylston Prize Essay on New England diet in which he sagely remarks "the Yankee Citizen . . . encounters his dinner as he would any other necessary work that has to be accomplished." In 1848 he wrote *On a Form of Disease Resembling Some Advanced Stages of Mania and Fever*. Hereafter this type of insanity was recognized as Bell's Disease or Bell's Mania. After his retirement from hospital work he was often called upon as a medico-legal expert. As a witness he was concise and practical and carried great weight with judge and jury. During his active years he frequently appeared as a lyceum lecturer. His talks, usually on mechanical problems, "showed a bent of mind adapted to the conveyance of profitable instruction in a lively way." He was always an adherent of the Whig party. In 1850 he was an executive councillor to Gov. Briggs of Massachusetts. As a delegate to the Whig national convention of 1852 he advocated the candidacy of Daniel Webster. At the outbreak of the Civil War, in spite of poor health, he at once enlisted. He was appointed surgeon to the 11th Massachusetts Regiment but was soon promoted and became Hooker's brigade surgeon. In February 1862, at Budd's Ferry, Maryland, he died, probably from some complication of pulmonary tuberculosis. He was married to Frances Pinkerton, daughter of James Pinkerton, of Derry, N. H., in 1834.

[Isaac Ray, in *Am. Jour. of Insanity*, Oct. 1854; G. Alder Blumer, in *Albany Medic. Annals*, June 1908; Andrew McFarland, *Am. Jour. of Insanity*, Jan. 1878; Geo. E. Ellis, *Proc. Mass. Hist. Soc.*, ser. 1, vol. VII, p. 27; John Carroll Chase, *Hist. of Chester, N. H.* (1926).]   G. B.

BELL, PETER HANSBOROUGH (Mar. 11, 1808–Mar. 8, 1898), soldier, governor of Texas, congressman, was born in Culpeper County, near Fredericksburg, Va., the son of James Madison Bell, of Scotch-Irish stock, and Elizabeth (Hansborough) Bell. Such education as he received was probably in the local schools.

When news of the Texas Revolution came early in 1836 he hastened to take part. He arrived just in time to join Sam Houston's little army before the decisive battle of San Jacinto in which he participated as a private in Karnes's cavalry company. He remained in the army where he soon attracted favorable notice. In May 1837 he was appointed by President Houston assistant adjutant-general; in 1839–40 he served as assistant adjutant and inspector general. In 1842 he went with Gen. Somervell as aide-de-camp on his fruitless expedition to the Rio Grande. In 1845 he was commissioned a captain of rangers and was in this service when the war with Mexico began. He then became lieutenant-colonel of rangers under the celebrated Col. Jack Hays and with a portion of the regiment kept guard over the Rio Grande frontier. After the close of the war he was placed in command of the ranging companies maintained by the state on the Indian frontier. He had acquired great popularity, and when he became a candidate for governor in 1849 against the incumbent, George T. Wood, he defeated him by means of the western vote. When he assumed office in December 1849 the country was in the midst of the great political crisis which had been precipitated by the Wilmot Proviso; but in Texas public interest centered upon the dispute which had arisen between the state and the United States authorities concerning jurisdiction over the Santa Fé region. The situation was really dangerous, for President Taylor was immovable and Gov. Bell stood stiffly upon the rights of Texas and threatened to call out volunteers to maintain her claims by force. Even after this controversy had been settled amicably, Bell had many difficult problems to deal with; the settlement of the heavy public debt; the defense of the frontier against the Indians; the improvement of transportation facilities; and the establishment of a public school system. Though none of these was settled during his administration, his conduct of his office met popular approval and he was reëlected in 1851. Just before the close of his second term he was chosen as congressman from the western district to succeed Volney E. Howard, an able man who had held the place for four years. In Congress Bell voted with the state rights and pro-slavery men. His only speech of consequence was on the Texas debt bill, Feb. 5, 1855; but he voted for the Kansas-Nebraska bill and he was reëlected over a strong Know-Nothing opponent, Judge John Hancock. In 1857 he married Mrs. Ella Eaton Dickens of North Carolina, removed to that state, and thereafter lived quietly on her plantation in Warren County. Despite his former political attitude, he seems to have been opposed to secession in 1861 —probably on the ground of expediency—and he refused a commission as colonel proffered him by Jefferson Davis. His fortune swept away by the war, he lived thereafter in retirement, his heart in the past "with his adopted state, Texas." In his prime, he was a man of strong physique, soldierly bearing, and kindly manner. He lies buried in Littleton, N. C.

[The biographical sketch of Bell in the *Tex. State Hist. Ass. Quart.*, III, 49, has been much discredited by other evidence adduced, *Ibid.*, XIII, 325. There is no adequate account of his whole career in Texas, but some information may be had in the following: *Southwestern Hist. Quart.*, vols. XXIII, XXVIII; W. C. Binkley, "The Expansionist Movement in Tex.," *Univ. of Cal. Pubs. in Hist.*, vol. XIII, the best account of the Santa Fé controversy; D. G. Wooten, *A Comprehensive Hist. of Tex.* (1898), vol. II; and contemporary Texas newspapers, esp. the *Daily Express* (San Antonio), Mar. 12, 1898.]   C. W. R.

BELL, ROBERT (*c.* 1732–Sept. 23, 1784), publisher, bookseller, and book-auctioneer, was a native of Glasgow, Scotland, and served his apprenticeship there as a bookbinder. Later he went to work at this trade for Samuel Taylor at Berwick-upon-Tweed, and from there moved to Dublin where he set up a bookselling and bookbinding business for himself. This venture did not prove successful, and he came to America (*c.* 1766). His employer and other acquaintances in Berwick had come to Philadelphia, so it was natural for him to locate in that city. In the spring of 1768 his advertisements as "Bookseller and Auctioneer" begin to appear in the Philadelphia newspapers. He offers to buy "Libraries or parcels of books," or owners "may have them exhibited with a regular catalogue by auction . . . where the intrinsic merit and excellence of each book shall be rationally expatiated upon with truth and propriety" (*Pennsylvania Journal*, Apr. 7, 1768). One such library "consisting of Law, History and Entertainment" he announces he will begin to sell "by Auction," on June 13, "From four o'clock to seven each evening" (*Ibid.*, June 9, 1768). As an auctioneer this "stout, chunky man" appears to have been very successful, his drollery attracting buyers. "It was as good as a play," one writer says, "to attend his sales at auction. There were few authors of whom he could not tell some anecdote which would get the audience in a roar. He sometimes had a can of beer aside him and would drink comical healths." (William McCulloch, "Additions to Thomas's History of Printing," *American Antiquarian Society Proceedings,* n. s., XXXI, 232).

Not only in Philadelphia but in other large towns and cities along the Atlantic seaboard Bell plied his vocation, sending a supply of books ahead of him; he thus became "well known for diffusing of literature" (*Pennsylvania Gazette,* Oct. 6, 1784). He liked to call himself "Provedore to the Sentimentalists in America" (*Illumination for Legislators and for Sentimentalists,* 1784, title page). When the British were occupying Philadelphia in the Revolutionary War Bell kept a circulating library and was patronized extensively by the officers; his rule was a deposit of a guinea for each book, the money to be returned with a sum deducted for the loan when the book was returned. After the Revolution when the State of Pennsylvania was contemplating legislation that would provide for the office of book-auctioneer for the city of Philadelphia, Bell issued a pamphlet entitled *Memorial on the Free Sale of Books,* arguing that no one should be "restricted and fettered in a Free-State in the Propagation of Literature" (p. 6). He would object to being appointed to the "Office of Book Auctioneer" himself, he says (p. 6), and he aims to strengthen his cause by reprinting John Dickinson's *Sentiments on What is Freedom, and What is Slavery,* Raynal's *Sentiments on Liberty,* and Rousseau's *Sentiments on Government, Law, Arbitrary Power, Liberty, and Social Institutions.* Nevertheless the Pennsylvania Assembly passed (May 4, 1784) what Bell called "a tyrannical embargo" on his selling books "By Auction," which impelled him to issue *Bell's Address to Every Free-Man,* in the course of which the Commonwealth is portrayed saying to him (p. 5).

"Pray stop, Master Bell, with your selling of Books,
 Your smart witty Sayings, and cunning arch Looks:
 By Auction, I mean—'tis a shocking Offence
 To sell Wit or Humor, or e'en common Sense,
 Unsanction'd by Law, on any Pretence."

The expression "common Sense" which he brought into his versification had more than the ordinary meaning to his readers because it was Bell who, in 1776, had brought out the first edition of Paine's *Common Sense.* Previously (1770) Bell had published in three volumes the first American edition of Robertson's *The History of the Reign of Charles the Fifth, Emperor of Germany,* and this was followed by an American edition of Blackstone's *Commentaries.* Publishing appeared to increase rather than diminish Bell's zeal as a seller of books, and he was on the way to Charleston, S. C., for one of his auction sales when he was taken ill and died in Richmond, Va., where also he was interred. He married in Dublin and left his wife and two children (son and daughter) there

when he came to America. The son joined his father later in Philadelphia but went back after his death. Another daughter (illegitimate) survived him in Philadelphia.

[There is a brief sketch in Isaiah Thomas, *Hist. of Printing in America* (1810), II, 68–69. Bell's individuality appears in his *Memorial on the Free Sale of Books* (1784), his *Address to Every Free-Man* (1784), and his many advertisements in the columns of the *Pa. Gazette* and the *Pa. Jour.*]

A. E. P.

BELL, SAMUEL (Feb. 8, 1770–Dec. 23, 1850), lawyer, governor of New Hampshire, senator, was the son of John and Mary Ann (Gilmore) Bell, and a grandson of John Bell, a Scotch-Irishman who settled in Londonderry, N. H., in 1720. He was born and brought up in Londonderry, working on his father's farm and attending the district school in the winter months. Later he studied at New Ipswich Academy, taught school, and graduated from Dartmouth in 1793. He was admitted to the bar in 1796 and began practise at Francestown, later removing to Amherst, and finally about 1812 to Chester where he maintained a residence henceforth. He was twice married: on Nov. 26, 1797, to Mehitable Dana of Amherst, who died in 1810, and on July 4, 1828, to Lucy Smith, also of Amherst. He was successful in his law practise from the outset and rapidly acquired a competence, although meeting severe losses in the failure of the Hillsborough Bank in 1809. His presidency of this ill-fated institution was afterward used against him as a Federalist campaign argument (*New Hampshire Gazette,* Feb. 3, Mar. 2, 1819). As a Jeffersonian Republican, he represented Francestown in the legislature 1804–06, being speaker in the last two years. He was president of the state Senate 1807–08 and member of the Executive Council in 1809 (*New Hampshire Register,* 1805–10). After several years' retirement from public affairs, due to ill health, he was appointed associate justice of the superior court in 1816, where he served for three years. In 1819 he was chosen governor. The Federalist party was now moribund, and his election was welcomed by its leading organ as a "harbinger of peaceful times" (*Portsmouth Oracle,* Mar. 13, 1819). He was reëlected in the three succeeding years with only scattering opposition. The most important enactment during his administration was the Toleration Act of 1819, which ended the power of the towns to tax for the support of clergymen. He advocated and secured the enactment in 1821 of an important statute conferring chancery powers on the superior court in matters affecting the trusteeship of charitable and other foundations. He was a pioneer in calling attention to the evils of intemperance and demanding a stricter licensing system. In the emphasis laid in his annual messages on the need of developing manufactures and diversifying the economic life of New Hampshire, it is easy to perceive the principles which later made him an ardent supporter of the tariff. He expressed disapproval of internal improvements by the national government, however, and in 1822 the legislature memorialized Congress against the practise. Beginning in 1823 he served two successive terms in the United States Senate. His career in that body was undistinguished, although he appears to have had the respect and confidence of his associates, including Webster. He spoke infrequently, but his speeches against the abolition of imprisonment for debt (*Register of Debates in Congress,* 20 Cong., 1 Sess., cols. 85–87), against a bill settling the claims of Revolutionary officers (*Ibid.,* cols. 436–40), against the preëmption and graduation of the prices of public lands (*Ibid.,* 21 Cong., 1 Sess., pp. 8, 416 ff.), and his stalwart opposition to President Jackson's bank policy(*Ibid.,* 23 Cong., 1 Sess., cols. 566–69, 1538–41), throw considerable light on his principles and show that he possessed some of the characteristics of the Ulster Scot. His longest congressional speeches were on tariff subjects, including one in support of the compromise measure of 1833 (*Ibid.,* 22 Cong., 2 Sess., cols. 742–45). By 1834 the tide of Jacksonian Democracy was running strongly in New Hampshire, and the legislature of that year passed resolutions which declared that he was misrepresenting the state and demanded his resignation (*Ibid.,* 23 Cong., 1 Sess., cols. 2064, 2067). At the expiration of his term the following March, he retired to his farm in Chester where he spent the remainder of his life.

[Chas. H. Bell, *Bench and Bar of N. H.* (1894); Wm. Cogswell, in the *N. H. Repository* (1846), I, 264; Benj. Chase, *Hist. of Old Chester* (1869).]

W. A. R.

BELLAMY, EDWARD (Mar. 26, 1850–May 22, 1898), author, was born at Chicopee Falls, Mass., the third son of Rufus King Bellamy and Maria Louisa (Putnam) Bellamy. His father had served as Baptist minister at Chicopee Falls uninterruptedly for thirty-five years. A preference for a settled habitat and home sights also appeared in Edward Bellamy, who spent practically all his life in Massachusetts—most of it in Chicopee Falls, his residence there being broken only by short periods in Boston, New York, and Colorado—and who chose American villages as the setting for most of his earlier fiction. He was educated almost wholly in the local schools, though he was for a short time at Union College with an older brother, pursuing a special course of study in literature, largely self-selected. At eighteen he went abroad for a year, spending most of the time in Germany. The reticence that characterized him as a man was already evident in college, and during his European travels appears for the first time that interest in the relief of social ills which was to mark the rest of his life. "It was in the great cities of Europe and among the hovels of the peasantry," he wrote later, "that my eyes were first fully opened to the extent and consequences of 'Man's inhumanity to man.'" On his return he studied law and was admitted to the bar, later joining the editorial staff of the *Springfield Union,* and working for a few months on the New York *Evening Post.* In 1880, with his brother Charles, he founded the Springfield *Daily News;* but his heart was never in journalism and he took little part in the editorial direction of the paper. In 1879 he began publication in a country paper of his unfinished historical novel, *The Duke of Stockbridge,* which was eventually completed by another hand and appeared as a book only after Bellamy's death. His choice of subject, Shays's Rebellion, plainly foreshadowed the social interests which produced *Looking Backward.* He had already begun to contribute to the magazines the short stories which were collected and published after his death as *The Blind Man's World and Other Stories* (1898). When his *Dr. Heidenhoff's Process* appeared, in 1880, he was acclaimed as the lineal descendant of Hawthorne, and Howells described the book as "one of the finest feats in the region of romance." This work, like the "romance of immortality," *Mrs. Ludington's Sister* (1884) which followed, made use of Bellamy's study of psychic phenomena, a subject in which he always had a lively, though in no sense morbid, interest.

A purely literary career, above all others that which appealed to Bellamy most strongly, now opened before him. In 1882 he had been married to Emma Sanderson, of Chicopee Falls, and a few years after his marriage he began to concern himself seriously with social questions. "According to my best recollection," he writes, "it was in the fall or winter of 1886 that I sat down to my desk with the definite purpose of trying to reason out a method of economic organization by which the republic might guarantee the livelihood and material welfare of its citizens on a basis of equality corresponding to and supplanting their political equality." Two years later, *Looking Backward* was published.

In spite of the undeniable charm of his earlier stories, Bellamy's permanent reputation rests on this utopian romance, and perhaps in less degree upon its sequel, *Equality.* When he wrote the book which was speedily to bring him national—and even international—fame, the fiction he had already published had won scant attention, and he deliberately made up his mind to undertake a new genre. The mild form of utopian socialism expounded in *Looking Backward* was by no means new to the American public. Numerous editorial writers had paved the way, there was a small socialist literature, and there had already been at least one socialistic novel, now forgotten. The sensation created by *Looking Backward* was due to its intrinsic qualities, to a charming style, and to an adroit fashion of presenting its socialist—or "nationalist," since it advocated nationalization—doctrine as after all no more than "an enlightened self-interest or wholesale common sense." The book achieved a popularity which endured for several years, sold a million copies, and has been fairly steadily in print ever since. Bellamy Clubs were organized to discuss the social implications of the romance, which became a kind of Bible to many people. As William Dean Howells later wrote (Preface to *A Hazard of New Fortunes*), "the solution of the riddle of the painful earth through the dreams of Henry George, through the dreams of Edward Bellamy, through the dreams of all the generous visionaries of the past, seemed not impossibly far off." The success of *Looking Backward* wrought a singular change in its author. He, whose most marked characteristic had been his modesty and a reticence which had been his from boyhood, now took a vigorous and enthusiastic share in the propaganda for nationalism, being firmly convinced that the conversion of a capitalistic society to his own utopianism was possible, by the method of peaceful persuasion, in the immediate future. In 1891 he founded in Boston the *New Nation,* a weekly supported almost wholly by the owner-editor's income from his sucessful book, then in its three hundred and seventy-first thousand. The *New Nation* continued publication for a few years only, after which Bellamy, whose health had suffered from his exertions, went into retreat, publishing little except a few magazine articles, but working steadily upon his second utopian romance, *Equality,* which was published in 1897. During the years in which he worked to complete this book his health was steadily failing, but he absolutely refused to leave his home in Chicopee Falls until it was finished. His jour-

ney to Colorado, in a vain effort to resist tuberculosis, was too long delayed, and when it was obvious that his life could not be saved, he was brought back to Chicopee Falls, where he died.

[No biography of Edward Bellamy has ever been published. His cousin, Francis Bellamy, contributed a short sketch as an introduction to the posthumous edition of *The Duke of Stockbridge* (1900). Henry Austin wrote an obituary article "Edward Bellamy," for the *National Magazine,* Oct. 1898, which contains some personal reminiscences and a portrait. Another portrait and further biographical facts are included in the 1910 edition of *Equality.* William Dean Howells wrote a prefatory sketch for *The Blind Man's World* (1898) and Sylvester Baxter an introduction for the memorial edition of *Looking Backward* (1917). The most vivid account is Caroline Ticknor's in her *Glimpses of Authors* (1922). There is a short critical discussion of Bellamy's ideas in Rudolf Blueher's *Modern Utopien* (1920). The controversial literature is, of course, voluminous.]

J.B.

BELLAMY, ELIZABETH WHITFIELD CROOM (Apr. 17, 1837–Apr. 13, 1900), author, was born near Quincy, Fla., the daughter of William Whitfield and Julia Stephens Croom. Her education in Philadelphia and New York gave her a life-long interest in music and literature. She was married in 1858 to her cousin, Charles E. Bellamy, who was a native of North Carolina. They had two children, neither of whom survived infancy. Dr. Bellamy died in 1863 while acting as a surgeon in the Confederate Army. Mrs. Bellamy, left destitute, began teaching in Mobile, Ala., and continued there, so occupied all her life. In 1870, calling herself "Kamba Thorpe," but permitting herself before long to be referred to in advertisements as "a Southern lady," she published a novel, *Four Oaks.* This was followed in 1876 by *The Little Joanna.* Both of these are romantic stories of the South, vaguely localized. The realistic impulse so far mastered her in 1888 that her *Old Man Gilbert,* published in that year, disclosed not only the real name of its author but the definite scene and time of its action, Tallahassee, Fla., 1857. The central character, Gilbert, is a typically humorous negro, domineering but indulgent and unexpectedly capable. *Penny Lancaster* (1889), the story of a Georgia farm, turns still faithfully upon affairs of the heart, but is freighted with different implication—it tells, in fact, how a woman without sacrificing any of her charm and virtue—and the consequence of those qualities, a satisfactory husband—may none the less at need be a thorough-going person of affairs, turning events to her own will. The writing of these four novels and stories which appeared in the better magazines of the country, together with her teaching, did not suffice to fill Mrs. Bellamy's time during the many years which she spent at the home of her brother. She was an enthusiastic student of Shakespeare, about whom she regularly gave courses of private lectures. The newspapers at the time of her death referred to her as a "typical Southern woman," who would leave a very gracious memory.

[T. McA. Owen, *Hist. of Ala. and Dict. of Ala. Biog.* (1921); *Mobile Reg.*, Apr. 14, 15, 1900; *Who's Who in America*, 1899–1900.]

J. D. W.

BELLAMY, JOSEPH (Feb. 20, 1719–Mar. 6, 1790), theologian, was born in Cheshire, then part of Wallingford, Conn., the fifth child and fourth son, of Matthew and Sarah (Wood) Bellamy. They were of English stock, though the name would indicate a French ancestor further back. A remarkably bright farmer's boy, he went to Yale, a few miles away, where he graduated in 1735 when he was but sixteen. After two years' study of theology, partly with Jonathan Edwards, whose ardent disciple he became, he was licensed to preach, though even yet only a few months over eighteen. After preaching in various churches he went in November 1738 to supply the pulpit in the newly organized parish of Bethlehem, Conn., then part of the town of Woodbury on the northwestern outskirts of the colony. A church was organized, of which he was pastor until his death over fifty years later. He married on Apr. 27, 1744, Frances Sherman of New Haven, who died in 1785; in 1786 he married, as his second wife, a lady already twice widowed, whose maiden name was Abiah Burbank. He was full of enthusiasm for the Great Awakening, and for the New Light theology, inaugurated by Jonathan Edwards, which had been the occasion of the revival, since it enabled the preacher to call men to repentance, as the older Calvinism had not. In this vein he preached with fervor, cogency, and success, first to his own parish, and from 1742 on, from place to place in and around Connecticut for a part of the year, during several years. He was a man of commanding presence with a fine voice and a keen mind and was regarded as even more powerful as a preacher than he was later as a writer. He was, however, domineering and censorious of any that stood in his way, with a biting wit, although he mellowed somewhat as he grew older.

Settling down at the close of the revival he began writing in defense of this new theology, his first notable work being *True Religion Delineated* (1750). Its important points were first, his definition of religion, in accordance with Edwards's theory of virtue, as love to God; second, his clarifying of the distinction between natural and mor-

al inability which was the foundation of the New Light theology; third, a more humane theory of the atonement, developed from Grotius, which made it universal instead of being limited to the elect, and based it on the moral government of God rather than on the satisfaction of his offended dignity as a sovereign. This work brought him into prominence. Young men came to him to study for the ministry, and a sort of theological seminary grew up in this tiny backwoods settlement. In 1758 appeared his work on *The Wisdom of God in the Permission of Sin*. God, he argued, did not ordain, but only permitted sin, and that because he foresaw it to be the means to the greatest good. This work also attracted attention and aroused controversy. His last important theological work was a series of pamphlets from 1762 to 1770 in opposition to that curious anomaly, the Halfway Covenant, which the New Light theology had made superfluous. He was a striking example of bold, independent thinking in early New England. His published writings consist of the two mentioned (the treatise on Sin being part of a volume entitled *Sermons . . . on The Divinity of Christ. The Millenium. The Wisdom of God in the Permission of Sin*, 1758), together with sermons and controversial pamphlets.

[A complete list of Bellamy's publications with a sketch of his life and a list of authorities may be found in F. B. Dexter, *Biog. Sketches Grads. Yale Coll., 1701–1745* (1885), pp. 523 ff. See also Frank Hugh Foster, *A Genetic Hist. of the New Eng. Theology* (1907).]

T. D. B.

BELLEW, FRANK HENRY TEMPLE (Apr. 18, 1828–June 29, 1888), caricaturist, illustrator, was born in Cawnpore, Hindustan, the son, it is said, of an English officer. He spent some years in France and England, and in 1850 came to the United States, where he was active in New York City for over thirty-five years. He brought into our comic journalism a bit of the flavor of *Punch*, to which he contributed some small drawings in 1860, when he revisited England. In various attempts to found an American comic paper there appeared drawings signed by his familiar triangle which was sometimes blank, sometimes enclosed the name Bellew or the initials F. B. Such publications were the *Lantern*, his full-page political cartoons in which were quite in the *Punch* manner; *Yankee Notions; New York Picayune; Nick-Nax; Vanity Fair* (New York); *Punchinello; Wild Oats; Texas Siftings*. He has been credited with having had a hand in the founding of some of these journals. Last-page "comics" in *Harper's Weekly* and *Scribner's Monthly* also bore his signature, and for the *Fifth Avenue Journal* (1872) he drew a series of *portraits-chargés,* as the French call them—"slightly tinged with the tincture of caricature," that *Journal* had it—somewhat like those in the London *Vanity Fair,* or the "Puckographs" in *Puck* (New York). He even wrote and illustrated a volume on *The Art of Amusing* (1866), containing suggestions for parlor amusements of a somewhat elementary order. "His forte," we are told, "was writing and sketching stories for children." As an illustrator he appeared in *Harper's Magazine,* T. W. Strong's *Illustrated American News* (1851), the first noteworthy publication of its kind here—and in books such as T. B. Gunn's *Physiology of the New York Boarding-House* (1857), Stephen C. Massett's *Two Logs, by Jeemes Piper* (1864), and John T. Irving's *The Attorney* (1853). The last was a not highly successful attempt to illustrate by etching, in the manner of the plates by Phiz and others in the Dickens-Ainsworth period in England. Bellew, it was said, had an inexhaustible fund of ideas. His son Frank P. W. (1862–94), better known as "Chip," likewise had a "limitless invention," to which John Ames Mitchell paid tribute. The son drew many droll designs for *Life* and other publications, a number being republished in volumes such as *Chip's Dogs* (1895). The work of both father and son provided amusement without slapstick vulgarity.

[Material on Bellew is somewhat contradictory in statement. Perhaps the best biog. sketch is that in *Appleton's Ann. Cyc.* for 1888. *Wild Oats* published a humorous account, accompanied by a clever caricature portr. of Bellew by Livingston Hopkins. See also obituaries in *N.Y. Times* and *N.Y. Tribune* for June 30, 1888, and F. Weitenkampf's *Am. Graphic Art* (1924). Tom Masson wrote of the son in *Munsey's Mag.,* XXXIII, 601–7.]

                 F.W.

BELLINGHAM, RICHARD (*c.* 1592–Dec. 7, 1672), colonial governor of Massachusetts, son of Frances (Amcotts) Bellingham and William Bellingham of Manton and Brombye ("Lincolnshire Pedigrees," *Publications of the Harleian Society,* L, 118), was born at Boston, Lincolnshire, England, probably in 1592. Trained as a lawyer, he was made a freeman in 1625 (*New England Historical and Genealogical Register,* XXVIII, 14) and served as recorder of the borough from 1625 to 1633 (Pishey Thompson, *History and Antiquities of Boston,* 1856, p. 428). He was also a member of Parliament for Boston in 1628 (*Accounts and Papers, Members of Parliament, Part I, Parliaments of England, 1213–1702, Commons Return No. 69, 1878,* p. 476), and in the following year became one of the patentees of the Massachusetts Bay Charter. Together with his first wife (Elizabeth, daughter of Samuel Backhouse) and his son, Samuel, who was to be a

graduate of Harvard's first class (1642), he came to New England in 1634 and settled at Boston, where he was elected deputy governor in 1635. The General Court seems to have appreciated his legal knowledge, for on more than one occasion he was ordered to examine and criticize the laws of the colony. He served as assistant, 1636–40, 1642–53; as treasurer, 1637–40; as deputy governor, 1635, 1640, 1653, 1655–65; as governor, 1641, 1654, 1665 until his death in 1672 (W. H. Whitmore, *Massachusetts Civil List* (1870). Contemporary writers agree on his honesty and marked legal ability, but consider him of slow and difficult speech. Bellingham's espousal of the popular cause, which brought him into conflict with Gov. Winthrop, probably dates from the "Stoughton affair" in 1635 (*Massachusetts Historical Society Proceedings,* LVIII, 450). By the time of the trial of Nicholas Trerice in 1639 there had developed an open breach, and in the election of 1641 Bellingham was chosen governor by a majority of six votes over Winthrop. His administration was marked by disputes with the other magistrates, and it is significant that the annual allowance of £100 to the governor was withdrawn by the Court. In the same year he further irritated the magistrates and clergy by his unique marriage to Penelope Pelham, in which he not only violated the law by neglecting the previous publication of his intentions, but performed the ceremony himself. As governor, he refused to leave the bench to stand trial, and the perplexed magistrates dropped the case. During the confusion following the Restoration, Bellingham rendered valuable service to the colony. He had succeeded Endicott as governor upon the latter's death in 1665, and was in office during the visit of the Royal Commission to Boston in that year. With others he was appointed to receive the Charter for safe keeping, and under his leadership the General Court denied the authority of the Commission, on the grounds that the Charter did not require the recognition of that body. As a result, Bellingham with several others was summoned to England in 1666 to explain his action, but the tactful present of a shipload of masts to the Royal Navy enabled him to ignore the order. He died on Dec. 7, 1672, and his peculiar will, which provided for the eventual entrusting of his large estate to the care of the clergy, produced litigation lasting over 100 years (*Collections of the Massachusetts Historical Society,* ser. 5, vol. VI, p. 197; *New England Historical and Genealogical Register,* XIV, 237).

[For Bellingham's political life see the *Records of the Governor and Company of Mass. Bay* (1853). Winthrop's *Hist. of New Eng.* (esp. Savage's edition of

1853) shows Bellingham in an unfavorable light. A favorable impression of him is gained from Wm. Hubbard's *Gen. Hist. of New Eng.* (pub. in 1815 as *Mass. Hist. Soc. Colls.*, ser. 2, vols. V, VI, and separately in 1848), while Edward Johnson in his *Wonder-Working Providence* (1654) is decidedly eulogistic. There is a short biog. by E. H. Goss in the *Mag. of Am. Hist.*, XIII, 262.]

H. P. S.

BELLOMONT, Earl of. [See COOTE, RICHARD, 1636–1701.]

BELLOWS, ALBERT FITCH (Nov. 29, 1829–Nov. 24, 1883), landscape painter, etcher, born in Milford, Mass., was the only son of Dr. Albert J. and Pamela (Fitch) Bellows, and was descended from John Bellows who emigrated to Massachusetts on the *Hopewell* in 1635. At an early age he was placed in a boot and shoe store, but at the age of sixteen he moved to Boston, with the consent of his parents, and entered the architectural office of A. B. Young. In 1849 he went into partnership with an architect named J. B. Toule, but abandoned architecture for painting at the end of a year. On Aug. 5, 1851, he married Candace J. Brown of Fall River. He was the principal of the New England School of Design in Boston, 1850–56. Upon his resignation from this position, he visited Paris during the Exposition and then lived in Antwerp where, after studying at the Royal Academy, he was elected an honorary member of the Royal Society of Painters of Belgium in 1858. Upon his return he lived in New York City and was elected a member of the National Academy in 1861. In 1865 he began painting in water-colors. In 1867 he returned to Europe, painting in England, France, and Belgium, and being elected an honorary member of the Royal Belgian Society of Painters in Water Colors in 1868. Moving to Boston shortly after, he remained in that city until the great fire of 1872, in which his studio and with it much of his work was destroyed. He then settled in New York City. He was one of the early members of the American Society of Painters in Water Color. This association published his book entitled *Water Color Painting; Some Facts and Authorities in Relation to Its Durability* (1868). The subjects of his paintings in this country were rural scenes, painted with homely fidelity, in the vicinity of New York, Boston, and Windsor, Conn. His technique both in oils and water-colors was of the early painstaking type. Some of his later oil paintings were carried out with the palette knife instead of a brush. Besides displaying at the National Academy, he showed his work in 1876 at the Philadelphia Centennial, and in 1878 at the Paris Exposition. "The First Pair of Boots," "A New England Village," "The Notch at Lancaster" are some of the titles of his paintings. Toward the end of his career he devoted much time to etching, and was one of the first in this country to attempt large etched plates. Of some fifteen etchings the most important were "The Inlet," "The River-side Inn," and "The Mill-stream." He was a member of the New York Etching Club, the Philadelphia Society of Etchers, and the Society of Painter-Etchers of London.

[Thos. Bellows Peck, *The Bellows Geneal.* (1898) ; H. T. Tuckerman, *Book of the Artists* (1867) ; H. W. French, *Art and Artists in Conn.* (1879) ; G. W. Sheldon, *Am. Painters* (1879) ; W. Montgomery, *Am. Art* (1889).]

T. B.

BELLOWS, GEORGE WESLEY (Aug. 12, 1882–Jan. 8, 1925), painter, lithographer, illustrator, was the son of George and Anna (Smith) Bellows, and traced his descent to Benjamin Bellows who founded the town of Walpole, Vt., during the eighteenth century. His grandfather was a seafaring man, a whaler who lived at the Montauk end of Long Island. His father was a builder and something of an architect in Columbus, Ohio. Bellows once wrote of the "two Sunday freedoms" of his boyhood, the freedom to read and the freedom to draw, and he went on to describe the Sundays when he created ambitious compositions with his pencil while his mother read to him. At school he was received with "a certain deference" because of his talent and was called "the artist." After graduation from the Ohio State University in 1903 he went to New York in 1904 and began the study of oil painting under Robert Henri. He also studied with Kenneth Hayes Miller and H. G. Maratta. Later he became fascinated with the idea of dynamic symmetry. "Ever since I met Mr. Hambidge," he said of the man who developed the theory, "and studied with him, I have painted few pictures without at the same time working on his theory." Henri helped him to develop his artistic personality. From Maratta he learned the importance of setting his palette. From Hambidge he took what he needed to help him in his composition. For the rest, he studied the paintings and prints of Goya and Daumier; and constantly experimented on his own account. But the study of the manifestations of life itself held more interest for him than the study of art. He liked to watch crowds of every-day people, he liked to draw the children in the streets, he liked to attend the prize fights at Tom Sharkey's who was once a boxer and staged encounters after he was too old to "stay in the ring." This life Bellows presently began to depict. One of the first of his paintings to win recognition was called "Forty-Two Kids" (1907), an animated canvas representing boys bathing along the New York river front. "Rain on the River" (1908),"Sharkey's" (1909), "Warships on the Hudson" (1909), and "Polo Game at Lakewood, New Jersey" (1910) are the titles of paintings that followed this first success. In 1908, five years after he began his studies, he exhibited a landscape that won a prize at the National Academy of Design. The next year he was elected an associate member of the National Academy. He was the youngest man ever to receive such recognition, being twenty-seven at the time. He now began to be taken more seriously by the older men. The late John W. Alexander predicted that he would become the foremost artist of the younger generation. In 1910 he became one of the teachers at the Art Students League, teaching there again in 1918 and 1919. He also taught at the Art Institute in Chicago during 1919. Although he never left the United States, he frequently exhibited his work abroad, in Buenos Aires, Munich, Venice, Berlin, Paris, and London. In 1910 he married Emma Louise Story of Upper Montclair, N. J., and made his home at 146 East Nineteenth St., New York City. Here he remained the rest of his life except for summers spent at Monhegan and Ogunquit, Me.; Newport, R. I.; Camden, Me.; Carmel, Cal.; Santa Fé, N. Mex.; and Woodstock, N. Y. Of his studio in New York City he made a splendid painting during the winter of 1919. The picture represents the artist working at a portrait of his wife while his two small daughters, Anne and Jean, play about on the floor; his mother-in-law and the maid stand by the telephone; and a printer bends over a lithographic press on the floor above. He painted a great variety of themes. The Brooklyn water front is the subject of "Men of the Docks" (1912); a dancer on horseback viewed by a Goya-like crowd is the subject of "The Circus" (1912); while "The Cliff Dwellers" (1913) is a picture of several layers of humanity on an East Side street in New York. As time went on, he felt more and more drawn from the city and by 1915 he was painting during the summer at Ogunquit, Me. But humanity he always painted, figures almost invariably playing an important part in his landscapes even along the Maine coast. "The Sand Team" (1917) was painted in California; "Fishermen's Huts" (1918) was painted at Newport. He then painted two large canvases with the horrors of war as the subject. One called "Edith Cavell" (1918), possibly his greatest work, received the sharp criticism of Joseph Pennell. The other, called "The Return of the Useless" (1918), represents a train load of French peasants returned by Germany as unfit for work. In 1916 he made his first experiments in lithog-

raphy in which he became more and more absorbed. Sometimes he made lithographic replicas of his paintings; but most of his lithographs are original scenes—in the men's gymnasium, at a prayer meeting, a shipwreck, or a prize fight— or studies of the nude figure; in short, as was the case in his paintings, he drew every-day scenes and plain houses by preference. "I am sick," he once said, "of American buildings like Greek temples and of rich men building Italian homes." In 1921 he induced his friend, Bolton Brown, to undertake the printing of his lithographs, an association lasting four years. He also undertook book illustrations, among them a series of drawings for "The Wind Bloweth" by Donn Byrne, which appeared in the *Century Magazine* from November 1921 to October 1922. Another series, appearing in *Hearst's International Magazine* from November 1922 to June 1923, illustrated a novel by H. G. Wells entitled "Men Like Gods." Several of these illustrations he redrew on the lithographic stone. A huge painting of "The Crucifixion" (1923), which caused a great stir when it was shown at first, was the subject of a drawing, then a lithograph. It was painted at Woodstock, N. Y. The next year he painted a vigorous picture of Jack Dempsey being knocked through the ropes in his fight with the Argentine boxer, Firpo. "Ringside Seats," "The Pic-nic," "River Front," and finally "Two Women," the latter a new treatment of Titian's "Sacred and Profane Love," were all painted the last year of his life. Prizes of one sort or another were awarded to his paintings at the National Academy of Design (1908, 1913, 1915, 1917); the Pennsylvania Academy (1913, 1917, 1921); the Carnegie Institute, Pittsburgh (1913, 1914, 1922); the National Arts Club (1921); the Corcoran Gallery of Art (1923); the International Exposition, Buenos Aires (1918); the Panama Pacific Exposition (1915); the Chicago Art Institute (1915, 1921, 1923); Newport Art Association (1918). Every important American museum owns examples of his work. He died of appendicitis at the Post Graduate Hospital, New York City, survived by his wife and two daughters, Anne and Jean. "In appearance," writes Frank Crowninshield, "he was tall, shambling and a little ungainly. By nature he was of a firm and elevated character; determined, enthusiastic and honest to the point of bluntness. He liked inordinately, baseball, music and reading."

Technically the earliest work of George Bellows shows a restricted color scheme in which blacks, whites, grays, with reds and yellows, predominate, as witness his portrait "The Cross-Eyed Boy" (1906), where the influence of Goya

and Hals are obvious. Seven years later he painted his splendid full-length portrait of Dr. Thompson, which ranks with the full-length portraits of
Whistler, Velasquez and Henri. As time went
on, the Goya influence became fused with that of
Daumier; and, finally, with Greco and Renoir;
and there was likewise a noticeable improvement
in color. His picture of "The Pic-nic" (1924)
is an exquisite harmony of form, color, and composition. But the foregoing is a tabulation of influences merely. Everything that Bellows painted was stamped with his own personality. His
work ranks with the most significant art of his
epoch.

[*Metropolitan Museum of Art, Memorial Exhibition
of the Work of Geo. Bellows* (1925); *N.Y. Times,* Jan.
9, 1925; *Am. Mag. of Art,* Dec. 1925; *Arts and Decoration,* Aug. 1914; *Century Mag.,* Oct. 1923; *N.Y.
Times Mag.,* Jan. 25, 1925; *Am. Architect,* Dec. 29,
1920; *Internatl. Studio,* May 1925; *Scribner's Mag.,*
May 1928; *Geo. W. Bellows: His Lithographs* (1927),
comp. by Emma S. Bellows, with a biog. sketch by Thos.
Beer.]   T.B.

BELLOWS, HENRY WHITNEY (June 11,
1814–Jan. 30, 1882), Unitarian clergyman, was
born in Boston, the son of John and Betsey
(Eames) Bellows. The family home was at Walpole, N. H. He attended the Round Hill School
at Northampton, where George Bancroft the historian was one of the principals, entered Harvard College at fourteen, and graduated in 1832.
During his college career his father suffered
financial reverses, and upon graduation Bellows
at once began to teach, first at Cooperstown, N.
Y., later as a private tutor in a wealthy family in
Louisiana. He graduated from the Harvard Divinity School in 1837. His first preaching was
at Mobile, Ala., but in 1839 he was invited to
take charge of the First Unitarian Church in
New York City. This was a severe task for a
man of twenty-four, but Bellows was equal to it
and soon won a conspicuous place in the civic,
social, and religious life of New York. He was
one of the founders of the Century, Union League,
and Harvard Clubs of New York, and was often
found at these and other clubs, always the center
of a group that admired his brilliant conversation.
His church grew rapidly in numbers and influence and soon had to find new quarters, building
the Church of All Souls on Fourth Avenue. In
his preaching he was always springing some
surprise on the community, sometimes a bold
theological heresy, sometimes the advocacy of an
unpopular reform, sometimes the championship
of a misunderstood class. He was often called
upon to deliver occasional addresses. In 1847
he began publication of the *Christian Inquirer,*
which he continued to edit until it was merged
with the *Christian Register* of Boston. He also

gave freely of his time, thought, and devotion to
establishing Antioch College at Yellow Springs,
Ohio. The Civil War afforded him opportunity
for the exercise of his varied gifts. He was the
originator, founder, and president of the United
States Sanitary Commission, the great national
organization which cared for the sick and wounded. By his personal appeal he raised in the North
millions of dollars for this work and directed it
with great skill and unflagging zeal. The end
of the war found him with a fund of unspent energy at his disposal. He applied his powers first
to the reorganization of his own religious fellowship, founding the National Conference of Unitarian Churches in 1865, the Ministers' Institute
in 1866, and then a series of state and local conferences. If the church to which he belonged had
proved more plastic to his shaping hand, it might
well have grown into one of the large Christian
bodies. He was editor of the *Christian Examiner,*
1866–77. Then he threw himself into the work
of Civil Service Reform, attacking the spoils system in every shape and on every hand and organizing state and national associations. He naturally found himself frequently in conflict not
only with a misled public opinion, but also with
vigorous personalities, and in these encounters
proved himself a stalwart fighter.

Bellows was not technically a scholar but he
was a man of wide reading, quick insight, and
great power of interpretation. He published numerous books, sermons, and articles, of which the
best known are: *The Treatment of Social Diseases* (1857), *Restatements of Christian Doctrine*
(1860), *The Old World in Its New Face* (1868–
69), and *Twenty-four Sermons* (1886). Conservative in feeling, he was often radical in
thought. He did his most effective work as an
inspirer of men in common purposes and aims.
With exceptional talents for public action and
for social and religious organization, he had, too,
a genius for friendship and domesticity. His first
wife, whom he married Aug. 13, 1839, was Eliza
Nevins Townsend of New York. She died Aug.
27, 1869, and on June 30, 1874, he married Anna
Huidekoper Peabody of Boston. He died at his
home in New York, Jan. 30, 1882.

[J. W. Chadwick, *Henry W. Bellows: His Life and
Character* (1882); *Bellows Geneal.* (1898), ed. by J. B.
Peck; articles in *Unitarian Rev.,* Mar. 1882, and in
Christian Reg., Feb. 2, 9, 16, 23, 1882; C. J. Stillé, *Hist.
of the U. S. Sanitary Com.* (1866); *U. S. Sanitary Com.
Bull.* (3 vols., 1866); W. E. Barton, *Life of Clara Bar-
ton* (1921).]   S.A.E.

BELMONT, AUGUST (Dec. 8, 1816–Nov.
24, 1890), banker, diplomat, patron of art, sportsman, of Jewish descent, the son of Simon and
Frederika (Elsaas) Belmont, was born in the

small town of Alzei, in the Rhenish Palatinate. His father, a wealthy landed proprietor, was able to permit his son to choose his own career. In this choice there was no hesitancy, and at the age of fourteen the youth entered, without pay, the office of the Rothschilds, at Frankfurt-am-Main, to learn the business. His first duty was to sweep the offices, but his industry and his remarkable talent for finance won quick promotion, and after three years' service at Frankfurt he was sent to the branch office at Naples. Here he gave continued proof of his unusual capacity, and, among other accomplishments, carried on successful negotiations with the Papal Court. In Naples much of his leisure was spent in the galleries, where he laid the foundation for an appreciation of art that was to make him one of the foremost collectors of his generation. His duties in Naples completed, he was sent by his employers to Havana, Cuba. While he was at sea the financial panic of 1837 began in the United States. Belmont was quick to sense the possibilities in the financial chaos then prevailing. Having executed his commissions in Havana, he notified the Rothschilds that he was entering business on his own account and sailed for New York on the first available ship. He rented a small office on Wall St., and there established, practically without capital, the foundations of the great banking house of August Belmont & Company. His only tangible asset—that, indeed, a great one—was the agency in the United States for the Rothschilds. Belmont's success was immediate and undisturbed; within a few years he was one of the leading bankers of the country. In August 1841 he fought a duel at Elkton, Ind., with William Hayward of South Carolina and as a result carried a wound with him throughout life. Securely established in business, he became, as speedily as possible, a citizen. Joining the Democratic party, he cast his first vote, in 1844, for Dallas and Polk. In the same year he was appointed consul-general for Austria in the United States. This post he held until 1850, when he resigned as a protest against the severe treatment of Hungary, and especially of the patriot Louis Kossuth, by the Austrian Government. This official position, combined with the charm of his personality, and his great wealth, which he spent freely, made him a conspicuous figure in the social life of New York. In 1849 he added to his prestige by marrying Caroline Slidell Perry, daughter of Commodore Matthew Calbraith Perry, who "opened" Japan to the Western nations. Belmont's political services and influence were rewarded in 1853 by his appointment by President Pierce as minister to the Netherlands. This post

he held with conspicuous success until the expiration of Pierce's term in 1857. He was now recognized as one of the most influential of the younger leaders of the Democratic party. He was opposed to slavery as an institution, but supported the policies of Stephen A. Douglas rather than those of the abolitionists. Following the split in the Democratic party at Charleston in 1860, he took an active part in the Baltimore convention of the same year. Although he strongly opposed the nomination and election of Lincoln, there was no faltering in his devotion to the Union. "I prefer," he said in a letter to John Forsyth of Mobile, Ala., in 1860, "to leave to my children, instead of the gilded prospects of New York merchant princes, the more enviable title of American citizen, and as long as God spares my life I shall not falter in my efforts to procure them that heritage" (*Letters, Speeches and Addresses*, 1890, p. 39). With the outbreak of war, he supported the Government with the greatest vigor. He aided in raising and equipping the first German regiment sent from New York City. In other ways he aided the Union cause, but his most valuable service, perhaps, was a constant correspondence with influential friends in Europe, the Rothschilds and others, in which he set forth forcibly the Northern side in the great conflict. He visited London in 1861 and Paris in 1863. In England he urged upon Palmerston and others the ethical and political claims of the North, and from Paris wrote to Seward that the Emperor Napoleon was the real center of French sympathy for the South. His influence upon public opinion in financial and political circles, both in England and throughout continental Europe, was of value to Lincoln and his advisers. Belmont continued to be a power in his party until 1872, when, the Democrats having accepted Horace Greeley as their nominee, he retired from active political life. His interest in party politics never ceased and he was a constant attendant at state and national conventions as a delegate, and often as presiding officer. Belmont was an eager and intelligent collector of paintings, porcelains, and other objects of art. His collections were sold by auction after his death. He was also a lover of horses and of horse racing, and was, for many years, president of the American Jockey Club.

[*N.Y. Sun*, Nov. 25, 1890; R. J. H. Gottheil, *The Belmont-Belmonte Family* (1917); A. Belmont, *A Few Letters and Speeches of the Late Civil War* (1870).]

A. L. C.

BELO, ALFRED HORATIO (May 27, 1839–Apr. 19, 1901), Confederate soldier, Texas journalist, was born at Salem, N. C., the son of Edward and Amanda (Fries) Belo. He opposed secession by separate state action, but when North Carolina withdrew from the Union he volunteered in the Confederate Army, raised the 1st Company Forsythe Riflemen and became its captain. His company was made part of the 55th Carolina Regiment under Col. J. Connally and Belo became quartermaster. He was promoted to major and then was made colonel when Col. Connally became brigadier-general. He was wounded twice at Gettysburg and again when Grant attacked Cold Harbor, but remained with the colors until Lee surrendered. After the war he rode horseback from North Carolina to Texas, where he joined the *Galveston News,* in September 1865, as bookkeeper. In March 1866 he became one of the owners in the firm of W. Richardson & Company. He was married to Nettie Ennis of Galveston on June 30, 1868. In 1875 he bought out Richardson's interest in the publishing firm and changed its name to A. H. Belo & Company, incorpora*t*·ng under that name in 1881. Until his death he was president of the corporation. Stern and austere, a quiet, conscientious worker, Belo used his military training in forming rules and methods of discipline on his publications, adopting an unrelenting and vigorous stand against the old style of personal journalism and entangling alliances. Believing in the future of his adopted state, he regarded it as the mission of the *News* "to furnish people with news and labor for the development of Texas." With his associates he contracted in 1883 with the Galveston, Houston & Henderson Railroad to run a special mail car every day in the year to carry papers out into the state. This is said to have been the first daily newspaper service of its kind in the world. Also in 1883 Belo built what is reported to have been the first modern exclusive newspaper plant in the United States, which was also the first fireproof building in Texas. He conceived the new and bold idea of duplicating the *Galveston News* simultaneously at Dallas to facilitate early delivery in all sections of Texas. The *Dallas News* was started Oct. 1, 1885, and the venture proved successful beyond expectation, setting a precedent in journalism. The *Dallas News* was the third paper of consequence in America to own its own home devoted exclusively to the publication of a newspaper. Belo was one of the incorporators of the Associated Press and served two terms as vice-president.

[The chief sources of information are the files of bound volumes of the *Dallas News* at the time of his death and newspaper clippings from the scrap-book of G. B. Dealey, now president of the A. H. Belo Corporation.]

A—oJ.

BEMAN, NATHAN SIDNEY SMITH (Nov. 26, 1785–Aug. 6, 1871), Presbyterian clergyman, college president, was born at New Lebanon, N. Y., the son of Samuel and Silence (Douglass) Beman, of German and Scotch ancestry, from whom he acquired a taste for learning and an interest in theology. Matriculating at Williams College in 1803, he withdrew at the end of the second term and entered Middlebury College a year later. During the interim he taught at Fairhaven, Vt.; upon graduation, in 1807, he became preceptor at Lincoln Academy, Newcastle, Me. In 1809 he accepted a tutorship at Middlebury. He was pastor of the First Presbyterian Church, Portland, Me., during 1810–12. He then established a school at Mount Zion, Ga., where, with the exception of a year (1818) which he spent as president of Franklin College, he remained until he was called to Troy, N. Y., in 1823, as minister of the First Presbyterian Church. There he became associated with Rensselaer Polytechnic Institute. In 1842 he was elected vice-president and, in 1845, president, a position which he held until 1865. Although he was professor of philosophy until his retirement, and although he served as director during 1859–60, succeeding Benjamin Franklin Greene, he does not appear to have aided him in the reorganization linked with his name. In the city, however, he was a power during the forty years of his ministry. His first independent publication, reprinted in England, consisted of *Four Sermons on the Doctrine of the Atonement* (1825). Although he published other addresses, his influence was due primarily to his impressiveness in the pulpit. Reserved and even arrogant, he nevertheless held his congregations by an eloquence wrought of emotion as well as intellect. Many of his discourses—especially his Thanksgiving orations—were pugnaciously controversial. He assailed relentlessly the doctrine of the apostolic succession maintained by the Protestant Episcopal Church. Even more biting were his attacks on the claims of the Roman Catholic hierarchy, which he challenged in his *Letters to Rev. John Hughes* (1851). His chief battlefield, however, was the Presbyterian Church. In 1826 he initiated a series of revivals which aroused the antagonism of conservative clergymen. Although he was rebuked by a convention summoned in the same year, he was chosen moderator of the General Assembly in 1831. By 1837, however, he had become head of the New School movement; and, as such, he was largely responsible for the disruption of 1838. Without slighting his parochial duties, he acquired a reputation as a publicist that was more than local. In his advocacy of abolition, especially, he incurred the enmity which is the lot of every reformer.

[Beman's career as an educator is reflected in the minutes of the Board of Trustees of Rensselaer Polytechnic Institute and in the catalogues and registers, 1842–65. Palmer C. Ricketts, *Hist. of Rensselaer Polytechnic Institute* (1895) contains a note of his services. A fuller sketch occurs in Henry B. Nason's *Biog. Record of the Officers and Grads. of the Rensselaer Polytechnic Institute* (1887). Beman's ministry in Troy is treated in the *Proc. Centennial Anniv. First Presbyt. Ch., Troy* (1891). His conduct is criticized severely in Josephus Brockway's *Delineations of the Characteristic Features of a Revival in Troy* (1827). Although equally biased, Marvin R. Vincent's *Memorial Sermon* (1872) and the addresses and notices printed with it contain much valuable information.]

R. P. Ba—r.

BEMENT, CALEB N. (1790–Dec. 22, 1868), agriculturist, inventor, publicist, was for many years a resident of northern New York state. It is well authenticated that the Bements, who were of English, Dutch, and French extraction, honorably assisted in the early settlement of New York, but it is uncertain to which branch of the family Caleb belonged. Prior to 1834 he is known to have been a printer by trade and also to have engaged in the hotel business. In April of that year, he purchased his subsequently celebrated "Three Hills Farm" near Albany, and thereafter for a number of years intelligently devoted himself to agricultural theory and practise. Quickly becoming dissatisfied with the crude farm apparatus of the day, before the end of 1835 he invented, and shortly afterward offered to the public, two implements, designated as Bement's Expanding Corn Cultivator and Bement's Turnip Drill. These machines, which he manufactured himself and placed on sale in Albany and New York, were improved from time to time in the next half-decade, and came into considerable use among farmers. Simultaneously with these inventive and manufacturing efforts, Bement began to display his long-continued interest in improved live stock, by importing, breeding, and distributing through sale, blooded Berkshire and China hogs, Southdown and Leicester sheep, Hereford, Devon, Ayrshire and Shorthorn Durham cattle, and poultry. After 1834 he frequently exhibited his animals at the annual fairs of the New York State Agricultural Society and won numerous prizes. Not content with these enterprises, Bement at the same time commenced offering his opinions and ideas upon farming to the agricultural press. These original contributions not only presented the results of his own careful and extended experiments at "Three Hills," but frequently added, by way of preface, informing historical summaries gained from a wide reading of ancient and contemporary agricultural writers in Europe and America. In this period and later

Bement also showed a notable generosity of spirit, as well as vision, by publicly calling attention to every new machine, improvement in live-stock, or agricultural practise, which came within range of his inquiring mind. Bement's pioneer activities along these and similar lines did much to encourage the introduction of better machinery and improved breeds of live stock in New York and other states.

Having tasted of the fruits of authorship through his published correspondence, Bement in January 1844 became one of the editors of the *Central New York Farmer,* but because of the competition with other agricultural papers the *Central Farmer* perished of financial atrophy at the end of the year. In the meanwhile in July 1844 he gave further proof of his diverse abilities. Turning over "Three Hills," which by now had become a show place, to a manager, who continued to breed and sell improved live stock under his supervision, he reëntered the tavern business by leasing the American Hotel in Albany for a number of years. This hostelry, under his guidance, soon became the rendezvous of all the agricultural notables who came that way. Bement's table, supplied from his farm, was justly famed, and many pleasant agricultural gatherings took place under his hospitable roof. One of the most valuable of Bement's activities consisted of the completion and publication of his *American Poulterer's Companion* in 1844. This book was proclaimed by the editor of the *Cultivator* as the most complete and practical treatise on the subject of poultry which had appeared up to that time, and was long regarded as a classic by agriculturists. Engaged with his hotel and his farm, Bement did not undertake any new enterprise until the beginning of the year 1848, at which time he purchased the *American Quarterly Journal of Agriculture and Science,* announced himself as editor, and offered it to the public. This second attempt at editorship, like the first, ended in disaster, the publication discontinuing for lack of financial support at the end of 1848. In the following year, possibly due to financial losses, Bement advertised his live-stock at "Three Hills" at public auction. In 1853 he appeared before the public as the proprietor of the Albany Steam Mills, where he manufactured and sold Bement's Compound, a substitute for yeast. In 1855 he added *The Rabbit Fancier* to his *Poulterer's Companion,* a work which increased his reputation as an author. Shortly afterward, he left Albany and took up his residence at Springside in Dutchess County, N. Y. Here he farmed again and continued his writings for the agricultural press, devoting much of his attention to poultry. In 1867 he moved to Poughkeepsie, and died in that city the next year.

As indicated by his career, Bement was a man of unusual intelligence, wide interests, and varied talents, accompanied by great industry. Lacking in humor, he atoned for this fault by an equanimity of temperament which enabled him to face the vicissitudes of a long life with unfailing courage. His numerous articles and his books are simply and clearly written but lack distinction of style. Frequently derived from his own extended researches they contain much detailed and valuable information. The practical tone which characterizes the writings of his early years is mellowed with a philosophic attitude in the later period. Bement's chief claim to be remembered proceeds from his vision and breadth of spirit as a pioneer agriculturist in a changing period of American farming, from his influence in encouraging his contemporaries to improve their agriculture, and from the very considerable addition which he made to our knowledge of live stock, including poultry.

[Among the chief sources are the *Cultivator*, 1835–47; *Central N. Y. Farmer*, 1844; *Am. Agriculturist*, 1843–47, 1859; *Genesee Farmer*, 1846–47, 1859–60, 1862; *Am. Quart. Jour. of Ag. and Sci.*, 1848; *Am. Farmer*, 1847–48, 1853; *Southern Planter*, 1845–46, 1859; *Pa. Farm Jour.*, 1853; *Valley Farmer*, 1857, 1859; *Prairie Farmer*, 1847, 1849–50; *Country Gentleman*, 1857, 1859–60, 1864–67, 1869; *Rural Annual*, 1862; *Trans. N. Y. State Ag. Soc.*, 1842, 1847, 1853; *Poughkeepsie Daily Eagle*, Dec. 24, 1868.]   H. A. K.

BEMENT, CLARENCE SWEET (Apr. 11, 1843–Jan. 27, 1923), collector, born in Mishawaka, Ind., was descended from John Bement who was settled in Massachusetts in 1635; another of his ancestors was the *Mayflower* passenger, Francis Cooke. Clarence Sweet Bement was the son of Emily (Russell) Bement and of William Barnes Bement, the celebrated manufacturer and inventor of machine tools and patron of fine arts. Early in life he identified himself with his father's business in Philadelphia, and in 1870 he entered the firm which then became William B. Bement & Son. On Dec. 19, 1871, in Philadelphia, he was married to Martha Shreve Ridgway, by whom he had four children. Seventeen years later, the retirement of his father made him the senior partner in the firm and he held that position until August 1899, when the firm of Bement, Miles & Company was merged into the Niles-Bement-Pond Company. Primarily a business man for many years, Bement nevertheless had diversified tastes and pursuits. He was prominent among a small group of Americans who found relaxation from their occupations in the pursuit of some branch of art or science. It was to minerals that he devoted

the most of his leisure and the greatest care, his interest in this subject beginning when he was still a lad in school. His collection of minerals became the foremost of its class in America, being rated "the finest ever made by a private individual," and a medal of appreciation was conferred on its owner by the University of Munich. It was purchased by the late Mr. J. Pierpont Morgan for the American Museum of Natural History, New York City. Among its more than 12,000 treasures, the four hundred specimens of meteorites stand out prominently. Another pursuit, perhaps the second to find expression, was Bement's search for rare books, which resulted in the formation of one of the most noted private libraries in the country. A portion of this library passed into the hands of Harry Elkins Widener, forming the nucleus of the Widener Library at Harvard University. Bement's interest was not merely acquisitive however, and he was one of the original founders of, and a silent partner in the Rosenbach Company of Philadelphia and New York, dealers in rare books. During the latter years of his life he became interested in numismatics. At first this interest extended to both ancient and modern coins, including the American series and paper money. He concentrated later on Greek and Roman coins, of which his collection in time became one of the finest in America. It was sold in Lausanne, Switzerland, in January 1924. The extreme diversity of Bement's artistic and other interests can be judged by the societies of which he was a member. These included the American Philosophical Society, the Academy of Natural Sciences, the Numismatic and Antiquarian Society, the Pennsylvania Academy of the Fine Arts, the Philobiblon Club, the Franklin Institute, the Historical Society of Pennsylvania, the Colonial Society, and the Pennsylvania Society of the Sons of the Revolution.

[MSS. of the late J. Granville Leach; *A Descriptive Cat. of Greek Coins from the Bement Coll.* (Am. Numismatic Soc., 1921); A. S. W. Rosenbach, *Books and Bidders* (1927); *Phila. Inquirer* and *Public Ledger* (Phila.), Jan. 28, 1923; *Col. Soc. of Pa., Charter, Constitution*, etc. (1914), p. 38.]   A. S. W. R.

BEMIS, GEORGE (Oct. 13, 1816–Jan. 5, 1878), lawyer, publicist, was a member of a well-known Massachusetts family. Joseph Bemis, the original immigrant, had come from England and settled at Watertown in 1640, his descendants for 150 years continuing to live there. Seth Bemis, a Watertown manufacturer and Harvard graduate, married Sarah Wheeler of Concord and moved to Waltham, Mass., where their youngest child, George, was born. Having been fitted for college at the school of the Rev. Samuel Rip-ley in Waltham, he proceeded to Harvard where he graduated with distinction in 1835. Entering the Harvard Law School he obtained the degree of LL.B. in 1839, and on being admitted to the Boston bar in the same year, commenced practise in that city. While at the Law School he had been a Sunday-school teacher at the State Prison at Charlestown, and had become keenly interested in the subject of crime, punishment and reform. On becoming a lawyer one of his first steps was to attack the system of cumulative punishment of offenders which then prevailed in Massachusetts. As a result of his efforts the whole system of punishment in the state was radically changed. In the meanwhile he was becoming known as an expert in the more difficult phases of criminal law. The case which established his reputation was that of the Commonwealth *vs.* Rogers, a convict who was tried in 1844 for murder of the warden of the prison in which he was confined. Involving the law of insanity and uncontrollable impulse as an excuse for homicide, it attracted wide attention and his defense was considered masterly (*7 Metcalf*, 500). In 1850 he was associate counsel with the attorney-general for the prosecution in the trial of Dr. Webster for the murder of Dr. Parkman, most of the heavy detail work being undertaken by him. After the trial he published a complete report of the proceedings. In 1858 he was compelled to retire from active practise owing to a severe hemorrhage of the lungs, and thereafter his health continued so impaired that he spent the remainder of his life abroad. He never married. Financially independent, he turned his attention to public international law and rendered valuable assistance to the United States Government in connection with the *Alabama* claims. He also contributed to the public discussion of the rights and duties of neutrals in the following pamphlets: *Precedents of American Neutrality, in Reply to the Speech of Sir Roundell Palmer in the British House of Commons* (1864); *Hasty Recognition of Rebel Belligerency and Our Right to Complain of It* (1865); *American Neutrality, Its Honorable Past, Its Expedient Future* (1866); and *Mr. Reverdy Johnson: The Alabama Negotiations, Their Just Repudiation by the Senate of the United States* (1869). Though necessarily controversial in character these writings were distinguished for their uniformly high level of thought and an absence of prejudice which stamped their author as a publicist of outstanding merit. He died at Nice, France, Jan. 5, 1878. Under a bequest in his will, the present Bemis Professorship of International Law at Harvard was established and endowed.

[Details respecting the Bemis family are contained in T. W. Draper, *The Bemis Hist. and Genealogy* (1900) and Henry Bond, *Genealogies and Hist. of Watertown, Mass.* (1860). The only article which does justice to the main currents of his life appeared in the *Am. Law Rev.*, XII, 599.]
H. W. H. K.

BENAVIDES, ALONZO DE (fl. 1600–1664), Franciscan friar, was the son of Pedro Alonzo Nieto and Antonia Murato de Benavides. His birthplace was the Island of San Miguel (probably São Miguel of the Azores). He made his vows in the Franciscan convent in the City of Mexico in 1603 and was afterward made Master of Novices in the monastery of Puebla. In 1621 New Mexico was erected into the "Custodia de la Conversion de San Pablo" and Benavides was appointed Father Custodian. He arrived in New Mexico in the following year taking with him at royal expense twenty-six or twenty-seven friars. Their work was among the Apaches of the Upper Gila in what is now the southwestern part of New Mexico. Shortly after his arrival in Santa Fé, Benavides began to build a suitable convent and church for the chief town of the province. Before he had presented his now famous *Memorial* he had initiated mission or convent buildings in no less than ten places. One was at Picuries, among the Tiwas where the natives were at first unfriendly. Another was the mission of San Gerónimo at Taos, among the same people. At Ácoma the Queres submitted to indoctrination in 1629 and accepted a missionary. Among the fourteen Pira towns Benavides established missions in 1626 at Pilabo, Senecú, and Sevilleta. In addition to this, and efforts to indoctrinate the Moquis, Benavides, while at Senecú, made a convert of Sanaba, a chief of the Gila Apaches, a circumstance which opened opportunity for missions in the river country. Among the Tiwas he founded on Sept. 17, 1629, a convent and church at Santa Clara de Capoo, a Tiwa town on the edge of the Apache country; it became the center of work in teaching and converting the powerful and warlike Navajo Apaches. The New Mexico missions are believed to have had more than 16,000 converts. In 1629, it seems, Benavides was relieved of his custodianship and returned to Mexico and in 1630, to Spain, where his *Memorial* was presented to the king. It is this document that has done the most to keep the name of Benavides alive. It shows him to have been a zealous religious propagandist, of an enthusiastic personality, and of considerable courage and fortitude. The *Memorial* is entitled, "Memorial which Fray Juan de Santander of the Order of Saint Francis, Commissary-General of the Indies, presents to His Catholic Majesty, the King, Philip IV, Our Lord, made by the Father

Fray Alonso de Benavides, Commissary of the Holy Office and Custodian that was of the Provinces and Conversions of New Mexico. In It are Treated the Treasures spiritual and temporal, which the Divine Majesty hath manifested in those Conversions and New Discoveries by means of the Priests of this Seraphic Order." Its object was to persuade the king to send more missionaries to New Mexico and to erect more churches, and in this it succeeded. The *Memorial* won great favor, as is evidenced by the translations that were made within the three following years into four languages—French, Dutch, Latin, and German. In 1634 Benavides wrote, at the request of Pope Urban VIII, a revision of the *Memorial*, a copy of which in his own handwriting and bearing his signature is in the Propaganda Archives in Rome. This revision, having as its object the granting of more extensive privileges and being to an even greater extent than the original *Memorial* a work of propaganda and promotion, emphasizes the difficulties of the labors and the sufferings of the missionaries, which Benavides with characteristic modesty and self-abnegation had almost ignored in the original *Memorial*. It is a more interesting work, giving the history of the missions and making the descriptions of the physical aspects of the country incidental to the story of what the missionaries were doing. In 1631 Benavides had written to the Fathers in New Mexico expressing the hope "to go back there to finish my days if He will allow me to do so in the company and service of your Reverences." Acording to Figueroa in his *Bezerro General,* Benavides returned to Mexico in 1632, and went to New Mexico again in 1633 or 1634. He states that there is a record of the Mexican province having sent him 100 pesos while there in 1634. Probably in the spring of 1634 Benavides was appointed assistant to the Archbishop of Goa in Portuguese India, and on the death of the latter he succeeded to the office.

[The chief sources of information about Benavides are his *Memorial* of 1630, tr. into English by Mrs. E. E. Ayer, with annotation by Frederick W. Hodge and Chas. F. Lummis (1916); his manuscript *Memorial* of 1634, discovered by the Rev. Peter Guilday in the Propaganda Archives at Rome after the publication of the Ayer edition of the 1630 *Memorial*—a photographic reproduction of the former together with several collateral documents, being in the Am. Hist. Dept. of the Cath. Univ. at Washington; the "Bibliography of Fray Alonso de Benavides," by F. W. Hodge, pub. in vol. III of *Indian Notes and Monographs* (1919); Lyman P. Powell, *Historic Towns of the Western States* (1901), pp. 453–54; Francisco Palou, *Life of Junipero Serra,* tr. by C. Scott Williams, with notes by Geo. Wharton James (Pasadena, 1913), containing Benavides's letter, "Tanto que se sacó . . . ," p. 327; J. G. Shea, *Hist. of the Cath. Ch. in the U. S.* (1892).]

H. I. P.

BENBRIDGE, HENRY (May 20, 1744–February 1812), early American portrait painter, was born in Philadelphia, the only child of James and Mary (Clark) Benbridge. When he was seven years old, his mother, who had been left a widow, was married to Thomas Gordon, a wealthy Scotchman. The boy's artistic talent was encouraged. He made for his stepfather's drawing-room decorative designs which were much admired. When he was fourteen years old he may have watched John Wollaston [*q.v.*] paint Mr. Gordon's portrait. It has been plausibly urged (Charles Henry Hart, "The Gordon Family, painted by Henry Benbridge," *Art in America,* VI, 191–200), that young Benbridge had instruction from Wollaston, since his earliest known portrait, that of his half-sister Rebecca Gordon, "seems to hark back to Wollaston." In his twenty-first year Benbridge was sent to Italy where he studied with Batoni and Raphael Mengs. In 1769, on order from James Boswell, biographer of Dr. Samuel Johnson, he made in Corsica a portrait of Pascal Paoli which he took to London. It was exhibited (1769) at the Free Society of Artists, and from it three mezzotints were scraped and published with the artist's name signed "Bembridge." Like other young Americans he was encouraged by Benjamin West. He wrote, Dec. 7, 1769, to his stepfather: "Upon my arrival I waited upon Mr. West who received me with a sort of brotherly affection, as did my cousin, Mrs. West." Impelled, apparently, by a longing to rejoin his family, he left England in 1770, bearing from West the following note of recommendation to Francis Hopkinson: "By Mr. Benbridge you will receive these few lines. You will find him an Ingenous artist and an agreeable Companion. His merit in the art must procure him great incouragement and much esteem. I deare say it will give you great pleasure to have an ingenous artist resident amongst you."

At Philadelphia Benbridge married a Miss Sage and was admitted Jan. 18, 1771, to membership in the American Philosophical Society, of which Franklin was a founder. He painted the large portrait of the Gordon family, with six figures, one of his masterpieces. Suffering, however, from asthma, he sought a more congenial climate and removed to Charleston where he succeeded Jeremiah Theus (d. May 18, 1774) as the popular portrait painter of South Carolina. He there made many likenesses of southern men and women, several of which have been popularly attributed to John Singleton Copley, an artist who never painted in the South and who left America in 1774. About 1800 Benbridge settled at Norfolk, Va., whence he made frequent visits to his native city. At Norfolk he gave to Thomas Sully [*q.v.*] his first lessons in oil painting. He had previously instructed Thomas Coram, of Charleston. Sully (as quoted by Dunlap, *History of the Arts of Design*, I, 167) describes his master as "a portly man of good address—gentlemanly in his deportment." Benbridge's health is said by Hart to have declined in middle age. Dunlap's assertion that his last years were passed "in obscurity and poverty" has been disputed.

As a technician Benbridge drew well and painted solidly, exhibiting many characteristics of the late Italian masters. His contemporary Charles Fraser (quoted by Dunlap) said that "his shadows were dark and opaque and more suitable to the historical style." Hart says "Benbridge was impregnated by the brownish sameness of Batoni's palette and his shadows were too opaque, and although later he was somewhat emancipated from these errors, all his work belongs to the late Italian school." His paintings, nevertheless, were notably good in respect of their black-and-white values and some of his miniatures are exquisite. His Italianate mode was much appreciated in the Middle and Southern states during his lifetime.

[The detailed but somewhat unreliable acount of Benbridge given by Wm. Dunlap in his *Hist. of the Rise and Progress of the Arts of Design in the U. S.* (1834) is corrected by F. W. Bayley and C. E. Goodspeed in a footnote in their revised edition (1918), I, 164. A brief notice of Benbridge, his self-portr. and his painting of Mrs. Thomas Hartley and Family was given by F. W. Bayley in his undated pamphlet *Little Known Early Am. Portr. Painters, No. 4*. Chas. Henry Hart, whose researches disclosed many heretofore unknown data concerning Benbridge, contributed to his cat. of the Herbert L. Pratt collection a succinct account which was amplified in his article, cited above (*Art in America*, VI, 191–200), in which he supplemented and corrected meager information concerning "An Early American Artist: Henry Bembridge," by William Roberts, of London (*Art in America*, VI, 96 ff.).]

F. W. C.

BENEDICT, DAVID (Oct. 10, 1779–Dec. 5, 1874), Baptist clergyman, historian, was born in Norwalk, Conn., the eldest child of Thomas Benedict, a farmer, and of Martha Scudder. He joined the Baptist Church in Stamford, Conn., in 1799, was a shoemaker's apprentice, and went to school at Mt. Pleasant (now Ossining), N. Y. Here he met expenses by tutoring younger pupils, among whom was Francis Wayland, later president of Brown University. After two years Benedict himself entered Brown and graduated in 1806, delivering an earnest oration on "Ecclesiastical History." He issued his first publication, anonymously, while he was still in college —a pamphlet entitled *The Watery War, or a Poetical Description of the Controversy on the Subjects and Mode of Baptism, by John of Enon*. It was widely circulated, and was reprinted in 1843. After graduation, he accepted his first and only

pastorate, at a salary of $400 a year, with the newly organized First Baptist Church of Pawtucket, to whose people he had preached when he was a student. He led them effectively for twenty-three years. On May 5, 1808, he married Margaret Hubbel Gano, daughter of Stephen Gano [*q.v.*], who was pastor of the First Baptist Church of Providence. They lived together sixty years and had twelve children.

Deeply engaged in the study of Baptist history, which he deemed his real vocation, Benedict ultimately gave up his pastorate. In a day of heavy postage he wrote hundreds of letters of inquiry and traveled nearly 4,000 miles on horseback throughout New England and as far west as the Mississippi. He rightly claimed a wider acquaintance with Baptist men and affairs than any one else then living. His chief works were: *A General History of the Baptist Denomination in America and Other Parts of the World* (2 vols., 1813), not free from defects or infelicities, but a pioneer work, widely used; *Abridgment of Robinson's History of Baptism* (1817); *History of All Religions* (1824); *A General History of the Baptist Denomination in America and Other Parts of the World* (1848), a different work from the previous one bearing the same title; *Fifty Years among the Baptists* (1860), his last personal publication. As a nonagenarian, with good health and eyesight, he still worked assiduously, and before his death had practically completed a "Compendium of Ecclesiastical History" for popular use, and a *History of the Donatists* which was published posthumously. In his pastorate he wrote and collected hymns for church use, publishing them in editions reaching 20,000 copies. He pioneered in founding Sunday-schools throughout the Blackstone Valley, with paid teachers in various churches. Elected a trustee of Brown University in 1818, from 1858 he was senior member of the Corporation, and, until his last year, was absent from but one meeting in fifty-five years. He was sometime postmaster of Pawtucket. Though hale to the last, he survived but a few days the deaths of his oldest daughter and of a beloved sister in the same week late in 1874.

[H. C. Graves, "Sketch of the Life and Work of Dr. Benedict" in *Hist. of the Donatists* (1875); H. M. Benedict, *Genealogy of the Benedicts in America* (1870); *Proc. R. I. Hist. Soc.*, 1874–75, pp. 89–90; *Baptist Encyc.* (1881); *Providence Jour.*, Dec. 7, 1874.]

C. M. G.

BENEDICT, ERASTUS CORNELIUS (Mar. 19, 1800–Oct. 22, 1880), lawyer, educationist, was a descendant of Thomas Benedict of Nottinghamshire who emigrated to New England in 1638, remaining for a time in Massachusetts and finally settling in Norwalk, Conn., with which place his descendants were long associated. Erastus Cornelius was the son of Joel Taylor Benedict, a clergyman, and of Currance, daughter of Deacon Adin Wheeler of Southbury, Conn. He was born at Branford, Conn., but the family moved to New York State in 1803, residing successively at New Windsor, Franklin, and Chatham, where young Benedict received his early education in the district schools. In 1816 he became a teacher, and in September 1818 entered Williams College, graduating in 1821 with high honors. He then became in turn principal of the Johnstown and Newburgh Academies, later joining the teaching staff at Williams College, and studying law in his leisure hours. He was admitted to the New York bar in 1824 and removing to New York City, obtained a position as deputy clerk in the United States district court of southern New York. In this office he acquired an intimate knowledge of admiralty law, which later induced him to resign his appointment, and enter into practise, devoting his attention to admiralty cases. He quickly became known as a specialist, and built up an extensive connection, gradually acquiring a reputation as one of the foremost admiralty lawyers of his day. On May 7, 1833, he was married to Caroline Margaret, daughter of Moses Bloodgood. In 1840 he was elected a member of the city common council, and in 1842 he was appointed a school trustee. For nearly forty years thereafter he was a prime factor in the development of education both in the city and state. In 1848 he became for one term a member of the state legislature. In 1850 he was elected a member of the board of education of the City of New York of which he became president. During the thirteen years for which he remained a member of the board he initiated and carried through reforms which resulted in the public schools of the city being consolidated into a harmonious and flexible system of high efficiency. In the course of this work he was mainly instrumental in establishing the Free Academy, which subsequently developed into the College of the City of New York. In 1855 he had been appointed by the state legislature to the board of regents of the state university. He resigned from the board of education in 1863, and in the following year was again elected a member of the Assembly, serving one term. In 1872 as a reform candidate he was elected to the state Senate, and was nominated a member of the court of impeachment before whom the charges against the members of the New York judiciary which arose out of the exposure of the "Tweed Ring" were heard. In 1878 he was selected as chancellor of the state

university, continuing to hold that position till his death, which occurred in New York City, Oct. 22, 1880. Despite his absorption in educational problems, he had continued the active practise of his profession, and in 1850 had published a treatise, *American Admiralty*, which was for years recognized as the standard work on the subject in the United States, passing through a number of editions. He also wrote *A Run Through Europe* (1860), being an account of a holiday trip which he had taken in 1854. The most striking testimony to the versatility of his culture is, however, found in his metrical translations from the French, German, and Latin, *The Hymn of Hildebert and Other Mediæval Hymns* (1861) attracting wide attention. In one of his translations of *"Dies Irae"* he used only words of Gotho-English derivation. He was the author of numerous addresses on historical and educational subjects.

[H. M. Benedict, *The Genealogy of the Benedicts in America* (1870) contains full details of the family history, in addition to a sketch of Benedict's career. Information will also be found in *Hist. of the Bench and Bar of N. Y.*, ed. by D. A. McAdam et al. (1897), I, 259, and *Am. Annual Cyc. and Reg.*, 1880, p. 56; long obituaries in *N. Y. Times* and *N. Y. Tribune*, Oct. 23, 1880.]

H. W. H. K.

BENEZET, ANTHONY (Jan. 31, 1713–May 3, 1784), philanthropist, author, was born in San Quentin, in Picardy, France, the son of Jean Étienne Benezet. The family were Huguenots. Increasing persecution, following the revocation of the Edict of Nantes, caused the parents in 1715 to take refuge in Rotterdam, soon leaving Holland, however, for London, where they remained sixteen years. Here the young Anthony received a liberal education, served an apprenticeship in a mercantile house, and coming under Quaker influence, joined that sect at the early age of fourteen. In 1731 the family removed to Philadelphia, bringing with them the lad of eighteen, "well recommended by divers Friends." For a brief time, Anthony appears to have been in business with his brothers, John, Philip, and Daniel, who later were successful importers of goods from London, Philip Benezet's advertisements being frequent in the *Pennsylvania Gazette* about 1759–60. In May 1736 Anthony Benezet married Joyce, daughter of Samuel and Mary Marriott of Burlington, N. J., and began a happy married life of forty-eight years. Dislike for the merchant's life to which he had been brought up, after a brief experience as a manufacturer in Wilmington, Del., determined him to follow his inclination to teach. Going first to the Germantown Academy, in 1742 he became a teacher in the Friends' English Public School in Philadelphia, now the William Penn Charter School, where he remained for the next twelve years. In this profession, to which the rest of his life was devoted, Benezet found congenial occupation, and an outlet for the energies of his active and altruistic mind. Finding female education defective, he established a girls' school in 1755.

At this time Benezet, always an omnivorous reader, began to be greatly interested in the amelioration of conditions among the slaves, and the reports of travelers and agents in the West Indies and in Africa aroused his pity and indignation. John Woolman of New Jersey, although seven years younger than himself, had completed his first tour among the slaveholders of the South, and their life-long intimacy resulted in Benezet's carrying on the remarkable pioneer work of Woolman, after the death of the younger man. He began to publish articles in almanacs and the papers of the day, and issued pamphlets, usually gratuitously distributed, on the subject of slavery. His knowledge of French led to a voluminous correspondence abroad with such men as the Abbé Raynal in France, and Granville Sharp, Wilberforce, and Clarkson in England. He also corresponded with Benjamin Franklin while the latter was abroad. He wrote Frederick the Great on the unlawfulness of war, and sent letters acceptably to the queens of England, France, and Portugal.

In 1766, finding himself absorbed in too many activities to carry out his philosophy of the simple life of studious leisure, and in frail health, he retired to Burlington, N. J., the early home of his wife, and sought a quieter existence. But the urge toward alleviation of at least some of the sufferings of his fellow-beings was too great to be resisted, and at the end of less than two years he was again in Philadelphia, teaching, and writing voluminously. It was probably while in Burlington that he wrote what is perhaps his most important work—*A Caution and Warning to Great Britain and Her Colonies on the Calamitous State of the Enslaved Negroes* (1766). This was examined and approved by the Yearly Meeting of Philadelphia in 1766, and many copies were distributed in England. It was shortly followed by his *Historical Account of Guinea; Its Situation, Produce and the General Disposition of Its Inhabitants* (1771), a publication which gave to Thomas Clarkson his first facts on the slave trade, and was the source of the impulse to begin his long and active protest against it.

It was natural, when the French in 1756 were expelled from Acadia, that the 500 who made their way to Philadelphia should find in Anthony Benezet their chief friend. The whole Quaker body joined him for their relief, together with the French residents, and in Philadelphia many of the Acadians found a permanent home. Benezet established and taught for the last two or three years of his life, a school for the "Blacks," which, after the death of his wife, he left his slender fortune to endow. The Overseers of the Friends' Public Schools were made the trustees. This school has been fostered ever since by the Quakers, and, merged with other and similar charities, is now (1927) the "Benezet House" of 918 Locust St., Philadelphia. In 1774 Benezet published his essay on the immoderate use of liquor, *The Mighty Destroyer Displayed,* which suggested to his friend, Dr. Benjamin Rush, the latter's pamphlet in 1776, *Sermons to Gentlemen on Temperance and Exercise.* In 1780 appeared Benezet's *Short Account of the People Called Quakers; Their Rise, Religious Principles and Settlement in America.* Just before his death the Indians, for whom he had long labored, and their injustices under the new Government, were engaging Benezet's attention, and he wrote *Some Observations on the Situation, Disposition, and Character of the Indian Natives of This Continent* (published anonymously, 1784). This is thought to have been intended as a prelude to a more extended work on the subject.

[Roberts Vaux, *Memoirs of the Life of Anthony Benezet* (1817); Wilson Armistead, *Select Miscellanies* (1851), I, 119, 133, 148 ff.; Marquis de Chastellux, *Travels in North-America* (London, 1787), pp. 278 ff.]

A. M. G.

BENHAM, HENRY WASHINGTON (Apr. 8, 1813–June 1, 1884), engineer, soldier, was born in Quebec, Canada. His mother, Rebecca Hill, born in Quebec in 1783, was the daughter of Lieut. Joseph Hill of the British army. His father was Jared Benham, the son of Darius Benham of Meriden, Conn., and a descendant in the seventh generation of Joseph Benham, one of the first settlers of Wallingford, and probably the son of John Benham, who is believed to have come over in the *Mary and John* in 1630 (*New England Historical and Genealogical Register,* XXXIX, 92). Jared Benham died while his son Henry was young, and his widow then married Liberty Perkins of Meriden, Conn. Henry's attempts to acquire a schooling met with opposition from his stepfather. Hidden in a garret, and helped by his loyal and devoted mother, he surreptitiously acquired sufficient education to enter Yale in 1832. Disliking the menial duties by which he attempted to defray his expenses at college, he sought and obtained an appointment to West Point. Entering on July 1, 1833, he graduated first in his class, and on July 1, 1837, was commissioned brevet second lieutenant of engineers. Until 1847 he was engaged in engineering duties, principally in connection with coast defenses. Promoted first lieutenant of engineers on July 7, 1838, he entered the Mexican War with that rank. He took part in the battle of Buena Vista, Feb. 22–23, 1847, being employed in making reconnaissances, and in carrying information and orders. Slightly wounded, he was highly commended by Gen. Wool, and was brevetted captain for gallant and meritorious conduct. Promoted captain of engineers on May 24, 1848, he was in charge, from 1848 to 1853, of the repairs of the defenses of New York Harbor, of sea-wall construction in Boston Harbor, of building the Buffalo Lighthouse, and of the Washington Navy Yard. From Mar. 29, 1853, to Nov. 1, 1856, he was assistant in charge of the United States Coast Survey Office at Washington, his duties calling him to Europe. From 1856 to 1861 he was in charge of engineering work connected with the defenses of Boston Harbor, New Bedford Harbor, Newport Harbor, and Sandy Hook, and in charge of the building of the Potomac Aqueduct.

On May 14, 1861, he was appointed chief engineer of the Department of the Ohio. In McClellan's West Virginia campaign he commanded the advance guard of Gen. T. A. Morris's column which pursued the Confederates under Gen. R. S. Garnett from Laurel Hill, defeating them at Carrick's Ford on July 13, 1861. This campaign won for him a brevet as colonel, high praise from Morris and McClellan, a commission as brigadier-general of volunteers, and the command of a brigade in West Virginia (*Official Records*, ser. I, vol. II: reports of Gen. Morris, p. 68; Gen. McClellan, p. 207; Capt. Benham, pp. 222–23. *Battles and Leaders of the Civil War*, vol. I, pt. I: "McClellan in West Virginia," by Major-General J. D. Cox, p. 126). The aggressiveness and energy which gained this advancement brought reverses when injudiciously exercised. On Sept. 10, 1861, he incurred the displeasure of Gen. Rosecrans by too rapidly developing the engagement at Carnifex Ferry, W. Va. Rosecrans also held him responsible for the failure to capture Floyd's Confederate forces after their demonstration at Gauley Bridge on Nov. 1, 1861, and charged him with disregarding orders (*Ibid.*, ser. I, vol. V: reports of Gen. Rosecrans, pp. 129 and 253; Gen. Benham, pp. 133 and 278). Gen. Hunter claimed that Benham's unsuccessful attack on Secessionville, James Island, S. C., on June 16, 1862, was in violation of orders, and relieved Benham of his command. On Aug. 7, 1862, his appointment as brigadier-general of volunteers was revoked; and on Sept. 8 he was placed in charge of coast defense work at Portsmouth Harbor, N. H. (*Ibid.*, ser. I, vol. XIV: reports of Gen. Hunter, Gen. Benham, etc., pp. 41 ff. and see also Appendix).

An appeal to President Lincoln resulted in the cancellation, on Feb. 6, 1863, of the revocation of his appointment, and his detail, in the spring of 1863, to command the engineer brigade of the Army of the Potomac. Until June 8, 1865, excepting about ten months passed in command of the Ponton Depot at Washington, D. C., he rendered valuable service with that brigade, particularly in the construction of ponton bridges for the army, and in the construction and command of the defenses of City Point, Va. He had been commissioned major of engineers on Aug. 6, 1861, and lieutenant-colonel on Mar. 3, 1863. His gallant, meritorious, and faithful services during the Civil War were rewarded by the brevets of brigadier-general United States Army, major-general United States Volunteers, and major-general United States Army. On Jan. 15, 1866, he was mustered out of the volunteer service; and on Mar. 7, 1867, was commissioned a colonel, corps of engineers. From June 17, 1865, until his retirement from active service, June 30, 1882, he was in charge of the construction of the defenses of Boston Harbor and New York Harbor. He had married on Oct. 3, 1843, Elizabeth Ann McNeil of New Hampshire; and she, two daughters, and a son, survived him.

[G. W. Cullum, *Biog. Reg.* (3rd ed., 1891) contains a succinct account of Benham's military record. Interesting details can be found in "Recollections of Mexico and the Battle of Buena Vista" and "Recollections of West Virginia Campaign," written by himself, published in the monthly magazine, *Old and New*, June, July 1871, June 1873, respectively, and reprinted as pamphlets. Obituaries may be found in the *N. Y. Tribune*, *N. Y. Herald* and *N. Y. Times*.]

W.S.G.

BENJAMIN, ASHER (June 15, 1773–July 26, 1845), architect, author, was born in Greenfield, Mass., June 15, 1773, and twice married; first to Achsah Hitchcock, Nov. 30, 1797, and second to Nancy Bryant, on July 24, 1805. It is likely that Greenfield was his home during his early professional life, as much of his work was in places easily accessible from there, and as his first book, *The Country Builder's Assistant* (1797), was published near-by in Deerfield. A second edition, enlarged, was printed in Boston, but sold especially by Alexander Thomas, in Worcester, in 1798, which may indicate a residence there as well. It is certain that Benjamin lived for some time in Windsor, Vt., as records show that he owned a house there for two years, and designed at least two houses, the Hatch and Jones houses, as well as (probably) the Old South Congregational Meeting House, which resembles much of the work published in his various books. He also evidently worked in various places in the Connecticut Valley prior to 1803, when he appears in the Boston directory. During this period we find him striving for another outlet for his desire to popularize architecture in America, for several times in 1802 there appeared in the Windsor local paper an advertisement by Benjamin proposing the start of a school of architecture (A. J. Wardner, *Old South Meeting House, Windsor, Vt.*). In Boston he appears to have prospered, as he owned two houses at the time of his death and left one to each of his daughters, Sarah Smith Benjamin and Elizabeth Augusta Bliss (Alexander J. Wall, *Books on Architecture Printed in America 1775–1830,* 1925, p. 6). There is evidence that he fulfilled at least to some extent his ambition to teach architecture, for Robert Henry Eddy of Boston writing in 1872 for the Historical and Genealogical Society states that he "studied architecture with the late Asher Benjamin, architect" (*New England Historical and Genealogical Register,* XLII, 214). This was probably prior to 1833. Benjamin died in Springfield, Mass., on July 26, 1845 (*Boston Daily Evening Transcript,* July 30, 1845).

Besides the buildings mentioned above, Benjamin has been credited with the design of the Carew House, Springfield; the Hollister House, Greenfield; the Alexander House, Springfield; the Colton House, Agawam (1806); the West Church, Boston; the First Congregational Church, Bennington, Vt. (1806), similar to plate 33 of *The Country Builder's Assistant;* the First Parish Church, Bedford, Mass., exactly like plate 39 of *The American Builder's Companion;* and the old Congregational Church of Northampton, burned many years ago, but shown on a Bartlett drawing published in 1839, and illustrated by figure 212 in *The American Spirit in Architecture,* by Talbot Faulkner Hamlin, being volume XIII, 1926, of *The Pageant of America.*

It was, however, even more as author than as architect that Benjamin was important. Through his books "late colonial" details and designs were broadcast throughout New England, as English ideas had been broadcast by English books in colonial times, and there is scarcely a village which in moulding profiles, cornice details, church spire, or farm-house does not reflect his influence. How much of the designs he published were original with him is not known; certainly he copied widely and eagerly. Aymar Embury, who published in 1917 a reprint of some of his work, notes a cornice type (plate 12, *The Amer-*

ican Builder's Companion) common in Litchfield, Conn., long before the date of the book, and Fiske Kimball states that Benjamin "codified Bulfinch's innovations" (*Domestic Architecture of the American Colonies and of the Early Republic,* 1922). Yet original or not, Benjamin's plates formed a collection harmonious and almost always in perfect taste.

The series of his books serves, too, as an excellent criterion of popular taste, which they both recognized and stimulated; the earlier works, up to 1814, contain only the refined delicacies of the typical New England "late colonial"; but in *The Rudiments of Architecture* (1814) Greek orders appear, and in *The Practical House Carpenter* (1830) he remarks, "Since my last publication, the Roman School of Architecture has been entirely changed for the Grecian." His influence was thus great in popularizing the Greek Revival. His publications include *The Country Builder's Assistant,* with thirty plates (Deerfield, 1797); *The Country Builder's Assistant,* with thirty-seven plates (Boston, 1798); *The American Builder's Companion,* with forty-four plates, by Asher Benjamin and Daniel Reynard (1806), of which a second edition, revised and enlarged, with fifty-nine plates, was published in 1811 and a third in 1816, while fourth, fifth and sixth "revised and enlarged" editions, the fourth with sixty-one plates, the fifth with sixty-three, and the sixth with seventy, appeared in 1820, 1826, and 1827; *The Rudiments of Architecture* (1814, and a second edition 1820); *The Practical House Carpenter* (1830, frequently republished). A portrait of Asher Benjamin exists in the possession of a great-grand-daughter, Mrs. Chester W. Bliss of New London, Conn.; it shows a strikingly handsome man of about fifty, smooth shaven, with a long slender face.

[In addition to the references above, see Thos. E. O'Donnell, "Asher Benjamin," in *Architecture,* Dec. 1926, pp. 375 ff.; Howard Major, *The Domestic Arch. of the Early Am. Republic* (1926); John Bullock, *The Am. Cottage Builder* (1854); Jos. E. Chandler, *The Colonial House* (2nd ed., 1924); Chas. A. Place, *Chas. Bulfinch: Architect and Citizen* (1925); Harold D. Eberlein, *The Architecture of Colonial America* (1915); *House Beautiful,* Sept. 1912, p. 114.]   T.F.H.

BENJAMIN, GEORGE HILLARD (Dec. 25, 1852–Nov. 10, 1927), lawyer, engineer, and patent expert, was born in New York City, one of the sons of Park Benjamin [*q.v.*] and Mary Brower (Western) Benjamin. His descent was from John Benjamin, who migrated from England to Watertown, Mass., in 1632. His father was a well-known poet and editor who had been associated with Horace Greeley on the *New Yorker* (before the founding of the *Tribune*).

The boy was fitted for college at Phillips Andover Academy and entered Union College, Schenectady, N. Y., in 1868; but left before the graduation of his class to begin his professional studies at the Albany Medical College. He was keenly interested in branches of science and technology outside his profession; to familiarize himself with advanced work in those fields he studied at the University of Freiburg, Germany, later receiving his doctorate in philosophy from that institution. For four years (1876–80) he practised medicine at Albany, N. Y.; but in 1880, at the age of twenty-eight, he removed to New York City, joining the staff of *Appleton's Cyclopædia of Applied Mechanics,* of which his brother, Park Benjamin II [*q.v.*], was editor. In his editorial work the legal aspects of engineering commanded more and more of his attention. Thus he was led to study patent law and in 1884 he was admitted to practise. Still he always had far more than a merely legalistic interest in engineering and technical problems. His counsel was sought in the organization of large corporations, notably the Western Electric Company, the General Railway Signal Corporation, and United States Steel. As a technical engineer, Benjamin long represented the German firm of Siemens and Halske. He frequently appeared as an expert witness in important patent litigation and other suits in which the Government was interested. He was a contributor to the technical journals and at times to the daily newspapers. His mind was unusually versatile in technical directions and so keen that the mere suggestion of an idea could be converted by him into a patentable invention literally over night. He was the patentee of a great many devices as well as the joint assignee of many of his clients' inventions. The same year that he was admitted to practise patent law he devised and patented an underground electric conduit; the following year a glass-melting furnace; the next year he was assignee with a Swiss client of a dynamo-electric machine; and the following year secured three patents on pipe couplings and expansion joints. A tin-plate manufacturing process was patented by him in 1892, and in 1893 he patented and assigned to his client, the Siemens Halske Company, Berlin, Germany, an incandescent electric lamp and an electric street-railway trolley. Benjamin's inventive work extended over the chemical and metallurgical fields as well. He devised a process of manufacture of diethyl ether in 1900; secured four patents for a metallurgical furnace in 1905; one for a regenerative gas furnace in 1910; for a by-product coke oven in 1920; for a metal casting furnace as late as 1923; and during the last ten years of his life was much interested in and invented processes for curing, preserving, and drying tobacco, beet sugars, and fruits. The United States Government employed him as an expert on high explosives. During the World War he served as chairman of the executive committee of the Mayor's Committee on National Defense in New York City. He was interested in the perfection of sound-detecting devices on American war-ships to detect approaching submarines. For many years he gave attention to problems in the detection and prevention of crime. He was thoroughly conversant with the Bertillon system of measurements and its application. He was consulted by Scotland Yard in difficult cases of crime detection, particularly such as involved chemistry. His reputation in this field, as well as in technical engineering, was international. Benjamin married, first, Jane Seymour of Ogdensburg, N. Y., in 1875; second, Mrs. Grace (Smith) Tremaine of Buffalo, N. Y., in 1901.

[Benjamin wrote little outside of professional reports and briefs, cyclopedia articles, and short contributions to the technical journals. Obituaries were published in the New York newspapers of Nov. 11, 1927. See also *Who's Who in America, 1926–27.*]

W. B. S.
C. W. M.

BENJAMIN, JUDAH PHILIP (Aug. 6, 1811–May 6, 1884), lawyer and statesman, was born in the island of St. Thomas, British West Indies. His parents (Philip Benjamin, an English Jew, and Rebecca de Mendes, of a family of Portuguese Jews) removed to Charleston, S. C., when their son was a mere lad. He was sent later to the Fayetteville Academy, Fayetteville, N. C., and thence to Yale. He entered college in 1825, but left without taking a degree in 1827. The next year he found a position with a commercial house in New Orleans. He was poor but resolute, with a cheerful and attractive personality which enabled him to make friends rapidly. In French New Orleans he eked out his slender resources by giving lessons in English. There is a tradition that one cautious gentleman refused to employ him as tutor for his daughter for fear the girl would fall in love with him. This was what happened in the case of a pupil of his, Mademoiselle Natalie St. Martin, whom he married in 1833. Meanwhile he had prepared himself for the legal profession through hard work in the office of a notary by whom he had been employed as clerk. A considerable reputation as a lawyer was promptly attained, and in 1834 it was greatly enhanced when he issued in coöperation with Thomas Slidell a *Digest of the Reported Decisions of the Superior Court of the Late Territory* *of Orleans and of the Supreme Court of Louisiana* (2nd ed., 1840). His reputation became national through his participation in the celebrated case of the brig *Creole,* involving delicate questions of international law. His brief in this case, a review of the status of slavery under international law and the United States domestic law, was printed as a pamphlet and widely circulated. So rapid was his rise at the bar that he soon became wealthy, purchased a sugar plantation, and for a time was even more concerned in his activities as a planter than as a lawyer. His eager and acute mind was applied with energy to the problems of sugar chemistry; he had Rillieux, inventor of a new process, install it at his plantation, and in 1846 and 1848 he wrote for *De Bow's Review* a series of articles setting forth the new theories and methods in the industry. The failure of a friend whose note for $60,000 he had indorsed cost him his plantation and threw him back upon his law practise. Thereafter until the end of his life, his devotion to the law, in which he attained the highest eminence, was tempered only by his interest in politics.

Being naturally a conservative he had joined the Whig party; in 1842 he had been elected to the state legislature; in 1844–45 he was a delegate to the constitutional convention; in 1848 he was a presidential elector on the Whig ticket; in 1852 he was elected by the Whigs to the United States Senate; and in the summer of that year was the leading spirit in the convention which drew up the constitution of 1852. At this time Benjamin had great dreams about the future development of American commerce. He was one of the foremost organizers of the Jackson Railroad, now the Illinois Central, and projected the great Tehuantepec Company to build a railroad and ultimately a canal across the Isthmus of Tehuantepec. "What have we before us?" he wrote, "The Eastern World . . . Its commerce makes empires of the countries to which it flows, and when they are deprived of it they are as empty bags, useless, valueless. That commerce will belong to New Orleans" (*Picayune,* Jan. 7, 1852, in Butler, p. 126).

This vision of Southern greatness with Asia as its source, following close upon the Southern attempt in 1850 to get an outlet to the Pacific, gives the keynote of Benjamin as a politician during the fifties. He shared the general Southern belief that foreign expansion of some sort was the one way to repair the defeat of the South through the upsetting of the sectional balance in the Compromise of 1850. Gradually he reached the conclusion accepted by many Southern Whigs that the new conditions had put the South on the de-

fensive and that a confessed "Southern party" ought to be formed. This chain of reasoning formed the intermediary through which he passed from the Whig to the Democratic party. On May 2, 1856, he made a speech in the Senate on the Kansas Bill and confessed himself a Democrat. He became an ardent partisan of Buchanan, that year, and on the expiration of his term in the Senate was returned for a new term by his new friends.

During the stormy events of the late fifties Benjamin took a leading but hardly a commanding part as a Southern advocate. He was one of the earliest of the Southern senators to advise secession, following the election of Lincoln. On Dec. 8, 1860, he advocated separate secession by Louisiana; on Dec. 14, he signed the famous address of Southern members of Congress "To Our Constituents." This was followed by a very able defense of the right of secession and of the Southern policy (speech in the Senate, Dec. 31, 1860, *Congressional Globe,* 36 Cong., 2 Sess., pp. 212–17), which further enlarged his reputation as a defender of Southern rights. Shortly after the secession of Louisiana he made his brilliant last speech to the Senate (Feb. 4, 1861, *Ibid.,* pp. 721–22), and withdrew.

Three weeks later Jefferson Davis appointed him attorney-general of the Confederacy. Politically the appointment was eminently appropriate. No other Southern leader could rival Benjamin as a lawyer. It is probable, however, that personal reasons of a sort peculiarly effective with Davis contributed to direct his choice. The nature of the Confederate President was intensely susceptible to ideas of honor. At one time during the heat of debate he had used words about Benjamin to which the latter had replied by a note demanding a duel. Davis, his anger having passed, was deeply sensitive to the wrong he had committed, declined the duel as not justifiable, and made a public recantation. Both men, in this quarrel, bore themselves so scrupulously according to the code which both accepted, that the incident proved to be the beginning of intimacy. Davis trusted far his estimates of men. Through the troubles which they now had to meet in common Davis and Benjamin developed close personal affection which no opposition was able to break.

Until his entrance into the Confederate cabinet Benjamin had enjoyed popularity. The tenor of his story now with singular rapidity changes. His brief tenure of the attorney-generalship afforded him no opportunity to display his legal powers. But it appears to have cemented his friendship with Davis. In these days, J. A. Jones set down in his *Diary,* "Mr. Benjamin is a frequent visitor at the [War] department and is very sociable; some intimations have been thrown out that he aspires to become, some day, Secretary of War. Benjamin unquestionably will have great influence with the President, for he has studied his character most carefully. He will be familiar not only with his likes, but especially with his 'dislikes'" (*A Rebel War Clerk's Diary,* 1866, I, 71). Without taking too seriously Jones's innuendo it is plain that Benjamin was just the man to be a consolation to the nervous and excitable Davis. It is also plain that he understood how to get on subtly with individuals. At the same time he appears to have lacked that instinct for men in the mass—at least for Americans in the mass—without which it was predestined that he should fail as a leader of the Confederacy. It is possible that his preoccupation during formative years with the legal and social genius of a Latin community, Louisiana, may have made it hard for him to sense the typically Anglo-Saxon community which formed the greater part of the South.

It was part of Benjamin's ironic fate to enter upon great offices under conditions that made it impossible to succeed in them. When Davis translated him to the War Department, Sept. 17, 1861, the tragedy of his life began. The first main division of Confederate history was nearing its end. The central, but secret, event of that period had been the competition of Southern and Northern agents in Europe in attempting to corner the munitions market. Benjamin's predecessor, Leroy P. Walker [*q.v.*], had failed lamentably to equip the Southern armies through purchases abroad; the financial credit of the Confederacy was not equal to its needs; and the shipment of such arms as were purchased had been ruinously interrupted by the Federal blockade. So inadequate were the supplies of the Confederate army that Davis, at a conference of generals in July, had refused to authorize a movement northward to follow up the victory of the First Manassas.

The real condition of the War Department was not generally known when Benjamin became secretary. The government would not take the people into its confidence and rested its defense of inaction on the avowed theory that the war should be entirely defensive so as not to estrange through invasion those Northerners who, it was believed, were at heart for secession. The result of this lack of candor was a furious tension in which many people sought nervously for some point of attack upon the government. They found it in what seemed to be a blunder of the Secretary of War. There appears, now, to be little if any

ground for holding him directly responsible for the loss of Roanoke Island early in 1862, almost coincident with the loss of Forts Henry and Donelson. These disasters were the match in the magazine, and there was an explosion of popular rage. Roanoke Island in particular became the shibboleth. Its defenders, was the cry, had been unable to hold their ground through the incompetence of the Secretary of War who had failed to equip them adequately, and had disregarded urgent appeals for more ammunition. A motion was introduced in the House of Representatives asserting that Benjamin had "not the confidence of the people of the Confederate States, nor of the Army" and requesting his retirement from the War Office.

By this time the relations between Davis and Benjamin had become very close. The attack upon the Secretary moved the President to indignation. Furthermore, he construed the criticism of the War Office as a criticism of the Administration. To his haughty and sensitive spirit both personal and public obligation made it necessary for him to stand firm against the popular clamor. The course which he took was perhaps Benjamin's greatest misfortune. It made permanent his estrangement from the Southern people.

The Secretary of State, R. M. T. Hunter [*q.v.*], had recently resigned. While a committee of Congress was investigating the affair of Roanoke Island and it was practically certain that the result would be an indictment of Benjamin, Davis appointed him secretary of state. Congress, cheated of its prey, could do nothing but delight in the report of the committee, which held "the late Secretary of War" largely responsible for the defeat at Roanoke Island.

Why Benjamin, who generally was astute, should have allowed himself as secretary of state to be put in such a false position before the Southern people is a mystery. He never revealed his inner life. He may truly be called the sphinx of the Confederacy. The only plausible explanation is that his point of view was irreconcilable with those of the people surrounding him. Apparently he had an innate attitude toward government, and toward all phases of public policy, which in certain respects, the planter type with its romantic mixture of individualism, class consciousness, and idealistic patriotism, found bewildering. Despite a surface geniality his mind was coldly realistic. It could not understand sentimental glamour, and it was firmly bureaucratic. This led to small errors of judgment that had large result, as when he scoffed at the emotionality inspired by barefoot soldiers, saying that they had doubtless traded their shoes for whiskey. He did not perceive how certain it was that a storm was going to break upon him as a result of Davis's rashness and his own lack of insight.

It broke in the midsummer of 1862 when Edward A. Pollard [*q.v.*] published *The First Year of the War*. This was a stinging attack upon the administration, especially the War Office. Pollard furiously denounced the elevation of Benjamin to secretary of state as an "ungracious and reckless defiance of popular sentiment." Powerful newspaper connections were behind Pollard, and from this time forward Benjamin's situation leads Prof. Dodd to speak of him as "the hated Jew" whom Davis kept in office despite the thousand and one protests of the Southern people. This unpopularity made no impression upon Benjamin's exterior. He was always the same calm, amused, smiling person whose equanimity in the dark days of the latter part of the war gave offense to many ardent natures. He was the very opposite of the over-strained and over-sensitive Davis, and seems to have been the chief mainstay, among men, of his afflicted chief.

There can be little doubt that no other Southern leader saw the problems of the desperate Confederate government with the same objectivity, the same relentless detachment, that Benjamin did. Probably he was the first to face the fact that the war could not be won on the basis on which it had been commenced. The vision of pure state rights together with the patriarchal system of slaveholding would have to go. Doubtless, he did not care if it did. State rights had not for him the sanctity they had for the born Southerner. They were mechanism only. Slavery, too, was for him a mere social device that was being made over by the crisis through which the South was passing. It is scarcely fanciful to suspect that the crisis was bringing out in him the Latin element assimilated in his youth and stripping him of certain Anglo-Saxon views acquired in middle life. At any rate, it was still early in the war that the idea of using the negro as a weapon, and at the same time facing toward a new relation of the black and white races in the South, found a place in his thoughts. It was first expressed in connection with the imperative problem of the reinforcement of the armies. That Benjamin was adroitly feeling the pulse of the hour may be inferred from his letters, such as one written late in 1864 (*Official Records*, ser. IV, vol. III, p. 959) urging the enrolment of slaves as soldiers, advising a campaign of education in the newspapers, and adding to all this a startling

new suggestion. Very delicately he intimated that a dictatorship on the Roman model might be the Confederacy's only salvation. There can be no doubt that he had Davis in mind.

During the winter of 1864–65 Benjamin kept himself in the background. His plan for arming the slaves was on every tongue. It aroused widespread terror. The President, at first, held off from committing himself and then rather suddenly and quite unwisely became an advocate. Despite the natural prejudice of the slaveholding community against such a measure, the peril of the Southern armies compelled its serious consideration. Bills were introduced into Congress providing in one way or another for black soldiers. At last Benjamin decided that it was time for him to come to the front. On Feb. 9, 1865, he made a public address, destined to be his last. His purpose was to fill his audience with a sense of the desperate situation of Lee's army (Benjamin to Lee, *Official Records*, ser. I, vol. XLVI, pt. 2, p. 1229), and after this impressive picture to pass triumphantly to the conclusion that the only way to relieve the situation was to enrol as soldiers those slaves "who might volunteer to fight for their freedom."

But even then, ignoring the desperation of the hour, a movement was forming to resist at all cost the proposal to enrol black soldiers. Benjamin's phraseology in his last speech drew the lines sharp. He assumed that emancipation would follow military service. That was the crux. The bills in Congress while they permitted black enrolment held out no promise of emancipation. A variety of reasons lay back of this attitude, ranging all the way from questions purely constitutional to the blunt exclamation of Senator Hunter, "If we didn't go to war to save our slaves what did we go to war for?" The constitutional enemies of black enrolment and the uncompromising devotees of slavery now drew together in a party of opposition that fixed upon Benjamin as its chief enemy. At this critical moment he was unable to restrain his tongue. There was quick reaction in both houses of Congress. On Feb. 13, 1865, the Senate divided evenly on a resolution declaring that "J. P. Benjamin is not a wise and prudent Secretary of State, and has not the confidence of the country" (*Journals*, IV, 550, 552, 553); on the fifteenth a third of the House sustained a similar resolution of censure (*Journals*, VII, 582). Though Benjamin enlisted Lee in the cause of enrolment with emancipation, and though Davis and others accepted the idea as inescapable, the only bill which Congress passed was a virtual defeat for Benjamin. It provided for slave soldiers but did not provide for emancipation (*Journals,* VII, 611–12, 729).

Benjamin was now entirely possessed by his idea, and so was Davis. As a last stroke, in January 1865 they sent Duncan F. Kenner [*q.v.*] to London with a proposal to effect general emancipation as the price of British intervention and the raising of the blockade. Kenner was told that he came too late (see J. M. Callahan, *The Diplomatic History of the Southern Confederacy,* 1901).

It is evident that Benjamin had hopes of the Hampton Roads Conference, but what connection he had with it is uncertain. It is also uncertain just what share he had in rejecting the indirect overtures made to the Confederate government through semi-official agents earlier in the winter. Considering his activity for black enrolment and his international policy, it seems fair to conclude that like Davis he continued hopeful almost to the moment when Richmond fell. He probably agreed with Davis in refusing to make concessions.

The tremendous energy of the Northern armies in January and February 1865 shattered all his hopes. He left Richmond in the President's party and was present in the council of the fugitive cabinet, at Greensboro, Apr. 12, when he approved the granting of permission to J. E. Johnston [*q.v.*] to open negotiations with Sherman. Continuing with the President in his flight southward, Benjamin's last official act was his advice given in writing during the short stay of the party at Charlotte where the cabinet discussed the terms of Johnston's surrender. Very characteristic was his cool and resolute acceptance of the accomplished fact. A few days later he left the presidential party and struck off for the coast, thus escaping capture along with Davis when the latter was overtaken by Federal cavalry at Irwinsville.

Benjamin made good his escape, reaching the West Indies and passing thence to England, having decided to attempt a career at the English bar. With this object in view he entered as a student at Lincoln's Inn, Jan. 13, 1866. His circumstances were such as to cause him much uneasiness, for he had lost practically all his fortune. It was customary with all aspirants to the bar to read with some eminent counsel and he had been fortunate in being received into Charles Pollock's chambers, but this fact only increased his financial responsibilities. He was driven to newspaper work in order to eke out his depleted exchequer, and the editor of the London *Daily Telegraph* employed him as a leader writer, particularly on international subjects. Then followed a unique recognition of his standing in the legal world, *viz.,* the action of the Benchers of his Inn of Court in dispensing with the three-year rule and calling him to the bar June 6, 1866, after less than five months as a student. The selection of his circuit became a matter of vital importance. The choice was decided by his Southern affiliations. Liverpool was the market whither the major portion of the pre-war cotton crop of the Southern states had been exported and sold, and its merchants and lawyers were in close touch with the leaders of the shipping industry of New Orleans and New York and presumably aware of Benjamin's high standing in his profession. He accordingly joined the northern circuit which at the time included that town. As anticipated his first retainers were from Liverpool solicitors, but progress was slow, and in the year of his call to the bar he lost the remnant of his private fortune in the failure of his bankers. Meantime he had been engaged on the preparation of a *Treatise on the Law of Sale of Personal Property,* which was published in 1868. This work, ostensibly based upon Blackburn's treatise of an earlier date, was so much wider in scope, and displayed such profound familiarity with the authorities in both English and Civil law that it at once became standard, being accepted "whenever cited, without the usual objection that it was the work of a living author" (*Law Times,* Feb. 17, 1883). From the day of its appearance, retainers poured in upon him. In 1869 he became a "Palatine silk," being made a Queen's Counsel for the County Palatine of Lancaster, and, though for some unexplained reason his name was not included among those who were created Q. C. in January 1872, his argument in Rankin *vs.* Potter (*Law Reports,* E. & I. App. Cas., VI, 83)— his first reported case in the House of Lords— so impressed the Lord Chancellor, Lord Hatherley, that the latter directed a patent of precedence to be issued to Benjamin, who was thus placed in a position equivalent to that which he would have occupied if the dignity had been actually conferred. Practising in all the courts of common law and equity, in an incredibly short time he established himself as without a superior in appeal cases, and such was the volume of work which came to his chambers that he was at length compelled to confine himself to the court in banc, court of chancery, and appeal courts, declining *nisi prius* retainers. Even then he was unable to accept all the briefs which were proffered him and ultimately he went "special," declining to appear before any court other than the House of Lords or the Judicial Committee of the Privy Council, unless he received a special fee of 100 guineas. Between June 1872 and December 1882, he appeared as counsel in no less than 136 reported cases heard before the two last-named tribunals of last resort—every one of which involved questions of great legal significance or affecting momentous financial interests. He was seen at his best perhaps in Privy Council appeals, whose infinite variety enabled him to exhibit his wide familiarity with different systems of law. His briefs dealt with appeals from such diverse courts as the Supreme Courts of Canada and New Zealand, the High Court of Griqualand West, the Consular Courts of Constantinople and the Court of Appeals of Malta, and involved, *inter alia,* difficult points of French law in Quebec, native African law and custom, Scots law, and the constitutional law applicable to almost every British dependency (see *Law Reports, E. & I. App. Cas.,* vols. VI–VII; *Law Reports, H. L. Scotch Ap.,* vol. II; *Law Reports, App. Cas.,* vols. I–VIII). Among the more important cases involving legal principles in which he was counsel were: Ashbury Railway Carriage and Iron Company *vs.* Riche, deciding that a company created a corporation under the Companies Act of 1862 is not thereby created a corporation with inherent common law rights (*Law Reports, E. & I. App. Cas.,* VII, 653); Debenham *vs.* Mellon, defining the circumstances under which a wife has authority to pledge her husband's credit for necessaries (*Law Reports, App. Cas.,* VI, 24); Lord Advocate *vs.* Lord Lovat, dealing with a salmon fishery on a Scotch river as purtenant to barony land and title (*Law Reports, App. Cas.,* V, 273); Charles Russell *vs.* The Queen, the "local option" case, deciding that the Canada Temperance Act of 1878 was within the legislative competence of the Dominion Parliament (*Law Reports, App. Cas.,* VII, 829). Benjamin also held briefs for the Liquidators of the City of Glasgow Bank throughout the prolonged litigation arising from the collapse of that institution. Perhaps his greatest triumph was achieved in The Queen *vs.* Keyn —the Franconia Case—where, appearing for the defense, he obtained an acquittal on the ground that the British courts had no criminal jurisdiction over a foreigner for acts committed on foreign ships within British territorial waters—two members of the Court of Crown Cases Reserved expressly adopting Benjamin's major contention (*Law Reports, Exchequer Div.,* II, 63). This case and that of Thomas Castro *vs.* The Queen (*Law Reports, App. Cas.,* VI, 229), where he was leading counsel for the Tichborne claimant in the latter's fruitless appeal to the House of Lords against his conviction, were among the few criminal cases with which Benjamin was associated in his English career. His life during these years

was divided between Paris, where from even before the Civil War he had maintained a home for his wife and daughter, and London, which during term claimed him for five days in the week. In May 1880, stepping off a moving streetcar in Paris, he was thrown to the ground, his right arm torn from its socket, his shoulder-blade broken, and the left side of his forehead fractured. Contrary to the orders of his physician, upon partial recovery he resumed his practise, but early in 1883 the state of his health compelled him finally to retire. This was the occasion of an unprecedented "collective farewell" which the Bar of England took of him at a public banquet in his honor given in the Inner Temple Hall, June 30, 1883. He died ten months later in Paris.

As a lawyer his preëminence was displayed in many specialized fields. It has been claimed that he was not successful before a jury or in the handling of witnesses, yet the fact remains that a large proportion of his early cases were of this character. Undoubtedly his chief sources of strength, apart from his profound acquaintance with the principles of law, were his capacity for logical analysis and the extraordinary facility with which he expressed his arguments in impressive convincing sequence and form. No superfluous words obscured the clarity of his contentions, his language was choice, his manner was deferential yet confident, and confidence carried with it conviction. He was particularly effective before the Judicial Committee and the House of Lords, where the gravity of the issues and the exceptional intellectual strength of the tribunal appeared to call forth all that was in him of mental endowment and argumentative power.

[The only biography is *Judah P. Benjamin* (1907) by Pierce Butler, good but partisan. There is a useful article in the *Jewish Encyc.,* and one in the *Dict. of Nat. Biog.* Benjamin figures, of course, in all the political literature of the Confederacy, as in Davis, *Rise and Fall of the Confederate Government* (1881), but has had no such consideration as he deserves. The *Cong. Globe* and the *Jour. of the Cong. of the Confederate States* (1904–05) are important as sources; also Jas. D. Richardson, *Messages and Papers of the Confederacy* (1905); *Official Records of the Union and Confederate Armies;* Dunbar Rowland, *Jefferson Davis, Constitutionalist* (10 vols., 1923). See also *Times* (London), Mar. 9, 1884; Chas. Pollock, "Reminiscences of Judah Philip Benjamin," *Fortnightly Rev.,* Mar. 1898; "Judah P. Benjamin: a Bibliography" in *Menorah,* Nov. 1902; Gustavus H. Wald, "Judah P. Benjamin," in *Harvard Grads. Mag.,* June 1928.]

N. W. S.
H. W. H. K.

BENJAMIN, NATHAN (Dec. 14, 1811–Jan. 27, 1855), missionary, the son of Nathan Benjamin, a Revolutionary soldier of distinction, and of Ruth (Seymour) Benjamin, was born in Catskill, N. Y. The father dying when the son was two years of age, the family moved to Williamstown, Mass., which now became their home. Nathan attended the old Academy at Bennington, Vt., but his college preparation was chiefly under Prof. Ebenezer Kellogg of Williams College. He graduated at Williams in 1831, studied theology two years at Auburn, and graduated at Andover in 1834. During the latter year, after a severe struggle at the prospect of sundering home ties, he accepted an appointment as a foreign missionary. After spending one winter in New Haven and another in New York in the study of medicine, and a few months in Vermont as an agent of the American Board of Commissioners for Foreign Missions, he was ordained at Williamstown, Apr. 21, 1836, and sailed at once for Greece. After eighteen months at Argos, he removed to Athens, where he remained till 1845. He was then transferred to the Armenian mission at Trebizond, but eighteen months later returned to America on account of his wife's health. On the improvement of the latter he returned to the Armenian mission and was at Smyrna from 1847 to 1852, when he removed to Constantinople, where he died of typhus fever three years later. He was wonderfully successful as a preaching and teaching missionary. He preached in both Greek and English and exerted a marked influence on educated Greeks through his Bible classes and through personal contact. But his chief work was that of an editor and translator engaged in supplying the country through the mission press with the Bible and evangelical literature in the vernacular. On his return from America he took up the same work for Armenia, acquiring a new language after he was thirty-five. He possessed remarkable executive ability and had large financial and administrative responsibilities in connection with the missions. During his last two years in Athens he was acting American consul, and he founded the *Morning Star,* the first Armenian newspaper. On Apr. 25, 1836, he was married to Mary G. Wheeler of New York City.

[The *Missionary Herald,* May 1855, contains a full account of Benjamin, by Rev. H. G. O. Dwight, a fellow missionary. Another excellent article is found in Hewlitt's *Williams Coll. and Foreign Missions* (1914). The facts of his life in briefer form are given in Calvin Durfee's *Biog. Annals of Williams Coll.* (1871).]

F. T. P.

BENJAMIN, PARK (Aug. 14, 1809–Sept. 12, 1864), editor, poet, was the son of Parke Benjamin, a sea-captain and trader of old New England stock who had extensive interests in Norwich, Conn., and Demerara, British Guiana. His mother, Mary Judith Gall, was a native of Barbados. He was born in Demerara, and remained there until the age of four, when he was sent to Norwich to receive treatment for an affliction which, nevertheless, left him permanently lame, with shrunken limbs. The rest of his life was spent in the United States. His early schooling was received at Colchester, Conn., and Jamaica Plain, Mass. In 1825 he entered Harvard, but two years later, in accordance with his father's wish, he transferred to Washington, now Trinity, College, at Hartford. After his graduation in 1829 he founded the *Norwich Spectator,* which survived but ten issues—the first of a long list of editorial and publishing ventures. In 1830 he entered the Harvard Law School but with characteristic restlessness removed to the Yale Law School in 1832. For a time he lived in Boston, nominally practising law, on friendly terms with the literary set. He had already written much verse. *The Harbinger,* published in 1833 in aid of a charitable fair, was made up of poems which Benjamin, his former Harvard classmate O. W. Holmes, and John O. Sargent had previously contributed to magazines. In 1834 he was employed by Joseph T. Buckingham on the *New England Magazine,* and in 1835 he became editor and owner. At the close of the year the magazine was discontinued and merged with the *American Monthly Magazine* in New York, and Benjamin became associated with Charles Fenno Hoffman in the editorship. After various vicissitudes this periodical came to an end in 1838. For a short period Benjamin was literary editor of Horace Greeley's *New Yorker.* By this time he had come to be known as a caustic literary critic. After a brief connection with the *Evening Tattler,* a one-cent daily, and the *Brother Jonathan,* a literary weekly, he withdrew to found in 1839 journals of his own on the same plan—the *Evening Signal* and the *New World.* R. W. Griswold was at first associated with the *New World,* but Benjamin frequently had difficulties with his colleagues, and Griswold remained for only five issues. The *New World,* the most important and the longest-lived of Park Benjamin's publishing experiments, was one of the fairly profitable but much censured journals which throve by reprinting British writings without remuneration to the authors. Besides the material in the regular numbers Benjamin issued "extras" containing novels and other longer works. Under the lax postal laws these could be mailed at the periodical rate; a revision of the law that conferred this privilege hastened the downfall of the *New World.* Besides British books the extras included a few American writings of no value, the one famous one being Walt Whitman's temperance novel, *Franklin Evans.* In both the editorial conduct and the selling methods of the *New World* and the *Evening Signal*

Benjamin adopted the sensational devices of personal journalism. He was especially noted for his vituperative abuse of rival editors and conspicuous authors, the *Signal* winning a place in the list of papers that were successfully sued for libel by James Fenimore Cooper. After the suspension of the *New World* in 1845 Benjamin planned a number of undertakings, literary and other, some of which were never begun and none of which were of long continuance. One of his many publishing ventures was a literary weekly in Baltimore. An example of his methods of attracting attention is afforded by a special Fourth-of-July issue of the *Constellation,* "The most gigantic paper the world has seen," printed on a single sheet 72 by 100 inches. For some time he conducted a literary agency; and he went on the lyceum platform, sometimes lecturing, more frequently reading didactic and mostly satiric treatises in heroic couplet composed for the purpose. In 1848 he married Mary Brower Western of Dosoris Island, L. I., and spent the remainder of his life rather quietly in New York.

Benjamin wrote much verse, and held a prominent place in earlier American anthologies. His poems are as yet uncollected, and few survive now even as fugitive pieces. His literary criticisms and comments on public affairs are often biting; in estimating them allowance must be made for the slashing editorial manners of the time. An apparent acerbity of temper, which showed itself not only in his writings but in his frequent quarrels with associates, has been ascribed by some to sensitiveness over his physical deformity. It should be remembered, also, that he had warm personal friends. His importance in American literary history comes more from his relationship with others than from the permanent value of anything he wrote.

[A biography prepared by Merle M. Hoover of Columbia University after access to the Benjamin family papers is in manuscript and, through the courtesy of Mr. Hoover, has been available for the preparation of this article.]

W. B. C.

BENJAMIN, PARK (May 11, 1849–Aug. 21, 1922), author, patent lawyer, was born in New York City, the son of Park Benjamin [*q.v.*] and Mary (Western) Benjamin, and brother of George Hillard Benjamin [*q.v.*]. He was graduated from the United States Naval Academy in 1867, and in the same year brought out his first book, *Shakings: Etchings from the Naval Academy.* After several cruises with Admiral Farragut he resigned from the Navy to take up the study of law. He was admitted to the bar in 1870 after a year's study at the Albany Law School. It was as a patent solicitor that he spent most of the time which he devoted to his practise. Due to an unusual knowledge of both technical and legal matters, and to a large store of information on scientific subjects, he was most valuable as an expert witness or technical adviser on matters relating to patents. For many years he served a large and wealthy clientele in this capacity and his testimony as an expert witness is written into many cases involving patent rights and patent infringements. His legal work was done in New York City, but he possessed a summer home in Stamford, Conn. He was thrice married—to Helen Campbell, to Isabel Torrans, and to Ida Crane, his daughter by whom, Dorothy, became the wife of Enrico Caruso. He was associate editor of the *Scientific American, 1872–78,* and took charge of the production of *Appleton's Cyclopædia of Applied Mechanics, 1881–92,* as its editor-in-chief. Many articles from his pen on technical or scientific subjects appeared in the *Scientific American* and other technical publications. During his connection with the *Scientific American* he published his *Wrinkles and Recipes* (1873), compiled from the magazine. This was probably the best seller of all his books. Other works written by him include *The Age of Electricity* (1886); a history of electricity called *The Intellectual Rise in Electricity* (1895); *The United States Naval Academy* (1900); and *The Voltaic Cell* (1893). Until the very time of his death, he was also a frequent contributor to nontechnical periodicals, particularly the *Independent.* Scores of articles from his pen, for the most part on subjects pertaining to our own or foreign navies and naval affairs, appeared in this magazine. He believed that the American navy was inadequate and in 1881 launched out into the realm of highly imaginative fiction to help get this idea into public consciousness. His short story, "The End of New York," picturing vividly the destruction of that city as a result of inadequate naval defenses, made a great impression at the time of its publication and is included in Volume V of *Stories by American Authors* published by Scribners in 1884. During the World War the *Independent* still held its columns open to Benjamin's discussions of naval policies. In conjunction with R. M. Thompson and E. J. Berwind, he collected a valuable library of books, particularly on scientific subjects, which he presented to the library of the United States Naval Academy at Annapolis.

[Material for this biographical sketch has been gathered from various sources in the N. Y. Pub. Lib., such as newspaper and magazine files, and verified by Mr. Walter Benjamin, a brother of Park Benjamin, and by contemporaries of Benjamin in the field of patent law, particularly Mr. A. Parker-Smith.]

E. Y.

BENJAMIN, SAMUEL GREENE WHEELER

BENJAMIN, SAMUEL GREENE WHEELER (Feb. 13, 1837–July 19, 1914), author, painter, diplomat, called himself a free-lance. Routine and a fixed abode did in fact make him ill. Accustomed to hardship on land and water, able to face undaunted a winter storm on a mere chip of a boat and to pass untouched through epidemics of typhus and cholera, he broke down completely when immured for a few years (1861–64) as an assistant in the New York State Library at Albany. He had no capacity for self-discipline. Quick, energetic, versatile, romantic, not without conceit, he tried his hand at many things, saw much of men and manners, climates, governments, enjoyed them all hugely, and left behind him a small residue of lasting achievement.

Born at Argos, Greece, the son of an exceptionally able and cultured missionary, Nathan Benjamin [*q.v.*], and of Mary Gladding Wheeler, he passed his first eighteen years in Greece and the Levant, chiefly in Athens, Smyrna, Trebizond, and Constantinople. He reveled in the picturesque, occasionally dangerous, life around him, picked up several languages, attended school in Smyrna and learned Latin from his father, got his lifelong passion for the sea and for sailing ships during a voyage to the United States in the winter of 1847–48, acquired the elements of drawing from various teachers—German, Dutch, Armenian, and Italian, and made sufficient progress in it to send acceptable pictures to the *Illustrated London News* during the Crimean War in 1854. When the elder Benjamin died of typhus, Jan. 27, 1855, the family returned to the United States. Benjamin graduated from Williams College in 1859, taught school for a while, married Clara Stowell of Brookfield, Mass., Oct. 20, 1863, was an assistant librarian in Albany for several years, made a trip to Europe to regain his health, and until 1882 lived in succession in Brookfield, Salem, Boston, and New York. About 1870 he established himself in Boston as a marine painter. In this work he aimed, he says, at boldness and force rather than refinement; his pictures sold at prices ranging from $60 to $600. While an undergraduate at Williams he had begun writing for the magazines; although such tasks irked him he turned out numerous articles, chiefly on art and travel. As an author he was conscientious in gathering his materials but sometimes careless in composition. One book *The Multitudinous Seas* (1879) he wrote in four days; sometimes he would dictate an article while painting. His first book had appeared in 1860: *Constantinople, The Isle of Pearls, and Other Poems*. Other characteristic volumes are: *Ode on the Death of Abraham Lincoln* (1865); *The Turk and the Greek* (1867); *The Choice of Paris: a Romance of the Troad* (1870), which he considered his best book; *Contemporary Art in Europe* (1877); *Art in America* (1879); *The World's Paradises* (1879); *Troy: Its Legend, History, and Literature* (1880); and *The Cruise of the Alice May* (1884). Much of his time was spent at sea; of his forty-five voyages across the Atlantic the majority were made in sailing ships. Even in the roughest weather he was never seasick; he set great store by his use of whiskey and tobacco, and drank water rarely, sometimes not for months. Generally sociable, he was particularly fond of mariners and Turks, and distrusted missionaries. His first wife having died, he married Fannie Nichols Weed in November 1882. He was the first American minister to Persia, 1883–85. He made a wily, pertinacious diplomat, quite capable of taking care of himself and of the missionaries whose tactics furnished the principal subject of his negotiations. The Persians liked him. He drafted the diplomatic code used by the American legation in Persia. On his return to the United States at the close of President Arthur's administration he published *Persia and the Persians* (1886) and *The Story of Persia* (1887), both of which are still useful to English readers. The rest of his life was comparatively uneventful. He made his home first on Staten Island, later in Washington, D. C., and finally in Burlington, Vt.

[The chief source is Benjamin's autobiography *The Life and Adventures of a Free Lance* (1914), posthumously published, badly edited; see also *Who's Who in America*, 1914–15.]

G.H.G.

BENNER, PHILIP

BENNER, PHILIP (May 19, 1762–July 27, 1832), merchant and ironmaster, was born in Chester County, Pa., the son of Henry and Dinah (Thomas) Benner. His father, an ardent Whig, was imprisoned by the British during the Revolution, and Philip, a youth in his early teens, enlisted as a private under his neighbor and relative, Gen. Anthony Wayne, and served through the war. At the conclusion of the conflict he engaged in the iron business at Coventry in the northern part of Chester County and at the same time conducted a store in Vincent township. Believing that there was a brighter future toward the west he purchased in 1792 the Rock Forge lands on Spring Creek, Centre County, and in the following year commenced his improvements by erecting a house and saw-mill. In 1794 he set up what was probably the first forge in Centre County, in 1799 he erected a slitting-mill, and in 1800 a second forge and a nail-mill. These early enterprises were carried on under great difficulty, for it was necessary to transport from Chester

County not only his workmen but also the provisions to maintain them. From the time of his arrival at Spring Creek, however, until his death forty years later, Benner was the leading iron manufacturer of that region, greatly extending his operations and building up a large fortune. His first iron had been shipped to the East, but impressed with the rising importance of the West, he struck out in a new channel by opening up an iron trade with Pittsburgh. As a result of this he engaged without competition for many years in the transportation of "Juniata iron" to Pittsburgh and the Western country.

Benner was a man of many interests. Not only did he manufacture and transport iron by his own teams, but he maintained stores in Ferguson township and at Bellefonte. Like most wealthy men of the time he speculated heavily in real estate and accumulated a large amount. In 1824 he commenced operating the Logan's Branch Woolen Factory. As the leading shipper of Centre County he was naturally interested in transportation facilities, and among the foremost in the movement for their development. He was the first president (1821) of the Centre and Kishacoquillas Turnpike Company and with two others represented Centre County as commissioner of the Bellefonte, Aaronsburg and Youngstown Turnpike Company, created by a law of Apr. 11, 1825. One of the founders of Bellefonte, he contributed largely to the construction of the waterworks in 1808 and erected a number of the best houses in the village, his own residence being among those still standing (1927). Interested in politics, he established in 1827 the *Centre Democrat* to promote the Jacksonian democracy but he did not personally edit this newspaper, and sold it in 1831 to John Bigler, later governor of California. A man of great industry, alert mind, and indomitable will, Benner represented the type of frontiersman who, already in possession of some capital, moved westward to enlarge his fortune and contribute prominently to the upbuilding of a community. He married Ruth Roberts (1765–1825) by whom he had a large family, eight of the children surviving him. His religious affiliations were with the Quakers.

[John Blair Linn, *Hist. of Centre and Clinton Counties, Pa.* (1883) contains the fullest account. See also Sherman Day, *Hist. Colls. of the State of Pa.* (1843). There is an incomplete file of the *Centre Democrat* in the office of that paper at Bellefonte.]   H.U.F.

BENNET, SANFORD FILLMORE (June 21, 1836–June 11, 1898), physician and song writer, was born in Eden, N. Y., the son of Robert and Sally (Kent) Bennet. The family moved to Lake County, Ill., when the boy was six years

old, living first in Plainfield, and three years later moving to a farm near Lake Zurich. His family was distinguished by more than ordinary ability. Two brothers became physicians and the father served as assessor, town trustee, school director, and for eight years as a justice of the peace. Young Bennet, who had been attending district school, was sent to the Academy at Waukegan, Ill., at sixteen, and in two years was teaching school at Wauconda. He entered the University of Michigan in 1858 but left before graduation to take charge of the public schools at Richmond, Ill. Two years later he was married to Gertrude Crosby Johonnatt and they moved to Elkhorn, Wis., where he became joint owner and editor with Frank Leland of the *Elkhorn Independent*. But toward the end of the Civil War he sold his interest to serve a three months' term as second lieutenant in the 40th Regiment of Infantry, Wisconsin Volunteers (May 25–Sept. 16, 1864). Returning to Elkhorn he opened a drug-store and took up the study of medicine. It was during this period that the verses which he had been writing in a desultory fashion most of his life began to acquire a vogue. Most of them were set to music, and "The Sweet By and By," his most popular hymn, for which J. P. Webster wrote the music, has been translated into many languages, including Chinese. In 1871, with Webster, who was a gifted musician, he published *The Signet Ring*, an anthology of hymns, of which the 100 or more from his own pen formed a substantial portion. At thirty-eight he received a degree from Rush Medical College in Chicago and moved to Richmond, Ill., where he established a flourishing practise. He was a frequent contributor to the *Richmond Gazette*, and for a time was one of its editors and publishers. In the year of his death he published *The Pioneer, an Idyll of the Middle West*, which tells of frontier experiences during the thirties and forties, especially in Lake and McHenry counties, Ill.

[H. A. Kelly and W. L. Burrage, *Am. Medic. Biogs.* 1920; *Wis. Hist. Soc., Newspaper Cat.*, 1911; *Wis. State Jour.* (Madison), June 14, 1898.]   M.A.K.

BENNETT, CALEB PREW (Nov. 11, 1758–May 9, 1836), Revolutionary soldier, governor of Delaware, was born in Kennett township, Chester County, Pa. His father was Joseph Bennett, a respectable Chester County farmer who came from English stock, and his mother was Elizabeth Prew Wiley, a widow, who was the daughter of Caleb Prew, for whom the son was named. When young Caleb was three years of age, the father moved to Wilmington and engaged in sailing vessels to and from the Bahamas. The education of the son was limited, as at fifteen years of age, at the breaking out of the Revolutionary War, he enlisted as a private. Near the close of his life he wrote an interesting account of the Delaware Regiment, in which he served. Presumably owing to his youth, he reached the rank of first lieutenant only. He was at Brandywine and at Germantown and rendered heroic service in the disastrous Southern campaign in the 1780's under Generals Greene and Gates when the Delaware Regiment was so badly cut to pieces and lost so many of its officers that Bennett was next in rank to the commanding officer, at the close of the battle of the Cowpens. The story of the war, "all of which he saw and part of which he was" is modestly told, but is convincing of the fact that, youth as he was, he served with bravery and efficiency. At the surrender at Yorktown, he was in command of one of the batteries, and in close touch with Washington.

At the close of the struggle the Delaware Regiment was disbanded and Bennett was honorably discharged and resumed his residence in the city of Wilmington, Del. He was then but twenty-three years of age. For some years he conducted the public ferry that crossed the Christiana River, in that city, on the Kings Road, leading from Philadelphia to New Castle, and engaged with his father in the shipping trade. On Apr. 5, 1792, he was married at Tinicum Island, near Philadelphia, to Catherine Britton, daughter of Richard Britton of Delaware County, Pa. Taking his bride to Wilmington he continued to reside there, for ten years or more, and then moved to New Castle, Del., and for a time was an inn-keeper at that place. He was an active member of the Delaware Society of the Cincinnati. In 1813 he was appointed major of artillery in the Delaware militia and during the War of 1812 was in command of the port of New Castle. In 1807 he was elected, by the Levy Court, treasurer of New Castle County, Del., and by successive elections, from year to year, continued in that office for a period of twenty-six years. In the state campaign of 1832, he was the nominee of the Jackson Democrats for the office of governor. His opponent was Arnold Naudain. Bennett received a total vote of 4,220, Naudain a total of 4,166—giving a majority of 54 votes to Bennett. The latter was the first Democrat elected governor of the state. His administration started under happy auspices. His inaugural address showed his loyalty to Andrew Jackson, emphatically announcing unflinching adherence to the Union and the Constitution and strongly condemning the nullification doctrine at that time rife in South Carolina. Unfortunately his administration was of short duration.

He was inaugurated governor on Jan. 15, 1833, and died at his home in Wilmington on May 9, 1836. He was interred in the graveyard adjoining the Friends Meeting House at the corner of Fourth and West Sts., in Wilmington.

[Records of births, marriages, and deaths, from the family Bible of Caleb P. Bennett, in possession of the Pub. Archives Commission of Del. For Bennett's "Brief Account of the Del. Regiment in the Revolution," see *Pa. Mag. of Hist. and Biog.*, vol. IX, no. IV (1885).]

H.C.C.

BENNETT, CHARLES EDWIN (Apr. 6, 1858–May 2, 1921), classical scholar, was born at Providence, R. I., the son of James and Lucia (Dyer) Bennett. He was graduated from Brown University in 1878, after which he taught for a year in a school at Milton, Fla., and for two years at Sing Sing, N. Y. He then studied for a year (1881–82) at Harvard University and for two years in Germany (Leipzig, 1882–83; Berlin, 1883–84; Heidelberg, 1884). He was principal of the preparatory department of the University of Nebraska for five years, after which he was professor of Latin in the University of Wisconsin (1889–91) and professor of classical philology at Brown University (1891–92) before his election, in 1892, to the professorship of Latin in Cornell University, which he held to the end of his life. He married, June 29, 1886, Margaret Gale Hitchcock, of Lincoln, Nebr. He was president of the American Philological Association, 1907–8, and was a member of the American Philosophical Society. From 1892 until his death he was editor of the *Cornell Studies in Classical Philology* and from 1895 to 1905 of the *College Latin Series* published by Allyn and Bacon. In addition to a very considerable number of articles in periodicals his published writings comprise: *A Latin Grammar* (1895, with many later editions), *Appendix to Bennett's Latin Grammar* (1895), *A Latin Composition* (1896), *The Foundations of Latin* (1898), *The Quantitative Reading of Latin Poetry* (1899), *The Teaching of Latin and Greek in Secondary Schools* (1900, with George P. Bristol), *Latin Lessons* (1901), *Preparatory Latin Writer* (1905), *The Latin Language* (1907), *First Year Latin* (1909), *Syntax of Early Latin* (vol. I, 1910, vol. II, 1914), and *New Latin Composition* (1912), besides annotated editions of *Cæsar's Gallic War,* books I–IV (1903), *Cicero, Selected Orations* (1904), *Virgil, Æneid,* books I–IV (1905), and also translations of *The Characters of Theophrastus* (1902, with William A. Hammond), *Horace, Odes and Epodes* (1914, Loeb Classical Library), and *Frontinus, The Stratagems and the Aqueducts of Rome* (1925, Loeb Classical Library). Most of these books are text-books for the use of pupils in secondary schools, but Bennett's scholarship was such that even in text-books he embodied the results of original thought and research, making those books of value to professional scholars, as well as to teachers and pupils. His contributions to knowledge in the fields of Latin syntax (chiefly in his *Syntax of Early Latin*) and metric (chiefly in articles) gained him an international reputation among scholars, his text-books made him favorably known to great numbers of his countrymen, and men of letters honor him for his translations. He was one of the outstanding classical scholars of his time.

There was nothing spectacular in Bennett's quiet and studious career. He was primarily interested in enlarging human knowledge concerning the Latin language and literature, but he was also of marked ability as a teacher, especially of mature and competent students. His standards were high and exacting. He had a quick and versatile mind and was an entertaining talker, greatly interested in the arts, especially in ecclesiastical architecture, as well as in music, literature, and the culture of flowers. He was also an enthusiastic fisherman. He had in him a strong mystic vein, a reverent and religious spirit. During the great war he was active in relief work and was chairman of the Belgian Relief Committee of Tompkins County. His death was caused by heart failure and came suddenly, almost without warning.

[*Who's Who in America*, 1920–21; obituaries in the *Ithaca Jour.-News*, May 2, 1921, the *Cornell Daily Sun* and the *N. Y. Times*, May 3, 1921, the *Am. Jour. of Philol.*, XLIII, 189, *Classical Philol.*, XVII, 279, *Classical Jour.*, XVIII, 23, and the *Circuit*, the advertising medium of Allyn & Bacon, Aug., Sept. 1926.]

H. N. F.

BENNETT, DE ROBIGNE MORTIMER (Dec. 23, 1818–Dec. 6, 1882), freethinker, was born on a farm on the east shore of Otsego Lake in New York. As a boy of fourteen, while returning from a visit to an uncle in the Berkshires, he fell in with two members of the Shaker society at New Lebanon, N. Y., and after enjoying their kindness and good victuals for almost two weeks confessed such sins as he had on hand, was received into the sect, and wrote to his Methodist mother and sister to come and join him. At New Lebanon he worked in the seed gardens, learned the primitive pharmacy of roots, barks, and herbs, and rose to be the physician of the community; but on Sept. 12, 1846, together with his sister and several others, he left the Shakers and on Oct. 12 of that year married Mary Wicks, who had also been one of the seceders. For the next twenty-seven years he lived in vari-

ous places, usually as nurseryman, druggist, or both, prospering at times but in the end coming invariably to grief. In Cincinnati, for several years, he made as much as $10,000 annually as purveyor of "Dr. Bennett's Quick Cure, Golden Liniment, Worm Lozenges, and Root and Plant Pills." Meanwhile he had absorbed Paine's *Age of Reason,* had been converted to freethinking, and was nursing an ambition to write. Finally, at Paris, Ill., on Sept. 1, 1873, he launched his periodical, the *Truthseeker,* sending 12,000 copies broadcast over the country. In December he moved to New York, taking his new enterprise with him. The *Truthseeker,* devoted to a kind of inverted Fundamentalism, was written in a plebeian style, copious and clear, never elegant, and not always correct. At first it led a hand-to-mouth existence, but ultimately as the organ of village infidels scattered far and wide it enjoyed a mild efflorescence. Bennett thriftily republished much of the contents of the paper in the form of tracts and books and also dealt in freethinking and liberal publications of all kinds. At best his propaganda would have been galling to the orthodox, but the jocose indecorum and irony that he permitted himself in discussing the delinquencies of clergymen and the less edifying portions of the Biblical narrative proved unbearable, and Anthony Comstock undertook to dispose of him. The first two attempts failed, the cases not even coming to trial, but on June 5, 1879, before a judge friendly to Comstock, Bennett was convicted of sending indecent matter through the mails and was sentenced to serve thirteen months in the penitentiary and to pay a fine of $300. (The "indecent matter" was E. H. Heywood's pamphlet, *Cupid's Yokes.*) All efforts to get him off, including a petition to President Hayes, were unavailing, and Bennett, now over sixty years old, was sent to prison. On his release, Apr. 29, 1880, his friends gave him a reception in New York and sent him to Brussels as a delegate to a congress of freethinkers, but his health had been undermined. On July 30, 1881, he started from New York on a trip around the world and reached home on that day a year later. On Dec. 6, after a short illness, he died. He was an amalgam of quack, crank, and idealist. The quack and crank are somewhat excused by the hard conditions of his early life; the idealist, in spite of faults of taste and mistakes of judgment, was for almost a decade an effective popular spokesman for liberal ideas in religion and ethics.

[All accounts of Bennett derive from the autobiographical sketch in *The World's Sages, Infidels and Thinkers* (1876), which should be supplemented by the material in *A Truth Seeker Around the World* (4 vols., 1882) and by the files of the *Truthseeker.* See also S. P.

Putnam, *400 Years of Freethought* (1894) and Heywood Broun and Margaret Leech, *Anthony Comstock, Roundsman of the Lord* (1927).]

G. H. G.

BENNETT, EDMUND HATCH (Apr. 6, 1824–Jan. 2, 1898), jurist, legal writer, the son of Adaline (Hatch) Bennett and of Miles Lyman Bennett of Sharon, Conn., a judge of the supreme court of Vermont for a number of years, was born at Manchester, Bennington County, Vt. He received his early education at Manchester and Burlington Academies, proceeding thence to the University of Vermont where he graduated in 1843. After teaching for a time at a private school in Virginia, he returned to Vermont and commenced the study of law in his father's office at Burlington. He was admitted to the Vermont bar in 1847, but shortly afterward moved to Massachusetts and was admitted to the Suffolk County bar, July 3, 1848. He commenced practise at Taunton, and took an active part in the public life of the community. Politically he was an adherent of the Whig party. In May 1858 he was appointed judge of probate and insolvency for Bristol County and he continued to hold this office for twenty-five years. In 1864 when Taunton was incorporated as a city he was unanimously elected its first mayor, taking office Jan. 2, 1865, and being reëlected in 1866 and 1867. In 1870, 1871, and 1872 he lectured at the Dane School of Law at Harvard. In the latter year he was offered the position of dean of the Law School which had been established in connection with Boston University, but was unable to accept, joining the faculty, however, as a lecturer. In 1876 the offer was renewed and this time was accepted. Bennett now opened a branch law office in Boston. Developing great powers of organization, he administered the Boston Law School in a remarkably successful manner. As a lecturer he developed unsuspected strength. Some of his colleagues surpassed him in erudition and knowledge of the science of law, but his great command of language and ability to impart his knowledge to others combined with an innate courtesy to make him an effective teacher and source of inspiration to students. In 1883 he resigned from the judiciary. In 1891 he was appointed chairman of the Board of Commissioners for the Promotion of Uniformity of Legislation in the United States, and in 1896 he became chairman of the state commission on revision of the public statutes.

Throughout his life he was an incessant writer and the list of his published works amounts to over one hundred volumes. He prepared a *Selection of Leading Cases in Criminal Law* (vol. I, 1856) in conjunction with F. F. Heard; *Mas-* *sachusetts Digest, 1804–57* (1862), with F. F. Heard; *Massachusetts Digest, 1857–69* (1872), with H. W. Holland; *Fire Insurance Cases, being a Collection of All Reported Cases in England, Ireland, Scotland and America to Date* (1872–77); *Farm Law* (1880), a lecture on the legal rights of farmers; and *Massachusetts Digest, 1869–79* (1881), with R. Grey and H. W. Swift. He also edited many of Joseph Story's works. He was associated with the *American Law Register* of Philadelphia, and contributed a large number of articles to law periodicals. He had great literary ability, but little that he wrote was destined to be of any permanent value. He never concentrated his efforts, his labors were dissipated over an extent of subject-matter prohibitive of other than superficial results, and he will be remembered as a teacher, when his books are forgotten. He was married to Sally, daughter of Samuel L. Crocker of Taunton. His second son, Samuel C., succeeded him as dean of the Boston Law School.

[An excellent detailed review of his career will be found in *The Judiciary and the Bar of New Eng.* (1900), by Conrad Reno, I, 9. An appreciative sketch appeared in the *New Eng. Mag.*, IV, 225. See also *Green Bag*, I, 62; and *Hist. of Taunton, Mass.* (1893), by S. H. Emery.]

H. W. H. K.

BENNETT, EMERSON (Mar. 16, 1822–May 11, 1905), poet, novelist, who produced more than fifty novels and serials and some hundreds of short stories, was born at Monson, Mass., and was educated in the district schools and Monson Academy. At seventeen he set out to see the world, and was soon drawn to New York, where he began his literary career in 1840. He was still in that city as late as October 1842 and about this time published there his first book, *The Brigand,* which was justly ridiculed as a "little 'poeticle pamphlick'" (*Knickerbocker*, December 1842). In 1843 he was in Philadelphia, and his first brief novel, *The Unknown Countess,* was written in competition for a prize offered by a newspaper there; but he soon continued his migration westward, this time by way of Baltimore and Pittsburgh to Cincinnati, where he arrived in the spring of 1844. Soon he was busy contributing to newspapers and magazines, and in 1846 conducted a quarto weekly, the *Casket.* In the same year he made substantial contributions to all of the four issues of the *Quarterly Journal and Review,* whose editor described him as a writer of power, and commended his poems for their purity, but warned him that in his prose he made his readers too familiar with desperate characters. In 1847 he married Eliza G. Daly of Philadelphia.

He seems to have remained at Cincinnati as late as September 1850; in December of that year, however, he was back at Monson, Mass., and soon afterward he must have established himself at Philadelphia, where he spent the apparently uneventful remainder of his life. During the early fifties the Jameses at Cincinnati and T. B. Peterson at Philadelphia were kept busy publishing his novels. Some of them, before appearing in book form, were printed as serials in the *Saturday Evening Post,* and were reputed to have swelled the circulation of that periodical; but perhaps the best proof of popular success was the announcement by Robert Bonner in 1856 (*New York Ledger,* Sept. 6) that Bennett was now engaged to write exclusively for his paper, which then claimed the largest circulation in America. Here the romancer appeared in the congenial company of such writers as Sylvanus Cobb and Mary Gibson. For years Bennett continued to produce a great quantity of fiction; but he lived to be an old man, and eventually found himself forgotten by the reading public. In 1901 he entered the Masonic Home in Philadelphia, where he died after a long illness (*Telegraph,* Philadelphia, May 12, and *Press,* Philadelphia, May 13, 1905).

The evolution of Bennett as a writer of fiction seems comparatively simple. *The League of the Miami,* published in its first form in 1845 (*The League of the Miami,* n. d., preface of 1850 and p. 116), though still, like *The Brigand* and *The Unknown Countess,* concerned with intrigue for the possession of an inheritance—a theme which long remained attractive to Bennett—and employing too the device of concealed identity, is unlike the earlier poem and novel in its western setting, which from this time was so commonly used by Bennett that he came to be known almost entirely as a romancer of frontier life. *The Bandits of the Osage* (1847) and *Mike Fink* (1848) are quite in the style of *The League of the Miami,* but carry the reader still farther westward. *The Prairie Flower* (first published in 1849) and its sequel, *Leni Leoti,* perhaps the two most popular novels of Bennett to be printed in book form —no less than 100,000 copies of each are said to have been sold—exemplified a third stage: adventures among the Indians were now his staple materials. Henceforth, though a few of his novels, like *Ellen Norbury* and *The Orphan's Trials,* deal with city life and social problems, possibly under the influence of Dickens, Bennett generally combined the tradition of Cooper, who was just at this time ending his career, with the artless tradition of the tale of Indian captivity, known throughout America since the time of Mary Rowlandson. He dealt with the pioneer Virginia of Nathaniel Bacon's day, and he fol-

lowed the changing frontier thence westward step by step to the Pacific. He sent his characters to Oregon and to California and into Texas when men were eager to hear of those places. But in spite of his professed devotion to realism and to history, his appeal was undoubtedly due chiefly to his inexhaustible flow of crude, melodramatic incident and to his frankly sentimental plots and obvious moralizing. The flimsy fictions which he wrote had not the vitality to keep them alive to the end of the author's lifetime. But they were a landmark in that era in which the dime novel was the dominant sub-literary type.

[The best available accounts are those in W. H. Venable's *Beginnings of Literary Culture in the Ohio Valley* (1891); *Who's Who in America,* 1903–05; and Bennett's *Villeta Linden* (1874). All these are based, partly at least, upon information derived directly from Bennett himself. The most important sources are the newspapers and magazines of Bennett's own day and the prefaces of his books.]

R. L. R.

BENNETT, FLOYD (Oct. 25, 1890–Apr. 25, 1928), aviator, was born near Warrensburg, N. Y., the son of Wallace and Henrietta Bennett. Quitting school at seventeen, he worked for a year in a lumber camp and then took a course in automobile engineering at Schenectady. He found employment in the People's Garage at Ticonderoga and out of his earnings bought a half interest in the business. In the war year of 1917 he grew restless, sold his share in the garage, and after some months of indecision enlisted for aviation duty in the Navy. While in the service he was married in February 1918 to Cora Lillian Orkins of Ticonderoga. In 1925, during his second enlistment, he was among the men assigned to Richard Evelyn Byrd on the Donald B. Mac-Millan expedition to northwestern Greenland. "It was in this group," Byrd wrote, "that I discovered Floyd Bennett. . . . Up to the time of the Greenland expedition he had been an obscure aviation mechanic aboard a man-of-war, not even specially well known on his ship. Once he had his chance, he showed that he was a good pilot and one of the finest practical men in the Navy for handling an airplane's temperamental mechanisms, and above that a real man, fearless and true —one in a million." Almost immediately Bennett became his commander's trusted friend and adviser. Together they made a series of remarkable flights, from Etah over Ellesmere Island. Once during a flight the oil in the tank heated up and threatened to kill them both by exploding, but Bennett crawled out on the wing of the plane in the Arctic gale and unscrewed the cap on the tank, thereby relieving the pressure. When their ship turned southward at the end of August, the two discussed the possibility of a flight to the North Pole. Next summer they realized their plan. On May 9, 1926, with Bennett as pilot and Byrd as navigator, the three-engine Fokker monoplane, *Josephine Ford,* flew 1,360 miles from King's Bay, Spitzbergen, to the Pole and back in fifteen and one-half hours. Bennett also took a leading part in the incredibly difficult and hazardous preliminary work of landing the plane from the ship at King's Bay and of building a suitable runway for the take-off. For his share in the achievement he received the Congressional Medal of Honor and a gold medal from the National Geographic Society and was promoted by an act of Congress, Jan. 5, 1927, to warrant machinist. Under the auspices of the United States Department of Commerce and the Guggenheim Foundation he took the *Josephine Ford* on a tour of forty-four cities without missing a single engagement. Byrd and Bennett had begun to plan a trans-Atlantic flight the very hour they hoisted anchor at Spitzbergen. Bennett was to be the pilot. Their plane, the *America,* was of the same type as their previous one, but larger and equipped with some new devices, including a switch designed by Bennett for cutting out all three engines simultaneously. On her first flight, over Hasbrouck Heights, N. J., Apr. 20, 1927, the *America* proved nose-heavy and crashed on landing. Bennett's switch probably saved Fokker, Byrd, Noville, and Bennett from the fate that a short time before had befallen René Fonck's two men. Bennett, with a thigh, a shoulder, and a rib broken, was near death for a week and was unable to participate in the trans-Atlantic flight, but Byrd saw to it that the public realized how much Bennett had done to make the exploit possible. Bennett's pride in his chief and devotion to him were matched by Byrd's admiration and affection for Bennett. Second-in-command of Byrd's expedition to the South Pole, Bennett was in charge of all details relating to transportation when death cut short his career. In April 1928 a newspaper syndicate engaged him and Bernt Balchen to fly a plane from Detroit to Greenly Island, in the Strait of Belle Isle, where Köhl, von Hühnefeld, and Fitzmaurice had landed from their flight from Ireland. Bennett and Balchen left Detroit Apr. 20, both men suffering from heavy colds. When they reached Lake Ste. Agnes, Bennett was too ill to proceed and was rushed to the Jeffrey Hale Hospital at Quebec. His wife and his friend were with him when he died. Mourned everywhere in America, he was buried in the Arlington National Cemetery. He was regarded by experts as one of the most skilful, courageous, and intelligent of American air pilots, and his sterling personal qualities made him a popular hero.

[R. E. Byrd, *Skyward* (1928); Navy Records; newspapers—see *N. Y. Times Index.*]

G. H. G.

BENNETT, JAMES GORDON (1795–June 1, 1872), editor, was born in Keith, Banffshire, Scotland. The year of his birth is frequently misstated; the name-plate placed on his coffin by his family gave it as 1795, but the month was unknown. Bennett himself declared that his paternal line was traceable to the Norman invasion, and was identified with the family of the Earls of Tankerville. He was named after the Rev. James Gordon, pastor of a church at Strathbogie (Pray, *post,* p. 31). His family being Catholic, after attending school at Keith he was sent to a Catholic seminary at Aberdeen for several years to be trained for the priesthood. From his own statements late in life it may be inferred that as a youth he was not devotionally inclined, but was warmly interested in literature. Among the books which impressed his boyish imagination were Byron's poems, Franklin's autobiography, and the Waverley novels, then just appearing. *Rob Roy* led him to visit Glasgow, and he declared long after that "I remember to this hour every nook and corner of that enchanting place so beautifully described by Walter Scott" (*Ibid.,* p. 33). In the spring of 1819, upon a sudden impulse, he left Aberdeen and emigrated to Halifax, Nova Scotia, where he earned his living by teaching. He shortly made his way to Portland, Me., and thence to Boston. Without friends, money, or work, he suffered for food, and was at one time rescued from two days of starvation by finding a shilling on the ground.

His first important employment was solicited of Henry W. Dutton, foreman of the publishing office of Wells & Lillie in Boston; Bennett stated that he was not a printer, but wished to be about the office to enjoy its facilities for mental improvement (*Boston Transcript,* June 3, 1872). He was given a position as copyholder, and by his diligence soon won promotion to a clerkship in the firm's bookstore in Court St. He was a constant attendant at the sermons of the best Boston ministers and missed no opportunity for self-improvement. In 1822 he went to New York, and made a slender living by writing for the press (Pray, *post,* p. 46). The following year A. S. Willington, proprietor of the Charleston (S. C.) *Courier* was attracted by him and took him to Charleston for miscellaneous work, including translating from Spanish-American newspapers. Here he saw slavery in practise, and formed impressions which always made him sympathetic with the Southern point of view. Returning to New York in October 1823, he advertised the opening of a "permanent commercial school" in Ann St., where he would teach elocution, algebra, geometry, history, political economy, English composition, commercial law, bookkeeping, and other subjects; the school to be conducted "according to the inductive method of instruction" (*Ibid.*, p. 50). Dr. J. S. Bartlett, long editor of an English journal in New York called the *Albion,* was named as reference. This school, however, seems never to have been opened, Bennett lacking the necessary capital. He continued to make a living by desultory newspaper writing, and delivered a course of lectures on political economy in the vestry of the Old Dutch Church.

Little by little Bennett advanced to responsible posts in New York journalism. He was employed for a time in 1825 at a low salary upon a Sunday journal called the *New York Courier,* owned by John Tryon. Bennett purchased this paper upon credit, but failing to make it pay restored it to Tryon. During 1826 he became a regular contributor to Thomas Snowden's *National Advocate* and to the *Mercantile Advertiser.* Here and in the *Courier* he attracted attention by a series of attacks upon speculators and sharpers in the mercantile community, and by his informative reports of the trials of some of them, notably Jacob Barker and Henry Eckford. His exposure of the excesses of the joint-stock fever of the time aroused much resentment. At the same time he affiliated himself with Tammany Hall, and gave support in politics to Martin Van Buren. An opportunity for promotion came when in November 1826 the associate editor of the *New York Enquirer,* W. W. Graham, fell in a duel, and the editor and owner, the eccentric and versatile Mordecai M. Noah, found it necessary to replace him. Bennett was forthwith employed, and spent the years 1827–28 on the staff of that newspaper, partly in New York and partly in Washington.

As Washington correspondent of the *Enquirer,* Bennett soon won a national reputation by a series of articles, modeled in style upon Horace Walpole's letters, in which he pungently and boldly sketched the leading figures in Washington politics and society. Abounding in personalities, they were much attacked but eagerly read. He was assiduous in attending Congressional debates, and by his application to work even injured his eyesight. In New York and Washington he dealt with a multitude of subjects: the tariff, the Federal bankruptcy bill, the Greek rebellion, the theatrical appearances of Macready and Forrest, the French, English, and Italian opera companies, and the new books. With the approach

of the presidential election of 1828 he devoted himself to the support of Andrew Jackson's candidacy. His description of the inauguration of Jackson in March 1829 was in a vein of rapturous enthusiasm. On returning from Washington he sought James Watson Webb, the chief proprietor of the *Courier,* and suggested that Webb should purchase the *Enquirer* and make the combined journals the leading Eastern newspaper. This purchase was effected, the first issue of the *Morning Courier and New York Enquirer* appearing May 25, 1829. When Democratic politicians showed doubt of Webb's loyalty, Bennett visited Saratoga Springs and Washington to secure the support of such leaders as Silas Wright, Edwin Crosswell, Jesse Hoyt, and Van Buren. The result was an arrangement by which the *Courier and Enquirer* was made a staunch Jacksonian organ, and Bennett was installed in the fall of 1829 as associate editor. Since Webb was a vain, irascible, unstable man, the shrewd and enterprising Bennett was the paper's real head.

From the autumn of 1829 till the autumn of 1832, three years, Bennett gave the *Courier and Enquirer* vitality as a newspaper and power as a party organ. His report of the famous trial of the Crowninshields at Salem, Mass., for the murder of Capt. Joseph White, added materially to his reputation. Bennett maintained against Attorney-General Percy Morton the right of the press to report the trial without permission of the court, and vindicated his contention that the newspapers are "the living jury of the nation." During 1830 he engaged fiercely in the United States Bank controversy, supporting President Jackson throughout. In April 1831, however, a share was bought in the *Courier and Enquirer* by M. M. Noah, representing United States Bank interests, and Bennett's articles against that institution ceased to appear. He continued to deal with political subjects. At the beginning of 1832 he was responsible for the *Courier and Enquirer's* proposal that Martin Van Buren be nominated for the vice-presidency with Jackson, while he warmly supported William L. Marcy for nomination as governor of New York. During the summer the newspaper carried the names of Jackson, Van Buren, and Marcy at the head of its editorial columns. On Aug. 18, 1832, however, Noah left the firm, Webb assumed full control, and the *Courier and Enquirer* was suddenly made a Whig organ. The result was the immediate resignation of Bennett.

Thirty-seven years old, possessing a little capital and a remarkably varied experience of journalism, Bennett now resolved to set up an independent establishment. On Oct. 29, 1832, he issued the first number of the New York *Globe,* a two-cent morning newspaper which endured for only one month. He then went to Philadelphia, and purchasing a small share in a newspaper called the *Pennsylvanian,* became its editor. Needing a loan of $2,500 to obtain complete control, he applied to his old political associates—Jesse Hoyt, Martin Van Buren, and others—but they closed their purses. The party leaders had marked his growing independence and feared he would prove unreliable. Bennett's bitterness was great; he wrote Hoyt that Van Buren could aid him as easily as he could drink a glass of Saratoga water, and yet treated him as if he were "a boy—a child—cold, heartless, careless, and God knows what." For lack of funds, Bennett retired from the *Pennsylvanian* in December 1833, but he was still undaunted.

Meanwhile there had occurred, in September 1833, the establishment of the penny press of New York City, in the emergence of the astonishingly successful *Sun,* founded by Benjamin H. Day and sold for one cent a copy (Frank M. O'Brien, *The Story of the Sun,* 1918, p. 25). Bennett was impressed by the sudden rise of the *Sun* to a circulation, in the spring of 1834, of 8,000. He applied during the summer of 1834 for a position in association with Day but was refused. Thereupon he began laying plans for a journal of his own. Arranging a business connection with two printers of 34 Ann St., Messrs. Anderson and Smith, he began the publication, May 6, 1835, of the *New York Herald,* a four-page newspaper, four columns to the page, which sold for $3 a year or one cent a copy. His publishing office was in the cellar of 20 Wall St., where a plank across two flour-barrels served as business and editorial desk. Possessing but $500 in capital, and no party support, his poverty compelled him to serve as editor, reporter, proof-reader, folder, and cashier. It was in truth "one poor man in a cellar against the world" (James Parton, *Famous Americans of Recent Times,* 1867, p. 277).

Yet a combination of reasons gave the *Herald* immediate success. Most important of these was the fact that it redeemed Bennett's promise to "give a picture of the world," its local news being comprehensive, piquant, and bold, and covering many neglected subjects. Its editorials were brief, pungent, independent, and lighted up by a vein of Mephistophelian mockery. Bennett disclaimed all political ties, saying that "We shall support no party, be the organ of no faction or coterie, and care nothing for any election or any candidate, from President down to constable. We shall endeavor to record facts on every public and proper subject, stripped of verbiage and coloring, with comments, when suitable, just, independent, fearless, and good tempered." The *Herald's* boldness in laughing at churches, politicians, and pompous public characters, and exposing financial rogues, appealed to all. In its second issue, delayed till May 11, it printed the first money-market report, and three days later ran a table of sales on the Stock Exchange. It printed also the first reports of religious conventions. By rejecting the credit system, and demanding cash, Bennett kept his financial independence. Working fifteen or sixteen hours a day, at the end of three months he made the *Herald* profitable, and was able to engage a cheap police reporter. When the great fire of December 1835 occurred, Bennett again showed his enterprise by giving the city the fullest reports, and published a picture of the burning Exchange and a map of the devastated district.

His labors continued arduous and his career stormy. During 1836 he closed a lucrative advertising contract with Dr. Benjamin Brandreth, the pill-maker; and in the fifteenth month of the *Herald* he felt able to raise its price to two cents. He was then able to boast a circulation of 30,000 to 40,000 daily. His flings at the financial operations of James Watson Webb and Nicholas Biddle aroused Webb's ire, and twice during the year, in January and May, Webb assaulted him in the street. Bennett published full accounts of these affairs, and in reply to editorial attacks declared that he would not be daunted: "I am building up a newspaper establishment that will take the lead of all others that ever appeared in the world in virtue, in morals, in science, in knowledge, in industry, in taste, in power, in influence" (*N. Y. Herald,* Oct. 29, 1836). He was viciously attacked by other journals for the flippancy, impudence, and sensationalism of his columns. His treatment of the murder of Helen Jewett (April 1836) and the trial of Richard P. Robinson for the crime, the *Herald* propounding a theory to show Robinson's possible innocence, even set afloat a story that his columns had been bought. This charge was frequently repeated (see Bennett's editorial, *Herald,* Feb. 25, 1855). Meanwhile, the editor's labors continued incessant. He rose at five, wrote his leading editorials, squibs, and sketches before breakfast, spent the hours from nine to one reading newspapers and editing copy, wrote a column of news, received callers, went to Wall St. and wrote his money article, dined at four, read his proofs, took in cash and advertisements, and went to bed at ten o'clock. But he gradually assembled an adequate staff, and after a few years could give himself more leisure.

On May 1, 1838, he sailed for a combined pleasure and business trip to Europe, and returning to New Mill, Scotland, found his mother and sister alive, but his father and brother dead. Visiting Paris and the principal British cities, he established six European correspondents for the *Herald*. During his five months' absence he wrote a series of letters to the paper. Early the next year he made a tour of the South, perfecting the *Herald's* news and business arrangements. Already he was opposing the renomination of President Van Buren, and during the campaign of 1840 he combated both Van Buren and Gov. W. H. Seward. The year 1840 was marked also by Bennett's marriage in St. Peter's Church in Barclay St. to Henrietta Agnes Crean, a descendant of the Crean Lynch family of Ireland, who had come to America with her family in 1838. She was a linguist and composer of some ability, and Bennett published an editorial of astounding vulgarity upon her virtues. On their return from their wedding trip to Niagara Falls they found that Bennett's enemies had unsuccessfully tried to induce Charles Stetson, manager of the Astor House, to bar his doors against them. During 1840–41 the press campaign against Bennett, partly inspired by the Van Burenites, reached new heights. Park Benjamin [*q.v.*] called him an "obscene foreign vagabond, a pestilential scoundrel, ass, rogue, habitual liar, loathsome and leprous slanderer and libeller" (C. H. Levermore, p. 463).

Yet the *Herald* was increasingly prosperous. In 1841 Bennett, attending Harrison's inauguration in Washington, organized a corps of reporters, at a cost of almost $200 a week, and commenced a fight, ultimately successful, to obtain their entry at will to the galleries of Congress. The newspaper boasted (Oct. 20, 1841) an annual revenue of $130,000; its weekly edition circulated 1,550 copies in Boston, 500 in New Orleans, and 450 in Pittsburgh. The following May it removed to a new building at Fulton and Nassau Sts., with facilities for printing 50,000 to 60,000 copies daily. Bennett's organization was now excellent, his chief lieutenant being Frederic Hudson, whom the elder Bowles called the best newspaper manager in America. In 1843 Bennett and his family made a tour of the British Isles and France. While in Dublin he clashed violently with Daniel O'Connell, who had been given a prejudice against him through some misstatements by the lecturer, James Silk Buckingham; and Bennett set forth the facts in a dignified letter to the London *Times* of Aug. 28, 1843. He returned to London on Oct. 21, announcing that he found himself "fresh, vigorous, renovated." His quarrel with O'Connell now gave fresh intensity to an old feud with Bishop John Hughes of the Catholic Church in New York, whom he accused of meddling with party politics and of hostility toward the public schools. As a result, Bennett treated with great cordiality the new Native American or Know-Nothing party (John Hughes, *A Letter on the Moral Causes That Have Produced the Evil Spirit of the Time*, 1844); but in the presidential election of 1844 he and the *Herald* supported James K. Polk.

For the next twenty years Bennett's life was comparatively uneventful, being identified with the steady rise of the *Herald* to preëminence as a news-gathering sheet. His corps of correspondents, European and American, was unrivaled. He kept a fleet of dispatch boats cruising outside Sandy Hook, at a distance of from 50 to 250 miles, to intercept steamers from Europe and hasten their news to shore (Pray, p. 375). The *Herald* was the first newspaper to make lavish use of the telegraph. On Dec. 26, 1844, it announced an overland express service from New Orleans to carry the Texas news, and upon the outbreak of war in 1846 this service was made weekly or oftener. The New York news of the *Herald* was the fullest to be had; and particularly valuable, as the slavery question grew prominent, was its comprehensive Southern intelligence.

Editorially, the *Herald* was for the most part on the Democratic side. In the campaign of 1848 it supported Gen. Taylor, whom Bennett had proposed for the presidency as early as 1846. Four years later it advocated the election of Franklin Pierce. Already Bennett was charged with being under the influence of Southern leaders. In 1856, however, he surprised his readers by aligning the *Herald* with the new Republican party for John C. Frémont. Four years later, alarmed by the prospect of civil war, and influenced by the sentiment of the commercial community in New York, he supported Douglas against Lincoln. The course which Bennett gave the *Herald* just before the outbreak of the Civil War excited much indignation among patriotic men. He was frankly in favor of letting the seceding states go, and even proposed a reorganization of the Union under the new Southern constitution, with the New England states left out. With the actual firing on Fort Sumter, however, Bennett grasped the demands of public opinion, and began to make the *Herald* a newspaper of acceptable loyalty, though sometimes copperhead in tone. After some hesitation, it gave Lincoln warm support for reëlection in 1864. During the war the *Herald* reached the height of its fame as an enterprising and exhaustive purveyor of the news. Its average week-day circulation in December 1860 was about 77,000; this rose steadily, and of one issue in 1864 more than 132,000 copies were sold. The newspaper employed sixty-three war correspondents in different theatres, and spent a total of $525,000 in gathering war news (Allan Nevins, *The Evening Post: A Century of Journalism,* 1922, pp. 267–83). Its dispatches from the front were rivaled only by those of the *Tribune,* and its European dispatches were unequaled. Lincoln constantly read it, and but for the fact that its editorials maintained what John Bright called "a reckless tone," its repute would have been high.

Bennett spent much time during the late forties and the fifties traveling in Europe, the United States, and the West Indies, and was presented (January 1847) at the court of Louis Philippe. Despite frequent absences, his supervision over the *Herald* was constant until 1867, when he retired; and he not merely directed its policy but wrote steadily for its columns. Its circulation when he resigned it to his son was 90,000 daily; its advertising revenue was surpassed only by that of the London *Times,* and its annual profits approached $400,000. Honors outside journalism had no appeal to him, and in 1864 he refused the offer of appointment as minister to France, made by Lincoln. He lived with increasing luxury, owning a country residence at Washington Heights, with ample grounds, a town house at the corner of Fifth Ave. and Thirty-eighth St., and a yacht which at the outbreak of the Civil War he gave to the Government. Even after he quitted active control of the *Herald* he gave the newspaper much attention. Gradually becoming feebler, on May 25, 1872, he was attacked by a convulsive seizure, with epileptic symptoms. On June 1, after receiving the last sacrament from Archbishop McCloskey, he died. The softening of the old ill-feeling against him was indicated by the list of pall-bearers at the funeral (June 12), which included Horace Greeley, George Jones of the *New York Times,* Charles A. Dana, D. M. Stone, Robert Bonner, and George Childs of the Philadelphia *Public Ledger.* He was buried in Greenwood Cemetery, Brooklyn. It was realized that, with all his errors, he had been perhaps the chief figure in a great and democratic revolution in journalism, a natural and beneficial concomitant of the rise of Jacksonian democracy. In person he was more than six feet tall, broad-shouldered, florid of complexion, with hair at first sandy and later silver, with eyes of grayish blue, and an air of command. His modesty of bearing in private was in strong contrast with the audacious vanity and even vulgarity with

which he had been wont to parade his affairs in the *Herald.*

[The fullest source of information upon Bennett's life is the files of the *Herald,* in which he wrote frankly and at times boastfully of his successes, reverses, and ambitions. Isaac Pray's *Memoirs of Jas. Gordon Bennett and His Times, by a Journalist* (1855) contains many inaccuracies which might have been corrected but for the author's resolve not to consult Bennett or any one connected with him. It is, however, the best single volume for the period covered. An illuminating interpretation, with some information, is furnished by C. H. Levermore in "The Rise of Metropolitan Journalism," *Am. Hist. Rev.,* VI, 446–65. There is a chapter upon "The Jas. Gordon Bennetts and Their Newspaper" in Oswald Garrison Villard's *Some Newspapers and Newspapermen* (1923); there is a sketch with some facts not easily available elsewhere in Jas. Melvin Lee, *Hist. of Am. Journalism* (1917), pp. 193–200, and Don C. Seitz has written a somewhat journalistic volume in *The Jas. Gordon Bennetts* (1928). A collection of obituaries appeared in the *N. Y. Herald,* June 2–14, 1872.]

A.N.

BENNETT, JAMES GORDON (May 10, 1841–May 14, 1918), editor, capitalist, was born in New York City, the son of James Gordon Bennett [*q.v.*] and Henrietta Agnes Crean, who two years previous to her marriage had arrived with her family from Ireland. The first of three children, he was born in Chambers St., then a fashionable place of residence. He was educated under the supervision of his mother, chiefly in Europe, to escape the atmosphere of calumny surrounding his father (Isaac Pray, *Memoirs of James Gordon Bennett,* 1855, p. 281); following a course with private tutors, he attended the École Polytechnique in Paris. In 1861 the outbreak of war brought him back to the United States, and to emphasize the loyalty of the Bennett family, he entered the navy, receiving a commission as lieutenant. From this service arose his lifelong interest in nautical affairs, which made the *Herald* long unrivaled in its attention to ship, naval, and military news. With the close of the war Bennett began a thorough training in the more important departments of the *Herald.* On the retirement of Frederic Hudson in 1866 he became managing editor, and the following year, when his father ceased to give the paper constant attention, he became its chief executive officer (*Literary Digest,* June 1, 1918). He combined a busy social life, moving in the faster set of young New York bachelors, with an erratic but energetic attention to the newspaper. Its achievements in reporting the Civil War had lifted the *Herald* to the height of its fame. The younger Bennett was responsible for several news exploits of importance. In 1867 he dispatched Henry M. Stanley, whose reports of Gen. W. S. Hancock's expedition against the Indians had attracted attention, to be *Herald* correspondent with the British army against the Emperor Theodore of Abyssinia. Stanley's success in sending back the first news of the capture of Magdala secured Bennett's special favor, and Bennett gave him a roving commission. In 1869 he met Stanley in Paris, and informed him that he was to go to Africa to search for David Livingstone. An expedition was outfitted from Zanzibar, and the result was a journalistic feat of the first importance, Stanley finding Livingstone at Ujiji on Nov. 10, 1871 (*The Autobiography of Sir Henry Morton Stanley*, 1909). This achievement was set forth in detail in the *Herald*.

Meanwhile, under Bennett's management of the *Herald*, Aloysius MacGahan had made his remarkable reputation as a reporter of the Franco-Prussian War and the Commune. Bennett, always ready to pay lavishly for unusual news, sent him to the Crimea, to Geneva for the sitting of the Alabama Claims Arbitration Commission, and with the Russian expedition of 1873 against Khiva; and MacGahan's heroic exploits in Central Asia were recounted in full in the *Herald* (J. Aloysius MacGahan, *Campaigning on the Oxus*, 1874). In 1875 Bennett, joining hands with Capt. Allen Young and Lady Franklin, financed an expedition in the bark *Pandora* under Capt. Young to search for the Northwest Passage. It was a failure, but MacGahan, who accompanied it, wrote some excellent letters to the *Herald* (MacGahan, *Under the Northern Lights*, 1876). During the panic year 1873–74, Bennett and the *Herald* opened kitchens for the poor in the slum districts of New York, where Delmonico's served soup and other food. The newspaper was at this time active in other charitable enterprises. Its most important benevolence was the Herald Relief Fund for Irish sufferers, established in 1882 at the time of the agrarian outrages. Bennett, always impulsively generous, headed the subscription list with a gift of $100,000 and thus earned the enduring gratitude of Irish-Americans.

In these early years he showed a capacity for gathering about him men of unusual ability. His staff included Charles Nordhoff, who in the early seventies became Washington correspondent, John Habberton, Ivory Chamberlain, John Russell Young, and George W. Hosmer. Unfortunately, Bennett, always eccentric, temperamental, and irascible, developed a jealousy of the men who gained great prominence on the *Herald*, and this led to the departure of Stanley and an open rupture with MacGahan (F. L. Bullard, *Famous War Correspondents*, 1914, p. 140). Bennett early made two ventures in the establishment of fresh journals. In 1867, with his father's support, he founded the *Evening Telegram*, which adopted a light and sensational tone, and for years

showed a heavy deficit; at one time, in the fall of 1897, Bennett resolved to discontinue it and published a notice to that effect, but repented and kept it alive. More important was his establishment in 1887 of the Paris edition of the *New York Herald*. Always a warm lover of France, Bennett found that nation misunderstood and disliked in the United States following the Franco-Prussian War. He designed his Paris edition not as a business enterprise but as an institution for fostering friendship between the two nations. It was seldom profitable financially; it was badly edited, presenting little news except scrappy cablegrams and social gossip; but it attained a circulation before the World War of almost 25,000 and as a gesture of amity it was greatly appreciated by the French public.

The year 1877 marked a sharp turning point in Bennett's life, witnessing his virtual expatriation. The cause lay in a scandal which made America repugnant to him. He had become engaged to be married to Edith May, of a prominent Washington family; the engagement was abruptly broken off by the May family under mysterious circumstances; his fiancée's brother, Fred May, attacked Bennett with a horsewhip on Jan. 3, 1877, as the latter was emerging from the Union Club on Fifth Avenue; and a duel followed immediately on the Delaware-Maryland border-line, shots being exchanged harmlessly. The stories circulated about the affair made New York unbearable to Bennett, and he took up his residence abroad. He maintained three homes in America: the old Bennett homestead on Washington Heights, Manhattan, a house at 37 West Forty-seventh St., and a villa at Newport. But except for flying visits he spent his entire time in his Paris home, his shooting lodge at Versailles, his villa at Beaulieu, or on his yacht. His management of the *Herald* and *Telegram* was by cable, and became more explosive, erratic, and domineering than ever.

Under these circumstances he did less and less to maintain the *Herald's* reputation for news enterprise. His last great effort to create "exclusive" news was his expenditure, 1879–81, of large sums in supporting the expedition of George Washington De Long to the Arctic. De Long had proposed this trip as early as 1873. His ship, the *Jeannette*, was caught in the polar pack, crushed, and sunk, and most of the crew, including the commander, perished (George W. Melville, *In the Lena Delta*, 1884). In 1883 Bennett and John W. Mackay established the Commercial Cable Company, which laid a line across the Atlantic and broke the grip of the existing cable monopoly. This undertaking proved very profitable, the association of the *Herald* and the cable company being of mutual benefit, and it supported for some years the *Herald's* reputation for preëminence in foreign news, but in the nineties this was gradually lost. In 1893 Bennett moved the paper from its old home at Broadway and Ann St. to a beautiful new structure at "Herald Square" (Broadway and Sixth Ave.), a stroke which did much to sustain the prestige of the journal.

In his ambition to remain editor of the *Herald* and *Telegram* in fact as well as name, Bennett refused to delegate adequate authority to the home staff. The city editor, who was actually managing editor, had certain powers, but was always subject to unexpected orders. The chief incumbent of this office was William C. Reick, through whom in the Spanish-American War Bennett spent $300,000 for news service. Bennett hired, promoted, demoted, and discharged men with lightning rapidity and frequently without reason. On a sudden whim he once made the first reporter to meet him coming up New York Bay the city editor. He issued eccentric orders with regard to editorial and news policies. These erratic acts did both the morale of the staff and the *Herald's* reputation for reliability great damage. The circulation of the paper was also badly injured in 1884 by a disastrous war with the news-dealers (Don C. Seitz, *Joseph Pulitzer*, 1924, p. 146); while the rise of the *World* under Pulitzer, the reinvigoration of the *Times* under Adolph S. Ochs, and the emergence of "yellow" journalism under William Randolph Hearst, all struck it heavy blows. By 1900 the *Herald* had declined seriously in circulation, revenue, news-enterprise, and prestige. In 1907 Hearst instigated the indictment of Bennett, with his advertising manager and the *Herald* corporation, on the ground that the personal column of advertisements was used for immoral purposes and violated the postal laws. Bennett pleaded guilty and paid fines aggregating $31,000—a humiliating episode. By the outbreak of the World War the newspaper's position was so precarious that only the sudden prosperity of the *Telegram* enabled the joint establishment to pay its way.

Bennett remained a prominent figure in European society and in the world of sports. He had introduced polo to Newport in the seventies, had been an ardent yachtsman from youth, and a leader in coach-driving. In 1870 he sent his yacht *Dauntless* to England and raced her against the British yacht *Cambria* to America, losing by the narrowest of margins. He was for a time commodore of the New York Yacht Club. His steam yacht *Lysistrata,* the largest ever built on

the Clyde (1900), carried a crew of 100 men and was long famous. When the automobile was still in process of early development, he offered the James Gordon Bennett cup to be competed for by the best international types. This was followed by the gift of cups for balloon-racing (1906) and aeroplane-racing (1908). One of his ambitions was to stimulate an interest in sports among the French, and for this purpose he offered numerous trophies; it is not too much to say that his name became the most prominent in France of those identified with sports. It has been estimated that during his long ownership of the *Herald* he drew from it and spent $30,000,-000.

In every sense Bennett was a man of the world. He entertained lavishly, his circle of friends becoming more and more European as his connections with America grew weaker. His point of view became European rather than American, a fact which injured the *Herald*. He made little effort to escape scandal. Much attention was at one time attracted by a series of unsuccessful suits brought by Mlle. Juliette Schettler, daughter of a French actress, Mlle. Camille Clermont, to prove that he was her father and should support her. Many stories were told during his lifetime of his personal peculiarities—his lavish tips; his intense hatred for a few men, notably Jay Gould and William Randolph Hearst; his love for owls; his fondness for dogs, which made him devote the *Herald* to a long campaign against vivisection; and his strange mixture of canniness and naïveté. He became one of the most picturesque figures of two continents.

Apparently a confirmed bachelor, Bennett used to remark: "I suppose no woman who ever lived could get along with me as wife." But on Sept. 10, 1914, he was married in Paris to the Baroness de Reuter, widow of Baron George de Reuter; at the same time becoming a member of the Protestant Episcopal Church. His wife had been Maud Potter of Philadelphia. During the next four years he was preoccupied with the war. His newspapers, which he now governed through a series of committees, were vigorous partisans of the Allies. At his death, which was caused at Beaulieu by heart disease, he left the greater part of his fortune to found the James Gordon Bennett Memorial Home for New York journalists; a shelter, in memory of his father, for indigent newspaper men who had been connected for at least ten years with some daily published in Manhattan. His estate was found to be much reduced and heavily involved, and the number of annuities provided for various persons prevented the prompt establishment of this home.

[The only volume devoted to Jas. Gordon Bennett, Jr., is Albert Stevens Crockett's *When Jas. Gordon Bennett Was Caliph of Bagdad* (1926), a sketchy book of reminiscences by an associate and employee. A chapter is given to the two Bennetts in Oswald Garrison Villard's *Some Newspapers and Newspapermen* (1923). Reminiscences by James B. Townsend were published in the *N. Y. Times* of May 19, 1918; by "Spillane" in the *N. Y. Evening Mail,* May 14, 1918; and by Arthur H. Warner in the *Evening Post* of July 6, 1918. Six chapters are devoted to him in Don C. Seitz's *The Jas. Gordon Bennetts* (1928).]

                                       A.N.

BENNETT, NATHANIEL (June 27, 1818– Apr. 20, 1886), lawyer, jurist, was born at Clinton, Oneida County, N. Y., and passed his youth on his father's farm. In 1832, having spent two years at Partridge's Military School, Buffalo, he entered Canandaigua Academy, where one of his schoolmates was Stephen A. Douglas, passing from there to Hamilton College, and completing his education at Yale University, where, however, he did not graduate. He then studied law at Buffalo, and having been admitted as an attorney in 1840 and a counsellor in 1843, practised there for eight years, at the same time actively interesting himself in politics. He became an ardent supporter of the "Barnburners" cause, and was a member of the convention at Buffalo in 1848 which nominated Van Buren for the presidency. His health had never been strong, necessitating periodical vacations during which he had sought relief in extensive travel, and on the discovery of gold in California in 1849 he determined to settle on the Pacific Coast. Journeying by way of Panama, he landed in San Francisco June 30, 1849, and proceeded to the mining camps. Locating on the Tuolumne River, he made a lucky strike and in three months had realized a considerable fortune. He thereupon returned to San Francisco in October, and opened a law office in partnership with John Satterlee who subsequently became a judge. California had just adopted a constitution preparatory to admission as a state, and at the ensuing elections Bennett was returned as a senator for San Francisco. The first matter to come before the new legislature was the basic law of the new state, as a strong feeling had been manifested in favor of the Louisiana Civil Code in preference to the English Common Law. A Senate judiciary committee, on which Bennett served, was appointed to investigate, and it reported, Feb. 27, 1850, recommending that the courts be governed in their adjudications by the English Common Law as received and modified in the United States. This report—able and exhaustive—in the preparation of which Bennett exercised a weighty influence, was accepted and acted upon. In the meantime he had been elected by the legislature as associate justice of the new supreme court of California. At the request of

his colleagues he assumed the task of reporting the decisions of the court and in 1852 published *Reports of Cases Determined in the Supreme Court of California,* vol. I, embracing all decisions of the court from its organization in March 1850 to the end of June term, 1851. His preface contains an authoritative account of the conditions in California previous to the organization of the state government. He retained his position but a short time, resigning Oct. 3, 1851, and paying an extended visit to the East. On his return to San Francisco in 1853 he resumed practise and acquired an extensive clientele, chiefly associated with "big" business. Affiliating himself with the Republican party, he officiated as chairman of the first Republican state convention at Sacramento, and was nominated in 1857 for judge of the supreme court on the party ticket but met with defeat. Thenceforth he devoted himself to his profession, being for some years prior to his death admittedly the leader of the state bar. He became very prominent in connection with the notorious litigation known as the "Bonanza Suits." In May 1878, action was brought against John W. Mackay, James G. Fair, and others, alleging misappropriation of funds of the Consolidated Virginia Mining Company, and other suits followed involving approximately $36,000,000. He acted as attorney for the plaintiff in some of these actions, which were ultimately compromised on terms which were never divulged. He died in San Francisco, Apr. 20, 1886. Somewhat paradoxically, though "a slow deliberate pertinacious man," he was a brilliant speaker, frequently called upon on great public occasions. As a lawyer he acquired a wide reputation, enjoying the confidence of leading financial and industrial institutions. In a pioneer community his scholarship and general culture were considered remarkable.

[The only adequate biography is in *Hist. of the Bench and Bar of Cal.,* ed. by Oscar T. Shuck (1901), p. 445, which work also describes the genesis of the judicial system of the state. See also *Cal. Supreme Court Reports,* vol. I, preface and notes; files of the *Alta California, San Francisco Chronicle,* and *Evening Bull.*]

                                     H.W.H.K.

BENNING, HENRY LEWIS (Apr. 2, 1814– July 10, 1875), jurist, statesman, soldier, was born on a plantation in Columbia County, Ga., the son of Pleasant Moon and Matilda Meriwether (White) Benning, the third of eleven children. He attended Franklin College (University of Georgia), where he graduated with first honors at the age of twenty. Upon his graduation he moved to Columbus and there made his home for the rest of his life. At twenty-one he was admitted to the bar, and two years later was appointed solicitor-general for his judicial circuit. He afterward served a term in the General Assembly. On Sept. 12, 1839, he married Mary Howard Jones of Columbus, by whom he had ten children, of whom five daughters survived him. His only son died of wounds received in the Civil War. Able, logical, industrious, and of the highest integrity, he had not a few of the qualities of Calhoun. He was convinced that to free the negroes would create such social chaos in the South as to make civilization impossible and life for the whites unendurable. He believed emancipation, and the subsequent enfranchisement of the slaves, inevitable if the South remained in the Union. He therefore became an ardent secessionist. But while he felt secession necessary he considered it by no means the solution of the problem. He feared some of the northernmost slave states might, from economic reasons, develop a sentiment against the institution, and he would protect the lower South from the chaos of emancipation by the formation of a "consolidated" Southern Republic, with strong centralized powers, so that slavery could be put "under the control of those most interested in it" (letter to Howell Cobb, "Toombs, Stephens and Cobb Correspondence," *American Historical Association Annual Report,* 1911, II, 171).

In the crisis of 1850 he was for immediate withdrawal from the Union, and became an enthusiastic supporter of the movement to hold a Southern conference at Nashville. In the election held in Georgia to name delegates to this conference he was successful, but most of the other secessionist candidates were overwhelmingly defeated, and the small number of votes cast showed that the vast majority of the people were not aroused. Indeed, the fact that Georgia, generally regarded as a pivotal state, had thus decisively repudiated the "Southern-rights" movement, foredoomed the convention to failure. But Benning was persistent and resourceful. Ostensibly in an effort at compromise, he introduced at Nashville a resolution to the effect that nothing less than the Missouri line could be accepted by the South as a settlement of the territorial problem. He believed the South could be persuaded to demand this as an ultimatum; that the North would promptly reject it; and that secession would then be the only alternative. The resolution was duly passed, but the result was not what he had hoped it would be. Meeting in December, the Georgia Convention, instead of ratifying the action of Nashville, accepted Clay's compromise measure, "being impelled thereto" (in the language of the resolution) "by an earnest desire to save the American Union." In 1851 Benning accepted the nomination of the Southern-rights Democrats as one of their candidates for Congress and, although he ran ahead of his party, was defeated in the Constitutional Union "landslide" of that year. In 1853 he was elected by the General Assembly as an associate justice of the Georgia supreme court, where he delivered, in the case of Padleford *vs.* Savannah (14 *Georgia,* 438), an exhaustive opinion in support of the principle that a state supreme court is not bound by the decisions of the Supreme Court of the United States on constitutional questions. The two courts he held to be "coördinate and co-equal." This remarkable decision, comprising eighty pages, is perhaps the most vigorous and elaborate exposition of the doctrine of "strict construction" ever set forth in a judicial pronouncement. At the expiration of his term in 1859 the General Assembly failed to reëlect him, largely because of the activities of an influential and disgruntled litigant.

Benning is generally regarded as having acted always with the Southern extremists, but in 1860 he refused to follow Yancey out of the Democratic party upon the disruption of the Charleston Convention; on the contrary he was vice-president of the adjourned convention of the "regulars" which met at Baltimore and nominated Stephen A. Douglas for the presidency. But in 1861 he took an active part in the Georgia Convention which adopted the Ordinance of Secession, and was sent by that body as its commissioner to the Virginia Convention. There he delivered a carefully prepared address on the race problem and secession.

Thomas R. R. Cobb said (*American Historical Association Annual Report,* II, 544) that Benning was seriously considered for a cabinet position in the newly established Confederacy, but he volunteered in the army, and was made colonel of a regiment which he organized in Columbus. His record as a field officer and as brigadier-general was distinguished. His steadfastness in critical situations earned for him the sobriquet "Old Rock." At Sharpsburg his defense of a bridge over Antietam Creek was heroic. At Chickamauga he had two horses shot from under him; cutting a third from an army wagon, he rode bareback into the fight at the head of his brigade. He went through the heavy fighting on Little Round Top at Gettysburg unscathed, but was severely wounded in the Wilderness. At Petersburg, during a fierce Federal assault, his brigade for hours withstood the whole attack alone. Throughout the varying fortunes of war he seems never to have lost hope that the South would win, and when a courier notified him at Appomattox that Gen. Lee was going to offer terms of surrender, it is said that he was heart-broken.

Returning home he found his houses burned, his goods and money vanished, and his dependents increased by the widow and children of his wife's brother, who had fallen in the war, and by his sister's orphans. He resumed the practise of law. On July 8, 1875, having spent the preceding night upon a case in which he was interested, he was stricken with apoplexy on his way to the court, and the next day he died.

[R. H. Shryock, *Ga. and the Union in 1850* (1926); A. R. Lawton, "Judicial Controversies on Appellate Jurisdiction," in *Report of the 38th Ann. Sess. of the Ga. Bar Ass.* (1921); a short biography of Benning by his daughter in *Men of Mark in Ga.*, vol. III (1911). Benning's judicial opinions are to be found in volumes XIV to XXIX, inclusive, of the *Ga. Reports.* See also *Atlanta Constitution,* July 11, 1875.]
                                                      B.F.

BENSON, EGBERT (June 21, 1746–Aug. 24, 1833), Revolutionary leader, was the son of Robert Benson and Catherine Van Borsum. He was graduated from King's College in 1765, read law in the office of John Morin Scott, and was admitted to the bar in the January term of the New York supreme court, 1769. Commencing the practise of his profession at Red Hook in Dutchess County in 1772, he soon became prominent in that region in promoting activities for the patriot cause, organizing revolutionary proceedings there and in the province generally, and taking a leading part in launching and maintaining the new state government. He was a member of the Provincial Congress, 1776, and of the Council of Safety, 1777–78, attorney-general 1777–87, and a member of the first legislative assembly, elected in 1777, wherein, according to Chancellor Kent, he "drafted much of the legislation passed by that body and was the most confidential and efficient adviser of the elder Clinton." He was active in the political development of the American union, being a delegate to the Congress of the Confederation, 1781–84, and serving on commissions for managing the embarkation of Loyalists for Nova Scotia, for adjusting boundary disputes betwen the states, and for promoting the power of the union government. With Hamilton, he was a delegate from New York to the Annapolis Convention in 1786, and was a zealous advocate of the adoption by his state of the draft from the Philadelphia Convention. As a representative from New York in the first two Congresses under the Constitution, he was a strong and conspicuous supporter of the Administration, being especially identified with Hamilton's measures for the public credit, and with the framing of the fundamental statutes organizing the Executive Department. In 1794 he was appointed a justice of the supreme court of New York, and is described by Chancellor Kent as having in his seven years' tenure of that position done more to reform the practise of that court than was ever done before or since. His service here was terminated in 1801 by the "midnight appointment" from President Adams as chief judge of the second United States circuit court. Owing to the repeal shortly thereafter of the law establishing this court, Benson retired from public life, except for a service of a few months in 1813 as representative from New York in the United States Congress. His reputation for legal learning was second only to that of Hamilton. He received the degree of Doctor of Laws from Union, 1779, from Harvard, 1808, and from Dartmouth, 1811. He was a regent of the University of the State of New York, 1787–1802, and a trustee of Columbia College, 1804–15. He was one of the founders of the New York Historical Society in 1804, and was its first president from 1805 to 1815. He never married. In his later years he lived at Jamaica, N. Y., where he died. He was the author of *Cases and Queries Submitted to Every Citizen of the United States* (1809), *A Vindication of the Captors of Major André* (1817), and *A Memoir on Dutch Names and Places* (published posthumously, 1835).

[Jas. G. Wilson, *Memorial Hist. of N.Y. City* (1892); B. F. Thompson, *Hist. of Long Island, N. Y.* (1918), IV, 249 ff.; *Memoirs and Letters of Jas. Kent* (1898), pp. 20–23.]
                                                      C.W.S.

BENSON, EUGENE (Nov. 1, 1839–Feb. 28, 1908), painter, was born at Hyde Park, N. Y., the youngest son of Benjamin P. Benson. When he began his study of art he was poor, but increased his small income by contributing to several New York dailies and to various periodicals, signing the name "Proteus" to his articles in the New York *Evening Post.* In 1856 he was studying at the National Academy of Design, at the same time taking up portrait work in the studio of J. H. Wright. He moved to New Haven in 1869 and remained four years, residing near East Rock. In 1873 he went abroad to study in France and Italy. He established a studio in Florence, spent a number of years in Rome, and moved to Venice in 1888, where he continued to live until his death. His paintings were chiefly of story-telling and symbolic subjects, though his portraits were successful. His modeling and color were effective. He exhibited frequently at the Royal Academy in London, and at the National Academy in New York, of which he was elected an associate in 1862. He contributed to the Centennial Exposition at Philadelphia in 1876, to the Paris Exposition in 1878 and to the Mechanic's Fair in Boston. His "Strayed Maskers" at the Royal Academy in 1873, his "Bazaar at Cairo," exhibited in the National Academy, and his "Slaves Tower" were especially noted at the time of their exhibition, and were afterward purchased by private collectors. He was the author of two books—*Gaspara Stampa, the Story of Her Life* (1881) and *Art and Nature in Italy* (1882). He married Mrs. Henriette (Malan) Fletcher, a daughter of Dr. César Henri Malan of Geneva, Switzerland. Her daughter was Julia Constance Fletcher, the novelist, author of *Kismet*.

[Clara E. Clement and Laurence Hutton, *Artists of the 19th Cent.* (1916); H. W. French, *Art and Artists in Conn.* (1879); E. Benezit, *Dictionnaire Critique et Documentaire des Peintres et Sculpteurs*, vol. I (Paris, 1911); obituary in *Il Secolo, Gazzetta di Milano*, Mar. 11, 1908.]   H.W.

BENT, CHARLES (Nov. 11, 1799–Jan. 19, 1847), the eldest of four brothers whose activities fill a large space in the annals of the Colorado-New Mexico frontier, was born at Charleston, Va. (now W. Va.). His father was Silas and his mother Martha (Kerr) Bent. In 1788 the family moved to western Virginia, where Silas became a judge of the court of common pleas, and in 1805 to Marietta, Ohio. Appointed principal deputy surveyor of the new Territory of Louisiana, Silas moved with his family to St. Louis, arriving there Sept. 17, 1806. Both Charles and his brother William [q.v.], ten years his junior, became interested in the fur trade, and it is probable that both of them were in the Sioux country, as employees of the American Fur Company, as early as 1823. In the following year the brothers, with Ceran St. Vrain, who for many years was to be their associate, visited the upper Arkansas on a fur-trapping expedition and built a stockade in the vicinity of the present Pueblo. Charles was probably a member of the expedition, led by St. Vrain, which in June or July 1826 visited Santa Fé and trapped the New Mexican streams. In 1828 the three associates, now organized as Bent & St. Vrain, began the building of what was to become the most famous of the old trading posts, Bent's Fort, at a point on the Arkansas near the present La Junta. In 1829 and again in 1832 and 1833 Charles captained a trading caravan to Santa Fé from the American settlements.

The fort was completed in 1832, and thereafter Charles and St. Vrain made their permanent homes in New Mexico and gave most of their time to the New Mexican business of the company, leaving to William and to the two younger brothers, George (1814–46) and Robert (1816–41), the management of the fort. In 1835, at San Fernando de Taos, Charles married Maria Ignacia Jaramillo (whose younger sister, Josefa, subsequently married Kit Carson) and fixed his residence there. Gen. Kearny, after his bloodless conquest of New Mexico, appointed Charles civil governor (Sept. 22, 1846) and left for California. The departure of the troops gave occasion for an attempt by Mexicans and Indians in certain localities to overthrow the American rule. In the uprising at Taos, Jan. 19, 1847, Charles and several others were killed. He was everywhere loved and admired for his sterling character, and the tragedy of his death was deeply felt throughout the frontier. Kit Carson, linking his name with that of St. Vrain, in a statement dictated in 1857, regretted that he could not pay an adequate tribute to them for their kindness. "I can say only," he continued, "that their equals were never in the mountains."

[Sources: Geo. B. Grinnell, "Bent's Old Fort and Its Builders," *Kansas State Hist. Soc. Colls.*, vol. XV (1923); Blanche C. Grant (ed.), *Kit Carson's Own Story of His Life* (Taos, 1926); Edwin L. Sabin, *Kit Carson Days* (1914); Stella M. Drumm (ed.), *Down the Santa Fe Trail and into Mexico*, the Diary of Susan Shelby Magoffin, 1846–47 (1926); Allen H. Bent, *The Bent Family in America* (1900).]   W.J.G.

BENT, JOSIAH (Apr. 26, 1771–Apr. 26, 1836), manufacturer, was born at Milton, Mass., the son of John (1746–1817) and Hannah (Coller) Bent (1746–1816). The father, a Revolutionary soldier, had been among those who responded to the Lexington alarm and had taken part in the siege of Boston. Josiah, the eldest of eight children, was a Milton farmer until the age of thirty, but like many Yankees of his generation was little interested in agriculture and sought to escape into manufacturing. His name is associated with the manufacture of water-crackers which appear to have been "made first in this country" by him (A. K. Teele, *History of Milton*). Beginning with the Dutch oven of his own home in 1801 and peddling the crackers himself, he continued with a constantly increasing output until he retired in 1830. These crackers, made simply of flour and water, without salt or shortening, and baked in Dutch ovens by the heat of hard wood fagots, became almost a household necessity in New England and attained an international reputation. Almost a century later they were still made by hand, and by essentially the same process. Concerning the founder of the industry little is known. He was evidently a man of persistence, energy, and ability. While his neighbor manufacturers were turning to textile manufacturing he continued to bake crackers. After his retirement in 1830 he served as representative in the state legislature for one term, 1832–33. He married, Mar. 28, 1794, Susanna (1776–1857), daughter of Samuel Tucker, Jr., of Milton, by whom he had eight children.

[A. H. Bent, *The Bent Family in America* (1900), pp. 105–06; W. R. Cutter, ed., *New Eng. Families: Geneal. and Memorial* (1913), II, 845; A. K. Teele, ed., *Hist. of Milton, Mass., 1640 to 1887* (1887), 386–87.]

H.U.F.

BENT, SILAS (Oct. 10, 1820–Aug. 26, 1887), naval officer, oceanographer, was born in South St. Louis, the eleventh child of Judge Silas Bent and Martha (Kerr) Bent, and brother of Charles and William Bent [*q.q.v.*]. Appointed a midshipman in the navy at the age of sixteen, he spent the following twenty-five years in that service, rising to the grade of lieutenant. During these years he served in various waters and became familiar with the oceanography of the seven seas, rounding Cape Horn four times and the Cape of Good Hope once, and crossing the Atlantic five times and the Pacific twice. In 1849 he was with Commander James Glynn when the latter sailed the U. S. Brig *Preble* into the harbor of Nagasaki and in the face of hostile demonstrations demanded and succeeded in securing the release of eighteen American sailors who had been shipwrecked and had been imprisoned by the Japanese authorities. As flag lieutenant aboard the *Mississippi,* which carried Commodore Matthew C. Perry on his well-known Japan Expedition, between the years 1852 and 1854 he made hydrographic surveys in Japanese waters, the results being incorporated in a publication issued by the government entitled *Sailing Directions and Nautical Remarks: by Officers of the Late U. S. Naval Expedition to Japan* (1857). In connection with these oceanographic labors he carried out a study of the great Pacific current known as the Kuro Siwo, which was printed in Perry's official report of the Japan Expedition ("Report on the Kuro-Siwo or Gulf Stream of the North Pacific Ocean" by Lieut. Silas Bent, in Narrative of the Expedition of an American Squadron to the China Seas and Japan, 1856, *House Executive Document 97,* 33 Cong., 2 Sess.).

In 1860 Bent was detailed to the Hydrographic Division of the Coast Survey, but on Apr. 25 of the following year he resigned his commission because "his sympathies were with his native state" (Allen H. Bent, *The Bent Family,* 1900, p. 129). In 1857 he had married Ann Eliza Tyler of Louisville, Ky., and on resigning his commission he returned to St. Louis and assumed the management of the Tyler estate. Oceanography still claimed his interest, as evidenced by an address before the St. Louis Historical Society in

1868 on "The Thermometric Gateways to the Pole" which was printed in St. Louis the following year. In this and in a later publication (1872) he maintained that the Gulf Stream from the Atlantic and the Kuro Siwo from the Pacific maintained an open sea about the North Pole. At this time considerable interest in North Polar exploration was manifested both in Europe and in America and while Bent's conclusions with regard to an open Polar Sea were not accepted by the leading authorities, his thesis encouraged discussion of the problems of polar exploration. He died on Aug. 26, 1887, at Shelter Island, L. I., and was buried in Louisville, Ky.

[Allen H. Bent, *The Bent Family* (1900), pp. 128–29, which contains also an excellent photograph; Silas Bent, *Gateways to the Pole* (1872); the official records of the Navy Dept.]

H.A.M.

BENT, WILLIAM (May 23, 1809–May 19, 1869), the son of Silas and Martha (Kerr) Bent and brother of Charles Bent [*q.v.*], was born in St. Louis. In his fifteenth year he appears to have been with a trapping expedition on the upper Missouri. From 1824, when with his brother and Ceran St. Vrain he trapped the upper Arkansas, the Colorado frontier was his home. Though the planning of Bent's Fort was predominantly the work of Charles, its building (1828–32) was mainly under his own direction. Owing to the long absences of the other partners he had most to do, moreover, with its management, and it was often, in his honor, called Fort William. He was the general director of the company, the vast business of which included the gathering of robes and peltries, the trading of goods to the Indians, the raising of horses and mules, and often the transportation of government supplies. He became the sole owner by the retirement of St. Vrain at about the end of 1848. By this time, however, the fort had become associated in his mind with many distressing memories. The death of his brothers—Robert, who was killed by the Comanches in 1841; George, who died of consumption in 1846, and Charles, who was killed in the Taos uprising in 1847—with the death in the same year of his wife, Owl Woman, a Cheyenne, whom he had married in 1835 and who had borne him four children—preyed upon his mind and decided him to remove to other scenes. He offered to sell the fort to the government, but in the negotiations that followed the price offered was so low that he indignantly rejected it. He thereupon (summer of 1849) packed up all his possessions, and after his new wife—Yellow Woman, the sister of Owl Woman—his children, his employees, and his stock had all been safely removed, he blew up the structure with gunpowder.

Thirty-eight miles downstream he built a new trading post. In 1859 he leased it to the government, whereupon it became the first Fort Lyon. In the same year he built a stockade at the mouth of the Purgatoire (Las Animas), took up land and began ranching, though serving also for the year as an Indian agent. After the death of Yellow Woman, he married at Westport, in 1867, Adalina, the daughter of Alexander Harvey and a Blackfoot woman, and returned with her to the Purgatoire. To the neighborhood, beginning with the fall of 1867, other settlers came, Kit Carson among them (for the last few months of his life), and the town of Boggsville, named for a nephew of Bent's, was born. Here, in the frequent company of men whom he had known for many years, he spent his last days. According to Sabin (*Kit Carson Days,* 1914, p. 635) he died at the home of Judge R. M. Moore, his son-in-law.

William Bent—he was usually "Col." Bent after August 1846, when he guided Kearny's column from the fort to Santa Fé—was the first permanent white settler in Colorado and in later days came to be regarded as its most prominent citizen. Perhaps no frontiersman of the trans-Mississippi West was more widely known. His reputation for probity and fair dealing equaled that of his two partners and could hardly have been greater. The tributes of respect paid to these three men have generally not discriminated among them: what has been given to one has been given to all. Yet it seems likely that William was regarded as the special friend and helper of the trapper and hunter, and it is certain that he held the confidence of the Indians to a degree unshared by any other trader.

[See bibliography following sketch of Charles Bent.]

W.J.G.

BENTLEY, WILLIAM (June 22, 1759–Dec. 29, 1819), Unitarian clergyman, author, was born in Boston, Mass., the son of Joshua and Elizabeth (Paine) Bentley. Through the generosity of his maternal grandfather he was educated at Harvard, graduating in 1777. After graduation he taught school for three years, and then returned to the college as a tutor in Latin and Greek, holding this position until his ordination over the East Church at Salem in September 1783. Here he remained until his death thirty-six years later. He was never married. Distinctly a liberal in theology and politics, he became a pioneer in Unitarianism, at a time when New England was still Calvinistic. While the educated clergy were almost wholly Federalist he was a Jeffersonian Republican. His church was a notable center of liberalism, to be attributed both to the leadership of its pastor and to the presence in its membership of many merchants and shipmasters, freed from New England parochialism by the broadening influence of foreign commerce and travel. Bentley was naturally in a somewhat isolated position, and this, combined with personal limitations, prevented his exercising a greater influence on the thought of the day. He was, however, an important factor in New England affairs, not only in the pulpit but through his regular contributions to the *Salem Register,* which entitle him to a recognized place in the history of American journalism. He delivered occasional public addresses and anniversary orations, the style of which appears somewhat turgid and bombastic to a later age. He was an active worker in Freemasonry. He also conducted an extensive correspondence with scientists, writers, and men of affairs in both Europe and America. In his insatiable fondness for books, in his interest in all kinds of natural phenomena and scientific experimentation, and in his taste for philosophical discussion, he had qualities in common with Thomas Jefferson, with whom he regularly corresponded, and who unsuccessfully tried to lure him from New England with an offer of the presidency of the projected University of Virginia. Bentley was one of the few great linguists in America, speaking fluently the chief languages of Europe, and having a reading knowledge of many others, including Arabic and Persian. He was a member of the Massachusetts Historical Society, and began a history of Salem, part of which was published in its collections. The historical and natural curiosities which he collected he afterward bequeathed to the American Antiquarian Society and other institutions. His library, remarkable considering his scanty resources, was left to Allegheny College, Meadville, Pa.

Bentley will, however, be longest remembered through his voluminous diary covering the period from Apr. 30, 1784, to Dec. 29, 1819, which, after lying in the custody of the American Antiquarian Society for many years, was finally published by the Essex Institute, 1905–14. The four bulky volumes with their accumulation of parish gossip, shipping news, vital statistics, and petty miscellany, are a joy to the local antiquarian and genealogist. Scattered through the mass of trivialities there is real history, and in the aggregate the diary constitutes a unique and invaluable picture of a New England seaport in the formative years of the new republic. It also reveals the sturdy qualities of mind and character, the manifold interests, and the numerous eccentricities of the author.

[The *Diary of William Bentley,* vol. I, contains a sketch by Jos. D. Waters, originally written in 1868, a list of Bentley's MSS. and miscellaneous papers in possession of the Am. Antiquarian Soc., and a bibliography. The essay on "Ecclesiastical Origins of Unitarianism in Salem," included in *Social Equilibriums and Other Problems Ethical and Religious* (1887), by Geo. Batchelor, discusses Bentley's influence. J. T. Buckingham in *Specimens of Newspaper Literature: with Personal Memoirs, Anecdotes and Reminiscences* (1850), II, 341–50, has an excellent sketch.]
W.A.R.

BENTON, ALLEN RICHARDSON (Oct. 1, 1822–Jan. 1, 1914), college president, was born in Ira, Cayuga County, N. Y., and was the son of Allen Benton of the vicinity of Albany. His mother was Deborah Willey of East Haddam, Conn. His early training was on the farm. He had his primary education in the common schools of his home; his secondary at Elbridge Academy in Onondaga County and Fulton Academy in Oswego County; his collegiate at Bethany College, Va., graduating in 1847. He taught five terms in the common schools of his home community and after graduating opened a private school in Cincinnati. While on a visit to Rush County, Ind., in 1848, he met Elder Henry R. Pritchard of the Christian Church, through whom he was appointed principal of Fairview Academy (*History of Rush County,* 1888, p. 814). After serving as principal here for six years he was called to Indianapolis in 1855 where he conducted a select school for a few months while rooms were being prepared for the opening of the Northwestern Christian University (*Indianapolis Daily Journal,* July 25, Nov. 2, 1855). He taught here from 1855 till 1861 as professor of ancient languages. In the latter year he became president of the institution, serving till 1868, continuing also to teach the ancient languages. From 1868 to 1871 he taught Latin in Alliance College, Ohio, being president the last two years. In 1871 he was called to Lincoln to organize the new University of Nebraska. After serving five years as chancellor of the University he returned in 1876 to North Western Christian (since 1877, Butler) University as professor of philosophy and Biblical literature. In 1886 he again became president of Butler, serving till 1891, after which he resumed his professorship till 1900. At the death of his wife in 1900 he withdrew from active teaching and engaged in church work. In 1909 he went to Lincoln, Nebr., and made his home with his daughter, Mrs. J. S. Dales, until his death. His life and influence were positive but quiet. Although his life had been spent in the service of

the classical tradition, he did not seriously oppose the elective system which encroached upon it. Personally Benton would have passed among strangers as a prosperous business man, or a lawyer. He preached and taught and smoked his pipe with equal ease and dignity. There seem to have been no rough corners to his character, and no sharp turns in his life. He wrote nothing for publication, took no prominent part in politics, and belonged to no organization other than the Christian Church. He was married in 1851 to Silence Howard of Oswego, N. Y., a cousin of W. C. Bryant.

[*Butler Alumni Quart.,* vol. III; *Pictorial and Biog. Memoirs of Indianapolis* (1893), p. 91; *Indianapolis News,* Jan. 2, 1914; *Indianapolis Star,* May 6, 1906, Jan. 2, 1914; *Indiana School Jour.,* 1856–1900, *passim.*]
L.E.

BENTON, JAMES GILCHRIST (Sept. 15, 1820–Aug. 23, 1881), ordnance expert, was born in Lebanon, N. H., the son of Calvin and Mary (Gilchrist) Benton. His father was postmaster of Lebanon for many years, a wool merchant, and the first to introduce merino sheep into New England. Benton graduated from the United States Military Academy at West Point, July 1, 1842, was promoted to brevet second lieutenant in the Ordnance Corps, and assigned to Watervliet Arsenal, Troy, N. Y. He was promoted to second lieutenant, Mar. 3, 1847. The following year he was promoted to first lieutenant and assigned to duty in the Ordnance Office at Washington, and assisted in the preparation of *A System of Artillery for the Land Service* and the *Ordnance Manual.* From 1849 to 1857 he served at various arsenals and at Washington, where he was engaged in making experiments to determine the model of a new rifled musket to replace the smooth-bore then in use, and from 1857 to 1861 he was an instructor in ordnance and gunnery at the United States Military Academy. While there he published *A Course of Instruction in Ordnance and Gunnery, for the Use of Cadets at the United States Military Academy,* and he also designed for the Seacoast Service a wrought-iron gun-carriage that was adopted by the government. He was promoted captain, July 1, 1856, after fourteen years' continuous service. He was assigned, Apr. 28, 1861, to duty as principal assistant to the Chief of Ordnance, and retained this position until Sept. 15, 1863, when he was promoted to major, and assigned to the command of the Washington Arsenal, where he remained until June 1866. Soon after he assumed command, an explosion took place in one of the storerooms. He entered the building, and, with the assistance of a single man, extinguished the flames. In July 1864, on the occasion of another explosion, he entered a magazine, stripped off his coat, threw it over an open barrel of powder that was dangerously close to the flames, and carried the barrel in his arms to a place of safety. He was assigned to the command of the National Armory at Springfield, Mass., in 1866, where he remained until his death. The various improvements in the Springfield rifle, in the models known as the 1866, 1868, 1873, and 1879, were made under his direction and were largely due to his inventive skill. Among his inventions were the electro-ballistic machine or "chronograph" for determining the velocity of projectiles, an improved caliper for inspecting shells, a velocimeter, a spring-dynamometer, a cap-filling machine, a reinforcing cap for cartridge cases, and the electro-ballistic pendulum. He also devised a system for loading and maneuvering barbette guns under cover from the enemy's fire, by depressing the muzzle of the piece and using a jointed rammer. He never took out a patent on his inventions, holding that the government that had educated him was entitled to benefit in every way by his time and talents. He was brevetted lieutenant-colonel and colonel, Mar. 13, 1865, for "faithful and meritorious services in the Ordnance Department" during the Civil War. He received his promotion to lieutenant-colonel, June 23, 1874, and to colonel, May 29, 1875.

Benton served on many special details, among which were the boards on ordnance; on seacoast rifles, cannon, carriages, projectiles, etc.; to examine ordnance officers for promotion; to consider the Protocol of the International Military Commission relative to the use of certain projectiles in war; on superintending the arming of certain seacoast fortifications; to determine the proper caliber of small arms; on the manufacture of Rodman's 15-inch guns; to examine ordnance and ordnance stores in various countries in Europe; on army revolvers; on selection of a magazine gun for the United States Service. He was married, Aug. 17, 1859, to Catherine L., daughter of Gen. J. Watson Webb. Benton was a man of dignified deportment, frank, genial, of unassuming manners, kind, and sympathetic.

[G. W. Cullum, *Biog. Reg.* (3rd ed., 1891); *Reports of the Chief of Ordnance, U. S. Army*; records in the Adjutant-General's Office, Washington, D. C.; obituary by Gen. Benét in *Army and Navy Jour.*, Aug. 27, 1881; obituary in *Springfield* (Mass.) *Republican*, Aug. 24, 1881.]

C.F.C.

BENTON, JOEL (May 29, 1832–Sept. 15, 1911), journalist, poet, was the son of Simeon Blackman and Deborah (Hallock) Benton. Almost all of his ancestors were members of a group which emigrated from England in 1639, and after landing at New Haven settled the town of Guilford, Conn. The Bentons lived in Guilford for five generations; in 1794 Caleb Benton, Jr., with his family, moved to Amenia, N. Y. Here Joel, great-grandson of Caleb, was born, and was educated in the local Amenia Seminary. On leaving school at the age of nineteen he was placed in charge of the weekly *Amenia Times,* which started publication in that year, and is still published under the name of the *Harlem Valley Times.* In 1856 he laid down his irksome editorial duties, and spent the next fifteen years in farming and miscellaneous literary work, including some lecturing. He acted as principal of the Academy, was town supervisor and a delegate to Democratic conventions; as candidate for the state Assembly he was defeated. He took special satisfaction in the conduct of a notable lyceum course, in which he enrolled the leading lecturers of the day. He was a natural hero-worshipper, and his happiest hours were spent in association with his literary acquaintances. His admiration for Horace Greeley led him back in 1872 to the editor's chair, in support of Greeley's presidential campaign; he was also in constant demand as a speaker at rallies. His father's death in 1883 left him burdened with debt, which he strove manfully to pay off. He spent two years in Minnesota, where he wrote for papers in Chicago and St. Paul. Returning east in 1885, he made his home for the rest of his life in Poughkeepsie as a professional writer. He died in the Vassar Brothers Hospital at Poughkeepsie, and was buried in the Poughkeepsie Cemetery.

Launched on a journalistic career at an early age, Benton always wrote with ease. His work is marked by keen observation, a pleasant humor, and a gift of phrase; his style is allusive, and tends to be over-literary. His spirit—except in political discussion, when he could be caustic—was gentle, and he was at his best in writing of out-of-door life or of the great men whom he had known. His verse is pleasing and expressive of his love for nature, but it is on the whole conventional and lacking in power. He was apparently susceptible to feminine charm, but he never married, and his poetry is marked by sentiment rather than emotion. His life and his work belonged to the Hudson River School, but he was always in a backwater, a local rather than a national figure. In addition to magazine articles and much verse, some of which has been included in the anthologies, he published the following books: *Emerson as a Poet* (1883); *The Truth about Protection* (1892); *Greeley on Lincoln* (1893); *In the Poe Circle* (1899); *Life of*

P. T. Barnum (1902); *Persons and Places* (1905); *Memories of the Twilight Club* (1909). He also edited the volume entitled *Amenia Seminary Reunion* (1907). He was a man of medium height, with luxuriant black hair and beard and expressive black eyes; he had a natural distinction of carriage and was fastidious in dress. In his later years he cultivated a resemblance to the poet Tennyson, in which he took great satisfaction.

[*Daily Eagle* (Poughkeepsie), Sept. 16, 1911; Chas. E. Benton, *Caleb Benton and Sarah Bishop, Their Ancestors and Descendants* (1906); Chas. E. Benton, *Troutbeck, a Dutchess County Homestead* (1916); letters from Chas. E. Benton, Rochester, N. Y., Joel E. Spingarn, Amenia, N. Y., and A. S. Frissell, New York City.]   F.H.C.

BENTON, JOSIAH HENRY (Aug. 4, 1843–Feb. 6, 1917), lawyer, a descendant of Andrew Benton who came from England about 1630 and settled in Milford, Conn., was the son of Josiah Henry and Martha (Danforth) Benton. He was born in Addison, Vt., and was educated in the common schools and at Bradford (Vt.) Academy, and at the New London (N. H.) Literary and Scientific Institute. When nineteen he became a private in Company H of the 12th Vermont Volunteers, serving from August 1862 to July 1863 in the Civil War. He graduated from the Albany Law School in 1866, and was admitted to the New Hampshire bar on May 5 of the same year. On May 19, 1866, he married Josephine Emery Aldrich, who died on Apr. 8, 1872, and on Sept. 2, 1875, he married Mary Elizabeth Abbott. From 1866 to 1872 he carried on a successful law practise in Lancaster, N. H. He was assistant clerk of the New Hampshire House of Representatives in 1868, and clerk of that body in 1870 and 1872; in 1869 he was private secretary to the governor of New Hampshire.

He settled in Boston in 1872, and was actively identified from that time with the development of the city. He served as counsel for the Old Colony Railroad and allied companies (1878), until the lease of those properties to the New York, New Haven & Hartford Railroad Company (1893), when he became the Massachusetts counsel for that corporation. In 1879 he became a director of the Northern Railroad of New Hampshire. He lectured on corporations and railroad law at the Law School of Boston University for twenty years. In 1894 he became a member of the board of trustees of the Boston Public Library, giving conspicuous service as president of the board during the last nine years of his life. From 1909 to 1913 he was chairman of the board of trustees of the Massachusetts

State Library. From 1910 to 1917 he was a trustee of Boston University. Throughout his life he collected editions of the English Prayer Book and related material to show its origin and growth. At his death this unique and valuable collection of six hundred and twenty-one items was bequeathed to the Boston Public Library. Besides numerous pamphlets Benton was the author of *Samuel Slade Benton; His Ancestors and Descendants* (1901); *The Story of the Old Boston Town House, 1658–1711* (1908); *Voting in the Field; a Forgotten Chapter of the Civil War* (1915).

[*Sixty-sixth Ann. Report Trustees Boston Pub. Lib.,* 1917–18, pp. 2–7; unpublished notes for an autobiographical sketch; *Boston Transcript, Post, Jour., Globe, Herald,* Feb. 7, 1917; *New Eng. Hist. and Geneal. Reg., Supplement to Apr. 1918.*]   C.F.D.B.

BENTON, THOMAS HART (Mar. 14, 1782–Apr. 10, 1858), statesman, was born at Hillsboro, N. C. He was the son of Jesse Benton, a Loyalist, who had been secretary to Gov. Tryon, and of Ann (Gooch) Benton, of excellent Virginia stock. Upon the death of his father, Thomas became at the age of eight the head of the family. After some preliminary study with a friend of his father, a short term in grammar school, and a partial course at the University of North Carolina, he undertook the supervision of the "Widow Benton's Settlement," a farm of 3,000 acres with a claim to some 40,000 acres near Nashville, Tenn. He was in 1809 a state senator in Tennessee, and took much interest in land tenure, and the rights of slaves in capital trials. He was admitted to the bar in 1811. Five of his seven brothers and sisters succumbed to tuberculosis, and Benton himself was in the incipient stages when the régime of camp life in the War of 1812 rebuilt his vigor, though all his life undue exertion of his throat would induce a hemorrhage. Benton at this time won the permanent friendship of Sam Houston, and the temporary enmity of Andrew Jackson. The trouble with the latter grew out of a tavern brawl in which Thomas supported his brother Jesse in a mêlée of knives, pistols, and clubs. Jackson long carried a bullet fired by Jesse or perhaps by Thomas. Notwithstanding his excellent prospects in Tennessee at the close of the war, Benton removed in 1815 to St. Louis, where, as editor of the *Missouri Enquirer* and in the enjoyment of a lucrative law practise, he speedily identified himself with his adopted state. The most regrettable incident of his career occurred on Sept. 27, 1817, when, in the second of two duels with Charles Lucas, a young United States district attorney, he shot down and killed his opponent. The record in the case is not favorable to Benton who, contrary to the wishes of the seconds and in violation of the accepted duelling code, after he had already wounded his antagonist, by whom he had been challenged, in turn forced a later meeting in which, as the inferior marksman, Lucas was almost certain to be killed (see *Switzler's Illustrated History of Missouri,* 1879, pp. 481–86).

Nominated by the son of Daniel Boone, and with the support of David Barton, his co-senator, Benton was first elected to the United States Senate in 1820, and took his seat in 1821. Also at this time he married Elizabeth McDowell, of a prominent Virginia family. In the Senate he became involved almost immediately in his life-long legislative interest, the defense of sound money. He favored settlers and discouraged land speculators. He deplored the sacrifice of Texas in 1819, and lauded to an uncomprehending public the significance of Oregon. He brought salt within the reach of western farmers, and in the interest of Missourians, defended a tariff upon lead. He promoted the navigation of the Mississippi, and advocated a national highway to New Mexico. In the election of 1824, Benton originally favored Henry Clay. He afterward opposed John Quincy Adams, though he did not believe in the "corrupt bargain" with Clay. Long estranged from Jackson, he now renewed his friendship with him. In the debate on the Panama Congress, he held that the Monroe Doctrine applied solely to the defense of our own territories. In the duel between Clay and Randolph growing out of the Panama debate, he acted as a friend of both parties, though more attached to Randolph. Meanwhile he was working steadily for Jackson in the approaching campaign of 1828. Success achieved, he became the administration spokesman in the Senate. His views on slavery now materially changed. While in 1820 he had opposed all slavery restriction in Missouri, by 1828 he had come to favor gradual abolition. Slavery was apparently hindering settlement—which to a westerner and expansionist was a serious indictment. Even when a discussion on Foot's resolution restricting land sales widened into the celebrated Webster-Hayne debate, Benton did not immediately perceive the issue between Union and Disunion. To defeat the Foot Resolution, he attacked the Webster speech in words he afterward regretted. Convinced at last of Calhoun's secession plans, he henceforth fought for Jackson and the Union. On the rejection by the Senate of Van Buren's nomination as minister to England, Benton actively championed the former secretary, and urged him to stand for nomination as vice-president on the

Jackson ticket in 1832. In the nullification crisis, he favored a repeal of the offensive tariffs of 1828 and 1832, but disliked the compromise tariff of 1833, desiring to keep the issue more clear-cut between nullification and submission.

Benton was the Senate floor leader in the war upon the National Bank. Always a "hard money" man, he favored a gold and silver coinage, but no bank of issue with its paper currency. In February 1831 he introduced a resolution opposing the re-charter five years later of the National Bank. His anti-Bank speeches, then and later, won a popular support which enabled Jackson finally to veto the re-charter. Benton thoroughly indorsed removal of the government deposits, prior even to the expiration of the charter. When hard times followed, he insisted that they were artificially created by the Bank. A resolution of censure against Jackson he capitalized into a contest for expunging. Just before the administration closed, he won his point, Jan. 16, 1837 (Rogers, *Benton,* p. 159). His method of holding his followers together by culinary and bibulous inducements has often been described. Excitement ran so high that it was feared his life was in danger from toughs who were said to have been hired by the Bank. Jackson's debt to Benton was immense, and the influence of the latter was now at its maximum.

In his attack upon the Bank, Benton was destructive; in championing "hard money," he worked creatively. His first move was to change the ratio between gold and silver from 15 to 1, as established by Jefferson, to the more accurate 16 to 1. Gold coins, dubbed "Benton's mint drops," returned to circulation. Further impetus was lent by the "specie circular" of Jackson, stipulating that public lands be paid for in hard money, an action sponsored by Benton and carried through by Jackson against the unanimous opposition of his cabinet. The most constructive financial legislation of that generation grew out of Benton's struggle for "hard money." On this issue the Democratic party divided into "Hards" and "Softs," and Benton was nicknamed in derision "Old Bullion," a name which stuck, and gave him satisfaction. Such profound changes in the financial structure nevertheless hastened the panic of 1837, which Benton attributed to the machinations of the Bank, a malicious explanation unworthy of his better judgment. Meanwhile, the country marched steadily toward a specie basis along the line of Benton's policy (*Ibid.,* 184).

Another economic issue on which Benton held strong views was the distribution of the public lands, a vital concern in the days when the Government was doing a "land office" business. On this question, as on that of the Bank, Benton's position was democratic. He favored reduction in the cash price for land, and advocated the grant of free homesteads of 160 acres based on five years' settlement and improvement. "He was," says Rogers, "the father of the cheap land system," thus anticipating Abraham Lincoln in one respect at least.

As a Democrat, Benton was naturally a Van Buren man in 1840. Again as a Democrat, he instinctively took sides with Tyler in the latter's conflict with the Whigs. But when his ancient enemy, Calhoun, received the State portfolio, and the acquisition of Texas became an avowed policy, Benton was opposed. He seems honestly to have felt that the time for Texan annexation had been in 1819, and that the Spanish treaty of that year sacrificed the interests of the West. But having done so, it was, in Benton's estimation, a fact accomplished, and he viewed the absorption of Texas at this late date as an unwarranted affront to Mexico. In 1845, annexation being finally determined by joint resolution, Benton sought to conciliate Mexico by treating the boundary as still a subject for negotiation. He was angered when Tyler anticipated the Polk Administration by sending a single commissioner to adjust the issue, without regard to varying shades of opinion within the United States.

Benton's attitude toward Oregon, the exploration of which owed much to Frémont, his own son-in-law, paralleled his attitude toward Texas. Always a Westerner, and one of the first to call his countrymen's attention to the territory, when the issue reached a climax he preferred compromise to war. In 1842 he criticized the Webster-Ashburton Treaty for its failure to include a settlement as to Oregon. But in 1844 he had no fondness for the campaign slogan, "54° 40' or fight," and he counseled Polk against adhering to it afterward. The 49th parallel was the boundary he wished, and the boundary secured. Never was Benton more bitterly assailed. His pioneering to arouse opinion, and then refusing to follow that opinion into extremes, seemed utterly inconsistent to the frontier mind, in other words, to Benton's own constituents in Missouri.

Yet when the Texan issue really led to war, Benton not only upheld the Government, but even sought a high command. Polk was willing to name him general, a sort of chief of staff to determine military policy, but Buchanan and other Democrats opposed. Though Benton finally declined a major-generalship, his military ambitions were achieved vicariously through the work of Frémont in taking California previously to the actual declaration of war.

This intellectual detachment of Benton's, curious in a man personally so dynamic, dictated his attitude toward slavery. Here again, as has been noted in connection with his earlier legislative attitudes, Benton was essentially a moderate. As abolitionism gained converts in the North, and as Calhounism threatened secession in the South, Benton's moderate position grew increasingly difficult of maintenance. But moderate he was, and moderate he remained. Extension and agitation he equally opposed; abolitionists he scorned. His cry was peace, peace, when there was no peace. Notwithstanding abolitionists and their wiles, Benton's belief in the essential fairness of the North was confirmed by his success in gaining an extension of Missouri on the northwest by an area equal to Delaware, wrested from free territory without any Northern protest. But whatever good-will Benton may have felt for slavery was entirely subordinate to his loyalty to the Union. In 1847, notwithstanding specific instructions from the Missouri legislature, he refused to uphold the Calhoun Resolutions in the Senate, because he regarded them as subversive of the Union. In the great debates on the Compromise of 1850, he maintained consistently his opposition to what he deemed too generous a concession to secessionists. He desired the admission of California as a free state. He objected to the scheme of Calhoun's followers to divide California by the Missouri Compromise line extended. He believed that secessionists could not be satisfied with any solution short of complete control of the Government, and hence he deemed the Compromise a hollow sham. During the debate, Senator Foote of Mississippi drew a pistol on Benton—the greatest indignity the Senate had ever suffered. Throughout the session Benton found himself in active opposition to his colleague, Atchison.

His opposition to the Compromise was his last important act as senator. In the breach within the Democratic ranks in 1848, caused by the decision of Van Buren to run as an independent against Lewis Cass, the party's nominee, he had avoided taking sides—a fatal error. Henceforth he was a man without a party, and his political career was doomed. When in 1850 he opposed the Compromise, he offended his constituents past all forgiveness. Notwithstanding his championship of essential Western interests, such as the pony express, the telegraph, and the railroad, of which latter Benton was an early and influential spokesman, advocating federal aid by means of land grants for a transcontinental line with its terminus at St. Louis, Missourians could not forgive their senator's defection on the major issue, slavery. In 1850 a Whig senator was chosen from Missouri. Undiscouraged, Benton secured election to the House of Representatives, where he vainly fought the Missouri Compromise repeal. He now lost his seat in Congress, and in 1856 failed of election as governor. Though his political career was over, a test of party allegiance remained in his support in 1856 of Buchanan as against Frémont. Indeed on this as on other issues, Benton displayed remarkable consistency.

To quit the forum he so long had graced was a heavy blow. Indeed, his death from cancer in 1858 was probably hastened by his political dethronement; possibly, also, by the burning of his house and papers while he was in the midst of preparing his memoirs. For in his retirement, Benton composed at top speed, made possible by his remarkable memory, the elaborate *Thirty Years' View* (1854–56), in which he surveyed the whole course of politics as he had seen it intimately from 1820 to 1850—one of the outstanding autobiographies of politics. Side by side with this book, he completed another monumental work, *Abridgement of the Debates of Congress from 1789 to 1856* (1857–61).

[Theodore Roosevelt, *Thos. Hart Benton* (1886); Wm. M. Meigs, *Life of Thos. Hart Benton* (1904); Jos. M. Rogers, *Thos. H. Benton* (1905); sketch by Benton's daughter, Mrs. Frémont, in John C. Frémont, *Memoirs of My Life*, vol. I (1887); Clarence Henry McClure, "Early Opposition to Thos. Hart Benton," *Mo. Hist. Rev.*, X, 151–96.]

L. M. S.

BENTON, THOMAS HART (Sept. 5, 1816– Apr. 10, 1879), educator, was of English-Scotch ancestry, his grandfather being Jesse Benton, who in 1765 came from England to North Carolina as private secretary to William Tryon. Of Jesse's four sons, the eldest, Thomas Hart Benton [*q.v.*], uncle of the subject of this sketch, became a distinguished statesman. Samuel, father of Thomas, Jr., was also a man of more than ordinary ability, well educated for his time, a leader among his fellows, active in the Texas Revolution, and a member of congress in that republic. Young Thomas was born in Williamson County, Tenn. First instructed by his father, he later attended an academy at Huntington, Tenn., and then Marion College in Missouri, attaining proficiency in the classics. He went into the Iowa country in 1837 while it was yet a part of Wisconsin, and settled in Dubuque, a frontier town of 1,200 inhabitants. Here in 1838–39 he conducted what was probably the first classical school in Iowa. On the organization of the State of Iowa, 1846, he was elected to the Senate, serving as chairman of the committee on schools, and securing the legislation upon which has been built the public-school system of the state. In

1848 he was elected to the office of state superintendent of public instruction. He served for two terms, six years, declined reëlection, and entered the banking business in Council Bluffs and Omaha. He married, 1851, Susan Culbertson of Boalsburg, Pa. In 1857 Iowa adopted a new constitution, in which public education was organized under a state board with an executive secretary. To this secretaryship Benton was called in 1858, a position which he filled until 1862, when he was commissioned colonel of the 29th Iowa Infantry. He served throughout the Civil War and was mustered out in 1865 with a brevet title of brigadier-general. He immediately accepted nomination for the governorship of Iowa on a soldiers' platform, opposed to negro suffrage, and though defeated by the Republican candidate, received a large vote. In 1866 he moved to Marshalltown as collector of United States revenue in the sixth congressional district, serving during the administration of President Johnson. For several years after the death of his wife, 1869, he lived in Cedar Rapids, as auditor of a railroad. He died at the home of his sister in St. Louis, Mo., and was buried with Masonic honors at Marshalltown, Ia.

[T. S. Parvin, "Thos. Hart Benton, Jr.," *Ia. Hist. Record*, vol. XVI (1900); Benj. F. Gue, *Hist. of Ia.*, vol. IV (1903); Clarence R. Aurner, *Hist. of Ed. in Ia.*, vols. I, II, III, IV (1914); educational reports of Thos. Hart Benton as superintendent of public instruction in *Jour. of Ia. House and Senate*, 1850–54, and his reports as secretary of state board of education, in *Ia. Legislative Docs.*, 1860–64.]

F. C. E.

BERG, JOSEPH FREDERIC (June 3, 1812– July 20, 1871), Dutch Reformed clergyman, was the son of Rev. Christian Frederic Berg, a native of Jutland, Denmark, and his wife Hannah Robinson Tempest, an Englishwoman, who were Moravian missionaries at Grace Bay on the island of Antigua, B. W. I. He was the first white child born on the island. At the age of four he was placed in a Moravian school at Fulneck, England, and in 1825 he came to the Moravian Academy at Nazareth, Pa., where he studied theology and was licensed to preach at nineteen. On Oct. 2, 1835, he was ordained and installed pastor of the German Reformed Church at Harrisburg, Pa. Two years later he went to the Race Street Church, Philadelphia. After a notable pastorate of fifteen years he withdrew from the German Reformed Church because of his opposition to what he considered the latitudinarian and Romanizing tendencies of the Mercersburg theology, and went to the Second Dutch Reformed Church of Philadelphia, taking a large part of his congregation with him. In June 1861 he was elected to the chair of didactic and polemic theology in the Theological Seminary at New Brunswick, N. J.; he was also professor of the evidences of Christianity in Rutgers College from 1862 to 1867.

He was master of many languages and his general information was encyclopedic. While a student at Nazareth, at the age of seventeen, he taught chemistry. During his Harrisburg pastorate he taught the classics at Mercersburg and declined a permanent professorship there. While at Race Street he obtained the degree of M.D. at the Jefferson Medical College. His preaching was not characterized by display, but he used his learning in a telling manner, with a wealth of well-chosen illustration. He engaged in much controversy with the Roman Catholics, edited an anti-Papal magazine, *The Evangelical Quarterly,* and wrote several books against Rome, such as *Lectures on Romanism* (1840); *Papal Rome* (1841), and *The Inquisition; Church and State; or, Rome's Influence upon the Civil and Religious Institutions of our Country* (1851). He was also a prolific contributor to periodicals and newspapers and wrote a number of story-books for children. His portrait in oil is the property of the Theological Seminary at New Brunswick. On Feb. 4, 1835, he married Eleonora Pomp of Easton, Pa.

[E. T. Corwin, *Manual of the Reformed Ch. in America* (3rd ed., 1879); *Centennial of the Theol. Sem. of the Reformed Ch. in America* (1885); *Reformed Ch. Messenger,* July 26, 1871. The writer is also indebted to Dr. Berg's daughter for much personal information.]

F. T. P.

BERGER, DANIEL (Feb. 14, 1832–Sept. 12, 1920), United Brethren clergyman, was born near Reading, Pa., the son of Daniel and Esther Boda Berger. His great-grandparents on both sides were emigrants from Germany. When Daniel was six years old, his parents, impelled like their ancestors to seek larger freedom and opportunity, sold their property and fell into line with the stream of immigration westward. A four weeks' journey by wagon brought them to Springfield, Ohio, where Daniel's father bought a farm on which was a log cabin. This the family occupied until a more comfortable home could be built. The two sons and daughters attended the district school, the boys spending their summers in hard work upon the farm. At the age of eighteen, Daniel entered the Ohio Methodist Conference high school, where he remained for two years, when he was made assistant principal of an academy at New Carlisle, Ohio. After serving here for three years he was appointed principal of one of the two large district schools in Springfield, and later, principal of the newly established high school. On July 28, 1853, he married Mary Frances Merry, a cousin of Cardinal Merry del Val. Brought up a devout Catholic, she had already become a Protestant, and later wrote a good-tempered booklet, entitled *In and Out of Catholicism.* During the six years Berger had been teaching, he had been preparing himself privately for the ministry, and in 1854 had been licensed by the Miami Conference of the Church of the United Brethren in Christ. He served in the pastorate from 1858 to 1864, at which time he was chosen editor of the *Religious Telescope,* the chief periodical of the United Brethren Church, published at Dayton, Ohio. This office he filled until 1869, when he became editor of the Sunday-school literature of his denomination. His work in this capacity covered a period of twenty-six years, and was marked by careful scholarship and lucid presentation. Beginning with a single children's paper, the publications came to include a complete line of literature for pupils, teachers, and officers. He also served for twelve years as a member of the International Sunday School Lesson Committee. He was a contributor to the *Schaff-Herzog Encyclopædia* and to the American Church History series, and was the author of a *History of the Church of the United Brethren in Christ,* published in 1897.

[Articles in the *Religious Telescope* for Oct. 2, 1920, and A. W. Drury's *Hist. of the United Brethren in Christ* (1924).]

A. W. D.

BERGH, CHRISTIAN (Apr. 30, 1763–June 24, 1843), shipbuilder, the third of his line in America to bear his name, was a son of Christian II, and Catrina (Van Benschoten) Bergh. He was born in Dutchess County, N. Y., near Rhinebeck, where his family had lived since the beginning of the eighteenth century. As a thirteen-year-old lad he experienced some of the harsh realities of civil war; for at the outbreak of the Revolution his father was penalized for Loyalist leanings by confiscation of his farm and homestead. The family took refuge within the British lines at New York City and at the end of the war migrated with thousands of other Loyalists to the Canadian provinces. The Berghs were among those who joined the new settlement at Shelburne, Nova Scotia, a community made up almost entirely of immigrants from the United States and numbering within three years after its founding, in 1783, about 10,000 persons. Fishing and shipbuilding were leading industries in the new town almost from the first and young Bergh, who was nearing his majority, had a good opportunity to master the ship-wright's trade. After a few years, when Shelburne's first prosperity had declined and the Berghs returned to

New York, he opened a shipyard on the East River and began to build merchant vessels. Through the first third of the nineteenth century he continued that industry with marked success. The United States frigate *President,* one of the men-of-war that achieved fame in the War of 1812, was a product of the Bergh yards. When she was badly crippled in a sea fight with four British ships and compelled to surrender, her captors considered her a model of naval architecture and recommended the method of her construction to British shipbuilders (James Barnes, *Naval Actions of the War of 1812,* 1896, p. 227). Bergh's only absence from New York was the period from 1812 to 1815, during which he was engaged in building war vessels for the United States on Lake Ontario. During those years work at the New York yards was suspended, but was resumed after peace, when many packet ships were built there and one war vessel, the *Hellas,* for the Greek government. Until 1837, when Bergh retired, the sailing ships built at his yards were unsurpassed in design or construction and won wide repute. One of his London packets made the Atlantic passage to England in fourteen days and ten hours, leading the *Great Western* (which was under steam) to Cape Clear. The "close rudder" was early a feature of the Bergh ships. Some of the swiftest of pilot boats used in that period were products of the Bergh yards. Bergh was six feet four inches in height and in his latter years was a well-known figure in the Corlears Hook section of New York, where his yards were located. He sometimes presided at political rallies in Tammany Hall. In politics he was a Jackson Democrat; his patriotism was never questioned. Somewhat late in life he married Elizabeth Ivers of Connecticut. He had two sons, one of whom, Henry [*q.v.*], was the founder of the American Society for the Prevention of Cruelty to Animals.

[A brief sketch of Christian Bergh, written by his son, Henry Bergh, *N. Y. Times,* Mar. 18, 1888; "The Berghs of New York," by Rev. Beverley R. Betts, *N. Y. Geneal. and Biog. Record,* XIX, 122; *Concerning the Van Bunschoten or Van Benschoten Family in America,* by Wm. Henry Van Benschoten (1907).]

W. B. S.

BERGH, HENRY (Aug. 29, 1811–Mar. 12, 1888), was America's outstanding pioneer and propagandist in work for the humane treatment of animals. The early history of the anti-cruelty movement in this country is his biography. His father, Christian Bergh [*q.v.*], was a prominent New York shipbuilder. His mother, Elizabeth Ivers, was of old Connecticut stock, with Knickerbocker affiliations. Henry received his formal education in New York City, studying at Colum-

bia College, from which, however, he did not graduate. In his twenty-fifth year he was married to Catherine Matilda Taylor, daughter of a wealthy English architect and builder residing in New York. Shortly after, in 1837, he and his brother Edwin undertook the management of their father's shipyard, which they continued until after the death of Christian Bergh in 1843. Having received a comfortable fortune under his father's will, Bergh and his wife spent the next years traveling in Europe and the East. While in Europe in 1863 he was appointed secretary of legation at St. Petersburg, an office he was obliged to resign in 1864 owing to Mrs. Bergh's inability to endure the severe winter climate of Russia. While in St. Petersburg he became interested in the prevention of cruelty to animals, which was strikingly prevalent. On occasion he intervened in behalf of suffering horses in ways which would have been violently resented but for his official connection. His interest in anti-cruelty work was stimulated through acquaintance with the Earl of Harrowby, president of the Royal Society for the Prevention of Cruelty to Animals. He returned to New York following the Civil War, and after a brief rest began to mature plans for an American organization modeled upon the English one. At the start he met with sneers and rebuffs. He persisted, however, and from time to time interested prominent citizens in his efforts. He lost no opportunity to make a popular appeal, often calling for help from bystanders in cases of cruel treatment of horses on the streets of the city. Many a street sermon was thus preached, and in this way his presence and mission became familiar to a widening circle. On the night of Feb. 8, 1866, he delivered a lecture in Clinton Hall on statistics relating to the cruelties practised on animals, with a view toward founding a society for their prevention. Offers of assistance were freely made to him after the lecture. As a result of ensuing efforts the state legislature, on Apr. 10, 1866, granted a charter of incorporation to the American Society for the Prevention of Cruelty to Animals. This act legalized a body, independent of existing constituted authorities, to enforce local laws for animal protection. Bergh was elected its president, and during the next two decades he gave his energies to the building up of the society and to the extending of statutory provision against a long array of animal abuses. In 1875 he was instrumental with Elbridge T. Gerry and others in forming a Society for the Prevention of Cruelty to Children, thus inaugurating a movement which in its growth has far outstripped its parent. The latter, however, always commanded

Bergh's main interest, and when he died in 1888 he left the animal protective movement a matured and vigorous one. Countless cruelties had been suppressed or minimized, the idea had spread to other cities, states, and countries, and hundreds of auxiliaries had sprung up in all parts of the world.

Bergh's figure was, of course, a very familiar one about the city. His appearance was striking, lending itself easily to caricature. He was tall and spare, but of vigorous muscular development. His face was long and thin, resembling pictures of Don Quixote, with sunken eyes and prominent cheek bones. His attire was always faultlessly neat.

Aside from his activities as an anti-cruelty propagandist, he found time to indulge literary and artistic inclinations. He wrote several plays, as well as a volume of tales and sketches entitled *The Streets of New York*. In middle life he wrote some verses designed to show the folly of scheming mothers with marriageable daughters (*"Married Off," A Satirical Poem*, London, 1860). As literary achievements none of these efforts deserve particular notice. Bergh's fame rests on his work as a friend of dumb beasts.

[The above data were obtained largely from former officials of the American Society for the Prevention of Cruelty to Animals, who knew Bergh during the period of his greatest activity. Extensive obituaries were published in the *N. Y. Herald, N. Y. Times*, and *N. Y. Tribune* of Mar. 13, 1888; the *N. Y. Times* of Mar. 18, 1888, contains J. H. Tooker's reminiscences of Henry and Christian Bergh. See also R. C. McCrea, *The Humane Movement* (1910); "Henry Bergh and His Work," in *Scribner's Mo.*, Apr. 1879; and Clara Morris, "The Riddle of the Nineteenth Century: Mr. Henry Bergh," in *McClure's Mag.*, Mar. 1902. Most accounts give the year of his birth as 1823; the date given above is from Wm. H. Van Benschoten, *Concerning the Van Bunschoten* or *Van Benschoten Family in America* (1907), pp. 669–76.]   R. C. M.

BERGMANN, CARL (Apr. 11, 1821–Aug. 10, 1876), orchestral conductor, was born at Ebersbach in Saxony. His parents later removed to Breslau, where he studied under A. Hesse. Between 1842 and 1848 he was an orchestral leader in Vienna, Budapest, Warsaw, and Venice. Implicated in the Revolution of 1848 he was obliged to leave Germany and in the autumn of 1849 came to New York. There he joined the Germania Orchestra, originally made up of twenty-four German musicians, which had set a new high standard of orchestral playing in this country. Bergmann started in as violoncellist, but soon became conductor. From 1852 to 1854 he conducted the Handel and Haydn Society in Boston, but in the latter year he returned to New York as conductor of the Männergesangverein Arion. In 1858 he became for a year conductor of the New York Philharmonic Society. In 1858-

59 he was again conductor, from 1859 to 1865 alternate conductor with Theodore Eisfeld, and from 1865 to 1876 sole conductor of the Society. In this period he introduced to this country many works by Wagner, Liszt, Rubinstein, Berlioz, Brahms, and other composers of the romantic school. "It was in fact Bergmann . . . who created an interest for the works of those masters. He did not play these works with the intention merely of bringing forward novelties, but from a conviction that he was promoting the new art-aspirations as engendered by our modern art-spirit" (F. L. Ritter, *Music in America*, 1883, p. 350).

In the field of opera Bergmann conducted apparently the first complete performances in German in this country of Beethoven's *Fidelio* (New York, Dec. 29, 1856), and Wagner's *Tannhäuser* (New York, Aug. 27, 1859). He had previously performed the *Tannhäuser* overture, first with the Germania Orchestra on Dec. 3, 1853, and with the Philharmonic Society in April 1855. The *Lohengrin* prelude and *Rienzi* overture had also appeared on Germania Orchestra programmes prior to 1854, doubtless for the first time in this country. In addition to his activity in conducting orchestral concerts and opera, Bergmann conducted the New York Harmonic Society (choral), and its successor the Mendelssohn Union. He was associated as 'cellist with William Mason, Theodore Thomas, and others in chamber music performances in 1855–60. After the death of his wife in 1875 mental depression made him so morose, moody, and at times childish, that he was finally in February 1876 obliged to resign his position with the Philharmonic Society, and a few months later he died. His compositions, few in number and now forgotten, were for orchestra. Theodore Thomas said of him: "Bergmann gave the impression that he never worked much, or cared to do so. He lacked most of the qualities of a first-rank conductor, but he had one great redeeming quality for those days which soon brought him into prominence. He possessed an artistic nature, and was in sympathy with the so-called 'Zukunftmusik'" (George P. Upton, *Theodore Thomas*, 1905, I, 36). According to F. L. Ritter, Bergmann was "at the height of his American career, the most respected and admired musical leader in the country" (*Music in America*, p. 349).

[Cesar Saerchinger, "Musical Landmarks in N. Y.," *Musical Quart.*, Apr. 1920; Wm. Mason, *Memories of a Musical Life* (1901); H. E. Krehbiel, *The Philharmonic Soc. of N. Y.* (1892); *Grove's Dict. of Music and Musicians* (1904), I, 308–09; good obituaries in the *N. Y. Staats-Zeitung*, Aug. 13, 1876; *N. Y. Times*, Aug. 13, 1876; *N. Y. Tribune*, Aug. 14, 1876.]   C. N. B.

BERKELEY, JOHN (d. Mar. 22, 1622), English ironmaster, was the hereditary owner of Beverstone Castle, Gloucestershire. He was married to Mary, daughter of John Snell, Esquire, had ten children, and undoubtedly suffered economic pressure. In 1597 he sold his ancestral castle, possibly to enter the iron industry, for the man recommended in 1621 to erect and conduct ironworks on the Virginia frontier could have been no industrial novice. The Society of Southampton Hundred, holding patents under the Virginia Company of London and obliged by it to employ an anonymous gift of £550 in educating Indian children as Christians, determined to augment the sum and use it in erecting "an ironwork" in Virginia, promising for Indian education the returns *pro rata* on the gift. By 1621, £4,000 was ventured and Capt. Bluett was sent with eighty workmen to Virginia. Bluett died shortly after reaching Jamestown, and the authorities, accepting Berkeley's terms, gave him Bluett's privileges with means to hire twenty additional mechanics and to transport them, himself, his son, and three personal servants from the Isle of Wight before August. Berkeley was appointed to the Virginian Council; he built ironworks on the west side of Falling Creek, south of James River, seven miles below Richmond, and early in 1622 sent word to England that he expected to make iron by Whitsuntide. But when the Londoners voted to meet his expenditures, Berkeley and his workmen lay dead in Virginia surrounded by ruined machinery. On Mar. 22, under crafty Opechancanough the Indians massacred 347 white persons in Virginia. Maurice, John's son, survived, and the company, powerless to provide funds to recreate the works, granted his petition to release him from their service and give him the 800 acres formerly promised him and his father for their service in the ironworks. John Berkeley ended tragically and his work perished with him. But he built for himself a home in men's minds. The Virginia Historical Society preserves slag from his furnace; and though Virginian ironmaking was not rooted until after 1710, Berkeley's furnace constitutes him the first American ironmaster and Virginia the seat of the first iron smelted in America.

[The chief sources of information in America about John Berkeley are *The Berkeley MSS.*, by John Smyth of Nibley, ed. by Sir John Maclean (3 vols., 1883–85), and *The Records of the Va. Co. of London . . . from the MS. in the Lib. of Cong.* (2 vols., 1906), ed. by Susan Myra Kingsbury. Similar information but no new material of significance is in the *Va. Hist. Soc. Colls.*, n. s., vols. VII and VIII (1888–89); Edward D. Neill, *Hist. of the Va. Co. of London* (1869); Alexander Brown, *The First Republic in America* (1898); *Va. Mag. of Hist.*, vols. I–XXXIV (1893–1926); and the *William and Mary Coll. Quart.*, 1st ser., vols. I–XXVII (1892–1919), 2nd ser., vols. I–VI (1921–26). The material in the last two publications does not always tally with that of the two chief sources cited above.]   K. B.

BERKELEY, NORBORNE. [See BOTETOURT, NORBORNE BERKELEY, BARON DE, c. 1718–1770.]

BERKELEY, Sir WILLIAM (1606–July 9, 1677), colonial governor of Virginia, the son of Maurice Berkeley of Bruton, Somerset, and the brother of John, first Lord Berkeley of Stratton, was a member of a celebrated family which during several centuries had enjoyed great influence at the English Court. He matriculated at Queen's College, Oxford, Feb. 14, 1623, and received the degree of B.A. from St. Edmund Hall, July 10, 1624, and that of M.A. from Merton College, July 10, 1629 (Joseph Foster, *Alumni Oxonienses*, 1892, p. 114). While still young, he had a seat in the Privy Chamber; was known at Whitehall as a polished courtier; and in London at large, as a playwright of merit. He was knighted by King Charles I at Berwick, July 27, 1639. His first colonial office was a commissionership of Canadian affairs (*Calendar of State Papers, Colonial Series, America and West Indies, 1574–1660*, 1860, p. 9), but its powers were exercised in England. It was not until 1642 that he went out to Virginia to take over its government; and there he remained, with the exception of a rare visit to England, down to the year 1677. He found the colony on his arrival torn by factions; but he soon quieted these by his unwearied promotion of the best interests of the community. His disinterestedness was illustrated in his offering no objection to the grant to the General Assembly of the right to act as a final court of appeal in Virginia, even from the decisions of the General Court, over which he himself presided. To encourage diversification of crops, he cultivated flax, cotton, and rice, on his own lands. He also experimented with silk production; and, during one year, was able to send 300 pounds of silk to the King as a gift (*Ibid., 1661–68*, 1880, No. 1805, pp. 594–95). He encouraged the manufacture of cloth by using his own looms to provide his family and his slaves with material for garments. He built his own mansion of brick, and urged others to follow his example. He sent a band of explorers to discover the easiest route to the country beyond the mountains; and, on one occasion, was prevented only by heavy rains from leading a large party of gentlemen in person into the wilderness for the same purpose. Naturally bold and resolute, he mustered a small army in 1644, the year of the second great massacre of the whites by the Indians, and, marching at its head to the frontier, completely crushed the savages lurking in the forest, and wrested a peace from them that lasted for a generation. His courageous spirit was even more conspicuously exhibited in the war with the Dutch in 1665. When hostilities began in European waters, he placed the colony in an attitude of defense by strengthening the forts, and arming and drilling every person available for military service. When the Dutch war-vessels arrived off the Virginia capes, they found the merchant ships fully manned, and equipped, and concentrated in a single fleet (*Ibid., 1661–68,* 1880, No. 1193, p. 380). It was not Berkeley's fault that some of these ships were captured. The defense on land, which was under his immediate eye, was so firm that the invasion stopped at the water's edge.

His administration, during its early years, was characterized by only two serious defects: he was relentless in persecuting the Quakers and the Puritans (*Hening's Statutes,* II, Acts of 1661–62), and he showed little appreciation of learning. He actually thanked God that there was neither a printing-press nor a free school in Virginia—a groundless assertion, in the latter case, as there were two excellent free schools in the colony, which still survive. He had always been animated by a spirit of almost preposterous loyalty to the throne. When the Civil War began in England, he expressed himself with violence in opposition to the movement, and influenced the General Assembly to condemn it in language equally embittered (*Ibid.,* I, 335). He encouraged the Cavaliers to come over in large numbers, and gave an asylum to the persecuted clergy of England. The King's execution aroused him to a fury of hatred and resistance. Parliament called upon him to submit to the Commonwealth, but he defiantly refused to do so; and when the Parliamentary fleet arrived in Virginia, it found the colony fully armed to meet it. Surrender took place only after a compromise had been effected (*Calendar of State Papers, Colonial Series, America and West Indies, 1574–1660,* 1860, No. 46, p. 376). The deposed Governor remained quietly on his plantation until the Restoration, when he was promptly put back in office.

From this time, his conduct was not at all consistent with the spirit of his earlier administration. It is true that he protested personally against the damage which the Navigation Act inflicted on the colony; and he also urged the adoption of a temporary cessation of tobacco culture as a means of raising the price of that staple; but he was too much inclined to repeat in Virginia the irregular policies that had been introduced in England under the reactionary influences then prevailing. Thus he established a Long Parliament of his own, which became a mere tool of his will. The former independent vestries and county courts fell under his thumb. So did the Council. And so did the General Court. The people had little share in the administration, even of their local affairs. There were other grave causes for popular discontent, and the whole number combined culminated in the insurrection of 1676. The spark that started this conflagration was an Indian invasion, accompanied as usual by murders and robberies. The leader in the uprising against the Governor was the younger Nathaniel Bacon [*q.v.*] to whom Berkeley had declined to give a commission. Without the commission Bacon marched against the Indians and destroyed their stronghold; but on his return to Jamestown, he was arrested by Berkeley and compelled to submit. While engaged in enlisting troops to carry out a second expedition, he was proclaimed an outlaw; but advancing on Jamestown in force, he compelled Berkeley to give him a commission. Later, Berkeley sought safety in flight across the Bay; but having captured a large vessel in Bacon's possession, he returned to Jamestown, only to be driven out again after a pitched battle. It was not until Bacon's death that Berkeley found a permanent foothold at Jamestown. He then entered upon a course of execution and confiscation too violent to be approved by the English Government, and a commission was sent out to Virginia to report upon the conditions that prevailed there. Berkeley declined to yield his place to his newly appointed successor, and withdrew only when his health had become shattered. He died in England a short time afterward, without having been able to talk with the King. But perhaps little would have been gained had he done so, for Charles is reported to have remarked, "The old fool has killed more people in that naked country than I have done for the murder of my father."

[A full account of the English Berkeley family will be found under the head "Berkeley" in the *Dict. Nat. Biog.* Indices of British Colonial Papers from 1642 to 1677 reveal a long series of reports relating to his administration. Many of these papers have been reprinted in the *Va. Mag. of Hist. and Biog.* and *Wm. and Mary Coll. Quart. Mag.* For the executions and confiscations, see *Hening's Statutes,* II, 547–50. See also John D. Burk's *Hist. of Va.* (1805), II, 250–53, 259–64.]
P. A. B.

BERKENMEYER, WILHELM CHRISTOPH (1686–1751), Lutheran clergyman, was living in Hamburg in May 1724 when the Lutheran Consistorium of Amsterdam inquired whether he would receive ordination and go to New York to succeed the late Justus Falckner as pastor of the Lutherans on Manhattan Island and in its vicinity. At first he demurred; but falling dangerously ill he resolved that if his life were spared he would go. On May 24, 1725, he was ordained at Amsterdam and proceeded to England to take ship for America. Of his earlier life little is known. He had been born at Bodenteich in the then Duchy of Lüneburg, the son of Jürgen Berckenmeyer, and had studied at the University of Altdorf under a Dr. Christoph Sonntag whose principal maxim, *Quo proprior Luthero eo melior Theologus,* Berkenmeyer took with him to New York. Toil and trouble were the customary lot of the colonial Lutheran ministers; in Berkenmeyer's case the trouble began ahead of time while he was still at Cowes in the Isle of Wight. There a letter was forwarded to him from the church council in New York, stating that they had already chosen a "God-fearing and able man" as pastor. Berkenmeyer, however, did not turn back. On his arrival, Sept. 22, 1725, he called together the council, presented his credentials, made a brief speech, and was thereafter master of the situation. The interloper, Dieren (Düren, Dören) by name, was a Pietistically inclined tailor with an uncontrolled impulse to clamber into unoccupied pulpits. He was unordained, uneducated, and theologically so ambidextrous that he could be either Lutheran or Reformed as the situation required. To a man like Berkenmeyer, with his solid learning, staunch orthodoxy, and high conception of the ministerial office, no one could have been more offensive, but he was by no means rid of him. Berkenmeyer had to minister to several congregations in New Jersey, to others scattered along the Hudson Valley as far north as Albany, and even to one or two along the Mohawk. Opportunities for an agile wolf to intrude into the fold were numerous, and Dieren availed himself of them whenever he got a chance. On Oct. 25, 1727, Berkenmeyer married Benigna Sibylla, eldest daughter of the late Josua von Kocherthal. On June 29, 1729, he consecrated a new church, Trinity, in New York. In 1731 he divided his immense parish in two and, leaving the southern half to Michael Christian Knoll, made his home thereafter at Loonenburg, now Athens, N. Y., whence he made regular visits to congregations at other points. On Aug. 20, 1735, at Raritan, N. J., he presided over a special meeting of three clergymen and nine laymen; this meeting has been described, though erroneously, as the first Lutheran synod in America (H. E. Jacobs, *A History of the Evangelical Lutheran Church in the United States,* 1893, pp. 125–26). Until 1743 he was the only

regularly called and ordained Lutheran minister in upper New York. He preached in Dutch, German, and English, and corresponded in Latin with the Swedish clergymen on the Delaware. He was a bitter opponent of Calvinism without and of Pietism within the Lutheran Church. He was consequently openly hostile toward Johann Christoph Hartwig, writing several pamphlets against him as he did against Dieren, and somewhat aloof in his attitude toward Mühlenberg, who called on him in New York once in 1750 and was courteously received. With his own congregations he was popular in spite of a certain gruffness of manner. Like his parishioners he kept negro slaves, but he gave conscientious attention to their spiritual welfare. We last hear of him on Aug. 25, 1751, when he baptized two children, although himself sick unto death. He is buried at Athens, N. Y.; his widow was still living in 1775.

[W. J. Mann, B. M. Schmucker, W. Germann, eds., *Nachrichten von den vereinigten Deutschen Evangelisch-Lutherischen Gemeinden in Nord-America,* Erster Band (Allentown, Pa., 1886), usually cited as the *"Hallesche Nachrichten"*; E. B. O'Callaghan, ed., *Doc. Hist. of N. Y.,* vol. III (1850); *Eccl. Records State of N. Y.,* see index volume (1916); A. L. Gräbner, *Geschichte der Lutherischen Kirche in America* (St. Louis, 1892); for MSS. see Gräbner's "Vorwort."]

G.H.G.

BERKOWITZ, HENRY (Mar. 18, 1857–Feb. 7, 1924), rabbi, son of Louis and Henrietta Berkowitz, was a native of Pittsburgh, Pa. He received his elementary and secondary education in the public schools of that city, graduating from the Central High School in 1872. Then he attended Cornell University for one year. In 1876 he entered the Hebrew Union College of Cincinnati, the theological seminary of liberal Judaism, and at the same time matriculated at the University of Cincinnati. He graduated from the latter institution with the degree of B.A. in 1881 and was a member of the first class of rabbis, four in number, to be ordained in the United States, which event took place July 14, 1883. During the latter year he was married to Flora Brunn of Coshocton, Ohio. He assumed charge of the congregation Sha'are Shomayim of Mobile, Ala., where he remained until 1888 when he was called to the pulpit of the B'nai Jehuda congregation of Kansas City, Mo. He made the third and last change of pulpits in 1892 when he accepted the call to the historic Rodeph Sholem congregation of Philadelphia, Pa., serving as rabbi for thirty years until ill health compelled his retirement two years before his death. A man of fine sensibilities, he was active while in Mobile in the organization of a humane society for the prevention of cruelty to children and animals, and in Kansas

City he was chiefly instrumental in the creation of its first bureau of charities. In recognition of this service the governor of the commonwealth appointed him to represent the state at meetings of the National Conference of Charities and Corrections. When a Vice Commission was appointed in Philadelphia in 1912, the mayor of the city named him a member of the commission; his contribution to the work consisted of a personal investigation of vice conditions and their solutions in European cities, whereof he made an able report to the municipal executive. He served his city also as a member of the Board of Recreation and as a vice-president of the Universal Peace Union and Social Purity Alliance.

Deeply impressed by the work of the Chautauqua Assembly, he instituted a movement along similar lines in Jewish circles when he founded the Jewish Chautauqua Society in 1893. This effort to stimulate popular education constitutes Berkowitz's chief contribution to Jewish institutional and educational activity in the United States. He served as chancellor of the society from the date of its foundation. In his own special rabbinical field he stood among the leaders. When the Central Conference of American Rabbis was organized at Detroit, Mich., in 1889, Berkowitz was a charter member and served as secretary of the meeting for organization. He functioned as chairman of the committee to draft a formula for the reception of proselytes and the committee on arbitration to adjust differences between congregations and rabbis. He was also a member of the Conference committee on a "Union Prayer Book." The Conference publications, "Prayers for Private Devotion" and "The Union Hagadah," were made possible by his guidance. His career as author began during his student days at the Hebrew Union College when, in collaboration with his classmate Joseph Krauskopf, he published in 1883 three text-books for Jewish religious schools, namely, *Bible Ethics, First Union Hebrew Reader,* and *Second Hebrew Reader.* His other published works were *Judaism on the Social Question* (1888); *The Open Bible* (1896); *Kiddush, or Sabbath Sentiment in the Home* (1898); *The New Education in Religion* (1913), and *Intimate Glimpses of the Rabbi's Career* (1921). This last-named book reveals the man himself and makes clear the reason why Berkowitz was acclaimed during his lifetime the best-loved rabbi in the United States.

[The *Am. Jewish Yr. Bk.,* XXVI, 448–58; *Yr. Bk. Central Conference of Am. Rabbis,* XXXIV, 174–77; obituaries in the Phila. newspapers of Feb. 8, 1924.]
D.P.

BERMUDEZ, EDOUARD EDMOND (Jan. 19, 1832–Aug. 22, 1892), lawyer, jurist, was the son of Judge Joachim Bermudez of New Orleans and his wife, Emma Troxler. The family, of French and Spanish blood, had wide connections in Latin America, in France, and in Spain. The father became a noted citizen, as judge of the probate court, and the son was familiar from his youth with several languages, French, Spanish, German, in addition to English. His formal education was received in Spring Hill College near Mobile (B.A. 1851) and in the office of Justice Thomas B. Monroe of Kentucky, with whom, after the custom of those days, he read law. Returning to New Orleans after his course with Justice Monroe, he passed his examinations creditably and received his degree in law from the University of Louisiana (now Tulane) in 1852. Though not yet of legal age to practise, he was presented for the bar by Judah P. Benjamin. In January 1853 he married Amanda Elizabeth Maupassant.

A well-established practise of his profession was interrupted by the political disturbances preceding the Civil War. Bermudez was a member of the Convention of 1860, and was one of the minority who opposed the secession of Louisiana from the Union. When the war began, however, he entered the Confederate army as a lieutenant in the 1st Louisiana Infantry. He became judge-advocate of the brigade; served as adjutant, provost-marshal-general, and post commandant at Mobile; and after the cessation of hostilities held the position of assistant city attorney of New Orleans. He was removed from office (1867) as "an impediment to reconstruction," by order of Gen. Sheridan. Resuming the private practise of law, he became very successful, and his office was the training school for such men as Charles T. Soniat, C. F. Claiborne, Edward Douglass White. With the gradual passing of the evil days of "radical" rule, the people of Louisiana set about the reorganization of the government. Gov. Wiltz made a fortunate and wise selection of Edouard Bermudez to fill a place on the bench of the supreme court of the state. He was appointed (April 1880) for a term expiring in 1892. A man of great vigor, of most scholarly tastes, he was favorably known to both the French and English elements in the state. He was of high temper, but patient, clear-headed, and firm on the bench. During the very bitter conflict regarding the Louisiana lottery, it was characteristic of him that he held firmly to the principle that he was a jurist and not a politician, and that he would not as chief justice take an active part in the controversy, but would decide points of law according to the law when cases were brought before him. It was always understood that Bermudez was a lottery man, but it was perfectly clear that the more sinister elements in the lottery camp could not make use of him. The severe strain told upon his health, however; with unflinching courage and devotion he was able barely to complete his term upon the bench. He died in New Orleans, Aug. 22, 1892.

[The only printed sources of information are the notices in the press (*Times-Democrat, Picayune,* etc.) of New Orleans, Aug. 23, 1892, and the memorial tribute in the *Louisiana Annual* for 1892.]   P.B.

BERNARD, BAYLE. [See BERNARD, WILLIAM BAYLE, 1807–1875.]

BERNARD, Sir FRANCIS (July ?, 1712–June 16, 1779), colonial governor, the only child of the Rev. Francis Bernard and his wife, Margery Winlowe, came of an old and well-connected English county family. The date of his birth is unknown, but as he was baptized July 12, 1712, and as baptism usually took place a few days after birth, he probably was born in that month. He became a scholar of St. Peter's College, Westminster, in 1725, proceeding thence to Christ Church, Oxford. In 1733 he became a member of the Middle Temple, was called to the bar in 1737, and soon after settled at Lincoln as a provincial counsel. In 1740 he was appointed commissioner of bails for Lincoln, York, Nottingham, etc., and in 1741 married Amelia Offley, daughter of Stephen Offley of Norton Hall, Derbyshire. The marriage ended the first phase of his career. His aristocratic tastes and a rapidly growing family made an increased income essential. His wife was a niece of the first Viscount Barrington and of Col. Shute, formerly governor of Massachusetts. Bernard soon became intimate with her cousin, the second Lord Barrington, who thenceforward was to be his political sponsor in England. Through Barrington's influence he was appointed governor of New Jersey, arriving there on June 14, 1758. His short term of office was successful and uneventful and was ended by his transfer to Massachusetts. His commission as governor of that colony was dated Jan. 14, 1760, and he arrived in Boston the 2nd of the following August.

The nine years which he spent there were among the most turbulent in the history of the colony. The problems with which he had to grapple were beyond the power of English statesmen to solve and well beyond that of Bernard. On his arrival he wrote that he found the political parties so equally divided that it would be "madness for me to have put myself at the head of either." On account of the necessity of exercising his appointing power he was at once, however, drawn into the arena, and in the stead-

ily growing bitterness of the disputes with the mother country it was inevitable that the representative of the Crown should incur the resentment of the colonial patriots. To indicate the delicacy of Bernard's task it is only needful to point out that his years of office covered the attempted enforcement of the new Sugar Act, the issuance of the hated Writs of Assistance, the Stamp Act, and the quartering of troops in Boston. Had his lot fallen on less troublous times he might have made a good record. He was by no means devoid of ability, and more open than many governors to the colonial point of view. In the trying months of 1763 and 1764 he showed wisdom and a liberal tendency. He realized as few did that the old triangular problem of New England, Old England, and the West Indies, which had taken legislative shape a generation earlier in the Molasses Act, was in reality more of a dispute between England and the island planters than between England and the American continental merchants. He strove hard by sensible arguments sent to his superiors to procure a lowering or abolition of the duties under the Sugar Act, and he regarded the Stamp Act as most inexpedient. As representative of the home Government, however, he was forced to carry out their policies. He did not always do so judiciously and as the turmoil became greater he lost what balance of judgment he may have possessed. He misread the signs of the times and did not understand the people he governed. Innocently but disastrously, he misrepresented conditions to the Government in England, and began to flounder in his own local policies. In October 1768, Commodore Hood, writing to Grenville, said of the Governor, "his doubles and turnings have been so many, that he has altogether lost his road, and brought himself into great contempt." Bernard's ideas on colonial trade were for the most part sound and favorable to the colonists, but his political ideas were fantastically opposed to the wishes and instincts of the people. For example, his scheme for dividing New England into new governments, one of which should embrace Massachusetts, New Hampshire, Rhode Island, and half of Connecticut, showed a doctrinaire obliviousness to colonial psychology. In 1769 a number of letters from him to officials at home were published in Boston and completed his unpopularity. The Assembly sent charges against him to England and he was removed from his post, sailing from Boston Aug. 1, 1769, amid somewhat ungenerous exhibitions of popular rejoicing. The accusations against him of underhand dealings do not bear examination and the English Government finally rejected the Assembly's complaint as "groundless, vexatious, and scandalous." Meanwhile, he had been made a baronet, becoming Sir Francis Bernard of Nettleham, Lincolnshire, by patent dated Apr. 5, 1769. His later years were spent in England and marred by disappointments. A promised pension of £1,000 a year was not paid, though he seems to have received £500 annually, and was appointed commissioner of customs for Ireland. He never resided there and resigned the post in 1774. A pleasant recognition came on July 2, 1772, when he was made an honorary D.C.L. by Oxford but his closing years were spent in almost complete retirement at his place at Aylesbury, where he died June 16, 1779, leaving eight children.

[The first two volumes of *The Bernards of Abington and Nether Winchendon* (1903), by Mrs. Napier Higgins, form practically a biography of the Governor. The letters which did so much to bring his career to an end were published at Boston, 1769, as *Letters to the Right Honourable the Earl of Hillsborough from Gov. Bernard, Gen. Gage, and the Honourable his Majesty's Council for the Province of Massachusetts Bay.* His *Select Letters on the Trade and Government of America* were published in two editions in London in 1774. His commission as governor of New Jersey is given in *N. J. Arch.,* ser. I, vol. IX, pp. 23 ff.; that for Massachusetts in *Pubs. Col. Soc. Mass.,* II, 146 ff. There are thirteen volumes of his correspondence in manuscript in the Harv. Coll. Lib. from which a selection of letters was published by the University Press at Cambridge in 1912 as *The Barrington-Bernard Correspondence.* Alden Bradford's *Speeches of the Governors of Mass. from 1765 to 1775 and the Answers of the House of Representatives* (1818), should also be consulted as well as Hutchinson's *Hist. of Mass. Bay,* vol. III (London, 1828).]

J. T. A.

BERNARD, JOHN (1756–Nov. 29, 1828), actor, theatrical manager, the son of John Bernard, an Irish lieutenant in the British navy, and of Ann Bernard, the daughter of a post captain (J. H. Bernard, *The Bernards of Kerry,* 1922), was born at the naval station at Portsmouth, England. As a boy of ten he began attending the local theatre, where London actors sometimes appeared. At the Latin Academy near Chichester, to which he was sent, he displayed great zeal for acting, and his success as Hamlet at the age of sixteen fired him with determination to make the stage his career. Accordingly he found employment with a strolling company until his mother broke up a performance and marched him back home. All efforts to direct him into the naval or the legal profession proving fruitless, his parents finally allowed him to follow his desire. He was soon engaged as a light comedian by the able Norwich company. At the age of nineteen he married Mrs. Cooper, a fellow player six years his senior. Subsequently he saw service in various provincial companies, including a season at the famous Bath Theatre, until in 1782

he and his wife made a professional visit to Ireland. Two years of Irish hospitality proving too much for his constitution, he accepted another engagement at Bath. Thence he was summoned in 1787 to Covent Garden, the *Ultima Thule* of his dreams, where he played second to Lee Lewis, one of the leading comedians of his day. Experiments with a summer theatre in the provinces led Bernard to form a theatrical circuit in 1791, with playhouses at Plymouth, Dover, and the Isle of Guernsey. This undertaking eventually entailed considerable financial loss, while membership in various convivial clubs, including the celebrated Beefsteak Club, further depleted his resources. Consequently an offer from Wignell, the Philadelphia manager, to come to America at a salary of £1,000 for the first year proved irresistible.

He arrived in the summer of 1797 accompanied by the second Mrs. Bernard, formerly Miss Fisher of the Guernsey company. After making his American début in New York on Aug. 25, as Goldfinch in *The Road to Ruin,* he established himself at Philadelphia, where he remained for six years, playing comedy parts and occasionally more serious rôles, such as Shylock and Hotspur. In 1803 he signed for Boston, and in 1806 he became joint manager of the Federal Street Theatre there. He visited England in the latter year to secure additional players, and, being again a widower, married a Miss Wright as his third wife. After five seasons of unprofitable management at Boston, he withdrew in 1811. A tour of Canada was followed by some performances at the Thespian Hotel at Albany. In January 1813 Albany's first regular playhouse was opened under Bernard's management. Retiring from this position in 1816, he renewed his connection with the Boston theatre and there made his final American appearance, Apr. 19, 1819, in *The Soldier's Daughter.* He then returned to England, where he died in poverty nine years later.

Although Bernard was in error in looking upon himself as one of the founders of the American stage, he was, nevertheless, the most finished comedian this country had yet seen. The Prince of Wales (later George IV) said of him that he could make one laugh heartily without feeling that one had got into low company. His figure, countenance, and manner were marked by a light neatness admirably adapted to the rôles in which he specialized (John Genest, *Some Account of the English Stage from the Restoration in 1660 to 1830,* 1832, VII, 274). America regarded him with general approval. Dunlap called him "a great comedian" (*A History of the*

American Theatre, 1832, p. 183). Other commentators bore testimony to the distinction of his acting and the excellence of his character (William B. Wood, *Personal Recollections of the Stage,* 1855, pp. 46, 72, 88; W. W. Clapp, *A Record of the Boston Stage,* 1853, p. 80; H. P. Phelps, *Players of a Century—a Record of the Albany Stage,* 1880, pp. 44, 45, 51; J. N. Ireland, *Records of the New York Stage,* 1866, I, 160). Socially he achieved a success here, largely because he honestly liked the Americans and showed no trace of condescension toward them.

[Aside from two or three dramatic trifles Bernard's writing consisted of an extensive autobiography, three volumes of selections from which were printed after his death: *Retrospections of the Stage* (2 vols., 1830), ed. by his son [Wm.] Bayle Bernard; and "Early Days of the Am. Stage," ed. by Bayle Bernard, published in *Tallis's Dramatic Mag.,* 1850–51, and republished, with additions from manuscripts prepared by Mrs. Bayle Bernard, as *Retrospections of America* (1887), ed. with an introduction by Brander Matthews and Laurence Hutton. These works, which are the chief source of information about his life, are full of amusing stage anecdotes; they make it clear that Bernard took pleasure in his profession and keenly enjoyed life.]

O. S. C.

BERNARD, SIMON (Apr. 22, 1779–Nov. 5, 1839), French military engineer, was born at Dôle, in the Department of Jura, France. His boyhood was spent in extreme poverty. Graduating at the École Polytechnique, he was appointed lieutenant of engineers in 1797, served in the Army of the Rhine and then in Northern Italy, and was made captain in 1800. He was brought to the personal attention of Napoleon through his success in a secret mission through South Germany and Austria in 1805, collecting information for the campaign which culminated in the battle of Austerlitz. On Mar. 10, 1809, he was married to Marie de Lerchenfeld. From 1810 to 1812, having acquired a high reputation as a military engineer, he was charged with the design and construction of the fortifications of Antwerp. In 1813 he was appointed colonel and aide-de-camp to the Emperor, with whom he served the greater part of the time until the abdication. He distinguished himself by his defense of Torgau during the siege of 1813. Remaining in the army of the Restoration, he was appointed *maréchal de camp* (brigadier-general) in 1814, but rejoined Napoleon on his return from Elba and remained with him till the end. According to Barras, he was the "last officer whom Napoleon had seen by his side at Waterloo" (*Memoirs,* English translation, 1896, IV, 363–64). He then sought and received employment in the United States, on Lafayette's recommendation, a resolution of Congress authorizing the President "to employ a skillful assistant" for the corps of engineers.

Bernard was given the pay and the courtesy title of brigadier-general, and placed on the board for planning the coast defenses. Although nominally only an assistant, he was actually allowed such independence that the chief of engineers, Col. Joseph G. Swift, finally found his situation intolerable and resigned from the army in 1818, and was followed a few months later by the senior officer of the board, Lieut.-Col. William McRee (a fort in Pensacola harbor, projected by Bernard, was afterward named Fort McRee). Thereafter the board consisted of Gen. Bernard and Maj. Joseph G. Totten, with other officers temporarily assigned. The two permanent members, both great engineers, preserved harmony by working independently of each other as a rule, and gradually worked out a complete system of defense, including not only plans for modern forts on the coast, but also a project for extensive development of interior communication by roads and canals. The fortifications were largely completed sooner or later. The work of the board also served as the basis on which several canals were constructed, before the railroad era rendered the comprehensive plan of communications obsolete. Upon the accession of Louis Philippe, Bernard gave up his position and returned to France. His work in the United States had been of incalculable value, though it is unfortunate that he was employed in such a way as to force out of the army two of its ablest engineers. His chief monument is Fort Monroe, in Virginia—the greatest fortress in the country when planned, and still preserved in all its perfection. Restored to the army in France, he was appointed lieutenant-general in 1831, and served as aide-de-camp to the King and then as inspector-general of engineers. He was minister of war for a short time in 1834, and again from 1836 to 1839. He was created baron shortly before his death.

[Article by Gen. W. H. Carter in *Jour. of the Mil. Service Institution* (1912), LI, 147–55, republished (1913) in *Professional Memoirs, Corps of Engineers,* V, 306–14; L. A. F. de Bourrienne, *Life of Napoleon Bonaparte* (English translation, 1831), II, 380–82; G. W. Cullum, *Biog. Reg.* (3rd ed., 1891), I, 55, 61, 65, for mention of Bernard's relations with Swift, McRee, and Totten.]

T. M. S.

BERNARD, WILLIAM BAYLE (Nov. 27, 1807–Aug. 5, 1875), dramatist, biographer, a son of the English actor John Bernard [*q.v.*], was born in Boston. His mother had been a Miss Wright, whom his father had married as his third wife shortly before leaving London and who had previously been the governess of his motherless children. The entire family returned to England in 1819, and that country was thenceforth Bayle Bernard's home. Many years later, in his biography of Samuel Lover with whom he had been "intimate for several years from the period of his first arrival in London," he refers to his native country in these words: "Born in America—where I had traveled in my youth—I was able to enlarge from my own memory many of his necessarily hasty jottings upon western scenery and cities." Later on in the same book he recalls the "look of Boston" as "unequivocally English." In addition to this life of Lover, which was declared by the *Spectator* to "fill an undeniable blank in biographical literature," he prepared from manuscript papers his father's *Retrospections of the Stage, by the late John Bernard, Manager of the American Theatre and formerly Secretary of the Beefsteak Club,* which was published in two volumes in London in 1830, and two years afterward in Boston. From other manuscripts he compiled and edited "Early Days of the American Stage," which appeared serially in *Tallis's Dramatic Magazine* in 1850 and 1851. A portion of these papers, with additions from manuscripts prepared by his widow, appeared in book form in 1887 under title of *Retrospections of America* (*1797–1811*), edited with an introduction by Brander Matthews and Laurence Hutton. His association with the stage as an actor was brief, but he was all his life a constant and successful writer of popular plays which he had begun to produce while serving as a clerk in the Army Accounts Office from 1826 to 1830. During that period he also wrote a novel entitled *The Freebooter's Bride.* He made one of the early dramatic versions of *Rip Van Winkle* (1832) which was acted by James H. Hackett both in England and in this country (its first performance was at the Park Theatre in New York, Sept. 4, 1833). The same actor also played the leading part in another of his comedies, *The Kentuckian.* He wrote plays for Yankee Hill, Josh Silsbee, and other American actors, and may therefore be considered the popularizer, if not the inventor, of the eccentric rural American on the stage. Many of his plays were farces, among them *His Last Legs* (1839), one of the most popular pieces of its kind both in England and in America, in which Hackett, John Brougham, and other famous actors for many years played the once familiar comic character of O'Callaghan. Bernard made a stage version of *Faust,* produced with Spohr's music at Drury Lane in London with Samuel Phelps as Mephistopheles and Mrs. Hermann Vezin as Marguerite. This play was acted many times by Lewis Morrison on the American stage after Sir Henry Irving's production of W. G. Wills's version of *Faust* had re-created a theatrical interest in the

old story. Among Bernard's more than one hundred plays are *The Dumb Belle* (acted at the Olympic Theatre in 1831 with Madame Vestris in the title rôle), *The Tide of Time, The Nervous Man, The Old Style and the New, The Evil Genius, The Middy Ashore,* and *The Man with Two Lives.* He was an active participant in the literary, theatrical, and bohemian life of London for nearly half a century, and there is scarcely a book of theatrical reminiscences of his period in which he is not frequently mentioned. His biographical works about his father make him a valuable contributor to the annals of the early American stage.

[*Retrospections of the Stage* (1830) and *Retrospections of America* (1887) furnish important information about Bayle Bernard, as does also *The Life and Times of Edward Leman Blanchard* (London, 1891), by Clement Scott and Cecil Howard. A valuable article in the *Era* (London) Dec. 2, 1899, contains material about Bayle Bernard's version of *Rip Van Winkle*; further information upon the same subject is given by William Winter in *The Jeffersons* (1881). In Bernard's *Life of Samuel Lover* (1874) are scattered autobiographical bits.]

E. F. E.

BERNAYS, AUGUSTUS CHARLES (Oct. 13, 1854–May 22, 1907), surgeon, was born at Highland, Ill., the son of Dr. George Bernays and Minna Döring, German Jews from Hesse-Darmstadt. His father later locating in St. Louis, the young Augustus obtained his primary education in public and private schools there. He received the degree of B.A. from McKendree College, Lebanon, Ill., in 1872 and his medical degree from Heidelberg in 1876. Following special courses under Von Langenbeck in Berlin and Billroth in Vienna he qualified for membership in the Royal College of Surgeons of London in 1877. Returning to St. Louis he took up the practise of medicine with his father. His is credited with being the first in that city to devote himself exclusively to surgical practise. From an association with Lister in London he became a pioneer in antiseptic and later in aseptic surgery. A daring operator, confident and resourceful, he excelled in the difficult field of plastic surgery. He successively occupied the chairs of surgery at the St. Louis College of Physicians and Surgeons and at Marion Sims College; his undoubted popularity as a teacher lay in his mastery of the basic medical sciences and in his enthusiastic earnestness. His writings were mainly case reports in medical periodicals, illustrating special pathology, surgical anatomy, or surgical technique. In his *Golden Rules of Surgery* (1906) he summarized his earlier observations on the science and art of his craft. In 1903 he suffered a stroke of apoplexy, after which he practised little, devoting his time to travels and writing. He died suddenly at the age of fifty-two from rupture of a cardiac aneurism.

Bernays was of the romantic temperament, emotional, impulsive, lacking in tact, and given to forceful and extravagant language. He was an outspoken and aggressive agnostic. In his early career these traits, together with questions of ethics, brought him into controversy with the St. Louis Medical Society. The gambling spirit was inherent in him. His diversions were attending horse races, betting on them, keeping a stable, and training the horses. His portraits show an aggressive face of Oriental cast, high, broad forehead, prominent eyes, and full lips. He never married but always made his home with a sister, to whom he was devotedly attached.

[A detailed biography with bibliography of Bernays's writings is contained in *Augustus Charles Bernays; a Memoir,* by Thekla Bernays (1912). This work contains portraits at different times of life. The various biographical sketches written at the time of Bernays's death add nothing to the data contained in his sister's book.]

J. M. P.

BERRIEN, JOHN MACPHERSON (Aug. 23, 1781–Jan. 1, 1856), congressman, was a native of New Jersey. His forebears were men of some prominence, his grandfather, John Berrien, having been a judge of the supreme court of New Jersey, and his father, also named John, a major in the American Revolution. The family was of Huguenot descent. His mother, Margaret MacPherson, of Scotch lineage, was the sister of John MacPherson, who, as aide-de-camp to Montgomery, was killed in the battle of Quebec. His parents removed to Georgia in 1782. After preparatory schooling in New York, Berrien matriculated at Princeton and was graduated in 1796. Returning to Savannah he studied law in the office of Joseph Clay, a federal judge; was admitted to practise in 1799; elected solicitor of the eastern circuit (1809); a year later became judge of the same circuit and held office until 1821; served one term (1822–23) in the state Senate; and, in 1824, was elected United States senator. He was an adherent of the Jackson faction of the Democratic-Republican party. In his speeches he advocated the current Georgia views in the controversy over the final Creek land cession. He opposed the Tariff of 1828, presenting a protest of the Georgia legislature against it. In 1829 he resigned to take office as attorney-general in Jackson's first cabinet, but, becoming estranged from the President on account of the Eaton affair, resigned on June 22, 1831. After ten years in private life he was returned to the Senate in 1841 as a Whig and served until May 28, 1852.

The period of his second session in the Senate was a momentous one in American history, and Berrien, then in the prime of his intellectual powers, became an outstanding leader in his party. He was a man of commanding personal appearance, a learned and skilful advocate, and an orator of unusual power. He supported the Whig positions on the Bank question, protective tariffs, territorial extension, and compromise of the slavery issue. Thus he at first opposed the annexation of Texas (*Congressional Globe,* 28 Cong., 2 Sess., pp. 383–87), alleging unconstitutionality in the attempted mode of admission. But in the next session, after the joint resolution of Congress had been passed committing the United States to the admission of Texas on certain conditions, and after these conditions had been met, he felt obliged to sustain the pledge of the country. Furthermore, he was then able to discover good reasons why Texas should be admitted, and so voted. He opposed the Mexican War, speaking against the bill declaring war and refusing, though present, to cast a vote on the final passage of the bill (T. H. Benton, *Abridgment of the Debates of Congress from 1789 to 1856,* XV, 505, 510). On the bill to provide $3,000,000 to be used in effecting a peace with Mexico, Berrien introduced an amendment (*Congressional Globe,* 29 Cong., 2 Sess., pp. 325–330) against taking any territory from Mexico, basing his opposition on the ground that the free states, by reason of their numerical superiority, would exclude slavery and thus deny to the South equal participation in the benefits of such acquisition of territory. He appealed to senators to exclude "this direful question" (slavery) from the national councils. When it began to look as if all factions in the anti-slavery North would combine to adopt the Wilmot Proviso, excluding slavery from the new territories, Calhoun called a caucus of Southern representatives and senators, Democrats and Whigs, and sought to form a Southern party (December 1848). Calhoun's *Address* was adopted, the Whigs voting against it. Berrien also issued an *Address to the People of the United States* (February 1849) in which he pleaded for a compromise of the slavery problem. The next year, however, he altered his position. He came out against Clay's Compromise, abandoning his long-sustained position of moderation and shifting over to a strong pro-Southern attitude. On the final passage of the various component parts of the Omnibus Bill he voted against the admission of California and the abolition of the slave trade in the District of Columbia, and for the organization of territorial government in New Mexico and Utah and the new Fugitive Slave Law. Convinced that the Whig party could no longer be relied on to protect Southern interests, he withdrew from the party in 1850. He strongly advocated "Non-Intercourse" in a business way as a form of resistance against Northern encroachment on Southern rights. He rejected secession, but believed resistance within the Union a necessity. In the stirring gubernatorial campaign in Georgia in 1851, in which the "finality" of the Compromise of 1850 was the issue, Berrien, in a half-hearted manner, accepted the "Georgia Platform," on which the Union candidate, Howell Cobb, ran, but took no active part in the campaign. A few weeks after the election it became incumbent upon the legislature to elect a United States senator, Berrien's term approaching a close. Berrien at first declined to become a candidate for reëlection, but later on announced that he would accept, if elected. The Union Democrats and Whigs combined to defeat him and elected Robert Toombs in his place (Nov. 10, 1851). Berrien thereupon resigned his senatorship. When the American or Know-Nothing party was organized, he joined it; and his last political activity was to preside over a state convention of the new party held at the Capital in December 1855. Shortly after this meeting, he died on Jan. 1, 1856. Thus passed from the stage one of the last of the elder statesmen, for many years regarded as the ablest constitutional lawyer in the Senate.

[U. B. Phillips, *Ga. and State Rights* (1902), and R. H. Shryock, *Ga. and the Union in 1850* (1926), discuss briefly Berrien's positions on political questions. Chas. C. Jones's address delivered before the Ga. Bar Ass. (*Report*, 1891) is devoted largely to an account of Berrien's personal traits and his career as a lawyer. There is a contemporary sketch of considerable importance in S. F. Miller, *Bench and Bar of Ga.* (1858), vol. I, ch. 3.]

R. P. B–s.

BERRY, HIRAM GREGORY (Aug. 27, 1824–May 3, 1863), Union soldier, was a native of Thomaston (now a part of the city of Rockland), Me. His parents were Jeremiah and Frances (Gregory) Berry. He came of fighting stock, as his grandfather was a soldier of the Revolution, and his father a veteran of the War of 1812. He began life as a carpenter, but rose to be a builder and a business man, and president of a bank. He was a Democrat in politics, a member of the legislature, and one of the early mayors in the new city of Rockland. Having been a captain of militia before the Civil War, at its beginning he was chosen colonel of the 4th Maine. He led this regiment, and afterward a brigade, and finally a division in the Army of the Potomac, and served from the first battle of Bull Run until

his death. He was commissioned brigadier-general of volunteers Mar. 17, 1862, and commanded a brigade in Gen. Kearny's division during the Peninsula campaign. He was particularly distinguished at the battles of Williamsburg (May 5) and Fair Oaks (May 31–June 1, 1862), and was commended by the division commanders Kearny and Hooker, by the corps commander Heintzelman, and by McClellan. Suffering from injury and ill health he was on furlough at Rockland, but returned in time for the battle of Fredericksburg, having been commissioned major-general of volunteers Nov. 29, 1862. A picturesque incident is related in regard to this battle: the Confederate general, A. P. Hill, is said to have presented his compliments to Berry, with the remark that his command was the "best behaved brigade that he ever saw under fire" (Gould, p. 221).

In February 1863, after Hooker had succeeded Burnside in command of the Army of the Potomac, Berry was promoted to a division (formerly Hooker's division) in the 3rd Corps. As general of this division he had an important part in the battle of Chancellorsville, May 2 and 3, and was killed in the crisis of the struggle. "The damage incurred in the rout of the Eleventh Corps, great as it was, had been almost repaired before the morning of the 3rd by the readiness and energy of Pleasonton, Sickles, and Hiram G. Berry . . . " (Nicolay and Hay, *Abraham Lincoln, A History*, 1890, VII, 104). According to a fellow-officer, "He was a plain, straightforward man, tall and broad-shouldered. His blue flannel blouse and his whole dress gave him very little of a military air. But whoever judged him from his appearance would have judged badly . . . he was not the less a good officer, as faithful to his duty as he was devoted to his soldiers. . . . In him the moral energy strove against physical weakness" (Regis Trobriand, *Four Years with the Army of the Potomac*, 1889, p. 370). Berry's gallantry and bearing under fire—as at the battle of Fredericksburg—and his personal relations with his men, are illustrated by a variety of anecdotes.

[Edward K. Gould, *Major-General Hiram G. Berry* (1899); Nathaniel Butler, *Discourse at the Funeral of Major-General H. G. Berry* (1863); Alexander Webb, *The Peninsula: McClellan's Campaign of 1862* (1881); F. B. Heitman, *Hist. Reg.* (1903).]

E. K. A.

BERRY, JAMES HENDERSON (May 15, 1841–Jan. 30, 1913), governor of Arkansas, senator, was born in Jackson County, Ala., son of James M. and Isabella Jane (Orr) Berry. His mother was a descendant of John Orr, who settled in Pennsylvania early in the eighteenth century. James was the fourth of ten children. When he was seven years old his father moved to Carrollton, Carroll County, Ark. His educational advantages were very meager, the best being one year at the Berryville academy. He enlisted in the Confederate army in 1861 and was elected second lieutenant in Company E, 16th Arkansas Infantry. He fought at Pea Ridge (Elk Horn), Iuka, and Corinth, losing a leg at the last-named place. On his recovery he went to Texas and remained there until the war closed. In returning home he stopped at Ozark, taught school a while, read law, and married Lizzie Quaile. Going back to Carrollton, he was elected to the legislature in 1866, being the youngest member of that body. As soon as the legislature adjourned he took up the practise of law at Carrollton, but moved to Bentonville in 1869 and formed a partnership with Sam W. Peel. His political career began in 1872, when he was elected to the legislature as a Democrat. A bitter struggle was on in the effort to recover the state from carpet-bag rule. At first the legislature had a Republican majority, but several resigned to accept appointments and enough Democrats were elected to give them control. When the Republican speaker, C. W. Tankersly, sided with Brooks at the called session of 1874 in the Brooks-Baxter war, he was deposed and Berry was elected in his place (Dallas T. Herndon, *Centennial History of Arkansas*, 1922, I, 312–13). In 1878 he was elected judge of the circuit court of the fourth district, serving for three years. In 1882 he was nominated by the Democratic convention as candidate for governor and was elected by a considerable majority. A leading plank in the Democratic platform was the demand for the re-submission of the Fishback amendment repudiating the bonds issued by the carpet-bag government to aid in building railroads and levees and the "Holford" bonds ($500,-000) issued in 1838 to the Real Estate Bank. This had failed to get the necessary majority in 1880. Berry now championed the amendment and in his inaugural address advocated re-submission. The amendment was re-submitted and this time was carried by a large majority (Fay Hempstead, *Pictorial History of Arkansas,* 1890, pp. 281–83). The Holford bonds had been disposed of in violation of law, but all really due on them except $67,967.33 had been paid by this time (W. C. Evans, "History of the Public Debt of Arkansas," a master's thesis in manuscript, Library of the University of Arkansas). Berry's administration also marked the beginning of labor legislation in the state.

In 1885 he was elected to the United States Senate and served continuously until 1907, when he was defeated by Jeff Davis. While senator, he supported Senator Beck's bill to prohibit members of Congress from serving as attorneys for any government-aided railroad, was on the committee on public lands, and was chairman when the Democrats had a majority. In this position he sought to protect the public interests, especially against fraudulent entries and timber thieves. He took a lively interest in Indian affairs and introduced a bill creating the Territory of Indianola for the region occupied by the Indians with a view to allotting the lands in severalty. His bill failed, but later some of his ideas were incorporated in the bill providing for the Dawes Commission. In October 1910 Berry was appointed, at the request of President Taft, to mark the graves of Confederate soldiers who had died in Northern prisons, and he carried the work to completion in 1912.

[Berry's *Autobiography* (1913) is undoubtedly the most reliable source for the bare facts of his life. See *Cong. Record,* 1885–1907, for his career in Congress. A portrait of him appears in John Hallum's *Biog. and Critical Hist. of Ark.,* vol. I (1887).]
D. Y. T.

BERRY, NATHANIEL SPRINGER (Sept. 1, 1796–Apr. 27, 1894), governor of New Hampshire, son of Abner and Betsey (Springer) Berry, was born at Bath, Me. The accidental death of his father, a ship-builder, when Nathaniel was six years old, meant a boyhood of hard work and meager educational opportunity. When about fourteen he moved to Lisbon, N. H., and soon afterward to Bath, in the same state. He served an apprenticeship in the tannery business, afterward settling in 1818 at Bristol, N. H., where he established a tannery which he operated for many years. He had personally investigated improved methods and equipment used in tanneries in the state of New York and was reported to be the first tanner in New England to use hot liquids, a method which greatly reduced the time required for the treatment of hides. He was henceforth identified with many activities, business, political and religious, in the town of Bristol, and in its records his name constantly appears on committees, directorates, and programs. He was twice married: on Jan. 26, 1821, to Ruth Smith, who died in 1857; and in January 1860 to Mrs. Louise Farley.

Berry represented Bristol in the legislature 1828, 1833, 1834, and 1837, and the neighboring town of Hebron in 1854. He was senator from the 11th district in 1835 and 1836. Beginning with 1841, he was associate justice of the court of common pleas and in 1856 began five years' service as probate judge of Grafton County. He was a Democrat in his earlier years and a delegate to the Baltimore Convention of 1840, but with the rise of the slavery issue he became increasingly dissatisfied with the Democratic attitude toward that question and by 1844 had definitely severed his connection with the party. In 1846 he was supported for the governorship by the Liberty party and a group of independent Democrats. The question of the annexation of Texas was disrupting the existing parties, and Berry received enough popular votes to force the decision into the legislature where, however, he failed of election. In the following years he devoted himself to the organization of the Free-Soil movement and was unsuccessfully supported for the governorship by the new party and sundry coalitions in 1847, 1848, 1849, and 1850.

He was generally regarded as an extremist and too closely allied with the abolitionist wing of the Anti-Slavery movement. In 1861, when nominated for the governorship by the Republican party into which he had naturally gravitated, he was denounced by the leading Democratic organ as "one of the fossils of the old abolition party who has been scarcely heard of for ten years past . . . a man who had been regarded as too ultra and fanatical even for the radical tone of their party during the last six years. . . . To vote for Berry is to vote to aggravate present difficulties, to oppose all concessions for the preservation of the Union, to invite and hasten the untold woes which must attend the fratricidal strife, the bloody civil war, which their policy is sure to precipitate upon the country" (*New Hampshire Patriot and State Gazette,* Jan. 16, 1861). Elected nevertheless, Berry in his inaugural message, June 4, 1861, made a spirited call for men and money to meet the crisis, declaring his confident expectation that "the principles upon which the republic was founded will be vindicated and made permanent; the Constitution will be sustained; the Constitutional rights of all American citizens, in all the States, will receive new guaranties; the freedom of speech and of the press everywhere in our land will be effectually secured; and the Government will come forth purified and strengthened" (*New Hampshire Statesman,* June 8, 1861). He threw himself into the difficult task of getting the state on a war footing, and proved an energetic and inspiring executive, ranking high among the "war governors." From the first he strongly advocated emancipation. In September 1862 he attended the conference of loyal governors at Altoona, and his name appears on the formal address which the conference presented to President Lincoln. After his retirement from the governorship in 1863, he moved in the following year to Massachusetts, where he resided for some time with members of his family at Andover and Worcester; later, for several years, he resided with a daughter in Milwaukee, Wis. His last years were spent at the home of a son in Bristol, N. H. Although some had considered his age a disqualification for the strenuous duties of the governorship in 1861, he survived his retirement from that office for more than thirty years, dying at the age of ninety-seven.

[A brief biography, with portrait, in *Hist. of the Town of Bristol* (1904), by R. W. Musgrove; obituary in the *Concord Evening Monitor,* Apr. 27, 1894.]

W. A. R.

BERTRAM, JOHN (Feb. 11, 1796–Mar. 22, 1882), sea-captain, merchant, was born in the parish of Saint Sauveur in the island of Jersey, the son of John and Mary (Perchard) Bertram. In 1807 the family moved to America, settling by chance at Salem where young John continued the education commenced in Jersey and in England. Late in 1812 he went to sea as cabin-boy in the merchantman *Hazard* at five dollars a month, and then served in two privateers, the *Monkey* and the *Herald,* the latter being captured by the British. Returning from prison at the close of the war, he continued at sea, sailing to various parts of the world. By 1821, he had risen to mate, and his first command was the schooner *General Brewer,* which he chartered for a profitable venture to St. Helena. His eyes were constantly open for trading opportunities, and his fortune began to rise after two successful years of gathering hides on the coast of Patagonia. His last voyage as captain was to Zanzibar in the *Black Warrior* in 1830. He was able to buy from the sultan a cargo of gum copal. This was much in demand by the varnish makers at home and was the beginning of a very lucrative trade. Upon his return in 1832, Bertram stayed ashore as shipowner and merchant, continuing the Zanzibar trade and later developing a lively commerce with Para. The first ship sent to California from the United States at the time of the gold rush was the brig *Eliza* which he dispatched in December 1848. At the same time he and his associates gave rush orders for the construction of a large clipper ship which bore his name. This, with several other clippers, brought him large profits from the Pacific trade. During the fifties, he foresaw the decline in American shipping and gradually restricted his scope of commerce to Zanzibar. By 1856 he was becoming interested in western railways and subscribed heavily to several lines. During his later years, he was much interested in philanthropy. "I want to live so long as I can do good, no longer," he once said. The Bertram

Home for Aged Men and the Salem Fuel Fund were among his special benevolences, but he gave generously to dozens of others. He was the last of the merchants of the old type, holding a position similar to that of Derby, Crowninshield, and Peabody at the beginning of the century. His portrait shows a keen but kindly face with much white hair and white whiskers. He was married three times: in 1823 to Mary G. Smith, in 1838 to Mrs. Clarissa Millett, and in 1848 to Mary Ann Ropes.

[The best account of Bertram's life is the detailed memorial in the *Essex Institute Hist. Colls.*, XXI, 81–96. There is a shorter sketch in the same series, XV, 308, with a portrait, and scattered references to his ships will be found throughout the collections. An excellent portrait, with a short account, is in R. D. Paine's *Ships and Sailors of Old Salem* (rev. ed., 1923), pp. 440–45.]

R.G.A.

BESSEY, CHARLES EDWIN (May 21, 1845–Feb. 25, 1915), botanist, was born in a log house on a farm in Wayne County, Ohio. His father's family was of Huguenot extraction, the name having originally been Bessé. The family is supposed to have fled from Alsace in the seventeenth century, first to England, then to Pennsylvania. His father, Adnah, taught school in Ohio, and married Margaret Ellenberger, one of his pupils. Charles Bessey received his early training from his father; he entered an academy at Seville, Ohio, in his seventeenth year, but the death of his father caused him to take a teaching position at Wadsworth. He soon reëntered the academy, only to be a spectator of its dissolution. At last, largely self-taught, he entered the Michigan Agricultural College in 1866, graduating in 1869 with the degree of B.S. He intended to prepare himself for a career of civil engineering, but his noticeable love of plant life caused President Abbott and Prof. Prentiss to persuade him to become a botanist. After graduation he accepted an instructorship in botany and horticulture at Iowa State College of Agriculture. He was active the following year in the famous meetings of the Farmers' Institute held in Iowa, and in 1875 and for several years after was president of this organization. In 1872 he met Asa Gray at the meeting of the American Association for the Advancement of Science at Dubuque, and in the winter of 1872–73 he studied under Gray. He returned to Harvard for another period of study under him in 1875–76. The strict and formal training imparted by the leader of American botany was a lasting influence in Bessey's career, balancing his strong practical inclinations with a grounding in the theory of botany.

In 1884 he accepted the invitation of the University of Nebraska to take the chair of botany, but only after he had made a visit, had found the institution without plans or equipment for botanical courses, and had, by a tentative refusal, inaugurated favorable changes in the new institution. From then on till his death his name was associated with that of agriculture and botanical science in Nebraska. He threw himself at once into the work of agricultural organization, and into the investigation of the state's vegetation. The popularity of his teaching methods, untechnical and well illustrated, was immediate, and when he received his crowning honor, in his election as president of the American Association for the Advancement of Science in 1910, his return from the meeting was celebrated by an ovation from the entire body of the University. In the closing years of his life he assumed heavy administrative duties as dean and chancellor.

During the years 1883–1914 he issued seven text-books of botany; and the number of his miscellaneous articles is well above a hundred, of which the most suggestive are those dealing with the reconstruction of the evolutionary tree of the plant phyla and families. (See his "Evolution and Classification," in *Proceedings of the American Association for the Advancement of Science,* vol. XLII; "The Phyletic Idea in Taxonomy," in *Science,* n. s., vol. XXIX, 1900; and "The Phylogenetic Taxonomy of Flowering Plants," in *Annals of the Missouri Botanical Garden,* vol. II, 1915). Whatever the limitations of Bessey's view-point, he set the mind of the botanical fraternity in motion, after it had lain too passive on the vital subject of classification, and his influence ultimately reached European circles. One of his last and most philosophic addresses was his prophetic "Some of the Next Steps in Botanical Science," in *Science,* n. s., XXXVII, 1–13 (1913).

[R. J. Pool, *Am. Jour. Bot.,* II, 505–18, with portrait and bibliography.]

D.C.P.

BETHUNE, GEORGE WASHINGTON (Mar. 18, 1805–Apr. 28, 1862), Dutch Reformed clergyman, was born in New York, the son of Divie (afterward Richard) Bethune, of Huguenot extraction, and his wife, Joanna Graham, both being natives of Scotland. The boy was reared in a home of wealth and piety, was instructed by private tutors and at the academy at Salem, N. Y., and entered Columbia in 1819. After three years there he went to Dickinson College, Carlisle, Pa., where he graduated in 1823. After studying theology at Princeton, he was ordained by the Second Presbytery of New York, Nov. 10, 1827, and immediately entered the Dutch Reformed Church, where he remained throughout his life. His pastorates were: Rhinebeck, N. Y., 1827–30; Utica, 1830–34; the First and Third churches in Philadelphia, 1834–49; Brooklyn Heights, 1850–59; and the Twenty-first Street Church, New York City, 1859–62. He made several extended trips to Europe, and died of apoplexy at Florence, Italy, where he had gone for the recovery of his health.

At various times in his life the way was opened to him to become chaplain and professor of moral science at West Point, chancellor of New York University, and provost of the University of Pennsylvania. But he preferred to remain in the pastorate. While in Brooklyn he was for a time lecturer on pulpit oratory in the Theological Seminary at New Brunswick. His pulpit work was distinguished for its oratorical power and its devotional qualities. He was an exact student, a musician, a poet, the author of several well-known hymns and many publications on religious themes. He published a volume of his own poems, entitled *Lays of Love and Faith* (1848), and edited *The British Female Poets, with Biographical and Critical Notices* (1848). In 1846 he issued the first American edition of Walton's Complete Angler, in which the volume of the work itself was nearly equaled by that of the editor's introduction and appendix containing ballads, music, and papers on American fishing, with the most complete catalogue of books on angling ever printed. Owing to the public feeling against the propriety of such a book by a clergyman, it was published anonymously. An untiring fisherman, Bethune also collected about 700 works on angling and kindred subjects. In politics he was a staunch Democrat, was opposed alike to slavery and Abolitionism and was a prominent member of the Colonization Society. He was the author of a letter to President Buchanan urging him to suppress the pro-slavery propaganda of the South, and when the Confederacy was formed he stood firmly for the Union. On Nov. 4, 1825, he married Mary Williams, to whom he was deeply devoted. Mrs. Bethune, who survived her husband, was an invalid for most of her life, and there were no children.

[*A Memoir* (1867) of Dr. Bethune was written by Dr. A. R. Van Nest, his colleague in his last pastorate. Briefer accounts are found in Henry Fowler's *Am. Pulpit* (1856) and Edward T. Corwin's *Manual of the Reformed Ch. in America* (3rd ed., 1879). All the foregoing have portraits, and in the last there is a full bibliography of Bethune's published works.]   F. T. P.

BETTENDORF, WILLIAM PETER (July 1, 1857–June 3, 1910), inventor, manufacturer, was born in Mendota, Ill., the eldest of the four children of Michael and Catherine (Reck) Bettendorf. His meager schooling was acquired in the common schools of Missouri and Kansas, where his parents made their home, and at St. Mary's Mission School, an Indian school in Kansas. When about fifteen he began work as a machinist with the Peru Plow Company (Peru, Ill.), later being employed with the Moline Plow Company (Moline, Ill.), and with the Partin & Orendorff Company (Canton, Ohio); in 1882 he returned to the Peru Plow Company as superintendent and remained with them until 1886. In 1879 he married Mary Wortman, who died in 1901; and in 1908 he married Mrs. Elizabeth Staby. His career as an inventor began in 1878 with the invention of the first power-lift sulky plow. A few years later he invented the Bettendorf Metal Wheel (for wagons and farm implements) and the machinery for its manufacture. In 1886, in conjunction with his brother, J. W. Bettendorf, he undertook the manufacture of this wheel at Davenport, Ia., and was successful. The further use of steel for farm implements intrigued his imagination, and in 1892 he developed a steel gear for farm wagons. New machinery for its manufacture had to be designed and built, and he gave all his time to the task. In 1905 this machinery was sold to the International Harvester Company, but his own company at Davenport, which was manufacturing steel gears in addition to the metal wheels, continued the manufacture of gears under contract. The next step conceived in Bettendorf's fertile brain was to enter the railroad field, where steel was fast being substituted for wood. His Davenport plant was large and in many ways adapted to this kind of manufacturing; so he soon began to add railway-car parts to its production. A new car bolster designed and patented by him, using two commercial I-beams shaped and joined together with a few small parts, had an immediate sale and is found today under railway cars all over the country. After this came a new cast-steel side-frame truck and then the Bettendorf integral journal-box. Eventually he was manufacturing complete railway cars. His aim was always toward simplification—fewer parts, less weight, greater strength. At the time of his death he was working on a complete steel freight car. With success in the manufacture and sale of railway car parts assured, a new plant was built three miles from Davenport in a town called Gilbert. The name of this town was changed to Bettendorf, and he took an active interest in the development and welfare of this community. His success was due not only to his inventive ability but to the confidence which he justly inspired and to the business ability which, combined with that of his brother, made it possible for him to weather the competition which was so keen a part of the manufacturing life of his day.

[Material for this sketch has been obtained from the *Railway Age Gazette*, XLVIII, No. 23 ; *Farm Machinery*, June 7, 1910 ; *Farm Implement News*, June 9, 1910 ; and from Mr. Henry Bellinghausen, attorney for the Bettendorf Co.]

E. Y.

BETTS, SAMUEL ROSSITER (June 8, 1786–Nov. 3, 1868), jurist, son of Uriah and Sarah (Rossiter) Betts, was born at Richmond, Berkshire County, Mass. He was first educated in the rural school, then tutored for college at Lenox Academy, Lenox, Mass. In 1806, after four years of study, he graduated from Williams College. Removing to Hudson, N. Y., he began to study law and was admitted to the bar in 1809, opening a law office in Monticello in the newly organized Sullivan County. His legal practise was disrupted by the War of 1812 when he enlisted in the army and served in the defense of New York Harbor until appointed by Gov. Tompkins as division judge-advocate in that vicinity (Daniel D. Tompkins, *Public Papers . . . Military*, I, 720). After the war he was elected to Congress in 1815 from Sullivan and Orange counties but declined reëlection in 1817 and resumed the practise of law at Newburgh. While a congressman, on Nov. 4, 1816, he married Caroline A. Dewey of Northampton, Mass. For two years he served as district attorney of Orange County. His genial disposition, industry, and ability brought him into prominence, and led to his appointment in 1823 as a circuit judge of the supreme court of New York. Three years later in 1826 he was elevated by President John Quincy Adams to the United States district court for the southern district of New York—a position he filled till 1867, more than forty years, with urbanity, kindness, wisdom, and legal erudition. When he moved to New York City in 1827 the admiralty court had few cases but under Judge Betts its work was quadrupled. He is generally credited with an authoritative restatement of American admiralty law, and his decisions in numerous cases of maritime law gave him such a high standing as a judge in that branch of law that for a score of years none of his rulings were appealed. With the outbreak of the Civil War such problems as slavery, neutrality, blockade, prize, and contraband, involving both national and international law, came before him as new questions and were settled on cogent reasoning and fundamental legal principles. In addition to these cases in admiralty law, violations of the national criminal law and cases of patents and bankruptcy were presented to him for adjustment. His decisions were characterized by learned research, clarity,

and logical statement. Many of his opinions, accepted as fundamental statements of the law, were written after the age of seventy-five.

[The best biography of Betts has been written by two of his descendants in a privately published pamphlet, *Thos. Betts and His Descendants* (1888). An appreciation of his life and work by his legal colleagues is given in Benedict, *Reports*, vol. II, App., pp. 559–62. In 1838 Betts published an authoritative work on *Admiralty Practice*. His legal opinions are published in Blatchford and Howland, *Reports*, vol. I (covering the period 1827–37) ; Olcott, *Reports* (covering the period 1843–47) ; Abbott, *Reports of Cases in Admiralty* (covering the period 1847–50) and Blatchford, *Prize Cases* (covering the period 1861–65). See also Blatchford, *Reports* (covering the period 1845–67), and Benedict, *Reports* (Eastern District N. Y., 1845–67). *The Civil List* of N. Y. contains data on his political service.]

A. C. F.

BEVERIDGE, ALBERT JEREMIAH (Oct. 6, 1862–Apr. 27, 1927), senator, historian, was born on a small farm in Highland County, Ohio, the son of Thomas H. and Frances (Parkinson) Beveridge. In 1865 the father, after the loss of his property, moved the family to a farm in Illinois. Young Beveridge's early life was one of privation and hardship. He was a plowboy at twelve, a railroad hand with a section gang at fourteen, a logger and teamster at fifteen. Before he was sixteen, however, he managed to enter a high school. His yearning for knowledge led him to determine to go to college, and with a loan of $50 from a friend, in the fall of 1881 he entered Asbury College, now DePauw University, at Greencastle, Ind. During his college course he won the inter-state oratorical honors and prizes sufficient to provide for two of his college years. He graduated in 1885. He was twice married : in 1887 to Katherine Langsdale of Greencastle, Ind., who died June 18, 1900; in 1907 to Catherine Eddy of Chicago. Admitted to the bar in 1887, for twelve years Beveridge practised law in Indianapolis. Meanwhile he had become well known in his state as a political orator. In every campaign for fifteen years, beginning while yet a college boy, as early as the Blaine campaign of 1884, he had stumped the state from end to end. In a deadlock among the leading senatorial candidates in 1899 the Republican legislative caucus turned to him as a compromise candidate, and he was elected to the United States Senate at the age of thirty-six, being among the youngest members ever to sit in that body. In 1905 he was reelected without opposition within his party, but in 1911, chiefly because of party schism, he was defeated for a third term, after which he never again held public office. The twelve years of his senatorial service were a period of agitation, of party revolt and insurgency, leading to the rise of the Progressive party. Beveridge was one of the Senate "insurgents," one of the original Progressive Republicans. He supported the Roosevelt policies, such as equal industrial opportunities, prevention of trust abuses, government regulation of public service corporations, a strong navy, the meat inspection law (which he drafted), conservation of national resources, and extension of nominating primaries. He was outstanding and effective in his opposition to injurious child labor, proposing an amendment (to a pending bill on child labor in the District of Columbia) prohibiting inter-state commerce in the product of factories and mines where children under fourteen years of age were employed. His speech on this amendment, occupying parts of three days (Jan. 23, 28, 29, 1907), was a notable contribution to the controversy (*Congressional Record,* 59 Cong., 2 Sess., pp. 1552–57). He favored a tariff commission, to be conducted on non-partisan lines, in the hope of taking the tariff out of politics and thus sparing the country from the business uncertainty resulting from frequent revisions. It was on the Payne-Aldrich Tariff Act, in the first year of President Taft's administration (1909), that the disruption in the Republican party occurred. Beveridge was in the forefront of the insurgent senators in opposition to this party bill. He believed that the "Old Guard" leaders cared nothing for the well-being of the masses but were working constantly for the protection of selfish interests, and that the Aldrich tariff was a "revision upward" and was, therefore, a betrayal of party pledges. Because of his independence of his party, the "stand-pat" Republicans in Indiana helped the Democrats to defeat him for the Senate in 1911.

With this senatorial experience and his democratic disposition it was easy and natural for him to go with Roosevelt into the Progressive party in 1912. In the Progressive National Convention in Chicago in that year it was Beveridge, as temporary chairman, who sounded the "keynote" in a campaign address, entitled "Pass Prosperity Around." During the same year he was nominated by the Progressive party of Indiana as its candidate for governor. He received 10,000 more votes than the Republican candidate, but was defeated by the Democratic candidate, Samuel M. Ralston. In 1914, after the adoption of the Seventeenth Amendment, the Indiana Progressives nominated Beveridge as their candidate for the United States Senate, but Progressive support had fallen away, and he came in third in the popular vote. In 1916, together with Roosevelt, he rejoined the Republican party, and supported Charles E. Hughes for the presidency. In 1922 he was nominated for the United States Senate

by the Republicans of Indiana in a state-wide popular primary, defeating Harry S. New, the sitting senator, but in the ensuing election he was again defeated by Samuel M. Ralston, the Democratic nominee. This closed his political career.

He was a pronounced nationalist, suspicious of foreign countries, with some anti-British feeling, a stout opponent of America's having anything to do with the League of Nations; at times disposed toward jingoism in speech, declaring himself for "America first! Not only America first, but America only!" He was somewhat temperamental, but his finer qualities greatly overtopped his minor defects. He had a rare political aptitude, and no man ever questioned his public integrity or his political courage.

But he was even more distinguished as a historical writer than as a politician. In his early service in the Senate he already showed an overwhelming desire to get information at first hand, even traveling to the Philippines in order to make a personal investigation of the Philippine problem. During the Japanese and Russian struggle in order to satisfy himself as to the situation he took a trip to Siberia and Russia, the outcome of which was *The Russian Advance,* published in 1903. In 1905 he brought out *The Young Man and the World,* in 1906 *The Bible as Good Reading,* in 1907 *Meaning of the Times,* in 1908 *Work and Habits* and *Americans of Today and Tomorrow,* —volumes intended especially for young men and women. In 1915, while spending a year as a war correspondent in Germany he produced his *What Is Back of the War,* which was regarded in America as distinctly pro-German, and brought the author some unpopularity. Beveridge's greatest work, however, was his biography of Chief Justice John Marshall, designed as an historical and political interpretation of the Supreme Court and of Marshall's part in giving that court its place in American history. This task he accomplished in a way that gained the universal approval of scholars and critics. As a biographer Beveridge showed his characteristic industry in gathering his materials, a discriminating mind in sifting and evaluating, a painstaking care in revising and rewriting until the facts took on their right relations and proportionate importance, and "the picture stood out as an historic and artistic whole." Bringing to his task sympathy for his subject, the art of eloquent and effective writing, and an undimmed historical imagination, he produced an outstanding historical biography. The first two volumes of *The Life of John Marshall* appeared in 1916, the second two in 1919. Beveridge then turned his attention to what he considered a harder and more important task, a similar biography of Lincoln in four volumes. At the time of his death two of these volumes had been substantially completed. He brought to this task the same qualities that had been applied to his *Marshall*. He had a horror of mistakes and his completed chapters had been read in manuscript by many historical scholars and were carefully revised and rewritten, some of them as many as fifteen times. His death was regretted on many accounts, but above all because of the loss to the world of his uncompleted Lincoln.

[*Pearson's Mag.*, Oct. 1910; *Am. Mag.*, Oct. 1910; *Saturday Evening Post*, Apr. 2, 1910; *Our Day*, July 1899; *Outlook*, July 18, 1917; *Am. Rev. of Revs.*, June 1927; *N. Y. Times*, Apr. 28, 1927; the *Indianapolis Star*, and *News*, same date.]

J.A.W.

BEVERLEY, ROBERT (*c.* 1673–1722), historian of Virginia, was the second son of that Robert Beverley (*c.* 1641–1687), representative of a "cavalier" family of the minor gentry of Yorkshire, who had emigrated to Virginia in 1663, and there played a conspicuous part in quelling Bacon's Rebellion. His mother, probably daughter of a Hull merchant, is recorded prior to her Beverley marriage in 1666 as the widow of George Keeble, a Virginia planter and magistrate. The future historian was born on his father's dwelling plantation in Middlesex County, and was sent thence, for education, to England. On his return to Virginia after his father's death he enrolled himself a volunteer scrivener in the provincial secretary's office, where his parts soon recommended him for service as clerk of a legislative committee; and by 1696 he had achieved the important posts of clerk of the General Court, clerk of the Council, and clerk of the General Assembly. As an incident to this employment at the statehouse he had become a freeholder in Jamestown, and on that footing sat as the burgess for the capital in the Assemblies of 1699, 1700–2 and 1705–6. In June 1703 he went to England to protect his interest in a litigation there pending before the Privy Council, and was detained for eighteen months. Being invited by a bookseller to criticize the MS. of Oldmixon's *British Empire in America,* he found the account of Virginia so jejune that he was moved then and there to put together his own *History and Present State of Virginia* (1705); a little book which has survived for two centuries by reason of its tonic originality, shrewd observation, and humorous commentaries upon the foibles of the Southern planter. Racy of the soil of Virginia, it is distinguished from other early American books by its freedom from any effort to ape a literary Oxford manner. During this sojourn in England,

Beverley sent home several indiscreet letters on public affairs, one of which persuaded the Assembly to formulate an Address to the Crown, preferring what proved to be frivolous charges against Robert Quarry, the surveyor general of customs. The reply to this Address, a mortifying rebuke to the Assembly, ended Beverley's political career within a year after his return to Virginia. He now retired to Beverley Park, an estate on the upper waters of the Mattapony in King and Queen County, and there lived the remainder of his life, presiding in the county court, experimenting with viticulture, and speculating boldly in frontier lands. A call for a new printing of his *History* induced him to revise the book, though he did not improve it; and with the new edition he published also *The Abridgement of the Public Laws of Virginia* (1722), which he had compiled for his own use as a working magistrate. He died shortly after and was buried at Beverley Park, leaving one of the largest landed estates in contemporary Virginia. He was married to Ursula, second daughter of the first William Byrd of Westover, who died after a year of marriage in her seventeenth year, leaving a son, William (1698–1756), who built the notable house, "Blandfield," on the Rappahannock, where his descendants persist to this day.

[The sources for Beverley's life, now available, are his own prefaces and the public documents of the colony, principally the contemporary journals of the Council and the House of Burgesses, pieced out by scraps of county and other local records. His family, interesting for its sustained public service throughout the colonial period and for its alliances, is fortunate in having its generations recorded and fully documented by Dr. W. G. Stanard, in *Va. Mag.*, vols. II, III, XX, XXI, XXII.]

F.H.

BEWLEY, ANTHONY (May 22, 1804–Sept. 13, 1860), Methodist clergyman, was born in Tennessee, the son of a local Methodist preacher. He was a member of the Tennessee Conference 1829–37 and then moved with his wife and children to southwestern Missouri. He joined the Missouri Conference in 1843 but declined to go with it into the Methodist Episcopal Church South in 1845. With a few others of like convictions he maintained a loose association and preached to a handful of sympathizers until 1848, when the group was reorganized as the Missouri Conference of the Northern Church and Bewley was assigned to the Washington Mission in Arkansas. There for ten years he worked amid social ostracism and petty persecution, his children excluded from the schools and his sisters so intimidated that they did not dare attend his preaching. In 1858, as a reward for this devotion to his Church and its principles, he was sent on missionary work to Johnson County, Tex., just south of Fort Worth, in territory dangerous for an abolitionist or a supposed abolitionist to enter. For two years he held his ground, and then Bishop Ames, as if bent on making a martyr, reassigned him to the same post. Bewley made a visit to his old friends in Missouri and then returned reluctantly to Texas. Serious trouble arose immediately through the publication of a letter, dated July 3, 1860, purporting to be addressed to Bewley by a W. H. Bailey at Benton Creek. The letter gave a long list of "fellow workers," and discussed the certain election of Lincoln, the underground railroad, combustible material for firing buildings, plans for destroying towns and mills, and methods of coöperating with "our colored friends." The letter contained nothing that could have been news to Bewley if he had been implicated in such a plot, but it sounded every note calculated to excite mob fury. Church as well as secular papers republished the letter. With his wife and children, Bewley fled north through Indian Territory to Arkansas and on across the Missouri line. Meanwhile rewards totaling $1,000 had been offered for his capture, and a posse led by A. G. Brayman and Joe Johnson of Fort Worth was in pursuit. On Sept. 3, 1860, he was overtaken near Cassville, Mo. He was not allowed to say good-by to his wife, but a bundle of clothes which she sent after him was given to him, and at Fayetteville, Ark., where he was held Sept. 4–7, he was allowed to write her a farewell letter. From Fayetteville he was taken to Fort Worth, where a mob hanged him to a tree that had been used on similar occasions. His murder terminated the activities of the Methodist Episcopal Church in Texas.

[C. Elliott, "Martyrdom of Bewley" in *Meth. Quart. Rev.*, Oct. 1863; M. Phelan, *A Hist. of Early Methodism in Texas 1817–66* (1924); L. C. Matlack, *The Antislavery Struggle and Triumph in the M. E. Ch.* (1881).]

G. H. G.

BIARD, PIERRE (*c.* 1567–Nov. 17, 1622), Jesuit missionary, was born at Grenoble, France. He entered the Society of Jesus, June 5, 1583, and in 1608, while professor of theology and Hebrew at Lyons, was named by the Royal Confessor head of the Acadia Mission founded in 1603 by the Huguenot, De Monts. In spite of Calvinist opposition, two Jesuits, Biard and Massé, sailed on Jan. 26, 1611, with the expedition financed largely by the Marquise de Guercheville, and after violent storms, graphically described in Biard's Letter, reached Port Royal on May 22. Here, with only scanty supplies, they held religious services and instructed the Indians. With difficulty they learned the language and endeavored to convey some general spiritual concepts to a people whose ideas were solely of sensible objects. By means of the material helps of the Church and by aiding the Indians in illness, Biard won their confidence. He visited the French trade-posts of the St. John and the St. Croix and also the later Castine where he saw the Penobscots, "the finest assemblage of savages." On a trip along the coast from Port Royal to Kinnibéqui (Kennebec) to see the English fort, as he entered the Great Bay of the "very beautiful river Pentegoet" (Penobscot) he was in grave danger of attack; yet soon he was performing a cure on a sick native.

In 1613 with La Saussaye he helped found a settlement at St. Sauveur, now Bar Harbor, which was soon plundered by the English under Samuel Argall [*q.v.*], later governor of Virginia. The carrying off of Biard and another priest to Virginia, their escape from hanging, their forced return to witness the destruction of Port Royal, their second storm-tossed voyage with their captors, the drifting to the Azores and to Wales, and the final landing in France all make a thrilling tale. Lescarbot, the parliamentary advocate and historian, differs, however, from Biard in his account of the sacking of the settlements, and intimates that dissensions had arisen between Biard and Saint-Just, the head of the colony, which provoked Biard in resentment to tell the Governor of Virginia that colonists had captured an English vessel and were about to fortify the post with thirty cannon (See Marc Lescarbot, *Histoire de la Nouvelle France,* 1617; an English translation of the fifth book, relating to Acadia, in *Forerunners and Competitors of the Pilgrims,* 1912, pp. 523–62). Yet Lescarbot calls Biard "a very learned man—highly spoken of." In his own account Biard appears as a keen observer of new lands; a single-minded worker for the Faith: a writer direct and vivid in pictures of Indian ceremonies and fighting; a sympathetic analyst of Indian nature; a healer claiming no personal merit for "cures" wrought by prayer; and finally the courageous voyager forgiving his piratical captain and even rescuing him from death on the hazardous journey homeward. On his arrival in France, Biard was accused of having been in league with the marauders who destroyed the settlements (*Factum du Procès, Entre Messire Jean de Biencourt . . . et Pierre Biard,* 1614), and set to work upon his *Relation* which constitutes his defense (see Pierre Biard, *Relation de la Nouvelle France,* 1616; translated in *The Jesuit Relations,* ed. by R. G. Thwaites, 1897, vols. III, IV). Upon its publication he returned to his work as professor of theology; later, he served as spiritual adviser in an army campaign and, as a result of its privations, died at Avignon while resting among simple novices of the order.

[In addition to references given above see H. P. Biggar, *The Early Trading Companies of New France* (1901); *Cath. Encyc.*; Street's *Hist. of Mt. Desert,* ed. by S. A. Eliot (1905). There is uncertainty as to the exact dates of Biard's birth and death; those given in *Jesuit Relations* are the ones followed in this sketch.]

M. C. H.

BIBB, GEORGE MORTIMER (Oct. 30, 1776–Apr. 14, 1859), lawyer, senator, the son of Richard and Lucy (Booker) Bibb, was born in Prince Edward County, Va. He early went to college, graduating from both Hampden-Sidney and William and Mary, and in his old age held the sentimental distinction of being the oldest living graduate from each. Not caring for the ministry, he made the very natural choice of the law and soon began its study under Richard Venable. After beginning his practise in Virginia, in 1798 he took up his residence in Lexington, Ky. His profound and exact legal ability, together with a courtly manner, won him when only thirty-two years old (1808) an appointment to the bench of the court of appeals, the highest court in the state. The next year he was elevated to the chief justiceship, but resigned in 1810. In 1811 he was elected to the United States Senate. Here, as one of the "War Hawks," he took a prominent part in forcing war against Great Britain and in loyally upholding President Madison in carrying it on. But his Kentucky law practise and associations had greater attractions for him than being a senator in the muddy village of Washington, so in 1814 he resigned, and took up his residence in Frankfort. For the next ten years and more he was closely associated with state politics and party maneuvers. In 1816 Gov. George Madison died and the lieutenant-governor, Gabriel Slaughter, became governor. Immediately the question arose on the interpretation of the constitution concerning the succession: whether the lieutenant-governor should serve out the unexpired term of his predecessor or a special election should be held. The peace of the state was soon upset, and Bibb, becoming a member of the lower house of the legislature in 1817, did all within his power to unseat Slaughter and to question the validity of his acts. The movement to oust Slaughter, however, failed. In 1822 Bibb and Henry Clay were appointed commissioners to Virginia to plead before the legislature there for an agreement which would straighten out the complicated land claims which had become more confounded by certain occupying-claimant laws passed by Kentucky, which the United States Supreme Court had declared unconstitu-

tional in the case of Green *vs.* Biddle. Clay and Bibb visited Virginia and addressed the legislature but to no effect. The next year both were appointed to uphold Kentucky before the Supreme Court in a re-hearing. They argued the case in Washington but failed to win the decision. In the devastating fight between the Relief and Anti-Relief parties, Bibb stood behind the radicalism of the latter group, and when violent hands were laid on the court of appeals, resulting in setting up a new court, Bibb supported the latter and practised before it. In his attempt to compose the judicial squabble, Gov. Joseph Desha appointed Bibb chief justice in 1827. Bibb resigned the next year to become again a United States senator, serving this time the full six years. In national politics he was at first a supporter of Andrew Jackson. In 1824 he had opposed Clay on the ground that he could not be elected president, and when he reached the Senate he stood behind President Jackson in opposing the Maysville Road Bill. A few years of close association with Jackson convinced him, however, that the President was a tyrant who refused other people the right to an opinion. He especially disagreed with Jackson on the bank question. When his term as senator had expired in 1835 he returned to Kentucky and became chancellor of the Louisville court of chancery, holding this position until 1844 when President Tyler appointed him secretary of the treasury. Bibb went out of office with Tyler on Mar. 4, 1845. He remained in Washington and Georgetown for the rest of his life, practising before the District courts and serving as chief clerk in the attorney-general's office. He was a typical "gentleman of the old school," ever refusing to discard knee-breeches for pantaloons. Twice married, he was the father of seventeen children.

[Mrs. Chapman Coleman, *The Life of John J. Crittenden* (1871); T. M. Green, *The Spanish Conspiracy: A Review of Early Spanish Movements in the Southwest* (1891); Lewis Collins, *Hist. of Ky.* (1874), II, 277; *Reg. of Ky. State Hist. Soc.* (1903), I, 43; *Louisville Daily Courier,* Apr. 19, 1859.]

E. M. C.

BIBB, WILLIAM WYATT (Oct. 2, 1781– July 10, 1820), governor of Alabama, was born in Amelia County, Ga. His grandfather was one John Bibb, a Huguenot from Wales who located in Hanover County, Va.; his father was William Bibb, a captain in the Revolutionary Army. His mother, Sally Wyatt, a descendant of Gov. Francis Wyatt of Virginia, was the daughter of William and Sallie Wyatt, and a relative of Martha Custis Washington. William Wyatt Bibb was educated at the University of Pennsylvania, graduating in medicine in 1801, and

His mother, Sally Wyatt, was a descendant of the Rev. Hawte Wyatt, minister at James-town, and a daughter of Joseph and Sallie Wyatt

went at once to Petersburg, Ga., where he practised his profession. He served in both the House and Senate of the state legislature, and, elected as a Democrat to the United States Congress, he continued there from Jan. 26, 1805, to Nov. 6, 1813, when he resigned. He was then elected to fill the vacancy in the Senate caused by the resignation of William H. Crawford and served for three years, when he again resigned before the expiration of his term. His second resignation was due to a nation-wide disapproval of the congressional measure fixing the salaries of congressmen and senators at $1,800 a year, the services of these officials prior to that time having been paid *per diem* during the sittings of the Congress. President Monroe appointed Bibb, in April 1817, governor of the newly formed Territory of Alabama. He entered upon his duties at St. Stephens, and when the territory was admitted to the Union as a state his administration was indorsed by a popular vote which continued him as governor. The power of the Creek Indians having been broken by the army led by Andrew Jackson, following the massacre of Fort Mims, the administration of Bibb was pacific. His experience in public life was regarded as of great value in the formative period of the state's political history and especially in the framing of the constitution. He was married in 1803 to Mary Freeman, known as "the beauty of Broad River," daughter of Col. Holman Freeman of Wilkes County, Ga., a Revolutionary hero and Whig leader under Gov. Elijah Clark. Bibb died in Autauga County, Ala., from the effects of a fall from a horse frightened by a violent thunder storm. He was succeeded as governor by his brother, Thomas Bibb, who was at the time serving as president of the Alabama Senate.

[A. J. Pickett, *Hist. of Ala.* (1851); G. R. Gilmer, *Sketches of Some of the First Families of Upper Ga.* (1859); C. E. Jones, "Gov. William Wyatt Bibb," *Pubs. Ala. Hist. Soc.*, III, 1899; *Pubs. Ala. Hist. Soc. Misc. Coll.*, I, 1901; L. L. Knight, *Standard Hist. of Ga. and Georgians*, VI (1917); T. M. Owen, *Hist. of Ala. and Dict. of Ala. Biog.*, III (1921).]   M. B. O.

BICKEL, LUKE WASHINGTON (Sept. 21, 1866–May 11, 1917), mariner-missionary, eighteen years captain of the ship *Fukuin Maru,* planned and developed under the auspices of the American Baptist Missionary Society a notable work of evangelization and education on the islands of the Inland Sea of Japan. He was of German descent, his father, Philipp, one of the young revolutionists of 1848, having fled to this country, married Katherine, daughter of Rev. Samuel R. Clarke, become a Baptist minister, and served in the Civil War. At the time of Luke's birth, he was publishing German Christian literature in Cincinnati, Ohio; but when the former was about twelve years old he returned to Germany with his family to carry on publishing work for the Baptists there. The son graduated from the Reformed Church Academy, Hamburg, in 1880, took three years' collegiate work at Soest, and then spent a year at Wandsbeck Gymnasium.

Although interested in religious activities, he was passionately fond of the sea, and at eighteen he was apprenticed for a term of four years on an English merchant sailing ship. By the time he was twenty-eight, he had become a captain, holding, though an American, a British Board of Trade certificate as master mariner. In 1893 he married Annie Burgess, a native of Norwich, England, and established a home in London. Soon, yielding to his wife's persuasions, he gave up the sea, and assumed control of the business of the London Baptist Publishing Society. The American Baptist Missionary Society, having been offered means to build a vessel for work among the Inland Sea islanders, asked him to captain the ship and the work. He consented, took a brief course at Spurgeon's College, and started for Japan, arriving in May 1898. The *Fukuin Maru* was built for him and dedicated Sept. 13, 1899. On this vessel and its successor, of the same name, built some fourteen years later, he traveled among the islands, establishing and directing missions for the rest of his life. He was a man of large proportions, great strength and courage, and as capable in mind as in body. His physical ability, nautical knowledge, and unselfish services, won the respect and confidence of the people. Selecting a strategic center in each group of islands, he made that a nucleus, arranging that from that center work should be carried on in every village in the group. Weakened by his strenuous life and a siege of typhoid fever, he failed to rally from a minor surgical operation and died at the age of fifty-one, but so well had his plan and work succeeded, that at his death there were sixty-two regular preaching places, fifty-two Sunday-schools with 3,500 pupils, and 400 villages in which services were occasionally held; while all denominations regarded his achievement as among the most notable in the missionary annals of the Japanese Empire.

["The Mission Ship 'Fukuin Maru'," ch. X in *The Christian Movement in Japan*, 1908, was written by Bickel. See also Chas. K. Harrington, *Captain Bickel of the Inland Sea* (1919); J. A. Foote, "Luke W. Bickel: An Appreciation," *The Standard*, June 30, 1917; F. C. Briggs, "Luke W. Bickel," *The Christian Movement in the Japanese Empire*, 1918; C. K. Harrington, "A Missionary Captain and His Gospel Ship," *Missionary Review of the World*, Sept. 1917; *Ann. Report of Am. Bapt. Foreign Missionary Soc.*, 1917.]   H. E. S.

BICKERDYKE, MARY ANN BALL (July 19, 1817–Nov. 8, 1901), "Mother Bickerdyke," one of the most capable and beloved of the women who ministered to the sick and wounded during the Civil War, was born in Knox County, Ohio, near what is now Mount Vernon. She was the daughter of Hiram and Anna (Rodgers) Ball, and came of rugged, fighting stock. David Ball, her first American ancestor on the paternal side, emigrated to this country from England some time before 1700 and settled at Newark, N. J. Three of his sons were in the War of the Revolution. Mary's grandfather, David, had gone to Ohio the year it was admitted as a state, and become a well-to-do citizen. On her mother's side she was descended from Thomas Rodgers who came over in the *Mayflower*. John Rodgers, her grandfather, as a lad of sixteen had gone into the battle of Bunker Hill and fought through the seven years of the war. In his household her early years were spent, for her mother died when she was seventeen months old. Later she lived with her uncle, Henry Rodgers. Brought up on a farm and fond of outdoor life, she developed physical hardiness, and became a frugal, competent housekeeper. At the age of sixteen she entered Oberlin College and spent four years there. An epidemic caused her to leave before graduating, and the removal of her uncle's family to Cincinnati prevented her return. Here she took a course of training for nurses under Dr. Reuben D. Mussey [*q.v.*], and became familiar with hospital work. On Apr. 27, 1847, she married a mechanic, Robert Bickerdyke, who was a widower with children. Several children were born to her. In 1856 the family moved to Galesburg, Ill., where her husband died two years later. In 1861 she was listed in the Galesburg directory as a "botanic physician."

When the war broke out, the patriotic women of her town, recognizing her peculiar fitness, urged her to attach herself to the army. With $500 worth of supplies which were put at her disposal she began work in the regimental hospitals at Cairo, Ill., and continued her service until Mar. 20, 1865. She was in nineteen hard-fought battles in the departments of the Ohio, Tennessee, and Cumberland armies. Whether ministering to men on the field, assisting at the operating table, running diet kitchens where she generally did the cooking herself, superintending hospitals, or foraging for supplies, she was equally efficient. A surgeon of the 22nd Illinois Infantry, Dr. Woodward, describes her as "a large, heavy woman of forty-five years, strong as a man; muscles of iron; nerves of steel; sensitive but self-reliant; kind and tender; seeking all for others, nothing for herself" (Julia A. Chase, *Mary A. Bickerdyke*, 1896, p. 11). She made the enlisted men her special care, and fought for their rights like a tigress, and they loved her as a mother. She was a terror to incompetent and dissipated officers, and invariably effected their discharge. She cut through red tape ruthlessly and sometimes violated army procedure, but though called to account by subordinate officials she was always sustained by their superiors. She was an especial favorite of Gen. Grant and Gen. Sherman; the former gave her a pass to and from any point in his military division with free transportation at all times, and after the battle of Vicksburg she became a special attaché of Sherman's corps. The Sanitary Commission made her its agent and had implicit confidence in her management. Her executive ability was of a high order, and her native economy saved the Commission and the Government an incalculable amount. One of her achievements was the establishment of army laundries. Previously the clothing and bedding of wounded soldiers had been destroyed. She procured washing machines, portable kitchens, and mangles, and with the aid of contrabands, who were devoted to her, she cleansed and prepared for redistribution what formerly had been a total loss. She also made her contrabands salvage accoutrements left on the battlefield. Innumerable stories are told of her resourcefulness in overcoming obstacles. Because of the uniqueness of her character and work, she was one of the most picturesque as well as efficient women of the army.

Her career after the war was a varied one. She became a legally admitted pension attorney and helped nurses and veterans secure pensions. Gen. Logan voiced a general feeling when he wrote to the chairman of the pension commission, "I desire to introduce Mother Bickerdyke. What she wants is right, and what she says will be the truth." For a year she was housekeeper in the Chicago Home for the Friendless. In 1867 she initiated a movement to get ex-soldiers to go West and through her influence some 300 families migrated to Kansas. She herself settled in Salina, and opened a hotel under the patronage of the Kansas Pacific Railroad. For four years she did missionary work in New York, under the direction of the Board of City Missions. In 1874 she returned to Kansas to live with her two sons, and at the time of the locust plague went to Illinois and secured relief for the sufferers. Later she was in California, working in the United States Mint. Congress in 1886 granted her a pension of twenty-five dollars a month. She died at the home of her son at Bunker Hill, Kan., and was buried in Galesburg, Ill., where by means of an appropriation of $5,000 made by the State in 1903 a monument has been erected to her memory.

[Mary A. Livermore, *My Story of the War* (1888); L. P. Brockett and May C. Vaughn, *Woman's Work in the Civil War* (1867); Mary A. G. Holland, *Our Army Nurses* (1895); Florence S. Kellogg, *Mother Bickerdyke* (1907); "Diary of Mrs. E. C. Porter," *U. S. Sanitary Commission Bull.*, Sept. 1, 1864.]   H.E.S.

BICKETT, THOMAS WALTER (Feb. 28, 1869–Dec. 28, 1921), governor of North Carolina, was born in Monroe, N. C., the son of Thomas Winchester and Mary (Covington) Bickett. Receiving his preparatory education in the public schools, he entered Wake Forest College in 1886 and received the bachelor's degree in 1890. He taught for two years, first at Marion and then at Winston-Salem, reading law at the same time, and in 1892 entered the law school of the University of North Carolina. He was admitted to the bar in February 1893 and practised for a time in Monroe and later in Danbury, but in 1895 moved to Louisburg. There, on Nov. 29, 1898, he married Fannie N. Yarborough. At the bar Bickett was quickly successful and won a great though local reputation, not only for professional ability, but for the satisfying human qualities which distinguished him through life. Inheriting a full share of Irish wit, he was a gifted teller of anecdotes which were racy of the soil and full of good humor which made him widely popular. But he had at the same time convictions which were passionately held and sternly followed. In his sympathy for the unfortunate and the oppressed was to be found the key-note of his real nature.

He took no active part in politics until 1906 when he was elected to the lower house of the state legislature, serving one term and taking a rather prominent part, for a new member, in the advocacy of legal reforms, an enlarged educational program, and more adequate care of the unfortunate. The next year he so distinguished himself in the Democratic state convention by a speech nominating an unsuccessful candidate for governor that he was nominated for attorney-general, a position which he filled for eight years. During this time he represented the state in five cases before the Supreme Court of the United States, the most notable being the Tennessee boundary dispute, and won all of them. In great demand always as a speaker he became widely known during these eight years and in 1916 he was nominated for governor in the first state-wide primary and was elected by a large majority over Frank A. Linney, the Republican candidate.

He proved himself, in spite of small executive powers, capable of vigorous and highly successful executive leadership. During his four-year term he recommended to the legislature forty-eight measures, forty of which were enacted into law. Among these were statutes providing for a six-months school term with increased salaries for teachers, for broader agricultural education, for more liberal support of the state's institutions, both educational and charitable, for an improved system of state highways, for more humane prison administration, and for tax reform. He believed that it was the major function of government to improve the economic and social condition of the mass of the people, and throughout his term he sought to improve the lot of the tenant-farmer class, to encourage home ownership, to elevate the negro, and to better the relations of capital and labor. During the war Bickett threw himself passionately into the task of leading the state to the exertion of its utmost power. Every agency of the state was brought into action and by proclamations and public addresses, in which were combined wit, sentiment, idealism, and deep conviction, he interpreted the struggle as he conceived it in terms that all could understand.

Bickett was short of stature and of thick-set frame. His ruddy face was frequently lighted by a smile of compelling charm and his blue eyes furnished a clear index to his quick turns of feeling. He died suddenly of apoplexy less than a year after his retirement from office, and was survived by his wife and one son.

[*Pub. Letters and Papers of Thos. Walter Bickett* (1923), comp. by Santford Martin and ed. by R. B. House; memorial sketch by Jas. S. Manning in *Proc. of the N. C. Bar Ass.*, 1922; *Who's Who in America*, 1920–21. The N. C. newspapers about the dates of his nomination for governor and of his death contain much material relating to him.]   J.G.deR.H.

BICKMORE, ALBERT SMITH (Mar. 1, 1839–Aug. 12, 1914), educator, was born in Tenant's Harbor, Me., the son of John and Jane (Seavey) Bickmore. The great event of his childhood was a voyage with his father, a sea-captain and ship-builder, to Bordeaux. Prepared for college at the New London (N. H.) Academy, he was graduated from Dartmouth in 1860. His bent toward natural history then led him to the Lawrence Scientific School of Harvard University to study under Agassiz. Soon appointed an assistant in the Museum of Comparative Zoology, in 1862 he accompanied an expedition of P. T. Barnum's to Bermuda, where he made an extensive collection of marine animals for the museum. In 1862–63 he served with the 44th Massachusetts Volunteers, a nine-months regiment, and upon being mustered out returned to Cambridge with "a very fine collection" which he had made upon the North Carolina coast while detached from his regiment upon special hospital duty (*Annual Report of the Trustees of the Museum of Comparative Zoology,* 1862, 1863). Having received his B.S. from Harvard in 1864, in January 1865, financed in part by "friends of science in Boston and Cambridge," he embarked upon a voyage to the East. He traveled through the Malay Archipelago and the Dutch East Indies collecting shells and bird-skins, penetrated into a part of China unexplored by "foreigners" (see "Sketch of a Journey from Canton to Hankow," *Journal of the Royal Geographical Society,* XXXVIII, 1868, and *American Journal of Science,* July 1868), and visited the little-known Ainos of Japan. Returning to Boston in December 1867, during the following months he published several papers: "A Description of the Banda Islands" (*Proceedings of the Royal Geographical Society* 1867–68, pp. 324 ff.), "Some Remarks on the Recent Geological Changes in China and Japan" (*American Journal of Science,* March 1868), "The Ainos, or Hairy Men of Yesso" and "The Ainos, or Hairy Men of Saghalien and the Kurile Islands" (*Ibid.,* May 1868), and completed his *Travels in the East Indian Archipelago* (London 1868; New York 1869; Jena 1869). In 1868–69 he served as professor of natural history in Madison (now Colgate) University.

Meanwhile, for several years Bickmore had been elaborating a plan, conceived while he was a student under Agassiz, for a great natural-history museum, to be located in New York. Upon Bickmore's return from the East William E. Dodge 2nd, with whom he had been in correspondence, introduced him to Theodore Roosevelt (father of the President), who immediately took an active interest in the project. Under Roosevelt's leadership a series of informal conferences in the fall of 1868 led to a meeting of prominent citizens at the home of Benjamin H. Field in January 1869, at which the first board of trustees of what was to become the American Museum of Natural History was elected. Bickmore contributed the title of the institution—national in scope, the definition of its relations with the municipality, the plan adopted for its financing, and not least, the enthusiastic arguments which won the support of Tweed and Tilden and secured from the legislature, without amendment, the charter as it had been drawn by Joseph Choate. Appointed superintendent in 1869 he served in that capacity till 1884, when he resigned to become curator of the Museum's Department of Public Instruction. The educa-

tion of the public had been one of the ideals of the founders, and under Bickmore's curatorship the schools of both city and state were brought into organized relation with the Museum, and Bickmore's lectures, illustrated by stereopticon slides from collections made by himself, became an increasingly important annual institution. In 1904, incapacitated for active service by chronic rheumatism which confined him to a chair, he was made curator emeritus of his department, but he continued in the office of trustee, which he had held since 1885. He died in August 1914 at his summer home in Nonquitt, Mass. A colleague has referred to Bickmore's "unflagging industry, his unshakable resolution" which were "supported by an almost sublime optimism." During his lifetime a division of the new building was named in his honor, and since his death he has been acclaimed "Father of the Museum."

Bickmore was married in 1873 to Charlotte A. Bruce of New York.

[*Am. Museum Jour.,* 1900–01, Nov. 1911, Apr. 1914, Feb. 1915, May 1917; *Forty-sixth Annual Report Am. Mus. Nat. Hist.,* pp. 15, 95; *Fifty-eighth Annual Report,* p. 1; *Watchman-Examiner,* Aug. 27, 1914; George H. Sherwood, *Free Education by the Am. Mus. of Nat. Hist.* (1918); *Bull. Geol. Soc. of America,* Mar. 1915; *Who's Who in America,* 1914–15; *Who's Who in N. Y.,* 1914; *N. Y. Times,* Aug. 14, 1914.]

E. R. D.

BIDDLE, CLEMENT (May 10, 1740–July 14, 1814), Revolutionary soldier, merchant, was descended from William Biddle, a shoemaker and colonel in Cromwell's army, who came to America in 1681 and by purchase from William Penn established himself as one of the proprietors in West New Jersey. His grandson, John, removed to Philadelphia in 1730 and six years later married Sarah Owen. Five children were born of this marriage, of whom Clement was the second. While still a boy he entered his father's shipping and importing business, and in 1771 his name appears as a partner in the firm. His commercial life was soon interrupted by the approach of the Revolutionary War. With his older brother, Owen, he signed the non-importation agreement of 1765, and for the next ten years was active in the patriotic cause in Philadelphia. In 1775 he helped to raise in Philadelphia a company of volunteers, the "Quaker Blues," and on July 8, 1776, was appointed by Congress deputy quartermaster-general for the militia of Pennsylvania and New Jersey with the rank of colonel. He took part in the battle of Trenton and was delegated by Washington to receive the swords of the surrendering Hessian officers. He also participated in the battles of Brandywine, Germantown, and Monmouth. In November 1776 Gen. Greene made him his aide-de-camp, and in

July 1777 appointed him commissary-general of forage. In this position he served until June 1780, when he resigned in order to give attention to his business affairs. In September 1781, at the urgent request of Greene, the supreme executive council of Pennsylvania appointed him quartermaster-general of the state militia with the rank of colonel. After the Revolution Biddle continued in his business as a merchant and importer in Philadelphia and came to hold many positions of honor and trust under both state and federal governments. He was in continual correspondence with Washington, whose factor he was in Philadelphia and with whom he was on terms of friendship. In 1788 he became a justice of the court of common pleas and in 1789 Washington appointed him United States marshal of Pennsylvania, in which office he continued until 1793. Biddle was twice married. His first wife was Mary Richardson, who died in 1773 without surviving children. In 1774 he married Rebekah Cornell, whose father at the time of his death in 1765 was lieutenant-governor and chief justice of Rhode Island. Of this marriage there were born thirteen children, of whom five died before reaching maturity.

[The chief source of information about Biddle is the manuscript "Washington Correspondence with Clement Biddle" in the Pa. Hist. Soc. Lib. in Philadelphia. See also *Pa. Mag. of Hist. and Biog.*, vols. XLII, XLIII. The genealogy of the Biddle family is given in "Col. Clement Biddle with a genealogy of the Biddle Family" in *Boogher's Repository* (1883), I, 101. Other sources are "A Sketch of William Biddle and Thomas Biddle" in *Pa. Mag. of Hist. and Biog.*, vol. XIV; "Owen Biddle," *Ibid.*, XVI; and Henry D. Biddle, *Notes on the Genealogy of the Biddle Family* (1895).]

R.S.C.

BIDDLE, HORACE P. (Mar. 24, 1811–May 13, 1900), jurist, writer, was born in what is now Hocking County, Ohio, the son of Benjamin and Abigail Converse Biddle. His parents came to Ohio from Connecticut and built a home in what was then Fairfield County on the Hocking River. Here Horace Biddle was born and reared on a backwoods farm. Like most boys of the time, he attended the country school for a few weeks during the winter months and worked on the farm during the summer. His school days were numbered but he read everything that came his way. He scorned the mere form but cherished the content of an education. Looking upon honors, titles and degrees as "burdens rather than buoys," he used to say that a man's name should float him without prefixes or suffixes. He finally determined to study law and entered the office of Hocking H. Hunter, a successful lawyer and striking personality of Lancaster. Admitted to the Ohio Bar in 1839, in October of the same year he began to practise in Logansport, Ind. It was here that

he spent the major part of his active life and built up his legal reputation. He dabbled in politics somewhat but was in no sense a politician. He was a useful and influential member of the convention which drafted the Indiana constitution of 1851. In 1846 he was elected president judge of the eighth Indiana district, and in 1857 he was elected to the supreme bench but was denied his commission as it was decided that no vacancy existed at the time. At a later time (1874) he was again chosen to the supreme court of Indiana, this time by an unprecedented majority. In 1881 he returned to private life to devote himself to literary pursuits. His home was on "Biddle's Island" in the Wabash River. Here, an adept in woodcraft and an expert fisherman, he spent many happy days communing with nature and reading the books of his splendid library—said to be the largest private library in Indiana at that time. He had a decided bent for language. He made translations from French and German poets and was a regular contributor to leading periodicals. He could also translate from the Portuguese, Spanish, and Italian. He was familiar with Latin and had some knowledge of Oriental languages. He published several volumes of poems, among them *American Boyhood* (1876) which a reviewer in the *Nation* (XIII, 15) pronounced an original and interesting book which would have been vastly better in prose. His most ambitious book was *The Musical Scale* (1860), in which he sought to explain the law governing the arrangement of the musical scale. With his long white beard and patriarchal appearance, he was a striking figure in Indiana for many decades. He was individual and not without his eccentricities. When he was elected to the supreme court he disposed of his law books so that, as he said, the lawyers could not borrow them and forget to bring them back. He remained a student of philosophy, science, literature and music throughout his entire life.

[Eva Peters Reynolds, *Horace P. Biddle* (1890); Jacob P. Dunn, *Indiana and Indianians* (1919), III. 1220; *Encyc. of Biog. of Ind.*, ed. by Geo. I. Reed (1899), II, 170; *Hist. of Cass, Miami, Howard, and Tipton Counties* (1898), I, 1–4; *Biog. Hist. of Eminent and Self-Made Men of Ind.* (1880), II (10th Dist.), 4.]

T.F.M.

BIDDLE, JAMES (Feb. 18, 1783–Oct. 1, 1848), naval officer, was born in Philadelphia, the son of Charles and Hannah (Shepard) Biddle, the family, of the Quaker faith, having been one of prominence since early colonial times. After finishing a course of study at the University of Pennsylvania, where he showed particular interest in literature, he and his younger brother, Edward, in the year 1800 received warrants as midshipmen in the navy, and were attached to the frigate *President,* which sailed for the West Indies in September of that year, upon a cruise during which the younger brother died of fever. On the termination of our misunderstanding with France, James Biddle, as one of the few who escaped the effect of the radical reduction of the navy, was retained as midshipman. During 1802 he served aboard the *Constellation,* in the squadron engaged in the protection of American shipping in the Mediterranean against Tripolitan vessels. On returning home in the spring of 1803, he was transferred to the *Philadelphia,* under the command of Capt. William Bainbridge [*q.v.*], and in her shared in the disaster of her grounding near Tripoli on Oct. 31, 1803, and her surrender to the enemy, as well as in the subsequent imprisonment of the ship's company for nineteen months. Upon the conclusion of peace with Tripoli, Biddle returned to the United States with Capt. Bainbridge, and was given command, with the rank of lieutenant, of a gunboat engaged in protecting the South Atlantic Coast against marauding privateers. In 1807, obtaining leave of absence, he made a voyage to China as first officer of a merchant ship, and upon his return he was detailed to the Delaware flotilla employed in enforcing the embargo. In 1809 he became second lieutenant of the *President* under his old commander, Bainbridge, and in 1810 obtained his first independent command, that of the sloop-of-war *Syren.* He subsequently served for short periods in the *Constitution* and again in the *President,* and in 1811 was bearer of dispatches from the American Government to its minister to France, remaining nearly four months in Paris.

On the breaking out of the second war against Great Britain, Biddle was appointed first lieutenant of the sloop-of-war *Wasp,* commanded by Capt. Jacob Jones [*q.v.*], and took part in the desperate close-quarters fight which ended in the boarding and capture of the British brig *Frolic,* the boarding party being led by Biddle, who sprang into the rigging and tore down the British ensign with his own hands. He was left in charge of the prize with orders to make his way to Charleston, but the appearance of the powerful British ship-of-the-line *Poictiers,* 74 guns, resulted in the capture of both vessels, the American officers and crew being taken to Bermuda and paroled in March 1813. Both Jones and Biddle were promoted for the capture of the *Frolic,* Biddle to the rank of master-commandant. Given command of the sloop-of-war *Hornet,* he started to accompany the *Peacock,* the *Tom Bowline,* and the ill-fated *President,* to the rendezvous desig-

nated by Commodore Stephen Decatur [*q.v.*], at Tristan d'Acunha. Becoming separated from his consorts, he fell in with the British brig *Penguin,* of more than the *Hornet's* armament and crew, and a severe engagement ensued terminated by the *Penguin's* surrender. Capt. Biddle, who had been promoted to this rank before taking the *Penguin,* was destined, in what proved to be the last regular naval action of the war, to bring his actual warlike experience to a close by a dramatic escape from a British line-of-battle ship which appeared and was approached unawares by the *Hornet,* Apr. 27, 1815. Discovering his mistake at 9 p. m., Biddle changed his course away from the enemy, and a long chase began, lasting until the next evening, the Briton occasionally getting within firing distance. By dint of throwing overboard stores, extra boats, spars, ammunition, sheet-anchor, and at last every gun save one, the determined American captain had the satisfaction of saving his ship, which he brought into New York in July 1815, after peace had been signed.

Continuing in active duty after the war, Biddle was sent on the sloop-of-war *Ontario* to the Columbia River in 1817 to take possession of the Oregon territory. In 1822 he commanded the *Macedonian* on the West India station as commodore, and from 1826 to 1832 he cruised in South American waters and in the Mediterranean. His services in protecting American shipping in South America, at a time when revolutionary disorders particularly menaced it, earned him the gratitude of American merchants. From 1838 to 1842 he was at the head of the Naval Asylum at Philadelphia, and as commodore of the East Indian Squadron, he negotiated, in 1846, the first treaty between the United States and China. His last command was on the Pacific Coast during the war with Mexico. He died in Philadelphia.

[Jas. Fenimore Cooper, *Hist. of the Navy of the U. S.* (1839); J. H. Brown, *Am. Naval Heroes* (1899); Chas. Biddle, *Autobiography* (1883); *Cumming's Evening Telegraphic Bull.,* Oct. 2, 1848; Navy Registers, 1816–48; A. T. Mahan, *Sea Power in Its Relations to the War of 1812* (1905); T. Roosevelt, *The Naval War of 1812* (1882).]

E. B.

BIDDLE, NICHOLAS (Sept. 10, 1750–Mar. 7, 1778), naval officer, was the sixth son of William Biddle, a member of an old, originally Quaker family of New Jersey, and his wife, Mary Scull, daughter of Nicholas Scull, for many years surveyor general of Pennsylvania. Nicholas was born in Philadelphia some years after his father had moved to that city, and was bred to the sea, his first voyage being made to Quebec at the age of thirteen. After a short but eventful career in the merchant service, in which he experienced his full share of hardship and even shipwreck, showing on several occasions uncommon determination and pluck, he decided to enter the British Navy. Proceeding to London with letters of recommendation from Thomas Willing of Philadelphia, president of the Bank of North America, to Willing's brother-in-law, Captain, afterward Admiral, Sterling, R. N., Nicholas served for some time as midshipman in the latter's sloop-of-war *Portland* in 1772. In the autumn of that year, his cruise having come to an end, he asked to be transferred to one of the ships which the Royal Geographical Society sent out in 1773 under Capt. Phipps, afterward Lord Mulgrave, to discover the polar limits of navigation; but, his application being refused, he abandoned his career in the navy, and shipped before the mast on board one of the vessels of the polar expedition. Here he found himself in the company of young Horatio Nelson, afterward England's greatest naval hero, who, like himself, had made the sacrifice of his rank in order to indulge his spirit of adventure. Both were eventually appointed coxswains, in spite of their youth. The expedition penetrated as far north as 81° 39', and experienced the usual hardships and vicissitudes of an Arctic voyage. Upon his return to England, Biddle, owing to the strained relations between England and her American colonies, resigned his commission, returned to Philadelphia, and offered his services to the Continental Congress.

He was given charge of the *Franklin,* a "Provincial Armed Boat" or galley, fitted out by the Pennsylvania Committee of Safety for the defense of the Delaware, on Aug. 1, 1775, but in December of the same year he was placed in command of the brig *Andrea Doria* (14 guns and 130 men) with the rank of captain, and ordered to join the squadron of Esek Hopkins, commander-in-chief of the naval forces of the United Colonies, with which he took part in the expedition against New Providence. During and for some time after this service the efficiency of his vessel was greatly reduced by a violent epidemic of smallpox, to which many of his crew fell victims. On the breaking up of the fleet he cruised in the North Atlantic and took a large number of prizes laden with arms and ammunition, which thus fell into the hands of Washington, then at Cambridge, instead of those of the British forces. Off the coast of Newfoundland he was fortunate enough to capture two armed transports with 400 Highlanders destined for the British army at Boston. J. F. Cooper (*History of the Navy,* 1839, I, 114) thus refers to this period of Biddle's career:

"This vessel, a little brig, carrying 14 fours, actually took two armed transports filled with soldiers, and made prizes of so many merchantmen, that, it is affirmed on plausible authority, when she got back into the Delaware, but five of the common men who composed her original crew were in her; the rest having been put in the prizes, and their places supplied by volunteers from among the prisoners. Captain Biddle gained much credit for this cruise, and on his return, he was appointed to the command of the *Randolph* 32, then recently launched."

Ordered by the Marine Committee to Martinique (February 1777), the *Randolph* encountered a violent storm after leaving the Delaware capes, and lost her masts, which, as appears in a letter from Biddle to his brother, were made of rotten timber, for he writes from Charleston, "A person of credit declares to me that he knew those spars our masts were made of to have lain these eighteen years in the water at the mast yard." Repairs being quickly made, Biddle undertook a successful cruise to West Indian waters, capturing among other prizes the English ship *True Briton,* 20 guns, which, with three merchantmen that she was convoying, he carried into Charleston harbor, occasioning great satisfaction throughout the South. During the remainder of the season the *Randolph* was blockaded in Charleston by a superior British force, but in late February, 1778, in company with four small war-vessels fitted out by the State of South Carolina and placed under Biddle's command, he put to sea in quest of several British ships which had been cruising off Charleston for some time. About three o'clock on Mar. 7 a sail was made out to windward, whereupon the squadron hauled on the wind and stood for her. Unfortunately she proved to be the "two-decker" *Yarmouth,* carrying 64 guns. Awaiting the approach of the American vessels, Captain N. Vincent of the *Yarmouth* ranged up on the weather quarter of the largest, the *Randolph,* which, upon the British demand to show her colors, hoisted the American ensign and poured in a broadside. There is no authoritative report from an American source on the scene which followed, but we have the report of the British captain, dated Mar. 17, 1778, in which he says: "A smart action now commenced and was maintained with vigor for twenty minutes, when the stranger blew up. The two ships were so near each other at the time that many fragments of the wreck struck the *Yarmouth....* Early in the engagement Commodore Biddle was wounded, but, ordering a chair, was placed in it on the quarter-deck, and continued to direct the battle and encourage the crew. His fire was constant and well directed. . . . Just then while a surgeon was examining his wound, the *Randolph* was blown up and the commander, with 311 of her 315 officers and men perished" (*Ibid.*, I, 146). Such was the heroic end of a man of whom Cooper wrote (*Ibid.*, I, 148) : "His death occurred at the early age of twenty-seven, and he died unmarried, though engaged, at the time, to a lady in Charleston. There is little question that Nicholas Biddle would have risen to high rank and great consideration, had his life been spared. Ardent, ambitious, fearless, intelligent, and persevering, he had all the qualities of a great naval captain, and, though possessing some local family influence perhaps, he rose to the station he filled at so early an age, by personal merit. For so short a career, scarcely any other had been so brilliant; for though no victories over regular cruisers accompanied his exertions, he had ever been successful until the fatal moment when he so gloriously fell." In personal appearance Biddle was of athletic frame and strikingly handsome, while his manner was animated and entertaining. His brother Charles pays tribute to his temperate mode of life in these words, "I believe he never drank a quart of liquor in his life" (Charles Biddle, *Autobiography*, 1883, p. 108).

[S. P. Waldo, *Biog. Sketches of Am. Naval Heroes* (1823) ; Edward Biddle, "Capt. Nicholas Biddle," *Proc. U. S. Naval Institute*, Sept. 1917 ; G. W. Allen, *A Naval Hist. of the Am. Rev.* (2 vols., 1913).]

E.B.

BIDDLE, NICHOLAS (Jan. 8, 1786–Feb. 27, 1844), litterateur, scholar, statesman, financier, was born and died in Philadelphia. He came of an old Quaker family of some wealth that followed William Penn into West Jersey early in 1681. William Biddle of the third generation in West Jersey married Mary, the daughter of the Pennsylvania surveyor, Nicholas Scull, and became a resident of the newer colony across the Delaware. It was a son of this marriage, Charles Biddle, a vice-president of Pennsylvania under the constitution of 1776, who gave the name of Nicholas to his own son, born of Hannah Shepard of Beaufort, N. C. At the age of ten years, Nicholas Biddle entered the University of Pennsylvania and was ready to graduate when he was thirteen, but was not allowed to receive his degree because of his youth. He immediately entered the College of New Jersey at Princeton in 1799, where he took advanced work, especially in the classics, and graduated in 1801 as valedictorian, dividing honors for first place with another student. It was during this year that Joseph Dennie established in Philadelphia the *Port Folio*, the first periodical avowedly devoted to making an American literature, and young Bid-

dle was among the young men who caught Dennie's outlook and enthusiasm. Though he was devoted to the study of the classics and French literature, he selected the law as his profession. He seems to have studied the latter under his elder brother, William S. Biddle, and the well-known jurist William Lewis, both of whom recognized his ability as a scholar of unusual grasp and as a writer. Indeed his family expected him to become a writer rather than a lawyer.

When Gen. John Armstrong was sent as minister to France in 1804, he took Biddle as his secretary. They sailed for France in August and were present on Dec. 2 at the self-coronation of Napoleon at Notre Dame. Among the tasks which fell to the legation was the settlement of the claims of those who had been despoiled by French privateers in the Napoleonic wars. Although but eighteen years old, Biddle was intrusted with the auditing and payment of these spoliation claims, allowed by the French Government, which were to be met out of the Louisiana purchase fund. He began the study of French law and continued his study of European languages and history, winning notable French friendships that continued throughout his life. Late in 1805 he began to travel in Switzerland and Southern France, and in 1806 proceeded through Italy and Sicily to Greece. In August he retraced his steps, with more travel in France, Germany, and Holland, and, having been chosen by Minister James Monroe to be secretary of legation at London, he was soon established in that diplomat's family, and so remained until August 1807, when he returned to Washington and Philadelphia. Monroe used to tell with delight of a visit to Cambridge University when Biddle conversed with the dons on the difference between classic and modern Greek. All were impressed with the young man's knowledge, and the friendship of minister and secretary was destined to have an important influence on the latter's future career.

On his return from abroad Biddle resumed his legal studies with his elder brother; but he was not admitted to the bar until Dec. 11, 1809. He was still primarily the student, caring little for the practise of law. Early in 1809 he became a member of the "Tuesday Club" established by Joseph Dennie to encourage contributions to the *Port Folio*, and some notable articles on the fine arts were among his earliest papers, although he had written for it as early as 1806—had become indeed Dennie's favorite coadjutor. From his entry into the "Tuesday Club," for the next five years, he led the life of a man of letters, interrupted only by a short service in the House of

Representatives of Pennsylvania in the winter of 1810–11, and by his marriage, Oct. 4, 1811, to Jane, the daughter of John Craig of "Andalusia" on the Delaware—if either of these events could be called an interruption. As early as February 1810, Gen. William Clark, after the death of Capt. Meriwether Lewis, had asked Biddle to write the narrative of their expedition into the Louisiana country. He consented and with the aid of Clark's oral statements undertook to weave the mass of notes and journals into a coherent narrative. This he did with a high degree of success. During the year or more of his work on this narrative (March 1810–July 1812), he was increasingly active in the editorial management of the *Port Folio,* partly because of the illness of Dennie during most of 1811; and upon the latter's death, at the beginning of 1812, Biddle became editor of what was then the leading literary periodical in America. His election to the legislature, however, forced him to give up this post and to turn over the work of carrying through the press his *History of the Expedition of Captains Lewis and Clark* (1814) to Paul Allen, a journalist of Philadelphia. As a writer Biddle was quite as skilful in verse as in prose, with a lightness of touch and mixture of wit, humor, and sentiment worthy of more publication than his modesty and more serious purposes permitted. His brilliant bit of humor, entitled *Ode to Bogle,* dedicated to his little daughter "with a mint stick," an account of a "colorless colored man" who had local fame as both a caterer and undertaker, was published in his own day (1829) and republished long after his death.

From this scholarly life so much to his taste, Biddle was drawn by the predicament of his old friend, James Monroe, then secretary of war, and of his country, paralyzed by lack of funds to carry on the war. He not only aided in getting loans for the War Department, but entered the state Senate in 1814 and initiated measures for the protection of Philadelphia. He was in thorough sympathy with Secretary Monroe and President Madison in securing the re-charter of the second Bank of the United States in 1816, even though his own father was a director of a powerful rival bank. The most notable feature of his four years' service in the state Senate, however, was his remarkable report on the Hartford Convention of January 1814, which had proposed seven amendments to the Constitution. This report, published on Mar. 7, 1815, was a cogent reply to the New England proposals and an able defense of the Constitution as it was.

Near the close of Biddle's service in the state Senate President Monroe asked him to prepare a digest of international exchange, which was issued in 1819, entitled *Commercial Regulations.* The President also invited him to become one of the five government directors of the Bank of the United States. Biddle had hoped to resume his studies, and had refused to become a director for the majority stockholders; but looking upon the call of President Monroe as the summons of his commander-in-chief to public service, he accepted the appointment. With characteristic energy, he threw himself into the study of banking and soon became one of the best informed and most efficient members of the board. It was a crucial period in the history of the Bank. The conservative policy of President Cheeves, however prudent for the stockholders of the institution, had only accentuated the hostility of state banks and bankers in the South and West. Yet with all its embarrassments, as Biddle wrote in 1822, it had sustained the national currency and rescued the country from the domination of irresponsible banks and their depreciated currency. In this year Cheeves retired from the presidency and Biddle was elected in his place. He promptly stated what he considered the true policy of the Bank in a letter to Robert Lenox (R. C. McGrane, *Correspondence of Nicholas Biddle,* 1919, p. 31): "We have had enough & more than enough of banking in the interior. We have been crippled & almost destroyed by it. It is time to concenter our business—to bank where there is some use & some profit in it, and therefore (while anxious to do business in the interior the moment there is clear prospect of doing it usefully & safely) to make at present the large commercial Cities the principal scene of our operations." It is generally admitted that Biddle's management of the Bank for the next five years was wise. It did a successful business, extending its own operations conservatively, and it did much to establish itself in public confidence by furnishing a stable currency and by restraining state banks which were inclined to do unsound business. Yet the Bank always had its enemies. Some, holding to a strict construction of the Constitution, denied the power of Congress to charter such an institution; others, like Martin Van Buren, aided those who desired to make New York the financial capital of the country, and were bent upon breaking the power of "Chestnut Street"; still others strove to make political capital out of this rivalry. Although Biddle had made it an absolute rule that the Bank of the United States should be neutral in politics, he had become, through accident, a stockholders' director, with proxies among their four-fifths (the government had one-fifth), so that he not only represented their capital rather than that of the government, but had the power to protect their interests against the government. When, then, President Jackson declared in his inaugural address that not only the constitutionality and expediency but also the success of the Bank in creating a sound and uniform currency were open to question, Biddle, as leader of the vast number of those who regarded the Bank as a necessity, was instantly alert to the menace, as was the whole financial world. President Biddle, the financier, became at once Mr. Biddle, the editor, and almost every prominent friend of the Bank offered his services on his staff; for they believed as their editor-financier believed, that only a lack of knowledge of currency, finance, and economics could be the basis of a real antagonism to the system. Probably the best article was that written by Albert Gallatin, at Biddle's suggestion, which appeared in the *American Quarterly Review* in December 1830, and which the Bank republished and distributed widely.

The decision to apply to Congress for a new charter in 1832, four years before the expiration of the old, was probably Biddle's. He had been warned that this course would project the Bank as an issue into the presidential campaign of 1832, but he thought this hazard offset by others. This now seems to have been an error of judgment. But on the failure of the Bank to secure a new charter, it did what the Bank of North America had done when its right to a national charter was questioned, namely, secured a state charter; and on the expiration of the old national charter on Mar. 1, 1836, it became "The Bank of the United States of Pennsylvania" and continued its operations almost uninterruptedly, functioning very much as the old Bank had done and as the Bank of North America had done under similar conditions.

In March 1839 Biddle resigned, and retired to "Andalusia," his country seat on the Delaware. "Andalusia" became the scene of an intellectual and social life which was not then common in the United States. Distinguished European exiles were often his guests, and records of their conversations on great events abroad were preserved by him. His interest and aid in all branches of internal development did not diminish his love for classic Greece and her freedom. His active mind not only determined the character of education in Girard College, of whose board he was president, but its architecture. Both the college and the Bank of the United States, as well as his remodeled seat at "Andalusia" followed classic Greek lines. His later papers and addresses were notable for their peculiarly modern tone, one of them advocating shorter hours and higher wages for workmen as sound economic truth. With his death at the age of fifty-eight, there passed a great gentleman and scholar.

[The only sketch of Nicholas Biddle is an excellent one by R. T. Conrad in Jas. Herring's *Nat. Portrait Gallery* (1854), reproduced in the *Autobiography of Chas. Biddle* in 1883. See also *The Second Bank of the U. S.* by Ralph C. H. Catterall (1903); and the Biddle Papers, Lib. of Cong.]

BIDLACK, BENJAMIN ALDEN (Sept. 8, 1804–Feb. 6, 1849), diplomat, was born at Paris, Oneida County, N. Y. His father, Benjamin Bidlack, was the great-grandson of Christopher Bidlack, who settled at Windham, Conn., in the late seventeenth century. His mother's name was Lydia Alden. His parents were among those Connecticut pioneers who settled in the Wyoming Valley north of Philadelphia, a great many of whom were martyrs to their patriotism in the massacre during the Revolution—an event which Bidlack vividly portrayed in an address delivered on Washington's birthday, 1839, at Wilkes-Barre (published in 1842). He received his early education at Wilkes-Barre and read law in the office of Garrick Mallery. An early marriage with Fanny, daughter of James Stewart, proved of short duration, and on Sept. 8, 1829, he married Margaret, daughter of William Wallace. Shortly after his admission to the bar, he was appointed deputy attorney for Luzerne County. In 1833 he participated in the purchase of the newspaper *Republican Farmer,* upon the subsequent sale of which he established and edited the *Northern Eagle,* the first paper published in Pike County. A brief period (1835–36) in the Pennsylvania legislature as the representative of Luzerne County gave him a taste for legislation which eventuated in two terms in the federal Congress (1841–45) as a Democrat. Failing to be reëlected in 1844, he secured, through the influence of a fellow Pennsylvanian, the new secretary of state, Buchanan, an appointment as chargé d'affaires in New Granada, one of three republics formed by the splitting up of the United States of Colombia. It is significant that the principal pending business of the mission consisted of the claims of American citizens, including Simeon Toby, president of the Insurance Company of the State of Pennsylvania, who was interested in the *Brig Josephine* claim. Leaving his wife and the rest of his family, Bidlack arrived at his post in company with one son on Dec. 1, 1845. He immediately set to work upon the settlement of the claims with remarkable success. Six months later in the course of negotiations looking toward the abolition of differential duties the question of interoceanic communication came to the fore. British and French interests were active in their attempts to secure rights for the construction of a macadamized road or a railroad. Bidlack repeatedly wrote the State Department for instructions, but through the impossibility of rapid communication with the Department and the latter's distraction to more pressing affairs nearer home in Mexico, he was forced to proceed with the negotiation of a treaty concerning trans-isthmian communication or let the matter go by default to one of the other countries. He chose the former alternative and on Dec. 2, he concluded and signed a general treaty of peace, friendship, commerce, and navigation between the United States and New Granada, including the abolition of differential duties—a concession which had unsuccessfully been urged for twenty years—and the right of way across the Isthmus of Panama by any mode of communication in return for a guarantee of neutrality and of Granada's sovereignty over the Isthmus. This did not reach the Department until Jan. 28. Meanwhile (Jan. 2), the Department had authorized Bidlack to negotiate a treaty about the differential duties only. Consequently President Polk was surprised and at first inclined to consider the treaty an "entangling alliance," but eventually (June 10, 1848) it was ratified. Buchanan, in notifying Bidlack of this action, congratulated the latter "upon the association of your name with this instrument. It has been most favorably received by the public, and, I doubt not, will be of great and lasting advantage to both countries" (MSS. Department of State, Instr., Col., XV, 117). Repeated requests for leave of absence to visit his wife and family having been denied or ignored, Bidlack died at his post in the following February. The American residents of Bogota erected a monument to his memory, but a far more lasting monument he erected in his own memory when he negotiated, without power or instructions, the Treaty of 1846.

[A few of the more important official letters to Bidlack are printed in the *Works of Jas. Buchanan,* collected and edited by John Bassett Moore (12 vols., 1908–11). Most of the details of Bidlack's life, especially while chargé d'affaires, have been taken from manuscript dispatches in the Department of State. There is a good sketch in G. B. Kulp, *Families of the Wyoming Valley,* III (1890), pp. 1134–38.]   H. F. W.

BIDWELL, BARNABAS (Aug. 23, 1763–July 27, 1833), writer, lawyer, the son of Rev. Adonijah Bidwell and Jemimah Devotion Bidwell, was born in Tyringham (now Monterey), Mass. He graduated from Yale in the class of 1785. During his senior year he wrote and published a tragedy, *The Mercenary Match,* which was acted by his college mates. Immediately after graduation he began teaching in a young ladies' school at New Haven, and in October 1787 he was appointed to a tutorship at Yale, a position from which he resigned in September 1790. He then took up the study of law and began to practise at Stockbridge, Mass. He was appointed treasurer of Berkshire County in September 1791. After serving as state senator from 1801 to 1805, he was elected to Congress, but here he disappointed those who expected leadership from him. President Jefferson, however, found him useful as a member of committees by which he aimed to carry out his plans, especially those having to do with the purchase of Florida from Spain. In this connection Bidwell, "timid indeed, but cunning, supple, and sly," as one historian describes him, incurred the contempt of John Randolph, who branded him and his kind as Jefferson's "back stairs favorites" and "pages of the presidential water-closet." When the abolition of the slave trade came up for discussion in the House in 1806, Bidwell strongly opposed a bill that would substantially make the government a dealer in slaves (Richard Hildreth, *History of the United States of America,* 1851, V, 566–71, 630).

In 1807 he accepted an appointment as attorney-general of Massachusetts in place of returning to Congress. Three years later, at a time when President Madison was considering him for the Supreme Court of the United States, an investigation of his accounts as county treasurer, an office he had held for nineteen years, put an end to all further political aspirations by disclosing a shortage of about $10,000. In order to avoid trial Bidwell absconded to Canada and settled with his family on the north shore of Lake Ontario. Being an alien, he was barred from practising in the Canadian courts, and for the same reason he was not permitted to serve in the legislature, although elected to that body. In his last years he was described as "a profound jurist, a man of great culture and attainments outside the law as well as in it." Before his disgrace his abilities had won for him the honorary degrees of master of arts from Yale and Williams and of doctor of laws from Brown. He was married in 1793 to Mary Gray, a native of Stockbridge.

To-day Bidwell is known chiefly as the author of an undergraduate tragedy. *The Mercenary Match* is a not unimportant specimen of early American drama. Designed, like other school plays of the time, to display the oratorical powers of the performers, it is filled with long, declamatory speeches as artificial as the improbable plot. It is distinguished, however, by the general smoothness of the blank verse and the occasional felicity of the phrasing—qualities seldom found in eighteenth-century American plays. Aside from this drama Bidwell's published writings consist of a few orations and political speeches. He is also said to have contributed eleven sketches to Robert Gourlay's *Statistical Account of Upper Canada* (1822).

[Edwin M. Bidwell, *Genealogy to the Seventh Generation of the Bidwell Family in America* (1884); *Reminiscences of the Rev. Geo. Allen* (1883); *The Lit. Diary of Ezra Stiles* (1901), ed. by Franklin B. Dexter; John F. Schroeder, *Life and Character of Mrs. Mary Anna Boardman* (1849); Franklin B. Dexter, *Biog. Sketches of the Grads. of Yale Coll.*, IV (1907), 387 ff.]

O. S. C.

BIDWELL, JOHN (Aug. 5, 1819–Apr. 4, 1900), California pioneer, politician, was born in Chautauqua County, N. Y., the son of Abram and Clarissa (Griggs) Bidwell. In 1829 the family moved to Erie County, Pa., and two years later to Ohio, stopping first in Ashtabula County and in 1834 going to Darke County. In the fall or early winter of 1836 young Bidwell, determined upon getting an education, walked 300 miles to Ashtabula in order to enter Kingsville Academy. Here he made such rapid progress in his studies that in the following year he was elected principal of the institution. In 1838 he returned home and spent the winter teaching, but in the following spring decided to seek his fortune in the West. After some wandering he took up a land claim near Weston, Mo., in the vicinity of Fort Leavenworth, and for something more than a year supported himself by teaching. Losing his land to a claim-jumper because he was still a minor, and hearing of the wonders of the Pacific slope from one of the noted Robidou brothers, he now resolved to make his way to California. In May 1841, at Independence, Mo., he started with Bartleson's party of sixty-nine persons, including Josiah Belden [*q.v.*]. At Fort Hall the party divided, about half going to Oregon. The California contingent, thirty-two strong, after suffering great hardships, including the loss of their wagons, reached the foot of Mt. Diablo Nov. 4, the first emigrant train to make the journey from the Missouri.

Bidwell found work with Sutter at Fort Sutter and remained with him for several years. In 1844 he was naturalized and received a grant of land. On the outbreak of the revolt of Alvarado and Castro against Micheltorena, in December 1844, Bidwell and Sutter took the field in defense of the Governor, and after his defeat at Cahuenga, Feb. 22, 1845, both were for a time imprisoned, but soon made their peace with the victors. The Bear Flag revolt of the following June (1846) found Bidwell reluctant to join, but on July 4 he served

as one of the committee that drew up the resolution of independence from Mexico. He accompanied Frémont to Monterey, where he was made a second lieutenant of the California Battalion, and then to the south. After the surrender of Los Angeles he was appointed magistrate of the San Luis Rey district. On the revolt of the Californians he fled to San Diego, later serving under Stockton as a quartermaster, with the rank of major, in the reconquest of Los Angeles. On the conclusion of peace he returned to Sutter's Fort. Following Marshall's discovery of gold, he prospected for a time and was the first to find gold on Feather River. In 1849 he acquired the extensive Rancho Chico, of 22,000 acres, north of Sacramento, and for the remainder of his life he was a cultivator of the soil, bringing his ranch to a high state of development and becoming the most noted agriculturist of the state. He maintained, however, a keen interest in public affairs and for many years was active in politics. In the same year that he took over the ranch he was chosen a member of the constitutional convention (though he learned of the fact too late to serve) and was also elected to the state Senate. In the following year he was one of the commission to carry to Washington a block of gold-bearing quartz as California's contribution to the Washington Monument. In 1854 and again in 1860 he was one of the vice-presidents of the Democratic state convention, and in the latter year he was also a delegate to the Charleston convention, where he supported Douglas. He was a strong defender of the Union and after 1861 affiliated with the Union party. In 1863 Gov. Stanford appointed him a brigadier-general of militia, doubtless in recognition of his services in thwarting the secessionists of the state. In the following year he was a delegate to the Baltimore convention, at which Lincoln was nominated; and was also elected to the House of Representatives. He declined a renomination in 1866, and in the following year was an unsuccessful candidate for governor on the Republican ticket. Later he became an independent, running for governor as an anti-monopolist in 1875. He was the candidate of the Prohibition party for governor in 1890 and two years later its candidate for president. He did not again engage actively in political affairs, but spent his remaining days in the supervision of his ranch. He was one of the early regents of the University of California, and in 1888 he donated the land on which a State Normal School was subsequently built. He was a constant advocate of internal improvements and was one of the first proponents of a transcontinental railway. To the Indians, many of whom he had in his employ, he was a friend, helper, and teacher. He died suddenly of heart failure following over-exertion in cutting down a tree.

Bidwell was married in Washington in 1868 to Annie, daughter of J. C. G. Kennedy, superintendent of the Census of 1850 and of 1860. She was a woman of many accomplishments and an efficient partner in all her husband's activities. Bidwell Park, a tract of 1,900 acres, said to be one of the most beautiful natural parks of California, given by the widow to the city of Chico, commemorates his life and career.

[E. M. Bidwell, *Genealogy to the Seventh Generation of the Bidwell Family in America* (1884), p. 92; H. H. Bancroft, *Hist. of Cal.*, II (1885); C. C. Royce, *John Bidwell* (1906); Marcus Benjamin, *John Bidwell, Pioneer* (1907); John Bidwell, "The First Emigrant Train to Cal.," *Century Mag.*, Nov. 1890; *A Journey to Cal.* (pamphlet, published probably in Weston, Mo., about 1843, from a MS. sent from California by Bidwell). Most of his writings, which are largely autobiographical, are collected in the Royce volume. A smaller collection appears in a pamphlet, *Echoes of the Past About Cal.* (Chico, probably 1900); *San Francisco Chronicle*, Apr. 5, 1900.]   W. J. G.

BIDWELL, MARSHALL SPRING (Feb. 16, 1799–Oct. 24, 1872), lawyer, politician, was descended from Richard Bidwell, a pioneer settler of Windsor, Conn., in 1630, and was the son of Barnabas Bidwell [*q.v.*], and Mary (Gray) Bidwell. Born at Stockbridge, Mass., he obtained his early education there and, after his father's flight to Canada, at Bath, Ont., where his father established a school. On the family's subsequently removing to Kingston, he studied law there and was admitted to the bar of Upper Canada in April 1820, opening an office in Kingston and later in Toronto. He was married to Clara Willcox of Bath. In 1821 his father, elected that year as Reform member of the House of Assembly for the united counties of Lennox and Addington in the legislature of Upper Canada, was, as an alien, not permitted to serve. Marshall Bidwell thereupon became a candidate for his father's seat. Canadian politics had become exceedingly bitter and he was strongly opposed by the "Family Compact" or Government party. He contested the constituency three times and was ultimately elected in 1824, the Reform party having meanwhile procured the passing of an act relaxing the conditions under which persons who had resided in or taken an oath of allegiance to a foreign state could be excluded. Bidwell at once became a prominent figure in the political arena, having early developed strength as a forceful debater with an intimate knowledge of constitutional law and precedent. His reputation as an able attorney was materially assisted

by his success as chief counsel for the plaintiff in the celebrated suit of McKenzie *vs.* Jarvis *et al.*, "the type-riot case." In 1828 he was re-elected member for Lennox and Addington, and was chosen speaker of the House in 1829, being now one of the acknowledged leaders of the Reform party whose head was William Lyon Mackenzie. The following year the legislature was dissolved and Bidwell's party suffered defeat in the general election, but he was again returned. Growing discontent at the arbitrary actions of the Government party had been manifest for some time, and at length culminated in a victory for the Reform party at the elections of 1834, Bidwell becoming speaker of the House in 1835 for the second time. Another general election took place in 1836 and he lost his seat, having represented Lennox and Addington for eleven years. Political feeling in Upper Canada had now reached such a pitch that its repercussions had aroused the British Government to the necessity of conciliating the extreme factions, and the lieutenant-governor, Sir Francis B. Head, was instructed to appoint Bidwell to the first vacant judgeship of the Court of King's Bench. This Head deliberately refused to do, and in the meantime what is known as "the Upper Canada Rebellion" broke out under the auspices of William Lyon Mackenzie. Bidwell, a republican in principle, took no part in the rising and was not implicated in it. He refused to be a member of the proposed provincial convention, and announced his withdrawal from public life. The authorities became, however, suspicious of his good faith, and Sir Francis Head determined to compel him to leave the country. The circumstances under which this was brought about have been a matter of great controversy. The truth appears to be that Bidwell was led to believe that a charge of treason would probably be made against him upon which, in the disturbed condition of the province, he would not get a fair trial. In any event he wrote, Dec. 8, 1837, to Head that he had determined to leave the province forever, and he departed two days later. He went at once to New York City and was admitted by courtesy to the New York bar, where he speedily acquired a good practise. A case which brought him into prominence there was the libel suit by Fenimore Cooper against W. L. Stone, editor of the *New York Commercial Advertiser*, relative to the conduct of Commander Perry at the battle of Lake Erie in September 1813. Bidwell specialized in the law of real property, trusts, and construction of wills and in his later years appeared almost exclusively in the higher trial and appellate courts. In New York he became very popular, socially and professionally, being a man of great personal charm and equable temperament, and interesting himself actively in religious and charitable institutions. It was gradually realized in Canada that Sir Francis Head's action in procuring Bidwell's practical expulsion had been inexcusable, and, after the constitutional troubles of Upper Canada had been adjusted, vain efforts were from time to time made to induce him to return. Bidwell died in New York City.

[Edwin M. Bidwell, *Genealogy to the Seventh Generation of the Bidwell Family in America* (1884); H. J. Morgan, *Sketches of Celebrated Canadians* (1862); J. C. Dent, *The Canadian Portrait Gallery* (1880), II, 108; E. F. De Lancey, "Marshall S. Bidwell," *N. Y. Geneal. and Biog. Record* (1890), XXI, 1; *In Memoriam, Marshall S. Bidwell* (N. Y. Bar, 1872); J. C. Dent, *The Upper Canada Rebellion* (1885), containing an extended account of Bidwell's political career; *Hist. of the Bench and Bar of N. Y.*, ed. by D. McAdam et al. (1897), I, 261.]

H. W. H. K.

BIDWELL, WALTER HILLIARD (June 21, 1798–Sept. 11, 1881), editor, publisher, was the son of William Bidwell of Farmington, Conn., and his wife, Mary Pelton. The family ancestry had mingled strains of English, Scotch, and French blood. He lived the usual life of the son of a Connecticut farmer till he was twenty-one, when he prepared for Yale, entering as a sophomore and graduating in 1827. In 1833 he graduated from the Yale Divinity School, having meanwhile married Susan M. Duryea of New York, and his course having been interrupted by a year spent in Europe for his wife's health. On Sept. 19, 1833, he was ordained and installed pastor of the Congregational Church at Medfield, Mass., but on account of the failure of his voice he retired from the ministry four years later. Moving to Philadelphia, he became in 1841 editor and proprietor of the *National Preacher and Village Pulpit*, which he continued for nineteen years, publishing sermons from about 500 preachers of all evangelical denominations. In 1843 he also became editor and proprietor of the *New York Evangelist*, which he conducted for nearly twelve years. From 1846 to 1849 he was proprietor and editor of the *Biblical Repository and Classical Review* and also of the *Eclectic Magazine; Foreign Literature*. He edited the latter till 1868 and owned it till his death, or for a period of about thirty-five years. In 1860 he became publisher and proprietor of the *American Theological Review*, whose editor was Prof. Henry B. Smith of Union Theological Seminary. Two years later it passed into other hands and was merged with the *Presbyterian Quarterly Review*. At one time Bidwell was the owner of five periodicals. Between 1848 and

1854 he published a series of seven missionary maps, of which his brother O. B. Bidwell was the maker. In 1864–65 he suffered a serious breakdown due to the mental strain of overwork, and spent two years abroad in the recovery of his health. After this, his sole editorial work was in connection with the *Eclectic Magazine* till 1868, when he retired from all active duties. He made six extensive tours in foreign countries partly for reasons of health, but mainly in the interests of the *Eclectic Magazine*. In 1867 he was appointed by Secretary Seward a special commissioner of the United States to various countries of Western Asia, and in this connection he made an extensive tour through Egypt, Greece, and the Levant. After his retirement he made several additional trips abroad, but the home of his latter years was mainly at Oberlin, Ohio, where he found the religious atmosphere congenial. He spent the last year of his life in Chicago, but died at Saratoga Springs, N. Y. His life was one of great activity and usefulness, and he had a very extensive acquaintance in America and abroad, especially with Protestant ministers of all denominations.

[*Obit. Record Grads. of Yale Univ.* (1890), p. 78; *Eclectic Mag.*, LXIII, and a fuller account in the latter publication for Nov. 1881. There is a briefer notice and estimate in the *Evangelist*, Sept. 20, 1881. Portraits are to be found in the *Eclectic Mag.*, XLII, LXIII.]

F. T. P.

BIEN, JULIUS (Sept. 27, 1826–Dec. 21, 1909), lithographer and map engraver, was born in Naumburg near Cassel, Germany, the son of Emanuel M. Bien, lecturer and lithographer. He attended the Academy of Fine Arts at Cassel and the Städel Art Institute at Frankfurt-am-Main, where he studied painting and specialized in the graphic arts. Having participated in the revolutionary movement of 1848, he came to the United States in the following year, settling in New York City. There he began business on a small scale with one lithographic hand press. Some of his early major commissions were to prepare the illustrations for the report on European railways by Zerah Colburn and A. L. Holley (*The Permanent Way and Coal-Burning Locomotive Boilers of European Railways*, 1858), and to produce a chromo-lithographic edition, by transfer from the original copper plates, of Audubon's *Birds of America*. The latter undertaking had to be abandoned soon after its inception because of the Civil War.

Having observed and reflected on the generally low standard of maps being produced in the country of his adoption, Bien saw in this deficiency an opportunity to apply his knowledge. He sought an interview with President Pierce, who referred him to the Secretary of War, Jefferson Davis, who was at the time the responsible head of the Pacific Railroad surveys. The reports were being published, and the engraving of a number of the maps was entrusted to Bien. Outstanding among these was the general map of the territory between the Mississippi and the Pacific on the scale of 1 : 3,000,000 (accompanying Lieut. G. K. Warren's memoir in Volume XI), which first adequately represented the relief of this vast area, in its various editions successively incorporated new explorations, and remained the standard map of the West for more than twenty-five years.

From then on to the end of the century there was scarcely a major geographical or geological publication issued by the Government for which maps were not engraved and printed by Bien. Nor were these merely translations on stone of author's drawings; often it was due alone to the method of representation devised by Bien that the geographical significance of the facts they portrayed became fully apparent. This is especially true of the maps and atlases accompanying the decennial census reports, of which Bien engraved those for the Ninth to the Twelfth Census (1870–1900). Noteworthy among these was a series of maps in the text volumes of the Tenth Census showing population density in the different sections of the country on larger scales than have ever been attempted since. Other outstanding cartographic productions by Bien were: the *Geological and Geographical Atlas of Colorado* (1877), by F. V. Hayden; the *Geological and Topographical Atlas Accompanying the Report of the Geological Exploration of the Fortieth Parallel* (1876), by Clarence King; the numerous map sheets on the scale of four or eight miles to the inch issued by the United States Geographical Surveys West of the One Hundredth Meridian under G. M. Wheeler (the representation of relief by hachures or shading on the topographic sheets of this series represented a degree of technical excellence in that domain not surpassed in this country before or since); and the atlases accompanying the following United States Geological Survey reports: C. E. Dutton's *Tertiary History of the Grand Canyon District* (1882) with W. H. Holmes's masterly drawings; G. F. Becker's *Geology of the Comstock Lode* (1882); S. F. Emmons's *Geology and Mining Industry of Leadville, Colorado* (1883–86); and *Geology of the Yellowstone National Park* (1899) by Arnold Hague and others. The monumental *Atlas to Accompany the Official Records of the Union and Confederate Armies* (War Department, 1891–95) contains no less

than 175 plates consisting of plans of battles and other military operations. It also includes a useful general map of the eastern half of the country on an exceptionally large scale (ten miles to the inch). During the Civil War itself Bien had made an active contribution by equipping a field map printing outfit for Sherman on his march to the sea. Many maps were also engraved and printed for state geological surveys, including the "Hand Atlas" for the *Second Geological Survey of Pennsylvania* (1884–85) by J. P. Lesley and the atlas for the *Geology of New Hampshire* (1878) by C. H. Hitchcock. Of a number of atlases Bien was publisher in his own name, *viz.*, Westchester County, N. Y. (1893), New York State (1895), Pennsylvania (1900), and the excellent topographic *Atlas of the Metropolitan District Around New York City* (1891). The total production of the Bien establishment amounts literally to thousands of different maps. During his long career Bien did more than any other to create and establish scientific standards in American cartography.

On the personal side the outstanding traits of Bien's character were breadth of view, tolerance, and love of his fellow man. Kindly and modest in personal relations, his life was characterized by many deeds of unobtrusive philanthropy. In 1863 he married Almira M. Brown of Philadelphia, who survived him until 1918.

[On Bien's life printed sources are practically limited to entries in *Who's Who in America* (last in volume for 1908–09, the *Jewish Encyc.*, III (1902), and an obituary in the *National Lithographer*, Jan. 1910. In addition this sketch is based on his son Julius's personal recollections.]   W. L. G. J.

BIENVILLE, JEAN BAPTISTE LE MOYNE, Sieur de (Feb. 23, 1680–Mar. 7, 1767), governor of Louisiana, founder of Mobile and New Orleans, was the eighth son of Charles le Moyne, Canadian pioneer, ennobled by the King in 1676 for his great services, and granted the seigneury of Longueuil. There Jean Baptiste was born; his mother was Catherine Tierry, called Primot from an adoptive father. Both parents dying while the boy was young, his elder brother Charles, Baron de Longueuil, gave him a father's care. When in 1691 his brother François, Sieur de Bienville, was killed in the Iroquois wars, the title was bestowed upon Jean. Of all the Le Moynes, Pierre, Sieur d'Iberville [*q.v.*], nineteen years older than Jean, was most illustrious; the boy longed to follow in his elder's footsteps, and at the age of twelve became *garde-marine* in the royal navy, and entered service on his brother's vessel. In the naval battles in the North Atlantic and Hudson Bay from 1695 to

1698 Bienville took his part, and was seriously wounded, Sept. 5, 1697, while serving a battery on the frigate *Pélican*.

King William's War having closed with the peace of Ryswick in 1697, the French government sent Iberville to re-discover the mouth of the Mississippi, attempted formerly by La Salle, and there to form a French colony. Bienville accompanied the expedition which left Brest on Oct. 24, 1698, in two small vessels, and six weeks later landed on an island in the Gulf of Mexico, off what is now Biloxi. He was very useful to the exploring party, because of his aptitude for learning Indian languages, and his ability in conciliating the tribesmen. Exploring a great stream near their landfall, he secured from a chief a letter, written some years before by Henry de Tonty, La Salle's faithful friend, which assured the adventurers that they had found the Mississippi.

The first settlement was made on the coast at Old Biloxi, where Iberville, May 24, 1699, left his infant colony to the care of Sauvole, with Bienville second in command. Twice in 1699 the latter explored the lower reaches of the Mississippi, and in October boarded and ordered off a British vessel, which had come to found a colony, saying that this river was appropriated to Louis XIV. (Alvord and Carter, "The New Regime," *Illinois Historical Collections*, XI, 417–19, gives the log of the English captain, Bond.) Early in 1700 the colony of Biloxi was cheered by the arrival of Tonty, who came from Illinois to cast in his lot with the Canadians on this southern shore. This same year, March to May, Bienville explored the Red River as far as Natchitoches, making alliances with the Indians of that region. In 1701 Sauvole died, leaving Bienville in command; Iberville, visiting his colony, brought his young brother a commission as king's lieutenant. The next year Bienville determined to remove headquarters to a better site, and on Mobile Bay built Fort Louis. which was in 1710 removed to the present site of Mobile. He was much engaged in Indian negotiations, when Queen Anne's War made it necessary to carry help to the Spanish settlements in the Gulf of Mexico. From them he imported into his colony the dread scourge of yellow fever, from which Tonty died in 1704 and Iberville in 1706.

After Iberville's death the colony declined, and Bienville had to contend with enemies within and without. Supporting the Jesuits, he was attacked by the Seminary priests and by Nicolas de la Salle, the commissary, who made such serious charges against him that a new governor was sent to replace him. This successor having died en route, Bienville remained in office and was later exonerated and restored. The colony, however, lacked workers and Bienville suggested that Indian prisoners brought by his allies be exchanged in the West Indies for negro slaves. In 1712 the King granted Louisiana to a company founded by Antoine Crozat, who displaced Bienville as governor and sent Cadillac to supplant him. The former governor was left as second in command, during Cadillac's administration (1713–16). He at first contemplated marrying a daughter of the new governor (see his letter in King, *Sieur de Bienville*, 198–205). The relations of the two officials soon became strained, however, and Bienville never married. In 1716 Cadillac sent him against the Natchez Indians, whom he reduced to obedience by stratagems of doubtful utility. When Cadillac was recalled, Bienville hoped to succeed him, but was disappointed, for Crozat sent another governor, who remained but a year, when Crozat's company was dissolved. Louisiana in 1717 passed into the hands of the colonization company founded by the financier, John Law, and became the object of wild speculation. Law restored Bienville to the command of the province, and secured for him the cross of the Order of St. Louis. Large accessions of colonists now began to be poured into Louisiana. Bienville had to furnish provisions for all of these, and to aid in the settlement of the great concessions granted to noblemen by the company. He saw the importance of changing the colony's base to the Mississippi, and in 1718 had New Orleans laid out; it did not, however, become the capital until 1722. In 1719 when Spain and France went to war, Bienville twice captured Pensacola. Soon after this Law's "Mississippi bubble" burst and its promoter fled from France. The Company of the Indies, however, continued to govern Louisiana until 1731. After removing his capital to New Orleans, Bienville promulgated the "Black Code," a series of regulations for the negroes, for which he has been blamed by a more humane age.

Louisiana's difficulties with the Natchez, with whom a second war was fought in 1723, and the lack of support by the Company brought ruin upon Bienville. In 1724 he was accused before the court; and the next year was summoned to France, with his brother and nephew. For the first time since its inception Louisiana was without any of the Le Moyne family. In Paris Bienville made a notable defense of his administration, and in a state paper of great force exposed the difficulties of the colonial life. Nevertheless he was degraded and deprived of all his offices. He dwelt quietly in Paris until 1732 when, Louisiana having been brought to the verge of ruin by the inadequacy of the governor and the rebellion of the Natchez, Bienville was implored to return. Upon his arrival in 1733 as royal governor he was received "with a joy and satisfaction without parallel."

The final decade of his governorship was disturbed by Indian wars. The Natchez had fled to the Chickasaw, who refused to give them up, and went to the English to trade. In 1736 Bienville ordered an expedition against these Indians, the Illinois contingent of which was overwhelmed by the tribesmen, and its commander, chaplain, and twenty other Frenchmen were burned at the stake. Bienville, then advancing from Mobile, was forced to retreat. To avenge this catastrophe another expedition took place in 1739–40, when a Canadian contingent met Bienville's near Memphis, and forced a peace, which in the end proved undecisive. Worn with these and other troubles, the governor asked for release from his heavy responsibilities. His request was granted, and on May 10, 1743, he left Louisiana never to return. His declining years were spent in Paris, where he lived on his pension and maintained his interest in his former colony. When in 1766 Jean Milhet came as envoy from the Louisianians to protest the cession to Spain, Bienville accompanied him in his futile audience with the minister. He himself suffered the pain of seeing France cede the colony he had striven to build.

Bienville has been extravagantly praised and unjustly blamed. His was a difficult, at times almost a hopeless, task; his resources were meager and his support poor. That he succeeded at all is proof of his ability. Not a man of the highest qualities, he was none the less loyal to his King and to his kinsfolk; and without him French Louisiana could hardly have been maintained.

[The sources for Bienville's career are numerous and full. Official and other documents are in Pierre Margry, *Découvertes et Établissements des Français dans l'Amérique Septentrionale* (Paris, 1880–86), IV, V, VI ; Le Page du Pratz, *Histoire de la Louisiane* (Paris, 1758) ; Bernard de la Harpe, *Journal Historique de l'Établissement des Français à la Louisiane* (New Orleans, 1831) ; Dumont de Montigny, *Mémoires Historiques sur la Louisiane* (Paris, 1753) : all written by travelers or colonists of Bienville's time. For modern works see Chas. Gayarré, *Hist. of La.* (4th ed. 1903), I ; Grace King, *Jean Baptiste le Moyne, Sieur de Bienville* (Makers of America series, 1892) ; Alcée Fortier, *Hist. of La.* (1904), I ; Frédéric de Kastner, *Héros de la Nouvelle France*, 1st ser. (1902), and *Le Moyne de Bienville et l'Etablissement de la Louisiane* (Quebec, n. d.) ; Pierre Heinrich, *La Louisiane sous la Compagnie des Indes* (Paris, 1908) ; Marc de Villiers, "Hist. of the Foundation of New Orleans," translated for *La. Hist.*

Quart., Apr. 1920 ; Peter J. Hamilton, "The Private Life of Jean Baptiste le Moyne, Sieur de Bienville," *Papers of the Iberville Hist. Soc.*, No. 1.]   L. P. K.

BIERCE, AMBROSE GWINETT (June 24, 1842–1914?), journalist, author, youngest of the numerous children of Marcus Aurelius and Laura (Sherwood) Bierce, was born in a log cabin on Horse Cave Creek, Meigs County, Ohio, whither the family had migrated from Connecticut. His parents were farmers—poor, obscure, and eccentric. Bierce was reticent concerning his humble origins, and of his childhood little is known. He received no general education beyond that afforded by his father's small library. At the outbreak of the Civil War he joined the 9th Indiana Infantry and served with distinction through many of the most difficult campaigns of the western armies. He twice risked his life in rescuing fallen companions from the battlefield and at Kenesaw Mountain was himself severely wounded. The war over, he became custodian of "captured and abandoned property" at Selma, Ala., resigning in 1866 to accompany Gen. W. B. Hazen on an inspection tour of the northwestern army posts. This completed, Bierce, discouraged with his prospects for advancement, joined his brother Albert in San Francisco, and while working with him in the Mint contributed paragraphs to the weeklies, especially the *Argonaut* and the *News Letter*. In a period of very bitter personal journalism his caustic wit and courage quickly brought him recognition and with it the editorship of the *News Letter*. The *Overland Monthly* published his first short story, "The Haunted Valley," in 1871. On Christmas Day of that year he married Mary Day of San Francisco and several months later they went to England.

During the next four years Bierce was on the staff of *Fun;* he edited for the Empress Eugénie the two numbers of the *Lantern* and contributed articles to *Figaro* and *Hood's Comic Annual*. He found stimulating associates in a bohemian group that included George Augustus Sala, W. S. Gilbert, and Tom Hood the younger. In 1872 he published, under the pseudonym of "Dod Grile" and in confessed collaboration with Satan, *The Fiend's Delight,* a "cold collation of diabolisms," and *Nuggets and Dust Panned Out in California*. Both books were collections of mordantly humorous sketches he had contributed to various California journals, while two years later a third volume, *Cobwebs from an Empty Skull*, containing many articles that first appeared in *Fun,* established the reputation of "Bitter Bierce" as a vitriolic wit.

Returning to San Francisco in 1876, he wrote

for the *Wasp* and the *Argonaut* until William Randolph Hearst took over the *Examiner* in 1887. From March of that year until he went East Bierce conducted a column of "Prattle" on the editorial page of the Sunday *Examiner*. This was the most active and fruitful period of his life. He became the literary dictator of the Pacific Coast; his keen wit and fearless satire

"Exposed the fool and lash'd the knave."

Although journalism gave him freedom of expression and a livelihood it was "frankly low and rotten" and was hateful to him. In his art he found a refuge from the newspapers and in the midst of much potboiling wrote a little for posterity. His first volume of short stories, *Tales of Soldiers and Civilians,* "denied existence by the chief publishing houses of the country," was published by a merchant friend, E. L. G. Steele, in 1891. These grim and vivid stories, without humor and without sentiment, attracted little attention and were soon forgotten. In 1892 Bierce revised and rewrote G. A. Danziger's *The Monk and the Hangman's Daughter,* a medieval romance. This, his longest piece of sustained narrative, fully reveals his deep feeling for beauty and his power of subjective analysis. As a world of rogues and fools provoked his bitter satire and at length wearied him, so a spirit world of masques and shadows fascinated him and brought forth his best art. *Can Such Things Be?* (1893), weird stories of the supernatural, rousing terror and pity, mark the perfection of his power and style.

Sent by Hearst to Washington in 1896, Bierce was instrumental in defeating Huntingdon's proposed refunding bill. The next year he returned East and became Washington correspondent of the New York *American*. His *Devil's Dictionary* (1906), sardonic comments on a world he knew too well, addressed to "enlightened souls who prefer dry wines to sweet, sense to sentiment, wit to humor, and clean English to slang," was a collection of earlier work. He continued writing but the creative period was over: his satire was milder and his stories less effective. In his *Collected Works* (1909–12) he achieved the success of one of his own characters who "sought obscurity in the writing and publishing of books." Those twelve volumes did little to promote his own reputation and perhaps much to hasten the financial disaster which now, as usually, soon overtook his publishers.

At length, in 1913, lonely and weary of the world, he asked a few friends to "forgive him in not 'perishing' where he was," and having settled his affairs, disappeared into warring Mexi-

co. "Goodbye," he wrote, "if you hear of my being stood up against a Mexican stone wall and shot to rags please know that I think it a pretty good way to depart this life. It beats old age, disease, or falling down the cellar stairs. To be a Gringo in Mexico—ah, that is euthanasia!" (*Letters,* pp. 196–97). Many and weird are the stories concerning his fate, but all agree that at last he found "the good, kind darkness" that he sought.

Bierce was not a disciple of Poe, but evolved his own type of the short story: brilliant, witty, and climactic. His situations often unusual and abnormal, with cruel and ironic motifs, he wrote some of the most terrifying and hauntingly suggestive stories in our literature. Bierce learned much from Poe and Bret Harte and, in his turn, influenced Stephen Crane and O. Henry. That "soul" and sentiment notably absent in his stories did find expression in his life and its rich friendships. His many social criticisms were independent and aggressive. Fiercely individualistic, he fought socialists as well as "mobocrats" and while greatly admiring Jesus as "a lightning moral calculator" hurled his sharpest shafts at priests and theologians.

[*Letters of Ambrose Bierce,* ed. by Bertha Clark Pope, with a memoir by Geo. Sterling (1922); "Bits of Autobiography" in vol. I of *Collected Words*; Vincent Starrett, *Ambrose Bierce* (1920), repr. in *Buried Cæsars* (1923); Percy Boynton, *More Contemporary Americans* (1927); Geo. Sterling, "Shadow Maker" in the *Am. Mercury,* Sept. 1925, and his introduction to *In the Midst of Life* (Modern Lib., 1927); Percival Pollard, *Their Day in Court* (1909); Paul Jordan Smith, *On Strange Altars* (1924); Van Wyck Brooks, *Emerson and Others* (1927); Vincent Starrett, *Bibliography of Ambrose Bierce* (Centaur Press, 1928); Fred Lewis Pattee, *The Development of the Am. Short Story* (1923); introduction by Herman George Scheffauer to the translation of a selection of Bierce's short stories, *Physiognomien des Todes* (Munich, 1922); private information.]

F. M.

BIERSTADT, ALBERT (Jan. 7, 1830–Feb. 18, 1902), landscape painter, was born of German parents, Henry and Christiana M. Bierstadt, at Solingen near Düsseldorf on the Rhine. His parents brought him to the United States as a child in arms. Educated in the schools of New Bedford, Mass., he turned to art and when twenty-one determined to start as a painter. When twenty-three he visited the land of his birth. He studied in Düsseldorf four years under Achenbach and Lessing; thence he departed for Rome which at that time was sought by American painters and sculptors as well as German, British, and French. In 1857 he was back in the United States and the following year joined a surveying expedition for an overland wagon route under Gen. F. W. Lander. The grandeur of landscape in the Far West did not daunt him; with sketches he laid the foundation of a score of big canvases painted in following years. In 1861 he exhibited "Laramie Peak," now in the Buffalo Academy of Fine Arts; in 1863 "Lander's Peak, Rocky Mountains"; in 1864 "North Fork of the Platte," bought by Judge Henry Hilton of New York City for his private gallery, and in 1865 "Looking down Yosemite Valley," bought by W. H. Crosby. In 1866 Lucius Tuckerman bought "El Capitan, Merced River" and the Lenox Library, "Valley of the Yosemite," now in the New York Public Library. For his private collection the senior August Belmont purchased "Burning Ship." The Boston Athenæum has an early painting, "Arch of Octavian, Italy."

Bierstadt made visits to Europe in 1867, 1878, and 1883. In France he was made a member of the Legion of Honor (1867) and in Austria of the Order of St. Stanislas (1869), while Prussia, Bavaria, and Belgium granted him medals. In 1870 Mrs. A. T. Stewart bought "Emerald Pool, Mount Whitney." Other large landscapes are: "In the Rocky Mountains" (1871); "Great Trees of California" (1874); "Valley of Kern's River, California" (1875), bought for the Hermitage, St. Petersburg, Russia. In 1877 Lewis Roberts bought "Mount Whitney, Sierra Nevada," and the Earl of Dunraven, "Estes Park, California." In 1878 the Corcoran Gallery, Washington, D. C., purchased "Mountain Lake, Mount Corcoran, Sierra Nevada." A large studio which Bierstadt had at Irvington-on-the-Hudson was burned down in 1882; he then opened a studio in New York City. In 1883 he painted "Geysers" and in 1884 "Storm on the Matterhorn, Switzerland" and "View on Kern River." For the Capitol at Washington he painted "The Discovery of the Hudson River" and "Entrance into Monterey." Not content with all these big landscapes he began in 1885 the painting of wild animals of North America, following in the footsteps of Audubon, James E. de Kay, Wilson, and others.

Bierstadt was a handsome man of polished manners and distinguished bearing. In 1886 he married Rosalie Osborne who died in 1893. In 1894 he married the widow of David Stewart. The great size of most of his canvases did not fit them for rooms of ordinary wall space. Düsseldorf pictures of moderate dimensions at moderate prices sold far and wide in the United States, so that Bierstadt found a receptive atmosphere, though his pictures have the same defects as theirs—lack of warmth and little technical cleverness. It was not till his later years, however,

that amateurs deserted him for landscapists gifted with deeper mentality and equipped with stronger technique. The formal dignity of Bierstadt, the size of the canvases he covered, the convincing quality of his personal address gave him for a long time advantage over his contemporaries. The present fashion finds his huge canvases singularly dull and monotonous, wanting in personal charm like stage painting, without dramatic vigor or imagination.

[*Zeitschrift für Bildende Kunst,* vol. V (1870), pp. 65–74; H. T. Tuckerman, *Book of the Artists* (1867); Samuel Isham, *Hist. of American Painting* (1905); *Current Lit.,* Apr. 1902; *Outlook,* Mar. 1, 1902; Chas. E. Fairman, *Art and Artists of the Capitol* (1927).]

C. De K.

BIGELOW, ERASTUS BRIGHAM (Apr. 2, 1814–Dec. 6, 1879), inventor and economist, was born in the town of West Boylston, Mass., the second son of Ephraim and Polly (Brigham) Bigelow. His father had a small farm and also plied the trades of wheelwright and chairmaker, but the family resources were scanty, and the son was soon faced with the problem of earning his own living. Between the ages of ten and twenty he found many different kinds of employment. He worked on a neighboring farm; he played the violin in the orchestra of the Lancaster Orthodox Church, and also at country dances; he was a clerk in S. F. Morse's retail dry-goods store in Boston; he taught penmanship at Newark, and wrote a small pamphlet of twenty-five pages called *The Self-Taught Stenographer* (1832); having sold copies to the value of $75 in Boston within ten days, he had a larger edition printed and attempted to distribute it throughout New England and the Middle States, but emerged from this venture $400 in debt and with a large portion of the edition still unsold. During these early years he gave constant proofs of his ardent longing for an education. At the age of eight he had mastered the early stages of arithmetic without the aid of his teacher, who stoutly maintained that he was still too young; he passed a winter at Leicester Academy in preparation for the study of medicine; he had visions of entering Harvard. But his ambitions for a literary or professional life were never to be realized; before he had reached his twenty-fifth year it had become evident that he was destined to be an inventor.

His first considerable invention came in 1837, in the shape of a power loom for the production of coach lace; this machine contained most of the essential features subsequently developed in the more permanently important carpet looms which were to follow. Its immediate success brought him promptly to the fore. A company was formed for the building and operating of the new looms, and was incorporated by act of the legislature on Mar. 8, 1838; it was named by the inventor "The Clinton Company," apparently because of his fondness for the Clinton House in New York, at which he was in the habit of staying; and "Factory Village" near Lancaster, the home of the new plant, soon came to be called "Clintonville," and finally "Clinton." During the next twenty years the number and importance of Bigelow's mechanical discoveries multiplied apace. He will always be principally remembered as the inventor of power looms for the production of Brussels, Wilton, tapestry, and velvet carpetings, and has been justly described as the originator of every fundamental device of a distinctive character which appears in these machines; but he also greatly improved the methods of manufacturing ingrain carpets, and invented looms for the making of counterpanes and ginghams, silk brocatel, pile fabrics, and wire cloth. Many of the plants for the production of these articles were set up at Lowell, and a few at Humphreysville (now no longer extant) near Derby, Conn., but Clinton continued to be the principal center of the various "Bigelow mills." The importance of his inventions was widely recognized before the middle of the nineteenth century, not only in the United States but also in Europe, which he visited frequently, beginning in the year 1841; six large volumes of his English patents between 1837 and 1868 are preserved with the original drawings in the Massachusetts Historical Society.

Bigelow's reputation does not rest solely on his mechanical inventions; he also deserves an honorable place on the roll of American economists. In *The Tariff Question Considered in Regard to the Policy of England and the Interests of the United States,* a large quarto volume with careful statistical tables, which was published in 1862, and in the smaller monograph, *The Tariff Policy of England and the United States Contrasted* (1877), he maintained "that there is no ultimate principle of universal application involved either in free trade or protection; they are questions of policy"; and gave reasons why it would be unsafe at that time for the United States to abandon its import duties. In 1860 he was nominated as candidate for Congress by the Democrats of the Fourth Massachusetts (Suffolk) district, but was defeated, after a close contest. In his later years he was much interested in the progress of scientific education, and was a leading member of a committee of twenty-one, appointed Jan. 11, 1861, to carry into effect proposals which led to the foundation of the Massachusetts Institute of Technology (*Memorial His-*

tory of Boston, edited by Justin Winsor, IV, 274 n.).

Bigelow was of medium stature, with a tendency to stoop in later years; his complexion fair, his eyes gray, with massive overhanging brows, his forehead broad and high. His chief mental trait was an intense power of concentration. It is a curious fact that he was almost totally unable to make anything with his own hands, and had the greatest difficulty in drawing even the simplest sketches of the different parts of his machines; he was consequently always obliged to employ a draftsman in preparing the plans of his inventions. His character was marked by uprightness, conservatism, generosity, and kindliness; he was a most genial host, "and never seemed so happy as when he had guests at his table," both at his country estate in the White Mountains, and in his house in Boston, where he died. He was twice married, first, to Susan W. King, who died in 1841, and second, to Eliza Frances Means.

[Genealogical details may be found in Gilman Bigelow Howe's complete but often inaccurate *Genealogy of the Bigelow Family of America* (1890). The fullest and most sympathetic account of Bigelow's early and middle life is that of his intimate friend and kinsman Nehemiah Cleaveland, in *Hunt's Merchants' Mag.,* Feb. 1854, pp. 162–76. Andrew D. Ford's *Hist. of the Origin of the Town of Clinton, Mass.* (1896), pp. 192 ff. and references there, is the best authority on his later years, and his relations to Clinton. A memoir by Delano A. Goddard is printed in *Proc. Mass. Hist. Soc.,* XIX, 429–37. *A Century of Carpet and Rug Making in America,* published by the Hartford-Bigelow Carpet Co. (1925), also contains much useful information. The most recent account of Bigelow's whole career was printed in the *Clinton Item,* Apr. 12, 1927, by Francis H. Sawyer of Clinton, who is probably better informed than anyone else now living, in regard to the origin and development of the Bigelow mills in that town.]   R.B.M.

BIGELOW, FRANK HAGAR (Aug. 28, 1851–Mar. 2, 1924), meteorologist, was the only son of Francis Edwin and Ann Hagar Bigelow and seventh in descent from a John Bigua, or Biglo, whose marriage was recorded in Watertown, Mass., in 1642. He attended both the primary and the high school of Concord, Mass., his birthplace, and also, for three years, a Latin school in Boston. His mother was interested in astronomy and had a small telescope, a circumstance that helped to arouse in her son his lifelong interest in astronomical problems. After graduating from Harvard College in 1873, Bigelow took a position as assistant astronomer at the Cordoba Observatory, Argentina. There he remained three years, returning to the United States in 1876 to study for the ministry. Receiving his degree of B.D. from the Episcopal Theological School at Cambridge, he became for a short while, 1880–81, rector of St. Paul's Church, Natick, Mass. His lungs soon became affected, however, and he had to give up active ministerial work. He then returned to his former place in Argentina, 1881-83. After this he held many posts, notably that of chief of the climatological division in the United States Weather Bureau (1906–10), that of editor of the *Monthly Weather Review* (1909–10), and lastly that of professor of meteorology, Oficina Meteorologica, Cordoba, Argentina (1910–21). He also was professor of solar physics at George Washington University (1894–1910) and served as assistant rector of St. John's Church. He had an active part in the United States Eclipse Expedition to West Africa, 1889; to Newberry, S. C., 1900; and to Spain, 1905. Naturally, too, he was a member of several scientific societies. After retiring at the age of seventy due to failing eyesight incident to diabetes, he went first to Marseilles, then to London, and, finally, to Vienna where he died. His wife, Mary E. Spalding, whom he married in 1881, survived him only a few days.

His voluminous writings cover a wide range in the fields of climatology, meteorology, and kindred subjects. Among the best are two ponderous volumes, *Report on the International Cloud Observations,* based on records made throughout the United States in 1896–97, and *Report on the Barometry of the United States, Canada, and the West Indies,* published as Reports of Chief of Weather Bureau for 1898–99, and 1900–01, respectively. He demonstrated the fact that the centers of extra-tropical cyclones are neither all warm nor all cold, but occur on a line of separation between adjacent warm and cold masses of air. This discovery attracted very little attention until years afterward when it was elaborated by others, explained, and made a powerful aid in foretelling the coming weather. In 1904 Bigelow elaborated and urged a plan for the study of atmospheric electricity and terrestrial magnetism and their relation to solar conditions. As his wishes in this matter could not be closely followed he became discouraged, and being quite reserved, was soon seeing too much of himself and too little of others. Presently he felt an urge to rewrite meteorology, an urge that resulted in many papers, two books, and five supplements, the last appearing shortly before his death and bearing the title *The New Must Replace the Old, Delenda est Carthago, Atmospheric Physics as Applied to a Reformed Meteorology.* But all this reforming effort produced little or no effect. His real contributions to meteorology had long been made.

[*Monthly Weather Review,* Mar. 1924; *Who's Who in America,* 1922–23; G. B. Howe, *Genealogy of the Bigelow Family* (1890).]

W.J.H.

BIGELOW, HENRY JACOB (Mar. 11, 1818– Oct. 30, 1890), surgeon, the oldest son of Jacob Bigelow [*q.v.*], an eminent physician of Boston, and of Mary Scollay, is noted for important contributions to surgery and for having published the first account of the use of ether in a surgical operation. He was born and spent his youth in the stimulating atmosphere of his father's house on Summer St. in Boston, and received his early education at Chauncey Hall. He was prepared for college at the Boston Latin School, entered Harvard at the age of fifteen, and was graduated with the class of 1837. After leaving college he studied with his father as preceptor, and attended lectures at the medical schools of Harvard and Dartmouth. In 1838–39 he was house surgeon at the Massachusetts General Hospital (Boston). Owing, however, to pulmonary symptoms which had threatened him from time to time for several years, he passed the winter of 1839–40 in Cuba, and in the spring went from there to Europe where he remained, except for a short visit home in 1841 (when he took his degree from the Harvard Medical School), until 1844. During these years Bigelow came under the influence of Louis in Paris, who was then at the height of his powers, and under his instruction laid an excellent foundation for work in surgical pathology and in clinical medicine. On returning to Boston he soon acquired a large practise, but to broaden his experience established a charitable out-patient clinic in the basement of the First Church on Chauncey Place, an action which unfortunately made him the object of much ridicule.

An important event in Bigelow's career was his association with the discovery of surgical anæsthesia. During the summer of 1846 W. T. G. Morton [*q.v.*], a Boston dentist, studied the effects upon animals of the inhalation of sulphuric ether, and on Sept. 30, 1846, after learning that Prof. Charles T. Jackson [*q.v.*] had inhaled it without subsequent ill-effect, Morton employed ether successfully on a human being during the extraction of a tooth. On Oct. 16, 1846, Morton, probably through Bigelow's influence (Hodges, p. 139), was permitted to give ether to a patient at the Massachusetts General Hospital who was to have a tumor removed from his neck by Dr. John Collins Warren. Ether anæsthesia proved successful with this and other cases. Bigelow read a preliminary communication concerning Morton's results to the American Academy of Sciences on Nov. 3, 1846. The first printed account appeared on Nov. 18, 1846, in the *Boston Medical and Surgical Journal* under the title: "Insensibility during Surgical Operations, Produced by Inhalation."

Bigelow also made important surgical contributions. Through his Boylston Prize Essay, *Manual of Orthopedic Surgery* (1844), he directed attention to a field of surgical endeavor then neglected in this country. According to Garrison (*History of Medicine*, 1913, p. 538) he was the first in America to excise the hip joint (*American Journal of the Medical Sciences*, 1852, XXIV, 90). In 1869 he described the ilio-femoral (Y–) ligament and its mechanism, and demonstrated the importance of the structure in reducing dislocation of the hip by the flexion method (*The Mechanism of Dislocation and Fracture of the Hip*, 1869). William W. Reid [*q.v.*] had clearly described the flexion method of reducing dislocation of the hip in 1851 but, though his results were published in the *Boston Medical and Surgical Journal* Bigelow gave him no credit. Bigelow also improved an instrument (lithotrite) for crushing stones of the bladder and perfected an evacuator of large caliber to secure immediate removal of the fragments. He designated the operation "litholapaxy" (*American Journal of the Medical Sciences*, 1878, LXXV, 117–34). In 1871 he published his *Medical Education in America*, a work which reflected little credit upon his reputation.

In forming an estimate of Bigelow one cannot forget that he was unscrupulous at times and became, especially in later life, something of a martinet. In his dealings with students he gained the reputation of being something of a poseur, but as he was exceptionally skilful, quick, and resourceful, there were few who did not admire him. For nearly forty years he was the dominating figure in New England surgery and stood on an equal footing with S. D. Gross [*q.v.*] of Philadelphia. As a lecturer he was terse and epigrammatic, and being ambidextrous and an exceptional draftsman, he had no difficulty in holding the attention of his students. He left the stamp of his striking personality upon all of his younger associates many of whom have recalled his exacting ways with a feeling of gratitude. "In personal appearance he was tall and rather slight, his elastic step betraying a nervous organization. He had well-moulded features which were unobscured even by a full beard, and his agreeable voice and manner always attracted attention." He was married on May 8, 1847, to Susan Sturgis, daughter of William Sturgis. She died in 1853 leaving one child, William Sturgis Bigelow [*q.v.*]. An excellent full-length portrait of Bigelow hangs in the Boston Medical Library.

[The chief source of information is *A Memoir of Henry Jacob Bigelow* prepared anonymously in 1900 by his son, William Sturgis Bigelow, as a fourth volume in a collected edition of his works. The memoir of

Bigelow by Oliver Wendell Holmes in the *Proc. Am. Acad. of Arts and Sci.*, 1890, vol. XVI, is particularly happy in its estimate of his character. A later notice by G. H. Monks is to be found in *Surg. Gyn. and Obstet.*, July 1924, pp. 112–16. All of the Bigelow letters and manuscripts have been deposited in the Boston Medical Library. The best account of the ether episode is probably that of R. M. Hodges, *A Narrative of Events Connected with the Introduction of Sulphuric Ether into Surgical Use* (1891). The extensive literature on the introduction of anæsthesia is listed with copious annotations in the *Bibliotheca Osleriana*, ed. by W. W, Francis (1928).]　　　　J.F.F.

BIGELOW, JACOB (Feb. 27, 1787–Jan. 10, 1879), botanist and physician, was of Massachusetts ancestry, the son of Jacob Bigelow, a Congregational minister, and of Elizabeth (Wells) Bigelow (*Vital Records of Sudbury, Mass.*, 1903; *Genealogy*). He entered Harvard at the age of sixteen and graduated in 1806. In 1809 he matriculated in the medical department of the University of Pennsylvania, studying under Dr. B. S. Barton [*q.v.*], botanist and physician, whose work on the medicinal plants of the United States exerted a strong influence on Bigelow's subsequent career. He received his M.D. from Pennsylvania in 1810. On returning to Boston (1811) he formed an association with Dr. James Jackson [*q.v.*] whose successor he ultimately became. Whilst building up his medical practise, Bigelow had not forgotten his botanical interests, and in 1812 gave, in conjunction with a Dr. Peck, a series of botanical lectures at Harvard. He was the first native botanist to collect and to systematize the knowledge of the New England flora in a thorough-going way. In connection with his botanical lectures and in the preparation of drugs for his medical practise, he commenced the intensive study of the flora of the Boston region, and in 1814 published a modest book, *Florula Bostoniensis*. The first edition of this work dealt only with the flora within a ten-mile radius, but by 1824 Bigelow had, with Dr. Francis Booth, explored the mountains of New Hampshire and Vermont, so that he was able to reprint his book, retaining its unassuming title, but now enlarged, corrected, popularized, and in a general way made useful for all New England. The *Florula Bostoniensis* remained the standard manual of New England botany till the appearance of Gray's *Manual* (1848). Bigelow's most important botanical contribution, the *American Medical Botany*, in three volumes, began to appear in 1817; the second volume was published in 1818, and the last in 1820. This work contained sixty plates colored by a special process of the author's own invention. Bigelow also took an important part in preparing the first *American Pharmacopœia*, which appeared in 1820. He departed from Continental usage in insisting upon the utmost simplicity in nomenclature. In 1822 was issued his *Treatise on the Materia Medica,* which was intended as a sequel to the *Pharmacopœia.*

In 1815 Bigelow had been made professor of materia medica in the Harvard Medical School, a post which he continued to hold until 1855. During these years his medical fame was increasing, for not only was his position at the Massachusetts General Hospital and the Harvard Medical School conspicuous, but his lectures, delivered before various medical organizations, were often revolutionary and always of enduring influence. It was he who made the first effective protest in America against ill-chosen drugs and large doses, and against excessive blood-letting. He embodied in his *Discourse on Self-limited Diseases* (1835) the idea that many disorders if left to the natural recuperative powers of the patient would disappear more rapidly than from excessive medical treatment. Of this lecture Dr. Oliver Wendell Holmes (*Proceedings of the American Academy of Arts and Sciences,* 1879, p. 16) said that it exerted more influence upon medical practise in America than any work that had ever been published in this country. In his *Address on the Limits of Education* (1865) Bigelow attacked classical education, denying that the dead languages were the indispensable preliminaries to all useful training. He was the more entitled to do this because he was himself a classical scholar of brilliant attainments.

In 1832 he was sent to New York with a committee to study the newly arrived Asiatic cholera. Upon his return his native state refused to readmit the committee, so great was the terror of Boston, but Bigelow eluded the quarantine and hastened back to his patients. For some years (1816–27), beside all his other duties, he had been holding the chair of application of science to the useful arts, established by Count Rumford, and in connection with his teaching of mechanics, for which he had a passion, he invented the term "technology." In 1829 he published his Rumford lectures under the title *Elements of Technology,* and they were again expanded in 1840 in a work *The Useful Arts.* From 1847 to 1863 he was president of the American Academy of Arts and Sciences, of which he was a member for sixty-seven years.

One of the many acts of his vigorous life was the foundation of Mt. Auburn Cemetery (1831), in Cambridge, Mass., in an effort to protect the health of the community which was then often imperiled by injudicious interment. He is often asserted to have been the first to conceive that cemeteries might receive the attention which is ordinarily devoted to private gardens. An act of

doubtful æsthetic value, but well intended, was his erection of a great stone sphinx in the cemetery, to commemorate the dead of the Civil War. His dominant personality caused its erection in spite of opposition, but in the blindness (cataract) that came upon him he could not see the monument he had raised, and had to be lifted to trace with his fingers the enigmatic countenance. Before his death, which occurred in Boston, his intellectual faculties became somewhat impaired. But even in his mental uncertainties a sort of playful genius exhibited itself in the clever doggerel by which he translated Mother Goose into Latin under the title of *Chenodia.* His early metrical reflections in English and the classic tongues had been privately and anonymously printed. In addition to the works already mentioned, he wrote: *Nature in Disease* (1854); *Eolopœsis, American Rejected Addresses* (1855); *Brief Expositions of Rational Medicine* (1858); and *Modern Inquiries* (1867). He was married in 1817 to Mary Scollay, daughter of Col. William Scollay.

[The most comprehensive authority is G. E. Ellis's *Memoir of Jacob Bigelow* (1880), with portrait, but it is inaccurate, poorly arranged and unattractively written. Asa Gray evaluated Bigelow's botanical work in *Am. Jour. Sci.,* Apr. 1879, pp. 263–66. L. H. Bailey's memorial in *Bot. Gazette,* May 1883, pp. 217–222, is based upon Gray's, but contains some incidents not mentioned by the older botanist. For a colorful popular account see H. A. Kelly, *Some Am. Medic. Botanists* (1914). Oliver Wendell Holmes's obituary of Bigelow in the *Proc. Am. Acad. Arts and Sci.,* 1879, is a classic in this kind of writing. See also J. G. Mumford, "Jacob Bigelow: A Sketch," reprinted from the *Johns Hopkins Hospital Bull.* (1902) in his *Surgical Memoirs* (1908), and G. B. Howe, *Genealogy of the Bigelow Family of America* (1890). All of the Bigelow manuscripts, including the original plates of the botanical works, were deposited in the Boston Medic. Lib., Jan. 1927, by the executors of William Sturgis Bigelow, grandson of Jacob Bigelow.]   D. C. P.
                                                             J. F. F.

BIGELOW, JOHN (Nov. 25, 1817–Dec. 19, 1911), editor, diplomatist, author, was born at Bristol, now Malden, N. Y., the son of Asa Bigelow and Lucy Isham, both natives of Connecticut. He attended Washington, now Trinity, College, at Hartford, Conn., but left in his junior year with a slight opinion of his teachers, and graduated at Union College, Schenectady, N. Y., in 1835. Three years later he was admitted to the New York bar. His first public office was that of an inspector of Sing Sing prison. In 1844, apparently through the influence of Samuel J. Tilden, he joined the Free-Soil Democrats. In 1848 he was invited by William Cullen Bryant to share in owning and editing the New York *Evening Post,* a connection that continued until 1861, when the paper was sold to Parke Godwin. On the questions of anti-slavery and free trade, to both of which the paper was devoted, his editorial attitude was outspoken and uncompromising. A visit to Jamaica afforded material for a series of newspaper letters later published (1851) as *Jamaica in 1850*. The same year (1850) saw his marriage to Jane Poultney of New York, formerly of Baltimore. In 1853–54 he visited Haiti to study "the African as he had developed in freedom," a later by-product of the visit being his *Wit and Wisdom of the Haytians* (1877), a collection of proverbial sayings. Incidentally the journey introduced him to the writings of Swedenborg, whose doctrines he presently accepted. Two of his later writings, *Molinos the Quietist* (1882) and *The Mystery of Sleep* (1897), reflect indirectly his interest in Swedenborg's philosophy. A campaign *Memoir of the Life and Public Services of John Charles Frémont* (1856) is still of some value for its California documents. A visit to Europe in 1858 won him the friendship of Sainte-Beuve, Cobden, Bright, Thackeray, and many others, and paved the way for his later success as a diplomatist.

Returning to the United States in 1860, he was appointed in 1861 consul-general at Paris, and in April 1865, was made minister to France, a post he held until September 1866. He established close personal relations with the French, German, and Austrian press, then mainly dependent upon London for American news and inclined to sympathize with the Confederacy, and exposed and defeated plans intended to secure effective French support for it. A summary sketch of American history bearing his name was published at Milan in 1863 under the title *Gli Stati Uniti d' America nel 1863*. Letters and papers of Slidell and others that he purchased at this time, supplemented by the Slidell-Benjamin correspondence found in the Confederate archives, form the documentary basis of *France and the Confederate Navy, 1862–68: An International Episode* (1888), one of the most valuable of his writings, but his charge, later elaborated in *Lest We Forget* (1905) and the *Retrospections,* that Gladstone subscribed to the Confederate cotton loan appears to have been unfounded (E. D. Adams, *Great Britain and the American Civil War,* 1925, II, 163). Bigelow skilfully warned Napoleon III of the folly of supporting an imperial program in Mexico, at the same time successfully urging a waiting policy upon the Administration at Washington. In the American diplomacy of the Civil War his work ranks second in importance only to that of Charles Francis Adams at London. Following his return to the United States, in 1867, he held no public office until 1875, when Gov. Tilden placed him on the commission which broke up

the New York canal ring. The same year he was elected secretary of state for New York, where he served one term.

The remainder of his long life was devoted to writing and editing, although he was United States commissioner to the Brussels Exposition in 1888 and a delegate to the New York constitutional convention in 1893. His special interest in France had already produced *Some Recollections of Antoine Pierre Berryer* (1869), *Beaumarchais the Merchant* (1870), and *France and Hereditary Monarchy* (1871), and to these he added *Some Recollections of the late Edouard Laboulaye* (1889). His *Life of Benjamin Franklin* (1874; 2nd ed., revised and corrected, 1879) reproduced the famous *Autobiography,* the manuscript of which he had discovered and correctly printed for the first time (1868). *The Complete Works of Benjamin Franklin* (10 vols., 1887–88), although incomplete, displaced all previous editions in its chronological arrangement and exact reproduction of the original texts. Bigelow's abilities as an editor and his limitations as a biographer appear in sharply contrasted light in his *Writings and Speeches of Samuel J. Tilden* (1885; supplemented by *Letters and Literary Memorials,* 1908), and the later *Life of Samuel J. Tilden* (1895). The *Writings* are carefully edited, but the *Life,* while of primary importance, is marred by numerous errors apparently due to hasty writing or lax revision, and by biased judgments of many of Tilden's contemporaries, notably Grover Cleveland. A report to the New York Chamber of Commerce on the Panama Canal (1886); a life of Bryant in the American Men of Letters series (1890); *The Supreme Court and the Electoral Commission* (1903), an open letter to Joseph H. Choate; *Our Ex-Presidents: What shall we do for them? What shall they do for us?* (privately printed, 1906); *Peace Given as the World Giveth—or, The Portsmouth Treaty and its First Year's Fruits* (1907); *A Substitute for the Tariff upon Imports* (1908), an open letter to Charles E. Hughes; *The Panama Canal and the Daughters of Danaus* (1908); and occasional articles in periodicals, showed the wide range of his intellectual activity. *Toleration, and Other Essays and Studies,* a posthumous collection, appeared in 1926.

[The chief authority to 1879 is Bigelow's *Retrospections of an Active Life* (5 vols., 1909–13), of which vols. IV and V were prepared by his son, John Bigelow. The work, often exceedingly discursive, contains many letters and documents. A sketch by Henry Van Dyke is to be found in a collection of *Memorial Addresses* delivered before the Century Association, New York, Mar. 9, 1912. Obituaries were published in the N. Y. papers, Dec. 19, 20, 1911.] W. M.

BIGELOW, MELVILLE MADISON (Aug. 2, 1846–May 4, 1921), educator, legal writer, was descended from Mary Warren and John Biglo of Watertown, Mass., who were married on Aug. 30, 1642. The son of William Enos Bigelow of Michigan, a Methodist clergyman, and Daphne F. Madison of New York, he was born near Eaton Rapids, Mich. His early education was received in the public schools wherever his father happened to be stationed within the territory embraced by the Detroit Conference, much of which was sparsely populated frontier country. Inheriting many of the characteristics of his mother, a remarkable woman, he was able to overcome the somewhat crude educational facilities of Milford, Port Huron, and Ypsilanti. Proceeding to the University of Michigan at Ann Arbor, he graduated A.B. in 1866, and LL.B two years later. He studied law at Pontiac for a short time, and went from there to Memphis, where his uncle, Joseph Enos Bigelow, was practising. In March 1868 he was admitted to the Tennessee bar. He had become interested in the historical development of the law and now determined to undertake research work in that line in preference to the actual practise of his profession. With this end in view he removed to Boston in 1870, and was admitted a member of the Boston bar. At that time the trustees of Boston University were considering the advisability of establishing a law school in the University and Bigelow was in 1871 appointed a member of a committee to investigate and report. The report, which he himself prepared, was favorable, and in September 1872 the Boston University Law School was opened, Bigelow being appointed a member of the faculty (*Green Bag,* I, 54). Thus commenced a connection which was maintained throughout fifty years as lecturer, professor, and dean. He was now engaged in a work for which by the nature of his previous studies he was admirably fitted, which coincided with his own inclinations and yielded the opportunity to indulge in research which was his chief delight. "Bigelow was not fit for a practising lawyer. He had not the litigious instinct, nor had he the instinct for business, nor for money. He was a scholar, if ever a pure scholar was born on earth, and he was an instructor and not a denizen of courts" (Brooks Adams, in *Boston University Law Review,* I, 169). At the outset, in addition to his lecturing duties, he undertook a post-graduate course at Harvard, receiving the degree of Ph.D. in 1879.

His initial publication was the first volume of *Reports of all the Published Life and Accident Insurance Cases, American Courts* (1871), the series being continued in four subsequent volumes, the last of which appeared in 1877. His next work, *The Law of Estoppel and its Application in Practice* (1872), at once attracted attention by its masterly handling of an extremely technical and difficult branch of the law, as well as by its attractive style. It established Bigelow's reputation as a legal writer and passed through many editions. Then followed *An Index of Cases overruled, reversed . . . by the Courts of America, England, and Ireland* (1873), a supplement to which was issued in 1887, a scientific selection of *Leading Cases on the Law of Torts* (1875), and a text-book, *The Law of Fraud and the Procedure pertaining to the Redress thereof* (1877), both of the latter being in the nature of preparatory work for two treatises which were to come from his pen later. Next to appear was his *Elements of the Law of Torts* (1878), a work intended for students, covering a field which had hitherto been greatly neglected. It became the standard text-book in all American law schools, and its inclusion by the University of Cambridge, England, in the list of works recommended for study, led ultimately to the preparation by Bigelow of an English edition which was published by the Cambridge University Press in 1889. This was the first instance of such an honor being accorded to an American text-book and indicated the high academic standard which Bigelow had attained. He had not confined his labors, however, to the law as it existed, but, pursuing a line of research which always had for him a particular fascination, read deeply in the ancient English records, the early results of which were embodied in his *Placita Anglo-Normannica: Law Cases from William I to Richard I preserved in Historical Records,* published in London in 1879, and republished in Boston two years later. His cases "are gleaned almost without exception from monkish chronicles, from diplomata, from Domesday Book, from anything in fact except what would be called a law book at the present day" (P. H. Winfield, *The Chief Sources of English Legal History,* 1925, p. 146). It was a bold experiment on Bigelow's part but the result justified the risk. In undertaking this work he entered a field—the study of legal history—which had been considerably neglected. Then came *Elements of Equity* (1879) and the *Law of Bills, Notes and Cheques illustrated by leading cases* (1880)— both students' books—which were followed by *History of Procedure in England from the Norman Conquest: the Norman Period 1066–1204* (1880), another excursion into legal antiquities, which confirmed previous estimates of the depth of his scholarship and the ability of his pen. This work also met with a hearty reception in English university circles. The succeeding eight years were devoted to assiduous work at the Law School and to the preparation of a monumental treatise on the *Law of Fraud on its Civil Side* which appeared in two volumes in 1888–90, and immediately became recognized as the most valuable work on that subject which had been produced in America. Bigelow subsequently published *Elements of the Law of Bills, Notes and Cheques and the English Bills of Exchange Act* (1893), *Cases on the Law of Bills, Notes and Cheques* (1894), and a treatise on *The Law of Wills* (1898), the latter exhibiting all the qualities which had made his *Estoppel* and *Torts* so conspicuously successful. In 1903 he wrote articles on "The Declaration of Independence" and "The Constitution," for *The Cambridge Modern History,* vol. VII. He contributed to and wrote a preface for a collection of essays entitled *Centralization and the Law* (1906). Other later works of his were *A False Equation—The Problem of the Great Trust* (1911), and *Papers on the Legal History of Government; difficulties fundamental and artificial* (1920). In addition, he contributed many articles on legal and kindred subjects to current periodicals, including the *Law Quarterly Review.* He died in Boston after a long illness, being the last survivor of the original faculty of the Boston Law School. He was three times married: (1) in 1869 to Elizabeth Chamberlin, daughter of Alfred Bragg of Milford, Mass., who died in 1881; (2) in 1883 to Cornelia Frothingham Read, who died in 1892; (3) in 1898 to Alice Bradford Woodman, who survived him.

[Particulars of Bigelow's ancestry are to be found in *Genealogy of the Bigelow Family of America* (1890), by Gilman Bigelow Howe, and in *Memoirs of the Judiciary and Bar of New Eng.* (1901), by Conrad Reno, II, 635, which also contains a sketch of his life. The best accounts of his activities are in *Boston Univ. Law Rev.*, I, 153, "Memorial of Melville Madison Bigelow," and II, 17, "Melville M. Bigelow and the Legal Profession"—the latter being a brilliant characterization study by Chas. W. Eliot.]   H. W. H. K.

BIGELOW, WILLIAM STURGIS (Apr. 4, 1850–Oct. 6, 1926), physician, orientalist, was the son of Henry Jacob Bigelow [*q.v.*], and grandson of Jacob Bigelow [*q.v.*,], eminent physicians of Boston. An only child, he was left solitary by the early death of his mother, Susan Sturgis, whose loss he felt severely, and he grew to manhood shy and retiring. He passed through Harvard College (class of 1871) without special distinction, and then took up the study of medicine. In the course of his work he developed a keen interest in the purely scientific aspects of medicine, the more practical phases of a practitioner's routine being distasteful to him. After graduating from the Harvard Medical School in 1874, he went abroad for five years. He studied first in the clinics at Vienna in company with Frederick C. Shattuck of Boston. He spent a year or more with Pasteur, acquiring an intimate knowledge of bacteriological technique. He was much influenced by Ranvier, the professor of histology, and also by Waldeyer, with whom he passed the summer of 1878 in Strassburg. He returned to Boston in 1879 with great enthusiasm for bacteriology, and set up a private laboratory in Pemberton Square. His father, however, gave him no encouragement in his investigations and prevailed upon him to take the post of surgeon to out-patients at the Massachusetts General Hospital, and as this gave him little opportunity for developing bacteriological interests his laboratory had to be discontinued. Few men could have had less taste for surgery than the sensitive Bigelow, and it was not long before he gave up entirely all thoughts of practise. In 1882 he left for Japan in order to divert his mind, and there spent seven years without break, collecting works of art, and studying the language, philosophy, and religion of a race which was then little known in the western world. Largely as a result of his activities in collecting, the Boston Art Museum now possesses the richest collection of Japanese works of art to be found anywhere in the world, not excepting Japan. While in the East, he also became interested in Northern Buddhism and devoted himself to a study of its philosophy. In 1908 he delivered his Ingersoll Lecture on *Buddhism and Immortality,* which helped to bring to the western world an understanding of Buddhistic philosophy. In recognition of his attainments, the Japanese Government made him a Commander of the Imperial Order of the Rising Sun. He never married. Bigelow published two scientific papers: "Notiz über den Theilungsvorgang bei Knorpelzellen, sowie über den Bau des Hyalinknorpels" (*Archiv für mikroskopische Anatomie,* 1879, XVI, 457–63), after his association with Waldeyer, and "The Study of Bacteria and their Relation to Disease" (*Boston Medical and Surgical Journal,* 1882, CVI, 248–50), published during his service at the Massachusetts General Hospital. Short discussions by him are also to be found in the *Boston Medical and Surgical Journal,* 1879, CI, 23 and 1881, CV, 233.

[An appreciation by Dr. Frederick C. Shattuck is to be found in the *Proc. Mass. Hist. Soc.,* Nov. 1926. The *Boston Evening Transcript* contained notices on Oct. 6, Oct. 8, Oct. 9, Oct. 11, 1926. Further information has been supplied by Dr. Frederick C. Shattuck and Dr. Harvey Cushing.]   J. F. F.

BIGGS, ASA (Feb. 4, 1811–Mar. 6, 1878), North Carolina jurist and politician, was born at Williamston, Martin County, N. C., the son of Joseph Biggs, merchant and elder of the Primitive Baptist Church, and Chloe Daniel, his third wife. His parents were poor and uncultured but strong in moral and religious qualities. Growing rapidly in mind and body, the boy at fifteen quit the Williamston Academy, clerked in neighboring stores, and, having read law privately, began its practise in 1831. Next year he attended a party convention, traveled to New York, and married Martha Elizabeth Andrews, who brought him some slaves and eventually bore him ten children. Until 1845, and intermittently thereafter until 1858, he was primarily a lawyer, painstaking, honest and financially successful. It was politics, however, that brought him into public notice. He had espoused the cause of Andrew Jackson early, and was sent to the state constitutional convention of 1835. Here he said nothing, learned much, and voted as planter interests and sectional jealousies required. Then he went to the House of Commons for two terms and to the Senate for one (1840–45). A single term in Congress immediately followed. These honors, far from being thrust upon him, were won by hard-fought campaigns in which he made a reputation by refusing either to "treat" or to trim on public issues. In the Democratic state convention of 1850 he attracted state-wide attention by attempting to commit the party against state internal improvements. Desisting, however, in the interest of party harmony, he was the next year appointed joint codifier of the state's laws by Gov. Ellis, whom the convention of 1850 had nominated. There followed four years of quiet, dignified and congenial labor, only slightly seasoned with politics, after which he returned to the Senate, saw Moore and Biggs's *Code* safely adopted, and was elected, along with Gov. Ellis, to the federal Senate. Here, because of his stand for economy in government, place was made for him on the Finance Committee. But the tall, black-haired and somber-faced North Carolinian was not happy in Congress: his political reading was inadequate; his health became impaired by severe labor without exercise; the Government was corrupt and growing worse; his domestic affairs and religious life—he had had a remarkable religious experience in 1851—were upset. Accordingly he resigned to become district judge of North Carolina (1858–61). Decidedly pro-Southern in his views, he was active in the Secession Convention until called to the duties of Confederate district judge (December 1861–

April 1865); and he supported the Confederacy whole-heartedly and prayerfully to the end. His fortune swept away by war and his law practise handicapped by the hostility of the state supreme court (to which, characteristically, he refused to apologize for signing a certain famous "Solemn Protest"), he began life anew in 1868 in Norfolk, Va.; and there he died ten years later.

[Biggs's *Autobiography,* ed. by R. D. W. Connor in *Pubs. N. C. Hist. Commission, Bull. No. 19,* 1915, was written for his children in Mar. 1865, with a short conclusion on July 1, 1865. Bound with it is his *Journal of a Trip from Williamston to N. Y. and Back in 1852.* His constitutional views may be found in *Cong. Globe,* 34 Cong., 1 Sess., p. 1962, and in appendices to his *Autobiography.* F. S. Spruill, *Address on Presentation of Portrait of Hon. Asa Biggs, Jan. 18, 1915,* is thoughtful, suggestive, eulogistic. Samuel A. Ashe in his *Hist. of N. C.,* vol. II (1925), and J. G. de Roulhac Hamilton in his *Reconstruction in N. C.* (1914) furnish background. An obituary is in the *News and Observer* (Raleigh), Mar. 7, 1878. A portrait hangs in the federal court-room at Raleigh.]

C.C.P.

BIGGS, HERMANN MICHAEL (Sept. 29, 1859–June 28, 1923), one of the pioneers of preventive medicine, was born in Trumansburg, N. Y., the son of Joseph Hunt and Melissa (Pratt) Biggs. The family was of English stock tracing its descent from a George Biggs who had come to America in 1690. Hermann Biggs received his elementary education at Ithaca, N. Y., graduated from Cornell University in 1882, and in the next year received his M.D. degree from Bellevue Hospital Medical College— an achievement which although it testifies to his brilliance also indicates the lax state of medical education at that time. After a year as interne at Bellevue Hospital, Biggs went to Germany for post-graduate work and spent the next two years in Berlin and Greifswald. Upon his return, he was put in charge of the newly opened Carnegie Laboratory of the Bellevue Hospital Medical College. From then on promotion at the college was rapid: he was lecturer on pathology, 1886; professor of pathology, 1889; professor of materia medica and therapeutics, 1892; professor of therapeutics, 1898; professor of the practise of medicine, 1912. On Aug. 18, 1898, he married Frances M. Richardson of Hornellsville, N. Y.

He began the practise of medicine at the time when the "germ theory" was rapidly developing into what has since become the science of bacteriology. One cannot realize Biggs's service to public health unless one is familiar with the unsatisfactory state of things at the time he began. Little progress had been made for fifty years. Matters changed rapidly after 1892, when Biggs organized the department of pathology and bacteriology of the New York City Health Department and became pathologist and director of the laboratories. These laboratories are said to have been the first municipal bacteriological laboratories in the world, and the methods inaugurated there have been widely followed. He introduced the use of bacteriological methods in the sanitary surveillance of infectious disease. In 1894 he introduced the use of diphtheria antitoxin in this country, and he obtained the necessary legislation and appropriations which enabled the department to produce, use, and sell biological products. The formulation and direction of the work in New York City for the prevention of tuberculosis was another notable achievement. Biggs successively established the notification of tuberculosis, the examination of sputum, the visitation of cases by nurses, the disinfection of premises, the compulsory segregation of careless cases, tuberculosis clinics, the Otisville Sanatorium for incipient cases, and the Riverside Hospital for advanced cases. Throughout his twenty-two years of service, his knowledge, sincerity, and tact enabled him in spite of all the vicissitudes and turmoils of New York politics to carry out his plans unhindered.

Early in 1914 he was appointed state commissioner of health and chairman of the public health council of the State of New York, a body recently created by the legislature and clothed with broad powers of sanitary control. As commissioner he reorganized the work for children, and very soon developed an efficient state-wide division of infant and maternity welfare. At the time of his death it was one of the most effective ministers to the public health. Among his other activities, Biggs wrote works dealing with Pasteur's prophylactic treatment of rabies, the outbreak of cholera in New York in 1893, the treatment of tuberculosis, and the use of antitoxin in the treatment of diphtheria, and other subjects, and contributed frequently to periodical literature.

[*Monthly Bull. N. Y. State Dept. of Health*, July 1923; *Science*, Nov. 23, 1923, p. 413; *Am. Medicine*, July 1923, p. 530.]   B.H.

BIGLER, JOHN (Jan. 8, 1805–Nov. 29, 1871), governor of California, was born near Carlisle, Pa. The son of Susan (Dock) Bigler and Jacob Bigler, a farmer, he came of a German family which had been in America for over a hundred years and had been represented by both paternal and maternal grandfathers in the Revolutionary War. His education was interrupted after his entrance into Dickinson College (at Carlisle) by the removal of the family to Mercer County, where his father apprenticed him to a printer. This training led him at the close of his ap-

prenticeship in 1827 to undertake the editorship of the *Centre County Democrat,* located at Bellefonte, where he remained for the next five years. He then took up the study of law and after having been admitted to the bar, removed some years later to Mount Sterling, Ill., where he continued his practise. Caught by the spirit of the Gold Rush in the spring of 1849, he set out with an overland company bound for California. With him he took his wife, a woman none too strong for the severe undertaking, and his infant daughter. The journey, made by ox-team and covered wagon, ended at Sacramento on Aug. 31. To Mrs. Bigler belonged the honor of being the first white woman to make her home in Sacramento. Bigler found no opportunity in the small, disorganized community to practise his profession; and, as he was without funds with which to maintain his family, he turned his hand to whatever came along. He found employment with an auctioneer for a time; later he cut wood in the adjoining country, bringing it into town for sale; he unloaded river steamers; and finally secured a contract with a Sacramento merchant to make up a number of calico comforters, for which he received in partial remuneration calico for dresses for his wife and daughter.

Bigler's position in the community appears not to have suffered because of his humble pursuits, and in November 1849 he was elected to the Assembly of the first state legislature. This body convened at San José on Dec. 16, 1849, and proceeded to complete the organization of the state government. Bigler served as assemblyman for two terms and was twice chosen speaker of that body. In 1851 he was elected governor on the Democratic ticket and two years later was reëlected. He ran for a third time, but was defeated. President Buchanan, shortly after his inauguration, appointed Bigler United States minister to Chile. This post Bigler held for four years, during which he was instrumental in effecting the settlement of a number of long-standing and troublesome questions. In 1861 he returned to California and resumed the practise of law. A year later, he was persuaded to run on the Democratic ticket for Congress but was defeated. He never again held public office but remained active in the affairs of his party and served three times as delegate to the national Democratic convention. His death occurred on Nov. 29, 1871. During his lifetime he had commanded general respect. His sympathetic understanding of the needs of the new settlers had made him also much beloved; and his achievements in the field of politics had added materially to the success of the party to which he gave his loyalty.

[A very full account of the life of Bigler is to be found in *Representative and Leading Men of the Pacific* (1870), ed. by Oscar Shuck. Some additional material is to be found in the *Pubs. Hist. Soc. of Southern Cal.* (1903), in H. H. Bancroft, *Hist. of Cal.* (1890), vols. VI, VII, and in the *Sacramento Daily Union,* Nov. 30, 1871.]

R. G. C—d.

BIGLER, WILLIAM (Jan. 1, 1814–Aug. 9, 1880), governor of Pennsylvania, senator, was born at Shermansburg, Cumberland County, Pa. His parents Jacob and Susan (Dock) Bigler, Pennsylvania Germans, decided soon after his birth to attempt to lift the burden of poverty from their shoulders, purchased a large tract of wilderness land in Mercer County, and migrated thither. But misfortune pursued them: the title to the tract was bad, and they lost their investment. For a few years Jacob Bigler attempted to support his family on a small farm, but discouragement and labor were too much, and he died when William was small. Hard work and little schooling were the lot of the latter, and at fourteen he entered the printing office of his brother John [*q.v.*] at Bellefonte, Center County. In 1833 he decided to set out for himself; so, acquiring a second-hand printing outfit and borrowing twenty dollars, he moved to Clearfield, where he established the *Clearfield Democrat,* "an eight by ten Jackson paper intended to counteract the influence of the seven by nine Whig (*sic*) paper." On Mar. 23, 1836, he married Maria J. Reed, daughter of a local magnate, and soon thereafter sold his paper and entered a partnership with his father-in-law, in which he amassed a fortune as a lumberman. In 1841 he was elected to the state Senate, where he served six years, twice as speaker. In the legislature he was mainly concerned in keeping the state solvent and in providing adequate railroad transportation to the westward counties. His political influence reached its high point in 1851 when he was nominated and elected governor. As executive he pursued a course in opposition to wholesale chartering of banks, in one message vetoing eleven bank charters. He also was successful in his fight against "omnibus" bills, the legislature passing a law which provided that each bill should deal with only one subject. He was renominated in 1854 but the Know-Nothing enthusiasm made his reëlection impossible. He was immediately made president of the Philadelphia & Erie Railroad Company, and a year later he was elected to the United States Senate, Jan. 14, 1856, as a vindication which he demanded for his sorry defeat in 1854. He

promoted the nomination of Buchanan, who had become estranged from him during the governorship largely because Bigler saw fit to recognize Buchanan's enemies and to remain inactive in 1852 when the latter was endeavoring to obtain the presidential nomination. In the Senate he was more active in committee than on the floor. He favored Buchanan's Lecompton policy after a visit to the Territory of Kansas in the summer of 1857. He was active in behalf of a Panama canal and a Pacific railroad and was opposed to the tariff of 1857. In the trying days of 1860–61 he protested against secession and favored the Crittenden compromise, serving as one of the committee of thirteen appointed in the Senate. His retirement in 1861 was of course inevitable. He remained a Democrat as long as he lived, made one campaign for Congress, attended most of the national conventions, and was one of the visiting statesmen who went to Louisiana after the election in 1876 to look after Tilden's interest. He was also prominent in the state constitutional convention of 1872–73 and active in the promotion of the Centennial in 1876. Most of the last twenty years of his life however were spent as a railroad promoter and capitalist in Clearfield. His stature was commanding and his face full and genial; he has been characterized as wise rather than brilliant, a politician destroyed by the disaster of 1861 which he had so long labored to prevent.

[Wm. C. Armor, *Lives of the Governors of Pa., 1609–1872* (1872); L. C. Aldrich, *Hist. of Clearfield County, Pa.* (1887); obituaries in *Phila. Press* and *Record,* Aug. 10, 1880. A number of Bigler's letters are in the possession of the Pa. Hist. Soc.]

R. F. N.

BILLINGS, CHARLES ETHAN (Dec. 5, 1835–June 5, 1920), manufacturer, tool-maker, was born in Wethersfield, Vt., son of Ethan Ferdinand and Clarissa (Marsh) Billings. His great-grandfather, Joseph Billings, had settled in Windsor, Vt., in 1793. Shortly after the birth of Charles Billings, the family moved to Windsor where he received a brief education in the public schools. At the age of seventeen he was engaged as an apprentice in the gun department of the old Robbins & Lawrence shop in Windsor, which made guns and machine tools and which markedly influenced American shop practise by training men destined to distinction. After serving three years, he became a journeyman machinist and a year later, when he was twenty-one, having gained a fundamental knowledge of machine-shop practise, he went to Springfield, Mass. A few months later he moved to Hartford, Conn., where for six years he was employed at the pistol factory of Samuel Colt, serving as tool-maker and die-sinker and for three years as foreman of the die-sinking department. While at Colt's he became an expert in drop-forging—a process for forging between dies by a drop-hammer. This process, which was coming into popularity as a means of manufacturing tools and machine parts, was a step in the replacing of hand work by standardized quantity production. In 1862 he was engaged by E. Remington & Sons of Ilion, N. Y., and, despite the criticism of conservative associates, he developed a process of treating drop-forgings that caused extraordinary saving of labor in manufacturing pistols. A single adaptation of drop-forging to the shaping of pistol frames by machinery saved this company many thousands of dollars in labor. As these improvements in firearms came at the time of the Civil War, they were particularly important. In 1865, at the close of the war, Billings returned to Hartford, and for three years was superintendent of manufacturing for the Weed Sewing Machine Company, which had taken over the old Sharps rifle works built by Robbins & Lawrence. While there he devised a method for making sewing-machine shuttles by drop-forging—a decided improvement over the old method of brazing the parts together. This was patented in 1867. In 1868 he became president and superintendent of the Roper Sporting Arms Company at Amherst, Mass., in association with C. M. Spencer. During the next year the business was moved to Hartford and reorganized as the Billings & Spencer Company. The sale of Roper sporting arms suffered a severe setback and in 1870 the firm took up the manufacture of drop-forgings in general, including machinist's small tools. The business prospered and grew, largely because of the inventive ability of Billings, the president. Among the outstanding inventions was the Billings commutator-bar for electric dynamos, made from drop-forged copper and invented in 1886. Other inventions included drills, chucks, pocket-knives, wrenches, etc., all made by machinery instead of by the old slow hand methods. Billings served as president of the American Society of Mechanical Engineers in 1895, as alderman and city councilman at Hartford, as president for twelve years of the board of fire commissioners, as high dignitary in the masons, as a bank trustee, etc. He was twice married; first to Frances M. Heywood on Jan. 5, 1857; second to Evalina Case Holt on Sept. 9, 1874.

[An excellent source on the general development of modern machine-shop practise and the men who influenced it is *English and American Tool Builders* (1916), by Joseph W. Roe. An interesting obituary of Billings is to be found in the *Trans. Am. Soc. Mech. Engineers* (1920), vol. XLII.]

P. B. M.

BILLINGS, FREDERICK (Sept. 27, 1823–Sept. 30, 1890), lawyer, railroad president, philanthropist, was born at Royalton, Vt., the fourth child of Oel and Sophia (Wetherbe) Billings, both of whom were of New England descent (Dana, *History of Woodstock*, pp. 594–97). In 1835 young Frederick moved with his parents to Woodstock, Vt., and a few years later entered the state university at Burlington, graduating in 1844. He then read law, and for two years, 1846–48, held a minor appointive state office. In 1848 he caught the gold fever from a seafaring relative, and early in 1849 went via the Isthmus to California. Here he had the good judgment to open a law office rather than to dig for gold, and reaped a rich harvest when the inevitable demand for legal talent set in. A partnership which he early formed with another lawyer grew rapidly into the leading law firm of San Francisco. Billings soon acquired wealth, prominence, and political influence. The latter he used in 1861 to prevent the loss of California to the Union. He was for a time attorney-general of the state, and could doubtless have had a political career. As attorney for Gen. Frémont in the matter of the Mariposa estate, Billings went to England in 1861. Returning to the United States, he was married on Mar. 31, 1862 to Julia, daughter of Dr. Eleazer Parmly, of New York City, and attempted to resume his law practise in San Francisco. Ill health prevented and in 1864 he went back to his old home in Woodstock, where a few years later he purchased the famous Marsh estate. This he enlarged and improved until, according to the local historian, "his home on the hill has come to resemble one of the baronial estates of the old world."

Billings's interest in the Northern Pacific railway was aroused by a trip to the Far Northwest in 1866. He bought one of the original twelfth interests in the company, and for many years its affairs claimed his chief attention. He organized its land department, and, knowing that the grant of lands received from Congress must be made to yield settlers rather than profits, kept the price of land low and inaugurated an extensive campaign of advertising. The results were highly gratifying, and the Northwest boomed until the panic of 1873 brought things to a standstill. Billings devised a plan of reorganization by which the prostrate Northern Pacific might be set on its feet, persuaded the directors to accept his plan, secured court assent to it, and put it into effect. In May 1879 he became president of the reorganized company. With the hard times at an end, he found money to begin construction westward from Bismarck, Dakota Territory, where the terminal had been since 1873, and eastward from the navigable waters of the Columbia River. The earnings of the company grew, its credit rose, and finally, in 1880, Billings persuaded a syndicate of bankers to purchase $40,-000,000 of its first mortgage bonds, enough to secure the completion of the road. This was regarded at the time as a financial triumph, and the Northern Pacific was described by a high authority as "the most important enterprise before the country, prosecuted by a single corporation, with a distinct purpose, and independent of entangling alliances" (*Commercial and Financial Chronicle,* XXX, 650; XXXI, 560, 579, 589; XXXII, 335–36). "Entangling alliances," however, were not easily avoided. Henry Villard, president of the O. R. & N., which operated a road along the southern bank of the Columbia River, feared the competition of the advancing Northern Pacific, and sought an agreement with it. Finding Billings "lukewarm and hard to satisfy," Villard determined to secure for himself a voice in Northern Pacific affairs. The result was his famous "blind pool," through which he was able to buy a large block of Northern Pacific stock. Villard now expected representation on a revised directorate, but this Billings sought to forestall. A struggle ensued, Billings at last capitulated, and an agreement was reached. In September 1881 the presidency was turned over to Villard, and Billings, although continuing as a director, ceased to take an active part in the company's management. The road was completed under Villard's leadership, but the credit for making its completion possible belongs chiefly to Billings (Villard, *Memoirs,* II, 291–300; *Commercial and Financial Chronicle,* XXXII, 313, 368, 421).

In spite of Billings's ill health, his fortune, now materially increased, commanded his attention. He was one of the active promoters of the Nicaraguan canal project. He devoted himself to philanthrophy, finding an outlet for his religious zeal in constructing a chapel for the Congregational Church of Woodstock, and in rebuilding its church and parsonage. He built a church, also, in Billings, Mont., a town named for him. He purchased for the University of Vermont the valuable George P. Marsh collection of 12,000 volumes, and built and en-

dowed at a cost of $250,000 a library building for the same institution. His numerous other benefactions included generous gifts to Amherst College and to Moody's School at Northfield, Mass. Billings's active business life did not prevent him from cultivating a fine appreciation of art and literature. He was devoted to the cause of public education, and was once considered for the presidency of the University of California. He was a forceful public speaker. His success in business came from an admirable compound of ability to plan and of ability to act. Commanding in appearance, gifted with the social graces, he won friends for himself and for his projects. For a long time he conquered his own ill health as he conquered other obstacles, but in 1890 death overtook him.

[Obituaries in *N. Y. Times* and *N. Y. Tribune,* Oct. 1, 1890, in *Univ. of Vt. Obit. Record,* No. I, 1895, and in *Appleton's Ann. Cyc. for 1890,* p. 634; longer sketches are by H. A. Hazen, in the *New Eng. Hist. and Geneal. Reg.,* XLV, 259–65, and by J. W. Buckham, in *Sunset,* XVI, 487–91. H. S. Dana's *Hist. of Woodstock, Vt.* (1889) contains some useful material. Billings's railway achievements are set forth in his address *The Northern Pacific R. R.: Its Hist. and Equitable Rights* (1880), and in E. V. Smalley, *Hist. of the Northern Pacific R. R.* (1883). *The Memoirs of Henry Villard* (1904), II, give a good account of the Billings-Villard controversy, and an article by J. B. Hedges, "The Colonization Work of the Northern Pacific R. R.," in the *Miss. Valley Hist. Rev.,* XIII, 311–42, tells of the activities of the land department under Billings.]

J. D. H.

BILLINGS, JOHN SHAW (Apr. 12, 1838–Mar. 11, 1913), librarian, surgeon, was descended from William Billings of Somersetshire who migrated to New England about the middle of the seventeenth century. In the course of six generations the family removed through New York State to Switzerland County in southeastern Indiana, where John was born to James Billings and his wife, Abby (Shaw) Billings, the latter descended from one of the *Mayflower* Pilgrims.

As a boy John read voraciously, learned Latin with a little aid from a clergyman of the neighborhood, and later made an agreement with his father to waive all claim to an inheritance in favor of the other child, a sister, if the father would help him through college. He prepared himself, and at the age of fourteen entered the sub-freshman class of Miami University at Oxford, Ohio, some fifty miles from his home. Five years later he received the degree of B.A. with honors and in the fall of the following year began his professional studies at the Medical College of Ohio. In the spring of 1860 he obtained his M.D. and in the fall was appointed demonstrator of anatomy in the medical college at which he had studied. A year later he went before the medical examining board of the regular army, then being rapidly enlarged to meet the demands at the opening of the war, and passed at the top of the list. He received his commission the following spring and was put in charge of a hospital. At the end of the summer he became executive officer of a Philadelphia hospital filled with thousands of sick and wounded, and at that post developed a facility in disposing of official business by which he was ever after characterized. In April 1864 he was assigned to duty with the medical director of the Army of the Potomac and during the Wilderness campaign was a medical inspector in fact if not in title for that army. He wrote: "I am to be what you might call the Medical Statistician of the Army of the Potomac. I am to collect and consolidate all sorts of reports—and when a battle comes off I am to wander round from Hospital to Hospital collecting records—overseeing the surgery in an unofficial way— . . . the sort of work just suits me" (Garrison, p. 76). In July he was invalided back to Washington and in December he was transferred to the surgeon-general's office where he remained until his retirement from active duty thirty years later. During the first few years of this period his time was occupied largely with routine departmental duties in connection with the closing of many great army hospitals and the discharge of civilian physicians and surgeons.

During his student years in the Medical College Billings had been aroused to the need of a great medical library in the United States. His graduating thesis had been on "The Surgical Treatment of Epilepsy." The six months which he spent in writing it, ransacking the while the libraries of Cincinnati and of eastern cities for material, showed him that there were more than 100,000 printed volumes of medical books and journals to search, that no medical library in the United States possessed the majority of these books, that under the circumstances it was an immense task to collect the information he needed, and that the burden of work was greatly increased by the fact that many of the volumes were not indexed or were badly indexed. This experience led him after peace came "to try to establish for the use of American physicians a fairly complete medical library and in connection with this to prepare a comprehensive catalogue and index."

Soon after beginning his Washington life Billings was put in charge of the Surgeon-General's Library and much of his time thereafter was devoted to fostering its growth. A sum of $80,000, turned in from the army hospitals after the war, was made available, and, energetically using this opportunity, he increased the library from 600 entries in the catalogue of 1865 to more than 50,000 entries in that of 1873. After he had seen the Surgeon-General's Library thus grow under his hands, he printed in 1876 a Specimen Fasciculus of a Catalogue and submitted it to the medical profession for suggestions. It was well received and four years later Congress provided for printing Billings's monumental work, the *Index Catalogue,* in the preparation of which he was ably assisted by Dr. Robert Fletcher. The first volume appeared in 1880. The reception it had from those professionally qualified to pass judgment is indicated by a contemporary estimate. "The prospective labour still before the compilers of this valuable work is so gigantic and the standard of those who have undertaken it so high that the accomplishment seems almost unattainable" (*Lancet*). One volume of the *Index Catalogue* including about one thousand pages royal octavo appeared each year thereafter until 1895 when the sixteen volumes had been printed and Billings, retiring from the service, left his successors to produce a second series, 1896–1916, even more voluminous, and to begin upon a third. In 1879 the *Index Medicus,* planned by Billings and Fletcher as a monthly guide to current medical literature and a companion publication to the *Index Catalogue,* began to appear, and it was continued without a break until after the retirement of Billings in 1895. By these two great works physicians and surgeons throughout the world were afforded a guide to the literature of their profession past and current far superior to the guides available to the members of any other profession. The *Index Catalogue* is probably the most important contribution yet made to American medicine (Welch) and the work which constitutes Billings's "float through posterity" (Osler). The Surgeon-General's Library is now without a serious rival since it comprises nearly one million books and pamphlets and the largest collection of medical periodicals in the world.

As Billings in 1873 was beginning his work at cataloguing and indexing the Surgeon-General's Library, Johns Hopkins of Baltimore died, leaving a generous endowment for a great hospital. The trustees asked five experts in hospital construction to submit sketch plans for the construction, heating, ventilation, and administration of the proposed group of buildings. The plans of Billings were accepted, the architects' plans were adapted to them, and Billings, with the consent of the Surgeon-General, was appointed medical adviser to the trustees. In this capacity he presented a series of reports upon hospital construction and organization, and the relation of hospitals to the training of nurses and medical men, which have become classical. In one of them he wrote: "A sick man enters the Hospital to have his pain relieved—his disease cured. To this end the mental influences brought to bear upon him are always important, sometimes more so than the physical. He needs sympathy and encouragement as much as medicine. He is not to have his feelings hurt by being, against his will, brought before a large class of unsympathetic, noisy students, to be lectured over as if he were a curious sort of beetle. . . . In this Hospital I propose that he shall have nothing of the sort to fear" (Garrison, p. 185). With these words, says his biographer, Billings swept away the old-fashioned clinical lecture and showed how to overcome the well-founded horror of hospitals existing at that day among nearly all classes. The plans for which he was so largely responsible "influenced hospitals in a way unparalleled in the history of hospital construction" and gave "a tremendous impetus to better hospitals" (H. M. Hurd in *Johns Hopkins Hospital Bulletin,* August 1914, p. 245). The new hospital was to be an integral part of the Medical School which Hopkins also endowed and both were to aim at raising the level of medical training in the United States. That Billings selected first William H. Welch, whom he met as a student in Germany, and later William Osler for the staff of the medical school illustrates his power of judging not merely performance but promise in younger men.

Perhaps the greatest change in medicine during the present generation has been a shift in emphasis from curative to preventive medicine, from caring for the individual patient to caring for community health; in this change Billings was a pioneer. He was one of the original members of the American Public Health Association which was formed in 1872 and to that organization he gave much time and energy. In 1878 a report which it received about the recent alarming epidemics of yellow fever was referred to a committee of which he was chairman, and the report urged that the work be broadened so as to include a search for the cause of yellow fever, a search which could best be prosecuted in Havana. It was more than twenty years before this hint was followed, with results now known to the world. A few months later the wide alarm over the ravages of yel-

low fever resulted in the creation of a National Board of Health mainly to aid localities menaced or decimated by that pestilence. Billings was made its vice-chairman and proved most efficient first in confining the disease to Memphis where it had gained headway and then in crushing it at that focal point. This victory was a main cause of his election the following year to the presidency of the American Public Health Association.

However it may be with curative medicine, for preventive medicine vital statistics is an indispensable foundation. Billings's first publication used the statistical method and in later years whatever the theme upon which he was writing he was likely to try the same method upon it. He was in charge of the vital statistics of the federal censuses of 1880 and 1890 and although the imperfections of his material prevented him from making in those reports any contributions of the first importance, the soundness of judgment, professional knowledge, and statistical acumen there displayed contributed much to rescue American work in this field from well-deserved reproach and to point out the one open path toward improvement, voluntary collaboration between the federal government and the states, a path which has been trodden with success now for half a century. Billings was informed about the best current European work in vital statistics and applied the approved methods so far as they could be adapted to the refractory American material. He introduced corrected death rates and life tables for unselected populations wherever the American figures were accurate enough to justify those refinements; he was the first to suggest the possibility of the mechanical methods of tabulation which were successfully employed in the United States census of 1890 and which since then have spread through the civilized world.

Five years before the date upon which Billings was to retire from active duty in the army the University of Pennsylvania with the permission of the Surgeon-General appointed him director of its University Hospital and professor of hygiene; after his retirement he removed to Philadelphia to give himself more fully to these duties. One year later, however, after securing the reluctant consent of the University authorities he resigned to accept a greater and more congenial task in New York City where the remaining seventeen years of his life were spent. Three libraries and library endowments in that city, the Astor, Lenox, and Tilden foundations, were consolidated in 1895 by common agreement and with the hope that a library worthy to be compared with the best in Europe might result from the union. The many problems involved in the execution of the plan required a director of energy and expert knowledge, and it was natural that Billings should be chosen. The city gave land in a central location and constructed upon it a library building following the plan which Billings originally sketched. While it was being erected, Billings supervised the reclassification and recataloguing of the books in the three libraries and the consolidation of New York's numerous free circulating libraries into branches of this central library. He also persuaded Carnegie to provide the $5,000,000 needed for building these branches, now more than forty in number, on condition that the city would furnish the necessary land, which was done. Of the New York Public Library as it stands to-day he was "in a very real sense the creator." It now contains more than 3,000,000 books and pamphlets.

In his last eleven years Billings was active in the organization and guidance of the Carnegie Institution of Washington, designed to encourage research, especially in the fields of pure and applied science. For most of that time he was chairman of the board of trustees and member of the executive committee and "he gave a surprisingly large amount of time and attention to the affairs of the Institution" and "rendered invaluable services during this formative period" (President Woodward in *Carnegie Institution of Washington Year Book,* 1913, pp. 8–10).

Billings was high-spirited and imperious in temper and in his later years the recurrent physical pain of which he never spoke added at times an edge to his words. His absorption in matters of large moment interfered with his enduring fools gladly; his army training developed an innate self-reliance and domination which to some were repellent; his achievements were not such as to split the ears of the groundlings; and his humor, at times somewhat grim, was not always understood by little men. During his lifetime his work won perhaps more honor abroad than at home because medical knowledge and skill in many countries of Western Europe then stood higher than they did in the United States. At the seventh meeting of the International Medical Congress in London he was invited as a representative of American medicine to give one of the four general addresses, the others being by selected representatives of France, Germany, and England. This was the first time American medicine had been so recognized and his address on "Our Medical

Literature" was his best public effort. It was received with great enthusiasm. The *Lancet* spoke of it as "remarkable even among all those of the past week (*sc.* by Virchow, Pasteur, Huxley, Paget, *et al.*) for its great ability, practical value and wit." "Tall and largely built, he was . . . a commanding presence, with flow of wholesome English, ready wit and humor. . . . The figure of athletic build, the large blue eyes, a certain happy sense of easy competence, won regard and held the respectful attention" (Mitchell, p. 382). Billings was married on Sept. 3, 1862, at Georgetown, D. C., to Katharine Mary Stevens, daughter of Hestor L. Stevens who had been a representative in Congress from Michigan, 1853–55, and had settled in Washington after his term in Congress was ended. Of this marriage six children were born of whom a son and four daughters survived.

[The main source of information is Fielding H. Garrison's *John Shaw Billings: A Memoir* (1915), which contains a good bibliography, omitting, however, one important article, "The Diminishing Birth Rate in the U. S.," in *Forum,* XV (1893), pp. 466–77. Other sources are H. M. Lydenberg's *John Shaw Billings* (1924), S. Weir Mitchell's "Memoir" and F. H. Garrison's "Scientific Work of John Shaw Billings" in the *Nat. Acad. of Sci. Biog. Memoirs,* vol. VIII (1919), and W. F. Willcox, "John Shaw Billings and Federal Vital Statistics" in *Am. Statistical Ass. Jour.,* XXI (1926), pp. 257–66.]   W. F. W.

BILLINGS, JOSH. [See SHAW, HENRY WHEELER, 1818–1885.]

BILLINGS, WILLIAM (Oct. 7, 1746–Sept. 26, 1800), early singing-master and composer of hymn tunes, was born in Boston, the son of William and Elizabeth (Clark) Billings. He was a tanner by trade and wholly untutored in music, except for a very limited knowledge of reading notes, which he probably acquired in one of the singing-schools of his period. He may also have gained some information through reading the *Introduction to Singing* in the English hymn-tune collections or perhaps in Tansur's *Musical Grammar,* though his style shows no resemblance to that pedantic work. His schooling was equally meager, but he was a music enthusiast, zealous in self-praise and possessing some musical talent on which he relied to such an extent that he had no hesitancy in entering the field of composition. He appeared at a time when church music was in an utterly crude though transitional state. Singing by rote ("lining-out") had lost its hold and had been largely superseded by psalm-tune books (psalms were the only texts permitted in the church music of New England), but the only available books were small compilations made by foreign-trained ministers who had some knowledge of harmony. The number of tunes was very limited and the choirs, weary of the monotonous repetition of the old music, were eager for something new. Billings, who was himself an ardent choir-singer, was keenly alive to this situation. In writing his first tunes he merely imitated those that pleased him and in the absence of paper chalked them on the board walls of the tannery and on sides of leather. In attempting to gain a hearing for his music he had every disadvantage, for he was not only eccentric, but deformed; one leg was shorter than the other and one arm withered, he was blind in one eye, his appearance was slovenly, and his voice loud and rasping. But his earnestness and enthusiasm attracted the attention of Gov. Samuel Adams and Rev. Dr. Pierce of Brookline, both music-lovers, who encouraged his efforts and sang beside him in the choir, though they well knew that his voice easily drowned their own. He soon abandoned his trade in order to enter upon a musical career, becoming a singing teacher and the trainer of the choirs of some of the important churches in Boston, notably the Brattle Street Church and the Old South Church. In this field his influence was deep and far-reaching. He did much to improve the rhythmic singing of the choirs and insisted on more exact pitch. Instruments were not as yet used in the churches, and the "striking-up" of the tune was a very uncertain and hazardous matter, often resulting in distressing and disastrous efforts to find the correct pitch. To remedy this situation he was the first to introduce the pitch-pipe. For the purpose of maintaining the pitch he also introduced the "viol" (violoncello). During his early years in music he had written many tunes that were sung by the choirs and had caught the popular fancy. His first published book, which he affectionately called his "Reuben" (being his first-born) appeared in 1770, engraved on copper by Paul Revere and bearing the following title-page: *The New England Psalm-Singer: or American Chorister. Containing a number of Psalm-tunes, Anthems and Canons. In four or five Parts. (Never before published.) Composed by William Billings, a Native of Boston in New England. Matt. XXI, 16. "Out of the Mouth of Babes and Sucklings hast thou perfected Praise." James V, 13. "Is any merry? Let him sing Psalms."*

> *O praise the Lord with one consent.*
> *And in this grand design*
> *Let Britain and the Colonies*
> *Unanimously jine!* [join].

Boston, New England. Printed by Eades and Gill.

Billings had been much impressed by the contrapuntal style of some of the English music, though he knew nothing of the rules of counter-point. Notwithstanding this, he made bold efforts at "fuguing" and, crude and discordant though they were, they met with approbation, possibly because of their originality and greater melodic freedom. Billings says of this "fuguing" that "it has more than twenty times the power of the old slow tunes, each part straining for mastery, the audience entertained, their minds surpassingly agitated and extremely fluctuated, sometimes declaring for one part, and sometimes for another . . . O ecstatic! Rush on ye sons of harmony!" In 1778 his second book, *The Singing Master's Assistant or Key to Practical Music,* was published, disclosing that in the intervening eight years he had learned much. This book, which was really an abridgment of his first book, had sixty tunes, some of which were new; some had words adapted from the Psalms by Watts and others, and some were by Billings himself, although he knew as little about poetry as he did about music. But this book was a great improvement over the first and was known as "Billings' Best." A second edition appeared in 1779 and a third in 1780. On the outbreak of the Revolution he became an ardent patriot and several of his patriotic songs, besides being sung in the homes, followed the Continental soldiers to camp. His "Chester" was the most popular of these and was played by the army fifers. The following is the first stanza:

> "Let tyrants shake their iron rod,
> And Slavery clank her galling chains;
> We fear them not, we trust in God;
> New England's God forever reigns."

Other books of his were: *Music in Miniature* (1779), *The Psalm Singer's Amusement* (1781), *The Suffolk Harmony* (1786), and *The Continental Harmony* (1794). His influence was not confined to Boston but extended beyond its borders. He started a singing-school of forty-eight members in Stoughton in 1774, and from this was developed the oldest musical organization in America. On Nov. 7, 1786, it was merged into the Stoughton Musical Society, which is still in existence. Important among the members of the original singing-school and heading the singers of "the treble" was Lucy Swan, daughter of Major Robert Swan, who became the second wife of Billings on July 26, 1774. His first wife had been Mary Leonard, whom he had married on Dec. 13, 1764. Crude and grotesque as was much of his music and poetry, his great sincerity as well as the fewness of musicians gave him temporarily a large influence. He was close enough to the comprehension of his generation to be appreciated, where a finer creative genius might have failed. He died, however, poor and neglected.

Some of his tunes survived for a time, but were gradually replaced by better ones.

[Frank J. Metcalf, *Am. Writers and Compilers of Sacred Music* (1925), pp. 51–64; Louis C. Elson, *Hist. of Am. Music* (rev. ed., 1915), pp. 12, 26; Louis C. Elson, *Nat. Music of America* (rev. ed., 1924), p. 67; Frederic L. Ritter, *Music in America* (1883), p. 58; *Grove's Dict. of Music and Musicians, Am. Supp.* (1920), p. 386 under "Tune-Books."]

F. L. G. C.

BILLY THE KID (Nov. 23, 1859–July 15, 1881), desperado, born in New York City, was William H. Bonney, the son of William H. and Kathleen Bonney. In 1862 the family moved to Coffeyville, Kan., where the father died. The mother, with her two children, moved to Colorado, where she married a man named Antrim. About 1865 the family moved to Santa Fé and in 1868 to Silver City, N. Mex. The boy had some schooling, but by the time he was twelve had become a frequenter of saloons and gambling places and an adept at cards. It was at this age that he is said to have stabbed to death a man who had insulted his mother. At sixteen he and a partner, near Fort Bowie, Ariz., killed three peaceful Indians for the furs they were transporting. After various spectacular adventures on both sides of the border, with a supposed record of twelve killings, he appeared in the Pecos Valley in the fall of 1877 and became an employee of J. H. Tunstall, a cattleman. On Feb. 12, 1878, he witnessed from a distance the opening scene in the Lincoln County cattle war, when his employer was killed by a posse of the Murphy faction. He became the fighting leader of the McSween faction, took part in several savage combats, was one of the party of six that on Apr. 1 killed Sheriff James A. Brady and a deputy, and in July figured conspicuously in the battle at Lincoln. With the arrival in August of Gen. Lew Wallace, whom Hayes appointed governor under instructions to end the war, a tacit truce began. Wallace issued a provisional amnesty to those not under indictment for crime, and in a conference with the Kid urged him to surrender, promising him a pardon in case he were convicted. The Kid, declaring that he should be murdered the moment he laid down his arms, refused the terms; and later, with a band of twelve companions, started on a career of wholesale cattle stealing with incidental killings. In 1880 a number of cattlemen, headed by John S. Chisum [*q.v.*], a former friend of the Kid, induced Pat Garrett, also a former friend, to accept the nomination for sheriff. Garrett was elected, and at once began a campaign to break up the Kid's band. In a fight at Fort Sumner, on Christmas Eve, 1880, one of the band was killed. The others fled, but a few days later the Kid, with three companions, was compelled to surrender. At Mesilla, in March, he was convicted of killing Sheriff Brady and was sentenced to be hanged at Lincoln on May 13. Conveyed to Lincoln, he was kept in confinement until Apr. 28, when, though shackled with handcuffs and leg irons, he contrived to kill the two deputies who guarded him and escaped. Two months and a half later he was trapped at the home of Pete Maxwell, in Fort Sumner, and shot and killed by Garrett.

Billy the Kid was the most famous outlaw of the Southwest. He had a score of twenty-one killings and is said to have expressed a wish to add two more to the list. He was about five feet eight in height, slender and well proportioned. His hair was light brown, and his eyes were gray. His face was long, and except for its thick coat of tan, colorless. His front teeth were large and slightly protrusive. He was left-handed. His manner was quiet and unassuming, and he had an unstudied grace of movement. On the range he dressed roughly, but he was something of a dandy in town. He danced well, was a frequenter of balls and fandangoes and was a notable favorite among women. His mood was cheerful and carefree, even in the greatest stress of danger. He had many friends, most of whom found excuses for his outlawry, and a certain glamour invests his career. He was, nevertheless, a cold-blooded killer who as a rule shot down his victims without shadow of provocation and who probably never felt a twinge of remorse.

[Pat F. Garrett, *The Authentic Life of Billy the Kid* (1882); G. B. Anderson, *Hist. of New Mexico* (1907); C. A. Siringo, *Hist. of "Billy the Kid"* (1920); W. N. Burns, *The Saga of Billy the Kid* (1926).]

W. J. G.

BIMELER, JOSEPH MICHAEL (*c.* 1778–Aug. 27, 1853), founder of the Separatist Society of Zoar in Ohio, was born in Germany, presumably in Wurttemberg, where for some ten years he labored as a teacher among a persecuted sect of Pietists, living meekly and changing his abode from time to time in order to avoid the eye of the government. He was of lowly origin, had been a weaver, was lame in one leg, and was disfigured by an enlarged, protruding eye, but he had educated himself rather successfully, and his intelligence, energy, and character were those of a superior man. In addition he had the spiritual power of a genuine religious leader. In 1817 he joined a company of about 300 Separatists from Wurttemberg, Bavaria, and Baden, who sailed from Hamburg to find a home in America. A woman mystic named Barbara Grubermann had been their moving spirit, but she died before they left Germany. On the voyage Bimeler—or Bäumler, to give him his original name—doctored the sick, cheered the downhearted, imparted religious and secular instruction, and by sheer force of character made himself their indispensable leader. Thereafter his career was the history of the company. They landed in Philadelphia on Aug. 14, 1817, and were hospitably received and cared for by members of the Society of Friends, who also enabled them, through Bimeler as their agent, to buy 5,500 acres of wooded upland in Tuscarawas County, Ohio. Bimeler with a few others preceded the main party, cleared ground for crops, built a cabin, and laid out the village of Zoar, named for the little city to which Lot had fled from Sodom and Gomorrah. Drastic measures were necessary to preserve the life of the colony. In order to pay for their land they agreed that no one was to marry and that husbands were to live apart from their wives. Community of goods was also adopted, although against Bimeler's own judgment. Under his benign autocracy the colony slowly got on its feet and finally reached prosperity. When the land was paid for marriage was reintroduced, Bimeler himself taking a wife. The brewery, flour mill, woolen and linen manufactory, and other communal enterprises throve; ironworks failed to pay, but Bimeler kept the plant in operation for several years so that outsiders employed in it would not lose their livelihood. Meanwhile he showed himself as successful in guiding the religious life of the community as he was in developing its material resources. No member of the Society was ever convicted of crime; the village jail was used exclusively by visitors. No one begrudged Bimeler the mansion which he lived in or the extra comforts that he allowed himself, with the exception of a few malcontents, whose suit to have the property partitioned ultimately reached the United States Supreme Court. The Court in its decision upheld the Society, vindicated Bimeler's administration as "not only not fraudulent but above reproach," and described him as "a man of great energy and high capacity for business." Toward visitors to the community Bimeler showed himself affable and remarkably open-minded; toward his own people his position compelled him to be somewhat reserved and decisive. After his death he was venerated as one of the saints, and written versions of his discourses took on an almost sacred character; but without his intelligence and driving power the Society stagnated and finally disintegrated.

[E. O. Randall, *Hist. of the Zoar Soc.* (2nd ed., Columbus, Ohio, 1900); C. Nordhoff, *The Communistic Societies of the U. S.* (1875); W. A. Hinds, *Am. Communities and Co-Operative Colonies* (2nd revision, 1908); G. B. Landis, "The Soc. of Separatists of Zoar" in *Annual Report of the Am. Hist. Ass. for 1898* (1899);
Penny Mag., VI, 411–12 (London, 1837); Henry Howe, *Hist. Colls. of Ohio*, III, 387–89 (1891); J. B. Mansfield, *Hist. of Tuscarawas County, Ohio* (1884). Bimeler's addresses fill three massive volumes: *Die Wahre Separation, oder die Wiedergeburt, Dargestellet in Geistreichen und Erbaulichen Versammlungs-Reden und Betrachtungen* (Zoar, Ohio, 4 pts. in 2 vols., 1856–60); *Etwas fürs Herz! oder Geistliche Brosamen von des Herrn Tisch Gefallen* (Zoar, Ohio, 2 pts., 1860–61).]

G. H. G.

BINGHAM, AMELIA (Mar. 20, 1869–Sept. 1, 1927), actress, was born at Hicksville, Ohio, the daughter of John B. and Marie (Hoffman) Smiley. Her father kept the local hotel. In 1890, while at home for the summer from Ohio Wesleyan University, she took part in amateur theatricals, and a guest of the hotel conceived a good opinion of her acting. He was Lloyd Bingham, manager of a theatrical road company. At his persuasion she went on the stage, toured the Pacific Coast as a member of McKee Rankin's company, and on Dec. 18, 1893, made her New York début in *The Struggle for Life* at the People's Theatre. Meanwhile she had married her discoverer. During the following years she acted in a series of melodramas: *The Power of Gold, The Shaughraun, The Colleen Bawn, The Village Postmaster, The Mummy, Captain Impudence,* and *Nature.* In 1897, under the management of Charles Frohman, she starred in *The White Heather* and was later seen in *The Pink Dominos, On and Off, The Proper Caper, At the White Horse Tavern, The Cuckoo, His Excellency the Governor,* and *Hearts are Trumps.* Her road tours took her in time into every state in the Union, and with her statuesque beauty and vibrant voice she became one of the most popular of American actresses. Year after year she and her husband returned for their vacation to Hicksville, where she gradually overcame the prejudices of her Methodist relatives and friends, the final proof of her uprightness coming when she lent money to a fellow-townsman in distress. In the summer of 1900 she went to Europe for rest and change. On her return she found herself without an engagement and, taking her cue from several English actresses, decided to become her own producer. She took over the Bijou Theatre in New York, accepted Clyde Fitch's *Climbers* after every important manager in the city had declined it, assembled an excellent company, and produced the play, Jan. 15, 1901, with great success. She herself took the part of Mrs. Sterling. In 1902 she produced *Lady Margaret* and *The Modern Magdalen* and in 1903 *The Frisky Mrs. Johnson,* another conspicuous success. Later she acted in *Olympe, Mlle. Marni,* and *The Lilac Room.* At various times she was a member of stock companies, including engagements in St. Louis in 1907, 1909, 1910, and 1911. Later plays in which she appeared were: *One of Our Girls, A Contented Woman, The Eternal City, A Modern Lady Godiva, My Wife's Husbands, Her Other Self, The New Henrietta,* a revival of *The Climbers* (Academy of Music, May 1914), *Mama's Affairs,* the 1925 revival of *Trelawney of the Wells,* and *The Pearl of Great Price,* to her part in which she objected because, as she said "for years I have played decent women on the stage." In 1909 she fulfilled a vaudeville engagement in London, appearing in an act called *Great Moments from Great Plays.* Her husband, who had been her manager, died at sea while a member of the Ford Peace Party Dec. 22, 1915. Her home in later years, 103 Riverside Drive, was a veritable museum of mirrors, armor, statuary, coins, bric-a-brac, antiques, and thirteen striking clocks, some collected by her husband, others the gifts of admirers. It was there that she died of heart disease aggravated by a touch of pneumonia.

[*Who's Who on the Stage,* 1908; J. Parker, ed., *Who's Who in the Theatre* (5th ed., London, 1925); L. C. Strang, *Famous Actresses of the Day in America,* Second Series (1902); *N. Y. Times,* Dec. 23, 1915; *N. Y. Times,* and *Herald Tribune,* Sept. 2, 4, 1927; M. J. Moses and V. Gerson, *Clyde Fitch and His Letters* (1924); F. W. Faxon, ed., *The Dramatic Index 1910–27* (1911 ff.).]

G.H.G.

BINGHAM, ANNE WILLING (Aug. 1, 1764–May 11, 1801), Federalist society leader, was one of the thirteen children born to Thomas Willing and Anne (McCall) Willing of Philadelphia. Her inheritance on both sides was enviable and was undoubtedly an important factor in her later success. Thomas Willing was a wealthy merchant of English descent and education, who had become a power in colonial politics and who is said to have resembled his friend Washington in character. Mrs. Willing, whose beauty was not eclipsed even by that of her daughter, belonged to the influential McCall family of Philadelphia. Already an acclaimed beauty in a city famous for its beautiful women, Anne Willing at the age of sixteen was married (Oct. 26, 1780) to William Bingham [*q.v.*], one of the wealthiest men in the American Colonies. In 1783 Mr. and Mrs. Bingham sailed for Europe, where the appearance, charm, and wit of the twenty-year-old wife became the subject of flattering attention. Mrs. Bingham was presented at the court of Louis XVI, and, writing of her at this time, Miss Abigail Adams said, "Mrs. Bingham gains my love and admiration more and more every time I see her; she is possessed of greater ease and politeness in her behavior than any person I have seen." After five

brilliant years in Paris, London, and The Hague, Mrs. Bingham returned home admirably prepared to reign over the "Republican Court" in Philadelphia. During the decade when her salon was at its height no single character of political importance but came to some extent under the influence of her personality. There was nothing of the democrat and nothing of the Puritan about Mrs. Bingham. Her vocabulary and taste in anecdote are reported to have been those of her contemporary the Duchess of Devonshire, and the extravagance of her entertainments surprised, and, in the case of Brissot de Warville at least, shocked European visitors. "Mansion House," built by the Binghams on their return from Europe, was modeled on the residence of the Duke of Manchester, "the dimensions of the original being somewhat enlarged in the copy." If Harrison Gray Otis was pained to find Mrs. Bingham's daughter clad only in her dress and chemise on a January day in Philadelphia; if there was amusement at a long line of Bingham servants, hurtling the names of arriving guests across the sidewalks, up the stairs, and along the corridors; if it leaked out that Mrs. Bingham had a protracted quarrel with a theatre manager over the owning of a box; these were but shallow ripples on a deep stream of admiration that flowed steadily in the conversation, letters, and diaries of the period. While it was probably her wealth and beauty that brought important personages to Mrs. Bingham, it was certainly her intelligence, sagacious wit, and a flair for analysis that made them listen to her. Shortly after the birth of her only son, in her thirty-seventh year, she insisted upon attending a sleighing party, and the resultant exposure caused an attack of lung fever which rapidly grew so serious that her physicians advised a milder climate. Carried from her luxurious home upon a palanquin which drew the eyes of hundreds, she was placed aboard her husband's elaborately appointed yacht and taken to the Bermuda Islands. There after a few weeks the lovely Anne Bingham died in unaccustomed exile.

[Thos. Willing Balch, *Willing Letters and Papers* (1922); Rufus W. Griswold, *The Republican Court* (1864); Samuel E. Morison, *Life and Letters of Harrison Gray Otis* (1913), I, 135–39; Henry Wansey, *An Excursion to the United States* (1798), p. 136 (description of the "Mansion House"); Jean Brissot de Warville, *New Travels in the United States* (Bowling Green, Ohio, 1919), p. 190; Claude Bowers, *Jefferson and Hamilton* (1926).]

G. G—m.

BINGHAM, CALEB (Apr. 15, 1757–Apr. 6, 1817), pioneer writer of text-books, was born in Salisbury, Conn., of Daniel Bingham and his wife, Hannah Conant. After attending district school he was prepared for college by the local minister and entered Dartmouth in 1779. At graduation in 1782 he had the honor of the valedictory address (in Latin). In that year he became master of Moor's Indian Charity School which President Wheelock of Dartmouth had founded in 1754 and maintained as an appendage to the college. After several years he moved to Boston, where he was, according to the city records of 1784, "approbated by the selectmen to keep a private school for the instruction of young ladies in the useful branches of reading, writing, etc." He published his first text-book primarily for use in this school, under the title, *The Young Lady's Accidence or a Short and Easy Introduction to English Grammar: Designed Principally for the Use of Young Learners, more especially of the Fair Sex, though Proper for Either* (1785). This was the second English Grammar published in the United States, that of Noah Webster having preceded it by one year. It was but a little book of sixty pages characterized by simplicity and clearness, and was long and widely used in the schools. In 1789 a reorganization of Boston's public schools was made, and Bingham had an important part in effecting the innovations then started. Appointed to be master of one of the three new Reading Schools he gave up his private school and served the city for seven years. Then he set up as a bookseller and occasional publisher at 44 Cornhill, remaining there for twenty-one years. "His bookstore was the favorite resort of all the Boston teachers, and education was continually discussed there" (*American Journal of Education,* X, 597). It was here that agitation for free primary schools centered, Bingham being prominent in advocating them, though they were not fully established till after his death. His store was also the headquarters of the local Jeffersonian Republicanism of which he was a disciple. Several times he ran unsuccessfully for the state Senate. During the governorship of Elbridge Gerry he was appointed director of the state prison and served for several years. In 1794 he first published a "Selection of Lessons for Reading and Speaking" entitled *The American Preceptor.* Three years later he brought out *The Columbian Orator* "designed for a Second Part of the American Preceptor." Few, if any, of the selections which these books comprise are from his pen; many of them are of a deeply religious sort, reflecting truly the spirit of their times, for until the appearance of these readers and those of Webster, the Bible and the psalmbook had been the principal school reading-books. Others of the selections are strongly patriotic, and were both expressions and developers of

the growing enthusiasm for the young American republic. For a quarter of a century, especially in the district schools, these readers surpassed in popularity all their competitors and made their author nationally known. Other text-books of his were: *The Child's Companion, being an Easy and Concise Reading and Spelling Book, for the Use of Young Children* (1792); *Juvenile Letters, being a Correspondence between Children, from Eight to Fifteen Years of Age,* a joint production of Bingham and one of his daughters, and designed to introduce children to English composition. His *Astronomical and Geographical Catechism* (1803) was based on the *School Geography* of Jedidiah Morse and comprised a set of questions and answers, both of which, according to the practise of those days, were to be committed to memory and recited verbatim. In 1796 he published for teachers of writing the first set of copy-slips printed in this country. He was a good French scholar and published his own translation of Chateaubriand's *Atala* (1802). On his native town he bestowed a generous gift of books to be the beginning of its public library and he was active in promoting town libraries in many other places. In religion he was a conservative Congregationalist, adhering to the older form of this faith when the churches of Boston became Unitarian. Of attractive appearance, nearly six feet in height and well proportioned, he impressed his contemporaries with his dignity, geniality, and integrity. He was fond of music and a member of the choir of the churches with which he was connected. At his death, in Boston, he was survived by his wife, Hannah (Kemble) Bingham, and by two daughters.

[The chief source of information is a biographical sketch by Wm. B. Fowle, Bingham's employee and successor, in Henry Barnard's *Am. Jour. of Ed.,* V, 325; in a biographical sketch of Fowle, *Ibid.,* X, 597, additional material is to be found. Bingham's text-books are best described in Clifton Johnson, *Old-Time Schools and School-Books* (1904); Geo. E. Littlefield, *Early Schools and School-Books of New England* (1904); Justin Winsor, *Memorial History of Boston* (1880–81).]

W. J. C.

BINGHAM, GEORGE CALEB (Mar. 20, 1811–July 7, 1879), portrait and genre painter, was born on a plantation in Augusta County, Va., the son of Henry Vest and Mary (Amend) Bingham. He was of mixed stock, chiefly Scotch and German. In 1819 the family emigrated to Franklin, Mo., then on the frontier, and in Missouri Bingham spent most of his life. He began early to copy engravings and to paint with home-made pigments, learned to roll cigars, worked as a cabinet-maker's apprentice, read law and theology, but was encouraged by Chester Harding [*q.v.*] to persist with his painting, and by 1834 had definitely made art his vocation. About 1837 he studied for a short time at the Pennsylvania Academy of Fine Arts. He lived in Washington, D. C., 1840–44, was in Europe, with his headquarters at Düsseldorf, 1856–58, returned to Germany for a few months in 1859, and made numerous short trips to various parts of the United States, but Missouri was his home. At different times he set up his studio in Arrow Rock, Columbia, Jefferson City, St. Louis, and Kansas City, where he died. His first genre painting to receive much attention was "Jolly Flatboatmen," which was selected by the American Art Union in 1846 for its annual engraving. His other noteworthy pictures include "Raftsmen Playing Cards" (by 1847), "Canvassing for a Vote" (by 1851), "Emigration of Daniel Boone" (1851), "County Election" (1851–52), "Stump Speaking" (1853–54), "Verdict of the People" (1854), "Gen. Lyon and Gen. Blair Starting for Camp Jackson" (about 1862), "Major Dean in Jail" (1866), "Order No. 11" (about 1868), and "The Puzzled Witness" (1874). His portraits, which vary noticeably in execution with his interest in the sitter, were once a standard article of furniture in prosperous Missouri homes. As the list of his genre pictures indicates, Bingham's avocation was politics. In 1846 he was elected to the legislature as a Whig by a margin of three votes; his opponent, one Sappington, contested the election and was sustained by the Democratic majority in the House. In 1848 Bingham declined the nomination at first but accepted it when he heard that Sappington would run against him; this time he beat him by twenty-six votes. He was a conspicuously honest and efficient state treasurer 1862–65, and was made adjutant-general of Missouri in 1875. He married Elizabeth Hutchison of Boonville in 1836, Eliza K. Thomas of Columbia in 1847, and Mrs. Mattie Lykins of Kansas City in 1878. He was small and delicate in appearance and, having lost all his hair from a severe attack of measles when he was nineteen, always wore a wig. In his genre work, although his coloring is never satisfactory and his drawing sometimes faulty, he has preserved, with realism and humor, certain characteristic scenes in old-time Missouri life.

[F. H. Rusk, *George Caleb Bingham, the Missouri Artist* (Jefferson City, Mo., 1917) is detailed, discriminating, and carefully documented.]   G. H. G.

BINGHAM, HARRY (Mar. 30, 1821–Sept. 12, 1900), lawyer, politician, traced his descent from Thomas Bingham of England, one of the landed proprietors of Norwich, Conn., in 1659. The son of Warner Bingham, a prosperous farm-er, state senator, and judge of Essex County, Vt., and of Lucy (Wheeler) Bingham, he was born in Concord, Vt. His early education having been obtained at the common schools, he entered the Lyndon Academy in 1838, proceeding thence in 1839 to Dartmouth College, where he graduated in 1843. He had taught school on vacations, and this he continued to do, on commencing the study of law. He passed a short time in law offices at Concord and Lyndon, but completed his studies at Bath, N. H., being admitted to the New Hampshire bar at Lancaster in May Term 1846. The same year he opened an office in Littleton, N. H., and practised there all his life. He was an ardent Democrat, and, being the only lawyer of that persuasion in the town, quickly obtained the nucleus of a thriving practise, which ultimately became one of the largest in the state. In 1861 he was elected to represent Littleton in the New Hampshire House of Representatives, and became Democratic leader in the legislature. Although a strong partisan he did not countenance machine politics, and he was able—apart from purely party measures—to exercise an influence in the House disparate to the numerical strength of his political following. He was reëlected no less than seventeen times between 1861 and 1891, in addition to being state senator for Grafton District 1883–87. When in the House he was always a member of the judiciary committee, being its chairman in 1871 and 1874. In 1865 and 1867 he was Democratic nominee for Congress, and was candidate for the United States Senate on seven occasions. He was a delegate to the national Democratic conventions at New York in 1868, Baltimore in 1872, Cincinnati in 1880, and Chicago in 1884 and 1890. An unswerving Gold Democrat, he declined to follow Bryan, and from the first refused to support the Chicago platform. He attended the Philadelphia peace convention of 1866, and took a conspicuous part in the proceedings of the state constitutional convention of 1876, being chairman of the committee on the legislative department.

The only office he ever held was that of United States treasury agent, to which he was appointed by President Johnson in 1867. He was nominated by Gov. Weston in 1874 chief justice of the superior court of judicature, but the appointment failed of confirmation by the Council. Retained in most of the heavy local litigation of his time, he was not an outstanding advocate, but his briefs were always prepared with the utmost attention to detail, and his manner of presenting his cases in clear, unpretentious style before judge or jury, his manifest sincerity and his scrupulous accuracy, were very attractive and had no small share in the attainment of many notable successes. For thirty years he was an acknowledged leader of the New Hampshire bar, and in 1893 was elected president of the Grafton and Coos Bar Association. He was unmarried.

[A detailed acount of his career by H. H. Metcalf appeared in the *Granite Mo.,* V, 277. Other information is contained in the *Judiciary and the Bar of New England,* ed. by Conrad Reno (1901), II, 41 ; *Green Bag,* XIII, 105 ; *Am. Law Rev.,* XXXV, 434, and *Dartmouth Coll. Ass. Alumni, Memorials of Judges* (1881), pp. 25–30. See also obituary in *Manchester* (N. H.) *Union,* Sept. 13, 1900.]

H. W. H. K.

BINGHAM, HIRAM (Oct. 30, 1789–Nov. 11, 1869), missionary, translator, was the seventh of thirteen children of Calvin and Lydia (Denton) Bingham, of Bennington, Vt. His father was a farmer. The son's early education was received in the local schools. In his twenty-third year he entered Middlebury College, and graduated in 1816. With the Christian ministry in mind, he went to Andover Theological Seminary and while there decided to offer himself for foreign-mission service in the Sandwich Islands. He graduated from Andover in 1819, and in the fall (Sept. 29) of that year was ordained at Goshen, Conn., for the work abroad under the American Board of Boston. At the ordination service he met Sybil Moseley, of Westfield, Mass., whom he married on Oct. 11, 1819, at Hartford. They joined a large company which sailed on the brig *Thaddeus* out of Boston harbor on Oct. 23, 1819, bound for the Sandwich Islands and the establishment of mission work. Admitted by the king "for a year," the party divided itself by royal permission and arrangement between Kailua on Hawaii and Honolulu on Oahu. Mr. and Mrs. Bingham were among those who disembarked at Honolulu on Apr. 19, 1820. For many months they lived in a native hut, until he erected in February 1821 a frame house which was sent out from America. Bingham and the others addressed themselves at once to the acquisition of the language, and to its reduction to writing. An alphabet of twelve letters was soon devised, and the missionaries set themselves the task of teaching a people to read, a task much simplified by the king's suggestion that his people learn. In 1822 Bingham issued his *Elementary Lessons in Hawaiian,* and thereafter came a steady output of works composed by various members of the mission. In October 1825 Bingham began the translation of the New Testament into Hawaiian, and by 1839 the entire Bible had been done by him and his associates, he himself contributing Luke, Colossians, Hebrews, Leviticus, Psalms 1–75, and Ezekiel. In 1828 the Gospel of Matthew, translated by himself and Thurston, was published, and in 1829 his own Luke. In 1831 he issued his *First Book for Children* and his *Scripture Catechism.* The services were first held in the open under immense hau (*hibiscus Titiaceus*) trees. In August 1821 a church was erected. Slowly the mission became fully organized. In February 1823, Bingham, Thurston, and Ellis, the ordained men, signed an article of incorporation of the Hawaiian Clerical Association which continued in power until 1863, when the Hawaiian Evangelical Association was formed. During 1826 Bingham made a one-hundred-mile preaching tour of the island in company with Kaahumanu, wife of the first great king, and chief pupil of the Binghams, who herself occupied the throne from 1823 to 1832. She had become Christian early in 1825 and was now urging the new faith upon her subjects. On June 1, 1840, the Mission "reluctantly, yet on the whole cheerfully, recommended that Brother and Sister Bingham make a visit to the United States," on account of Mrs. Bingham's health. Accordingly the parents and their small children left Honolulu Aug. 3, 1840, for New York. Mrs. Bingham's health continued poor and she died at Easthampton, Mass., on Feb. 27, 1848. Since the American Board thought it unwise for Bingham to return, he occupied himself in America with preaching and writing. For a time he served in New Haven as pastor of an African Church. On Aug. 24, 1854, he married Naomi Emma Morse. His voluminous and generally reliable *Residence of Twenty-one Years in the Sandwich Islands; or The Civil, Religious, and Political History of Those Islands* was published in 1847. In 1863 certain friends put an annuity at his disposal. Shortly after passing his eightieth birthday he died in New Haven.

[Wm. Ellis, *Jour. of a Tour Around Hawaii* (1826) ; Sheldon Dibble, *Hist. of the Sandwich Islands* (1843) ; R. Anderson, *Hist. of the Sandwich Islands Mission* (1870) ; O. H. Gulick, *Pilgrims of Hawaii* (1918) ; *Hawaiian Mission Centennial Book* (1820) ; E. C. Hawley, *Introduction of Christianity into the Hawaiian Islands* (1922) ; *Missionary Herald,* 1820–41.]

J. C. A.

BINGHAM, HIRAM (Aug. 16, 1831–Oct. 25, 1908), missionary to Micronesia, was the sixth child of Hiram Bingham [*q.v.*] and Sybil (Moseley) Bingham. He was born in Honolulu, where his elementary education was obtained in the Honolulu school for missionary children. A fortnight before his ninth birthday he started for America with his parents and two sisters. Some time after his arrival he entered Williston Academy, Easthampton, Mass. From there he went to Yale, where he graduated in 1853. For one year he served as principal of the Northampton

(Mass.) High School. The next he spent abroad as a private tutor. Then with his mind turned toward a missionary career he entered Andover Seminary, but ill health compelled him to leave in the spring of 1856. On Nov. 9, 1856, he was ordained in New Haven, on Nov. 18 he was married to Minerva Clarissa Brewster of Northampton, and on Dec. 2 he and Mrs. Bingham sailed from Boston on the brig *Morning Star,* the first of several missionary vessels of that name, bound for Honolulu and Micronesia. They arrived at Ponape, Gilbert Islands, Sept. 23, and established a missionary station at Apaiang. The Gilbert Islands lie along the equator and were then as now almost unendurable to white men. Proper food was scarce, epidemics of disease frequently broke out amongst the islanders, and unscrupulous traders were bitter in their opposition to mission work. Yet Bingham remained seven years. His work was destined to be mainly with the language. (Up to 1870 scarcely fifty good converts were numbered by the mission.) He put in his seven years to good advantage, and when ill health compelled his withdrawal he was equipped to proceed with the creation of a Gilbertese literature. He visited the United States in 1865 and on Nov. 12, 1866, sailed from Boston in command of the second *Morning Star,* a small two-masted schooner. As commander of this vessel he visited the Marquesas Islands mission of the native Hawaiian churches and made the tour of Micronesia, returning to Honolulu Dec. 16, 1868. Taking up his residence in the Hawaiian capital, he gave his time to work on the Gilbertese Bible. On Friday evening, Apr. 11, 1873, at "a joyful gathering at Honolulu" Bingham announced the completion of the translation of the entire New Testament, and had copies for distribution. Sharing the honor of the occasion was Moses Kaure, a Gilbert Islander who assisted Bingham in his translations.

On June 9, 1873, Mr. and Mrs. Bingham sailed again for the Gilbert Islands and resumed their residence at Apaiang. He preached at least once every week in the church, taught in the school, and began work on a Gilbertese dictionary. New schools and churches were organized in inland regions, and many new members were received into the Apaiang Church. Early in April 1875, however, Bingham's health gave way again and he had to leave the Islands. Receiving some medical aid en route Mrs. Bingham was able to get her feeble husband back to Honolulu in November by way of Samoa and Australia. He did not venture again to Apaiang and Micronesia, but remained in Honolulu except for several trips to the United States (1887, 1892–93, 1908), on behalf of the printing of translation materials. By 1890 Bingham had finished the Gilbertese translation of the entire Bible, and before his death had seen seven editions of it. His Gilbertese dictionary was published in 1908. Bingham was also the author of a Gilbertese hymn and tune book (1880), and of commentaries on the Gospels and the book of Acts, and of a *Gilbert Islands Bible Dictionary* (1895). Mrs. Bingham published a book of *Bible Stories in the Gilbertese* (1875). No small result of their literary work was the amplification to 12,000 words of a poverty-stricken language of 4,000. Bingham's end came suddenly at the Johns Hopkins Hospital in Baltimore, where he had gone for an operation, Oct. 25, 1908.

[*Obit. Record Grads. Yale Univ. . . . for 1909* (1909) ; T. A. Bingham, *Genealogy of the Bingham Family in the U. S.* (1898), pp. 94, 138; O. H. Gulick, *Pilgrims of Hawaii* (1918) ; R. Anderson, *Hist. of the Sandwich Islands Mission* (1870) ; *Missionary Herald,* Dec. 1908.]

J.C.A.

BINGHAM, JOHN ARMOR (Jan. 21, 1815– Mar. 19, 1900), lawyer, Ohio politician, was born in Mercer, Pa., the son of Hugh Bingham, a carpenter. After securing such elementary education as his neighborhood offered, he spent two years in a printing office, a like period at Franklin College, then studied law, was admitted to the bar, and began practise at Cadiz, Ohio, in 1840. He soon became prominent as a stump speaker in Harrison's "log cabin, hard cider" campaign. In 1854 he was elected to Congress, and served continuously until 1873, except for the Thirty-eighth Congress, when, failing of reëlection, he was appointed judge-advocate in January 1864, and solicitor of the court of claims the following August. When political fortunes failed him again in 1873 he was solaced by the appointment as minister to Japan, a position he held for twelve uneventful years.

Bingham was a clever and forceful speaker, overflowing with invective, rhetorical phrases, and historical allusions of varying degrees of accuracy. In two of the most dramatic episodes of the immediate post-war period—the trial of the assassins of Lincoln, and the impeachment of Andrew Johnson—he played a leading rôle. In the conspiracy trial his part as special judge-advocate was to bully the defense witnesses and to assert in his summary of the evidence that the rebellion was "simply a criminal conspiracy and a gigantic assassination" in which "Jefferson Davis is as clearly proven guilty . . . as is John Wilkes Booth, by whose hand Jefferson Davis inflicted the mortal wound upon Abraham Lincoln" (Benn Pitman, *Assassination of President*

Lincoln..., 1865, pp. 351, 380). In defending the legality of the military court set up by President Johnson, he argued that the executive could exercise all sorts of extra-constitutional powers, even to "string up the culprits without any court"— an argument which was somewhat embarrassing when he was selected by the House as one of seven managers to conduct the impeachment of President Johnson. He had voted against the first attempt at impeachment and had opposed the second, holding the President guilty of no impeachable offense (D. M. DeWitt, *Impeachment,* p. 506), but he finally yielded to party pressure and voted for impeachment after the Senate had declared the President's removal of Secretary Stanton illegal. It fell to him to make the closing speech at the trial. For three days (May 4–6) he rang the changes on the plea of the defense that the President might suspend the laws and test them in the courts—"the monstrous plea interposed for the first time in our history" (*Trial of Andrew Johnson,* II, 389 ff.). His confident manner carried conviction to the galleries, who pronounced it one of his greatest speeches.

In the work of reconstruction, Bingham's chief contribution was the framing of that part of the first section of the Fourteenth Amendment which forbade any state by law to abridge the privileges or immunities of citizens of the United States, or to deprive any person of life, liberty, or property without due process of law or to deny the equal protection of the laws (Kendrick, *Journal,* p. 106).

Bingham was married to Amanda Bingham, a cousin, by whom he had three children. He died at his home in Cadiz, Ohio. He did not introduce the resolution at the Whig national convention of 1848 containing the spirited anti-slavery apothegm carved on his monument at Cadiz, the resolution ascribed to him having been introduced by Lewis D. Campbell. Stenographic reports fail to show that Bingham ever spoke on the floor of the convention (*North American and United States Gazette,* and *Public Ledger,* both Philadelphia, for June 8, 9, 10, 1848).

[B. B. Kendrick, *Jour. of the Comm. of Fifteen on Reconstruction* (1914); *Trial of Andrew Johnson,* pub. by order of the Senate as a supplement to *Cong. Globe* (1868); *Cong. Globe,* 1854–73, *passim*; *Ohio Arch. and Hist. Pub.,* X, 331–52; D. M. DeWitt, *The Judicial Murder of Mrs. Surratt* (1895) and *The Impeachment and Trial of Andrew Johnson* (1903); *Evening Star* (Washington), Mar. 19, 1900; *Cadiz Democrat Sentinal,* Mar. 22, 1900.]   T.D.M.

BINGHAM, WILLIAM (Apr. 8, 1752–Feb. 6, 1804), banker, legislator, son of William and Mary (Stamper) Bingham, was born in Philadelphia. The family had been prominent in England. James (great-grandfather of William), who died in December 1714, was the first Pennsylvania representative. William's father served in the French wars 1748–62 and was a vestryman at St. Peter's church until his death in 1769. The son graduated from the University of Pennsylvania in 1768 and in 1770 was appointed British consul at St. Pierre, Martinique. He continued until 1776, after which he served four years as Continental agent in the West Indies. This experience determined Bingham's future. Joint ownership of privateers and constant trade gave him unusual wealth for that period. Upon his return to Philadelphia he married Anne, daughter of Thomas and Anne (McCall) Willing on Oct. 26, 1780, the bride being described by Anna Rawle, her neighbor, as one who "might set for the Queen of Beauty." Certainly she was a leader in Philadelphia society and the Bingham mansion became at once an important political and social center of the national capital [see Anne Willing Bingham]. Washington writes frequently in his diary of having tea at this house, and later of promising Mrs. Bingham to sit for his portrait to Gilbert Stuart. She died in Bermuda, May 11, 1801. In 1780 Bingham enlisted in the Philadelphia "Associators," later becoming captain in the city cavalry, but his effective national service was as a founder and director of the Pennsylvania Bank under President Willing. Incorporated May 26, 1781, and chartered Dec. 31 as the Bank of North America, it was the first bank in the country and gave increased stability to American finance. During 1784–86 Bingham was in Europe. Here his *Letter from an American ... to a Member of Parliament,* in reply to Lord Sheffield (London and Philadelphia, 1784), and his friendship with Lord Shelburne strengthened Adams and Franklin in their contest for American commercial rights. On his return to Pennsylvania Bingham served in the Continental Congress 1786–89, the Pennsylvania Assembly 1790–95 and the United States Senate 1795–1801. His real-estate interests made him an advocate of internal improvements. The founder of Binghamton, N. Y., and the owner of considerable oil lands in Pennsylvania, he was the first president of the Philadelphia and Lancaster Turnpike Corporation, which built the earliest and for years the best turnpike in the United States. His two million acres of timberland in New England, pictured in his *Description of Certain Tracts ... in the District of Maine* (1793), and his West Indian experience made him see the importance of American shipping. He was vice-president of the Society for Political Inquiries until the death of Franklin in 1790, a trustee of the University of Pennsylvania, and a frequent host to Presidents Washington and Adams, as to other American and foreign statesmen. One of his daughters married (1) Comte de Tilly and (2) Henry Baring; another daughter married Alexander Baring, Baron Ashburton, who obtained Bingham's fine collection of American pamphlets published between 1755 and 1782.

[Bingham MSS. and papers in the Hist. Soc. of Pa.; the Robert Morris MSS., the Naval MSS. of the Revolution, and the Washington MSS. in the Lib. of Cong.; T. A. Bingham, *Genealogy of the Bingham Family in the U. S.* (1898) ; J. T. Scharf and J. Westcott, *Hist. of Phila. 1609–1884* (1884), I, II ; *Pa. Mag. of Hist. and Biog.*, vol. XLII, no. 3, vol. XLVII, nos. 2, 4 ; T. Westcott, *Historic Mansions and Buildings of Phila.* (1877), pp. 337–49.]

                                    C. H. L—n.

BINGHAM, WILLIAM (July 7, 1835–Feb. 18, 1873), educator, was the fourth child of William James and Eliza (Norwood) Bingham. His grandfather, the Rev. William Bingham, was a Scotch-Irish Protestant who came from Ireland after being involved in the plots which culminated later in Emmet's Rebellion. He taught at Wilmington, N. C., from 1789 until 1793, when he established at Pittsboro a school of his own which he removed, after serving for a time as professor of Latin in the University of North Carolina, first to Hillsboro and later to Mount Repose. He died at the age of seventy-two years after gaining an enviable reputation as scholar and teacher. His eldest son, William James Bingham, the second headmaster of the Bingham School, was also a successful teacher. Before the Civil War he was interested in plans for the emancipation of the negroes and for returning them to Africa, but when the War broke out he gave his whole heart to the Southern Confederacy. His son, the subject of this sketch, entered the University of North Carolina in 1853 and was graduated with highest honors in 1856. In December 1856, he married Owen White of Raleigh, N. C., and almost immediately joined his father as a partner in the school. His father being in delicate health and his brother Robert being only eighteen years of age, William became at once the controlling member of the partnership, and under his control the school grew in size, efficiency, and reputation. During the war he served the Confederacy untiringly, though prevented from joining the army. At the same time he carried on the work of the school, which was incorporated as a military academy in 1864, the principal receiving the rank of colonel. In December of that year Bingham moved the school to a place near Mebane in Orange County, and made it a boarding school in which the pupils lived entirely under his own care. In 1865 he bought out the interest

of his brother-in-law and his cousin and became the sole proprietor of the school, the reputation and influence of which was increased by his extraordinary teaching power and the merit of his books. He published *A Grammar of the Latin Language* (1863), *Cæsar's Commentaries on the Gallic War* (1864), *A Grammar of the English Language* (1868), *A Latin Reader* (1869), and when seized with his final illness was busy with a text-book on Latin composition.

[*Biog. Hist. of N. C.,* ed. by Samuel A. Ashe, vol. VI (1907), esp. pp. 74–82 by Mrs. Preston Lewis Gray; Walter P. Williamson, "The Bingham School" in *Our Living and Our Dead,* May 1875; *N. C. Presbyterian,* Dec. 24, 1896; Chas. L. Roper, *The Church and Private Schools of N. C.* (1898).]   H. N. F.

BINNEY, AMOS (Oct. 18, 1803–Feb. 18, 1847), zoologist, was born in Boston, the second child of Col. Amos Binney and Hannah (Dolliver) Binney, and came of a family traceable to John and Mercy Binney of Hull, Mass., who came from England in 1678 or 1679. Many members of this family were prominent in shipping, commerce, the professions and public affairs of New England. Binney was educated at Brown University, graduating in 1821. During his college years he became interested in the natural sciences. Like most young naturalists he collected birds' eggs, afterward taking up the collection and study of land shells and other mollusks. After beginning the study of medicine, ill health led him to a horseback trip to Cincinnati, followed by a year in Europe, where natural-history museums and art galleries were his favorite haunts. Restored to health he turned homeward, resumed his studies, and received the degree of M.D. from Harvard in 1826. This course of study was undertaken chiefly for the sake of scientific training, in those times not offered in college courses. He had no desire to practise medicine, preferring to become associated with his father in real estate and other business ventures. His leisure was always devoted to scientific studies. After his father's death he carried on the business with marked success until 1842.

In 1830 Binney, Augustus A. Gould, and several others founded the Boston Society of Natural History. From the outset Binney contributed freely to the resources of the Society, both scientific and financial. He gave papers on zoological and paleontological subjects, and was president of the Society from 1843 until his death. Elected to the state legislature in 1836, he was instrumental in obtaining state support for geological, zoological, and botanical surveys, resulting in the classical *Massachusetts Reports* by Gould, Harris, and others, useful far beyond the borders of the state. About 1835 Binney began the studies for his chief work, *The Terrestrial Air-Breathing Mollusks of the United States and the Adjacent Territories of North America.* Practically completed at the time of his death, it was published posthumously (1851) under the editorship of Dr. A. A. Gould, with an anatomical chapter by Dr. Joseph Leidy of Philadelphia. The illustrations were copperplates mostly engraved by Alexander Lawson. They have perhaps never been surpassed for scientific fidelity combined with artistic excellence. This scholarly and beautiful work gave Binney an international reputation in the scientific world of the time. It is generally recognized that the clarity and the high standard set by this work of Binney, and later by that of his son, served to preserve the literature of land mollusks from the confusion which is so apparent in American work on other molluscan groups of the middle decades of the last century.

Binney was a handsome man of dignified presence, over medium height, with dark eyes and black hair. A somewhat formal and reticent manner concealed a generous and friendly nature. "He possessed the art of writing amusing and descriptive letters to perfection." He was fond of pictures and a generous patron of art. In 1827 he married a cousin, Mary Ann Binney. Of their five children the third, William Greene Binney, continued and extended his father's scientific work with ability, succeeding him as the chief authority on American land mollusks.

[A. A. Gould, "Memoir of Dr. Amos Binney," in vol. I (1851) of Binney's *Terrestrial Air-Breathing Mollusks;* C. J. F. Binney, *Genealogy of the Binney Family in the U. S.* (1886).]

H. A. P.

BINNEY, HORACE (Jan. 4, 1780–Aug. 12, 1875), lawyer, son of Dr. Barnabas and Mary (Woodrow) Binney, was descended from Capt. John Binney, who came to Hull, Mass., about 1678. Horace was born in the Northern Liberties, Philadelphia, where his early education was obtained at the Friends Almshouse School and the Grammar School of the University of Pennsylvania. In 1788 he went to a classical school at Bordentown, N. J., but his father had died in 1787 and on his mother's subsequent marriage to Dr. Marshall Spring, the family removed to Watertown, Mass. After a short period of private tuition Binney entered Harvard College in July 1793, graduating in 1797 with high honors. At first he meditated taking up medicine but his stepfather dissuaded him, and going to Philadelphia, he endeavored to enter a mercantile office, but found no vacancy. He thereupon studied law in the office of Jared Inger-

soll, working steadily and eschewing social attractions though he could "play pretty well on the flute and sing an agreeable song." He was admitted to the Philadelphia bar in March 1800, and started practise in that city, but for the first five years made little progress. Politics had no attraction for him, but he was persuaded in 1806 to be a candidate for the legislature on a fusion ticket of Federalists and Independent Democrats, and headed the poll. His record in the legislature was undistinguished, but he was brought into contact with influential underwriters and merchants, and his legal ability was speedily recognized. At this period marine-insurance litigation was particularly heavy in Philadelphia, the maritime measures adopted by Great Britain and France against each other's trade during the Napoleonic War seriously affecting United States commerce, and continually raising new points in insurance law. The first important retainer Binney received was in Gibson *vs.* Philadelphia Insurance Company (1 *Binney,* 415) in 1808, involving the correct mode of adjusting a particular average under a clause in a respondentia bond, and the ability he displayed was such that he soon had all the business he could attend to. In 1809 appeared the first volume of his *Reports of Cases Adjudged in the Supreme Court of Pennsylvania,* undertaken at the suggestion of Chief Justice Tilghman. Ultimately extending to six volumes, covering all important cases down to September 1814, these reports have always been considered very valuable, their accuracy never having been challenged. Binney had in January 1808 been elected a director of the first United States Bank, and his first case in the Supreme Court of the United States—which he won—was United States Bank *vs.* De Veaux (5 *Cranch,* 6), respecting the right of a corporation composed of citizens of one state to sue a citizen of another state in the federal courts. In 1810 he was elected to the common council of Philadelphia, and reëlected in 1811, being appointed president of that body each term. A Federalist in politics, he attended as a delegate from Pennsylvania the convention at New York in June 1812 and unsuccessfully opposed the proposition of alliance with the Clinton Democrats. Four years later he was induced to return to the municipal arena, and was a member of the Philadelphia select council during the years 1816–19; but steadfastly declined to be a candidate for Congress. He was now recognized as one of the leaders of the Philadelphia bar, and his reputation extended beyond the limits of his state. In 1823 he argued the case of Lyle *vs.* Richards (9 *Sergeant & Rawle,* 322), one of the two great cases upon which his reputation as a lawyer rests. It dealt with the construction of a devise with contingent remainders in tail and the validity of a common recovery, involving an intricate discussion of the application of the common law to real property in the state, and his contention was upheld by the court. In 1827 the bar of Philadelphia almost unanimously recommended his appointment to the chief justiceship of Pennsylvania, and in 1829 President Jackson was urged to appoint him to the Supreme Court of the United States. Both movements were unsuccessful, but he had not been consulted on either occasion, and he had no inclination to take a seat on the bench, as was evidenced by his declining in 1830 an offer from Gov. Wolf, of a position on the supreme court of Pennsylvania.

He was now commencing to feel the continuous strain of court work, most of it involving heavy responsibilities, and he contemplated an early retirement. But powerful influences were brought to bear which induced him to become a candidate for Congress on the anti-Jackson ticket in 1832. He consented on the understanding that he would not be required to support a protective tariff, that a vote for him should only be considered a vote against Jackson, and that if elected he should not be bound to any party. After a stirring campaign he was elected and took his seat in Congress Dec. 2, 1833. In the House he was an outstanding figure, but he could effect nothing in the face of the majority which the President commanded. His bitter disappointment was expressed in the statement that "the spirit of party is a more deadly foe to free institutions than the spirit of despotism." As a debater he showed himself second to none in the House, and his speeches reached an unusually high level, but he disliked his environment, and declined a renomination. In May 1836 he undertook a European tour with his daughter and niece, visiting Great Britain, France, Holland, Belgium, Switzerland, and Italy, being away over a year. On his return in 1837 he definitely retired from court work, confining himself to giving opinions, particularly with regard to land titles, in reference to which he was, and still is, regarded as almost infallible. He was vehemently opposed to the amendment proposed in the Pennsylvania constitutional convention of 1837–38 making the tenure of judges for a term of years only instead of during good behavior, and he published an eloquent address to the people appealing to them to vote against it, but in vain.

In 1844 he emerged from his semi-retirement and appeared in the Supreme Court of the United States at the imperative call of the City of Philadelphia in connection with the case of Vidal *et al.* *vs.* Philadelphia *et al.* (*2 Howard,* 127), involving the validity of a bequest by Stephen Girard of large properties to the city upon trust to establish a college for poor white male orphans. Relatives of the deceased claimed, *inter alia,* that the City could not hold a trust and that the objects were too vague. The question was of momentous importance to the City inasmuch as it had large commitments, having sold part of the property and undertaken the erection of expensive buildings in connection with the gift. An appeal had been taken by Girard's heirs from a decision of the United States circuit court in favor of the trust, and after the argument in the Supreme Court a re-argument had been directed, for which purpose the appellants had retained Daniel Webster. Binney's argument, remarkable for its erudition and power, was perhaps the most brilliant that has ever been addressed to the Supreme Court, and carried the day. This was his last appearance in court and undeniably his greatest triumph. That same year the anti-Catholic riots occurred in Philadelphia—the worst disturbances ever experienced by that city —and the civic authorities through incompetence or timidity failing to rise to the occasion, Binney stepped in and by his bold advice and resolute action restored order and confidence. In 1846 he evidenced his indifference to public opinion and the complete detachment with which he could scrutinize a legal problem, when he advised the City of Philadelphia that it could not legally subscribe for shares in the Pennsylvania Railroad Company. In 1850 he began to experience trouble with his eyes, and decided to withdraw completely from practise. His temperament, however, was such that he could not remain unemployed. Earlier in his career he had, by his *Eulogium upon . . . William Tilghman, C. J. of Pennsylvania* (1827) and *Eulogy on the Life and Character of John Marshall* (1835), shown the possession of literary ability of high quality. He now turned to his pen again. His first publication was *The Alienigenæ of the U. S. under the Present Naturalization Laws* (1853), addressed to the question of citizenship of children born outside the United States. This was followed by an obituary, *Horace Binney Wallace* (1853); *Bushrod Washington* (1858); *The Leaders of the Old Bar of Philadelphia* (1859); and *An Enquiry into the Formation of Washington's Farewell Address* (1859). The outbreak of the Civil War found him ranged with the administration, though he did not approve all its acts. It however gave occasion for the first of his series of

"Habeas Corpus Pamphlets," *The Privileges of the Writ of Habeas Corpus under the Constitution* (1862), wherein he upheld the legality of the President's action in suspending the writ. Two subsequent pamphlets elaborate his argument, and the three together compose a very valuable constitutional treatise.

As a lawyer preëminent, he was for nearly thirty years the acknowledged leader of the Pennsylvania bar, and it is doubtful whether there was during that time his superior in the country. His devotion to principle, his sincerity, and his fearlessness in the discharge of what he conceived to be his duty, combined to give him a prestige and influence in Philadelphia which during the latter part of his life were unique. A convinced Federalist as long as that party was in existence, he later refrained from any party affiliations. He was married to Elizabeth, youngest daughter of Col. John Cox of Bloomsbury Court, Trenton, N. J., and he died at Philadelphia Aug. 12, 1875.

[His ancestry is traced in *Geneal. of the Binney Family in the U. S.,* by C. J. F. Binney (1886). The standard authority for particulars of his life and career is *The Life of Horace Binney, with Selections from his Letters* (1903) by his son, Chas. Chauncey Binney. See also, *In Memoriam H. Binney,* extract from minutes of Philadelphia contributorship for Insurance of Houses (1875); "A Discourse illustrative of the Life and Character of Horace Binney" by Wm. Strong, in *Proc. Am. Phil. Soc.,* XVI, 1–51; *Memorial Biogs. of the New Eng. Historic Geneal. Soc.,* VII, 163; *A Sketch of Horace Binney* (1907), by Hampton L. Carson.]

H. W. H. K.

BINNS, JOHN (Dec. 22, 1772–June 16, 1860), journalist, politician, author, was born in Dublin, Ireland. His father, John Binns, a prosperous hardware dealer, died in 1774. Mary (Pemberton) Binns, his mother, remarrying within a short time, did not provide her three children with the decencies justified by their inheritance, but she was lavish of her counsel regarding morality and social deportment. This regimen, together with a little schooling and much indiscriminate reading, constituted John's education. By 1794 he was in London, associated with William Godwin and other agitators. He joined and became president of the London Corresponding Society, the avowed object of which was the reform of Parliament on a basis of universal suffrage, but the suspected object of which was the establishment of a British republic. Identified by the officials with political principles then dominant in France, Binns was imprisoned several times before 1801, when there was a general release of political prisoners in England. He then emigrated to America, arriving in September 1801, and proceeding directly to Northumberland, Pa., at that time "capital" of the projected community of free spirits—Cole-

ridge and Southey among them—who talked of coming hither from Europe. Joseph Priestley and Thomas Cooper were already on the ground, but their thought was not so advanced as to prevent Binns, soon after his arrival, from engaging in a duel, or from marrying Mary Anne Boyster, with whom he joined the Church of the United Brethren, and by whom, in time, he had ten children. So much advanced thought did not prevent, either, his pride in certain physical characteristics—animation and grace, a fine person, a pleasing voice, all as nicely disciplined as one could wish. On July 4, 1802, Binns addressed his community on the glory of America, a subject which he further expatiated upon, from a Republican view-point, in a letter to the Federalist *Northumberland Gazette.* From 1802 to 1807, after a method considered perhaps too direct and personal even for those direct, personal times, he published the *Northumberland Republican Argus.* He suspended this activity and changed his residence in order to establish in Philadelphia the *Democratic Press,* a paper published from 1807 till 1829, always direct and personal, always one of the leading organs of its party in the state, but, at the outset, because of its name, *Democratic,* held even by its friends to be almost too daringly radical. Governed largely by his belief that Andrew Jackson was a "tyrant," Binns opposed his election to the presidency in 1828, and in spite of his Irishman's consistent antipathy for England, found himself supporting John Quincy Adams. As part of his campaign against Jackson he published and distributed everywhere pictures of eight imaginary coffins bearing inscriptions relative to the martyrdom of their all too real inmates, soldiers, who, retiring from service at the expiration of their enlistment, though before the military emergency was past, had been, at Jackson's command, executed. This shift of allegiance brought disaster to Binns. His home was attacked by a mob, and financial difficulties necessitated the discontinuance of his paper. In 1819 he published an elaborate engraving of the Declaration of Independence, "far surpassing anything that the pencil and the burin have hitherto accomplished in this country" (*Port Folio,* January 1819). The attendant circumstances included angry charges and counter-charges that involved plagiarism of the idea, at least, of making such an engraving, and charges also to the effect (not new to him) that Binns, being no native American, was unworthy of popular confidence. It is likely that the noise did not trouble him, for by now he doubtless thought controversy quite normal. He was an alderman of Philadelphia from 1822 till 1844, and he was for many years a ready orator for all occasions. It was said that no one could comprehend the phrase "Irish eloquence" without having heard him. He boasted that never till he was almost sixty did he write out a speech in advance—till then the inspiration of the moment had always been enough. In 1840 he published *Binns's Justice,* a manual of Pennsylvania law. The book passed through as many as six editions before his death. The last edition, the eleventh, was published in 1912. *Recollections of the Life of John Binns Written by Himself* was published in 1854. It is the discursive chatter of a forgotten old man.

[The chief sources of this article in addition to those already mentioned are J. Binns, *Monumental Inscriptions* (1828), *Oration* (1810); B. O. Tyler, *Declaration of Independence* (1818); D. P. Brown, *First Speech* (1818). Notices appear also in H. C. Bell (ed.), *Hist. of Northumberland County, Pa.* (1891); J. T. Scharf and T. Westcott, *Hist. of Phila.* (1884); E. P. Oberholtzer, *Phila.; a Hist. of the City and Its People* (n. d.).]

J. D. W.

BINNS, JOHN ALEXANDER (*c.* 1761–1813), Virginia farmer, was born in Loudoun County, Va., probably in the year 1761, the son of Charles and Ann (Alexander) Binns. His father was evidently a man of means, for in 1782 he presented his son with a farm of 220 acres upon which to begin his career. Agriculture at that time in Virginia and Maryland labored under serious difficulties. The separation from England had closed valuable markets, and "soil exhaustion" (the fruit of long-continued tobacco planting and poor methods) threatened to force the abandonment of large portions of the older sections. If agriculture was to be maintained and disaster avoided, fundamental changes were necessary. To this task young Binns set himself. His first step toward improvement, he tells us, was taken in 1784 when he purchased a small quantity of gypsum from a ship captain at Alexandria and applied it as a fertilizer to his crops. It was not the first time in America that this had been done, but it was the first trial by a common farmer and the first to give wide practical results. Enlarged yields encouraged further trials and in the years that followed Binns experimented with gypsum on clover, grass, and grains (sometimes applied to the soil, sometimes to the seed before planting, and sometimes to the growing plant) recording his findings with such care and detail as to warrant their acceptance even today, "as legitimate fertilizer experiments" (Rodney H. True, "John Binns of Loudoun," *William and Mary College Quarterly,* January 1922, pp. 20–39). The results which Binns obtained were startling. His timothy and corn crops doubled, his oats yielded twice as much as his neighbor's,

and fields once as barren "as the main roads" were by 1803 producing forty bushels of corn to the acre. In the course of time, doubters were convinced and before long the granaries of the county were glutted and threshing was being delayed because of heavy yields of grain. Soon "meadows [once] infested with sedge and broom grass," were "well-set with white and red clover" and "old fields" had become fruitful again. All this just at the time when the Napoleonic Wars were opening markets for grain in Europe and in the West Indies (A. O. Craven, "Soil Exhaustion as a Factor in the Agricultural History of Virginia and Maryland, 1606–1860," being vol. XIII, no. 1 of *University of Illinois Studies in the Social Sciences,* 1926). In 1803 Binns incorporated his ideas on agricultural improvement through gypsum, clover, deep plowing, etc., in a pamphlet called *A Treatise on Practical Farming.* In this way the "Loudoun System" became widely known and practised in Virginia and Maryland. Thomas Jefferson sent copies to his English friends, Sir John Sinclair and William Strickland, recommending them as the means whereby lands once "exhausted and wasted" had become the most productive in the state. As Jefferson said, "These facts speak more strongly . . . than . . . polished phrases."

[The chief source of information about John Binns is his own pamphlet, *A Treatise on Practical Farming,* a copy of which is in the Jefferson Collection, Lib. of Cong. Mention is made of his work in letters in the Jefferson Papers, Lib. of Cong. The exact date of his death is uncertain, but his will, dated Jan. 11, 1813, was offered for probate in November of the same year.]

A. O. C.

BIRCH, THOMAS (July 26, 1779–Jan. 14, 1851), pioneer landscape and marine painter, was the son of William Russell Birch [*q.v.*], miniaturist and engraver. English by birth, he had his professional training at and near Philadelphia. William Dunlap states that young Birch "from infancy (to use his own expression) 'could sketch a little,'" and intimates that the youth preferred, to his father's discipline, "the instruction of nature, and studied on the banks of the Schuylkill." His companions on sketching tours were John Wesley Jarvis, afterward a distinguished portrait painter, and Samuel Seymour, who became an engraver and who served as draftsman with Capt. Long's expedition to the Yellowstone River. Birch was married on June 1, 1802, to Ann Goodwin. He was presumably responsible for many of the views of country seats published by W. Birch & Son. His portrayals of architecture are praised by Anne Hollingsworth Wharton (*Heirlooms in Miniature,* 1898, I, 143); she writes: "To him [Thomas Birch] the present generation is indebted for the many paintings in water color which he made of old country seats and historic buildings in the middle and southern colonies, and especially in and around Philadelphia." Birch likewise painted snow scenes, and in 1807 he visited the Capes of Delaware and began to do marine views. He was an exhibitor, in 1811, at the first annual exhibition of the Society of Artists, held at the Pennsylvania Academy of Fine Arts (Helen W. Henderson, *The Pennsylvania Academy of Fine Arts,* 1911).

The War of 1812 turned Birch's attention to the artistic possibilities of the sea fight. "His first regular essays in this department," says Dunlap, "were made at the commencement of the late war between his adopted and his native country. England was known as his country, but he felt as an American. The desperate fights which could lower the flag and the pride of the boasted mistress of the ocean were his chosen subjects." Birch's first picture in this genre was his "Engagement of the Constitution and the Guerrière," made for James Webster, a Philadelphia publisher. It is now at the Naval Academy, Annapolis. Subsequently Nicholas Biddle, afterward president of the United States Bank, commissioned Birch to do "The Wasp and the Frolic." Then came "The United States and the Macedonian," portrayals of Perry's victory on Lake Erie and McDonough's on Lake Champlain, and a succession of similar subjects which, as Dunlap wrote, "furnished employment to his pencil in the path he had chosen, and in which he stands unrivaled in our country." Some of the best of the historical pictures of the *Naval Monument* (Boston, 1816), to which Michele Felice Corné was a principal contributor, were after designs by Thomas Birch. He also designed several coins for the United States Mint (*American Art News,* Feb. 22, 1808).

[Wm. Dunlap, *Hist. of the Rise and Progress of the Arts of Design in the U. S.,* with supplementary footnote by the editors, Frank W. Bayley and Chas. E. Goodspeed (1918 ed.); Clara Erskine Clement and Lawrence Hutton, *Artists of the Nineteenth Century and their Works* (1879). Birch's portrait by John Neagle was reproduced in the *International Studio,* Oct. 1924.]

F. W. C.

BIRCH, WILLIAM RUSSELL (Apr. 9, 1755–Aug. 7, 1834), painter and engraver, was born in Warwickshire and professionally educated at Bristol and London. He showed in 1775 (Thieme and Becker, *Allgemeines Lexicon der Bildenden Künstler,* 1910, IV) two miniatures, "Head of Psyche" and "Jupiter and Io" at the Society of Artists. In 1781 he exhibited an enamel miniature, "Mother and Child," at the Royal Academy (according to Samuel Redgrave, *Artists of the English School,* 1874) and in 1782 he

was represented at the Academy by a "Portrait of a Child Going to Bed." J. J. Foster (*Dictionary of Painters of Miniatures,* 1926) writes admiringly of Birch's enamel portrait of the first Earl of Mansfield, after Sir Joshua Reynolds, now in the Bentinck-Hawkins collection in the Ashmolean, Oxford. The *Dictionary of National Biography* notes that in 1785 Birch was awarded a medal of the Society of Arts for excellence in his art and improvements in its processes. His one work published in England was the *Délices de la Grande Bretagne* (1789), a portfolio depicting ancient buildings and scenery (copy in the Boston Public Library). Its stippled plates are beautifully rendered, with good feeling for romantic and dramatic effects. In 1794 he came to America bringing with him his seven-year-old son Thomas Birch [*q.v.*]. He engraved a series of twenty-eight *Views of Philadelphia* (1798–1800), and a smaller series, published in 1808, of plates depicting American country seats. He also designed a famous New York City view (1803) with white horse in the foreground (described by Frank Weitenkampf in *Print Connoisseur,* January 1924). Some of his prints are inscribed as "drawn, engraved and published by W. Birch, Springland, near Bristol, Pennsylvania"; others as "drawn and engraved by W. Birch & Son, Philadelphia." His miniatures on enamel, of which he made at least sixty in America, gave him his chief reputation. Justly celebrated is his miniature portrait of George Washington, which was among the historic relics inherited and collected by William Lanier Washington and dispersed after exhibition at the Anderson Galleries, New York, in 1917. Of this work Elizabeth Bryant Johnson, author of *Original Portraits of Washington,* is quoted in the exhibition catalogue as writing: "It is said in outline to be precisely like the first Stuart, though the unpleasant impression arising from the false teeth is happily avoided." This miniature, according to W. S. Baker (*Engraved Portraits of Washington,* 1880), was painted in 1796 from life by request of Mr. Van Staphorst of Holland, a friend of American independence. Birch's contemporary, William Dunlap, wrote of it, "I remember seeing a miniature of Washington, executed by him in enamel; which I thought very beautiful, and very like Trott's copy from Stuart's original picture. My impression is that it was copied from Trott. Birch could design." This brief estimate of Birch's ability coincides with twentieth-century opinion.

[Wm. Dunlap, *Hist. of the Rise and Progress of the Arts of Design in the U. S.* with supplementary note by the editors, Frank W. Bayley and Chas. E. Goodspeed (1918 ed.); J. J. Foster, *Miniature Painters, British* and *Foreign* (1903); Anne Hollingsworth Wharton, *Heirlooms in Miniature* (1898), which mentions an unpublished autobiographical sketch. A technical description of several of Birch's American plates is printed in *A Descriptive Catalogue of an Exhibition of Early Engraving in America*, Dec. 12, 1904–Feb. 5, 1905, Museum of Fine Arts, Boston.]

F. W. C.

BIRD, ARTHUR (July 23, 1856–Dec. 22, 1923), composer, belongs to that small but interesting group of American musicians who, for one reason or another, have elected to spend their mature life abroad rather than at home in America; so that, while in Europe they have been looked upon as Americans, in America they have been almost regarded as Europeans. In fact, Bird's works have been so uniformly published and performed abroad that to most Americans he is practically unknown. He was born at Cambridge, Mass., the son of Horace and Elizabeth (Homer) Bird; and even as a child showed great interest in music, being unusually gifted in improvisation. When nineteen years old he went to Europe and spent two years under Haupt, Loeschhorn, and Rohde in the study of theory and piano. In 1877 he returned to America and took up his residence in Halifax, Nova Scotia, where he served as organist and choirmaster in the Kirk and as head teacher of piano in the Young Ladies' Academy and the Mount St. Vincent Academy of that city. Here he remained until 1881, when he again repaired to Berlin for further study, this time with Heinrich Urban in composition and orchestration. He also spent a year or so in close social and musical contact with Liszt during the memorable last years at Weimar, where Liszt paid the young American composer the honor of having many of his compositions performed. In 1886 Bird gave his first Berlin concert with excellent success, the Berlin papers giving him high praise. Even more successful, however, was a later concert at Sondershausen, where the Allgemeine Deutsche Musik Verein, under the personal auspices of Liszt, played his "Carnival Scene" for full orchestra. Also in 1886 at the invitation of the committee of the North American Sängerbund in Milwaukee, Bird visited America and officiated as director of the Milwaukee Musical Festival of that year. Returning to Germany from this visit he spent the entire remainder of his life in and about Berlin, taking an interested part in all its musical activities. On Feb. 29, 1888, he married Wilhelmine Waldmann at Peterboro, England. He was a prolific composer in almost all forms, from symphony and opera down. Not least in importance among his numerous interests was his valuable service as Berlin correspondent for the *Musical Leader,* Chicago, and as writer on various musical topics for the *Etude, Musician,* and other musical magazines. In 1901, with his serenade for wind instruments, *opus 40,* he achieved the Paderewski prize, founded by the famous Polish pianist to encourage American musical composition. This serenade was first performed in America by the Longy Club, Mar. 31, 1902; later, in Berlin, Feb. 6, 1908. On the latter occasion the musical critic of the *Berliner Börsen Courier* wrote of it as "distinguished for the freshness and spontaneity of its invention, as well as the clever craftsmanship and the clear and compact disposition of its different parts." This might very well be taken as a summing up of Bird's style in general. Arthur Farwell (*Art of Music,* IV, 402) wrote, "Bird is a musician of German training and French sympathies and calls himself a 'conditional modernist.'" It is quite evident both from Bird's writings and from his compositions that these conditions loomed large. In fact, his work is characterized rather by a certain attractive and facile lyricism than by any great depth, and he seems to have been but slightly influenced by the modern trends of musical composition. A strange development of the last years of his compositional activity was a frequent writing for the harmonium.

Of Bird's numerous compositions the following are perhaps best known: for orchestra, "Symphony in A," *opus 8* (1886); "Carnival Scene," *opus 5* (1887); for piano, two hands, three "Waltzes," *opus 12* (1886); "Eight Sketches," *opus 15* (1887); "Puppentänze," four pieces, *opus 19* (1887); and two early suites, *opus 4* and *opus 6;* for piano, four hands, three characteristic "Marches," *opus 11* (1886); ballet music, *opus 13* (1886); introduction and fugue, *opus 16;* "Zwei Poesien," *opus 25;* two pieces for violin and piano, *opus 9;* numerous songs, of which perhaps the five songs, *opus 36* (1896), are the best; for organ, three "Oriental Sketches" (1903) and a "Concert Fantasia" (1905); a ballet, "Rübezahl"; the comic opera, *Daphne,* produced at one of Mr. Bagby's *Musicales* at the Hotel Waldorf-Astoria, New York, in 1897; and numerous compositions for the harmonium.

[*Musical Courier,* Dec. 7, 1898; *Musical America,* Feb. 9, 1924; *Musical Leader,* Mar. 2, 1922, Jan. 31, 1924.]

W. T. U.

BIRD, FREDERIC MAYER (June 28, 1838–Apr. 2, 1908), Lutheran and Episcopal clergyman, hymnologist, editor, was born in Philadelphia, the son of Robert Montgomery Bird [*q.v.*] and of Mary Mayer, whose father, Philip Mayer, was for fifty-two years pastor of St. John's Lutheran Church on Race St. Probably the influence of the grandfather accounts for the fact that after graduating from the University of Pennsylvania in 1857 Bird entered Hartwick Lutheran Theological Seminary at Hartwick, N. Y., but, as the scanty records of his life show, he had little genius for remaining long in one place. After one year at Hartwick 1858–59 he transferred to Union Theological Seminary in New York, graduated in 1860, was ordained to the Lutheran ministry Sept. 3, 1861, was pastor at Rhinebeck, N. Y., 1860–62, was chaplain in the United States Army 1862–63, was pastor at West Philadelphia 1865–66 and at Valatie, N. Y., 1866–68, was ordained a deacon of the Episcopal Church Oct. 25, 1868, and priest June 18, 1869, was rector at Spotswood, N. J., 1870–74, and in Indianapolis 1874, was temporary supply at Hightstown, N. J., 1875–76, was rector at Iowa City, Ia., 1877–78, and at Waterloo, Ia., 1879–81, and was chaplain and professor of psychology, Christian evidences, and rhetoric in Lehigh University 1881–86. In 1877 he married Frances Snowhill of Spotswood, N. J. He published *Charles Wesley Seen in His Finer and Less Familiar Poems* in 1867, with Beale Melancthon Schmucker [*q.v.*] did most of the work on *Hymns for the Use of the Evangelical Lutheran Church* (1865), which has had a wide and wholesome influence on American Lutheran hymnody, collaborated with Bishop Odenheimer on *Hymns of the Spirit* (1871) and contributed hymnological articles to the *Schaff-Herzog Encyclopedia,* to Jackson's *Concise Dictionary of Religious Knowledge,* and to Julian's *Dictionary of Hymnology.* His hymnological library included about 3,000 volumes and was said to be the largest in the United States; it was presented by Henry Day, Esq., to Union Theological Seminary in 1888. He also did much miscellaneous work for various encyclopedias, was interested in numismatics and philately, published two novels, *A Pessimist in Theory and Practice* (1888) and *An Alien from the Commonwealth* (1889)—the latter an agreeable study in local color—under the name of "Robert Timsol," was editor of *Lippincott's Magazine* 1893–98 and wrote for it various articles, including some breezy disquisitions on the art of fiction, and in 1893 brought out *The Story of Our Christianity.* During his latter years he made his home in South Bethlehem, Pa., where he died.

[*Who's Who in America,* 1908–09 ; *Union Theol. Sem. Gen. Cat. 1836–1918* (1919) ; *Gen. Alumni Cat. of the Univ. of Pa.* (1917) ; C. E. Foust, *Life and Dramatic Works of R. M. Bird* (1919).]

G.H.G.

BIRD, ROBERT MONTGOMERY (Feb. 5, 1806–Jan. 23, 1854), playwright, novelist, editor, physician, was descended on his father's side from Thomas Bird, an Englishman who settled in New Castle County, Del., about 1700, while his mother, Elizabeth von Leuvenigh, came from early Dutch settlers of the same period. He represented a stock which had been for a century substantial citizens and cultivated people. His father, John Bird, was a member of the state Senate and filled other public offices until his sudden death in 1810 left his family in straitened circumstances. Montgomery Bird, as he was called by his family, had been born in New Castle. After his father's death he was brought up by his uncle, Hon. Nicholas van Dyke, who had been president of the State of Delaware, and was one of its leading citizens. Bird's early schooling, either at Newcastle or Philadelphia, made little impression upon him, but his reading was wide, especially in romance. Fortunately, he came under the influence of an inspiring teacher, Walter Johnson, at Germantown Academy in Philadelphia, and here he prepared for entrance to the Medical School of the University of Pennsylvania in 1824. In April 1827 he took the degree of M.D., having studied with such men as Robert Hare, Philip Syng Physick, and John Redman Coxe. But his study of medicine was due rather to the belief of his family that he should enter a profession, than to any real ability as a physician. He practised medicine for about a year, in Philadelphia, but as he disliked taking fees, his career was brief. His interest in science remained keen, however, and when the Pennsylvania Medical College was established in 1841, Bird became professor of the institutes of medicine and materia medica. His notebooks, filled with references to his reading in chemistry, botany, and agriculture, as well as in history and literature, ancient and modern, reveal him as one who responded instinctively to intellectual stimulation. His comments show, too, that he studied creatively, and his knowledge of Latin, Greek, Spanish, French, and Italian was active and not merely a polite accomplishment.

With an unusual equipment, and a desire to create, Bird entered upon a career as a writer with two handicaps. He had the artist's disregard of financial returns, and he faced the conditions which at that time in America made the lot of an author who depended exclusively upon his writing almost hopeless. His first manuscript of any length, *'Twas All for the Best,* is dated May 1827, but fortunately he turned from this imitation of British comedy to romance, in which his forte lay. *The Cowled Lover* and *Caridorf,* romantic tragedies, and *The City Looking Glass* and *News of the Night,* comedies of life in Philadelphia, remain in manuscript. The first two reveal an imaginative power and *The City*

Looking Glass is an early example of the play of low life. But his first drama of significance was *Pelopidas,* a tragedy based upon the revolt of Thebes against her Spartan oppressors. Though not written for Edwin Forrest, it was purchased by him, with a promise of the payment of one thousand dollars. Forrest's comments upon the manuscript show why he never produced it. While the character of Pelopidas is well drawn, it is really surpassed in interest by that of others, notably Philidas, the Theban patriot who plays the dangerous game of the apparent traitor, and Sibylla, the wife of Pelopidas. So, probably by mutual agreement, Bird substituted *The Gladiator* for *Pelopidas.* In the character of Spartacus, the Thracian captive of Rome, forced into the arena as the price of reunion with his wife and child, Bird provided a part exactly suited to Forrest. It proved to be one of the most vital creations of the stage. The motives of self-preservation, of family love, and of personal honor are made concrete in one heroic character, which Forrest acted as long as he lived and which held the stage in other hands as late as 1893. *The Gladiator* was first performed Sept. 26, 1831, at the Park Theatre, New York, and scored an instant success. Contemporary criticism records the effect upon the audience in Philadelphia who "rose and cheered in their seats" (Durang). The British actor, Wemyss, states that "The effect at the closing of the second act, I do not believe was ever surpassed in any theatre in the world." Forrest chose *The Gladiator* for his opening bill when he played at Drury Lane, Oct. 17, 1836. Notwithstanding the severe test, for Forrest was playing the work of a young man in a repertoire composed almost exclusively of Shakespeare, Bird's merit was generally recognized, and he was elected an honorary member of the English Dramatic Authors' Society. *The Gladiator* brought him another distinction, for when in 1853 it was played for the thousandth time, it was the first play written in English to be given so often during the lifetime of the author.

Encouraged by the success of *The Gladiator,* Bird wrote the tragedy of *Oralloossa,* laid at the time of the assassination of Pizarro and the revolt of Diego de Almagro. He created the character of Oralloossa, the heir of the Incas, for Forrest, who produced the play at the Arch Street Theatre, Philadelphia, Oct. 10, 1832. While it has its fine moments, it has not the force of *The Gladiator,* and Forrest withdrew it from his repertoire after the second season. Bird was intensely interested in Mexico and South America, and in 1833 he and Forrest started for a tour of those countries. Owing to a cholera epidemic,

their expedition only reached New Orleans, but it gave Bird an opportunity to see many of the Southern cities, and to explore the Mammoth Cave of Kentucky. His best play, *The Broker of Bogota,* was produced by Forrest at the Bowery Theatre, New York, Feb. 12, 1834. It is a domestic tragedy, laid in Santa Fé de Bogota, in South America, in the eighteenth century. The character of Febro, the money-lender, whose heart is broken by the treachery of his oldest and best-loved son, is the product of even a finer art than that which created Spartacus. Febro is all the more heroic because he struggles and suffers without losing his middle-class character and meets the blows of fate with dignity. *The Broker of Bogota* was a stage success and was played by Forrest until the last years of his career. Among the Bird manuscripts, a letter from Forrest, written on the night of its first performance, prophesies that "it will live when our vile trunks are rotten." The last work Bird did for Forrest was the revision of *Metamora,* John A. Stone's Indian play. Then came a break between the friends, due to Forrest's refusal to keep his financial agreements, made orally to Bird, who trusted him without any written contract. Bird had sold *The Gladiator* to Forrest for one thousand dollars, with the understanding that two thousand more was to be paid if the play was successful, and he also believed that the same agreement held good for the later plays. He received, however, only one thousand dollars each for *The Gladiator, Oralloossa* and *The Broker of Bogota,* and nothing for *Metamora* or *Pelopidas,* while from *The Gladiator* alone, Forrest made a fortune.

Discouraged by these circumstances, Bird turned to novel writing. In 1834 he published *Calavar; or The Knight of the Conquest,* a romance of the expedition of Cortez in 1520, following this in 1835 with *The Infidel; or The Fall of Mexico,* which deals with events a year later. These novels are based on wide reading and have the virtues and faults of the romantic school. Before *Calavar* appeared, Bird paid a visit to England, where he found his hopes of securing any return for his work futile. In 1835 appeared *The Hawks of Hawk Hollow,* a novel laid in and near the Water Gap of Pennsylvania, toward the close of the Revolution. Bird's picture of the decaying fortunes of a once prominent family, and his establishment of a sense of impending doom hanging over a race that has proved disloyal to its native country, make it one of the best of his novels. It was not, however, the most popular. After an anonymous story, *Sheppard Lee* (1836), a curious study of metempsychosis, he wrote *Nick of the Woods, or The Jibbenainosay, A Tale of*

Kentucky (1837), which had a pronounced success, was reprinted at least ten times in London by 1900, and four times in Germany. In the character of "Bloody Nathan," the Quaker who takes his revenge upon the Indians for the murder of his family, he created a striking figure, and his picture of the Indians, drawn without the idealization of Cooper, but rather as cruel, savage, and treacherous, was based, at least, upon personal observation. *Peter Pilgrim; or a Rambler's Recollections* (1838) is a collection of sketches, including a realistic picture of a Mississippi River steamboat, and a detailed description of the Mammoth Cave. *The Adventures of Robin Day* (1839) is a picaresque novel, laid in Philadelphia, in the Southwest, in Florida, and upon the sea.

The intensity of Bird's mental labors, spurred on by necessity and inadequate recompense, led to a breakdown in health and his retirement to a farm on the Eastern Shore of Maryland in 1840, where his health was for a time restored. In 1841–42–43, he delivered courses in materia medica at the Pennsylvania Medical College, and, on account of his friendship for John M. Clayton, he became active in politics, declining proposals to be himself a candidate for office, but acting as Clayton's representative in the Whig convention at Baltimore in 1844. At Clayton's suggestion he purchased in 1847 a share in the Philadelphia *North American,* and became literary editor. After the retirement of George R. Graham in 1848 the paper continued to be published by the firm of McMichael and Bird, but the incessant labors attending the production of a daily newspaper, upon which he did more than his share, again undermined Bird's health. Anxiety, too, as to the conduct of the paper, in which his authority was not equal to his responsibility, brought on what was then called "suffusion of the brain." He died in Philadelphia and was buried in Laurel Hill Cemetery. He had married in 1837 Mary Mayer, daughter of Rev. Philip F. Mayer, rector of St. John's Lutheran Church, Philadelphia. He had one son, Rev. Frederic Mayer Bird [*q.v.*], who was editor of *Lippincott's Magazine,* 1893–98, and who completed and published in that journal in 1889 his father's unfinished manuscript of "Ipsico Poe," under the title of "A Belated Revenge."

Robert Montgomery Bird was tall, fair, and of a commanding presence. In his journals, his correspondence, his editorials, he reveals the most uncompromising integrity, and an almost quixotic sense of right. Driven by unfortunate conditions from dramatic authorship at the height of his success, his plays were kept from publication by the selfishness of Forrest, who, even as late as 1869, refused Frederic Bird permission to print them. Forrest's refusal was all the more churlish since an examination of the copyright records in 1916 failed to reveal any copyright taken out by him. The fact that Bird's plays remained unpublished until 1917 (see Bibliography) has prevented his sterling work from receiving its proper place in our literary history.

[The MSS. of the plays, poems, and biographical material were presented by Robert Montgomery Bird, grandson of the playwright, to the Lib. of the Univ. of Pa. Among these is a manuscript life of Bird, by his wife, which is the main source for his biography. In 1917, the present writer published for the first time *The Broker of Bogota,* in his *Representative Am. Plays,* and in 1919 Dr. Clement E. Foust issued his *Life and Dramatic Works of Robert Montgomery Bird,* which contains *Pelopidas, The Gladiator, The Broker of Bogota,* and *Oralloossa.* For discussion of the plays, see Jas. Rees, *The Dramatic Authors of America* (1845); F. C. Wemyss, *Twenty-six Years of the Life of an Actor and Manager* (1847); W. R. Alger, *The Life of Edwin Forrest* (1877), vol. I; A. H. Quinn, *A Hist. of the Am. Drama from the Beginning to the Civil War* (1923), ch. XI. For general bibliography, see Dr. Foust's *Life* and *The Cambridge Hist. of Am. Lit.* (1917), I, 493–94, 525–26.]   A.H.Q.

BIRD WOMAN. [See Sacagawea, c. 1787–1812.]

BIRGE, HENRY WARNER (Aug. 25, 1825–June 1, 1888), Union soldier, was born at Hartford, Conn., where the Birge family had been established as early as 1640. At the outbreak of the Civil War he was a merchant in Norwich, Conn. Appointed major of the 4th Connecticut Infantry, May 23, 1861, he served with it in Maryland, without contact with the enemy, until Nov. 13, 1861, when he resigned in order to take command of a new regiment being organized in his state. On Feb. 18, 1862, he reëntered the service as colonel of the 13th Connecticut. The regiment was at once assigned to the expedition which was being organized to take New Orleans, arrived at Ship Island on Apr. 13, and entered the city when it was occupied by Gen. Butler a few days later. For the next few months it was engaged in minor operations in Louisiana. Upon the reorganization of Gen. Banks's command (19th Army Corps), in preparation for the Port Hudson campaign, Birge was assigned to the command of the 3rd Brigade, 4th Division, to which his own regiment belonged. The investment of Port Hudson was completed on May 26, 1863. An assault the next day being repulsed with heavy loss, regular siege operations were begun. A second assault on June 14 also failing disastrously, the besieging army suffering terribly with sickness and heat, and a Confederate army threatening New Orleans in the rear, it became evident that the city must be taken quickly if at all. The siege works were pressed vigorously forward, and meanwhile an "élite storming party" was organized, in order to penetrate the defense at all costs. Birge was selected to command. The party was made up of carefully chosen volunteers, mostly from the 13th Connecticut, organized into two battalions of eight companies each, and daily trained for its undertaking. On June 28, Birge reported 67 officers and 826 enlisted men present for duty. On July 7, all preparations were made for springing two mines, to precede the assault, when word was received of the surrender of Vicksburg, which put an end to the garrison's hopes of holding out at Port Hudson. Articles of capitulation were signed on July 8, Birge being one of the commissioners on behalf of Gen. Banks. He was appointed brigadier-general of volunteers on Sept. 19, 1863. He commanded a brigade, and at times a division, in the Red River campaign in the spring of 1864. Gen. Banks, in his report of the campaign, wrote that "Gen. Birge, as in all actions in which he has been engaged, deserved and received the highest commendation." Soon after, a part of the 19th Army Corps, including his brigade, was moved to Virginia, arriving on the James River late in July. Immediately afterward, it was moved to Savannah. There it remained in garrison until March, when it became a division of the 10th Army Corps, with Birge as its commander, and joined Schofield's army in North Carolina. On the surrender of the Confederate forces, Birge was assigned to the command of the district of Savannah. He resigned on Oct. 18, 1865, and returned to civil life. After the war he engaged in cotton planting and in the lumber business in Georgia, and later engaged in various enterprises in Texas and the West. His last years were spent in New York City, where he died.

[F. B. Heitman, *Hist. Reg.* (1903), I, 219; *Official Records*, ser. 1, vols. XV, XXVI (pt. 1), XXXIV (pts. 1, 3, 4), XL (pts. 1, 3), XLIII (pt. 1), XLVII (pt. 3); Homer B. Sprague, *Hist. of the 13th Infantry Regiment of Conn. Volunteers* (1867); Richard B. Irwin, *Hist. of the Nineteenth Army Corps* (1892); *N. Y. Times, N. Y. Tribune, Hartford Courant,* June 2, 1888.]

T. M. S.

BIRKBECK, MORRIS (Jan. 23, 1764–June 4, 1825), Illinois pioneer, publicist, was born at Settle, England, the son of an influential Quaker, Morris Birkbeck, and of Hannah Bradford. By 1794, as leaseholder, he was farming an estate of 1,500 acres at Wanborough in Surrey, where he was the first man to raise merino sheep in England, and was master of the hamlet. On Apr. 24, 1794, he married Prudence, daughter of Richard and Prudence Bush of Wandsworth, Surrey, who died Oct. 25, 1804, leaving him with seven children. In 1814, accompanied by his friend George Flower [*q.v.*], he traveled in France; his *Notes on a Journey through France* (1814) reveals a good-tempered, fair-minded observer, well grounded in science and the humanities. A liberal in politics and religion, he found it increasingly irksome to be taxed by a government that denied him a vote and tithed by a church whose doctrines he disapproved, and in 1817, with a party consisting chiefly of his children, he emigrated to the United States, where George Flower, who had gone before, now joined him. During 1817–18 Birkbeck either for himself or others entered 26,400 acres of public land in Edwards County, Ill., while Flower was raising more money and colonists in England. Birkbeck's *Notes on a Journey in America from the Coast of Virginia to the Territory of Illinois* (1817) was published in Philadelphia, London, Dublin, and Cork, ran through eleven editions in English in two years, and appeared in German at Jena (1818). His *Letters from Illinois* (1818), published in Boston, Philadelphia, and London, went through seven editions in English besides being translated in 1819 into French and German. In directing settlers to the prairie lands of the west these two books exercised a widespread influence, and incidentally brought down on their author the hearty vituperation of William Cobbett, who was in the pay of eastern land speculators. In 1818 he laid out the town of Wanborough, which has since vanished. That same year he and Flower parted and were never reconciled; the cause of the feud, which did irreparable injury to their colonization scheme, remains conjectural. A little later he became president of the first agricultural society in Illinois and gave a great impetus to the raising of cattle and to the scientific tilling of the soil. In 1823, by cogent articles contributed to newspapers under the name of "Jonathan Freeman," he helped to consolidate the anti-slavery forces in Illinois and to save the state for freedom. In 1824 an old London acquaintance, Edward Coles, now governor of Illinois, appointed him secretary of state; for three months he served with conspicuous ability, and then was turned out by the pro-slavery element in the state Senate, who refused to confirm the appointment. On June 4, 1825, returning from a visit to Robert Owen at Harmony, Ind., he was drowned while swimming his horse across the Fox River. In person he was below middle stature, spare, muscular, and wiry, his face bronzed and lined by exposure to the weather. He was one of the ablest, most cultured, and most public-spirited men on the frontier. His services to his adopted country were ill requited and soon forgotten.

[R. Birkbeck, *The Birkbecks of Westmorland and Their Descendants* (London, privately printed, 1900); G. Flower, *Hist. of the English Settlements in Edwards Co., Ill.* (1882); *The English Settlement in the Illinois: Reprints of Three Rare Tracts on the Illinois Country* (1907), ed. by E. E. Sparks; J. Woods, *Two Years' Residence in the Illinois Country* (1822); W. Faux, *Memorable Days in America 1819–20*, being vol. XI (1905) of *Early Western Travels 1748–1846*, ed. by R. G. Thwaites; S. J. Buck, *Travel and Description 1765–1865*, being vol. IX of *Ill. State Hist. Lib. Colls.; Bibliographical Series*, II, (1914); S. J. Buck, *Illinois in 1818*, being the Introductory Volume (1917) of *Ill. Centennial Publications*; T. C. Pease, *The Frontier State 1818–48*, being vol. II (1918) of the *Centennial Hist. of Illinois*.]

G. H. G.

BIRNEY, DAVID BELL (May 29, 1825–Oct. 18, 1864), Union soldier, was the son of James G. Birney [*q.v.*], who was a native of Kentucky and a graduate of Princeton, but who later moved to Huntsville, Ala., where he became a successful planter as well as one of the leaders of the Alabama bar. Here it was that David Bell Birney was born. In the year 1838 the Birney family moved to Cincinnati—after the father had freed his own slaves and had actively identified himself with the emancipation movement. In 1844 James G. Birney became the national presidential candidate of the Anti-Slavery party. With such family influences, it was natural that the son should take an active part in the war between the states. Young Birney received his education at Andover, and after graduation, went into business, first in Cincinnati and later in Upper Saginaw, Mich., where he studied law and was admitted to the bar. But in the year 1848 he moved to Philadelphia and became a clerk in a mercantile agency, which position he held until 1856, when he engaged in law practise. The year preceding the Civil War found him a successful practitioner with many influential friends. He foresaw the outbreak of war, and late in the year 1860, entered upon an intensive study of military subjects. For some years he had been a member of the historic 1st Troop of Philadelphia City Cavalry, and in February 1860 he secured appointment as lieutenant-colonel of a regiment of Pennsylvania militia. The young civilian was better prepared for a military career than most of the inexperienced field-officers, hastily mustered into the United States service in the spring of 1861. Although it never assembled or paraded, his militia regiment formed the basis of the 23rd Regiment of Pennsylvania Volunteers, upon the President's call for volunteers; and, as such, performed guard duty north of the Susquehanna, and during the summer of 1861 engaged in minor operations along the upper Potomac. Birney received his baptism of fire at Falling Waters, West Va., and later his regiment occupied Winchester. The term of enlistment of the three-months volunteers expiring, a new regiment was formed from the old through consolidation and reënlistments; and within a few days after Aug. 17, 1861, due to his energy and leadership, the regimental commander was able to parade a new 23rd Regiment through the streets of Washington, its soldiers sworn in for three years' service. Then began a long period of drill and training, and such was the favorable impression created by Birney's capacity for command and proper ideas of discipline, that early in 1862 he was appointed a brigadier-general of volunteers. His first assignment was to a brigade of Gen. Kearny's division. As a brigade commander, he participated in the early operations of the Army of the Potomac, including Centreville and Manassas, and later in 1862 engaged with his brigade in the sanguinary battles of the Peninsular campaign—Yorktown, Williamsburg, Fair Oaks, Malvern Hill. At Fair Oaks, he was unjustly charged with having "halted his command a mile from the enemy," and was brought before a court martial. After careful consideration of the evidence, the court, composed in the main of regular officers, honorably acquitted him. Transported back to Alexandria, Va., Birney's brigade was pushed forward to the support of troops engaged in Pope's campaign, and on Aug. 31, 1862, took an active part in the Union victory at Chantilly, Va., where Birney's warm friend and military superior, Gen. Phil Kearny, lost his life. He succeeded Kearny as division commander, and led his division through the battles of the Army of the Potomac, until the middle of July 1864. At Fredericksburg, his division was in support of Meade; and although it was charged that Birney failed to comply with urgent instructions, careful investigation at the time failed to substantiate such charges, and Gen. Stoneman reported that Birney's division "probably saved the entire left wing from disaster." For his able leadership at Chancellorsville, Birney was promoted, May 5, 1863, to be major-general of volunteers. At Gettysburg, he commanded the 3rd Army Corps after Gen. Sickles was wounded, and was struck twice by enemy's bullets, but was only slightly injured (*New York Herald*, July 6, 1863). Thereafter, Birney's division followed Grant through his first campaign against Richmond until July 23, 1864, when Grant selected Birney to command the 10th Army Corps. After these major operations in which for months his system had been weakened by exposure and fatigue, Birney became seriously ill with malarial fever of an especially virulent type; and against his wishes to remain in the field, was ordered home for recuperation. He reached Philadelphia on Oct. 11, 1864, where, after acute suffering, he died on Oct. 18, in the thirty-ninth year of his age. His last words in delirium were, "Boys! Keep your eyes on that flag!" Resolutions of the Philadelphia Board of Trade characterized him as "an honest citizen, a gallant soldier, and a pure, chivalric, self-sacrificing patriot." So great was the esteem in which Birney's life and services were held, that during the fall of 1864 and the spring of 1865 a group of Philadelphia friends raised a trust fund of nearly thirty thousand dollars by popular subscription, which was wisely invested by trustees for the benefit of Birney's widow and six small children.

[Oliver W. Davis, *Life of David Bell Birney* (pub. anonymously, 1867) is the principal source; see also *Official Records, Army and Navy Jour.*, Oct. 22, 29, Nov. 19, 1864, and "Report of the Joint Committee on the Conduct of the War," *Senate Report No. 142*, 38 Cong., 2 Sess. The honorable acquittal of Birney by court martial is in General Order No. 135, Headquarters Army of the Potomac, June 19, 1862 (War Department files).]							C. D. R.

BIRNEY, JAMES (June 7, 1817–May 8, 1888), lawyer and diplomatist, the eldest son of James G. Birney [q.v.] and brother of David Bell Birney [q.v.] and of William Birney [q.v.], was born at Danville, Ky. His academic education was obtained at Centre College, Danville, and at Miami University, Oxford, Ohio, from which latter institution he graduated in 1836. In 1837–38 he taught in the Grammar School of Miami University; then he studied law at Yale for two years and began to practise at Cincinnati. He became a trustee of the Saginaw Bay Company, and in 1857 removed to Lower Saginaw (now Bay City), Mich., where he made his home until his death. In 1859 he was elected to the state Senate as a Republican, and successfully opposed the transfer to the state school fund of the proceeds of the sales of swamp lands given to the state by the federal government in aid of the construction of roads. From Jan. 1 to Apr. 3, 1861, he was lieutenant-governor, resigning that office to accept an appointment as judge of the eighteenth judicial circuit to fill a vacancy. Although his standing as a lawyer was high, he appears to have been somewhat wanting in judicial temperament, and at the end of four years, notwithstanding that he had been nominated to succeed himself, he failed of election. In the state constitutional convention of 1867, of which he was a member, he was made chairman of a select committee on procedure, and of a committee which reported the provisions for the executive department. In 1871 he established the Bay City *Chronicle,* changing the paper from a weekly to a daily in 1873. In 1876 he was a commissioner from Michigan to the Centennial Exposition at Philadelphia. To-

ward the end of that year he was appointed by President Grant minister resident at The Hague, a post which he retained until 1882, when he resigned. At the time of his death he was president of the Bay City board of education. He married, June 1, 1841, Amanda S., daughter of John and Sophia Moulton of New Haven, Conn., and cousin of Commodore Isaac Hull.

[There is a summary sketch of Birney's life in *Mich. Biogs.* (1924), I, 84; and there is a brief account by A. C. Maxwell in the *Mich. Pioneer and Hist. Colls.*, XXII, 227–30 (1893). See also the *Jour. of the Mich. Constitutional Convention of 1867.*]							W. M.

BIRNEY, JAMES GILLESPIE (Feb. 4, 1792–Nov. 25, 1857), anti-slavery leader, was the son of James Birney, an Irish expatriate who migrated to America in 1783 and in 1788 removed to Kentucky, where he eventually became one of the richest men in the state. Although a slaveholder, the elder Birney advocated a free state constitution for Kentucky and favored emancipation. He married about 1790 a daughter of John Read, also an Irish exile; she died in 1795. James Gillespie, the only son of the marriage, was born at Danville. He was educated at Transylvania University, Lexington, Ky., and at the College of New Jersey (now Princeton), where he graduated in 1810. He read law in the office of Alexander J. Dallas [q.v.] at Philadelphia, was admitted to the bar in 1814, and began what presently became an important practise at Danville. On Feb. 1, 1816, he married Agatha, daughter of William McDowell, United States district judge, and niece of Gov. George McDowell of Kentucky. The marriage brought him some slaves. In August 1816 he was elected to the lower house of the legislature. Two years later he removed to Madison County, Ala. He was not a member of the Alabama constitutional convention, but he seems to have been largely responsible for the inclusion in the state constitution, in amended form, of certain provisions of the Kentucky constitution permitting the legislature to emancipate slaves and prohibiting the introduction of slaves into the state for sale. In October 1819 he took his seat as a representative in the first General Assembly of Alabama, but his opposition to a resolution indorsing the candidacy of Andrew Jackson for president was unpopular, and he was not reëlected. He had already attained marked prominence as a lawyer, but by 1820 neglect of his plantation, together with gambling, brought financial embarrassment, and in January 1823 he removed to Huntsville, later selling his plantation with its slaves. At Huntsville his legal practise shortly recouped his finances, and thereafter, for most of his life, he was comparatively wealthy. For several years he acted as counsel for the Cherokee Nation. He had been brought up an Episcopalian, but in 1826, mainly through the influence of his wife, he became a Presbyterian. From about this time dated his interest in the colonization movement and the restriction of slavery and the domestic slave trade. A bill which he drafted to give effect to the provision of the Alabama constitution prohibiting the importation of slaves for sale, although passed by the General Assembly in January 1827, was repealed in 1829, following the election of Jackson. He was nominated a presidential elector on the Adams ticket in 1828, but Birney strongly disapproved of the policy of attacking Jackson personally, and urged the Northern element of the party to direct their opposition to the annexation of Texas and the issue of nullification. A visit to New York and New England in the fall of 1829 impressed him with the superiority of free institutions, economic and social, to those of the slave states, but he was not yet an abolitionist, and his growing reputation as an anti-slavery supporter rested upon his repugnance to slavery in general and his advocacy of gradual emancipation. For reasons not divulged he parted company politically with Henry Clay, one of his father's intimate friends, in October 1830. Another anti-slavery bill, the passage of which in Alabama he secured in January 1832, was repealed in December. In August of that year he accepted a commission as agent of the American Colonization Society, and for some months traveled and lectured in the South in behalf of that organization. An idea that Kentucky was "the best site in our whole country for taking a stand against slavery" (letter to Gerrit Smith, in W. Birney, *Life and Times of James G. Birney,* p. 131) led him in November to return to Danville. Several of his occasional writings, among them two letters on slavery and colonization addressed to Rev. R. R. Gurley (1832), essays on slavery and colonization contributed to the Huntsville *Advocate* (1833), and two letters to the Presbyterian Church (1834), belong to this period. The emancipation of his six slaves in 1834 was later described in detail in a letter (1836) to Col. Stone, editor of the New York *Spectator* (Birney, *op. cit.,* Appendix D). Convinced that colonization would increase the interstate slave-trade, and unable to reconcile it with his views of religion and justice, he resigned in 1834 the vice-presidency of the Kentucky Colonization Society, stating his reasons in a *Letter on Colonization* (first published in the Lexington *Western Luminary* and later reprinted in several editions), which added to his reputation and definitely allied him with

the more aggressive anti-slavery forces. March 1835 saw him active in forming the Kentucky Anti-Slavery Society, but the membership of the American Anti-Slavery Society, whose meeting at Cincinnati he attended, did not seem to him effective. In a speech at the New York meeting of the Society in May 1835 he forcibly urged united action by all opponents of slavery. A second visit to New England, after the New York meeting, was interrupted by news of outspoken hostility to the publication in Kentucky of an anti-slavery weekly, the first number of which he had planned to issue on Aug. 1. An attempt to mob him on his return was defeated, but the publication of the paper was delayed and his mail was repeatedly rifled. The continuance of opposition determined him to remove to Ohio, and at the beginning of January 1836 he issued at New Richmond, near Cincinnati, the first number of the *Philanthropist,* continuing the publication, with the editorial assistance of Gamaliel Bailey, until September 1837, when he removed to New York. In the *Philanthropist* Birney not only attacked both Democrats and Whigs for their attitude toward slavery, but also urged upon the abolitionists the necessity of political action. On July 30 another plan to assault him at a public meeting was frustrated; his *Narrative of the Late Riotous Proceedings,* published soon after, described the episode, and was followed in October by a letter *To the Slaveholders of the South.* On several occasions later he was exposed to personal danger, meetings at which he spoke were interrupted, and his paper suffered; his son and biographer, however, is authority for the statement that "no man ever laid an unfriendly hand upon him during his public career" (Birney, *op. cit.,* p. 252). The convention of the New England Anti-Slavery Society at Boston, May 30–June 2, 1837, which he attended, found him an open dissenter from the "no government" or political abstention views of Garrison's followers, and a champion of organized political action and voting. For harboring in his home an escaped slave, Matilda, who was subsequently claimed and returned as a fugitive, he was indicted in Cincinnati, was acquitted after pleading his own case, and presently published his argument. In September, having been elected executive secretary of the American Anti-Slavery Society, he removed to New York, and spent the winter of 1837–38 in visiting such of the state legislatures as were in session. A published letter to Representative F. H. Elmore of South Carolina, in response to a request for information regarding anti-slavery organizations, separated him still farther from the Garrisonians by establishing his position as an upholder of the Federal Constitution. A *Letter on the Political Obligations of Abolitionists,* prepared as a "report on the duty of political action" for the executive committee of the American Anti-Slavery Society in May 1839 (published in the Boston *Emancipator* May 2; replied to at much length by Garrison May 31; the two reprinted as a pamphlet), was an incisive criticism of the constitution of the Society and of the Garrisonian policy, and brought appreciably nearer the ultimate breach in the abolition ranks. For the next few years Birney was the most conspicuous representative and the ablest spokesman of those who sought to get rid of slavery by political means as well as by moral suasion. On Nov. 13, 1839, a state convention at Warsaw, N. Y., unanimously nominated him for president, but the nomination was declined, partly because the convention was not national in character, and partly because he thought it inexpedient to make an independent nomination until the candidate of the Whigs had been selected. In April 1840, the Whigs having nominated William Henry Harrison, Birney was again nominated at Albany, N. Y., by an anti-slavery convention representing six states. The new party, generally known as the Liberty party, had at first no name and adopted no platform. The popular vote polled was 7,069, drawn from the six New England states, New York, New Jersey, Pennsylvania, Ohio, Illinois, and Michigan (Edward Stanwood, *History of the Presidency,* I, 203). In the same year Birney went to England, where he was one of the vice-presidents of the World's Anti-Slavery Convention. His best-known work, *The American Churches the Bulwarks of American Slavery,* was written and published in England (1840; 2nd, and first American, edition, "By an American," 1842; 3rd ed., 1885). He had already, in 1839, emancipated twenty-one slaves, a part of his father's estate, at a cost of $20,000 in the form of compensation for the interest of a co-heir. His wife died in 1839, and in 1841 he married Miss Fitzhugh, sister-in-law of Gerrit Smith. The next year he removed to Bay City, Mich. In August 1843 he was again nominated for president, this time by a convention at Buffalo, N. Y., comprising 148 delegates from twelve states. The platform, by far the longest that any party had yet adopted, added to its denunciation of slavery an announcement of the purpose of the abolitionists, "whether as private citizens or as public functionaries sworn to support the Constitution of the United States, to regard and to treat the third clause of the fourth article of that instrument, whenever applied to

the case of a fugitive slave, as utterly null and void, and consequently as forming no part of the Constitution of the United States, whenever we are called upon or sworn to support it." No electoral votes were won, but the popular vote of the Liberty party, drawn from the same states that voted for Birney in 1840, with the addition of Indiana, was 62,300. The "Garland Letter," issued on the eve of the election and purporting to solicit for Birney a Democratic nomination for the Michigan legislature and stating his intention to defeat Clay, was a forgery. Horace Greeley's charge in the *New York Tribune* that Birney had sought a Democratic nomination in New York and tried to catch the Democratic vote was widely believed at the time but appears improbable (Stanwood, *op. cit.,* I, 224). In the summer of 1845 a fall from a horse, resulting in partial paralysis, made Birney an invalid and brought his public career to a close. His *Examination of the Decision of the Supreme Court of the United States in the case of Strader et al. v. Graham, concluding with an Address to the Free Colored People, advising them to remove to Liberia* (1852), was written in 1850: the decision in question was one much relied upon by Chief Justice Taney in the Dred Scott case (1857). About 1853 Birney removed from Michigan to Eagleswood, near Perth Amboy, N. J., and died there Nov. 25, 1857. In the history of the American anti-slavery movement he occupies a peculiar position. Never a supporter of slavery in principle, notwithstanding that he owned slaves, he accepted the institution for a time as he found it and worked earnestly to ameliorate its conditions. He early manifested an almost insuperable repugnance to selling slaves, and was at pains to explain and defend his course in disposing of the few that he held. Acquaintance with the North convinced him that the overthrow of slavery was as necessary for the whites as for the negroes, and he passed gradually, but on the whole rapidly, from advocacy of gradual emancipation, reinforced by colonization in Africa, to a conviction that abolition must be secured by constitutional political means. He was too reasonable, and perhaps too good a lawyer, to follow Garrison in the latter's denunciation of the Constitution, but he was nevertheless willing at last, as the party platform on which he stood in 1844 showed, to nullify so much of the Constitution as gave countenance to fugitive slave legislation or identified the federal government with the support or extension of slavery. The assertion of his biographer that he "voted Free Soil or Republican tickets, state and national, except Van Buren, as long as he lived," helps to explain the distrust with which Garrison and other radical abolitionists regarded him, although the statement could hardly have applied to the elections of 1840 and 1844.

[The chief authority, except for the presidential campaigns of 1840 and 1844, is *Jas. G. Birney and His Times* (1890), by his son, Wm. Birney. The book was inspired by what the writer believed to be the misrepresentations of W. P. and F. J. Garrison's *William Lloyd Garrison* (1885–89), with which its statements and comments should be compared; it is extremely hostile to Garrison and to much of the view of the abolition movement which Garrison's biographers present. The latter, in turn, are persistently hostile to Birney. A review of Wm. Birney's book in the *Nation* (New York), L, 206, is informing. An earlier life by Beriah Green, *Sketches of the Life and Writings of Jas. Gillespie Birney* (1844), written as a campaign document and laudatory, contains many extracts from Birney's writings; see especially pp. 100–04, a summary of Birney's letter of acceptance in 1840, and pp. 105–15, virtually the whole of the letter of acceptance in 1843, dissecting the claims of John Quincy Adams to the support of abolitionists. See also the anonymous *Tribute to Jas. G. Birney* (Detroit, Mich., n. d., c. 1865). References in the voluminous literature of the anti-slavery movement are many, but usually brief. Most of Birney's writings appeared first as contributions to newspapers or magazines, subsequently in pamphlets; to those already mentioned are to be added *Vindication of the Abolitionists* (1835), a reply to resolutions of an Alabama committee proposing drastic dealings with abolition agitators; *Addresses and Speeches* (1835); various articles in the *Quarterly Anti-Slavery Magazine* and the *Emancipator* (1837–44), and *Speeches in England* (1840).]

W. M.

BIRNEY, WILLIAM (May 28, 1819–Aug. 14, 1907), Union soldier, author, was born in Madison County, Ala., the son of James G. Birney [q.v.] and Agatha McDowell. At some time prior to 1845 he was practising law in Cincinnati, Ohio. In February 1848, being a member of a Republican student organization in Paris, he commanded at a barricade in the Rue St. Jacques during the revolutionary outbreak. In the same year he won in a competitive examination an appointment as professor of English literature at the Lycée at Bourges, where he remained for two years. During his five years' residence abroad he wrote for English and American papers, among other things reporting the first World's Fair at London (1851). He appears also to have paid some attention to the history of art and current activities in art education (see his *Art and Education,* a lecture before the Washington Art Club, Feb. 6, 1878). Upon his return to the United States he established the daily *Register* at Philadelphia (1853) and edited it for two years. At the outbreak of the Civil War he raised a volunteer company in New Jersey, and became in succession captain of the 1st New Jersey Infantry and major and colonel of the 4th New Jersey Infantry. In 1863 he was appointed one of the superintendents of the enlistment of colored troops, in which capacity he organized

seven regiments. On May 22, 1863, he was made brigadier-general of volunteers. While in command of colored troops he freed the inmates of the slave prisons at Baltimore. He took part in a number of important engagements, and after the battle of Olustee, Fla. (Feb. 20, 1864), aided in recovering the state from the Confederates. During the last two years of the war he commanded a division. On Mar. 13, 1865, he was made brevet major-general of volunteers "for gallant and meritorious service during the war," and on Aug. 24 was mustered out. After a residence of four years in Florida he removed to Washington, where he practised law, wrote fortnightly letters to the New York *Examiner,* and served for a time as United States attorney for the District of Columbia. His best-known writing, *James G. Birney and His Times,* appeared in 1890. In his later years he interested himself in religious controversy, publishing *Functions of the Church and State Distinguished: A Plea for Civil and Religious Liberty* (1897); *Revelation and the Plan of Salvation* (1903); *Creeds not for Secularists* (1906); *Hell and Hades* (Truth Seeker Tracts, New Series, No. 51, New York, n. d.), and *How Christianity Began (Ibid.,* No. 54, n. d.). He was twice married: in 1845 to Catherine Hoffman, and in 1891 to Mattie Ashby.

[*Who's Who in America,* 1899–1907; F. B. Heitman, *Hist. Reg.* (1903); *Official Records,* see Index; *Washington Post,* and *Evening Star,* Aug. 15, 1907.]

W. M.

BISHOP, ABRAHAM (Feb. 5, 1763–Apr. 28, 1844), politician, was born in New Haven, the son of Samuel and Mehetabel (Bassett) Bishop. His father was a respected and well-to-do citizen who exemplified the steady habits of his native state by more than fifty years' service as town clerk and representative in the Assembly, besides holding at different times several other local offices, including, late in life, that of mayor. Abraham graduated at Yale in 1778. Inasmuch as he was less than sixteen years of age at graduation it is not surprising that he led an unsettled life for some years following. In 1785 he was admitted to the bar but never attained any professional distinction, not even practising with any regularity. In 1787–88 he visited Europe and, like his classmate Joel Barlow, was profoundly influenced by its intellectual unrest and the political and religious skepticism of the revolutionary era. He returned, as President Stiles of Yale sourly remarked, "full of Improvmt and Vanity," but more likely merely impressed with the unprogressive and static character of Federalist Connecticut.

For several years he taught school, lectured, and engaged in miscellaneous activities. William Bentley records him in 1792 as "Alias J. Martin, schoolmaster, actor, excentric writer, traveler" (*Diary*, 1905, I, 391). Making all due allowance for political detraction such as that of the *Connecticut Courant*, Aug. 16, 1802, which described him as a man "whose life is but another name for deformity," he appears in his early life to have been somewhat dissipated. On Mar. 11, 1792, he married Nancy, daughter of the notorious Timothy Dexter of Newburyport. His eccentric and semi-illiterate father-in-law described him as the "two leged Conekett boull—short Neck, boull head, thik hare, big sholders, black Corlley hare," with comments on his character as unflattering as those on his appearance (J. P. Marquand, *Lord Timothy Dexter of Newburyport, Mass.*, 1925, pp. 363 ff.). This connection soon ended in a squalid family quarrel and the divorce of his wife. In 1802 he married Betsey Law of Cheshire, Conn., who died Sept. 11, 1817, and on Jan. 3, 1819, he married Mrs. Elizabeth (Nicoll) Lynde of New Haven, who survived him.

Soon after his marriage in 1792 he returned to New Haven, where he lived for the remainder of his life. He taught school and was in 1795 made clerk of the county court, in 1796 of the probate court, and in 1798 of the superior court. He became an ardent supporter of Jefferson, which in a Federalist community like Connecticut was the equivalent of moral and political treason, and by 1801 accordingly, he had been ousted from the last of these local offices. In 1801 President Jefferson removed the Federalist collector of the port and assigned the place to Samuel Bishop. As his father was in feeble health it was generally considered that the appointment was in effect that of Abraham himself, and indisputably a reward for political services. The protest of the New Haven merchants thereat, and President Jefferson's reply will always appear as landmarks in the history of American civil service (see C. R. Fish, *The Civil Service and the Patronage*, 1905, pp. 32–38). In 1803, on the death of his father, Bishop was formally appointed collector and held the place until removed by President Jackson in 1829. His official career thus coincided with a distinct epoch in the history of Federal patronage and he was first a beneficiary and then a victim of two great exponents of democratic administration. One of his contemporaries noticed the fact that the possession of a lucrative office quieted his radical tendencies and that his political activity quickly subsided after 1804 (S. G. Goodrich,

Recollections of a Lifetime, 1856, I, 125). He spent the rest of his life acquiring respectability, a belief in the protective tariff, and a fortune, apparently with marked success in each endeavor.

Bishop's political activity was largely concentrated in a period of six or seven years around the opening of the century and he unquestionably exercised an important influence both within his own state and in New England at large. He delivered a series of noteworthy addresses which were in several instances enlarged and printed for general reading. They were widely circulated and quoted. He had a command of simple, forcible English, a distinct satirical bent, and some sense of humor, a combination which made him a dreaded and hated opponent of that conservative, religious, legal, and propertied alliance which completely dominated Connecticut prior to 1818. The most noteworthy of these productions were *An Oration on the Extent and Power of Political Delusion* (1800); *An Oration delivered in Wallingford* (1801); *Proofs of a Conspiracy, Against Christianity, and the Government of the United States* (1802); *Oration in honor of the Election of President Jefferson and the Peaceable Acquisition of Louisiana* (1804). "Have mercy upon us! ye well-fed, well-dressed, chariot-rolling, caucus-keeping, levee-revelling federalists; for we are poor, and wretched, and ignorant and miserable" is the demagogic theme running through many of his pamphlets. Nevertheless, he performed a valuable service when he assailed the alliance of church and state, the clannishness produced by family alliances in business and politics and the exaggerated respect for wisdom of ancestors who as he said "fought, quarreled, sinned and punished, as often in proportion to their numbers as their posterity." Conservative Federalism also needed to be continually reminded that "everything valuable in our world has been at one time, innovation, illuminatism, modern philosophy or atheism" to those disturbed by it.

[Bishop's pamphlets are found in many of the older New England libraries. The best summary of his life is that by F. B. Dexter in *Biog. Sketches Grads. Yale Coll., IV*, (1907), pp. 17–24, which includes a list of his publications and a bibliography. Another brief sketch by the same author appears in *Mass. Hist. Soc. Proc.*, ser. II, vol. XIX, pp. 190–99. The studies by R. J. Purcell, *Conn. in Transition, 1775–1818* (1918); and M. L. Greene, *The Development of Religious Liberty in Conn.* (1905), show the political and social background of Bishop's career and contain considerable direct information. There are numerous references to Bishop in the *Lit. Diary of Ezra Stiles*, ed. by F. B. Dexter (1901), vols. II, III.]

W. A. R.

BISHOP, JOEL PRENTISS (Mar. 10, 1814–Nov. 4, 1901); lawyer, was born in Volney, Oswego County, N. Y., being a descendant in the direct male line from John Bishop, who, coming from England, settled at Guilford, Conn., in 1639. His father, Amos Bishop, a farmer of small means, son of Deacon David Bishop of Guilford, married Fanny Prentiss, of Paris, Oneida County, N. Y., and shortly after his birth the family moved to Paris. His youth was spent working on the farm, and his early education was obtained by intermittent attendance at Whitestone Seminary, Oneida Institute, and Stockbridge Academy. In 1830 he became a public school teacher, thus earning enough to continue his studies in his spare time. In 1835 he became associated with the New York Anti-Slavery Society, and for a time was its general business manager, assisting also to edit *The Friend of Man*. He removed to Boston in 1842, entered a law office, supporting himself by literary work outside office hours, and was admitted to the bar Apr. 9, 1844. Commencing practise in Boston, he slowly built up a connection, devoting his leisure to the collection of material for a treatise on the law of domestic relations. His *Commentaries on the Law of Marriage and Divorce, and Evidence in Matrimonial Suits* was published in 1852 and immediately attracted attention by its independent standpoint and freshness of treatment. Encouraged by its reception, and urged thereto by the profession, he thenceforward devoted himself to legal authorship, relinquishing active practise. His next work, *Commentaries on the Criminal Law,* in two volumes (1856–58), placed him in the front rank of contemporary legal authors, being distinguished for clarity of style, scrupulous accuracy and originality of thought. Additional editions of both these early books were quickly called for, and they continued in demand until long after his death. His subsequent publications included *Commentaries on the Law of Criminal Procedure; or, Pleading, Evidence and Practice in Criminal Cases* (1866); *First Book of the Law* (1868), an introduction to legal science, study, and practise; *The Law of Statutory Crimes* (1873); *Commentaries on the Law of Married Women* (2 vols., 1873–75); *Doctrines of the Law of Contracts in their principal outlines,* a small elementary work (1875); *Commentaries on the Written Law and their Interpretation* (1882); *Prosecution and Defence* (1885), a book of forms and practise; *Commentaries on the Law of Contracts* (1887), designed to supersede his smaller work on this subject; *Commentaries on the Non-contract Law . . . or the Everyday Rights and Torts* (1889); *New Commentaries on Marriage, Divorce and Separation* (2 vols., 1891), and *New Criminal Procedure* (2 vols., 1895–96). Occasionally he ventured into lay fields, with articles and pamphlets on current topics, the more noticeable of these being *Thoughts for the Times* (1863); *Secession and Slavery* (1863), *Look and Think: Strikes and their related Questions* (1886), and *Common Law and Codification* (1888). His life was uneventful. He never aspired to public office of any kind, and early in his career refused the appointment of chief justice of the Hawaiian Islands offered him by King Kamehameha III. He died at Cambridge, Mass.

Though Bishop's books varied greatly in merit, they maintained, considering the large and constant output, a surprisingly high standard of excellence, combining extreme accuracy and clear style with effective exposition. He always worked entirely independently of previous writers on the subjects he treated. His *Commentaries on Marriage, Divorce and Separation* and his *Criminal Law* have become classics. His early years were one long indomitable struggle in an environment of poverty, and his after life was characterized by incessant industry in his chosen vocation. An unfortunate peculiarity of an otherwise admirable personality was his inordinate self-esteem. A leading law periodical, criticizing one of his prefaces in his lifetime, did not hesitate to say that it was "characterized by the most enormous vanity, a quality in which this author surpassed every other man of distinction since the death of Cicero" (*American Law Review,* XXVII, 939).

[Bishop by request contributed to the *Central Law Jour.,* XX, 321, a brief resumé of the first forty years of his life—valuable as the only record of that period, but he gave no particular phases of his work and character; in *Am. Law Rev.* XXXVI, 1 is an article intimate and appreciative, which fills up the gaps in his autobiographical sketch.]
                                        H. W. H. K.

BISHOP, NATHAN (Aug. 12, 1808–Aug. 7, 1880), educator, philanthropist, was born in Vernon, N. Y., and died in Saratoga Springs, N. Y. He was the eldest son of Elnathan and Statira (Sperry) Bishop, both of New England stock. His education was secured by dint of great personal effort. When eighteen, as a student in the academy at Hamilton, he found time to teach the lower classes. In 1832 he entered Brown University, but, owing to school-keeping, private tutoring, acting as bell-ringer, milking the president's cows, and other activities, he did not graduate until 1837. The next year he served as tutor in mathematics; in 1842 he became a member of the board of trustees; in 1849–50 he coöperated with Dr. Wayland in plans for reorganization and served as solicitor of the $125,000 subscription sought; and in 1854–61 he was made a member of the Board of Fellows. In 1838 the public school system of Providence was reorganized, provision being made for a superintendent of public schools. To this Bishop was chosen, and from 1839 to 1851 he served so acceptably that it was said that the Providence schools ranked with the first in the country. His success gained recognition beyond the state; in 1851 he was appointed superintendent of public schools in Boston, where he served six years. Good judgment, scholarship, business ability, and kindliness contributed to his success in education and philanthropy. His *Reports* during his superintendency show the outstanding character of his work and were responsible for extending his educational influence beyond the confines of the state. By fortunate investment of his limited income from teaching he became independent. In 1857 he gave up teaching and moved to New York, where in 1858 he married Caroline (Cauldwell) Bleecker, widow of Garrat Noel Bleecker. Because of the financial stringency of the times, he did not enter the publishing business, as he had planned, but devoted his remaining years to denominational, educational, and philanthropic work. Several engagements of this nature came now in quick succession; during the Civil War he was chairman of the executive committee of the United States Christian Commission; in 1867 he was appointed a member of the Board of State Commissioners of Public Charities; he was one of the first trustees named by Matthew Vassar for Vassar College; and in 1865 he was elected to the board of managers of the American Bible Society. He took a leading part in the work of the New York Sabbath Committee (1859); the American Branch of the Evangelical Alliance (1866)—in the interests of which he was sent to Russia in 1870; the American Revision Committee—both as contributor and chairman of the finance committee; and the American Baptist Home Mission Society, to which he rendered conspicuous service. Being named by President Grant to the Board of United States Indian Commissioners in 1869, he went with others to visit certain tribes in the Southwest. While thus engaged, he contracted malaria, from which he never fully recovered.

[The best sources are: *A Layman's Ministry* (n.d.); *Baptist Home Missions in North America: 1832–82* (1883); the Necrology in the *Providence Daily Jour.*, June 15, 1881; and official records of Providence and Boston public schools, 1839–51 and 1852–57. Long obituaries appeared in the *N. Y. Eve. Post*, Aug. 7, 1880, *N. Y. Tribune*, Aug. 8, 1880. There are also sketches and appreciations in the *Baptist Weekly*, Aug. 12, 1880, and the *Examiner and Chronicle*, Aug. 12, Aug. 26, Sept. 9, 1880.]   T. W.

BISHOP, ROBERT ROBERTS (Mar. 30, 1834–Oct. 7, 1909), lawyer and jurist, was born in Medfield, Mass., the son of Jonathan Parker and Eliza (Harding) Bishop. The father was a country lawyer who lived on a farm and had sat in the state legislature. At the age of sixteen the boy entered Phillips Academy, Andover, working his way through school and learning the meaning of scholarship under a great teacher, Samuel H. Taylor. Graduating in 1854, he studied law with the firm of Brooks and Ball, in Boston, simultaneously pursuing the regular course at Harvard Law School, from which he took a degree in 1857. He married, Dec. 24, 1857, in Holliston, Mass., Mary Helen Bullard. In 1861 he moved to Newton, Mass., where he spent the remainder of his life.

For a brief period, while establishing himself in his profession, he was a law reporter for the *Boston Daily Advertiser*. In 1861 he associated himself with Thornton K. Lothrop in the firm of Lothrop & Bishop, which conducted many important litigations before its dissolution in 1879. Bishop entered public life as a Republican in 1874, through an election to the Massachusetts House of Representatives, but he declined a second term because of his duties as a member of the Newton Water Board, which was then completing a system of water-works for that city. He became a state senator in 1878 and was reëlected for three successive years, being the president of the Senate for 1880, 1881, and 1882. During his term of office he published *The Senate of Massachusetts: an Historical Sketch* (1882), which is the authoritative book on the subject.

In 1882, after a contest in the Republican convention at Worcester, Bishop received the nomination of his party for governor. The Democratic candidate was the aggressive Benjamin F. Butler, who, in an acrimonious campaign, defeated Bishop, 133,946 to 119,997. Various factors, including the prevailing discontent and a desire for a change of party at any cost, affected the result. On Mar. 7, 1888, Bishop was appointed associate justice of the Massachusetts Superior Court, a position which was most congenial to him. On the bench he was distinguished by his unfailing courtesy, his careful consideration of cases, his patience and open-mindedness, his dignity, and his complete impartiality. While still on the bench, he died in his seventy-sixth year, after a brief illness from pneumonia. He was a deliberate and thoughtful man, of conservative tendencies, who once said of himself, "I am not much for speed, but I think I have staying qualities." The *Boston Evening Transcript* said of him editorially, "In a judiciary justly renowned for integrity and acquirement he held deserved prominence."

[The *Green Bag* for Jan. 1911 (vol. XXIII, no. 1) has an excellent article on Bishop, written by Jos. T. Bishop. The *Proceedings of the Suffolk Bar and Superior Court in Memory of Judge Bishop*, Dec. 18, 1909, were printed and published in 1911. The *Boston Evening Transcript* for Oct. 8, 1909, has a full obituary.]

C.M.F.

BISHOP, SETH SCOTT (Feb. 7, 1852–Sept. 6, 1923), Chicago laryngologist, the son of Lyman Bishop by his wife, Maria Probart, was born at Fond du Lac, Wis., and obtained his early education at the Pooler Institute of his native town. He attended Beloit Academy (1872–73) and passed two academic years at Beloit College (1873–75), but was forced to leave college "on account of his eyes" and did not obtain an academic degree. Despite his eyes he evidently made rapid progress in medical work, for he obtained his M.D. from Northwestern University in 1876. He also studied medicine for a short time at New York University, and supported himself during his early years of practise by learning the printer's trade. Though at first a general practitioner, he later limited his work to the diseases of the ear, nose, and throat. In 1887 he was awarded first prize by the United States Hay-fever Association for an essay upon the etiology and treatment of hay-fever (*Journal of the American Medical Association*, July 23, 1887). He was later appointed to the chair of otology, rhinology, and laryngology at Loyola University School of Medicine, and he held a similar position at the Chicago Post-Graduate Medical School. He became surgeon to the Jefferson Park Hospital, the Illinois Charitable Eye and Ear Infirmary, and consulting surgeon to several other religious institutions. From 1912 until his death, Bishop was a member of the board of contributing editors of the New York *Medical Times*. He was also an early editor of the *Illinois Medical Bulletin,* which ran from 1902 to 1908. His chief contributions to medicine were his two well-illustrated text-books, *Diseases of the Ear, Nose and Throat and Their Accessory Cavities; a Condensed Textbook* (1897), the third edition of which appeared in 1904, and *The Ear and Its Diseases, a Textbook for Students and Physicians* (1906). In the preface of the latter work he refers to the unprecedented sale of his first text-book and states that both were based upon the case records of an active practise extending over twenty-five years. Though his works were well illustrated, his style of writing was not always lucid. On page 415 (Fig. 199) of his second text-book is a photograph of the author. He was married Mar. 23, 1885, to Jessie A. Button.

[*Medic. Times*, N. Y., LI, 243; *Jour. Am. Medic. Ass.*, Chicago, LXXXI, 945; *Ill. Medic. Jour.*, XLIV, 304; *Who's Who in America*, 1922–23; private information.]

J.F.F.

BISHOP, WILLIAM DARIUS (Sept. 14, 1827–Feb. 4, 1904), railway official, was the son of Alfred and Mary (Ferris) Bishop, and was born in Bloomfield, Essex County, N. J. Having been graduated from Yale in 1849, he shortly became a director of the Naugatuck Railroad, which Alfred Bishop, who was a railway contractor, had built through the Naugatuck Valley of Connecticut from Bridgeport to Winsted. W. D. Bishop was first made superintendent of this road and then in 1855 was chosen to its presidency. In 1850 he had married Julia A. Tomlinson of Bridgeport. He was elected in 1857 a Democratic member of the Thirty-fifth Congress; and when he failed of reëlection was appointed United States commissioner of patents by President Buchanan. During his brief term as commissioner (1859–60), he is said to have done good service, especially in putting in order the Patent Office records and in systematizing the work of his subordinates. In May 1866 he left the presidency of the Naugatuck to take up that of the New York & New Haven. Under his régime, the New York & New Haven acquired both the Hartford & Connecticut Valley and the Harlem & Port Chester, and leased the Shore Line. With this consolidation, the road became increasingly powerful. So late as 1885 there were as many as twenty-two railroads in Connecticut; and it must be said that from the earliest days of railway building in the state the influence of the numerous separate companies, as they contended or united with one another in order to control legislation and obtain special privileges, had been far from beneficial in public affairs. During Bishop's administration, the New York & New Haven system gained an ascendancy it never lost. While he was executive head of this system, Bishop was admitted to the Fairfield County bar (1870), represented Bridgeport in the General Assembly (1872), was a state senator, 1866, 1877, 1878, and had a conspicuous part in general railway legislation. Extensive and thoroughgoing improvements were made by him in local railroad conveniences at Bridgeport. He was a director of the Bridgeport Steamboat Company, operating between Bridgeport and New York; and also of the Housatonic Railroad, extending from Bridgeport to Pittsfield, Mass. In March 1879 he retired from the presidency of the New York & New Haven, but until his death he remained upon the board of directors. In 1883 he was once more called to be president of the Naugatuck, and he held this office until his retirement in October 1903. Although in over a half-century of busy life he engaged in many activities, yet primarily he was a railroad man, and it was in problems of railway construction and management that he found his chief interest. His formal practise of the law was largely confined to a few patent cases of more or less importance.

[The sources of information regarding Bishop are mainly: Lewis and Calhoun, *The Judicial and Civil Hist. of Conn.* (1895); N. G. Osborn, *Men of Mark in Conn.* (1906); *Geneal. and Family Hist. of the State of Conn.* (ed. by W. R. Cutter and others, 1911); *Obit. Record Grads. Yale Univ.* (1910).]   G.S.B.

BISPHAM, DAVID SCULL (Jan. 5, 1857–Oct. 2, 1921), baritone, was the son of William D. Bispham of old Jersey Revolutionary stock, and of Jane Scull, daughter of a Philadelphia Quaker family, who would not allow a piano in her home. David Bispham was born in the latter city, and one of his earliest recollections was "seeing men armed with shotguns jump on the Market Street horse-cars to take the first train to Gettysburg during Lee's invasion of Pennsylvania." An eight months' tour of Europe at the age of twenty-one fanned to flame the repressed musical leanings of his childhood, and in 1880 he began to appear as a singer in amateur stage performances and in the choirs of St. Mark's and Holy Trinity churches in Philadelphia. Returning to Europe, definitely committed to a musical career, he studied from 1886 to 1890 in Florence under Vannuccini and Lamperti, and in London under Shakespeare and Randegger. He made his début on Nov. 3, 1891, at the Royal English Opera House, London, as the Duc de Longueville in Messager's comic opera *La Basoche*. On June 25, 1892—he had continued to sing in comic opera in the meantime—he made his first appearance as a dramatic baritone in serious opera as Kurwenal in *Parsifal*, at the Drury Lane Theatre. This at once established his reputation as a "singing actor"; he continued to sing in opera in London, and from 1896 to 1909 divided his time between Covent Garden and the Metropolitan Opera House in New York. At the same time he achieved a reputation as a singer in oratorio and on the concert stage (the Christ in Bach's *The Passion According to St. Matthew*, and the baritone solos in the Perosi oratorios may be mentioned in the former connection); while his recitals in London and New York were so successful that, in a measure, they overshadowed his operatic achievement so that after 1909 he gave up the opera stage to devote himself almost exclusively to recital work. He had studied and sung in Bayreuth, however, and was considered one of the best Wagnerian baritones of his day: aside from Beckmesser, Wolf-

ram, Alberich, Wotan, and Hunding, his forty-odd rôles included Verdi's Falstaff, Boito's Mefisto, Mascagni's Alfio, and Humperdinck's Peter. In the United States he created the part of Chillingworth in Walter Damrosch's *Scarlet Letter*. Endowed with a personality of much charm, a thorough artist in every sense, and a man of the highest culture, Bispham's real histrionic gifts and command of a notably flexible and sonorous vocal organ were paired with an intense musical temperament. After 1918 he devoted most of his time to teaching, and published two volumes of "Bispham Songs." The singer's married life was not happy: and in 1908 he separated from his wife, Caroline Russell, daughter of the late Gen. Charles Russell, whom he had married on April 28, 1885. Though he wrote no "method," his autobiography, *A Quaker Singer's Recollections,* contains much information regarding his ideals and their development; and practical hints for the vocal student are contained in a series of three articles by Herbert Wilber Greene entitled "Quotations from a Conversation with David Bispham" in the *Musical Observer,* February, March, April, 1919. Bispham's service in establishing high standards in the American song recital field is beyond question. He gave recitals of Beethoven, Schubert, Schumann, and the best older and modern French and Italian songs in English (being the first to sing Brahms' *Four Serious Songs* in the United States). In the moot question as to whether foreign songs should be sung in their original tongues in the United States and Great Britain he advocated the use of English, writing "Ever since the production of 'The Vicar of Wakefield' in London (1906) . . . I have been more than ever addicted to the use of our own language in my concerts. . . . To all American singers I say, sing your songs in well-chosen English, if singing to an English-speaking audience, and sing them so that every one understands your words. . . . Get away from this foreign language fad and you will find yourself nearer the heart of the audience" (*A Quaker Singer's Recollections,* p. 342). Bispham's undeviating stand at a time when the artistic pros and cons of the question were hotly debated was influential in encouraging the employ of the vernacular in American song recital.

[The principal source is Bispham's enjoyable and humorous autobiography, *A Quaker Singer's Recollections* (1920). The articles in *Grove's Encyc. of Music and Musicians* (1904), I, 333, and *Am. Supp.* (1920), p. 133, are full and reliable, and the notice in Theodore Baker's *Biog. Dict. of Musicians* (3rd rev. ed., 1919) also calls for mention. A readable sketch of Bispham's life appeared in *Musical America,* Oct. 8, 1921, and his name frequently occurs in the memoirs of contemporaries: Hermann Klein, *Music and Mummers* (1925);

Walter Damrosch, *My Musical Life* (1923) ; James M. Glover, *Jimmy Glover, His Book* (3rd ed., 1911).]

F.H.M.

BISSELL, EDWIN CONE (Mar. 2, 1832–Apr. 10, 1894), Congregational clergyman, the son of George C. and Elizabeth (White) Bissell, was born in Schoharie, N. Y. He prepared for college at Monson Academy, graduated from Amherst in 1855, for one year taught at Williston Seminary, Easthampton, Mass., and then began his theological studies at Hartford Theological Seminary, finishing them at Union Theological Seminary, N. Y., in 1859. During the latter year he married Emily Pomeroy, daughter of Col. Oren Pomeroy of Somers, Conn. In September 1859 he was ordained to the ministry in West Hampton, Mass., where he remained as pastor of the Congregational church until 1864. During this pastorate he organized Company K of the 52nd Massachusetts Volunteers and for the year 1862–63 served as their captain at the front. In 1864 he became pastor of the Green Street Congregational Church in San Francisco, remaining until 1869 and serving also two years as editor of *The Pacific.* For a year after this (1869–70) he served as pastor of the Fort Street Church in Honolulu, H. I., but was called thence to the Congregational Church in Winchester, Mass., where he remained until 1873. His varied experience in the pastorate was then still further diversified by five years' service under the A.B.C.F.M. as missionary in Austria, working among the Bohemians of Gratz. He returned to America in 1878 and spent two years of special study at Boston and then spent a year or two more in Germany at the University of Leipzig. This diversion of his activities toward a teaching career may perhaps be ascribed to his having published during his pastorate at Winchester a small volume entitled *The Historic Origin of the Bible* (1873), which won for him in 1874 the honorary degree of D.D. from his alma mater, an honor later duplicated by Lake Forest University. In 1880 he published a revised translation with introduction and notes of *The Apocrypha of the Old Testament,* being Volume XV of the American edition of Lange's Commentaries and in the following year was made Nettleton professor of Hebrew language and literature in Hartford Theological Seminary. This position he held until 1892, when he resigned to become professor of Hebrew in McCormick Presbyterian Theological Seminary in Chicago, where he served until his death. He was a patient and painstaking teacher, interesting himself in the questions of historical criticism and documentary analysis which were then beginning to agitate the American church, and devot-

ing to them a large number of contributions to reviews and periodicals. His chief work, *The Pentateuch, Its Origin and Structure,* appeared in 1885, to be followed in 1888 by *Biblical Antiquities,* in 1891 by a text-book on Hebrew Grammar, and in 1892 by the Book of Genesis printed in colors. In all these works he defended the traditional view, applying his linguistic knowledge against the now dominant theory of the Graf-Wellhausen school.

[*Biog. Record Alumni Amherst Coll.* (1883) ; *Obit. Record Grads. Amherst Coll.* (1894) ; C. D. Hartranft, *Memorial Address* (1894) ; *Springfield Republican* and *Hartford Times,* Apr. 11, 1894.]

B.W.B.

BISSELL, GEORGE EDWIN (Feb. 16, 1839–Aug. 30, 1920), sculptor, was descended from Huguenot ancestors who came to America in 1632 and settled at Windsor, Conn. George was born at New Preston, Conn., to Hiram Bissell, a quarryman, and his wife, Isabella Jones. About 1853 the family moved to Waterbury, where George became a clerk in a store. His education was received partly at the Northville Academy and partly at the Gunnery, Washington, Conn. The latter school he entered when he came of age, intending to prepare for college. The Civil War, however, changed his plans, for, after teaching in a district school for a few months, he enlisted as a private in the 23rd Regiment of the Connecticut Volunteers, in which he served 1862–63. When his company was mustered out he became a paymaster in the United States Navy (1863–65). After the war he married, on Aug. 16, 1865, Mary E. Welton of Waterbury, and soon after joined his father and brother in the marble business in Poughkeepsie, N. Y. Without any previous training he took to making designs and models for monuments. His first commission (1871) was a life-size marble figure of a fireman for the Fire Department of Poughkeepsie. In 1875 he went to Europe, studying in Paris, Florence, and Rome. At Paris, either at this time or later, he worked under Aimé Millet and Tabar. In 1876 he was a pupil at the English Academy in Rome. On his return to Poughkeepsie he did a number of portrait busts. From 1878 dates the colossal granite figure for the John C. Booth family monument. From 1883 to 1896 his time was largely divided between Paris and Poughkeepsie. Among his works dating from this period are: "Soldiers' Monument" (1883–84) and "Col. John L. Chatfield" (1887), both in Waterbury; "Gen. Gates" on the Saratoga Battle Monument at Schuylerville, N. Y.; "Lincoln" (1893), Edinburgh, Scotland; "Standard Bearer," Winsted, Conn.; "Union," Salisbury, Conn.; "Chancellor John Watts," Trinity

Churchyard, N. Y.; "James Kent," in the Congressional Library. All these works show his realistic tendency, though in non-portrait figures, such as those on the Waterbury monument, his realism is somewhat tempered. In 1896 he settled in Mt. Vernon, N. Y., and in the same year did the "Abraham de Peyster" for New York City, a much reduced variant of which is in the Metropolitan Museum, where also is a marble bust of Mary Justina de Peyster. Though continuing to live at Mt. Vernon until his death, he kept a studio in Florence from 1903 to 1905 and from 1907 to 1909. In 1898 he made the "President Arthur," in New York; in 1899 the navy group on the colonnade of the arch temporarily erected on the occasion of Admiral Dewey's return; and in 1900 "Lycurgus" on the Appellate Court building. For the Pan-American Exposition he made "Hospitality," and for the Louisiana Purchase Exposition "Science" and "Music." At this latter exposition he received a silver medal. The Elton Memorial Vase in Waterbury at the entrance of Riverside Cemetery, where are a number of other monuments by him, was made in 1905. Among his remaining works many are widely scattered: "Lincoln" at Clermont, Ia.; "Burns and Highland Mary" (a relief) at Ayr, Scotland; a colossal bust of Admiral Dahlgren on the Civil War Memorial in Philadelphia; "Samuel Sloan" in Hoboken, N. J.; and "John Starin" in Fultonville, N. Y. Though he turned to sculpture somewhat late, his output, during his long life, was considerable. His works show a seeking for realism, often tempered, however, by a certain amount of idealization. In his best works there is dignity and restraint. He was a charter member of the National Sculpture Society. A genial, kindly person, in temperament and appearance, he was affectionately termed "Père Bissell" by the younger sculptors who knew him, and in his family the same traits made him beloved.

[*The Town and City of Waterbury,* ed. by Jos. Anderson (1896), III, 1037; *Who's Who in America,* 1920–21; *N. Y. Times,* Aug. 31, 1920; *Hartford Times,* Aug. 31, 1920; Lorado Taft, *Hist. of Am. Sculpture* (rev. ed., 1924, pp. 245–47; *Am. Art Annual,* ed. by F. N. Levy, XIV; *Internat. Studio,* vol. XXVIII (Apr. 1906), p. xliii.]　　　　　　　　　　　E. G. N.

BISSELL, GEORGE HENRY (Nov. 8, 1821–Nov. 19, 1884), promoter of the petroleum industry, was born at Hanover, N. H., the son of Isaac and Nina (Wempe) Bissell, of Norman and Belgian descent, respectively. He attended the military school at Norwich, Vt., the Kimball Union Academy at Meriden, N. H., and Dartmouth College, where he was graduated in 1845. For a short time he was professor of languages at the University of Norwich but soon resigned to go to Washington, D. C., as correspondent for the Richmond *Whig.* He then spent a short time in Cuba before going to New Orleans, where he was on the editorial staff of the New Orleans *Delta.* In 1846 he was elected first principal of the new high school and later became superintendent of the New Orleans schools. During this period he also studied law and graduated LL.B. from Jefferson College. Because of ill health he was compelled to return north, going to New York City, where he was admitted to the bar (1853) and began the practise of law in partnership with J. G. Eveleth. In 1855 he was married to Ophie Griffin of New York City. While on a visit to Dartmouth College his attention was drawn to a sample of petroleum from the Oil Creek region, Pennsylvania, which so interested him that he sent his partner to investigate the source. Finding a ready demand for petroleum, the bulk of which was then used for medicinal purposes, Bissell and Eveleth bought and leased 200 acres of oil lands for $5,000 and in 1854 organized "The Pennsylvania Rock Oil Company," the first oil company in the United States, with a nominal capital of $500,000. The company proceeded to develop the land by digging wells and trenching—the crude method then used—to collect the surface oil. Since the return from the sale proved insufficient to pay expenses, a sample of the petroleum was sent to Prof. Silliman of Yale for analysis in the hope that more valuable use for the oil would suggest itself. Prof. Silliman's report gave information concerning the fractional distillation of the crude and concluded with the belief that "the company have in their possession a raw material from which by simple and inexpensive processes they may manufacture very valuable products." When this report was published the company was reorganized with Prof. Silliman as president, and the work of trenching and digging continued until 1858. The next development was that of boring for oil in the manner of artesian wells, as is done to-day. There is no doubt that Bissell was the first to suggest this important innovation but the story of how it occurred to him has many versions. It is most probable that the salt wells in the oil district suggested oil wells of the same type. When the first drilled well had been sunk by the Seneca Oil Company, lessees of the Pennsylvania Rock Oil Company (1859), Bissell moved to Franklin, Pa., and with Eveleth invested more than $300,000 in oil lands. Returning to New York (1863), he devoted the rest of his life to the promotion of enterprises connected with the petroleum industry.

[*Hist. of Venango County, Pa.* (1879), ed. by J. H. Newton; *A Pop. Hist. of Am. Invention* (1924), ed. by W. B. Kaempffert; Ida M. Tarbell, *Hist. of the Standard Oil Co.* (1904); obituary in *N. Y. Herald,* Nov. 20, 1884.]

F. A. T—r.

BISSELL, WILLIAM HENRY (Apr. 25, 1811–Mar. 18, 1860), congressman, governor of Illinois, came of poor parents living in Yates County, N. Y., but he secured a fair common school education, graduated from Jefferson Medical School, Philadelphia, in 1834, and took up the practise of medicine in Monroe County, Ill. Known for his ability as a public speaker, he was induced to become a candidate on the Democratic ticket, for a seat in the lower house of the state legislature, and although the county was considered a Whig stronghold he was elected. The experience of two years proving agreeable, he then attended a law school in Lexington, Ky., in preparation for a political career. Meantime (1839) he married Emily James, who died the following year, and in 1841 he married Elizabeth Kane. As a lawyer at Belleville, Ill., he quickly took rank among the best in that circuit and was elected prosecuting attorney. It was said to be a hopeless task "to defend where he was prosecuting." Though modest and courteous in manner, he was capable of arousing the passions by his choice language, his keen humor, and his cutting satire. His legal career was interrupted by the Mexican War. Enlisting as a private, he was elected captain and then colonel of the 2nd Illinois, a regiment which was highly rated for its service at the battle of Buena Vista on Feb. 23, 1847. On his return Bissell was elected a representative in Congress, without opposition, in 1848 and again in 1850. Because of a speech during his first term he gained a national reputation. In reply to a Virginia member who claimed that it was a Mississippi regiment which saved the day at Buena Vista, Bissell declared that at the critical moment this regiment was not within a mile and a half of the scene of action (*Congressional Globe,* 31 Cong. 1 Sess., vol. XXII, pt. I, App. p. 228). For this assertion he was challenged to a duel by Jefferson Davis, colonel of the Mississippi regiment. The challenge was accepted, but President Zachary Taylor brought about an adjustment. In opposition to the Southern leadership of the national Democratic party, Bissell announced himself as an independent candidate for Congress in 1852 and was elected. Unable to take part in debate because of illness due to exposure in the army and a partial paralytic stroke, which forced him to go on crutches for the remainder of his life, he was now about to abandon politics. But in the first Republican convention at Bloomington, Ill.

(May 29, 1856), wherein were Abraham Lincoln, John M. Palmer, Gustav Koerner, and other well-known representatives from the several political parties, Bissell was the unanimous choice for governor. In the election, he led the state ticket to victory, receiving a plurality of 4,729 votes over the Democratic nominee. The Democrats, however, were in control in both houses of the legislature and united in their opposition to any policy proposed by the Governor. He was bitterly attacked at the opening of the session by John A. Logan on the ground that as a challenger or one who had accepted a challenge to a duel he had sworn falsely in taking the oath of office. In reply, Bissell stated that whatever occurred was outside the jurisdiction of the State of Illinois and therefore did not interfere with his taking the oath. Governor and legislature came to grips over his demand for a law providing for the redistricting of the state based on the census of 1855. The Democrats determined to keep their ascendancy by a bill which gerrymandered the state. Having passed both houses, the measure was sent to Bissell, who refused to sign it. Numbers of Republicans having withdrawn, the bill could not be passed over his veto, and the legislature was forced to adjourn without action on a large number of appropriation measures and on several hundred bills. Some ten months before the expiration of his term of office, Bissell's death occurred, due to an attack of pneumonia, and thus "it was not granted him to see the cause victorious for which he had so nobly fought" (*Memoirs of Gustav Koerner,* 1909, II, 80).

[Jos. Gillespie, *Recollections of Early Illinois,* Fergus Hist. Series 11–15; *Pubs. Illinois Hist. Lib.,* no. 9 (1904), no. 10 (1905); John M. Palmer, *Bench and Bar of Illinois* (1899); Arthur C. Cole, *Era of the Civil War* (1919).]

J. A. J.

BISSELL, WILSON SHANNON (Dec. 31, 1847–Oct. 6, 1903), lawyer, was born in Oneida County, N. Y., of Scotch-Irish stock, and at the age of five was taken to Buffalo by his parents, John and Isabella Jeannette (Hally) Bissell. Destined for the law, he was sent to school in New Haven, Conn., and he was graduated at Yale in 1869. Two years later he was admitted to the bar, and soon became associated with the firm of lawyers to which Grover Cleveland belonged,—in the same office from which Millard Fillmore had gone to the vice-presidency of the United States in 1849. Bissell's friendship with Cleveland, who was ten years his senior, lasted for the rest of his life. He accompanied Cleveland to Albany when the latter was inaugurated as governor of New York in 1883. He appears to have declined a position in the first cabinet that Cleveland formed, in 1885; but he accepted the post office in the second cabinet in 1893. His two years as postmaster general were not productive of novel results in administration, or of happiness to himself. After two years of a prosaic and honorable business administration, disliking the burdens of patronage and the publicity of office, he resigned and returned to his law practise. His permanent satisfactions came from his work as counsel for railroad and other corporations, and from his association with the non-political activities of Buffalo. The Buffalo Historical Society found in him an active, though non-producing member, and owes him much for his services in procuring the notable building that houses its collections. He was a friend to the struggling University of Buffalo, which had been no more than a group of professional schools until, about 1900, it prepared to launch a college of liberal arts. Bissell became chancellor of the University in 1902, holding a position which had generally been ornamental since the day when Millard Fillmore held it. He died in the second year of his office, and was survived by his widow, Louisa Fowler (Sturges) Bissell, whom he had married in 1889.

[*Obit. Record Grads. Yale Univ.* (1910); *Sixth Biog. Record Class of 'Sixty-Nine, Yale Coll.* (1895); H. W. Hill, *Municipality of Buffalo* (1923), II, 904; *Pubs. Buffalo Hist. Soc.,* VII, 488; *Buffalo Express,* Oct. 7, 1903.]

F.L.P.

BITTER, KARL THEODORE FRANCIS (Dec. 6, 1867–Apr. 10, 1915), sculptor, of sound burgher stock, arrived in New York in his twenty-first year, without money, without friends, without English. To offset these lacks, he had health, intelligence, energy, and a passion for art. He had also a valuable though brief experience in decorative modeling, gained at a time when his native Vienna was undergoing great changes, morally and intellectually, the historic city wall having been razed to make way for the famous Ring, with its façades blooming with sculpture. What Bitter brought with him made the foundation of his success. For, working obscurely with his mates to adorn Vienna, he had already formed ideals of coöperation, of leadership, of civic pride, of the importance of beauty in a city's life.

His father, Carl Bitter, was a Protestant who, with his journeyman's kit on his back, had come from Baden in South Germany to seek his fortune in Vienna, where later he became a chemist. He married Henriette Reitter, a Catholic, by whom he had three sons. Karl Theodore Francis, or as he called himself, Karl, was the second

of these, and grew up a headstrong, beauty-loving child, with his father's independence, his mother's idealism, and a keen mind of his own. After a period at the Volksschule, he went to the Gymnasium. Here, when he was ten years of age, his encounters with the all-important Latin grammar were markedly unsuccessful. In explanation to his parents, he declared, as an ingenious defense, that the Latin teacher was so ugly to look at that one simply could not learn. As Karl had the gift of eloquence and an interest in affairs, his father had planned for him a career in law, while his mother, a devout woman, had dreamed of the priesthood. But without Latin, what hope in either field? The boy was not sorry. Near his home was a stoneyard, where he had spent magical hours watching the workmen, until at length he was allowed to try his hand. He thereupon became an apprentice, of sorts, in his spare moments. When his anxious parents found it out, they concluded that it was better to let nature, which in Karl's case was art, take its course. He was entered at the Kunstgewerbeschule, the imperial school for applied arts, from which, when old enough, he passed to the Kunstakademie. Attending these schools from 1882 to 1887, he was eager, tireless, filled with delight in his work, and often an arrogant leader of rebellion against the less progressive instructors. When he was twenty, his studies, together with his labors as an obscure assistant in Vienna's adornment, were interrupted by his call to military service. Most of his comrades were regarded as professional students, and therefore were to serve but one year. Bitter, however, had left the Gymnasium too early to have the required certificate, and so was drafted for three years. This injustice he felt keenly. After serving faithfully one year, he took matters into his own hands, renounced his allegiance, and fled to Germany, where he picked up a living as best he might, en route for America. In Berlin he found a friend in a former comrade, Rudolph Schwartz, who aided him with money for his passage, and for his immediate needs in a strange land.

The day after he reached New York, Bitter found work at the first door at which he knocked. He had stumbled on a firm of architectural modelers. Having no English, he let his drawings and photographs speak for him. He was shown some clay, with a crude indication of an angel within it, and was motioned to go to work. He obeyed to such purpose that at the end of a week he received to his amazement a pay envelope of $48. His modeling in this shop met the kindly eye of Richard M. Hunt, the famous architect.

Hunt urged him to set up for himself, promising him considerable interior sculpture for the C. P. Huntington house, then under way. Bitter's talent and training made him just the sculptor Hunt had long been looking for, namely, a facile, imaginative modeler, versed in ornament. That Bitter's gift had also its serious side appears from the fact that in 1891, sixteen months after his arrival in New York, he won the competition for the most important of the three bronze gates of Trinity Church, provided for by the John Jacob Astor bequest, the subject of the competitive panel being "The Expulsion from Paradise." Then came the Chicago Exposition. As Hunt's protégé, Bitter distinguished himself in the elaborate scheme of sculptural decoration for Hunt's Administration Building at the head of the Court of Honor, a scheme in which battalions of forms at once decorative and functional embossed the whole structure with their impassioned story of "The Elements, Controlled and Uncontrolled" (1893). "The zest which he put into these themes," says Taft, "revealed a temperament of singular power and intrepidity, if not a mature taste." The public admired, the architects admired, and thereafter Bitter had no lack of orders for such work. A fifty-foot pediment in terra cotta over the main entrance to the Pennsylvania Railroad Station in Philadelphia, a thirty-foot panel in the waiting-room, and ten panels celebrating the cities along the line had an undisciplined grace that took the public eye (1894). His next achievement was a host of interior and exterior sculptures, of fluent technique and admirable variety, in relief and in the round, in stone, wood, bronze, and polished steel, created to adorn "Biltmore," the Vanderbilt villa in North Carolina (1895). During the following year he completed three colossal stone atlantes, representing the White, Negro, and Malay races, for the façade of the St. Paul Building, in New York, and three years later he undertook the four figures, Architecture, Sculpture, Painting, and Music, for the front of the Metropolitan Museum. In 1899 he made his contribution, a spirited naval group, to that extraordinary sculptural improvisation, the Dewey Arch.

In his bronze statue of Dr. William Pepper, provost of the University of Pennsylvania, a meditative seated figure in academic gown, Bitter expressed himself with a deeper significance than ever before (1898). But the architects were still clamoring for his decorative work, and his gift of leadership still kept him at the head of a group of assistants profitably turning out an amazing amount of architect's fodder, even while he himself longed to make some nobler use of his power. In 1896 he gave up his New York establishment for a romantic site at Weehawken, building there in due season, house, studio, stable. He was not only the maker of equestrian groups, such as the dashing "Standard Bearers" of the Buffalo Exposition (1901), called by Saint-Gaudens the finest of the Exposition sculptures, and the noble presentment of Gen. Sigel on Riverside Drive, New York (1907), he was also a lover of the horse; and his horseback exercise doubtless contributed to his soldierly erectness of bearing. Tall, slender, dark-haired, dark-eyed, dark-bearded, Bitter had nothing of the Teuton in his aspect. Perhaps his military experience was a help to him in his able leadership of the workers associated with him while he was director of sculpture at the Pan-American Exposition (1899–1901), at the St. Louis World's Fair (1902-04), and even at the Panama-Pacific Exposition, where his directorship was generally advisory rather than personal (1912–15). He was twice chosen president of the National Sculpture Society (1906, 1914), and was a member of the New York Municipal Art Commission from 1912 until his death.

On the happy conclusion of his task at the Buffalo Exposition, he was married (1901) to Marie A. Schevill of Cincinnati, Ohio, a lady of marked musical talent and of sensitive artistic appreciation. The pair went abroad for the ensuing summer, but as it was not until 1909 that Bitter received his amnesty from Franz Josef, he was obliged to meet relatives and friends outside the Austrian border. In 1910, however, he revisited his native city, and with great satisfaction renewed old ties, only to realize more fully than ever how dear to him was his American citizenship, which he had obtained as early as possible after his arrival in New York. His marriage was an ideal one. At the turn of the century, when he brought his bride to Weehawken, his first step was to reorganize his studio, "a flourishing decorative establishment," writes his biographer, Dr. Schevill, "fairly flooded with orders, and often with the appearance more of an industrial battlefield than of a retreat of an artist. One after another the helpers were dismissed, and further decorative orders, especially if they carried the unsavory odor of commercialism, rigorously refused." For Bitter, this meant temporary financial loss, and permanent spiritual gain. His draped "Thanatos," in his Hubbard Memorial at Montpelier, Vt. (1903), has often been compared with Saint-Gaudens's celebrated Rock Creek figure, but only as a lyric may be compared with an epic. In his marble Villard Memorial at Sleepy Hollow (1904) a more austere note is sounded by means of a handsome and unique architectural ensemble, the central feature of which is the undraped seated figure of a smith resting beside carved bay trees. These and other memorials reveal Bitter's valiant attempt at a farewell to the commercial element in his art. Happily he still retained the lessons learned in properly relating sculpture to architecture. He had not yet finished with expositional sculpture, however. As director of sculpture at the St. Louis Fair, he succeeded notably in evoking plastic unity of design from an assemblage of models from many hands. His own contribution is a great shaft swarming with history-telling figures. Of this work, one feature has been preserved in bronze for the Jefferson Memorial Building in St. Louis. It is a large relief in eighteenth-century vein, showing Livingston, Monroe, and Marbois signing the Purchase Treaty. The historical studies Bitter then made led him to an intense interest in early American heroes, especially Jefferson; a decade later, during the last three years of his life, he created in addition to other important works, no less than three bronze statues of Jefferson. The first was for the Jefferson Memorial Building; the second, a seated figure of heroic size, and flanked by a Hamilton, also from Bitter's hand, was placed in front of the Court House at Cleveland; the third, commissioned by his friend, Charles R. Crane, was unveiled on the grounds of the University of Virginia three days after Bitter's death. These three bronzes differ suitably in design. The first reveals Jefferson as pioneer, the last as patriarch, while the second chooses middle ground. Bitter's enormous productivity is shown by the host of works created by him and his assistants during the interval between the St. Louis Fair and the San Francisco Fair. Included are two important pediments and four heroic groups for the Wisconsin State Capitol at Madison (1908-12), four Chinese figures for the façade of the Brooklyn Museum (1909), statues of Lords Somers and Mansfield for the Court House at Cleveland (1910), and many portraits in relief or in the round. By frequent trips abroad, Bitter, master of many materials, kept himself abreast of all the new movements in art. In the granite panels for his finely conceived and nobly placed Schurz monument in New York (1913), as in the perforated marble screen behind his statue of Thomas Lowry, a leading citizen of Minneapolis (1915), and the sternly cut granite figures for the First National Bank Building in Cleveland (1908), he showed himself an adept in modern simplicity; while on the other hand, in his memorials to Dr. Angell

and to Dr. Tappan at Ann Arbor, Mich. (1910, 1913), he made a sober return to a generally useful realism of manner, not untouched by poetic idealism. The frieze of little children in his Prehn Memorial at Passaic, the graceful kneeling figure in the Kasson Memorial at Utica, the Goose Girl fountain at Pocantico Hills, and the unfinished studies for the Depew fountain for Indianapolis finely express their opposed emotions of joy and sorrow. In his relief portrait of Dr. Angell for Ann Arbor and in his bronze statue of President White of Cornell University (1915), Bitter enjoyed the opportunity, rare for sculptors, of studying his subjects from life rather than afterward.

Thus far, Bitter's gifts to his adopted country were: first, a swarm of decorative sculptures in the Viennese manner; next, a successful management of the sculptural elements in three World's Fairs, to be followed by a more permanent civic service, valuable in many directions; and last, his solid achievements as a many-sided sculptor of increasingly high ideals. He had received golden honors, including the Architectural League Medal of Honor in Sculpture (1914). Fond of music and reading, he took special pleasure in the study of history, of philosophy, of comparative religion. The headstrong youth had matured into the thoughtful, kindly man who had learned to persuade instead of to domineer. His last work, not yet put into bronze at the time of his tragic death, but faithfully completed by his friend Isidor Konti, is a calm and happy figure of "Abundance" crowning the great fountain in New York's Plaza. In a spirit of elation on the evening of the very day when he had put the last touches to his full-sized model, he and his wife attended the opera. The performance over, they started across Broadway, when suddenly an automobile out of control swept them down. Mrs. Bitter escaped with minor injuries, her husband lived but a few hours. His life was cut short before he had reached the fullness of his powers. In his latest work, every element attested and prophesied still further growth, still higher ideals.

[The most reliable information concerning Karl Bitter is found in the biography written by his brother-in-law, Dr. Ferdinand Schevill, and issued under the auspices of the National Sculpture Society in 1917. From 1891 until after Bitter's death, numerous articles in the press and in magazines chronicled his activities. See esp. *Sketch Book*, VI, 1; *Brush and Pencil*, XIII, 199, 466; *Am. Art News*, XIII, 4; *Am. Arch.*, CVII, 274; *Art and Progress*, VI, 285, 295; *Arch. Record*, XLII, 280. Bitter's work is described in Lorado Taft's *Hist. of Am. Sculpture* (1903), and in the same author's *Modern Tendencies in Sculpture* (1921).]   A. A—s.

BIXBY, HORACE EZRA (May 8, 1826–Aug. 1, 1912), Mississippi pilot, was born in Geneseo,

N. Y., the son of Sylvanus Bixby and his wife, Hannah Barnes, who had been the widow of Benjamin Kneeland. In his early teens he ran away from home and wandered as far as Cincinnati, where he found work in a tailor's shop. At eighteen he became a "mud clerk" on the river steamboat *Olivia* and two years later was made her pilot. The rest of his long life was passed on the Mississippi and her great tributaries. He soon was known as a "lightning pilot"—one whose courage, judgment, and knowledge of the uncharted, unmarked, ever changing river were equal to any emergency, and his services were usually required on the large boats plying between St. Louis and New Orleans. But in April 1857 he happened to be taking an "ancient tub" from Cincinnati to New Orleans when one morning a young printer, Samuel Clemens by name, invited himself into the pilot house, struck up an acquaintance, and did much of the steering for the remainder of the trip, while Bixby sat at his ease and nursed a sore foot. The rest of the episode has been recorded, though not with complete historical accuracy, in some of the most vivid pages of American prose. When Clemens received his pilot's license, Sept. 9, 1858, Bixby took him for a while as a partner, and the two friends met again long after in 1882 and 1902. In the years just before the Civil War Bixby was frequently engaged in the lucrative Missouri River trade, sometimes making almost $1,800 a month. So retentive was his memory that he learned the Missouri in an incredibly short time: for his trained intelligence it was enough to see each section of the river once in daylight and once by night. In 1860 he married Susan Weibling of New Orleans. She died in 1867, and on Jan. 2, 1868, he married Mary, daughter of Capt. Edwin A. Sheble of St. Louis, who outlived him. During the Civil War he was pilot on the gunboat *Benton* and rose to be chief of the Union River Service. For two or three years he was captain and owner of a boat that made trips to Fort Benton, Mont. Occasionally, in the upper reaches of the Missouri, the boat had to stop while a herd of buffalo swam the river; at other times there were meetings, more or less exciting, with Sioux Indians. Later he was one of the owners of the Anchor Line, which operated a fleet of palatial river steamers between St. Louis and New Orleans. He himself was captain of the *City of Baton Rouge*. At first the line prospered; later it lost many of its boats and finally disappeared from the river. Bixby, of small physique but wiry and tremendously energetic, stayed on the Mississippi long after the glory of its commerce had disappeared. He entered the

government service and at the age of eighty-six was commander of the snagboat *Wright*. At last, however, he decided that he was growing too old for active service, and two days after his decision he died suddenly at his suburban home in Maplewood, Mo.

[Letter to writer from Bixby's daughter Edwina (Mrs. Louis Tousard Pim) June 25, 1928; *St. Louis Globe-Democrat*, Aug. 2, 3, 1912; S. F. Kneeland, *Seven Centuries in the Kneeland Family* (1897), p. 345; A. B. Paine, *Mark Twain* (1912); Mark Twain, *Life on the Mississippi* (1883); *Official Records U. and C. Navies*, ser. I, vol. XXIII.]

G. H. G.

BIXBY, JAMES THOMPSON (July 30, 1843–Dec. 26, 1921), Unitarian clergyman, author, was born in Barre, Mass., the third child of Clark Smith Bixby, a merchant, and of Elizabeth (Clark) Bixby, daughter of Abijah and Elizabeth (Heald) Clark of Hubbardston, Mass. The family leaving Barre, the son prepared for college in the Cambridge High School and graduated from Harvard in 1864. After employment for three years in New York as a private tutor, he received the degree of A.M. from Harvard and entered the Harvard Divinity School, being the first to receive (1870) the degree of B.D. from that school. On Sept. 1, 1870, he was married to Emma Gibson of Boston. Ordained Sept. 20, 1870, he was pastor of the First Parish, Watertown, Mass., until April 1874, and from November 1874 to 1878 was pastor of the Independent Congregational (Unitarian) Church of Belfast, Me. He then became professor of religious philosophy and ethnic religions in the Meadville Theological School, serving also as pastor of the Unitarian Church of Meadville, Pa. From July 1883 to June 1885 he was in Europe, studying in the universities of Heidelberg, Jena, and Leipzig, and obtaining the degree of Ph.D. in Leipzig in March 1885. For a year after his return he supplied the Unitarian Church of Ann Arbor, Mich., and then was settled over the Unitarian Church in Yonkers, N. Y., from January 1887 until he retired in December 1903. During this pastorate he was prominent in New York in the activities of the Reform Club, the Authors Club, and the Liberal Ministers' Association, being chairman of the latter organization for twelve years (1891–1903). In such circles his genial disposition, his magnanimous judgments, and his unusual fluency of expression won him high favor. His preaching, though often too burdened with learning, was marked by deep spirituality and sensitive comprehension of human suffering. His first wife having died on Mar. 20, 1902, he was married on Feb. 24, 1906, to Clara Webster Parker of Yonkers, and continued to reside in Yonkers until his death.

In his earlier pastorates Bixby published in the *Unitarian Review* many vigorous discussions of the problems created for religion and ethics by the evolutionary science of Spencer, Darwin, and Huxley. In this connection he argued (1874) that science, to be complete as science, must apply its methods of observation, induction, and verification to the indisputable facts of religion in human experience. He was heralding a new "scientific theology." Other articles (1876,1877) advocated a Theistic Monism on the basis of evolutionary science. Bixby won distinction also as an early expositor of the philosophy of Lotze and of the physiological psychology of Fechner and Wundt (1877). A second stage in his career was marked by his interest in comparative religion, which bore fruit in many articles in the *Unitarian Review* (1880–90) and the *New World* (1892–1900) and in lectures before the Meadville Theological School (1887–1899) and the Greenacre Summer School. The most widely influential of his books was *The Crisis in Morals* (1891) which reappeared in larger revision as *The Ethics of Evolution* (1900), a searching criticism of the Hedonism of Spencer's *Data of Ethics,* followed by a constructive argument that the source of moral principles is found in the fundamental unity of life with its pressure to larger and higher existence. His other books were *Similarities of Physical and Religious Knowledge* (1876) ; *Religion and Science as Allies* (1889) ; *The New World and the New Thought* (1902) ; *The Open Secret; A Study of Life's Deeper Forces* (1912). In his last years, afflicted with blindness, he dealt with the question of immortality (*Bibliotheca Sacra,* October 1916; *Biblical World,* September 1920).

[W. G. Bixby, *Bixby Family Record,* pt. 3, p. 584; *Report of the Class of 1864, Harvard Coll.* (1919) ; F. A. Christie, *The Makers of the Meadville Theological School* (1927).]

F. A. C.

BJERREGAARD, CARL HENRIK ANDREAS (May 24, 1845–Jan. 28, 1922), mystical philosopher and librarian, born in Fredericia, Denmark, where his father was principal of the local Latin school or gymnasium, was the son of Janus Bagge Friis and Louise (Nielsen) Bjerregaard. He studied at his father's school, but did not graduate there or at the University (letter, Apr. 21, 1927, from Konst, Universitetsinspekter, København) ; served as a volunteer spy in the Schleswig-Holstein war, tried various occupations, went to St. Petersburg and other parts of Europe as a teacher in the household of the Danish minister to Russia, entered the Danish military service as a candidate for officer (in the reserve not the regular service) on July 2, 1866,

reached the rank of second lieutenant, and was dropped from the army rolls on Jan. 1, 1894. His actual connection with the army ceased many years earlier, however, for he left the service and the country without permission in the summer of 1873, on the eve of a police investigation into an alleged offense against the civil criminal code. The offense could scarcely have been of gravest character, as he was permitted to return on a visit in 1904, and on Sept. 11, 1920, the King made him a Knight of Danebrog. He explained his departure by saying he anticipated an assignment to garrison duty in the Danish West Indies, or by saying he had been seen with socialists while in uniform.

In August 1873, he landed in New York, penniless and friendless. A linoleum factory in Salem, N. J., gave him work for a month at starvation wages, but left him stranded when the panic of September 1873 closed its doors. Six years of distress and privation followed. He managed to bring over in the summer of 1874 his wife and the two children then born to them. In October 1879, the struggle for existence was lessened somewhat by his appointment to the staff of the Astor Library. He remained with that institution and its successor, the New York Public Library, until his death. He had been a reader and student wherever he found himself, and his connection with the library gave a welcome chance to work with books and to follow his scholarly instincts. Increasing command of English brought opportunities for self-expression on the lecture platform, and as his name became better known there came increased demand for his writings on philosophy and related topics. His books include *Lectures on Mysticism and Talks on Kindred Subjects* (1896) ; *Lectures on Mysticism and Nature Worship, Second Series* (1897) ; *Sufi Interpretations of the Quatrains of Omar Khayyam and Fitzgerald* (1902) ; *The Inner Life and the Tao-Teh-King* (1912) ; *The Great Mother: a Gospel of the Eternally Feminine* (1913). Lesser known sides of the man were his love of nature and his sense of artistic expression. He frequently took friends and fellow spirits on Sunday walks for combined exposition of flowers, mysticism, botany, oriental philosophy. Shortly before his death he took to painting in oil as another form of expression, and though he certainly was not a great artist his work was vibrant with a note of individuality.

He was married on Sept. 30, 1868, to Mathilde Georgina Thomsen by whom he had seven children.

[Dahl og Engelstoft, *Dansk Biografisk Haandleksikon,* I ; *Illustreret Familie-Journal* (Minneapolis), July

1905 ; *Norden* (Racine, Wis.), Sept. 1905 ; *Am.-Scan-dinavian Rev.*, June 1921 ; *N. Y. Evening Post,* Apr. 11, 1914, Jan. 8, 1921 ; *Sun* (N. Y.), Oct. 30, 1920 ; *N. Y. World,* Oct. 23, 1921 ; *N. Y. Herald,* May 24, 1915 ; *Bull. N. Y. Pub. Lib.,* Feb. 1922.]   H. M. L.

BLACK, FRANK SWETT (Mar. 8, 1853–Mar. 22, 1913), lawyer, governor of New York, the son of Jacob and Charlotte (Swett) Black, was born on a farm at Limington, York County, Me. He obtained such education as the rural community afforded, and upon the removal of his parents to Alfred, Me., where his father was keeper of the county jail, he prepared for college at Limerick and Lebanon academies, meanwhile working and teaching school to earn expenses. At eighteen, a slender young man six feet three inches in height, he entered Dartmouth College. Although forced by circumstances to earn his way, he graduated in 1875 as an honor man, having married in his senior year Lois B. Hamlin of Provincetown, Mass. Declining several school principalships, he accepted the editorship of the *Journal* at Johnstown, N. Y., devoting himself meanwhile to the study of law. Severing his connection with the *Journal* because of a difference of opinion with the owner over the Blaine-Conkling controversy, he located in Troy, N. Y., continued his legal studies, and supported himself and family meanwhile with newspaper and clerical work. Admitted to the bar in 1879, he joined the firm of Smith, Wellington & Black for a year and then set up his own office. Native ability, hard work, and the mastery of every case, quickly won for him a wide legal practise and a reputation as one of the leading attorneys in his section of the state. By 1888 his wit and eloquence as a public speaker brought him into prominence as a campaign orator for the Republican party of which he was an ardent member. As chairman of the Republican committee for Rensselaer County in 1893 his successful efforts to clean up certain election frauds resulted in his election to Congress in 1894 and in his reëlection two years later. Meanwhile as a delegate to the Republican National Convention he helped to nominate McKinley for the presidency and was active in his election. The Republican State Convention held at Saratoga Springs in 1896, captivated by his address as temporary chairman, nominated him for governor. After a spectacular campaign, he was elected by the largest plurality ever given in the state to a gubernatorial candidate. Serving but one term, from 1897 to 1899, he urged the completion of the capitol at Albany, the preservation of the forests, biennial sessions of the legislature, a sensible civil service code, reform in the election laws, and the improvement of roads. Most of his recommendations were enacted into law.

During his administration the Spanish-American War broke out and it was largely due to his efforts that New York responded so quickly with men and money. Upon retiring to private life he resumed the practise of law in New York City, where his services were in much demand by litigants with important cases. He was generally regarded as an able lawyer, a fearless and incorruptible statesman, and a man of charming manner.

[No complete biography of Frank Swett Black has been written. Brief sketches of his life are given in E. L. Murlin, *N. Y. Red Book* (1897), pp. 91–104 ; Chas. E. Fitch, *Official N. Y. from Cleveland to Hughes* (1911), I, 149–63 ; Rutherford Hayner, *Troy and Rensselaer Counties* (1925), II, 482 ; *Albany Jour.,* Mar. 22, 1913. His messages as governor are in Chas. Z. Lincoln, *State of N. Y., Messages from the Governors* (1909), IX, 738–886.]   A. C. F.

BLACK, GREENE VARDIMAN (Aug. 3, 1836–Aug. 31, 1915), dentist, was born on a farm near Winchester, Ill., a son of William and Mary S. (Vaughn) Black. When he was eight years old, the family removed to another farm near Virginia, Ill., where they made with their own hands the brick out of which their house was constructed. The little lad helped as his puny strength permitted. At seventeen he took up the study of medicine with an elder brother, Dr. Thomas G. Black of Clayton, Ill. Three years later he entered the office of Dr. J. C. Speer, Mt. Sterling, Ill., as a student of dentistry; in 1857 he began practise in Winchester, Ill., and in 1860 he married Jane L. Coughennower. In 1862 he enlisted in the 129th Illinois Volunteer Infantry, serving as sergeant, mostly on scout duty, until disabled by an injury to the knee, which led to his discharge in 1863. In 1864 he resumed the practise of dentistry, in Jacksonville, Ill., and in 1865, his first wife having died two years earlier, he married Elizabeth Akers Davenport. Shortly after he began practise in Jacksonville, he formed a class in chemistry among the school teachers and others which he continued for several years. From 1870 to 1880 he lectured in Missouri Dental College on pathology, histology, and operative dentistry. He was professor of dental pathology in Chicago College of Dental Surgery 1883–89, introducing the teaching of dental technics in 1887; professor of dental pathology and bacteriology in the University of Iowa 1890–91; and professor of dental pathology and bacteriology in Northwestern University Dental School from 1891 until his death, becoming in 1897 dean of the school and professor of operative dentistry in addition to his other professorships. Black's first important paper (*Missouri Dental Journal,* July 1869) reported his investigation into the cause of the loss of workability by cohesive gold when stored in the dental cabinet. Its demonstration of the cause, the remedy, and means of prevention has remained unquestioned, the successful rule of practise by dentists. Black's views on "Diseases of the Peridental Membrane," presented in a chapter contributed to the *American System of Dentistry* (1886), were sharply criticized at first but finally accepted. His next important dental investigation was reported in a series of papers (*Dental Cosmos,* January, February, May, June, July, 1891) entitled "Management of Enamel Margins," setting forth the doctrine of "Extension for Prevention," *i. e.,* the extension of the cavity in order to prevent further decay. The idea was bitterly assailed in some quarters, but is now the basis of the accepted method of preparing cavities for filling. In 1895 Black presented in the *Dental Cosmos* (May-September) "An Investigation of the Physical Characters of the Human Teeth in Relation to Their Diseases and to Practical Dental Operations, together with the Physical Characters of Filling Materials." In this he definitely destroyed two myths that had been everywhere accepted as true. The first was that some teeth were soft and prone to caries, while others were hard and practically immune. Black showed that neither the density of the tooth nor the percentage of lime-salts it contains has anything to do with its liability to caries. The second had to do with the idea expressed in the common saying, "for every child a tooth." Black showed that, contrary to the common belief even among dentists at that time, the teeth of women during pregnancy are not leached of their lime-salts. As a third result of this investigation, Black evolved a method of making alloys for amalgam that assured their stability. This method he taught to all who cared to learn. To-day practically all dental amalgam alloys are made by the Black method, and amalgam, then a despised outcast, has come to be valued second only to gold as a filling for tooth cavities. Dr. Black was a voluminous writer. Besides the reports of his investigations, of which only a few of the more important have been mentioned, he wrote several books and numerous papers. At a banquet tendered to him five years before his death by the Chicago Odontographic Society, and attended by several hundred dentists from this country and abroad, a pamphlet—admittedly incomplete—was distributed containing more than five hundred titles of books, reports, papers, and major discussions. His style was singularly clear and simple, a clean-cut statement of facts and of the logical deductions from them, with a notable lack of technical terms. He wrote for the understanding of the many, with an unusual faculty of making

his ideas available for practical application. His first book, *The Formation of Poisons by Micro-Organisms* (1884), is still looked upon as an authoritative statement of the subject as then developed. In 1887 came *A Study of the Histological Characters of the Periosteum and Peridental Membrane.* In 1891 he produced his *Dental Anatomy,* a minute study of the macroscopical structure of the human teeth, the recognized text-book of the dental colleges to-day. In 1893, as chairman of the committee on nomenclature of the Columbian Dental Congress, his comprehensive report laid the foundation for a scientific dental nomenclature. In 1908 his *Operative Dentistry* appeared in two volumes: Volume I—*Pathology of the Hard Tissues of the Teeth;* Volume II—*Technical Procedures in Filling Teeth.* In 1915 appeared a third volume to be grouped with the two just mentioned, entitled *Diseases and Treatment of the Investing Tissues of the Teeth and the Dental Pulp,* his final presentation of this subject. He was also an inventor. In 1871 he designed one of the first cord dental engines. Much of his experimental work took him into unknown fields and he was compelled to devise, in some cases to personally make, much of the apparatus he used. In 1904 he supplied the patterns for 102 "cutting instruments" for carrying out the exact measures he regarded as necessary to the proper excavation of cavities. He made the drawings for many of the illustrations in his books and papers, played several instruments with more than the touch of an amateur, and had a fine singing voice. His varied activities continued till within a few weeks of his death. The last article from his pen, a study in collaboration with Dr. Frederick S. McKay of "Mottled Teeth, an Endemic Developmental Imperfection of the Enamel," theretofore unknown in dental literature, appeared in July 1915. Physically, Black was tall though never robust in build, but capable of almost unlimited endurance, as was necessary in the strenuous life he led. Always he wore a full beard, its dark, almost black color bleaching with advancing years. Of a simple, unaffected personality, willing to learn from others, never failing in his willingness to help others, he had the respect and affectionate regard of all who came in contact with him. He steadily refused to commercialize his work, devoting his energies mainly to the elucidation of problems for the benefit of his colleagues, though he engaged in many scientific investigations outside of dental matters. He was accorded numerous honors, including the presidency of the National Dental Association in 1901, the first International Miller Prize in 1910, and honorary degrees from five institutions. The character of the man was not one whit below the level of his achievements. One of his biographers voiced the feeling of his profession in these words: "He was great in achievements, great also in his simplicity and sincerity. He climbed the heights, but he took his fellows with him every step of the way."

[The facts for this sketch of Dr. Black were gained from files of the dental magazines, transactions of dental societies, and from correspondence with his son, Dr. Arthur D. Black. There is a sketch by A. W. Harris in *Science*, n. s., XLII, 496–97.]

F.L.H.

BLACK, JAMES (Sept. 23, 1823–Dec. 16, 1893), lawyer, founder of the National Prohibition Party and its first candidate for president (1872), was born in Lewisburg, Pa., the son of John and Jane (Egbert) Black. His father, an engineer and contractor, had a leading part in building the Grand Trunk Railroad, and the first Croton (N. Y.) Dam. His grandfather, John Black, came to America in 1790 from Scotland, and settled in Union County, Pa., where the family lived for two generations. James Black moved with his parents to Lancaster in 1836, and there married (1845) Eliza Murray, daughter of William Murray. His formal schooling ended in 1843, after he had spent three years in Lewisburg Academy. Upon leaving the academy he read law and was admitted to the Lancaster County bar in 1846, at the time when Thaddeus Stevens and James Buchanan were the leading local attorneys. At sixteen he became a convert to the cause of temperance. According to the story that he and other temperance writers used to tell, he was forced on one occasion, when employed as a mule-driver on the Pennsylvania and Union Canal, to join the older men in a drinking orgy. Upon recovering from the effects and realizing what had occurred, he made a vow forever after to abstain from the use of intoxicating liquors. This marked a turning-point in his life. In 1840 he was one of the first in Lancaster to join the local branch of the "Washington Association." This association had recently been organized in Baltimore by members of a drinking club, who, after listening to a lecture on temperance, Apr. 6, 1840, decided to reform, and changed their name to the "Washington Temperance Society." In 1846 Black helped to organize the Conestoga Division of the Sons of Temperance in Lancaster. In 1855, because of his leadership, the Prohibition Party in Lancaster County elected two members to the Pennsylvania state legislature. In 1857 he was instrumental in organizing the Lancaster Lodge of Good Templars, of which in 1864 he was elected Right Worthy Grand Councillor. It was at the request of the Grand Lodge

that he prepared his celebrated "Cider Tract," which resulted in barring cider drinkers from the order. Following the Civil War, he worked more ardently than ever for prohibition. He early sensed the need for an extensive educational campaign, and at the National Temperance Convention in Saratoga, 1865, he presented a plan and had it approved, of establishing a National Publication House. He was responsible for the first state prohibition convention in Pennsylvania, held in Harrisburg in February 1867, and served as its chairman. In 1872 the National Prohibition Party decided to nominate a national ticket. At the convention in Columbus, Ohio, Feb. 22, six names were presented for the presidential nomination: Ben F. Butler, David Davis, Samuel P. Chase, J. D. Cox, Horace Greeley, and James Black. A majority of the committee on nominations voted for Black, and he was made the unanimous choice. In the election he polled 5,608 votes (Smull, *Legislative Handbook of Pennsylvania*, 1872, p. 393). From this time until his death, Black had a voice in virtually every platform, resolution, and official document written by the Prohibition Party. He was a member of the Lancaster Methodist Episcopal Church, and in 1869, he with twenty-seven other individuals organized the Ocean Grove (N. J.) Association. He was a life-long collector of books and pamphlets on temperance, and at the time of his death (1893) had probably the most complete temperance library in existence.

[The Hon. David F. Magee of Lancaster, an intimate friend and associate of Black, and now Secretary of the Lancaster County Historical Society, assisted in obtaining many of the facts used in this sketch. Black's son, William Murray Black, Major-General, U. S. A., retired, supplied the facts and dates regarding the family's genealogy. The story of Black's sudden decision to take up the cause of prohibition appears in numerous temperance publications; the earliest printed account is found in the *Daily New Era* (Lancaster, Pa.), Dec. 16, 1893, and was probably written by the late Hon. John H. Landis, a life-long associate and friend. Black himself was the author of three small volumes,—*Is There a Necessity for a Prohibition Party?* (1878); *Brief Hist. of Prohibition* (1880); and *Hist. of the Prohibition Party* (1885).]

J.W.O.

BLACK, JEREMIAH SULLIVAN (Jan. 10, 1810–Aug. 19, 1883), attorney-general, of Scotch-Irish, Irish, and German descent, the son of Henry and Mary (Sullivan) Black, was born near Stony Creek, Pa. He grew up in this pioneer agricultural community a quick-witted, homely, nervous boy. As his appearance made him a tempting object of ridicule, he early learned the utility of hard-hitting and tongue-lashing and gained skill in the art of self-defense; controversy became second nature. He went to various schools irregularly kept in the locality at Stoystown, Berlin, and Somerset, and "finished" at the academy in Bridgeport, Pa. But much of his preparation came from his own enterprise; his restlessness ever required something for his mind to feed upon. He had imagination and a feeling for rhythm; Horace, the Bible, and Shakespeare he read with a retentive memory, and throughout the remainder of his life he could startle or thrill with a variety of apt quotations. His inclination was toward medicine, but his father had other plans and at seventeen sent him to Somerset to study in the office of Chauncey Forward, leader of the bar and prominent politician.

Black's law apprenticeship had all the advantages arising from the patronage of a prominent man. Forward pushed him, and within three years he was admitted to the bar, Dec. 3, 1830. Thereupon his teacher went to Congress leaving him in charge of his extensive practise. Very shortly he was appointed deputy attorney-general for the county and in this manner found himself on one side or the other of nearly every case before the county court. It was a responsibility which weighed heavily upon Black because self-confidence came slowly and with difficulty, but in the constant matching of wits with the elder lawyers he learned to use effectively his mental agility and telling speech. Politics was of course inevitable to most lawyers in those days, and in the exciting 'thirties he marched with his teacher in the Jacksonian ranks. His relations with Forward were perhaps the greatest influence in his life. Besides following him in law and politics he married Forward's daughter, Mary, in 1836 and after his preceptor's death embraced his religious views, becoming an ardent Campbellite after a deep religious experience. In 1842 Gov. Porter solved a patronage tangle by using Black as a compromise appointee and placing him upon the bench as president judge of the court of common pleas for the sixteenth judicial district (Franklin, Bedford, and Somerset counties). After nine years' experience he was elected to the supreme bench of the state and was reëlected in 1854; by lot he served the first three years as chief justice. As lawyer and judge, Black does not seem to have studied widely, but rather to have reduced the law to a number of fundamental principles and to have based his arguments and his decisions on strikingly clear and convincing statements of these maxims. As judge his principal contribution is said to have been his clarity of reasoning and statement in defining the meaning of corporation charters when that problem first arose.

Black had been an active supporter of Buchanan for twenty years and in 1857 the latter appointed him attorney-general at the last mo-

ment as a compromise between Pennsylvania factions. So at forty-seven, Black went to Washington to begin his national career. Though not yet as eccentric as he was later to become, he was quite a "character." He was tall, rather slouching, and loose-jointed, given to quick and erratic movements. His clothes and his wig never seemed to fit, but his keen gray eyes and infectious laugh made him singularly attractive in some moods. He was temperamental and proverbially absent-minded; he could lose himself in a task completely and become perfectly oblivious of surroundings. His ability to love and hate was marked, and his usually sound judgment could be much distorted by his emotions; stubbornness in holding to his opinion was not the least apparent of his numerous decided characteristics. Thus equipped Black started on a very trying four years. His most important problem was connected with California land titles. The policy of Congress in forcing every one to prove his title in that region had caused innumerable suits. As many of the actions involved government titles and depended upon the widely dispersed Spanish archives, Black sent Edwin M. Stanton to California to collect the records and investigate. With local aid the latter uncovered a system of fraud which when presented to the Supreme Court caused it to reverse many decisions sent up from the district court. Black considered this the great achievement of his régime; H. H. Bancroft after his investigations is not so confident (*History of California*, 1888, VI, 573–74). The other important legal problem which confronted the attorney-general was that of enforcing federal laws locally unpopular. There were three classes of cases of this type, dealing with the slave trade, filibustering expeditions, and return of fugitive slaves. In directing these, Black sought to enforce the law both in the North and the South but without much success, for though to him law was law, this fact was not so potent among the laity.

An incomplete picture of his life in Washington would be presented, however, if consideration were given only to his legal duties. As a member of Buchanan's cabinet he had to be politician and minister as well as lawyer. As politician he must aid Buchanan in keeping the Democratic party solid. In this capacity his greatest task was his controversy with Douglas when the latter attacked the administration policy. He entered into a pamphlet war with the Illinois senator and ably attacked squatter sovereignty, basing his argument upon the ground that territorial legislatures could never make laws violating the fifth amendment. As cabinet minister, Black did his share in shaping the administration's Kansas policy, upholding the Lecompton Constitution as legally adopted, in the vain hope that statehood would bring to an end the turmoil. But the greatest problem was secession. Lincoln's election causing the administration to realize the imminence of secession, Black was called upon to give advice as to the proper course to pursue in the event of such action. The Attorney-General prepared an opinion wherein he argued that while the Executive might not coerce a seceding state, he was in duty bound to enforce the laws and protect federal property. Black urged that proper garrisons be placed in the federal forts in the South as precautionary measures; but these measures Buchanan would not take. For this reason, ostensibly, Cass resigned as secretary of state, and Buchanan chose Black to fill his place, commissioning him on Dec. 17, 1860. His brief tenure of this office witnessed little of note in our foreign relations, an abortive negotiation with Great Britain over the northwest boundary being the only action attempted; but the domestic difficulties were a continuous nightmare. How to maintain the authority of the federal government and yet not take any steps that would cause secession; this was the difficult problem which Buchanan and his advisers faced.

Almost the day Black entered the State Department, South Carolina seceded and immediately attempted to negotiate for the control of federal property within state limits. Buchanan refused to recognize South Carolina's pretensions, but in the course of correspondence with her commissioners the President made some statements which Black thought insufficiently explicit in denying South Carolina's contentions. He threatened to resign; Buchanan, however, accepted some of his suggestions and at length when the tone of the commissioners became too overbearing broke off correspondence with them and sent the *Star of the West* with supplies to aid Major Anderson in Charleston Harbor. Black was somewhat relieved at this outcome, but when the *Star of the West* was forced to return his hopes failed. He did what he could to urge further reinforcements and the mobilization of troops to protect Washington, but Buchanan was pinning his hopes upon the Peace Convention. With this disappointment came another: the Senate refused to confirm Black's appointment to the Supreme Court made by Buchanan Feb. 5, 1861; Republicans, Douglas Democrats, and the Southern sympathizers were all hostile to Black. On Feb. 28, the Secretary sent a circular letter to our foreign ministers urging them to do what they could to prevent any recognition of the Confed-

eracy by foreign powers and upon Mar. 4 he retired.

In the weeks and months following Lincoln's inauguration Black reached the lowest point of his career. He was not in good health; several times during his service in the cabinet he had been forced to leave his duties to conserve his strength. He had lost his savings, entrusted to a relative for investment. He was, besides, a member of a defeated and discredited party and the impending conflict was paralyzing normal business activity; there seemed nothing in the future. Black suffered as only a temperamental person can. He retired to York, Pa., in which vicinity he was to live the remainder of his days, and there his material fortunes began to mend. He was appointed United States Supreme Court reporter in December 1861 and prepared *Black's Reports,* vols. I and II. But his greatest good fortune was his knowledge of the California land cases. There was to be litigation for the next decade and his expert services proved generally successful to the side retaining them; hence enormous fees came his way and even his carelessness could not return him to poverty. During the war he was a sharp opponent of the administration's "unconstitutional" program of disregarding civil rights and confiscating Southern property. He continued his protest against secession, however, and paid lip service at least to the successful prosecution of the war. He supported McClellan in 1864 and undertook an unofficial mission to see Jacob Thompson in Canada on behalf of peace, a commission which Stanton afterwards repudiated. The close of the war found him deep in the Milligan and McCardle cases which gave him free rein for powerful forensic condemnations of the war despotism. He aided and advised Andrew Johnson in his constitutional law and was to be one of his counsel before the impeachment court but withdrew in a fit of pique because Johnson would not overrule Seward for one of his clients. During this period, in 1869, Black met with a serious accident which deprived him of the use of his right arm. Nothing daunted, he learned to use his left. Fame was his, pleasant surroundings, fortune; he had reached about as high a plane of freedom as one can attain; oblivious of any unconquerable situation, he lived a curiously egocentric, mentally active life that made him a renowned "character," the hero of many a comic anecdote, and a great controversialist. He defended Christianity, he defended Buchanan, he defended Tilden before the Electoral Commission, he participated in magazine-article wars, he championed unpopular causes, he helped revise the Pennsylvania constitution of

1873 where his chief activity was directed toward controlling and regulating railroads and corporations. He reveled in righteousness and expression. So his life increased in its satisfactions and its independence until he died in August 1883, his great mental energy unflagging to the end. For more than a quarter of a century he had played a dynamic and dramatic rôle upon the national stage as a defender of the Constitution, the Union, and the Ten Commandments.

[There is no life of Black. His son, Chauncey F. Black, edited his *Essays and Speeches* (1885), prefaced by a biographical memoir, while his daughter, Mary Black Clayton, was the author of *Reminiscences of Jeremiah Sullivan Black* (1887); both of these, however, are appreciations. Articles upon his career and its various phases are, Henry C. Niles, "Jeremiah S. Black and His Influence on the Law of Pennsylvania" in *Ninth Annual Report of the Pa. Bar Ass.* (1903); Margaret C. Klingelsmith, "Jeremiah S. Black" in *Great Am. Lawyers*, ed. by Wm. Draper Lewis (1909), VI, 1–75; Francis Newton Thorpe, "Jeremiah S. Black," in *Pa. Mag. of Hist. and Biog.*, L, 117–33, 273–86; Roy F. Nichols, "Jeremiah S. Black" in *Am. Secretaries of State and Their Diplomacy* (1928), VI. The papers of Jeremiah S. Black are in the Manuscript Division of the Lib. of Cong. and a number of his letters are in the Buchanan MSS. in the Hist. Soc. of Pa. His reminiscences were published by Frank A. Burr in the *Phila. Press*, Aug. 7, 14, 21, 28, 1881.]   R.F.N.

BLACK, JOHN CHARLES (Jan. 27, 1839–Aug. 17, 1915), lawyer, soldier, was the son of John C. Black, a Presbyterian minister, and of Josephine (Culbertson) Black, both originally of western Pennsylvania. He was born in Lexington, Miss., but his parents later moved to Midway, Ky., and then returned to western Pennsylvania. After the death of the father in 1844, the family of four, consisting of two boys and two girls, John being the oldest, were taken by their mother to Danville, Ill., where her brother resided. At the opening of the Civil War, John was a junior in Wabash College. He enlisted immediately after the fall of Fort Sumter, serving in a company of Zouaves which was organized and commanded by Lew Wallace. For three months after this company became a part of the 11th Indiana Regiment he served as sergeant-major of the regiment. Then returning to Danville, he recruited a company for the 37th Illinois Infantry and was made major. With this regiment, he took part in thirteen battles and was severely wounded, losing, permanently, the full use of his right arm at the battle of Prairie Grove, Ark., Dec. 7, 1862. Shortly after, he was made a colonel and for gallantry in action at the storming of Fort Blakely, Ala. (Apr. 9, 1865), he was brevetted brigadier-general. After studying law and being admitted to the bar, he began the practise of law at Danville, Ill., but soon moved to Champaign, Ill., where he attained prominence in his profession. In 1867 he married Adaline L.

Griggs. He is described as a man of medium height, fair complexion, handsome features and of graceful movements (*Memoirs of Gustave Koerner*, II, 563). Because of his ability as a public speaker, he was in demand on patriotic occasions and in the conventions of the Democratic party of which he was a member. In 1866, 1880, and 1884, he was a candidate of that party for membership in the House of Representatives and in 1879 opposed John A. Logan for a seat in the Senate. Meantime, in 1872, on a fusion of the Liberal Republicans with the Democratic party Gustave Koerner and John C. Black were the nominees of their respective parties for governor of Illinois and lieutenant-governor. But they were defeated by Richard J. Oglesby and John L. Beveridge representing the regular Republican party. Beginning in 1885, Black served for four years as commissioner of pensions, having been appointed by President Grover Cleveland. On retiring, he took up the practise of law in Chicago. While serving as congressman at large from Illinois, having been elected in 1892, he was once more rewarded by President Cleveland with appointment to office. Resigning his seat as a representative, he became United States attorney for the northern district of Illinois (1895–98). For ten years, beginning with 1903, he was a member of the United States Civil Service Commission, serving nine years of the period as president of the Commission. In 1913, he retired from public life, but continued to devote much time to the interests of the Grand Army of the Republic, of which he had served as commander-in-chief, 1903–04.

[Much of the information about the career of Gen. Black was secured in conversation with his son John D. Black. The chief sources of printed information are: *Memoirs of Gustave Koerner, 1809–1896* (2 vols., 1909), ed. by Thos. J. McCormack; *Bench and Bar of Illinois*, ed. by John M. Palmer (1899); obituaries in *Chicago Tribune* and *Chicago Record Herald*, Aug. 18, 1915.]
                                              J.A.J.

BLACK HAWK (1767–Oct. 3, 1838), Sauk war chief, named Ma-ka-tai-me-she-kia-kiak (Black Sparrow Hawk), was born in the great Sauk village on Rock River, Illinois, two miles above the outlet of that stream into the Mississippi, near the present city of Rock Island. During the period of actual Spanish rule on the Mississippi (1769–1804) the Sauks, Foxes, and other Indian tribes were accustomed to take furs to St. Louis, there to trade them for supplies, and it was at St. Louis that Black Hawk heard of the Americans, for whom, as dispossessors of the Spanish, he conceived a hearty dislike. In 1804, William Henry Harrison, on behalf of the United States, negotiated a treaty with a band of Sauks at St. Louis, under Quashquame and two other chiefs

—one a Fox—whereby the Sauk and Fox nations ceded to the government the whole of their country east of the Mississippi. Of this treaty Black Hawk in particular never recognized the validity, claiming that it was entered into without tribal warrant, by chiefs who had gone to St. Louis for quite other ends, and who were badly intoxicated. This contention modern scholarship is on the whole disposed to accept (T. C. Pease, "The Frontier State," 1918, *Centennial History of Illinois*, II, 153, citing Annie H. Abel, *Annual Report of the American Historical Association*, 1906, I, 267). The War of 1812 broke forth and Black Hawk joined the British as a leader under Tecumseh. He fought at Frenchtown, Fort Meigs, and Fort Stephenson, but whether or not he was at the battle of the Thames, where Tecumseh fell, is not altogether certain. Brooding over the injustice of the Treaty of 1804—a treaty which he himself (wittingly or unwittingly) was in 1816 brought to confirm—Black Hawk, between 1816 and 1829, sought to enlist support from the British in Canada. He formed relations with a Winnebago prophet (medicine man), Waubesheik or White Cloud, and the twain plotted a great Indian confederacy against American encroachment. In June 1831, with Black Hawk clinging defiantly to the village of the Sauks, Gen. Edmund P. Gaines, in response to an urgent request by the governor of Illinois (John Reynolds), was sent to Fort Armstrong on the island of Rock Island, and Black Hawk withdrew beyond the Mississippi to the mouth of the river Iowa. But in April 1832, encouraged by what he believed to be assurance of help from Canada, he recrossed the Mississippi, with perhaps two hundred warriors with their women and children, and set out for Rock River. Winnebagoes, Potawatomi, and Mascoutins had promised to join him, and this some of them now did. But before Black Hawk could repossess himself of his ancestral seat, now largely in the hands of white settlers, Gen. Henry Atkinson with a force of United States troops landed in Illinois, below Rock River. With the coming of Gen. Atkinson, the Black Hawk-White Cloud confederacy (so far as in existence) fell rapidly to pieces. "I concluded," says Black Hawk, "to tell my people that if White Beaver (Gen. Atkinson) came after us, we would go back. . . . I discovered that the Winnebagoes and Potawatomi were not disposed to render us any assistance." The Black Hawk War (so called) was precipitated through an assault by a body of Illinois volunteers on a flag of truce sent out by Black Hawk for a parley—two of the Indians being killed. The conflict lasted till Aug. 2, 1832, when at the mouth of the Bad

Axe River in Wisconsin, he and his warriors, with their families, were overwhelmed by Gen. Atkinson and the Illinois volunteers. Black Hawk himself, along with his two sons, the prophet White Cloud, and the prophet's follower Neapope, was made prisoner and taken to Prairie du Chien, whence, under charge of Lieut. Jefferson Davis, he was transferred to Fort Armstrong, now in the hands of Gen. Winfield Scott. In the spring of 1833, by order of the President (Andrew Jackson) the fallen chief and his party were carried East, met the President, and after a short confinement at Fortress Monroe were returned to their own country—Iowa. Here, under the supervision of the Sauk Chief Keokuk, Black Hawk spent the remainder of his days. On his trip to Washington, Black Hawk was shown marked attention, and the experience quite changed his attitude toward the Americans. He wished to set forth to them the reasons for his conduct, and his story, dictated to the United States interpreter at Fort Armstrong, Antoine Le Claire, was prepared for publication by an Illinois journalist, J. B. Patterson, and in 1833, "tenth moon," duly given forth. The book has become an American classic. On Oct. 3, 1838, Black Hawk, not long after a second visit to the East, died at his lodge on the river Des Moines. He was laid away, Sauk fashion, in a reclining posture, beneath a wooden shelter, and by his side were placed the many gifts,—swords, cane, and medals,—which had been made to him. Death, be it said, did not bring him rest. In 1839 his sepulchre was invaded, his head severed from the body, and, together with other parts of the skeleton, carried away to be put on exhibition. Ultimately the bones were recovered, but were consumed in the burning of the Historical Society Building in Burlington, Iowa, where, by consent of his family, they had been placed.

[*Autobiography of Black Hawk* (Rock Island, Ill., 1833; new ed., 1882, with *A Hist. of the Black Hawk War*, by J. B. Patterson; annotated ed., 1916, by Milo M. Quaife); Benj. Drake, *Life and Adventures of Black Hawk, with Sketches of Keokuk*, etc. (1839); Perry A Armstrong, *The Sauks and the Black Hawk War* (1887); Frank E. Stevens, *The Black Hawk War* (1903); Jacob Van der Zee, "The Black Hawk War and the Treaty of 1832," *Iowa Jour. of Hist. and Politics*, XIII, 416; I. B. Richman, "Black Hawk, Keokuk and their Village," *John Brown Among the Quakers and other Sketches* (3rd ed., Hist. Dept. of Iowa); *Bull. 30, Bureau of Am. Ethnology*.]

                             I. B. R.

BLACKBURN, GIDEON (Aug. 27, 1772– Aug. 23, 1838), Presbyterian clergyman, missionary to the Indians, was born in Augusta County, Va., the son of Robert Blackburn. In his boyhood his family moved to eastern Tennessee where he attended Martin Academy and studied for the ministry under Dr. Robert Henderson.

In 1792 he was licensed to preach by the Abingdon Presbytery and began his ministry by holding services for some soldiers whom he had accompanied on an expedition against the Indians. Soon he established the New Providence Church and was given charge of another ten miles distant. On Oct. 3, 1793, he married Grizzel Blackburn, a distant cousin, by whom he had eleven children. His most notable work was the establishment of a mission to the Cherokee Indians. When he was unable to interest his own presbytery in the subject, he took his plea to the General Assembly, which, in 1803, voted $200 for the support of the work. Blackburn collected additional funds on the outside and having secured the approval of President Adams and the Secretary of War, opened a school for the Cherokee children in 1804. A teacher was employed, and Blackburn had general supervision in addition to his regular church services. This work he continued until 1810, by which time the hardships of the frontier had so undermined his health and the demands of the mission work so strained his finances that he felt compelled to resign. During the next twenty-three years he continued his teaching and preaching, was president of Harpeth Academy, and of Centre College, served as pastor of churches in Louisville and Versailles, Ky., and did much itinerant preaching. He is described as "the best type of backwoods eloquence," a commanding figure, above average height, with strongly marked features and flowing black locks.

Because of his success as a money raiser he was invited, in 1833, to go to Illinois by some persons interested in education in that region, and in 1835 was given the task of raising funds for Illinois College. Later he conceived a unique plan for raising an endowment for a school at Carlinville, Ill. The government was placing large tracts of land on the market and Blackburn offered to enter lands for friends of the cause at the rate of two dollars an acre. After paying the $1.25 per acre to the government, twenty-five cents was to go to him for his services and fifty cents for lands for the school. In this way he raised funds to enter a little over 16,656 acres for the institution. In the following year, 1838, he died. The institution he planned for was not opened until 1857. Beginning as a primary school, it later became Blackburn Theological Seminary and, when the theological courses were discontinued, Blackburn College.

[Sketches in W. B. Sprague's *Annals of the Am. Pulpit*, vol. IV (1858), and E. H. Gillett's *Hist. of the Presbyt. Ch. in the U. S.* (1864). In the *Panoplist*, June, July, and Dec. 1807 and Feb., Mar., May, and Dec. 1808, are letters from Blackburn describing his mission work. For endowment plan see *Blackburn Coll. Bull.*, 1915.]

B. R.

BLACKBURN, JOSEPH (fl. 1753–63), colonial portrait painter, is represented in art museums and private collections by distinguished and beautiful canvases, but left almost no other record of himself. His name in several publications and on museum labels has been given as "Jonathan B." Blackburn, but since 1919 it has been generally accepted that he was Joseph Blackburn, resident at Boston and Portsmouth, N. H., and perhaps elsewhere in the colonies. His paintings were usually signed "I (or J) Blackburn" with the date appended. Several writers, apparently accepting without scrutiny H. W. French's statement to that effect, have said that the artist signed himself "J. B. Blackburn." Examination of more than eighty canvases attributed to Blackburn has disclosed no such signature. One signature "Jos Blackburn" has been found. William Dunlap, in his *History of the Arts of Design in the United States* (1834), wrote: "All we know is that he [Blackburn] was nearly contemporary with Smibert, and painted very respectable portraits in Boston." Augustus T. Perkins, contributing to *Proceedings of the Massachusetts Historical Society* (1878) his list of portraits attributed to Blackburn, admitted that his own, and others', investigations had not shown "whence Jonathan B. Blackburn came and where he went on leaving Boston." Perkins conjectured that Blackburn taught Copley and that chagrined by his pupil's superiority he went away. Neither of these assumptions is probable. In *Art and Artists in Connecticut* (1879) French stated that Christopher B. Blackburn, an itinerant painter and jack-of-all-trades who worked in several towns, had a son, J. B., possibly born in Wethersfield, probably about the year 1700. This conjecture has frequently, and uncritically, been reprinted as if it were fact. Frank W. Bayley (1917) noted in a Portsmouth newspaper the name of Joseph Blackburn as that of one for whom posted letters were held. The same name was found in a Boston list. Following this clew Lawrence Park examined Blackburn signatures and (1918) discovered at Brooklyn a portrait signed "Jos Blackburn 1755." Soon after this John Hill Morgan came upon a receipted bill for the Mrs. Nathaniel Barrell portrait signed by Joseph Blackburn at Portsmouth, 12 July, 1762. These discoveries were published in the *Boston Sunday Herald*, in September 1919, and subsequently in several other publications. Research since 1919 has revealed few additional data concerning Blackburn. His name, as "Mr. Blackburn," occurs in two letters written, 1757, by Mrs. Richard Russell and now at the American Antiquarian Society, Worcester. The three Tucker family portraits, owned in Baltimore, appear to have been painted at Bermuda, 1753, indicating that Blackburn may have come thence to America. No Blackburn portrait dated later than 1763 has been found. Mr. Morgan reasonably conjectures that the painter went to Jamaica with his sitter, Sir Alexander Grant, who in 1764 became governor of that colony. Blackburn evidently came to America with a well-formed style, painted industriously among wealthy colonial families and, apparently, had no purpose to remain. His manner somewhat resembles that of the English painters Thomas Hudson (1701–79) and Joseph Highmore (1692–1780). No record of his British connections has been disclosed. One writer has assumed, without supporting evidence, that he traveled under an assumed name. As a painter Blackburn had admirable feeling for graceful gesture and sumptuous textures. He was perhaps inferior as an artist to Robert Feke, but was a better draftsman than Smibert or Badger. Among notable portraits attributed to him are those of Jeffery Amherst, Theodore Atkinson, Sr., Theodore Atkinson, Jr., Joshua Babcock, Mrs. Joshua Babcock, Mrs. Nathaniel Barrell, Mrs. John Bours, Rev. Peter Bours, Mrs. Thomas Bulfinch, Mrs. Wiseman Claggett, Mary Holyoke Cutts, Samuel Cutts, Mrs. Thomas Deering, Mary Faneuil, Mary Brown Greenleaf, Mrs. Thomas Hancock, Daniel Henchman, William B. Johnson, Lady Pepperell and Sister, James Otis, Joshua Warner, Joshua Winslow.

[Lawrence Park, "Joseph Blackburn, a Colonial Portrait Painter," *Proc. Am. Antiquarian Soc.*, n. s. XXXII, 1922; John Hill Morgan, "Notes on the Portrait of Lettice Mitchell," *Brooklyn Museum Quart.*, 1919; Lawrence Park, "Two Portraits by Blackburn," *Art in America*, Feb. 1919.]

F. W. C.

BLACKBURN, JOSEPH CLAY STYLES (Oct. 1, 1838–Sept. 12, 1918), Confederate soldier, senator from Kentucky, belonged to a family that had been prominent in the political history of Kentucky from the formation of the state. Several members served in the legislature; his father, Edward Blackburn, was a prosperous and well-known planter of considerable local influence; and a half-brother, Luke P. Blackburn [q.v.], was governor 1879–83. J. C. S. Blackburn was born near Spring Station in Woodford County and was educated at Centre College, from which he graduated in 1857. He read law in a private office and was admitted to the bar in 1858. For the next two years he practised in Chicago but returned to Kentucky in 1860 in order to work for the election of Breckinridge.

For Blackburn the Civil War interrupted a legal career not over-rich in promise. He joined the Confederate army and fought throughout the war with valor but without distinction. For a year he served on the staff of Brigadier-General Preston as volunteer aide-de-camp with the rank of captain and received special mention by that officer for good conduct at Chickamauga. Later he served as a lieutenant under Polk and in March 1864 was authorized to raise a cavalry company for special service along the Mississippi. His company was virtually independent, and its activities were such as to make it equally obnoxious to friend and foe (*Official Records*, ser. 1, vol. XLIX, pt. 1, p. 1010). After the war, Blackburn lived for a few years in Arkansas but returned to Kentucky in 1868. Family influence and the enthusiasm for Confederate veterans in the general reaction against military interference in Kentucky soon carried him into public life, sending him to the legislature in 1871 and again in 1873. This was followed by ten years 1875–85, in the national House of Representatives and twelve, 1885–97, in the Senate. He failed of re-election in 1896 because of his ardent advocacy of free silver and his support of Bryan, but was elected for the third time in 1901. Beaten in 1907, he retired to private life and held no more offices except by appointment. Roosevelt appointed him governor of the Canal Zone, but he resigned after two years. In 1914 Wilson appointed him resident commissioner of the Lincoln Memorial and this position he held till his death. For twenty years "Joe" Blackburn was probably the most popular man in Kentucky. This was due to his genial disposition, his perfervid oratory, his war record, and his astonishingly retentive memory, which enabled him, it is said, to call by name the majority of the voters of his state. As a legislator he cannot be placed in the first rank and his name is not connected with any great measure. He was a vigorous debater, whose powers of vituperation often provoked his opponents to physical violence. In the House he gained notoriety for his filibuster against accepting the decision of the electoral commission in 1877 and by his activity in unearthing the scandals of Grant's administration. In the Senate his debating powers and continued service combined to make him of considerable influence. He was twice married; in 1858 to Therese Graham of Danville, who died in 1899; in 1901 to Mrs. Mary E. Blackburn of Washington, D. C.

[Blackburn's career in Congress may be followed in the *Cong. Record*. The *Official Records of the Union and Confederate Armies* make only meager mention of him and it is possible that in some instances they confuse him with his numerous relatives. O. O. Stealey, *130 Pen Pictures of Live Men* (1910) contains a character sketch of him by a reporter who was perhaps not unbiased. The *Biog. Cyc. of Ky.* (1896) gives the outstanding facts of his life, while all histories of Kentucky devote some attention to his career. Cf. also *Who's Who in America,* 1899–1918; O. O. Stealey, *Twenty Years in the Press Gallery* (1906); W. E. Connelley and E. M. Coulter, *Hist. of Ky.* (1922), vol. II; *Louisville Evening Post,* Sept. 12, 1918.]			R. S. C.

BLACKBURN, LUKE PRYOR (June 16, 1816–Sept. 14, 1887), physician, surgeon, governor, the son of Edward M. and Lavina (Bell) Blackburn, was born in Fayette County, Ky., although his parents' home was in Woodford County. His grandfather George Blackburn moved to Kentucky about 1780 from Culpeper County, Va., and settled in Woodford County, calling his estate "Blackburn's Post." His father was prepared for the law but chose rather to engage in farming and breeding thoroughbred horses, for both of which he became well-known. Luke P. Blackburn, determining on the study of medicine, took advantage of Transylvania University to prepare himself. He graduated in 1834 with the M.D. degree and immediately began his practise in Lexington, Ky. The next year he married Ella Guest Boswell, and before the year was over, cholera having broken out in Versailles, Ky., he offered his services free to a people almost completely deprived, by death or desertion, of medical attention. Here he developed characteristics and interests that were to constitute his chief claim to distinction: generosity with his medical skill and services, and a profound knowledge of epidemics and their control. So grateful were the people of Versailles that they prevailed upon him to settle in their town. Here Blackburn attempted to supplement his income by a venture into the manufacture of rope and bagging, but in 1839 he failed with considerable financial losses. Though not greatly interested in politics at the time, he represented Woodford County in the legislature in 1843. Three years later flush times in Mississippi drew him to Natchez, where he soon began a work destined to tax his capacities and to make him known to the whole nation. He assumed general control of the yellow fever epidemics which broke out in the lower Mississippi Valley in 1848 and 1854, and became so much interested in the welfare of the rivermen that at his own expense he set up a marine hospital in Natchez. Later he induced Congress to take charge and to erect others. In his efforts to control yellow fever, he held that a quarantine station on the Mississippi below New Orleans would be of inestimable value. To aid him in carrying out this plan Mississippi commissioned him a representative to Louisiana to induce her to erect such a station, and while on this visit he addressed both the Louisiana House and Senate and secured favorable action. He later induced the federal government to assume control. In 1856 while he was on a visit to New York, yellow fever broke out on Long Island and at the request of the mayor he assumed control, refusing to make any charges for his services. In 1857 he visited the principal hospitals of England, Scotland, Germany, and France, and while in Paris met Julia M. Churchill of Louisville, Ky., whom he married on his return, his first wife having died in 1855. He made his home in New Orleans until the Civil War broke out. Being a strong secessionist, he offered his services to the Confederacy. He was attached as a surgeon to the staff of Gen. Sterling Price, with $50,000 given by Mississippi to be used in caring for the sick troops of that state. To secure medical supplies for the Confederacy he visited Canada and was prevailed upon by the governor-general to go to the Bermuda Islands to relieve distress there. In 1867 he moved to Arkansas to live on a plantation but returned to Kentucky in 1873 and made his home in Louisville. Two years later he assumed control of the yellow fever situation around Memphis and in 1878 gave free his services to Hickman, Ky., suffering under a like epidemic. He had long held an ambition to be governor of his native state and in 1879 secured the Democratic nomination and election. His administration was conspicuous for the large number of pardons which he granted in order to relieve bad prison conditions. He died in Frankfort, Ky.

[For a physician's account and estimate of Blackburn see *Ky. Medic. Jour.,* vol. XV, no. 11 (1880). Other sources of information are, Appleton's *Annual Cyc.,* 1887; L. and R. H. Collins, *Hist. of Ky.* (1874), vol. I; *Lexington Morning Transcript,* Sept. 15, 1887; *Biog. Cyc. of the Commonwealth of Ky.* (1896); *Louisville Courier-Journal,* Sept. 15, 1887; H. A. Kelly and W. L. Burrage, *Am. Medic. Biogs.* (1920).]			E. M. C.

BLACKBURN, WILLIAM MAXWELL (Dec. 30, 1828–Dec. 29, 1898), Presbyterian clergyman, son of Alexander and Delilah (Polk) Blackburn, was born at Carlisle, Ind. He was educated in the Academy of La Porte, Ind., and later at Hanover College, graduating in 1850. After spending a year in teaching he entered Princeton Theological Seminary. Here he spent four years, pursuing theological studies, but not graduating. He was licensed to preach by the Presbytery of New Brunswick in April 1853, and was ordained by the Presbytery of Lake on Sept. 28, 1854. His first charge as a minister was the church at Three Rivers, Mich., where he preached from 1854 to 1856. From this work he was called to Erie, Pa., to take charge of the newly organized Park Presbyterian Church. The following year he was installed as pastor of this church and continued as such until 1863. When he left this field it was in order to supply the pulpit, and then become the pastor, of the Fourth Presbyterian Church of Trenton, N. J. On Aug. 16, 1864, he was married to Elizabeth Powell. In 1868 he was called to the professorship of Biblical and ecclesiastical history in the Seminary of the Northwest (later McCormick Theological Seminary), Chicago. This position he occupied until 1881. Meantime in addition to his labors as professor in the seminary he served as acting pastor of the Fullerton Avenue Presbyterian Church of Chicago (1869–71). In 1881 he accepted a call to the Central Presbyterian Church of Cincinnati, Ohio, which he served until 1884. From this pastorate he was called to the presidency of the Territorial University of North Dakota. He served in this position, however, only until the next year, when he was transferred to the presidency of Pierre University in South Dakota (removed in 1898 to Huron, S. Dak., and renamed Huron College). From 1885 to the day of his death Blackburn was not only president of the University, but also professor of mental, moral, and political science, and from 1886 to 1890, and again from 1892 to 1894 he had charge of the local Presbyterian Church at East Pierre, S. Dak.

Blackburn early developed aptitude for and facility in writing. His first effort, a translation of Gerhard's *Sacred Meditations,* was followed by *The Holy Child* (1859), a story for use in Sunday-schools, which proved successful and was republished in England. This was followed by a series of six juvenile tales under the general title of the "Uncle Alick Stories." In the same popular vein but of wider interest, Blackburn produced a large number of historical and biographical works designed to disseminate knowledge concerning the important personalities and events of the world's religious life, especially those of the Reformation period. He also published a comprehensive treatise on church history under the title: *History of the Christian Church from its Origin to the Present Time* (1879), which received wide recognition, and was used as a text-book in the study of the subject, though recent advances in this field of knowledge have practically superseded it. Great energy characterized all his numerous activities: his writing, his labors as pastor, teacher, and college president, his work on committees of Presbytery and Synod. In personal appearance and bearing he was dignified and even courtly, producing the impression of one who was a force-

ful thinker but was indisposed to impose his thoughts upon others.

[*Princeton Theol. Sem. Alumni Cat.* (1909); *McCormick Theol. Sem. Gen. Cat.* (1912); Le Roy J. Halsey, *Hist. of the McCormick Theol. Sem.* (1893); the *Minutes of the Gen. Assembly of the Presbyt. Ch. and of the Synod of S. Dak.* (1886–98); Thos. L. Riggs, "Wm. Maxwell Blackburn," *S. Dak. Hist. Colls.,* I, 25–36.]

A. C. Z.

BLACKFORD, CHARLES MINOR (Oct. 17, 1833–Mar. 10, 1903), lawyer, came of a family of which there is no American record prior to Benjamin Blackford who was born in New Jersey Oct. 31, 1767, and went to Virginia in 1789. His son, William Matthews Blackford, editor and part owner of the *Lynchburg Virginian,* married Mary Berkeley Minor, daughter of Gen. John Minor, and their second son, Charles Minor Blackford, was born at Fredericksburg, Va. He obtained an excellent education from his father, who was a noted scholar, and at private schools at Fredericksburg and Lynchburg. Entering the University of Virginia Oct. 1, 1850, he passed to the Law School, graduating LL.B. in 1855. The same year he commenced practise in Lynchburg. "My success," he wrote later, "was not particularly brilliant but it was sure and steady." He married Susan Leigh, daughter of Thomas M. Colston of Fauquier County, Va., Feb. 19, 1856. On the outbreak of the Civil War he was commissioned first lieutenant in the 2nd Virginia Cavalry, the first mounted regiment organized in Virginia, and took part in the battles of Manassas, Slaughter's Mountain, and Fredericksburg. During the winter of 1863 he was appointed judge advocate of the 1st Army Corps under Longstreet and was present at Gettysburg, Chickamauga, and the Wilderness. On the conclusion of the war he resumed practise at Lynchburg, being "the only lawyer in town who kept his office open, for there were no courts and no business." In 1866 he entered into partnership with Col. T. J. Kirkpatrick and the firm gradually acquired the most extensive legal connection in Virginia, being engaged in much heavy corporation litigation, including Gilbert *vs.* Washington City Virginia Midland Electric Railway Company (*33 Grattan,* 586, 645), which involved the powers and duties of a court of equity in dealing with foreclosure and receivership where there was a plurality of mortgages on different parts of a railway—the largest case up to that time tried in a Virginia court. His cases were always elaborately prepared and in court he was strong and aggressive, though ever courteous to his opponents and deferential to the bench. In his early years a Whig and later a Democrat, he never aspired to office; and the adoption of the free silver plank at the Chicago convention caused him to vote for McKinley at the ensuing presidential election. He always took a keen interest in local administration, occupying the position of city solicitor from 1869 to 1881 and being for a time a member of the city council and school board. He was also an influential and active supporter of the Protestant Episcopal Church. An original charter member of the Virginia State Bar Association, he was elected its president in 1894. He died at Lynchburg, Mar. 10, 1903.

Of pronounced literary tastes, possessing exceptional culture, and widely read, he was the author of *Memoirs of the Army in Virginia* (1894–96); *Legal History of the Virginia Midland Railway Company* (1881); *Campaign and Battle of Lynchburg* (1900); *Historical Sketch of the Book of Common Prayer*; and a number of articles and addresses, including a masterly "Trials and Trial of Jefferson Davis," read before the Virginia State Bar Association, 1900. All his writings were distinguished for their attractive style and effective handling of material.

[The chief authority for the more important features of his life is his own autobiographic sketch in his war memoirs. See also *Va. State Bar Ass. Report*, 1903, p. 67.]

H. W. H. K.

BLACKSTONE, WILLIAM (1595–May 26? o. s., 1675), New England colonist, was descended from a family of some distinction near Salisbury, England. Attending Emmanuel College, Cambridge, he took the degrees of B.A. in 1617 and M.A. in 1621, and took orders in the Church of England. About 1623 he came to Massachusetts and was the first settler to live on the land where Boston now stands. He continued there after the Puritan immigration but in April 1633 the new settlers limited him to fifty acres. Neither he nor the Puritans liked each other. It was enough for them that he was a Church of England man, and his own most famous remark is that he left England because he did not like the lord-bishops and would not now be under the lord-brethren. In 1634 he decided to remove, sold his property, except six acres, and settled at Study Hill, as he called his place, in what is now Cumberland, about three miles from Pawtucket. In 1659 he married Sarah, widow of John Stevenson of Boston, Endicott performing the ceremony. By her he had a son John. She died in June 1673 and Blackstone himself was buried May 28, 1675. He was a man who has perhaps gained in interest from a certain mystery attaching to him. He lived the life of a recluse, was cultured and devoted to his library of 186 volumes, and at the same time was thoroughly at home with the Indians, whom he much preferred

to the Bostonians. He planted the first orchards in Massachusetts and seems to have had some property. In King Philip's War, soon after his death, his house and library were burned. His son, who was no credit to him, married, and the family is still extant.

[L. Bliss in his *Hist. of Rehoboth* (1836), is the best source of information, with references to all contemporary sources. L. H. Tilton in *Hist. of Rehoboth* (1918) gives a few additional facts as to descendants. S. C. Newman's letter in S. G. Arnold, *Hist. of R. I.* (1860), II, 568–70 should be consulted. There is a good brief account by C. F. Adams, *Three Episodes in Mass. Hist.* (1892), I, 322–38. See also L. M. Sargent, *The Blackstone Family* (1857), and J. W. Blackstone, *Lineage and Hist. of Wm. Blackstone* (1907).]

J. T. A.

BLACKWELL, ANTOINETTE LOUISA BROWN (May 20, 1825–Nov. 5, 1921), reformer, was born in Henrietta, Monroe County, N. Y., the daughter of Joseph and Abby (Morse) Brown, both of New England descent. At the age of nine she joined the Congregational Church and soon was speaking publicly in meetings; at sixteen she was teaching school; later she attended Oberlin College, completing the literary course in 1847 and the theological course in 1850. Refused a ministerial license, because of her sex, she preached wherever churches, of any creed, would receive her until in 1852 she became the regular pastor of the Congregational Church in South Butler, N. Y. She had already joined the movements for abolition, prohibition, and woman's rights—three reforms which, however illogically, usually drew the same supporters. Her efforts at first were devoted mainly to harmonizing these reforms with the teachings of the Bible, but theological difficulties grew upon her until she resigned her pastorate in 1854 and, eventually, became a Unitarian. In the summer of 1853 she came into national prominence when although a regularly authorized delegate to the World's Temperance Convention in New York City she was refused permission to speak; her "unwomanly conduct" in striving quietly for three hours to be heard, amid a tumultous group of angry, shouting men, was severely criticized by many newspapers, although Horace Greeley in the *New York Tribune* succinctly characterized the convention's achievements toward temperance as consisting in "First Day—Crowding a woman off the platform; Second Day—Gagging her; Third Day—Voting that she shall stay gagged" (*New York Daily Tribune*, Sept. 9, 1853).

Miss Brown was married on Jan. 24, 1856, to Dr. Samuel C. Blackwell, brother of Elizabeth Blackwell and Henry Brown Blackwell [*qq.v.*]. She became the mother of six children. During the early years of the Civil War she was prominent in the movement for the immediate emancipation of the slaves and until the end of her life remained active in the causes of woman suffrage and prohibition. A very effective speaker, she habitually devoted her eloquence to the presentation and support of particular resolutions rather than to mere general inspiration. Although far from unemotional, her appeal was mainly to the reason, and to considerations of practise. The same qualities appeared in her numerous books: *Shadows of Our Social System* (1855); *Studies in General Science* (1869); *A Market Woman* (1870); *The Island Neighbors* (1871); *The Sexes Throughout Nature* (1875); *The Physical Basis of Immortality* (1876); *The Philosophy of Individuality* (1893); *Sea Drift; or Tribute to the Ocean* (1902); *The Making of the Universe* (1914); *The Social Side of Mind and Action* (1915).

[*Who's Who in America*, 1899–1921; Frances E. Willard and Mary A. Livermore, *A Woman of the Century* (1893), later included in their *Portraits and Biogs. of Prominent Am. Women* (1901); *Hist. of Woman Suffrage*, ed. by Elizabeth Cady Stanton, Susan B. Anthony, and Matilda Joslyn Gage, I (1881), 119, 152, 186, 449 (portrait), 473, 524, 553, 624, 723, 862; II (1882), 723, 862; obituary in *Newark Evening News*, Nov. 5, 1921.]

E. S. B.

BLACKWELL, ELIZABETH (Feb. 3, 1821–May 31, 1910), the first woman doctor of medicine of modern times, was born in Bristol, England, one of nine children of Samuel Blackwell, a sugar refiner, and his wife, Hannah Lane. Henry Brown Blackwell [*q.v.*] was her younger brother; another brother, Samuel, was to become the husband of Antoinette Louisa (Brown) Blackwell [*q.v.*]. At the age of twelve (August 1832), she sailed with her family in the merchant ship *Cosmos* from Bristol to New York, where the family remained for six years and then moved to Cincinnati, Ohio. Elizabeth had attended local schools at Bristol and New York, but her formal education was cut short by the death of her father (1838) a few months after reaching Ohio. This calamity left the family unprovided for, and consequently when twenty-one (1842) Elizabeth began to teach school, her first position being in Henderson, Ky., but her ardent antipathy to slavery caused her after a year to seek another post. In 1844 she first thought of studying medicine, and during the next year, while supporting herself by teaching at Asheville, N. C., she began to read medical works, and in 1847 continued her medical studies under the guidance of Dr. Samuel H. Dickson, professor at Charleston Medical College. The problem of securing entry into a medical school proved difficult; she was refused at Philadelphia and New

York, but in October 1847 the Geneva Medical School of Western New York accepted her application. Through tact and dignity she succeeded in overcoming the prejudice of undergraduates and instructors, but in the world at large she was regarded "as either mad or bad." She received her M.D. in 1849, which led to much comment in the public press both in America and abroad (see *Punch*, XVI, 226, 1849). After graduation she sailed immediately for England and was courteously received, but she regarded the opportunities on the Continent as more favorable and accordingly went to Paris, where, on June 30, 1849, she entered La Maternité and had six months of obstetrical experience in that institution. A purulent ophthalmia contracted at the end of her service there caused her to lose the sight of one eye, which put an end to the surgical aspirations which she had previously entertained. She then studied at St. Bartholomew's Hospital in London and was permitted to practise in all branches of medicine except, ironically enough, gynecology and pediatrics. At this time she received congratulations from Florence Nightingale, Lady Byron, the Herschels, Faraday, and others of note. She returned to New York in 1850 to practise, and, on encountering prejudice, opened a private dispensary of her own which later (May 1857) became incorporated into the New York Infirmary and College for Women, a hospital entirely conducted by women. In this venture she was joined by her sister, Emily, who had also become qualified in medicine, and by Marie Zakrzewska, and they were supported by the Quakers of New York. During the Civil War, Dr. Blackwell was active in the organization of a unit of field nurses which did much to win sympathy for the feministic movement in medicine. In 1869 she decided to settle permanently in England where, as in America, she aimed to secure free and equal entrance of women into the medical profession. Later (1875) she became professor of gynecology in the London School of Medicine for Women which had just been established, and continued her activities there until 1907 when she became enfeebled following an accident in Scotland. She had taken a house in Hastings where she died, May 31, 1910. She was buried at Kilmun, Argyllshire. An excellent portrait of her hangs in the London School of Medicine for Women.

Dr. Blackwell was an active writer and her works had a wide circulation. The *Laws of Life* (New York, 1852) was reissued in London in 1859 and again in 1871. She was active in public health, and several of her popular lectures—"How to Keep a Household in Health" (1870),

The Laws of Life with Special Reference to the Physical Education of Girls (1852), *The Religion of Health* (1871), and *Counsel to Parents* (1879)—did much to arouse popular interest in the subject. She wrote extensively also on problems of sex and moral education of the young. Her other writings are listed in the *Index Catalogue of the Surgeon-General's Library* and in the *Dictionary of National Biography.*

[Elizabeth Blackwell, *Pioneer Work in Opening the Medical Profession to Women; Autobiographical Sketches* (London, 1895); *The Times* (London), June 2, 1910; *N. Y. Evening Post,* June 1, 1910; Mesnard, *Miss E. Blackwell et les femmes médecins* (Paris, 1889); Frances Hays, *Women of the Day* (London, 1885); *Brit. Medic. Jour.,* 1910, I, 1523; *Del. State Medic. Jour.,* 1916, VII, 3–24; *Lancet* (London, 1910), I, 1657; *Medic. Mag.* (London), IX, 117–25; *Medic. Record* (N. Y.), LXXVII, 1016; *Woman's Medic. Jour.* (Cincinnati), XX, 155, 174, 188, 208.]

J. F. F.

BLACKWELL, HENRY BROWN (May 4, 1825–Sept. 7, 1909), editor, one of the earliest advocates in America of woman suffrage, was born in Bristol, England, the son of Samuel and Hannah (Lane) Blackwell and brother of Elizabeth Blackwell [*q.v.*]. Samuel Blackwell was an advanced Liberal and a great admirer of American institutions. In 1832 the family came to New York City where the father engaged in sugar refining. The Blackwells took an active interest in the anti-slavery movement and their Long Island home was soon a refuge for persecuted abolitionists. In 1838 they moved to Cincinnati, Ohio. A short time after, Samuel Blackwell died and left his widow with nine children to support. Henry became an office boy, later drifting into milling and then into the hardware business. In 1853 he made his first speech for woman suffrage at a convention in Cleveland, Ohio. During the same year he attended a legislative hearing in Massachusetts at which Lucy Stone spoke in support of a woman suffrage petition. This meeting was the beginning of his courtship of Lucy Stone. After promising to devote himself to the work of advancing woman suffrage, he obtained Miss Stone's consent to marriage. On the day of their marriage, May 1, 1855, they published a joint protest against the inequalities in the marriage law. This protest was widely distributed and attracted much attention (*Woman's Journal,* Sept. 11, 1909). Soon after his marriage Blackwell moved with his wife to New Jersey where he engaged in book-selling, sugar refining, and real estate, making money in each venture. With the exception of one year at Kemper College in St. Louis he obtained most of his education through reading. In 1858 while in the book business, he introduced many agricultural libraries into the Illinois schools. In 1867 he wrote a message to the Southern legislatures proposing the extension of woman suffrage in the South as a counterbalance to negro suffrage (*What the South Can Do,* 1867). When the American Woman Suffrage Association was organized in 1869, Blackwell was financially able to devote most of his time to it. In 1870, when the *Woman's Journal* was founded in Boston, he contributed a substantial sum of money. Later when an editor was needed who would work without salary, he consented to fill the place and remained editor of the *Journal* until his death, which occurred in Dorchester, Mass. He was interested not only in woman suffrage, but in other liberal movements such as activity against the deportation of political refugees, the Armenian massacres of 1895, and the Russian pogroms. His interest in economic affairs was shown by his activity in favor of reciprocity with Canada (*Reciprocity, a Republican Issue,* 1904). He was a kindly, sympathetic person, always willing to aid humanitarian causes.

[Most of Henry Blackwell's writing, aside from the pamphlets mentioned above, appears in the form of signed editorials in the *Woman's Journal* from 1870 to 1909. Obituaries appeared in the *Woman's Journal,* Sept. 11, 1909, and in the *Boston Transcript, Boston Post,* and *Boston Daily Globe,* Sept. 8, 1909.]

M. S.

BLACKWELL, LUCY STONE. [See STONE, LUCY.]

BLADEN, WILLIAM (Feb. 27, 1673–August 1718), publisher, was born at Hemsworth, Yorkshire, England, the son of Nathaniel Bladen and his wife Isabella, daughter of Sir William Fairfax, a general of Cromwell's time. Bladen came to Maryland in 1690, and soon became active in public affairs. In 1692 the Archives of Maryland record an allowance of 4,000 pounds of tobacco to Bladen for transcribing the laws. In 1695 he was recompensed for "fair Copy of the Laws sent for England, 2 Journalls, 2 Copyes of the Court house act" (*Archives of Maryland,* XIX, 198), and in 1696 the records again reveal his clerical activities. Meanwhile (*c.* 1695), he was made clerk of the House of Assembly, and in 1696 he proposed to the Assembly the advantages of a printing-press for printing the laws and offered to send for press and appurtenances if the governor would give his permission for their use. Upon receiving the sanction of assembly, council, and governor, Bladen, "at Great Charge and Trouble," as he informed the officials on May 4, 1700, finally procured "printing press Letters papers Inck printer &c." (*Ibid.,* XXIV, 22). For his assistance an ordinance was passed making obligatory the use of legal papers printed by Bladen and fixing the price thereof. The printing of the "body of Laws . . . soe that every person might easily have them in their houses without being troubled to goe to the County Court house to have recourse thereto" was arranged for, and it was also ordered that "every County be Oblidged to take one faire Coppy endorsed and Titled to be bound up handsomly" (*Ibid.,* XXIV, 83) for which Bladen was to receive from each county 2,000 lbs. of tobacco. Evidently an inefficient printer had been obtained, as the committee that compared the printed laws with the original found many errata, and Bladen was required to have these printed and sent to the several counties. In 1698 he became clerk of the governor's council and Gov. Nicholson paid him tribute in a letter to the Board of Trade. Apologizing for his delay in forwarding journals, etc., Nicholson says: "Another Reason is the great scarcity of good Clarks; (so that I am allmost forced to make according to the proverb Bricks without straw) only Mr. Wm. Blaiden whome I have found the most capable in all Respects, I have removed from being Clark of the House of Delegates, to that of the Council" (*Ibid.,* XXIII, 489). Collector of port and district of Annapolis, surveyor of port, register of court of admiralty, clerk of the free school, attorney-general of Maryland at a salary of £100 a year, and clerk of council of state at a fee of 12,000 lbs. of tobacco, are titles indicating some of the other offices in which Bladen served his generation. He married Anne Van Swearingen in 1696; a son, Thomas, became proprietary governor of Maryland. The exact date of Bladen's death is uncertain, but he was buried on Aug. 9, 1718.

[The *Archives of Maryland,* particularly Vols. VIII, XIX, XXIII, XXIV, and XXV, are the primary source; among secondary sources may be mentioned J. T. Scharf, *Hist. of Md.* (1879), I, 362, L. C. Wroth, *Hist. of Printing in Colonial Md.* (1922), and Christopher Johnston, "Bladen Family," *Md. Hist. Mag.,* Sept. 1910.]

A. E. P.

BLAIKIE, WILLIAM (May 24, 1843–Dec. 6, 1904), lawyer, athlete, and promoter of physical training, was born in New York City, the son of Rev. Alexander and Nancy (King) Blaikie. He prepared for college at the Boston Latin School, graduated from Harvard in 1866, and from the Harvard Law School in 1868, being one of the two honor men of his class. After serving as pardon clerk in the United States Attorney-General's office (1869–70) and as assistant in the office of the United States district attorney, New York (1870–72), he established himself in practise in that city. He was twice married, first, to Isabella Stuart Briggs of Harrisburg, Pa., July 3, 1872; and second, to Rebecca Wynne Scott of Elk Horn, Ky., Oct. 6, 1891.

From boyhood he was an all-round athlete. When seventeen years old and weighing 133 pounds, he lifted a weight of 1,019 pounds. He was captain of a winning football team at the Boston Latin School, and in 1866 stroked Harvard's victorious crew. For ten years he held the amateur long distance walking record, having covered the 225 miles between Boston and New York in four and one-half days. Throughout his life his interest in physical education remained strong, and by lecturing and writing he added impetus to the rapid development in that field which took place in the eighties and nineties. In 1879 he published *How to Get Strong and How to Stay So,* the last edition of which appeared in 1902, a book of nearly 300 pages, interesting, untechnical, and not without charm of style. It had wide popularity in this country and in Europe. In 1883 he issued a manual entitled *Sound Bodies for Our Boys and Girls,* which in the form of safe and simple exercises embodies some of the suggestions in his earlier work. Its clarity and illustrations made it a book suitable for schools or private use. As has been the case with many athletes, Blaikie did not attain old age, but died suddenly of apoplexy in his sixty-second year.

[*Who's Who in America,* 1903–05; *Boston Evening Transcript,* Dec. 7, 1904; *N. Y. Tribune,* Dec. 7, 1904; *Harvard Grads. Mag.,* Mar. 1905.]

H. E. S.

BLAINE, JAMES GILLESPIE (Jan. 31, 1830–Jan. 27, 1893), statesman, was born at West Brownsville, Pa. He was the son of Maria Louise Gillespie and Ephraim Lyon Blaine, and fifth in descent from the first James Blaine who emigrated from Londonderry in 1745. His paternal ancestors were for the most part Scotch-Irish and Scotch Presbyterians. The Gillespies were Roman Catholics of Celtic Irish stock. In America the Blaines settled about Lancaster and Carlisle, Pa., were active in business, and played a prominent part in the Revolution. After the Revolution they crossed the Alleghanies and settled in the vicinity of Pittsburgh. In 1842 Ephraim Blaine was elected prothonotary of Washington County and thereupon moved to the county seat. At the age of thirteen James entered Washington College which his father and many other relatives had attended. His age at graduation is an indication of the limited nature of the college course. He secured, however, a sound grounding in the classics, in English, and in mathematics. He began at once to teach in the Western Military Institute, at Georgetown, Ky. He did not like the South, and was ambitious to study law. From 1852 to 1854 he taught in the Pennsylvania Institute for the

Blind, at Philadelphia, where he could study law at the same time.

On June 30, 1850, he secretly married Harriet Stanwood, at that time teaching in Kentucky, but belonging to an old Massachusetts family, one branch of which settled in 1822 at Augusta, Me. As the legality of this marriage was in doubt, they were remarried on Mar. 29, 1851, at Pittsburgh, Pa. Through this connection came, in 1854, an opportunity to enter journalism at Augusta. Through the financial assistance of Mrs. Blaine's brothers he was able to purchase an interest in the *Kennebec Journal*. For several years he also served on the editorial staff of the *Portland Advertiser*. Although he left journalism in 1860, it was, aside from politics, his profession, and he may be said to have been one of the most prominent of American statesmen to receive their training from that calling. He settled in Augusta, joined the Congregational church, and from 1854 was identified with Maine, illustrating a migration unusual in American history. Augusta remained his home, and here he raised a family of seven children, of whom four survived him. Much of his time, however, was spent at Washington, and in his later years, his summers at Bar Harbor.

Blaine was of a stalwart, well-proportioned physique, with a large, fine head; distinctly a commanding figure. His eyes were particularly brilliant; his voice effective and attractive. His manner had much of the dignity of his generation of statesmen. Much more striking, however, was his magnetic quality, which gave charm to his social intercourse, and which made his oratory perhaps the most thrilling of his day. It was probably the exhaustion coming after demonstrations of such power, which caused his complaints of ill health, which often puzzled his friends. Undoubtedly he had much of what is called temperament. It followed that he was at his best with a crowd or audience. He was not a club man, and had more followers than intimates.

His mental characteristics were decidedly those connected with mathematical talent. His speeches were carefully prepared and contained much exact information. One of his greatest political assets was his ability to remember names and faces. He was an expert in the interpretation of election returns. He had in addition an intuitive talent for political leadership. It was this talent, combined with an imagination which gained in power as he gained confidence in himself, which distinguished his foreign policy; but by the time he put this forward, when fifty, he had, perhaps, lost his earlier zest for the exact study upon

which he based his domestic policies. His humor, which must have been native, was slow to develop and was assiduously cultivated. Developed by the repartee of debate, it became one of his effective political weapons.

Blaine came to his leading political ideas by nature and by inheritance. His family were Whigs. Thomas Ewing of Ohio was a cousin of his mother. He was a great admirer of Henry Clay, on whose famous Lexington speech of 1847 he took notes. To advocate measures of a nationalizing character was, therefore, natural to him. His interest in the question of slavery was equally keen. In 1854, his first year of editorship, he abandoned the name Whig, and was instrumental in causing those Maine voters, who, under many political titles, were opposed to the Kansas-Nebraska bill, to adopt the new Western cognomen of Republican; thus giving that name currency in the East. In 1856 he was a delegate to the first national Republican convention, and one of its secretaries. He was, therefore, one of the genuine founders of that party, which he expected to carry on Whig measures as well as to oppose slavery.

While Maine was located so far to one side of the country as to miss that strategic importance of a central position which has counted for so much in American politics, nevertheless Blaine found there two advantages. The Maine elections were, during most of his career, held a month earlier than those elsewhere, and were consequently watched eagerly all over the country. More important was the fact that the number of men of exceptional ability in the politics of the state was particularly large. The editor of the rival newspaper at Augusta was Melville W. Fuller, later chief justice of the United States. The strength of the Maine politicians helped him not only by rivalry, but also by support. He was always surrounded by a strong group of local supporters, such as William Pierce Frye, Thomas Brackett Reed, and Nelson Dingley. The Maine habit of keeping such men long in office made them an increasingly powerful group. In a new party young men have an exceptional opportunity. In 1859 he was made chairman of the Republican state committee. He kept this post until 1881, and made himself the accepted and acceptable dictator of his party in the state.

In 1858 he was elected to the state legislature and was twice reëlected. During the last two terms he was Speaker of the House of Representatives. This success was won by his editorial skill and ability in political management and in legislative business. It was not until 1860 that he began his career as a public speaker. He entered Congress in 1863, serving in the national House of Representatives until July 10, 1876. In 1869 he was elected speaker, serving until the Democratic House of 1875 took office; after which he became leader of the Republican opposition. On July 10, 1876, he became senator, holding that office until Mar. 5, 1881.

During these years Blaine rose to be a national figure. He exhibited an unusual level-headedness, and changed his views less often than most men during the trying period of Civil War and Reconstruction. These views were sufficiently direct and clear-cut to arouse enthusiasm, but did not share the radicalism and vindictiveness of the extremists. He was firmly a Lincoln man, although in 1860 most of his Maine associates preferred Seward. Before he entered Congress he helped to win a victory in the state election of 1863 on Lincoln's program of Unionism, dropping in that election the designation of Republican, and doing much to organize the large Union majorities of that year, so necessary to offset the Democratic gains of 1862.

Early in the Reconstruction period he came out for negro suffrage, but accepted the lead of neither Thaddeus Stevens nor Charles Sumner. Rather he began to make connections with certain Western leaders, like Bingham and Garfield. He first attracted wide notice by joining with Bingham in adding as an amendment to Stevens's bill for the military government of the South, a provision for reconstruction. This amendment was characterized by the extreme Radicals as "making universal suffrage and universal amnesty" the basis of reconstruction (J. F. Rhodes, *History of the United States,* 1906, VI, 19). After a severe fight the amendment was attached to the bill, though its amnesty feature was modified.

This was a notable victory for a youngster over the venerable Republican floor leader. Stevens's death Blaine regarded as "an emancipation for the Republican party." Asked who could take his place, Blaine replied, "There are three young men coming forward." He pointed to Allison of Iowa, Garfield of Ohio, and, looking up into the dome of the Capitol, said, "I don't see the third" (G. F. Hoar, *Autobiography,* 1903, I, 239). He remained opposed to the extreme coercive measures of the Grant administration, helping to defeat a new Force Bill. On the other hand, in 1875, when the Democrats had gained control of the House, he opposed a general amnesty bill, making a violent attack on Jefferson Davis which left no doubt of his genuine Unionism. On the whole he came well through this trying period with the reputation

of a liberal who could nevertheless be trusted even by the Grand Army.

During these years he built up also a strong popularity in the West. His associates were Garfield and Allison. He assisted in 1872 in a reduction of the tariff (Horace White, *The Life of Lyman Trumbull,* 1913, pp. 354–55). His position on the currency was that of a moderate, with tendencies toward sound money. He was regarded as loyal to the principles and practises of his party, but was not an extremist. As important as the friendships which he made was one lasting enmity. This was with the brilliant representative from New York, Roscoe Conkling. In April 1866 they became engaged in a violent personal encounter, when Blaine was presenting a report from the committee on military affairs. Words ran very high, and Blaine accused Conkling of editing his remarks for the *Congressional Globe* in a way to place Blaine's rejoinders in a false light. This break was never healed. Conkling became one of the leading supporters of Grant, and Blaine became the head of opposition within the party. Gradually there formed two Republican factions, the Stalwarts, or Grant men, and the Half-Breeds, among whom Blaine was most conspicuous—a rivalry kept before the country by the wit of Conkling and the dramatic instinct of Blaine. The probable retirement of Gen. Grant from the presidency in 1876 left the field open to many candidates. Circumstances seemed to have made Blaine the leading candidate for the Republican nomination when a dramatic episode occurred which probably barred the door of the presidency to him forever, as the cry of "Bargain and Corruption" had barred it to his hero Clay. The Democratic committee investigating the charges of railroad graft brought charges of corruption against Blaine. The proof of their truth or falsity was supposed to rest in a collection known as the "Mulligan Letters." These letters Blaine secured. He refused to hand them over to the committee of "southern brigadiers," but he himself read from them to the House in a brilliant and dramatic speech.

The facts seem to be that a decision of Speaker Blaine saved a land grant for the Little Rock and Fort Smith Railroad in 1869. Blaine, thereupon, on the basis of this favor, asked the favor of the railroad managers. He received the privilege of selling bonds on a commission that was secret and certainly generous. He claimed that he lost money on the transaction, as the bonds fell, and he felt under obligation to reimburse his friends. This loyalty to his friends and disregard for the public interest was characteristic of the time.

The fact that he conferred the favor before, and not after, receiving the return favor, differentiated him from many public men. It was, nevertheless, true that Blaine became wealthy without visible means of income, and that he resisted all attempts "to expose his private business." His standards were not below those of many public men of his time, but they rendered him anathema to those who were endeavoring to raise the public standards, particularly to the group headed by Carl Schurz, whose independence of party rendered them so powerful in politics from 1868 to 1895. (The best statement of the charges against Blaine is in Carl Schurz, *Speeches, Correspondence, and Political Papers*, 1913, IV, 239–48; the most considered historical judgment is F. L. Paxson, *Recent History of the United States*, 1921, pp. 90–91.)

It was under such circumstances that Blaine was first a candidate for the presidency. As always with him the striking accidental combined with the well-earned weight of facts to influence the result. Five days before the convention he was prostrated by the heat of Washington, and the uncertainty of his recovery became a factor in the voting. His name was presented by Robert G. Ingersoll in a speech which has generally been considered the most brilliant nomination in the history of our conventions, and which designated Blaine as the "Plumed Knight," a title which always clung to him. In this convention he had the strongest initial vote, 285, to 125 for his nearest rival, Oliver P. Morton of Indiana who was among those favored by Grant. In addition the anti-Grant forces were in a majority in the whole convention. It was felt, however, that the feeling of the administration against Blaine was so strong that the support of powerful men would be lacking in the campaign should he be nominated, and that the Schurz group would turn to the Democrats. The vote of Rutherford B. Hayes, governor of Ohio, grew steadily, and when New York transferred its vote from Conkling to Hayes, Blaine telegraphed Hayes his congratulations, although Hayes was not nominated until the seventh ballot. It was by such impulsive and generous gestures that Blaine won the widespread affection which was his great political asset.

During the Hayes administration Blaine, now senator from Maine, was preparing for the next campaign. He supported the administration against the attacks of Conkling, their brilliant exchanges keeping both constantly in the public eye. It was a contest for tactical advantage but Blaine strengthened his reputation for moderation and for consideration of the West.

President Hayes was not a candidate for renomination. The Stalwarts concentrated their attention upon again nominating Grant himself, securing a solid block of over three hundred delegates who never wavered. Blaine was again the leading candidate in opposition, with an initial 284 delegates. The others were divided among other Half-Breed leaders, the most important being Senator John Sherman of Ohio and Senator George F. Edmunds of Vermont. Again Conkling's extreme bitterness against Blaine was feared as a factor in the subsequent campaign, and on the thirty-sixth ballot, Gen. James A. Garfield, a friend of Blaine, was nominated. Again Blaine took the result with good nature and worked in the closest intimacy with Garfield in the subsequent campaign. To assuage the disgruntled Stalwarts, Chester A. Arthur of New York was nominated for the vice-presidency.

Garfield appointed Blaine as secretary of state and the administration might almost be called that of Garfield-Blaine. Among its lesser political measures were a series of appointments which violently angered the Stalwarts. After Garfield was shot and died, and Arthur, the friend of Conkling, succeeded, Blaine's influence in the administration was gone, and he tendered his resignation, Sept. 22, 1881. At the request of President Arthur, however, he continued to serve as secretary until Dec. 19, 1881.

The division in the Republican party still remained, but on the whole the Half-Breeds gained. However much Blaine was a politician, it seems to be the fact that from 1876 he was the choice of the majority, or of the largest faction of Republicans, who believed that he had been kept from nomination by political expedients and who felt that his time had now come. Remaining in Washington, he wrote the first part of his *Twenty Years of Congress* (Volume I published 1884) and articles setting forth his position. He was also in daily touch with his political associates. As the presidential year approached President Arthur received the support of the Stalwarts for renomination, but that faction was steadily losing power. In the convention of 1884 Blaine was nominated for the presidency on the first ballot, and Gen. John A. Logan of Illinois was chosen as candidate for vice-president.

His Democratic opponent was Grover Cleveland, who as governor of New York had attracted the favor of those particularly interested in certain reforms, as that of the civil service. This fact, combined with the suspicion clinging to Blaine as a result of the affair of the Mulligan Letters, caused the group led by Carl Schurz, which had up to this time coöperated with the Republicans, to shift to the support of Cleveland. Their numbers were not large and some associated with them, as Theodore Roosevelt and Henry Cabot Lodge, refused to change. Nevertheless they were men of prominence and their desertion weakened the Republican hope of success. Popularly they were designated as Mugwumps.

The foreign policy which Blaine had developed while secretary of state, moreover, seems to have caused more apprehension than enthusiasm. His tilts with Great Britain, however, were popular with the Irish-Americans, and it was hoped that he could divide that vote. At the very end of the campaign, in a speech at the Fifth Avenue Hotel in New York, a supporter of Blaine, the Rev. S. D. Burchard [*q.v.*], referred to him as fighting the Democratic party as "the party whose antecedents are rum, Romanism, and rebellion." This expression, coming too late to be explained away, undoubtedly alienated many Irish Catholics, and in view of the closeness of the vote in New York, the key state, where a change of 600 votes would have turned the election, may well have meant the defeat of Blaine. He lost Connecticut, New York, New Jersey, and Indiana, and the election.

Blaine now resumed the writing of his *Twenty Years in Congress,* publishing the second volume in 1886. In the following year he published a collection of his speeches with the title *Political Discussions: Legislative, Diplomatic, and Popular.* He still remained the most powerful Republican, and expectation was general that he would be nominated again in 1888. Before the convention he went for a long trip to Europe. On Jan. 25, 1888, he wrote home from Florence stating that he was not a candidate, and that he could not accept unless he were to be chosen by an unanimity which was impossible. This decision was confirmed by other letters, and finally convinced his friends, although votes were still cast for him in the convention. He was, however, though still away, a powerful factor, and was instrumental, if not the chief influence, in causing the selection of Benjamin Harrison of Indiana, as candidate.

It was taken for granted, upon the election of Harrison, that the chief post in the cabinet would be offered to Blaine. The offer was made and accepted and Blaine entered upon the most fruitful part of his career. These were, however, unhappy years for Blaine. In 1890 he lost two children. His relations with the President became strained, and his health was not good. As the presidential year approached, again he announced that he would not be a candidate, which left the President the leading aspirant, but not a popular one. When the convention met, the President had almost, but not quite, a majority of pledged delegates. On June 4, three days before the convention, Blaine resigned in a curt letter, and his resignation was as curtly accepted. Such action can hardly be interpreted otherwise than that Blaine hoped for a miracle, for a demonstration of that enthusiasm which he still inspired so convincing as to sweep the convention off its feet. He received 182 ⅚ votes, but Harrison was nominated on the first ballot. With that generosity which always characterized him, Blaine returned to Washington, was reconciled with the President, and took what little part in the campaign his health allowed. His health, however, rapidly declined, and on Jan. 27, 1893, at the age of sixty-two, he died. In spite of this early death, Blaine seemed to have well rounded out a career. New times were calling for men of different training. He impresses one, moreover, as having lived at the height of his powers in the years between 1865 and 1885, and to have died an old man.

The permanent influence of Blaine on American life has been through his foreign policy. On Mar. 7, 1881, he first entered upon his duties as secretary of state. This position in American government has taken on a double significance; the secretary is, under the president, the leader of the administration, and is also the foreign minister. The general expectation was that in an unusual degree Blaine would emphasize the political aspects of the office. Intimate friend of the President, he was in the public eye a more considerable figure. This political reputation, moreover, had been built up on the basis of his leadership in domestic problems. It was not, therefore, supposed that he would do more than follow the routine policies of the country, perhaps with some tincture of his customary dash.

It is too little to say that this expectation was shattered. From the time he took office, Blaine made foreign affairs his leading interest. He made them the outstanding point in the appeal to the people for the presidency to which he constantly aspired. Nor does this seem to have been merely an intellectually contrived project for political advancement. Almost alone among the public men of his period, he saw in American foreign relations not merely a series of episodes, to be dealt with according to the fixed rules of the Monroe Doctrine and of international law, but a general situation calling for a constructive policy, to be adjusted to changing conditions. His rising interest in diplomatic problems may well have been due to native instinct. He had the qualities of a diplomat, and his personal conduct of such affairs was his strongest asset; though his personal feeling was perhaps too strong, as is evinced by his refusal while in London to meet Lord Salisbury, because of their acrimonious exchanges.

Blaine's generation in the United States was almost totally without the basic training for diplomatic thought or practise. It was the nadir of American diplomacy. This defect Blaine at fifty was not prepared to make good by study. His years of strenuous application had passed. He remained, therefore, lamentably ignorant of international law and of diplomatic history. In addition his major interest in politics often caused him to be careless in the selection of his agents in critical situations. These defects seriously affected his reputation. That they marred his success is more doubtful; he was a forerunner of American world interests, and so far in advance of the public that even perfect achievement would scarcely have won popular support in his time.

Blaine's first term as secretary lasted only from Mar. 7, 1881, to Dec. 19, 1881. On Mar. 7, 1889, however, he again entered the office, serving until June 4, 1892. In the interval, neither the Republican administration of President Arthur and Secretary Frelinghuysen, nor the Democratic administration of President Cleveland and Secretary Bayard, was in harmony with his views. Blaine, however, during this period, made his chief residence in Washington, with summers at Bar Harbor, and one visit to Europe. He was always in the closest touch with his group of Republican leaders in Congress, and his influence was very powerful. He remained thus constantly a force in determining United States policy, and this period of his life is distinctly a unit.

There were several closely interknit problems to which he devoted his attention. Ever since the Civil War the relations between the Latin-American countries and Great Britain had been growing more intimate at the expense of the United States. This was due in large measure to the supplanting of the latter's merchant marine by the British. Furthermore the competition of South American nations, particularly of Argentina, was encroaching upon the command of the European food trade by the United States, at the same time that the latter's manufactures, which were Blaine's chief concern, were reaching the point where foreign markets were deemed necessary. Lastly, the question of an inter-oceanic canal had assumed a new importance in the light of the successful forcing of the isthmus of Suez. From these factors Blaine evolved a policy well

coördinated and appealing. In form, this was much influenced by his admiration for Henry Clay. Like Clay he was not satisfied with the negative features of the Monroe Doctrine. He would unite the nations of America into a real system, with the United States as "elder sister." He would maintain peace among them by the use of the good offices of the United States and by arbitration. For constructive purposes he would call them all in joint conference to plan measures of mutual advantage. He would rally them to an extension of Clay's American system, "America for the Americans." That this policy might bring some occasion for dispute with Great Britain was politically an advantage, for any baiting of the British lion was pleasing to the Irish vote which was large and strategically placed. The traditional division of the world into two hemispheres, set forth in the Monroe Doctrine, would be maintained.

When Blaine took office in 1881 a concession for the building of a canal across the isthmus of Panama had already been obtained from the Republic of Colombia by a French company headed by the famous De Lesseps, the constructor of that at Suez. Both Secretary Evarts and President Hayes of the preceding administration had strongly taken a stand refusing to join in an international guarantee of the neutrality of such a canal, and insisting that such a canal must be built under the auspices and sole protection of the United States and the country through which it was constructed. Blaine promptly endorsed this policy, sending instructions to the American ministers in Europe, that the "guarantee given by the United States of America does not require re-enforcement, or accession, or assent from any other power." He stated that the passage of hostile troops through such a canal when either the United States or Colombia was at war was "no more admissible than . . . over the railroad lines joining the Atlantic and Pacific shores of the United States."

This was in fact a change in policy on the part of the United States, which had until the time of Evarts stood for an international control of such a canal. It was, in addition, in direct contravention of the Clayton-Bulwer treaty of 1850 with Great Britain, which had agreed to a canal under a joint international guarantee and had invited others to join in a guarantee of neutrality. On Nov. 1, 1881, Blaine took up this treaty. He argued that the treaty was void because of changed conditions, and contrary to the established policy of the United States. A lively interchange of notes, however, between the governments of the United States and Great Britain, failed to eliminate the treaty, nor was there any peaceful method of voiding the Colombian concession to the French company. Blaine, therefore, used his influence to promote the project of a United States canal through the nearby isthmus of Nicaragua. His canal policy was continued by Frelinghuysen, but negotiations with Nicaragua were brought to an end by President Cleveland, who reverted to the earlier United States policy, that such a canal "must be for the world benefit, a trust for mankind, to be removed from chance of domination by any single power." This matter continued as a subject of political and international controversy for twenty years. Ultimately the policy of Blaine was accepted by the United States. The plan for a Nicaragua Canal was not dropped until President Roosevelt succeeded in so modifying the Clayton-Bulwer treaty as to allow the canal at Panama to become a United States property, fortified by the United States.

A similar question confronted Blaine when he became secretary a second time, in 1889; that of the protection of the seal herds which bred on the Pribilof Islands of Alaska. The question of their destruction by Canadians and other deep-sea fishers had reached an acute stage under President Cleveland. Blaine at once took the stand that Bering Sea was a closed sea and part of the territorial waters of the United States. This position was historically unsound and was out of harmony with the previous policy of the United States as it had been evolved in the case of the northeastern fisheries. He negotiated, however, with the British minister in the United States, Sir Julian Pauncefote, a rather remarkable treaty by which legal rights were submitted to arbitration, and, in case the United States were to lose, for a scientific enquiry to be made to determine measures necessary to protect seal herds. Pending the arbitration they were placed under the protection of a *modus vivendi*. The United States lost its case but Blaine had raised the question of the protection of such animal life as migrates from country to country and uses the high seas. Since his day much has been done in this direction, by treaties between various countries interested.

The main constructive portion of Blaine's foreign policy had to do with South America. This had been foreshadowed before he became secretary by his support of subsidies to revive the United States's shipping connections with that continent (Blaine, *Political Discussions*, pp. 186–93). As secretary one of his first acts was to stand between Latin-American countries and Europe. To prevent the seizure of Venezuelan custom-houses by the French for payment of a claim,

he urged Venezuela to pay through the agent of the United States and threatened that should no payment be made within three months, the United States would herself seize the custom-houses and collect the money. He protested June 25, 1881, in a letter to Lucius Fairchild, minister to Spain, against the proposal of Colombia and Costa Rica, to submit a boundary dispute to Spain for arbitration. This was not a denial of right, but an expression of his hope, that the United States might become sole arbitrator in such disputes (see C. R. Fish, *American Diplomacy*, 1915, pp. 384–85).

He devoted much attention to keeping the peace in America by active mediation. Convinced that Guatemala was right in a dispute with Mexico, he wrote the latter: "This country will continue its policy of peace even if it cannot have the great aid which the coöperation of Mexico would assure; and it will hope at no distant day to see such concord and coöperation between all nations of America as will render war impossible." His greatest interest was in the war actually in progress between Chile and Peru, over the Tacna-Arica territory. His first agents to the two countries were diplomatically incompetent, but finally he sent William H. Trescot of South Carolina, an accomplished diplomat. Trescot was to warn Chile against an unwarrantable use of her victories, and to threaten her with intervention, not by the United States alone but by joint action of the American powers (*Ibid.*, p. 386). Already Blaine was making preparations to secure such American coöperation, by developing the idea of Pan-Americanism, which had been so dead since Clay's fiasco with the Congress of Panama. On Nov. 29, 1881, he asked all the independent nations of America to discuss arbitration, and inaugurate an era of good will. This invitation was withdrawn when, after the assassination of Garfield, Blaine was succeeded by Frelinghuysen. In fact his whole Latin-American policy was promptly dropped. It did not, however, cease to be discussed. It was attacked as partial and blustering and apt to bring hostility between Europe and America. Its errors of detail were severely arraigned. It seems to have served Blaine little politically, as the country was uninterested in foreign affairs. Blaine defended his policy in magazine articles, and urged it through his friends in Congress. In 1888 Congress passed a bill calling a Pan-American congress, which President Cleveland allowed to become a law without his signature (M. Romero, "The Pan-American Conference," *North American Review*, September, October, 1890). On Oct. 2, 1889, this Congress met at Washington, with a long program including arbitration and the facilitating of commercial intercourse; but avoidance of all exciting questions. While without power, it drew up, under the personal influence of Blaine, many desirable recommendations, and in particular laid the foundation of the Bureau of American Republics at Washington, which has proved a permanent contribution. The vitality of this coöperation was in Blaine's mind to rest upon increased commercial intercourse, which he planned to promote by reciprocity treaties authorized in 1884. The new McKinley tariff bill, then under discussion in Congress, put on the free list most of the agricultural products of Latin America, thus depriving the United States of any *quid pro quo* in bargaining. Blaine, on July 11, 1890, wrote Senator Frye of Maine: "There is not a section or a line in the entire bill that will open the market for another bushel of (American) wheat or another barrel of pork." His views received much support from the West, and were offered in an amendment, fixing a duty upon sugar and such commodities, but allowing the President power to remove such duties in the case of "all products of any nation of the American hemisphere upon which no export duties are imposed" in case the agreed products of the United States should be admitted free of duty. This amendment was not passed, but a "reciprocity" clause was introduced, which left the products in question on the free list, but allowed the President to impose a tax in case the duties imposed by any nation on articles from the United States appeared to him "unequal and unreasonable." This ignored Blaine's intention of specially cementing relations with American powers; nevertheless he concluded under it a number of treaties, which were in operation too short a time to demonstrate their possible effect.

As had been customary since the days of Webster, Blaine considered the Hawaiian Islands as part of the American hemisphere. He found them a kingdom closely bound to the United States by a reciprocity treaty, but with a government which he believed was strongly susceptible to foreign influences, especially that of Great Britain. In 1881 he wrote the American minister there that should the native population continue to decline, the United States would be obliged to take over the islands. On becoming secretary again in 1889, he sent as minister John L. Stevens, one of his closest friends and business associates. On Feb. 8, 1892, Stevens wrote Blaine that "annexation must be the future remedy or else Great Britain will be furnished with circumstances and opportunity to get a hold on these islands which will cause future serious em-

barrassment to the United States." After Blaine's retirement a revolution broke out, which was sympathetically supported by Minister Stevens and which could hardly have been beyond Blaine's vision of the possible.

While pursuing his policy of America for the Americans, Blaine did not stand apart from movements to improve general international organization. He negotiated an important treaty on extradition with Great Britain, joined in a general act for the suppression of the African slave trade, and made the United States's first treaties on international copyright.

Blaine is conspicuous as the only outstanding public figure between Seward and Hay who was really interested in foreign affairs. His contributions, the Pan-American Union and reciprocity, are of less importance than the fact that he attracted public attention to international problems, and in particular to certain lines of policy relating to America, which were followed out by Roosevelt, and are still (1927) developing.

[Blaine was not careful of his correspondence; letters of his, however, are found in the Lib. of Cong., in the McCulloch, W. T. Sherman, Staunton, and Israel Washburn MSS. Aside from official records, the chief source of information is his own *Twenty Years of Congress, from Lincoln to Garfield* (2 vols., 1884–86), which stands high in character among works of its kind. He also published: *Political Discussions, Legislative, Diplomatic, and Popular* (1856–86); an article on "The Foreign Policy of the Garfield Administration," *Chicago Weekly Magazine*, Sept. 16, 1882, and many other articles and editorials. Gail Hamilton, *Biog. of Jas. G. Blaine* (1895), p. 722, gives an account of his ancestry and intimate life. The biography by Edward Stanwood, *Jas. Gillespie Blaine* (1905) is the most complete account of his political career. The Mulligan Letters are discussed by J. F. Rhodes, *Hist. of the U. S.*, VII (1906), 193–206, and by F. L. Paxson, *Recent Hist.* (1921), pp. 90–91. In 1884 nearly a score of campaign biographies were published, containing many extracts of speeches and letters; perhaps the best is that of J. C. Ridpath, *Life and Work of Jas. G. Blaine* (1893). *Letters of Mrs. Jas. G. Blaine*, ed. by Harriet S. Blaine Beale, appeared in two volumes in 1908. See also Alice Felt Tyler, *The Foreign Policy of Jas. G. Blaine* (1927).]

C. R. F.

BLAIR, AUSTIN (Feb. 8, 1818–Aug. 6, 1894), governor of Michigan, was born at Caroline, Tompkins County, N. Y. His great-great-grandfather came from Scotland in 1756 and settled on land now covered by Worcester, Mass. In 1809, his father, George Blair, built the first log cabin in Tompkins County, N. Y. Blair's mother was Rhoda (Blackman) Mann, widow of Sabin Mann. Ardent advocates of the abolition of slavery, the parents lived to see their hopes realized, and their son an instrument in the accomplishment. Austin Blair was educated at Cazenovia Seminary and Hamilton and Union Colleges, graduating from the latter in 1837. He was admitted to the Tioga County bar in 1841, and removed to Jackson, Mich., where he became a Whig and an active supporter of Henry Clay. From 1845 to 1849 he was a member of the state legislature, where he incurred the hostility of leaders of his party by advocating the granting of the ballot to colored citizens, and of the clergy by aiding to secure the abolition of capital punishment. Cutting loose from the Whigs, Blair in 1848 was a member of the Buffalo convention of Free-Soilers that nominated Van Buren and Adams for president and vice-president. As a member of the mass convention of Whigs, Democrats, and Free-Soilers, held "under the oaks at Jackson," July 6, 1854, he participated in the formation of the Republican party. Republican leader in the state Senate from 1855, he led the Michigan delegation at the Chicago convention that nominated Abraham Lincoln. Michigan supported Seward, and Blair was one of the trio (William M. Evarts and Carl Schurz being the others) to whom the Seward cause was intrusted on the floor of the convention. An unsuccessful candidate for the United States Senate in 1857, when Zachariah Chandler displaced Lewis Cass, Blair was elected governor in 1860, and on Jan. 3, 1861, he declared in his inaugural address that "the Federal Government has the power to defend itself, and I do not doubt that that power will be exercised to the utmost. It is a question of war that the seceding states have to look in the face" (*Detroit Free Press,* Jan. 4, 1861). The news of the bombardment of Fort Sumter reached Detroit Saturday, Apr. 13; on Sunday the state sprang to arms; $100,000 was raised by subscription to equip troops, the treasury having been emptied by theft. On May 15, a week earlier than was required, the Michigan regiment was the first to reach Washington from the West. This initial energy continued unabated to the end; and by his energy, steadfastness, and good judgment Austin Blair came to be numbered with Andrew of Massachusetts, Morgan of New York, Curtin of Pennsylvania, Dennison of Ohio, Morton of Indiana, Yates of Illinois, and Kirkwood of Iowa in the illustrious band of "War Governors" who staunchly upheld President Lincoln. When Blair retired from the governorship in 1865, the end of the war was in sight. A year later he was elected to Congress, where he served from 1867 to 1873. In 1871, he was supported by the soldiers and the Republican newspapers in his candidacy for the Senate, but after a bitter contest the choice of the legislature was Thomas W. Ferry, with whom Blair had made an unsuccessful combination against Senator Chandler in 1869. Feeling that his public services had entitled him to election to the Senate, and chagrined over defeat as the result of (as he

believed) political trickery characteristic of his party, Blair joined the Independent Republican movement in 1872. He took the stump for Horace Greeley, and allowed himself to run for governor of Michigan on a fusion ticket. He was overwhelmingly defeated. Finding his new political bedfellows uncongenial, he was welcomed back to the Republican party, and in 1885 was nominated for justice of the Michigan supreme court on the ticket with Justice Thomas M. Cooley; but both were defeated by reason of venomous newspaper attacks on decisions of the court alleged to favor railroads. From 1882 to 1890 Blair served by election two terms as a regent of the University of Michigan. The controversies in which he had been engaged from boyhood had burned themselves out, and the latter days of his life were spent in the practise of his profession. He was married in February 1849 to Sarah L. Ford, and his son, Charles A. Blair, was a justice of the Michigan supreme court from 1904 until his death in 1912.

[H. M. Utley and B. M. Cutcheon, *Mich. as a Province, Territory and State* (1906), vols. III, IV; J. F. Rhodes, *Hist. of the U. S.,* vols. II (1894), VI (1906); Chas. Moore, *Hist. of Mich.,* vol. I (1915); E. W. Leavitt, *The Blair Family in New Eng.* (1900); *Evening News* (Detroit), Aug. 4, 1894.]

C. M.

BLAIR, FRANCIS PRESTON (Apr. 12, 1791–Oct. 18, 1876), journalist, politician, was descended from John Blair, a Scotch-Irish immigrant to America in the early eighteenth century, who settled in Bucks County, Pa., and held the first chair of theology in Princeton College. John's son, James, a Virginia lawyer, early moved to Kentucky where he served as attorney-general of the state (1796–1816). Francis Preston, born at Abingdon, Va., was one of the sons of James Blair. He was a sickly lad with a consumptive tendency which he later outgrew. Educated at Transylvania University, he graduated with honors (1811), studied law, was admitted to the bar (1817), but owing to a vocal defect never practised. In 1812 he volunteered for service against Great Britain to act as aide to his uncle George Madison, then governor of Kentucky. At Vincennes he was seized with a hemorrhage from his lungs which forced him to return to Frankfort. To improve his health he tried to farm but his liking for politics led him to make farming an avocation and politics his profession. This he did when Kentucky was agitated over relief measures, mainly financial and judicial, and convulsed with the New Court *vs.* Old Court struggles. Blair joined the relief party and became clerk of the new court of appeals. He, Maj. W. T. Barry, and Amos Kendall were bosom friends and political allies. He assisted Kendall, who edited in Frankfort, Ky., the *Argus of Western America* and the *Patriot,* and his editorials and pamphlets were pungent condemnations of the Old Court party. He finally emerged from this singularly bitter political controversy as clerk of the state circuit court, editorial contributor to the *Argus of Western America,* and president of the Commonwealth Bank. He assisted his father in the preparation of the argument for the right of a state to tax the Bank of the United States (1811) and opposed its recharter.

In spite of their divergent views Blair in 1824 wanted Clay for president of the United States, and even after the election of Adams he remained hopeful until late in 1825 that Clay would mould the Administra'on's policy in the interests of the West. The publication of the first presidential message to Congress, however, definitely alienated him from the Administration. He joined the ranks of Jackson where he served whole-heartedly as a member of the Jackson committee at Frankfort. He advocated direct election of the president by the people, legislative control of judicial decisions, cheap lands for settlers, and the abolition of imprisonment for debt. His articles in the *Argus of Western America,* after the election of 1828, attacking the Bank of the United States and nullification, received considerable notice. He answered, editorially, Cheves and McDuffie of South Carolina on the tariff and nullification. Blair maintained that Congress had the power to levy a tariff, and that the tariff should be regulated downward, and that the country was fortunate in having a president who said: "The Union must be preserved." At the same time he was arguing that the Bank of the United States was trying to ruin the democratic Commonwealth Bank of Kentucky, of which he was president. When Maj. W. T. Barry and Amos Kendall were established in offices at Washington, they, upon President Jackson's request for advice, suggested Blair for the editor of the proposed Administration organ to replace Duff Green's *Telegraph.* Jackson called Blair to Washington where he established the *Globe* in 1830.

Blair adopted the significant slogan: "The World is governed too much." He received the patronage of the Administration and with the able John C. Rives as a business manager the *Globe* was made a financial success. Nullification, the United States Bank, and Clay's "American System," were viciously and effectively attacked while he warmly advocated Jacksonian measures and championed the cause of Jackson and Van Buren in their respective campaigns.

Few men exerted a political power more potent than Blair through the *Globe* during 1832–41. Being eager to supply their readers with daily proceedings in Congress, Blair and Rives also published the *Congressional Globe.* Blair became a confidential member of the Kitchen Cabinet. He accompanied President Jackson on vacation trips, talked with him about public policies before he had breakfasted, and then hurried to the *Globe* office to pursue his adopted policy of "shooting the deserters" and to give the cue to the Administration papers throughout the country. He constantly used his vitriolic pen against men who opposed "the democracy." His editorials were so skilfully written that he often goaded the opposition to madness. Blair believed that a political party existed primarily to carry out the will of the people, that every man should be a defender of the sacred Constitution of the United States. "The Constitution" and "the Union" were his watchwords. When the question of the annexation of Texas became a campaign issue he joined the Benton-Van Buren wing of his party, thereby alienating a majority of the annexationists. Even though he supported Polk after the Baltimore Convention (1844), and offered to conduct the *Globe* as strongly for Polk's administration as he had for Jackson and Van Buren, Polk felt that he must have a new editor. He forced Blair to sell his interests in the *Globe* to Thomas Ritchie of the Richmond *Enquirer* (1845), offering Blair the Spanish mission as a sop. Blair refused the post.

Silver Spring, Blair's country estate, near Washington, D. C., became a political shrine when he retired from the *Globe.* He had expected to live a quiet life but reëntered politics in 1848 when he joined Van Buren in advocating Free-Soilism. In 1852 he supported Pierce, believing that Jacksonian Democracy would be revived. Pierce made overtures to Blair early in 1853, but Blair thought Pierce broke his promises in his cabinet appointments and failed to adopt the methods of Jackson and "the [true] democracy." Finding himself bitterly disillusioned, he denounced the Kansas-Nebraska Act as a violation of the Missouri Compromise. Still hoping to see a revival of "the Democracy" he became one of the principal organizers of the Republican party, and used his influence to effect the nomination of Frémont. By 1858 he was rejoicing over Buchanan's accusation that he was in rebellion against the Democratic party. He wanted a Democrat of the old faith to resist the Southern influences but, caught in the political drift, he joined his sons in the campaign for Lincoln, and was an active member of the Chicago convention in 1860. After 1861 his advice was offered to the President and welcomed by him. Blair's love for Southern friends, desire for peace, and concern for the Union, caused him to go unofficially to Richmond to confer with Jefferson Davis in 1864. He proposed peace on the basis of a joint effort to be made by the North and South to expel Maximilian from Mexico. The Hampton Roads Conference (1865) was the result. Blair fully embraced Lincoln's plan of reconstruction, and after the President was assassinated, the Radicals drove him back into the Democratic party. He wanted Grant to head the Democratic party in 1867; he supported Seymour in 1868, and Greeley in 1872. He died believing that he had been a true Jacksonian Democrat and a disciple of Lincoln. He was married to Eliza Violet Gist, daughter of Nathaniel Gist and grand-daughter of ~~Sir~~ Christopher Gist; his sons, Montgomery [*q.v.*] and Francis Preston [*q.v.*], were both prominent in politics.

[The chief sources of information are found in the Blair Papers (unpublished); Jackson Papers (in process of publication); Van Buren Papers (unpublished); and in various newspapers. The *Globe* (Washington, D. C., 1831–45); *Argus of Western America* (Frankfort, Ky., 1827–30); *Nat. Intelligencer* (Washington, D. C., 1830–45); *Spectator* (Washington, D. C., 1844); *Kentuckian* (Frankfort, Ky., 1828) are especially good for information during the years indicated. "Annals of Silver Spring" by Gist Blair in *Records of the Columbia Hist. Soc.*, XXI (1918), contains a vivid description of Silver Spring. *Thirty Years' View* (1858) by Thos. Hart Benton has an interesting account of the establishment and disestablishment of the *Globe*. Glimpses of Blair's impressions of Washington and men in 1830 may be had in Thos. M. Clay's article, "Two Years with Old Hickory," in *Atlantic Mo.*, LX, 187–99. It is now certain that Blair was the author of the *Life and Public Services of Gen. Wm. O. Butler* (1848), a work generally ascribed to his son, Francis Preston Blair, Jr. Blair wrote a number of political pamphlets, among which are: *Gen. Jackson and Jas. Buchanan* (1856); *A Voice from the Grave of Jackson* (1856); *To My Neighbors* (1856); and *To the Working Men* (1869). An obituary notice appears in the *N. Y. Herald*, Oct. 19, 1876.]

W. E. S.

BLAIR, FRANCIS PRESTON (Feb. 19, 1821–July 9, 1875), Union soldier, statesman, was born at Lexington, Ky., the third and youngest son of Francis Preston Blair [*q.v.*]. While a child he was taken to Washington, D. C., by his father and there he attended a select school. As a young man he contributed to the editorial columns of the *Globe*, edited by his father, who took great pride in educating his son for a political career. Blair graduated at Princeton (1841) and then entered the law school at Transylvania University. After graduating there, and upon admission to the bar at Lexington, Ky., he went to practise with his brother, Montgomery [*q.v.*] in St. Louis (1842). Three years

of intense study and practise of law injured his health. While he was seeking rest and recreation in the Rocky Mountains the Mexican War broke out; consequently, he joined a company of Americans which was commanded by George Bent. When Gen. Kearny took New Mexico Blair was appointed attorney-general for the territory.

Upon returning from the West Blair was married on Sept. 8, 1847, to Appoline Alexander of Woodford County, Ky., and resumed his law practise in St. Louis. Having pronounced views on the extension of slavery he established a Free-Soil paper, the *Barnburner,* to further the interests of the cause in Missouri. He organized and led the Free-Soil party in that state and voted for Van Buren in 1848. Henry Clay found supporters in him, his father, and Montgomery, for his Compromise of 1850. Though a slave owner, Blair denounced the Kansas-Nebraska Act as a violation of the Missouri Compromise, and his views on slavery, so clearly and forcefully expressed, marked him as a character dangerous to slave interests. Two terms in the Missouri legislature (1852–56) gave him opportunity to express his Free-Soilism and prepare himself for Congress. He was like Thomas Hart Benton in his methods, although in 1856 he refused Benton's request to retract some of his public statements on slavery. Benton was defeated for governor of Missouri in that year, while Blair, who voted for Frémont, was the only Free-Soiler elected to Congress from a slave state. In his first speech in Congress he warned the South that slavery was bound to die. He urged the South to adopt the policy of gradual emancipation by deportation and colonization. He was defeated for reëlection to Congress (1858). In 1859 he published an argumentative "address" on colonization, entitled, *The Destiny of the Races on This Continent.*

The years 1858 to 1861 were eventful years for Blair. He opposed the extension of slavery on the basis that it was an economic hindrance to the development of the West, as well as socially and morally wrong. His family connections, his brilliance, his ability as an extemporaneous speaker, and his courageous frank manner, made him one of the popular orators of the day. As a speaker he was in demand in Minnesota and Vermont where he campaigned for the Republicans, in Illinois where he hoped to ruin the political fortunes of Douglas, and in Missouri where he battled against the "Nullificationists" and Benton's old enemies, especially the "Fayette Clique." He organized the Union party in Missouri and largely transformed it into the Republican party; in the latter he became the "leading spirit and chief adviser" in his own state. Like his father, he was a constitutionalist and an unyielding unionist. He was a Democrat-Republican who used parties merely as a means to an end.

The speeches and letters of Blair indicate that he feared a coming catastrophe long before the Civil War. The spectre of "Nullification" haunted him. He tried in vain to convert Northern men to his scheme of colonization. He supported Edward Bates for the presidential nomination through fear of secession early in the campaign of 1860, but he turned to Lincoln on the third ballot in the Chicago convention. After the convention few men labored as faithfully as he in the campaign. Consequently, he was ready to act quickly and decisively when civil war loomed. He organized the "Wide Awakes" in St. Louis, had men secretly drilled, secured ammunition and arms, kept himself informed of movements at Washington, and as a friend and supporter stood well in Lincoln's favor.

Blair was elected to Congress in 1860. In the spring of 1861 he determined to save Missouri for the Union. After much political maneuvering and "Home Guards" organizing, he and Gen. Lyon marshalled their forces sufficiently to compel the surrender of Camp Jackson, a camp of state militia sympathetic with the Confederacy. It was a play of Blair and his Unconditional Unionists against Gov. Jackson and his confederates, who desired to carry Missouri into the Confederacy. The capture of Camp Jackson drove thousands of Missourians into the Confederate cause, but the issue was now sharply drawn in the state; the United States arsenal at St. Louis was saved, and the state remained Unionist. Blair was offered a brigadier-generalship but refused in order to avoid political complications in Missouri.

In the Thirty-seventh Congress, as chairman of the Committee on Military Defense, Blair's policy was to crush the rebellion as quickly as men and money could do it. His policy included the acceptance of all volunteer troops for service, government control of railroads and telegraph lines, and the construction of a ship canal from Lake Michigan to the Illinois River for commercial and military purposes. He caused Frémont to be sent to Missouri to command the forces in that region but soon became disgusted with Frémont's policy, criticized him, and was, in turn, arrested and imprisoned by him. Blair's father and brother attempted unsuccessfully to stop the quarrel. For this and other reasons Lincoln removed Frémont. Blair's enemies in Mis-

souri increased in number, particularly while he was in the army. In 1862, when the Union cause looked dark, an appeal was made to Blair to raise troops and lead them to the front. He immediately raised seven regiments, received the appointment of brigadier-general, and saw his first hard fighting at Vicksburg where he showed bravery and leadership. He was in many engagements, was raised to the rank of major-general, and completed his military career with Sherman on the march through the South. As commander of the 15th and 17th Corps, respectively, he received the praises of Generals Sherman and Grant. Blair was considerate of his officers and men and was popular among them. While in the army he made his own opinions and the wishes of Gen. Sherman known to his brother, the Postmaster General, who in turn communicated the information to the President. In 1864 Blair was recalled from the battlefield to help organize Congress and to defend Lincoln's plan of reconstruction. On Feb. 5 and 27, 1864, he made two provocative speeches: one defending the President's policy; the other, against Secretary Chase and the Radicals whom he derisively called Jacobins. A storm of condemnation from the Radicals fell on his head. Chase threatened to resign, and Blair returned to his command.

When the war closed Blair was financially ruined as he had spent much of his private means in support of the Union. His attempt to retrieve his lost fortune on a cotton plantation in Mississippi failed. He then turned his attention to politics in Missouri where a set of Radical Republicans had gained control within the party. He opposed the registry laws, test oaths, the policy of sending carpet-baggers to the South, and the disfranchisement of the whites and the enfranchisement of the negroes. He wished to allow the states to return to the Union to work out their own problems if they recognized abolition as an accomplished fact and swore allegiance to the Constitution. President Johnson nominated Blair for collector of internal revenue at St. Louis, and then to the Austrian mission, only to see the Senate refuse to confirm his appointment in each case. Blair was then appointed as commissioner on the Pacific Railroad but Grant removed him as soon as he became president. The Radicals in Missouri caused Blair to defend the conservatives and ex-Confederates. He began his work of reorganization of the Democratic party in 1865, supported Johnson in 1866, and received the nomination for vice-president with Seymour in 1868. In the latter year his public utterances and his notorious

Blair

"Broadhead Letter," addressed to J. O. Broadhead, declaring that it would be the duty of the Democratic candidate if elected to abolish the Reconstruction governments, gave the opposition an opportunity to distort Blair's meaning when he advanced his plan of reconstruction. He maintained that the Constitution had been perverted. To restore it, he would have the people, by their mandate expressed at the polls, declare the acts of the Radical Congress "null and void"; compel the army to undo its usurpations of power in the South; disperse the carpet-bag governments; allow the whites to reorganize their own governments and elect senators and representatives. After the Democratic defeat in 1868 he coöperated with the Liberal Republicans, secured election as representative to the Missouri legislature; and was, by that body, chosen United States senator. He helped to secure the nomination of Horace Greeley for president (1872), and through coöperation with the Liberal Republicans saw the Radicals ousted from power in Missouri. He was defeated for reëlection to the United States Senate in 1873. During the same year Blair was stricken with paralysis, never to recover. He was generous to a fault, cordial, and seldom held a personal grudge against a political enemy. His scathing denunciations of his political opponents antagonized them but his faculty for remembering names and his sociability endeared him to many people. He was nominally state superintendent of insurance when he died. His friends erected a fitting monument to his memory in Forrest Park (St. Louis) and Missouri placed his statue in the United States Capitol.

[The chief sources are the Blair Papers (unpublished). Two biographies of a political and biased nature are: Jas. Dabney McCabe (Edward Martin), *The Life and Public Services of Horatio Seymour Together with a Complete and Authentic Life of Francis P. Blair, Jr.* (1868); David Goodman Croly, *Seymour and Blair: Their Lives and Services* (1868). A manuscript copy of a sketch of the life of Blair, presumably written by Montgomery Blair, is in the Blair Papers. Short sketches exist by: Wm. Van Ness Bay, in *Reminiscences of the Bench and Bar of Mo.* (1878); Augustus C. Rogers, *Sketches of Representative Men North and South* (1874); Chas. P. Johnson, "Personal Recollections of Missouri's Statesmen" in *Proc. Mo. Hist. Soc.*, Jan. 22, 1903; and John Fiske, *The Mississippi Valley in the Civil War* (1900). The best account of Blair's services in Missouri during the early part of the Civil War is found in *Gen. Nathaniel Lyon and Missouri in 1861* (1866) by Jas. Peckham.]
W.E.S.

BLAIR, HENRY WILLIAM (Dec. 6, 1834–Mar. 14, 1920), congressman, the son of William Henry and Lois (Baker) Blair, of Scotch-Irish descent, was born at Campton, N. H. When he was only two years old his father died as the result of an accident, and his mother being unable to provide for the entire family, several children, including Henry, were brought up by neighbors. His mother died in 1846. Until the age of seventeen he lived with a neighboring farmer, attending school in the seasons when farm work permitted. He studied several terms at Plymouth Academy and New Hampshire Conference Seminary, his attendance being irregular because of the necessity of self-support. The strain on his health proved so severe that he was unable to enter college. In 1856 he began the study of law in the office of William Leverett of Plymouth, was admitted to the bar in 1859, and in the following year was appointed solicitor for Grafton County. He was married on Dec. 20, 1859, to Eliza Ann Nelson. On the outbreak of the Civil War he promptly offered his services but was twice rejected as physically unfit, and it was not until the following year that he was accepted. Going to the front as captain in the 15th New Hampshire Volunteers he rose to the rank of lieutenant-colonel, but was invalided home after being severely wounded at Port Hudson. He resumed practise but was handicapped by bad health for a number of years as a result of his army experience. He represented Plymouth in the lower house in 1866, and in the two succeeding years was chosen senator from the 11th district. Entering the Forty-fourth Congress in 1875, he was for the next twenty years a prominent figure in national affairs. He was a member of the House in the Forty-fourth, Forty-fifth, and Fifty-third Congresses, and senator from 1879 to 1891. Declining an appointment to the federal bench on his retirement from the Senate, he accepted President Harrison's offer of the post of minister to China. He was recalled while on his way to the Pacific Coast, however, on representations from the Chinese Government that his attitude on the immigration question had rendered him *persona non grata* (*Congressional Record*, 52 Cong., 1 Sess., 3151 ff.). On his retirement from active politics in 1895, he settled in Washington, D. C., where he resumed the practise of law.

Blair had the orthodox Republican faith in sound money, the tariff, and the pension system, and his arguments on these subjects were frequently printed in quantity for circulation as campaign documents. He also had, however, a strong humanitarian bent, firm religious convictions, and an enthusiasm, sometimes almost visionary, which frequently put his views far ahead of those of his contemporaries. In 1876, he introduced in the House a joint resolution amending the Constitution by prohibiting the manufacture, importation and sale of distilled liquors after Jan. 1, 1900, a plan which he claimed would have some of the merits of the slave-trade clause of 1787, permitting time for the necessary educational work and the adjustment of property rights. He asked "the considerate attention of all men now, for the time is coming when it will be forced upon them" (*Ibid.*, 44 Cong., 2 Sess., App., p. 16). He was a pioneer in the effort to interest the National Government in public education and in 1876 introduced a bill for the purpose of applying the proceeds of public land sales to education (*Ibid.*, 44 Cong., 1 Sess., App., pp. 235 ff.). As chairman of the Committee on Education and Labor in the Senate he gave earnest support to the project of national aid to the public schools. In 1881 he introduced in the Senate a bill proposing to "extend and vitalize" the common school system of the country by distributing among the states, on the basis of illiteracy, the sum total of $120,000,000 in annual instalments covering a period of ten years. This measure, or a substantially similar one, passed the Senate on three different occasions, only to die in committees of the House. Blair also introduced a constitutional amendment requiring the states to maintain free non-sectarian schools, and prohibiting religious establishments (*Ibid.*, 50 Cong., 1 Sess., p. 4615). In 1890 he introduced in the Senate a resolution requesting the President to summon an international conference to deal with the suppression of the slave-trade, the traffic in alcohol and weapons with backward peoples in Africa and Asia, and more important, to consider the problem of reduction and disbandment of existing military and naval establishments and the creation of tribunals for the peaceful settlement of controversies. An ardent supporter of woman suffrage, he repeatedly championed a constitutional amendment. He was concerned at the growing importance of labor problems and his activity in this field eventually resulted in the creation of the Department of Labor. More than once he demanded that the people of the District of Columbia be enfranchised and granted representation in Congress. Sabbath observance, the interests of the colored race, pension legislation, the prevention of railroad monopoly, the proper utilization of the public lands, were also topics in which he was deeply interested.

[A sketch of Henry W. Blair appears in Ezra S. Stearns, *Hist. of Plymouth, N. H.* (1906); another, with portrait, in David L. Perkins, *Manchester Up to Date* (1896); another in Emily W. Leavitt, *The Blair Family of New England* (1900).]

W. A. R.

BLAIR, JAMES (1655–Apr. 18, 1743), founder and first president of William and Mary College, was born in Scotland. The names of his parents are not known. He attended the University of Edinburgh, receiving the degree of Master of Arts in 1673. He was ordained in the Church of England and for several years preceding the year 1682 was rector of the parish of Cranston in the diocese of Edinburgh, serving with "exemplary diligence, care and gravity." Due to the disfavor of the Church of England in Scotland, he left his native land for England. We have no record that he continued his connection with the Church in England after his removal. For part of the three years preceding his departure for Virginia, he was employed in the office of the Master of the Rolls in London where he became acquainted with Dr. Henry Compton, Bishop of London, who prevailed upon him to go as a missionary to Virginia. He reached Virginia in 1685, and accepted the rectorship of the parish known as Varina at that time, but after 1720 always referred to as Henrico. The Bishop of London, whose diocese included Virginia, had no representative, with official title, in Virginia until Dec. 15, 1689, when he appointed Blair his commissary or deputy, with authority to supervise the clergy in a general way, but without the power of ordination or confirmation. As commissary, Blair began the custom of calling the clergy of the colony together occasionally in conventions. In the first convention, which met in 1690, he urged that the clergy take the initiative in the establishment of a college. Although there were other prominent men in the colony, who supported the project of a college, the chief burden of its promotion fell upon Blair. He well deserves, therefore, the title of founder of the College of William and Mary. In the spring of 1691 the General Assembly considered the establishment of a college, and Blair was selected May 20, 1691, to proceed to England and to present a memorial in behalf of the projected college to their Majesties King William and Queen Mary. The Assembly had previously asked him to assist a committee in drawing up the memorial. He reached London Sept. 1, 1691. Dr. Henry Compton, Bishop of London, Dr. Edward Stillingfleet, Bishop of Worcester, and Dr. John Tillotson, Archbishop of Canterbury, were all exceedingly interested in the college, and befriended Blair to the utmost. On Nov. 12, 1691, introduced by the Archbishop, he presented his memorial to the King, by whom it was graciously received and referred to proper officials for further consideration. Blair had to wait patiently for months while the charter was passing through the routine of the different offices. In the meantime, he was busy in the solicitation of funds. On Feb. 27, 1692, he wrote home that the Bishop of Salisbury had succeeded in getting two hundred pounds from the Boyle bequest for the college. Through his own direct efforts he assisted in obtaining an order in council that certain seized property of former pirates should be returned to them if they would give 300 pounds to the college. The charter was finally granted on Feb. 8, 1693, and in this document Blair is named as the first president "during his natural life." This clause of the charter carried out the wish of the General Assembly in its memorial which had named James Blair "as a fit person to be president." He was also named in the charter as rector of the board of visitors for the first year. He laid the charter before the Virginia Assembly on Oct. 20, 1693. By request of the board of visitors, he resigned his living in Henrico, and became minister of the Jamestown church in 1694. As Middle Plantation, later Williamsburg, the site selected for the college, was only seven miles from Jamestown, he was near enough to watch the construction of the college building, and to supervise the early instruction. He retained the charge at Jamestown until 1710, when he was appointed rector of Bruton parish in Williamsburg. This parish he retained until his death in 1743. He was appointed by the King to the council in the spring of 1694. The executive journal of the council shows that he was first present on July 18, 1694. His position as commissary therefore did not seat him *ex officio* in the council. He remained a member of the council until his death, though he was suspended by Andros for purely personal reasons from Apr. 19, 1695, to Aug. 12, 1696. On the latter date by order of the King he was again seated in the council. There were some opponents to the college, and Sir Edmund Andros, the governor, becoming the leader of the opposition, hindered the erection of the building and annoyed Blair in many ways. There was a hearing in London before the Archbishop of Canterbury and the Bishop of London upon charges brought against Andros, Dec. 27, 1697, when Blair himself was present. Blair was sustained, and Andros was recalled. The succeeding governor, Francis Nicholson, though at one time most friendly to Blair and the college, was no better than Andros. He used every means to obstruct the work of Blair both as commissary and president. With five other members of the council on May 20, 1703, Blair petitioned the Queen to remove Nicholson. This petition was sustained and Nicholson was recalled in 1705. Blair lived in harmony with the other governors, Nott, Spotswood, Drysdale, and Gooch, except in the later years of Spotswood's administration, when a quarrel arose over the rights of the governor and the commissary in regard to the appointment

of ministers. Due not only to Blair's unfriendliness, but to other causes, Spotswood was removed in 1722. In 1726 Blair was again in England attending to college business. On Feb. 27, 1729, the transfer of the property of the college from the trustees was made to the faculty. After overcoming the determined opposition of two governors, the indifference of some of the prominent and wealthy in the colony, and the supreme misfortune of a disastrous fire in 1705 which destroyed the main building, Blair at last saw the college well established. At the time of his death it had three substantial buildings. From December 1740 to July 1741, Blair, as president of the council, was acting governor of the colony in the absence of the governor. His death occurred Apr. 18, 1743. A determined independence and firm assertion of his personal and official rights were his characteristics. He was somewhat inclined to be pugnacious, but justly so. He represented the church and the college in the midst of self-seeking politicians, and was therefore somewhat suspicious and impatient. He had many bitter enemies. The charges against him are variations of these two: first, that, being a Scotchman, he befriended his countrymen in church preferment; second, that he was particular in expecting payment of his salary as president and commissary. The careers of Andros and Nicholson, both before and after they came to Virginia, sustain Blair's charges against them. M. C. Tyler in his *History of American Literature* speaks of Blair as "the creator of the healthiest, and the most extensive intellectual influence that was felt in the southern group of Colonies before the Revolution." He married June 2, 1687, Sarah Harrison, the daughter of Col. Benjamin and Mrs. Hannah Harrison, of Wakefield, Surry County. He left an estate of about £10,000 to the family of John Blair [1687–1771, *q.v.*], his nephew and he left his library and £500 to the college. Blair was joint author with Henry Hartwell and Edward Chilton of *The Present State of Virginia and the College . . . to Which is Added the Charter,* originally written for the Board of Trade in 1697 but not published at that time. It was printed in London by J. Wyat in 1727 and has been reprinted in the *Calendar of State Papers, Colonial, 1696–97,* pp. 641–66, and in the *Massachusetts Historical Collections,* ser. 1, vol. V, pp. 144–60. Blair's sermons upon *Our Savior's Divine Sermon on the Mount* were published in five volumes in London in 1722. Copies of this edition may still be seen in some of the older houses in Virginia. A second edition in four volumes, with a prefatory note by Dr. Daniel Waterland, highly complimentary to Blair, was published in London in 1740. A Danish edition of the sermons translated by Dideric de Thurah was issued in Copenhagen in 1761, in four volumes.

[The only life of Blair is D. E. Motley's "Life of Commissary Jas. Blair" (*Johns Hopkins Univ. Studies in Hist. and Polit. Sci.*, XIX, no. 10, 1901). The author drew extensively upon the documents in Bishop W. S. Perry's *Papers Relating to the Hist. of the Ch. in Va., 1660–1776* (1870). These documents were copied from the archives at Lambeth and Fulham, and from the letter books of the Society for the Propagation of the Gospel in Foreign Parts. Bishop Perry's *Hist. of the Am. Epis. Ch., 1587–1883* (1885) also should be consulted; see in this work, I, 113–28, "The College at Williamsburg and President Blair," with illustrative and critical notes. The following works also are useful: J. S. M. Anderson, *Hist. of the Ch. of Eng. in the Colonies and Foreign Dependencies of the Brit. Empire* (1856); W. Meade, *Old Churches, Ministers and Families of Va.* (1856); L. G. Tyler, *Williamsburg, the Old Colonial Capital* (1907), *The Cradle of the Republic* (1900), and *The College of William and Mary* (1907); Frederick Horner, *Hist. of the Blair, Banister, and Braxton Families* (1898).]

E. G. S.

BLAIR, JOHN (1687–1771), acting governor of Virginia, the son of Archibald Blair, brother of James Blair [*q.v.*], was probably born in Virginia. His father was a student at the University of Edinburgh in 1685; he married three times, and John Blair was the son of the first wife, whose name is unknown. John received his education at the College of William and Mary, and as early as 1713 held the position of deputy auditor-general *pro tem*. His uncle and father were both prominent in the political affairs of the colony, and he doubtless owed much to their influence. His father was a member of the House of Burgesses, 1718–34. On Feb. 5, 1727, John Blair was appointed naval officer for the upper district of James River, and on Aug. 15, 1728, he took oath as deputy auditor-general, which position he filled until his death in 1771. From 1734 to 1740 he was a member of the House of Burgesses. According to Gooch, Blair was in narrow circumstances until he and his children received about £10,000 by the will of his uncle James Blair, who died in 1743. On Feb. 26, 1745, Gooch recommended John Blair for appointment to the Council and this recommendation was approved by the board of trade. Among Blair's activities was an interest in lands in the western part of the colony. As early as Nov. 4, 1745, a grant to him and his associates of 100,000 acres west of the Fairfax line was voted by the council. In addition to his services as councillor, Blair was appointed in 1746 on the committee to revise the laws, and was one of the committee of correspondence with the colonial agent Montague in England. As president of the Council he was twice called upon to act as governor, from January 1758, the time of Dinwiddie's

departure, until the arrival of Fauquier, June 7, 1758; and again from Fauquier's death, Mar. 3, 1768, to the arrival of Botetourt in October 1768. As governor, he seems to have been agreeable to all political factions. His letter to the King's attorney of Spotsylvania County, July 16, 1768, in regard to the treatment of Baptists, gives us a most favorable view of his character. Instead of countenancing persecution of this sect, he advocated a liberal and sympathetic policy. In the Two Penny Act controversy he took the popular view and supported the act by his vote in council. He fully approved of the doctrine expressed by the General Assembly Mar. 31, 1768, that only the Assembly could make laws regarding the colony's internal policy of taxation. When Gov. Botetourt died Oct. 15, 1770, the duties of governor would again have devolved upon Blair but in order to avoid this, he resigned his seat in the Council. His death occurred in his eighty-fifth year. He was married to Mary Monro, daughter of Rev. John and Christian Monro, of St. Johns Parish, King William County, by whom he had ten children. Aside from his official papers as governor, we have nothing remaining of a literary nature, except his diary for the year 1751. This reveals him as a typical Virginia public man of that day, interested in the minor affairs of the town and colony, conscientious in his official duties, and not averse to the pleasures and amusements of the time.

[Blair's official career as burgess and councillor may be traced in the *Jours. of the House of Burgesses* and in the *Legislative Jours. of the Council of Colonial Va.* Transcripts of his letters as president of the council to the secretary of state and to the board of trade are in the Force Transcripts in the Lib. of Cong. For his letters to Washington, see S. M. Hamilton, *Letters to Washington*, vol. V. His diary for 1751 is printed in full in the *William and Mary Quart.*, VII, 134–53, and VIII, 1–17, accompanied by valuable notes of the editor, Lyon G. Tyler. Frederick Horner's *Hist. of the Blair, Banister and Braxton Families* (1898) has a chapter entitled "John Blair, Sr." which adds little to our information about him, but the letters of his children printed therein tell us much of their family life and of the general social conditions in Williamsburg in the eighteenth century. In this chapter may be found Blair's well-known letter to the King's attorney of Spotsylvania County.]

E. G. S.

BLAIR, JOHN (1732–Aug. 31, 1800), jurist, was born in Williamsburg, Va., son of John Blair [*q.v.*] and Mary Monro, daughter of Rev. John and Christian Monro of King William County. He attended William and Mary College, and later studied law at the Middle Temple in London in 1755. He entered the House of Burgesses in 1766, being elected to represent the College of William and Mary. His service began while his father was president of the Council. He continued to represent the College through the session of 1770. He probably became clerk of the Council after the close of the legislative session, June 28, 1770, for we find Washington in a letter of Oct. 5, 1770, referring to him as clerk. He retained this position as late as June 24, 1775. He signed the association entered into by the gentlemen of the House of Burgesses and the body of merchants, June 22, 1770, in which the signers agreed not to import certain specified goods from Great Britain until the Act of Parliament which imposed a duty on tea, paper, glass, and painters' colors was totally repealed. He was also a signer of the association of May 27, 1774. He probably succeeded his father as deputy auditor. In the convention of May 6, 1776, which met at Williamsburg for the purpose of drawing up a constitution for the new commonwealth of Virginia, John Blair was a representative, elected by the College of William and Mary. He was a member of the committee of twenty-eight which framed a declaration of rights and a plan of government. On June 30, 1776, he was elected a member of the Privy Council of the new state and was reëlected on May 29, 1777. On Jan. 23, 1778, he was elected one of the judges of the general court, by joint ballot of the Assembly. His successor in the Council was not elected till May 29, 1778. He may have served therefore on both Council and court for a time. He later became chief justice of this court. In 1780 upon the death of Robert Carter Nicholas he was elected a judge of the high court of chancery, and by virtue of both positions became judge of the first court of appeals of Virginia. In the important case of Commonwealth of Virginia *vs.* Caton *et al.,* in November 1782, which brought up the respective rights of the judicial and legislative branches of the government, Blair with the rest of the judges was of the opinion that the court could declare any act or resolution of the legislature unconstitutional. On Dec. 4, 1786, he was selected by the General Assembly one of the delegates to the convention in Philadelphia for framing a constitution, and he was one of the three from Virginia who voted for the acceptance of the document. He was returned from the county of York to the convention which met in Richmond in 1788 for the consideration of the proposed constitution. In this convention he was a firm supporter of the new constitution. On Sept. 30, 1789, he was appointed by President Washington an associate justice of the Supreme Court. On Jan. 27, 1796, he resigned. He was "blameless of disposition, pious, and possessed of great benevolence and goodness of heart." His wife, who was Jean Balfour, died Nov. 22, 1792. After his resigna-

tion from the Supreme Court he returned to Williamsburg and lived there until his death on Aug. 31, 1800. "He was about five feet ten inches in height, of erect and imposing stature, with a noble forehead, blue eyes, a well formed nose, and hair inclining to be red" (Robert Bolling, *Memoir of a Portion of the Bolling Family in England and Virginia,* 1868, pp. 33–34). He was a sincere and consistent patriot in the American Revolution. In his judicial career he was a conservative. His support of Madison and Washington in the struggle to frame and adopt a constitution showed him to be a firm believer in a strong federal government. No speeches of Blair have been preserved.

[*The Jours. of the House of Burgesses, 1766–1770,* and the *Jour. of the Convention of 1776* give us Blair's record in the Revolutionary cause and the Minutes of the Council, in manuscript, in the Va. State Lib., his career as a councillor. The most noted cases in which he took part on the Supreme Bench were Hayburn's Case, *2 Dallas 409;* State of Georgia *vs. Brailsford 2 Dallas 415;* Chisholm *vs.* Georgia, *2 Dallas 419;* Penhallow *vs.* Doane's admr., *3 Dallas 54.* The sketch of Blair in Hugh Blair Grigsby's *Convention of 1776* (1853) is useful. In Frederick Horner's *Hist. of the Blair, Banister, and Braxton Families* (1898) there is a chapter on Judge Blair, in which there are printed some interesting letters from him to his sister, Mrs. Braxton.]

E. G. S.

BLAIR, JOHN INSLEY (Aug. 22, 1802–Dec. 2, 1899), capitalist, philanthropist, the son of James and Rachel (Insley) Blair, was born on a farm on the banks of the Delaware, two miles below Belvidere, N. J. His school instruction, obtained during a few brief months in the winters, ceased when he was eleven years old, and he went to work in a country store. It is said that when ten years of age, he exclaimed to his mother, "I have seven brothers and three sisters. That's enough in the family to be educated. I am going to get rich." At eighteen he was his own master and owner of a store. At twenty-seven he had a chain of five general stores in the northern part of New Jersey and ran four flouring-mills. He married, Sept. 20, 1828, Ann Locke of Frelinghuysen, N. J., grand-daughter of a Revolutionary captain. In 1833 he became interested with Col. George W. Scranton and Seldon T. Scranton in the mines at Oxford Furnace. Success in this enterprise led in 1846 to his participation in the founding of the Lackawanna Coal & Iron Company. Mining led to railroad promotion, and it was in this enterprise that he amassed the greater part of his fortune and reputation. In 1852 the Delaware, Lackawanna & Western Railroad, so named at Blair's suggestion, was organized. He became one of the largest stockholders and served as a director from the organization of the road until his death.

He was always keenly interested in politics, state and national. He attended every national convention of the Republican party from its founding till 1892. In 1868 he was the unanimous choice of the New Jersey state Republican convention for governor, but lost the election to Gov. Randolph. The campaign cost Blair over $90,000 personally. In 1860, when attending the convention at Chicago, Ill., which nominated Abraham Lincoln, Blair's attention was attracted to the great possibilities of Western development through the extension of railroads. He joined with Oakes Ames and others in getting the charter of the Union Pacific Railroad, and personally built the first one hundred miles west from Omaha, having been responsible for the adoption of that route. His operations in the West extended in succeeding years to Iowa, Wisconsin, Kansas, Nebraska, Dakota, Missouri, and Texas. He was at one time president of sixteen different railroads, and is said to have been the individual owner of more miles of railroad property than any other man in the world. He laid out sites for more than eighty towns, and owned lands equal to half the area of his native state. He was a man of unusual energy and possessed a remarkable physique. He told friends that it had been his custom to travel about 40,000 miles a year and that he reduced this to 20,000 only when he reached the age of eighty-five. When ninety-two years old, he would often be at his desk at 5:30 a. m., and business would then claim his attention during the greater part of the day. His habits were always simple, and his acquisition of millions made little change in his mode of living. He continued to reside in New Jersey in his beloved Blairstown, his enormous enterprises being directed from this inaccessible little village. One of the institutions which claimed his special favor and attention was the Blair Presbyterian Academy at Blairstown. Blair Hall at Princeton University, of which institution he was made a trustee in 1886, is another monument to his liberality. Grinnell and Lafayette Colleges were also special recipients of his benevolences. He was a most liberal benefactor of the Presbyterian Church, of which he was a life-long member. In the eighty towns in the West, whose sites he was instrumental in selecting, he helped erect, by gifts of land and money, more than one hundred churches. The value of his estate was roughly estimated at the time of his death at $70,000,000 and he was said to have given away over $5,000,000.

[*N. J. Hist. Soc. Proc.*, 3rd ser., vols. III and IV; the *Sun* (N.Y.), *N. Y. Herald, Times, Tribune*, Dec. 3, 1899; C. M. Knapp, *N. J. Politics during the Period of the*

Civil War and Reconstruction (1924); letters of J. I. Blair in Princeton Univ. Library.]

C. R. E.

BLAIR, MONTGOMERY (May 10, 1813–July 27, 1883), lawyer, statesman, eldest son of Francis Preston Blair, Sr. [*q.v.*], was reared in Franklin County, Ky., amidst the scenes of political strife between "relief" and "anti-relief" and "Old" and "New Court" factions. The schools of Kentucky gave him his early education. He was appointed by President Jackson to West Point in 1831; after his graduation in 1835 he received a lieutenancy in the army in time to serve in the Seminole War. The next year he resigned his commission in order to study law in Transylvania University. He settled in St. Louis in 1837 as the protégé of Thomas Hart Benton. After practising law two years he was appointed United States district attorney for Missouri, only to be removed for political reasons by President Tyler. He served in St. Louis as mayor (1842–43) and as judge of the court of common pleas (1845–49). In 1849 he resigned to resume his law practise. In 1853 he moved to Maryland where he practised law chiefly before the Supreme Court of the United States. President Pierce made him the first solicitor for the court of claims of the United States (1855) but President Buchanan dismissed him because of his pronounced views on slavery. He was a Free-Soiler in principle, believed slavery could be peaceably settled, generally held the political views of border statesmen, and had sympathy with the interests of the West. After joining the American party he left it because of its silence on slavery and became a Democratic-Republican in the Republican party. His prestige was greatly increased among anti-slavery people when he became counsel for Dred Scott. His sense of fairness led him to help secure a defense attorney for John Brown after the Harper's Ferry incident. He was a delegate to the Democratic national conventions in 1844, 1848, and 1852. In 1860 he presided at the state Republican convention at Baltimore and attended the Chicago national convention as a delegate from Maryland. Because of his services to the Republican party, his family connections, and his political views and experiences he was made postmaster general in Lincoln's cabinet, where he belonged to the Bates-Welles-Blair group. He strongly urged the reënforcement of Southern forts, particularly Fort Sumter, which he believed could be held against the Confederates, and threatened to resign if that fort were not reenforced. Without being obsequious he was a staunch supporter of Lincoln. He strongly opposed Secretary Chase's views, befriended Mc-

Clellan, and insisted from the beginning of the incident that the seizure of Mason and Slidell was illegal. In his own department he organized the postal system for the army, introduced compulsory payment of postage and free delivery in cities, improved the registry system, established the railway post-office, organized the postal draft plan which his successor put into operation, stopped the franking privileges of postmasters, and was instrumental in bringing about the Postal Union Convention at Paris (1863). In the Union national convention (1864) the Radicals succeeded in passing a resolution which virtually demanded the dismissal of Blair from the cabinet. The President, after a fair assurance of victory at the polls, bowed to political expediency and requested Blair's resignation, which was cheerfully given. Blair continued, however, to work loyally for Lincoln. After the assassination of Lincoln, Blair advised Johnson to dismiss the old and appoint a new cabinet. He sought moderation for the South, asserting and believing that Lincoln's plan of reconstruction was just and best. He decried the disfranchisement of the Southern whites and enfranchisement of the negroes. His views brought him into conflict with those held by the radical reconstructionists. He drifted back to the Democratic party, where he supported Seymour in 1868 and Greeley in 1872, and championed Tilden's cause in 1876. With the financial aid of W. W. Corcoran he established a newspaper, the *Union* (Washington, D. C.), to uphold Tilden's claims to the Presidency. As Tilden's counsel he appeared before the Electoral Commission. He declared Tilden represented "the one issue"—reform. Being elected to the Maryland House of Delegates (1878) and immediately made chairman of the judiciary committee, Blair proposed the resolution which denied the right of President Hayes to office. Though honest in his belief that Hayes was illegally chosen president, he aroused the intense enmity of many people by his method of agitating the question. He unsuccessfully ran for Congress in 1882. Blair was tall and spare, clean-shaven, with light hair and bluish-grey eyes. His speech was slow, his voice calm. Few men were more courteous and genial than he, but he was temperamentally combative and obstinate when he thought he was right. Though deeply religious he held anti-ritualistic sentiments. As a lawyer he used persuasive argument which was the result of research and logical reasoning. While he had strong prejudices, he was shrewd, frank, and thoroughly honest. He was twice married: to a Miss Buckner of Virginia, who died in 1844, and to a daughter

of Judge Levi Woodbury of New Hampshire. He was an inveterate worker and died while engaged in writing a life of Andrew Jackson.

[The Blair Papers (unpublished); Levi Woodbury Papers (unpublished); "Montgomery Blair" in *Maryland in National Politics* (1915) by Jesse Frederick Essary; "Montgomery Blair" in *Sketches of Representative Men North and South* (1872), ed. by Augustus C. Rogers; "The Public Career of Montgomery Blair, Particularly with Reference to His Services as Postmaster General of the United States" by Madison Davis in the *Records of the Columbia Hist. Soc.*, XIII (1910), 126–61; *Diary of Gideon Welles* (1911); J. G. Nicolay and John Hay, *Abraham Lincoln* (10 vols., 1890).]

W. E. S.

BLAIR, SAMUEL (June 14, 1712–July 5, 1751), Presbyterian clergyman, was born in Ulster, Ireland, the son of William Blair. He came to America in early youth and was drawn into the movement headed by William Tennent for a broader and more aggressive evangelicalism in the young Presbyterian Church. With Tennent's four sons and a few other young men of talent and devotion he entered the academy at Neshaminy, near Philadelphia, founded by Tennent for the education of ministers and nicknamed by his critics the "Log College" because of its crude domicile and equipment. Blair was licensed to preach by the presbytery of Philadelphia at the early age of twenty-one, Nov. 9, 1733, and in the following year was settled as pastor of the double charge consisting of the churches at Middletown and Shrewsbury, N. J. While occupying these pulpits he joined with some others in the organization of the Presbytery of New Brunswick (1738). His success as a preacher called attention to him and he was invited to the leadership of the more important work at New Londonderry, Chester County, Pa. (known also as Fagg's Manor). He began his labors here in 1739 and was installed in 1740. During his ministry of twelve years in this field, he threw himself into a number of enterprises of importance. First of all, in addition to his pastoral labors he conducted a rudimentary theological seminary. Among his pupils some came to prominence and leadership in the church, notably Samuel Davies, successor to Jonathan Edwards in the presidency of the College of New Jersey (Princeton), and John Rodgers, first moderator of the General Assembly of the Presbyterian Church. In 1740 the evangelistic fervor aroused by George Whitefield's visit and preaching in America reached Blair's parish and found him ready to place himself in the forefront of the movement. His gifts as a preacher made his pulpit one of the conspicuous centers of the revival. When Whitefield's manner became the subject of criticism and controversy, Blair was called upon to take part in the defense of the movement. In this work he had the coöperation of his old fellow-student, Gilbert Tennent. The struggle became acute and from the mere defense of the revival Tennent and Blair assumed an aggressive attitude, bringing before the Synod of 1740 charges against the ministry of negligence in the performance of their duties and of lack of interest in their spiritual functions. On being challenged to produce their evidence they were obliged to confess that they had not based their charges upon adequate investigations. In the division of the Presbyterian Church which resulted from this controversy, Blair, like all the other followers of Tennent, went with the "New Side" (Synod of New York), became its chief spokesman, and wrote its declaration of principles. He is described as "grave and solemn, yet cheerful, pleasant, and witty."

[*The Works of the Rev. Samuel Blair, Late Minister of the Gospel at Fagg's Manor, in Chester County, Pa. Containing a Collection of Sermons on Various Subjects: together with several Treatises, in a Vindication of the Brethren etc., the Doctrine of Predestination, etc., a Sermon on his death by Rev. Mr. Finley* (1754), ed. by John Blair; A. Alexander, *Biog. Sketches of the Founder and Principal Alumni of the Log College* (1851); E. H. Gillet, *Hist. of the Presbyterian Ch. in the U. S.* (1864); J. S. Futhey and Gilbert Cope, *Hist. of Chester County, Pa.* (1881).]

A. C. Z.

BLAKE, ELI WHITNEY (Jan. 27, 1795–Aug. 18, 1886), inventor, manufacturer, son of Elihu and Elizabeth (Whitney) Blake, was born in Westborough, a small village in Massachusetts sixteen miles east of Worcester. In Westborough lived his famous uncle, Eli Whitney, and also his maternal grandfather, the latter, in good Yankee fashion, being both farmer and mechanic, and having not only a complete kit of cabinet-making tools but a turning-lathe as well. In this environment Blake was reared. His life differed, however, from that of the average youth of his day and was more like that of a young man of the twentieth century in that his parents apparently were fully resolved from his birth to enable him to be well educated. His mother probably had not had time to forget the firm opposition of both her father and stepmother to her brother's ambition to obtain a college education. At all events, young Blake was prepared for Yale at Litchfield Academy, entered college at the age of seventeen, and graduated with the class of 1816. After spending the year succeeding graduation in the Litchfield Law School, at the request of his uncle, Eli Whitney, he abandoned a professional career and entered his uncle's employ in the manufacture of firearms at Whitneyville, a suburb of New Haven. Upon the death of Whitney in 1825, Blake with one of his brothers

carried on the armory business at the same place until 1836. During this time he made several important inventions having to do with the manufacture of arms, which were immediately adopted in armories throughout the country. In 1836 the armory was given up, and with two brothers, Blake established in Westville, another suburb of New Haven, a manufactory of domestic hardware, which was the pioneer establishment in this field in the United States. He continued as the directing head of this establishment for thirty-five years and then retired at the age of sixty-six. While assistant to his uncle in the armory, Blake married Eliza Maria O'Brien of New Haven, on July 8, 1822. They had twelve children, ten of whom lived to maturity. Each of their six sons attended Yale and five graduated, the sixth being prevented from completing his course by ill health. Among the patents granted by the United States Patent Office to the Blake brothers, Philos, Eli, and John, for inventions made during the period of their hardware manufacturing business, were a door lock and escutcheon (Dec. 31, 1833), thumb latch (July 21, 1840), castors for bedsteads (June 30, 1838), button, plate, and turn for fastening cupboard and other doors (Mar. 21, 1843). In 1855 Blake served on a committee of townsmen who had charge of the macadamizing of one of the principal streets of New Haven. His attention was drawn to the need of a machine to perform the labor of crushing the various sizes of stone used in this type of paving. He apparently devoted all of his energies and inventive genius to the solution of the problem, and on June 15, 1858, United States patent No. 20,542 was granted him for a stone crusher. It is for this invention that Blake is best known. For originality, simplicity, and effectiveness the Blake type of crusher has not been surpassed for general use and is still employed the world over. All of his life Blake was a profound student of mathematics and physics, and in his later years, particularly after his retirement from active business, found his happiness in studying problems of aerodynamics. He was one of the founders and several times president of the Connecticut Academy of Sciences, and wrote many valuable papers for the *American Journal of Science* and other scientific periodicals. Just four years before his death he gathered together a number of these papers and published them in a single volume, under the title *Original Solutions of Several Problems in Aerodynamics* (1882), which was probably his most valuable contribution. After an old age of honored retirement, he died at his home in New Haven, Conn., in his ninety-second year.

[W. H. Doolittle, *Inventions in the Century* (1902), being vol. XVI of the Nineteenth Century Series; *Biog. Sketches of the Members of the Class of 1816, Yale Coll.* (1867); *Obit. Record Grads. Yale Univ.* (1887); obituaries in *New Haven Evening Reg.,* Aug. 18, 1886, and in *New Haven Morning Jour.,* Aug. 19, 1886; Records of the U. S. Patent Office.]   C. W. M.

BLAKE, FRANCIS (Dec. 25, 1850–Jan. 19, 1913), inventor, physicist, was born in Needham, Mass., a descendant of William and Agnes Blake, who came to America in 1630 from Somersetshire, England, and settled in Dorchester, Mass. They were leaders in colonial affairs. Francis Blake was of the eighth generation. His father, also Francis Blake, was a business man and for many years United States appraiser at Boston. His mother was Caroline Burling, daughter of George Augustus Trumbull. Blake attended the public schools until he was sixteen years old, when he left Brookline High School to accept a position as draftsman in the United States Coast and Geodetic Survey in Washington, the position having been secured for him by an uncle, Commodore George Smith Blake. It was in this service for thirteen consecutive years that he acquired the scientific education which led to his later successes in civil life. During this time he assisted in many of the most important scientific achievements of the Survey, including hydrographic surveys of the Susquehanna River, the west coast of Florida, and the north coast of Cuba. He assisted in the determination of the transcontinental longitude between the observatory of Harvard College and San Francisco. A metallic circuit of 7,000 miles with thirteen repeaters was employed and the experiment resulted in a signal being sent from Harvard Observatory to San Francisco and back again in eight-tenths of a second. In 1870 he was temporarily detached from the Survey to serve as astronomer of the Darien Exploring Expedition, under Commander Selfridge. This expedition was undertaken primarily to determine routes for a ship canal across the Isthmus of Darien. His final work with the Survey was in the determination of differences in longitude between the observatories at Greenwich, England; Paris; Cambridge, Mass.; and Washington. Upon the completion of this work he retired to his home in Weston, Mass. His work with the Survey developed his interest in physics and electrical communication, and at an early period he began devoting his leisure moments to experimental physics, building up at the same time a well-equipped laboratory in his home. Within a month of his retiring in 1875, he began experimental work on a telephone transmitting instrument, and in 1878 received a United States patent for a transmitter the mechanical features of which made practical the fundamental principles of the Berliner microphone. This patent was purchased in November 1878 by the Bell Telephone Company, and Blake was immediately employed to perfect it. It was the adoption of the Blake transmitter that enabled the Bell Telephone Company to succeed in an intensely competitive field. Blake continued his laboratory work, particularly in electrical communication, and between 1878 and 1890 received twenty patents. He married Elizabeth L. Hubbard on June 24, 1873, in Weston, Mass. He was a Fellow of the American Association for the Advancement of Science, a member of the American Institute of Electrical Engineers, of the corporation of the Massachusetts Institute of Technology, and also of several historical societies.

[D. H. Hurd, *Hist. of Middlesex County, Mass.,* vol. I (1890); E. W. Byrn, *The Progress of Invention in the Nineteenth Century* (1900); *Who's Who in America,* 1912–13; *Report of the Supt. of the U. S. Coast Survey 1867–74;* Records of the U. S. Patent Office; F. W. Wile, *Emile Berliner, Maker of the Microphone* (1926); *Boston Transcript* and *Daily Globe,* Jan. 20, 1913.]   C. W. M.

BLAKE, HOMER CRANE (Feb. 1, 1822– Jan. 21, 1880), naval officer, son of Elisha and Marilla (Crane) Blake, was born in Dutchess County, N. Y., but the next year his parents removed to Hancock County, Ohio. After serving as acting midshipman on board the frigate *Constellation* for some time, he was warranted as midshipman on Aug. 20, 1842, in accordance with the recommendations of his commanding officers. He saw service on several war-ships and in many seas, and enjoyed one year, 1845–46, at the Naval School, Annapolis. He became passed midshipman, 1846, lieutenant, 1855, and lieutenant commander, 1862, commanding the steamer *Hatteras* in the Western Gulf Blockading Squadron. On Jan. 11, 1863, he was ordered by signal to chase a sail to the southeastward, which, when approached and hailed, at first pretended to be a British war-ship. Before a boat could be lowered the suspicious stranger hailed in her turn, announcing that she was the Confederate ship *Alabama*. A broadside immediately followed, to which the *Hatteras* replied. Commander Blake endeavored immediately to close with the enemy, which was of greatly superior power, in order to take her by boarding. This intention was frustrated by the *Alabama's* captain, and, after a sharp fight in which several shells exploded in the *Hatteras,* depriving Blake of the power of maneuvering his vessel or working the pumps to quench the fire which broke out, he was no longer able to continue the unequal battle, and surrendered his ship, which sank ten minutes after her crew had been taken off by the *Alabama.* After being exchanged, Blake was exonerated and commended by the Navy Department, and received command of the gunboat *Eutaw* in the North Atlantic Squadron, taking part in several actions in the Virginia rivers. An interesting letter is extant in the Navy Department from representatives of the crew of the *Hatteras,* petitioning the Secretary of the Navy to place their "brave and excellent commander" in command of a "fast and well-armed steamer, and that in company with him we may seek out and capture our former foe," a request which it was impossible to fulfil, as measures had already been taken which eventually resulted in the destruction of the *Alabama.* Blake was commissioned commander Mar. 3, 1866, captain May 25, 1871, and commodore in 1879. He was married to Mary Flanagan, by whom he had two children.

[Sketch and portrait in Ellery Bicknell Crane, *Genealogy of the Crane Family,* II (1900), 151–54; obituary in *Army and Navy Jour.,* Jan. 24, 1880; *Official Records,* ser. 1, vol. XIX; Navy Registers, 1823–80.]

E. B.

BLAKE, JOHN LAURIS (Dec. 21, 1788– July 6, 1857), Episcopal clergyman, author, was born in Northwood, N. H., the son of Jonathan and Mary (Dow) Blake. He worked on his father's farm in summer and went to the district school in winter, attended Phillips Exeter Academy, and graduated in 1812 from Brown University. He was licensed as a Congregational minister in 1813, but soon turned to the Episcopal Church. He married Louisa Gray Richmond June 25, 1814, who died Jan. 3, 1816; on Dec. 6 of the same year he married Mary Howe. Upon his ordination as an Episcopal deacon in 1815 he organized St. Paul's parish in Pawtucket, R. I., and was its rector until 1820. He then took charge of parishes in Concord and Hopkinton, N. H., and at Concord started a girls' school that succeeded so well that in 1822 he moved it to Boston, where he continued to maintain it until 1830. In Boston he was also rector of St. Matthew's 1824–32 and editor of the *Gospel Advocate,* which in January 1827 was merged with the *Episcopal Watchman.* The rest of his life was given chiefly to literary work of one sort or another. He made his home in New York for a time and about 1846 moved to Orange, N. J., where he died. He seems to have been an amiable, dutiful man, a diligent though decidedly uncritical student and writer. As cleric and schoolmaster he had acquired a varied stock of information, which he purveyed at first in small packages as text-books and later in whole tomes as one-volume encyclopedias. He wrote in all more than forty books, most of them texts of geography, the natural sciences, and Christian evidences, together with various reading books and other miscellaneous productions. The farmer being especially dear to his heart, he endeavored to further scientific agriculture and rural education in general with *A Family Text-Book for the Country, or the Farmer at Home, Being a Cyclopædia of the More Important Topics in Modern Agriculture* (1853), an alphabetization of definitions, anecdotes, homilies, and tidbits of information not altogether trustworthy. The same characteristics reappeared in his larger work, *A Family Encyclopedia of Useful Knowledge* (1852). Somewhat better was the book by which he was most widely known, his *General Biographical Dictionary* (1835, 13th ed., rev. and enlarged, 1856), which enjoyed for almost a generation a good reputation and a useful career as a reference book.

[*Hist. Cat. of Brown Univ. 1764–1904* (1905); E. C. Cogswell, *Hist. of Nottingham, Deerfield, and Northwood, N. H.* (1878), pp. 645–47; *Church Rev. and Ecclesiastical Reg.,* Oct. 1857.]

G. H. G.

BLAKE, LILLIE DEVEREUX (Aug. 12, 1835–Dec. 30, 1913), author, reformer, was descended on both sides of the family from Jonathan Edwards. George P. Devereux, her father, was a wealthy gentleman of Raleigh, N. C., where Lillie was born; her mother, Sarah Elizabeth Johnson, of an old New York and New England family, was descended from the Hon. William Samuel Johnson. Her mother moved to New Haven on the death of her husband when Lillie was two years old, and the child attended Miss Apthorp's school for girls and later was tutored in college subjects by Yale professors. At twenty she married Frank G. Q. Umsted, Philadelphia attorney. They had two children. She now began to write, but without the definite social and political bias which characterized her later work. A short story was published in the *Atlantic Monthly* and there was a novel, *Southwold* (1859). Four years after their marriage her husband died, leaving her with a depleted fortune and two small children to support. She wrote feverishly during this period, completing a book of stories, and two novels in the *New York Mercury,* "The Orphan or The Mystery of Maple Cottage" and "Ireton Standish or the False Kinsman." During the first year of the Civil War she was Washington correspondent of the *New York Evening Post.* She published *Rockford, or Sunshine and Storm* in 1863. Under various *noms de plume,* one of which was Tiger Lily, she also contributed to the *Galaxy* which was later merged with the *Atlantic Monthly.* She was

married again, in 1866, to Grenfill Blake, a merchant of New York City, where she lived from
that time. Her interest in the rights of women
crystallized a few years later and she became active in agitation for enfranchisement and economic reforms for women. She arranged conventions, addressed committees, presided at public meetings, and made extensive lecture tours.
In her spare time she wrote articles for newspapers and periodicals, and fiction which carried her message. The best known of her novels
is *Fettered for Life, or Lord and Master* (1874,
republished in 1885), "designed to illustrate the
subject condition of women" (*Testimonial to
Mrs. Blake, National Pageant and Dramatic
Events in the History of New York,* Union
Square Theatre, Nov. 25, 1889). She was one
of the delegation from the National Woman's
Suffrage Association which presented the Declaration of Rights at Independence Hall, Philadelphia, on July 4, 1876; she was president of the
New York State Woman's Suffrage Association
for eleven years; and in 1900 she founded the
National Legislative League. She championed
measures which established matrons in police
stations, women census takers, seats for sales-
women, and women physicians in insane asylums
admitting women patients. One of her most important activities was in behalf of the school suffrage laws for women in New York State, in the
passage of which in 1880 she was largely instrumental. In reply to Dr. Morgan Dix's *Lectures
on the Calling of a Christian Woman* (1883) she
herself gave a series of lectures, published as
Woman's Place Today (1883), which created a
sensation in the current press and did much to
waken women and convert them into active workers. She was president of the New York City
Suffrage League from 1886 until 1900. A woman of unusual beauty and charm, she was not an
easy prey for the cartoonists who amused themselves at the expense of the early suffragists.

[*Who's Who in America,* 1899–1912; *N. Y. Times,*
Dec. 29, 31, 1913; *N. Y. Tribune,* Dec. 31, 1913; *Sun,*
Dec. 31, 1913; manuscript letter from Mrs. Blake's
daughter, Miss Katherine D. Blake.]
                                                    M.A.K.

BLAKE, LYMAN REED (Aug. 24, 1835–
Oct. 5, 1883), inventor, was born at South Abington, Mass., the son of Susannah Bates and Samuel Blake, directly descended from William and
Agnes Blake who came to Dorchester, Mass.,
from Plymouth, England, in 1630. Lyman, the
youngest of ten children, eight of whom were
girls, received the usual district school education
of the period. During his school vacations he
worked for the shoemakers of Abington and at
sixteen was regularly employed by his older

brother Samuel, who was manufacturing shoes
in a small way. From Samuel's "factory" the
cut-out parts of shoes were given to the shoemakers, who worked on them at home and then
returned the finished shoes. Lyman's duties at
the factory were to give out the stock, receive the
finished shoes, and keep account of these. Following this he worked with Edmund Shaw, agent
for the Singer Sewing Machine Company at
Abington, setting up sewing machines in the
shoe factories and teaching operators their use.
By 1856 he had saved money enough to purchase
an interest in the shoemaking firm of Gurney &
Mears, which became Gurney, Mears & Blake.
Here he immediately organized a stitching room,
put in machines, and taught the operators in what
was probably the first such room to be run on the
"contract" system. At that time the machines
were able to sew only the seams of the uppers
which were then hand-sewed or pegged to the
sole. Blake entertained the idea of a machine
capable of sewing the soles of shoes to the uppers. His partners thought this a bit visionary
and suggested that any work on the machine
should be done on his own time. Blake went
ahead at night and first designed a shoe that could
be sewed. This shoe is essentially the present-
day shoe and is considered by many as Blake's
most important invention. It is described in Patent No. 29,561. He then whittled a wooden model of a machine that would, in his opinion, sew
such a shoe. He had the parts made for a metal
machine, put them together, and found that it
worked. He immediately patented the machine
(Patent No. 20,775, July 6, 1858) and through
his patent attorney met Gordon McKay (1859),
who was able and willing to promote it. McKay
paid Blake $70,000 for this patent, $8,000 in cash,
and $62,000 from the profits of the company. Be-
cause of poor health Blake then moved to Staunton, Va., where with the $8,000 he was able to
open a retail shoe store, though the Civil War
very soon forced him to leave his store and return
to the North. In 1861 he rejoined McKay and
to promote the introduction of his machine, did
all in his power to improve it. With McKay he
worked out the details of the factory system which
made the machine available and traveled over
New England introducing the machine and instructing manufacturers in its use. Blake's machine, when finally perfected, came into almost
universal use, as is indicated by Blake's own
statement that in fifteen years (1861–76) over
177,000,000 pairs of shoes had been sewed on the
McKay machines at a saving of $14,000,000. To-
day, with many refinements, it is an important
link in the series of machines that allows the shoe

to be completely machine made. Unfortunately for the fame of Blake the machine has always been known in this country as the McKay machine, although in Europe, where his patents were handled so carelessly that he received very little from them, he did have the satisfaction of having it known as the Blake machine. The product and process patents on the shoe were reissued to Blake in 1874 and reassigned by him to the McKay Association, for which he received a large sum of money. He then retired from active business and spent most of his remaining years in travel. He was married on Nov. 27, 1855, to Susie V. Hollis of Abington.

[B. Hobart, *Hist. of the Town of Abington, Plymouth County, Mass.* (1866); *Vital Records of Abington, Mass., to the Year 1850*, vol. I (1912); B. E. Hazard, *Organization of the Boot and Shoe Industry in Mass. before 1875* (1921); F. A. Gannon, *Short Hist. of Am. Shoemaking* (1912); *Supt. and Foreman*, Oct. 27, 1896; obituary in *Boston Evening Transcript*, Oct. 6, 1883; *Shoe and Leather Reporter*, Mar. 13, 1884; A. Getchel, *In the Matter of the Application of Lyman Blake for Extensions of Letters Patent No. 29,561* (1874).]

F.A.T—r.

BLAKE, MARY ELIZABETH McGRATH (Sept. 1, 1840–Feb. 26, 1907), author, daughter of Patrick and Mary (Murphy) McGrath, was born in Dungarven, Ireland, and died in Boston. Her father came to Massachusetts about 1850 and settled in Quincy. There, prospering as a worker in marble, he was able to send his children to the best schools and to devote much of his own time to reading. Mary completed her formal education at Emerson's Private School in Boston (1859–61) and at the Academy of the Sacred Heart, Manhattanville (1861–63). In 1865 she was married to John G. Blake, a Boston physician who had known her first through the poems which she had already begun publishing in the newspapers. She was the mother of eleven children, to whom she was thoroughly attentive, but her maternal duties did not check either the steady flow of verse which "welled from her heart spontaneously" (Conway, "M. E. Blake," p. xiii), or the "Rambling Talks" which she contributed regularly for many years to the *Boston Journal*. A devout Catholic, she wrote many articles for the *Catholic World*, but she published also in *Scribner's* and even in *The Congregationalist*. From time to time she published collections of her poetry. Her *Poems* (1882) contains matter written as early as 1863. *Verses along the Way* appeared in 1890, and *In the Harbour of Hope*, 1907. She wrote also two books of poems for children, *The Merry Months All* (1885), and *Youth in Twelve Centuries* (1886). Her writing was so esteemed in the Boston of her time that she was invited by the city to prepare memorials

for Wendell Phillips and other celebrities. But the artistic value of her work is not commensurate with her reputation. She published in prose three volumes of travel, *On the Wing* (1883)—dealing with the western United States; *Mexico* (1888)—in collaboration with Margaret F. Sullivan; and *A Summer Holiday in Europe* (1890). "She had visited Europe," it is reported, "five times; thrice on walking trips of educative purpose with her three younger children; and in every land she could make herself at home with its people" (Conway, "M. E. Blake," p. xvi). She opposed militarism, and in 1887 denounced it in her pamphlet, *The Coming Reform*. Of her six children who reached maturity, she sent five sons to Harvard and one daughter to Radcliffe.

[K. E. Conway, "Mary Elizabeth Blake," in M. E. Blake, *In the Harbour of Hope* (1907); J. B. Cullen, *Story of the Irish in Boston* (rev. ed., 1893); *Who's Who in America*, 1906–07; *Publishers Weekly*, Mar. 9, 1907; *Boston Globe*, Feb. 27, 1907.]

J.D.W.

BLAKE, WILLIAM PHIPPS (June 21, 1825–May 22, 1910), geologist and mining engineer, was born in New York City, the son of Adeline (Mix) Blake and of Elihu Blake, a prominent surgeon dentist and lineal descendant of William Blake who settled in the Massachusetts Bay colony about 1630. W. P. Blake was fitted for college at private schools in New York and entered the Sheffield Scientific School to graduate in the course in chemistry in 1852. He then became chemist and mineralogist of the New Jersey Zinc Company and chemist of the chemical works at Baltimore, Md. In 1854–56 he was one of the geologists of the Pacific Railroad surveys. On Dec. 25, 1855, he was married to Charlotte Haven Lord Hayes. From 1856 to 1859 he was engaged in investigating the mineral resources of North Carolina and adjacent regions and in the last-named year became editor and proprietor of the *Mining Magazine*, the name of which he subsequently changed to the *Mining Magazine and Journal of Geology, Mineralogy and Metallurgy, Chemistry and the Arts*. The venture did not prove a success, in part owing to the approach of the Civil War, and the publication was suspended in 1860. In 1861–63 Blake was employed as mining engineer by the Japanese government and in company with Raphael Pumpelly he organized the first school of science in Japan and taught there both chemistry and geology. In 1863 he returned to the United States by way of Alaska and explored the Stickeen River region, discovering and describing the Stickeen glacier. Returning to California he resumed his profession of mining engineer, making special studies of the Comstock Lode, and in 1864 he was appointed mineralogist of the state board of agriculture, and also professor of mineralogy and geology in the College of California (afterwards the University of California at Berkeley). In 1867 he was appointed commissioner for California to the Paris Exposition and was editor of the six volumes of reports of the United States Commissioners. In 1871 he was chief of the scientific corps of the United States to Santo Domingo, and in 1873 he was commissioner of the United States to the Vienna International Exposition. His manifest efficiency in this capacity led to his appointment by the Smithsonian Institution to collect and install the government exhibit, illustrating the mineral resources of the United States, at the Philadelphia Centennial Exposition of 1876. His work in the preparation of this exhibit was enormous but highly successful. These collections, in connection with those of several foreign governments turned over at the close of the exposition, formed the basis of the New National Museum's collections begun in 1879–80. To Blake also fell the somewhat onerous task of editing the notes and describing the fossils collected long before by the French-American geologist, Jules Marcou, who, through a falling out with the then secretary of state, had relinquished his work, leaving his collections in confusion, and had returned to France. Blake was for some fifteen years engaged in sundry economic surveys in the West, and in 1895, although already in his seventieth year, he became professor of geology and mining, and director of the School of Mines at the University of Arizona at Tucson. This position he resigned in 1905, but retained until his death the honorary and non-salaried appointment of territorial mineralogist and geologist, to which he had been appointed in 1898. Blake stood all of six feet in height and with his strong features and abundant growth of beard and snow-white hair made a very striking appearance. He is stated to have been an ideal teacher, a strong, aggressive fighter, fair and above board in all things. He died from pneumonia brought on by exposure when receiving the degree of LL.D. at Berkeley in 1910.

[R. W. Raymond, biographical sketch in *Trans. Am. Inst. Mining Engineers* (1910), containing full bibliography of Blake's publications; G. P. Merrill, *First 100 Years of American Geology* (1924).]

                             G.P.M.

BLAKE, WILLIAM RUFUS (1805–Apr. 22, 1863), actor, was born in Halifax, N. S., of Irish parentage, his father being a descendant of the Blakes of Galway. Early attracted to the stage, he made his first appearance with a company of strolling players in Halifax as the Prince of Wales in *Richard III*. He was first seen in this country in 1824 when as a light comedian he ap-

peared on July 12 at the old Chatham Theatre, New York, as Frederick Bramble in *Poor Gentleman* and as The Three Singles in *Three and Deuce, or Which Is He?* He remained several seasons at this house, appearing in *Pizarro, Speed the Plough, The Rivals, Damon and Pythias,* and *Three and Deuce.* On Aug. 26, 1826, he married Mrs. Caroline (Placide) Waring, a member of the famous Placide family of actors. The following year he went into theatrical management, assuming successively the direction of the Tremont Theatre, Boston, 1827; of the Walnut Street Theatre, Philadelphia, 1829; and, with H. E. Willard, of Mitchell's Olympic Theatre, New York, which he opened in 1837. In 1839 he went to England, appearing at the Haymarket Theatre in *Three and Deuce.* Returning to America, he was for a time stage manager of the Walnut Street Theatre, Philadelphia, and in 1848 he accepted a like position at the Broadway Theatre (Wallack's), New York. Afterwards he was a member of the stock companies at Burton's, Laura Keene's, and Wallack's, with which last theatre he was chiefly identified, "receiving, as we have heard, the heaviest salary of any actor on the stock list" (J. N. Ireland, *Records of the New York Stage,* 1866, I, 448). His last appearance in New York was on Apr. 16, 1863, as Geoffrey Dale in *The Last Man* and he was seen for the last time on any stage Apr. 21, 1863, at the Boston Theatre as Sir Peter Teazle.

T. Allston Brown says of him: "In his early days he was a really handsome man. He excelled in the old comedies, and his performance of Young Dornton in *The Road to Ruin* was considered one of the best ever known to the stage. As his bulk increased with his years, he was compelled to abandon light-comedy parts and adopt the portraiture of the old comedy uncles and fathers, and also some parts purely sentimental. In the former he was undoubtedly one of the most mirth-provoking of actors, and his Lord Duberly in *The Heir at Law* always attracted large audiences to Wallack's, Burton's, and at Laura Keene's, where he played the most brilliant engagements of his life" (*A History of the New York Stage,* 1903, I, 280). William Winter speaks of the "richly humorous Blake, so noble in his dignity, so firm and fine and easy in his method, so copious in his natural humour" (*Shadows of the Stage,* 1892). J. N. Ireland says of him: "In certain characters he surpassed all who had attempted them. His Jesse Rural, Geoffrey Dale, Hardcastle, Old Dornton, Admiral Kingston, Sir Peter Teazle, Sir Willoughby Worrett, Sir Anthony Absolute, Governor Heartall, etc., were examples of perfection.

... In the line of 'old men' we doubt if he has ever been excelled on the New York boards." Ireland also refers to "the immense rotundity which, independent of other causes, ultimately placed him among the greatest of modern comedians. He experienced the usual vicissitudes of an actor's lot—at one time enjoying the greatest popularity, and at another visited with undeserved neglect" (*Records of the New York Stage*, I, 447). According to T. Allston Brown, he was the first actor ever called before the curtain in America— an incident which occurred at Boston in 1827.

[In addition to the references given above see obituaries in *Boston Evening Transcript,* and *Evening Post,* Apr. 23, 1863.]   A.H.

BLAKELOCK, RALPH ALBERT (Oct. 15, 1847–Aug. 9, 1919), landscape painter, the son of R. A. Blakelock, a homeopathic physician, was born in New York City. His father desired him to study medicine, but he turned to music and the fine arts and entered the school of Cooper Union (F. W. Morton, "Work of R. A. Blakelock," *Brush and Pencil, post*). He attended classes there for a time but soon took his own course. The rich color schemes and enamel-like technique of Albert Pinkham Ryder fixed his attention. Ryder had sometimes used Indian figures and groups imaginatively as vehicles for moods. Blakelock followed suit on somewhat larger canvases, with a special liking for trees in silhouette against rather irrelevant skies, afterward widening his scope to woodland dreams and moonlights. Colors of rich deep timbre fascinated him; he used them like themes in music. At the Metropolitan Museum, New York, his "Pipe Dance" shows umbers and reds in a late afternoon effect with tree masses somber against a yellowish cloudy sky. "Indian Encampment" in the same museum is lighter in tone but with the strong impasto of A. P. Ryder; an effect of pale sunlight in early autumn. The St. Louis Museum has a foreign theme: "From St. Ives to Lelant." Blakelock's devotion to landscapes with groups of Indians has suggested that he made an early trip to the West, but probably this is an unsafe inference; his Western landscapes belong to a later date. Realism was not his aim. Similar tones with strong impasto are seen in paintings by George Bogert and Julian Rix. In 1892 Blakelock received an Honorable Mention at the exhibition of the Pennsylvania Academy, and in 1899 in New York he took the first Hallgarten Prize at the National Academy of Design. It was just then, when beginning to appeal to a wider circle of amateurs, that he experienced a mental breakdown. While in an asylum at Bennington, N. Y., he was elected associate of the National Academy in 1913 and three years later academician. Partly owing to his unhappy condition, which precluded further output, partly to the publicity consequent thereon, Blakelock's paintings, which hitherto had found little favor among the dealers, began to grow scarce and rise in value. At auctions they were competed for; a group of collectors, including the late Senator W. A. Clark of Montana and New York, bid them up, a large "Moonlight" with foliage etched on a dark sky fetching $20,000. These honors reacted to a very limited extent on the painter who had found it difficult in the eighties and nineties to dispose of his work. But in 1916 his health improved so distinctly that he left the asylum and came to New York where his return created much interest, not only owing to the signal appreciation of his pictures shown by high prices but because of sympathy for a man with an attractive personality who had been overtaken by disaster at the high tide of his career. Unfortunately the improvement did not persist. He tried to paint but the results were inadequate. Perhaps realization of his plight preyed on his mind, already shattered by his infirmity. In 1918 he had to return to the asylum, and in the following year he died at a camp in the Adirondacks.

There is something childlike and winning in Blakelock's moods; they recall many of the colorful dreamy pictures by eighteenth-century Hollanders and English landscapists influenced by Rembrandt. Rich mellow tones that salute the eyes as organ tones appeal to the ears may leave the intellectual votary of art cold, but to the sensuous they are a joy. Blakelock's gift was not wide. His was not a nature to formulate themes of tragedy, nor did he lean toward the religious or sublime. Though born in a great city his affections were rustic, not urban, as if the spirit of Barker of Bath or Old Crome had returned to earth and sought a painter like in tastes, simplicity, and unpretence. The names given his pictures signify little, for he was not telling a story, he was expressing a mood or a dream or a memory. Among his notable works are: "Shooting the Arrow"; "Bannock Wigwam in Peaceful Dale"; "Autumn" bought by Mrs. Kurtz; "Moonlight," 1886, bought by Catholina Lambert for his collection in "The Castle," Paterson, N. J.; "Sunset, Nevarra Range" bought by Wm. T. Evans; "Colorado Plains" in the Corcoran Gallery, Washington, D. C.; "October Sunshine" in the Art Museum of Worcester, Mass.; "The Capture" in the Brooklyn Art Institute; "Canoe Builders," "Sunset," and "Moonrise" in the National Gallery of Art at Washington.

[Elliott Daingerfield, *Ralph Albert Blakelock* (privately printed, 1914); Frederick Fairchild Sherman, *Landscape and Figure Painters of America* (privately printed, 1917), pp. 23–30; Frederick W. Morton, "Work of Ralph A. Blakelock," *Brush and Pencil*, IX, 257–69; N. N. (E. Pennell), "Blakelock," *Nation*, Aug. 23, 1919.]

C. De K.

BLAKELY, JOHNSTON (October 1781– October 1814), naval officer, was born near the village of Seaford in the County of Down, Ireland, whence, when he was two years old, his father, John Blakely, emigrated with his family to America, settling at Wilmington, N. C. Johnston was prepared for college at a school in Flatbush, L. I. He attended the University of North Carolina in 1797, and about this time his father died, leaving Edward Jones, an eminent lawyer of Wilmington, guardian of his son. A few years later Johnston lost his patrimony and was forced to suspend his education. On Feb. 5, 1800, he accepted the appointment of midshipman in the Navy. Serving in the Mediterranean squadron on the *President, John Adams,* and *Congress,* he took part in the operations of the squadron before Tripoli. On Feb. 10, 1807, he became a lieutenant. In 1811–13 he commanded the brig *Enterprise,* in which he cruised off the coast of the United States, capturing the armed schooner *Fly.* On July 24, 1813, he was commissioned master commandant and given command of the sloop-of-war *Wasp.* In December he married Jane Ann Hoope (or Hooper), daughter of a New York merchant. On May 1, 1814, he sailed from Portsmouth, N. H., on the *Wasp,* and after capturing a number of enemy vessels, fell in with the British brig *Reindeer* on June 28 in the English Channel. In the ensuing close-quarters battle, the *Reindeer,* gallantly fought by her commander, Capt. William Manners, and his crew, was badly worsted by the superior gun power of the *Wasp,* and hauled down her flag when her captain was shot dead in a vain attempt to board the American vessel. The *Reindeer* was burnt, and Blakely proceeded to L'Orient, France, in order to land his numerous prisoners and to refit. Here he remained seven weeks, resuming his cruise on Aug. 27, and taking three more enemy vessels by Sept. 1, one of which was cut out from a convoy and burnt under the eyes of the convoying 74-gun ship. In the late afternoon of Sept. 1, he fell in with four sails, one of which proved to be the British brig *Avon,* slightly inferior in force to the *Wasp.* Blakely at once attacked, even surrendering the weather position in order to force the enemy to fight before her consorts could close. After an hour's combat the *Avon* answered Blakely's hail with the announcement that she

had struck, but, before possession of the prize could be taken, a second enemy brig was observed approaching with two more coming up in the offing, and Blakely was obliged to abandon his prize. In this fight the *Wasp* was much damaged in sails and rigging, while the *Avon* sank two hours after the engagement. "The course of the *Wasp* after this event," says Mahan (*post,* II, 257), "is traced by her captures. The meeting with the *Avon* was within a hundred miles of that with the *Reindeer.* On Sept. 12 and 14, having run south three hundred and sixty miles, she took two vessels; being then about two hundred and fifty miles west from Lisbon. On the 21st, having made four degrees more southing, she seized the British brig *Atalanta,* a hundred miles east of Madeira. This prize being of exceptional value, Blakely decided to send her in, and she arrived safely at Savannah on Nov. 4, in charge of Midshipman David Geisinger, who lived to become a captain in the navy. She brought with her Blakely's official despatches, including the report of the affair with the *Avon.*" Three weeks after the capture of the *Atalanta,* the *Wasp* is known to have been nine hundred miles farther south but nothing more was ever heard of her. Blakely was commissioned captain on Nov. 24, 1814, before the loss of the *Wasp* was known and was also tendered the thanks of Congress and a gold medal for his victory over the *Reindeer.* A sword awarded him by the General Assembly of North Carolina was presented to his widow, accompanied by a resolution "That Capt. Blakely's child be educated at the expense of this State; and that Mrs. Blakely be requested to draw on the Treasurer of this State, from time to time, for such sums of money as shall be required for the education of the said child."

[John H. Wheeler, *Hist. Sketches of N. C.* (1851); Wm. Johnson, "Biog. Sketch of Capt. Johnston Blakely," *N. C. Univ. Mag.,* Feb. 1854; K. P. Battle, "A N. C. Naval Hero and his Daughter," *N. C. Booklet,* Jan. 10, 1902; John Frost, *Am. Naval Biog.* (1844); Jas. Fenimore Cooper, *Hist. of the Navy,* II (1839); Theodore Roosevelt, *The Naval War of 1812* (1882); A. T. Mahan, *Sea Power in its Relations to the War of 1812* (1905).]

E. B.

BLAKESLEE, ERASTUS (Sept. 2, 1838– July 12, 1908), Congregational clergyman, was the son of Joel and Sarah Maria (Mansfield) Blakeslee, and was born in Plymouth, Conn. In his boyhood he attended the district school and worked on his father's farm and in his carriage shop. Deciding to enter the ministry, he prepared for college at Williston Seminary, Easthampton, Mass., and entered Yale in the class of 1863. On Oct. 9, 1861, he joined Company A, 1st Connecticut Cavalry, and received rapid promotion for bravery and distinguished service. In 1864 he obtained his degree at Yale and was enrolled with his class. On Mar. 13, 1865, he was commissioned brevet brigadier-general "for gallant conduct at Ashland, Va., June 1, 1864." He was the only brigadier-general from Connecticut who had enlisted as a private and had held every rank from second lieutenant up. From 1865 to 1876 he engaged in business in New Haven and in Boston. In the fall of 1876 he entered Andover Seminary and graduated in 1879. While a graduate student at Andover, he was called to the Second Congregational Church in Greenfield, Mass., and was ordained there, Feb. 11, 1880. In July 1883 he became pastor of the Second Church, Fair Haven, Conn. (now the Pilgrim Church, New Haven). In the fall of 1887 he declined the presidency of Atlanta University, but accepted a call to the First Congregational Church of Spencer, Mass. As a business man he was successful, and patented a number of valuable inventions. As a pastor he was far-seeing and resourceful. At Greenfield he organized the Connecticut Valley Congregational Club. In New Haven he became a prominent promoter of the Christian Endeavor movement, then in its infancy, was the first president of the New Haven Union, and wrote the Christian Endeavor constitution of Connecticut. Realizing the inadequacy of the Sunday-school "helps" of the time, he devised for his own school in Spencer, in 1888, a system of lessons designed to impart a more comprehensive knowledge of the Bible, and graded to meet the needs of pupils of various ages. These lessons were so successful that in 1891 he began their publication for wider use, and in 1892 resigned at Spencer and organized in Boston the Bible Study Publishing Company. He formed also the Bible Study Union, composed of prominent religious educators, as a sort of advisory board, so that his publications became known as the *Bible Study Union Lessons*. During his lifetime about 170 volumes of these lessons, for all grades, were published. They have been widely used and translated into many languages, doing much to bring biblical instruction in the Protestant Churches into harmony with pedagogical principles. Blakeslee was a member of the Council of the Religious Education Association, of the Society of Biblical Literature and Exegesis, and of the Victoria Institute of London. He wrote a history of his regiment, and originated the scheme of the *Harmony of the Gospels*, later worked out by Stevens and Burton (Dr. Frank K. Sanders in *Sunday School Times*, Aug. 23, 1908). He was an able speaker, a strong and positive character, and a

gentle and lovable personality. He was married on Mar. 30, 1865, to Mary Goodrich North of New Haven. From 1892 until his death he made his home at Brookline, Mass.

[Shortly after Blakeslee's death, a pamphlet, *In Memoriam*, was issued, containing much biographical material. Cf. also *Congreg. Yr. Bk.*, 1909; *Congregationalist*, July 23, 1908; *Obit. Record Grads. Yale Univ.*; *Boston Evening Transcript*, July 13, 1908; *Triennial Meeting and Biog. Record of the Class of '63 in Yale Coll.* (1869); *Official Records*, ser. I.]   F. T. P.

BLALOCK, NELSON GALES (Feb. 17, 1836–Mar. 14, 1913), physician, agriculturist, at the time of his death was recognized as the foremost citizen of the State of Washington. This, no doubt, was due to the fact that his career was far more than that of the physician who confines himself exclusively to medical practise. After working his way through academy and college in Mitchell County, N. C., the place where he was born, young Blalock moved to Philadelphia and secured his medical education in Jefferson Medical College of that city, graduating in March 1861. He then took up the practise of medicine in Decatur, Ill., but soon joined the 115th Illinois Volunteers as a surgeon and served with ability during the Civil War. He returned to Decatur after the war and practised his profession successfully for twelve years until 1873, when he went West with a wagon train and settled in Walla Walla, Wash. He at once established a remunerative and important practise, performing on an average a surgical operation each day and delivering during the course of his career some five thousand babies. He was of the old-time practitioner type, seldom keeping his books in good condition, so that when he died he had over $40,000 in outstanding bills unpaid. Nevertheless he was the first practitioner in Walla Walla to establish modern electric equipment in his office, including X-ray. Blalock was also widely known for his interest in civic and educational affairs, serving for many years as a member of the board of trustees and later as president of the board of trustees of Whitman College. He was a member of the board of trustees of the public schools and for a number of terms mayor of his city. He aided in calling the constitutional convention of Washington in 1889, and was instrumental in framing the constitution. In the development of the agricultural factors of Washington state he aided much by inaugurating the fluming of lumber from the mountains, raising wheat in the uplands, and establishing a large orchard for the raising of fruit and vegetables which is still known as the Blalock orchard. From his first marriage, to Panthea A. Durham who died in 1864, there was a son who succeeded his father as a physician in Walla Walla. From a second marriage, to Marie G. Greenfield, there were two daughters. The death of Blalock at the age of seventy-seven closed a long career of service to his community and to the state.

[*Memorial Address, Joint Session of Senate and House, 14th Legislature of the State of Washington,* 1915, pp. 45–50; *Post Intelligencer* (Seattle), Mar. 15, 1913; *Spokesman-Review* (Spokane), Mar. 15, 1913; Wm. D. Lyman, *Lyman's Hist. of Old Walla Walla County* (1918), II, 5–8.]   M. F.

BLANC, ANTOINE (Oct. 11, 1792–June 20, 1860), Catholic archbishop, a native of Sury near Lyons, France, was among the first ecclesiastical students raised to the priesthood after the religious restoration in France. Bishop Du Bourg of New Orleans who had come to France for the purpose of securing priests for the missions of the Mississippi Valley ordained him on July 22, 1816. With several young seminarians Blanc landed at Annapolis in 1817 and after being entertained by Charles Carroll of Carrollton was sent to the Mississippi Valley where for nearly fifteen years he labored in the missions. In 1831 Bishop de Neckère of New Orleans appointed him vicar-general, and when the Bishop died in 1833 Blanc was named administrator and on Nov. 22, 1835, was consecrated bishop of the diocese, which included the states of Louisiana, Mississippi, and, in 1838, Texas. In 1842 the question of the authority of the Bishop to appoint the rector of the Cathedral brought Bishop Blanc into conflict with the trustees of the church. When the latter refused to accept the rector appointed by the Bishop the church was for a few months placed under the ban of the interdict. Finally the trustees took the matter to court asking $20,000 damages. They were represented among others by Pierre Soulé and Christian Roselius. The court dismissed the petition and the decision was sustained by the Supreme Court. During this same period the Bishop with a number of prominent Catholic laity worked strenuously to counteract the influence of the Know-Nothing party. In 1850 Pius IX established the Archdiocese of New Orleans, and Bishop Blanc was raised to archepiscopal dignity in 1851. His principal services were in building new churches to meet the demands of the growing population, in the establishment of schools and orphan asylums, and in the systematizing of church affairs in general. In order to provide priests for the diocese he invited the Jesuits and the Lazarists to establish seminaries. To care for the free colored orphans and the aged he founded the Sisters of the Holy Family, the first colored sisterhood in the United States. When Bishop Blanc took charge of the diocese the only churches in

New Orleans were the Cathedral, St. Patrick's, and the chapel attached to the old Ursuline convent. In 1854 there were eighteen churches. The Archbishop was one of the American delegates to Rome in 1855 when the dogma of the Immaculate Conception was proclaimed. In January 1860 he was taken seriously ill but rallied and apparently regained his usual health. He died suddenly June 20, 1860, and was buried in the St. Louis Cathedral. According to contemporary accounts, he was a man calculated to win the esteem and affection of all who made his acquaintance. He was remarkably gentle and mild in his manners and affable with all (*New Orleans Daily Crescent*, June 22, 1860).

[Alcée Fortier, *Louisiana* (1909), vol. I; *Daily Picayune* (New Orleans), Jan. 9, 14, 1844, Apr. 17, 1850, June 22, 1860, and other New Orleans papers of June 21, June 22, 1860; Archives of the St. Louis Cathedral, New Orleans.]   S. H.

BLANCHARD, JONATHAN (Jan. 19, 1811–May 14, 1892), Presbyterian clergyman, college president, the son of Jonathan and Mary (Lovel) Blanchard, was born in the little town of Rockingham, Vt., of pure English ancestry. His early education was obtained in the common schools of the town and from private instructors. He was a school-teacher at the age of fourteen and entered Middlebury College at the age of seventeen, graduating in 1832, when he was twenty-one years old. For two years he taught at Plattsburg Academy and afterwards studied at Andover and at Lane Theological Seminary in Cincinnati. In the latter city he was ordained pastor of the Sixth Presbyterian Church in September 1838. From the beginning Blanchard was a strong temperance advocate and in 1834, at the age of twenty-three, he became a violent abolitionist. In 1843 he attended the World's Anti-Slavery Convention in London and was elected American vice-president of that body. On his return from England he delivered a series of spirited lectures on the wrongs of Ireland. In spite of the fact that Cincinnati was almost as strongly pro-slavery as any southern community, he never hesitated to attack that institution in sermons, in articles, and in private conversation (see *A Debate on Slavery ... Between the Rev. J. Blanchard and N. L. Rice,* 1846). Almost as violent was his hatred of secret societies and especially of the Masonic order. This, too, he attacked in every way and at every opportunity. As the Civil War approached he more and more coupled Masonry and slavery and declared that the Masonic order was concerned in the attempt at disunion. During his Cincinnati pastorate he founded and edited a church paper later known as the *Herald and Presbyter*.

In 1845 he was elected president of Knox College, at Galesburg, Ill., and held that position until 1857. Under his administration the financial condition of the college was greatly improved and the number of students practically doubled. Blanchard's outspoken attitude on many subjects, however, brought him into frequent controversies, and the later years of his administration were full of strife and difficulty. After resigning the presidency he served for a year as acting president and teacher, at the same time conducting the *Christian Era* which he had founded. In 1860 he took the presidency of Wheaton College, at Wheaton, Ill. While there he published *Freemasonry Illustrated* (1879) and founded and edited the *Christian Cynosure*. He became president emeritus in 1882 and died on May 14, 1892. He was married in 1838 to Mary Avery Bent, by whom he had twelve children, five sons and seven daughters. One son, Charles Albert, succeeded his father as president of Wheaton College, and died on Dec. 20, 1925.

[J. W. Bailey, *Knox College* (1860); Rufus Blanchard, *Hist. of Du Page County, Ill.* (1882), pp. 174 ff.; T. S. Pearson, *Cat. of Grads. of Middlebury Coll.*; *Chicago Tribune*, May 15, 1892.]

A. B.

BLANCHARD, NEWTON CRAIN (Jan. 29, 1849–June 22, 1922), lawyer, governor of Louisiana, the son of Carey H. and Frances Amelia (Crain) Blanchard, was born in Rapides Parish, La. He was reared on his father's cotton plantation in that parish and was educated in private schools and the Louisiana State Seminary of Learning (now the Louisiana State University). He was granted the LL.B. degree by the University of Louisiana (now Tulane) in 1870 and in the next year began the practise of law at Shreveport, La. He soon entered politics, and through a period of over forty years he achieved considerable success in that field. He first became prominent for the part that he took in resisting the reconstruction policy of the national government in Louisiana and, with a number of other men in his parish (Caddo Parish), he was arraigned before the federal authorities in New Orleans on the charge of intimidating the negroes from voting. Popular sentiment, however, was with them and they were acquitted. In 1879 he was elected as the representative of Caddo Parish to the Louisiana state constitutional convention and served on many of its more important committees. In 1880 he was chosen to represent the fourth Louisiana district in the Forty-seventh Congress and was reëlected to the five succeeding congresses (1881–93). He was chairman of the Rivers and Harbors Committee of the lower house under Speaker Crisp and was active in se-

curing legislation for the improvement of the Mississippi levees. In 1893 he was appointed by the governor of Louisiana, and in 1894 he was elected by the Louisiana state legislature, to the United States Senate to fill out the unexpired term of Edward Douglas White who had been appointed to the United States Supreme Court by President Cleveland. As senator he was especially interested in getting such tariff legislation as would benefit Louisiana's agricultural interests. On the expiration of his term in the Senate, he was appointed associate justice of the supreme court of Louisiana and served in that capacity from 1897 to 1904. From this position he was elevated in 1904 by the vote of the people of the state to the governorship of Louisiana for a term of four years. His administration as governor was marked by the creation of several state boards and departments, including a board of charities and corrections, a board of equalization, and a reform school; by the revision of the system of taxation so as to lay a heavier burden upon the corporate interests in the state; by the encouragement of education; by making elective by popular vote a large number of state and local officers heretofore appointed by the governor, such as the supreme court justices, the register of the state land office, the parish assessors, the members of the parish school boards and the state tax collector of New Orleans; and by providing for state-wide primaries for all state and national offices. At the close of his term as governor, he resumed the practise of law at Shreveport. That did not bring his public career to an end, however. In 1913 he was elected to the Louisiana state constitutional convention which had been called primarily to fund the public debt of the state, and he was chosen by that body as its president. In this position he did much to shape the work of the convention. He was a delegate-at-large to several Democratic national conventions and also served several times as national Democratic committeeman for Louisiana. He was twice married, first, on Dec. 16, 1873, to Emily Barret of Shreveport, who died on July 27, 1907, and second, on Jan. 29, 1909, to Charlotte Tracy of Baton Rouge. He was a man of large physique and presented a rather striking and somewhat pompous appearance. His state papers, especially his judicial decisions, were marked for their clarity of expression and intelligent comprehension of the subject in hand.

[Brief biographical sketches may be found in the daily newspapers of New Orleans and Shreveport, La., for June 23, 1922, and also in Alcée Fortier, *Louisiana* (1909), I, 100–106.]

E. M. V.

BLANCHARD, THOMAS (June 24, 1788–Apr. 16, 1864), inventor, son of Samuel and Susanna (Tenney) Blanchard, was born in Sutton, Worcester County, Mass. He came of very old New England stock, and his father was a farmer. Early in life he evinced a fondness for mechanical subjects, his tools being limited to a knife and a gimlet. At the age of thirteen he invented an apple-parer which made him a favorite at the "paring bees" of the neighborhood. When quite young he went to reside with an elder brother who made tacks by hand. The youthful Thomas invented a counter with a bell for keeping tally on production. He worked on a tack-making machine which could turn out 500 tacks a minute—one of the first automatic machines. The perfecting of this device required several years' labor. He sold his patent rights for this invention for $5,000—a large sum for that period. Next he turned his attention to the turning of gun barrels. He devised a lathe which not only turned the barrel externally but, when the breech was reached, by means of a special mechanism cut both the flat and oval portions. Here we have an important step—one machine performing two dissimilar operations. Blanchard now entered the employ of the great Springfield Arsenal, for which he invented a machine which would not only cut in a straight line but would bore and mortise so neatly that when the operation was complete the lock would fit closely to the stock. While puzzling over the problem of how to turn a gun-stock, the whole principle of turning irregular forms from a pattern burst upon Blanchard's mind. Models were constructed which worked so well that a shoe last, a gun-stock, spokes of wheels, hat-blocks, or other articles of irregular shape could be produced at will. The invention consisted of a friction-wheel which touched the pattern and a cutting-wheel secured to the same shaft. A large driving drum allowed the belt which turned the two wheels to slide up and down so that power was supplied irrespective of the position of the cutting-wheel to the wood being shaped. The friction-wheel followed the contour of the pattern and pushed the cutting-wheel in and out of contact with the wood being machined. The machine not only duplicated but made articles longer or shorter, larger or smaller, and right and left. The importance of this invention can hardly be overestimated and many machine tools, as well as woodworking machinery, depend on this principle; even dies for medals employ the same idea.

Blanchard worked for the Government for five years and in the meantime his invention was extensively pirated. He received a royalty of "nine cents" on each musket produced at Harper's Ferry and Springfield. When his patent expired in 1833 he petitioned Congress for a renewal which was granted on the ground that this was an original machine, standing among the "*first* American inventions." The renewal was granted in 1834. This patent contained mistakes which well-nigh caused Blanchard to lose all his rights; but Congress finally rectified the mistakes and Blanchard was upheld in the courts. He also invented machines for cutting and folding envelopes. In 1825 he built a steam carriage and secured a patent on it, and in 1826 he tried to promote a company to build railroads. The legislature of Massachusetts approved the plan, but capitalists considered it visionary. Blanchard went to New York and tried to get Gov. Clinton interested, proposing to build a railroad from Albany to Schenectady; but Clinton was of the opinion that it was too soon after the completion of the Erie Canal. Finding himself ahead of the times, Blanchard abandoned the project, and devoted his attention to steam navigation of rivers where there were shoal rapids. He constructed a boat with a stern wheel placed far astern where the greatest eddy is found; this boat made trips between Hartford and Springfield. Blanchard also designed and built several kinds of shallow-draft steamers which were introduced on western rivers, making the upstream trip possible,—a type of boat which later came into universal use.

[E. W. Byrn, *Progress of Invention in the Nineteenth Century* (1900), pp. 368–69 ; Henry Howe, *Memoirs of the Most Eminent Am. Mechanics* (1844) ; W. Kaempffert, *A Pop. Hist. of Am. Invention* (1924), I, 136 ; II, 412, 413, 416 ; J. W. Roe, *Eng. and Am. Tool Builders* (1926), pp. 6, 140, 142, 219, 220–221 ; Asa H. Waters, *Biog. Sketch of Thos. Blanchard and His Inventions* (1878) ; *Boston Evening Transcript,* Apr. 18, 1864.]

A. A. H.

BLANCHET, FRANÇOIS NORBERT (Sept. 3, 1795–June 18, 1883), Catholic missionary and first archbishop of Oregon City, was the son of Pierre and Rosalie Blanchet, Canadian land owners, who traced descent from the earliest adventurers of New France. Well connected with the best families, the Blanchets had given a number of sons and daughters to the Church and one of them had founded the *Canadien,* an influential journal. Educated at the parish school of St. Pierre, Rivière du Sud, Quebec, and at the Sulpician petit seminary of Quebec, Blanchet in 1816 entered the major seminary where he won distinction in theological studies. Ordained in 1819, Abbé Blanchet was assigned to the Cathedral for a year. He was then sent as a missionary to the Acadians and Micmac Indians of New Brunswick, where in addition to the native dialect he learned English in order to serve a group of Irish immigrants. For seven years, Blanchet labored zealously in this vast, wild region where he built three churches and made visitations by horse, snow-shoes, canoe, and dog-sledges, according to seasonal demands. With regret he left this perilous work and his primitive communicants for the rectorship of a well-established parish at the Cedars near Montreal. During the cholera (1832), the abbé was presented with loving cups by non-Catholics in admiration of his courageous service which knew neither creed nor race. It was here that he came into contact with the fur-traders and learned of the need for priests among the trappers, traders, and Catholic Iroquois in the Oregon region. The French petition for a priest through Dr. McLoughlin, chief factor of the Hudson's Bay Company, was heard by the bishops of the Red River Valley and of Quebec. Blanchet was ready and was thereupon appointed vicar-general to Archbishop Signay of Quebec with jurisdiction over the whole Oregon region though cautioned to establish his missions north of the Columbia River. Accompanying the annual Hudson's Bay Express, he preached at all posts on the route and at the Red River was joined by Abbé Modeste Demers, a newly ordained priest. The French and half-breeds at Vancouver and in the settlement of St. Paul's in Willamette Valley welcomed the missionaries for whose reception they had built a log church. From the first these missionaries were successful, aided as they were by Catholic half-breeds and Iroquois from whom they learned the various native dialects and who popularized their work among the pagan redmen. Demers with his chapel at Fort Nesqually as a center labored among the northern tribesmen as far as Alaska, and Blanchet served missions at St. Paul's, Astoria, Walla Walla, Vancouver, Cowlitz, and the Cascades. Their work was made easier with the conversion of Judge Peter Burnett, and the American official Secretary Long.

All this success aroused bitterness. Methodists circulated the "disclosures of Maria Monk," which Blanchet answered by citing the American Protestant exposé. Religious, political, racial, and fur trading rivalries combined to separate the Catholic and Protestant missionaries. Blanchet had little interest in Oregon politics, but he did not discourage the projected if extra-legal settlers' government. Later charges that Catholics inspired the Indian uprising which resulted in the murder of Marcus Whitman's party have been disproven. The Indians were actually aroused by the loss of hunting lands, stories of rival traders, absurd belief that Methodist settlers had poisoned the game and brought smallpox, by the murder of a chief by an American, and the whipping of Indians for thefts from the Metho-

dist mission. The younger Blanchet and Abbé Brouillet visited the Indians assembled in Walla Walla to aid the factor in quieting them and in obtaining the release of prisoners (1847). They also consoled the survivors, and risked death by burying the dead. Blanchet, however, did not hesitate to attend the five Indians who were executed for supposed complicity in the Whitman murder after a dubious trial (1849).

In the meantime Blanchet, who in 1843 had been made vicar apostolic and titular bishop at the joint suggestion of the archbishops of Quebec and Baltimore, learned on the way to Paris of his elevation to the archbishopric of the newly established see of Oregon City (1846) with his brother Augustine as bishop of Walla Walla and his faithful friend Demers as bishop of Vancouver, a recognized part of Canada. Blanchet visited Rome, France, and the German states in the interest of his archdiocese and obtained the services of several priests and Notre Dame nuns. While abroad, he was received in audiences by the courts of Belgium, Bavaria, Austria, and France and was presented with a purse by Louis Philippe and the Leopoldine Society. On his return he consecrated Bishop Demers and held a provincial council. At his invitation, the Oblate Fathers soon sent a mission band (1848). The diocese faced bad years with the seizure of McLoughlin's estate in Oregon City, the withdrawal of communicants for the California mines, and Cayuse and Rogue Rivers Indian Wars of which the Whitman massacre was a prelude; yet the bishop was of good heart at the First Plenary Council of Baltimore. In 1855 he visited Peru, Bolivia, and Chile where he collected enough money to meet the diocesan debts, because of the enthusiasm aroused by his Spanish publication of the story of Oregon. Four years later he was in Canada seeking aid and enlisting thirty-one priests and nuns, including the Sisters of Holy Names of Jesus and Mary, for service in Oregon. By 1862 when the bishop moved his see to Portland, conditions had become normal as the Civil War had little effect on the Coast. In time he built a cathedral, St. Michael's College (1871), and a hospital under the Sisters of Providence (1875).

Bishop Blanchet representing the Catholic hierarchy protested against the unfairness of Secretary Delano of the Interior in applying Grant's Indian policy of assigning the Indian agencies to "such religious denominations as had hitherto established missions among the Indians." Of thirty-eight reservations only four were assigned to Catholics, although on the basis of Indian desires and the number of active stations fully two-thirds might have been allotted with justice. The Yahima tribesmen seem to have been assigned to Methodists who showed marked hostility to Catholic priests, though Methodist missions were inactive and regarded as unsuccessful by Indians and candid observers. At any rate, Blanchet's heated correspondence with Delano aroused the Catholic hierarchy to establish a permanent Catholic Indian Commission at Washington to deal with the Commissioner of Indian Affairs and assume general supervision over Catholic missions.

Soon after celebrating his golden jubilee, Blanchet journeyed over the new transcontinental railroad from San Francisco and accompanied Bishop John Ireland to the Ecumenical Council in Rome (1870) where he was appointed an orator and warmly supported the formal declaration of infallibility. Worn by age, he obtained the Alaskan missionary Charles Seghers as coadjutor bishop (1879). Two years later he resigned and as titular archbishop of Amida retired to the hospital which he had founded. Here he lived two years, rounding out sixty-four years as a priest and forty-five as a missionary apostle on the Pacific Coast.

His writings include: *Fiftieth Jubilee Sermon* (1869); *Letters on Catholic Indian Missions together with Reply of Secretary of Interior* (1871); *Chinook Dictionary and Catechism* composed (1838) by M. Demers and revised (1867) by F. N. Blanchet with corrections by Rev. L. N. St. Onge (1871); *Historical Sketches of the Catholic Church in Oregon* (1878, 1910); and *Historical Notes and Reminiscences* (1883).

[Archbishop C. Seghers, *Life and Labors of F. N. Blanchet* (1883); R. H. Clarke, *Lives of Deceased Bishops of Cath. Ch. in U. S.* (1872), III, 438–502; E. V. O'Hara, *Pioneer Cath. Hist. of Ore.,* based on manuscript journals and letters in Portland Cathedral archives (1911); F. V. Holman, *Dr. John McLoughlin, Father of Ore.* (1907); H. M. Chittenden and A. T. Richardson, *Life, Letters and Travels of Pierre-Jean De Smet, S. J.* (1905); Katherine Hughes, *Father Lacombe, the Black-Robe Voyageur* (1911); M. de Baets, *Mgr. Seghers, Lapôtre d'Alaska* (Paris, 1896); C. A. Snowden, *Hist. of Washington* (1909), II, 159–72; J. G. Shea, *Hist. of the Cath. Ch. in U. S.* (1892), IV; Peter Burnett, *Recollections and Opinions of an Old Pioneer* (1880).]
                                                    R.J.P.

BLAND, RICHARD (May 6, 1710–Oct. 26, 1776), statesman, was the son of Richard Bland of Berkeley and Jordan's Point, Va., and his second wife, Elizabeth, daughter of William Randolph I of Turkey Island. His paternal grandfather, Theodorick Bland of Westover, was the immigrant ancestor of the family in Virginia. Both father and grandfather were successful planters, and influential in the government of the colony. Richard Bland was educated at William and Mary College. It is sometimes stated that he also attended the University of Edinburgh, but of this we have no proof. In 1742 he first took his seat from Prince George County in the House of Burgesses, and served continuously from that time until 1775. As early as 1753, in his discussion of the pistole fee demanded by the governor, he became the champion of public rights. It is likely that he was the author of both the "Two Penny" bills. In the controversy which raged after the passage of the bills, he opposed the clergy most vigorously. In *A Letter to the Clergy of Virginia* (1760) and in *The Colonel Dismounted* (1764) he supported the right of the General Assembly to enact this legislation, which was in effect a reduction of the salaries of the clergy. He was a member of the committee of the House of Burgesses, in the October 1764 session of the Assembly, to draw up an address to the king, a memorial to the lords, and a remonstrance to the House of Commons respecting taxation imposed on Virginia by any other power than its own legislature. In 1766 he printed in Williamsburg *An Inquiry into the Rights of the British Colonies,* the earliest published defense of the colonial attitude in regard to taxation. This was reprinted in the *Political Register,* London, 1769. He was a sincere advocate of colonial rights, but wished to avoid a break with the mother country, until every effort had been made for conciliation. In 1765 he opposed Henry's resolutions against the Stamp Act, and in March 1775 was not in favor of Henry's plan of immediately arming the colony. Though he was somewhat conservative at this critical time he was sent by his constituents to the revolutionary conventions of March 1775, July 1775, and May 1776. After the adoption of the state constitution, he was a member of the first House of Delegates, and served until his death. In his legislative career, he was a member of leading committees, and was always in demand for drawing up memorials. Due to his careful study of the ancient records of the colony, he was considered the best authority of the time on its history. When the non-importation agreement was drawn up in 1769, he was one of the first to sign. On Mar. 12, 1773, he was appointed by the House a member of the committee of correspondence with the sister colonies. He was placed on the committee of safety by the convention of July 1775. Elected as a delegate to the First Continental Congress, he was present throughout the session. He was elected to the Second Congress, but was present a few days only. Upon his third election on Aug. 11, 1775, he declined to serve. Jefferson refers to him as "the most learned and logical man of those who took prominent lead in public affairs, profound in constitutional lore, a most ungraceful speaker," and again he speaks of him as "one of the oldest, ablest and most respected members." He was "staunch and tough as whitleather," writes Roger Atkinson, "he has something the look of old parchments, which he handleth and studieth much." To Bland's industry in collecting old records, we are indebted for the preservation of valuable historical documents. He was thrice married: first to Anne, daughter of Col. Peter Poythress, by whom he had twelve children; second to Martha Macon, widow of William Massie; third to Elizabeth Blair, widow of John Bolling, and daughter of John Blair, president of the Council. His writings include: *A Fragment on the Pistole Fee, Claimed by the Governor of Virginia, 1753* (edited by W. C. Ford, 1891); *A Letter to the Clergy of Virginia* (1760); *The Colonel Dismounted, or the Rector Vindicated* (1764); *Inquiry into the Rights of the British Colonies* (1766; a new edition, edited by E. G. Swem, 1922); *A Treatise on Water Baptism against the Quakers* (title mentioned by Atkinson, but no copy known); *On the Tenure of Land in Virginia* (no copy known).

[The sketch of Bland by Hugh Blair Grigsby in his *Convention of 1776* (1855), pp. 57–67, is the best we have. The reader should also consult the preface to the reprinted edition, 1922, of *Bland's Inquiry into the Rights of the British Colonies*, ed. by E. G. Swem. In the *William and Mary Quarterly*, XIX, 31–41, Dr. L. G. Tyler discusses "Bland's constitutional argument in *The Colonel Dismounted*." For the controversy between Rev. Samuel Shield and Bland see Dixon and Hunter's *Va. Gazette*, July 8, July 22, and Aug. 5, 1775.]

E. G. S.

BLAND, RICHARD PARKS (Aug. 19, 1835–June 15, 1899), congressman, known to both friends and opponents as "Silver Dick," was throughout the last quarter of the nineteenth century the leader of the group in Congress favoring the bimetallic standard of currency or "Free Silver," a leadership for which his earlier life and environment were peculiarly appropriate. Born near Hartford, Ky., the son of Stoughten Edward and Margaret Parks (Nall) Bland, he was self-supporting as a mere boy. After a year at Hartford Academy he taught school in Kentucky, and after his removal to Missouri in 1855, in Wayne County on the Ozark border. The next year he went to California and for ten years lived in the mining camps of California, Colorado, and Nevada, prospecting, working as a miner, teaching school, and, after his admission to the bar, serving as treasurer of Carson County, then in Utah Territory. He returned to Missouri in 1866, and in 1869 opened his office at Lebanon, a little Ozark town, his home until his death. Though the boundaries of his Con-

gressional district were repeatedly changed, they always included much of the Ozark country. Thus he was intimately acquainted with the problems of the silver miners and of the more primitive frontier farmers, the two economic groups most devoted to Free Silver.

He prospered as a lawyer, making many friends by his gratuitous aid to Democrats disenfranchised under the test oath, and in 1872 he was nominated for Congress without much effort on his part, and was elected with the help of the Liberal Republicans; save for one Congress, 1895 to 1897, he served continuously until his death. His first term in Congress was only normally eventful, but in the Democratic House of 1875–77 he was appointed chairman of the Committee on Mines and Mining and began his life-long fight against the "Crime of '73" and the demonetization of silver. Bland's bill for the free coinage of silver passed the House in the second session but was smothered in the Senate. His leadership in the fight was recognized by his appointment to the congressional "Silver Commission" of 1876–77. In 1879 he became a member of the Committee on Coinage, Weights and Measures, and its chairman in 1883, serving in that capacity whenever the Democrats controlled the House. He became a national figure with the passage over Hayes's veto in 1878 of the compromise Bland-Allison Act remonetizing silver and providing for a limited coinage. The Bland Bill as it had passed the House provided for free coinage. He succeeded in defeating the repeal of the Bland-Allison Act in 1886, but again failed to secure a free coinage act. In 1890 he bitterly opposed the Sherman Silver Purchase Act as a travesty on bi-metallism and again fought in vain to secure a free coinage act. The climax of his fight for free coinage came in his leadership of the unsuccessful opposition in 1893 to the repeal of the Sherman Act unless accompanied by the passage of a free coinage bill. In his famous "Parting of the Ways" speech of Aug. 11, 1893, he served notice that the western Democrats would put Free Silver above party loyalty. Defeated for the first time in 1894 (by 70 votes) because of Democratic disgust with Cleveland and the presence of a separate Populist candidate, he preached Free Silver from the lecture platform and in 1895 was the leader of the Pertle Springs convention where the Free Silver wing secured control of the Missouri Democracy. The similar control of the national party at Chicago made him admittedly the logical candidate for president in 1896. But his long career and a certain lack of appeal to the public imagination and to the crusading zeal of the Free-Silverites were fatal handicaps. After leading on the first three ballots, Bland withdrew his name when the set toward Bryan was unmistakable. He emphatically negatived the movement to nominate him as vice-president and later just as decidedly the proposal of nomination for governor; instead he was triumphantly reëlected to Congress in 1896.

While Bland's views on the currency were quite unorthodox, his speeches and debates show wide reading and a real, if frankly one-sided, study. Unlike many of the free-silver inflationists he recognized the evils of a fiat paper money inflation. He also saw the desirability of an international agreement on bi-metallism; he believed however that an independent adoption by the United States would soon force the other nations into line, though this would involve, he admitted, a considerable temporary wrench to the bankers and investors. Throughout he urged the advantages of Free Silver to the "producing classes" in general rather than primarily to the agrarian group. This real interest in the common people was also clearly reflected in his denunciation of monopolies and his arguments against the protective tariff; he vigorously supported the Mills Bill and took the lead in opposing the McKinley tariff. At the very end of his career he was an extreme anti-imperialist. Not a brilliant speaker or debater, he was effective through his mastery of his data, his clear-headedness and self-control, and a certain blunt honesty and sincerity. In a period of rather low standards in public life he was unusually sensitive as to personal and official honesty, withdrawing from the practise of law when first elected, refusing a silver service presented by the miners, and actually persisting in his refusal of his back pay under the "Salary Grab" act and of his mileage for a few days' recess between sessions. In 1873 he married Virginia Elizabeth Mitchell of Rolla. Both at Washington and on his farm near Lebanon he lived very simply on his salary, and died probably poorer than when he entered public life. In his virtues and even in his failings, he suggests the better type of ante-bellum Jacksonian Democrat.

[W. V. Byars, *An American Commoner* (1900); W. R. Hollister and H. Norman, *Five Famous Missourians* (1900), pp. 95–172; *Cong. Record,* 56 Cong., 1 Sess., pp. 3894 ff.; *Globe-Democrat* (St. Louis), June 16, 1899.]

J. V.

BLAND, THEODORICK (Mar. 21, 1742– June 1, 1790), Revolutionary soldier, was born in Prince George County, Va., the son of Theodorick Bland of Cawsons on Appomattox River and Frances Bolling, only daughter and heir of Drury Bolling. Through his mother he was a descendant of Pocahontas. At the age of eleven he was sent to school in Wakefield, Yorkshire, England, where he remained until 1758. In 1759 he was in Liverpool, attending an infirmary as a student of physic. He entered the University of Edinburgh in 1761, and received the degree of M.D. in 1763. After graduating he spent some time in London, and probably also in Leyden and Paris. He was back in Virginia in 1764, and began the practise of his profession in his native county. He continued in active practise until 1771, when he retired and became a planter, his health having suffered from the exposure incident to a country practise. In the conflict between England and the Colonies, he took a determined stand against the mother country. On June 24, 1775, he was one of a party of twenty-four gentlemen who removed the arms from the governor's palace in Williamsburg to the powder magazine. Toward the end of this year he wrote some bitter letters in the *Virginia Gazette* against Lord Dunmore under the signature of "Cassius." He was ambitious to help his country in the field, and on June 13, 1776, was appointed captain of the 1st Troop of Virginia Cavalry, and on Mar. 31, 1779, was made colonel of the 1st Continental Dragoons. He was with the main army in New Jersey and Pennsylvania in 1777, and was present at the battle of Brandywine on Sept. 11. In referring to Bland's services at this battle, Gen. Henry Lee says "Col. Bland was noble, sensible, honorable, and amiable, but never intended for the department of military intelligence." On Nov. 5, 1778, Washington ordered Bland to assume command of an escort to conduct the Convention troops (the Saratoga prisoners) from Connecticut to Albemarle County, Va. He was placed in command of the post at Charlottesville which guarded these prisoners, but in November 1779 he received permission to retire from this station. In 1780, the General Assembly of Virginia elected him a delegate to Congress, a position which he filled with honor for three years. At the conclusion of his term, he returned to his plantation, Farmingdale or Kippax, in Prince George County, which had been plundered by the enemy. He was in the House of Delegates in the sessions of 1786–87, 1787–88, and 1788. In the Assembly of 1786 he was an unsuccessful candidate for governor, against Edmund Randolph. He was a member of the Virginia convention of 1788 for the consideration of the proposed Federal Constitution, and voted against its adoption. He was elected a member of the first House of Representatives and served until his death. He was married to Martha Dangerfield, probably a sister of Col. William Dangerfield of Belvidera near Fredericksburg. Chastellux speaks of him as a "tall, handsome man." Campbell remarks that he was a man of most agreeable manners, and strict integrity of conduct. He was not "distinguished for extraordinary exhibitions of genius, but for plain, practical qualifications."

[*The Bland Papers,* ed. by Chas. Campbell, and published in two volumes in 1840, with a memoir by Campbell prefixed, is the principal source of information. Selections from the Chas. Campbell papers, now in the Va. Hist. Soc., have been printed in the *Va. Mag. of Hist.,* IX, 59–77, 162–92, 298–306, and constitute important documents. Bland's will is published in the *Va. Mag. of Hist.,* III, 315. His thesis at Edinburgh was entitled *De Concoctione Alimentorum in Ventriculo.* There are two letters of Bland in R. H. Lee's *Life of Arthur Lee* (1829). There are some interesting references to Bland's career in the Continental Congress in Hunt's edition of Madison's works, vol. I.]

E. G. S.

BLAND, THOMAS (Oct. 4, 1809–Aug. 20, 1885), naturalist, was born at Newark, Nottinghamshire, England, the son of Dr. Thomas Bland. His mother was a Shepard, niece of Richard Shepard, the conchologist. He was educated at the Charterhouse School, London, where he was a classmate of Thackeray. He then studied law, and after practising in London for a time, emigrated to Barbadoes (1842) and later to Jamaica, where he became interested in the *Mollusca* through a visit of Prof. Charles B. Adams of Amherst (1848–49) and plunged at once into a study of the rich fauna of the West Indies. In 1850 he became superintendent of a gold mine at Marmato, New Granada (now Colombia), where he continued his study of shells. He settled in New York in 1852 and becoming acquainted with William G. Binney, who was just starting to complete the work of his father, Amos Binney, on *The Terrestrial Air-Breathing Mollusks of the United States,* etc. (1851–78), the two collaborated in a number of papers on terrestrial mollusks, the most important of which was Part I of "Land and Fresh-Water Shells of North America," published in the *Smithsonian Miscellaneous Collections,* vol. VIII (1869). "It systematized, expanded and put in manual form the knowledge of the land shells of this continent and placed this information within the reach of students everywhere. For many years it was the chief authority in its particular field, and even at this late date it must still be consulted by all who study this fauna" (letter of William B. Marshall, Conchologist of the United States National Museum). During his scientific career Bland produced seventy-two papers on the *Mollusca* of the United States and region of the Antilles, most of which were published in the *Annals of the Lyceum of Natural History of New York* and in the *American Journal of Conchology.* They dealt not only with description of species, but anatomy, classification, geographic distribution, and the development of the *Mollusca* as well.

Bland was a fellow of the Royal Geological Society of London, a member of the American Philosophical Society, and of a number of other societies devoted to natural history.

[A complete bibliography of Bland's scientific works was compiled by Arthur F. Gray and published in 1884; see also biographical sketches in *Science,* Nov. 13, 1885, and in the *Am. Jour. of Sci.,* Nov. 1885.]

F. E. R.

BLANKENBURG, RUDOLPH (Feb. 16, 1843–Apr. 12, 1918), mayor of Philadelphia, was born in Barntrup, Germany, the son of the Rev. Ludwig and Sophie (Goede) Blankenburg. He spent his early years in Hillentrup, where his father's church was, and it was there that he was educated under private tutors and at the Real Gymnasium. He preferred business to the ministry and went to an uncle in Lipstadt where he received the basis of what was to prove an uniquely successful business career. What he had heard of America, and especially his reading of *Uncle Tom's Cabin,* gave him an interest in this country which could only be satisfied by making it his home, which he did in 1865, seeking naturalization at the earliest possible day. On arriving in Philadelphia he secured a position with an importer and manufacturer of yarns and notions. Then he became successively a traveling salesman and European buyer for the concern. He was married on Apr. 18, 1867, to Lucretia, daughter of Dr. Hannah Longshore of Philadelphia. In 1875 he established the firm of R. Blankenburg & Company, at the head of which he remained until it was incorporated in 1905. After that he continued as a member of the board of directors. Blankenburg achieved fame,—city, state, and national, as an impassioned tribune. He was a champion of the rights and privileges of the people rather than a reformer, although he possessed a large measure of reforming zeal. He early manifested an interest in public affairs, an interest that was increased and fashioned by his association with the Society of Friends shortly after his arrival in the United States. His voice was early heard in behalf of the downtrodden and oppressed, and this led him to oppose those forces in public life which he believed to be responsible for their condition. In 1881 he was one of the leaders in the formation of the famous "Committee of 100" in Philadelphia, from which however he promptly resigned when it endorsed the sitting mayor (William D. Stokley) for another term. Within a month he was invited to return to the Committee, which reconsidered its endorsement of Stokley and nominated Samuel G. King, a Democrat, who was elected. This action established Blankenburg as a leader among the reform forces. He had a ready wit, a fearless courage, a commanding presence and personality and an imagination that added fire and color, if not always accuracy, to his addresses. So picturesque was he as a crusader that he was popularly known by the sobriquet "The Old War Horse of Reform." He was an accomplished phrase-maker and his designation of his opponents as "the powers that prey" has become a part of the language of politics.

A Republican in national affairs, he was in almost constant opposition to the dominant Republican organization in Philadelphia and Pennsylvania. His most picturesque fight was his organized attack on Quay in 1897 and 1898. Quay supported Boies Penrose and Blankenburg supported John Wanamaker in his unsuccessful attempt to win the election to the United States Senate. In 1906 he was compelled, against his wishes and vigorous opposition, to accept the Independent nomination for county commissioner. He and his colleagues were elected over the regular Republican candidates, he leading the ticket by a majority of over 50,000. In 1911 he was persuaded to become an Independent candidate for mayor and was elected over the regular Republican candidate by the narrow margin of 5,000 votes. During his four years of office he earned for himself the title of the "Old Dutch Cleanser." Public administration, however, did not appeal to him for he was essentially an advocate and was more at home in arousing interest than in organizing and directing it. Nevertheless, his administration was characterized by many improvements especially in the department of public works presided over by Morris L. Cooke to whom he gave hearty support. Another phase of public activity to which Blankenburg made a large contribution was in the realm of public charity. He it was who organized the Citizens' Permanent Relief Committee which contributed largely to affording relief in disasters like the Charleston earthquake, the Russian famine, and the Johnstown flood. He was the animating leader of the warfare on the "loan sharks," recovering many thousands of dollars for those who would otherwise have been helpless. He also organized a philanthropic pawn shop. A big, dominating man glowing with health, with a rich, powerful voice, he was a jovial companion who played as hard as he worked.

[*Who's Who in America,* 1916–17; Geo. E. Mapes,

"An Uncompromising Fighter," *Outlook,* LXXXIII, 220; *Am. Mag.,* LXXVI, 58; *Yr. Bk. of the Pa. Soc.* (1919), p. 172; *Phila. Inquirer* and *Public Ledger,* Apr. 13, 1918; personal knowledge.]
C. R. W—f.

BLASDEL, HENRY GOODE (Jan. 20, 1825– July 26, 1900), governor of Nevada, the son of Jacob and Elizabeth Blasdel, was born in Dearborn County, Ind. His mother was of German descent, a native of Virginia. His father's ancestors came from Scotland to New England in the early seventeenth century and two hundred years later his grandfather went with the westward tide of emigration to the Old Northwest, settling at the site of the present Cincinnati in 1804. A large amount of land was acquired a short distance to the west in Dearborn County, Ind. There the grandfather and father engaged in farming and to this occupation Henry Goode was born and bred. At the age of seventeen, while as yet possessed of only a common school education, the death of his father took from him the opportunity for further study in the schools, but he read such law books as were accessible. On Dec. 9, 1845, he married Sarah Jane Cox, of Southern parentage, and eighteen months later they removed to Aurora, Ind., where Blasdel as a produce merchant shipped goods to New Orleans and later entered the steamboat business. In January 1852 he went as a prospector to Yankee Bar on the American River in California, then shortly tried farming in Santa Cruz County, and soon afterward entered the mercantile produce business in San Francisco. Here his family joined him. Here also he became financially prosperous but the crisis of 1860 deprived him of his fortune and he went with the rush of miners to Virginia City, Utah Territory. There he built the Empire and the Hoosier State Mills, which were respectively the second and the third mills. He was the first superintendent of the Potosi mine and later was in charge of the Hale and Norcross. He also was associated with ex-Governor Colcord in mining operations in Aurora. So long as he supervised a property it was closed on Sunday and at one time, although in especial need of money, he left a quartz mill of which he was manager because he was required to keep it running on the first day of the week.

In politics he was an Old Line Whig until in 1860 he joined the Republican party. In 1864 when on a visit to the old home in Indiana he attended the convention that nominated Abraham Lincoln for a second term and was an unofficial representative of Nevada in the convention of the National Union League as well as a member of that body's committee which informed President Lincoln of his nomination by the

League. In the fall of 1864, upon his return from the East, he was drafted by the National Union League of Nevada as a candidate for governor of this new-born state. He was elected by a large majority and was reëlected in 1866, serving until 1870, after which he turned again to the business of mining. He was six feet, five inches in height; he had keen intelligent eyes, handsome features, and a smile that won all hearts. Until old age he retained his youthful appearance. In character he was unswerving. At one time he failed in a wheat deal for $80,-000 but he later paid all his debts, even to the extent of forcing money upon his creditors when it was not collectible in law. His creditors then presented him with a watch which he carried till his death. Inside the cover was engraved: "Presented by a few friends, who can appreciate integrity." He was buried in Mountain View Cemetery in Oakland.

[Files of the *Gold Hill News*, 1864, 1866, and of the *Reno Evening Gazette*, 1900; Alonzo Phelps, *Contemporary Biog. of Cal.'s Representative Men* (1881), II, 122–24; *Hist. of Nev.* (1881), ed. by Myron Angel, pp. 87, 89, 679; H. H. Bancroft, *Hist. of Nev., Colo., and Wyo.* (1890), p. 184; *Statutes of Nev.*, 1864, 1866, 1868; *Jour. of the Nev. Assembly*, 1864–65, 1866.]

J. E. W—r.

BLATCHFORD, RICHARD MILFORD (Apr. 23, 1798–Sept. 4, 1875), lawyer, was the ninth of the seventeen children of Samuel Blatchford, a Nonconformist minister from Plymouth Dock, Devon, England, who came with his wife Alicia (Windeatt) to the United States in 1795. Born at Stratford, Conn., Richard attended the common schools, and completed his education at Union College, Schenectady, where he graduated in 1815. He then became a school teacher at Jamaica, L. I., studying law in his spare time. On his admission to the New York bar in 1820, he commenced practise in New York City, devoting himself more particularly to mercantile law and finance. In 1826 he was appointed counsel and financial agent of the Bank of England in the United States and shortly afterwards was retained in a similar capacity by the Bank of the United States. When the charter of the Bank of the United States expired in 1836, to him was confided the adjustment of all outstanding matters between it and the Bank of England. His services were also requisitioned on occasion by the Bank Commissioner of the State of New York. In politics he was a prominent adherent of the Whig party of that time, was an intimate friend of W. H. Seward, and in 1855 was elected a member of the state Assembly, serving one term. When the war broke out in 1861 Blatchford was indefatigable in organization work in the New York area, and President Lincoln appointed him one of the Committee of Three to superintend the disbursement of the public monies appropriated to the purpose of raising troops for the Union. In 1862 he was appointed United States minister to the States of the Church at Rome. Though he held this post only until the following year, his conduct of his delicate diplomatic duties at a critical period earned unstinted praise from the Administration.

Blatchford always manifested an intense interest in the public park system of the City of New York. In 1859 he had been appointed commissioner of Central Park, continuing as such until the new city charter came into operation in April 1870. In December 1872 he became commissioner of public parks of the city, but impaired health shortly compelled him to retire. He died at Newport, R. I., after a long illness. He was married three times: first on May 17, 1819, to Julia Ann, daughter of J. P. Munford of New York City, who died in 1857; second, on Nov. 8, 1860, to Angelica, daughter of James A. Hamilton of Nevis, Westchester County, N. Y., who died in 1868; third, on Jan. 18, 1870, to Katherine, daughter of Philip Hone. His son by his first marriage, Samuel, became successively United States district judge of the southern district of New York, United States circuit judge of New York, and finally associate justice of the Supreme Court of the United States. A man of spotless integrity, high ideals and single-hearted devotion to public service, Richard Blatchford enjoyed unreservedly the respect and confidence of his fellow citizens.

[A brief account of his immediate antecedents will be found in *Abridged Compendium of Am. Genealogy*, ed. by F. A. Vickers (1925). Various incidents of his life are recounted in *Blatchford Memorial II, A Geneal. Record of the Family of Rev. Samuel Blatchford*, by E. W. Blatchford (1912). Obituaries appeared in the *N. Y. Times*, *N. Y. Tribune*, *N. Y. Herald*, Sept. 5, 1875.]

H. W. H. K.

BLATCHFORD, SAMUEL (Mar. 9, 1820–July 7, 1893), lawyer and jurist, was the grandson of a dissenting minister who had come to the United States in 1795 from Devonshire and after trying several different localities had settled in Lansingburg, N. Y. His father, Richard Milford Blatchford, was born in Stratford, Conn., graduated from Union College, was admitted to the bar of New York, was counsel for the Bank of England and the Bank of the United States, and served in the New York legislature. His mother, Julia Ann, daughter of John P. Mumford, a well-known publicist, was a noted belle. Samuel was born in New York City. His first education was received at Pittsfield, Mass., at the school of William Forrest; later he attended an academy in New York City and the grammar school of Columbia College. He learned rapidly and showed a marked studious bent, although his devotion to books did not keep him from spending some time on outdoor sports. At thirteen he was ready to matriculate at Columbia College. He graduated in 1837 and then became private secretary to William H. Seward, a post which he held until he reached his majority. Association with Seward was in itself not inadequate legal training. Blatchford was admitted to the bar in 1842, and the next year began to practise with his father. He married Caroline, daughter of Eben Appleton of Lowell, Mass., Dec. 17, 1844. Meanwhile he served as military secretary on Gov. Seward's staff and in November 1845 went to Auburn as a partner of Seward and Christopher Morgan. When this firm was dissolved in 1854 he returned to New York and formed his own firm of Blatchford, Seward & Griswold, Seward being an adopted son and nephew of the ex-Governor. The firm prospered. Blatchford became particularly expert in international and maritime law and had many notable successes at the bar. He remained a consultant of the firm until 1862 (David McAdam and others, *History of the Bench and Bar of New York,* vol. I, 1897).

On May 3, 1867, President Grant appointed him a district judge of the southern district of New York. Here he was confronted by a number of international and admiralty matters that arose as a result of the Civil War. Five years later he was made a circuit judge for the second judicial district. Here though he specialized in patent law, his opinions on bankruptcy, copyright, libel, and maritime torts gave him a great reputation for learning. Many of his opinions, published in the reports which he himself edited, are extremely learned discussions of the points involved. His decisions were rarely reversed. He was appointed to the Supreme Court of the United States by President Arthur and was confirmed by the Senate, Mar. 2, 1882, taking the place of Judge Hunt who had been incapacitated for five years. On the Supreme Court bench Blatchford was one of the hardest working judges, rivaled only by Justice Miller. He gave opinions in 430 cases. During his ten years on the Supreme Court his most elaborate decision was probably Pennsylvania Railroad *vs.* Miller (132 *United States Reports,* 75). This case held that a corporation was bound by a new constitutional provision imposing burdens not contemplated by the corporation's charter. He also decided the famous case of Terry *vs.* Sharon (131 *United States Reports,* 40) and spoke for the majority of justices in the much

more important case of Cunningham *vs.* Neagle (135 *United States Reports,* 1)—a case which contributed materially to the supremacy of federal authority. (See W. H. Taft, *Our Chief Magistrate and His Powers,* 1916, chap. 4). In several important cases (Dobson *vs.* Hartford Carpet Company, 114 *United States Reports,* 439, and Dobson *vs.* Dornan, 118 *United States Reports,* 10) Blatchford announced the status of design patents and laid down rules for infringement of design. These decisions were influential in determining the nature of the statute that Congress later passed (Act of Feb. 4, 1887; 24 *United States Statutes at Large,* 387), to afford special remedies for the infringement of design patents. Of somewhat austere personality and of studious temperament, Blatchford was one of the most respected justices on the bench. If his judicial style sometimes lacked concision and suffered from dullness, of his learning there was no question. If was difficult to be interesting in discussing patents and trademarks. As Chief Justice Fuller said of him, Blatchford "was at home in every branch of the jurisdiction of the courts in which he sat. It may be justly said that he displayed uncommon aptitude in the administration of maritime law and of the law of patents, his grasp upon the original principles of the one, and his mastery of details in the other aiding him in largely contributing in the development of both." His death occurred at Newport, after a short illness.

[H. L. Carson, *The Supreme Court of the U. S.* (1892); A. Oakey Hall, "Justice Samuel Blatchford," in the *Green Bag,* Nov. 1893; Chas. Warren, *The Supreme Court in U. S. Hist.* (1922); *Minnesota Law Jour.,* July 1893; *Am. Law Reg.,* Sept. 1893; *Albany Law Jour.,* Nov. 18, 1893; *N. Y. Tribune,* July 8, 1893; David McAdam *et al., Hist. of the Bench and Bar of N. Y.,* I (1897); *Am. Law Rev.,* Nov.–Dec. 1893; "The Supreme Court of the U. S. Memorial for Samuel Blatchford," in *150 U. S. Reports,* p. 707; S. Blatchford, *The Blatchford Memorial* (1871); E. W. Blatchford, *The Blatchford Memorial,* vol. II (1912).]   L. R.

BLAUSTEIN, DAVID (May 5, 1866–Aug. 26, 1912), rabbi, educator, social worker, was born in Lida, Province of Vilna, Russian Poland, the youngest son of Isaiah and Sarah Natzkovsky Blaustein. He received his early education in the Hebrew school of his native town, but, longing for larger opportunities, he ran away from home at the age of seventeen, and, crossing the Prussian frontier, entered the Hebrew academy at Memel. After a brief sojourn in this border town he settled in Schwerin, the capital of Mecklenburg-Schwerin, where he attended a teachers' preparatory school. His stay here terminated in 1886 when Bismarck promulgated the decree forbidding Russian Jews to live in Germany. He emigrated to the United States and landed at

Boston. His career as an educator began shortly after his arrival when he established a German and Hebrew school. He matriculated at Harvard College in 1889 and graduated with the degree of B.A. in 1893. While attending Harvard, he founded the Sheltering Home for Immigrants, his earliest service to the immigrant Jews, to whose welfare he devoted much thought and time throughout his life. In 1892 he was elected rabbi of the congregation of Sons of Israel and David at Providence, R. I., and for a number of years taught at Brown University as assistant professor of Semitic languages. He received the degree of M.A. from Brown in 1898, in which year he resigned as rabbi to accept the superintendency of the Educational Alliance of New York City. This proved the beginning of his real work. The Educational Alliance was the educational and social center of New York's East Side Ghetto. His selection for the post was unwelcome to many of the East Side leaders, and to allay their fears he determined to institute no definite policy until he had studied the situation. As the first step toward this end he undertook a survey of the neighborhood and with it as a guide set himself to fit the activities of the Alliance to the needs of the people. He strove to bring the opposing leaders and factions into harmony, and to make the building a common educational and social center for all groups. Thus the Educational Alliance became a true community house and set an example for Jewish settlements in other cities. The Americanization of the immigrant had been the chief purpose of the founders of the Alliance, but other problems, serious and complicated, enlisted the attention of the superintendent, among them the constantly widening breach between the older and the younger generation. He was unable to satisfy the ultra-radical group who in 1901 founded a new institution, known as the Educational League, with an absolutely free platform, as a protest against what this group considered Blaustein's reactionary policy. Largely because of this dissension Blaustein resigned his position in 1907. A year later he went to Chicago to assume the superintendency of the Chicago Hebrew Institute. Here too he fell into disfavor with the radical element, who boycotted the institution when he refused to let Emma Goldman speak in its hall. After he resigned the superintendency in 1910 he devoted the remaining two years of his life to social studies. On Sept. 18, 1911, he married Miriam Umstadter of Norfolk, Va. During a five-months tour of the country, from October 1911 to February 1912, he made studies of the immigrant Jewish problem and the Jewish situation generally. He may be considered the first in

the line of trained Jewish social workers. Original in thought and method he left a deep impression on the development of social thought and endeavor in Jewish communal activity.

[Miriam Blaustein, *Memoirs of David Blaustein* (1913); Boris D. Bogen, *Jewish Philanthropy* (1917), pp. 39, 231 ff., 240, 286; *N. Y. Times, Sun* (N. Y.), Aug. 28, 1912; *Secretary's Fifth* and *Sixth Report, Harvard Coll., Class of 1893* (1913, 1918); *Reform Advocate,* Aug. 31, 1912.]
                     D. P.

BLAVATSKY, HELENA PETROVNA HAHN (July 30, 1831–May 8, 1891), founder of the Theosophical movement, was born at Ekaterinoslav in Southern Russia. She was the daughter of Col. Peter Hahn and grand-daughter of Gen. Alexis Hahn von Rottenstern Hahn of old Mecklenburg stock. Her mother, Helena Pavlovna Fadeev, a distinguished novelist writing under the pseudonym of "Zinaida R-va," was an aunt of the celebrated Count Witte and a daughter of Privy-Councillor Andrey Fadeev and Princess Helena Dolgoruki. Further back, her ancestors were allied with the royal family. She passed an undisciplined childhood, at one time with her father in an army camp, and then, after the death of her mother, with her maternal grandparents. Their old country mansion at Saratov, much like a feudal castle, in the midst of parks and forests, fed the high-spirited girl's naturally romantic disposition. Hysterical and subject to hallucinations, she lived in a world of her own fancy when she was not quarrelling with her various governesses. "The slightest contradiction brought on an outburst of passion, often a fit of convulsions" (her aunt, Nadejda Fadeev, quoted in Sinnett, *post,* p. 27). In 1844 her father took her to Paris and London where she received some instruction in music, in which she showed remarkable talent, but he soon found his thirteen-year-old daughter too much for him and returned her to her grandparents. She grew up as reckless, self-willed, and erratic a young person as was to be found in all Russia. On July 7, 1848, she was married to Gen. Nikifor Vasilevich Blavatsky, at one time vice-governor of Erivan, who according to her statements was then seventy-three years old, although forty-five years later he was said to be still alive. She soon deserted her husband and returned to her grandfather who immediately shipped her to her father, but on the way she escaped and got to Constantinople. Here she seems to have formed a liaison with the Hungarian revolutionist and opera-singer Metrovich (or Mitrovich) which was followed by another with an unknown Englishman (S. Y. Witte, *Memoirs,* 1921, pp. 5–6). Then ensued a long period of wanderings about European capitals and gambling-places, in the

Near East, in Egypt, and possibly even to America (1851, 1853) and India (1853, 1856, 1869). No accurate record of these years can be pieced together from her own utterly unreliable and contradictory statements. Thus, in her first interview in America in 1874 (*New York Graphic,* Nov. 13) she made no mention of having been to India but claimed to have made a fortune by selling ostrich feathers in Africa and, on another occasion, to have penetrated into the Sudan and lived for four months without seeing a white face, while incidentally translating Darwin and Buckle into Russian! Later, in the information which she gave A. P. Sinnett for his *Incidents in the Life of Mme. Blavatsky* (1886), the ostrich feathers, Darwin, and Buckle were forgotten, but three trips to India and a residence in Tibet were substituted. In 1858 she was, according to her own statement, "converted to spiritualism" by the celebrated medium, Daniel D. Home, in Paris. In 1860 she was again in Russia, seeking reconciliation with her family and, at Pskov and Tiflis, creating a local sensation by her exhibitions of spirit-rapping. The arrival of Metrovich in Tiflis led to a renewal of their former relations and a new scandal. The two hastily went to Kiev whence they were ejected for pasquinades by Mme. Blavatsky against the Governor-General (Witte, *op. cit.,* pp. 7–8). Her statement that she was with Garibaldi in the battle of Mentana, Nov. 3, 1867, seems to have been without other foundation than her romantic imagination. She was in Odessa at some time between 1867 and 1871, still with Metrovich whom she supported by making and selling artificial flowers. In 1870 she was ship-wrecked off Spezzia. The next year she was investigating and practising spiritualism in Cairo. In 1872 she was back in Russia, in 1873 again in Paris, and in July of the latter year she crossed to New York by steerage and settled in one of the poorer quarters of the city. Her once attractive appearance was now a thing of the past: she had grown enormously corpulent, was slovenly in dress, gorged herself on fat meat, smoked incessantly, and swore like a trooper. Her personal duplicity and profound contempt for humanity were, however, concealed beneath an engaging frankness of manner. Her unconventionalities attracted the unconventional. Above all, her large mystical blue eyes magnetized and fascinated. She was about to start a new religious movement.

In the summer of 1874 the alleged spiritualistic phenomena of the Eddy brothers at Chittenden, Vt., received great publicity through the favorable articles of Henry Steel Olcott [*q.v.*] in the *New York Graphic.* Mme. Blavatsky visited Chittenden, met the receptive Olcott, and soon convinced him of her own psychic powers. During the ensuing year they became very intimate and wrote numerous articles in defense of spiritualism. But in the winter the disastrous exposure of the medium, Mrs. Nelson Holmes, in Philadelphia, caused public interest in spiritualism to wane. Mme. Blavatsky, up to this time under the "control" of the famous spook, "John King," shifted her allegiance, announced that she was in touch with certain Egyptian masters, "the Brothers of Luxor," and strove to found a society for the study of Egyptian occultism. This took form eventually in the Theosophical Society, started on Sept. 7, 1875, with sixteen members, Olcott as president, and herself as corresponding secretary. The aims of the Society were later enlarged to embrace the promotion of the brotherhood of man, the study of comparative religion, and the study of occultism in general. In the autumn of 1877 Mme. Blavatsky published in New York her celebrated *Isis Unveiled,* a two-volume work on occultism, largely made up of unacknowledged quotations. In this she denounced spiritualism as bitterly as she had formerly denounced its opponents. In 1878 a branch of the Theosophical Society was formed in London. Meanwhile, and very incidentally, claiming to be a widow, Mme. Blavatsky had been again married, to a Russian named M. C. Betanelly, from whom she was divorced on May 25, 1878.

The parent society in New York failing to prosper, Olcott and Mme. Blavatsky now decided to try their fortunes in India. They sailed on Dec. 18, 1878, and arrived in Bombay, Feb. 16, 1879. Even before this they had affiliated with the Arya Samaj, a group headed by a Hindu mystic, Dayananda Saraswati, but within a short time they and the venerable Hindu were denouncing each other as "humbugs." Mme. Blavatsky supported herself and Olcott by writing, under the pseudonym of Radda-Bai, for the *Russky Vyestnik,* a series of exceedingly able travel sketches (translated into English under title *From the Caves and Jungles of Hindostan,* 1892). Meanwhile her production of "psychic phenomena" converted A. P. Sinnett, editor of the leading Anglo-Indian paper, the *Allahabad Pioneer,* in whose pages the Theosophical movement was widely advertised. The two founders established their own magazine, the *Theosophist,* and began to gain adherents throughout India; in 1880 they carried the movement to Ceylon; in 1882 they fixed the permanent headquarters of the Society at Adyar, a suburb of Madras, in a bungalow fitted up with an "occult room" and a "shrine." By means of these, Mme. Blavatsky received over the astral telegraph mysterious letters from her latest masters, two Tibetan Mahatmas named "Morya" and "Koot Hoomi." In 1883, however, it was brought out that one of Koot Hoomi's letters, published in Sinnett's *Occult World* (1881), was taken verbatim from a spiritualistic address delivered by a certain Mr. Kiddle in America. This discovery led to numerous resignations from the London branch, and the situation became so serious that early in 1884 Olcott and Mme. Blavatsky paid a trip to Europe. Hardly had they departed before her secretary, Mme. Emma Coulomb, together with her husband, both residents in the Theosophical bungalow, began to circulate stories of wholesale trickery on Mme. Blavatsky's part. These were published in the *Christian College Magazine* at Madras in the fall, and the much-harassed Theosophical leaders now hurried back to India, closely followed by Richard Hodgson, come to make an investigation on behalf of the British Society for Psychical Research. This investigation was carried on for three months; when it became known that the investigator's report would corroborate the Coulomb charges, Mme. Blavatsky resigned her position as corresponding secretary of the Society and sailed once more for Europe.

In April 1885 she arrived at Naples, desperately ill, impoverished, and all but universally discredited. But her spirit was indomitable. She settled down to an obscure life in Würzburg, Germany, where as soon as her health was a little better she devoted herself to her most important piece of writing, *The Secret Doctrine* (1888), in two large volumes, an elaborate exposition of the basic ideas of Theosophy. Toward exposures of her past she adopted the attitude of a religious martyr persecuted by unbelievers, and this rôle gradually gained her more followers than she had lost. In the spring of 1886 she moved to Ostend and in the summer of 1887 to London. There in September 1887 she organized the Blavatsky Lodge; in October 1888 she established the Esoteric Section of the Theosophical Society with herself as head; in August 1890 authority over the entire European Theosophical organization was given to her. During all this time she was suffering from a variety of diseases any one of which, in the opinion of her physician, would have sufficed to kill an ordinary person. Nevertheless, in these years, besides her other activities, she edited a monthly Theosophical magazine, *Lucifer* (1887–91) and wrote the *Voice of the Silence* (1889), a Theosophical rhapsody; *The Key to Theosophy* (1889); a *Glossary of Theosophical Terms* (1891); and *Nightmare Tales* (published posthumously, 1892), a collection of semi-mystical short stories. At the time of her death, on May 8, 1891, she was once more the recognized head of a great religious movement. Although unquestionably a charlatan, with a superficial knowledge of the Oriental philosophy which she advocated and a character the reverse of her own teachings, she made a deep appeal to the childish love of mystery and magic still latent in most human beings. She possessed the rare power of temporarily believing whatever she wanted to believe. Thus she hypnotized others, having first hypnotized herself, and, although one of the most unspiritual of women, she gained from her followers a veneration amounting almost to idolatry.

[There are several biographies of Mme. Blavatsky but none satisfactory. A good sketch in Russian by Zinaida Vengerova will be found in the *Kritico-biograficheskii slovar russkikh pisatelsi i uchenikh* (St. Petersburg, 1889–1904, vol. III), on which the sketches in other Russian encyclopedias are mainly based. The best account in English of her early life is in A. P. Sinnett, *Incidents in the Life of Mme. Blavatsky* (1886), ch. I–VI, based largely on a narrative in Russian by her sister, Mme. Vera Jelihovsky. For a discussion of her travels see Arthur Lillie, *Mme. Blavatsky and Her "Theosophy"* (1895), ch. II, III; for her residence in America: H. S. Olcott, *Old Diary Leaves, First Series*, published first and in fuller form in the *Theosophist*, 1891; for her residence in India: the Hodgson report in *Proc. British Soc. for Psychical Research*, vol. III (1885); Mme. E. Coulomb, *Some Account of My Intercourse with Mme. Blavatsky from 1872 to 1884* (Lond. 1885); Franz Hartmann, *Observations during a Nine Months Stay at the Headquarters of the Theosophical Society* (Madras, 1884); *Mahatma Letters to A. P. Sinnett* (1923); John N. Farquhar, *Modern Religious Movements in India* (1915); for her later life: V. S. Solovyoff, *A Modern Priestess of Isis* (1895); *Letters of H. P. Blavatsky to A. P. Sinnett* (1924); A. P. Sinnett, *Early Days of Theosophy in Europe* (1923); Countess Constance Wachtmeister, *Reminiscences of H. P. Blavatsky and "the Secret Doctrine"* (1893); Alice L. Cleather, *H. P. Blavatsky: Her Life and Work for Humanity* (Calcutta, 1922); *The Theosophical Movement 1875–1925* (1925). The recent *Life of Madame Blavatsky* (1927) by Baseden Butt is negligible. A good brief account of the teachings of Theosophy is that by A. P. Warrington, *Encyc. Americana* (1925), XXVI, 517–22.]

E.S.B.

BLECKLEY, LOGAN EDWIN (July 3, 1827–Mar. 6, 1907), jurist, the son of James and Catherine (Lutes) Bleckley, was born in Rabun County, Ga., shortly after that mountainous region had been quitted by the Cherokee Indians. His father, a native of North Carolina, was a man of influence in the community, being successively sheriff, clerk, ordinary, and county judge. His mother was of German ancestry and through her Bleckley is supposed to have inherited his love for the abstruse. He was a frail lad, but studious, and from the age of eleven, when he became a sort of clerical assistant in his father's office, his youth was largely spent in reading such law books and legal documents as he could lay hands upon. In this manner he prepared himself for the bar to which he was admitted shortly before he was nineteen. When twenty-one he moved to Atlanta where, at the age of twenty-six, he was elected solicitor general (prosecuting attorney) for the judicial circuit. At the outbreak of the Civil War he became a Confederate soldier, but his service in the field was cut short by ill health and he was transferred to the law department of the army where he remained until 1864. He then was made reporter for the Supreme Court of Georgia, resigning in 1867 to resume active practise. In 1875 he was appointed an associate justice of the State Supreme Court and thus, in his forty-ninth year, began the career which was to make him distinguished. Overwork forced his retirement in 1880, but he went back upon the bench in 1887 when appointed chief justice and remained for seven years, after which failing strength again compelled him to resign. He was married twice; first in 1857 to Clara Caroline Haralson; again, in 1893, to Chloe Herring. Five children were born of each marriage.

During all of his life he was a student,—of law, philosophy, metaphysics, mathematics. His general reading and intellectual interests were extensive. But save for a few years' meager instruction in early youth and a short course in higher mathematics at the University of Georgia in his old age, he had no schooling. He wrote many essays of a philosophical nature and not a few poems. One of his poems, "In the Matter of Rest," he read from the bench upon the occasion of his first retirement. In 1892 the University of the South conferred upon him the degree of D.C.L. Few of his decisions established novel principles. No great political or constitutional question was presented to the court while he was a member. But owing to his profound knowledge of the law, his sound reasoning, his faculty for making the complex simple, and his delightful literary style,—which abounds in quaint phrases, pertinent witticisms, and humorous allusions,—his opinions have taken high rank, and have been widely quoted in the United States, in Canada, and, to less extent, in Great Britain. He captured the imagination of his contemporaries no more by the unusual quality of his judicial decisions than by his engaging and unconventional personality. His dress was of Quaker-like simplicity; his manners were gentle; his countenance was serene. Well over six feet in height, spare, but of large frame, with flowing beard and long white hair, he had in his latter years the appearance of a patriarch.

[The chief source is the *Memorial of Logan E. Bleckley* (1907), containing sketches by Jos. R. Lamar, Wal-
ter B. Hill and others, a brief autobiography, several of Bleckley's essays, a number of his poems, and an article by Alfred H. Russell entitled "Wit and Wisdom of Chief Justice L. E. Bleckley in the Georgia Reports." See also *128 Ga. Reports,* 849; *Men of Mark in Ga.,* IV (1908), 80–88; *Green Bag,* IV, 49, 72, X, 530, XV, 555; *Atlanta Georgian,* Mar. 6, 1907; *Augusta Chronicle,* Mar. 7, 1907. Bleckley's personal appearance is described from memory.]   B.F.

BLEDSOE, ALBERT TAYLOR (Nov. 9, 1809–Dec. 8, 1877), Confederate official, editor, author, was the grandson of Rev. William Bledsoe, who, because of the persecution of the Baptists in Virginia by the then established church, removed from Orange County into the wilds of Kentucky in the later years of the eighteenth century. William's son, Moses Ousley Bledsoe, in 1816 founded and edited in Frankfort, Ky., the *Commonwealth.* He married Sophia Childress Taylor, who was related to President Taylor. Of their union Albert Taylor Bledsoe was the firstborn. He graduated in 1830 at West Point Military Academy, where he was a fellow student of Jefferson Davis and Robert E. Lee. For a while he was stationed at the Indian forts in the West, but returned east to study law, theology, and philosophy in Kenyon College, Ohio. He was adjunct professor of mathematics and teacher of French in Kenyon College, 1833–34, and was professor of mathematics in Miami University, 1835–36. In the latter year he married Harriet Coxe of Burlington, N. J., and in 1838 moved to Springfield, where for ten years he practised law in the same courts with Lincoln and Douglas. His continued interest in theology led to the writing of an *Examination of President Edwards' "Inquiry into the Freedom of the Will"* (1845). From 1848 till 1854 he was professor of mathematics at the University of Mississippi and from 1854 to 1861 he held the same chair at the University of Virginia. The results of his studies during those years are found in *A Theodicy: or Vindication of the Divine Glory* (1853) and the *Essay on Liberty and Slavery* (1856). On account of his training at West Point he entered the Confederate army as colonel in 1861 and then became assistant secretary of war. Believing that Bledsoe's brain could be of more service than his arm, President Davis sent him to London to investigate certain historical problems involved in the issues between the North and the South and perhaps to influence English public opinion. When he returned in February 1865, he had collected the material which he soon used in his volume, *Is Davis a Traitor?, or Was Secession a Constitutional Right Previous to the War of 1861?* (1866). In this book, which proved to be a mine of material for the lawyers who were defending Davis, Bledsoe restated with real clearness and force the position of Calhoun and other Southern leaders and laid the basis for much of his future writing. In 1867 he became the founder and editor of the *Southern Review,* published in Baltimore. For ten years he was the fiery protagonist of the Lost Cause. The magazine was dedicated to "the despised, disfranchised, and down-trodden people of the South." "Shall we bury in the grave of the grandest cause that has ever perished on earth," asks the editor, "all the little stores of history and philosophy which a not altogether idle life has enabled us to amass, and so leave the just cause merely because it is fallen to go without our humble advocacy? We would rather die." In a later volume he writes: "To abandon the *Review* would be like the pang of death to me. It is the child of my affection. Money is not my object. I am willing to be a slave for the South." In this spirit he toiled unceasingly, writing nearly always three to five articles for each number, and for one number of 250 pages all but one article. But so poverty-stricken were the Southern people and so seemingly indifferent to his efforts to plead their cause that he received but little compensation and was dependent for the support of his family on the salaries of his daughters, who were school-teachers.

The historical significance of Bledsoe's writings, now buried in the files of the old *Review,* is that they represent the attitude of the unreconstructed Southerner in the ten years after the Civil War. Although he often quoted the words of Gen. Lee to him, "You have a great work to do; we all look to you for our vindication," his spirit was exactly opposite to that of the man who moved out of the shadows of Appomattox into the dawn of a new day, and who urged all Southerners to become Americans, and to "unite in the restoration of reason, the allayment of passion, and the dissipation of prejudice." Bledsoe interpreted the war as a conflict between principle and brute force. He justified secession as a constitutional right and slavery as a moral right sanctioned by the Bible. He seemed like a Titan fighting against all the tendencies of modern life and thought. Democracy, he contended, is an impossible form of government because it enthrones the tyranny of the mob; it is the result of the infidel doctrinaires of the eighteenth century, including Jefferson, whom he bitterly denounced as the source of the South's woes; instead of being the last hope of the world, it is the last madness of a self-idolizing nation. Industrialism is the enemy of chivalry and beauty, and science is the enemy of faith. The new doctrine of Evolution destroys the story of the Fall of Man, which is the corner-stone of theology. German

philosophy and higher criticism are responsible for the reign of rationalism, which can only be overthrown by the religious faith of the South. Because "we can no longer trust the mental and moral training of our sons and daughters to teachers and books imported from abroad," Bledsoe advocated a series of text-books to be written for the most part by professors in the University of Virginia. The South must maintain its higher education against the whole tendency toward the uniformity and standardization of the infidel and utilitarian public school system. All along the line there must be "a renewal of the old fortifications," "a return to the old paths." Ever a fighter, Bledsoe was engaged in continuous controversy, not only with other editors and authors, but, in his later years, with various denominational leaders in the South over such questions as infant baptism, predestination, the mode of baptism, etc. It is little wonder that he gave way under the strain of financial burdens, excessive work, and bitter disputation. He died at Alexandria, Va., Dec. 8, 1877. His daughter, Sophia Bledsoe Herrick, who had helped him with his editorial duties, later became one of the editors of *Scribner's Magazine.*

[Sketch by Sophia Bledsoe Herrick in the *Lib. of Southern Lit.,* vol. I (1907); Jas. W. Davidson, *Living Writers of the South* (1869); Edwin Mims, "Southern Mags." in *The South in the Building of the Nation,* vol. VII (1909).]

                 E. M.

BLEECKER, ANN ELIZA (October 1752–Nov. 23, 1783), poet, was born in New York City, the posthumous daughter of Brandt Schuyler and Margareta (Van Wyck) Schuyler. Belonging on her father's side to one of the most aristocratic families in the colony, she came into the world an heiress of considerable fortune. With her one brother and two sisters she was brought up in an atmosphere of comfort and culture, and while still very young began to write creditable verse. She was married, Mar. 29, 1769, to John J. Bleecker, a gentleman of good family in New Rochelle. They first went to Poughkeepsie for two years and then removed to Tomhanick, near Schaghticoke, N. Y., a frontier village where Bleecker possessed some landed property. Here he "built him an house on a little eminence, which commanded a pleasing prospect" of orchard, meadow, stream, and hill. Although Mrs. Bleecker sometimes became a little weary of her rustic neighbors and compared herself to Orpheus

> Impatient trees, to hear his strain
>   Rent from the ground their roots:—
> Such is my fate, as his was then,
>   Surrounded here—by brutes

she really had many friends of her own class, and

her familiar verse of this period is full of glee. When misfortunes came, however, they came fast. In the summer of 1777 the approach of Burgoyne's army counseled withdrawal to a safe community and Bleecker went to Albany to arrange for accommodations there. During his absence, Mrs. Bleecker, alarmed at the breakfast table by news that hostile Indians were within two miles of the village, rushed impetuously from the house, carrying a young baby on her arm and leading a four-year-old daughter. Joining a stream of refugees, she was able to secure a place in a wagon for the children, but was obliged to walk, herself, all the way to the nearest settlement of Stony-Arabia. This town proved itself to deserve its name by refusing shelter to the fugitives, but finally one of its richest citizens did permit Mrs. Bleecker to spend the night on the bare floor of an attic. The next morning her husband found her and they proceeded to Albany and thence down the Hudson to Red Hook where her mother was awaiting them. On the journey, however, her baby sickened and died; it was buried on the riverbank in a coffin hastily prepared from a dining-table. A few days later, her mother also died, and within a few weeks her only surviving sister.

After Burgoyne's surrender, the Bleeckers returned to Albany where prudence would have bade them remain. But Albany, in Mrs. Bleecker's words "that unsociable, illiterate, stupid town," proved insupportable, and in spite of danger they went back to their beloved Tomhanick. From this time until the end of the war Bleecker, like his fellow-townsmen, was away much of the time on militia duty, and although the adjacent forest swarmed with Indians and Tories the village was often left without a single male defender. Mrs. Bleecker consoled herself as best she might during these years of loneliness and terror by the reading of Homer, Virgil, Theocritus, Ariosto, and Tasso. During the winter of 1779 she was again obliged to save her life by flight, this time to the settlement of Coeymans, but in the ensuing spring returned once more to Tomhanick. In 1781 her husband was captured by Tories and for six days she was in doubt as to his fate; at the end of that time he reappeared, having been unexpectedly rescued by a party of Vermonters, but the emotional reaction was too great for Mrs. Bleecker's health, worn out by constant nervous strain; a severe illness followed from which she never really recovered. After peace was declared, her husband took her on a visit to New York, hoping that old scenes would revive her waning interest in life,

but the city had been devastated, family and friends were gone, and she returned to Tomhanick to die. "My days have been few and evil," she had written in 1780, and in 1783 she wrote "I die of a broken heart." She died on Nov. 23 in the latter year.

Mrs. Bleecker's poems, published in the *New York Magazine* but not collected in book form until after her death, show much variety of subject-matter and some technical proficiency; although her emotion is too unrestrained for modern taste, she does at time invest the meters of Pope with lyrical quality. Her letters reveal a personality of much charm and grace, with a lightly satirical wit and gayety until overclouded by her later melancholy.

[*The Posthumous Works of Ann Eliza Bleecker,* containing her letters and a memoir by her daughter, Margaretta V. Faugeres (1793); Geo. W. Schuyler, *Colonial N. Y.,* II (1885); J. Munsell, *Annals of Albany,* vol. VI (1855), containing inscription on Mrs. Bleecker's tombstone.]

E. S. B.

BLENK, JAMES HUBERT (July 28, 1856–Apr. 20, 1917), Catholic archbishop, the youngest of the sixteen children of James Blenk and Catherine Wigman, was born in Neustadt, Bavaria. His parents were Protestants and died in that faith. The family came to America when he was a baby. Environmental influences were responsible for his conversion to Catholicism. He attended services at the Cathedral with his Catholic playmates and the ritual of the Church appealed to him so strongly that he was baptized at the age of twelve. His early education was received in New Orleans and later he attended a Franciscan school in New York. Ill health interfered with his desire to join the Redemptorist order. He secured a position as teacher of mathematics at Jefferson College, Convent, La. The college was under the control of the Marists and when his health improved he applied for admission to that order. His ecclesiastical training was received in France and Ireland. On Aug. 16, 1885 he was ordained. His first assignment was to Jefferson College, of which he became president in 1891. Under his leadership the college progressed rapidly and in order to better utilize his talents the general of the Marists sent him to visit the various houses and missions of the order in France, England, and Ireland. Upon his return to New Orleans in 1897 he was put in charge of the Holy Name Church in Algiers. Archbishop Janssens appointed him on the board of consultors of the diocese. When after the Spanish-American War Archbishop Chapelle of New Orleans was appointed apostolic delegate to Cuba and Porto Rico to adjust matters pertaining to the church, Father Blenk was selected as auditor and secretary of the delegation. As a result of his excellent work, he was named first bishop of Porto Rico in January 1899. In Porto Rico he Americanized the Catholics, provided for education, and adjusted the affairs of church and state very satisfactorily. He became archbishop of New Orleans on July 2, 1906, and devoted his energies to systematizing and unifying the activities of the church. A common system of parochial schools with uniform text-books and teaching was organized. Catholic high schools were established and the Jesuits were aided in organizing Marquette University. Provision was made for the training of priests. The Fathers of the Congregation of the Holy Ghost and the Josephites were invited to come to the diocese in order to establish churches and schools for the negroes, and through his influence Mother Catherine Drexel established a school for their higher education. When priests and nuns were driven out of Mexico, Archbishop Blenk gave them shelter. His last work was when he accompanied Dr. Kelly of the Church Extension Society to Cuba and to New York in the interests of the Mexican refugees. The diocese gained both spiritually and materially under the leadership of Archbishop Blenk, due not only to his executive ability but to his untiring energy and the fact that he was—"approachable, companionable and democratic" (*Times-Picayune*, New Orleans, Apr. 21, 1917).

[Archives of the St. Louis Cathedral, New Orleans; *Daily Picayune* (New Orleans), July 2, 3, 7, 10, 1899, Apr. 25, 1907; *Daily States* (New Orleans), Apr. 21, 1917; *Morning Star* (New Orleans), Apr. 21, 1917.]
S. H.

BLENNERHASSETT, HARMAN (Oct. 8, 1765–Feb. 2, 1831), associate of Aaron Burr, son of Conway Blennerhassett, an Irishman, was born in Hampshire, England, where his mother, a daughter of Thomas Lacy, was temporarily visiting. Educated at Trinity College, Dublin, he was admitted to the Irish bar in 1790. Afterward he spent several years in travel on the continent, being in Paris at the first anniversary of the taking of the Bastille and at the Festival of Confederation in the Champ de Mars. Influenced by his reading of Voltaire and Rousseau, he became an ardent republican. He was a cultured man with some talent for music and a flair for science, and was gifted, according to contemporary report, with "all sorts of sense except common sense." In 1796 he married Margaret Agnew and brought his bride to America. Two years later they settled on an island in the Ohio River near Parkersburg, then in the state of Virginia. In undertaking to make this a sylvan retreat he sunk a large part of his patrimony. "Foreign

frescoes colored the ceilings,—the walls were hung with costly pictures, and the furniture, imported from Paris and London, was rich, costly, and tasteful. Splendid mirrors, gay colored carpets, and elegant curtains embellished their apartments. Massive silver plate stood on the sideboard. The drawing-room resembled the richest Parisian *salon* in the heyday of Louis XIV" (E. O. Randall, *Ohio Archæological and Historical Society Quarterly*, I, 132).

Blennerhassett's reputation rests upon his connection with Aaron Burr. This began in May 1805, when he may have casually met Burr at Marietta. In that year the latter twice visited the island establishment. Blennerhassett's apparent means, his enthusiasm, and his desire to escape from his wilderness home commended him to one who hoped to profit from the disturbed conditions of the southern frontier. On his own part Blennerhassett eagerly responded to Burr's vague proposals. In the following year when Burr journeyed westward the second time, Blennerhassett's island became a center for his activities. In a measure the master of the island proved too enthusiastic a recruit. To him are attributed a series of articles, published in the *Ohio Gazette,* under the pseudonym "Querist," which discussed the probability of a separation of the western states from the Union. One fails to see how they could have helped Burr's main plan, which was to prepare the West for an invasion of Mexico, unless he intended through the publication to deceive the Spanish authorities as to his real purpose.

Blennerhassett supervised operations on the island and on the nearby Muskingum, contributed liberally of his means, and also assisted in making the first payment on the Bastrop Purchase which Burr proposed to colonize. He interviewed John Graham, the agent of the federal government sent to watch Burr, and assured him that their plans were not illegal. Later such recruits as assembled on the upper Ohio made the island their headquarters. These preparations, coupled with the enmity that Blennerhassett had already excited among his neighbors, led the militia of Wood County, Va., to make a descent on the island, Dec. 11, 1806. Blennerhassett and Comfort Tyler, another prospective colonist, had hurriedly left the island the night before. The militia thereupon looted the mansion and outbuildings. The fugitives succeeded in passing the various militia groups stationed along the river and ultimately joined Burr at the mouth of the Cumberland. In company with Burr and other leaders Blennerhassett was detained by the authorities of Mississippi Territory, but after a hearing before the district judge, he was released. He was arrested again in Kentucky and brought to Richmond for trial. When the government failed to convict his principal, either for treason or for misdemeanor, the court entered a *nolle prosequi* also against Blennerhassett's indictment. His appearance at the trial elicited from Wirt a famous oratorical gem. His island residence was ruined, and in a few years fire and the floods swept away what the militia had spared. For a time he became cotton planter in Mississippi and spent three years, 1819–22, as a lawyer in Montreal. Then he returned to Europe and died on the island of Guernsey. His wife, a prepossessing woman of considerable talent, attempted to recover from Congress the value of the property but died shortly after she came to this country for the purpose.

[Wm. H. Safford, *Life of Harman Blennerhassett* (1853); Wm. H. Safford, ed., *The Blennerhassett Papers* (1864); *Century Mag.*, July 1901.]   I. J. C.

BLINN, HOLBROOK (Jan. 23, 1872–June 24, 1928), actor, was born in San Francisco, the son of Col. Charles H. and Nellie (Holbrook) Blinn. His father was a surveyor, his mother an actress. The boy caught his first glimpse of theatrical life in 1878, when he appeared as a child in *The Streets of New York*. The year 1891–92 he spent not too successfully at Leland Stanford Jr. University and then went on the stage, playing Corporal Ferry in *The New South* at Stockwell's Theatre, San Francisco, Sept. 12, 1892, under the management of William A. Brady. He made his New York début in the same play at the Broadway Theatre, Jan. 2, 1893, and continued to act in it for two seasons. Later he returned to California, got together a company of his own, and took it to Alaska. One member of the troupe was Ruth Benson, whom he married. She was the daughter of Maj. Henry McKinley Benson, U. S. A., appeared with her husband in several plays, and outlived him. Blinn made his London début as Wing Shee in *The Cat and the Cherub* at the Lyric Theatre, Oct. 30, 1897. He was popular in London and until 1903 had more engagements in England than in the United States. He was a life governor of Charing Cross Hospital. In 1900, in New York, he acted with Maurice Barrymore in *The Battle of the Strong*. In 1907–08, under the management of Arnold Daly [*q.v.*] he acted in *The Shirkers, How He Lied to Her Husband, The Van Dyck, After the Opera, The Hour Glass,* and *Candida;* later he was to be seen with Daly in *The Regeneration.* For three seasons 1908–11 he was leading man with Mrs. Minnie Maddern Fiske in *Salvation Nell, The Pillars of Society, Hannele,*

The Green Cockatoo, Becky Sharpe, and *Mrs. Bumpstead-Leigh.* In 1913 he organized the Princess Theatre, New York, and produced thirty one-act plays, with which he later went on tour. Always a competent player, he enjoyed steady employment; yet, except while with Daly and Mrs. Fiske, he acted in few plays of distinction. His best work was done in the last decade of his life, but he remained a popular and superficially brilliant, rather than a distinguished, actor. In 1919 he starred as Henry Winthrop in *The Challenge;* in 1920 he was Jeffrey Fair in *The Famous Mrs. Fair* and joint star with Mary Nash in *Man and Woman;* for three seasons 1920–23 he played Pancho Lopez in *The Bad Man* with gorgeous comic verve; he starred in *The Dove* 1925–26 and produced and starred in Molnar's *The Play's the Thing* 1926–28. His home was at Croton-on-Hudson. There, while riding a new horse, he was thrown June 16, 1928, and badly bruised. Infection set in, and he died after a week's illness. He was buried in the old Sleepy Hollow Cemetery, in Scarborough, N. Y.

[*Who's Who in America,* 1928–29; J. Parker, ed., *Who's Who in the Theatre* (5th ed., London, 1925); *Leland Stanford Jr., Univ. Alumni Dir., 1891–1910* (1910); *N. Y. Times,* June 25, 26, 28, 1928. See also *N. Y. Times Index* under *Blinn* and *Plays; San Francisco Chronicle,* Sept. 12, 1892; F. W. Faxon, ed., *The Dramatic Index 1910–28* (1911 ff.).]   G. H. G.

BLISS, AARON THOMAS (May 22, 1837– Sept. 16, 1906), governor of Michigan, was born at Peterboro, Madison County, N. Y. He was the seventh child of Lyman Bliss, who traced his ancestry back to Thomas Bliss, a settler in Hartford, Conn., in 1636. His mother was Ann (Chaffie) Bliss. From his dry-goods store at Bouckville Aaron T. Bliss enlisted, Oct. 1, 1861, in the 10th New York Volunteer Cavalry, and went to the front as a first lieutenant, becoming captain a year later. Wounded while stubbornly defending the retreat of Wilson's Raiders, he was captured and suffered imprisonment in Salisbury, Andersonville, Macon, Charleston, and Columbia prisons, escaping from the latter in November 1864. Broken health caused his resignation three months later. In 1865 he went to Saginaw, Mich., and in the pine forests began a career that took him from a driver of logging teams to the head of one of the successful lumber firms of the Saginaw Valley. A paying farm of a thousand acres afforded recreation. His wife, Allaseba, daughter of Ambrose Phelps of Madison County, N. Y., shared both early privations and later success, and in philanthropy had a life all her own. Taking a leading part in the Michigan department of the Grand Army of the Republic, Bliss was elected first to the state Senate in 1882, and next as a member of the Fifty-first Congress, 1889–91. He was defeated for reëlection to Congress; but in 1900 he wrested from six other candidates the Republican nomination for governor. He succeeded the spectacular H. S. Pingree, and was reëlected in 1902. His name is linked with the establishment of the Indian School at Mt. Pleasant and the Michigan Soldiers' Home at Grand Rapids. He was a good administrator, and during his service as governor the educational and charitable interests of the state advanced steadily. He stood for the equal taxation of railway properties, and without being a reformer was a sound progressive. His gifts to Saginaw and to the Methodist Episcopal Church were extensive.

[J. H. Bliss, *Geneal. of the Bliss Family in America* (1881); H. M. Utley and B. M. Cutcheon, *Mich. as a Province, Territory and State* (1906), IV, 252; *Mich. Biogs.* (1924), ed. by the Mich. Hist. Commission; J. C. Mills, *Hist. of Saginaw County, Mich.,* II (1918), 24–28.]   C. M.

BLISS, CORNELIUS NEWTON (Jan. 26, 1833–Oct. 9, 1911), merchant, politician, was the son of Asahel Newton Bliss and of Irene Borden (Luther) Bliss. He was born in Fall River, where his father died at the age of twenty-six when the son was still very young. His mother, re-marrying, removed to New Orleans with her husband, Edward S. Keep, and the boy was left in the competent care of his grandmother. He attended the public schools of Fall River, and Fisher's Academy, working at odd jobs in his spare time. At the age of fourteen he joined his mother in New Orleans, and for a short time was clerk in the dry-goods store of his stepfather. Seeing little opportunity for a business career in the South, he returned to New England, and in Boston sought employment from James M. Beebe, then the leading dry-goods merchant of New England. He was given a beginner's place, from which he steadily rose until he became a member of the firm. There was in the employ of J. M. Beebe & Company during these years another young man, who was destined to large things in business and politics. This was Levi P. Morton, and the friendship between him and Bliss lasted as long as they both lived. In 1866 Bliss became convinced that manufacturing offered greater opportunities than wholesaling, and, severing his connection with J. M. Beebe & Company, he became the New York partner in the house of J. S. & E. Wright of Boston, operators of large textile mills. Soon the New York branch outstripped the mother house in volume of business, and the firm of Wright, Bliss & Fabyan became one of the most important in its line in the United States. On the death of the Wrights,

the firm took the name of Bliss, Fabyan & Company, and Bliss remained its head until his death. On becoming a citizen of New York he took an immediate and intelligent interest in the civic and political affairs of the city. He was a Republican of the conservative type, but he frequently opposed with vigor the policies and performances of Thomas C. Platt, then the Republican leader of the state. In 1884 he supported Chester A. Arthur for the presidency, and in 1887 served as chairman of the Republican state committee. He began in 1892 his long service as treasurer of the Republican national committee. In this capacity he served with great ability in the presidential campaigns of 1892, 1896, 1900, and 1904. In the last year Alton B. Parker, Democratic candidate for the presidency, charged that Bliss, as treasurer of the Republican national committee, had procured excessively large contributions from corporations, and especially from those benefited by a high protective tariff. To these charges Bliss made no reply, and refused in any way to be drawn into the controversy. He declined, however, to serve longer as treasurer. In 1896 he was urged by McKinley to accept the Treasury portfolio, but refused. He agreed, however, in order to relieve the President in an awkward political complication, to become secretary of the interior. This office he filled most competently for two years. He had, however, little liking for the routine of political office, and resigned in 1898 to return to the management of his business. President McKinley urged him in 1900 to accept the nomination for the vice-presidency, but he declined. Had his decision been otherwise, he, and not Theodore Roosevelt, would have become president in 1901. Bliss refused repeatedly to be a candidate for state and municipal offices, including those of mayor of the city and governor of the state. Nevertheless, he gave his services freely as a member of civic and political committees. He was a consistent advocate of a high protective tariff, and was for many years president of the Protective Tariff League. He was an official in many large financial and industrial organizations, and served for a short time as president of the Fourth National Bank. He was married, on Mar. 30, 1859, to Elizabeth Mary Plummer of Boston.

[J. H. Bliss, *Geneal. of the Bliss Family in America* (1881); *Who's Who in America,* 1910–11; *Tribute of the Chamber of Commerce of the State of N. Y. to the Memory of Hon. Cornelius Newton Bliss* (1911); obituaries in *N. Y. Times, N. Y. Tribune, N. Y. Herald,* and *Sun* (N. Y.), Oct. 10, 1911.]   A. L. C.

BLISS, DANIEL (Aug. 17, 1823–July 27, 1916), missionary educator, founder and first president of Syrian Protestant College (now the

American University) of Beirut, was born in the village of Georgia, Vt. He was one of the seven children of Loomis and Susanna (Farwell) Bliss. His early lot was cast on various farms in his native state and in Ohio. His devout and loving mother died when he was nine years old. He spent his youth in the neighborhood of Painesville and Kingsville, Ohio, living with relatives and others, and supporting himself from the age of sixteen by farming, tanning, and tree-grafting. He attended the district schools and in 1846 entered the Kingsville Academy, studying and teaching therein until graduation in 1848. On Nov. 7, 1848, he arrived at Amherst College, Mass., in the middle of the fall term and was admitted upon examination to the freshman class. He was strong-minded, robust in physique, and a liberal in religion,—testifying, however, years afterward that he "never opposed what he believed to be true Christianity." What modest debts he accumulated in making his way through Amherst he cleared from the proceeds of a private school which he conducted in Shrewsbury, Mass., during the summer of 1852. He graduated from Amherst in the latter year and during 1852–55 attended Andover Seminary in preparation for the ministry and foreign missions. On Oct. 17, he was ordained at Amherst, and in November was married to Abby Maria Wood, of Westminster, Mass. Receiving appointment by the American Board and being assigned to Syria, Mr. and Mrs. Bliss sailed from Boston on Dec. 12, 1855, for Malta, Smyrna, and Beirut. After a short stay in Beirut they left on Apr. 15 for Abeih, a Lebanon village 2,500 ft. above the sea, where they worked for two and one-half years among the few hundred Christian and Druse villagers. This was Bliss's apprenticeship, and under his hand the school which Dr. Van Dyck had opened in 1843 grew rapidly into an academy of importance. The Syrian work at the time was almost exclusively amongst non-Moslems, for while Turkey was tolerant of Christian missionaries, she did not guarantee immunity to Moslem converts to Christianity. For four years from Oct. 16, 1858, the Blisses were in charge of the Girls' Boarding School in Suq al-Gharb, five miles above Abeih. It was there he preached his first Arabic sermon on Dec. 12, 1858, and displayed further his fitness for educational work. When the Syrian Mission voted on Jan. 27, 1862, to recommend the founding of a "Literary Institution," Bliss was assigned the task and privilege of organizing and presiding over it. He and Mrs. Bliss came at once to America, where he took the first steps in the new assignment. Syrian Protestant College was chartered in 1864 by New

York State, and began an independent career under its own trustees with Bliss as president. Enough endowment was raised to enable the Institution to open in Beirut on Dec. 3, 1866, the aim being to serve "all conditions and classes of men without regard to colour, nationality, race, or religion." Arabic was the medium of instruction for the first seventeen years; thereafter, English. After existence in various quarters until 1873 the present site was occupied, where the corner-stone of the main building had been laid on Dec. 7, 1871. Bliss acted also as professor of Bible and ethics, and as treasurer. He was the active head of the College for thirty-six years and saw its enrolment grow from sixteen to over six hundred students. In 1902 he resigned, being succeeded by his second son, Dr. Howard Sweetser Bliss [q.v.], but after his retirement he still continued his daily classes, attended faculty meetings, and preached an occasional sermon. A hall of the Beirut institution bears his name, and his memory is preserved by Arabic text-books of his own composition in moral and in natural philosophy.

[*Reminiscences of Daniel Bliss* (1920), ed. by his eldest son, F. J. Bliss; C. A. Hoppin, *The Bliss Book* (1913); J. H. Bliss, *Geneal. of the Bliss Family in America* (1881); contemporary numbers of the *Missionary Herald*.]   J. C. A.

BLISS, EDWIN ELISHA (Apr. 12, 1817– Dec. 20, 1892), missionary, was born in Putney, Vt., the son of Henry and Abigail (Grout) Bliss. He was one of eight children, and one of three who became missionaries. A sister, Emma (Mrs. Van Lennep) went to Turkey, and a brother, Isaac Grout, to Turkey and Egypt. Edwin's early education was finished at the High School in Springfield, Mass., where his parents then dwelt. Thence he went to Amherst College, graduating in 1837. For two years following graduation he taught in Amherst Academy, and then entered Andover Seminary, from which he received his diploma in 1842. On Feb. 26, 1843 he married Isabella Holmes Porter, of Portland, Me. His ordination had taken place on Feb. 8, 1843, and on Mar. 1 he and Mrs. Bliss sailed from Boston on the bark *Emma Isadora* with a notable company bound for Smyrna.

After arrival in the East the Blisses proceeded to Trebizond instead of to Kurdistan and the Nestorian Mission, for they learned of trouble in the Kurdish mountains and could secure from the government (Turkey) only permissive passports and not protective *firmans*. They never, in fact, went into Kurdistan. Instead, they were "permanently connected with the Mission to the Armenians," and labored from 1843 to 1851 at Trebizond and from 1851 to 1856 at a new station opened by Bliss at Marsovan. At both stations the evangelical work suffered severe persecution at the hands of the orthodox Armenians. In February 1856 Bliss was transferred from Marsovan to Constantinople to give his time to literary work, and for thirty-six years he labored quietly and effectively in the department of publication. He edited the *Avedaper* (*"Messenger"*) from 1865 to 1892, a newspaper which had become in 1855 a weekly issued in three forms: Turkish in Armenian characters, Turkish in Greek characters, and Armenian in Armenian. It had 1,500 subscribers and some ten thousand readers throughout Turkey, and was a fruitful agent of inspiration to Christian workers, and of social and religious reformation. Its editor declared one of its important offices to be the exposure of "the shameless misstatements" made in other papers about the work of the American Board. Bliss edited, also, a monthly children's paper issued in the three forms mentioned above. In addition to this editorial work he wrote pamphlets and tracts, "helps in Bible study, narratives of Christian life and experience." He was the author of a *Bible Handbook* (in Armenian), and frequent articles in the *Missionary Herald*. He visited the United States four times on various errands, including the quest of health. While located at Marsovan he had contracted malaria from which he was never thereafter free. Before his death he had been for some time in feeble health and unable to work.

[Geo. Washburn, "Rev. Edwin E. Bliss," *Missionary Herald,* Feb. 1893; *Congreg. Yr. Bk.*, 1893; *Andover Theol. Sem. Necrology*, 1892–93; J. H. Bliss, *Geneal. of the Bliss Family in America* (1881).]   J.C.A.

BLISS, EDWIN MUNSELL (Sept. 12, 1848–Aug. 6, 1919), missionary, editor, was born at Erzerum, Turkey, the son of Isaac Grout and Eunice (Day) Bliss, and nephew of Edwin Elisha Bliss [*q.v.*]. His father was agent of the American Bible Society for the Levant and missionary of the American Board. Edwin's early years were spent in Constantinople where his education was begun as one of the first students of Robert College under Cyrus Hamlin. In 1866, after four years in the College, he entered the Springfield, Mass., High School. After two years there he entered Amherst College from which he graduated in 1871 as valedictorian of his class. He spent the year 1871–72 in the Yale Divinity School and had begun his second year when called back to Constantinople because of his father's failing health. During the next three years he served as an assistant agent of the Bible Society, traveling extensively in Turkey, Egypt, Persia, and the Holy Land. In 1875 he resumed his

studies at Yale and received in 1877 the B.D. degree. He was ordained in New Haven on May 18 of his senior year. Returning to the Levant, he served again as assistant agent of the Bible Society. He was married in Urumia, Persia, on June 5, 1885, to Marie Louise Henderson of New York City, and for two years thereafter resided in Constantinople as assistant agent of the Society. The health of Mrs. Bliss failed and in 1887, together with her daughter, Elizabeth Labaree, she returned to America, where she died on Dec. 12 of that year. Because of this loss Bliss resigned his post in 1888 to the great regret of the Bible Agency, and took up his residence at home.

From 1889 until 1891, the year of publication, Bliss was editor of the *Encyclopædia of Missions,* and filled the office with distinction. It was for this work in particular that his alma mater bestowed upon him in 1896 the honorary degree of D.D. From 1891 to 1901 he was associate editor of the *Independent,* New York City, serving also during one year (1898–99) as lecturer on foreign missions in the Yale Divinity School, and one year (1900) as editorial writer for the *New York Times,* and *Harper's Weekly.* He was chairman of the Press Committee and the Committee on Publication of the Ecumenical Foreign Missions Conference, New York City, 1900. On Nov. 8, 1900, he married his second wife, Theodora Crosby of Georgetown, Mass. During 1902–04 he was field agent for New England of the American Tract Society, in 1904 joint editor of a second edition of the *Encyclopædia,* and in 1905 general secretary of the Foreign Missions Industrial Association. In 1907 he was called to Washington for special work in the Bureau of Census— as expert on religious bodies—and remained at this post until his death at the age of seventy-one.

Bliss was the author of *The Turk in Armenia, Crete, and Greece* (1896); *Turkey and the Armenian Atrocities* (1896); *Concise History of Missions* (1897); *The Missionary Enterprise* (1908), and a series of historical sketches of the sects of Christendom for the World Conference on Faith and Order (1920), in addition to miscellaneous writings and his work in the Bureau of Census (see especially *Religious Bodies,* 2 vols., 1916). He was a rapid writer, quick in thought, and of a nervous temperament. While never very robust he was seldom ill. He was impulsive and generous.

[*Who's Who in America,* 1918–19; *Amherst Coll. Biog. Record,* 1821–1921; *Reports of the Am. Bible Soc.*; files of the *Missionary Herald*; information from Bliss's widow, Mrs. T. C. Bliss.]   J.C.A.

BLISS, ELIPHALET WILLIAMS (Apr. 12, 1836–July 21, 1903), manufacturer, was one of the six children of John Stebbins Bliss, a physician and farmer whose ancestors had settled in Springfield, Mass., and of Ruby Ann (Williams) Bliss. He was born at Fly Creek, Otsego County, N. Y. Educated in the public schools and at Fort Plain Seminary, the boy spent his life on a farm. A pronounced mechanical bent, however, led him to an apprenticeship in a machine shop in Otsego County, where he remained until the age of twenty-one. Seeking wider mechanical opportunities he moved to New England and obtained work in the Parker gun factory in Meriden, Conn., where he was soon advanced to the position of foreman which he held for seven years. During the Civil War he served as a corporal in Company I of the 3rd Connecticut Volunteers. An older brother, Lucien Wood Williams Bliss, was a major in the Confederate army. Following the war Bliss returned to Fly Creek, N. Y., married Anna Elizabeth Metcalf on June 19, 1865, and in the following year located permanently in Brooklyn, N. Y., where he was employed for a short time with the Campbell Printing Press Company. In 1867 he founded the machine shops which through his ingenuity and perseverance were to grow into the E. W. Bliss Company and the United States Projectile Company, concerns which at his death employed 1,300 men. Bliss's mechanical interests developed along two lines: the manufacture of tools, presses, and dies for use in sheet metal work, and the manufacture of shells and projectiles. For the former numerous patents were taken out, either his own inventions or patents assigned to him. Under his own name are machines for manufacturing and soldering metal cans and for shaping and casting sheet metal. One of the important orders which the company obtained was for part of the material used in the Brooklyn Bridge. From the time when Bliss had worked in the Parker gun factory, he had been interested in projectiles, and with the development of his machine shops he naturally turned to this phase. The E. W. Bliss Company obtained control of the patents for the manufacture of the Whitehead torpedo in use in the navy, while the United States Projectile Company during his later life manufactured most of the shells in use in the large guns in the navy. In addition to his machine shops Bliss was deeply interested in the development of Brooklyn. He invested heavily in real estate, was vice-president of the Brooklyn Heights Railroad and of the Brooklyn Gas Fixture Company, and was a director of the Kings County Trust Company. His residence, "Owl's Head," located on the heights of Bay Ridge, contained an observatory which swept the harbor and was long one of the "show estates" of Brook-

lyn. In his later years Bliss devoted much of his time to club activities. He was an active member of the leading New York and Brooklyn social and athletic organizations, particularly the latter, maintaining a membership in five important yacht clubs. The bulk of his large estate went to his widow, with some provisions for the Episcopal Church of Bay Ridge, of which he was a member, and for the maintenance of the E. W. Bliss Kindergarten which he had supported during his life.

[*Who's Who in America*, 1903; J. H. Bliss, *Geneal. of the Bliss Family in America* (1881); *N. Y. Tribune*, July 22, 1903, Aug. 14, 1903; *Sun* (N. Y.), July 22, 1903; *Brooklyn Daily Eagle*, July 22, 1903.]

H.U.F.

BLISS, GEORGE (Apr. 21, 1816–Feb. 2, 1896), merchant, banker, was a descendant of Thomas Bliss, who was driven from England by religious persecution and settled at Braintree, Mass., in 1635. The son of William and Martha (Parsons) Bliss, George Bliss was born at Northampton, Mass. The straitened means of his parents compelled him in his eighth year to leave school in order to aid in the farm work. His education thereafter was sporadic and broken. At sixteen, he took a clerkship in the dry-goods store of Harvey Sanford, in New Haven, and soon became a trusted agent of the owner. At eighteen years, he was the purchasing representative of the shop and was admitted into partnership in 1837, when only twenty-one years old. Three years later he married Catherine Sanford, the daughter of his partner. In 1844, having accumulated some small savings, he removed to New York and there joined John J. Phelps and S. B. Chittenden, forming the firm of Phelps, Chittenden & Bliss, at No. 12 Wall St., and engaging in the wholesale dry-goods trade. In 1853, upon the retirement of Chittenden, Bliss himself became the head of the firm, being joined by James H. Dunham and others, as George Bliss & Company, with headquarters at No. 340 Broadway. In spite of difficulties in the panic of 1857 and later, the firm was able to maintain itself. At the opening of the Civil War, Bliss recognized that the issue of irredeemable paper would result in advance of prices. He greatly extended his purchases, taking on long lines of goods which became immensely enhanced in selling value. He was also able to foresee the close of the war and sold heavily. Thus he laid a substantial foundation for his large fortune of later years. His first wife having died on Mar. 13, 1862, he married Augusta H. Smith of New Haven on July 22, 1868. The second phase of his career opened in 1869, when he retired from the dry-goods trade and joined Levi P. Morton in the banking business under the firm name of Morton, Bliss & Company. The new enterprise did a large and profitable business up to the panic of 1873, then suffered some moderate reverses but recovered its prosperity during the extensive government refunding operations between 1875 and 1879 in which it had an important part. Bliss was one of the comparatively few business men who believed that specie payments should and could be inaugurated at an early date. In April 1878, he personally advised the House Banking and Currency Committee to that effect. He correctly foresaw the great improvement in business conditions which would follow resumption and was able to take advantage of it in his regular routine of banking transactions. He was a Republican but by no means a mere partisan. He regarded the tariff bill of 1890 as a blunder and severely criticized the attitude of the Republican politicians on the silver question. During his later years, he made many public benefactions, including the stone church on Blackwell's Island and similar buildings elsewhere.

[The most complete source of information is a memoir written for private circulation by the late James Cross who was associated with Bliss in business; this is now in possession of the Bliss family. There is a good sketch in H. Hall, *America's Successful Men of Affairs,* vol. I (1895), and there are good obituaries in the *N. Y. Times, N. Y. Tribune,* and *Sun* (N. Y.), Feb. 3, 1896.]

H. P. W.

BLISS, GEORGE (May 3, 1830–Sept. 2, 1897), lawyer, was descended from Thomas Bliss, a farmer of Belstone, Devonshire, England, who left Plymouth for Boston in 1635 and settled at Braintree, Mass. Seventh in direct line of descent from Thomas, George Bliss of Springfield, Mass., was a leading lawyer, speaker of the lower house and president of the Senate of the state legislature, subsequently becoming prominent in western railway circles. He married Mary Shepherd Dwight, and their only son, George Bliss, Jr., was born at Springfield. He received his early education at home, and in May 1846 went to Europe, spending eighteen months in travel. In 1848 he entered Harvard College, graduating in 1851. While there he assisted David A. Wells in the preparation of two volumes of *The Annual of Scientific Discovery.* In 1851 he again went to Europe, remaining there two years, traveling extensively and studying at Paris and the University of Berlin. In 1853 he commenced the study of law at Springfield, and after a year at the Harvard Law School (LL.B. 1856) completed his course in New York City, being admitted to the New York bar in 1857. A strong Republican, he took an active interest in politics. In January 1859, he became private secretary to E. D. Morgan, the governor of New York, and at the outbreak of war in April 1861 joined the latter's staff. In 1862 he was appointed paymaster of the state with the rank of colonel. In that year he was also commissioned captain in the 4th New York Heavy Artillery. With the authority of the Secretary of War he, on behalf of the Union League Club, organized the 20th, 26th, and 31st Regiments of New York colored troops. At the close of the war he returned to law practise and, in 1866, was appointed attorney for the newly constituted Metropolitan Board of Excise and Board of Health. In this capacity he carried to a successful conclusion the heavy litigation involving the constitutionality of the legislation which created the boards, the New York court of appeals finally holding that the Acts were valid. In December 1872 Bliss was appointed United States attorney for the southern district of New York, retaining the position till Jan. 24, 1877. During his tenure of office he conducted the prosecutions which followed the disclosure of serious frauds in the customs service involving a loss to the government of over $1,000,000. He drafted, on behalf of the Republican general committee, the New York city charter of 1873, and remained closely in touch with all subsequent amendments, being also the promoter and draftsman of the original Tenement-House Act for the city. In 1879 he was appointed by the state legislature a member of the commission which, in that and the succeeding year, compiled *The Special and Local Laws Affecting Public Interests in the City of New York.* This was followed by *The New York City Consolidation Act* of which he was the draftsman. In 1882 he was retained by the federal government as special prosecutor to assist the Attorney-General in the celebrated "Star Route" postal conspiracy cases against Senator Stephen W. Dorsey, ex-Assistant Postmaster-General Brady, and others. In 1884, in association with F. R. Coudert, he represented the Roman Catholics of the state of New York before the constitutional convention in opposition to a proposed amendment forbidding state aid to religious and charitable institutions. In recognition of this and other services rendered to the Catholic Church, to which he had become a convert, Pope Leo XIII in 1895 conferred upon him the title of "Commendatore of the Order of St. Gregory the Great." He withdrew from active participation in politics toward the end of 1893. An intimate friend of President Arthur, and one time supporter of Roscoe Conkling, he had always refused, except during the stress of civil war, to be a candidate for or hold public office. Nevertheless, he occupied a dominant position in the Republican party counsels both federal and state. He died at Wakefield, R. I., Sept. 2, 1897.

As a lawyer in a broad sense he was always adequate, painstaking, and reliable, safe rather than brilliant. From the overthrow of the Tweed Ring down to the day of his death, he was intimately associated with all legislation affecting the interests of New York City, and his skill as a legislative draftsman was demonstrated in his work upon the city charter and as a codifier. He was the author of *The Law of Life Insurance* (1872); *The New York Code of Civil Procedure* (1877), of which there were several editions; and *The General Rules of Practice of all the Courts of Record of the State of New York* (1881). He was an occasional contributor to the *North American Review* and wrote much for the *New York Times* and *New York Tribune*. He was twice married: on Oct. 22, 1856, to Catherine Van Rennselaer Dwight of Springfield, who died in 1884; and on May 25, 1887, to Anais Casey, who survived him.

[His ancestry is traced in *Genealogy of the Bliss Family in America* (1881), by J. H. Bliss. A sketch of his lif_ is contained in *Hist. of the Bench and Bar of N. Y.*, ed. by D. McAdam *et al.*, II, (1899), 44–46. Obituaries appeared in the *N. Y. Times, N. Y. Tribune, N. Y. Herald,* and *Sun* (N. Y.), Sept. 3, 1897.]

H.W.H.K.

BLISS, HOWARD SWEETSER (Dec. 6, 1860–May 2, 1920), missionary educator, was born at Suq al Gharb, Syria, the second son of Rev. Daniel Bliss [*q.v.*], and Abby (Wood) Bliss. Soon after his birth the family moved to Beirut in connection with the founding (1862–66) of Syrian Protestant College (now the American University of Beirut) under the father's presidency. In the cosmopolitan atmosphere of city and college Howard obtained his early education from his parents and from mission schools. He continued his studies in America in the Amherst (Mass.) High School, and in 1878 passed into Amherst College, from which he graduated in 1882 with honors. He served as instructor in Latin in Washburn College, Kansas, 1882–84 and then entered Union Theological Seminary, New York City. He graduated from the seminary in 1887 with the award of a traveling fellowship which enabled him to continue his studies in Mansfield College, Oxford, 1887–88, and in Göttingen and Berlin Universities, 1888–89. Returning to America in the fall of 1889, he was married on Nov. 7 to Amy, daughter of Eliphalet W. Blatchford of Chicago, Ill. In January 1890 he was ordained and then served with Dr. Lyman Abbott as assistant pastor of Plymouth Church, Brooklyn, until 1894. Thereafter until 1902 he was pastor of Union Congregational Church, Upper Montclair, N. J. In

1902 the trustees of Syrian Protestant College selected him to succeed his father in the presidency of that institution. He was formally inducted in May 1903. During his administration the campus area was considerably extended, the number of buildings doubled, the enrolment increased to about one thousand, and the teaching and adminstrative force increased to about eighty. Students were drawn from many lands— as widely separated as Russian Tartary and Newfoundland—and from the ranks of many different religious bodies. Bliss maintained the predominantly Christian character of the institution, but so liberal was his policy that toward the close of his administration non-Christian students were slightly in the majority. His tact, fearlessness, and perfect frankness in dealing with the Turkish Government during the World War enabled the college to continue its work with honor and dignity and almost without interruption. The four and one-half year strain, however, told severely upon Bliss's health. In 1919, while in Paris appearing before the Peace Conference on behalf of Syrian and Near Eastern affairs, he contracted his last illness. A short stay in his American home in Jaffrey, N. H., renewed his strength for a time and he went about filling public engagements until stricken with hemorrhage in Bridgeport, Conn. He died at Saranac Lake, N. Y., and was buried at his own request in Jaffrey, under the shadow of Mt. Monadnock. He was a man of fine personal presence and distinguished bearing, fearless yet patient, firm yet tactful. His Christian statesmanship is best seen in his remarkable paper on "The Modern Missionary," in the *Atlantic Monthly,* May 1920.

[J. H. Bliss, *Geneal. of the Bliss Family in America* (1881); *Who's Who in America,* 1919–20; Frederick J. Bliss, *Reminiscences of Daniel Bliss* (1920); *Amherst Coll. Biog. Record* (1921); annual reports of Syrian Protestant Coll.]

J.C.A.

BLISS, JONATHAN (Oct. 1, 1742–Oct. 1, 1822), jurist, was born in Springfield, Mass. Descended from Thomas Bliss of Belstone, Devon, he was the son of Capt. Luke and Mercy (Ely) Bliss. His parents were well-to-do, and he received a good education, entering Harvard College where he graduated in 1763. He then read law in the office of Lieutenant-Governor Hutchinson, where he was a fellow student of Sampson Salter Blowers [*q.v.*], and on his admission to the provincial bar, commenced practise in Boston. He acquired a good connection and quickly came to the front. In 1768 he was elected to the General Court of Massachusetts from Springfield, and was one of the minority of seventeen who were in favor of acceding to a demand of the home Government that a certain obnoxious vote should be rescinded—hence the reproachful term "rescinder." He was a consistent supporter of the British Government throughout the pre-revolutionary troubles. At the outbreak of hostilities in April 1775, he accompanied Earl Percy on his march to Concord following the skirmish at Lexington. Later in the same year he removed to England and resided there for nine years, joining the New England Club of Loyalists in London. His name appeared in the Massachusetts Proscription Act, 1778, as an enemy of the State, and as such he was forbidden to return thither. In 1785 he was appointed by the Crown attorney-general of the newly formed province of New Brunswick, and leaving England, took up his residence at St. John, N. B., where he practised for twenty-four years. The year of his arrival he was elected member for St. John in the House of Assembly, and was intimately associated with all the legislation of New Brunswick's formative period. His legal ability gave him a leading position at the bar, and he appeared as counsel in most of the important causes of his time. He was retained in 1790 by Benedict Arnold in the suit for slander which the latter brought against Manson Hart. In a test case on the subject of slavery heard in 1800 before the full bench, he appeared for the master. His speech "was divided into thirty-two heads" (J. W. Lawrence, *post*), despite which the court was divided in opinion. In 1809 he was appointed chief justice of New Brunswick and retained this position till his death at Frederickton, N. B. He married a daughter of Hon. John Worthington of Springfield, Mass. As a lawyer he ranked high in the estimation of his contemporaries, and in his public career he consistently adhered to the principles of loyalty to the Crown which he had imbibed in his youth. As attorney-general and chief justice he enjoyed the unreserved confidence and respect of the people of New Brunswick.

[His ancestry is fully detailed in *Genealogy of the Bliss Family in America* (1881), by J. H. Bliss, which also contains a short sketch of his life, p. 75. See also *The Judges of N. B. and Their Times* (1907), ed. by A. A. Stockton, p. 155; *The Am. Loyalists* (1847), by Lorenzo Sabine, I, 233; *1783–1883 Footprints, or Incidents in Early Hist. of N.B.* (1883), by J. W. Lawrence; and *Jour. and Letters of the late Samuel Curwen* (1842), ed. by G. A. Ward, p. 508; "Extracts from the Jour. of Edward Oxnard," *New Eng. Hist. and Geneal. Reg.*, XXVI (1872).]

H. W. H. K.

BLISS, PHILEMON (July 28, 1814–Aug. 24, 1889), congressman, jurist, was born in North Canton, Conn., of early Puritan stock through both parents, Asahel and Lydia (Griswold) Bliss. The family moved to Whitestown, N. Y., in 1821, where Philemon attended the local academy and Oneida Institute, but lack of funds compelled him to withdraw from Hamilton College in his sophomore year, and ill health cut short his training in a local law office. He began the active practise of law at Elyria, Ohio, in 1841, and two years later married Martha W. Sharp. His public career began in 1849 with his election by the Ohio legislature as judge of the 14th judicial district where he served until 1852. Of Federalist and Whig antecedents, he had campaigned actively for Clay in 1844, but his pronounced anti-slavery views carried him into the Free-Soil party in 1848 and later into the Republican. In 1854 he was elected to Congress from a formerly Democratic district and was reelected in 1856. His dislike of controversy and his weak voice—he struggled all his life against bronchial and pulmonary weakness—unfitted him for debate, but his set speeches are able statements of the advanced anti-slavery, anti-state-sovereignty views. In 1861 he accepted an appointment as chief justice of Dakota Territory, hoping that the drier climate would relieve his throat trouble. Two years later he resigned, and coming to Missouri with improved health, in 1864, he brought his family to St. Joseph. Here he served as probate judge and as a member of the county court of Buchanan County; in 1867 he was appointed a curator of the state university, serving until 1872 and taking an active part in its reorganization. In 1868 he was elected to the state supreme court for a four-year term on the Radical or Republican ticket, and won the respect and confidence of all parties in a time of great political bitterness. The dominance of the Democratic party after 1872 ended his political career. In that year the curators of the university appointed him first dean of the newly created department of law, which position he held until his death in 1889. He died at St. Paul, Minn., whither he had gone for his health, and he was buried at Columbia, Mo.

While a man of decided convictions and unquestioned intellectual courage—he was a lifelong Republican in a state and community intensely Democratic—he had an essentially judicial and peaceful temperament. In spite of his lifelong struggle against physical weakness and his retiring disposition, he gave a great and well recognized service in the training of the postbellum generation of lawyers, and in the restoration and advancement of the standards of the legal profession in Missouri. His sound legal knowledge is evidenced by his *Treatise upon the Law of Pleading under the Codes of Civil Procedure*

(1870), a text nationally used and frequently revised until superseded by the modern case method.

[J. H. Bliss, *Geneal. of the Bliss Family in America* (1881); *The Bench and Bar of St. Louis* (1884), pp. 376–79; W. F. Switzler, "Hist. of the Univ. of Mo." (MSS.).]

J. V.

BLISS, PHILIP PAUL (July 9, 1838–Dec. 29, 1876), singing evangelist, was the writer of gospel songs which have had extraordinary popularity. They appeared as an adjunct to the organized revivalistic enterprises of the last half of the nineteenth century, furnishing the emotional atmosphere which contributed much to the success of Moody and other evangelists, and breathing the breath of life into the social meetings of the churches. Judged by standards of art they are decidedly inferior, but the masses could understand and sing them, and their melody, martial note, joyousness, and hope produced the religious exhilaration desired.

Philip Bliss was a tall, well-framed man, with clustering black hair, full beard, easy manners, buoyant spirit, and gifted with a rich baritone voice of wide range. Grandfather and great-grandfather had been Seventh Day Adventist preachers. The most of his youth was spent in Pennsylvania, where in a log house in Clearfield County he was born to Isaac and Lydia (Doolittle) Bliss. Until he was sixteen he worked on farm and in lumber camp, but got enough learning here and there to enable him to teach in schools in New York and Pennsylvania. At J. G. Towner's singing school in Towanda, Pa., and at the normal academy of music in Geneseo, N. Y., he received a little training in music. On June 1, 1859, he married Lucy J. Young, one of a family of singers.

He began his professional career by teaching music in Bradford County, Pa., at two dollars an evening and his board. Acquaintance with the composer and publisher, George F. Root [*q.v.*], led to his association with the firm of Root and Cady of Chicago sometime about 1865, and for nearly ten years he traveled over Illinois conducting musical conventions and giving concerts. He became chorister of the First Congregational Church, Chicago, superintendent of its Sunday-school, and a frequent singer at religious gatherings. His song book, *The Charm* (1871), made him popular as a composer of Sunday-school music. This was followed by *The Song Tree* (1872), *The Sunshine* (1873), *The Joy* (1873). Dwight L. Moody and Maj. D. W. Whittle persuaded him to take up evangelistic work, and during 1874–75–76 he traveled through the West and South with the latter. In 1874, with Ira

Sankey, he brought out *Gospel Songs,* which contained "Hold the Fort," "Only an Armor Bearer," "Let the Lower Lights Be Burning," "Pull for the Shore," and other songs long unexcelled in popularity. Of the $60,000 profits he gave his share to charitable and evangelistic projects. The Ashtabula train disaster ended his career. Getting free from the wreck himself, he returned to his wife who was pinned down, and both were burned to death.

[J. H. Bliss, *Geneal. of the Bliss Family in Amer.* (1881); D. W. Whittle, *Memoirs of Philip P. Bliss* (1877); W. H. Daniels, *D. L. Moody and his Work* (1875); J. W. Hanson, *The Wonderful Life and Works of Dwight L. Moody* (1900).]

H. E. S.

BLISS, PORTER CORNELIUS (Dec. 28, 1838–Feb. 2, 1885), journalist, was the son of the Rev. Asher Bliss, for many years a missionary to the Indians, and of Cassandra (Hooker) Bliss. Born on the Cattaraugus Reservation of Senecas in New York, his chief interest in childhood was in observing the habits and life of the Indians. When a young man, he studied for a year at Yale and received the degree of B.A. at Hamilton. In 1860 he began his travels by a tour through Maine, New Brunswick, and Nova Scotia, in the service of several Boston societies, to investigate the condition of Indian tribes in that region. After fulfilling this commission in 1861, he went to Washington, hoping to secure a position in the Interior Department which would give him the opportunity to continue his studies of the Indians beyond the Mississippi. He failed to obtain more than a clerkship, but when Gen. James Watson Webb was made minister to Brazil in 1861, Bliss was appointed his private secretary. Gen. Webb surrendered his office in 1862. Bliss, instead of returning to the States, made a trip to Buenos Aires. Almost immediately he was commissioned by the Argentine Republic to explore the country known as the Grand Chaco, an immense desert inhabited by Indian tribes. He spent eight months in this service, acquainting himself with various Indian dialects and studying the antiquities of the country and the habits of the natives. The results of his explorations were published by the Argentine government and are standard works on the Indian tribes of the Grand Chaco. Then for a short time Bliss edited a monthly periodical in Buenos Aires called the *River Plate Magazine.* In 1866 he went to Paraguay and became private secretary to Charles A. Washburn, who was serving as United States minister. The same year President Lopez appointed Bliss to write a history of Paraguay. While this work was in progress, Lopez declared war against Brazil, Uruguay, and the Argentine Republic, and from this event the trouble of the young historian began. Knowing that he had come from Brazil the Paraguayans suspected him of hostility to Lopez. Soon the archives of the government were closed to him and he was told that his contract was ended and that he would not be paid for his work. At about this time, Washburn resigned his position as minister and with Bliss prepared to sail for the States. On their way to the boat, Bliss was seized by the police and thrown into prison. For three months he was subjected to severe torture in efforts to force him to admit a conspiracy against Lopez. He was finally released at the demand of the United States Government and returned to Washington, where he was made translator to the State Department. At his request, the committee on foreign affairs of the House investigated the charges made against him in Paraguay and declared them unfounded. In 1870 President Grant appointed Bliss secretary of the legation to Mexico, which position he held for four years. While there he found time to study and write on the history, geography, and condition of Mexico and on American enterprises in that republic. He became an active member of the Mexican Geographical and Statistical Society and was chairman of its committee on archeological explorations. Reports of the latter were published in the bulletin of the society. In 1874 Bliss went to New York City and became one of the editors of *Johnson's New Universal Cyclopædia*, taking charge of the biographical department. He contributed over 1,500 biographies to that publication. He also wrote for it articles on Sanskrit and Portuguese literature. When the *Cyclopædia* was completed in 1877, Bliss became editor of a literary periodical called the *Library Table,* which venture soon failed. In 1878 he wrote in collaboration with Dr. L. P. Brockett, a history of the Russo-Turkish War, entitled *The Conquest of Turkey*. It is a very detailed and carefully written history, including the causes of the war, and the principals that took part in it. During the same year Bliss became one of the editors of the *New York Herald* and in 1879 he again visited South America as correspondent for the *Herald*. The material he sent back to his paper contained many bits of forgotten lore and many pieces of quaint erudition. He was perhaps the best informed man of his time concerning the political situation of the South American countries. He returned to the United States and in 1881 went to Mexico on a gold-hunting expedition on his own responsibility and in behalf of some friends. After this trip he failed rapidly

in health and except for a few months, when he edited the *New Haven Morning News,* did no more active work. At the age of forty-seven he died, in New York City.

[The *N. Y. Herald,* Feb. 3, 1885, contains an obituary of Bliss. An interesting article dealing with his life and travels is found in the *N. Y. Times,* Jan. 5, 1885. *House Report No. 65,* 41 Cong., 2 Sess., gives a detailed account of his work and imprisonment in Paraguay; see also *Senate Exec. Doc. 5, Pt. 3,* 40 Cong., 3 Sess.]

M. S.

BLISS, WILLIAM DWIGHT PORTER (Aug. 20, 1856–Oct. 8, 1926), Christian Socialist, was the son of the missionaries, Edwin Elisha Bliss [*q.v.*] and Isabella Holmes (Porter) Bliss and was born in Constantinople, Turkey. He was educated in Robert College, Constantinople; Phillips Academy and Amherst College, Massachusetts, and the Hartford Theological Seminary, from the last-named of which he graduated in 1882. On June 30, 1884, he married Mary Pangalo, of Constantinople. As a Congregationalist he was for a time pastor of a church in Denver and later in South Natick, Mass. In 1886 he joined the Protestant Episcopal Church and for the years 1887–90 was the rector of Grace Church, South Boston. About this time he became deeply influenced by the Christian Socialist doctrines of Maurice and Kingsley, of which he continued an active exponent for the remainder of his life. In 1889 he organized the first Christian Socialist Society in the United States, and in the same year started a propagandist periodical, *The Dawn* (discontinued in 1896). In 1890 he founded the Church of the Carpenter, in Boston, of which for four years he was the rector. Other pastorates were at San Gabriel, Cal., 1898; Amityville, L. I., 1902–06, and West Orange, N. J., 1910–14.

His activities in social service covered a broad range. His lecture trips carried him to almost every state of the union. In 1887 he was the Labor party candidate for lieutenant-governor of Massachusetts; in 1894 national lecturer for the Christian Socialist Union and in 1899 president of the National Social Reform Union. From 1907 to 1909 he was an investigator for the United States Bureau of Labor and from 1909 to 1914 he was connected with Dr. Josiah Strong's American Institute of Social Service. His labors as writer, compiler, and editor were, when considered in the light of his other activities, prodigious. In 1891 he published collections of the social writings of Ruskin and Mill under the titles *The Communism of John Ruskin* and *Socialism, by John Stuart Mill,* and also an abridgment of Thorold Rogers's *Six Centuries of Work and Wages*. In 1895 he produced the

Handbook of Socialism, in 1897 the *Encyclopedia of Social Reform,* in 1906 (with W. H. Tolman) the third volume of *Social Progress, a Year Book,* and in 1908 a revised and greatly enlarged edition of the *Encyclopedia.* In collaboration with Dr. Strong he also produced *Studies in the Gospel of the Kingdom* and for a year (1895–96) edited a monthly periodical, *The American Fabian.* During the World War he was in charge of educational work among interned French and Belgian soldiers in Switzerland. From 1921 to 1925 he was rector of St. Martha's Church in New York City. Toward the end of his pastorate his health failed. He died, after a lingering illness, in St. Luke's Hospital, and his funeral was held in the Cathedral of St. John the Divine.

Bliss was an omnivorous reader and a tireless propagandist. Much of his editorial work, however, was too hurried to take first rank in scholarship. He was impatient to get things done; if the product was honest and a contribution to human welfare, it would do. He is best remembered for his moral force, his passion for justice, his crystalline sincerity and perfect disinterestedness. He believed what he professed; he was a missionary who carried his religion into the workaday world. Unaggressive, but persistent, he preached his gospel of social salvation to all who would listen or read, and did it with a sheer disregard of personal consequences. He died a poor man.

[*Who's Who in America,* 1926–27; obituaries in the *N. Y. Times* and the *N. Y. Herald Tribune,* Oct. 9, 1926; personal recollections of the writer.] W. J. G.

BLITZ, ANTONIO (June 21, 1810–Jan. 28, 1877), magician, is said to have been born in Kent, England, though his autobiographical *Fifty Years in the Magic Circle* (1871) mentions his seeing "white cliffs across the water" and his traveling to England from his birthplace. In this same work he tells of picking up tricks from passing gypsies, and of astonishing the countryside with them to such an extent that his father sent him out with a servant to make a fortune with his entertainment when he was thirteen years old. His first professional appearance was in Hamburg in 1823 and he was exhibited in central and western Europe for two years. Shortly after his return his mother died and he left home thereafter alone. His performances were often viewed with alarm by the superstitious country people, particularly as he was fond of playing practical jokes on the people wherever he happened to be. He had become a ventriloquist by this time and the ignorant were quite sure that the devil accompanied him. He married a Breton woman, whose first name was

Marie, and in the following year the first of their several children was born. In 1834 he came to New York, appearing at the Masonic Hall and at Niblo's Garden with much success. He toured the States, the West Indies, Canada, and finally had a long engagement in Philadelphia, where he resided thenceforward. He was a genial little man with a fringe of whiskers, and not at all the type of the traditional magician, but he was very popular as is proved by the fact that he had thirteen imitators who even took his name with little alteration. He was also a bird-trainer and his combination of sleight-of-hand, ventriloquism, and bird tricks gave a program that was varied enough to avoid monotony. He appeared for a long time in Philadelphia at one of the museums established in imitation of Barnum's. Having made a moderate fortune he gave much time to performances for charity. His autobiography is devoted entirely to personal anecdotes and is of no literary value.

[Antonio Blitz, *Fifty Years in the Magic Circle* (1871); H. R. Evans, *The Old and the New Magic* (1906)—somewhat inaccurate; J. W. Forney, "Anecdotes of Public Men" in *Washington Sunday Chronicle,* Jan. 19, 1873, reprinted in the *Press* (Phila.), Jan. 20, 1873; obituary in *Phila. Inquirer,* Jan. 29, 1877.]

K. H. A.

BLOCK, ADRIAEN (fl. 1610–1624), Dutch mariner and explorer, first emerges from complete obscurity about 1610, when he made a voyage to the Hudson River, in company with Hendrick Christiaensen. In the spring of 1614 he was placed in command of one of a fleet of five sail sent out by the merchants of Amsterdam and Hoorn. The fleet ascended the Hudson River, where Block's vessel was accidentally burned. probably near the site of Albany. He then constructed the *Onrust,* a yacht forty-four and one-half feet long, in which he explored the region to the east of New York Bay. He sailed through the "Hellegat," so named by him, into Long Island Sound, explored "Roodeberg" (New Haven Harbor), and the "Versche Rivier" (the Connecticut), as far as an Indian village near the site of Windsor, Conn. He explored the island which bears his name, calling it "Adrianbloxeyland," although it was probably discovered in 1524 by Verrazano, who compared a "triangular shaped island" in this region to the Isle of Rhodes. Proceeding across Buzzards Bay and around Cape Cod, which he named Cape Bevechier, Block then explored "Wyck" (Massachusetts Bay) as far north as "Pye Bay," 42° 30', which corresponds to Nahant Bay. Having exchanged vessels with Christiaensen he returned to Holland. The first detailed map of the southern New England coast, the "Figurative Map" of 1616, which became the basis of trading privileges to "New Netherland," was drawn as far as Cape Ann from data furnished by Block (thence northward being probably modeled after Champlain's map of 1607, or a common original). Block probably did not return to America. Early in 1615, in command of a whaling fleet, he sailed for Spitzbergen, and in December 1624 was still engaged in that industry.

[Our knowledge of Block's voyages is largely derived from Johan de Laet's *Nieuwe Wereldt* (1625) and N. J. van Wassenaer's *Historisch Verhael* (1624–1625). Translations of the pertinent parts of these works will be found in *N. Y. Hist. Soc. Coll.*, 2 ser., vols. I, II; E. B. O'Callaghan, *Doc. Hist. of the State of N. Y.*, vol. III (1850); and J. Franklin Jameson, *Narratives of New Netherlands* (1909). J. R. Brodhead, *Hist. of the State of N. Y.*, vol. I (1853), is the principal secondary authority. The Figurative Map is reproduced in Brodhead, *Docs. Rel. to the Col. Hist. of the State of N. Y.*, vol. I. A model of the *Onrust* may be seen in Congress Hall, Philadelphia.] R.H.

BLODGET, LORIN (May 25, 1823–Mar. 24, 1901), statistician, climatologist, publicist, was descended from Thomas Blodget, merchant, of London, England, who was one of the first sworn as freemen at the founding of Boston, 1632. His grandfather was a soldier in the Revolutionary War (American side), and his father served in the War of 1812. His parents, Arba Blodget (1789–1838) and Bebe (Bullock) Blodget, lived on a farm near Jamestown, N. Y. He was educated at the Jamestown, N. Y., Academy and at Geneva (now Hobart) College, but did not graduate, having to leave college because of his father's death. When a youth of but seventeen, he taught a country school in Chautauqua County, N. Y. He early developed an active interest in politics and in 1848 took the stump as a Whig against the nomination of Taylor for president, and was a delegate to the convention that nominated Van Buren. When about twenty years of age he became one of the voluntary meteorological observers of the Smithsonian Institution; and in 1851 was appointed "assistant professor" at the Institution, in charge of researches on climatology. In this capacity he prepared, and in 1857 published, his *Climatology of the United States,* a quarto of 536 pages, in which there are full comparisons of the climate of this country with those of Europe and Asia at the same latitudes. It was based on all the appropriate meteorological data that he could obtain; *viz.,* those which for years had accumulated in the Surgeon General's Office, those gathered by the Smithsonian Institution, and many furnished by individuals in various parts of the country. This first work of importance on the climatology of any portion of America was so carefully and thoroughly done that the subsequent myriads of observations have essentially but confirmed Blodget's major conclusions.

During 1852–56 he was employed on the Pacific Railroad survey for the War Department, and directed the determinations of altitudes and gradients by the use of the barometer. The latter portion of this time he was in the War Office to which he had been transferred. From 1857 to 1864 he was associate editor of the *North American* of Philadelphia, and wrote for it numerous editorials; and from 1858 to 1865 secretary of the Philadelphia Board of Trade. He originated the Bounty Fund of Philadelphia during the Civil War, raised $530,000, and was secretary of the Fund. In 1863 he was placed in charge of the financial and statistical reports of the United States Treasury; and in the following year published his *Commercial and Financial Resources of the United States.* From 1865 to 1877 he was United States appraiser of merchandise, appointed by Lincoln, and residing in Philadelphia. He prepared tariff acts and bills, and wrote reports on finance, revenue, industrial progress, and censuses of industry, which fill some 150 volumes and 350 pamphlets. In addition to his other and varied interests, he took an active part in the meetings and deliberations of several scientific societies, especially the American Association for the Advancement of Science and the American Philosophical Society, of which he was a member. In 1856 he married Mary Elizabeth Gibbs of Alexandria, Va.

[*Who's Who in America,* 1899–1900; *Phila. Inquirer,* Mar. 24, 25, 1901; *Public Ledger* (Phila.), Mar. 25, 1901; information from Mrs. John Molitor, Germantown, Philadelphia, Pa.] W.J.H.

BLODGET, SAMUEL (Apr. 1, 1724–Sept. 1, 1807), merchant, manufacturer, canal builder, was born in Woburn, Mass., the son of Caleb and Sarah (Weyman) Blodget. Caleb was an innholder, moderator of "proprietor's meetings," and the promoter of the first stage line between Haverhill and Boston. Very little is known of the early life of Samuel though his subsequent attainments indicate that he received the limit of the education then available. He served in the French and Indian Wars and was at Louisburg in 1745. He then bought and worked a farm in Goffstown for a short time before returning to the army as sutler to the New Hampshire Regiment, seeing action at Fort William Henry (1757). Shortly after this he successfully engaged in general merchandising in Boston, later manufacturing potash and pearl-ash, which part of his business he extended to Hempstead, Goffstown, New Boston, and other places, with his main establishment at Haverhill (1760).

In these places he continuously expanded his activities, establishing stores for his employees, purchasing lands and timber, and erecting sawmills. His lumber was sold in Haverhill and Newbury and his potash and furs in London where he had profitable business arrangements with Sir William Baker. In 1769 he moved with his family from Boston to Goffstown to be more conveniently located for business. Here he was prominent in the community and was given the first appointment of justice of the inferior court for the County of Hillsborough. About this time he began to consider the construction of a canal around the Amoskeag Falls of the Merrimac, to more conveniently connect his timber lands with the markets. But then the Revolutionary cause attracted him and in 1775 he joined Gen. Sullivan's Brigade as a sutler, remaining with it until the army left Boston when he returned to his farm. During the latter part of the war he developed a device for raising sunken ships, in the operation of which he spent four years in Europe with very little success. Returning to Amoskeag and his plans for the canal, he commenced actual construction on May 2, 1794. The work progressed rapidly to the point of the building of the locks, for which Blodget had an original design, but here he met repeated failure and in 1780 an unusually high freshet carried off the locks and ruined the work of five years, with a personal loss to Blodget of $20,000. In 1798 he had obtained a charter and now after agreeing to adopt a proven type of lock he was able to sell stock to raise funds. He then appealed to the legislature of New Hampshire and was authorized to raise $9,000 by lottery, but after expending $12,000 and failing to complete the canal he received another lottery grant of $12,000, with the managers of which he became involved in such a legal tangle that the project would have failed had not the Massachusetts legislature now aided him with lottery grants in that state. The locks were completed in December 1806, and the canal was officially opened on "May Day," 1807, to render valuable service to the community until supplanted by the railroad many years later (1842). Blodget married Hannah White of Haverhill in 1748. He died Sept. 1, 1807, at Derryfield, Mass.

[Isaac D. Blodgett, *Asahel Blodgett, his Am. Ancestors and his Descendants* (1906) ; G. W. Chase, *Hist. of Haverhill, Mass.* (1861) ; C. E. Potter, *Hist. of Manchester, N. H.* (1856) ; *Manchester Hist. Soc. Colls.*, I, 121–76.]

F.A.T—r.

BLODGET, SAMUEL (Aug. 28, 1757–Apr. 11, 1814), merchant, economist, architect, was born in Goffstown, N. H., the son of Samuel [*q.v.*] and Hannah (White) Blodget. The character of his father, a man of long business experience and much imagination, seems to have been reflected in that of the son. The latter served in the Revolution, as a captain of New Hampshire militia, resigning Dec. 22, 1777. He then engaged in business in Exeter, N. H., and, this proving unsuccessful, went into the East India trade in Boston, acquiring a fortune. In 1789 he removed to Philadelphia where in 1792 he became one of the directors of the Insurance Company of North America. This same year he married Rebecca Smith, the daughter of the Rev. William Smith, provost of the University of Pennsylvania. She was a notable beauty and wit, whose irrepressible remarks on her husband's "comical look" are borne out by his portrait in the office of the Superintendent of the Capitol at Washington.

Although not a professional architect, he designed the building of the first Bank of the United States in Philadelphia, still standing after having been occupied for a century by Girard's Bank. It was the first important building in America to be executed in marble, and was occupied in 1794. The design was taken from that of the Exchange in Dublin, a work of Thomas Cooley. Blodget may have known this through Malton's engraving, which had just appeared, or he may have seen the original, since he had more than once visited Europe. Of the Bank of the United States, B. H. Latrobe, though criticizing both the prototype and the execution of Blodget's design, admits that the columns have a very beautiful appearance (*Journal of Latrobe*, p. 84), and commends it as "a bold proof of the spirit of the citizens who erected it, and of the tendency of the community to *force* rather than *retard* the advancement of the arts" (*Anniversary Oration before the Society of Artists in Philadelphia,* May 8, 1811).

In 1792 Blodget began to be interested in the new Federal City. He commenced to buy Washington real estate in 1792 and from that date became very actively engaged in the promotion of its realty developments, the erection of public buildings, and the founding of a national university at the new capital, which he was the first to suggest. His time was completely engrossed in the interests of Washington. During a visit to Boston for the purpose of floating a loan to secure money for the erection of federal buildings Blodget prepared a competitive design for the Capitol, with a tall dome and four Corinthian porticoes modeled on those of the Maison Carrée. This was sent to the Commissioners of the Federal City in Philadelphia on July 1, 1792 (War

Department, Office of Public Buildings and Grounds, *Letters to Commissioners,* II, III). Although it arrived after July 15, the date of the closing of the competition, the design was considered at the Commissioners' meeting of August 27. In presenting this plan Blodget asked that it be considered only as a study. The Commissioners invited him to submit complete drawings, sending for his use a statement of some changes in requirements. Blodget seems, however, not to have availed himself of this opportunity for there is no mention of a second design. No example of his draughtsmanship remains, his first study having doubtless been returned to him. Another design for the city of Washington was that for a bridge over the Eastern Branch submitted to the Commissioners Nov. 27, 1795 (Department of State, *District of Columbia Papers,* II, 107). The record of its reception makes no comment on the features of the plan nor is there any further mention to show whether or not it was the one executed in 1804 (W. B. Bryan, *A History of the National Capital,* 1914, I, 427). On February 10, 1797, Blodget wrote the Commissioners of his success in executing an amphitheatre 249 feet in circumference on the scheme of the Halle aux Blés in Paris, and undertook to submit a model, with a view to the construction of the proposed dome for the Conference Room of the Capitol (Office of Public Buildings and Grounds, *Letters Received,* II, 1060). His efforts in design and his endeavors to erect numerous houses and a hotel were all a part of Blodget's sustained effort toward the development of Washington. In the year 1793 he held official position as "Superintendent of the Buildings," the active representative of the Commissioners. The office, however, was allowed to expire with the end of Blodget's term of one year.

In promoting the sale of Washington real estate Blodget's resort to lotteries, though they were at first sanctioned by the authorities, finally brought him into discredit. Moreover, the failure of both lotteries brought Blodget's financial ruin, since he had put up his property as security for the payment of the prizes. It is of interest to note that the principal prize of the first lottery was to be a hotel to cost $50,000. The plans for this building, known as Blodget's Hotel, were prepared by James Hoban, the architect of the President's House, and the structure was in part completed by Blodget. The prizes for the second lottery were houses to be erected in the city, the best one to cost $30,000. It was further proposed that such funds as were left after the payment of these prizes should go toward the founding of the national university. Although Blodget's schemes were economically unsound and impractical there is no evidence that he acted in bad faith, and the fact of his complete financial downfall attests the sincerity of his belief in the lotteries and other ventures. Even while imprisoned for debt he solicited funds for the national university, and upon his release after a short period this project seems to have been his principal interest. At his death he left a fund of $7,000 collected for this purpose. A general likeness is apparent between the fate of Blodget and that of Robert Morris and other too sanguine investors of the time. So completely did he finally drop out of public affairs that his death in a Baltimore hospital in 1814 received no notice in the Washington papers.

[The principal events of Blodget's career are documented in W. B. Bryan's *Hist. of the National Capital,* I (1914). His connection with the Bank of the United States is traced by J. T. Scharf and T. Westcott, *Hist. of Phila.* (1884), II, 1068; with the Capitol, by F. Kimball and W. Bennett in the *Jour. of the Am. Institute of Architects,* Jan., Mar. 1919, as well as by G. Brown, *Hist. of the U. S. Capitol* (1900). Some letters regarding him are printed in *Records of the Columbia Hist. Soc.,* XVII (1914). Details of his land speculations may be gleaned from the *Pa. Archives,* ser. III, vols. XXIV–XXV. His own published writings include two volumes on economics, *Thoughts on the Increasing Wealth and National Economy of the U. S.* (1801) and *Economica: a Statistical Manual for the U. S.* (1806), the latter including personal reminiscences and apologetics.]

W. B—t.

BLODGETT, BENJAMIN COLMAN (Mar. 12, 1838–Sept. 22, 1925), pianist, organist, music-teacher, composer, was born in Boston, Mass., the son of Henry and Louise (Allen) Blodgett. His first musical instruction was received from James Hooton, pianist, and W. R. Babcock, organist. At the age of twelve he became organist of the Essex Street Congregational Church, and three years later of the Eliot Church in Newton. In 1858 he went to Leipzig, where three years were spent in study with Moscheles, Plaidy, Richter, and Hauptmann. Then he returned to Boston, became organist of the Park Street Church, and was active as a teacher and concert pianist. He was married on Mar. 5, 1862, to Alethea E. Pulsifer of Newton, Mass. His work from 1865 as teacher of music at Maplewood Institute, Pittsfield, Mass., led to the organization of a separate music school in 1870, under Blodgett's direction. He became director of music and teacher of piano playing at Smith College, Northampton, Mass., in 1878, and two years later assumed the direction of the School of Music affiliated with the College. He remained in this position for twenty-five years until 1903. In 1904 he went to Leland Stanford University, Palo Alto, Cal., as organist and director of the choir, with a daily organ recital in the chapel as a part of his duties. The destruction of the chapel by the earthquake of April

1906 interrupted this series, and shortly afterward Blodgett retired from active musical work. His last years were spent with his family in Seattle, Wash.

The educational work done by Blodgett at Northampton was advanced and noteworthy. He gave frequent lecture-recitals, displaying marked powers as a pianist and ability in speaking. His organ playing was distinguished by an unusual talent for improvisation. A personal friend of Wagner, Blodgett attended the first performance at Bayreuth in 1876, and the first performance of *Parsifal* in 1882. His published compositions include études for the piano, church music, and a cantata, "The Prodigal Son" (1895). The unpublished works are headed by an oratorio on the Book of Job, written for women's voices for the Smith College commencement of 1889, and revised the following year (both versions with full orchestra).

[Sketch compiled chiefly from information supplied by friends and associates of Blodgett. Some personal reminiscences appeared in *Musical America*, June 2, 1917, and a short obituary was published in *Music and Musicians* (1925).]

C.N.B.

BLODGETT, HENRY WILLIAMS (July 21, 1821–Feb. 9, 1905), lawyer, was of English ancestry, the paternal family having been founded in Massachusetts in 1630. He was born at Amherst, Mass. His father, Israel Porter Blodgett, was a blacksmith; his mother, Avis (Dodge) Blodgett, is said to have been a woman of exceptional qualities and education. In 1831 the family removed to Illinois. His father was an abolitionist, whose house was a station on the underground railroad for escaped slaves. Many of his father's patrons were Indians, and many of his own early playmates were Indian boys. He was educated in the common schools, spending also one year in Amherst Academy. Thereafter he taught school, and finally in 1842 began the study of law. After his admission to the bar in 1844 he removed to Waukegan, Ill., which thenceforth remained his home. He was a delegate in 1848 to the Free-Soil Democratic convention which nominated Martin Van Buren; was the Free-Soil candidate for Congress from his district in 1850; was elected in 1852 as an anti-slavery man (the first ever so elected) to the Illinois state legislature; and helped to organize the Republican Party in the state. He remained a member of it from its beginning. From 1852 to 1854 he was a member of the Illinois House of Representatives, and from 1859 to 1863 a member of the state Senate. To him was largely due legislation giving married women independence in the control of their property. He was constantly in the front

line of anti-slavery agitation in the decade before the Civil War. In 1860 he was a delegate to the Republican national convention that nominated Lincoln. After this early dip into politics the law absorbed all his interest. He was associated, in particular, with the legal departments of several railroads, and of one, which became the important Chicago & Northwestern, he was the main promoter, attorney, director, and president. In 1869 he was appointed United States district judge for the northern district of Illinois, and in 1891 was chosen as one member of the newly established circuit court of appeals, seventh circuit. It seems probable that the allowance of priority to receivers' certificates over a railroad first mortgage originated with him (being derived from admiralty doctrine), though it was a fellow judge who first so held. Among the famous cases that came before him as a federal judge were the Whiskey Ring cases of 1876. He resigned his judicial offices in 1892 to act as one of the counsel for this country in the Bering Sea arbitration, an appointment amply justified by his great reputation as an admiralty lawyer. One unfortunate episode marked his judicial career. In 1877, upon the initiative of certain individual members of the Chicago Bar Association, inquiries were made by a Congressional committee in contemplation of his impeachment. They found that the Judge had borrowed money from his referees (though not out of the funds of bankrupt estates in their hands) but had repaid it all with interest; other charges were found unsupported. The committee acquitted him of dishonest intent and did not impeach him (*House Report No. 142* and *House Miscellaneous Document No. 22*, 45 Cong., 3 Sess.).

Blodgett was a truly distinguished lawyer. In common law, equity, criminal, patent, bankruptcy, and admiralty law he was equally a master. He had a keen logical, acutely analytical mind, great experience in large business problems, unusual insight into men, sound judgment in both law and practical affairs. To these ideal judicial qualities he added patient industry in research and an encyclopedic memory. His face was strong and commanding. An injury to one of his legs gave him a peculiar and ungainly gait; possibly owing to the same injury he was irascible, and sometimes impatient with tyros. He was also characterized by some prejudices—including a dislike of stenographers. He took very voluminous notes of cases in his court, made up his record according to them and his memory, regardless of the records of these "nimble-fingered gentry," and by his notes determined bills of exceptions and certificates of evidence. Such faults were compensated for by his ability, learning, conscientiousness in studying his cases, and abhorrence of subterfuges and delays in procedure. On the whole he was a unique personality and a very great judge. In his home surroundings he was a charming companion, in whom humor and a natural dignity, unconscious and never assertive, were strong characteristics. He married (Apr. 29, 1850) Althea Crocker of Hamilton, N. Y., by whom he had five children, of whom three daughters lived to maturity. In religious views he was first a Congregationalist, and finally a Unitarian.

[John M. Palmer, *Bench and Bar of Illinois* (1899), I, 245; *Portrait and Biog. Album of Lake County, Ill.* (1891); *Chicago Legal News*, Feb. 11, 1905.]
F.S.P.

BLOEDE, GERTRUDE (Aug. 10, 1845–Aug. 14, 1905), poet, was born in Dresden, Germany, the daughter of Dr. Gustavus Bloede, a German Liberal, and his wife Marie, half-sister of the Silesian poet Friedrich von Sallet. Dr. Bloede, after imprisonment in Dresden during the Revolution of 1848, escaped to America with his family and settled in Brooklyn, N. Y., where he was for years editor of the *New-Yorker Demokrat*, a Republican daily. Gertrude was privately educated, was a natural student, and became a musician and a linguist of ability. She spoke English, French, and German fluently and read Latin, Italian, and Dutch without difficulty. The Bloede home was a center for literary gatherings, frequented by such men as Stoddard, Stedman, Aldrich, and Bayard Taylor. With these associations, Gertrude Bloede early began to try her hand at writing. Her first published work was in the form of verses contributed to magazines under the pseudonym Stuart Sterne. A volume of *Poems* appeared in 1875 and was favorably reviewed by Richard Grant White, critic of the *New York Times*, who also helped to find a publisher for the narrative poem *Angelo* (1878). Three other volumes of verse followed; *Giorgio* (1881), *Beyond the Shadow and Other Poems* (1888), and *Piero da Castiglione* (1890). A novel, *The Story of Two Lives* (1891), was Miss Bloede's only sustained prose writing. She lived at the time of her death with her sister, Mrs. Susan T. King of Greene Ave., Brooklyn. She died while on a summer sojourn at Baldwin, L. I. Her small, large-eyed, serious face showed her tense, nervous temperament. She shunned general society and steadily refused membership in women's clubs and participation in other women's activities of Brooklyn. She cared for the companionship only of intimate friends whose pursuits were, like her own, intellectual. She loved city life, not for its diversions, but because

she could find in it greater retirement than in the country. Her poetry shows much feeling but little inspiration; the form is stiff, lacking in musical quality, and often inadequate to the thought. Her narrative poems are introspective and emotional, but undramatic. *Angelo* has for its subject the friendship of Michelangelo and Vittoria Colonna and ends with the death of Vittoria. *Giorgio* tells the story of the painter Giorgione and his unhappy love. *Piero da Castiglione,* her most facile long poem, is a story of struggle between love and priestly vocation during the time of Savonarola. Her shorter poems are subjective reactions to beauty in the outside world, common human experiences, and religious theories, and are perhaps more adequate in form than the longer poems. Her novel, *The Story of Two Lives*, written chiefly in the form of a journal, is slow in action, devoid of characterization, and conventional in phrasing.

[The chief sources of information about Gertrude Bloede are *Who's Who in America*, 1903–05, and her own works, including the prefaces, which reveal much of her personality. A sketch of her life appeared in *Am. Women* (1897), ed. by Frances Willard and Mary A. Livermore. An obituary notice was published in the *Brooklyn Daily Eagle*, Aug. 16, 1905.]
S.G.B.

BLOOD, BENJAMIN PAUL (Nov. 21, 1832–Jan. 15, 1919), philosopher, mystic, and poet, was descended on his father's side from Jeremiah Blood, an Irish emigrant of the middle of the eighteenth century. Jeremiah's son Robert was a thrifty farmer who acquired large holdings in Schenectady and Montgomery counties, N. Y.; he married Mary Simons (Simmons), by whom he had nineteen children, one of whom, John, was the father, by Mary Stanton, of Benjamin Paul Blood. On his mother's side the latter was descended from John Howland, the *Mayflower* Pilgrim. He was born and brought up in the town of Amsterdam, N. Y.; he attended the local schools of Amsterdam, Amsterdam Academy, and, for a time, Union College; in due course he inherited a farm which had been in the family for one hundred and thirty years. He was twice married: first to Mary E. Sayles, who died in 1873; and second to Harriet A. Lefferts. His long life, passed in and near his birth-place, was almost devoid of outward incident. Too self-sufficient to feel the need of travel, incurious as to the details of the world, he found in his inner life and in his reading of poetry and philosophy material for sufficiently rich experience. His career as an author began early. Before he was twenty-one he had completed *The Bride of the Iconoclast* (not published until 1854), a long Shelleyesque poem in Spenserian stanzas, and *The Philosophy of Justice* (1851), the writing of which converted

him, temporarily, from atheism to a very unorthodox Christianity. These works show an astonishingly precocious subtlety of thought and mastery
of style in both prose and verse. Blood had already elaborated a definite theory as to the relation of sound to sense, somewhat similar to the
theories of Plato, Swedenborg, and Burns (see
his valuable "Suggestions Towards the Mechanical Art of Poetry" in *The Bride of the Iconoclast,* partially reprinted in *Pluriverse* as a supplementary essay on "The Poetical Alphabet").
Some unknown cause now intervened, however,
to inhibit Blood's productivity. At long intervals
there appeared from his pen, *Optimism* (1860),
an attempted theodicy, and *The Colonnades*
(1868), a philosophical epic in blank verse. For
the rest he contributed when the mood took him
an occasional letter to "such far-from reverberant
organs of publicity as the *Gazette* or the *Recorder*
of his native Amsterdam, or the *Utica Herald* or
the *Albany Times*" (William James, "A Plural-
istic Mystic," *Hibbert Journal,* VIII, 738). Had
it not been for his personal experience with anæsthetics (nitrous oxide), an experience first obtained prosaically in a dentist's chair and then repeated poetically and voluntarily during a period
of twenty-seven years, Blood might have remained all his life in contented obscurity. Impressed by the quasi-mystical state of philosophic
certainty and peace induced by anæsthetics, seemingly an attainment of consciousness of pure being, he printed in 1874 *The Anæsthetic Revelation and the Gist of Philosophy,* which he mailed
to numerous authors in this country and in Europe. As a result there ensued a remarkably
fruitful correspondence, notably with Hutchison
Stirling, Alfred Tennyson, and William James.
In 1889 several of Blood's earlier letters to newspapers appeared in a revised form as quasi-He-
gelian "Philosophic Reveries" in the *Journal of
Speculative Philosophy,* XX, 1–53. He steadily
moved, however, toward a more dynamic and plu-
ralistic philosophy which found its final expression in his intransigeant *Pluriverse* (published
posthumously in 1920). Horace Meyer Kallen,
who knew Blood personally, writes (letter to author), "At heart he was, I think, a monist always." In that case, Blood's intellect triumphed
strikingly over his emotions, for his critique of
monism in *Pluriverse* was ruthless. He was a
keener reasoner than either James or Bergson,
and, if he entered late into the ranks of the prag-
matists, he brought to them a much-needed dia-
lectical ability. Poetry seems to have tempted
him less in later years, although he contributed
from time to time a number of short poems to
Scribner's Magazine (December 1888, July 1899,

March 1900, December 1901, January 1903,
March 1915, January 1919). His last acknowledged prose was an Introduction to the anonymous *A Capitalist's View of Socialism* (1916).
Old age did not break his serenity of spirit and he
could write "I am thankful at having seen the
show; and although, after eighty-five years, the
stars are flickering slightly, and the winds are
something worn, I am still clear and confident
in that religion of courage and content which
cherishes neither regrets nor anticipations" (*Pluriverse,* p. 245).

[The biographical material is singularly scanty. The
present sketch is chiefly based upon Horace Meyer Kallen's introduction to *Pluriverse* and upon information
supplied by Mr. Kallen and by Blood's daughter, Miss
Anna W. Blood of Amsterdam, N. Y.]   E.S.B.

BLOODWORTH, TIMOTHY (1736–Aug.
24, 1814), politician, was born in New Hanover
County, N. C., and died in Washington, N. C.
He had few social or educational advantages.
James and Thomas Bloodworth, politicians, are
mentioned as his brothers, but there is no further
record of his domestic relationships. He is reported to have adorned eight or ten occupations,
ranging, by way of the ministry, from cobbler
and wheelwright to United States Senator and
philanthropist at large. In January 1775 he was
a member of the New Hanover County Committee of Safety, and two years later he was one of
the eleven justices present at that county's first
non-royal court. As a state legislator, 1779–84,
he supported a relentless policy against all who
had remained loyal to England. In 1784 he was
elected to represent North Carolina in the Continental Congress in New York, but was given no
money for his expenses. This oversight did not
delay him, since at other times he had advanced
the state money out of his own pocket. He resigned from the Congress in August 1787 and returned to North Carolina to help dissuade the
state from ratifying the proposed Federal Constitution. His view was the popular one, but circumstances outside the state proved strong
enough to compel ratification. Locally he honored no such compulsion. As lieutenant-colonel
of the militia in the Wilmington district, he refused in 1793 to execute orders enforcing Washington's proclamation of neutrality in the war between France and England. He was intensely
radical, almost, said a North Carolina historian
writing of him in the 1870's, "a red Republican
in his views, and intolerant of opposition." At
the time, this attitude carried him to the United
States Senate, a haven which in 1789 he had
sought vainly. He was in the Senate Dec. 7,
1795–Mar. 3, 1801, but he evidently left no great
impression. That fervor, in fact, which was his

chief political merit, had never been conspicuous-ly operative in affairs of more than sectional in-terest. When he resigned his office in 1807 he had achieved something like venerableness, and he was settled off as collector of customs for the port of Wilmington. This place he filled placidly until he died. Almost all his life he stood against the main trend of history, and sixty years after his death even a newspaper editor in the North Carolina state capital was obliged to admit that he had never heard of him.

[The sources of this sketch are W. E. Dodd, "Timo-thy Bloodworth" in S. A. Ashe, *Biog. Hist. of N. C.* (1905); *Biog. Cong. Dir.* (1903); James Sprunt, *Chronicles of the Cape Fear River* (1916); A. M. Wad-dell, *Hist. of New Hanover County* (1909); J. H. Wheeler, *Reminiscences and Memoirs of N. C.* (1884).]
J.D.W.

BLOOMER, AMELIA JENKS (May 27, 1818–Dec. 30, 1894), reformer, was born in Ho-mer, Cortland County, N. Y., the daughter of Au-gustus Jenks who was killed at the battle of Get-tysburg. Her education was limited to a few terms at the district school. At seventeen she herself taught a short term. She then lived for several years with a married sister in Waterloo, N. Y. In 1837 she was governess and tutor of three small children in the family of Oren Cham-berlain near Waterloo. Three years later she was married to Dexter C. Bloomer, a young Quaker. Through the influence and encouragement of her husband who was much interested in current events, as editor and part owner of the weekly Whig newspaper, the *Seneca County Courier*, Mrs. Bloomer began to write unsigned articles for newspapers on the social, moral, and political questions of the time. At the first public meeting on woman's rights in 1848 in Seneca Falls, in which Lucretia Mott and Mrs. Stanton were ac-tive, she was an interested spectator. She took no part in it, however, and did not sign the resolu-tions or the declaration of independence. Her earliest activity as a reformer was in the temper-ance movement. In January 1849 she started the *Lily,* one of the first papers of its kind pub-lished by a woman. For six years she continued its publication, writing vigorous articles on edu-cation, on unjust marriage laws, and, later, on woman's suffrage. She was therefore one of the actual pioneers in the woman's rights movement. Mrs. Stanton became an early contributor, writ-ing over the name of "Sunflower." The sub-scribers increased in number from two or three hundred for the first issue to over 4,000 twice a month by 1853. From 1849 to 1853 Mrs. Bloomer entered a new field for women by becoming dep-uty to her husband who was postmaster of Seneca Falls. In 1850 the heading of her paper "pub-lished by a committee of ladies" was dropped and Mrs. Bloomer's name appeared alone as publisher and editor and a new heading "devoted to the interests of women" was substituted. But al-though throughout her life she devoted her ef-forts to temperance and woman's rights her name through newspaper publicity and ridicule is asso-ciated in the public mind with dress reform, which was actually first suggested by a conserva-tive rival paper. This was merely an episode in her life, though perhaps an important one. After the ridicule began she continued to carry out the idea in practise until after a period of six or eight years the matter was dropped by the papers. The circulation of the *Lily* was much increased by the notoriety given her. Because of the dress she wore—an ordinary bodice, short skirt, and full trousers, later called "bloomers"—large crowds came out to hear her speak in New York City and other towns in New York State where she talked in 1853, together with Susan B. Anthony, the Rev. Antoinette L. Brown, and other leaders in the woman's movement. Horace Greeley sat on the platform at one of her talks and she was fa-vorably reported in the *Tribune.* In this year, the Bloomers left Seneca Falls for Mt. Vernon, Ohio, where they lived for a year while Mr. Bloomer edited and was part owner of the *Western Home Visitor.* A year later they moved to Council Bluffs, Ia., which was their home until Mrs. Bloomer's death. The *Lily* was now sold, as Council Bluffs was too far from a railroad to make mailing it practicable, but Mrs. Bloomer kept up her interest throughout her life in the various questions it had advocated. She wrote and lectured and her home was always open to all friends of reform.

[D. C. Bloomer, *Life and Writings of Amelia Bloom-er* (1895); Elizabeth Cady Stanton, *et al., Hist. of Wo-man Suffrage,* vol. I (1881), vol. II (1887); *Bloomer-ism, or the New Female Costume of 1851* (1851); *Ia. State Reg.* (Des Moines), Jan. 1, 1895.] M.A.K.

BLOOMFIELD, JOSEPH (Oct. 18, 1753–Oct. 3, 1823), lawyer, soldier, was descended from Thomas Bloomfield, major in Cromwell's army, who emigrated from Woodbridge, on the river Deben in Suffolk, by way of Massachusetts to Woodbridge on Woodbridge Creek, Middlesex County, N. J. His descendants were noted for public spirit and in 1796 certain rural settlements in Essex County, N. J., were named "Bloomfield" (now an apartment-house suburb of Newark) after his great-great-grandson (J. W. Dally, *Woodbridge and Vicinity,* 1873, p. 1). The latter was born in Woodbridge, his father being Dr. Moses Bloomfield, a founder of the New Jersey Medical Society and a member of the colonial assembly and of the provincial congress, who freed fourteen slaves on July 4, 1783, to prove his belief in the Declaration of Independence. Joseph's mother was Sarah (Ogden) Bloomfield. He was educated at the Rev. Enoch Green's Classical Academy in Deerfield Street, Cumberland County, whence he went to study law in the home and office of Cortlandt Skinner, the Colony's royalist attorney-general, at Perth Amboy. Admitted to the New Jersey bar Nov. 12, 1774, he prepared to practise law at Bridgeton but in 1775 was commissioned captain in Col. Elias Dayton's Regiment (later the 3rd New Jersey) and took part in the Quebec expedition but got no further than the Mohawk Valley. As Gen. Schuyler's guard officer he brought the Declaration of Independence to Fort Stanwix, he became major and judge advocate of the northern army, and he fought at Monmouth and at Brandywine where "he was wounded in the bridle arm." Resigning in 1778, he married on Dec. 17, Mary, daughter of Dr. William McIlvaine of Burlington and Philadelphia. She died in 1818 but his second wife, Isabella (family name unknown), survived him. There were no children.

Settling in Burlington, the old capital of West Jersey, in 1794 Bloomfield commanded an infantry brigade of New Jersey militia and took an active part in suppressing the Whiskey Rebellion without bloodshed. He was mayor of the town, 1795–1800, clerk of the state assembly for several years, register of the court of admiralty, and attorney-general of New Jersey, elected in 1783, re-elected in 1788, resigning in 1792 when he served as a presidential elector, opposing John Adams. Changing his politics to Jeffersonism, he was elected governor by the New Jersey legislature, 1801, over Richard Stockton. In 1802 a tie vote emptied the governor's chair, but Stockton withdrew after defeats in 1803 and 1804 so Bloomfield was returned unopposed until 1812. As governor he signed, 1804, the gradual emancipation act, amended 1846, which reduced the slave population of New Jersey from six per cent of the total in 1800 to eighteen individuals by 1860. He was a leader in the work of legal and gradual emancipation. The Bloomfield Compilation of New Jersey Laws, 1811, was named in his honor. As governor he was *ex officio* chancellor, but no record was made of his decisions though a few of his opinions were published much later. "A particular friend of Burr's," Bloomfield, as governor, requested the prosecutor of Bergen County to enter a *nolle prosequi* to the indictment of Aaron Burr for shooting Hamilton in their duel at Weehawken. This was done, as urged by leading Republicans, and Burr thus left free to preside at

the impeachment trial of Justice Samuel Chase of the United States Supreme Court. In 1812 President Madison appointed Bloomfield brigadier-general in the United States Army. He commanded the 3rd Military District, headquarters at New York, organized and trained new troops, marched to Plattsburgh with eight thousand men, and, later, put Philadelphia "in a complete state of defence," largely by his own energy and money (*True American*, Trenton, Oct. 11, 1823). He was twice elected to Congress, sitting from Mar. 4, 1817, to Mar. 4, 1821.

In manner Bloomfield was of the old school, wearing always the ruffles, powdered hair and cue of Washington's day. Neither war nor politics ruffled his benevolent, courteous, and sensible good nature. His portrait in major-general's uniform, by W. H. Griffin, in the governor's office at Trenton, is a pleasing contrast to the dourness of other New Jersey patriots. Accounts describe him as housed and served "in the style of a gentleman of fortune," but he disliked his official title "Your Excellency." Bruised by the upset of his gig while viewing lands near Cincinnati, Ohio, in 1823, he was badly bled by local doctors and died on reaching home.

[There is a good sketch of Bloomfield by L. Q. C. Elmer, son of his friend and subaltern officer Jonathan Elmer, in his "Reminiscences," *N. J. Hist. Soc. Colls.*, VII, 114–37; also interesting notes by Wm. Nelson, *Ibid.*, IX, 36–40.]   W.L.W—y.

BLOOMFIELD–ZEISLER, FANNIE. [See ZEISLER, FANNIE BLOOMFIELD, 1863–1927.]

BLOOMFIELD, MAURICE (Feb. 23, 1855–June 13, 1928), Orientalist and philologist, son of Solomon and Bertha (Jaeger) Bloomfield, was born in Bielitz, Austria, whence his parents came to the United States when he was four years old. They made their home first in Milwaukee and then in Chicago, where the boy's early schooling was received. At sixteen he entered the University of Chicago, remaining there for three years (1871–74), and finished his collegiate education at Furman University, Greenville, S. C. (1876–77), obtaining the degree of M.A. It appears that during these Greenville days the young man was influenced by the well-known Biblical scholar Crawford H. Toy to turn his attention to Oriental studies, and he became a graduate student at Yale University for the academic year 1877–78, specializing in Sanskrit and comparative philology under the renowned William Dwight Whitney. On completing this year of advanced work he was awarded a fellowship in the newly opened Johns Hopkins University at Baltimore, where Charles Rockwell Lanman, five years his senior and afterward distinguished as professor of Sanskrit at Harvard, became his preceptor. He received from Johns Hopkins the degree of Ph.D. in 1879, the title of his dissertation being "Noun-formation in the Rig-Veda." After two fruitful years in Germany (1879–81), where he studied at the universities of Berlin and Leipzig under the acknowledged masters of his day in the field of Indology and Indo-European philology, he was called back to the Johns Hopkins University, in 1881, as professor of Sanskrit and comparative philology, and entered upon his long scholarly career, rendered famous by his teaching, researches, and publications.

Bloomfield was not only eminently successful as a teacher but the number likewise of his published writings, always recognized for their excellence and originality, was particularly large. The combined list (referred to in the bibliography below) comprises nearly two-hundred entries of articles and reviews contributed to learned journals on subjects relating to the languages, literature, history, and religion of ancient India, as well as on comparative and historical grammar. His chief fame rests on his important volumes concerned with editing, translating, or interpreting the sacred texts of the Vedas. His great *Vedic Concordance* (1906), which was crowned by the Royal Academy of Bavaria with the Hardy Prize, will ever remain a standard work, and of like value and usefulness are the two volumes of *Rig-Veda Repetitions,* published in 1916. A compact and very suggestive book, entitled *The Religion of the Veda* (1908), presents in admirable form a series of lectures which he delivered that year in the course of American Lectures on the History of Religion. While constantly engaged in the study and interpretation of the Rig-Veda, he devoted himself likewise to the exposition of the Atharva-Veda, on which he became the foremost authority, editing the *Kauçika-Sutra of the Atharva-Veda* (1890), followed by a translation of "Hymns of the Atharva-Veda" (1897, in the *Sacred Books of the East,* vol. XLII) and by an elaborate monograph "The Atharva-Veda" (1899, in the *Grundriss der indo-arischen Philologie und Altertumskunde,* vol. II, part 1 B). In 1901 there appeared the chromo-photographic reproduction in three volumes of the unique Tübingen manuscript of the *Kashmirian Atharva-Veda,* which he edited in collaboration with the German scholar Richard Garbe. He also published, in the latter part of his life, a number of valuable monographs on the subject of Hindu fiction, particularly his book on the *Life and Stories of the Jaina Savior, Parçvanatha* (1919). As a philologist, moreover, Bloomfield was particularly attracted by comparative

grammar, one of his many suggestive monographs being "On Adaptation of Suffixes in Congeneric Classes of Substantives" (published in the *Journal of American Philology,* 1891, XII, 1–29). He took a lively linguistic interest in the discoveries, made at the beginning of this century, of manuscript fragments among sand-buried ruins in Turkestan, Central Asia, which brought to light languages that were hitherto practically unknown, and later in the problem of the "Hittite" languages, evoked by remarkable finds of cuneiform tablets in Asia Minor, which captivated his fancy and inspired his pen. The high quality of his work throughout was recognized by universities at home and abroad through the bestowal of honorary degrees. He was a member of many learned societies and academies both in Europe and America, and was especially active in the American Oriental Society, serving as a director 1884–1928, a vice-president in 1906 and again later, and president 1910–11. He was a foundation member of the Linguistic Society of America in 1925, and its second president (1926), though ill health prevented him from taking the chair.

Bloomfield never lost his youthful enthusiasm, which he imparted to a large number of students, many of whom have since won distinction. His style of lecturing, like his writing, was clear and precise, and his manner of expression, which was unique in its way, was lightened by a subtle sense of humor that was sometimes tinged with a touch of irony. His capacity for work was remarkable, but he knew also how to play, finding recreation in social intercourse, music, novels, and walking. He was a distinctly human scholar and was very devoted in his home life. He was twice married, his first wife being Rosa Zeisler, of Vienna, whom he married on June 20, 1885, and who died on June 20, 1920, leaving a son and a daughter. On July 9, 1921, he married Helen Townsend Scott of Baltimore, who had been one of his graduate students in Sanskrit, and who survives him. His sister Fannie Bloomfield Zeisler [q.v.], a celebrated pianist, two years his junior, died in 1927. He himself retired from active service at the University in 1926 and became professor emeritus, having suffered from heart trouble during the preceding year. In 1927 he moved to San Francisco, where his son, Dr. Arthur Bloomfield, was head of the Leland Stanford Hospital. In that city he continued to lead quietly his normal life, keeping up research work, enjoying the theatre and social diversion, interested in new acquaintances and in all that the city offered. His death occurred, after a brief illness, on June 13, 1928.

[A biographical sketch, with a bibliography of his writings up to 1920, is prefixed to a volume of *Studies in Honor of Maurice Bloomfield by a Group of his Pupils*, New Haven (1920); consult later the obituary article in *Language*, IV, 214–17, and that by F. Edgerton in *Jour. of the Am. Oriental Soc.*, XLVIII, 193–99; compare also *Who's Who in America*, 1926–27. Some data were kindly furnished by Mrs. Bloomfield, supplemented by the present writer's memory of a long and cherished friendship with Bloomfield.]

A. V. W. J.

BLOOMGARDEN, SOLOMON (Mar. 1870–Jan. 10, 1927), writer, who was to enrich New York's East Side with his personality, his writings, and his philosophy, under his pen-name of Yehoash, was born in the town of Wertzblowo in Lithuania. He was the son of Caleb Bloomgarden, a Talmudic scholar, and his wife, Dobre-Chave. The poetry and scholarship of the Talmud which his father taught him to read and interpret were exactly the right basis for the development of his literary talent. Whatever else his mind needed of the world's intellectual wealth he chose himself and became not only a deep student of the literature of Jewish life and history, but a master of the great literature of the world and of languages as separate as Arabic, Russian, German, and English. In 1890 he came to America where he was obliged to end a brief business career and to retire to Denver on account of illness. But soon he was back in New York. From his earliest youth he wrote poetry and to the last day of his life he was an indefatigable, even a feverish, worker at varied forms of literary expression. Poems, essays, special articles, poured from his pen. For a short time, as a young man, he wrote in Hebrew and even in English, but the great portion of his work, all that best represents him, is in Yiddish. Besides his verse and his essays it includes translations of such works as *The Song of Hiawatha* from the English (1910), the *Sayings of the Fathers* (*Pirke Aboth*) from the Hebrew (1912), and the compilation of the *Yiddish Dictionary Containing all the Hebrew and Chaldaic Elements of the Yiddish Language* (1911), in collaboration with Dr. Charles D. Spivak. His greatest work was the translation of the Jewish Bible into Yiddish. A large part of this was published serially in a New York journal (the *Day*), to which he was a frequent contributor. Since his death the task has been completed and the Bible is being published in its entirety and with Bloomgarden's valuable commentaries by the Yehoash Publishing Company, New York. Only a few stray works of Bloomgarden's are available in English, *The Feet of the Messenger,* a translation by Isaac Goldberg (published by the Jewish Publication Society, 1923) of the book which Yehoash made as a record of his stay in Pales-

tine, cut short by the war; also "The Shunamite," translated by Henry T. Schnittkind and published (1925) in Frank Shay's collection, *Twenty-Five Short Plays, International.*

In August 1904 Bloomgarden married Flora Smirnow. They had one daughter, Evelyn.

[All of the Jewish newspapers published interesting accounts of Yehoash and his work at the time of his death. One of the best accounts in English is "The Passing of Yehoash," by Elbert Aidline Trommer, in the *Jewish Tribune* of Jan. 14, 1927. There is an extended criticism and appreciation by Charles Madison in *Poet Lore*, XXXVII, 537–50.]

E. J. R. I.

BLOUNT, JAMES HENDERSON (Sept. 12, 1837–Mar. 8, 1903), lawyer, congressman, diplomatic envoy, will be remembered chiefly as that special commissioner of President Cleveland to Hawaii, whose report largely determined the policy against annexation. Born in Jones County, Ga., the son of Thomas and Mary (Ricketts) Blount, he was graduated from the University of Georgia in 1857, studied law, and was admitted to the Macon bar. During the Civil War he served in the Confederate army as a private in the Floyd Rifles until he was invalided home. On partial recovery he organized a company known as Blount's Cavalry, of which he was made colonel, but soon came the news of Appomattox. During the troubled period of Reconstruction he took an active part in maintaining order, and his powers of persuasion or command were often called upon to control the passions of threatening mobs. In 1872 he was elected to the federal House of Representatives from the sixth congressional district, and retained his seat by successive elections until 1893, when he declined further nomination. He had served prominently on the Appropriations and the Ways and Means committees, and as chairman of the Committee on Post Office and Post Roads and the Committee on Foreign Affairs. His experience and competence in the field of foreign relations led to his appointment in March 1893, shortly after his last term had expired, as a special commissioner to Hawaii with paramount authority to represent the United States Government and to investigate the details of the crisis in the affairs of the islands. This episode proved the most conspicuous distinction of Blount's career.

Since early in the century a large majority of the white residents of the islands had been of American birth, and had largely influenced or controlled the native government. As early as 1853 and 1854 and again in 1866 suggestions of annexation to the United States had been favorably entertained by the native rulers. In 1891 however Queen Liliuokalani ascended the throne and soon inaugurated a policy tending to strengthen native rule and increase the power of the crown. Opposition fostered by the American element finally led to the setting up of a provisional government, which on Jan. 17, 1893, declared the queen deposed. Sanford B. Dole, the Hawaiian-born son of American missionaries, was head of the provisional government. The American minister to Hawaii was John L. Stevens. John W. Foster had just succeeded James G. Blaine as secretary of state. On Jan. 16 at the request of Minister Stevens the captain of the United States cruiser *Boston,* which by chance or design had anchored at Honolulu shortly before, landed 300 marines. It is a matter of dispute whether Minister Stevens and the marines aided the provisional government in overpowering or overawing the unhappy queen. Secretary Foster elaborately says they did not (perhaps protesting too much). Blount, Cleveland, and Gresham more than imply they did. At any rate the queen under protest yielded to *force majeure* and appealed to the United States Government for justice. Dole despatched five commissioners to negotiate a treaty of annexation. They reached Washington on Feb. 3; the treaty was drafted and sent to the president on Feb. 14, and submitted to the Senate on Feb. 15, with an urgent recommendation of "prompt action" (Message of Feb. 15). Mar. 4 however found it still unratified, and Cleveland's first official act was to withdraw it and send Blount out to investigate. Meanwhile at the request of the provisional government Stevens had accepted the islands as a protectorate of the United States, and raised the American flag over the Government House.

Commissioner Blount promptly arrived at Honolulu and, convinced by his early investigations of the complicity of American interests in the revolution, he ordered the flag lowered and the marines withdrawn, putting an end to the protectorate. Stevens resigned and was recalled in May, and Blount was appointed minister in his place, remaining in Hawaii until August. On his return the report of his investigations was accepted by the President as decisive. On Dec. 18 Cleveland sent to Congress a message which contained the words:

"By an act of war, committed with the participation of a diplomatic representative of the United States, and without the authority of Congress, the government of a feeble but friendly and confiding people has been overthrown. A substantial wrong has been done, which . . . we should endeavor to repair . . . "

The report and the President's action were received by the country at large with conflicting sentiments, and not a little excited opposition was expressed. The high motives of the commissioner, however, remain unimpeached. His outstanding characteristic seems to have been unswerving integrity and devotion to duty. This was recognized in the remarkable tributes paid him by his colleagues of the House on the occasion of his retirement (*Congressional Record,* 52 Cong., 2 Sess., 1207–08).

In appearance Blount is described by his daughter as "of medium stature, florid complexion, a penetrating steel-gray eye before which falsehood or deceit trembled. His fine head of hair became snowy white very early in life, giving him distinction among the members of the House." He spent the last decade of his life in the practise of law in Macon and in the care of his country estate. He was married to Eugenia Wiley, daughter of Dr. Jack Barnett Wiley and Ann Clapton Wiley.

[The chief sources of information about the public life of Blount are the *Cong. Record,* 1873–93; Sec. Foster's letter to President Harrison, Feb. 15, 1893, *Sen. Ex. Doc.* 76, 52 Cong., 2 Sess.; Sec. Gresham's Report, *House Ex. Doc.* 47, 53 Cong., 2 Sess.; Blount's Hawaiian Reports, *House Ex. Docs.* 47, 48, 76, *Sen. Ex. Docs.* 13, 46, 53 Cong., 2 Sess. Personal information from his daughter, Mrs. Walter D. Lamar.]

J. H. T. M.

BLOUNT, THOMAS (May 10, 1759–Feb. 7, 1812), Revolutionary soldier, merchant, politician, was born in Edgecombe County, N. C., the son of Jacob and Barbara (Gray) Blount. At the age of seventeen he enlisted in the 5th Regiment, and added his name to the Revolutionary annals of North Carolina that already included his father and two brothers, Reading and William [*q.v.*]. Late in 1777 he was taken prisoner by the British, carried to England, and held until the close of the war (J. K. Turner and J. L. Bridgers, *History of Edgecombe County, N. C.,* 1920, p. 106). Returning to his native state he joined his brother, John Gray, who was engaged in foreign trade, and opened a branch store at Tarboro, Edgecombe County. In 1786 they were agents and trustees for the state in the Martinique debt settlement. A republican in politics, Thomas participated in the second North Carolina convention called to consider the ratification of the national Constitution, opposed James Iredell's federalist amendments, but voted for ratification without amendment. Elected to the lower house of the state legislature in 1789, he served on the commission to locate and plan the state capital, gave his name to Blount St., Raleigh, and in general made himself so useful that he was rewarded with a seat in Congress in 1793. From then until the time of his death in 1812 he served continuously, except for the intervals of the Sixth, Seventh, and Eleventh Congresses. His achievements as a national legislator were not conspicuous. He was an adroit politician of the old Revolutionary school, who "wined and dined" for political support, discussed horse-racing more than political issues, and defended his loyalty by answering George Thatcher's charge of Francophil sympathies with a challenge to a duel. He married Jacky Sullivan Sumner, daughter of the Revolutionary general, Jethro Sumner.

[*N. C. State Records,* XVII–XXIV ; *The Harris Letters,* ed. by H. M. Wagstaff (Jas. Sprunt Hist. Pub., vol. XIV, 1916) ; J. H. Wheeler, *Reminiscences and Memoirs of N. C.* (1884), pp. 130–131 ; *National Intelligencer* (Washington, D. C.), Feb. 11, 1812.]

T. D. M.

BLOUNT, WILLIAM (Mar. 26, 1749–Mar. 21, 1800), territorial governor of Tennessee, senator, was descended from Thomas Blount, son of Sir Walter Blount, who came to Virginia shortly after the restoration of Charles II and settled on Pamlico Sound in North Carolina. Jacob Blount, grandson of Thomas, married Barbara Gray in 1748, and the first born of their eight children was William. Of the latter's youth we know little save that, as his letters of a later period witness, he received a good education for that day. On Feb. 12, 1778, he married Mary Grainger, daughter of Col. Caleb Grainger of Wilmington, N. C. (Family records). In 1776 he entered the service of revolutionary North Carolina, was paymaster of various units of North Carolina's troops during the Revolution, and thereafter, for the remainder of his life, was almost continually in public office. Between 1780 and 1789 he was four times member, and once speaker, of the state's House of Commons, and twice a member of its Senate. In 1782–83 and again in 1786 and 1787 he served as a delegate to the Congress of the United States. He was also a member of the Convention of 1787 that framed the United States Constitution. In this convention, aged thirty-eight, he thus impressed one of his colleagues : "Mr. Blount is a character strongly marked for integrity and honor . . . He is no Speaker, nor does he possess any of those talents that make Men shine ;—he is plain, honest, and sincere." He took no part in the debates in the Convention, and he signed his name to the completed constitution, not to signify his approval of it, but to "attest the fact that the plan was the unanimous act of the States in Convention" (Farrand, *Records of the Federal Convention,* III, 95 ; II, 645–46). Nevertheless, in the North Carolina convention of 1789 he voted for ratification of the Constitution. Ambitious for further political advancement, he desired elec-

tion to the United States Senate, but failed to secure it. He then turned to the trans-Alleghany region, with which for some years he had been familiar as a speculator in Western lands and as a representative of North Carolina in dealings with the Indians. In 1789 North Carolina had ceded to the United States her claims to transmountain lands, and in 1790 Congress provided a territorial government for this cession. Blount now actively sought the governorship of this territory, and in June of 1790 he secured the appointment from President Washington. With the governorship went also the office of Superintendent of Indian Affairs for the Southern Department. When he crossed the mountains to begin his administration of affairs Blount found the inhabitants divided into hostile factions and a clash threatened between frontier interests and the pacific Indian policy of the United States government. Blount handled the affairs of his dual office with tact and firmness, with a conscientious regard for the orders of his superiors and yet with sympathy for the frontier settlers, with an eye also to his own advancement, and with a considerable measure of political adroitness. He was on friendly terms with the leading men of the territory, and he sought and secured a personal popularity with the generality of settlers. He was president of the convention which met in January 1796 and proclaimed the transformation of the territory into the State of Tennessee, and by the first legislature of the new state he was elected to the United States Senate. His service in that body, however, was brief. As territorial governor, he had continued his dealings in Western lands. He now became involved in financial difficulties and entered into a plan to launch an attack, by Indians and frontiersmen in coöperation with a British fleet, upon Spanish Florida and Louisiana for the purpose of transferring the control of those provinces to Great Britain. Unfortunately for Blount a letter that he wrote to an interpreter in the Cherokee Nation, speaking in veiled language of the plan and of his desire to have the Indians put into a frame of mind to aid him, came into the hands of President Adams, who sent it on July 3, 1797, to Congress. This letter, wrote Blount, made "a damnable fuss" in Philadelphia, but he hoped the Westerners would "see nothing but good in it, for so [he] intended it" (*Wisconsin Historical Collections,* X, 411). The senators saw it otherwise and expelled him from their body, July 8, by a vote of twenty-five to one. In the House of Representatives impeachment proceedings were begun at once, but did not come before the Senate for final decision until January

1799, when the impeachment was dismissed for lack of jurisdiction. Blount, meanwhile, had returned to Tennessee. That he had lost nothing of the confidence of the people of that community was evidenced by his election, in 1798, to the state Senate and his elevation by that body to its speakership. Further political preferment, perhaps, he might have had but for his death in 1800.

[Information, including many of Blount's letters, may be found printed in the *State Records of N. C.* (16 vols., 1895–1905), in *Am. State Papers, Indian Affairs*, I (1832), in H. M. Wagstaff (ed.), *The Papers of John Steele* (2 vols., 1924), in M. J. Wright, *Wm. Blount* (1884), and in the *Am. Hist. Mag.* (Nashville), I–IV, VI, *passim*. Some unpublished letters are in the Manuscript Div. of the Lib. of Cong., in the Draper Papers at Madison, Wis., in the collections of the Tennessee Hist. Soc., and in the McClung Collection (Knoxville) of photostats from the Spanish Archives. His journal as territorial governor is printed in the *Am. Hist. Mag.*, II, 213–277. Frederick J. Turner has edited "Documents on the Blount Conspiracy, 1795–1797," with a detailed bibliographical note, in the *Am. Hist. Rev.*, X, 274, 574–606.]

P. M. H.

BLOUNT, WILLIE (Apr. 18, 1768–Sept. 10, 1835), jurist, governor of Tennessee, belonged to a family prominent in eighteenth-century North Carolina. Of the third generation in that colony was Jacob Blount who was three times married and the father of thirteen children. Willie, pronounced Wiley, was born of the second marriage, to Hannah Baker, née Salter, widow of William Baker. His father was a man of wealth and Willie received an education at the institutions that are to-day Princeton and Columbia Universities. When his older and more accomplished half-brother William Blount [*q.v.*] was appointed governor of the Southwest Territory, Willie followed him to that frontier community, served him as private secretary, and was by him licensed to practise law in the territorial courts. When the territory became the State of Tennessee in 1796, Willie Blount was elected by the first legislature one of the three judges of the superior courts of law and equity, a position, however, which he shortly resigned. Some time after 1802 he removed from Knoxville, where he had made his home, to Montgomery County and married Lucinda Baker. In 1809, after one term of service in the legislature, he was elected governor of the state, defeating William Cocke by a majority of about 3,000 votes (*Wilson's Knoxville Gazette*, Sept. 9, 1809). In 1811 and 1813 he was reëlected for the constitutional maximum of three successive terms. As governor, he pointed out the need of extinguishing Indian titles to land in Tennessee, of securing for the state improved facilities of communication and transportation, and of de-

voting the energies of the people to the development of the wealth of the state. "Attention in us in these things," he asserted to the legislature in 1811, is more "important to the future growth of our infant state, than time devoted to the idle whimsies of foreign relations . . ." Yet the last two of his three administrations fell largely within the period of the second war between the United States and Great Britain, including with it the war with the Creek Indians. To this war and to Gen. Andrew Jackson, Blount gave energetic support, and enjoyed a considerable measure of popularity as Tennessee's war governor. In 1815 he retired from office to assume the more leisurely duties of a planter in Montgomery County. One may assume that he did this with a sigh of relief, for earlier he had written, " . . . the trade of governing does not suit my genius as well as retirement; I am tired of it." In truth, as Blount himself realized and as many who knew him have testified, he was a man of only ordinary abilities. One cannot, perhaps, better estimate his mental worth than to quote the comment of a contemporary that "in writing, he would labor a great deal, and say but little" (Draper Papers, 3xx18). Yet he was patriotic and honest. Agreeable, even affectionate, and at heart a democrat, he had many personal friends and few, if any, enemies. Twice after 1815 he came from retirement. In 1827 he was a candidate for governor in opposition to Sam Houston and Newton Cannon and was overwhelmingly defeated (*Knoxville Enquirer,* Aug. 15, 22, 29, 1827). In 1834, the year before his death, he served actively in the Tennessee constitutional convention, sponsoring in particular the provision of the new constitution that directed the legislature to encourage internal improvements.

[Blount's official papers, together with most of his private papers, including a history of Tennessee in manuscript, appear to have been destroyed. Some letters from him and some extracts from his writings are in the Draper Papers in Madison, Wis. A few letters, relating mainly to his religious opinions, are owned by the Tenn. Hist. Soc., a few are in the Robertson Correspondence (*Am. Hist. Mag.*, V), and a number to Andrew Jackson have been printed in *Correspondence of Andrew Jackson,* I, II (1926–27), ed. by J. S. Bassett. A brief pamphlet by Blount, *A Catechetical Exposition of the Constitution of the State of Tenn.: intended principally for the use of Schools,* was printed in Knoxville (1803).]

P. M. H.

BLOW, HENRY TAYLOR (July 15, 1817–Sept. 11, 1875), capitalist, diplomat, congressman, was the son of Peter and Elizabeth (Taylor) Blow. When he was thirteen, his father, a Virginia planter of moderate circumstances, migrated to the West and settled in St. Louis. Henry enjoyed the best educational advantages of the time and locality and graduated with distinction from St. Louis University. He commenced the study of law but abandoned it in order to enter business with his brother-in-law. In the economic transformation of St. Louis from a frontier town to an industrial and commercial center, Blow was an important figure. He was a pioneer in the lead and lead-products business and was instrumental in the opening and development of the large lead mines of southwestern Missouri. He was also president of the Iron Mountain Railroad. The educational and cultural interests of St. Louis came soon to realize that in Blow they had a devoted friend and generous supporter; that he was, in every sense, a public-spirited citizen. In common with many of the leading business men of the city, he was a Whig. In 1854 he was persuaded to become a candidate for the state Senate and was easily elected. Here he became one of the party leaders in the turbulent sessions of the following four years when factionalism was at its height. As chairman of the important committee on banks and corporations, Blow represented adequately and effectively the commercial and financial interests of St. Louis, which were conservative. He had opposed since 1854 the extension of slavery and with the final disappearance of the Whig party, he became, successively, an American and a "black" Republican. Together with Blair, Brown, and others of similar views, Blow supported the Free-Soil movement and helped to organize the Republican party in Missouri. He was a delegate to the national convention of 1860. Laboring tirelessly to keep Missouri in the Union, in the early and critical months of the war he was active in the raising and equipping of troops for the support of the government. Lincoln appointed him minister to Venezuela in 1861 but he returned in 1862 to become a Republican candidate for Congress as a "charcoal," that is, a Republican who favored the immediate and uncompensated emancipation of the slaves in Missouri. He was elected, and was re-elected in 1864. His congressional career was marked by close application to committee work and to conferences; he rarely spoke on the floor of the House and took little part in the acrimonious debates which marked the early days of reconstruction. As a member of the joint committee on reconstruction, he supported the policies of Stevens during the first session of Congress in 1866, but during the second he was a follower of the more conservative John A. Bingham. He was singularly free from those bitter personal and political animosities which were dominant during the reconstruction period, especially in the border states. As a business man he was concerned with the restoration and rehabilitation of St. Louis and her markets. He retired from public life in 1867 and devoted himself to the development of his mining properties. Because of his thorough knowledge of the important interests involved, Blow was prevailed upon to accept in 1869 the appointment as minister to Brazil, a position which he held for two years and in which he did much to further closer relations between the two countries, before returning to St. Louis to his numerous business interests. With the reorganization of the District of Columbia government in 1874, Blow reluctantly accepted an appointment on the new board of commissioners and assisted in the reconstruction of the District. He announced his definite retirement from politics in 1875, and died suddenly on Sept. 15 of that year. He was married to Minerva, daughter of Col. Thornton Grimsley of St. Louis.

[The chief facts concerning Blow's political career can be found in the files of the *Mo. Republican*, the *Mo. Democrat*, and the *Mo. Statesman* during the years he was in public life. The *Cong. Record* for the 39th and 40th Congresses is useful for the years 1863–67. Blow's work on the joint committee on reconstruction is appraised in B. B. Kendrick, *Jour. of the Joint Committee of Fifteen on Reconstruction* (1914). There are general accounts of his life in W. B. Stevens, "Lincoln and Mo.," *Mo. Hist. Rev.*, X, 63 ff., and S. B. Harding, "Mo. Party Struggles in the Civil War Period," *Annual Report, Am. Hist. Ass.*, 1900; H. L. Conard, *Encyc. of the Hist. of Mo.* (1901), I, 305–06.]   T. S. B.

BLOW, SUSAN ELIZABETH (June 7, 1843–Mar. 26, 1916), kindergartner, the daughter of Henry Taylor Blow [*q.v.*] and of Minerva (Grimsley) Blow, was born in St. Louis, Mo. Her childhood was passed in a cultivated home, and the deeply religious character of her early training quickened a serious and reverent attitude toward life which led her very early to consecrate herself to education. A complete surrender to the mysticism and symbolism of Froebel's philosophy was the natural outcome of a prolonged study of Hegel, Schelling, Fichte, and Kant, a close association with the transcendental philosophy of the Concord School, and the influence and support of Dr. William T. Harris [*q.v.*], superintendent of schools in St. Louis and an able exponent of German idealism. After some acquaintance with the kindergarten methods of Germany, Miss Blow conceived the idea of opening a kindergarten in St. Louis. Dr. Harris received the suggestion with favor, and Miss Blow, in order to fit herself for this responsibility, went to New York to study for a year with Mme. Maria Kraus-Boelte, called the spiritual daughter of Froebel. Mme. Kraus-Boelte had established a class for mothers and kindergartners in that city in 1871. Miss Blow became the first kindergartner in America trained by Mme. Boelte and upon her return to St. Louis in 1873 opened the first public kindergarten in the Des Pères School in Carondelet, a suburb of St. Louis, and in 1874 opened a training school which played a significant part in the history of education in her time.

When Miss Blow began her teaching, no translation of Froebel's *Mother Play* had been made. Miss Blow assumed this task and translated these songs and plays from week to week for use in the kindergarten. The work was done, however, with an untroubled orthodoxy that did not take into account the theory of evolution which gave a new interpretation to the laws of growth and necessitated a revision of the plays and games of the kindergarten. When a more liberal group of students began such a revision in 1887, Miss Blow did not lend her support to the movement. The social significance of her work must not be underestimated, however, for her belief in the *Gliedganzes* or member-whole of Froebel's philosophy found expression in many pragmatic, correlated educational activities of social significance. She gave hearty support and direction to mothers' meetings, home visitation, school gardens, and nature study. She was an instinctive leader with strong personal power. The training which she offered was built upon a broad cultural background, awakening in her students an intellectual curiosity and a recognition of fundamental spiritual values which gave permanence and direction to the kindergarten as an educational institution. Ill health forced her to retire from active work during a period of about ten years. In 1895 she began to lecture again in Boston, conducting study classes in the Bible, Homer, Dante, Goethe, and Shakespeare. The last years of her life were spent in New York, where she was connected with the graduate department of the New York Kindergarten Association. A list of her publications includes: *Symbolic Education* (1894); *The Mottoes and Commentaries of Froebel's Mother Play* (1895); *The Songs and Music of Froebel's Mother Play* (1895); *Letters to a Mother on the Philosophy of Froebel* (1899); *Educational Issues in the Kindergarten* (1908); *Kindergarten Education* (1900).

[*Pioneers of the Kindergarten in America* (1924); G. Stanley Hall, *Educational Problems* (1911); Ilse Forest, *Preschool Education* (1927); *Kindergarten Mag.*, Oct. 1895; *Elementary School Teacher*, Dec. 1906; Nina C. Vandewalker, *The Kindergarten in Am. Education* (1908); Denton J. Snider, *The St. Louis Movement* (1920); David H. Harris, ed., *The Early St. Louis Movement* (1921).]

B. C. G.

BLOWERS, SAMPSON SALTER (Mar. 10, 1742–Oct. 25, 1842), jurist, was born in Boston, the son of Lieut. John and Sarah (Salter) Blowers. He was a descendant of Pyam Blowers—the name being indifferently spelled Blower or Blores —who settled at Cambridge, Mass., toward the end of the seventeenth century. Educated at the grammar school, Boston, and at Harvard College where he graduated in 1763, Sampson Blowers studied law with Lieut. Gov. Hutchinson, was admitted to the bar at Boston in 1766, and commenced practise in that city. In 1770 the so-called "Boston massacre" occurred, in which a party of British soldiers under Capt. Preston fired on a mob in the streets, killing and wounding a number of citizens. The soldiers were subsequently tried for murder. Blowers was retained for the defense, in association with John Adams and Josiah Quincy, and an acquittal was secured in all but two cases wherein verdicts of manslaughter were returned. Thus brought into public notice, Blowers was thereafter known as a strong supporter of the royal administration and incurred the active enmity of the local patriots. In 1774 he went to England, becoming in 1776 a member of the New England Club of Loyalists which was formed in London during that year. Returning to Boston in 1778, he found that his name was in the Proscription Act as an enemy of the new state. He was arrested and imprisoned for a short time, and on his release went to Halifax, Nova Scotia, whither a large number of Loyalists had preceded him, and commenced the practise of law there. From Halifax he returned to Newport in April 1779; and was there appointed judge of the Rhode Island court of vice-admiralty. On the evacuation of Newport by the British, in October 1779, he sailed for England to seek compensation for his financial losses. The next year he came back to America, this time with the appointment of solicitor-general for New York. Early in September 1783 he sailed for Halifax with his wife and her sister (A. W. H. Eaton, article in *Americana*, XI, 52–53). In September 1784 the province of New Brunswick was formed by dividing Nova Scotia, and on Dec. 24, 1784, Blowers was appointed attorney-general of Nova Scotia as reconstituted. He was also elected from Halifax County to the new House of Representatives in the following year, and when the Assembly met at Halifax, Dec. 5, 1785, he was elected speaker, continuing as such till his appointment, Jan. 3, 1788, as a member of the legislative council, when he vacated his seat in the House and the speakership. In the council he was distinguished for the broad-minded non-partisan manner in which he discussed all matters which came up for consideration, and his varied experience and robust patriotism combined to give him great influence. He was appointed chief justice of Nova Scotia and president of the council, Sept. 9, 1797, and occupied this position for thirty-six years. He was an excellent, conscientious judge, and performed his duties "with great assiduity" (letter of Wentworth to Secretary of State, see B. Murdock, *History of Nova Scotia or Acadie*, 1865–67, II, 214). The Lieutenant-Governor, Sir George Prevost, reported that "the Chief Justice is most deservedly and universally esteemed" (*Ibid.*, II, 286). At the same time he had a proper appreciation of the dignity of his office, as was evidenced by his abstention from attendance at Council during the absence of Sir George Prevost on the expedition to Martinique in 1808–9, his reason being that he was senior to the Hon. A. Croke who had been appointed *ad interim* president of the province during the Lieutenant-Governor's absence. He retired in 1833; and died at Halifax, Oct. 25, 1842, having thus passed the century by more than five months. He married in 1774 Sarah, daughter of Benjamin Kent of Boston, who was himself a Loyalist and refugee, and she survived him, dying in 1845 at an advanced age.

[Brief details of Blowers's ancestry will be found in Jas. Savage, *Geneal. Dict. of the First Settlers of New Eng.* (1860), I, 206, and Lucius R. Paige, *Hist. of Cambridge, Mass.* (1877), p. 489. A short sketch of his life appeared in Lorenzo Sabine, *Loyalists of the Am. Rev.* (1864), I, 233. There is a laudatory reference to him in the *Diary and Letters of Thos. Hutchinson* (1883), I, 341–42.]

H. W. H. K.

BLOXHAM, WILLIAM DUNNINGTON (July 9, 1835–Mar. 15, 1911), governor of Florida, was born almost within sight of the state capitol. His father, William, of English ancestry, was a native of Alexandria, Va., and moved with his wife, Martha Williams, to Leon County, Fla., in 1825. He became a planter, served in the Seminole War, and died in Tallahassee in 1862. The son, William, was educated for the bar at William and Mary College where he was graduated in 1856, but the state of his health forced him also to become a planter. An early and lively interest in politics led to his election to the Florida House of Representatives where he served in the important session of November–December 1861. In the following February he was elected captain of a newly organized infantry company which was at once mustered into Confederate service for three years; but, his health again becoming impaired, he did not complete this service and returned to his planting. After the war he took part from the beginning in the resistance of the Conservatives to the radical and negro government

of the state; became a candidate for presidential elector on that ticket in 1868 and supported it actively on the stump; and was elected lieutenant-governor in 1870, in a period of continual radical victories, but only after a noteworthy campaign in which, notwithstanding the lack of railroads, he spoke in almost every county. Again leading the party in the same fight in 1872 he was defeated for the office of governor; but, still a leader, he had a large share in the overthrow of the foreign and negro element in 1876, was appointed secretary of state, and was finally elected governor in 1880. The success of his administration (1881–85) was without precedent in the state. By 1883, for the first time in the state's history, there was no floating debt and no deficit; funds were in the treasury for current expenses, and the reduction of the large debt contracted by the radical government had begun. Hence, he recommended to the legislature a reduction in taxation from a levy of nine mills to five mills, and this was reduced by an additional mill the next year. His most serious and pressing problem was the relief of the Internal Improvement Fund which was overwhelmed by debt and litigation. By effecting a sale to Hamilton Disston, on June 1, 1881, of 4,000,000 acres of lands held under the Fund, at twenty-five cents per acre, nearly all in cash, the Board of Trustees, of which he was chairman, rescued the Fund from insolvency and prevented a forced sale by its creditors (*Message*, Jan. 2, 1883; Caroline M. Brevard, *A History of Florida*, 1924–25, II, 182–86).

After the close of his term as governor, Bloxham declined appointment as United States minister to Bolivia, but accepted that of United States surveyor-general of Florida, in which office he served four years, to 1889, when he was appointed state comptroller. Elected to that office the next year, he was reëlected in 1892 for the four-year term. His service as comptroller left its mark upon the financial history of Florida; his recommendations for reforms, dealing mainly with the cost of criminal prosecutions, the equalization of assessments, and payment of interest on state deposits in banks, were carried out by the administration, the legislature, and the people through constitutional amendment. In January 1897 Bloxham was again inaugurated as governor, the first to be elected to that office for the second time. During this term (1897–1901) occurred the Spanish-American War, when Florida became the principal theatre of encampment and embarkation of the army. Bloxham's public service had now covered a period of forty years and he had been all but continuously in office for twenty-five years. In 1857 he had married Mary C. Davis, who died in 1904. In 1907 he married Mrs. G. Moss Norvell, who survived him. He was above medium height, with erect carriage, a high, broad forehead, small bright eyes, and thin compressed lips. Though aggressive he was conservative, was uncommonly effective as an orator, and "a thoroughly likable man" (W. W. Davis, *The Civil War and Reconstruction in Florida,* 1913, p. 620).

[R. H. Rerick, *Memoirs of Florida* (1902), vol. I; and *Makers of America* (Fla. ed. 1911), I, 104–28.]

J. C. Y.

BLUE, VICTOR (Dec. 6, 1865–Jan. 22, 1928), naval officer, born in Richmond County, North Carolina, came of distinguished Scotch, Welsh, and Huguenot ancestry settled in the Carolinas before the Revolution. His father, John Gilchrist Blue, was a lieutenant-colonel in the Confederate army. His mother was Annie M. Evans, daughter of Williams Evans, a brigadier-general of South Carolina militia in the nullification trouble of 1833. A younger brother, Rupert Blue, was Surgeon-General, United States Public Health Service. After boyhood on his father's plantation, "Bluefields," Marion, S. C., and high-school work at Laurinburg, N. C., Victor was appointed to the Naval Academy, graduating in 1887 in the engineering branch of the service, from which five years later he was transferred to the line. In the Spanish War he was a lieutenant in the converted yacht *Suwanee.* Having had previous experience ashore in Cuba, May 31–June 1, 1898, in an effort to land munitions for the insurgents, Blue volunteered for two highly difficult scouting expeditions through the Spanish lines at Santiago. By the first, June 11–13, he established definitely that all Cervera's squadron was in the harbor, thus giving assurance for the transport of troops from Tampa. By the second, June 25–27, he identified and accurately located each enemy vessel for purposes of a projected torpedo attack. Accompanied only by insurgent guides, he traveled on each trip over sixty miles on mule-back, penetrating two miles or more within the Spanish lines to hills overlooking the harbor. On Admiral Sampson's recommendation he was promoted five numbers for "extraordinary heroism." In addition to other routine assignments, he served on the staff of Rear Admiral Cooper, in command of the Asiatic Fleet, 1903–04; as executive officer of the *North Carolina,* 1909; as commander of the *Yorktown* and later as chief of staff in the Pacific Fleet, 1910. On Mar. 26, 1913, while still in the grade of commander, he was appointed by Secretary Daniels chief of the Bureau of Navigation, with the temporary rank of rear admiral; and in this important office, controlling all matters relating to personnel, he worked harmoniously with the secretary in the expansion of the navy which preceded American entry into the World War. On Aug. 10, 1916, he left the bureau to command the battleship *Texas.* For the grounding of his ship on Block Island in the next year he was reduced ten numbers. The *Texas,* in January 1918, joined Admiral Rodman's squadron with the British Grand Fleet in the North Sea, and in this trying service Blue remained in her command until the close of the War. For a brief period, from December 1918 until his retirement, he was again chief of the Bureau of Navigation. He was made permanent rear admiral in April 1919, and was retired in the following July, owing to heart trouble. His later life was spent chiefly at Fort George, Fla., where he had extensive real estate interests. He died of heart failure on a train while going from Fort George to Washington for treatment. Blue was married, Oct. 17, 1899, to Eleanor Foote Stuart, a grandchild of Gen. David Stuart of Detroit. Of his two sons, John Stuart and Victor, the elder, John, became an officer in the navy. In addition to the bold spirit displayed in the Spanish War, Blue had the sound judgment and qualities of coöperation required for the important administrative duties of his later years. He was of dark complexion and large build, fond of social life, "a generous-hearted, lovable man," as a classmate and fellow officer describes him, "with a fund of quiet merriment which was a distinguishing characteristic."

[Sketch is based chiefly on information from family and naval sources, and from Navy Department records. See especially "Naval Operations of the War with Spain," *House Doc. No. 3,* 55 Cong., 3 Sess. Obituaries appeared in the *N. Y. Times,* Jan. 23, 1928, and *Army and Navy Record,* Jan. 28, 1928.]

A. W.

BLUM, ROBERT FREDERICK (July 9, 1857–June 8, 1903), painter, was the son of Frederick and Mary (Haller) Blum. His father was a native of Germany, born at Rohrbach, in the Rhine Palatinate of Bavaria, whence he emigrated in the early "fifties," coming in a sailing ship to New Orleans and up the Mississippi and Ohio rivers to Cincinnati, where at the time of Blum's birth he was occupied as a designer of insurance charts. Here Blum was born, his mother being also of German extraction. His school days began in 1864 while the Civil War was in progress. After passing through the various grades he entered high school in 1873. Chafing at its restraints he left it in 1874 to enter Gibson & Sons' Lithographic Establishment on Elm Street, Cincinnati, as an apprentice. In addition to his daily practise, he studied drawing in the evenings at the Mechanics' Institute and in 1875 entered the

McMicken School of Design where Alfred Brennan and Kenyon Cox were fellow pupils, sketching from the nude in pencil and pen and ink. As early as 1872 his eye had been attracted by some Japanese fans, which were being hawked in connection with the holding of a "Sänger-fest" in Cincinnati. He bought several of the best for study. He was also interested in reproductions of the Spanish painter Fortuny and others of that school. When he visited the Centennial Exhibition of 1876 at Philadelphia, in company with Kenyon Cox, he was able to study original works by masters of the Hispano-Roman School and the marvels of art in the Japanese section. He then resolved to visit Europe and Japan—ambitions which were afterward realized. He remained in Philadelphia with Cox to study nine months in the life classes of the Pennsylvania Academy of Fine Arts. Brennan soon joined them, a loft in Elbow Lane serving the three as a studio. In 1877 Blum returned to Cincinnati, but notwithstanding parental advice to stick to lithography, he returned to Philadelphia and soon after, in 1878, went on to New York, where he first lived at 91 Clinton Place (East Eighth St). After four months of struggle and privations, his clever sketches caught the eye of A. W. Drake, the art editor of *Scribner's Monthly* and *St. Nicholas,* who gave him commissions. An excursion to Alexandria and Yorktown, Va. (November 1879), in company with Lungren, and O'Donovan the sculptor, resulted in a series of clever sketches of old Colonial life in which the eighteenth-century costumes and poses recalled those preferred by Fortuny, whose works, light in subject but profoundly skilful in technique, strongly influenced Blum's manner at this time.

Working in a studio at 21 East Fifteenth St. in 1879 Blum saved enough money by spring to permit a four months' visit to Europe. Sailing from New York in company with A. W. Drake on the *Arizona,* he visited London, Paris, Genoa, and Rome, afterward going to Venice. Here he found Whistler occupied with his now famous etchings and pastels, living with Blum's fellow townsman, Duveneck, in the Riva Schiavoni, where he joined them. Martin Rico, the Spanish painter, was also in Venice, and these combined influences must have been invaluable to the young artist. Returning to New York in September 1880, Blum took a studio at the Sherwood Building, recently erected at 58 West Fifty-seventh St. A number of pen and ink studies of Joe Jefferson as "Bob Acres" and "Rip Van Winkle," as well as of other actors and actresses, appeared about this time in *Scribner's* and the *Century* magazines as evidences of his astound-

ing skill, and have been classed as *chef-d'œuvres* by Joseph Pennell in his *Pen Drawing and Pen Draughtsmen.* Decorations for Mr. Roberts's residence on the northwest corner of Washington Square and University Place were completed during April and May, 1881, and in June we find Blum again in Venice occupying rooms with his friend Baer. In 1882, he joined the jolly party of artists, including William Chase, Carroll Beckwith, Lungren, Quartley, A. A. Anderson, and F. P. Vinton, who passed the time in decorating the captain's cabin of the *Belgenland,* about which event Clarence Buel, of the *Century,* also on board, wrote an article, "Log of an Ocean Studio," five of the illustrations being by Blum. In July we find Blum at Madrid, where he made a copy of Velazquez's "Mœnippus." In 1883 he visited Long Meadows, Mass., with Durand, and passed August and September with Turcas at Ellenville, N. Y. A visit to Vinton was coïncident with a trip to Boston for the Century Company. The completion of another large decoration was the prelude to his sailing for Antwerp in July 1884, where he met Chase, Ulrich, and Baer, with whom he visited Brussels, proceeding to Haarlem and Zandvoort in Holland, where he remained at work for some time. The annual pilgrimage to Europe was repeated in 1885 with visits to Venice, Paris, and London, and on his return to New York in September, he took the studio lately vacated by Alden Weir at the Benedict Building, Washington Square, which he retained till 1893. In the meantime an opportunity came, in 1889, to make the long-deferred visit to Japan, with a commission to illustrate Sir Edwin Arnold's "Japonica," published serially in *Scribner's Magazine* (1890–91), and afterward in book form. Here he remained over two years, sending back a series of drawings of unequalled fidelity and beauty. He recorded his impressions in "An Artist in Japan," a series of papers published in *Scribner's Magazine* (1893). While engaged on the illustrations for "Japonica," he painted and sketched unceasingly, his most important work in oil colors being "The Ameya" or "Candy Blower," exhibited at the National Academy of Design (1892), and now at the Metropolitan Museum of Art, New York.

Soon after the return from Japan, Blum moved to 90 Grove St., where with his friend, Baer, he had renovated a house, arranging for convenient studios and living quarters, and thus they became the pioneers in the "Greenwich Village" migration of New York artists. It was here he designed and carried out the decorations for the Mendelssohn Glee Club Hall, which occupied almost five years to complete. This has been termed a "personal message of joyous freshness and sensitive rhythms." On one wall he painted "Moods of Music"—a frieze twelve feet high and fifty feet long,—a series of dancing figures, in light tones and colors, representing musical movements from the stately *andante* to the lively *allegro*. The costumes are of Grecian simplicity, and before painting the composition he modeled each figure separately in the nude and arranged the groups on an architectural background, with innumerable sketches in crayon and pastel. When this first frieze was completed, he took up the execution of "The Vintage Festival" on the opposite wall. Profiting by his first experience, he made this more positive in color and divided it into contrasting groups upon an architectural background of white marble. When the building for which they were painted was demolished some years ago, these decorations were happily preserved and they have found a fitting home on the side walls of the sculpture hall of the Brooklyn Museum of Art, having been generously donated by the heirs of Alfred Corning Clark who had been Blum's "perfect patron" in carrying out the work. Another important decoration for the Proscenium of the New Amsterdam Theatre, undertaken in collaboration with the artist A. B. Wenzell, was in progress at the time of Blum's death.

One is impressed by his versatile use of various mediums. Perhaps the early experiences with lithographic crayon led to his skilful use of pastels later on. Oscar Wilde happening into his studio one day said, in commenting on their delicacy, "Your pastels give me the feeling of eating yellow satin." Blum was one of the founders of the Society of Painters in Pastel, and became its president. Among the eleven etchings shown at the Memorial Exhibition at Knoedler's Galleries, New York, in April 1904, were "The Hag," a masterly character sketch of an old woman smoking a pipe, dated 1879; "The Etcher," showing William Chase at work in his Tenth Street studio; and a keenly characterized profile portrait of the artist himself, besides others, done at Venice and in Holland. Water-color he always found a particularly sympathetic medium; its fluid transparency and telling accents served in numerous studies at Venice, in Holland, and later in Japan. Although he seems to have found oil colors less pliable, even designating them at first as "a nasty medium," yet his "Lace Makers," which gained him a gold medal in New York and another in bronze at the Paris Universal Exhibition of 1889, gave no evidence of technical difficulties. The exhibition of his "Bead String-

ers" resulted in election as an associate of the National Academy of Design and gained a diploma at Philadelphia. "The Ameya" or "Candy Blower," which he classed as "the one important picture of my Japan trip," resulted in his election to full membership in the National Academy. He was also a member of the Society of American Artists and of the Water Color Society. In twenty-five years of unremitting toil, he had achieved a distinguished position. Honored with the friendship of some of the most notable artists of his time, both in America and abroad, he was singularly happy in intimate relations established with Whistler, Chase, Duveneck, Martin Rico, Carroll Beckwith, Bacher, Cox, and his lifelong friend, afterward the executor of his estate, William J. Baer. At the relatively early age of forty-six, an attack of pneumonia carried him off in five days at New York. He was buried at Cincinnati, and, appropriately, by the devoted efforts of his sister, Mrs. Haller, and of his friend, William J. Baer, a collection of his works which includes one hundred and forty originals and forty reproductions, has been placed in a special gallery at the Cincinnati Art Museum, with a bronze portrait bust by the sculptor, C. H. Niehaus.

[R. Bridges, *Lamp*, July 1903; Mrs. C. M. Fairbanks, *Metropolitan Mag.*, July 1904; Royal Cortissoz, *N. Y. Tribune*, June 30, 1895, *N. Y. Times*, Feb. 2, 1913, *N. Y. Herald Tribune*, Apr. 25, 1926; Clarence Cook, *Studio*, Dec. 5, 1891; Jos. Pennell, *Pen Drawing and Pen Draughtsmen* (1889, rev. ed. 1920); personal recollections, supplemented by information furnished by Mr. Wm. J. Baer.]   R. J. W.

BLUNT, EDMUND MARCH (June 20, 1770–Jan. 4, 1862), hydrographer, was born in Portsmouth, N. H., the son of William and Elizabeth (March) Blunt. His boyhood and early manhood were spent in his native city and in Newburyport, Mass., where he had many contacts with the life of the sea as both places enjoyed at that time a rather prosperous commerce. It was in Newburyport that he embarked on a business career, beginning in 1793, with Howard S. Robinson, the publication of the *Impartial Herald*. In the same year he married Sally Ross of Newbury. For three years he carried on newspaper publishing along with his bookstore which stood just a few doors below the Wolfe Tavern. This feature of his business had a steady growth until in 1802 there were 3,000 volumes available for circulation. The step which without doubt was the most important in his career was his decision in 1796 to publish the *American Coast Pilot*, compiled by Capt. L. Furlong. This book, which contained "directions for principal harbors, capes, and headlands of the coast of North and part of South America" (19th ed., title-page), filled a long felt need and found a ready sale not only in America but also in Europe where it was translated into the more important languages. The first edition was soon exhausted and others were called for. These Blunt personally sponsored and edited. Between the editions of the *Coast Pilot*, Blunt found time to publish in 1799 a *New Practical Navigator* which in turn was followed in 1801 by the publication of *Bowditch's New American Practical Navigator*.

These books together with nautical charts made Blunt's workshop the center of American nautical publications. An incident which arose in connection with the publication of the charts gives considerable insight into Blunt's character. In 1805 James Akin was engaged in engraving maps and charts for Blunt when the latter became infuriated in a dispute over some details of the work and seizing a heavy iron skillet threw it at Akin. In revenge Akin published a caricature called "Infuriated Despondency" representing Blunt in the act of throwing the skillet. This engraving he sent to England with instructions to have it reproduced on crockery. A large number of household utensils bearing the caricature were imported and sold in Newburyport but most of them were purchased by Blunt's friends and broken up. In July 1805 Blunt sued Akin for libel. A decision was rendered in favor of the defendant after a long and bitter contest. Shortly after the quarrel Blunt moved to New York City, where he continued to carry on his nautical publications, at first alone, and later with his sons E. and G. W. Blunt [*q.v.*]. A notable work of this period was his *Stranger's Guide to the City of New York* which appeared in 1817. His death, at Sing Sing (now Ossining), N. Y., was mourned by large numbers of his intimates among the old school of American shipmasters.

[The chief source of information is John J. Currier's *Hist. of Newburyport*, vol. I (1906), vol. II (1909). Much information regarding the character of Blunt's work and publications can be had from the prefaces of the various editions of the *Coast Pilot*. A notice of his death appeared in the *N. Y. Times*, Jan. 6, 1862.]

G. H. B.

BLUNT, GEORGE WILLIAM (Mar. 11, 1802–Apr. 19, 1878), hydrographer, was born in Newburyport, Mass., the son of Edmund March Blunt [*q.v.*] and Sally (Ross) Blunt. He inherited his father's love of the sea and left school at the age of fourteen to serve five years before the mast. On his return in 1821 he married Martha Garsett and settled in New York City, where he established with his brother, Edmund, a publishing house making a specialty

of nautical works. He immediately began marine surveys of the Bahama Banks and of New York Harbor for the purpose of revising existing charts. In 1833 he was appointed first assistant of the United States Coast Survey—a position which he held until the time of his death. He was the moving spirit of his publishing house, which was kept constantly busy printing nautical books and charts. He himself edited *The Young Sea Officer's Sheet Anchor* (1843), *Memoir of the Dangers and Ice of the North Atlantic Ocean* (1845), *The Way to Avoid the Center of our Violent Gales* (1868), *Pilot Laws, Harbor and Quarantine Regulations of New York* (1869). *Bowditch's Navigator* and *Blunt's Coast Pilot*, both of which were originally published by his father, continued to run into large and numerous editions. The chart business of the firm also grew rapidly; new charts were constantly added to the list and older ones were revised so that by 1863 the Blunts were publishing "charts of all the navigable world, from the best authorities" (preface to the nineteenth edition of *Blunt's Coast Pilot*). As a side line they handled all types of nautical instruments of American manufacture and by means of a dividing engine which was perfected "after a labor of over five years [were] enabled to divide astronomical and nautical instruments to a degree of precision which they [guaranteed] to be equal to the best of foreign make" (*Ibid.*). That Blunt's work was basic in the organization of the United States Hydrographic Office is borne out by the fact that, "The first important accessions to the stock of chart-plates came through purchase from the firm of E. & G. W. Blunt, nautical publishers, of New York City, under authority conferred upon the Secretary of the Navy by the Act of Congress establishing the Hydrographic Office. Twenty-four copperplate charts, relating mainly to the coast of America, were thus added to the list of issues; and besides these, the copyrights of *Bowditch's American Practical Navigator*, and a few volumes of *Coast Pilots and Sailing Directions* were also acquired by purchase" (Pamphlet dated Jan. 1, 1910 issued by the Bureau of Equipment, Navy Department). Even in the midst of his busy publishing career Blunt never lost his interest in the practical side of navigation. He served for thirty-two years on the Board of Pilot Commissioners; he and his brother constantly forwarded to Washington complaints of captains about the lighthouse service; and it was largely through their efforts that reforms in that bureau were instituted (Arnold B. Johnson, *The Modern Lighthouse Service*, 1889, p. 15). He found time to help organize the pilotage system in New York

Bay and from 1845 up to the time of his death except for a six months' period served as pilot commissioner. He was for a time a harbor commissioner and a trustee of the Seamen's Retreat. In 1852–54 he served as a commissioner of immigration. With his death which occurred in New York City, the American sailor lost an interested and devoted friend.

[In addition to the references given above, see J. J. Currier, *Hist. of Newburyport*, vol. I (1906), vol. II (1909), and an excellent obituary in the *N. Y. Times*, Apr. 20, 1878. Much information regarding the character of Blunt's work and publications can also be gleaned from the prefaces to the various editions of the *Coast Pilot*.]   G. H. B.

BLUNT, JAMES GILLPATRICK (July 21, 1826–July 25, 1881), physician, soldier, politician, was born in Trenton, Hancock County, Me., and after passing his earlier years in the little town of Ellsworth, yielded to his love of travel and adventure and went to sea. From his fifteenth to his twentieth year he was a sailor. Subsequently he decided to study medicine, and in the year 1849 graduated from the Starling Medical College, Columbus, Ohio. He practised his profession in New Madison, Ohio, where he married Nancy Carson Putnam, daughter of Ernestus and Elizabeth Putnam. In 1856 he moved to Kansas, where he settled at Greeley and continued the practise of medicine, but soon became actively interested in politics and took an active part in the anti-slavery movement. He was closely associated with John Brown, and his strong antipathy toward slavery took practical form in aiding Brown in secretly removing slaves from the United States into Canada. A member from Anderson County, of the now historic constitutional convention, which met at Wyandotte, July 5, 1859, and which framed the constitution of Kansas, Blunt was made chairman of the committee on militia,—an appointment which probably influenced his future military career. On July 24, 1861, he was mustered into the Union army as lieutenant-colonel of the 3rd Kansas Volunteers, and later was placed in command of cavalry attached to the brigade of Gen. James H. Lane. On Apr. 8, 1862, he was promoted brigadier-general, and placed in command of the military department of Kansas. He first distinguished himself with his brigade of Kansans and Cherokees, Oct. 22, 1862, in what is known as the battle of Old Fort Wayne, near the southwest corner of Missouri. Here he encountered the enemy, some 3,000 to 5,000 Indians under Col. Douglas H. Cooper, concentrated near Maysville and on their way north to invade Kansas. The Confederates were severely punished and gave up their northward march, and on Nov.

20, 1862, Gen. Schofield turned over to Blunt command of what was known as the Army of the Frontier (*Battles and Leaders of the Civil War*, III, 446–47). Continuing his active operations against the Confederates, Blunt attacked Gen. Marmaduke, Nov. 28, 1862, at Cane Hill, and signally defeated him. These successful operations were recognized by the Federal government by Blunt's promotion to major-general, Nov. 29, 1862. Still on the aggressive, Blunt again attacked the enemy under Gen. Hindman on Dec. 7, at Prairie Grove, and, with the coöperation of Gen. Herron, caused Hindman to fall back fifty miles to the Arkansas River and to abandon his objective of occupying Missouri. Following up his advantage, Blunt captured Van Buren on the Arkansas, Dec. 28, again defeated the Confederate forces, and destroyed four of their gunboats. In June 1863, having been relieved of command of the Department of Kansas. he took the field with the Army of the Frontier, and on July 16 defeated Gen. Cooper at Honey Springs, and opposed with his division the threatened invasion of Missouri by Gen. Sterling Price. At Newtonia, Mo., Oct. 28, 1864, he defeated Price, and in combination with Gen. Sanborn, engaged in a final skirmish with Shelby's cavalry. This ended what is known in history as the disastrous "Price Raid." Viewed in the light of a subsequent study of conditions obtaining at that period, it seems quite certain that had not Blunt and his veteran soldiers thrown themselves across Price's advance, he would undoubtedly have captured Kansas City and occupied southeastern Kansas. After Price's defeat, the latter crossed the Arkansas River above Fort Smith with a few pieces of artillery, and with his army reduced by captures and dispersion to some 5,000 demoralized men. Most of the noted guerrilla bands followed Price from the state (*Ibid.*, IV, 374–77). At the close of the Civil War, Blunt was honorably mustered out of the service, July 29, 1865, and settled in Leavenworth, Kan., where he resumed the practise of his profession. About the year 1869, he removed to Washington, D. C., where for twelve years he practised before the Federal departments as a solicitor of claims. On Apr. 9, 1873, Blunt and others were charged by the Department of Justice with conspiracy to defraud the government and a body of Cherokee Indians in North Carolina, but about two years later he was discharged by the United States Court in North Carolina, hearing the case (D. W. Wilder, *The Annals of Kansas*, 1875, pp. 609, 680). His health gradually giving way, Blunt was, on Feb. 12, 1879, admitted as a patient to St. Elizabeth's, the government hospital for the insane, where he finally died. His remains were sent to Kansas for interment.

[Besides the references cited above, see F. B. Heitman, *Hist. Reg.* (1903) ; Wm. E. Connolly, *Standard Hist. of Kan.*, II (1918) ; *Kan. State Hist. Colls.*, I, II ; *Evening Star* (Washington, D. C.), July 28, 1881.]

C. D. R.

BLYTHE, HERBERT. [See BARRYMORE, MAURICE, 1847–1905.]

BOARDMAN, THOMAS DANFORTH (Jan. 21, 1784–Sept. 10, 1873), pewterer, was born in Litchfield, Conn., the son of Oliver and Sarah (Danforth) Boardman. Oliver Boardman had served in the campaign against Burgoyne and at that time kept a diary now available in printed form in *Collections of the Connecticut Historical Society*, VII, 221–37. He removed from Litchfield to Hartford, where presumably Thomas was apprenticed. There, at all events, the latter began work in the ranks of craftsmen pewterers—possibly as early as 1807, though the date is not definitely known. On May 28, 1812, he was married to Elizabeth Bidwell Lewis of Glastonbury, who died in 1869. It is stated (Charlotte Goldthwaite, *Boardman Genealogy*, 1895, p. 448) that "Mr. Thomas D. Boardman and his family were all useful members of Dr. (Horace) Bushnell's church"— *i.e.*, the North Congregational, of which Bushnell was pastor from 1833 to 1859. During this period Boardman's shop was at 59 Main St., and his output included basins, ladles, porringers, and plates (ranging from six-inch through larger sizes). J. B. Kerfoot's *American Pewter* (1924, p. 58) has a picture of a T. D. Boardman communion flagon, thirteen and one-half inches in height. The recorded touch-marks employed by Thomas Boardman in his first period were: TDB in a rectangle; T. D. BOARDMAN in a rectangle; a spread-eagle with TDB; a spread-eagle surrounded by THOMAS D. BOARDMAN. He also occasionally used an X to indicate fine quality—this being uncommon with American makers, though standard practise in England. According to Kerfoot, Boardman stands out as the last pure representative of ancient traditions in pewter-making. A few specimens of his craftsmanship are in the Morgan collection of the Wadsworth Atheneum (*Bulletin of the Wadsworth Atheneum*, I, No. 2).

During Boardman's second period, he and his brother Sherman were in partnership, under the style of T. D. & S. Boardman, with an establishment on Main St., near Morgan. Pioneers in this country in the manufacture of britannia-ware and block-tin, they "carried on a successful business . . . for more than fifty years" (Goldthwaite). The old principles of craftsmanship were being affected by the rising tendency toward quantity production. The firm of Boardman brothers would seem to have led the way, and to have done much to set the patterns for new designs. It has been stated that the two Boardmans and William Calder of Providence, R. I., "are, between them, responsible for the great majority of the surviving porringers of early American origin" (Kerfoot, p. 44). "Offshoots" (Goldthwaite, p. 448)—affiliated concerns—appeared in New York and Philadelphia. The precise relation of these "offshoots" to the original firm has been considerably mooted. One view regards them as agencies for the sale of wares from the Hartford workshops, which thus found new outlets. The firm's own touch-mark was TD & SB in a rectangle.

[In addition to sources given above, see E. T. Freedley, *Leading Pursuits and Leading Men* (1856), p. 404.]

G. S. B.

BOAS, EMIL LEOPOLD (Nov. 15, 1854–May 3, 1912), was for thirty years the general manager for the United States of the Hamburg-American Steamship Line and for about five years its sole American director. He was born in Goerlitz, Germany, the son of Louis and Minna Boas. After attending the local schools he was sent to the Royal Frederick William Gymnasium, in Breslau, and then to the Sophia Gymnasium, in Berlin. He graduated at the unusually early age of eighteen and at once began work as a clerk in the banking office of C. B. Richard & Boas, of which an uncle of his was a member. In the following year (1873) he was transferred to the New York office of the firm, which was then the American representative of the Hamburg-American Steamship Company. By his close application to the interests of the company he attracted the attention of its heads and was promoted. He was married, Mar. 20, 1888, to Harriet B. Sternfeld, who afterward became prominent in various women's organizations. In 1892, when the steamship company established a separate office in New York, he was made one of the three directors and also the general manager. In 1907 he became the sole director, or "resident manager." For his services in the development of their commerce and in safeguarding the welfare of their subjects he was many times decorated by European rulers.

Boas witnessed the evolution of the ocean-going steamship from the packet type of the seventies to the huge liner of the present day. As a clerk in the Richard & Boas office he had made shipping his particular study and had become a master of technical detail. He took a leading part in building up the New York agency until it became the center and controlling pivot for a vast network of steamship routes, and he was energetic in all movements looking toward the improvement of commercial and traffic facilities. Following the *Titanic* disaster he was the first steamship manager to announce an intention of providing an adequate number of life-boats for passengers and crew. He also began an investigation of safety devices, but his study was stopped by his death, less than a month later, at his summer home in Greenwich, Conn.

Boas was one of the foremost business men of the metropolis. He was an incredibly active man, and the strain of work is said to have worn him down. His activities, however, extended far beyond his business. His range of interests was wide, and the number of organizations to which he belonged was exceptionally large. An advocate of Germanic culture, he was a leading figure in the German societies. He was also a music lover and a cultivator of rare flowers. Above all, he was a life-long student, and to his acquaintances he gave the impression of being a scholar rather than a business man.

[*Who's Who in America*, 1912–13; obituaries in the *Times, Sun, Tribune,* and *Herald* of New York, May 4, 1912.]   W. J. G.

BÔCHER, MAXIME (Aug. 28, 1867–Sept. 12, 1918), mathematician, born in Boston, was fortunate in his parentage. His father, Ferdinand Bôcher, born in New York City of Normandy parents, was one of the best-known teachers in the country, being for many years professor of French at Harvard, a man of all-round culture, and a great collector of books in the field of French literature, art, and history; his mother, Caroline Little, belonged to one of the oldest New England families, tracing her ancestry back to Richard Warren of the *Mayflower* company and maintaining the best of the intellectual and moral traditions of Boston and the East. Passing from the Cambridge Latin School to Harvard, where he graduated in 1888, Bôcher's education at home and in the schools was built upon a more secure foundation than came to the lot of most men in his day. In college he took a broad course but found his chief interest in mathematics; while he received the bachelor's degree *summa cum laude,* he at the same time had the distinction of highest honors in his chosen subject, his thesis being "On three systems of parabolic coördinates."

It was characteristic of the catholicity of view of his father and himself that his doctor's degree was taken at Göttingen. Family reasons might have suggested Paris, but scientific reasons in

the late eighties pointed clearly to Germany, and notably to Klein, who was then lecturing on the potential function and studying especially the series and integrals employed in the theory. It was in this domain that Bôcher began his most serious work. His paper, "Ueber die Reihenentwickelungen der Potential-theorie" (Göttingen, 1891) not only served as his doctor's dissertation but secured for him a prize offered by the University and hence bore upon the title-page the words "Gekrönte Preisschrift und Dissertation." Far from narrowing his interests, as is so often the case, his investigation broadened them, extending his work into the fields of theoretical physics, pure geometry, and higher analysis. His later work, however, was not so much in the field of pure geometry as in that of differential equations, series, and higher algebra. In September 1891 he became instructor in mathematics at Harvard, in September 1894 assistant professor, and in 1904 professor. As a teacher, he was unusually successful. He was clear in his lectures and stimulating in the suggestiveness of his assignments. His great influence on mathematics in America was exerted in the seminar where he did much to train some of the later leaders in mathematical research in this country. In the year 1913–14 he was exchange professor at Paris. His most important publications consisted of nearly a hundred memoirs and reviews in his field of interest, and an algebra (1907) which gave a new view of the higher domain of this important branch of mathematics. Less significant as mathematical contributions but very stimulating in the more elementary courses were his works on trigonometry (with Mr. Gaylord) and analytic geometry. On the completion of his course at Göttingen he had married Marie Niemann of that city, and she, with three children, survived him. His health began to fail at about the time of his lectures in Paris, and his closing years were a period of trial for one upon whose strength so many demands were made and who felt himself unable to give to his students the degree of assistance that had characterized his earlier days. His loss to American scholarship was severely felt, not alone in this country, but by the entire mathematical world.

[For the biography of Bôcher consult "The Life and Services of Maxime Bôcher" in the *Bull. Am. Mathematical Soc.,* XXV, 337–50, by his colleague Prof. Wm. F. Osgood. For a summary of his contributions consult "The Scientific Work of Maxime Bôcher," *Ibid.,* pp. 197–215, by Prof. Geo. D. Birkhoff. In the latter article will be found a complete list of Bôcher's publications chronologically arranged. The Minute on his life and services, placed upon the records of the faculty of arts and sciences of Harvard University, was printed in *Science,* Nov. 29, 1918.]   D. E. S.

BOCOCK, THOMAS STANLEY (May 18, 1815–Aug. 5, 1891), congressman, was born in that part of Buckingham County, Va., which later became a part of Appomattox County. He was one of the twelve children of John Thomas and Mary (Flood) Bocock. Receiving his preparatory work, as well as his later law course, from a brother, Willis P. Bocock, later attorney-general of Virginia, he ranked first among the B.A. graduates of Hampden-Sidney, in 1838. Elected to the General Assembly at the age of twenty-seven he remained until 1845, when he became county commonwealth's attorney. In 1847 he went to the United States House of Representatives, where he was appointed to the naval committee and was for a decade its chairman. His vote on the compromise measures of 1850 is not recorded, but he favored the Kansas-Nebraska bill and the Lecompton constitution. He developed great skill in what Congressman S. S. Cox called "parliamentary skirmishing" (Cox, *Union-Disunion-Reunion: Three Decades of Federal Legislation,* 1885, p. 74), and was the Democratic candidate for the speakership against John Sherman and fourteen lesser candidates. On the first ballot he received eighty-six votes—twenty more than Sherman, but still less than a majority. The balloting went on from Dec. 5, 1859, until Feb. 1, 1860, when, Bocock and Sherman both having withdrawn, Pennington was elected on the forty-fourth ballot. The story used to be told that after the war older members of the House sometimes absent-mindedly voted "Bocock" or "Sherman" instead of "Yes" or "No."

Following Virginia's passage of the secession resolution, Bocock, on May 7, 1861, entered the Provisional Congress of the Confederate States as a delegate from Virginia. He became, by unanimous vote, speaker of the Confederate House of Representatives in both the First and Second Congresses, and headed the delegation that presented to President Davis what the latter called "a warning if not a threat" that the House was in a mood to pass a vote of want of confidence in the President's cabinet (N. W. Stephenson, *The Day of the Confederacy,* 1919, p. 156). After the war Bocock entered the General Assembly, 1869–70, as a moderate Conservative; was a delegate to the Democratic national conventions of 1868, 1876, and 1880; and in the *post-bellum* contest between Virginia's "readjusters" and those who advocated the payment of the war debt, dollar for dollar, he came forward as a compromiser in the Bocock-Fowler bill which failed of passage (C. C. Pearson, *The Readjuster Movement in Virginia,* 1917, p. 79). He became attorney for two or three railroads,

held high rank as a practising attorney, and rendered great service to Hampden-Sidney College in its post-war financial difficulties (*Richmond Dispatch,* Aug. 7, 1891).

Bocock was a skilful parliamentarian, as is very evident from a perusal of the *Congressional Globe.* He was in great demand as presiding officer of conventions in Virginia. This is accounted for by his ability to preserve order, and by suggestion to call forth motions suited to the parliamentary situation. He was also in demand as a speaker. A lover of books, he collected one of the largest private libraries in Virginia. On Aug. 5, 1891, he died at "Wildway," six miles from Appomattox Court House. He was twice married, first to Sarah P. Flood, and, second, to Annie Faulkner.

[*Jours. of the General Assembly of Va.*; *Cong. Globe,* for the years 1847–61; *Jours. of the Confed. Cong;* *Sen. Doc. 654,* 61 Cong., 2 Sess.; Thos. Cary Johnson, *Thos. S. Bocock;* *Political Pamphlets,* vols. XXVIII, XXXI (Va. State Lib.).]   E. L. F.

BOEHLER, PETER (Dec. 31, 1712–Apr. 27, 1775), was a bishop in the *Unitas Fratrum,* commonly called the Moravian Church. The *Unitas Fratrum* of the eighteenth century was a revival of the old church organization in Bohemia and Moravia, dating from the time of John Hus. Refugees from Moravia found religious freedom on the lands of Count Zinzendorf in Herrnhut, Saxony, and developed there a community which became the center of a great spiritual awakening. Peter Boehler early felt the influence of the Moravian Brethren, and carried that influence to England and America as religious teacher and as organizer of other communities on the order of Herrnhut. He was born in Frankfurt-am-Main, son of John Conrad Boehler and his wife, Antonetta Elizabetha Hanf. The father was a worthy burgher, innkeeper and brewer, and at one time comptroller at the Corn Office (Lockwood, *Memorials,* p. 52). The child Peter began school at the age of four, started Latin at eight, and was ready for the Gymnasium in Frankfurt at ten. On the advice of his instructors he prepared for the study of theology instead of medicine as he had planned. In 1731 he went to the University of Jena where he yielded to the influences of the pietists, especially the lecturer Spangenberg. When Zinzendorf visited the University in 1732, Boehler made a sacred agreement with him to carry on the work of Christ. Boehler became Magister Legens in 1736 with the right to lecture as junior professor. Two years later he entered upon the missionary endeavors which occupied most of his life. According to a project arranged by Zinzendorf and the English Society for the

Propagation of the Gospel, Boehler was to organize missions among the negro slaves of South Carolina in the vicinity of Purysburg. At the same time he was to act as pastor to a group of Moravians in Savannah. Boehler spent several weeks in England on his way to America,— weeks significant for his contact with the founders of Methodism, the spread of Moravian doctrines, and the organization of classes. He preached frequently to groups in London, and visited Oxford twice in the company of the Wesleys, addressing both citizens and students. His success as an evangelist was due both to his personality and the clarity of his argument. A frank and open countenance with clear, fearless eyes gained the trust of his listeners, whether in public addresses or in private conversations. His discussions of the cardinal points in the doctrine of the *Unitas Fratrum* influenced the Wesleys at a time when they were still uncertain of their faith. When Boehler left England John Wesley exclaimed, "O what a work hath God begun since his coming into England."

The American mission of Boehler and his companion, Georg Schulius, began in September 1738. The possibilities for success were not promising, for the company of Moravians in Savannah had dwindled to nine, and there were practically no negro slaves around Purysburg. Boehler suffered a severe illness, and Schulius died. In the meantime the Moravians in Georgia were troubled by the warfare with the Spaniards, and decided to migrate to Pennsylvania. Boehler became their leader. At that time began his connection with George Whitefield when the Moravians took passage for Philadelphia in Whitefield's sloop. With some difficulty Boehler managed to hold his small group together after they reached Pennsylvania, for they were without funds. Whitefield had purchased land at the forks of the Delaware, and there the Moravians agreed to build a stone school-house for his use. The obstacles which the Brethren had to face that year in the wilderness tested the ability of their leader. The work was barely begun when winter set in, and doctrinal differences which had developed between Whitefield and the Moravians made him question the desirability of having the Brethren on his land. They stayed during the winter, however; then moved to the site of Bethlehem. They were later able to purchase the land at the forks from Whitefield. Before the permanent settlement was made Nitschmann had succeeded Boehler, and the latter had sailed for Europe in January 1741. While in England he preached for a while in Yorkshire, assisting Ingham. After a visit to his family in

Frankfurt he returned to England to organize a new company of emigrants to America, the "Sea Congregation." His wife, Elizabeth Hobson, whom he married in London on Feb. 20, 1742, accompanied him on this second expedition.

Boehler's varied experiences during his stay in America included a trip through the Indian country west of Bethlehem, and expulsion from New York in 1743 under a colonial law which forbade the teachings of papists and Moravians. For over a year he was in charge of the community at Bethlehem, and Syndic of the Pennsylvania Synod. Relieved of responsibility by the arrival of Spangenberg, he returned to Europe. Although his ship was captured by a French privateer, he was released in France and found his way into Germany through Holland. Six of the eight years which intervened before his next visit to America were spent in England where he acted as superintendent of the Moravian Church. He was consecrated bishop on Jan. 10, 1748. His genius for financial management saved the English branch of the Church from bankruptcy and placed it on a firm basis. Another opportunity to exercise his financial ability presented itself when he returned to Bethlehem in 1753 and rescued the mortgaged lands from threatened foreclosure. A period of eleven years of service in America ensued, during which time he was absent only six months when attending a General Synod in Germany. For eight of these years he was vice-superintendent of the American Province. The new community of Bethabara in North Carolina was organized during this time. Boehler's later years were filled with the duties of a member of the Directory, and then of the new board called the Unity's Elders' Conference. Official business often called him to England, and on one of these visits he was stricken with paralysis. He died on Apr. 27, 1775, and was buried in the Moravian cemetery in Chelsea.

[The two best accounts of the life of Peter Boehler are the ones included in Edmund de Schweinitz, *Some Fathers of the Am. Moravian Ch.* (Bethlehem, 1881) and *Memorials of the Life of Peter Boehler* by J. P. Lockwood (London, 1868). The relations of Boehler with the Wesleys may best be studied from the *Jour. of John Wesley* (Standard Ed. of his works, N. Y., 1909). A contemporary history of the Unitas Fratrum, *Alte und Neue Brueder-Historie oder kurz gefasste Geschichte der Evangelischen Brueder Unitaet in den aeltern Zeiten und insonderheit in dem gegenwaertigen Jahrhundert* by David Cranz (Barby, 1771) is invaluable for background and for many of the most important facts of Boehler's life. There is an English translation by Benj. La Trobe (London, 1780).]   D. M. C.

BOEHM, HENRY (June 8, 1775–Dec. 28, 1875), Methodist itinerant preacher, was born in Lancaster County, Pa., the son of Martin [*q.v.*] and Eve (Steiner) Boehm. His father was expelled from the Mennonites for his "too evangelical opinions" (Abel Stevens, *A Compendious History of American Methodism*, 1867, p. 352), and became a bishop of the United Brethren Church, the members of which were largely German Methodists. His home at Conestoga sheltered many of the itinerant preachers of the pioneer period of Methodism and in "Boehm's Chapel," built in 1791, their voices were heard. Henry Boehm's boyhood was passed under frontier conditions and amid these religious influences. He was a vigorous, daring, self-trained young man of twenty-five when he himself became an itinerant preacher, traveling circuits in Maryland, Virginia, and the regions beyond. Later he labored in Pennsylvania, introducing Methodism into Reading and Harrisburg. His success was augmented by his ability to preach fluently both in English and German. Before 1810 he had preached in German in fourteen different states. At Bishop Asbury's request he superintended the translation of the Methodist Discipline into the German language, thus giving material aid to the progress of the Methodist Episcopal Church among the Germans of the United States. As traveling companion of Bishop Asbury for five years he visited annually not only all the states along the Atlantic coast, but all the frontier settlements and many of the isolated homes. After he ceased to travel with Bishop Asbury he was appointed to various important districts of the rapidly growing denomination needing skilled leadership, and then to pulpits of commanding influence in Pennsylvania and New Jersey until old age compelled him to ask release from regular ministerial duties. After his one hundredth birthday he preached several times, and only a few days before his death gave an effective formal address.

[Boehm's *Reminiscences, Historical and Biographical, of Sixty-four Years in the Ministry*, ed. by Dr. John B. Wakeley (1865; republished with additional chapters in 1875 under title, *The Patriarch of One Hundred Years*); sketch by J. B. Good in Alex. Harris, *Biog. Hist. of Lancaster County* (1872), pp. 49–62; *Jour. of the Rev. Francis Asbury* (1832), vols. II, III; *Minutes of the Annual Conferences of the M. E. Ch. for 1876*; J. M. Buckley, *Constitutional and Parliamentary Hist. of the M. E. Ch.* (1912); J. G. Hurst, *Hist. of Methodism* (1902–04); Wm. H. Daniels, *Illus. Hist. of Methodism* (1880); the Wakeley Collection of MSS. in Drew Theological Seminary, Madison, N. J.]

E. S. T.

BOEHM, JOHN PHILIP (1683–Apr. 29, 1749), German Reformed clergyman, was born at Hochstadt, near Frankfurt-am-Main, Germany, the son of the local Reformed pastor, Philip Ludwig Boehm, and his wife Maria, and was baptized Nov. 25, 1683. He was schoolmaster of the Reformed congregation at Worms

Mar. 11, 1708–Nov. 22, 1715, and at Lambsheim, a short distance southwest of Worms, from then till 1720, when he emigrated with his family to Pennsylvania. Before moving to Worms he had been married to Anna Maria Stehler; his second wife was Anna Maria Scherer of Lambsheim. He settled as a farmer in Whitpain Township, Philadelphia (later Montgomery) County, and, being devoted to the Reformed Church, gathered his German neighbors together and conducted services for them. This beginning led to work that made him the founder of the German Reformed Church in Pennsylvania. At the earnest entreaty of friends who urged that he could not justify his refusal before God, he finally, with some misgiving, assumed the pastoral office. The territory that he covered in his ministerial visits extended from the Delaware to the Susquehanna and from Philadelphia to the Blue Mountains; every month, he wrote in a letter of July 9, 1744, he traveled over 100 miles preaching the gospel and administering the sacraments. He served the congregations of Falkner Swamp, Skippack, and Whitemarsh (1725); Conestoga, the older Tulpehocken congregation, and Philadelphia (1727); Egypt, probably (1734); Cocalico (1735); Oley (1736); the second Tulpehocken congregation (1738); Providence (1742); Coventry (1746); and Whitpain (1747); but he was not allowed to carry on this work in peace. In 1727 the Rev. George Michael Weiss, university educated and regularly ordained, appeared on the scene, denounced Boehm as a mere farmer unfit for the duties of the ministry, and attempted, with some success, to wrest his congregations from him. Boehm and his friends, recognizing that his position was irregular, appealed to the Classis of Amsterdam, which ruled that Boehm's call to the ministry was lawful and his acts valid but stipulated that he should receive ordination. He was accordingly ordained in New York on Nov. 23, 1729, by the Dutch Reformed clergymen, Henricus Boel and Gualtherus Du Bois. Weiss thereupon professed to be reconciled but later resumed his poaching on Boehm's preserves. Trouble of another sort came with Count Zinzendorf's visit to Pennsylvania (Nov. 29, 1741–Dec. 31, 1742). An honest sectarian, Boehm saw the results of his long, body-breaking labors melting away before the Count's unionistic movement and resisted furiously. His *Getreuer Warnungsbrief an die Hochteutsche Evangelisch Reformirten Gemeinden und alle deren Glieder in Pensylvanien* (Phila., A. Bradford, 1742) was part of his counter-propaganda. As old age came upon him, he found his duties increasingly onerous and begged the Dutch

Church authorities for aid. This came at last in the person of Michael Schlatter [*q.v.*], who visited Boehm, Sept. 7, 1746, the day after his arrival in Philadelphia. On Sept. 29, 1747, the Coetus of Pennsylvania was formed; at its second meeting the next year Boehm was elected president. By this time he had given up all his congregations except the one Schlatter had organized for him in Whitpain Township. Seven months later he died unexpectedly at his son's home at Hellertown. His funeral sermon, it would have chagrined him to know, was preached by a Mennonite. He was buried in the church now named for him in front of the pulpit under the altar. As a successful farmer, he left a respectable estate.

[W. J. Hinke, *Life and Letters of the Rev. John Philip Boehm* (1916); J. I. Good, *Hist. of the Ref. Ch. in the U. S. in the Nineteenth Century* (1911); J. I. Good and W. J. Hinke, eds., *Minutes and Letters of the Coetus of the German Ref. Congregations in Pa., 1747–92* (1903).]
                          G. H. G.

BOEHM, MARTIN (Nov. 30, 1725–Mar. 23, 1812), Mennonite bishop, United Brethren bishop, was the son of Jacob Boehm, one of the Mennonites from the Palatinate, who settled in Conestoga Township, Lancaster County, Pa., in the early eighteenth century (I. Daniel Rupp, *A Collection of Upwards of Thirty Thousand Names of German, Swiss, Dutch, French, and other Immigrants in Pennsylvania, 1727–76,* 1876, Appendix III, p. 436). Jacob married into the Kendig family, early settlers in the county, became a deacon in the Mennonite Church, and prospered as farmer and blacksmith. Martin Boehm received his early education at home. He knew both German and English. Though the former was his mother tongue and the language which he used in preaching, he possessed a library of English works which according to his son Henry [*q.v.*], he read "with great pleasure and profit; among others, Wesley's *Sermons* and Fletcher's *Checks*" (Henry Boehm, *Reminiscences, Historical and Biographical, of Sixty-four Years in the Ministry,* 1865, p. 383). His mind was strong and stored with learning, according to his friend, Bishop Asbury. Like his father, Martin Boehm was a farmer; but religion early became the main interest of his life. He inherited the paternal estate which he cared for until his own son Jacob was old enough to manage it. In 1753 he married Eve Steiner, a woman of Swiss ancestry. About three years later he was chosen by lot as a preacher for the Mennonites (Minton Thrift, *Memoir of the Rev. Jesse Lee with Extracts from his Journals,* 1823, p. 253). In 1759 he became a bishop. Because formalism characterized the Mennonite Church,

as it did many of the religions of the day, his task as preacher proved difficult. After experiencing a spiritual conversion he gradually broke away from the orthodox manner of worship, and was influenced to preach a more vital faith. During a preaching tour in the Shenandoah Valley he heard of the teaching of George Whitefield. Later, preachers of the "new light" movement found their way into Lancaster County where they were welcome in Boehm's home.

Of great significance in his later life was his connection with William Otterbein. The two preachers met sometime between 1766 and 1768 (A. W. Drury, *History of the Church of the United Brethren in Christ,* 1924, p. 88). Boehm was addressing an overflow congregation in an orchard not far from Lancaster. Otterbein was among the listeners, and at the close of the service he is said to have clasped Boehm in his arms, exclaiming, "We are brethren." Otterbein and Boehm were chosen at the first annual conference in 1800 as the first bishops of the Church of the United Brethren in Christ. Long before 1800, however, Boehm's connection with the Mennonites had been broken. The Mennonites had censured him for his doctrine and his method of preaching because they thought he was lacking in respect for the ordinances of the church, and because he associated with men of other denominations (John F. Funk, *The Mennonite Church and Her Accusers,* 1878, pp. 42 ff.). Reproofs failed to bring Boehm back into the narrow ways of the sect. Bishops, ministers, and deacons, in conference, therefore, decided to exclude him and his followers from communion and the counsel of the brotherhood. He continued his itinerant preaching, nevertheless, and became more and more successful. He still wore the long beard and plain costume of the Mennonites, and maintained also their simplicity of manner. These characteristics marked his appearance in the pulpit, but more impressive were the sweetness of his character and a quality common to successful revivalists, a peculiar magnetic force. He traveled widely through southern Pennsylvania, Maryland, and Virginia, holding service in barns when the regular meeting places failed to accommodate the crowds of Lutherans, Reformed, Mennonites, and Dunkards who flocked to hear him. Boehm often united in services with other preachers who laid emphasis upon the things of the spirit. He was present at the conference in Baltimore where the Church of the United Brethren in Christ was first organized. He also attended the second conference in 1791, the first annual conference in 1800, and every succeeding conference, with the exception of those in 1806 and 1808, until two years before his death (Drury, *op. cit.,* p. 208; and *Religious Telescope,* June 5, 1926). While thus playing an important part in the Church of the United Brethren, Boehm also formed a connection with the Methodists. A "class" was formed at his house in 1775, and Methodist ministers frequently preached in his father's home until the Methodists built a chapel on land which had belonged to the Boehms. In 1802 Boehm allowed his name to be placed on the class book to comply with Methodist rules of attendance, but evidence that he ever left the Church of the United Brethren is lacking. Boehm's liberality, which had caused his break with the Mennonites, made the dual connection with Methodists and United Brethren possible. In referring to his membership in the Methodist class he said, "For myself, I felt my heart more greatly enlarged towards all religious persons and to all denominations of Christians" (Francis Hollingsworth, *Methodist Magazine,* June 1823, VI, 212). Thus affiliated with two churches, he continued to serve in the ministry, preaching occasionally, though growing more and more feeble, till his death, Mar. 23, 1812.

[References given above.]　　　　　D. M. C.

BOELEN, JACOB (*c.* 1654–1729), silversmith, was born in the Netherlands and brought to America about 1659. The name of his master has not yet been discovered. He was married on May 21, 1679, to Catharina Klock. His brother Henricus (b. 1661) was associated with him in his work and later his son Henricus (b. 1697) carried on his business in the shop on lower Broadway. Judged by the excellence of his general workmanship and the skill of his engraving, he ranks as one of the best of the early silverworkers of New York City. He was admitted a freeman in 1698 but before that time had begun his public services, having been an assessor for the North Ward 1685–94, having been appointed "brant-master" in 1689, and being alderman from the North Ward 1695–97–98–1701. His name was signed to a petition for the restoration of the bolting monopoly to New York. His will was proved Mar. 23, 1729.

[E. Alfred Jones, *The Old Silver of Am. Churches* (1913); F. H. Bigelow, *Historic Silver of the Colonies and its Makers* (1917); Robt. Ensko, *Makers of Early Am. Silver* (1915); Stephen Ensko, *Am. Silversmiths and their Marks* (1927); Metropolitan Museum of Art Catalogues of Silver Exhibitions,—namely, the Clearwater Collection, the Hudson-Fulton Celebration Exhibition, and the 1911 Exhibition of Silver used in New York, New Jersey and the South.]　　K. H. A.

BOGARDUS, EVERARDUS (1607–Sept. 27, 1647), second minister of New Netherland, was born at Woerden, Netherlands, the son of Willem Bogardus. He matriculated in Leyden University, July 17, 1627, as a student of letters, but on Sept. 9, 1630, before he had finished his studies, he was sent by the Consistory of Amsterdam as a comforter of the sick to Guinea, whence he returned in 1632, with good testimonials. After having been examined and ordained for the ministry, he was, on July 15, 1632, accepted for service in New Netherland, as successor to Rev. Jonas Michaëlius, the first minister. He sailed the same month with Wouter van Twiller, the newly appointed director general, in the ship *Soutberg,* which arrived at New Amsterdam in April 1633. His advent in New Netherland marks the erection of the first church edifice at New Amsterdam, a plain wooden building, on the site of the present 39 Pearl Street, which took the place of the mill loft used by Michaëlius. Bogardus soon came into conflict with Van Twiller, whom he threatened to denounce openly from the pulpit. He was also antagonistic to Lubbert van Dincklagen, the public prosecutor, who on his return to Holland, in 1636, laid charges against Bogardus before the Classis of Amsterdam. On July 8, 1638, Bogardus petitioned the director and council of New Netherland for leave to go to Holland to defend himself, but it was felt that he could not be spared. Van Dincklagen renewed his accusations and, in 1640, requested the Classis to be relieved from the excommunication which had been passed upon him through the machinations of Bogardus. After some correspondence with the Consistory of New Amsterdam, the Classis, in 1644, resolved to postpone action until Bogardus could be heard. Meanwhile, in 1638, Bogardus married Anneke Jans, the widow of Roeloff Jansen van Masterland, an early settler of Rensselaerswyck. Through this marriage Bogardus came into possession of a farm of sixty-two acres on Manhattan Island, which in 1636 had been granted to Roeloff Jansen and which afterward became known as the "Domine's Bouwery." In 1642, at the wedding of Bogardus's eldest stepdaughter, Sara Roeloff, to Dr. Hans Kierstede, Director General Kieft secured subscriptions for a new church. From the pulpit in this church, Bogardus afterward severely criticized the director's Indian policy and made uncomplimentary allusions to his person. Kieft at first sent him a "Christian admonition," which Bogardus refused to receive, and then, on Jan. 2, 1646, in the name of the council, sent him a formal communication, in which among other things he accused him of having appeared in the pulpit while drunk and in which he threatened to prosecute him in a court of justice for stirring up the people to mutiny and rebellion. Bogardus admitted some facts, but demanded proof of others and denied that Kieft and his council had jurisdiction to try his case. The director and council offered to submit the matter to impartial judges. Bogardus, however, preferred to defend himself before the Classis of Amsterdam and requested that another minister be sent over in his place. On Aug. 17, 1647, he and Kieft and many other passengers sailed on board the ship *de Princesse* from New Amsterdam. The captain having missed his reckoning, the ship was wrecked during a violent September gale near Swansea, on the southern coast of Wales. Out of about one hundred persons on board, eighty-one perished, among them Kieft and Bogardus.

[Manuscript minutes of the Consistory and of the Classis at Amsterdam, the New York Colonial MSS. in the N. Y. State Lib. at Albany, and the letters and documents in the Sage Lib. at New Brunswick, N. J.; J. R. Brodhead and E. B. O'Callaghan, *Docs. Relating to the Colonial Hist. of the State of N. Y.*, I (1855), 206, 299, 345, 417, and XIV (1883), 12, 16, 59, 69–73, 82–87; *Ecclesiastical Records of the State of N. Y.*, I (1901), 81, 87, 126–27, 181, and VII (1916); *Van Rensselaer Bowier MSS.* (1908), pp. 77, 352, 404, 423, 431, 615, 648; J. R. Brodhead, *Hist. of the State of N. Y.*, I (1853); J. F. Jameson, *Narratives of New Netherland* (1909); E. T. Corwin, *Manual of the Reformed Ch. in America* (4th ed. 1902).]
A.J.F.V-L.

BOGARDUS, JAMES (Mar. 14, 1800–Apr. 13, 1874), inventor, was born in Catskill, N. Y., the son of James and Martha (Spencer) Bogardus. After attending school at irregular intervals until he was fourteen years old, Bogardus became an apprentice to a watchmaker, specializing from the very beginning in engraving and die-sinking. After completing his apprenticeship he left Catskill and went to New York City where he lived and worked for the rest of his life. The earliest record of Bogardus's inventive powers and mechanical skill is the award to him of the gold medal of the American Institute of New York at its first Fair in 1828, for an eight-day, three-wheeled chronometer clock. Two years later on Mar. 2, 1830, he received a patent for a clock which was a most complicated timepiece. The same year he perfected his first generally useful invention, patented May 25, 1830. It was a "ring flyer" and was largely used for fifty years or more thereafter in cotton-spinning machinery. This was followed the next year by another successful invention, namely, an eccentric sugar-grinding mill. From these two inventions Bogardus received sufficient remuneration to permit him to resume work in die-sinking and engraving and in 1831 he made an engraving machine capable

of turning imitation filigree work, rays radiating from a common point, and figures in relief, all in one operation. Its special use was for making engraved metal watch dials. About this time, too, he perfected a so-called transfer machine with which he introduced the production of bank-note plates from separate dies. Again on May 18, 1832, he received a patent for an improvement in the striking parts of clocks. By this time Bogardus was being recognized as an unusual technician, and besides his own work he was often called upon to develop the ideas of others. Thus on Mar. 19, 1833, Miles Berry received a patent for a dry gas meter which was devised by Bogardus. The latter improved the meter during the next two years and was again awarded the gold medal of the American Institute in 1835. On Sept. 17, 1833, he received a patent for a metal-cased pencil, the lead of which was "forever pointed." In 1836 Bogardus went to England and almost immediately accepted a public challenge to construct an engraving machine. This machine made not only an accurate facsimile of the head of Ariadne on a medal but from the medal engraved comic facial expressions. With the machine Bogardus, at her own request, engraved a portrait of Queen Victoria. In 1839 he won the award of $2,000 offered by the English Government for the best engraving machine and plan for making postage stamps. Upon returning to New York in 1840, Bogardus continued his inventive work and during the next seven years perfected a number of devices. These included a white lead paint grinding-mill, a rice grinder, a new eccentric mill, a dynamometer, and a portable horse power. Probably his greatest contribution was his introduction of the use of cast-iron for the frames, floors, and all supports of buildings. His first construction of this sort was his own five-story factory building erected in 1850. This is said to have been the first complete cast-iron building in the world. He patented his method and in the years following erected many other iron buildings throughout the United States and in Cuba. Amongst these were the office building of the Baltimore *Sun,* the Adams Express Building in Washington, the Birch Building in Chicago, and the Public Ledger Building in Philadelphia. Of his last inventions the more important were a machine for pressing glass, a machine for cutting India rubber threads for the production of shirred goods, a pyrometer of great accuracy, and a deep-sea sounding device. Bogardus married Margaret Maclay, the eldest daughter of Rev. Archibald Maclay, D.D., of New York, on Feb. 12, 1831. None of their children having lived to maturity, they adopted a niece, Harriet Hogg, who survived them.

[Sources of information on James Bogardus are *Scientific American*, May 2, 1874; Records Am. Inst., N. Y.; the *New York Herald*, Apr. 14, 1874; *Hist. of Greene County, N. Y.* (1884); U. S. Pat. Office Records; *Centenary Celebration of the First Commercial Gas Co.*: account published by Am. Gas Institute, 1912.]

C. W. M.

BOGART, JOHN (Feb. 8, 1836–Apr. 25, 1920), engineer, was descended from Dutch ancestors who settled in 1641 at Albany, N. Y., where he was born, the son of John Henry and Eliza (Hermans) Bogart. His formal education was received at the Albany Academy and at Rutgers College, from which he was graduated in 1853 with the degree of A.B. He commenced the study of law but, due to ill health, forsook it for the active exercise of engineering. His first position was a temporary one with the New York Central Railroad. He served as an engineer during the Civil War. In 1870 he was married to Emma Cherrington Jefferis of West Chester, Pa. His engineering life was remarkable for the diversity of its accomplishments. Probably he was best known for his work in connection with public park planning and improvement in New York City and many other American cities, and for his contribution to hydro-electric development in the United States and Canada. As consulting engineer for the Cataract Construction Company (later the Niagara Falls Power Company) he traveled all over Europe, studying existing methods of power generation and transmission, and at Domène, opposite the Grand Chartreuse in the Dauphiné Alps, where the power for a paper-mill was drawn from a glacial stream in the mountains four miles away, he found the precedent which had great influence in the final decision as to the system to be adopted at Niagara. Possibly his main contribution to hydro-electric development was in his work as chief engineer of the Chattanooga and Tennessee River Power Company on a 60,000 horse-power plant in the Tennessee River near Chattanooga. "This work was particularly difficult on account of the great variation in head on the turbines and the difficult foundations for the dam. It was found necessary to resort to reinforced concrete pneumatic caissons in making the excavation and afterward to incorporate these as part of the dam. As far as known, this was the first instance where pneumatic caissons had been used for this purpose" (*Transactions of the American Society of Civil Engineers*, LXVIII, 1349).

As advisory engineer for the original Rapid Transit Commission of New York, Bogart pre-

pared plans and contracts for the first subway system. He prepared plans for tunnels under the Hudson to Jersey City and Hoboken, and for the subway now operating between New York and Queens. He was delegated by the president to represent the United States at the international Navigation Congresses held in Düsseldorf, Germany, in 1902; in Milan, Italy, in 1905; and at St. Petersburg, Russia, in 1908. His technical work covered the field of engineering from railroads, canals, water-works, tunnels, parks, and bridges to hydro-electric development, dams, inland-waterway and irrigation projects. He earnestly believed that the great engineer was the man who, rather than specializing too deeply on any one phase of engineering, is capable of combining all essentials into a harmonious whole, and his varied work throughout a life of eighty-four years was a successful effort to realize this conviction.

[Files of the Am. Soc. of Civil Engineers, of which Bogart was, for years, secretary, especially biographical material prepared by Chas. A. Pohl, his partner, and by Herbert Spencer; article in the *Engineering News-Record*, vol. LXXXIV.]

E. Y.

BOGGS, CHARLES STUART (Jan. 28, 1811–Apr. 22, 1888), naval officer, was born at New Brunswick, N. J., the son of Robert Morris Boggs and his wife, Mary, a sister of the heroic Capt. James Lawrence, of "Don't give up the ship" fame. He was a descendant of Ezekiel Boggs who came from Ireland to Delaware about 1741. After several years in the well-known military school of Capt. Partridge at Middletown, Conn., young Charles was appointed a midshipman on Nov. 1, 1826, and was ordered to the sloop-of-war *Warren*, attached to the United States Squadron in the Mediterranean, at that time engaged in protecting American commerce against the Greek and North African pirates. Having served a short time on the ship-of-the-line *Delaware* in the same squadron, he was, in 1830, ordered to the schooner *Porpoise* of the West India Squadron, where he spent two years. On Apr. 28, 1832, having become passed-midshipman, he was attached to the receiving-ship at New York, and spent the next four years mostly on land duty. In 1836 he was appointed master of the ship-of-the-line *North Carolina*, and shortly afterward, as acting lieutenant, to the *Enterprise*. On Sept. 6, 1837, he was promoted to lieutenant, and, after returning home in the *North Carolina*, did notable service in the training of naval apprentices until 1842, when he joined the sloop *Saratoga* and took part in the hostilities against certain African slave ports. In 1846–47 he served on board the steamer *Princeton*, taking part in the bombardment of the castle of San Juan de Ulloa and the capture of Vera Cruz. The United States brig *Truxtun,* having been wrecked on a bar near that city and having fallen into the hands of the Mexicans, Boggs, in charge of a hazardous boat expedition, with great gallantry cut out and retook the ship. He was promoted commander Sept. 14, 1855. For the next three years, having received a furlough, he commanded the mail steamer *Illinois* in the service of the California Steamship Company. At the outbreak of the Civil War he was placed again on active service at his own request, and was given command of the steamer *Varuna,* which, as a unit of Farragut's fleet below New Orleans, was the first vessel to force its way past the batteries. Once beyond the fire of the forts, Boggs succeeded in doing great damage to the Confederate gunboats and auxiliaries. At dawn the next morning (Apr. 25, 1862) the *Varuna* was attacked by two powerful rams and run down by one of them, the *Stonewall Jackson.* Boggs was able, however, to beach the *Varuna,* and in a disabled and sinking condition she continued to fire, practically destroying her two adversaries, until her guns actually sank below the surface of the river. For his signal gallantry in this action Boggs was promoted to be captain, and given command of the *Sacramento* of the blockading squadron off Cape Fear; but, in consequence of overwork and exposure, he was obliged to return to shore duty, and during the rest of the war was in New York, superintending the building and fitting out of vessels for the navy. In 1866 he resumed sea duty as commander of the steamer *Connecticut,* and on a special cruise to the West Indies caused an international incident by demanding the surrender of the Confederate ironclad *Albemarle* in the harbor of Havana, an act resented by the Spanish government. In 1867–68 Boggs commanded the schooner *De Soto.* He was promoted to rear admiral on July 1, 1870, and placed in charge of the third lighthouse district. He commanded the European Fleet in 1871–72, and retired in 1872. He was married twice: on Dec. 4, 1834 to Sophia Dore, who died on Nov. 10, 1872; and on Apr. 8, 1875 to Henrietta Eugenie (Molt) Bull, a widow.

[*Official Records,* ser. I; David D. Porter, *The Naval Hist. of the Civil War* (1886); Wm. E. Boggs, *The Geneal. Record of the Boggs Family* (1916); Navy Registers, 1820–88; obituary in *Army and Navy Jour.,* XXV, 799–800.]   E. B.

BOGGS, LILLBURN W. (Dec. 14, 1792– Mar. 14, 1860), governor of Missouri, was born in Lexington, Ky., the eldest son of John M.

and Martha (Oliver) Boggs. In 1816 he came to St. Louis and soon married Julia, daughter of Judge Silas Bent, thus identifying himself with the fur trading group. [See sketches of Charles and William Bent.] He served as first cashier of their bank, the Bank of Missouri. Always drawn toward the frontier, after an unsuccessful venture at store-keeping at Old Franklin in 1818–19, he spent several years as deputy factor and Indian trader under George C. Sibley at Fort Osage and New Harmony Mission, finally again opening a general store at the new town of Independence. He married as his second wife in 1823 Panthea Grant Boone, grand-daughter of Daniel Boone. His public life began with his election to the state Senate in 1826. He was reelected in 1830, elected lieutenant-governor in 1832, and governor in 1836, defeating the popular W. H. Ashley. As governor he showed independence verging on unconventionality in his appointments. His policy on two other problems aroused widespread opposition and criticism—the "Mormon War" and the construction of the new capitol. When the Mormons, after their expulsion from Jackson and Clay counties, refused to be bound by the attempt to segregate them in a county of their own, and the people of the adjacent counties appealed to the governor for aid, he called out a formidable force of militia and expelled the Mormons from the state. He was bitterly criticized for the expense of the expedition and for his famous order that the Mormons must be exterminated or driven from the state if necessary for the public good. As originally authorized the new capitol was to cost $75,000; by 1840 $200,000 had been spent and the building was still unfinished. Moreover the panic had made the sale of bonds impossible and the governor had secured the funds on short term loans from the new state bank. Searching legislative investigation revealed no trace of fraud or mismanagement. The governor had simply decided (and wisely) on the type of building needed and had gone straight to his goal. During his administration and on his urgent advice and support, the Bank of the State of Missouri was chartered, a conservative and highly successful state bank. Boggs was also largely instrumental in the establishment of the state university and the passage of the first (if ineffective) public-school law. The panic effectually blocked his plans for railroads and public improvements. Shortly after his retirement as governor he was the victim of a murderous assault universally believed to have been instigated by the Mormons. He served in the state Senate from 1842 to 1846, where he was one of the few Democrats who voted against Benton in 1844. This closed his political career in Missouri.

Always attracted to the Far West, having (c. 1829) once engaged in the Santa Fé trade, and now with two sons in the Rocky Mountain fur trade, in 1846 he moved with his family to Napa Valley, Cal. With the breakdown of the Mexican régime he was appointed at once by the American military authorities *alcalde* of all California north of the Sacramento and was the sole civil authority there until the inauguration of the state government. At Sonoma the ex-Governor engaged once more in trade, and for the first time successfully, being just in time to profit by the gold rush. After paying his numerous debts and acquiring a competency he retired to his farm in Napa Valley, where he died.

["Lillburn W. Boggs," by his son (W. M. Boggs) *Mo. Hist. Rev.,* IV, 106–10; biographical sketch by Wm. Southern, Jr., in *Messages and Proclamations of the Governors of Mo.,* I, 303–6 (portrait); biographical sketch (probably by W. M. Boggs) in *Hist. of Napa and Lake Counties, Cal.* (1881), pp. 373–86; J. R. Cable, "The Bank of the State of Mo.," *Columbia Univ. Studies,* CII, No. 2; Jonas Viles, "Capitals and Capitols of Mo.," *Mo. Hist. Rev.,* XIII, 135, 232.]   J.V.

BOGUE, VIRGIL GAY (July 20, 1846–Oct. 14, 1916), civil engineer, the son of George C. and Mary (Perry) Bogue, was born at Norfolk, N. Y. He received his preparatory school education at Russell's Military School, New Haven, Conn., and then attended the Rensselaer Polytechnic Institute from which he was graduated with a degree in civil engineering in 1868. On Mar. 2, 1872 he married Sybil Estelle Russell of San Francisco. His death occurred on board the steamship *Esperanza* en route from Mexico to New York City.

Bogue's chief work was in connection with railroads, in both North and South America. As a young man, just a year out of college, he went to Peru where he had his first railroad experience. Part of that time was spent as assistant engineer (1869–77) on the construction of the Oroya Railway which, in crossing the Andes, reaches the highest altitude of any railway in the world. During his last years in Peru (1877–79) he was manager of the Trajilo Railway. While assistant engineer for the Northern Pacific Railroad (1880–86), in locating a line across the Cascade Mountains in Washington, he discovered and named Stampede Pass through which he drove a two-mile tunnel. At the completion of this work he became chief engineer for the Union Pacific System, serving in this capacity for five years; then, in 1891, he established himself as a consulting engineer with offices in New York City. Transportation problems very largely oc-

cupied his time during the twenty-five years he was engaged in private practise. He was a member of the commission appointed by President Harrison to investigate methods for improving the navigation of the Columbia River, and of the commission appointed by Mayor Strong to determine the feasibility of operating surface cars on Brooklyn Bridge. For three years he was consulting engineer for the governor of New Zealand on a route for a proposed railway across the South Island. From 1905 to 1909, the four years during which the Western Pacific Railway was constructed, he acted as both its vice-president and its chief engineer. The capacity which made him so valuable in railroad work was his combination of a practical constructive talent with a fine sense of the economic aspects of railway operation. Some of his most important work included economic studies of railroad problems. He investigated and made a report for the Canadian Pacific on the economies of the line that existed from Calgary to Vancouver, B. C., as compared with a proposed revised line and other routes. Another of his reports was on the costs of revisions and improvements of the Tehuantepec National Railway in Mexico, and of its port facilities. Water transportation problems also interested him and he made the plans for extensive water-front improvements at both Seattle and Tacoma. Another notable work was his report on the economics of the Denver, Western & Pacific Railway.

[Material for this sketch has been obtained from the *Railway Age Gazette,* Oct. 20, 1916, and the *Engineering News,* Oct. 19, 1916. There are obituaries in the *N. Y. Times, N. Y. Herald,* and *Sun* (N. Y.) for Oct. 16, 1916.]   E. Y.

BOGY, LEWIS VITAL (Apr. 9, 1813–Sept. 20, 1877), lawyer, senator, was the son of Joseph Bogy, a native of Kaskaskia, Ill., and a member of an early French pioneer family. Joseph Bogy was one of the secretaries of Gov. Morales during the Spanish occupation of the Louisiana Territory, and after the purchase, he removed to Sainte Genevieve, Mo., where he became a leading figure in the economic and political life of southeastern Missouri. Here he married Marie Beauvais, and several years later his son, Lewis Vital, was born. Because of limited facilities and ill health, the early education of the boy was seriously hampered. After much difficulty, he commenced the study of law and was graduated in 1835 from Transylvania University,—his studies being interrupted by service in the Black Hawk War. He removed to St. Louis in 1836 and within a decade had built up an extensive and lucrative practise. His attention and energy were largely occupied with the development of railroads and of iron mines. He suffered heavy financial losses in both ventures. From the first, he participated in Democratic politics, being elected in 1840 a member of the legislature from St. Louis. Returning in 1849 to Sainte Genevieve, he again became candidate for the legislature, representing the anti-Benton faction, but was defeated by a combination of Whigs and Benton Democrats. Two years later, he opposed Benton for Congress in a bitter and protracted contest but was unsuccessful (*Missouri Statesman*, May–August 1854). Dogged perseverance, a marked characteristic of Bogy, served him well during these campaigns, and he was elected in 1854 to the legislature. Here he became a leader of the anti-Benton forces and a supporter of D. R. Atchison for senator. Upon the outbreak of the Civil War, Bogy espoused the Southern cause, although he had no direct part in the spectacular events in Missouri during the spring and summer of 1861, which resulted in the military defeat and political elimination of the disloyalists. "During the war he kept very quiet," although it was well known that his sympathies were with the South. He did not subscribe to the oath of loyalty required of attorneys and abandoned his legal practise. In 1862, he became the Democratic, or "snowflake," candidate for Congress but was defeated by Francis Preston Blair, Jr., an ardent supporter of the Lincoln administration. The election district was under martial law and was administered by provost marshals. At the close of the war, he became a determined and relentless opponent of the Missouri Radicals and was a leader in the reconstruction of the Democratic party. He advocated the Liberal Republican movement in 1870 as a temporary expedient for the benefit of the Democratic party. In 1872 the Democrats gained complete control of the state and Bogy became a candidate for senator, as the successor to Blair. His chief support came from those pro-slavery Democrats who had remained at home during the war. He received the nomination after a spirited contest in the party caucus and was elected. Grave charges of bribery and of other irregularities were made subsequent to the election, but after a somewhat perfunctory investigation, Bogy was fully exonerated (*Missouri Statesman,* Feb. 28, 1873; *Senate Document, No. 186,* 49 Cong., 2 Sess.). He entered the Senate when the grave conditions in financial affairs and in the South were the foremost issues. His views of public questions were essentially Western and he strongly advocated the inflation bill of 1874. He was a severe critic of the policy of the Grant

administration in Louisiana during the troubles of 1874–75. In the deliberations of the Senate concerning the disputed election of 1876, he was one of the chief critics of the Louisiana Returning Board and of Packard. In his views both on the financial situation and on the election of 1876, he was supported by his constituents in Missouri. Neither an interesting speaker nor an effective debater, he stood in suggestive contrast to his colleague, Carl Schurz, with whom he was in complete disagreement on most political questions. Following a prolonged illness, he died during the fifth year of his term. He was married to Pelagie, daughter of Bernard Pratte, a member of one of the pioneer families of St. Louis.

[The public career of Bogy can be traced in the files of the *Mo. Republican* and the *Mo. Statesman.* The *Jefferson City Tribune* gives complete information concerning his election to the Senate. The *Cong. Record,* 43, 44, and 45 Cong., is useful for his senatorial career. Sketches of his life appear in W. V. N. Bay, *Reminiscences of the Bench and Bar of Mo.* (1878), and in L. U. Reavis, *St. Louis: The Future Great City of the World* (1870).]   T. S. B.

BOHM, MAX (Jan. 21, 1861–Sept. 19, 1923), painter, son of Henry Justus Edmond and Emilie (Stuhr) Bohm, was born at Cleveland, Ohio, where his father was a successful lumber merchant. His grandfather, Karl Christian Bernard Bohm, an eminent jurist, author, and a friend of Goethe and Schiller, left Saxony because of his political views and, coming to America in the middle of the nineteenth century, settled near Cleveland. Max Bohm in his early youth displayed a talent for painting and at the age of eleven was studying at the Cleveland Art School. In 1887 an artist aunt took him to Europe and for some years he worked at the Louvre and the Académie Julien and studied under Jean Paul Laurens, Lefebvre, and Benjamin Constant. His early work was marine canvases in which he depicted the vast salty sweep of the sea, sailors, fisherfolk, and their boats. He painted with a large, bold gesture; his conceptions were rugged and lofty. At the age of twenty-one his first picture was accepted by the Salon. His first notable success came about six years later with "En Mer," which was given a place of honor in the Paris Salon, and "Crossing the Bar." For twelve years Bohm taught and lectured in London and Paris. In 1898 he married Zella Newcomb of London. Herself an artist and a remarkable personality she did much to mould his life and his art. His "Golden Hours" and "The Family" attracted wide attention when exhibited in 1911; the following year the French government purchased "The Family," a group portrait of his wife and two children and one of the most successful of his paintings, for the Luxembourg Museum. Bohm executed the mural decoration in the Court House at Cleveland. A more notable achievement is the music room murals in the home of Mrs. Mary Longyear in Brookline, Mass. His paintings are included in the collections of the Metropolitan Museum, the National Gallery at Washington, the Boston, Detroit, and Minneapolis Museums, and in many private collections. While at work on important commissions he died suddenly of heart failure at his summer home in Provincetown, Mass.

Bohm's life was reflected to an extraordinary degree in his art. He conceived the world to be filled with active and joyous life, honest toil, and simple pleasures, the whole enhanced by sentiment and love, and filled with a lofty purpose. He eschewed realism and sought to portray ideas rather than the mere facts of nature. He possessed a deep reverence for what appealed to him as the beautiful and noble in life and these he symbolized in an art that was essentially romantic and idealistic. He believed in emotional painting only and maintained that if a man did not have "a deep urge to paint a great thought there was no use in trying to 'carry on' by the mere exercise of paint and brushes." He had a profound faith in the future of American art and constantly urged less reliance on European traditions and opinions and a greater confidence in native ideals.

[*N. Y. Morning Telegraph,* Sept. 30, 1923; *Art News,* Nov. 1, 1924; *Internat. Studio,* May 1924; Samuel Isham and Royal Cortissoz, *Hist. of Am. Painting* (1927); private information.]   F. M.

BOHUNE, LAWRENCE (d. Mar. 19, 1621), is notable as the first physician general of the London Company in Virginia, but the little that is known of him relates almost entirely to his interest in colonization. Contemporary accounts testify that he was "a worthy Valiant Gentleman, a long time brought up amongst the most learned Surgeons and Physitions in Netherlands" (Smith, II, 548). It cannot be said when he first came to America, but he was appointed on Dec. 13, 1620, to be physician general for the company, a position he had occupied before. He was concerned with the importation of fruit trees and of seed; and in connection with one James Smith he transported 300 colonists. The court of Virginia on recognizing him as one of its functionaries awarded him, for the prosecution of some plans of his, 500 acres of land and twenty laborers—this project had apparently been explained to the court most vaguely, but it seemed "to promise much benefit." Somehow he was in England in the winter of 1620–21,

and in the beginning of February he set out on his second journey to America. In the West Indies, the ship on which he had taken passage was attacked by a superior force of Spaniards. In the ensuing fight he took part valiantly, but was killed before the enemy was beaten off.

[Capt. John Smith, *Travels and Works* (1910), ed. by Ed. Arber; Caleb C. Magruder, *Interstate Medic. Jour.* (St. Louis), June 1910, reprinted in H. A. Kelly, *Cyc. of Am. Medic. Biog.* (1912); *Records of the Va. Co. of London* (ed. by S. M. Kingsbury, 1906).]   J. D. W.

BOIES, HENRY MARTYN (Aug. 18, 1837–Dec. 12, 1903), capitalist, of Puritan and Huguenot descent, the son of Joseph Milton Boies and Electa Caroline (Laflin) Boies, was born in Lee, Berkshire County, Mass. He graduated in 1859 from Yale, and two years later married Emma Brainerd, who died in 1868. During the six years after his graduation from college he undertook a number of business ventures, most of which were futile quests of fortune,—as sales agent in Chicago for a powder company, partner in a Hudson River transportation company, Wall Street speculator, newspaper writer, clerk, oil promoter in West Virginia. In 1865 he located at Scranton, Pa., as a member of a powder manufacturing firm, of which he later became president. In 1870 he married Elizabeth Linen Dickson, daughter of Thomas Dickson of Scranton, a noted manufacturer. Boies made extensive scientific studies of explosives, and invented a widely used device for enabling miners to use blasting powder more safely and effectively, together with machinery for its manufacture. He took the lead in the expansion and reorganization of his firm, and continued his connection with its business after the firm was merged with the Du Pont interests and after other enterprises demanded a large share of his attention. In 1872 he became one of the organizers and directors of the Third National Bank of Scranton. Ten years later he became president of the Dickson Manufacturing Company, and inaugurated a policy of expansion which gave the company an international position in the manufacture of engines and machinery. It was during his presidency of this company that he made a second important invention—a steel car wheel designed to meet the constantly increasing demands of weight and speed. He also devised machinery, organized a company, and built a plant for its manufacture (*Railway Gazette,* XXX, 338).

When he left college and went to Chicago in 1859 Boies became a member of the Ellsworth Zouaves, a prominent military organization. Although he was not a member of the combatant forces during the Civil War, his interest in military affairs continued throughout his life. In 1877, during the coal strikes and the national railway strike, he took the lead in the formation of the Scranton City Guard. Fear of public disturbances led to a public meeting presided over by Boies, and to the organization of a battalion of which he was chosen major. As might be inferred from his business connections, he was extremely hostile to the miners and the railway workers and he believed that military means should be available for the repression of industrial disturbances. When the battalion became the 13th Regiment of the National Guard of Pennsylvania, Boies became colonel of the regiment. He instituted the first rifle range, established the office of inspector of rifle practise, created a regimental school for officers, wrote articles on military subjects, and in other ways promoted efficiency in the military organization of the state and nation. His appointment in 1887 as a member of the Pennsylvania Board of Public Charities led to his principal ventures in the field of authorship, notably his *Prisoners and Paupers* (1893) and *Science of Penology* (1901), in which he took relatively advanced positions with respect to the humanitarian treatment and reformation of offenders. The book was used as a college text and was one of the pioneer attempts at a scientific treatment of a grave social problem. Boies traveled widely, read extensively, wrote and made public addresses on varied subjects, and had active connections with an unusually large number of business, civic, religious, social, and learned organizations.

[J. H. Odell (ed.), *Henry Martyn Boies* (1904); F. L. Hitchcock, *Hist. of Scranton and Its People* (1914); H. E. Hayden (ed.), *Geneal. and Family Hist. of the Wyoming and Lackawanna Valleys* (1906).]
W. B—n.

BOIES, HORACE (Dec. 7, 1827–Apr. 4, 1923), governor of Iowa, was born in a log cabin on a farm in Erie County, N. Y., and was educated in the country schools. His father, Eber Boies, who served in the War of 1812, was of French ancestry; his mother, Esther Henshaw, was the daughter of a soldier of the American Revolution who was of English ancestry. At the age of sixteen Horace Boies, carrying some clothes and other belongings in a red bandana handkerchief and one dollar in his pocket, boarded a lake boat at Buffalo, N. Y., bound for Wisconsin Territory. There he worked as a farm hand helping to put in crops, harvest the grain, and break the prairie sod. Late in the fall of 1844 the serious illness of his mother compelled his return to New York. But the lure of the frontier soon recalled him to the West—to Illinois and to Wisconsin Territory. Here he worked in the fields during the summer and gave some atten-

tion to schools during the winter. At the age of twenty-one he was back in Erie County, where he married Adella King, and at her suggestion entered upon the study of law in the office of a village attorney. In 1849 he passed the examinations and was admitted to bar. For fifteen years he practised law in the vicinity of Buffalo. His first wife having died in 1855, in 1858 he married Versalia M. Barber. Removing to Waterloo, Ia., in 1867 he entered into a law partnership with H. B. Allen. Like many another lawyer, Boies was drawn into politics. He was first a Whig, then a Republican, and finally a Democrat. In 1857 he had been elected by the Republicans to a seat in the lower house of the New York legislature, where he served for one term. When the Republicans of Iowa committed their party to prohibition by constitutional amendment, Boies left the party and voted with the Democrats. He opposed the amendment on the grounds that it would deprive individuals of property without compensation and would violate the fundamental principle of "the largest possible liberty of the individual consistent with the welfare of the whole." He denounced "as merciless in their severity many of the penalties inflicted by the prohibitory statutes of the State." On this issue he was elected governor of Iowa in 1889 and was reëlected in 1891. In his second campaign for governor he denounced the protective tariff as "unjustly burdensome to the agricultural interests of the country." Largely because the Republican party had modified its attitude on prohibition, he was defeated in his candidacy for a third term in 1893. Election and reëlection to the office of governor in a state in which the Republican party had never before been defeated since its organization in 1856 attracted to Boies nation-wide attention. Thus in 1892 he had a considerable following for the Democratic presidential nomination. At the convention in 1896 he was the second in the balloting with a good prospect of winning the nomination when Bryan captivated the delegates with his "cross of gold" speech. In 1893 Cleveland offered Boies the portfolio of secretary of agriculture. "This I declined," wrote Boies, "for the double reason that its acceptance would compel my resignation as governor of the state, and for the further reason that I did not believe myself qualified to discharge the duties of that office." He spent the later years of his life partly in Iowa and partly in southern California. Although he had given up the practise of law he retained an interest in farming. He owned thousands of acres of land in Iowa, Nebraska, and Canada.

A man of medium size, Boies walked erect to the end of his long life: he possessed the sturdiness of the pioneers. The dominant expression of his unseamed face was one of human sympathy. Free from ostentation in speech and manner, he was inclined to reticence. While moderate in his opinions, he was courageous in the expression of his convictions. In politics he was not a good mixer, and he shunned publicity. He lived simply and without pretense. He was a member of no church and belonged to no secret order. In view of his stand on the constitutional and statutory regulation of the manufacture and sale of intoxicating liquors it is an interesting fact that he was a member of the Good Templars, a worldwide fraternal society for the promotion of total abstinence.

[Unpublished autobiographical letters addressed to Benj. F. Shambaugh; autobiographical sketch dictated in 1914 upon the request of Edw. H. Stiles and published by him in *Recollections and Sketches of Notable Lawyers and Public Men of Early Ia.* (1916); autobiographical sketch published in the *Waterloo Tribune*, Apr. 6, 1923; Shambaugh's *Messages and Proclamations of the Governors of Ia.*, VI, 269–429.]   B.F.S.

BOISE, REUBEN PATRICK (June 9, 1819–Apr. 10, 1907), jurist, lawmaker, was the son of Reuben Boies (not Boise) Jr., and Sarah (Putnam) Boies. Born at Blandford, Hampden County, Mass., he was educated partly in the public schools of that place and graduated from Williams College in 1843. At Westfield, Mass., an uncle, Patrick Boies, practised law, and under his tuition young Boise was initiated into his future profession, being admitted to the bar in 1847. Previously he had spent one year in Missouri as a teacher. After practising several years in Chicopee, in 1850 he went to Portland, Ore., where he began his distinguished career as a lawyer. Beginning in 1851 as prosecuting attorney under the territorial legislature, he became code commissioner in 1853 and with two associates prepared the first Oregon code. In the constitutional convention, 1857, he was one of half a dozen leaders who were chiefly responsible for the character of the new state constitution. He was chairman of the committee on the legislative department and reported the article constituting it of fifteen senators and thirty representatives, with the power to double the respective numbers as population increased. The sessions were technically not restricted to a definite period of time; but members were to receive pay for only sixty days, which constituted an effective practical limitation. This article still remains in force. Boise took an active part in the discussion of every important feature of the constitution. He favored the policy of rigidly limiting the powers of corporations, which was good democratic doctrine in that day. He was concerned to make the cost of government for the new and impecunious commonwealth as light as possible. For that reason he voted to make the governor *ex officio* state treasurer. His influence upon the new constitution can be described as neither conservative nor radical. He was eminently practical, seeking a sound, workable system adapted to the conditions of the people. In 1857 he was appointed, by President Buchanan, a member of the Oregon territorial supreme court. After statehood he was elected to the supreme bench of the state, where he served with distinction for twelve consecutive years, being chief justice during two periods of two years each, and after an intermission of four years, he was again on the supreme bench for four years, till 1880. Thereafter he was judge of the third judicial district over whose court he presided for eighteen years, though not continuously. He practised law at Salem from 1892 to 1898 when he was once more elected to the judgeship in his eightieth year, serving the full term of six years, the oldest judge in Oregon.

He owned 640 acres of Willamette Valley land near Dallas which he developed into a valuable estate. He was always deeply interested in farming, in scientific training for agriculture, and in the development of social life among farmers. He was a frequent contributor to agricultural journals, was a member of the governing board of the Oregon Agricultural College (as well as of other educational institutions) and was chosen master of the state Grange during a succession of years. He also attended meetings of the national Grange. He was twice married: in 1851, to Ellen F. Lyon, who died in 1865; and, in 1867, to Emily A. Pratt.

Boise was a man of soldierly bearing, erect, and dignified. His eyes were hazel, his hair black and curly, and he wore a full close-cropped beard. He had a large head with very high forehead, and prominent Roman nose. In speaking and writing he was solid rather than brilliant. He was deliberate, definite, impressive, intent on facts and arguments, but little given to embellishment. His opinions delivered from the bench were marked by clearness, cogency, and brevity. In private he was chary of words but sympathetic and interested. The same spirit characterized his relations with his fellow-men in the mass. Generous views, a steady concern for the welfare of the people, and admirable judgment enabled him in a long active life to do much for the development of Oregon from a primitive western community to a modern commonwealth.

[*Ore. Reports*, vols. I–XLVII, for cases decided by Boise; *Ibid.*, XLIX, 23–29, "In Memoriam, Hon. Reuben P. Boise"; *Morning Oregonian*, Apr. 11, 12, 1907; short sketch in *Ore. Hist. Quart.*, VIII, 201–4; personal letter of Reuben P. Boise, Jr., Apr. 4, 1927.]   J.S.

BOISSEVAIN, INEZ MILHOLLAND

BOISSEVAIN, INEZ MILHOLLAND (Aug. 6, 1886–Nov. 25, 1916), reformer, was born in New York City, the daughter of John W. and Jean (Torrey) Milholland. Her father was a newspaper man. She received her early education at the Comstock school in New York, the Kensington High School, London, and the Willard School in Berlin, and obtained the B.A. degree at Vassar in 1909. As a student she was known as an active radical. She started the suffrage movement at Vassar, enrolled two-thirds of the students, and taught them the principles of socialism. With the radical group she had gathered about her, she attended socialist meetings in Poughkeepsie which were under the ban of the faculty. She was also devoted to athletics and held records in basket ball. After graduation she tried for admission at both Oxford and Cambridge with the purpose of studying law, but without success. She also failed to gain admission to the Harvard Law School, but was finally matriculated at the New York University Law School, from which she took her LL.B. degree. She was interested in every way in the working conditions and rights of women and took a prominent part in the shirtwaist strike in New York in 1912. She was a member of the Political Equality League, the Woman's Trade Union League, the Women's Political Union, the National Child Labor Committee, the Fabian Society, and the Women's Social and Political Union of England. On July 14, 1913, she was married in London to F. E. Boissevain, son of Charles Boissevain of Amsterdam. In December 1915 she joined the Ford Peace Party which, however, she left at Stockholm because she considered its methods undemocratic. Her most prominent work was done in connection with the movement for woman's suffrage. After the suffrage convention in Philadelphia in 1912 she organized a picturesque demonstration in Washington in which, mounted on a white horse, she led a parade of women down Pennsylvania Avenue. She was then called the American Joan of Arc. At the head of a department for women in *McClure's Magazine* which began in 1913, she wrote a number of articles on woman's rights. Her mind was full of ideas and she expressed herself well. Aligned with the radical wing which early in 1916 took the name of National Woman's Party, she took an active part in the presidential campaign of that year. She traveled through the twelve western states which at that time had given women the vote and appealed for help for the Republican party which had pledged itself to support an amendment granting woman suffrage. Unsparing of her strength, she collapsed in Los Angeles during a speech and after ten weeks died of anemia brought on by her over-exertions. The National Woman's Party held a beautiful and striking memorial service for her on Christmas Day 1916 in Statuary Hall in the Capitol at Washington.

[*Who's Who in America,* 1914–15; *World Today,* Mar. 1910; *McClure's,* July 1912, Jan., Feb., Mar., 1913; *Harper's Weekly,* May 30, 1914; *Photo Era,* Dec. 1916; *Good Housekeeping,* Aug. 1918; I. H. Irwin, *The Story of the Woman's Party* (1921); *Los Angeles Times,* Nov. 26, 1916; *N. Y. Times,* Nov. 26, 1916.]

M.A.K.

BOKER, GEORGE HENRY (Oct. 6, 1823–Jan. 2, 1890), was playwright, poet, patriot, diplomat. The ancestry and environment which shaped Boker's character were typical of the America which built a patrician caste upon the foundations of commercial success. He was descended from a Quaker family of Nottinghamshire, which had come to England, by way of Holland, from the French town of Nîmes, where the name had originally been Bocher. Charles Boker, father of the playwright, was a banker, who restored the Girard Bank to solvency after the panic of 1837. George Boker grew up among cultivated surroundings, in the Philadelphia which still preserved the Colonial tradition, social and architectural. From his boyhood, he was a reader of romance, and his philosophy of composition was expressed by his advice to R. H. Stoddard, "Get out of your age as far as you can."

Boker graduated from the College of New Jersey, as Princeton was then called, in 1842. His contributions to the *Nassau Monthly,* of which he was one of the founders, show an unusual maturity of thought, of which one sentence "if there is one offence in a nation which we should willingly forgive, it is the undue pride and admiration of its great men" is typical. After his marriage to Julia Mandeville Riggs of Georgetown, D. C., in 1844, and a foreign tour, he gave up his study of law and devoted himself to writing. His first volume of lyric and narrative verse, *A Lesson of Life* (1848), was only promising, but in *Calaynos,* published in the same year, he showed his power as a playwright. It is a blank verse tragedy, laid in Spain in medieval times, and based upon the Spanish horror of any taint of Moorish blood. Although *Calaynos* was written for the stage, Boker had to wait for foreign approval before he could secure a hearing from his own countrymen. Samuel Phelps produced *Calaynos* at the Sadler's Wells Theatre, in London, May 10, 1849, without the formality of asking Boker's consent. Encouraged by reports of the play's success, James E. Murdoch produced it at the Walnut Street Theatre, Philadelphia, Jan.

20, 1851, and it was later revived. But although Boker received overtures for his next play from managers here and abroad, *Anne Boleyn* (1850) never saw the stage. It was not as lofty in conception as *Calaynos,* or as charming as his romantic comedy, *The Betrothal,* which was first performed at the Walnut Street Theatre, Philadelphia, Sept. 25, 1850, with "as brilliant success as ever greeted any production within the walls of this edifice" (Durang, *The Philadelphia Stage,* ser. III, ch. 112). A love story of medieval Italy, the characters were better drawn than is usual in romantic drama, and the verse showed Boker's usual distinction. It was produced at Drury Lane, Sept. 19, 1853. Boker next attempted a social satire, laid in England in 1851, in *The World a Mask,* which was put on at the Walnut Street Theatre, Philadelphia, Apr. 21, 1851. This play, which still remains in manuscript, was well received, but the mingled prose and verse have not the dignity of Boker's poetic drama. *The Widow's Marriage,* a comedy in blank verse, of the days of George II, was a much better play, but the inability of Marshall, the manager of the Walnut Street Theatre, to find an actress capable of portraying the leading character of Lady Goldstraw, prevented its performance.

Boker was widely read in the history of Spain and he found in the career of Leonor de Guzman, the mistress of Alphonso XII, a fine subject for an heroic tragedy. In *Leonor de Guzman,* which was written for Julia Dean, and first produced at the Walnut Street Theatre, Oct. 3, 1853, he portrayed a striking contrast between the characters of Leonor and of Queen Maria, the two women who had loved the dead King, and he preserved the sympathy of the audience for both of them. Second only to his next play, *Leonor* is a powerful study of human passions of an exalted kind. The climax of Boker's achievement was his tragedy of *Francesca da Rimini,* first produced by E. L. Davenport at the Broadway Theatre, New York, Sept. 26, 1855. Taking the historic story of Francesca and Paolo, wife and brother of Prince Lanciotto of Rimini, who loved each other and who died by his hand, Boker created the character of the medieval prince who, misshapen and misunderstood, is yet "the noblest heart in Rimini." For the first time in literature, the husband became the most appealing figure, and so skilfully did Boker blend history and tradition, so powerful was his interpretation of the Italian spirit of the thirteenth century in terms of passion, pride, and brotherly affection, that he produced the greatest piece of dramatic poetry written in the English language and presented on the professional stage during the nineteenth century. Com-

pared with Boker's characters, vitally human either in love or hate, the creations of later writers in English seem pale and ineffective. Due to Davenport's mechanical interpretation, *Francesca da Rimini* was only moderately successful upon its first production. But when revived by Lawrence Barrett, who acted Lanciotto in 1882, with Otis Skinner as Paolo, and Marie Wainwright as Francesca, it made a profound impression, and provided Barrett with one of his best parts. In 1901 Otis Skinner again revived *Francesca,* taking the part of Lanciotto, Aubrey Boucicault playing Paolo and Marcia von Dresser, Francesca. This superb production proved, once more, the perennial appeal of this drama, truly "not of an age but for all time."

But the lack of recognition in 1855 of his real ability discouraged Boker, and when *The Bankrupt* was produced at the Broadway Theatre, Dec. 3, 1855, he did not allow his name to be attached to it. Perhaps it was a recognition on his part that the play, a prose melodrama, in which a much injured hero returns to Philadelphia in 1850 to revenge himself upon his persecutors, is the poorest of his dramas. Boker could not trifle and was primarily a poet.

In 1856 he collected his lyric and narrative verses and published them, together with *Calaynos, Anne Boleyn, Leonor de Guzman, Francesca da Rimini,* and *The Widow's Marriage,* in two volumes, entitled *Plays and Poems,* which have been five times reprinted. Among his lyrics, his sonnets are the most outstanding. He had a gift for the sonnet on public affairs, and those addressed to England, at the time of the Crimean War, were often reprinted during the World War as representative of his discriminating sympathy with Great Britain. His love sonnets, with their haunting beauty of phrase, gave him rank among American sonneteers second only to Longfellow. Seventy-seven sonnets were included in the *Plays and Poems,* but Boker wrote altogether three hundred and fourteen. Some of these have only recently been brought to light (see E. S. Bradley's *A Newly Discovered American Sonnet Sequence, Publications of the Modern Language Association of America,* vol. XL, 1925, pp. 910–20).

During the years immediately following his father's death in 1857, Boker's attention was turned from poetry through his brave and successful legal fight to rescue Charles Boker's name from calumny and his property from seizure. It was not until 1873 that a final judgment was rendered, which established the fact that his father had saved, not wrecked, the Girard Bank. Boker paid his respects to the vilifiers of his father's memory in his *Book of the Dead,* written between 1858 and 1860 but not published until 1882.

Both as a poet and a citizen, Boker rendered sterling service to his country during the Civil War. Like all war poetry, his is uneven, varying from the ill-considered attack on McClellan, "Tardy George," which he omitted when his *Poems of the War* were published in 1864, to his stirring "Black Regiment," his touching "Dirge for a Soldier," in memory of Gen. Philip Kearny, and his noble "Ode to America," written in March 1862, when the cause of the Union seemed dark. These were published in 1864 and on July 20, 1865, Boker read before the Phi Beta Kappa Society at Harvard College his "Our Heroic Themes," in which he paid one of the earliest and most discriminating tributes to Abraham Lincoln. It was the Philadelphia patrician who first spoke of Lincoln as "Lord of himself, an inborn gentleman."

Boker had been a Democrat, but when Fort Sumter fell, he recognized that there could be no question of divided allegiance. Knowing how close and intricate were the social and economic relations between Philadelphia and the South, he took an active part, in November 1862, in the foundation of the Union Club, which became on Dec. 27 the "Union League of Philadelphia," the first in the country. Boker was its first secretary and devoted a large share of his time to the organization of its activities. The services of the Union League in raising money, in encouraging enlistment and in combating the more subtle social influences which disturbed Philadelphia during the earlier days of the Civil War, were directed by Boker, and he remained secretary until 1871. During the years 1865 to 1871 he was quietly helping other poets who were not so securely established. Through him, Charles Godfrey Leland became managing editor of the Philadelphia *Press,* and Richard Henry Stoddard, William Gilmore Simms and Paul Hamilton Hayne were introduced to the pages of *Lippincott's Magazine* with which Boker was endeavoring to restore the lost primacy of Philadelphia in the magazine world.

In 1869 Boker published *Königsmark, The Legend of the Hounds, and Other Poems,* the first being a verse drama, written about 1857, dealing with the love of Queen Sophia of Hanover for a colonel of the guards. "The Legend of the Hounds," a stirring narrative, was based upon a tradition that an owner of a smelting furnace in the Lebanon Valley of Pennsylvania cast into the flames a dog who had displeased him. Boker's skill in transferring this incident to an English setting and his establishment of the supernatural, in the terrible effect upon a human being of the ghostly pack of hounds which hunt him to his doom, make this poem noteworthy. Among his other narrative poems, "The Ivory Carver," a celebration of faith, and "The Countess Laura," are the best.

Boker was appointed minister to Turkey, Nov. 3, 1871. By his dignity, his prompt courage and his tact, he reëstablished our diplomatic relations with the Porte. Two treaties were negotiated by him, one securing for the first time recognition by the Ottoman Government that Turkish subjects, when naturalized according to American law, became American citizens, and the other referring to the extradition of criminals. Hearing that his son George, who was military attaché to the Legation, had been insulted by Turkish soldiers in the Pera, or foreigners' quarter of Constantinople, Boker drove instantly to the Porte and protested so effectively that the foreign quarter was thereafter forbidden ground to the Turkish soldiery. With a capacity for detail, Boker also recognized the importance of dealing in a large way with the problems of diplomacy. When the Khedive of Egypt sought his aid in the establishment of judicial freedom from Turkish interference, Boker advised the United States Government at once to take a broad view of the request, but had the mortification of seeing his constant representations disregarded, while one by one the chief European nations took the proper steps. Boker's informal letters to Bayard Taylor reveal his sympathy with any nation that sought to respect itself, and his disappointment at being unsupported in his efforts to help Turkey in her desire to control her internal affairs without dictation from the powers of Europe embittered his stay in Constantinople. He disliked also the constant wrangles with the Turkish Government in which, however, he seems to have been unvaryingly successful. He welcomed, therefore, the promotion implied in his appointment as Envoy Extraordinary and Minister Plenipotentiary to Russia, leaving Constantinople on May 4, 1875, and presenting his credentials to Alexander II in St. Petersburg on July 24. There was something regal in Boker's nature, which had won him the regard of the Sultan and the Khedive and which established a personal friendship with the Czar. The immediate result was the change of attitude toward the Centennial Exposition, in which Russia had hesitated to participate. The account of the dinner given in his honor by the Commission on the Russian section of the Exposition reveals him in that happy attitude and tactful expression which won friends everywhere for him and for his country

(*Journal de St. Petersbourg,* LIII (1877), 68). But the administration of Hayes was unfriendly to Boker and despite the intimation from Alexander II that his continuance in office would be most agreeable to the Czar, Boker was recalled in January 1878. His return was a signal for Philadelphia to bestow such honors upon him as the presidency of the Union League and of the Philadelphia Club. In 1886 he became president of the Fairmount Park Commission and devoted his attention to the beautifying of the park system, remaining in the office until his death.

The impulse to write, which had been checked by the lack of appreciation of his work, was renewed by the success of the revival of *Francesca da Rimini* by Lawrence Barrett in 1882. He first revised *Calaynos,* but a disagreement with Barrett concerning the royalties on *Francesca da Rimini* prevented its production. In the meantime Boker had written *Nydia* in 1885 for Barrett, a blank verse tragedy which owes its central situation to Bulwer's *Last Days of Pompeii,* but which is entirely original in language and in feeling. The play was not produced, and Boker rewrote it under the title *Glaucus* in 1886, probably to give Barrett a more definitely leading part. These plays, still unpublished, contain some of his loftiest poetry. *Nydia,* especially, in its depiction of the passion of the blind girl for Glaucus, is one of the finest conceptions in our dramatic literature. It is evident from the manuscripts that Boker was preparing a revised edition of his works, but illness prevented his completion of the project. His death on Jan. 2, 1890, at his home in Philadelphia, from disease of the heart, brought forth renewed interest in his poetry and led to the publication of the fifth edition of his *Poems and Plays* and the reprinting of his *Poems of the War.*

The very qualities which made Boker so preeminently a patrician, defeat the attempt to draw any adequate portrait of him. He was tall, and long enjoyed the reputation of being "the handsomest man in Philadelphia." But, from his early days at college until his death, he guarded the privacy of his own emotions so well that his personality cannot be transferred to the printed page. It is only in the unguarded letters to Taylor that we discover the disappointment of the high-minded gentleman, who longed to devote his life to poetry, which his countrymen did not appreciate, or to playwriting, which the circumstances of the American Theatre made hazardous, or to the service of his country, to which the sordid politics of the day put an end. To the Philadelphia that would give him any honors except the one he craved, he presented the smiling unconcern which

never betrayed how deeply the iron had entered into his soul.

[The best and only biography is *Geo. Henry Boker, Poet and Patriot* (1927), by Edward Scully Bradley. This contains a complete bibliography. The present account is based also on the inspection of the manuscripts now at Princeton University and, until her death, in the possession of the daughter-in-law of the poet, Mrs. Geo. Boker, who furnished many of the details. From the personal side, interesting pictures are given by R. H. Stoddard, "Geo. Henry Boker," *Lippincott's Mag.,* June 1890; C. G. Leland, "Reminiscences of Geo. Henry Boker," *American* (Phila.), Mar. 1, 1890; an anonymous "Some Recollections of Boker," *Atlantic Mo.,* Mar. 1890; and Jas. Barnes, "Geo. H. Boker," *Nassau Lit. Mag.,* XLVI (1891), 90. Contemporary criticism of his plays is to be found in C. G. Leland, "Boker's Plays," *Sartain's Mag.,* June 1851; in Wm. Winter, *Wallet of Time,* I (1913), 312–22; and more recent studies in A. H. Quinn, "The Dramas of Geo. Henry Boker," *Pub. Mod. Lang. Ass.,* XXXII (June 1917), 233–66; J. W. Krutch, 'A Little Known Am. Dramatist,' *Sewanee Rev.,* Oct. 1917; A. H. Quinn, "Geo. Henry Boker, Playwright and Patriot," *Scribner's Mag.,* June 1923; Boker's services to the Union are treated in the *Reception Tendered by the Members of the Union League of Philadelphia to Geo. H. Boker, Dec. 22, 1871* (1872), and in *The League for the Union* (1888). An interesting foreign view of Boker is given in "Biographie du très honorable, Geo. H. Boker, Ministre des États Unis d'Amérique" in *L'Orient Illustré,* Constantinople, June 13, Aug. 22, 1874. Boker's works are now out of print, except *Francesca da Rimini,* included by A. H. Quinn in *Representative Am. Plays* (1917).]

A.H.Q.

BOLDT, GEORGE C. (Apr. 25, 1851–Dec. 5, 1916), hotelman, was born in the Island of Rugen, in the Baltic Sea. The son of a merchant, and educated in the common schools, he came alone to the United States at the age of thirteen, and went to work in a hotel in New York City. With his savings he started a chicken farm and sheep-ranch in Texas. This venture proving unsuccessful, he returned to the hotel service at Cornwall-on-Hudson, N. Y., afterwards taking a position in Parker's Restaurant, Broadway, New York City, where he advanced through successive stages from general-utility man to steward. His next post was as steward of the famous Clover Club in Philadelphia, where influential members helped him convert a large private residence on Broad St. into a hotel, called the Bellevue. His policy was to charge high prices for good things, which at the same time preserved its exclusiveness. Meanwhile, he turned a favor for William Waldorf Astor, and won his gratitude. When Astor decided to abandon his residence at Fifth Ave. and Thirty-fourth St., New York, Boldt was instrumental in persuading him to build on the site the Waldorf Hotel, then the most magnificent in the world, of which he was named manager. When it opened, in 1893, there were but thirty-two guests, and other hotelmen smiled at its apparent failure. But the public which demanded the best found that they could get it at the Waldorf. Within a few years it was too small for the great business Boldt had built up, and by 1898 the Astoria was completed, forming the Waldorf-Astoria, which Boldt made famous the world over as the acme of what a good hotel should be. By actual count some 20,000 people a day entered the Waldorf-Astoria, which had some 1,800 employees. While continuing as president of the Waldorf-Astoria Hotel Company, he again turned to Philadelphia, bought the old Stratford, adjoining the Bellevue, and on its site erected the new Bellevue-Stratford Hotel. He was president or a director of a number of insurance companies and other corporations; was president of the Holland Library, Alexandria Bay, N. Y., and of the Thousand Islands Country Club; a trustee of the Saturday and Sunday Hospital Association, and active head of the trustees of Cornell University, to which he gave $100,000, and for which he planned its comprehensive system of dormitories. He rode frequently in Central Park, and was a good judge of a saddle horse. Married to Louise, daughter of William Kehrer of Philadelphia, he had a winter home at Santa Barbara, Cal., and a summer estate of 1,000 acres on the St. Lawrence River. In 1909 Tammany Hall considered him as a possible candidate for mayor of New York. More than any other man he was responsible for the modern American hotel. He was a lovable, simple person, and when he died the flags on almost every New York hotel were placed at half-staff. Simeon Ford, dean of New York hotelmen, said of him: "George Boldt invented the theory that the public was right. . . . He trained his employes to give the patron something he would like, and he never let a man leave his doors unsatisfied." His place in the hotel business was peculiar to himself, there was none to dispute his preëminence, none who attended to the multifarious duties of the hotel proprietor with the same unflagging enthusiasm, or who did more to raise it from the dull routine of a business to something approaching a profession.

[The chief source is Simeon Ford's *Recollections*; see also the obituaries in the *N. Y. Times, Herald,* and *Evening Post,* Dec. 6, 1916. Trade journals such as the *Hotel Reporter* and the *Hotel Gazette* give technical and statistical information about the Waldorf-Astoria under the Boldt régime.]   R. R. R.

BOLL, JACOB (May 29, 1828–Sept. 29, 1880), Swiss-American geologist and naturalist, son of Henry and Magdalena (Peier) Boll, was born in Bremgarten, Canton Aargau, Switzerland. After two years at the University of Jena (which he left without a degree) he returned to his native town, married Henriette Humbel (1854), and settled down to a long career as apothecary in his own pharmacy in Bremgarten. His inter-

est in natural history had been awakened during his *gymnasium* days in Switzerland, and had been fostered at Jena. His persistent study of the natural history of his canton bore fruit in a number of now little-known papers, and in a thin book on the flora of Canton Aargau, published in 1869. In this year he visited Texas (whither his family had preceded him), and during 1870 collected so well in Texas for Louis Agassiz at Harvard that there are said to be Boll specimens in pretty nearly every department of the Harvard Museum. The winter of 1870 Boll spent with Agassiz at Harvard, returning to Switzerland in the spring. He remained in Switzerland until after the death of his wife, which occurred in August 1873. He then decided to accept the repeated invitations of Agassiz to become a staff-member of the Museum of Comparative Zoology at Cambridge, and came to America for the second time in January 1874. On reaching Cambridge, he first learned of the death of Agassiz on Dec. 14, 1873. At once he returned to Texas, and during the years 1874–80 he investigated the geology and natural history of that state. During the four seasons of 1877–80 he collected fossils and reptiles, chiefly in northern and northwestern Texas for Edward D. Cope [*q.v.*]. He died in the field while collecting fossils in Wilbarger County.

Boll first intelligibly identified the Permian rocks of northwest Texas (*American Naturalist,* XIV, 684–86). He discovered many new species of fossil plants and animals which were described by Cope in a series of contributions on the Permian vertebrates of Texas (1878–83). Many Boll specimens of recent Texas reptiles, batrachia, and fishes are referred to by Cope in his book entitled, *On the Zoological Position of Texas* (1880). Boll's large collection of microlepidoptera, embracing species from the entire world, passed at his death into the hands of B. Neumoegen and Dr. C. V. Riley, with whom he had worked on the United States Entomological Commission for the study of the Rocky Mountain locust (1877–80). He was an indefatigable collector in all groups of insects, and most of the European museums have specimens of his collecting. He was commissioned by European silk-growers to investigate American species of silk-worms, with an eye to the introduction into Europe of hardy species. His cantonal government commissioned him (1874) to make extensive collections of the Colorado potato beetle (just then becoming a pest in America), as well as to collect (1871) the seeds of woody plants, and the fresh-water and marine mollusks of Texas. During the last two years of his life he printed in the

American Naturalist (June 1879; September 1880) two papers that "were only the introduction to what promised to be valuable original contributions to the geology of Texas" (R. T. Hill, "Present Condition of Knowledge of the Geology of Texas," in *Bulletin XLV of the United States Geological Survey,* 1887).

[*Galveston News,* Oct. 10, 21, 1880; *Dallas Daily Herald,* Oct. 7, 19, 1880; *Dallas Morning News,* Oct. 21, 1928; a documented appraisal of Boll's contributions to the biology of the Southwest, to appear shortly in *Am. Midland Naturalist.*]   S. W. G.

BOLLAN, WILLIAM (*c.* 1710–*c.* 1776), lawyer, agent of Massachusetts, was born in England, probably about 1710. He came to America while young, studied law in Massachusetts with Robert Auchmuty, and became an able lawyer. As early as 1732 he was "Counsellour at Law" for Harvard College (*Harvard College Records,* II, 606, 619, 623), and the next year was retained by King's Chapel on behalf of "the suffering members of the Church of England" (Henry Wilder Foote, *Annals of King's Chapel,* vol. I, 1882, p. 462). As a prominent Anglican he was associated with John Checkley [*q.v.*]. He acquired land in both Massachusetts and Rhode Island. On Sept. 18, 1736, he made a motion before the court at Bristol in the case of Frost *vs.* Leighton, the motion being renewed at York on June 22 following. This interesting colonial case, arising from an incident connected with the King's rights to timber in New England, resembled in some respects the celebrated case of Marbury *vs.* Madison in the United States Supreme Court (*Publications of the Colonial Society of Massachusetts,* III, 254 ff.). In 1743 Bollan had become advocate general and on Sept. 8 he married Frances, the daughter of the governor, William Shirley. His wife died in childbirth and was buried Feb. 18, 1744/5 leaving a daughter, Frances Shirley Bollan. In 1745 he was sent as colonial agent to London to endeavor to obtain repayment to Massachusetts of £183,649 spent by that colony for the Louisburg expedition. In this he was successful, after three years' negotiating, the British government finally sending £200,000 in silver to Massachusetts. Bollan continued in England as agent and stood stoutly for the interests of the colony, opposing, for example, the attempts against the charters in 1749, resisting the order against erecting slitting mills in 1750, and the legislation forbidding paper money in 1751. In spite of this he does not seem to have been popular with the more radical patriots of the lower house, perhaps in part from his being a Churchman and in part from his too close connection with the governor, who was succeeded

by Pownall in 1757 (cf. James Otis's unfair opinion, *Massachusetts Historical Society Collections,* LXXIV, 76). In 1762 Bollan was rather curtly dismissed as agent of the colony although he continued to act as agent for the Council. In 1769, £300 allowed him for so doing was disallowed by the governor. In the same year he gained popularity with the Assembly by obtaining and sending to them thirty-three letters of Bernard and Gage, for which act he was denounced by Lord North. He wrote several pamphlets, published in London, in favor of the colonies and was for conciliatory measures in 1775. He was a man of property and at one time was lending nearly £5,000 to the colony (*Ibid.,* p. 37) where he had real estate at the time he died. He was a man of ability and loyal to his trust as agent. John Adams called him "a faithful friend to America" and Hancock spoke of the colony's great debt to him. The colony, however, delayed eight years before paying the salary due him to his daughter.

[There is neither biography nor extended notice of Bollan. A number of letters to and from him are given in the volume of the *Mass. Hist. Soc. Colls.,* cited above (separate title, *Jasper Mauduit*). There is also a short letter in *Col. Soc. Mass. Pubs.,* VII, 212–13. Official communications may also be found in the manuscript records of the two houses of the General Court. His work in England for Gov. Bernard in connection with the Mt. Desert Grant is noticed in *Col. Soc. Mass. Pubs.,* XXIV, 204 ff. A rather detailed account of his services in obtaining reimbursement for the colony's expenditures in the Louisburg expedition is given in Geo. A. Wood, *Wm. Shirley,* vol. I (1920), esp. pp. 399–407, 409–10.]   J. T. A.

BOLLER, ALFRED PANCOAST (Feb. 23, 1840–Dec. 9, 1912), civil engineer, was born in Philadelphia, the son of Henry J. and Anna M. (Pancoast) Boller. After a preparatory education at the Episcopal Academy, he entered the University of Pennsylvania and was graduated in 1858 with the A.B. degree. Three years later he received his C.E. from the Rensselaer Polytechnic Institute and then spent several years in bridge and aqueduct construction work for railroads. He was married on Apr. 28, 1864, to Katherine Newbold of Philadelphia. From 1866 to 1870 he was associated with Samuel Millikin as an agent for the Phœnix Iron Company. From 1871 to 1873 he was vice-president and engineer for the Phillipsburg Manufacturing Company, and in 1874 he opened an independent office in New York City where he soon acquired an important professional practise. A partnership was formed in 1898 with Henry M. Hodge. Later Howard C. Baird became a member of the firm. Boller was consulting engineer for various projects and improvements of the Lake Superior Company at Sault Ste. Marie in Canada and Michigan. He was an expert, too, in the matter of foundations and acted as consulting engineer on a number of deep and difficult foundations in New York City. Among the remarkable bridge designs made by him and his partners is the draw-span of the Thames River Bridge at New London, Conn. This span, 503 feet in length and weighing 1,200 tons, was the longest ever attempted up to that time. The Central Bridge over the Harlem River at 155th St., New York City, 4,500 feet long, costing over two million dollars, and having a draw-span weighing 2,400 tons, was said at the time of its construction to be the heaviest movable mass in the world. Other bridges designed and built by Boller and his partners include the bridge over the Monongahela River for the Wabash Railroad at Pittsburgh; the Municipal Bridge over the Mississippi at St. Louis; and the State Bridge over the Connecticut River at Saybrook, Conn. His firm acted as consulting engineers for the steel framework of the Singer Building and the Metropolitan Life Insurance Building in New York City. Boller was the author of a *Practical Treatise on the Construction of Iron Highway Bridges, for the Use of Town Committees* (1876). He was an expert in bridge engineering and stood in the front rank of structural engineers of his day. With sound judgment, he designed his structures skilfully and with great daring, and as much as any man of his day was responsible for the great progress during the latter half of the nineteenth century in the art of bridge design and building. Intuitively he was artistic. In his spare hours he used to do landscapes in water colors. This fondness for the artistic and an appreciation for architectural symmetry had a marked influence on his work. The 155th Street Bridge in New York City exemplifies his ability to combine technical principles and practical utility with beauty of outline.

[*Trans. Am. Soc. Civil Engineers,* LXXXV, 1653; *Engineering News,* Dec. 19, 1912.]   E. Y.

BOLLES, FRANK (Oct. 31, 1856–Jan. 10, 1894), nature writer, secretary of Harvard University, was born at Winchester, Mass., the son of John A. Bolles and his wife, Catherine Dix, a sister of John Adams Dix [*q.v.*]. His love of nature and of writing showed itself early. When his father was appointed solicitor of the navy in 1866, the family moved to Baltimore and the next year to Washington. Bolles studied law in Washington, spent the summer of 1879 in Europe, and entered the Harvard Law School, from which he graduated in 1882. While studying at Harvard, he founded and was first president of the Harvard Coöperative Society, compiled a genealogy of his mother's family, won the Bow-

doin prize for an essay on international arbitration, and with two other Harvard Law students brought out *A Collection of Important English Statutes* (1880). Two later, enlarged editions were entirely his own work. In October 1884 he married Elizabeth Quincy Swan, of Cambridge, Mass., by whom he had four daughters. After some journalistic and editorial experience on the *Boston Advertiser,* he became in 1886 a secretary to President Eliot of Harvard and in 1887 secretary of the University. The latter post, which up till then had been that of a glorified bookkeeper, Bolles made into an office of wide influence. He was kind, candid, and approachable, concerned for everything affecting the welfare of the University, and unremitting in his endeavor to make Harvard equally hospitable to the unknown poor boy and to the son of the affluent and influential alumnus. He built up a remarkably efficient employment bureau, helped to found the *Harvard Graduates Magazine,* and arranged for numerous loans to needy students. His memory retained names, faces, and personal histories beyond the capacity of the most elaborate filing system; his industry was unflagging, his resources of ideas and enthusiasm apparently inexhaustible. The tall, rugged man with bearded face and friendly eyes became one of the most popular men in the Yard.

As passionate as his devotion to Harvard and Harvard's sons was his love of nature. His official duties were confining, but on afternoons and holidays he would make short excursions on foot or by train to the open country and write up his notes on birds and flowers while returning at night on the cars. His summers were given to an abandoned farm at the base of Mt. Chocorua, in New Hampshire, where he could lie motionless behind a bush all day, when he chose, studying the habits of sparrow, wren, owl, and woodpecker. Encouraged by James Russell Lowell, he published a collection of sketches, *The Land of the Lingering Snow,* in 1891. He followed it with a similar volume, *At the North of Bearcamp Water,* in 1893. Early in January 1894, an attack of grippe developed into the pneumonia from which he died on Jan. 10. *From Blomidon to Smoky, and Other Papers* (1894) and *Chocorua's Tenants* (1895), in verse, were issued posthumously. Bolles's English is limpid, his attitude toward nature impersonal and yet sympathetic.

[W. R. Thayer, "Frank Bolles," in *Harvard Grads. Mag.,* VI (1893–94), 366–72; *Boston Advertiser, Jour.,* and *Transcript,* Jan. 11, 1894; *Harvard Coll., Report of President and Treasurer, 1893–94.*]   G. H. G.

BOLLMAN, JUSTUS ERICH (1769–Dec. 9, 1821), agent of Aaron Burr, was born in Hoya,

Hanover, studied medicine at Göttingen, and practised for a time in Carlsruhe and Paris. From the latter city in 1792 he fled to London and later went to Vienna for the purpose of locating and freeing Lafayette, who was then confined at Olmütz. He was assisted by F. K. Huger, a young American from South Carolina. Lafayette escaped but was recaptured and Bollman himself spent several months in prison. He was released on condition that he leave Austria. In 1796 he came to America where his attempted rescue of Lafayette assured him a cordial reception, and when after some years he failed in business, Jefferson, of whose friendship he seemed disposed to take advantage, offered him in succession the consulate at Rotterdam, the commercial agency at Santo Domingo, and the Indian agency at Natchitoches, La. (*Jefferson Papers 131, 132, 144, 153, 154*). The tender of the last-named position occurred in the latter part of 1805. Shortly afterward Bollman became a confidential agent of Burr and as such attempted to interest prospective settlers in the settling of the Bastrop land grant. He was entrusted with a copy of Burr's famous cipher letter, which, in December 1806, he delivered to Gen. Wilkinson at New Orleans. Shortly afterward he was arrested by military authority along with his fellow messenger, Samuel Swartwout, and hurried off by sea to Washington, where they were brought before the district court and, on the evidence afforded by Wilkinson's version of the cipher letter and Eaton's deposition, were remanded to prison. On a writ of *habeas corpus* they were brought before the Supreme Court. Chief Justice Marshall, in reviewing their case, laid down some of the principles that afterward guided him in defining "treason" at the Burr trial. The hearing attracted wide attention and influenced the discussion then going on in Congress over the proposal to suspend the writ of *habeas corpus*. The prisoners were released and were then and later recipients of many attentions from those who did not favor the arbitrary policy of the administration. On Jan. 23, 1807, Bollman secured a personal interview with Jefferson, at which Madison was present, and gave in detail the plans of Burr, which he claimed were in no way directed against the interests of the United States. Later at the request of the president and on the latter's assurance that this testimony should be kept inviolate, he committed his statements to writing. This document was given to George Hay, the district attorney who conducted the prosecution against Burr, and was produced in the court room at Richmond, together with a pardon for Bollman, when the latter was called as a witness. Bollman refused the pardon which would have been a virtual admission of guilt and his testimony was not unfavorable to Burr (A. J. Beveridge, *Life of John Marshall*, 1916–19, III, 450–453). The collapse of the case against the latter saved Bollman from any serious consequences. Later he was the author of some pamphlets dealing with the banking system of the United States between 1810 and 1816. After that date he resided for some years in London where he likewise wrote on the banking system of England and engaged in an extended discussion of Ricardo's theories. He died in Jamaica.

[Casual references to Bollman occur in the manuscript collection of the Jefferson Papers, vols. CXXXI–CLXIV. The last contains his statement of Burr's plans. For a general account of his connection with the conspiracy, see the references in the article on Burr, particularly those to the works of Beveridge and of McCaleb. Among Bollman's pamphlets may be mentioned, *Paragraphs on Banks* (1810), *Plan of an Improved System of the Money Concerns of the Union* (1816), *A Letter to Thos. Brand* (1819), and *A Second Letter to the Hon. Thos. Brand* (1819).]   I. J. C.

BOLTON, HENRY CARRINGTON (Jan. 28, 1843–Nov. 19, 1903), chemist and bibliographer, was descended from good English stock on his father's side, after whom Bolton Abbey, Priory, Woods, etc., were named. He was the only child of Dr. Jackson Bolton and Anna Hinman (North) Bolton, the daughter of Dr. Elisha North, one of the first American physicians to practise vaccination. He was born in New York City, and was educated at Columbia University, graduating in 1862; his studies in chemistry were continued under Wurtz and Dumas in Paris, Bunsen at Heidelberg, Hofmann at Berlin, and Wöhler at Göttingen where he took his doctor's degree in 1866, his thesis being on The Fluorine Compounds of Uranium. In connection with this work he isolated and preserved a material which was kept in phials. After his death these were found to give off radioactive rays, due to the presence in the material of radium, so that he very nearly anticipated the work of the Curies. After graduating at Göttingen he returned to New York and opened a private laboratory. In 1872 he became an assistant at Columbia, and in 1875 professor of chemistry in the Woman's Medical College. In 1877 he accepted the chair of chemistry at Trinity College, where he remained for ten years. He then retired and, having sufficient means, devoted his time to literary and scientific pursuits. In 1882 a visit to the "Singing Beach" at Manchester, Mass., interested him in this subject; he wrote several papers and with his wife traveled many thousand miles to investigate similar occurrences elsewhere. While at Columbia he published papers on the action of organic acids on minerals. He was interested in folk-lore, was one of the founders of the American Folk-Lore Society, contributed to the *Journal of American Folk-Lore,* and published *The Counting Out Rhymes of Children* (1888) and other similar works. He was also interested in alchemy and the history of chemistry and wrote *The Follies of Science at the Court of Rudolph II, 1576–1612* (1904), and the *Evolution of the Thermometer, 1592–1743* (1900). In 1874 he proposed and carried out a pilgrimage to the grave of Priestley at Northumberland, Pa. Here an acquaintance with Priestley's descendants enabled him to edit the *Scientific Correspondence of Joseph Priestley* (1892), an account of the Lunar Society, and an inventory of the contents of Priestley's laboratory destroyed by the rioters in 1791. In connection with his own work on uranium he published in the *Annals of the New York Lyceum of Natural History* (1870), an index of the literature on the subject; this was the beginning of an interest in bibliography which he cultivated with zeal and great success for the rest of his life. In 1885 he published a *Catalogue of Scientific and Technical Periodicals, 1865–82* (1885), and in 1893 the first part of his *Select Bibliography of Chemistry* which was continued in several volumes. He was chairman of a committee on the bibliography of chemistry of the American Chemical Society and wrote many annual reports. He married Henrietta Irving, a great-niece of Washington Irving, in 1893; died in Washington, D. C.; and is buried in the Irving plot at Tarrytown-on-the-Hudson. He was a man of medium height and rather stocky build, with blue eyes. His disposition was kindly and amiable and he was deeply religious, a great traveler, full of anecdote, and fond of funny stories. He had met most of the noted chemists of his generation, with whom he was a general favorite.

[Sketch by F. W. Clarke, in the *Proc. Am. Chemical Soc.,* 1904, p. 6; sketch in the *Pop. Sci. Mo.,* XLIII, 688 ff.; obituary in the *N. Y. Tribune,* Nov. 20, 1903; personal information.]   E. H.

BOLTON, SARAH KNOWLES (Sept. 15, 1841–Feb. 21, 1916), author and reformer, came of distinguished New England stock. Her father, John Segar Knowles of Connecticut, was descended, through his mother, Mary Carpenter, from Elizabeth Jenckes, sister of Joseph Jenckes, governor of Rhode Island 1727–32, and through his father from Henry Knowles, one of the earliest settlers of Portsmouth, R. I.; her mother, Elizabeth (Miller) Knowles, had among her ancestors, Nathaniel Stanley, treasurer of Con-

necticut Colony; Col. John Allyn, secretary of the colony and historian of the Pequot War; and Col. William Pynchon, one of the incorporators of Massachusetts Bay Colony. On the Knowles side the family had been Quakers for generations. Born at Farmington, Conn., Sarah Knowles passed her childhood in the country, where her fondness for pets, particularly hens, laid the foundation for her later interest in animal welfare. Losing her father when she was eleven, she and her mother went to live with an uncle, Samuel Miller, and later she resided with another uncle, Col. H. L. Miller, an able lawyer of Hartford, Conn. Here she became acquainted with Lydia Sigourney and Harriet Beecher Stowe. Her pen was early busy; she wrote verses, publishing some of them at the age of fifteen, and she had a passion for biographical writing. After graduating from the Hartford Female Seminary in 1860, she went with a Prof. Tenney to teach school in Natchez, Miss. Forced to return by the outbreak of the Civil War, she taught for a time in Meriden, Conn. At the age of twenty-three she brought out a volume, *Orlean Lamar and Other Poems* (1864), of which one reviewer said "Very well to have written but a great mistake to have published." She next produced "Wellesley," a novel on the insurrection of Kossuth, which was published in the *Literary Recorder* in 1865. In the following year (Oct. 16, 1866) she married Charles Edward Bolton of Cleveland, Ohio, a man of congenial humanitarian interests. They were drawn more and more into the temperance movement, and in 1874 they took a prominent part in tthe Woman's Temperance Crusade in Ohio. Mrs. Bolton also wrote for the cause a book called *The Present Problem* (1874), but only 250 copies were sold. During 1878–81 she was on the editorial staff of the *Congregationalist* in Boston. The next two years she spent in Europe, making a study of higher education for women and of the methods used by employers to better the condition of their employees. On her return she read an influential paper on the latter subject before the American Social Science Association at Saratoga. Secretary of the Woman's Christian Association and assistant corresponding secretary to Frances E. Willard in the Woman's Christian Temperance Union, Mrs. Bolton nevertheless found time for voluminous writing. In addition to two more volumes of didactic, sentimental poetry, *From Heart and Nature* (in collaboration with her son, Charles Knowles Bolton, 1887), and *The Inevitable and Other Poems* (1895), she published several works of fiction, and a long series of books designed to assist in popular education, their character indicated by titles such as *Poor Boys Who Became Famous* (1885), *Girls Who Became Famous* (1886), *Famous American Statesmen* (1888), *Famous Men of Science* (1889). Written with enthusiasm and a vigorous narrative power, these biographical works perhaps merited the large sale which they obtained. A reformer to the last, Mrs. Bolton rounded out her life by devoting herself to the welfare of the animals she had loved in youth. She was chiefly responsible for the Ohio law stopping the sport of pigeon-shooting and on several occasions she deterred the Cleveland city council from waging war on the faithful dog.

[*Sarah K. Bolton, Pages from an Intimate Autobiography* (1923), ed. by Chas. Knowles Bolton; *The Boltons in Old and New England* (1890), by Chas. Knowles Bolton; *Who's Who in America*, 1914–15.]

E. S. B.

BOLTON, SARAH TITTLE BARRETT (Dec. 18, 1814–Aug. 4, 1893), poet, born in Newport, Ky., was the daughter of Jonathan Belcher and Esther (Pendleton) Barrett, pioneer settlers of Indiana. Her grandfather, Lemuel Barrett, was an Englishman who emigrated to New Jersey some time before 1754, and her mother's father, a cousin of James Madison. Her early days were spent in the wilderness, about six miles from Vernon, Ind., where her father had staked a farm. Of this period her poems entitled "Our Pioneers" and "A Pioneer Grandmother" are reminiscent. When she was nine, her father sold his farm and moved to Madison. Here she got some knowledge in the schools, and as much outside. Before she was fourteen, verses from her pen had been published in the Madison *Banner,* and she soon became a regular contributor to the newspapers of her home town and Cincinnati. In her seventeenth year, October 1831, she married Nathaniel Bolton, a young newspaper man, and went to live in Indianapolis. Thereafter her life was shaped by her husband's fortunes until his death in 1858. He was first editor of the *Indiana Democrat;* then proprietor of a farm outside the city, his house there a tavern which became a stopping place for distinguished men and something of a social center, Mrs. Bolton acting as housekeeper and cook, besides running a large dairy. Later he was state librarian, then clerk of a United States Senate committee, and finally consul at Geneva, which appointment gave Mrs. Bolton opportunity for extensive travel. Two children were born to her. About five years after his death, she married, Sept. 15, 1863, at Keokuk, Iowa, Judge Addison Reese, and for the next two years lived with him at his home in Canton, Mo. The climate there was not favorable to her health,

and she returned to Indianapolis, where she made her home until her death, though she spent two or three years abroad. She was always known as Sarah T. Bolton, and used the name "Reese" only for business purposes.

Her writings and participation in public affairs made her a prominent figure in Indiana. She was interested in various reforms, and was an active aid to Robert Dale Owen [*q.v.*] in his effort to secure property rights for women in the constitutional convention of 1850. She was a true child of the rising West, an ardent democrat and champion of freedom, full of fiery patriotism and faith in the country's future. These characteristics are reflected in many of her poems. As a whole these are of no great literary merit, but have the melody, sentimentality, and moral and religious flavor relished by the fireside magazine readers of their day. *Paddle Your Own Canoe* and a few others had wide popularity. *Poems* appeared in 1865, and a collection of her writings with a sketch of her career was published in 1880 under the title, *The Life and Poems of Sarah T. Bolton.* A volume of selections, *Songs of a Life Time,* edited by John Clark Ridpath, was published in 1892. It contains an introduction by Lew Wallace and a proem by James Whitcomb Riley.

[*Ladies' Repository,* Feb. 1852, pp. 69–73; Wm. W. Woollen, *Biog. and Hist. Sketches of Early Indiana* (1883); J. P. Dunn, *Greater Indianapolis* (1910); obituary in *Indianapolis Sentinel,* Aug. 5, 1893; and information furnished by Mrs. Adah Bolton Mann.] H. E. S.

BOLTWOOD, BERTRAM BORDEN (July 27, 1870–Aug. 15, 1927), chemist, and physicist, was born in Amherst, Mass. His father was Thomas Kast Boltwood, a lawyer; his grandfather, Lucius Boltwood of English descent, was active in the founding of Amherst College, was secretary of its corporation (1828-64), and was also the first candidate of the Liberty Party for governor of Massachusetts, in 1841; the ancestors of his mother, Mathilda (Van Hoesen) Boltwood, were among the first Dutch settlers in Rensselaer County, N. Y. His boyhood was spent in Amherst, Castleton on Hudson, and Albany, N. Y. He prepared for Yale at the Albany Academy and entered Sheffield Scientific School of Yale University in 1889. As a freshman at Yale he received the first-rank prize in physics and as a senior he took the highest rank in chemistry, reading a dissertation at the commencement ceremonies. After graduation in 1892 he studied two years in Munich under Professor Krüss, giving special attention to rare earths and analytical methods; he spent part of 1896 in Leipzig in Ostwald's laboratory. At Yale he was assistant in chemistry, 1894–96; received the Ph.D. degree in 1897; and was instructor in analytical, later in physical, chemistry 1896–1900. During 1900–06, he conducted a private laboratory in New Haven and during this period he started the important work in radioactivity which he continued when he accepted an assistant professorship in physics in Yale College (1906–10). From 1910 to 1927 he was professor of radio chemistry. With the late Prof. H. A. Bumstead he devoted much time and energy to the building of the new Sloane Physics Laboratory (1912) of which he was, in 1913–14, the acting director in the absence of Prof. Bumstead. As the representative of the chemistry department it was also his lot to plan the construction and equipment of the Sterling Chemical Laboratory (1921). The work in connection with this undertaking proved so severe that his health broke down under the strain. He had two or three periods of nervous depression from which he apparently recovered; but there was a recurrence of this to some degree in the summer of 1927, when he ended his own life in Maine whither he had gone to recuperate.

While Boltwood contributed to laboratory technique and arts, his prominence was primarily in actual scientific contributions of the first magnitude in the realm of radioactivity. To him are due the following fundamentally important contributions: (1) The proof that radium is a disintegration product of uranium. (2) The discovery of a radioactive element, ionium, the parent substance of radium. (3) The experimental work showing the inseparability by chemical means of ionium and thorium, a fact which aroused interest among chemists and physicists the world over and is the basis from which the branch of science called isotopy has arisen. (4) The contribution of the experimental evidence that the "lead" found in uranium minerals must be the final product of disintegration in the uranium-radium series, a fact amply verified by others. (5) The statement of a theory and invention of a method for the calculation of the age of uranium minerals from their lead and uranium content—a method which, with some important modifications, constitutes our best method in determining the age of a geological formation. (6) The experimental evidence that actinium is also a genetic descendant of uranium but not in the same line as radium. Besides these important investigations, to Boltwood was due the first investigation in this country of the radioactivity of natural waters (Hot Springs Reservation) and the giving to the measurements obtained a quantitative significance in terms of uranium, there being at that time no radium standard. He also investigated the production of helium in minerals; as product

of alpha-ray emission from radium; and from ionium. Pointing out (1905) the significance of lead and helium and perhaps other elements as the disintegration products of one form or another, he raised the question about the origin of elements. In regard to his scientific work he was amazingly modest as is exemplified by his statement in *Who's Who,* where the only words bearing on his work are that he was a "contributor to chemical journals." He was unmarried; possessed great personal charm; and had a wide acquaintance with matters outside of his science.

[*Who's Who in America,* 1924–25; *Am. Men of Sci.* (3rd ed., 1921); scientific notebooks and personal papers left in Boltwood's estate to his heir, Lansing V. Hammond; scientific publications in *Am. Jour. of Sci.,* 3rd ser. L, 4th ser. XXVI (1895 to 1908) and 4th ser. L (1920); *Philosophical Mag.* (London), IX (1905) and XXII (1911); *Nature,* LXX (1904) and LXXV, LXXVI (1907), C (1918); *Physikalische Zeitschrift,* VII and VIII (1906–7); *Proc. Royal Soc.,* LXXXV (1911); *Science,* XLII (1917); *Yale Alumni Weekly,* Apr. 19, 1918; *Industrial and Engineering Chemistry,* XV (1923); Records, Yale University Secretary's office, and longer biographical sketches from these sources prepared for the *Yale Scientific Mag.,* II (1927), and for the *Am. Jour. of Sci.,* 5th ser., XV (1928); also personal acquaintance.]   A.F.K.

BOLTZIUS, JOHANN MARTIN (Dec. 15, 1703–Nov. 19, 1765), Lutheran clergyman, was twenty-nine years old and held the post of inspector-vicar in the Latin School connected with the Lutheran Orphanage at Halle, Germany, when he was called as pastor of a company of about one hundred Salzburgers who had agreed to emigrate to the English colony of Georgia. He had grown to manhood in the Orphanage, had studied at the University of Halle, and was imbued with the Pietism that emanated from those two institutions. He accepted the call, was ordained at Wernigerode Nov. 11, 1733, and proceeded to Amsterdam, where his congregation was ready to embark. With him went Israel Christian Gronau, a teacher in the School, who was ordained at the same time. The emigrants landed at Savannah on Mar. 12, 1734, and were welcomed with a salute of cannon and a gala dinner. Gen. Oglethorpe himself helped to select a site for their town of Ebenezer.

For the next thirty years Boltzius was the religious and business leader of the little colony. His charges were among the thousands of Protestants who had been driven from the archiepiscopal duchy of Salzburg because of their religion. They were simple folk, pious, industrious, uneducated, impoverished by confiscation and exile, and bewildered by their situation on the Georgia frontier. In spite of an excessively high death rate, the handicap of having to move their town in 1736 to a more wholesome locality, and the hardships incident to pioneer life, the Salzburgers ultimately attained a mild prosperity and were noted for their neatness, order, and industry. The religious life, after the manner of the Pietists, was cultivated assiduously, and perhaps to excess. There was no crime. Differences were settled by a committee of arbitration appointed by the chief pastor. As money was scarce tokens signed by Boltzius took the place of small coins and passed at their face value. The two pastors became brothers-in-law by marrying the daughters of a woman named Kroher. In 1737 John Wesley, on his visit to Georgia, became Boltzius' friend. Wesley, however, because of his High Church principles, refused to admit Boltzius to the Lord's Supper, and years later set down in his journal the appropriate comment on his own folly. Another visitor was George Whitefield, who took the Ebenezer orphanage as a model for his own, and was generous in his gifts of money, ironware, and church bells. In October 1742 Henry Melchior Muhlenberg, on his way to Pennsylvania, visited Boltzius, who accompanied him as far as Charleston, where, mindful of his frail wife and two sick daughters, he turned back. A son Boltzius sent home to Halle to be educated. To the Rev. Samuel Urlsperger of Augsburg, who collected the funds out of which the salaries of the ministers were paid, he wrote voluminous reports on all phases of the colony's life. In his last years he was ill a great deal, but he had able assistants in Hermann Heinrich Lemke and Christian Rabenhorst. After much suffering patiently borne he finally succumbed to dropsy.

[*Äusfuhrliche Nachrichten von der Königlich-grossbrittannischen Colonie Saltzburgischer Emigranten in America* (19 pts. in 3 vols., Halle, 1741 [1735]–1752); *Americanisches Ackerwerk Gottes,* etc. (5 vols. in 3, Augsburg, 1754–67); *Zuverlässiges Sendschreiben von den geist-und-leiblichen Umständen der Saltzburgischen Emigranten,* (Halle, 1736); *Ausführliche Nachrichten von den Saltzburgischen Emigranten, etc.* (Halle, 1744). The foregoing were compiled from Boltzius' letters, diaries, etc., by Samuel Urlsperger of Augsburg and are usually cited as the *"Urlsperger Nachrichten."* Cf. also *An Extract from the Journals of Mr. Commissary Von Reck . . . and of the Rev. Mr. Bolzius,* etc. (London, for the S. P. C. K., 1734, repr. in Peter Force, *Tracts,* Washington, 1836–46, vol. IV, 1846, No. 5); N. Curnock, ed., *The Jour. of the Rev. John Wesley, A.M.* (Standard Ed., London, n. d.). Good secondary accounts are P. A. Strobel, *The Salzburgers and Their Descendants* (Baltimore, 1855); C. C. Jones, Jr., *The Dead Towns of Georgia* (Savannah, 1878); A. Prinziger, art. in *Mitteilungen der Gesellschaft für Salzburger Landeskunde,* vol. XXII (Salzburg, 1882); A. L. Gräbner, *Geschichte der Lutherischen Kirche in America* (St. Louis, 1892).]   G.H.G.

BOMBERGER, JOHN HENRY AUGUSTUS (Jan. 13, 1817–Aug. 19, 1890), clergyman of the German Reformed Church, college president, the son of George and Mary (Hoffmeier) Bomberger, was born in Lancaster, Pa. His an-

cestors on both sides were German. His father was a merchant but his mother's father and two of her brothers were ministers and he himself was early destined for the ministry. He was educated at Marshall College (Mercersburg, Pa.) and was the only member of its first graduating class in 1837. He spent one year of theological study under Dr. Frederick A. Rauch, the first president of Marshall College and a professor in the Theological Seminary of the Reformed Church. On Dec. 27, 1838, he was ordained a minister of the (German) Reformed Church and immediately entered upon pastoral work at Lewistown, Pa., at a salary of "from $400.00 to $500.-00." His longest and most fruitful pastorate was that of the Old Race Street Church in Philadelphia (1854–70), which included a parochial school. Three congregations branched off from this church, and a tremendous impetus was given to church extension in Philadelphia. During the Civil War Bomberger was a radical abolitionist and an ardent supporter of the Union. Active in the Christian Commission he was a potent force in organizing patriotic impulse into forms of service. He was a dominant figure in the judicatories of the Church and served on most of its executive boards and important committees. He was president of the Board of Home Missions for many years, and represented his denomination in the Alliance of Reformed Churches at Belfast, Ireland (1884). He was a working member of the American Tract Society, the American Bible Society, and the American Sunday School Union. He was twice married: first, in 1839, to Marian Elizabeth Huston of Mercersburg, Pa., who died in 1855; and second, in 1863, to Julia Aymer Wight of Philadelphia, who died in 1889. His published works include *Kurtz's Text-Book of Church History* (2 vols., 1860–62), pronounced by Dr. John W. Nevin "among the most important contributions yet made to the theological literature of the country"; and *The Protestant Theological and Ecclesiastical Encyclopedia* (1858–60)—a condensed translation, with additions from other sources, of the first six volumes of *Herzog's Real Encyklopädia* then in course of serial publication. He was the founder and editor of the *Reformed Church Monthly* (1868–76). As the recognized leader of the so-called antiliturgical party, he was foremost in the movement that led to the establishment of Ursinus College and became its first president (1869–90), filling at the same time the chair of moral and mental philosophy and evidences of Christianity. The publications that best reveal his theological views are his articles in the *Mercersburg Review* and his articles in the *Reformed Church Monthly* and the *Christian World* (1861–90). He was a skilled controversialist and an able speaker. Even though at times his arguments appear to have been more personal than logical his sincerity need not be questioned. He had an engaging personality, great social talents, and a mind tempered with imagination and sentiment.

[*Franklin and Marshall Coll. Obit. Record,* vol. I; John H. A. Bomberger (Ursinus College, 1917); *New Schaff-Herzog Encyc. of Religious Knowledge* (1910); *Reformed Ch. Mess.,* Aug. 28, 1890.]   G. F. M.

BOMFORD, GEORGE (1782–Mar. 25, 1848), soldier, was born in the city of New York. His father was an officer of the Continental army in the Revolution. He was appointed a cadet in the army on Oct. 24, 1804, commissioned as second lieutenant of engineers, July 1, 1805, and for the next seven years was engaged upon fortification work in New York Harbor and Chesapeake Bay. He was promoted first lieutenant in 1806, captain in 1808, and major in 1812. Upon the outbreak of the war with Great Britain he was assigned to ordnance duty, for which he proved to have a special talent. Knowledge of the manufacture of ordnance was rare in this country, and his exceptional abilities made him indispensable. The howitzer or shell gun named the Columbiad, from Joel Barlow's epic poem, was Bomford's invention. He was appointed lieutenant-colonel of ordnance in 1815, and in 1832 was made colonel and chief of ordnance of the army. Upon the death of Mrs. Barlow, whose sister he had married, he bought the famous estate of Kalorama, which lay just outside the limits of the city of Washington as then constituted, between the present location of Florida Avenue and Rock Creek. It is commonly associated with Joel Barlow, who owned it, however, for only five years, during part of which time he was absent on a diplomatic mission in France, while it was Bomford's for nearly thirty. During his occupancy it was famous as the resort of statesmen and diplomats. The trees and plants collected there from all parts of the world, under Mrs. Bomford's judicious direction, made it one of the most notable botanical gardens in the country. The failure of a large cotton mill which Bomford had established on Rock Creek crippled his fortunes, already impaired by unfortunate investments in Washington real estate, and late in life he was obliged to sell Kalorama to settle his liabilities. He died at Boston, where he had gone to witness the casting of some heavy guns. Bomford was the greatest ordnance expert of his time in the United States, an inventor of note, and an able organizer and administrator. A good writer and speaker, his opinions carried great weight both in

the executive departments and in Congress. "His official papers in particular were models of reserve force, lucid argument, and fluent style" (Dutton). He was a public-spirited citizen, interested in religious, philanthropic, and artistic activities in the District of Columbia, notably in the movement which led to the building of the Washington Monument.

[G. W. Cullum, *Biog. Reg.* (3rd ed., 1891), I, 58–59; article by C. E. Dutton in *The Army of the United States* (1896), ed. by T. R. Rodenbough and W. L. Haskin; Corra Bacon-Foster, "The Story of Kalorama," in *Columbia Hist. Soc. Records,* XIII, 98–118.] T. M. S.

BONAPARTE, CHARLES JOSEPH (June 9, 1851–June 28, 1921), lawyer, municipal and civil service reformer, attorney-general, was the son of Jerome Bonaparte and Susan May Williams. His grandfather was that Jerome, King of Westphalia, who married Elizabeth Patterson of Baltimore [*q.v.*], and subsequently separated from her, at the command of his august brother, the Emperor Napoleon. Any pride of French ancestry that Charles Joseph might have paraded was inhibited by the good sense of his mother who came of New England stock and was intensely American. He was educated first in a French school near Baltimore, his birthplace, and then under private tutors. He was regarded as a brilliant scholar, a reputation which he seems to have sustained at Harvard College. Graduating in 1872, he at once entered the Harvard Law School where he took a keen interest in current politics as they were discussed in the debating society. Two years later he graduated from the Law School, was admitted to the bar, and began to practise in Baltimore. Possessed of ample wealth, he experienced none of the initial hardships of a young lawyer; and from the outset he put his legal talents at the service of litigants who, or whose causes, appealed to his ardent desire for justice. His fellow practitioners regarded him as a skillful and resourceful attorney. It was public causes, however, which appealed most strongly to him. He identified himself with the reform party which was trying to purge Baltimore of its corrupt ring; he was one of the founders of the Baltimore Reform League and became its chairman; he helped to found and support *The Civil Service Reformer,* the organ of the Maryland Civil Service League; and he was also one of the founders of the National Civil Service Reform League. His interest in civil service reform brought him into contact with Theodore Roosevelt, then civil service commissioner, who later as president repeatedly sought his services, first as member of the board of Indian commissioners charged with the investigation of conditions in the Indian Territory, and then as special counsel to prosecute alleged frauds in the postal service.

In 1905 he was invited to enter President Roosevelt's cabinet as secretary of the navy, with the expectation of succeeding to the attorney-generalship on the retirement of William H. Moody. The appointment stirred more than ordinary public interest. Even the Republican press indulged in good-natured raillery at the thought of the grand-nephew of the Little Corporal becoming head of the United States navy. He afterward described his manifold administrative duties in an article contributed to the *Century Magazine* (March 1910), which revealed not only his high ideal of public service but his unfailing good-humor in the discharge of duty. In December 1906 he was appointed attorney-general and transferred his abundant energies to the more congenial duties of the Department of Justice at a time when President Roosevelt needed a hard-hitter in his fight with "bad trusts." During his term of office he appeared personally before the Supreme Court in more than fifty cases. Aside from the prosecutions begun by his predecessors, he instituted twenty suits under the anti-trust laws, of which eight were eventually decided in favor of the government. His most notable achievement was the dissolution of the American Tobacco Company, though the decree was not issued until after he had left office.

Bonaparte went out of office with President Roosevelt in March 1909 and returned to his somewhat desultory law practise in Baltimore. His dominant interest was still good government. He was one of the founders of the National Municipal League and later its president. An effective public speaker, he was much in demand wherever the cause of civic reform needed a fearless champion. He was, in short, as Senator Gorman once contemptuously called him, a "professional reformer." Nominally a Republican, he did not hesitate to act as an independent in politics. He had attacked the war policy of President McKinley; he followed Roosevelt in the Progressive party of 1912; but he labored to prevent a rupture in the Republican party in 1916 when he believed that a united party was necessary to defeat the Wilson administration. Bonaparte bore little resemblance to his famous ancestor. He was taller, of sturdier build, with large strong neck and massive head. "A vast, round, rugged head," observed one of the newspaper correspondents who delighted to interview him, "with curious rises over the temples. . . . Beneath the forehead lurks the Bonaparte smile. It is there all the time" (*Baltimore Sun*, June

29, 1921). On Sept. 1, 1875, he had married Ellen Channing Day of Hartford, Conn., and a few years later he established a country estate at "Bella Vista," not far from Baltimore. There, after a lingering illness, he died as he had lived, a devout and loyal communicant of the Catholic Church.

[J. B. Bishop, *Chas. Jos. Bonaparte. His Life and Public Services* (1922) is a laudatory biography but gives the main facts of his career. There is an informing obituary in the *Baltimore Sun*, June 29, 1921, as well as an editorial comment. See also the *Baltimore American*, June 29, 1921, and the *Baltimore News*, June 28, 1921. The trust prosecutions are listed in *Administration of the Sherman Anti-Trust Law* (1926).]

BONAPARTE, ELIZABETH PATTERSON (Feb. 6, 1785–Apr. 4, 1879), wife of Jerome the brother of the Emperor Napoleon, was born in Baltimore, the daughter of William and Dorcas (Spear) Patterson. Her father emigrated to that city from County Donegal, Ireland, in 1766, dealt shrewdly in arms and munitions during the Revolution, and as merchant, banker, and land-owner became one of the wealthiest men in Maryland. His daughter was early famous for her beauty, and was ambitious and headstrong as well as beautiful. She made a conquest of the nineteen-year-old Jerome Bonaparte when he visited Baltimore; and on Christmas Eve, 1803, with the reluctant consent of her father, she married him. Expecting trouble, her father tried to protect her by a special marriage contract and, though himself a Presbyterian, had the ceremony performed by the ranking Catholic ecclesiastic in the United States. The father's foreboding was justified; Napoleon, refusing to recognize the marriage, ordered his brother to return to France alone. When the truant finally did return in 1805, it was on a ship of his father-in-law's and accompanied by his wife. At Lisbon they parted, Jerome hastening to Paris to negotiate a reconciliation, while Elizabeth, forbidden to land on European soil, proceeded ultimately to England, where her son, Jerome Napoleon Bonaparte, was born at Camberwell, July 7, 1805. In his brother's presence Jerome's resolution melted. Pope Pius VII declined to annul the marriage, but a French council of state was more pliable, and Jerome as the last reward of his compliance was married to the Princess Catharine of Württemberg and was made king of Westphalia. To his first wife, who wasted no pity on herself, Napoleon gave an annual pension of 60,000 francs, on condition that she stay in America and renounce the Bonaparte name. She vegetated in Baltimore until the Napoleonic fabric crashed in 1815. Then she secured a divorce from Jerome by a special act of the Maryland legislature and set out for Europe, where she spent most of her time until 1840, was made much of in society, and found an appreciative audience for her extraordinary beauty, caustic wit, and brummagem royalty. She spent lavishly to educate her son and to clothe herself, but was otherwise parsimonious. The second Jerome finally disappointed her by failing to make a brilliant European match and by condescending to marry a girl from Baltimore, Susan May Williams. With the Bonapartes her relations were prevailingly cordial; Napoleon himself she admired as a man after her own heart. The legitimacy of her son was recognized by Napoleon III but his right to succession disallowed. The last eighteen years of Madame Bonaparte's life were passed in Baltimore. She lived obscurely in a boarding house and by pinching economy and strict attention to her real estate was able to leave a fortune of approximately $1,500,000 to her two grandsons.

[All accounts of Mme. Bonaparte derive from E. L. Didier, *Life and Letters of Mme. Bonaparte* (1879).]

G. H. G.

BONAPARTE, JEROME NAPOLEON (Nov. 5, 1830–Sept. 3, 1893), soldier, was born at Baltimore of Susan (Williams) Bonaparte and the elder Jerome Napoleon Bonaparte, son of Jerome, King of Westphalia. He was educated in private schools, and for a short time was a student at Harvard, withdrawing upon his appointment to a cadetship at the Military Academy. He graduated at West Point in 1852, a classmate of Slocum, Crook, and Stanley, and was commissioned in the Mounted Riflemen (now the 3rd Cavalry). For the next two years he served in the United States army, and then, upon the invasion of the Crimea, resigned his commission, went to France, and was appointed a second lieutenant of dragoons in the army of his imperial cousin. He was assigned to duty as an aide to Gen. Morris, who commanded a cavalry division, and under him he served with credit throughout the war, seeing plenty of hard fighting at Balaklava and Inkermann, and during the siege. He received British and Turkish decorations, as well as the award of the Legion of Honor. At the end of the war, he did not return to his native country, but settled himself to the permanent career of a French army officer, probably not without some calculations as to what the turn of events might some day bring to a Bonaparte of recognized military achievement. He had been promoted to first lieutenant in 1855; he was a captain in 1859, a major in 1865, and a lieutenant-colonel in 1870. During this time his service was active and varied, including

a campaign in Algeria, and field service in the Austrian war, in which his conduct at Montebello and Solferino gained him a decoration from the King of Sardinia. The death of his father in 1870 recalled him to America for a brief period, but the declaration of war against Prussia brought him back to France almost immediately. Moving to the front in August, in command of his regiment, he was turned back by the news of the surrender at Sedan. Accompanying the Ex-Empress until she was placed in safety in England, he returned to Paris and served through the siege. But he was an imperialist rather than a Frenchman. The fall of the empire had put an end to any hopes he may have cherished, and he offered his resignation from the army which was no longer the Emperor's. Before he could leave Paris, the city was in the hands of the Commune, and as a Bonaparte he was of course proscribed. Barely escaping with his life, he returned to Baltimore. Thereafter he lived chiefly in Washington and Newport, with extended trips to Europe. He was married to Caroline Le Roy (Appleton) Edgar, widow of Newbold Edgar of New York. He died at Pride's Crossing, Mass.

[G. W. Cullum: *Biog. Reg.* (3rd ed. 1891), II 480–81; *Bull. Ass. Grads. Mil. Acad.* (1894), pp. 53–55.]

T. M. S.

BONARD, LOUIS (1809–Feb. 21, 1871), early benefactor of the American Society for the Prevention of Cruelty to Animals, was born in Rouen, France. About 1849 he left that country and after successful trading operations in South America and California, settled in New York City where he invested his gains in real estate. He was an eccentric individual, something of a genius in a mechanical way, parsimonius, but known to a few to be kind of heart. In the cellar of one of his tenement houses in Mulberry Street he had a workshop, equipped for doing the odd jobs necessary to keep his property in repair. Here, too, he worked on his inventions, which included a circular loom for weaving hats, a brick-making machine, and a machine for casting iron, all of which he patented. The newspaper report, which appeared after his death and has been perpetuated, that he was a miser, living in squalor in a single room, was unfounded. His apartment was in a large modern brick house in Wooster Street, and was clean, though modestly furnished (letter by Henry Bergh, *American Society for the Prevention of Cruelty to Animals, Fifth Annual Report*, 1871). He had a religion of his own, he confessed, "based upon justice and humanity." His agent declared that he was generous to unfortunate tenants, and fond of animals, his indignation being aroused by any act of cruelty toward them (*New York Times,* May 11, 1871). Having watched with admiration the activities of Henry Bergh [*q.v.*], founder of the American Society for the Prevention of Cruelty to Animals, Bonard, at his death, left all his property, amounting to about $150,000, to that society. The will was contested by alleged heirs in France, and by two persons claiming as legatees under a previous will, one of the grounds being that the testator entertained an insane illusion that upon his decease his soul would enter into the body of some animal, and that, influenced by this delusion, he executed the will with a view to the better security of his future existence. The case attained some celebrity (Austin Abbott, *Reports of Practice Cases Determined in the Courts of the State of New York,* new series, XVI, 1876). Ultimately the property went to the society, which erected a monument to his memory in Greenwood Cemetery, New York City, where he was buried.

[In addition to references above, see annual reports of Am. S. P. C. A. 1871–72; C. C. Buel, "Henry Bergh and His Work," *Scribner's Mo.,* April 1879; *N. Y. Times,* Feb. 28, 1871, Sept. 13, 1871.]   H. E. S.

BOND, ELIZABETH POWELL (Jan. 25, 1841–Mar. 29, 1926), educator, author, was a descendant of John Howland, the *Mayflower* Pilgrim, and of other New England ancestors. She was one of the four children of Townsend and Catherine (Macy) Powell. Born in Dutchess County, N. Y., when she was four years of age the family moved to Ghent, N. Y., where she attended a small country school until she was sixteen years old, after which she had one year at the State Normal School in Albany. Brought up in a Quaker environment, she passed a quiet childhood, the chief incidents of which were the frequent visits of anti-slavery advocates to her parents' home. From the age of fifteen she made visits to Boston where association with the families of the leading abolitionists and men of letters enriched her young life with interests and ideals which were, as she herself expressed it, "in some measure equivalent to the broadening influence of modern college life." In Boston she also attended Dr. Dio Lewis's school for physical culture. This training led to her appointment as "Instructor in Calisthenics" at Vassar College, 1866–70. On May 23, 1872, she married Henry Herrick Bond, a lawyer of Northampton, Mass. Her husband died in 1881, leaving her with one child, Edwin Powell Bond. Five years later, her abiding interest in higher education led her to accept a call to Swarthmore

College, where she became dean in 1890. Her special task was to preside over the students' social life, and she succeeded to an extraordinary degree in placing the college life in a home setting. Coeducation was still on trial in the East, and Dean Bond raised it from the stage of doubt and experiment to an assured success. She was the author of two volumes, entitled *Words by the Way* (first series, 1895; second series, 1901), which are collections of addresses made to the students of Swarthmore, to whom they are dedicated. She was also a frequent contributor in both prose and verse to current periodicals. In 1906, she retired from active service with the title of "Dean Emeritus," and resided for the remainder of her life in Germantown, Philadelphia. She continued her interest in education, and aided as she could such movements as the advancement of women, international peace, and especially the promotion of the negro race, whose problems had stirred her heart in youth and had not been wholly solved, she believed, by freedom from slavery. She lectured frequently, to school, club, and college audiences, on all of these topics. One of her favorite and most popular lectures was upon the reminiscences of her personal friendship with Emerson and Garrison, their families, and the literary and anti-slavery circles of which they were the center. She was a life-long member of the Society of Friends (Liberal Branch) and frequently shared in the ministry in its meetings for worship. Her simplicity and graciousness of demeanor, her dignity of bearing, her characteristic manner of dress, her gentleness of spirit, her delicacy of feeling, her culture and appreciation of the beautiful, her gifts of mind and heart, and her implicit obedience to the demands of an unusually sensitive Puritan-Quaker conscience, combined to create in her a personality whose impress left a permanent influence upon the ideals of her time.

[The chief sources of information about Elizabeth Powell Bond have been her own manuscripts, letters, and diaries. The manuscript of "Dean Bond of Swarthmore, A Quaker Humanist," by Emily Cooper Johnson, in process of publication, was also consulted, as were obituary notices in the *N. Y. Times,* and Philadelphia *Public Ledger,* Swarthmore *Phœnix, Friends' Intelligencer,* and accounts of a memorial meeting to Dean Bond, held in Swarthmore College on June 5, 1926.]   H. C. H.

BOND, GEORGE PHILLIPS (May 20, 1825–Feb. 17, 1865), astronomer, was the son of William Cranch Bond [*q.v.*], director of the Harvard College Observatory, and of Selina (Cranch) Bond. He graduated from Harvard in 1845 and was immediately appointed assistant observer. He himself said, in speaking of his brother William, "His natural bias toward astronomy was far stronger than mine. While I was in a manner pressed into the service, he entered of free choice." His strongest inclination was toward ornithology but he had a strong passion for all the beauties of nature, and he was very happy in his ability to make other people, especially children, see these beauties. He and his father worked together on many investigations. The method of determining parallax by measurements of right ascension, east and west of the meridian, was independently proposed by the Bonds and applied to Mars in 1849–50. On the death of his father in 1859 George Bond succeeded him as director of the Harvard College Observatory. He had no private resources at his disposal and the funds of the institution were wholly inadequate to its needs. The war broke out and further pinching economies became necessary. In spite of all these difficulties the work of the observatory was continued at the same high standard.

George Bond is usually credited with the discovery of Hyperion, the eighth satellite of Saturn, and of the crape ring. In the years 1847–56 a vast quantity of drawings and measurements of Saturn were accumulated. The observation of new divisions and of the transparency of the crape ring called for a revision of the theory of a solid structure of the rings. The facts were reviewed and the hypothesis of a fluid state of the rings advanced by George Bond in 1851. No memoir on comets approaches in completeness that of the Donati comet of 1858 by George Bond in the *Annals of the Harvard College Observatory,* vol. III (1862). Every phenomenon of the great comet was described, the text illustrated with a remarkable series of drawings, and many important conclusions drawn. George Bond should be regarded as the true founder of photographic astronomy. He quickly recognized and put to the test its possibilities in mapping the sky, in measuring double-stars, in determining stellar parallax, and in measuring the brightness of the stars. He saw clearly what certainly would be finally accomplished by the new process and fretted only at the necessary delay in discovering the means of increasing the sensitiveness of the plates. His researches in photometry were most suggestive. His photographs showed that the reflecting power of Jupiter is much greater than that of the moon; with his ingenious device of reflection from a silvered glass globe he determined the variation of the brightness of the moon with phase and compared the brightness of the moon with that of Venus, Jupiter, and the sun. At the

time of his death he was at work on the discussion of the drawings and measurements of the Orion Nebula which he had undertaken as a vindication of his father's work.

Bond was deeply religious, conscientious, and untiring. In appearance he was rather tall and slender, becoming in later years painfully thin. While modest and unassuming, he had a strong sense of justice and a due estimate of his own worth. The loss of his wife, Harriet Gardner Harris, of his youngest child, and of his father, all within a few months, and the contraction of the disease (tuberculosis) which destroyed him at the age of forty combined to make his path hard. Though repeatedly warned that the only remedy was rest, he could not leave his work.

[Edward S. Holden, *Memorials of Wm. Cranch Bond and of his Son, Geo. Phillips Bond* (1897); *Am. Jour. of Sci. and Arts,* Mar. 1865; *Proc. Am. Acad. of Arts and Sci.,* VI, 499–500; *Memoirs of the Am. Acad. of Arts and Sci.,* containing Bond's numerous scientific papers.]　　　　　　　R. S. D.

BOND, HUGH LENNOX (Dec. 16, 1828–Oct. 24, 1893), jurist, was born in Baltimore, the son of Christina (Birckhead) Bond and Dr. Thomas E. Bond, a physician and clergyman, one of the founders of the city's first medical school, and at one time editor of the *Christian Advocate.* In early childhood Hugh Bond was taken to New York, where he lived until he graduated from the University of the City of New York in 1848. He returned to Baltimore to read law, and was admitted to the bar in 1851. He married in 1853 Anne Griffith Penniman of Baltimore. In 1860 he was appointed by Gov. Thomas H. Hicks as judge of the criminal court, in 1861 he was elected to the same position. He was a valuable addition to the American Party in the conservative state of Maryland. Less radical than Henry Winter Davis, he was no less loyal to the Union. The attack of Apr. 19, 1861, on the 6th Massachusetts Regiment on its way through Baltimore gave him the first opportunity to exercise a fearless sense of right which was characteristic. According to his charge to the grand jury, those who took part in the riot had been guilty of murder. Other decisions during the war were his release on *habeas corpus* writs of seventy-five Unionists who had been arrested for displaying flags; his committal to jail of police commissioners appointed by Gov. Swann; his charge to the grand jury to indict military commissioners appointed by the national government who tried citizens for offenses against the United States when Maryland was not under military law; his release on *habeas corpus* writs of children of free colored people apprenticed to slaveholders under an old law.

At the same time he had active political and humanitarian interests. He was a supporter of Davis and when the latter's election to Congress was in doubt in October 1863, he wrote Secretary Stanton about the possibility of postponing the draft until the canvas of votes could be completed (B. C. Steiner, *Life of Henry Winter Davis,* 1916, citing the *Official Records,* ser. 3, vol. III). His protest gave an impetus to the support of emancipation by the non-slaveholding whites in Maryland through the resulting levy of slaves which released the whites. Impelled by a warm interest in the negro, he started and later helped support an educational plan (nicknamed "Timbuctoo") which developed into the "Association for the Improvement of Colored People." In 1868 schools for colored children were established in Baltimore through the efforts of this organization.

Rearrangement of the courts by the new state constitution of 1867 automatically retired Judge Bond from the criminal court bench and he took up private practise. In 1870 President Grant appointed him judge of the newly created fourth United States circuit court, including Maryland, Virginia, West Virginia, and the Carolinas. The Senate confirmed his appointment by a majority of four votes. Almost immediately he was called upon to hear the Ku Klux cases of South Carolina. His independence of judgment was conspicuous here. Fines and imprisonment which he imposed broke the reign of terror that had held nine counties of the state helpless. Five years later Bond gave the famous decision which made Hayes President of the United States when he released on *habeas corpus* writs the members of the state board of canvassers of South Carolina who had been illegally imprisoned by order of the South Carolina supreme court in the effort to force the electoral vote of the state for Tilden. For almost twenty-five years more he was an active and valuable judge in the fourth United States circuit. Many important civil and criminal cases were heard by him, among which the Virginia Coupon cases of 1886 (*Federal Reporter,* vol. XXIX), the receivership and sale of the Atlantic, Mississippi & Ohio Railroad, and the Navassa Island murder case were conspicuous.

[*Sun* (Baltimore), Oct. 26, 1893; *Weekly Sun* (Baltimore), Oct. 28, 1893; *Baltimore American,* Oct. 25, 26, 27, 1893; B. C. Steiner, *Life of Reverdy Johnson; Proc. in the Ku Klux Trials at Columbia, S. C., in the U. S. Circuit Court, Nov. Term, 1871* (1872).]

M. A. K.

BOND, SHADRACH (*c.* 1773–Apr. 13, 1832), governor of Illinois, belonged to a prosperous farm-owning Episcopalian family of Baltimore

County, Md. His father, Nicodemus Bond, a man of marked piety, became a Methodist, and on his death bed in 1804, manumitted his four slaves (*Baltimore Wills,* VII, 315). His mother, Rachel, was the daughter of a plantation-owner by the name of Richard King Stevenson. She bore her husband ten children, of whom Shadrach was the sixth. He retained the piety of his father but was captivated by the lure of adventure in the West. An uncle, also bearing the name of Shadrach Bond, had been a member of the gallant little band under George Rogers Clark which opened up the Illinois country in 1779; after roving the prairies several years he settled in the fertile American Bottom along the Mississippi below Kaskaskia. Here he was joined by his nephew about the year 1791. With avuncular aid the latter secured a number of land grants (*American State Papers: Public Lands,* II, 123, 132, 135, 204). His fondness for hunting was not allowed to interfere with prosperous farming and public service. In 1806, he became adjutant of the militia in St. Clair County and two years later, lieutenant-colonel. Having been elected in 1806 to his uncle's former seat in the territorial legislature, in 1807 he succeeded his uncle in the council. In 1808 he again succeeded his uncle as presiding judge of the court of common pleas for St. Clair County. In 1812 he was elected as first delegate to Congress from the territory of Illinois. His principal achievement at Washington was the preëmption law of 1813. Thousands of settlers had trespassed upon the public lands before these were offered for sale, and their great concern was to insure themselves against having their lands sold at a higher figure than the minimum of one dollar and a quarter per acre at the public auction or acquired by the holders of unlocated military grants. With the help of Jeremiah Morrow, of Ohio, Bond secured the passage of an act somewhat more generous than the preceding acts, granting preëmption of 160 acres up to two weeks before the public sale. He also increased his popularity at home by securing the passage of an act raising ten companies of rangers from the Western frontier and by his strenuous efforts to secure payment for the Illinois militia in the War of 1812.

Resigning in 1814 to accept the appointment of receiver of public moneys at Kaskaskia, Bond spent four years settling claims to lands in southern Illinois with fairness to his neighbors and loyalty to the federal government. He shrewdly avoided taking sides in the factional dispute between the Edwards group and the Thomas group which divided Illinois politics for two decades. Thus, although a man of no great ability, and a constant seeker after public office, his popularity was such that in 1818, when Illinois with a population of 35,000 reached statehood, he was elected governor. Although the possessor of fourteen slaves (Census of 1820) he had remained silent during the controversy over slavery which agitated the constitutional convention of 1818, and he now straddled the question during the struggle which culminated in the defeat of the pro-slavery attempt for a new constitution in 1824. He appears, however, to have been considerably under the influence of Elias Kent Kane, whom he appointed as secretary of state, and who became the leader of the pro-slavery movement. His administration was simple and honest. In his message to the first general assembly he had the foresight to recommend the construction of a canal connecting Lake Michigan and the Illinois River. Although bitterly criticized for his personal interest in the wildcat bank established by the legislature (*Illinois Emigrant*, Shawneetown, Apr. 3, 1819, p. 1), his financial record appears to have been sound (J. C. Pease, *The Frontier State*, 1918, II, 52–69). At the expiration of his four-year term, he resumed his occupation of farming. He continued his interest in politics, campaigning for Jackson and running for Congress in 1824, but being defeated. He supported internal improvements, being one of the incorporators of the Illinois & Michigan Canal Company in 1825 (*Illinois Intelligencer,* Springfield, Mar. 25, 1825). In 1825 he was appointed register of the land office at Kaskaskia and held this position at his death.

Bond prided himself on his generous hospitality. On his farm near Kaskaskia he built a large two-story brick house with broad verandas in Southern fashion, and received many guests. In 1810, he married a distant cousin, Achsah Bond, of Nashville, a woman of considerable character and charm, who accompanied him on his arduous journeys to Washington as delegate to Congress, and who shared his delight in sociability. A German writer who visited the frontier in 1819 has left a pleasing picture of the distinguished company and the courtesy that he found in the home of Gov. Bond (Ferdinand Ernst, *Reise durch das Innere der Vereinigten Staaten,* p. 32). One of his contemporaries describes Bond as of military bearing, six feet in height, erect and compact, with black hair and commanding appearance, a description comporting with his portrait which is in the possession of the Chicago Historical Society. The bad grammar of his letters as delegate to Congress bears witness of the limitations of his early edu-

cation. He was a man of business but not of original ideas. His state papers while governor were supposed to have been drafted by Kane.

[J. C. Smith, *Freemasonry in Illinois* (1903); John Reynolds, *Pioneer Hist. of Illinois* (1852), not always trustworthy; W. H. Brown, *Early Hist.* (1840); Henry Brown, *Hist. of Illinois* (1844); Thos. Ford, *Hist. of Illinois* (1854); E. B. Washburne, *Edwards Papers* (1884); E. B. Greene and C. W. Alvord, *Governor's Letter-Books* (1909).]

K. C.

BOND, THOMAS (1712–Mar. 26, 1784), physician, the son of Richard and Elizabeth (Chew) Bond, was born in Calvert County, Md. After studying medicine with Dr. Alexander Hamilton, of Annapolis, Md., he completed his medical education in Europe, chiefly at Paris. About 1734 he began practising medicine in Philadelphia where he was joined a few years later by his brother Phineas. "He was of delicate constitution," according to Thacher, "and disposed to pulmonary consumption, for which he went on a voyage when a young man, to the island of Barbadoes. By unremitted care of his health, the strictest attention to diet and to guard against the changes of temperature, and also by frequently losing blood when he found his lungs affected, he lived to an age which the greater part of mankind never reach." Although Bond's chief interest lay in medicine, especially in its application to hygiene and epidemiology, he was an excellent surgeon, performing amputations and operating for stone in the bladder with much success. His name is still applied to the splint he devised for use in fractures of the lower extremity of the radius. Benjamin Rush ascribed to Bond the credit for the introduction and general use of mercury in the practise of Philadelphia physicians. Bond was also a great believer in the efficacy of various forms of baths, hot, cold, and vapor, in the treatment of disease.

The best account of Bond's connection with the founding of the Pennsylvania Hospital, the oldest hospital in the United States intended solely for the reception of the sick, injured, and insane, and unconnected in any way with the idea of a poorhouse or almshouse, is given by Benjamin Franklin in his *Autobiography.* With great generosity Franklin disclaims the credit frequently ascribed to him of being the founder of the Hospital, and tells how Bond had conceived the idea and sought to obtain subscriptions for the project with but little success, largely because he was generally asked "Have you consulted Franklin on this business?" Bond had not heretofore spoken to Franklin on the subject because he felt it was one in which he might not be interested. When he finally in 1751 approached him Franklin entered into the plan with the greatest enthusiasm and with the aid of his shrewd advice and great influence the Hospital was soon launched on its beneficent career and was open for the reception of patients in February 1752. Bond was a member of the first staff and served as physician to the Hospital until his death. One of the objections raised to the establishment of the Hospital had been the expense incident to paying for the services of physicians. This was overcome when Bond, his brother Phineas, and Dr. Lloyd Zachary offered to give their services for nothing. In 1766 Bond began the delivery at the Hospital of the first course of clinical lectures to be given in the United States. He had previously secured the consent of the Managers of the Hospital to such a course by asking them to meet at his house where he read them an address in which he showed the value of such a course in connection with the newly projected plans of Dr. John Morgan and Dr. William Shippen, Jr., for a medical school in Philadelphia. The Managers not only permitted Bond to give his lectures but thought so highly of his remarks that they ordered them copied into the minutes. Bond was a member of the original board of trustees of the College of Philadelphia, as the University of Pennsylvania was then called, and took a great interest in the establishment of its Medical School in 1765. He was also one of the founders of the American Philosophical Society in 1768. Although sixty-four years old, he volunteered his services to the Committee of Safety in 1776 and did considerable service in the organization of the army. He was president of the Humane Society of Philadelphia which was founded in 1780 and took much interest in its affairs. Thacher gives the following as his contributions to medical literature: "An Account of a Worm bred in the Liver," *Medical Observations and Inquiries by a Society of Physicians in London,* May 1, 1754; "A letter to Doctor Fothergill on the use of the Peruvian Bark in Scrofula," *Ibid.,* vol. II. Bond's "Essay on the Utility of Clinical Lectures" is printed in T. G. Morton's *History of the Pennsylvania Hospital* (1895). He was married to Sarah Roberts by whom he had seven children, two of whom became physicians.

[Jas. Thacher, *Am. Medic. Biog.* (1828); G. W. Norris, *Early Hist. of Medicine in Phila.* (1886); manuscript ledgers and letters in the Lib. of the Coll. of Physicians of Phila.]   F. R. P.

BOND, WILLIAM CRANCH (Sept. 9, 1789–Jan. 29, 1859), astronomer, was born in Falmouth (now Portland), Me., where his father, William Bond, had settled in 1786 and engaged in the export of lumber. His mother was Hannah Cranch. The venture in the lumber business proving unsuccessful, William Bond moved to Boston and returned to his trades of silversmith and clockmaker. There followed years of struggle with poverty. It was necessary for young Bond to leave public school at an early age and share in the support of the family. His brother describes him as the best-tempered boy he knew and says that he was the best of the boys at making traps and snares. He soon became an admirable workman. At the age of fifteen he made a ship's chronometer and at about the same time, a quadrant. For many years preceding the War of 1812 the chronometers of most of the ships sailing out of Boston were rated by his instruments. He was entirely self-taught, at a time when astronomy was just starting in America. His brother describes the first transit instrument in the house at Dorchester—"a strip of brass nailed to the east end of the Champney house, with a hole in it to see a fixed star and note its transit." His mother shared his plans and sympathized with his high aspirations. His independent discovery of the comet of 1811 shows him to have been a constant observer at that time, though no one knew of his discovery until several months later. With what instruments he could make or procure he watched and recorded the positions of the heavenly bodies with no other apparent motive than a love of the occupation. In 1815 when preparing for a trip to Europe he was commissioned by Harvard College to visit the English observatories and gather data concerning instruments and mountings. While the building of an observatory in Cambridge had to be delayed for many years, Bond's report was satisfactory in every way and his contact with European astronomers was of great value to him. In 1819 he married his cousin, Selina Cranch, in Kingsbridge, Devonshire. She was the mother of his six children. After her death, in 1831, he married her elder sister, Mary Roope Cranch. Household expenses were willingly cut down to save money for the purchase of costly instruments and books. The only parlor in the house at Dorchester was sacrificed to science—a huge granite block rose in the middle of the room and the ceiling was intersected by an opening in the meridian. During this period Bond did pioneer work on the rates of chronometers and in meteorology and magnetism. The children were impressed into service as assistants and recorders. William Cranch Bond, Jr., a lad of great promise, was an especially devoted assistant until his death in 1841.

After thirty years of unremitting observation in Dorchester and at a time when he was beginning to be able to enjoy more leisure for astronomy, Bond consented in 1839 to move to Cambridge and take charge of what was then little more than a plan for an observatory. No salary was attached to the office until 1846. The last observation in Dorchester was made on Dec. 25, 1839. The first at Cambridge is dated Dec. 31. By the generosity of the citizens of Boston and the vicinity it finally became possible to order a 15-inch telescope, matching the one newly put into operation at Pulkovo. During the last twelve years of Bond's directorship this instrument was in constant use by him and his son George. It is difficult, and perhaps not important, to weigh the credit which should be given to each. During the administration of the elder Bond elaborate studies were made of the Orion and Andromeda nebulæ and of the planets. The photographic process, invented by Daguerre in 1839, was here first put to practical astronomical use. The regulating device which made the chronograph an instrument of precision is also to be attributed to the Bonds. In his later years William Bond was very frail in health. He is remembered in his last years as a gentle, kindly old man, serene and placid. He was deeply religious, modest, and retiring.

[Edward S. Holden, *Memorials of William Cranch Bond and of His Son, George Phillips Bond* (1897); *Annals of the Harvard Coll. Observatory*, vol. I, pt. 1, vol. II, pt. 1, vol. VII.]
R. S. D.

BONER, JOHN HENRY (Jan. 31, 1845–Mar. 6, 1903), editor, poet, the son of Thomas Jacob and Phœbe Elizabeth Boner, was born in Salem, N. C. After an academic education varied by rambles along the Yadkin River and prentice work at versifying, the youth was put to learn the printer's trade. At twenty-two he ventured to establish the *Salem Observer* but met with failure; in the same year he edited the *Asheville Pioneer*. Moved by Whig influence and anti-slavery sentiment among his Moravian ancestors, Boner early cast his lot with the Republican party. He was recognized by appointment as secretary of the constitutional convention (1868) and as clerk of the House of Representatives of North Carolina (1869, 1870). Feeling assured of his future, Boner now married Lottie Smith of Raleigh. But in the following year the Carpet-Baggers were routed at the polls, and Boner, refusing to modify his politics, found all doors closed to him in his own state. He had been worsted in his first encounter with partisan government. Removing to Washington, he entered the Government Printing Office as typesetter. His first publication, *Sparrows in the Snow* (1877), was negligible; but *Whispering Pines* (1883) won the poet recognition in New York, and friendship from Edmund Clarence Stedman. Although

Boner's lyrics of this period were entirely conventional, his sketches of life among Moravians and negroes were sincere and appealing. At this juncture, the Democratic party gained control of national affairs; Boner's activities in North Carolina were recalled; and he was dismissed from his position as proof-reader because of "offensive partisanship." For the second time the vagaries of politics had frustrated the poet.

Brought to New York by Stedman, Boner soon established himself as an editor, serving on *The Century Dictionary* (1887–91), *A Library of American Literature* (1888–90), the New York *World* (1891–92), and *The Standard Dictionary* (1892–94). His associates found him dignified and reserved: only his wife and a few intimates knew his gentle humanity. His lyrics were now surer in execution, deeper and wider in emotional range; but sentimentalism defeated his attempt at interpreting the metropolis in verse. Elated by appointment in 1894 as an editor on the *Literary Digest*, he began building a home for his old age, "Cricket Lodge" on Staten Island. But in the following year he disagreed violently with his editor and characteristically resigned rather than yield to his superior. Weakened in health, he struggled to support himself by hack-writing, particularly for *Appleton's Annual Cyclopædia* (1896–99). Out of disaster came his finest lyrics—his chief claim to more than local reputation. Such work, however, did not maintain the payments on "Cricket Lodge": his home was lost. Thus the poet, unable to concede or to conciliate, was finally broken by the discipline of journalism.

Ill and destitute, Boner was in 1900 reinstated in his former position in Washington, through the intervention of friends. His health did not allow him to remain at the desk: on the proceeds of *Some New Poems* (1901) he recuperated in North Carolina. In January 1903 he returned to Washington, where he died. Sensitive and high-spirited, kindly yet unyielding, Boner, like the three poets whom he most highly revered—Spenser, Keats, and Poe—had failed to adjust himself to the realities of a commercial civilization. His last volume, *Poems* (1903), was published by his widow. The Boner Memorial Association in 1904 removed his remains from the Congressional Cemetery in Washington to the Moravian burying-ground in his beloved Salem. Participation in this ceremony by the governor of the state indicated that the foremost poet of North Carolina was no longer an alien among his own people.

[The foregoing sketch is based primarily on the publications and records of the concerns with which Boner was associated and on a manuscript letter from Mr.

Frank Vizetelly. Scattered biographical data appear in the *South Atlantic Quart.*, Apr. 1904 ; *Memorial of John Henry Boner* (1905) ; *Charlotte Observer*, Jan. 6, 1906 ; *Lib. of Southern Lit.*, I, 415 ; *Who's Who in America*, 1901–2.]   G. T. M.

BONHAM, MILLEDGE LUKE (Dec. 25, 1813–Aug. 27, 1890), Confederate soldier and congressman, was descended from Nicholas Bonham, who was living in Barnstable, Mass., in 1659 when he was married to Hannah Fuller, grand-daughter of a *Mayflower* Pilgrim. James Bonham, fifth in the line of descent from Nicholas, moved to South Carolina after the close of the Revolution and married Sophie Smith. Their eighth child, Milledge Luke, was born at Red Bank, Edgefield District. His father died when he was two years old and under the care of his mother he was educated in the "old field" schools of Edgefield District, the academies of Edgefield and Abbeville, and the South Carolina College, graduating in 1834 under the presidency of the famous Dr. Thomas Cooper. He successfully practised law in the intervals of his public and military life. He was in command of the South Carolina Brigade in the Seminole War and was always interested in the militia, holding the office of major-general of militia for several years. He served in the state legislature from 1840 to 1844 representing Edgefield District. He was married Nov. 13, 1845, to Ann Patience Griffin. When war was declared with Mexico in 1846 he was appointed by President Polk lieutenant-colonel of the 12th Infantry. His adjutant was Capt. Winfield Scott Hancock, afterward major-general in the United States Army, and his brigade commander was Gen. Franklin Pierce, afterward president. He was an original member of the Aztec Club, was cited by Gen. Pierce for conspicuous service, and for a year served as governor of one of the conquered provinces. Upon his return to Edgefield he resumed his law practise and was elected in 1848 solicitor of the southern district in South Carolina, serving till 1857 when he was elected as States Rights Democrat to fill the unexpired congressional term of his cousin, Hon. Preston S. Brooks. He remained in Congress till the secession of South Carolina in 1860. Appointed commander-in-chief of the South Carolina troops around Charleston, at the request of Gov. Pickens he waived his rank and served under Gen. Beauregard of the newly created Confederate Army. In April 1861 he was appointed brigadier-general in the Confederate Army, and was in command of the first troops arriving in Virginia for the defense of Richmond. He led his brigade in the fighting around Fairfax, Centerville, Vienna, and First Manassas. He was one of the many officers who protested against President Davis's interpretation of the ranking of officers who had served in the "old army," and in 1862 he resigned his commission in the army and was at once elected to the Confederate Congress. Later in the same year he was elected governor of South Carolina and served with marked success in a period of internal difficulties. In February 1865 he was reappointed brigadier-general of cavalry and served under Joseph E. Johnston until he surrendered with Johnston's army. After the end of the Civil War he resumed his law practise, served in the legislature in the early days of Reconstruction, was a delegate to the national Democratic convention in 1868, but kept out of active politics till the "Red Shirt Campaign" of 1876, when he took an active and enthusiastic part in restoring white supremacy in the state government. He was appointed by Gov. Wade Hampton in 1878 as railroad commissioner and served in this capacity during the difficult days of building up the wrecked transportation system of the state until his death, which occurred suddenly on Aug. 27, 1890, from the bursting of a blood vessel.

[Bonham's personal papers and a manuscript sketch of the Bonham family, written by Judge M. L. Bonham, are now in the possession of Dr. M. L. Bonham of Hamilton College. There are other sources in the Pickens-Bonham manuscripts and the Hammond Papers in the Lib. of Cong. A life of Bonham is in preparation by his grandson, Dr. M. L. Bonham.]   J. E. W—y.

BONNER, JOHN (*c.* 1643–Jan. 30, 1725/26), mariner and mapmaker, born possibly in London, came to Boston about 1670. He began his career there in that year by purchasing the *Recovery*, in which his first extended venture was in 1671–72 from Boston to Virginia, Barbados, England, Ireland, and back to Boston, a charter-party with Henry Ashton and others. He became owner or master of many other vessels, including the *Amity, Speedwell, Crown, Mary* (in Phips's Canada Expedition of 1690), *Two Brothers, Three Friends,* and the brigantine *Hope* (a flag of truce to Quebec in 1706) in which he brought home the Rev. John Williams of Deerfield [*q.v.*], author of *The Redeemed Captive* (1707). He was a member of a committee on building the Province Galley in 1693 and of a committee on repairing a later Province Galley in 1709 ; chief pilot of Admiral Walker's disastrous expedition, 1711 ; maker of a draught of the entrance of Boston Harbor, 1716 ; and member of a committee to inspect another draught of the same and report on the necessity of a second lighthouse, 1718. He made a chart of Canada River before 1711, a plan of the Boston waterfront in 1714, and published "A Curious ingraven map of the town of Boston" during 1722. Only two copies of the original exist: one in possession of I. N. Phelps Stokes of New York, and the other at the Massachusetts Historical Society, Boston. A contemporaneous opinion of him from the *Boston Newsletter* of Feb. 3, 1726 (*i. e.,* 1725/26), reads as follows: "He was a Gentleman very Skillful and Ingenious in many Arts and Sciences; especially in Navigation, Drawing, Moulding of Ships, &c. One of the best acquainted with the Coasts of North America, of any of his time; of great Knowledge and Judgement in Marine Affairs; was very much consulted, improved and relyed upon by the Government as a Principal Pilate [*sic*], in our Marine Expeditions; and with diligent Care and Faithfulness discharged his Trust. In short, He was brave, hardy, healthy, sober, industrious, honest, good natur'd, as well as Religious; and much belov'd by all that knew him." He was married four times: (1) to Rebecca Greene; (2) to Mary Clark, who died Apr. 20, 1697; (3) to Persis Wanton, on Sept. 28, 1699; (4) to Susannah Stilson, on June 2, 1709, who died in January 1710/11.

[The principal sources of information are the *Boston Newsletter,* 1704–26; *Boston Gazette,* 1719–26; *New Eng. Courant,* 1721–26; *Reports of the Record Commissioners of the City of Boston* (1876–1909); *Calendar of State Papers, America and West Indies,* 1603–1714; *Vital Records of Cambridge, Mass.* (1914); *Pubs. Colonial Soc. of Mass.; Acts and Resolves, Public and Private, of the Province of the Mass. Bay,* vols. I, II, VII–XI; *Records of the Governor and Company of the Mass. Bay in New Eng.* (1853–54); *Records of the Court of Assistants of the Colony of the Mass. Bay* (1901–28); *Proc. and Colls. of the Mass. Hist. Soc.; New Eng. Hist. and Geneal. Reg.,* Apr. 1851, July 1860, July 1889; manuscript records in the Massachusetts Archives.]

                         J. H. E—s.

BONNER, ROBERT (Apr. 28, 1824–July 6, 1899), newspaper publisher and famous turfman, born near Londonderry, Ireland, came to America in 1839. Learning the printer's trade on the *Hartford Courant* in Connecticut, he became a remarkably fast compositor and early showed a fondness for fast horses. While still a typesetter for the *Courant,* he was constantly swapping horses to get one that had more speed. Believing that New York City offered greater opportunities for a practical printer than Hartford, he went in 1844 to the metropolis where in 1851 he purchased from the profits of his printing plant the *Merchant's Ledger,* a commercial sheet published in the interest of the dry-goods trade. Promptly shortening the name, he excluded all news of that business and turned the paper into a family newspaper by substituting popular fiction for quotations on stock for merchants. To secure circulation he became a lavish purchaser of advertising space in newspapers though he refused all advertisements submitted for publication in the *Ledg-*

er. He originated freak advertising and what is known to-day as "teaser copy." For example, he would purchase a whole newspaper page and then put in each column, "Read *The New York Ledger,*" repeated over and over again until the jumble filled all the space. When in 1860 his press room was "gutted" by fire he distributed the printing of his *Ledger* among a dozen other plants and advertised in the leading daily papers throughout the country, "Unless we are burned out more than once a week, *The New York Ledger* will be ready Monday mornings on all newsstands of the United States, the Sandwich Islands and New Jersey." Even in his personal advertising he was also spectacular. He once offered for sale his summer home from which he wanted to get away as fast as one of his famous horses could carry him because all his family and servants had the ague and fever. Cash was demanded because "any security would get the fever and ague and become shaky" (see advertisements in New York newspapers, September 1867). He advertised his stable by getting occupants of the White House to ride behind his horses. To the public he sold the *Ledger* as cheaply as possible, three dollars a year, but to authors—he had a mania for "big names"—he paid startling sums. To Mrs. James Parton, who, writing under the *nom de plume* of "Fanny Fern," was one of the "best sellers" of the day, he paid $100 a column and to Edward Everett, for a series of short articles, he gave $10,000. Obtaining contributions from Raymond of the *New York Times,* Greeley of the *New York Tribune,* and Bennett of the *New York Herald,* he put all three articles in one issue of the *Ledger.* Always he was seeking some new thing or an old thing that could be done in a new way. Even in producing his periodical he sought profits in a novel way for the time—from circulation alone (see editorial in the New York *Sun,* Mar. 13, 1875). He achieved his ambition and saw the weekly sales reach nearly the half-million mark. The profits from the *Ledger* went in part to establish racing records. For fast horses, which he never allowed to run again for money prizes, Bonner spent more than $500,000. Cornelius Vanderbilt had about everything he wanted except Bonner's Dexter, a great trotter. The end for both Bonner and his *Ledger* came at about the same time. An attraction at the 1926 National Horse Show in New York City was a racing sulky over which was this placard, "Once pulled by Maud S., owned by Robert Bonner."

[The files of the *N. Y. Ledger* constitute the best biography of Robt. Bonner. His influence on later periodicals of the family type is discussed by S. N. D. North in the eighth volume of the quarto series comprising the final report on the *Tenth Census* (1884), p. 119. His spectacular advertising campaigns are treated by Frederic Hudson in *Journalism in the U. S.* (1873), pp. 646 ff., but too much emphasis is put upon those inserted in the *N. Y. Herald* with which Hudson was connected. Briefer but more accurate is the mention made of Bonner by Augustus Maverick in *Henry Raymond and the N. Y. Press* (1870), p. 346. A letter about Bonner from "an old friend," printed in the N. Y. *Sun,* July 8, 1899, sets forth Bonner's views on horse racing and an editorial in the *N. Y. Times* for the same date reviews his career as a publisher.]   J.M.L.

BONNEVILLE, BENJAMIN LOUIS EULALIE DE (Apr. 14, 1796–June 12, 1878), soldier, was born in or near Paris, France, the son of Nicholas and Margaret (Brazier) de Bonneville. His father was a learned philosophical radical, an editor and pamphleteer, and an intimate friend of Lafayette, Condorcet, and Thomas Paine. His mother was educated and talented. Paine was for a time a dweller in their home and was godfather to one of the sons who was named for him. When he left Paris for America in the fall of 1802 it was agreed that the Bonnevilles should follow him. Mme. Bonneville and the children arrived in August of the next year, but Bonneville, who had incurred the wrath of Bonaparte, was kept under close surveillance and could not leave France until after the Corsican's downfall. Mme. Bonneville gave her children careful training. Benjamin entered West Point on his seventeenth birthday and graduated Dec. 11, 1815. He served in some of the New England garrisons and in recruiting service until 1820 and was then transferred to a force constructing a military road through Mississippi. His connection with the frontier, which was to continue throughout the greater part of his life, began with his assignment to Fort Smith, Ark., in 1821. After four years at this post and at Fort Gibson, Okla., he was detached (1825) to serve as aide to the nation's guest, Lafayette, and on the completion of the visit accompanied the Marquis to France. On Oct. 4 of that year he reached the rank of captain. In November 1826, he was back at Fort Gibson, where, except for some months at St. Louis, he remained four years.

The fur trade had long fascinated him, and he now resolved to reap some of the rewards it offered in fortune, fame, and adventure. In the fall of 1830 he took an eight months' leave of absence in New York, where he interested several capitalists, including Alfred Seton, a onetime Astorian, in a project for a thorough exploitation of the fur country. Astor, too, though the project involved certain competition with the American Fur Company, was friendly. Provided with funds, Bonneville asked for a two years' leave of absence for the purpose of exploration and the gathering of information. Leave was granted and on May 1, 1832, with an imposing force of 110 men,

he left Fort Osage, Mo., for Green River. He spent more than three years in the mountains, sending detachments of trappers and hunters in every direction, but the result was negative. He could not successfully compete with men who knew the field. Early in July 1835 he gave up the struggle and with a part of his force started for the settlements. Reaching Independence on Aug. 22, he learned that he had been dropped from the army on May 31, 1834, for overstaying his leave of absence. He hastened to report to Astor in New York and then went to Washington to begin a campaign for reinstatement. Against the protests of many of his fellow officers, President Jackson, on Apr. 22, 1836, restored him to his captaincy. He was again sent to Fort Gibson, but finding the social atmosphere uncongenial was soon detached for service at other posts. A major in 1845, he served with distinction in the Mexican War, winning a lieutenant-colonelcy for gallantry at Contreras and Churubusco. On Feb. 3, 1855, he was made a colonel. He was retired, Sept. 9, 1861, for disability caused by sickness and exposure in the line of duty, but immediately became active again in various services, continuing till after the close of the war. On Mar. 13, 1865, he was brevetted brigadier-general for long and faithful services. On Oct. 15, 1866, his connection with the army closed, and he moved to Fort Smith to spend his remaining days. He had married, early in his young manhood, Ann Lewis, who, with an infant daughter, had died in St. Louis. At Fort Smith, in 1870, he married Susan Neis, who survived him. He died at his home.

It is impossible to reconcile the familiar picture of Bonneville drawn by Irving with that drawn by Chittenden. To the engaging social qualities given his subject Irving further adds the moral quality of disinterestedness and the merit of high achievement as an explorer. Chittenden, on the other hand, regards Bonneville as "a history-made man," unentitled to the fame Irving brought to him; he was not a man of honor or he would not have pretended to the government that his purely commercial venture was an attempt at exploration, and he was not an explorer, since he gave to the world little that was new. Certain merits the historian allows him: he was a skilful commander, for he lost not a single life in any case where the men were under his personal control, and he showed an exceptional humaneness in dealing with the Indians.

[G. W. Cullum: *Biog. Reg.* (3rd ed., 1891); H. M. Chittenden, *The Am. Fur Trade of the Far West* (1902); Moncure D. Conway, *Life of Thos. Paine* (1892); Washington Irving, *The Adventures of Capt. Bonneville* (1837); Grant Foreman, *Pioneer Days in the Southwest* (1926).]   W.J.G.

BONNEY, CHARLES CARROLL (Sept. 4, 1831–Aug. 23, 1903), lawyer, educationist, reformer, son of Jethro May Bonney and Jane Charity Lawton, was descended from Thomas Bonney or Boney, a shoemaker of Sandwich, who came to New England in 1634 on the ship *Hercules*. He was named after the last surviving signer of the Declaration of Independence. Born at Hamilton, N. Y., he was brought up on his father's farm, attending the district school and Hamilton Academy. In 1847 he became a school teacher and intermittently attended Madison (now Colgate) University, studying law in leisure moments. In 1850 he removed to Peoria, Ill., and opened a school called the Peoria Institute. Continuing his law studies he was admitted to the Illinois bar Sept. 23, 1852, and commenced practise there. During 1852–53 he was public lecturer on education for Peoria County and later vice-president of the Illinois State Teachers Association, being also instrumental in the calling of the first state educational convention and contributing on scholastic matters to the press. On Aug. 16, 1855, he married Lydia A. Pratt of Troy, N. Y. He was a persistent advocate of legal and constitutional reforms, and a prominent speaker and writer on behalf of the Democratic party until the year 1860, when he relinquished active participation in politics. Having become well-known in the state through these activities, he moved in 1860 to Chicago, where he soon acquired an extensive legal connection as a general practitioner. His interests were wide, his energy unbounded, and his mind fertile in projects for the advancement of his fellows. During his early years in Chicago he wrote two law books: *Rules of Law for the Carriage and Delivery of Persons and Property by Railway* (1864), and *Summary of the Law of Marine, Fire and Life Insurance* (1865), primarily intended for the general public and not pretending to be exhaustive treatises. When the Civil War broke out he supported the Government in all its war measures, at the same time remaining, as he always had been, a convinced state's rights supporter. After the termination of the war, an important constitutional question arose as to the right of Congress to impose a tax on processes of states' courts, and he was successful in establishing the doctrine that Congress cannot destroy the agencies of the states through the exercise of its taxing power, and that similarly state legislatures cannot destroy or impair agencies of the federal government. In 1872–73 he lectured on medical jurisprudence at Hahnemann Medical College, Chicago. In 1882 he was president of the Illinois State Bar Association. He had

been one of the founders of the Citizens' Law and Order League of the United States and at its first national convention at Boston in 1883 he was elected president. Subsequently under the name of the International Law and Order League the organization held seven consecutive annual conventions in different centers, at each of which he officiated as president, contributing addresses of great value on various subjects of national importance. In 1887 he was prominently mentioned for a vacancy as associate justice of the United States Supreme Court, but political and other exigencies did not admit of the appointment. In 1889 he attracted great attention by his advocacy of the establishment of a permanent international court of justice, thus laying the foundation stone of the Arbitration Court at The Hague. When the project of holding the Columbian Exposition at Chicago in 1893 was launched, he conceived the idea of holding auxiliary congresses in conjunction with the larger undertaking, and it was mainly due to his initiative and organizing force that the project was carried out. As president of the Auxiliary, he was completely successful in maturing plans by which representatives of many nations were brought together for discussion of matters of common interest at the World's Fair, the most conspicuous success of which was the Parliament of Religions. The addresses he delivered to the latter and the religious denominational congresses were subsequently published under the title *World's Congress Addresses* (1900). The energy with which he devoted himself to this work and his untiring exertions at the congresses themselves undermined his health, ultimately bringing on paralysis, and compelling him to relinquish all his manifold activities. He died in Chicago Aug. 23, 1903.

Throughout his life he was distinguished for remarkable activity of mind and body, combined with methodical precision of work and great courtesy. He was "never known to be too busy to give a person a civil answer or to treat him otherwise than as a gentleman" (Judge J. B. Bradwell). His activities were spread over a wide field, though they could be summed up in a single phrase, the diffusion of knowledge. Practically self-educated, he was a pioneer in the fields of education and social reform. A ready and impressive speaker, he was much in request on anniversary and similar occasions, and many of his addresses and papers were published. He also edited a volume of the poems of Judge A .W. Arrington (1869).

[Bonney's ancestry is traced in Chas. L. Bonney, *The Bonney Family* (1898). Biographical details will be found in F. B. Wilkie, *Sketches and Notes of the Chicago Bar* (1871) and *The Bench and Bar of Chicago*

(1883), and appreciative notices appeared in the *Am. Bar Ass. Report*, 1903, p, 708, and *Proc. Ill. State Bar Ass.*, 1908, pt. 11, p. 125. The article in the *Am. Law Rev.*, XXXVII, 745, is discriminating and well-balanced.]   H.W.H.K.

BONNEY, WILLIAM H. (1859–1881). [See BILLY THE KID.]

BONWILL, WILLIAM GIBSON ARLINGTON (Oct. 4, 1833–Sept. 24, 1899), dentist, inventor, was the eldest son of Dr. William Moore Bonwill, descendant of an old Huguenot family of Camden, Del., and of his wife, Louisa Mason (Baggs) Bonwill. He attended an academy in Middletown, Del., "clerked" in a grocery store, and taught school, previous to taking, in his twentieth year, private instruction in dentistry with Dr. Samuel W. Neall of Camden, N. J. This was supplemented by studies under Dr. Chapin A. Harris and Dr. A. A. Blandy of Baltimore. In October 1854 he began the practise of dentistry in Dover, Del., and on June 13, 1861, he married Abigail E. Warren of Dover. He received the degree of D.D.S. from the Pennsylvania College of Dental Surgery in 1866, and later the M.D. from Jefferson Medical College. While he was on a visit to Philadelphia, Feb. 28, 1867, his attention was attracted by the tapping of a telegraph sounder in the old Continental Hotel. Then and there the idea of the electro-magnetic mallet was born. This, when perfected, became an important factor in the development of "contour" filling operations. In his earlier years Bonwill had been attracted by Dr. Arthur's idea of "permanent separations" for the prevention of tooth decay, and he invented the diamond drill for forming the separations without disfiguring the teeth. With the introduction of the electromagnetic mallet his views changed. It was patented in 1873 and in 1875 the Franklin Institute of Philadelphia awarded him the "Cresson" gold medal of the first class for its invention.

His regard for contour work became even more decided after he brought out his automatic engine-mallet. Thereupon he became as bitter an opponent of the old non-cohesive gold filling as he had before been its ardent advocate. The engine-mallet he esteemed more highly than the electro-magnetic, a preference probably due in some degree to bitterness engendered by the need for modification of the earlier appliance. He could conceive a stupendous, epoch-making mechanical idea and develop it to the point of practicality in his hands, but almost invariably his inventions had to be carried to their final perfection by others. His teeming brain would be busy with a new idea long before the mechanical details of an invention could be worked out. He was a

wonderful operator. It is doubtful if the combination of speed and skill with which he habitually worked has ever been surpassed. When at the height of his career as a gold operator he was attracted to amalgam work. After many experiments he devised an alloy which satisfied his requirements, and in its use he became as skilled as with gold. He originated the use of Japanese bibulous paper in the introduction of amalgam fillings; invented a double-disk device for reducing and pointing root-canal broaches, vulcanite and carborundum disks, a cervical matrix, and numerous attachments for the dental and surgical engines, several of which are still largely used. He invented two forms of dental engines, the last of which, of the cord type, became the progenitor of the Bonwill Surgical Engine.

He was equally distinguished as a prosthetic dentist. His method of selecting porcelain teeth for artificial dentures was original. Instead of choosing them by the set he picked them individually, sometimes breaking up several sets in order to get what he wanted. It cannot be denied that the sets so selected, as mounted by him, were remarkably artistic. He was the first to break away from the "barn-door hinge" articulator with which dentists had worked up to that time; the first to devise an anatomical articulator, with which to imitate the various movements of the mandible in mastication. This was founded on his belief in the geometrical construction of the human mandible. This postulate of geometrical construction, he believed, contained a basal truth, which, carried to its logical sequence, demonstrated the negation of the doctrine of organic evolution; and he wrote several papers in support of his idea. Outside of the dental field he made a number of inventions: improvements in grain reapers, kerosene lamps, shoe fasteners; was at work on an aerial trolley car; and claimed to have invented the "Giffard" injector four years before it was brought out in France.

Physically he was slightly above average height, and very slender, apparently unable to cope with the tremendous tasks he set for himself; but he was a tireless worker. It was his habit to place pad, pencil, and a night light near his bed that he might not lose any inspiration that came to him during the night. Kindly, generous, ready at all times to give of his best in knowledge or demonstration, to any one who asked it, he could not brook opposition. His faith in his ideas allowed no question, and he demanded unfaltering belief from others. As a teacher he was interesting and instructive, welcoming freely all who sought his help. As a writer, he was discursive. His bubbling thoughts ran away with him, often leading him into new paths before the old was cleared of the jungle. This oftentimes obscured his ideas to those who had not the patience to dig out their meaning. Notwithstanding his idiosyncrasies, his great abilities were honored at home and abroad. Russian, Dutch, German, Spanish, and French dental societies bestowed honors and decorations upon him. Some of his most notable papers were as follows: "The Electro-Magnetic Mallet" (1874), *Pennsylvania Journal of Dental Science*, I, 257; "The Air as an Anesthetic" (1875), *Ibid.*, III, 57; "The Salvation of the Human Teeth" (1881), *Transactions of the Odontological Society of Pennsylvania*, 1881, p. 107; "Plastic Gold Alloys" (1882), *Ibid.*, 1882, p. 143; "Geometrical and Mechanical Laws of Articulation" (1885), *Ibid.*, 1885, p. 119; "Regulators and Methods of Correcting Irregularities" (1887), *Ibid.*, 1887, p. 281; "New Method of Clasped Plates *vs.* Movable or Unmovable Bridge-Work" (1890), *International Dental Journal*, XIV, 86; "What Has Dentistry to Demonstrate Against the Hypothesis of Organic Evolution?" (read before the World's Columbian Dental Congress, Aug. 15, 1893), *Transactions*, I, 226.

[C. Newlin Pierce, "Memoir of Dr. Wm. G. A. Bonwill" in *Proc. Am. Phil. Soc.*, I, 206–09; *Dental Cosmos*, Oct., Nov., 1899; *Pub. Ledger* (Phila.), Sept. 25, 1899; B. W. Weinberger, *Orthodontics: an Hist. Rev. of Its Origin and Evolution* (1926); *Dental Digest*, Oct. 1899.]

                       F. L. H.

BONZANO, ADOLPHUS (Dec. 5, 1830–May 5, 1913), engineer, inventor, was born at Ehingen, Würtemberg, Germany. He received his education at the gymnasia in Ehingen, Blönsdorf, and Stuttgart, although his father and other members of his family had emigrated to Texas. In 1850 he came to Philadelphia for two years of further study, particularly aimed at the mastery of English. Recognizing the possibilities offered by the iron industry in the development of this country, he apprenticed himself to the Reynolds Machine Works in Springfield, Mass., in order to supplement his academic studies with practical shop experience. He became one of the skilled mechanical superintendents of his day. On July 2, 1857, he was married to Laura J. Goodell of Detroit. In 1865 he engaged himself with the Detroit Bridge and Iron Works and from that day until his retirement (1898) he was an influential factor in the bridge industry. "In the work of the pioneer and formative period of American bridge construction, Mr. Bonzano had no peer" (*Transactions of the American Society of Civil Engineers*, LXXVII, 1846). In 1868 he became a partner and chief engineer in Clark, Reeves & Company at Phœnixville, Pa. This firm dis-

solved in 1884 to be succeeded by the Phœnix Bridge Company which Bonzano served as chief engineer until 1893. His last five years of active professional practise were spent as a consulting engineer in New York City. Some of the bridges resulting from his professional activities are the Pecos Aqueduct which carries the Southern Pacific Railroad over the Pecos River; the Red Rock Cantilever Bridge over the Colorado River Canyon on the Atchison, Topeka & Santa Fé; the Chesapeake & Ohio Railroad Bridge over the Ohio River at Cincinnati; the Susquehanna River Bridge at Sunbury, Pa., and the Columbia Bridge in Fairmount Park, Philadelphia. Bonzano had a large share in the development of the modern draw-span. The construction of the turntable in the 274-foot double-track draw of the New York Central & Hudson River Railroad at Albany, built in 1870, embodied original features which he designed and which were later accepted as standard practise. He was one of the first engineers to recognize the merits of the Phœnix column and used it in the Sixth and Ninth Avenue Elevated structures in New York City. Bonzano gave many inventions to the world, chief of which is the rail joint which bears his name. In draw-span construction he was the first to use the locking roller with a pair of links at the draw end, and soon after modified this by the knuckle joint. The use of a vertical screw for operating the locking mechanism was also original with him. In addition to his accomplishments in mechanical lines he was a talented musician—an able pianist, organist, and choir master. He was a familiar figure at the opera, and a man of whom it was said, "he never had an enemy."

[*Trans. Am. Soc. Civil Engineers*, LXXVII, 1846; *Engineering News*, May 15, 1913; J. S. Futhey and Gilbert Cope, *Hist. of Chester County, Pa.* (1881), p. 484.]

                       E. Y.

BOONE, DANIEL (Nov. 2, n.s., 1734–Sept. 26, 1820), pioneer, Indian fighter, was born about eleven miles from Reading, Pa., the son of Squire and Sarah Morgan Boone. The family were Quakers. Daniel's grandfather, George, a weaver and small farmer, had come to America with his family from near Exeter, England, arriving in Philadelphia Oct. 10, 1717. To his father's vocations Squire Boone added blacksmithing and stock-raising, and Daniel from his early days was a general helper. At twelve, with a rifle which his father had given him, he became a hunter of game and furs. He probably had no regular schooling. In the spring of 1750 most of the Boones, Daniel among them, started for North Carolina, and after tarrying for perhaps a year in the Shenandoah Valley arrived at Buffalo Lick, on the north fork of the Yadkin, in 1751. For several years the youth continued to work for his father. In 1755, as a teamster and blacksmith, he accompanied a North Carolina contingent in the Braddock campaign. Here he met John Finley, a hunter, who told him stories of the Kentucky wilderness that fired him with the determination to see the land for himself. He was in the disastrous battle of July 9 and escaped on one of his horses. Returning to North Carolina, he resumed work on his father's farm. On Aug. 14 of the following year he married Rebeccah Bryan, the seventeen-year-old daughter of a neighbor. In 1765, following a visit to Florida, he resolved to settle in Pensacola, but on his wife's objection the project was given up.

His thoughts again turned to Kentucky, and in the fall of 1767, with a companion or two, he started westward, reaching a point in the present Floyd County, from which he returned in the spring. Finley, in the rôle of a peddler, wandered into the neighborhood the following winter, and the Kentucky venture was planned anew. On May 1, 1769, a party consisting of Boone, his brother-in-law John Stuart, Finley, and three others, started out and after traversing Cumberland Gap entered the present Estill County and set up their camp at Station Camp Creek. After many adventures Boone and his brother, who had joined the party late in 1769, returned to their homes in the spring of 1771. As an agent of Col. Richard Henderson, of the Transylvania Company, who had planned a great colony in Kentucky, he set out in March 1775 with the first division of settlers. On Apr. 1 he reached what was to become Boonesborough, where he at once began the erection of a fort. In the early fall he returned to North Carolina and brought back his family and twenty young men. Hunting, surveying, and Indian fighting occupied his time for the next two years. On the organization of Kentucky as a county of Virginia in the fall of 1776, he was made a captain of the militia, later becoming a major. In February 1778 he was captured by the Shawnees, but escaped in June, and in September rendered important service in the defense of Boonesborough. He spent a year in the east, but in October 1779 returned with a new party of settlers. The repudiation by Virginia of Henderson's land titles sent him east again in the following spring with $20,000 collected from the settlers for the purchase of land warrants, but on the way he was robbed of the entire amount. Returning to his home, he moved to Boone's Station. On the division of Kentucky the same year into three counties, he was made lieutenant-colonel of Fayette County, and in April of the following year

was chosen a delegate to the legislature. In 1782 he was made sheriff and county lieutenant and served also as a deputy surveyor. He moved to Maysville in the spring of 1786, and in the fall of the following year was elected to the legislature. He had taken up many tracts of land, but all of them had been improperly entered, and in 1785 the first of a series of ejectment suits by which he was to lose all his holdings was begun. In the fall of 1788 he abandoned Kentucky, moving to Point Pleasant, at the mouth of the Great Kanawha, in what is now West Virginia. A year later he was appointed lieutenant-colonel of Kanawha County and in 1791 was chosen its legislative delegate.

At some time in 1798 or 1799, with his last Kentucky holding lost, he moved to the present Missouri, where his son Daniel Morgan had preceded him, and obtained a land grant at the mouth of the Femme Osage Creek. On July 11, 1800, he was appointed magistrate of the district, a post he held until the cession of the territory to the United States. His land title was voided by the United States land commissioners, but after many delays was confirmed by Congress on Feb. 8, 1814. He journeyed to Kentucky, probably in 1810, to pay off his debts, an action that gave him one of the greatest satisfactions of his life, but left him, according to tradition, with a surplus of only fifty cents. His wife died Mar. 18, 1813, and his remaining years he spent mostly at the home of his son Nathan, where he died.

Boone's appearance has often been described, but with an unfortunate lack of agreement. To Audubon his stature "appeared gigantic," to the editor of the *Missouri Gazette* "common," to the Rev. J. E. Welch "rather low." Daniel Bryan, a relative by marriage, records it as "about five feet, eight or nine inches." His head was large, his eyes were blue (light according to some, dark according to others), and his look was sharp and alert. Originally his hair was light and his eyebrows were yellow. He had a wide mouth, thin lips, and a nose somewhat of the Roman type. The portrait of him painted by Chester Harding a short time before his death is probably the only authentic representation of him ever made. In his prime he was a man of great strength, lithe and quick in movement, and a fast runner.

Modern criticism has dealt destructively with the Boone legend. Boone first came into general notice by means of John Filson's *The Discovery, Settlement, and Present State of Kentucke* (1784), purporting to be told by Boone himself, but given in words that Boone could not possibly have used. It gained wide circulation in England through its inclusion in the second and third editions (1793, 1797) of Gilbert Imlay's *A Topo-*

graphical Description of the Western Territory of North America. The seven stanzas that Lord Byron devoted to him in the eighth canto of *Don Juan* (1823) made him a world-wide celebrity, and he gradually became the one overshadowing figure of the frontier. He was acclaimed the discoverer of Kentucky, its first explorer, its first settler, its chief military protector, and even, as the title of a reprint (1847) of Timothy Flint's biography hailed him, "The First White Man of the West." None of these distinctions belonged to him; nor did his services to the community, meritorious though they were, equal in importance those of certain other men. He had, however, his own ample titles to fame and the regard of posterity. In every duty he bore his part manfully. He had the qualities most needed on the frontier—courage in a rare degree, great fortitude, an iron endurance, a mastery of woodcraft, and signal expertness with the rifle. Though his letters reveal him as close to the border line of illiteracy, he had strong native intelligence; and though not a man of affairs, his counsels were always eagerly welcomed. He was loyal in friendship, honest, truthful, and modest. One of his prime characteristics was serenity of mind. He never seemed irritated or excited, and though often wronged he never harbored rancor. He was one of the most respected and beloved of the nation's heroes.

[The earlier biographies and sketches of Boone are all, in varying degrees, untrustworthy. *Daniel Boone* (1902), by Reuben Gold Thwaites, is based on the great mass of source material in the Draper collection, at Madison, Wis. Much valuable information is given in *The Boone Family* (1922), by Hazel Atterbury Spraker, which includes a sketch of Boone by Jesse Procter Crump; and other information, less critically examined, in *A History of the Pioneer Families of Missouri* (1876), by W. S. Bryan and Robert Rose. Stewart Edward White's *Daniel Boone, Wilderness Scout* (1922), though written for boys and deficient in detail, gives a clearer presentation of Boone and his environment than most of the lives written for adults. A searching examination of "the Boone Myth," by Clarence Walworth Alvord, is given in the *Jour. of the Ill. State Hist. Soc.,* Apr.–July 1926. Incidental references to early accounts of Boone are given in Ralph Leslie Rusk, *The Literature of the Middle Western Frontier* (1925).]   W. J. G.

BOORMAN, JAMES (1783–Jan. 24, 1866), merchant, railroad president, son of John and Mary (Colgate) Boorman, was born in the county of Kent, England, of Scotch ancestry. He came with his parents to New York in 1795; was apprenticed to Divie Bethune, and entered into partnership with him in 1805. In March 1813 he joined with a fellow Scot, John Johnston, in forming the New York mercantile house of Boorman & Johnston, which became successively, Boorman, Johnston & Company, and Boorman, Johnston, Ayres & Company. Adam Norrie be-

came a partner in 1828. A subsequent department of the business was conducted as Boorman & Clark. At first Boorman sold Scotch cloths from Dundee, and Virginia tobacco, handling virtually all of the latter that came from the Richmond market. Later the firm did an enormous business in iron from Sweden and England. From South St. the house moved to Greenwich St. The business became so large that the partners had to relinquish a part of it. They were the largest importers of Madeira wines, and they received large consignments from Italy. Their counting-room was over the Bank of the Republic. "A more remarkable man than James Boorman never lived" (Scoville, I, 157). In 1835 he received from Sweden a consignment of immense iron pillars, and the entire trade was much amused by Boorman's valiant effort to sell what no one wanted. Undaunted, he tore out the front of his store, put the pillars under the front wall, and with this increased support added several stories to the building. Aside from his own business he was made chief of every corporation with which he connected himself. He was the originator of the Hudson River Railroad, and as a director he led the board in bringing about the removal of Hon. Azariah C. Flagg as president of that road (*Communications from J. Boorman,* W. C. Bryant & Company, 1849, reprinted in the *Evening Post*). He himself succeeded Flagg. At this time he wrote to the directors: "It will, I hope, not be deemed impertinent for me to add that my services to you as president are gratuitous. . . ." He was chairman of a committee of the road that awarded a contract to Peter Cooper for rails to extend his road to Albany, was a large owner in the Troy & Schenectady Railroad, and was a founder of the Bank of Commerce. He retired in 1855. No New York merchant was more liberal in benevolence. He gave with great liberality to the Institution for the Blind, the Protestant Half-Orphan Asylum, the Southern Aid Society, the Union Theological Seminary, and Trinity Church, of which latter he was long an officer. His town house was at Waverley Place and Washington Square. He also owned No. 1 Fifth Ave., the fine home that was later the residence of the Duncans, and he possessed a country estate at Hyde Park, Dutchess County, N. Y. He married Mary Wells Davenport on Nov. 10, 1810, and they later adopted a daughter. He was inclined to be headstrong, he had little patience with incompetency, and none at all with shams; his integrity was of that rare sort that is never questioned.

[Boorman is mentioned prominently in J. A. Scoville, *The Old Merchants of New York City* (1863).

The lengthy pamphlet entitled *Communications from Jas. Boorman to the Stockholders of the Hudson River Railroad Co., in Reply to Mr. A. C. Flagg, late President of that Co.,* contains much valuable information. He gives some facts of his financial dealings in his *Statement of the Administration of the Estate of Jas. R. Smith* (1865). His will, made in 1862, is on file in the N. Y. Pub. Lib. Obituaries were published in the *N. Y. Times* and *N. Y. Daily Tribune,* Jan. 26, 1866.]

R. R. R.

BOOTH, AGNES (Oct. 4, 1846–Jan. 2, 1910), actress, was born Marian Agnes Land Rookes, daughter of Capt. Land and Sara Rookes, in Sydney, Australia. Her father was a British officer quartered there. She was early apprenticed to the stage as a child dancer, and in that capacity, at the age of twelve, appeared with Mrs. Wood's company in San Francisco, in 1858, under the name of Agnes Land. A little later she appeared with the company of the famous and much-married Ada Isaac Menken. Like so many young dancers of that day, her aim was the dramatic stage, and she began to act at Maguire's Opera House, in San Francisco, where she remained till 1865. During this period, in 1861, she married Harry Perry, a popular actor, who died in 1863. Joseph Jefferson wrote of him, "Youth, vivacity and a ringing laugh made him altogether one of the most captivating fellows in his line. . . . On the occasion I speak of he was quite intoxicated with happiness, being in the height of a honeymoon. His bride was Miss Agnes Land—a young lady who had lately arrived from Australia, and whose talents and beauty combined with his own made them valuable members of the theatrical profession" (*Autobiography,* 1890, p. 230). In 1865 Agnes Land—the name by which she was still known—heard the call of Broadway, and crossed the continent to appear at Booth's Theatre. She was then only nineteen. A little later she supported Edwin Forrest in *Richelieu,* and attracted so much attention that from that time on her services were in constant demand. In 1867 she married Junius Brutus Booth the younger (elder brother of Edwin), and thereafter always appeared as Agnes Booth. The marriage was a happy one. There were two sons—Junius Brutus Booth, III, and Sydney Barton Booth. Mr. and Mrs. Booth acted frequently together, but Mrs. Booth also appeared in support of other male stars, notably her brother-in-law Edwin Booth, McCullough, Wallack, Barrett, and E. A. Sothern. She also served, at different times, as leading woman of the Union Square and Madison Square Theatres, both under the management of A. M. Palmer, and as the star of *The Sporting Duchess* during its tour of the country in 1895–96. Booth died in 1883, and on Feb. 4, 1885, Mrs. Booth married John B. Schoeffel, owner of the Tremont Theatre in Boston. After this marriage, she was under no necessity to act, but continued to do so for a dozen years, her connection as leading woman with Palmer's company at the Madison Square Theatre following the new alliance. She was leading woman of this company in 1890, when the youthful Augustus Thomas, then a newspaper reporter in St. Louis, sent a one-act sketch to Maurice Barrymore, also a member of the company, which was used as a curtain raiser and led to Mr. Thomas's engagement to become dramatist to the theatre (at a salary of $50 a week). In his book, *The Print of My Remembrance* (1922, pp. 288 ff.), he tells how he wrote *A Constitutional Point* for Mrs. Booth—a one-act play twenty years later to become the third act of his noted drama *The Witching Hour.* A. M. Palmer, the manager, considered that the public would not understand this sketch, so he put it away, and wrote another, *Afterthoughts,* which Mrs. Booth acted. That she herself may not have been eager to do the more modern sketch is indicated by the fact, recorded by Mr. Thomas, that when his play, *Alabama,* a pioneer of the new American drama, was read to the company, in 1891, Mrs. Booth paused at the stage manager's desk as she was leaving the house and whispered, "Rotten, thank you." In fact, she at first refused her part of May Brookyn, but later reclaimed it, *and it was going to many* after the play was a sensational success. In 1892, she appeared in a sketch also written for her by Mr. Thomas, in which he supported her. Her last appearance of any moment was as Rose in *L'Arlésienne* at the Broadway Theatre, New York, Mar. 22, 1897. She retired from the stage to her home in Brookline, a suburb of Boston, and devoted the remaining years of her life to social activities.

Mrs. Booth as actress belonged to an earlier generation in training and style. She had no "line," but played all sorts of parts. Indeed, her versatility was exceptional. She was best liked, perhaps, in rôles calling for a mingling of light comedy and sentiment, but she was competent in tragedy and melodrama. Her style, however, was robust and had little in common with the naturalistic methods which in her later years were conquering the stage.

[*Who's Who in America,* 1910–11; J. B. Clapp and E. G. Edgett, *Players of the Present* (1899), pp. 43–47; L. C. Strong, "Agnes Booth," in *Famous Am. Actors of Today* (1896), ed. by F. E. McKay and Chas. E. L. Wingate; *Boston Evening Transcript,* Jan. 3, 1910.]

W. P. E.

BOOTH, EDWIN THOMAS (Nov. 13, 1833–June 7, 1893), actor, the fourth son of Junius Brutus Booth [*q.v.*] and Mary Anne (Holmes) Booth, was born on his father's farm near Bel

Air, Md. He was named after the actors Edwin Forrest and Thomas Flynn, but dropped the "Thomas" in later life. His formal education, such as it was, was obtained at various small private schools in the neighborhood, kept by a Miss Susan Hyde, by a Frenchman, M. Louis Dugas, and by a Mr. Kearney. Far more important for his development were the long theatrical journeys on which he early began to accompany his father. To see to it that that erratic genius did not break his engagements, murder some one, or commit suicide during his times of intoxication and half-insanity was a heavy responsibility for the fragile youth and made him grave, serious, and melancholy beyond his years. His wayward father loved him deeply and would yield to the lad's suasion when deaf to the entreaties of all others. But having derived more fame than happiness from his own theatrical career, he at first resisted his son's desire to go on the stage, although the extent of that resistance seems to have been much over-emphasized by the latter's biographers. Edwin Booth's first appearance, in the minor part of Tressel in *Richard III* on Sept. 10, 1849, at the Boston Museum, was featured on the program, and during the next two years he played occasionally with his father in such juvenile parts as Wilford in Colman's *The Iron Chest* and Titus in Payne's *Brutus* until in 1851 at the National Theatre, New York, the elder Booth one night without warning forced his son to appear in his stead as Richard III. Following these sporadic performances the younger Booth obtained an engagement, at a salary of six dollars a week, with Theodore Barton of Baltimore, but here he was a complete failure. He had not yet learned to overcome his smallness of stature, was awkward and ill at ease, and gave no indications of his future greatness.

In July 1852 he accompanied his father to California, where, under the management of his brother, Junius Brutus Booth, Jr., they had a profitable engagement at the Jenny Lind Theatre, San Francisco, and a very unprofitable one in Sacramento. At the latter place for his benefit Edwin Booth played Jaffier in *Venice Preserved* to his father's Pierre. California then suffering one of its intermittent states of financial depression, the elder Booth decided to return home but died during the long journey. Meanwhile Edwin together with the actor D. W. Waller attempted the theatrical conquest of Nevada County; the venture was not successful, their party was snowed in, barely escaping starvation, and Edwin returned to San Francisco in a penniless condition. Here he was again employed by his brother, in varying capacities ranging from utility man to

star, occasionally appearing in such rôles as Petruchio (never one of his best), Richard III, Macbeth, Hamlet, Sir Giles Overreach, Sir Edwin Mortimer; later he joined Mrs. Catherine Forrest Sinclair, who had newly opened the Metropolitan Theatre; and still later he played with James E. Murdoch [*q.v.*] and Laura Keene [*q.v.*], the latter attributing her failure to "Edwin Booth's bad acting." During most of this time Booth lived with another actor, D. C. Anderson, in a small shack on a tiny plot of ground which they jestingly named "the Ranch." In 1854, despite mutual dislike, Booth and Miss Keene, accompanied by Anderson, made a professional trip to Australia, during which, in Sydney, Booth appeared for the first time as Shylock, a character whom, contrary to his custom, he refused to idealize and presented, then and always, as a purely malevolent villain. At Melbourne the business alliance with Miss Keene ended in financial disaster; and Booth and Anderson returned to America, stopping on the way for two months at Honolulu, where, among other performances, they produced *Richard III* before King Kamehameha IV.

On his arrival in San Francisco, Booth was offered an engagement by Mrs. Sinclair at the Metropolitan and for a short time played Benedick to her Beatrice in *Much Ado;* then came a brief engagement at the American Theatre in the same city; and then, in August 1855, he was again in Sacramento, playing juvenile parts in comedies and melodramas at the Sacramento Theatre. During the fall he joined a company of strolling actors under one Moulton to visit the mining towns in the neighborhood, but each appearance was, by a curious coincidence, so uniformly followed by a fire after they left town that Booth became known as "the Fiery Star" and eventually the community rose against the dangerous intruders, who ignominiously dispersed and sought safety in the valley. Back in Sacramento, Booth obtained a brief engagement at the Forrest Theatre in November, but was soon dismissed for reasons of economy. He was once more saved from imminent starvation by Mrs. Sinclair, who opportunely started at the Sacramento Theatre a joint stock company which he joined as leading man. On Dec. 10 they produced for the first time in America *The Marble Heart or the Sculptor's Dream,* in which Booth created the part of Raphael. In February the company took over the Forrest Theatre where Booth continued to act, after the departure of Mrs. Sinclair for the East, until the end of April. By that time his popularity had become such that on Apr. 19 he received a "Grand Complimentary

Testimonial tendered by the Members of both Houses of the Legislature and the Citizens of Sacramento," on which occasion he presented *The Iron Chest,* repeating the performance on Apr. 22 by request of members of the legislature unable to attend the previous production. Then followed a week at the Sacramento Theatre, a two weeks' successful engagement in San Francisco, another run at the Sacramento Theatre, May 15–June 7, and a final farewell appearance in San Francisco, in *King Lear*—in the Nahum Tate version, which he later abandoned—prior to his departure for the East. (The above paragraph, which differs materially from the accounts given by William Winter and Asia Booth Clarke, is based largely upon the Sacramento play-bills of the period.)

He had left the East a callow youth hardly started in his profession; he returned to it an accomplished actor. His style was inevitably moulded by that of his father and by the whole Kean tradition but it was marked by an intellectuality and a sustained power which the elder Booth never achieved. Not super-eminent as a comedian, in tragedy the younger Booth was soon to reach the level of Kean himself. On his arrival in the East he played at the Front Street Theatre in Baltimore and then toured the South in preparation for a momentous engagement in Boston, the city which was still considered the arbiter of American taste. He made a triumphant appearance there as Sir Giles Overreach on Apr. 20, 1857, and immediately repeated the triumph in numerous rôles at Burton's Metropolitan Theatre, New York. Subsequent tours in the West and South maintained his newly-established position at the very top of his profession in America. On July 7, 1860, he was married to Mary Devlin, a young actress of great charm who had played Juliet to the Romeo of Charlotte Cushman but who now after her marriage retired from the stage. In September of the following year he appeared at the Haymarket, London, in the rôles of Shylock, Sir Giles, and Richelieu, but aroused intense enthusiasm only in the last-named part, which was probably his greatest rôle. There followed relatively unsuccessful engagements at Liverpool and with a stock company at Manchester of which the youthful Henry Irving was a member. In 1862 and 1863 Booth was seen at the Winter Garden, New York, the latter engagement being interrupted by the sudden death of his passionately loved wife on Feb. 21 at their home in Dorchester Mass., leaving him with the care of a daughter, Edwina, then only two years old. After a temporary retirement, Booth undertook the management of the Winter Garden, also purchasing in conjunction with his brother-in-law, John S. Clarke [*q.v.*], the Walnut Street Theatre, Philadelphia. On Mar. 28, 1864, he scored a notable success at Niblo's Theatre, New York, in the rôle of Bertuccio in Tom Taylor's *The Fool's Revenge,* an adaptation of Hugo's *Le Roi S'Amuse.* The next season saw his famous run of one hundred nights as Hamlet, a rôle particularly well adapted to his own melancholy, intellectual, and lofty temperament. The assassination of Lincoln by Booth's younger brother, John Wilkes Booth [*q.v.*], on Apr. 14, 1865, sent the actor into a long retirement. But he himself had been entirely loyal to the Northern cause and when he returned to the stage on Jan. 3, 1866, at the Winter Garden, although threats had been made against his life, he found that his audience was equally loyal to him. He now put on a series of the most lavishly staged performances which had yet been seen in America, terminated on Mar. 23, 1867, by the disastrous burning of the Winter Garden in which his scenery and costumes, his library, and a valuable gallery of theatrical portraits were completely destroyed. Booth almost at once started plans for a new theatre to be the most beautiful in America, and the building, known as Booth's Theatre, at the corner of Twenty-third St. and Sixth Ave., was opened on Feb. 3, 1869, with a performance of *Romeo and Juliet.* On June 7, 1869, Booth was married to his leading woman, Mary McVicker, an actress of more ambition than ability; she left the stage after her marriage, but her restless energy fed upon itself until she became insane, dying on Nov. 13, 1881. Meanwhile in the midst of increasing domestic and financial misfortune, Booth reached his high-water mark as an actor. The seasons 1869–74 at Booth's Theatre were an epoch in the history of the American stage. Booth's most notable performances in his own theatre were as Romeo (a study in adolescence), as Othello (emphasizing the poetic aspect of the character), as Benedick (for the first time in New York, Mar. 6, 1871), as Macbeth (Charlotte Cushman objecting to his idealistic interpretation because "Macbeth was the great ancestor of all the Bowery ruffians"), as Hamlet, as Richelieu, and at various times as Brutus, Cassius, and Mark Antony. Other players at Booth's Theatre were Joseph Jefferson, John S. Clarke, Edwin L. Davenport, John McCullough, John E. Owens, Lawrence Barrett, Mrs. Emma Waller, Charlotte Cushman, and Kate Bateman. But Booth had no head for pecuniary details, his business associations were unfortunate, and the most artistic theatre in America met financial disaster during the panic of 1873–74. Booth withdrew from it in 1873 and the next year he went into bankruptcy. The theatre itself continued to function until Apr. 30, 1883, when it was closed and a little later was torn down.

Booth soon paid off his debts but his career henceforth was that of a traveling actor without a permanent theatrical home. After the age of forty his powers slowly began to decline. His health, possibly injured by excessive drinking in early manhood and by excessive smoking at all times, was gradually undermined by the strain of an actor's life augmented by his long series of personal disappointments. In his acting he often seemed tired; his voice, always his weakest point, tended to become monotonous; his gestures became more formal. Yet he carried on gallantly for almost twenty years, and even to the very end he remained one of the greatest actors of his day. In 1877 he arranged for publication the text of fifteen of his usual plays, which were brought out in 1878 as *Edwin Booth's Prompt Book* under the editorship of William Winter. This work, invaluable for students of the acting drama, includes *Richard II, Richard III, Henry VIII, Hamlet, Macbeth, Othello, Lear, Merchant of Venice, Much Ado, Katherine and Petruchio, Richelieu, The Fool's Revenge, Brutus, Ruy Blas,* and *Don Cæsar de Bazan.* Booth's courage and his dramatic sincerity were well shown by his not stepping out of his rôle when twice fired at by a lunatic during a performance of *Richard II* at McVicker's Theatre, Chicago, on Sept. 23, 1879. (Wags said that the attempted assassination was due to anger at Booth's temerity in reviving so poor a play.) In the season of 1880–81 he had a brilliant repertoire engagement of 119 nights at the Princess's Theatre, London, shortly followed by an engagement in *Othello* at the Lyceum with Henry Irving, the two alternately playing Othello and Iago. In 1882 Booth reappeared at the Princess's, toured the British Isles, and gave extraordinarily successful performances at Berlin, Hamburg, Hanover, Leipsic, and Vienna. After his return to America, when not traveling he made his home at No. 29 Chestnut St., Boston, until his retirement from the stage, after which he lived in the building at 16 Gramercy Park, New York, which he had presented to the Players' Club founded by him in 1888. In the years just prior to his retirement Booth played continuously with Lawrence Barrett, from 1887 until the latter's death in March 1891, with the exception of a single season, 1889–90, with Mme. Helena Modjeska. His last performance was in *Hamlet* at the Academy of Music, Brooklyn, on Apr. 4, 1891. A slight stroke of paralysis two years earlier had left his health

permanently enfeebled, and he now sank steadily until his death on June 7, 1893.

"Booth was marked out by fortune for honour and despite. He felt the strangeness of his lot, and reflected much upon the mysteries of life and death. Helped by his religion, a kind of stoical Christianity, he came to some definite conclusions in the face of all the mysteries. 'All my life,' he wrote to Mr. Winter, in 1886, 'has been passed on picket duty, as it were. I have been on guard, on the lookout for disasters—for which, when they come, I am prepared. . . . Why do not you look at this miserable little life, with all its ups and downs, as I do? At the very worst, 'tis but a scratch, a temporary ill, to be soon cured, by that dear old doctor, Death—who gives us a life more healthful and enduring than all the physicians, temporal or spiritual, can give'" (Copeland, pp. 149–50). Booth expressed his brave, beauty-loving personality almost as fully with the pen as on the stage; he was among the best of American letter-writers. Unfortunately the largest collection of his letters, those addressed to William Winter, was sold at auction after the latter's death and hopelessly scattered. The much-needed edition of Booth's letters will probably never appear.

[Wm. Winter's tedious but usually accurate *Life and Art of Edwin Booth* (1893, rev. ed., 1894) is the chief source. See also Asia Booth Clarke, *The Elder and the Younger Booth* (1882); Laurence Hutton, *Edwin Booth* (1893); Lawrence Barrett, "Mr. Edwin Booth" in *Actors and Actresses of Gt. Brit. and the U. S.* (1886), ed. by Brander Matthews and Laurence Hutton; Edward Robins, *Twelve Great Actors* (1900), pp. 279–311; Lyman Abbott, *Silhouettes of My Contemporaries* (1921), pp. 16–27; Edwina Booth Grossman, *Edwin Booth, Recollections by His Daughter* (1894); Ella V. Mahoney, *Sketches of Tudor Hall and the Booth Family* (Bel Air, Md., 1925); Henry A. Clapp, "Edwin Booth," *Atlantic Mo.,* Sept. 1893; Wm. Bispham, "Memories and Letters of Edwin Booth," *Century Mag.,* Nov., Dec. 1893; Mrs. Thos. Bailey Aldrich, *Crowding Memories* (1920), *passim.* For Booth's interpretation of Shakespearian rôles see his notes contributed to *Othello* and *The Merchant of Venice* in H. H. Furness's Variorum Edition, and also Chas. Townsend Copeland's excellent *Edwin Booth* (1901).]

E. S. B.

BOOTH, JAMES CURTIS (July 28, 1810– Mar. 21, 1888), chemist, was born in Philadelphia, the son of George and Ann (Bolton) Booth. His early education was obtained in the public schools of his native city and in Hartsville (Pa.) Seminary. Entering the University of Pennsylvania in 1825, he studied chemistry with Hare and Keating. Upon receiving the A.B. degree in 1829 he continued to study chemistry for a year or more at the Rensselaer Polytechnic Institute, Troy, N. Y., taught chemistry in Flushing, L. I., in the winter of 1831–32, and then went to Germany, where he studied analytical chemistry with

Wöhler in Hesse-Cassel and with Magnus in Berlin. He also attended lectures in Vienna and visited chemical plants on the continent and in England. On his return to Philadelphia in 1836, he started a student-laboratory where men could obtain practical training in chemistry—especially analytical chemistry—by personal instruction. With him were associated successively Martin H. Boyé [q.v.], Thomas H. Garrett, and Andrew A. Blair. In 1878 the firm became Booth, Garrett & Blair. Many men of this period received their technical education in this unique training school, and several became distinguished chemists. From 1836 to 1845 Booth was professor of chemistry applied to the arts in the Franklin Institute, from 1842 to 1845 he taught chemistry in the Philadelphia Central High School, and from 1851 to 1855 he was professor of chemistry applied to the arts in the University of Pennsylvania. While teaching in the Central High School he analyzed sugar and molasses with the polariscope—probably the first chemist in America to use the polariscope for this purpose. Owing to his knowledge of chemistry, mineralogy, and geology he was made a member of the first geological survey of Pennsylvania. Later he became state geologist of Delaware. Although he subsequently abandoned geology he retained his interest in mining and metals, especially iron. In 1849 he was appointed melter and refiner at the Philadelphia mint, and for thirty-nine years he devoted his skill and energy to the exacting duties of this position. Meanwhile he found time to prepare the reports of the Franklin Institute Committee on Science and Arts, a report on *Our Recent Improvements in the Chemical Arts* (1851), and numerous papers for scientific periodicals. In conjunction with Martin H. Boyé, Campbell Morfit, and R. S. McCulloh he wrote an *Encyclopædia of Chemistry, Practical and Theoretical* (1850). Two years later he edited T. R. Belton's translation of Regnault's *Elements of Chemistry*. In 1860 he tried to interest iron manufacturers in a system of control analysis of iron ores, and although unsuccessful he and his business associates (Garrett and Blair) continued to study iron ores and ultimately one of them (Blair) wrote the *Chemical Analysis of Iron,* which has gone through many editions and is authoritative to-day in its field. Booth was an active member of the following organizations: the American Philosophical Society, the Academy of Natural Sciences, the Maryland Institute for the Promotion of Mechanic Arts, the Philadelphia Society for the Promotion of Agriculture, the Historical Society of Pennsylvania, and the American Chemical Society (president in 1883

and 1884). He was married, on Nov. 17, 1853, to Margaret M. Cardoza. As an analyist he was skilful and accurate, and as a consulting chemist he was indefatigable and resourceful, especially in metallurgical processes. As a teacher of practical chemistry he was unsurpassed by his contemporaries; a course in his laboratory was considered indispensable to the chemists of his day.

[The chief source of information is a brochure, *Jas. Curtis Booth,* by Edgar F. Smith, presented at a meeting of the Am. Chem. Soc., Sept. 9, 1922: see also "Jas. Curtis Booth," by Paterson Du Bois, in *Proc. Am. Phil. Soc.,* XXV, 204, and obituary in the *Press* (Phila.), Mar. 22, 1888.]   L.C.N.

BOOTH, JOHN WILKES (1838–Apr. 26, 1865), actor, assassin of President Lincoln, was the brother of Edwin Booth [q.v.] and the son of Junius Brutus Booth [q.v.] and Mary Ann (Holmes) Booth. He was named after the celebrated English agitator, a distant relative of his grandfather. Born and brought up on his father's farm near Bel Air, Md., he received an irregular schooling in neighboring academies. The taint of his father's insanity perhaps appeared in his unbalanced disposition. As a boy he would charge through the woods on horseback, holding an old lance, and shouting battle-cries; more than once he ran away from home and school to mingle with the oyster fishermen on Chesapeake Bay; on one occasion in order to win a bet he drove a sleigh in July across the dirt roads to Bel Air and back. Aside from a detestation of cats which led him to violate his father's benevolent principles by exterminating all those on the farm, his character was marked by great kindliness. In a large family of brothers and sisters he was always his mother's favorite. His courtesy, gayety, care-free generosity, and extraordinary beauty—black eyes, black hair, and a face which resembled Poe's but was far handsomer—fascinated his acquaintances. It is said that he had the physical defect of markedly bowed legs but was accustomed to conceal it by wearing a long cloak. Although of less than medium height, he was athletic, a skilful horseman and fencer, and a crack pistol-shot. Early attracted to the stage, he made his début at the age of seventeen in the rôle of Richmond at the St. Charles Theatre, Baltimore. During the season of 1857–58 he played subordinate rôles at the Arch Street Theatre, Philadelphia, then under the management of his brother-in-law, John Sleeper Clarke [q.v.]. Here he was frequently hissed for his neglect to learn his parts adequately. He developed rapidly, however, into an actor of distinction; in the next year he played leading Shakespearian rôles in a stock company at Richmond, Va.; and in 1860 he began a meteoric career as star. After his opening appearance at Columbus, Ga., in September of that year, he toured the South and Southwest and then successfully invaded the North. Women proved particularly vulnerable to his charm, on and off the stage, and he was reputed to be the hero of numerous amours. In May 1861 at Madison, Ind., an actress, Henrietta Irving, attacked him with a dirk, and then stabbed herself almost fatally (*Courier*, Madison, May 10, 1861). In 1862 and 1863 he was enthusiastically welcomed at the Boston Museum (which then possessed the most critical audience in America); his performance of Romeo was declared by the *Chronicle* (Washington, D. C.) to have been the best ever rendered in that city; his contemporaries, Edwin Booth and Joe Jefferson, declare that he was one of the most promising actors of the day, and the veteran manager Ellsler even asserted that "John has more of the old man's power in one performance than Edwin can show in a year" (Clara Morris, *Life on the Stage*, 1901, p. 103). His acting was marked by inspiration rather than finish, and he was given to daring innovations, rendering the death of Richard III, for example, in a realistic manner that astounded his contemporaries. Although careless in his enunciation and prone to slur minor passages in his haste to reach the big scenes, his fire and passion more than atoned for these defects. His repertoire included *Richard III, Romeo and Juliet, Hamlet, Macbeth, Othello, The Merchant of Venice, Katharine and Petruchio, The Lady of Lyons, Money, The Robbers, The Marble Heart, The Apostate, The Stranger,* and *The Corsican Brothers.* Had his temperament permitted wholesouled attention to his art, he would probably have become one of the leading figures in American theatrical history. But in 1863 a slight bronchial trouble led to his temporary retirement from the stage, and the investment of a part of his theatrical earnings in oil speculations; and in 1864–65 his notable appearance at the Winter Garden, New York, on Nov. 25, in *Julius Cæsar* in which he played Antony to Edwin Booth's Brutus and J. B. Booth, Jr.'s Cassius, and his equally notable last performance, on Mar. 18, at Ford's Theatre, Washington, in the part of Pescara in *The Apostate* at John McCullough's benefit were, both of them, mere interludes in the great political conspiracy which the young actor now had in hand.

From even before the beginning of the Civil War Wilkes Booth's sympathies, unlike those of the rest of his family, had been with the South. Slavery he sincerely regarded as "one of the greatest blessings (both for themselves [the slaves] and us) that God ever bestowed upon a favoured nation. Witness heretofore our wealth and power, witness their elevation and enlightenment above their race elsewhere" (letter of Booth in Clara E. Laughlin, *The Death of Lincoln,* 1909, p. 21). In 1859 he had been a member of a Virginia militia company, which took part in the arrest and execution of John Brown. He had not enlisted in the Confederate army—ostensibly because of a promise to his mother, more probably because of an unwillingness to serve in a subordinate capacity—but as the war proceeded he came to see it more and more violently as a simple struggle between tyranny and freedom. "That he was insane on that one point, no one who knew him well can doubt" (Edwin Booth to Nahum Capen, in Ella V. Mahoney, *Sketches of Tudor Hall and the Booth Family,* 1925, p. 38). As early as the fall of 1864 he formed a daring project to abduct President Lincoln and carry him to Richmond, thereby, as he hoped, either to end the war or at least to secure an exchange of Southern prisoners. In September he enrolled his first recruits, two former schoolmates named Samuel Arnold and Michael O'Laughlin, both ex-Confederate soldiers, who after two years of service had returned to their native Maryland and were living in Baltimore. Booth shortly thereafter divested himself of his oil holdings and proceeded to Montreal in order to put his valuable theatrical wardrobe in safe custody and to place between seven and eight hundred dollars in a Canadian bank. The efforts made by the prosecution in the conspiracy trial to show that he was at this time in communication with the so-called "Canadian Cabinet" of the Confederacy rested entirely on the later discredited testimony of the spies, Sanford Conover and Richard Montgomery. In reality Booth was the last man to have sought orders from above, and throughout gloried in the fact that he was acting on his own responsibility. During November and December he was much in Washington, engaged in exploring the roads in lower Maryland. On Dec. 23 he made the important acquaintance of John H. Surratt, son of a widow, Mary E. Surratt, who had kept a tavern in Surrattsville, Md. John Surratt in 1862 had left St. Charles's College, where he was being educated for the Catholic priesthood, and had become a secret dispatch-rider for the Confederacy, carrying messages between Richmond and the North. His mother had meanwhile sold her tavern and moved into Washington where she kept a boarding-house. Surratt entered with eagerness into Booth's plot and soon gained two other adherents, David E. Herold, a feeble-minded youth of nineteen, and George A. Atzerodt, a middle-aged coach-maker at Port Tobacco on the Potomac, who was secretly engaged in ferrying Confederate sympathizers back and forth across the river. Arnold and O'Laughlin moved into Washington in February. On Mar. 1, Booth added the last and most noted conspirator to his band, Lewis Thornton Powell, calling himself Payne, son of a Baptist minister in Florida, Confederate soldier at the age of sixteen, wounded at Gettysburg, captured and escaped, now adrift in the North, penniless and half-mad. The band, thus constituted, lay in wait, on the afternoon of Mar. 20, to seize the President while driving near the Soldiers' Home in the outskirts of the city but their plans were frustrated by his not appearing. Learning that their plot was suspected, the conspirators separated, Arnold and O'Laughlin returning to Baltimore, and Surratt going first to Richmond and then to Canada. During the next few weeks the capture of Richmond and the surrender of Lee ended all possibility of Lincoln's abduction. Booth's six months of plotting had come to naught.

Just when he decided upon the assassination cannot be absolutely determined but it was probably after Lincoln's speech from the White House window on Apr. 11, in which the President advocated limited negro suffrage. Not until noon of Apr. 14, when Booth learned that Lincoln was to attend Laura Keene's performance of *Our American Cousin* at Ford's Theatre that night, were the details definitely arranged. Of his remaining accomplices, Atzerodt was deputed to murder Vice-President Johnson in his room at the Kirkwood Hotel; Payne, guided by Herold, to assassinate Secretary Seward in his home; while Booth reserved to himself the more difficult and spectacular task of killing the President. Atzerodt, however, lost his courage and did nothing. Payne, a young gladiator, fulfilled his part of the agreement to the extent of seriously wounding Seward and three others who sought to capture him, but being deserted by the frightened Herold, fled to the woods north-east of the city, whence he returned three nights later to be arrested at Mrs. Surratt's. Meanwhile Booth, having prepared the President's box in the afternoon so that its door could be barred to prevent pursuit, during the performance, at a little after ten o'clock entered the theatre, coolly surveyed the audience, and made his way to the box. Coming in noiselessly, he shot the President through the head, wounded with his dagger Major Henry R. Rathbone, who strove to seize him, and leaped to the stage, shouting *"Sic semper tyrannis! The South is avenged!"* But his spur, caught in the

folds of the flag that draped the box, caused him to fall, breaking his left leg. He managed, nevertheless, to limp swiftly across the stage and down the stairs to the rear of the theatre, where he mounted a horse kept in readiness and fled through the night. After crossing the Navy Yard Bridge he was joined by Herold; toward morning the pain from his leg became so intense, the splintered bone "tearing the flesh at every jump" (Booth's Diary), that the two turned eight miles out of the way to go to the house of Dr. Samuel A. Mudd, a Confederate sympathizer, who set Booth's leg and gave him rest and refreshment. Precious time, however, had been lost, and after leaving Mudd's the two wandered all night in the marshes, only reaching their goal, the Potomac, on the morning of Apr. 16, twelve hours behind schedule. Here they were secreted for six days and five nights in a pine thicket, virtually surrounded by pursuing Union troops, but secretly supplied with food and newspapers by Thomas A. Jones, a farmer and Confederate underground-mail carrier, who waited the chance to put them across the river. This man risked his life, when he might instead have obtained the $100,000 reward offered for the criminals, not so much, as he testifies, through loyalty to the Confederacy as through sympathy for Booth, who even in his agony and despair retained his old power of fascination (Thomas A. Jones, *J. Wilkes Booth*, 1893). Finally the two fugitives on Apr. 23 succeeded in crossing the Potomac, and the next day crossed the Rappahannock, proceeding three miles farther on to the residence of Richard H. Garrett, who took them in under the guise of Confederate soldiers. Here, in Garrett's barn, in the early morning hours of Apr. 26 they were surrounded by a band of soldiers and detectives from Washington who had traced them beyond the Rappahannock. Owing to the fact that the three officers in charge, Lieut. Edward P. Doherty (Regular Army), Lieut.-Col. Everton J. Conger (Secret Service), and Lieut. Luther B. Baker (Secret Service), gave conflicting testimony in a subsequent unsavory squabble over the rewards, it is difficult to make out in every detail just what happened, although the main outline is clear. Summoned to surrender, Herold soon came out and gave himself up, but Booth maintained an undaunted attitude. Theatrical to the end, he called out in the darkness, "Captain, give a lame man a chance. Draw up your men before the door and I'll come out and fight the whole command." This being refused, his voice was again heard, "Well, my brave boys, you can prepare a stretcher for me." The barn was set on fire, Booth was dimly seen for a moment in the blaze erect on his crutch, then fell just as a shot was heard. His captors were divided as to whether he shot himself or was struck by a bullet fired just at that moment by Sergeant Boston Corbett, a religious monomaniac who justified himself in disobeying the order not to fire by saying, "Providence directed me." As Corbett stood some thirty feet from the barn and fired through a mere crack, unless Providence also directed the bullet, the probability is that Booth shot himself. The dying man was pulled out from the barn and carried to the porch of the house where he lingered until about seven o'clock, having recovered consciousness sufficiently to murmur, "Tell Mother—tell Mother—I died for my country," words which she was destined first to receive through that day's newspaper.

That the man who was slain in this encounter was indeed Booth was rendered reasonably certain by his words and actions and by the diary and a Canadian bill of exchange found in his pocket. The body was taken on board the monitor *Montauk*, where it was identified by Dr. John F. May, who had operated for a tumor upon Booth's neck in the previous year (John F. May, "The Mark of the Scalpel," *Columbia Historical Society Records*, XIII, 51). It was then secretly buried under the floor of one of the warehouses in the Arsenal Grounds on Greenleaf's Point where at that time it was customary for felons to be buried.

The other victims of Booth's mad act, his various accomplices, met an even more hapless fate than his own. They were all soon captured and imprisoned, together with Mrs. Surratt, Dr. Mudd, and Edward Spangler, a scene-shifter at Ford's Theatre who was accused of preparing the President's box for the assassination and of assisting Booth to escape. With the possible exception of Mrs. Surratt, all were loaded with irons and their heads covered with flannel bags devised by the ingenuity of Secretary Stanton. The trial, which lasted from May 10 to June 29, was before a military commission headed by Major-General David Hunter. Joseph Holt [*q.v.*], the judge-advocate general of the army, led the prosecution, assisted by Hon. John A. Bingham [*q.v.*] and Col. Henry L. Burnett [*q.v.*]. All the prisoners were accused of conspiring with Jefferson Davis and Confederate officials in Canada to murder the President of the United States, and the death penalty was demanded for all. The determination to implicate the Confederacy in the assassination governed the proceedings of one of the most irregu-

lar trials known to history. All manner of irrelevant testimony was introduced; the counsel for the defense, Hon. Reverdy Johnson [*q.v.*] and Gen. Thomas Ewing [*q.v.*] were bully-ragged and insulted; witnesses were intimidated; and evidence in the possession of the Government was deliberately suppressed, notably Booth's diary, which would have overthrown the theory of a general plot to assassinate. (See *The Assassination of Abraham Lincoln*, 1909, by David Miller DeWitt, and *The Judicial Murder of Mary E. Surratt*, 1895, by the same author. The full account of the proceedings in *The Conspiracy Trial*, 3 vols., 1865–66, edited by Benjamin Perley Poore, should be compared with the officially expurgated *Assassination of Lincoln*, 1865, compiled by Benn Pitman. Cf. also the lame defense of the Military Commission in *The Assassination of Lincoln*, 1892, by Gen. T. M. Harris, a member of the Commission). The authority of the tribunal was unsuccessfully attacked by Reverdy Johnson on grounds identical with those later upheld by the Supreme Court in the Milligan case (Bernard C. Steiner, *The Life of Reverdy Johnson*, 1914, pp. 115–16). All of those accused, with the exception of Spangler, were adjudged guilty "of combining, confederating, and conspiring with . . . Jefferson Davis . . . to kill and murder . . . Abraham Lincoln," at the very time when the Government was preparing to abandon the case against Davis (Roy F. Nichols, "United States *vs.* Jefferson Davis," *American Historical Review*, January 1926). In the rendering of the sentences, however, a half-hearted and capricious effort was made to recognize varying degrees of guilt among the prisoners. Spangler, convicted only of abetting Booth's escape, was given six years' imprisonment, while Dr. Mudd, actually proven guilty only of the same crime, was condemned to life imprisonment, as were also Arnold and O'Laughlin, actually guilty of the attempt at abduction but innocent of any complicity in the murder. (All of these were pardoned by President Johnson by Mar. 4, 1869, with the exception of O'Laughlin who died of yellow fever, Sept. 23, 1867, at Fort Jefferson, Dry Tortugas Island, Fla.) Herold, Payne, and Atzerodt, who were clearly the most guilty, were condemned to be executed together with Mrs. Surratt, against whom the evidence was the weakest of all, it not even being absolutely proven that she knew of the abduction plot. To be sure the same tribunal that sentenced Mrs. Surratt signed a petition to President Johnson to commute the sentence to life imprisonment, but, according to the

President, Judge Advocate Holt never showed him this petition, and all mention of it was carefully excluded from the official Pitman report. Mrs. Surratt was hanged with the others on July 7, 1865. All this time her son, John H. Surratt, probably ignorant of the events of the trial, was kept in hiding by a Roman Catholic priest at St. Liboire, Canada. He later went to Europe, became a member of the Papal Zouaves in Rome, was apprehended, made a daring escape, was again apprehended, and was finally returned to America in December 1866. The Government, holding that he had been a ring-leader in the conspiracy to assassinate, made every effort to obtain his conviction, but at the end of his trial, before a civil court and lasting from June 10 to Aug. 10, 1867, the jury stood eight to four for acquittal. Surratt was kept in prison until June 22, 1868, when he was released on bail, and three months later the indictment against him was nolle-prossed. During the trial the Government promised to place in evidence Booth's manuscript diary but it again failed to do so. The existence of the diary had become known through an indiscreet remark in La Fayette C. Baker's *History of the United States Secret Service* (1867), and in May 1867, during the impeachment proceedings, Johnson ordered Stanton to produce it. Its publication (*Daily Morning Chronicle*, Washington, May 22, 1867) led Gen. Butler on the floor of the House to charge John A. Bingham with having deliberately perverted justice in the case of Mrs. Surratt, a charge to which Bingham made a very weak reply. The tragic diary, consisting of a few pages jotted down in physical and mental agony at hurried moments during Booth's flight, gives convincing evidence that his fevered mind, seeing the world through an emotional cloud, envisaged his act as that of a Brutus or William Tell; that he was amazed at the public reception of the crime; that his insane deed, productive of nothing but woe to himself, his friends, and the whole South, was initiated solely by his own gallant but disordered spirit.

In February 1869 the bodies of the conspirators, who had been buried beside Booth, were restored to their families; that of Booth himself was reinterred, on Feb. 20, in an unmarked grave in the Booth lot in Greenmount Cemetery, Baltimore, a number of his fellow-actors serving as pall-bearers (see "Lincoln Obsequies," a volume of newspaper clippings in the Library of Congress). While in the undertaker's shop in Baltimore the body had again been identified, in various ways, by Mrs. Rogers, an old Bel Air friend; by Col. William M. Pegram, Henry C.

Wagner, and other acquaintances; and by a dentist who recognized his filling in one of the teeth (Mahoney, p. 48). Despite all this positive identification, humanity was loth to part with so picturesque a character as Booth, and a widespread legend arose that he had escaped capture and was still alive. Report had it that he was seen in London, Paris, and India, and was even masquerading as a minister in Atlanta, Ga. Many believed that John St. Helen, an erratic personage moving about Mexico, Texas, and Oklahoma in the years after the war, finally committing suicide in 1903 at Enid, Oklahoma, under the name of David E. George, was in reality the escaped John Wilkes Booth. (For St. Helen's claims, see Finis L. Bates, *The Escape and Suicide of John Wilkes Booth,* 1908; W. P. Campbell, *The Escape and Wanderings of J. Wilkes Booth,* 1922, and documents in the possession of Mr. Clarence True Wilson, Washington, D. C.; for a refutation of these claims see William G. Shepherd, "Shattering the Myth of John Wilkes Booth," *Harper's Magazine,* November 1924.) St. Helen's mummified body was exhibited in Chicago, Memphis, and elsewhere, and those who so desire may still examine it at Venice, Cal.

[In addition to the references cited above, see, for Booth's acting, theatrical criticisms in the Boston newspapers, May 12–24, 1862, and Jan. 19–Feb. 14, 1863. Booth's diary, the boot taken from his broken leg by Dr. Mudd, and other personal articles are in the possession of the War Dept., Washington, D. C.]

E.S.B.

BOOTH, JUNIUS BRUTUS (May 1, 1796– Nov. 30, 1852), English actor, of Jewish descent (see below), was born in London, the son of Richard Booth, a lawyer, and the grandson of John Booth, a silversmith. His mother had been a Miss Game or Gam. The Booths were related to the Wilkes family and shared the radical views of John Wilkes. In his youth Richard Booth ran away from home to join the American Revolutionists although he only got as far as Paris; in his later years he is said to have kept in his drawing-room a picture of George Washington before which he insisted that all visitors should bow in reverence. Junius Brutus Booth early showed an embarrassing multiplicity of talents, especially for painting, poetry, sculpture, and female seduction. After learning the art of printing, studying a little law, and contemplating the career of a midshipman, he finally, when seventeen years old, and much against his father's will, went on the stage. His first appearance was with an amateur company in a temporary theatre in Tottenham Court Road in the part of Frank Rochdale in Colman's

John Bull, but he soon obtained regular employment with a company of comedians under Penley and Jonas at Peckham and later at Deptford. His début with them was in the rôle of Campillo, a minor character in *The Honeymoon,* on Dec. 13, 1813. During the next year, after a severe illness, he accompanied the same company on a tour of some months in Holland and Belgium. On May 8, 1815 he was married, in London, to Marie Christine Adelaide Delancy, with whom he had eloped from Brussels; later, he deserted her after she had borne him a son, Richard Junius, who served in the Confederate army, and a daughter, who died in infancy. In the summer of 1815 he filled an engagement with the Worthing and Brighton Theatres, in the ensuing season played unimportant parts at Covent Garden, and then filled another engagement at Worthing and Brighton. His appearances as Fitzharding in the comedy of *Smiles and Tears,* as Bertram in *Bertram,* and as Sir Giles Overreach, all aroused favorable comment so that he was engaged to appear at Covent Garden in the rôle of Richard III on Feb. 12, 1817. His striking similarity in appearance and manner to Edmund Kean challenged comparison with the most famous actor of the day, and a furious discussion arose in the public press between the "Boothites" and the "Keanites." There seems to have been no just ground for the charge of imitation which was brought against Booth: both actors belonged to the realistic school of Cooke, but Booth gave his lines differently from Kean and his emphasis was more intelligent (for examples see *The Actor,* 1846, pp. 36–37). After a successful repetition of the performance of Richard III, Booth not unnaturally asked for an increase of salary at Covent Garden; this being refused, he was persuaded by Kean to join the latter at Drury Lane on a three years' contract, but after a single notable performance of Iago to Kean's Othello, he became convinced on good grounds that he was going to be kept subordinate to Kean; forthwith he promptly returned to Covent Garden and signed a three years' contract with that house. This unprecedented struggle between the two leading theatres of England for the services of an actor of twenty-one, together with Booth's carelessness in regard to legal ties, made him the temporary center of English theatrical history. His reappearance at Covent Garden was the signal for a riot in the theatre, and the play was given entirely in pantomime, as no words could be heard above the storm of cat-calls, hissings, and applause. His subsequent appearances were marked by similar scenes but with decreas-

ing vehemence; gradually the excitement subsided, and Booth now paid the penalty for his previous notoriety by having to play to smaller houses; nevertheless he ended the season with an established reputation as one of the leading actors on the English stage.

In the following year he toured the provinces and in the autumn returned to Covent Garden where he repeatedly appeared as Richard III and as Iago and also added the innovation of playing Shylock in Jewish dialect. In 1820 his most important activities were an engagement as King Lear (Nahum Tate's version) at Covent Garden, a long run at the Cobourg Theatre in *The Lear of Private Life* and another in *Horatii and Curiatii,* an engagement at Drury Lane where he played Iago to Kean's Othello, Edgar to his Lear, and Pierre to his Jaffier and a particularly noteworthy performance of *Julius Cæsar* at Drury Lane in which Booth played Cassius to the Brutus of James W. Wallack and the Antony of John Cooper.

On Jan. 13, 1821, Booth was married to Mary Anne Holmes, and shortly afterward the couple visited France and Madeira and then in April sailed on the ship *Two Brothers* for America. Landing at Norfolk, Va., Booth immediately obtained an engagement at Richmond, followed by one in the Park Theatre, New York, and others in Boston, Philadelphia, and the leading Southern cities. In the following summer he purchased a large farm in a beautiful secluded tract of woodland near Bel Air, Harford County, Md., twenty-three miles from Baltimore. Here in a comfortable log cabin, with his vegetable garden, orchard, and vineyard, his fish-pond and herd of sheep, the actor spent as much time each year as he could steal from his profession. Here his father soon joined him and here were born his children, Junius Brutus, Edwin [*q.v.*], Asia Frigga, and John Wilkes [*q.v.*], besides several others who died in childhood. The most important events in Booth's long stage career in America were his performance of Pescara, a part expressly written for him, in Sheil's *Apostate* at the Park Theatre in June 1827; his stage management of the Camp Street Theatre, New Orleans, in 1828, when he also appeared at the Théâtre d'Orléans as Oreste in Racine's *Andromaque* in French (Booth being a remarkable linguist familiar also with German, Dutch, and Hebrew); his management in 1831 of the Adelphi Theatre in Baltimore when he first introduced Charles Kean to an American audience, in *Hamlet,* he himself gracefully taking the minor part of the Second Grave Digger; and his playing of Pierre to Edwin Forrest's

Jaffier and of Othello to Forrest's Iago in September 1831 at the Park Theatre. He made tours of England in 1825–26 and in 1836–37, the first unsuccessful because of the hard times, and the second saddened by the death of a favorite son. Booth now became increasingly subject to temporary fits of insanity; in one of these during a trip to the South in 1838 he attempted to drown himself and also one night attacked his manager, Thomas Flynn, with an andiron, receiving in the encounter a broken nose which permanently marred his handsome countenance and somewhat nasalized his melodious voice. From this time he appeared in the theatre less frequently, although he played every year in Boston and New Orleans where he was an especial favorite. In the spring of 1852 he and Edwin Booth, who had now been on the stage for several years, joined the younger Junius Brutus Booth, also an actor, in California; after some weeks of fairly successful performances in San Francisco and Sacramento, the elder Booth decided to return home. He stopped on the way at New Orleans, where he played for the last time, in a series of six performances at the St. Charles Theatre. Having overtaxed his strength, he caught a severe cold and died alone in his cabin on the steamboat *J. S. Chenoweth* on the way to Cincinnati. His funeral in Cincinnati was attended by great crowds of people, including throngs of negroes. The body was later removed to Greenmount Cemetery, Baltimore.

Owing to his attacks of madness, his intemperance, and his general irresponsibility, Booth broke his theatrical engagements with reckless frequency, and on more than one occasion, when irritated, came forward to the footlights and expressed his contempt of the audience. But the public always forgave him because of his unquestioned ability. He was easily the foremost tragedian of his day in America. Although short in stature, he dominated the stage by the passion and fire of his performance. His best rôles were those of villains and semi-villains; Richard III, Iago, Shylock, Sir Giles Overreach, Pescara, Luke in *Riches* (an adaptation of Massinger's *City Madam*) and Sir Edward Mortimer in Colman's *The Iron Chest,*—to which somber list should be added, curiously enough, the comic rôle of Jerry Sneak in Foote's farce, *The Mayor of Garratt.* He was essentially an emotional rather than intellectual actor, depicting best of all the passions of ambition, jealousy, hatred, fear, and revenge. His own blank verse tragedy of *Ugolino,* piously produced by John Wilkes Booth at the Boston Museum in 1863 (published in French's *American Drama,* No.

CXX), is a mediocre work. An amateur student of the Koran, Catholic theology, and occultism, he believed in the transmigration of souls and the equality of man. He was a vegetarian both in theory and practise, on his farm he refused to permit even the most noxious animals to be killed, and at least on one occasion he went to the length of arranging an elaborate funeral for some of his dumb friends (James Freeman Clarke, "My Odd Adventure with Junius Brutus Booth," *Atlantic Monthly,* VIII, 296–301, who also states that Booth told him he was of Jewish ancestry). Equally noteworthy, despite Booth's irascibility and moodiness, was his erratic kindness toward every type of human being.

[The standard biography, *The Elder and the Younger Booth* (1882), by Asia Booth Clarke, is largely based upon an anonymous but generally accurate work, *The Actor: Passages in the Lives of Booth and Some of His Contemporaries* (1846). See also Oxberry's *Dramatic Biog.,* IV (1826). For an elaborate but somewhat amateurish study of Booth's acting see *The Tragedian* (1868), by Thos. R. Gould. The sketch by Jos. Knight in the *Dict. of Nat. Biog.* (1921–22), based mainly on Oxberry, is unfair to Booth in several particulars.]　　　　　　　　　　　E.S.B.

BOOTH, MARY LOUISE (Apr. 19, 1831–Mar. 5, 1889), author, translator, editor, was the daughter of William Chatfield Booth, descendant of Ensign John Booth, who came to this country from England in 1649. Her mother was a grand-daughter of one of the exiles driven from home by the French Revolution. From her father she inherited a high measure of single-mindedness and integrity, and an enthusiasm for books; while her mother endowed her with the brilliancy and vivacity of the old French émigrés. She was born at Yaphank, on Long Island, N. Y. Mentally precocious, she learned English and French simultaneously, reading the Bible and Plutarch at the age of five, Racine at seven, Hume and Gibbon before she was ten. At fourteen she became a teacher in a school established by her father in Brooklyn, but she did not pursue the vocation. She devoted herself instead to study, acquiring a thorough knowledge and fluent use of German, Italian, and Spanish, in addition to French which had been one of her two mother tongues. Her translations from the French of *The Marble-Workers' Manual* (1856) and the *New and Complete Clock and Watch-Makers' Manual* (1860) were long recognized as valuable works of reference in their respective fields. In 1859 she published a *History of the City of New York,* which was the first complete work upon the subject. It sold for many years and was revised and enlarged by her in 1880. The outbreak of the Civil War gave her an opportunity for the use of her talents which she eagerly seized. In a single week she translated Count Agénor de Gasparin's *The Uprising of a Great People* (1861), working almost twenty-four hours a day. The appearance of the book met with a remarkable outburst of enthusiasm. Charles Sumner wrote to her: "It is worth a whole phalanx in the cause of human freedom," and he said of her translations of Augustin Cochin's *Results of Slavery* (1863) and *Results of Emancipation* (1863) that they were "of more value to the North than the Numidian cavalry to Hannibal." President Lincoln sent her a letter of thanks for her achievement in stimulating and encouraging the people of the Union. She gave herself to this work with ardor and energy, producing other translations, corresponding with friends of the Union cause in France, and publishing their replies in the press and in pamphlets. In later years she said that "all hours have since seemed thin and poor beside those of that glowing and stormy epoch." During this period of her life she produced about twenty volumes of translations. In 1867 Harper & Brothers invited her to become the editor of *Harper's Bazar,* which they were just establishing. She edited it with conspicuous success for twenty-one years, attracting to its pages many of the most prominent novelists, story writers, and essayists of England and America. She prized lofty standards of womanhood and lent her influence to the cause of higher education for women, but the activities of the so-called woman's movement were distasteful to her and in spite of the urging of many of her friends, she remained unconvinced of the desirability of woman suffrage. Though not conventionally beautiful, she was possessed of a majestic bearing, large and soft dark brown eyes, a luminous smile and "hands as exquisite as if carved in ivory." She was described by an intimate associate as "a sagacious and energetic woman, with as cool judgment as brilliant foresight . . . full of both critical power and of imagination, of the love of nature and of beauty in every form."

[Obituary by Harriet Prescott Spofford in *Harper's Bazar,* Mar. 30, 1889; other obituaries in *N. Y. Times* and *N. Y. Tribune,* Mar. 6, 1889.]   H.H.

BOOTH, NEWTON (Dec. 30, 1825–July 14, 1892), governor of California, senator, the son of Beebe and Hannah (Pitts) Booth, was born in Salem, Washington County, Ind. Little is known of his life up to the time of his graduation from Asbury (now DePauw) University in 1846. He entered upon the study of law and was admitted to the Indiana bar three years later. The lure of the West, however, was strong and 1850 found

Booth answering its call and moving westward with the pioneers who sought gold and opportunity on new horizons. He settled in Sacramento where he engaged in a mercantile and grocery business. In 1856 he returned to Indiana, but 1860 saw him again in Sacramento. His interest in literature and history, and his extensive reading on those subjects, now brought him increasingly into demand as a lecturer and writer. As early as 1862 he began to contribute to the *Sacramento Union,* a paper wielding a remarkable influence in California during the years 1850–75. His strong support of the Union cause at the time of the Civil War, together with his ardent devotion to the Republican party, led him into political life, and resulted in his election in 1863 as state senator from Sacramento, an office which he held for one term. In the years immediately succeeding, he threw himself whole-heartedly into the cause of his party, and helped to carry the state for Grant in the presidential election of 1868. In 1871 he became the eleventh governor of California. He went into office on a platform whose chief feature was opposition to the granting of subsidies to the railroad. This issue was then the source of bitter controversy, but it died down to some extent following the election. Booth's administration was notable for a genuine attempt at economy in public affairs and also by a successful revision of the statute law. The resignation of Eugene Casserly as senator from California in 1873 led Booth, while still governor, to seek appointment at the hands of the legislature for the unexpired term. In this move he was unsuccessful. His defeat, however, was only temporary; for at the next election the legislature returned him to the United States Senate for the full term of six years. In March 1875 he accordingly resigned the governorship, a position which he had retained even in the face of criticism while he was seeking election, and took up his duties in the national capital. There, during his single term, he was active in accomplishing the adoption of the silver certificate and the redemption of the subsidiary coins, secured the passage of a bill for the settlement of land titles in California, and was a member of the committees on Public Lands, Patents, Manufactures, and Appropriations. It is generally agreed that he was a man of exceptional ability and unquestioned integrity. His strong partisanship, together with his eloquence and literary talent, made him a leader in the political life of California from the days of early statehood almost up to the time of his death. This occurred at Sacramento on July 14, 1892, when he was sixty-seven years of age. He was married on Feb. 29, 1892, to Mrs. J. T. Glover.

[The most complete record of the life of Newton Booth is to be found in the *Hist. of Cal.* (1898), by Theodore H. Hittell. Additional material appears in *Cal. and Californians* (1926), ed. by Rockwell D. Hunt, and in an excellent obituary in the *Sacramento Record-Union*, July 15, 1892.]   R.G.C—d.

BOOTH-TUCKER, EMMA MOSS (Jan. 8, 1860–Oct. 28, 1903), Consul of the Salvation Army, at the age of ten converted a little Jewish playmate to Christianity and thus inaugurated an extensive career of salvation. She was born in Gateshead, England, a daughter of William and Catherine (Mumford) Booth. There were six children in the family, of which Harold Begbie says in his *Life of General William Booth* (1920) that outside the pages of Dickens it was probable that no other such household ever existed. William Booth had begun night street-preaching at seventeen, and a year after Emma's birth resigned from the New Connection Methodist Church in order to devote himself entirely to evangelical preaching. Unlike her brothers and sisters, Emma, who was a nervous, delicate child, made no attempt at public speaking for some time, contenting herself with conducting a children's Bible class where she had "frequently a row of weeping penitents" to her credit (F. St. G. de L. Booth-Tucker, *The Consul*, 1903). But at sixteen she spoke before a meeting at St. Leonard's and five souls sought salvation; after this experience she became a frequent speaker. Booth founded the Salvation Army two years later, as a means to his complete independence, and in 1880 Emma was made Mother of a training home to prepare women cadets for officership. The organization flourished under her administration, for she had a winning personality and a capacity for hard work. She spent much time with individual cadets, praying with them and advising them, and when they left each carried an inscribed photograph of her. When the campaign of the Army in India expanded under the impetus of a $25,000 donation she met Frederick St. George de Lautour Tucker, who was summoned from India to head the fifty officers to be sent there. Emma selected the group and helped him organize them. They became engaged, but Tucker departed without her, to return a year later for their wedding, which was celebrated before five thousand spectators in Clapton Congress Hall in London. A second collection of $25,000 was raised on this occasion and fifty more officers ("The Wedding Fifty") set out for Bombay, this time under the joint command of Tucker and his bride, who was given the title of Consul. The Consul assumed native costume and manners, and was soon embarked on a career of lectures which took her to inland villages in Southern In-

dia, and to Ceylon. The illness of her mother recalled her to England after a few years, but on Mrs. Booth's death in 1890 she returned to India only to find her own health failing. With her husband she went to England once more and in 1896 Tucker was made Commander in charge of the work in America. An assembly of four thousand received them at Carnegie Hall in New York. They settled in Mt. Vernon, a suburb of New York, with their children, of whom there were seven at the time of Mrs. Booth-Tucker's death. The work in America took a more practical turn, perhaps because of the criticism with which Gen. Booth's book *In Darkest England* (1890) had been met. Much of the Consul's time was spent in organizing industrial homes providing temporary employment, rescue homes for women, workingmen's hotels, orphanages, and country homes for city poor; much of it also was spent in the care of the Salvation Army's three farm colonies. But she continued her speaking: her most famous lecture, "Love and Sorrow," describing the activities of the Army, was delivered for two years in fifty cities. She liked to lead marches through the slums at midnight to "stir things up" and gather the "roughs" about her for prayer. In the midst of her duties she visited the sick, wrote innumerable letters of exhortation and encouragement, and articles for the official publication, the *War Cry*. She was on a speaking tour when her train was wrecked near Dean Lake, Mo., and she and Col. Thos. C. Holland, in charge of the Colorado farm colony, were fatally injured. Thousands crowded Carnegie Hall for her funeral services. Her published work is *The League of Love, Being the Assistant Rescue Branch of the Salvation Army* (1896).

[In addition to references given above, see Commander F. St. G. de L. Booth-Tucker, "Farm Colonies of the Salvation Army," *Bull. U. S. Bureau of Labor*, No. 48; Albert Shaw, "A Successful Farm Colony in the Irrigation Country," *Rev. of Revs.*, Nov. 1902; "Commander Booth-Tucker and His Work in America" (editorial), *Rev. of Revs.*, Nov. 1904; *St. Louis Globe-Democrat*, Oct. 30, 1903.]   M.A.K.

BOOTT, KIRK (Oct. 20, 1790–Apr. 11, 1837), manufacturer, was a son of Kirk Boott, an English merchant, originally of Derbyshire, who settled at Boston after the American Revolution, and of Mary (Love) Boott. He studied at Rugby Academy, England, whence he entered Harvard College in the class of 1809. There he "sowed an abundance of wild oats but never graduated" (Charles Cowley, *A Handbook of Business in Lowell, with a History of the City*, 1856, p. 72). Being militarily inclined he was sent to England where a commission had been procured for him. He served in the Peninsular War under Wellington, commanding a detachment at the siege of San Sebastian. His regiment was ordered in 1813 to New Orleans, but Boott, unwilling to join an expedition against his native land, secured a detail to a military academy for more instruction (*History of Middlesex County, Mass.*, edited by S. A. Drake, 1880, II, 74). He married, at about this time, Ann Haden of Derby. In 1817 Boott's father died, and soon after this the son, who had been dependent on a subaltern's meager salary (*Reply to a Pamphlet recently Circulated by Mr. Edward Brooks*, p. 49), entered his father's firm in Boston expecting a good living from it. In this he was disappointed. The business was in such shape that he found himself practically without employment. In 1821, while passing a day at Nahant with Patrick Tracy Jackson [*q.v.*], he applied for a position as manager of an enterprise then projected by several Boston capitalists at East Chelmsford, afterward Lowell. When, later, negotiations for control of the holdings of the Proprietors of Locks and Canals on Merrimack River were completed, young Boott was engaged as agent of the newly incorporated Merrimack Manufacturing Company. Boott did not originate the cotton manufacture (as is explained in a letter written by his associate Nathan Appleton to John A. Lowell and quoted in Drake's *History*, II, 58–62), but after the enterprise was under way he became its dictator. He enlarged the Pawtucket Canal, which had been opened Oct. 18, 1796, for conveying logs around Pawtucket Falls, and he dug a lateral canal to bring power to the Merrimack Company's first unit. Other canals followed, and on them other cotton factories. Boott inaugurated a machine-shop which, with Maj. George Washington Whistler as superintendent, began the making of locomotives in America. He brought to his mill village much of the best mechanical talent of his time. Brick boarding-houses were built for the operatives, most of them young women from the nearby farms, and elaborate rules and regulations for their conduct were adopted. St. Anne's Church, Episcopal, was erected after the design of an English parish church, and all operatives were at first taxed for its support. Boott built for himself a mansion,—still standing in upper Merrimack St., and used as a corporation hospital. In these and many other undertakings he proved himself an indefatigable worker. "He gave his whole zeal and strength to promote the prosperity of the new village. He watched its growth with a personal interest, resolving here to live and die" (Henry A. Miles, *Lowell as it Was and as it Is*, 1845, p. 87). To the new place,

when in 1826 it was about to be set off from Chelmsford as a separate township, Boott wished to give the name of Derby, after his English ancestral home, but he was overruled by his directors, who chose the name of Lowell in honor of Francis Cabot Lowell [*q.v.*]. Boott's surname is still perpetuated in one of its chief manufacturing corporations; his Christian name in a down-town street (Frederick W. Coburn, *History of Lowell and its People*, 1920, I, 149).

Boott carried more burdens than one man should. To his friend, Edward Brooks, he wrote, Sept. 29, 1830 (*Correspondence between Edward Brooks and John A. Lowell, with Remarks by Edward Brooks*, p. 15): "I am almost worried out. Committee after committee keep coming up in relation to the increase of the Appleton works, or a new concern, for all of which many calculations are required, taking all my time and, since this unhappy disclosure [of his brother's mismanagement of the family property] I get neither rest nor sleep." His nerves tense, Boott quarreled with his chosen director, Rev. Theodore Edson, D.D., over a difference of opinion regarding the public school system (Charles C. Chase, "Lowell," in D. H. Hurd's *History of Middlesex County, Mass.*, 1890, II, 116). When the town meeting voted to sustain Dr. Edson and built two modern school-houses, Kirk Boott withdrew from St. Anne's and for a time attended the Unitarian Church. Before his death, however, he returned to his pew in the Episcopal Church whose forms he loved. He died while driving his chaise in Merrimack St., on Apr. 11, 1837.

Boott's personality, projected upon the town and city of Lowell, considerably determined the character of many American industrial communities. He was a pioneer of industrial feudalism, a benevolent despot, a driver of men and women, an emotional, opinionated, and well-meaning man who was endowed with constructive imagination and ability to organize.

[In addition to the references given above, see *Proc. in the City of Lowell at the Semi Centennial Celebration* (1876); Frank P. Hill, *Lowell Illustrated, a Chronological Record of Events* (1884); Wilson Waters and Henry Spaulding Perham, *Hist. of Chelmsford, Mass.* (1917); the various and numerous publications of the Old Residents' Hist. Ass. and its successor, the Lowell Hist. Soc.]

F. W. C.

BORDEN, GAIL (Nov. 9, 1801–Jan. 11, 1874), surveyor, inventor, the eldest son of Gail and Philadelphia (Wheeler) Borden, was born on his father's farm at Norwich, N. Y. He was of the seventh generation descended from Richard Borden who settled at Pocasset (now Portsmouth), R. I., in 1638. His mother was the great-great-grand-daughter of Roger Williams.

His youth was that of a farmer's son of the times, with the additional interest of surveying taught him by his father. When he was fourteen his parents moved to what is now Covington, Ky., and within a year, they moved again, into the Territory of Indiana. Here Borden obtained his only schooling, totaling one and one-half years. During this time he farmed, practised surveying, became an expert rifleman, and captained a company of militiamen. Almost as soon as he stopped being a pupil he began teaching school and from nineteen to twenty-one taught in the backwoods schools of the territory. Because of poor health he left home in 1822 and proceeded further south, settling shortly thereafter in Amite County, Miss. Here he taught school and was county and United States deputy surveyor for six or seven years, after which he went with his bride of less than a year to join his parents in Stephen A. Austin's colony in Texas. Borden's first employment here was farming and stock raising. He was subsequently appointed by Gen. Austin to superintend the official surveys of the colonies. He represented his district at the convention held in 1833 at San Felipe to seek separation from Mexico and during the war he and his brother published the only newspaper issued in the territory. When the republic was founded Borden compiled the first topographical map and made the surveys for and laid out the city of Galveston, and was made collector of customs there. From 1839 to 1851 he was agent for the Galveston City Company, a corporation owning large areas of land on which the city was built. At an age when many men are desirous of reducing the number of their activities, Borden, who for fifty years had led the varied and rugged life of a pioneer, began the most important work of his life. His greatest pleasure lay in doing something for his fellow-man and it was this characteristic that led to his new and wholly different work. One of the greatest hardships of the pioneer was that of securing and carrying sufficient food on his migrations, and Borden set to work with the fixed idea of preparing food in concentrated form. He first developed a meat biscuit. Its value was quickly recognized, and Borden invested all that he had in a plant for its manufacture. A strong and influential competition of Army food contractors, however, resulted in the failure of the undertaking and Borden lost everything. He had an exhibit of his meat biscuit at the London Fair in 1851 and received "the great council medal" and was elected an honorary member of the London Society of Arts. It is said that on his way back from Europe he was impressed by the plight of the immigrant children on board

ship because of the impossibility of giving them wholesome milk. So, when his meat biscuits failed he thought of concentrating milk. He left Texas and went north to New Lebanon, N. Y., where he had friends in the Shaker Colony. He began at once experimenting in their laboratory and condensing milk, using, particularly, a vacuum pan of the type used in making sugar. He applied for a patent in May 1853 "on a process of evaporating milk in vacuum." For three years the process was questioned by the Patent Office until Borden's contention that the important function of the vacuum was to protect the milk from air and to keep it clean while it was being condensed was scientifically proven. On Aug. 19, 1856, Borden received Patent No. 15,553 for "the concentration of milk." He endeavored to go into production immediately after the issuance of his patent but until he met Jeremiah Milbank, he failed to secure enough money to build a plant. Manufacture was started in 1858 and the first big condensary was opened in 1861 at Wassaic, N. Y. But for the Civil War it might have taken years to introduce this new product. It was found, however, to be a very valuable food for soldiers, nourishing and easily carried, and the public learned from the soldiers. After the business was established on a firm basis Borden returned to Texas and in the town of Borden he turned his attention to the concentration of other foods, including fruit juices, tea, coffee, and cocoa. On July 22, 1862, the Patent Office granted him Patent No. 35,919, "for concentrating cider and other juices and fruits." He continued his experimental work thereafter until the end of his life. Borden's first wife was Penelope Mercer of Amite County, Miss., whom he married in 1828. She was the mother of all his children and died in 1844. He later married Mrs. A. F. Stearns, and some time after her death he married in 1860 Mrs. Emeline Eunice (Eno) Church. He died at his home in Texas at the age of seventy-three.

[*Hist. and Geneal. Record of the Descendants . . . of Richard and Joan Borden* (1899), compiled by Hattie Borden Weld; Records of the Borden Co., N. Y.; U. S. Pat. Office Records; obituary in *N. Y. Tribune*, Jan. 14, 1874.]

C. W. M.

BORDEN, RICHARD (Apr. 12, 1795–Feb. 25, 1874), manufacturer and executive, was descended from the Quaker, Richard Borden, who settled at Pocasset (now Portsmouth), R. I., in 1638. He was born in Freetown, Mass., the ninth child of Thomas and Mary (Hathaway) Borden. His scholastic training was obtained during the winter terms of the district school, while strenuous work on his father's farm and in his father's grist and saw-mills contributed to the sturdy physique with which he was endowed. As manager, between the ages of eighteen and twenty-five, of his father's grist-mill, he was accustomed to sail down the river in the sloop *Irene and Betsey* and collect the grain to be milled. These voyages suggested to Richard Borden and a shipbuilder, Maj. Bradford Durfee, the possibility of enlarging the operations, and under their supervision several vessels were constructed for the river trade. The making of nails and other metal accessories for sloops resulted in the formation in 1821 of the Fall River Iron Works, destined to a leading place among Fall River industries. Its original capital was $18,000; without a single outside dollar added to the original investment it had attained in 1845 a capitalization of $960,000 with a plant valued at half a million. Richard Borden took an active part in the formation of this company, "was appointed treasurer and agent, a position which he filled ably and satisfactorily up to the day of his final withdrawal from business, a period of over fifty years" (F. M. Peck and H. H. Earl, *Fall River and Its Industries*, 1877, p. 48).

Borden's connection with cotton milling originated from his position in the Fall River Iron Works. The immense success of the enterprise led the company into schemes for the development of water power and cotton milling. In this way the iron works company became an owner in the Watuppe Reservoir Company, in the Troy Cotton and Woolen Manufactory, in the Fall River Manufactory, in the Annawan Mill built by it in 1825, in the American Print Works built by it in 1834, in the Metacomet Mill built in 1846, and in various transportation enterprises. In most of these concerns, which were pioneers in the cotton industry, Borden took a prominent part, as well as in others. He was president and director of the American Print Works, the American Linen Company, the Troy Cotton and Woolen Manufactory, the Richard Borden Mill Company, and the Mount Hope Mill Company, and was a director of the Annawan and Metacomet Mill Companies. He was also president of the Fall River National Bank and of the Watuppe Reservoir Company. Not only was Borden a leading entrepreneur and magnate in the development of Fall River cotton, but to him must be given credit for breaking the geographical isolation of that city and achieving direct connections with Boston and New York. Borden's interest in transportation never died after his early experience, and we find the Fall River Iron Works under his inspiration inaugurating a regular line of steamers in 1827 between

Fall River and Providence. In 1846 mainly through his personal efforts a railroad line from Fall River to Myricks was constructed to connect with the New Bedford & Taunton Railroad and thence by the Providence Railroad to Boston. Subsequently he built to South Braintree, striking the Old Colony Railroad at that point. He also projected the Cape Cod Railway Company, of which he was president, and which built from Middleborough down the Cape. Simultaneously with the railroad enterprises Richard and his brother Jefferson organized (1847) a steamship line between Fall River and New York which was enormously successful from the start. In 1864 Borden planned a better rail connection with Boston and secured a charter for a railroad. The opposition, however, of the Old Colony Railroad, and Borden's advanced age led him to sell both his charter and the steamship company to that railroad. He was a man of strong physique, of handsome and commanding presence, and of generous disposition. In private life he is described as a "sincere outspoken Christian," as "one of the leaders in the Central Congregational Church," and as an active worker in Sabbath School Missions (*Ibid.*, p. 52). He was married, on Feb. 22, 1828, to Abbey Walker Durfee by whom he had seven children.

[The best sketch of Borden's life is in the *Biog. Encyc. of Mass.* (1883), II, 89–96. See also Hattie Borden Weld, *Hist. and Geneal. Record of the Descendants . . . of Richard and Joan Borden* (1899), pp. 166–69, and the obituary in the *Boston Morning Jour.*, Feb. 26, 1874.]   H. U. F.

BORDEN, SIMEON (Jan. 29, 1798–Oct. 28, 1856), skilled mechanic and civil engineer, was the oldest son of Simeon and Amy (Briggs) Borden and was of the fourth generation born on the Borden estate established by his great-grandfather, Joseph, at Fall River, Mass. When Simeon was eight his family moved to Tiverton, R. I., to take over the farm left to his mother, and it was here that the boy acquired a rudimentary education in the country schools. When he was thirteen his father died, whereupon he stopped school to assist his mother in the management of her farm. Within six years his mother also died, and Borden at nineteen had thrust upon him the full responsibility of the estates of both parents. He was successful in this, settling and dividing the estates after some years. From the time he stopped school he studied applied mathematics at home as best he could, and also mastered the metal and wood-working crafts. His interests lay in the latter direction, so when freed of the farm responsibilities he entered a machine shop, becoming superintendent in two years when he was thirty years old.

When the legislature of Massachusetts in 1830 passed a law requiring Boston and the several towns of the state to make accurate maps by trigonometrical survey Borden was engaged to construct the base bar for the measurement of the base line. This he completed in the winter of 1830. It was fifty feet in length, was inclosed in a metal tube, and was so compensated as to remain constant in length at all temperatures. Four compound microscopes were employed with it for taking constant readings. This instrument was, at the time it was constructed, the most accurate of its kind in the United States and brought Borden much recognition. He had nothing to guide him in its construction and it was entirely through his own resources and by repeated experiments that he succeeded so admirably. Borden assisted in the survey for the season of 1831, particularly in the measurement of the base line, and again in 1832, after which he continued with it until its completion in 1841, having full responsibility following the resignation of the chief surveyor in 1834. He prepared and read an account of the survey at a meeting of the American Philosophical Society in 1841 which was subsequently published (*Transactions of the American Philosophical Society*, n. s., IX). During the succeeding ten years Borden served as engineer and surveyor for several railroads in New Hampshire, Maine, Massachusetts, and Connecticut. He also made the survey of the line between Rhode Island and Massachusetts which was used in the United States Supreme Court case of Rhode Island *vs.* Massachusetts in 1844. In 1851 he published his computations and methods for running curves for railroads under the title, *A System of Useful Formulæ*. This was based upon a paper read before the Boston Society of Civil Engineers in December 1849. His natural ability and acquired knowledge of the principles of mechanics brought him into prominence in the closing years of his life when he was often called upon to testify as an expert in the courts. Besides his other duties he represented Fall River in the state legislature in 1832–33, 1844–45, and 1849. He never married, and died at the age of fifty-eight at the home of his brother, Congressman Nathaniel B. Borden.

[Hattie B. Weld, *Hist. and Geneal. Record of the Descendants . . . of Richard and Joan Borden* (1899); *Proc. Am. Phil. Soc.*, vol. II (1841–43).] C. W. M.

BORDLEY, JOHN BEALE (Feb. 11, 1727–Jan. 26, 1804), lawyer, agriculturist, was the posthumous son of Thomas Bordley, by his second wife, Mrs. Ariana Vanderheyden Frisby. His father came from Yorkshire, England, in 1694, settled in Maryland, and was attorney-general there in 1712. John Bordley was born at Annapolis, and after his mother's death was brought up by Col. Hynson at Chestertown, Md. He studied law under his eldest brother, Stephen, and also did much general reading of history, philosophy, science, and arts. In 1750 he married Margaret Chew, who died Nov. 11, 1773. Their joint property included several farms, on one of which, near Joppa, Md., they resided twelve years. In 1753 Bordley was appointed prothonotary of Baltimore County, and after resigning this office and moving to Baltimore, he was appointed a judge of the Maryland Provincial Court in 1766, and the following year also judge of the Admiralty. In 1768 he was one of the commissioners to determine the boundary between Maryland and Delaware, and was also member of the Governor's Council during the administrations of Governors Sharpe and Eden. In 1770 he came into possession of 1,600 acres on an island at the mouth of Wye River, and resided there. He also purchased Pool's Island, near Joppa. From this time he farmed on a large scale and endeavored to improve practises with the aid of imported machinery, seeds, and treatises on husbandry. He rotated crops and grew wheat, as a substitute for tobacco, together with hemp, flax, cotton, and many kinds of vegetables and fruits. He made bricks, salt, and beer, the last, as better than whiskey, for his farm people. He was on the side of the colonists in their contest with Great Britain and helped to supply the American army with food. On Oct. 8, 1776, he married Mrs. Sarah Fishbourne Mifflin, of Philadelphia, and moved to that city in 1791. Believing that agriculture might be advanced by a society of "well informed men of liberal minds" he brought about the formation of the Philadelphia Society for Promoting Agriculture in 1785, and was its vice-president and active in its affairs until his death. He was of large frame, is characterized as "beneficent, vigorous and original," was interested in painting and music, and was a member of the Protestant Episcopal Church.

Results of his farm operations and studies were published at first on written cards, and then on handbills and as essays. Among these are: *A Summary View of the Courses of Crops, in the Husbandry of England and Maryland* (1784), and *Sketches on Rotations of Crops and other Rural Matters* (1797). His *Essays and Notes on Husbandry and Rural Affairs,* published in 1799, and with additions in 1801, is a book of 566 pages describing a system of farming based on rotation of crops and deals with the several kinds of crops, fruits, and animals grown on English and Maryland farms (particularly his own), manures, farm buildings, dairy products, food and diet for farm people, etc. American and foreign practises are compared and results of experiments are given. The style is clear and practical, an effort evidently being made to give such data as would enable the intelligent farmer to make use of the information thus conveyed. Bordley also published an essay on *Money, Coins, Weights and Measures* in 1789 and a supplement to this in 1790.

[Mrs. Elizabeth Bordley Gibson, *Biog. Sketches of the Bordley Family of Md.* (1865); the *Minutes of the Phila. Soc. for the Promotion of Agriculture, 1785–1810* (1854); Robt. Wilson, "Wye Island," in *Lippincott's Mag.,* Apr. 1877.]   A. C. T.

BORÉ, JEAN ÉTIENNE (Dec. 27, 1741– Feb. 2, 1820), sugar planter, is generally credited with having established the sugar industry in Louisiana. The family belonged to the old Norman nobility and some of its members had risen high in the service of the French kings. One Michel de Boré had been a *conseiller de roi* as well as a postal official under Louis XIII, and Robert Louis de Boré, the great-grandfather of Étienne, had performed like services for Louis XIV. For some reason not explained, Étienne's father had turned from the life at court and had sought his fortunes in the far-off French possessions in America. There he married one Céleste Thérèse Carrière, and there his son was born. The stay in America, however, was short, and, at the age of four years, the boy was taken to France to be educated, and, when his age permitted, to take his place as a member of the *Mousquétaires du Roi*, the king's own household troops in which the private held the rank of captain. For ten years he remained in the service, then accepted the command of a company of cavalry, only to resign and turn his face westward toward the land of his birth,—prompted, no doubt, by his recent marriage to Marguerite Marie Destrehans, daughter of the former royal treasurer in Louisiana who had large possessions in that province. Establishing himself upon a plantation situated six miles above the city of New Orleans he shared the hopes and disappointments of the native planters in the search for a profitable staple and at length, like the others, turned his major attention to the cultivation of indigo. For a time all went well but in the early seventeen-nineties insects ravaged the crops with disheartening regularity and slaves used in the work sickened and died. In despair the planters were forced back into the old search for a staple ("Memoir of the Present State of Louisiana by Chevalier de Champigny," in B. F.

French, *Historical Memoirs of Louisiana,* 1852, V, 145). Under such conditions Étienne Boré resolved upon a new attempt at the hitherto unsuccessful making of sugar. Purchasing cane from the planters Solis and Mendez, who raised it for syrup and tafia, he planted his fields, built a sugar house, and in 1795 was ready for a trial. Amid intense excitement the time for the strike was awaited, and the cry of the sugar maker, "It granulates," was carried far and wide as the announcement of a new day for the province. Louisiana had at last found a staple. From this time on Boré's fame and fortune expanded. Profits took the place of losses; his fields widened and his negroes, under semi-military discipline, grew in numbers and contentment. His great house with its moat and ramparts, reminiscent of old France, opened its doors with equal hospitality to the exiled brothers of Louis XVI or to the American generals who were serving with Andrew Jackson. Throughout the province he was honored and revered as the great benefactor of agriculture. When Louisiana was transferred from Spain to France in 1803 Boré was appointed mayor of the city of New Orleans and continued to serve on into the American period. He was then appointed a member of the first Legislative Council under the new government, but, consistent with his opposition to the form of government imposed, he refused to serve, and returned to his rural life. He died at the age of seventy-nine years, requesting that his funeral be conducted with the greatest simplicity, so that the money saved thereby might be given to the Charity Hospital of New Orleans. The wish was characteristic of the man.

[Chas. Gayarre, *Hist. of La.* (1854); Grace King, *Creole Families of New Orleans* (1921); *De Bow's Rev.,* XXII, 615–19; G. H. V. Collot, *Voyage Dans L'Amérique Septentrionale* (1826); obituary in *Courrier de la Louisiane,* Feb. 4, 1820.]   A. O. C.

BOREMAN, ARTHUR INGRAM (July 24, 1823–Apr. 19, 1896), governor of West Virginia, senator, was the grandson of John Boreman, a native of Manchester, England, who became a merchant in Philadelphia and assistant paymaster of the Revolutionary army. John Boreman's son, Kenner Seaton Boreman, was a successful merchant in Waynesburg, Pa., and married Sarah Ingram by whom he had seven children, among them Arthur Ingram. The latter prepared for law by a course of reading and observation largely under the direction of his brother William, a distinguished lawyer and member of the Virginia legislature. He was admitted to the bar in 1845 and removed the following year to Parkersburg, where he became prominent in the practise of his profession. In

1855–61 he represented Wood County in the Virginia House of Delegates, being a member of the famous extra session of 1861 which called a convention, without popular referendum, to consider the subject of secession. Boreman had opposed secession in all its phases and especially that by Virginia under the existing circumstances. When the Virginia convention voted to secede, Apr. 17, 1861, he became active in efforts to hold western Virginia in the Union. He was president of a convention that met in Wheeling, June 11, 1861, and reorganized the government of Virginia with a complete set of loyal officials, including United States Senators. Soon after he became a judge of a circuit court of the reorganized government, which office he held for two years. Meanwhile political events in western Virginia moved rapidly. The reorganized government consented to the dismemberment of Virginia, and West Virginia was admitted to the Union. Officers of the former moved to Alexandria, giving place to those of the new state, among them Boreman, the unanimous choice for governor. He was reëlected in 1864 and again in 1866, but before his third term expired, he resigned to accept a seat in the United States Senate, which he occupied from Mar. 4, 1869, to Mar. 4, 1875. In the Senate he served with ability as a member of the committees on Manufactures and Claims and as chairman, in turn, of the committee on Political Disabilities and Territories. The national political upheavals of the seventies carried West Virginia into the Democratic column and retired Boreman to private life. He resumed the practise of law, and devoted himself to home and church, having married in 1864 Mrs. Laurane Bullock, daughter of Dr. James Tanner of Wheeling. In 1888 he was reëlected to the judgeship which he filled years before and which he continued to hold until his death.

[G. W. Atkinson and A. F. Gibbons, *Prominent Men of W. Va.* (1890) ; T. C. Miller and H. Maxwell, *W. Va. and Its People,* vol. III (1913) ; *Jours. of W. Va. Leg.,* 1863–69 ; *Wheeling Daily Intelligencer,* Apr. 20, 1896.]

C. H. A.

BORGLUM, SOLON HANNIBAL (Dec. 22, 1868–Jan. 31, 1922), sculptor, fourth child of Dr. James de la Mothe Borglum and Ida (Michelson) Borglum, was born in Ogden, Utah. There were six sons and three daughters. The father and mother were Danes, who came to this country in the early sixties, settling for a time in Ogden. From them Solon derived many of the sturdy traits characteristic of the North Danish stock. His feeling for form and his instinct for anatomical structure were a two-fold inheritance from his father, who, arriving here as a wood-

carver, later became a physician, practising at Fremont, Nebr. Since his work carried him far and wide into the country, Dr. Borglum had many horses, and these young Solon loved better than his school-books. The boy spent some not too happy years in the public schools of Fremont and Omaha, and in Creighton College, but at sixteen he was sent to western Nebraska as cowboy on his father's 6,000-acre ranch. Afterward, he took charge of a larger outfit. During many years of close, sympathetic watching of animals he developed an extraordinary sense of animal form and movement. His vision and memory were swift, fine, true. Often he spent his leisure jotting down on stray bits of paper his visual impressions of man and beast in action, in repose, in transition. His artist brother, Gutzon, returning from study abroad, was amazed by the vitality and truth of these rude sketches, and urged the ranchman to turn artist.

Solon, like his father before him, had the courage to make a complete change in his way of life. He was then twenty-six, and without any knowledge whatever of art as taught in schools. He joined his brother in the Sierra Madre mountains, studying under him for some months, passing then to Los Angeles, and later to Santa Ana, where he rented a so-called "studio" at two dollars a month. The confinement irked him. He therefore set on his door a sign, "In Studio Saturdays Only." The rest of the week he spent roaming the mountains, living among the lawless, meeting with the disinherited, and eating with the uncivilized,—Indians, half-breeds, white men, types noble or ignoble. Being spiritually-minded, he was strengthened, not coarsened, by contact with the wild free life he loved and studied. A sound instinct had told him that "Saturdays Only" would appeal to clients who might be indifferent to unrestricted privileges of visit. Promptly appeared a manly sitter, an Eastern school teacher, whose portrait he painted for five dollars. Acquaintance ripened into friendship, interest was aroused, other clients came. Ladies took lessons at a dollar apiece. Encouraged by friends, he exhibited his work, made sixty-five dollars, and with this, fortified by a railroad pass received from a brother, he went to Cincinnati to study at the Art Academy, joining both day and evening classes.

In his narrow rented room he knew the loneliness of cities. But not too far away were the United States Mail stables, lit all night, and these he frequented in the early morning hours, to study the horses. He learned from veterinaries, he worked at dissections. Experimenting in clay, he modeled a sketch of a horse pawing its dead mate, and showed it to Mr. Rebisso, director of sculpture at the Academy. Rebisso recognized the young man's gift, invited him to work in his (Rebisso's) own studio, and made it possible for him to go to Paris. At last, after obstacles that would have daunted a man of less intrepid mind, Borglum had found in sculpture his true lifework. "All this," writes Mrs. Borglum, "with no money, and at the cost of much suffering. At the Art School he won a scholarship so small that it was not expected to be used abroad; still, Solon went to Paris with it. A horse which he had modeled with Rebisso was cast, and copies were sold, mostly to students, thus giving him enough money for his steamer ticket. Later the school bought another horse, which allowed him to remain another year; they also prolonged the scholarship. Then Theodore B. Starr began taking up his work, and life became more easy."

Borglum's stay in Paris gave him larger advantages for special study and a wider horizon of general culture. At "l'Académie Julien" he studied six months under Denys Puech, then one of the new forces in French sculpture. Frémiet, veteran master of animal form, was his constant adviser, correcting the ardent young American's work out of his own inexhaustible lore. "Mon ami," said M. Frémiet, "you're lucky! You lived, you had something to say before you studied art." And Solon Borglum, wherever he went, had the advantage of a rare personal charm springing chiefly from native goodness, from his quick and abounding sympathy toward all life. To his first Salon he sent two spirited groups, both well received, especially his "Lassoing Wild Horses." The next year, 1899, he won honorable mention at the Salon, for his "Stampede of Wild Horses," and in 1900 a silver medal at the Paris Exposition. On Dec. 10, 1898, in Paris, he married Emma Vignal, daughter of a French Protestant clergyman. The couple spent the following summer in Crow Creek Reservation, among the Sioux Indians.

After one more year in Paris, they remained near New York, making at Silvermine, Conn., their studio home, Rocky Ranch. Here during a period of seventeen years Borglum's art found natural and varied expression in works ranging from busts to equestrians, from small bronzes such as the "Bulls Fighting" and the "Border of White Man's Land" in the Metropolitan Museum to the four large groups modeled for the St. Louis Exposition, 1904, and the "Pioneer Group," Court of Honor, San Francisco Exposition, 1915. Made a member of the National Sculpture Society in 1901, he received a silver medal at Buffalo, 1901, a gold medal at St. Louis, 1904, and a silver

medal at Buenos Aires, 1910, becoming an associate member of the National Academy of Design the same year. His sculpture is impressionistic, deeply felt, soundly constructed. He is at his best in frontier themes such as "Burial on the Plains," "Pioneer in a Storm," "Snow Drift," "The Blizzard," "The Intelligent Bronco," "The Rough Rider," "Cowboy at Rest." Among his works are two fine equestrians, the "Bucky O'Neill," Prescott, Ariz., the "Gen. John B. Gordon," Atlanta, Ga. Other works of note are "Soldiers and Sailors Monument," Danbury, Conn., the "Hurley Monument," Topeka, Kan., the "Washington, 1753," owned in Canada, the austere "Schieren Memorial," Greenwood Cemetery.

"Solon never lost the spirit he put into a sketch," wrote Gutzon Borglum, justly extolling as a rare creative gift the power to retain in a long-considered heroic group all the vitality and charm of the first swift rendering. Nor was Solon Borglum one of those sculptors whose labors end with the completion of a clay model turned over to the practitioners. He could, and when advisable did, carve in marble and in wood, with a hand not enfeebled by super-civilization. A photograph which shows him carving his marble group, the "Command of God," indicates well this sculptor's aspect; his frame, not tall, but powerful, his intellectual head, his eager, friendly countenance.

On the entrance of the United States into the World War, Borglum, by reason of age refused as a soldier, went to France with the "Y." His service abroad was of indomitable heroism. Frequently under fire, escaping when a shell blew up his canteen, gassed twice, continuing in the saddle before complete recovery, he won the hearts of the French officers with whom he worked shoulder to shoulder in the Foyer du Soldat. "He was the first American to enter Rheims when the German Army fell back," declared Raymond V. Ingersoll in a personal tribute (*New York Times*, Feb. 13, 1922). "He and a French co-worker were there with a small donkey to carry the materials for hot drinks." The citation for his Croix de Guerre honors him for what the French commandant calls his *"âme d'apôtre."* George S. Hellman, Lloyd Warren, and Ernest Peixotto (*Sun*, New York, Feb. 19, 1922) laud his work as director of sculpture at the A. E. F. art training center at Bellevue.

After his return home, he founded a school of sculpture based on principles set forth in his *Sound Construction* (copyright 1923), a book of six hundred drawings, the fruit of his life's observations in comparative anatomy, and in the basic forms of all nature as seen in all great art.

He was an inspiring teacher of fundamental truths. One of his last works of sculpture is the "Little Lady of the Dew," a kneeling figure in marble. Here, as in his two standing figures of the same period, "Aspiration" and "Inspiration," the ideal theme is a departure from his usual choice. It would seem that a new chapter in his artistic life was opening when he died, a few days after an operation for acute appendicitis.

The main body of his work, depicting as it does a vanishing phase in American life, has a unique historic value. More than any other of our artists, he himself was part of all he tells. His frontier groups form an epic,—an epic sculptured in free verse. They reveal clearly their open-air origin; often they are enveloped in the elements (see the "Burial on the Plains," the "Mare and Foal in a Snow Drift"). Subtleties of modeling, academic nobility in composition, the grand style of past ages, were outside Borglum's purposes and powers. His passion in sculpture was to impart the very essence of things seen and felt; hence, and not because of Rodin's influence, he became a master of elimination. Surely no man knew better than he every strap and buckle horse or rider might wear; but he was an artist and not a harness-maker in shaping his bronze and marble tales. In its own large, unacademic way, his sculpture has saved for our contemplation certain swiftly-passing moments in the march of American frontier life.

[Chas. H. Caffin, *Am. Masters of Sculpture* (1903); Lorado Taft, *Hist. of Am. Sculpture* (1903); Arthur Goodrich, "The Frontier in Sculpture," *World's Work*, III, 1857; Louise Eberle, "In Recognition of an American Sculptor," *Scribner's Mag.*, Sept. 1922; Gutzon Borglum, letter in *N. Y. Times*, Mar. 5, 1922, reprinted, with illustrations, in the *Am. Mag. of Art*, Nov. 1922.]

A. A—s.

BORIE, ADOLPH EDWARD (Nov. 25, 1809–Feb. 5, 1880), merchant, financier, was the eldest of the twelve children of John Joseph Borie, a Frenchman who established himself early in the nineteenth century as a merchant and manufacturer at Philadelphia and of Sophia Beauveau, a refugee from Haiti. He graduated from the University of Pennsylvania in 1825, and studied and traveled in Europe. In 1839 he married Elizabeth Dundas McKean. Upon his return from Europe in 1828, he entered his father's mercantile business. His firm carried on trade with Mexico, the West Indies, and the Far East, engaging particularly in the silk and tea trade. His mercantile career extended over a period of about thirty years, during the epoch of the clipper ships, when Philadelphia's foreign trade was in its prime. The magnitude of his operations is indicated by his complaints of property damages amounting to $100,000 in China during the dis-

turbances of 1857–58. He was a pioneer in seeking the diplomatic and naval support of the government for safeguarding his interests abroad. Gradually he became interested in financial and railroad enterprises, serving from 1848 to 1860 as president of the Bank of Commerce, and becoming director in several leading business institutions of Philadelphia. Before the Civil War, his connection with political affairs was slight. In 1843 he was consul to Belgium. He was a champion of Whig policies, particularly protection. He supported Lincoln in 1860, and upon the outbreak of the Civil War became an ardent Unionist. His activities in this connection were mainly as an organizer and vice-president of the Union League, which assumed national importance because of its influence in promoting similar organizations in other cities. He was the moving spirit in the recruiting and equipping of a number of regiments, as well as in promoting Unionist sentiment. His war-time acquaintance with Gen. Grant developed into an intimacy, and led to the appointment of Borie in 1869 as secretary of the navy. With no experience and little interest in public life, with varied business connections and fragile health, his tenure of office was largely nominal, and he resigned June 25 of the same year. According to one of his colleagues in the cabinet, "he often said, 'The department is managed by Admiral Porter, I am only a figure head'" (G. S. Boutwell, *Reminiscences of Sixty Years in Public Affairs*, 1902, II, 212). He held no other important public office.

Borie was a noted patron of art and learning. His collection of paintings received considerable recognition (*Lippincott's Magazine*, X, 221–26). His philanthropies were varied and extensive. His continued intimacy with Grant resulted in his being invited to join the Ex-President's party which toured the world in 1878–79. Shortly before the conclusion of the tour his age and ill health caused him to withdraw from the party, and early the next year he died in the city of his birth.

[Obituaries were published in the *Press*, the *Inquirer*, the *Public Ledger*, the *Bulletin*, and other Philadelphia journals, and in some other newspapers, notably the *N. Y. Times* of Feb. 6, 1880. An extensive biographical sketch of Borie's family by F. W. Leach appeared in the *North American* (Phila.), Jan. 5, 1913. The record of his connection with the Union League is available in *Chronicle of the Union League* (1902), and in the archives of the League's Library. For anecdotal accounts and reflections, see J. R. Young, *Around the World with Gen. Grant* (1879). Some of his correspondence is preserved in the manuscript collections of the Pa. Hist. Soc.]

W. B—n.

BORLAND, SOLON (Sept. 21, 1808–Jan. 1 or 31, 1864), senator, diplomat, Confederate soldier, was born near Suffolk, Va., received an elementary education in North Carolina, studied medicine, and then located in Little Rock, Ark. When the Mexican War opened he volunteered and served until the capture of the City of Mexico. On Apr. 24, 1848, he took his seat in the United States Senate by appointment in the room of A. H. Sevier, resigned. Later he was elected for the regular term beginning in 1849. At first he seems to have played no conspicuous part in the proceedings of the Senate, taking very little part in the debate on such important matters as the compromise measures of 1850, but later he took considerable interest in foreign affairs. On Apr. 3, 1853, he resigned from the Senate and fifteen days later was appointed minister to Nicaragua and the other Central American states, vice John Slidell, declined. By this act Honduras was recognized as an independent state (J. B. Moore, *Digest of International Law,* 1898, I, 92). Borland entered upon his official duties on Sept. 14, 1853. In a little over six months he started home, coming to Punta Arenas on the Accessory Transit Company's steamer *Routh.* At this time the Transit Company (Cornelius Vanderbilt) was engaged in a controversy with the authorities at Greytown. While Borland was waiting for transportation home the authorities of Greytown came to arrest Capt. Smith, of the *Routh,* on the charge of having murdered a native boatman, but Borland told them that the United States did not recognize their right to arrest an American citizen and ordered them to leave. This produced great excitement and later in the day, when he went to visit the American consul, a crowd attempted to arrest him. In the fracas some one threw a broken bottle and struck him in the face. On reaching Washington Borland reported the matter to President Pierce, who sent the U. S. S. *Cyane,* Capt. Hollis, to the scene of trouble. The captain demanded $24,000 damages for the Transit Company and an apology for the indignity to our minister. Satisfaction not being forthcoming he completely destroyed the town next day (July 13, 1854) by bombardment and fire, although there had been a complete change in the city government and the offenders could not be found. His actions met with protest from Great Britain, but were approved by President Pierce (Moore, II, 414–416; VII, 112–14; W. O. Scroggs, *Filibusters and Financiers,* 1916, pp. 75–76). On July 13, Borland was offered the governorship of New Mexico, but declined and resumed his practise in Little Rock. While the secession convention was in session, but before it took final action, Borland raised a company of militia and with the approval of Gov. Rector proceeded by steamer to Fort Smith to demand the surrender of the fort, but

Capt. S. D. Sturgis learned of his approach and abandoned the fort shortly before his arrival. Borland raised the Third Arkansas Cavalry, of which he was made colonel. He participated in several battles east of the Mississippi River and was involved in the disaster at Port Hudson. He rose to the rank of brigadier-general, but was forced to give up service on account of his health and died in or near Houston, Tex. He was thrice married: to Mrs. Huldah Wright of Suffolk, who bore him two sons; to Mrs. Hunt of Tennessee, no issue; and to Mary J. Melbourne of Little Rock, who bore him one son (died in 1862) and two daughters.

[In addition to references above, see Fay Hempstead, *A Pictorial Hist. of Ark.* (1898).]   D.Y.T.

BOSS, LEWIS (Oct. 26, 1846–Oct. 5, 1912), astronomer, was born in Providence, R. I., the son of Samuel P. and Lucinda (Joslin) Boss. He studied at Dartmouth, graduating in 1870 with the A.B. degree. After graduation he held a position in the government Land Office and was often at the Naval Observatory. In 1871 he was married to Helen Hutchinson of Washington. From 1872 to 1876 he was assistant astronomer with the survey party of the United States-Canada boundary. The need of more precise places of stars for his latitude work led him, during his evenings in camp, to an investigation of the systematic errors of star catalogues; to a discussion of instrumental errors and methods of reduction; and finally to the construction of a new homogeneous declination system. The discussion of nearly one hundred star catalogues, which this involved, showed clearly the attention to detail and the critical handling of observational material which made him the foremost American authority on star positions. It told severely upon his health and eyesight and the resulting catalogue of five hundred standard stars was not completed until after his appointment in 1876 as director of the Dudley Observatory in Albany (Lewis Boss, *Report on the Declination of the Stars Employed in Latitude Work with the Zenith Telescope . . . and a Catalogue of Five Hundred Stars for the Mean Epoch 1875,* 1878). The catalogue finished, he undertook the observation of one of the zones of the Astronomische Gesellschaft program of star positions on which another observatory had defaulted. He made all the observations himself and minutely investigated the graduation errors and his magnitude equation. Begun ten years after some of the other zones were started, his zone was the first completed for publication. The catalogue also contained the proper motions of the stars, compiled from a comparison with older catalogues, and a valuable discussion of the sun's motion. Boss observed the solar eclipse of 1878, and in 1882 was chief of a government expedition to Chile to observe the transit of Venus. Later he became the editor and manager of an Albany newspaper, and entered actively into civic matters and into the presidential campaign of 1884. He was state superintendent of weights and measures of New York from 1883 to 1906. Meanwhile he was maturing his plans for a great catalogue to contain standard positions and proper motions of about twenty-six thousand stars, involving re-observation with a single instrument and a critical discussion of all catalogue positions. Observations were begun at Albany and carried nearly to completion for the northern stars, while the arduous labor of reduction and discussion went on. A grant from the Carnegie Institution in 1904 made it possible for Boss to secure much needed clerical aid, and to transfer the meridian circle to Chile for the observation of the southern stars. This monumental work is being carried to completion under the direction of his son, Benjamin Boss. *The Preliminary General Catalogue of 6188 Stars for the Epoch 1900* was published by Lewis Boss in 1910 as Carnegie Institution of Washington Publication No. 115. In discussing the proper motions of these stars, he detected the community of motion of the Taurus cluster and thus opened the way to a powerful method of measuring distance; he made a determination of precession and of the sun's motion; he studied the average proper motions of stars of various spectral types and the average motion of stars in various galactic latitudes.

[Benj. Boss in *Nat. Acad. of Sci. Biog. Memoirs*, vol. IX (1920); R. H. Tucker in *Astron. Nachrichten*, CXCIII, 29–32; *Pubs. Astron. Soc. of the Pacific*, XXIV, 256–60, and *Pop. Astron.*, Nov. 1922; *Astron. Jour.*, Nov. 13, 1912; *Jour. Brit. Astron. Ass.*, Oct. 1912.]   R.S.D.

BOSWORTH, EDWARD INCREASE (Jan. 10, 1861–July 1, 1927), Congregational clergyman, educator, the son of Franklin S. and Sarah (Hunt) Bosworth, was born in Elgin, Ill. The first ancestor in this country on his father's side was Benjamin Bosworth, a major in the Revolutionary War. Edward Bosworth was a student at Oberlin College, 1879–1881, but graduated at Yale in 1883. In the same year he returned to Oberlin to enter the Theological Seminary, on graduating from which in 1886 he was ordained to the Congregational ministry and served for a year as pastor of the Mt. Vernon Congregational Church. He was then elected professor of English Bible in the Oberlin Theological Seminary (1887), a title changed to professor of New Testament Language and Litera-

ture in 1892. He was the dean of the Seminary, 1903–23, and acting president of the College in the difficult war year, 1918–19. His career was diversified by several years abroad: he was a student in the University of Leipzig, 1890–91; spent the winter of 1891–92 in Athens; lectured in Japan in 1907, in Turkey in 1911, and in Athens in 1927. He was married to Bertha McClure of Elgin, Ill., on Oct. 1, 1891.

It was the influence which Dr. Bosworth exerted upon Oberlin College and through it upon the religious life of his time that imparts to his career its larger significance. Working in closest harmony with his life-long friend, President King, he shaped the ideals and determined the fortunes of Oberlin for almost half a century. Under these two men the institution rapidly and healthfully expanded into one of the strongest colleges in the country. Dr. Bosworth was a sound and accurate scholar, but his real power lay in the classroom. He had that best gift of a teacher, the ability at once to stir curiosity and to check undisciplined speculation. His life-work fell at a time of transition in theological thinking and when the process of secularization and materialization in our colleges was going on at a rapid rate. His own religion was intellectually well fortified, salted with shrewd common sense, but in its essence mystical. He became one of the chief influences which enabled Oberlin College to effect a change from the older to the more modern points of view in theology without loss of a vital interest in religion. His books which have had a world-wide circulation have contributed to the same end. Among them are: *Studies in the Acts and Epistles* (1898); *Studies in the Teachings of Jesus and His Apostles* (1901); *Studies in the Life of Jesus Christ* (1904); *New Studies in Acts* (1908); *Christ in Everyday Life* (1910); *Thirty Studies about Jesus* (1917); *Commentary on Romans* (1919); *What It Means to Be a Christian* (1922); *The Life and Teaching of Jesus* (1924).

[*Who's Who in America*, 1926–27; *Oberlin Alumni Mag.*, July, Oct., 1927; personal recollections.] K.F.

BOSWORTH, FRANCKE HUNTINGTON (Jan. 25, 1843–Oct. 17, 1925), laryngologist, the son of Daniel P. Bosworth, merchant, and Deborah Wells, both of New England ancestry for many generations, was born in Marietta, Ohio. His primary education was received in the schools of his native town and from 1858 to 1860 he attended Marietta College. In 1860 he entered the junior class at Yale, graduating in 1862. During the Civil War he was in active service in West Virginia under Gen. Rosecrans and was also sent to the Peninsula where he joined in opposing the raids of Gen. Morgan. After the war he settled in New York and graduated in 1868 from Bellevue Hospital and Medical College as valedictorian of his class. In 1873, after his internship at Bellevue, he was appointed lecturer on diseases of the upper air tract and in 1881 was made full professor, a position which he retained after Bellevue became united with New York University and until his final retirement from active work. He issued a *Handbook upon Diseases of the Throat for the Use of Students* (1879), and in 1881 he published the first edition of his celebrated *Manual of the Diseases of the Throat and Nose.* In 1878 J. Solis-Cohen [*q.v.*] of Philadelphia had published his monograph on laryngology, and later Sir Morell MacKenzie issued another work on the same subject (1882). The contributions of these three men may be said to have created the science of laryngology. Bosworth's most extensive work, *A Treatise on Diseases of the Nose and Throat,* appeared in two volumes in 1889 and 1892 and it is to be noted that during his ten years of active practise he changed his emphasis from the throat to the nose by reversing their order in the title of his later publication. His shorter text-book of the *Diseases of the Nose and Throat* was brought out in 1896 and enjoyed great popularity for nearly a generation. Bosworth wrote easily and his text-books and scientific papers were always eagerly awaited by those engaged in his specialty. He presented original ideas and was responsible for many contributions to the physiology and the pathology of the sinuses and nasal obstruction. Soon after the introduction of cocaine he devised a nasal saw by means of which septal spurs and other obstructions could be readily removed. His studies were promptly recognized in this country and abroad, and in consequence he was elected honorary fellow of the British, French, and German Laryngological Societies. He was also one of the founders (1873) of the New York Laryngological Society. It has been well said that Bosworth "more than anyone who had gone before, gathered the disjointed and scattered fragments of laryngological knowledge, developed the science of rhinology and, welding all into a perfectly coördinated form, established them as definite and distinguished departments of medical science." He was a man of wide interests and literary tastes. He was well known among dramatists and actors of note and was fond of horses and racing. For many years he studied art and acquired more than an amateur's knowledge of painting. On Sept. 12, 1871, he married Mary Hildreth Putnam, and two children survived their father: a son, F. H. Bosworth, Jr.,

dean of the School of Architecture at Cornell, and a daughter, wife of Hon. Walter R. Herrick of New York.

[*The Twenty Years' Record of the Yale Class of 1862* (1884); *Yale Univ. Obit. Record of Grads. Deceased during the Year Ending July 1, 1926;* Dr. D. Bryson Delavan, obituaries in the *Medic. Jour. and Record,* 1926, CXXIII, 125–126 (with portrait), and in the *Laryngoscope,* 1925, XXXV, 950–60; obituary in the *N. Y. Herald Tribune,* Oct. 18, 1925.] J.F.F.

BOTELER, ALEXANDER ROBINSON (May 16, 1815–May 8, 1892), congressman, Confederate soldier, was the son of Dr. Henry Boteler, a graduate of Dr. Rush's medical school, Philadelphia, and of Priscilla (Robinson) Boteler, whose father was a successful Baltimore ship owner and merchant and whose mother was a daughter of the artist Charles William Peale. Boteler's mother having died when he was four years old, he lived with his grandmother in Baltimore. At eighteen he entered Princeton and roomed with the poet-novelist Philip Pendleton Cooke [*q.v.*]. Graduating in 1835, in the following year he married Helen Macomb Stockton of Princeton and they went to live at his father's estate, "Fountain Rock," in Shepherdstown, Va. (now W. Va.). In addition to his agricultural interests Boteler entered politics, as a Whig, and as a presidential elector voted for Winfield Scott in 1852. In 1859 he was elected to the United States House of Representatives, succeeding Charles J. Faulkner who was appointed minister to France. During the sectional struggle in Congress, in 1860, Boteler sought to avoid disunion and secured the passage of a resolution creating a committee of one from each state to consider the "perilous condition of the country" (*Congressional Globe,* 36 Cong., 2 Sess., p. 6). He made an appeal for the Union so effectively that a fellow member, S. S. Cox, considered it "the most eloquent speech, next to that of Sergeant S. S. Prentiss in his own case, ever delivered in Congress" (see S. S. Cox, *Union-Disunion-Reunion, Three Decades of Federal Legislation,* 1885, p. 93; *Congressional Globe,* 36 Cong., 1 Sess., p. 583.) With Virginia's passage of the secession resolution Boteler left Congress and was elected to the General Assembly of Virginia; but in the meantime his district elected him as its delegate to the Confederate Provisional Congress, which he entered on Nov. 27, 1861. He was also a member of the first Confederate Congress, presenting a design for the flag and being influential in the selection of the seal. In the summer of 1862 he was serving as volunteer aide on the staff of his friend, Stonewall Jackson, who upon more than one occasion appealed, through Boteler, to the Congress.

After Jackson's death, he became aide to J. E. B. Stuart (*Official Records,* ser. IV, vol. II, p. 718). Later he was aide to Governors Smith and Letcher. He was West Virginia's commissioner at the Philadelphia Exposition 1871–76; he was appointed by Arthur as a member of the Tariff Commission in 1881; he was assistant attorney in the United States Department of Justice in 1882 and 1883; he was clerk of pardons in the same department, 1884–89.

Boteler was the author of a number of pamphlets and articles. His description of John Brown's Raid (which occurred near his home and to part of which he was an eye-witness) appeared in the *Century Magazine,* July 1883. He wrote "My Ride to a Barbecue," and presented in writing the claims of James Rumsey as the inventor of the steamboat. He probably had much to do with the placing of the memorial to Rumsey on the Potomac near Shepherdstown. He was also an artist. In 1887 the Military Historical Society of Massachusetts purchased "The Boteler Collection" composed of oil sketches of Robert E. Lee, Longstreet, Jefferson Davis, Wade Hampton, Pickett, and John H. Morgan, and a pencil sketch of John Brown.

[A sketch of Col. Boteler's life was written by his grand-daughter, Miss Helen B. Pendleton, for the *Shepherdstown Register,* Aug. 14, 1924. References to the friendship of Stonewall Jackson and Boteler are found in R. L. Dabney, *Life and Campaigns of Lieutenant-General Thos. J. Jackson* (1866), John Esten Cooke, *Stonewall Jackson* (1863) and H. A. White, *Stonewall Jackson* (1909). His legislative career can be followed in the *Cong. Globe,* 36 Cong., and in the "Jours. of the Cong. of the Confederate States," *Senate Doc. No. 234,* 58 Cong., 2 Sess.]

                                   E. L. F.

BOTETOURT, NORBORNE BERKELEY, Baron de (*c.* 1718–Oct. 15, 1770), colonial governor of Virginia, was sprung from the family which, in Sir William Berkeley, had already furnished the colony of Virginia with one governor. He was the son of John Symes Berkeley. It was not until 1764 that he acquired his title. He had already served as colonel of the Gloucestershire militia and as a member of Parliament. He was appointed governor of Virginia in 1768, and unlike his predecessors subsequent to Howard, he went out to the colony in person, instead of sending a deputy to perform his duties. He brought over with him, for gala occasions, a resplendent coach and a team of cream-white Hanoverian horses, a present to him from the Duke of Cumberland (*William and Mary College Quarterly Magazine,* XIII, 87). Disembarking at Hampton, he journeyed to Williamsburg overland, and was received on its outskirts by a concourse of citizens; the town at night was illuminated; and a grand banquet in his honor

was given. A eulogistic ode was also composed and published in the *Gazette.*

Botetourt promptly summoned the General Assembly, and, dressed in a light red coat, decorated with gold braiding, drove to the Capitol in his glittering coach, drawn by his Hanoverian horses in their silver mounted harness,—the whole a counterpart of King George's equipage at the opening of Parliament. And it was also observed that the Governor, in delivering the address, imitated the mannerisms of his royal master when reading his speech from the throne. But the burgesses were not so awed by all this state as to refrain from passing resolutions upholding the colonists' rights, which had recently been grossly violated by the transportation of Americans oversea to be tried by English juries. So frankly did they express themselves that Botetourt summoned them to the council chamber, and having rebuked them for their boldness, dissolved them as a body. But most of the burgesses reassembled in the Raleigh Tavern, and adopted a resolution, offered by Washington, but really drafted by Mason, that they would neither import nor buy any article that was subject to a parliamentary tax. When the general tax was repealed by Parliament, the tax on tea was retained. The merchants of the colony, in concert with the burgesses, at a meeting at Williamsburg formed an association which bound its members to purchase no tea, no British manufactures, and no slaves, imported into the colony in British vessels, until all the regulations subjecting colonial imports to a tax had been revoked. It is said that Botetourt was so much mortified by his inability to restore good feeling between the colony and the mother country, after these causes of difference arose, that he sank into a fever and died. The people of Virginia made allowance for the difficulties of his position, and remembered only his good intentions in their favor. His administration was, on the whole, so beneficent that, after his death, a marble statue was erected in his honor. This still stands in the quadrangle of the College of William and Mary.

[L. G. Tyler, *Williamsburg the Old Capital* (1907); Indices of *Brit. Col. Papers,* 1768–70; *Minutes of Virginia Council* and *Minutes of House of Burgesses,* 1768–70.]

                                  P. A. B.

BOTSFORD, GEORGE WILLIS (May 9, 1862–Dec. 13, 1917), historian, was descended from Henry and Elizabeth Botsford who came from Leicestershire, England, and settled in Milford, Conn., in 1636. He was the son of William Hiram and Margaret (Johnson) Botsford, who were living in West Union, Ia., when he was born. He received his early education in public schools and was graduated as bachelor of arts at the University of Nebraska in 1884. The same university conferred upon him the degree of A.M. in 1889. After a short period of teaching and a brief sojourn at Johns Hopkins University he entered Cornell University as a graduate student, where he attained the degree of Ph.D. in 1891. Meanwhile he had been professor of Greek at Kalamazoo College, 1886–90. He married Lillie M. Shaw, of Kalamazoo, Mich., Aug. 30, 1891. He was professor of Greek in Bethany College, 1891–95; then was appointed instructor in the history of Greece and Rome at Harvard University, where he remained six years, until 1901. He was appointed lecturer on ancient history at Columbia University in 1902, instructor in 1903, adjunct professor in 1905, and professor in 1910, and was thus one of the few professors of ancient history in the United States. In the year 1909–10, and again in 1913, he was engaged in historical research in Italy. He was a member of the American Philological Association and the American Historical Association and at the time of his death was a member of the board of editors of the *Political Science Quarterly*.

Botsford was a scholar of unusual ability, extraordinary industry, and great singleness of purpose. His original contributions to historical knowledge were made, for the most part, in articles published in periodicals, but his books, even when they were designed primarily as textbooks for schools, not only contained the generally known and accepted facts, but also embodied the results of serious original research. The titles of his books are as follows: *The Development of the Athenian Constitution* (1893); *A History of Greece for High Schools and Academies* (1899); *A History of Rome for High Schools and Academies* (1901); *An Ancient History* (1902); *The Story of Rome as Greeks and Romans tell it* (1903; with Lillie S. Botsford; an elementary source-book); *Ancient History for Beginners* (1904); *The Roman Assemblies* (1909); *History of the Ancient World* (1911); *A Source-book of Ancient History* (1912; with Lillie S. Botsford); *Hellenic Civilization* (1915; with E. G. Sihler); and, published after his death, *Hellenic History* (1922). Most of these books have been widely used in schools and colleges, and the reputation of their author is deservedly great.

Botsford was powerfully built and perhaps of somewhat less than the average height. Apart from the intellectual quality of his face, there was nothing especially striking in his appearance. He was rather shy and not greatly interested in general society. Indeed he was so devoted to his work as to be almost a recluse. He was very highly esteemed and admired by his colleagues on account of his scholarly achievements, but had comparatively little social intercourse with them. On the last day of his life he came from his home at Mt. Vernon to take up his appointed work at the University, and immediately upon his arrival complained of feeling unwell. He was escorted to his study where, before a physician could reach him, he died of acute indigestion. Death came upon him in the midst of his activity as a teacher and while his capacity for productive scholarship was at its height.

[*Who's Who in America*, 1916–17, and *Who's Who in New York*, 1918; obituaries in N. Y. papers, Dec. 14, 1917.]   H. N. F.

BOTTA, ANNE CHARLOTTE LYNCH (Nov. 11, 1815–Mar. 23, 1891), author, hostess to literati of New York, was the daughter of Patrick Lynch, who, having been imprisoned in England for taking part in the Irish Rebellion of 1798, refused allegiance to the British Government, and, in the first decade of the nineteenth century, came, an exile, to America. In Bennington, Vt., he carried on a dry-goods business, and married, in 1812, Charlotte Gray, daughter of Lieut.-Col. Gray, an officer in the Revolution. Anne Charlotte Lynch inherited from her father, who died when she was not yet four, an ardent, poetic temperament and keen perceptions; from her mother, energy and good judgment. What success she had in her career she attributed to learning early her own limitations. Diligent in her studies and artistic in her tastes, she found her power to do creative work less than her ability to stimulate others. People, she confessed, were the main passion of her life. As soon as she was able to make a home for her mother, after graduating from the Albany Female Academy in 1834, teaching for a time there and in a private family on Shelter Island, N. Y., she settled in Providence, R. I. Here, in her own household, she continued to educate young women, and her home became a gathering-place for the more cultured people of the community. After the year 1845, when Miss Lynch moved to New York, taking a position as teacher of English composition in the Brooklyn Academy for Women, her home in Waverley Place was a center for the most brilliant intellectual and artistic life of the city. Her personal charm, intuitive sympathies, and skill at repartee attracted to her modest drawing rooms, among others, Bryant, Horace Greeley, Margaret Fuller, Willis, and Poe; and hither came Bayard Taylor and R. H. Stoddard for their introduction to the literati of New York. In 1851 Miss Lynch spent a season in Washington while occupied in seeking through Congress delayed payment for her grandfather's military services. The paying of this debt by the Government brought easier circumstances to her and to her mother; and during 1853 she traveled abroad, giving some time to the study of art, particularly sculpture. In 1855 she married Prof. Vincenzo Botta [*q.v.*]. Guests from home and abroad were entertained at their residence at 25 West Thirty-seventh St., which Emerson called "the house of the expanding doors."

Anne C. Lynch Botta's literary work was for the most part poetic, elevated in theme, simple and direct in style, as in the sonnets, "The Ideal," "The Ideal Found," and "Vita Nuova." Her personal charm is more evident, perhaps, in occasional verse, such as "To Juliette's Twins." During her residence in Providence and later she contributed poetry to various magazines, particularly to the *Democratic Review.* Her collected poems, first published in 1849, went through three editions, but it could hardly be said that Mrs. Botta stood out with distinction from the host of sister poets composing verse in the same period. In 1860, however, she published *A Handbook of Universal Literature,* which has gone through many editions, and was a notable achievement for a woman of her time. She was modest in character, devoted to family and friends, and, according to Willis, "equally beloved of man and woman" (*Memoirs of Anne C. L. Botta,* p. 321). Slender, with dark hair and eyes, she bore herself with a certain grace and freedom of movement in harmony with a spirit of perpetual youth. A hostess, presiding with tact and simplicity over the first important salon in the history of American letters, she is a figure to be remembered in the social and literary life of the mid-nineteenth century.

[The chief source of information is *Memoirs of Anne C. L. Botta with Selections from her Correspondence and from her Writings in Prose and Poetry,* ed. by Vincenzo Botta (1893). A description of Mrs. Botta's salon may be found in Hervey Allen, *Israfel, The Life and Times of Edgar Allan Poe* (1926), pp. 677–80, and an appraisal of her literary work in Poe's *Works,* ed. by Stedman and Woodberry (1894–96), VIII, 124–26. Obituaries appeared in the *N. Y. Times* and *N. Y. Tribune,* Mar. 24, 1891.]   M. A. W.

BOTTA, VINCENZO (Nov. 11, 1818–Oct. 5, 1894), scholar, was born at Cavallermaggiore, Piedmont, Italy. Destined for the Church, he gave up all thought of the priesthood shortly after he entered upon his ecclesiastical studies. Graduating from the University of Turin, he taught philosophy at his *Alma Mater,* at Cuneo,

and then at Turin. From this university he received the degree of doctor of philosophy. In 1849 he was elected to the Sardinian Parliament where he rendered important service in the cause of Italian unity. In conjunction with Dr. Parola he was appointed in 1850 by the government to examine into the educational system of Germany. His report was printed by the State. In 1853 he came to the United States to study our public school methods and was so attracted by the country and the opportunities offered here that he settled in New York City and became a naturalized citizen. He was called to teach Italian language and literature in the University of the City of New York, a position he held until a few years before his death. In 1855 he was married to Miss Anne C. Lynch, brilliant daughter of an Irish exile. Possessing ample means they entertained generously and their "evenings" became widely known for the distinction and wit of the people assembled. During the Civil War Botta championed in the Italian press the cause of the Union. As 1865 approached when Italy and the world were to celebrate the six hundredth anniversary of the birth of Dante, he wrote as his contribution a book entitled *Dante as a Philosopher, Patriot and Poet* (1867), republished as *Introduction to the Study of Dante* (1886). The first portion of the volume is an excellent interpretation of the character and peculiar genius of the great Italian, and the latter part an analysis of the Divine Comedy, based upon Cary's translation. In 1871 Victor Emmanuel made Botta a Commander of the Order of the Crown of Italy, and in 1879 King Humbert sent him a gold medal struck in honor of his services to Italy in the United States. On the night of Oct. 3, 1894, in his seventy-sixth year, Botta fell from the window of his bedroom in the third story of his house and died two days after from his injuries. In his will he left his library and his own bust in marble to the University of the City of New York, and his works of art to the National Academy. His published works include *Public Instruction in Sardinia* (1858); *Discourse on the Life of Count Cavour* (1862); "An Historical Account of Modern Philosophy in Italy" in F. Ueberweg, *History of Philosophy* (1874); *Memoirs of Anne C. L. Botta* (1894).

[Obituaries at the time of Botta's death in the *N. Y. Tribune* and *N. Y. Times*; article by Ernest G. Sihler in *N. Y. Univ.* (1901).]   C. A. D.

BOTTINEAU, PIERRE (*c.* 1817–July 26, 1895), Chippewa half-breed, has been called the Kit Carson of the Northwest. He was born about 1817 in the Red River country near Bear Point at the mouth of the Turtle River, the son of Joseph Bottineau, a fur-trader of French ancestry, and Clear Sky, a Chippewa woman. He early gained experience as a guide on overland expeditions in the north country. In the winter of 1837 he conducted three members of the abortive James Dickson filibuster from the Selkirk settlement to Fort Snelling, a hazardous trip in the course of which two members of the party perished in a blizzard. At Fort Snelling Bottineau was employed by Henry H. Sibley, agent of the American Fur Company. In 1841 he settled on a claim in what is now the heart of St. Paul; five years later he bought a tract of land near the Falls of St. Anthony, later a part of Minneapolis.

From 1850 to 1870 Bottineau guided many civil and military expeditions into the West. These trips took him to the Red River Valley, to the mining country of Montana, to the Frazer River in British Columbia, and to other regions. In 1853 he served as guide for the Pacific Railroad expedition of Gov. Stevens, leading the party across the prairies, then swarming with buffaloes, as far as Fort Benton; and sixteen years later he led the directors of the Northern Pacific on a re-survey of this route. In 1862 he guided the James L. Fisk expedition to the Montana mining country; and the next year he was a trusted scout on Gen. Sibley's military expedition to the Missouri River in pursuit of hostile Sioux. During an attack on Fort Abercrombie he slipped out through the Sioux lines as a messenger to secure aid for the fort.

Bottineau lived until 1895, a quarter of a century after he retired from the active life of the frontier, most of this time at Red Lake in northwestern Minnesota. In addition to French and English, he spoke Chippewa and Sioux and is said to have had some knowledge of Mandan, Winnebago, Cree, and other dialects. He knew the wilderness, was a straight shooter and skilled hunter, and won wide fame for his daring exploits. Gov. Stevens said that he surpassed "all his class in truthfulness and great intelligence," had the "broadness of view of an engineer," and was "the great guide and voyageur of Minnesota" (Hazard Stevens, *The Life of Isaac Ingalls Stevens*, 1900, I, 310).

[Information on Bottineau may be found in diaries and other accounts of the various expeditions which he accompanied, as, for example, Isaac I. Stevens, "Narrative and Final Report of Explorations for a Route for a Pacific Railroad," *House Ex. Docs.*, *No. 56*, 36 Cong., 1 Sess.; the Martin McLeod Diary and the Samuel R. Bond Journal, in the manuscript division of the Minn. Hist. Soc.; and Daniel S. B. Johnston, "A Red River Townsite Speculation in 1857," in *Minn. Hist. Colls.*, XV, 411–34. An unpublished paper on Bottineau by Margareth Jorgensen is in the manuscript division of the Minn. Hist. Soc.]   T. C. B.

BOTTOME, MARGARET McDONALD (Dec. 29, 1827–Nov. 14, 1906), writer, organizer of the International Order of the King's Daughters and Sons, was the daughter of William and Mary (Willis) McDonald. Born in New York City, she spent her childhood in Brooklyn and was educated at Prof. Greenleaf's school, Brooklyn Heights. After her marriage to the Rev. Frank Bottome, a Methodist Episcopal clergyman, her interest in religious questions crystallized. For twenty-five years she gave informal talks on Bible subjects, and was an associate editor of the *Ladies' Home Journal*. Her most important work germinated from a gathering of nine women at her house on Jan. 13, 1886, met to talk over means of coöperation "for their own greater advancement in true Christian living and usefulness in practical good works." This small group became the nucleus of the King's Daughters, which subsequently added men to its membership and altered its name accordingly. Each of the original ten women organized another group and each member of each succeeding group did the same until in 1907 the membership was conservatively estimated at 500,000 in twenty-six states and five Canadian provinces. Men and boys were admitted in 1887, in 1889 the order was incorporated under the laws of New York state and in 1891 the term "International" was added to the name. For sixteen years the founder of the order conducted a department in the *Ladies' Home Journal* called "Mrs. Bottome's Heart to Heart Talks with the King's Daughters." The organization devoted itself chiefly to the development of character and training for Christian service. No sectarian lines were drawn. Groups of ten met to read and pray once a month. The work, which progressed quietly and without newspaper notice, included a variety of philanthropic undertakings, including work for the aged, for seamen, home and foreign missions, outings and vacations for women and children. Some notable institutions were established in the United States, among them the Frank Bottome Memorial Settlement in New York, the Day Nursery of Los Angeles, the National Junior Republic in Washington, D. C., the Gordon Rest for working women and girls in New England. University Extension work was done without a fee, professors and others giving their services. Mrs. Bottome herself was constantly writing for the *Silver Cross*, the monthly magazine of the order, which was first published in October 1888. In 1896 she was elected president of the Medical Missionary Society. She published *A Sunshine Trip: Glimpses of the Orient* in 1897, and from time to time other little books of a definite religious bent. *Heart to Heart Letters, being Extracts from the Letters of Margaret Bottome to a Son* (1909) was published after her death.

[*Who's Who in America*, 1906–07; "The Story of the King's Daughters," by Herbert O. McCrillis, *New Eng. Mag.*, Jan. 1907; *Silver Cross*, esp. Jan. 1907; obituaries in N. Y. papers, Nov. 15, 16, 1906.]

M. A. K.

BOTTS, CHARLES TYLER (1809–1884), editor, was born in Virginia (either at Dumfries or Fredericksburg) in the year 1809, the fourth son of Benjamin and Jane (Tyler) Botts. His father was a lawyer of some importance, being conspicuous in the trial of Aaron Burr, and had just moved to Richmond when both he and his wife perished in the great theatre fire of Dec. 26, 1811. Two of the sons thus left to the care of relatives were trained for the law; Charles Tyler and his older brother John Minor [*q.v.*], but both early abandoned it for the pursuit of agriculture. The older brother became a gentleman farmer mainly interested in politics, while Charles Tyler was more practical and cast his lot with that group who were struggling to restore "the exhausted fields of old Virginia." He took an active part in the work of the Henrico County agricultural society and showed a keen understanding of the problems faced. His interests were ever practical and the invention of an improved straw-cutting machine indicates the trend of his efforts (*American Agriculturist*, III, 309; *Cultivator*, X, 93). In 1841 he decided to establish a journal to help forward the new agriculture. Virginia's first agricultural paper, the *Virginia Planter*, had long ago ceased to exist and Edmund Ruffin's *Farmer's Register*, by refusing to accept advertising, had kept its price beyond the reach of common men. Botts now proposed "a plan . . . of publishing an agricultural paper at so small a price as to bring it within the reach of all . . . " and to present his materials "in simple and condensed style" which all could understand. The *Southern Planter* was a success from the beginning. Its suggestions, like its editor, were practical. Crop rotation and diversification, improved stock, the use of better machinery, together with the application of manure and other fertilizers, were advocated in and out of season. So sound were its policies that it alone of all the papers established in this period has survived, to boast to-day of being "the oldest agricultural journal in America."

In December 1846 Botts sold his paper to P. D. Bernard, remaining for a period as a contributor, but in 1848 catching the California fever and going to Monterey as keeper of United States naval stores. He soon drifted to the mines and,

after experiencing the lawless interregnum, was sent to the constitutional convention of 1849. Here he took a prominent part, opposing Gwinn, King, and others in their effort to extend the boundaries of California to include all the lands acquired from Mexico in an attempt to solve the entire question of slavery extension. To Botts this was but to entangle California's affairs with an insolvable national problem and thus destroy the hope of permanent local government. His wisdom is apparent to-day. Failing by one vote of being elected attorney-general in 1849, he became a member of a San Francisco law firm and in the years following was conspicuous in many important cases in the new state. He served as judge for a time in the Sacramento district and then returned to editorial work as publisher of the *Standard* at Sacramento. In 1861 he was appointed state printer. After the Civil War he returned to the South but was soon back in California practising law. His last years were spent in Oakland where he died in 1884. He was married to Margaret Marshal of Fredericksburg, Va.

[*Southern Planter*, Richmond, Va., 1841–46; Geo. A. Goode, *Va. Cousins* (1887); *Tyler's Quart. Hist. Mag.*, V, 252; H. W. Bancroft, *Works*, XIX, 725–26; XXIII, 271, 288; T. H. Hittell, *Hist. of Cal.*, II (1885), 769, 771, 789, 811.]

A. O. C.

BOTTS, JOHN MINOR (Sept. 16, 1802–Jan. 7, 1869), congressman, lawyer, author, the son of Jane (Tyler) Botts and Benjamin A. Botts, well-known Virginia lawyer, one of Aaron Burr's counsel, was born at Dumfries, Prince William County, Va. He lived for a short time at Fredericksburg, and was living in Richmond when both his parents perished in the Richmond Theatre fire in 1811. His education was confined to Latin, Greek, and mathematics, as taught in the private schools of the day. At eighteen, with six weeks' private study, he was admitted to the bar, and practised law with fair success for six years. He married Mary Whiting Blair and soon became a successful farmer. In 1831 he entered politics as a Whig candidate for the legislature, was elected in 1833, serving till 1839, when he entered Congress as a member from the Richmond district. He served till 1843, and again in the session 1847–49. Powerful in build, aggressive, often violent in speech, distrusting and denouncing the Democrats as a party of disunion led by John C. Calhoun, he was an outstanding opponent of every measure advocated by Democrats, standing with them only in opposition to Northern abolitionists. He ably supported John Quincy Adams in his fight against the "Gag Law" of 1836. He considered President Tyler guilty of treachery to the Whig party

in his bank veto and ever after opposed him un-
relentingly. Botts was a member of a select committee which criticized Tyler's veto of the Whig
Tariff, declaring that his reasons were "feeble,
inconsistent, and unsatisfactory" (*Congressional
Globe,* Aug. 16, 1842). He opposed strenuously
the annexation of Texas and the Mexican War,
but as chairman of the Committee on Military
Affairs, did his part in bringing the war to a
successful conclusion. He was a member of the
Virginia constitutional convention of 1850 which
struggled with the question of a mixed basis of
representation in proportion to the number of
white inhabitants and also to the taxes raised.
He advocated a division of the state at the Blue
Ridge Mountains with equal representation in
both houses of the legislature (*Journal of the
Constitutional Convention 1850–51,* Appendix).
Called to Washington by Henry Clay to aid in
the compromise measures of 1850 he played a
vital part in their passage. In 1852 he resumed
his law practise in Richmond, making it a matter of principle to take only cases in which he
was satisfied with the justice of his position. He
was a member of the Whig convention of 1852,
at Baltimore, casting the only vote from the
South for Scott on the first ballot. After the
collapse of the Whig party he was an unsuccessful candidate for Congress on the Know-Nothing
ticket in 1854.

From this time he gave himself to opposing
what he believed to be a conspiracy of certain
"Democratic bosses" to bring on secession rather
than yield control, and from this time his hostility to Jefferson Davis grew more intense. He
was especially violent in his characterization of
Gov. Wise, of Virginia, "The Unwise Henry
A.," asserting that the John Brown affair was
deliberately used to further the secession conspiracy. As a member of the reorganization
movement of 1859, against the Democrats, he
supported Goggin against Letcher for governor
of Virginia, and was considered as a presidential
nominee of the "Opposition" in 1860. He
claimed, in what was one of his greatest speeches,
at Lynchburg, October 1860, that the Democratic
party deliberately split in order to make inevitable the election of Lincoln and the success of
the secession plot (*Political Pamphlets, IV, No.
48,* Virginia State Library). Nominated for the
convention called in Virginia to decide on secession, and defeated, as he claimed, by fraud, he did
what he considered his greatest piece of work in
trying to prevent the secession of Virginia.
There followed the most disputed act of his life
when he said on the basis of personal knowledge
that President Lincoln offered through J. B.

Baldwin to stop the fleet which was about to sail
for Charleston if the Virginia convention would
adjourn *sine die.* This offer was not reported to
the convention and in his testimony before the
Reconstruction Committee, Feb. 10, 1866, Baldwin testified that no such offer had been made
(Botts, *Great Rebellion,* pp. 194–202). After the
passage of the Ordinance of Secession, Botts, believing that secession was now inevitable, wrote
a series of letters to Attorney-General Edward
Bates, at Washington, proposing a constitutional
amendment in accordance with which the Southern States could withdraw peacefully. With the
ratification of the action of the convention by the
people, Botts withdrew from public life to his
farm near Richmond, and rarely left his premises,
though he talked freely. On Mar. 1, 1862, President Davis proclaimed martial law in and near
Richmond, and before daybreak next morning
Botts was arrested and confined for eight weeks
in a negro jail. After the transfer of Benjamin,
secretary of war, whom Botts cordially hated, to
the State Department, Randolph, the new secretary of war, had him released on parole. In January 1863 he purchased a farm and located in
Culpeper County, entertaining officers of both
armies and suffering from depredations of soldiers of both armies. He was offered the nomination for United States Senator by the "Restored
Government" in 1864, but refused. In 1866 he
proposed a plan of reconstruction which was rejected. He presided over the organization meeting of the "Union Republican Party of Virginia"
at Alexandria, in May 1866, and opposed manhood suffrage strongly, but finally accepted it. He
led the Virginia delegation to the "Convention of
Southern Loyalists" at Philadelphia in 1866.
Representing the conservative element of the
Unionists, remembered as one of those who had
signed Jefferson Davis's bail bond, he lost control of the party to the radicals. Afterward to the
disappointment of his older friends he accepted
the radical position, was defeated for the constitutional convention by a conservative from his
own county, and for the last two years of his life
took no active part in politics.

[The chief source of authority for John Minor Botts
is his *Great Rebellion,* autobiographical to an extent,
started in 1861, and published with a voluminous appendix of speeches and letters in 1866. A short sketch
by Clyde C. Webster was published in the *Richmond
Coll. Hist. Papers,* I, No. 1, June 1915. A sketch written by his son-in-law, D. S. Lewis, and published in the
Spirit of the Valley (Harrisonburg, Va.), is out of
print. The collected Political Pamphlets in the Va.
State Lib. contain his outstanding speeches. The files
of the Richmond *Whig,* which in general supported his
politics, are also in the State Lib.]   J. E. W—y.

BOUCHER, JONATHAN (Mar. 12, 1737/8–
Apr. 27, 1804), Loyalist, Anglican clergyman,

was born in the village of Blencogo in the county of Cumberland, England, the third child of James and Ann Barnes Boucher, who kept an alehouse. In after years he recalled rather bitterly the penury and hardships of his boyhood; but the father, though a ne'er-do-well, had native ability and some education, and eked out a livelihood as village schoolmaster. From him Boucher learned to read and spell, so that he could go to school and begin the study of Latin at the age of six. Both parents desired to make a scholar out of the lad. He was first sent to a little free-school at Bromfield and then to a school at Wigton where at sixteen he himself did some teaching in a night school. Having found his *métier,* he became two years later an usher in a school at Saint Bees kept by the Rev. John James. This kindly and generous master did much for the further education of his usher and finally procured for him a position as tutor to a gentleman's sons at Port Royal, in Virginia. Thither Boucher sailed in April 1759.

He was at first somewhat disdainful of his new surroundings, finding the manners and conversation of the Virginians "almost in everything the very opposite to my taste" (Letter to Rev. James in *Maryland Historical Magazine,* VIII, 4). That he never did find himself wholly at one with his associates in the colonies was, in a large measure, the cause of his later misfortunes. He was soon living beyond his means, beginning an indebtedness to Mr. James which was not discharged for many years. To better his fortunes, he returned to England in 1762 to take orders, having been assured of the vacant rectory in Hanover Parish. He was ordained without any further preparation and returned the following summer. Subsequently he removed to the rectory of St. Mary's in Caroline County, where he bought a small plantation and took nearly thirty boys as pupils, "most of them the sons of persons of the first condition in the colony" (*Reminiscences,* p. 41). Among these boys was "Jacky" Custis, the son of Mrs. Martha Washington, for whose proper training his step-father, Col. George Washington, was much concerned (*Writings of Washington,* Ford edition, II, 257). Thus began an acquaintanceship which Boucher improved to the utmost. In 1770 he was appointed to the rectory of Saint Anne's in Annapolis, which he had solicited for several years. Thither he removed with some of his slaves and two of his pupils, one of whom was Master John Parke Custis.

Annapolis was then, in Boucher's opinion, "the genteelest town in North America." He took an active part in its social life; patronized the local theatre; "wrote some verses on one of

the actresses and a prologue or two"; became the first president of the Homony Club, a literary organization; and enjoyed an intimacy with Gov. Eden and his family. As chaplain of the lower house of the Assembly, he had no little influence in shaping legislation, according to his own account (*Reminiscences,* p. 92); but he was unable to prevent a reduction in the stipend of the clergy. His efforts in their behalf, however, and his persistent advocacy of the establishment of an American Episcopacy, were rewarded by King's College of New York with the degree of Master of Arts. When the desirable rectory of Queen Anne's Parish in Prince George's County fell vacant, it was bestowed "unsolicited" upon him by Gov. Eden. Shortly after, he married a Miss Eleanor Addison who brought him a comfortable dowry. He bought a plantation on the Potomac and prepared to settle down to a comfortable existence, when he became involved in the controversy of the colonies with the mother country.

Ever a firm supporter of established authority, Boucher regarded as seditious all the various extra-legal organizations, which the colonists devised to resist the acts of Parliament. When the provincial convention proclaimed a solemn fast-day by way of protest, he announced his intention of preaching against active resistance, but was forbidden to enter his pulpit by a body of armed men. From this time on, believing his life in danger, he never preached without a pair of loaded pistols lying on the cushion (*Ibid.,* p. 113). He was under constant surveillance by the local committee of safety; grew more and more unpopular; and was burned in effigy. Finally, fearing the worst, he and his wife abandoned their home and property and departed for England in September 1775.

Boucher never returned. Friends procured for him the curacy of Paddington and a pension from the government, while he added to his income by tutoring and writing for journals. During the last nineteen years of his life he was vicar of Epsom. He never recovered his property in Maryland, but he shared in the compensation which the royal government allotted to loyalists. In 1797 he published thirteen discourses preached in America, with a lengthy preface under the title *A View of the Causes and Consequences of the American Revolution*—a book of considerable historical interest. He spent the latter part of his life making a glossary of obsolete and provincial words, a part of which was published after his death as *A Supplement to Dr. Johnson's Dictionary of the English Language* (1807). Another edition with the title

Boucher's Glossary (1832–33) contains a discursive introduction on philology.

[Boucher's autobiography was published in 1925 by his grandson Jonathan Bouchier under the title *Reminiscences of an Am. Loyalist 1738–1789.* It should be supplemented by "Letters of Rev. Jonathan Boucher" printed in vols. VI–IX of the *Md. Hist. Mag.,* and by *Letters of Jonathan Boucher to Geo. Washington* (1889), ed. by W. C. Ford.]   A—n.J.

BOUCICAULT, DION (Dec. 26, 1820–Sept. 18, 1890), dramatist, actor, was born in Dublin. His mother was Anne Darley Boursiquot, sister of George Darley, poet, who went from Dublin to London and was admired by Carlyle. She married Samuel Smith Boursiquot, a Dublin merchant of French ancestry, but was divorced from him in 1819. Dion was apparently the natural son of Dionysius Lardner, then boarding at her house, whom Dion in later life physically resembled. Lardner wrote popular science articles and was a man of some ability. He supervised and paid for Dion's education, and the boy was named after him "Dionysius Lardner" Boursiquot. Dion went to school in England and entered London University, but experience in school plays had given him such a passion for the theatre that in 1837 he got jobs acting in provincial theatres, under the name of Lee Moreton, and in 1840 came back to London determined to shine as author and actor. The first play he submitted to Charles Mathews and Madame Vestris at Covent Garden was rejected, but a second was accepted. This was *London Assurance,* based in part, at least, on a suggestion from John Brougham [*q.v.*]. Produced Mar. 4, 1841, it was a striking success, Mrs. Nisbet as Lady Gay Spanker being particularly popular. It is said Boucicault wrote the part in for her after the original MS. had been completed. The play was burlesqued by Thackeray (*Sketches and Travels*) but coming in an age of inflated rhetorical drama it seemed to have a freshness and high spirits very welcome to the people, and it foreshadowed to some slight extent the modern drama. But Boucicault was not a conscious reformer, and his next plays were either imitations of eighteenth-century English styles still persisting on the stage or adaptations from the French. He turned them out in rapid succession. Lack of international copyright made it cheaper for managers to put on French adaptations than to pay for original plays, and Boucicault, to live in the style he had adopted, had to do a vast amount of hack work. From 1844 to 1848 he was in France, where he married a French woman who died while they were on a tour of the Alps. Boucicault said she fell over a precipice. In 1848 he returned to London and became an assistant to Charles Kean at the Princess's Theatre, for whom he adapted *Pauline* (1851) and *The Corsican Brothers* (1852) from Dumas, and *Louis XI* (1853) from Delavigne. He also made other adaptations, now quite forgotten.

In September 1853 he sailed for New York, where many of his plays were already familiar. On a different boat sailed Agnes Robertson (born in Edinburgh, 1833), an actress and singer also from Kean's company. It was generally assumed that she had married Boucicault. She made her début at Burton's Theatre, N. Y., Oct. 22, 1853, in *The Young Actress,* a musical interlude adapted by Boucicault, and was immediately a sensational success. In Boston the following January crowds trailed her through the streets and she played for nine weeks to capacity business. A tour followed, Boucicault acting with her. In 1856 they were back in New York. Pleased with America, and quick to adapt himself to new conditions, Boucicault turned out *The Poor of New York,* "a superficial but graphic picture" of the panic of 1857, and it had a long run at Wallack's. The next year he wrote *Jessie Brown, or the Relief of Lucknow,* with his wife as Jessie and himself as the Sepoy villain. Again a great success. The same year (1858) he opened a theatre in Washington, in partnership with William Stuart, and the next year, with Stuart, directed the Winter Garden in New York, for which he "adapted from the French" a play that turned out to be simply a dramatization of Dickens's *Cricket on the Hearth.* He called this play *Dot,* and assigned the rôle of Caleb Plummer to Joseph Jefferson, who records in his *Autobiography* (p. 209) how much Boucicault helped him to act it. Presently he made a stage version of *Nicholas Nickleby,* and then followed (1859) one of his greatest successes, and something of a milestone in the American theatre—*The Octoroon,* a problem play about slavery. The subject was gunpowder, of course, but Boucicault escaped offending either side (see Jefferson's *Autobiography,* pp. 213–15). Possibly that is not the highest merit in a problem play. Boucicault next formed an alliance with Laura Keene, and produced in 1860 a stage version of Gerald Griffin's Irish novel, *The Collegians.* This play, *The Colleen Bawn,* was the first of a long series of Irish comedy dramas. He had tapped a new vein, and one in which he worked with more sincerity than in any other. On this play, perhaps, and on *Arrah-na-Pogue* (1864), *The O'Dowd* (1873), and *The Shaughraun* (1874) his fame as a dramatist now largely rests.

Boucicault returned to London in 1862 and in

1865 made the version of *Rip Van Winkle* used by Jefferson. He remained in London for ten years, then returned to the United States and continued to write, act and produce plays here till his death in 1890. But after *The Shaughraun* either his powers declined or public taste changed, and his fortunes steadily sank. In 1885 he went to Australia and there married Louise Thorndyke. Miss Robertson at once sued for and obtained a divorce. At the time of his death he was teaching in a school of acting in New York for $50 a week. Boucicault's talent was that of a stage manager and dramatic technician rather than that of a sincere creative artist. He had a fatal facility. He wrote or adapted 132 plays, an average of much more than two a year, seeking always immediate popularity. He also originated the system of casting a play entirely in New York and taking the whole company around the country, thus inaugurating the so-called "long run" system, and sounding the knell of the older stock companies. Fond of good living, a gay, careless spender, his money went as fast as it came. He had a broad, bald forehead, a delicate, white skin, a Celtic wit, and as actor excelled in parts, especially Irish parts, calling for high spirits, dash, and a flavor of romantic tenderness. It may justly be said that more than any other one man he kept the American drama lively and popular during the mid-nineteenth century, while waiting the birth of a realism he was not quite artist enough to bring about.

[Townsend Walsh, *The Career of Dion Boucicault* (1915); Geo. Wm. Curtis, remarks on Boucicault's Irish drama in the "Easy Chair," *Harper's Mag.*, July, 1875; *North Am. Rev.*, Sept. 1877, and scattered issues during the next twelve years, containing Boucicault's own articles on the art of playwriting; Wm. Winter, *Other Days* (1908); Montrose J. Moses, *Famous Actor-Families in America* (1906), pp. 115–40.]   W.P.E.

BOUCK, WILLIAM C. (Jan. 7, 1786–Apr. 19, 1859), governor of New York, was of German ancestry, his great-grandfather having been one of the first of a company of German Palatines to settle in the Schoharie Valley beyond the Helderbergs. William Bouck, William C.'s grandfather, was the first male child born of white parents in the valley, and it was he who established the old Bouck farm in Schoharie County on which the future governor was born. The latter's father was Christian Bouck and his mother before her marriage was Margaret Borst who, like her husband, was a descendant of one of the first settlers of the Schoharie district. Bouck's father, a man of abundant means, planned to give him an extensive schooling but the demands of the farm, the scarcity of labor, and the habit of frugality so characteristic of the German pioneer frustrated this plan and the boy did not get beyond the district school. "Until I was twenty-two years of age," he wrote, "no common laborer on my father's farm did more work than myself either in clearing land or in the harvest field. Often have I gone to the plough before daylight, and from it after dark." In 1807 he was married to Catherine, daughter of Jacob Lawyer, by whom he had eleven children. He early became interested in politics and, like the majority of farmers of his day, was an ardent and zealous adherent to the principles expounded by Thomas Jefferson. During his lifetime he was an undeviating Democrat and a loyal party-man. Before his election as governor he held several offices including town-clerk, supervisor, sheriff, and state assemblyman. His opposition to De Witt Clinton and his lack of confidence in Clinton's views on internal improvements were perhaps the chief reasons why Bouck was at first skeptical about the wisdom of building the Erie and Champlain canals. He was one of the first of the unconvinced, however, to change his mind and to give the Clintonian proposal whole-hearted support. In 1821 he was named as canal commissioner and assigned to superintend construction of the most difficult section of the Erie Canal—that from Brockport to its western terminus. He was also selected to take charge of the work on the Cayuga & Seneca, the Crooked Lake, the Chemung, and the Chenango canals. After serving nineteen years as canal commissioner he was removed by the Whig legislature in 1840 for political reasons.

His removal, if anything, increased his popularity with the people of the state, and in the autumn of 1840 he was unanimously nominated as the Democratic candidate for governor, but was defeated by Gov. Seward by a small majority of about 5,000 votes. His party became seriously split into two factions—the conservatives or Hunkers and the radicals or Barnburners—largely over the allied questions of internal improvements and state finances. Bouck, a leader of the former faction, was again unanimously nominated for the governorship in 1842 and was elected by a majority of about 22,000. From the outset, his administration was a stormy one despite his efforts to conciliate and harmonize the conflicting party factions. Toward its close he was obliged to call out the militia to protect Columbia County from the riots incited by the "Anti-Renters" (Smith, *post*, II, 311). Failing of renomination, he returned to Schoharie County where he was chosen as a delegate to the constitutional convention of 1846. While the convention was in session he was appointed by President Polk federal assistant treasurer in the City of New

York. He discharged the duties of this office until removed by President Taylor in May 1849. Once again he retired to his Schoharie farm where he died at the age of seventy-three. He was regular and frugal in his habits and was blessed through life with good health. The official honors bestowed upon him he owed not so much to the backing of powerful friends as to his native talent and strength of character.

[John S. Jenkins, *Lives of the Governors of the State of N. Y.* (1851), pp. 689–721; Ray B. Smith, ed., *Hist. of the State of N. Y., Political and Governmental* (1922), vol. II, ch. XVII; Chas. Z. Lincoln, "The Governors of New York," *Proc. N. Y. Hist. Ass.*, IX, 87; Jeptha R. Simms, *Hist. of Schoharie County and Border Wars of N. Y.* (1845); *N. Y. Times*, Apr. 21, 1859.]

H. J. C.

BOUDINOT, ELIAS (May 2, 1740–Oct. 24, 1821), Revolutionary statesman, was the fourth of the same name in direct descent, and has been often confused with his younger brother, Elisha (1749–1819), and with this brother's son, Elias E. (1791–1863). Driven out of Marans, Rochelle, France, by the revocation of the Edict of Nantes (1685), Elias Boudinot the first, a prosperous merchant, elder in the Reformed Church, Seigneur de Cressy, went to London, thence to New York about 1687, joined in protest against Leisler's maladministration, bought extensive lands in Bergen County, N. J., and died in New York in 1702. Elias the second (1674–1719) married Marie Catherine Carrée, and through their daughters was built up a remarkable matrimonial network of the Boudinot family with the Ricketts, Chetwood, Chandler, Clayton, Vergereau, Tennent, and other families noted in colonial law, church, and business affairs. Elias the third (1706–70), postmaster and silversmith of Princeton, married Catherine Williams of Antigua, British West Indies; their daughter, Annis, married Richard Stockton, signer of the Declaration of Independence, father-in-law of Benjamin Rush and grandfather of Richard Rush. Elias the fourth, born in Philadelphia, married, Apr. 21, 1762, the signer's sister, Hannah Stockton (July 21, 1736–Oct. 28, 1808), whom he had long courted, and urged to "press forward toward a heavenly goal." Their courting names "Eugenia" and "Narcissus" were in use thirty years later. Neither a classical academy education, baptism by George Whitefield, nor early and arduous study of law, could mar the serenity of Elias's temper or the poise of his good sense. Licensed counsellor and attorney-at-law, 1760, sergeant-at-law, 1770, he became a leader in his profession (hon. LL.D. Yale, 1790) and a trustee of Princeton (1772–1821). Two fellowships founded by him are extant there. He is described as tall, hand-

some, "every way prepossessing," elegant, eloquent and emotional. He could use tears to good effect but his advice to his only child, Susan Vergereau (1764–1854), married to William Bradford, attorney-general (1794–5), was: "take the world as you find it" and convert even prejudices to usefulness.

Supporting gentry rule, legal government, and property rights, he was a conservative Whig in politics but followed the liberal trend of his Colony and his connections, and entered on revolution chiefly by opposing Gov. William Franklin. On June 11, 1774, he became a member of the Committee of Correspondence for Essex County, N. J., but felt a "firm dependence in the mother country essential." In March 1775, with William Livingston, he hurried the New Jersey Assembly into approving the proceedings of the first Continental Congress at Philadelphia (*New Jersey Archives*, ser. 1, vol. X, p. 575). In August 1775 he, then a member of the New Jersey Provincial Congress, procured from Elizabethtown eight or ten half-casks of powder for Washington's army at Cambridge, the forces there being down to eight rounds per man. In April 1776 at New Brunswick he quashed Dr. John Witherspoon's queer attempt to rush New Jersey into declaring for independence. On June 6, 1777, by commission dated May 15, Congress appointed him commissary-general of prisoners, with the pay and rations of a colonel, five deputies, and full power even to altering the directions of the board of war. Thus he was drawn into "the boisterous noisy, fatiguing unnatural and disrelishing state of War and slaughter" (to his wife July 22, 1777). This he did, not only to "be of some service to the Prisoners" but also "to watch the Military and to preserve the Civil Rights of my Fellow Citizens" (*Journal*, p. 67). He organized the care of the American prisoners despite great difficulties, and put in $30,000 of his own money to do it. On William Duer's insistence he recovered most of this despite New England opposition. Washington offered to stand half the loss, corrected Boudinot's judgment as to treason and military tactics, and relied on him to reconcile Steuben to other officers and for certain secret service information. Their relations were close and, on Boudinot's part, extremely reverential.

On Nov. 20, 1777, he was elected delegate to Congress, and wrote of Philadelphia, "This City is enough to kill a horse" (to his wife July 9, 1778). He did not attend Congress until July 7, 1778, and then only on Washington's insistence that it was his only chance to be reimbursed in "hard money," *i.e.*, out of the cash captured from Burgoyne (*Journal*, p. 69). Rechosen to Congress until 1784, president Nov. 4, 1782, acting also as secretary of foreign affairs from June 16, 1783, he served on over thirty committees and usually as chairman, while his social grace and legal acumen were invaluable in dealing with representatives of other countries. He signed the treaties of peace with Great Britain and of alliance with the French king, the proclamations for cessation of hostilities, thanksgiving, discharging the army, and removing the Congress to Princeton, and presided at that session in Nassau Hall when Washington was thanked for his services "in establishing the freedom and independence of your country." His benevolent good sense went far to neutralize the acidities of our peace commissioners abroad.

As a strong Federalist he helped ratify the Constitution in New Jersey and conducted Washington into New York for the first inauguration. Elected to the House of Representatives in the first, second and third Congresses, he fathered many essential measures and took part in practically all important debates. In the great assault of February 1793 on Hamilton's conduct of the federal Treasury, Boudinot led the defense. In 1795 he succeeded David Rittenhouse as director of the United States Mint and reorganized the enterprise with "great industry as well as ability" (J. R. Snowden, *A Description of the Medals of Washington*, 1861, p. 185). Some of his rules are still in force. His technical skill and his care for the employees are shown by his letters to Jefferson of June 16, 1801, and Apr. 17, 1802. He resigned July 1, 1805, to study the Bible at his home in Burlington, N. J. His religious works, *The Age of Revelation* (1801), *Memoirs of the Life of the Rev. William Tennent* (1807), *The Second Advent* (1815), *A Star in the West* (1816), may be read by those curious to do so. His guiding thought was "I am satisfied that the grace of God is not confined to Sect or Party." He was the first counsellor named by the United States Supreme Court (Feb. 5, 1790) and seems never to have lost either his taste for the practise of his profession or his acute and sensible interest in public affairs. Save when absent on duty, he spent his entire life in New Jersey, living successively at Princeton, Elizabethtown, and Burlington. His will, July 3, 1821, disposed of a large property, including several tracts of wild land in Pennsylvania, to innumerable dear ones and good causes. He seems to have had few quarrels, and no enemies.

[Boudinot's letters and papers have not been published. His *Journal* (1894) deals only with selected "American Events during the Revolutionary War" but affords interesting side-lights on the man. *The Life, Public Services, Addresses and Letters of Elias Bou-*

dinot (1896) by a collateral descendant, Jane J. Boudinot, includes much material but the selection and arrangement are not impressive. This is the chief source. His public activities are reflected in the *Journals of the Continental Congress*, the *Annals* of the first, second, and third Congresses, and in the published letters of leading men of the period.]

W. L. W—y.

BOUDINOT, ELIAS (*c.* 1803–June 22, 1839), Indian editor, was born in Georgia among his people, the Cherokees, who, due to contact with the whites, were rapidly becoming civilized. His Indian name was Galagina (pronounced Killke-nah). In 1818 he, with two other young Cherokees, was sent by the missionaries to the mission school at Cornwall, Conn. While there he took the name of the benefactor of the school, Elias Boudinot [*q.v.*]. Meanwhile George Guess (Sikwaji, or Sequoyah), a young man of Cherokee-German blood, who could not read, invented a Cherokee syllabary of eighty-six characters. This was immediately followed by a great increase of interest in Indian education and in 1824 the National Council decided to establish a newspaper, the *Cherokee Phœnix,* and employed young Boudinot as editor at $300 a year. The greater part of the paper was printed in English, but a fourth or more was in Cherokee and it was very popular among the natives. In his editorial work Boudinot was assisted by the Rev. Samuel A. Worcester, a medical missionary. The paper appeared weekly, except for occasional omissions, from Feb. 21, 1828, until October 1835, when it was suppressed by the Georgia authorities for unfavorable remarks about the attitude of the state (Rachel C. Eaton, *John Ross and the Cherokee Indians,* 1921, pp. 33, 37, 57). In 1833 the United Brethren's Missionary Society published in Cherokee characters at New Echota a book by Boudinot called *Poor Sarah or the Indian Woman.* From 1823 until his death Boudinot collaborated with Worcester in translating several books of the New Testament into Cherokee. In 1831 the Council elected John Ross, who was bitterly opposed to removal to the West, chief executive for an indefinite term. This seemed to John Ridge, cousin to Boudinot, a death blow to his own political ambitions and he gradually, under pressure and persuasion from government agents, became an advocate of removal. In 1835 Boudinot joined him and a few others in signing, without any authority, a treaty for removal, and on June 22, 1839, after arrival in the Indian Territory, Boudinot was treacherously murdered in revenge for his part in the transaction. He was twice married: in 1826 to Harriet Ruggles Gold, who bore him six children, and, after her death in 1836, to Delight Sargent, who died without issue.

[Bureau of Am. Ethnology, Bull. 30, I, pp. 162–63; Wilson Lumpkin, The Removal of the Cherokee Indians from Ga. (1907); L. L. Knight, Georgia and Georgians (1917) and Georgia's Landmarks, Memorials, and Legends (1913), vol. I. Incomplete files of the Cherokee Phœnix may be found in the N. Y. State Lib., another more nearly complete in the British Museum.]   D. Y. T.

BOUDINOT, ELIAS CORNELIUS (Aug. 1, 1835–Sept. 27, 1890), Indian lawyer, was born in the Cherokee Nation, near the site of Rome, Ga. He was the son of Elias Boudinot [q.v.] 1803–39 and Harriet Ruggles Gold, whom Elias had married at Cornwall, Conn. On the assassination of his father (1839) all the children were sent to Cornwall and distributed among Harriet Gold's sisters, Elias Cornelius going to Manchester, Vt. He first tried engineering and spent one year with a railroad in Ohio, but gave that up and settled in Fayetteville, Ark. Here he studied law under A. M. Wilson and was admitted to the bar in 1856. While practising law he gave a part of his time to editorial work on the *Arkansian*. In 1860 he was made chairman of the Democratic state central committee and went to Little Rock, where he became chief editorial writer for the *True Democrat*. In 1861 he was elected secretary of the secession convention. After the state seceded he went to the Indian Territory, where he helped Stand Waitie raise an Indian regiment, in which he rose to the rank of lieutenant-colonel. In 1863 he was elected delegate for the territory to the Confederate Congress and served until the end of the war. After the war he took part in restoring peaceful relations between the Cherokees and the United States. Soon after this he started a tobacco factory in the Territory, but in 1868 it was seized by the government under an act of that year. Boudinot then spent many years in Washington, trying to recover his property and working for the good of the Indians. The court of claims finally allowed a part of his claim. He was an ardent advocate of education for the Indians, of breaking up the tribal relations, and of allotting the lands in severalty. For this he incurred the enmity of his tribe, but lived to see his policy put partially into effect and to regain the good will of his people. He was a man of striking appearance, a very forceful speaker, a good writer, and an amateur musician of no mean attainments. In Washington he became acquainted with many distinguished men. There he married Clara Minear, and brought her to Fort Smith in 1885. He practised law, gave entertainments, and farmed in the Territory until his death.

[E. C. Starr, Hist. of Cornwall, Conn. (1926), pp. 156, 378; S. W. Harman, Hell on the Border (1898);

Ark. Gazette (Little Rock), Sept. 28, 1890. A portrait of him appears in In Memoriam: Elias Cornelius Boudinot (n. p., n. d.).]   D. Y. T.

BOULIGNY, DOMINIQUE (c. 1771–Mar. 5, 1833), legislator, born in New Orleans, La., was the son of Francisco Bouligny and Marie Louise le Senechal d'Auverville. The family was of Italian origin and was founded in Milan in the fourteenth century by Mateo Atendolo, the first count of Bolognini. The family name was changed in its spelling from Bolognini to Bouligny in the early seventeenth century when a member of the family, then in the service of the Spanish king, was captured by the French and taken to Marseilles. In the early eighteenth century, Joseph Bouligny, the progenitor of the Louisiana Bouligny family, settled in Alicante, Spain. His son, Francisco, the father of Dominique, was born there in 1736 and came to Louisiana in 1769 with O'Reilly, the first Spanish governor of Louisiana. Dominique Bouligny attained considerable political prominence in Louisiana in the first three decades of the nineteenth century. He was elected to the first legislature of the Territory of Orleans in 1805 as one of the ten representatives of the parish of Orleans. In 1813 he was one of a number of New Orleans citizens who subscribed $10,000 to secure the safety of the state during the war that was then going on between the United States and England. In the following year he was chosen by the people of New Orleans as one of a committee of nine to counteract the effects of an appeal which an English army officer by the name of Col. Nicholls had issued from Pensacola, calling upon the people of Louisiana who were of Spanish, French, Italian, and British descent to rebel against the "usurpation" of the Americans in their country. The committee issued a stirring address to the people, urging them to remain loyal to the American government. Bouligny was elected to the United States Senate in 1824 to succeed Henry Johnson who had been elected governor of Louisiana, and he served in that body until 1829. He married Arthemise Le Blanc, and on his death in New Orleans he left six sons and six daughters. Many of his descendants are still living in New Orleans.

[Grace King, Creole Families of New Orleans (1921), ch. XVIII, deals with the Bouligny family and is the best source of information concerning its history. There are scattered references in Chas. Gayarré, Hist. of La., vol. IV (1866), and Alcée Fortier, Hist. of La., vol. III (1904).]   E. M. V.

BOUNETHEAU, HENRY BRINTNELL (Dec. 14, 1797–Jan. 31, 1877), miniature painter, was born in Charleston, S. C., son of Peter Bounetheau, an officer of Huguenot descent who fought in the American Revolution. Little is known of his life except that he devoted his entire time to art for a period only and remained to the end a business man who spent a portion of each day painting excellent miniatures. He managed to produce a considerable amount of work and although his likenesses never went above a high respectable average, he will be remembered as a competent craftsman who carried on the tradition of his fellow townsman, Charles Fraser. At a first glance, indeed, his miniatures might be taken easily for those painted by Fraser during his later years. The miniatures of both men are generally rectangular in shape. Both men posed the sitter in about the same position. Both frequently introduced a conventional column in the background. Fraser's work, however, became more vigorous and he painted with dashing, straight strokes as he grew older, while Bounetheau from beginning to end generally used an effective method of stippling.

Bounetheau had the advantage of Fraser in his early training. Fraser while still a boy was condemned to the study of law whereas Bounetheau studied art early in life. About the age of sixteen, he went into business and worked for the firm of Dart & Spear. His reliability, accuracy, and general personal integrity were recognized by his fellow citizens and he later became an officer in the Bank of Charleston. After leaving the firm of Dart & Spear, he went into business for himself, becoming a partner in the firm of Hamilton, Son & Company. It is not known for what reason, but it is a matter of fact that the partnership was dissolved at the end of two years. Bounetheau then took "to miniature painting for support, and displayed so much skill that his pictures soon became the rage," according to a newspaper obituary. He finally became the chief accountant for the C. N. Hubert Company, holding this position for the rest of his life. He was married to Julia Clarkson Dupré, and died in Charleston, S. C. Their son, Henry Dupré Bounetheau, lost his life in the great fire at Jacksonville, Fla., 1901, in which, also, many miniatures by his father were burned.

But in spite of this disaster there still remain numerous miniatures by Bounetheau. Among the portraits which he painted, two, those of Charles C. Pinckney and Nathaniel Greene, were engraved, the first being engraved by Longacre and the second by A. B. Durand. Other portraits by Bounetheau are those of Charles Austin Pringle, Dr. T. L. Ogier, Henry Heyward Manigault, William Ravenel, and the Hon. James R. Pringle.

[The principal source of information concerning Bounetheau is the extended obituary notice in the *News and Courier* (Charleston, S. C.), Feb. 1, 1877. A summary of this account is given in Theodore Bolton, *Early Am. Portrait Painters in Miniature* (1921), where seventeen of Bounetheau's miniatures are listed and one of these, the portrait of Henry H. Manigault, is reproduced. The engravings after Bounetheau's portraits mentioned in the text above appeared in Jas. Herring and Jas. B. Longacre, *The Natl. Portrait Gallery of Distinguished Americans* (1834–39).]   T. B.

BOUQUET, HENRY (1719–Sept. 2, 1765), British officer, was born of a good French Protestant family at Rolle, Canton Vaud, Switzerland. In 1736 he entered the service of the States General of Holland as a cadet in the regiment of Constant, and two years later was commissioned as lieutenant. During the war of the Austrian Succession he served the King of Sardinia, and displayed such coolness and resourcefulness in action that the Prince of Orange engaged him as captain-commandant, with the rank of lieutenant-colonel, in a newly-formed regiment of Swiss Guards. In 1748 he accompanied the officers who received from the French the evacuated forts in the Low Countries, and shortly after traveled through France and Italy with Lord Middleton, from whom he acquired the foundations of his excellent knowledge of English, which he wrote with grace and precision. On his return he devoted himself to a thorough study of his chosen profession of arms, especially in the mathematical branches, and throughout his career continued to enjoy scientific discussion.

In the fall of 1755 James Prevost, supported by the urging of Joseph Yorke, British minister at The Hague, succeeded in gaining Bouquet's consent to take the lieutenant-colonelcy of the first battalion in the newly-planned Royal American Regiment (later the King's Royal Rifle Corps), and in the spring of 1756 Bouquet left for North America, where he contributed to the remarkable recruiting success the regiment enjoyed in 1756 among the Germans of Pennsylvania, and had his first experiences of the unwarlike but obstinate temper of the Quakers, which he never ceased to impugn. The center of the quartering dispute in Philadelphia in the winter of 1756, he met greater resistance in quartering regulars in 1757 in Charleston, S. C., where he commanded a small force of provincials, Royal Americans, and, later, Montgomery's Highlanders. This was the only independent command assigned him by a commander-in-chief during the war.

Promoted to be colonel in America only in January 1758, he served as second under Brigadier John Forbes in the weary expedition against Fort Duquesne, and his rare patience and tact were largely responsible for overcoming the delays of provincials and the uncertainties of transportation, for building new forts, and for cutting through western Pennsylvania the great highway known as "Forbes' Road," which resulted in the evacuation of Fort Duquesne by the French. His foreign birth prevented Amherst from giving him the command in the west at Forbes's death (*Northcliffe Collection,* Ottawa, 1926, p. 114), and he served for the remainder of the war under Stanwix and Monckton, occupied chiefly in the supervision and strengthening of the western forts, Pitt, Venango, and Presqu'isle. He was commissioned colonel by brevet in 1762, and was naturalized by Maryland and by the Supreme Court of Pennsylvania. Neither the attractions of domestic life upon his estate at Long Meadow, Md., nor the importunities of his many warm American friends could lure him from the army during the war (*Pennsylvania Magazine of History and Biography,* III, 121–143), and leave of absence was denied him in 1761. He continued, therefore, to exploit to the full his long experience on the frontier, by adapting the discipline of European armies to the exigencies of wilderness warfare, and by drilling his own first battalion in the principles of open-order combat and extreme mobility of action.

In Pontiac's conspiracy he proved the worth of his methods. In 1763 he marched a small army of Royal Americans and Highlanders towards Fort Pitt, and at Edgehill, within a short distance of Braddock's fatal field, repulsed a considerable number of Delawares and Shawnees. The following day, Aug. 6, the Indians again attacked at Bushy Run, and Bouquet, drawing up his troops in circle to protect his convoy, lured them from cover by the feigned retreat of one segment, and crushed them by a bayonet charge when they rushed into the gap. Henceforth the Indians respected him, perceiving, as not many contemporaries did, that he was the most brilliant leader of light infantry the war produced, and incomparably in advance of the military practise of the day. The following year he commanded the southern of the two expeditions sent to pacify the Indians, led a small force of provincials and regulars to the forks of the Muskingum, and, by an admirable mixture of firmness and justice, forced the surrender of all prisoners in Indian hands and concluded a general peace. Publicly thanked by the king in general orders, and by the assemblies of the southern provinces, he received the unexpected rank of brigadier in 1765, and the command of the southern district. At Pensacola, the same year, fever carried him away prematurely.

[The sole authority for Bouquet's European career is C. G. F. Dumas's biographical preface to the French edition (1769) of Wm. Smith's *Hist. Account of the Expedition against the Ohio Indians in 1764* (1765) reprinted in *Ohio Valley Hist. Ser., No. 1* (1868). The chief sources for his American career are the thirty manuscript volumes in the British Museum, transcribed for the Canadian archives, and calendared in Douglas Brymner's *Report on Canadian Arch.* (1889), as the Bouquet Collection. Some letters are printed in full in Mary C. Darlington, *Hist. of Col. Henry Bouquet and the Western Frontiers of Pa.* (1920) and in *Mich. Pioneer and Hist. Colls.,* XIX, 27–295. Bouquet's military abilities are appraised in Sir Edward Hutton, *Henry Bouquet* (1911); Lewis Butler, *Annals of the King's Royal Rifle Corps,* vol. I (1913); and Col. Jas. F. C. Fuller, *British Light Infantry in the Eighteenth Century* (1925). American appreciations are Cyrus Cort, *Col. Henry Bouquet and his Campaigns* (1883) and J. C. Reeve, "Henry Bouquet," in *Ohio. Arch. and Hist. Quart.,* XXVI, 489–506. Parkman's *Conspiracy of Pontiac* (1851) is the charming and classic account.]

S. M. P.

BOUQUILLON, THOMAS JOSEPH (May 16, 1840–Nov. 5, 1902), Catholic theologian, was born at Warneton, Belgium. He was the second of five children. The family had owned land in the vicinity of Ypres and Warneton for 200 years. Search made at the time of his death failed to bring to the surface any records that might have a bearing on the hereditary background of his life. Bouquillon entered the College of St. Louis at Menin in 1854. He studied philosophy and related sciences at the Preparatory Seminary at Roulers where his ability attracted much attention. He entered the Theological Seminary at Bruges in 1861. Two years later he went to the Gregorian University at Rome where he completed his theological studies. While there he formed an intimate and enduring friendship with Rampolla del Tindaro who later as cardinal became secretary of state for Pope Leo XIII. Bouquillon was ordained to the Catholic priesthood at Rome in 1865. He then took up graduate studies in theology and received the degree of D.D. in 1867. He was at once appointed professor of moral theology in the Seminary at Bruges where he remained in that capacity until 1877. During that period he developed a plan of extension courses for laymen interested in theological studies. In August 1877 he accepted appointment to the chair of theology in the Catholic University of Lille in France. Eight years later he gave up active work as professor and retired to the Benedictine Monastery at Maredsous, Belgium, where he devoted himself entirely to theological and historical research. In 1889 he was asked to take the chair of moral theology in the newly founded Catholic University at Washington, D. C. After some hesitation he accepted the position and entered upon his duties as graduate professor in the same year. He taught there until his death at Brussels in 1902 following a surgical operation. He was buried at Croix, Nord, France.

Bouquillon's chief service to Catholic thought lies in his effort to restore to moral theology the scientific and historical prestige with which Saint Thomas and other early theologians had invested it. In the *Summa Theologica* of the former the theological sciences appear as related aspects of the body of revealed truth, and contemporaneous natural and social sciences are woven into one complete system with it. Bouquillon brought to the task of restoring moral theology to its historical and scientific prestige, unusual command of the whole field of theological literature, a well-balanced knowledge of ecclesiastical and secular history, a philosophical temperament, untiring research, and a gift of balanced exposition. His *Theologia Moralis Fundamentalis* (3rd edition, Bruges, 1903) is the finished product of his gifts and industry. It did much to rehabilitate moral theology in harmony with his great ideal. His special treatises, *De Virtutibus Theologicis* (2nd edition, Bruges, 1890) and *De Virtute Religionis* (Bruges, 1880), displayed the same scholarship and breadth of treatment in their respective fields. Bouquillon exerted far-reaching influence upon the development of the Catholic University at Washington. Shortly after he began to teach there he published a series of lectures in which he discussed the theoretical principles that govern the relations of church, state, and family in the field of education (*Education, to Whom Does It Belong,* Baltimore, 1891). He took the position that "education belongs to men taken individually and collectively in legitimate association, to the family, to the state, to the Church, to all four together and not to any one of these four factors separately." It was his purpose to show "that the doctrine of the Church is not opposed to a reasonable liberty or to the just prerogatives of the state in matters of education" (*Education, a Rejoinder to Critics,* Baltimore, 1892). His views were opposed by some Catholic leaders and a controversy resulted in 1891 and 1892. Against him it was argued that no one "has the right to educate the children of anybody unless the parents give him the power" (Holaind, *The Parent First,* 1891). The issue that arose resulted from differences of approach to the problem. Bouquillon maintained his original position without modification: a purely abstract exposition of principles independent of circumstances of time and country. In the course of the controversy he published a third pamphlet, *Education, A Rejoinder to the Civilta Cattolica* (Baltimore, 1892). All of these pamphlets appeared simultaneously in French. (See also

"The Catholic Controversy about Education" in the *Educational Review,* April 1892.) Aside from the original works mentioned Bouquillon edited and annotated numerous Latin and French works, and contributed twenty-one articles in Latin and in French to the *Revue des Sciences Ecclésiastiques,* and fifteen to the *American Catholic Quarterly Review* and the *Catholic University Bulletin.*

[A short account of Bouquillon's life is contained in *Thos. Bouquillon, Notice Bio-Bibliographique par le Chanoine H. Rommel* (Bruxelles, 1903). Some of the material contained there will be found in the *Cath. Univ. Bull.,* Jan. 1903. There is also a biographical sketch by Wm. J. Kerby in the *Cath. Encyc.,* vol. II (1907).]

W. J. K.

BOURGMONT, ÉTIENNE VENYARD, Sieur de (*c.* 1680–*c.* 1730), French explorer, was the son of Charles de Venyard, Sieur de Vergié, a Norman physician. Of an undisciplined and adventurous nature, Étienne early sought New France, where he was at first merely a *voyageur.* Having obtained the rank of ensign in the army, he was stationed at Detroit and in 1705 he was temporarily in command upon the retirement of Alphonse de Tonty. As commandant he became embroiled in an Indian revolt in 1706, and the next year deserted, probably because of a love affair with Madame Tichenet, called "La Chenette," who followed him to an island in Lake Erie. There with other deserters he lived a dissolute life, until a detachment was sent to arrest the band. Bourgmont, who was befriended by Cadillac, was allowed to escape, and fled to Louisiana, where he lived for a decade among the Indians of the Missouri River. The extent of his explorations is not certain; in 1717, however, he wrote an article called *La Description* detailing the courses of the Missouri as far as the Arikara villages in the later Dakota. For his services as an explorer and pacifier of Indians, Gov. Bienville asked for him a captaincy and sent him to France in 1719 to report his discoveries. The Company of the Indies granted him permission to build a fort on the Missouri, and to make peace with the Padouka (now the Comanche) Indians on the borders of Spanish territory. Bourgmont came back to Louisiana in 1723 and late in that year built the post called Fort Orléans on the Missouri just above Grand River. Thence in 1724 he undertook an expedition westward in which he penetrated to the western border of the present state of Kansas, held a council with the Padouka, and formed an alliance. After his return he persuaded a number of chiefs to accompany him to Paris, among whom was the Michigami named Chicagou. They were received with great éclat, and entertained by royalty. Bourgmont did not return to Louisiana with them; he is said to have married a rich widow and to have remained in France. The date or place of his death is not known.

[The most recent account of Bourgmont, founded on documentary sources, is that of Baron Marc de Villiers, *La Découverte du Missouri et l'Histoire du Fort d'Orléans* (Paris, 1925). Brief but excellent sketches are in *Mich. Pioneer and Hist. Colls.*, XXXIV, 306–7; Louis Houck, *Hist. of Mo.* (1905), I, 258. Pierre Margry, *Découvertes et Établissements des Français dans l'Amérique Septentrionale* (Paris, 1876), VI, 388–448, gives several documents concerning Bourgmont and the journal of his western expedition. For its route see *Kan. Hist. Trans.*, IX, 255–57, and *Kan. Hist. Colls.*, XIV, 450–55. The account in Le Page du Pratz, *Histoire de la Louisiane* (Paris, 1758) is believed to be apocryphal.]

L. P. K.

BOURKE, JOHN GREGORY (June 23, 1846–June 8, 1896), soldier, ethnologist, was the son of Edward and Anna (Morton) Bourke, natives of Galway, Ireland, and is said to have been descended from the Norman De Bourgh family and from Godfrey de Bouillon. His birthplace was Philadelphia. His family had great ambitions for his education, putting him at eight years of age to studying Latin, Greek, and Gaelic with a Jesuit priest. At sixteen, pretending he was eighteen, he ran away from home in 1862 and joined the 15th Pennsylvania Cavalry with which he served during the rest of the Civil War. He then obtained an appointment to the United States Military Academy, where he graduated in 1869. For the next fourteen years he served under Gen. George Crook in the Southwest with the 3rd United States Cavalry, with which he remained for the rest of his life. Becoming interested in the study of the Indian, he observed the habits and customs of many tribes, hostile and peaceful, and methodically reduced what he heard or saw to careful notes. Primarily necessary in campaigning and in diplomacy with the Indians, these data formed the basis of his scientific and historical writings, often accomplished in the field. He first wrote *The Snake Dance of the Moquis of Arizona* (1884), the pioneer publication on the subject, containing much of interest to ethnologists. Detailed to Washington to work up his notes, he wrote ten ethnological papers for the *American Anthropologist* and completed *The Medicine Men of the Apache* (1892), a major paper published by the Bureau of American Ethnology. Meanwhile he had also produced *An Apache Campaign* (1886), *Mackenzie's Last Fight with the Cheyennes* (1890), *On the Border with Crook* (1891), and *Scatalogic Rites of all Nations* (1892). Bourke's historical writings are unusually vivid, as he was a good story teller and had a generous fund of

wit and humor, while his scientific writings, compiled from his notes and unmarred by immature generalizations, will always be storehouses upon which workers may draw with profit. Bourke had deep-set gray eyes under bushy eyebrows, a prominent nose, well-formed chin, and the heavy mustache of the period. Of average height, his frame well-muscled, he gave the impression of endurance. This ensemble was informed by a lively, kind, shrewd, and attractive spirit.

[G. W. Cullum, *Biog. Reg.* (3rd ed., 1891); F. W. Hodge, "John Gregory Bourke," *Am. Anthropologist*, IX, 245–48; information from Bourke's daughter, Mrs. Sara Bourke James; personal recollections of the writer.]

W. H.

BOURNE, BENJAMIN (Dec. 9, 1755–Sept. 17, 1808), soldier and jurist, was born in Bristol, R. I., the son of Shearjashub and Ruth (Bosworth) Church Bourne. He was graduated from Harvard College in 1775. In January 1776 he was appointed quartermaster of the second regiment of the Colony Brigade under command of Col. Henry Babcock, who was later succeeded by Col. Christopher Lippitt. He was later appointed ensign in Capt. Arnold's company and under date of Dec. 4, 1776, volunteered to cross the North River. He received his final pay at Chatham, N. Y., and returned to King's County, R. I., on Jan. 18, 1777. In February 1780 he was elected a deputy or representative in the legislature from Bristol. At the following session in May he was a deputy and also clerk of the General Assembly and in the same month he became a member of the Council of War. He retained the position of clerk until May 1786, and then became a deputy from Providence, serving from May 1787 to May 1790. During his term of office he became deeply interested in the ratification of the Federal Constitution on the part of Rhode Island and was a member of the General Assembly when a petition was received from the town of Providence requesting that the General Assembly call a convention to consider the acceptance of the Constitution of the United States. The General Assembly refused the request of the petitioners, but as in the interval the new government had been recognized in New York the situation in Rhode Island was far from satisfactory, and again the town of Providence chose a committee, of which Bourne was a member, to draft a petition to Congress asking for due consideration to Rhode Island in the emergency. This petition was transmitted to Congress by the hands of President Manning of Rhode Island College, and Bourne. In November 1789 Rhode Island was the only state remaining outside of the Union and at the January session in the following year Bourne renewed his motion for the calling of a convention and it was carried in the lower house by a strong majority. It afterward was passed by the state Senate with a very close vote. Bourne was sent as a delegate to the convention for the ratification of the Constitution, which occurred on May 29, 1790, in the town of Newport. In August of the same year President Washington visited Providence, and Bourne served as a member of the committee to receive him. Doubtless on account of his activity in connection with the Constitution, the State chose him as her first representative to the Congress of the United States and he served in the First, Second, Third, and Fourth Congresses. In September 1801 he became judge of the United States district court for the district of Rhode Island. He was married to Mrs. Hope (Child) Diman, widow of Capt. Benjamin Diman of Bristol.

[W. H. Munro, *Hist. of Bristol, R. I.* (1880); W. R. Staples, *Annals of the Town of Providence* (1843); *Biog. Cong. Dir.* (1911); manuscript records, State Record Commissioner's Office.]   H.O.B.

BOURNE, EDWARD GAYLORD (June 24, 1860–Feb. 24, 1908), historian, educator, the son of Rev. James Russell and Isabella Graham (Staples) Bourne, was born in Strykersville, Wyoming County, N. Y. His father, a Congregational pastor, was descended from Richard Bourne who settled in Plymouth Colony about 1626, the family homestead being at Bourne, formerly in the town of Sandwich. His mother's mother was a Sears whose family was of Mayflower stock. His early life was spent mainly in New England rural parishes. A long illness in boyhood left him permanently lame. He prepared for college at Norwich Free Academy, ranking first in his class. In both school and college his love of books had no rival and he read widely in excess of all requirements. At Yale, where he graduated with the degree of B.A. in 1883, he distinguished himself in the classics until senior year when his interest was aroused in economics by Sumner and he won the Cobden medal. Declining a scholarship for classical study at Athens, he remained a graduate student of economics and history for five years, holding a Foote fellowship, being instructor in medieval history (1885–87) and lecturer on political science from 1886 to 1888. He then became instructor in history and economics in Adelbert College (1888–90) and professor of history there during the following five years. In 1892 he received the degree of Ph.D. from Yale, and in 1895 returned to New Haven as professor of history. In 1895, also, he was married to Annie Thomson Nettleton, daughter of William A. and Eliza Lyman (Thomson) Nettleton of Stock-

bridge, Mass. For the first two years of his professorship he taught European history, thereafter mainly American history. Preëminently a master of historical criticism, Bourne in his articles, reviews, and books revealed rare keenness in the application of its principles to problems of authorship and veracity, and to detection of plagiarism and legend. He tried for the Porter prize and his essay, suggested by Sumner, was developed into his first book, *The Surplus Revenue of 1837* (1885), the standard monograph on the subject. In Cleveland began a long friendship with J. F. Rhodes for whose history he collected materials and rendered valuable advice, services acknowledged by Rhodes in a grateful tribute (Rhodes, *Historical Essays*, 1909, pp. 191–200). From student days he contributed constantly to various periodicals. Thirteen of his more important articles appeared as his second book: *Essays in Historical Criticism* (1901). Here his critical sense was skilfully revealed in "The Legend of Marcus Whitman," wherein he distinguished between fact and myth, a revelation which evoked much protest from devotees of legend (see Myron Eells, *Reply to Professor Bourne's "The Whitman Legend,"* 1902; also, favorably to Bourne, W. I. Marshall, *History vs. The Whitman Saved Oregon Story . . . ,* 1904). Bourne's conclusions, however, "impressed scientific scholars as conclusive" (J. F. Jameson, *American Historical Review,* VII, 745–7). The period of discoveries and Spanish Colonization enlisted Bourne's chief interest in later years. His historical introduction to Blair and Robertson's *Philippine Islands* appeared in 1903. His third and best-known volume was *Spain in America* (1904; Spanish translation, 1906) wherein he gave an appreciative recognition of the work and purposes of Spain. The narrative was interwoven with shrewd criticism and original conclusions. If the book created too favorable an impression of Spanish institutions and culture (see M. Oppenheim, *American Historical Review,* XI, 394–97), that may have been owing to excessive reliance upon official documents and laws. Bourne edited Woolley's *Journal* (1902), Fournier's *Napoleon* (1903), Roscher's *Spanish Colonial System* (1904), and narrative sources for *De Soto* (1904), *The Northmen, Columbus, and Cabot* (1906), and *Champlain* (translated by Mrs. Bourne, 1906). As an early and energetic member of the American Historical Association, he was chairman (1901–8) of its historical manuscripts commission which published the diary and part of the correspondence of Chief Justice Chase (1903). For the New England History Teachers' Association, of which he was president in 1901, he served on the committee of five who prepared *Historical Sources in Schools* (1902). In recognition of rare editorial ability he was considered for editor of the Massachusetts Historical Society and his appointment was prevented only by declining health (Rhodes, *Historical Essays*, p. 199). His last undertaking was a life of Motley which he did not live to complete. Suffering nearly two years from hip-joint disease, he died in New Haven, in his forty-eighth year.

[Correspondence and materials for a life of Bourne possessed by his brother, Henry Eldridge Bourne; appreciations by A. B. Hart, A. G. Keller, and others, including a bibliography of Bourne, in *Yale Alumni Weekly*, Mar. 25, 1908 (*Yale Reprints*, No. 2); F. H. Herrick in *Western Reserve Univ. Bull.*, XI, 96–103.]

F.W.P.

BOURNE, GEORGE (June 13, 1780–Nov. 20, 1845), Presbyterian and Dutch Reformed clergyman, abolitionist, was born in Westbury, England, and was educated at Homerton Seminary in London. From there he came to Virginia and Maryland. He was pastor of a Presbyterian church in South River, Va., in 1814. As a result of his strong reaction to his direct contact with the institution of slavery, he was one of the first in the United States to advocate immediate emancipation (*The Book and Slavery Irreconcilable*, 1816). He was bitterly persecuted by the advocates of slavery and called before a Presbyterian council where he was condemned on a charge of heresy for his anti-slavery views. He was finally compelled to leave the Southern states. For a while he lived in Germantown, Pa. (*Manual of the Reformed Church*), a little later in Sing Sing, N. Y., where he was principal of an academy as well as pastor of a Presbyterian church. In Quebec from 1825 to 1828, he had two Presbyterian churches, and here he became a strong opponent of Catholicism. Two years later he was back in New York, but without a church. Presbyterian records list him as an editor in 1831 and in 1832 Garrison writes of him as publishing "a spirited journal, entitled, *The Protestant*." The following year saw him a member of the Dutch Reformed Church, which had perhaps the greatest tolerance for his extreme anti-slavery principles. He supplied the Houston Street Chapel and vacant churches, and at the same time contributed to periodicals and the press, and was the author of a number of works which expressed his views. Garrison said of him, "Bourne thunders and lightens," and he frequently recognized his courage and the vigor and strength of his mind. He was among the fifty or sixty delegates present at the Philadelphia convention for the formation of the Anti-Slavery Society in 1833 (*Garrison*). At an anniversary meeting in 1837, he offered a resolution censuring clergymen who during the past year had defended slavery and opposed the enlightening of their congregations "without the advice and consent of the pastors and regular ecclesiastical bodies" (*Ibid.*). He was opposed to "woman's rights," and felt certain that no woman would be allowed a seat in the world anti-slavery convention, although Lucretia Mott had been appointed as a delegate by the American society. Naturally belligerent, he had no patience with the policy of non-resistance. He wrote Garrison in 1838 that he anticipated no peace from his "non-resistance oppugnation" but foresaw in it only mischief to the anti-slavery cause. He lived at West Farms from 1839 to 1842, and at the time of his death in 1845 was employed on the *Christian Intelligencer* in New York. His published works are: *The History of Napoleon Bonaparte* (1806); *The Spirit of the Public Journals; or, Beauties of the American Newspapers for 1805* (1806); *The Book and Slavery Irreconcilable* (1816); *The Picture of Quebec* (1829); *An Address to the Presbyterian Church, Enforcing the Duty of Excluding All Slave-holders from the "Communion of Saints"* (1833); *Lorette, The History of Louise, Daughter of a Canadian Nun, Exhibiting the Interior of Female Convents* (1834); *Man-Stealing and Slavery Denounced by the Presbyterian and Methodist Churches* (1834); *Picture of Slavery in the United States of America* (1834); *Slavery Illustrated in Its Effects upon Woman and Domestic Society* (1837); *A Condensed Anti-Slavery Bible Argument* (1845).

[*Minutes of General Assembly of the Presbyt. Ch.*, vols. III, V, VI, VII; *Manual of the Reformed Ch. in America* (1879); *Liberator*, vols. I, II; *Wm. Lloyd Garrison, Told by His Children* (1885–89); *N. Y. Herald*, Nov. 22, 1845; *N. Y. Tribune*, Nov. 21, 1845.]

M.A.K.

BOURNE, NEHEMIAH (*c.* 1611–1691), ship builder, British rear admiral, was born in London, the son of Robert and Mary Bourne. His father, a Wapping shipwright, desired in his will that Nehemiah become a scholar and be brought up at Cambridge University, but the son cared more for the father's trade than for the father's wishes. He married young and in 1638 migrated to Massachusetts, where he was a ship-builder and merchant first at Charlestown, later at Dorchester, and finally at Boston. He had the distinction of building Gov. Winthrop's ship, the *Trial*, the first vessel of any size to be laid down at Boston. The *Trial* was of between 160 and 200 tons burden, was ready in June 1641, but had to wait another year until her rigging arrived from London. The subsequent career of her builder, though not known in detail, is full of interest.

He was a major in the Parliamentary army, returned to Massachusetts to take back his family, and in 1650 became commander of the frigate *Speaker* in the Parliamentary navy. In this ship he brought to London the Scottish records, insignia, and regalia taken at Stirling Castle, for which he received a gold medal worth £60. As commander of a squadron near the mouth of the Thames, he notified Admiral Blake on May 18, 1652, that Van Tromp with forty sail was off Southend-on-Sea. In the battle of the following day he and his squadron played a prominent part. On that same day he was appointed "Rear Admiral of the Fleet of the Commonwealth of England and Captain of the ship (*St. Andrew*) of 60 guns." In less than a year he was made Commissioner of the Navy charged with refitting, victualing, and manning ships sent to Harwich and Yarmouth from the main fleet. At the same time he appears to have engaged in mercantile pursuits, probably in a way that legitimately combined public service with private profits. At the Restoration he decamped to the continent, was later pardoned, and spent his last years in England. He was buried in Bunhill Fields beside his beloved wife, Hanna, by whom he had four sons and a daughter. His will, dated Feb. 11, 1690/91 and probated May 15, 1691, shows that the doughty old merchant, sea fighter, and Puritan died in comfortable circumstances.

[I. J. Greenwood, "Rear Admiral Nehemiah Bourne," *New Eng. Hist. and Geneal. Reg.*, Jan. 1873, pp. 26–36; article "Nehemiah Bourne" in *Dict. of Nat. Biog.*, vol. VI (1886).]   G.H.G.

BOURNE, RANDOLPH SILLIMAN (May 30, 1886–Dec. 22, 1918), essayist, was born in Bloomfield, N. J., the son of Charles and Sara (Randolph) Bourne. Owing to a fall in infancy, he was deformed,—hunchbacked, with a stunted body, large head, and heavy features; only those who recognized the keenness of his mind and the beauty of his spirit could forget his physical appearance or write of it like Van Wyck Brooks, "I shall never forget . . . that odd little apparition with his vibrant eyes, his quick bird-like steps"; less appreciative observers could see only a painful outward ugliness. Bourne attended the public schools of Bloomfield, earned his living for a time as an assistant to a manufacturer of automatic piano music, and in 1909 entered Columbia University where he graduated in 1913. In 1913 also he published *Youth and Life,* a book of radiantly idealistic essays inspired by the thought of an approaching "youth movement" in America. Enabled by a Gilder Fellowship to spend a year in European travel and study, on his return he submitted to Columbia a remarkably

incisive report on European cultural conditions, modestly entitled "Impressions of Europe 1913–14." Profoundly influenced by the educational theories of John Dewey, he produced, somewhat in their vein, *The Gary Schools* (1916) and *Education and Living* (1917), but the failure of liberal pragmatism to meet the issues raised by the World War gradually drove him to a more radical philosophy. He became a pronounced pacifist and in the *Masses* and the *Seven Arts* vigorously attacked America's entrance into the war. With the suspension of the *Seven Arts* in September 1917 his chief organ of expression was gone; in extreme poverty he held on his lonely way; and at the time of his death he was engaged in a work upon the State the published fragments of which present a close analysis and scathing indictment of that institution. He died in the influenza epidemic of 1918. Of his two posthumously published works, *Untimely Papers* (1919), edited by James Oppenheim, and *The History of a Literary Radical* (1920), edited by Van Wyck Brooks, the former constitutes the most trenchant expression which we have of the attitude of the suppressed minority during the World War. In his early death America lost a writer of great promise, a critic at home in philosophy, education, politics, and literature but homeless in his contemporary world.

[Introductions by Brooks and Oppenheim to the volumes mentioned above; *Who's Who in America,* 1918–19; personal acquaintance.]   E.S.B.

BOUTELL, HENRY SHERMAN (Mar. 14, 1856–Mar. 11, 1926), lawyer, diplomat, was born at Boston, Mass., the son of Lewis Henry and Anna (Greene) Boutell. A colonial ancestry entitled him to membership in the Sons of the American Revolution and in the Society of Colonial Wars. His college education was secured at Northwestern (A.B. 1874, M.A. 1879) and Harvard (A.B. 1876, A.M. 1877). After studying law in an office, in 1879 he was admitted to the bar and began practise in Chicago. Although both able and prominent as an attorney (representing, for example, the Baltimore & Ohio Railroad in securing a right of way into Chicago, and in the erection of its terminal therein), his tastes from the beginning ran to public life, and he was soon both active and useful as a worker in the Republican party. In 1884 he was a member of the lower house of the state legislature, and from 1897 to 1911 a representative of Chicago districts in Congress. There he was a member of the committees on Rules, and on Ways and Means, and was chairman of the Committee on Expenditures of the Navy. He was an effective speaker and of considerable influence, but his

tariff views were unacceptable to business interests in Chicago, which forced his retirement. President Taft then appointed him to the post of envoy extraordinary and minister plenipotentiary to Portugal, on Mar. 2, 1911. He never assumed its duties, and on Apr. 24, 1911, he was given a similar appointment to Switzerland. In this post he served from May 17, 1911, to July 31, 1913. He did not find the diplomatic service to his liking, and resigned. Before he did so he had declined the chief-justiceship of the United States court of claims tendered him by President Taft (January 1913). With this his public career ended, except for service (November 1913) as chairman of a board of arbitration which settled an important dispute between the operatives and officers of the Chicago, Burlington & Quincy Railway. From 1914 to 1923 he taught constitutional law and international law in Georgetown University, in Washington, D. C. He was short of stature, very erect and dignified of carriage, alert in movement. Distinctly of the scholarly type, he was very widely read, and active, so long as he resided in Chicago, in the Literary Club of that city. His speeches, which reflected his reading, were always graceful and sometimes eloquent. In his political opinions he was fairly liberal, but in the regulation of purely personal affairs and conduct he was notably conservative. He was a rare combination of force and urbanity. Although unfailingly careful to avoid giving offense to anybody with whom he came in contact, invariably gracious, and charming in manner, his opinions were not lacking in definiteness, and he was not in any way colorless. These qualities should have won him great distinction either in law or diplomacy, but in politics they left him merely a staunch and dependable "party" man, whose mental independence and natural talents were hampered by party platforms. He did not win in public life the renown of which his abilities and early professional success gave promise. On Dec. 29, 1880, he was married to Euphemia Lucia Clara Gates of Providence, R. I. He died at San Remo, Italy. Several children survived him.

[The chronology of Boutell's life is given, inadequately, in *Who's Who in America*, 1908–09; and in the *Biog. Cong. Dir. 1774–1911*; see also obituaries, Mar. 13, 1926, in the *Chicago Daily Tribune* and the *Washington Post*, as well as the sketch in *Harvard Coll. Class of 1876, Tenth Report* (1926).]   F.S.P.

BOUTELLE, CHARLES ADDISON (Feb. 9, 1839–May 21, 1901), naval officer, journalist, congressman, was the son of Charles and Lucy Ann (Curtis) Boutelle. He was born in Damariscotta, Me. When he was nine years old his parents moved to Brunswick. There he received a common school and academic education. His parents wished him to go through college but he had a strong craving for a seafaring life and preferred to accompany his father on his voyages. On returning from a voyage in 1862 he found the country in the midst of the Civil War and promptly enlisted in the navy and took part with credit in various operations. In 1863 he was acting master on board the U. S. S. *Sassacus*. On May 5 he showed great coolness and courage in a desperate conflict of the *Sassacus* with the Confederate iron-clad *Albemarle* and for his gallant conduct was made an acting volunteer lieutenant, the highest position attainable by a volunteer. In the winter of 1864–65 he took an active part in the operations at Mobile. In 1866 he was discharged from the service at his own request. Boutelle received high praise from his superiors. One said, "I regarded him as one of the best of the volunteer appointments, officer-like in his bearing, intelligent and exhibiting an interest in his professional improvement, gunnery and small arms, unusual in one not bred to the service." Another officer in reply to a request for a recommendation for a special appointment wrote: "He is brave to a fault; he is intelligent and possesses the adornments of a cultivated gentleman." After leaving the service Boutelle fitted out and commanded a steamer plying between New York City and Wilmington, N. C., and later he engaged with the shipping commission firm of Walsh & Carver in New York City. From boyhood Boutelle had been interested in journalism, he had already contributed to political journals, and in 1870 he became managing editor of an old and influential paper, the *Whig and Courier* in Bangor, Me. In 1874 he became principal owner. In 1880 he was nominated on the Republican ticket for Congress, made a whirlwind campaign, and greatly cut down the majority of the Democratic sitting member at the previous election, but failed of success. He then took an active part in the national campaign in Ohio and New York. He was renominated for Congress in 1882, was elected, and was reëlected for nine successive terms. As editor and politician as well as soldier Boutelle was a hard though clean fighter and a foe to compromise. He was an intense Republican of the reconstruction school, an ardent protectionist, always ready to do battle for the legal rights of the negroes, for a high tariff, and for liberal pensions. He vigorously opposed the conciliation policy of Hayes, the reinstatement of Fitz-John Porter, and the removal of the disabilities of Jefferson Davis. But as the years passed he softened and at the close of his career he was highly regarded by his political opponents. A strong sound-money man, he opposed the war with Spain, fearing that it would be used to drive the country to a silver basis. His most individual work was his championship of a modern and stronger navy in the period between the Civil and the Spanish wars when the public took little interest in the question of sea power. He was an ardent admirer of James G. Blaine and his constant and unflinching supporter for the presidency. As editor, Boutelle kept his paper free from yellow journalism; late in life it was sold, first to a friendly syndicate and then to a journalistic and political rival. In 1899 Boutelle had an attack of congestion of the brain from which he never recovered. He was, however, reëlected to Congress but resigned and died in 1901. His Maine colleagues in the House placed in the Central Church of Bangor a stained glass window as a memorial in his honor. Boutelle was married to Elizabeth Hodsdon, daughter of Adjutant-General Hodsdon of Augusta, who predeceased him.

[*Hist. of Penobscot County, Me.* (1882), pp. 766, 915; *Biog. Encyc. of Me.* (1885), ed. by H. C. Williams, p. 308; *Bangor Daily News,* May 22, 1901; *Daily Eastern Argus,* May 22, 1901.]   L. C. H.

BOUTON, JOHN BELL (Mar. 15, 1830–Nov. 18, 1902), author, was born in Concord, N. H., where for more than forty years his father, Rev. Nathaniel Bouton [*q.v.*], was pastor of the First Congregational Church. He was of French descent through Jean Bouton, who came to this country from England in 1635 and settled in Connecticut. His mother, Mary Anne Persis Bell, daughter of Gov. John Bell of New Hampshire, was of Norman origin, though after the Conquest the Bells settled in the south of Scotland and later in the north of Ireland, from which country John Bell emigrated to New Hampshire in 1720. John Bell Bouton grew up in a home where interest in public service and literary pursuits was fostered. He graduated from Dartmouth College in 1849, having taken high rank as a scholar. He studied law, but in 1851 became editor of the *Cleveland Plain-Dealer.* In 1857 he removed to New York, and was for many years one of the editors and owners of the *New York Journal of Commerce.* For about ten years he was also an editor of *Appleton's Annual Cyclopedia.* On Dec. 4, 1873, he married his cousin Eliza, daughter of John and Eliza (Bell) Nesmith of Lowell, Mass. Severing his business connections in 1889, he made his home in Cambridge, Mass., and spent his time in travel and writing. His publications include a volume of essays, *Loved and Lost* (1857); *Round the Block, an American Novel* (1864), which, though long and tedious,

portrays rather well some of the manners of the time in New York, and reveals skill in character portrayal; *A Memoir of General Louis Bell* (1865); *Roundabout to Moscow, an Epicurean Journey* (1887), a good-humored and entertaining narrative of travels in Europe; *The Enchanted, an Authentic Account of the Strange Origin of the New Psychical Club* (1891); *Uncle Sam's Church: His Creed, Bible and Hymn-book* (1895), a plea for the development of a patriotic cult. He also edited the *Autobiography of Nathaniel Bouton* (1879).

[*Dartmouth Coll. Cat.* (1910); obituaries in *Boston Evening Transcript,* Nov. 18, 1902, and information supplied by Hollis R. Bailey, Esq.]   H. E. S.

BOUTON, NATHANIEL (June 29, 1799–June 6, 1878), Congregational minister, historian, was a descendant in the sixth generation of Jean Bouton, a French Huguenot, who came from England to New England in 1635, and in 1651 became one of the founders of Norwalk, Conn. Nathaniel was born in Norwalk, the fourteenth and youngest child of William and Sarah (Benedict) Bouton. His father was a farmer who could provide no more than a common school education for his children; but Nathaniel aspired to something more, and succeeded at fourteen in becoming an apprentice to a printer who was also the editor of a weekly paper at Bridgeport, a few miles away. The boy was bright, conscientious and affectionate, though somewhat quick-tempered and fond of disputation. Beside learning his trade, he occasionally wrote contributions for the paper. At a time of special religious interest, when he was sixteen, his own religious nature was aroused and he became active and successful in evangelistic work among those of his own age. This turned his thoughts to the ministry and, with the help of those whose interest had been aroused by his activity, he procured his release from his apprenticeship, prepared himself for college, and made his way through Yale (where he graduated in 1821) and through Andover Seminary (graduating in 1824). He was called almost immediately to the First Congregational Church of Concord, N. H., then the only church in the place. He spent the rest of his life in Concord, for forty-two years as a notably successful pastor, and for ten years thereafter as state historian. He was thrice married; first, on June 11, 1825, to Harriet Sherman; second, on June 8, 1829, to Mary Ann Persis Bell; and third, on Feb. 18, 1840, to Elizabeth Ann Cilley. He is described by his son John B. Bouton [*q.v.*] as "a medium-sized man, spare and sinewy, with a clean-shaven face, regular features, piercing, gray-blue eyes and shaggy eyebrows."

Incidentally to his pastoral work he became a student of New Hampshire history and a zealous member of the state historical society, editing in 1850 Volumes VII and VIII of its *Collections*. In 1856 he published his *History of Concord, N. H.*, and in 1861 he brought out an annotated edition of *Lovewell's Great Fight at Pigwacket, 1725*. After his resignation of his pastorate the office of state historian was created for him in order that he might edit and publish the entire documentary history of New Hampshire, from the beginning of the settlement in 1623 to the adoption of the constitution in 1784. This he did in ten volumes averaging over 850 pages apiece, which appeared annually from 1867 to 1877. It was an arduous task, four-fifths of the manuscript being written out in his own hand. Though not his chief interest, which was the ministry, this labor of his old age is his chief claim to remembrance, and his enduring monument. He contributed also to religious journals and published a number of sermons, and addresses, largely biographical and historical. Though not a man of great originality, he was kindly and lovable, and an indefatigable worker, who well served his day and generation.

[The chief sources are Bouton's *Autobiography* (1879), ed. by John Bell Bouton, and the latter's *Sketch of the Character and Life-Work of Rev. Nathaniel Bouton* (1902) ; see also obituary in the *Concord Daily Monitor*, June 7, 1878.]   B.W.B.

BOUTWELL, GEORGE SEWALL (Jan. 28, 1818–Feb. 27, 1905), politician, born in Brookline, Mass., was the son of Sewall and Rebecca (Marshall) Boutwell, both of old Massachusetts stock. His boyhood was passed in Lunenburg, Mass., where from the age of thirteen to seventeen he was employed in a small store with the privilege of attending school during the winter months. When he was seventeen he became clerk in a store in Groton, Mass. He devoted much of his time to self-education in the hope of becoming a lawyer, and at an early age began to write articles for the newspapers on political topics, and to make addresses. In 1841 he was married to Sarah Adelia Thayer. He was an active Democrat, and during seven sessions between 1842 and 1850 represented Groton in the lower house of the state legislature. Through his useful work there he became one of the leaders of the younger element of the party, whose anti-slavery leanings made possible the coalition with the Free-Soilers which in 1850 defeated the Whigs. As a result of this coalition, Boutwell was elected by the legislature governor for the year 1851, and Charles Sumner, representing the Free-Soilers, was elected senator; the same po-

litical combination effected Boutwell's reëlection for 1852. After the expiration of his term he pursued legal studies with the purpose of becoming a patent lawyer ; from 1855 to 1861 he was secretary of the state board of education. In January 1862 he was admitted to the Suffolk bar.

The important part of Boutwell's career lies in the field of national politics. He had been one of the organizers of the Republican party in Massachusetts in 1855, and he consistently represented its radical wing,—more, however, on the side of practical politics than in its idealistic aspect. From July 17, 1862, to Mar. 3, 1863, he was commissioner of internal revenue, and in that short period did effective work in organizing this new branch of the government. His activities as a radical Republican were most conspicuous during his terms of service as representative in Congress from 1863 to 1869 in connection with the problems of reconstruction. As a member of the Joint Committee on Reconstruction he helped in framing the Fourteenth Amendment; his belief in the necessity of full suffrage for the negro led to his advocacy of the Fifteenth Amendment. His support of the congressional plan of Reconstruction involved persistent, vigorous, and even fanatical opposition to President Johnson and his policies. In the movement for the impeachment of the President he was among the leaders, being chosen by the House of Representatives as one of its seven managers to conduct the impeachment. His suggestion that a suitable punishment for Johnson, the "enemy of two races of men," would be his projection into a "hole in the sky" near the Southern Cross, drew the ridicule of William M. Evarts, counsel for the defense. Boutwell's efforts on behalf of the radical Republicans were rewarded by a place in Grant's cabinet as secretary of the treasury. To this position he brought qualifications chiefly of a political nature, and he was not a supporter of civil service reform; but he labored diligently in improving the organization of the department and in reducing the national debt. Before the end of his four years as secretary he had effected the redemption of 200 millions of six per cent bonds and sold an equal amount bearing interest at five per cent (*Report of the Secretary of the Treasury*, December 1872, iii). Early in his administration occurred the famous "Black Friday," on which day an attempted corner in gold was broken by his release of Treasury gold.

From March 1873 to March 1877, he served a four-year term as senator from Massachusetts. On his failure to be reëlected by his party he was appointed commissioner to revise the statutes of the United States. In 1880 he became counsel and agent of the United States before a board of international arbitrators for the settlement of claims of French citizens against the government of this country, and of American citizens against the government of France. In his practise as a lawyer, which he resumed after his retirement from the Senate, he handled numerous cases involving questions of international law. The independence of spirit which at various times in his career he had manifested,—in marked contrast to his general disposition for party regularity—showed itself in his last years in his opposition to the policy of the Republican party on the Philippine question, and led to his withdrawal from the party; he was president of the Anti-Imperialist League from its organization in November 1898 until his death in 1905. He was the author of *Thoughts on Educational Topics and Institutions* (1859); *A Manual of the Direct and Excise Tax System of the United States* (1863); *Speeches Relating to the Rebellion and the Overthrow of Slavery* (1867); *The Constitution of the United States at the End of the First Century* (1895); *The Crisis of the Republic* (1900).

[Boutwell's *Reminiscences of Sixty Years in Public Affairs* (1902) contains interesting though guarded accounts of the public men of his time; to it is prefixed a biographical sketch which appeared in the *Memoirs of the Judiciary and the Bar of New Eng.*, Jan. 1901. For his connection with the impeachment of Johnson see D. M. DeWitt, *The Impeachment and Trial of Andrew Johnson* (1903); E. P. Oberholtzer, *Jay Cooke* (1907) has numerous references to Boutwell as secretary of the treasury.]   H. G. P.

BOUVET, MARIE MARGUERITE (Feb. 14, 1865–May 27, 1915), linguist, writer of books for young people, was born in the French city of New Orleans, of French parents. Her father, Jean François Bouvet, was a descendant of François, Comte de Bouvet d'Asti in Piedmont. Her mother, Adelphine Bertrand Bouvet, daughter of a cavalry officer of Charles X, attended the Convent of the Sacred Heart, Paris, and took a degree at the Sorbonne. The parents were married in New Orleans and there the father died in 1870, after having suffered loss of fortune in the Civil War. In early childhood Marguerite spent seven years with her father's parents in their home near Lyons, France, and memories of this period are embodied in several of her books. She attended Loquet-Leroy Female Institute, New Orleans, in which her mother was a teacher, and was graduated from St. Mary's College, Knoxville, Ill., in 1885. After graduation she became a teacher of French and compiled a book of French quotations, *Fleurs des Poètes et des Prosateurs Français* (1900). Soon her interest in teaching was shared, if not overshadowed, by

the interest of authorship. She wrote books for young people, with quiet narratives, simply but not childishly told, so that many older people have found them interesting. Most of the settings are European and quaint foreign characters and customs are well described. *Sweet William* (1890), which is located at Mont St. Michel, in Normandy, and introduces the character of William the Conqueror, is the one of her books which best meets the approval of children's librarians. *Little Marjorie's Love Story* (1891), *Prince Tip Top* (1892), *My Lady* (1894), and *Pierrette* (1896) are less successful. *A Child of Tuscany* (1895) is a story of child life in Florence. *A Little House in Pimlico* (1897) has a London child for its central figure. *Tales of an Old Château* (1899) recounts incidents of the French Revolution, told to Marguerite Bouvet during her childhoood in France. *Bernardo and Laurette* (1901) has good atmosphere of the Savoy Mountains and the Rhone Valley. *Clotilde* (1908) is a story of child life in New Orleans. *The Smile of the Sphinx* (1911), with setting divided between Baltimore and France, is artificial. According to later standards, sentimentality is the chief fault of all Marguerite Bouvet's work. Two extended visits in Europe, after she had begun to write, enabled her to make her European stories realistic. For some years before her death she and a friend of St. Mary's College days made their home together in Reading, Pa. She was a member of the Woman's Club there and her adaptability, gracious manner, and Gallic vivacity won her many friends.

[*Who's Who in America*, 1914–15; *Woman's Who's Who of America*, 1914–15; *Men and Women of America* (1910); private information.]   S. G. B.

BOUVIER, JOHN (1787–Nov. 18, 1851), judge, legal writer, was born at Condognan, Department of Gard, in France, of French-Quaker parentage. At the age of fourteen he emigrated from France with his parents, John and Marie (Benezet) Bouvier, to Philadelphia, where members of his mother's distinguished family already lived. The following year his father died. A friend of his family, Benjamin Johnson, who was a printer and bookseller, took him into business. When he became twenty-one his friends set him up in the printing business in Philadelphia, whence he moved to West Philadelphia, later to Brownsville where he edited and published a weekly newspaper, the *American Telegraph,* and still later to Uniontown where he published the *Genius of Liberty,* also continuing the *American Telegraph.* In 1818, he was admitted to the bar in Uniontown, and in 1822, was admitted to practise before the supreme court of Pennsylvania. In the following year he returned to Philadelphia. While studying law he made an abridgment of *Blackstone's Commentaries*. During his years of study he had discovered the handicap under which the student and lawyer labored at that time due to the lack of a dictionary containing legal information logically and conveniently compiled. He began work on a great dictionary and indefatigably applied himself to it, in spite of increasing duties. In 1836 he was elected recorder of Philadelphia, and on the abolition of the mayor's court in 1838, he was made associate judge of the court of criminal sessions. Nevertheless, in 1839, he was able to give his completed dictionary to fill the need of the profession. It was entitled, *A Law Dictionary Adapted to the Constitution and Laws of the United States and the Several States of the American Union*. He sought to cover all legal subjects and terms arising under such a title, giving citations from federal and state courts. Eminent jurists such as Kent and Story, to the latter of whom the work was dedicated, attested its value and importance, and received it with unqualified commendation, stating that it would receive a response from the bar all over the United States. The dictionary passed through three editions during the twelve years following, and Bouvier was preparing a fourth at the time of his death. In these subsequent editions he not only rewrote many of the earlier articles, but added copiously to them, covering omissions and new developments. By the year 1886, when it was first revised, there had been fifteen editions. Since that revision there have been two others, with many editions. In 1841–45 Bouvier issued a new edition of *Matthew Bacon's Abridgment of the Law* in ten volumes, making its first index. In 1851 he published the *Institutes of American Law* in four volumes, which was a compendium of American law based upon the system of Pothier, which he greatly admired. Of this work there was a second edition in 1870.

[*North Am. Rev.*, July 1861; *Law Reporter*, XIV, 466; *Legal Intelligencer*, XXIV, 373; Henry Simpson, *The Lives of Eminent Philadelphians* (1859), pp. 111–23.]   G. R.

BOWDEN, JOHN (Jan. 7, 1751–July 31, 1817), Anglican clergyman, educator, the son of Thomas Bowden, an officer in the British army, was born in Ireland where his father was serving at the time. He came to America in the care of a Church of England clergyman, following his father who had come here with his regiment, and for two years he was a student at the College of New Jersey (afterward Princeton). When his father's regiment was ordered home young Bowden returned with him. But in 1770 he came back to America to carry on his studies. This time he entered King's (afterward Columbia) College, and graduated in the class of 1772. He then studied for holy orders, and in 1774 was ordered deacon by the Rt. Rev. Frederick Keppel, Bishop of Exeter, and advanced to the priesthood the same year by the Rt. Rev. Richard Terrick, Bishop of London. In the fall of this year he returned to New York, and accepted an invitation to serve as an assistant minister in Trinity Church. During the troublous times of the Revolution he resigned his position and remained without a parish until the close of the war when, in December 1784, he became rector of St. Paul's Church, Norwalk, Conn. Here he remained until the fall of 1789, when the condition of his health made it imperative that he should seek a change of climate, and he accepted an invitation to take charge of the church in St. Croix in the West Indies. He did not obtain the benefit which he had anticipated, and after a stay of about two years he returned to this country and made his home in Stratford, Conn., where he established a small school. Among the Connecticut Episcopalians, who were now forging ahead under the vigorous leadership of Bishop Seabury, a movement was inaugurated as early as 1792, looking to the founding of an institution of learning within the bounds of the Diocese of Connecticut, which should be under Episcopal control, but not narrowly sectarian. The result was the Episcopal Academy of Connecticut located at Cheshire, which opened its doors for the admission of pupils in June 1796. The constitution provided that "female education may be attended to under this institution," and that was the policy of the school until 1836, when it became exclusively a boys' school. For the first principal of this academy Bowden was unanimously chosen. He accepted and took with him most of the pupils who were under his charge at Stratford. He administered the affairs of the Academy with marked distinction and success until April 1802, when he resigned to become professor of moral philosophy, belles lettres, and logic in Columbia College, which position he held until his death. When the Diocese of Connecticut was called upon to choose a successor to Bishop Seabury, who died Feb. 25, 1796, Bowden was unanimously elected to that office, Oct. 19, 1796. He requested that he might delay his answer until the annual convention in the following June. At that time he signified his unwillingness to accept, the condition of his health being not the least of the reasons which governed him in making his decision. The testimony of Bowden's contemporaries is that he was a man of fine scholarship, an effective teacher, a true gentleman. He lived in times of ecclesiastical controversy, when to give and take in the form of pamphlets was the recognized and orthodox mode of warfare. In the defense and exposition of his cherished principles of church doctrine and government, he struck vigorous blows. These controversial pamphlets constitute, for the most part, his literary production. Among the more important are: *A Letter to Ezra Stiles [on] Church Government* (1788); *An Address from John Bowden, A.M., to the Members of the Episcopal Church in Stratford* (1792); *Two Letters to the Editor of the Christian's Magazine* (1807); *A Full Length Portrait of Calvinism* (1809). He was married to Mary Jervis, and one of his three sons graduated from Columbia in the class of 1813, and became a clergyman in the Episcopal Church. He died at Ballston Spa, N. Y., and was buried there.

[*Christian Jour.*, Jan. 1818; Rev. John McVicar, *Address before the Alumni of Columbia Coll.* (1837); Rev. Wm. Berrian, *Sketch of Trinity Ch. N. Y.* (1847); W. B. Sprague, *Annals of the Am. Pulpit*, vol. V (1859).]
W.A.B.

BOWDITCH, CHARLES PICKERING (Sept. 30, 1842–June 1, 1921), archæologist, was the son of Jonathan Ingersoll Bowditch and Lucy O. Nichols, and the grandson of Nathaniel Bowditch [*q.v.*]. He received the A.B. degree from Harvard College in 1863 and the A.M. degree three years later. He served in the Civil War as second lieutenant, first lieutenant, and captain of the 55th Massachusetts Volunteer Infantry and as captain of the 5th Massachusetts Volunteer Cavalry. On June 7, 1866, he was married to Cornelia L. Rockwell. His broad interests are shown in his membership in learned societies connected with the fields of art, science, archæology, anthropology, geography, history, and genealogy and in many of these he held the highest offices. He was treasurer of the American Academy of Arts and Sciences from 1905 to 1915 and president from 1917 to 1919. As trustee of the Hopkins Fund and as member of the faculty of the Peabody Museum his affiliation with Harvard University was a very close one. He was the greatest benefactor the Museum ever had. Two large exhibition halls are filled to a great extent with the results of frequent expeditions to Yucatan and Central America, planned and financed by him. By his own individual studies he occupied at the time of his death a commanding position in American archæology. He was the greatest scholar of Maya hieroglyphic writing and no one working in this field can disregard his pioneer work. Special mention should be made of

his book, *The Numeration, Calendar Systems and Astronomical Knowledge of the Mayas* (1910). This work was a landmark in the study of the Central American writing and served to focus attention on the subject as no other book had done. His mental agility in working out the dates of the inscriptions and his feats of rapid calculation were received with wonder and admiration by his friends and colleagues. He collected and presented to the Peabody Museum one of the best working libraries in Maya studies and he was responsible for the publication of several ancient documents in facsimile. He also gave the Museum over fifty thousand pages of photographic reproductions of manuscripts and rare books dealing with the languages of Mexico and Central America. This collection comprises practically everything in manuscript form now extant on the languages of these regions. His benefactions included the founding of fellowships and instructorships in Central American archæology. There is perhaps no other instance in American anthropology where an effort in one field of interest was so long sustained, so intense, and so productive of results. Following in the footsteps of his illustrious grandfather who translated Laplace's monumental *Mécanique céleste*, he translated numerous Spanish works the most important of which were Landa's *Relación de las Cosas de Yucatán* and Avendaño's *Relación*. His mind was an analytical one; he was a worthy foe of speculative theories and his studies and deductions in the Maya field were based on sound mathematical calculations. He was of striking appearance with a commanding figure. He had a very strong personality, trying to carry out the letter of the law and expecting others to do so. He was forceful yet full of modesty, always with opinions but willing to reason, wrathful before underhandedness but just to all.

[*Am. Anthropologist*, n.s., XXIII, 353–59 (portr.); *Proc. Am. Acad. of Arts and Sci.*, LVII, 476–78; *Report of the Class of 1863 Harvard Coll.* (1903, 1913); *Who's Who in America*, 1920–21.]
A.M.T.

BOWDITCH, HENRY INGERSOLL (Aug. 9, 1808–Jan. 14, 1892), physician and abolitionist, third son of Nathaniel Bowditch [*q.v.*] and Mary (Ingersoll) Bowditch, was born in Salem, Mass., where he resided until 1823 when his family moved to Boston. He received his early education at the Salem Private Grammar School, but when fifteen he entered the Boston Public Latin School. As a boy he exhibited no evidence of precocity, though at fourteen he won a diploma for Latin. He entered Harvard College in 1825, graduating in 1828, but did not distinguish himself as an undergraduate; his diary (*Life*, I, 12) at that period, however, shows a serious-minded young man, deeply religious and conscientious. With some misgivings he entered the Harvard Medical School (M.D., 1832), and went from there to the Massachusetts General Hospital (Boston) where he served during 1831–32 as a house-officer under James Jackson [*q.v.*]. He went to Paris in 1832, and his father's international reputation brought him at once into contact with many of the best minds of France. For two years Bowditch studied under Louis and followed him in his wards at *La Pitié,* from time to time in company with other young Boston physicians. He became deeply attached to Louis and looked upon him as the greatest leader of that day in medical science. When Bowditch went to England the contrast between Louis and the English physicians whom he met seemed so great that he left London in disgust (*Life,* I, 55) and returned to Paris for an extra year. While in England he attended and was deeply moved by the funeral of Wilberforce, whose writings had stirred him and were largely responsible for stimulating his desire for freedom of the slaves. His letters from Europe (*Life,* I, 32) are those of an alert and discerning fellow with much tact and a broad understanding of human nature. His religious turn of mind, however, always showed itself in his letters, and they exhibited little humor. In 1834 he returned to Boston where he soon acquired a moderate practise. At that time William Lloyd Garrison was thundering his denunciations of slavery. Bowditch listened and became at once an ardent follower. He severed his connection with Warren Street Chapel because the "pillars" of this institution refused to listen to abolitionist sermons. In 1842 Massachusetts opinion was acutely aroused by the arrest in Boston of George Latimer, a runaway slave. William F. Channing, Frederick S. Cabot, and Bowditch formed themselves into a "Latimer Committee" and edited the *Latimer Journal and North Star,* a tri-weekly publication issued from Nov. 11, 1842, until May 10, 1843. Bowditch's ardor in the cause of Latimer threatened to unbalance his mind. Later he assisted other runaway slaves, and no one did more than he to foster anti-slavery feeling in the North. Consequently this pious Christian did much to bring about the Civil War into which he entered with the spirit of a crusader of old. When his son, Nathaniel, was killed (1863) he said, "This summoned me like the notes of a bugle to a charging soldier" (*Ibid.,* II, 16). It led him to write *A Brief Plea for an Ambulance System for the Army of the United States; as drawn from the Extra Sufferings of the Late Lieut. Bowditch and a Wounded Comrade* (1863). The feeling

created by this pamphlet eventually caused the government to establish an ambulance unit of men trained to care for the wounded,—one of the great services rendered to the Northern armies.

Bowditch's other medical contributions were numerous and important. His training with Louis had aroused his interest in the diseases of the chest, and in 1846 he published *The Young Stethoscopist,* a work used by medical students for fifty years. Puncturing of the chest (paracentesis thoracis) for removal of pleural effusions was advocated by Bowditch in 1851 in a paper read (Oct. 20) to the Boston Society for Medical Observation (*American Journal of Medical Science,* April 1852). The use of the trocar and suction pump for this operation had been suggested by Dr. Morrill Wyman of Cambridge, Mass., but the world is indebted to Bowditch for bringing the procedure to the attention of physicians and, through repeated efforts, convincing them of its value. The operation was not new, having been employed spasmodically since the time of Hippocrates, but substitution of a hollow needle for a lancet made the procedure safe and simple. As a student of tuberculosis, also, Bowditch became distinguished. In 1836 appeared (in Boston) his English editions of Louis's two monographs on *Fever* [typhoid] and on *Phthisis.* The latter work greatly amplified Laennec's classical treatise (1819) on the pathology of tuberculosis. For many years Bowditch collected evidence concerning the influence of damp soil upon the spread of tuberculosis, which was carefully tabulated case by case and analyzed after the numerical method of Louis, but he did not publish his conclusions until 1862 (*Consumption in New England; or Locality One of Its Chief Causes*). Tuberculosis was a subject which occupied his mind until his death, his last published work being on the open-air treatment of the disease (*Transactions of the American Climatological Association,* VI, reprinted, XXVIII). In this paper one finds the modern conception of tuberculosis therapy clearly enunciated.

Bowditch's greatest service lay in the public health measures which were instituted through his efforts, and with the lapse of time his work in this field assumes ever-increasing significance. In 1869 was established the first Massachusetts State Board of Health (*Life,* II, 217–39) on which Bowditch served until 1879 preparing reports upon general questions relating to public health. The Massachusetts Board was the second in this country, the first having been established in Louisiana (1855). Bowditch's most important contribution in the field was his book, *Public Hygiene in America* (1877), in which is given a history of preventive medicine and a summary of sanitary law in various parts of the world. Bowditch's influence in stimulating the public health movement in the country was probably greater than that of any other man of his time. From 1859 to 1867 he was Jackson Professor of Clinical Medicine at the Harvard Medical School. He was a Fellow of the American Academy, an active member of the Massachusetts Medical Society (in which he held secretarial offices from 1849 to 1854), and was associated with the Massachusetts General Hospital from May 6, 1838, until the end of his life. He was also instrumental in founding the Boston Medical Library. In 1838 he married Olivia Yardley, an English girl of great charm whom he had met six years before at his lodgings in Paris. She died in December 1890, and he in January 1892 at the age of eighty-three.

[The numerous letters and diaries of Bowditch have been collected by his son, Vincent Yardley Bowditch, in a two-volume work, *Life and Correspondence of Henry Ingersoll Bowditch* (1902). A bibliography of his scientific works is to be found in the *Index Catalogue of the Surgeon General's Library,* ser. 1, 2, and 3. See also *Boston Medic. and Surgic. Jour.,* CLXVII, 603–07. All of Bowditch's numerous case-books have been deposited in the Boston Medic. Lib.]   J.F.F.

BOWDITCH, HENRY PICKERING (Apr. 4, 1840–Mar. 13, 1911), physiologist, came of Massachusetts families remarkable for scientific ability. His father, Jonathan Ingersoll Bowditch, a Boston merchant, who wrote on navigation and published nautical tables, was the son of the famous Nathaniel Bowditch [*q.v.*], the translator of Laplace and author of the *New American Practical Navigator* (1802). His mother, Lucy Orne Nichols, a grand-daughter of Col. Timothy Pickering (Washington's secretary of state), was related to John Pickering, an authority on Indian languages; to the astronomers, Edward and William Pickering; and to the mathematician, Benjamin Pierce;—a group of intellectuals who might have found a place in Francis Galton's "Noteworthy Families." Born in Boston, young Henry Bowditch was raised in the austere fashion of the place and period, but like other boys played on the Common and skated on the Frog Pond, and after the removal of his family to an estate at West Roxbury (1853) became expert in swimming, diving, sailing, and boat-building, through the attractions of Jamaica Pond nearby. He was prepared for college at the school of Epes S. Dixwell and entered Harvard in 1857, having already evinced an aptitude for medicine by setting up a complete articulated skeleton from the cadaver of one of his father's horses. Upon his graduation (1861), he entered the Lawrence Scientific School (Cambridge), where his studies in

chemistry and natural history were interrupted by the Civil War. In November 1861 he was commissioned second lieutenant in Company G, 2nd Battalion, 1st Massachusetts Cavalry. He participated in a number of raids and engagements, was wounded in the right forearm while leading a charge at New Hope Church (Nov. 27, 1863), entered Richmond with Weitzel (Apr. 3, 1865) as a major of the 5th Massachusetts Cavalry, and was honorably discharged from his command on June 3, 1865. At this period, he was described by Maj. H. L. Higginson as handsome, refined, homegrown, "with a fondness for keeping face clean and clothing neat when those attributes were a rarity," reserved and unbending in manner, of unequivocal loyalty and courage, yet with no particular liking for army life. Directly upon leaving the army, he resumed his studies at the Lawrence School, this time under the stimulating influence of the eminent comparative anatomist, Jeffries Wyman. While pursuing this course, he fulfilled the requirements of the Harvard Medical School, from which he was graduated M.D. in 1868. In the late summer of the same year, he proceeded to Paris, to follow physiology under Claude Bernard, histology under Ranvier, and neurology under Charcot. A chance meeting with the physiologist, Willy Kühne, in March 1869, led Bowditch to enter the laboratory of Carl Ludwig (Leipsig) in September. Ludwig was the greatest trainer of physiologists who ever lived, in Heidenhain's view, "the only physiologist who ever did anything." Under such a leader, Bowditch acquired the formative and directive stimuli which were to determine his subsequent career. Upon entering the Leipsig laboratory he delighted the old master by promptly inventing an automatic contrivance for registering the time relations of the blood-pressure tracings made on the revolving smoked drum attached to Ludwig's kymograph (1869). Under Ludwig, Bowditch made two investigations which are now classical. The first (1871) demonstrated the *Treppe* or step-wise increase of contraction of cardiac muscle under successive uniform stimuli, and the fact that, independently of the strength of stimulus, it will either contract to the maximal limit or not at all ("All or None" law). The second demonstrated that delphine will make the apex of an isolated heart beat rhythmically (1871), a discovery ten years in advance of the introduction of Ringer's solution (1880). A third paper, on the effect of variations of arterial blood-pressure upon the accelerator and inhibitory nerves of the heart, followed in 1872. Meanwhile, Charles W. Eliot, the new president of Harvard, had proposed that Bowditch give a course of university lectures on physiology in the second Harvard term (1871). This proposition Bowditch declined, as interrupting his studies, but Eliot's subsequent invitation "to take part in the good work of reforming medical education," with the offer of an assistant professorship of physiology (April 1871), was accepted, and Bowditch took ship from Liverpool on Sept. 14. Five days before sailing, he was married to Selma Knauth, the daughter of a hospitable Leipsig banker.

Bowditch came to his Harvard chair with a complete outfit of novel apparatus, purchased abroad at his own expense, but could only get the use of two small attic rooms in the old Medical School building on North Grove Street. Here, however, the first physiological laboratory in our country was started (1871), and Bowditch soon made it a going concern, imbued with the spirit of his great teacher. He invented new apparatus and gathered around him, as pupils, some of the best experimenters of his time, notably: C. S. Minot, W. P. Lombard, J. J. Putnam, William James (physiology), Isaac Ott and R. W. Lovett (experimental pharmacology), Stanley Hall and E. E. Southard (psychology), J. W. Warren (experimental pathology) and O. K. Newall (experimental surgery). With Minot, he showed the superiority of chloroform over ether in depressing vaso-motor reflexes (1874); with G. M. Garland, the effect of respiratory movements on the pulmonary circulation (1879–80); with Southard, the relative accuracy of sight and touch in estimating spatial relations (1880–82); with Stanley Hall, various optical illusions relative to moving objects (1880–82); with Warren, the effect of varying stimuli upon contraction and relaxation of blood-vessels (1883–86), and the effect of voluntary effort and external stimuli in reënforcing and depressing the knee-jerk (1890). In 1885 Bowditch made an investigation of the utmost practical importance, viz., his conclusive proof that nerve fibre cannot be tired out. Bernstein (1877) had concluded that the nerve in a nerve-muscle preparation can be tetanized (exhausted) by 5–15 minutes' stimulation, but Wedensky (1884) and Maschek (1887) had gotten response after 1–9 hours' stimulation by blocking the nerve by means of a galvanic current applied between the point of stimulation and the muscle (Wedensky) or by etherizing the same area (Maschek). Bowditch completed the proof by producing a functional nerve-block with curare and got muscular twitchings after 1–4 hours' stimulation in warm-blooded animals. He concluded that a nerve is like a telegraph wire and the passage of a nerve-current analogous to that of light

or electricity. This method of proof was the rationale of the conduction anæsthesia (nerve-blocking) subsequently introduced into surgery by Halsted, Cushing, and Crile. A minor experiment of 1876 illustrates Bowditch's originality of approach, namely his proof that ciliated epithelial cells can move weights up an inclined plane in one minute (unit) time with a force equal to the amount of work required to lift their own weight 4.25 metres. Of a piece with his skill in devising experiments was his talent for mechanical invention. He was the inventor of the Bowditch clock, the comfortable "Bowditch chair," a new induction coil, a new plethysmograph and many other ingenious devices used in the Harvard Laboratory. He was a pioneer in composite photography, to which he contributed a memorable early paper (McClure's Magazine) in 1894. Perhaps his most important work, apart from physiological experimentation, was his study of the rate of growth in school children (1872–91). In anthropometry, a Chinese invention, Bowditch was a pioneer. His measurements showed, in opposition to Quetelet's findings, that up to 11–12, boys are heavier and taller than girls, girls larger at 13–14, after which boys are again larger up to manhood; that large children begin to grow earlier than small children, that growth is more dependent upon environment (optimum nutrition) than upon race; and that loss of weight in growing children is a warning signal of approaching illness or decline in health. These data, in which Galton's percentile grades were utilized, are but little known apart from school hygiene, in which they are of paramount importance. With Bowditch's appointment to the Harvard chair, physiological teaching came into its own, and ceased to be a subordinated subject in the medical curriculum. Five years before, the few lectures given were delivered by the Parkman professor (O. W. Holmes), as part of his anatomical course. Five years later, Newell Martin brought the methods of Huxley and Michael Foster to Johns Hopkins University (1876). Bowditch taught the subject for thirty-five years, was appointed full professor in 1876 and George Higginson professor in 1903, and resigned this chair in 1906. Although a pioneer in laboratory instruction, he held fast to the didactic lecture and declared that "a good teacher with a bad method is more effective than a bad teacher with a good method." As early as 1900, he saw clearly that, apart from base-line instruction in the fundamental disciplines, elective courses would become a necessity in the crowded medical curriculum of the future. During the decade 1883–93, he was dean of the Harvard Medical Faculty, introduced a four-year course and a chair of bacteriology (H. C. Ernst), was a prime mover in the planning of the new school in Boylston St. (1881) and of the splendid later units which he lived to see completed in 1906. In 1896, he filed a strong brief against the anti-vivisectionists and did important public service through his reports on the alcohol problem in 1872, 1894, and 1903 (Committee of Fifty). He was a founder of the American Physiological Society (1887), succeeded Weir Mitchell as its second president (1888), and was reëlected during 1891–95. In 1877, he became a coeditor of Sir Michael Foster's *Journal of Physiology,* in which the investigations of the Harvard Laboratory were published up to 1898, when the *American Journal of Physiology* was established and financed by Bowditch's assistant, W. T. Porter. Bowditch was elected to membership in most of the leading scientific societies and received honorary doctorate degrees from the Universities of Cambridge (1898), Edinburgh (1898), Pennsylvania (1904), and Harvard (1906). Before his resignation from his chair (1906), he had become afflicted with a hopeless form of paralysis agitans. He quietly passed away on Mar. 13, 1911.

In his particular period, Bowditch was unquestionably the foremost American physiologist after Beaumont. His findings on the *Treppe,* the "All or None" principle, and the indefatigability of nerve are truly classical. Such features of conduction anæsthesia as shockless surgery or auto-surgery (operating upon oneself before a mirror) really derive from his nerve-blocking experiment of 1890. The rationale of school lunches and of the "Watch me grow" cards of school inspectors is to be found in his acute reasoning from the data of juvenile anthropometry. His mechanical ability ranged from prompt insight into the workings of complex apparatus, to such modes of handicraft as glass-blowing, turning the lathe, kite-flying, photography, and the making and repairing of furniture. In person, he was a sturdy, gallant, well-set-up figure of medium height, with aquiline features, pointed beard, cavalry mustache and shrewd, penetrating, humorous glance; serious and austere *au fond* rather than witty, yet full of fun and fond of a hearty laugh. The athletic habits of his boyhood were maintained and at his summer camp in the Adirondacks, where he entertained the leading physiologists of Europe for twenty years, he knew how to play. He was happy in his married life, and left a family of two sons, five daughters, and ten grandchildren. Recalling his visits to the Surgeon General's Library with his charming wife, it was a pleasure to see him enter an office room. He seemed to light up the musty atmosphere, as Osler may be said to have warmed it. His blithe, buoyant personality radiated joy of life and good will toward his fellow men.

[The authoritative biography of Bowditch is that of his Harvard successor, Prof. W. B. Cannon (*Memoirs Nat. Acad. Sci.,* XVII, 183–96). Appreciative memorials in *Science,* Apr. 21, 1911, p. 598, and *Boston Medic. and Surgic. Jour.,* Mar. 23, 1911, p. 438, cover much the same ground.]

F. H. G.

BOWDITCH, NATHANIEL (Mar. 26, 1773–Mar. 17, 1838), astronomer and mathematician, born in Salem, Mass., was the fourth of seven children of the shipmaster and cooper, Habakkuk Bowditch, by his wife Mary Ingersoll. His Bowditch ancestors were residents of Thorncombe, Dorsetshire, England, for at least one hundred and fifty years before the American founder of his family, a clothier, arrived at Salem, Mass., in 1671. So straitened were the family's circumstances that Nathaniel left school shortly after his tenth birthday to assist in his father's cooper shop. At about the age of twelve he became a clerk or apprentice in a ship-chandlery, an occupation which he continued until his first voyage in 1795. During these years he was constantly reading and studying. With a very retentive memory (except for people and their names) he acquired a vast fund of general information by reading every article in the four folio volumes of *Chambers' Cyclopædia* and *Supplement.* He began the study of algebra when fourteen years of age, constructed an almanac for 1790 when he was fifteen, studied French, and Euclid's *Elements,* and commenced at seventeen the acquisition of Latin in order to read Newton's *Principia,* which with volumes of the *Transactions of the Royal Society of London,* and many other scientific works was for him a source of constant inspiration and delight. During this period he also made a sun-dial and assisted in making a survey of Salem. Between Jan. 11, 1795, and Dec. 25, 1803, he made five voyages, the first in the capacity of clerk, the next three as supercargo, and the last as master and supercargo. In this way, being a keen observer, he became somewhat acquainted with many peoples in such places as Lisbon, Cadiz, Madeira, Réunion, Sumatra, Batavia, and Manila, and his journals of the voyages contain many interesting passages. Although every spare moment was devoted to study, he was popular with the crews and always ready to talk to them about the subjects engrossing his attention. He improved his knowledge of languages, especially Spanish, continued mathematical reading, and, on the suggestion of a publisher at Newburyport,

Mass., checked up the accuracy of the popular English work of J. H. Moore, *The Practical Navigator* (1st ed., London, 1772; 20th, 1828). From the thirteenth English edition of this work was prepared, in 1799, the first American edition "improved . . . revised and corrected by a skilful mathematician and navigator" (no name). This was Bowditch's first publication (in which his brother William collaborated). A second edition appeared in 1800. After preparing copy for a third edition, the additions to the original work were so numerous that it was decided to issue the volume under a different title, *The New American Practical Navigator,* as if Nathaniel Bowditch alone were the author; the book was mostly printed, but not published, in 1801. The printed copy was sold for 200 guineas to the English publishers of Moore's work on condition that the American and English editions should appear simultaneously in June 1802. The English edition was edited by Thomas Kirby (2nd ed., 1806; 3rd ed., 1809). A thirty-six page appendix to the first American edition was published in 1804. Nine other editions appeared during Bowditch's life, the last being the tenth in 1837. At least fifty-six further editions or reprints have since appeared under various auspices and editing. A few sections were translated into German by A. Hirsch (Giessen, 1863). In 1844 *Bowditch's Useful Tables* were reprinted from the work and of these there have been at least seventeen editions or reprints. During the first third of the nineteenth century the Bowditch-Moore work was the best of its kind in the English language. Bowditch's practical knowledge of this subject, acquaintance with various tables published, and his gift of clear exposition, accuracy in computation, and thoroughness, contributed notably to this result. After his third voyage, in 1799, Bowditch was elected a Fellow of the American Academy of Arts and Sciences of which he was afterwards to be president for the last nine years of his life. In 1802, shortly before he started on his fifth voyage, Harvard University conferred on him the honorary degree of Master of Arts, greatly to his surprise and gratification. It was about this time that he won the ardent admiration of a prominent Salem captain by translating a Spanish business document; this resulted in 1804 in his appointment as president of the Essex Fire and Marine Insurance Company, an office which he conducted with great sagacity and success till his removal to Boston in 1823 to become (at more than three times his previous salary) actuary of the Massachusetts Hospital Life Insurance Company, a position which he held till his death.

To the period of Bowditch's residence in Salem belongs practically all of his scientific activity. Apart from the work already mentioned, and a dozen problems proposed and solved in the five numbers of Adrain's *Analyst* (1808 and 1814), he made an admirable chart of the harbors of Salem, Beverly, and Manchester from a survey taken during 1804–06 (published 1806; second ed. 1834). But much more important were the twenty-three papers published (1804–20) in the *Memoirs of the American Academy of Arts and Sciences,* and the preparation of the translation, with much of the commentary, of the first four volumes (Paris, 1799–1805) of Laplace's *Mécanique céleste.* Indeed this latter work was done before 1818, although publication did not take place till 1829–39. The delay was caused by the fact that in wishing to preserve his entire independence Bowditch declined both the suggestion to publish his work by subscription, and the offer of the American Academy of Arts and Sciences to publish it at its own expense, and had to arrange his finances so as to have $12,000 available for publication expenses. So elaborate were the notes, in elucidation and in attempting to bring the subjects up to date, that the completed work contained nearly four thousand quarto pages and was considerably more than double the size of the original. This was Bowditch's most notable piece of scientific work and "made an epoch in American science by bringing the great work of Laplace down to the reach of the best American students of his time" (Newcomb, *Side-Lights on Astronomy,* 1906, p. 282). Most of Bowditch's twenty-three papers mentioned above dealt with astronomical and nautical matters. Those on the orbits of the comets of 1807, 1811, and 1819 were based on an enormous mass of calculations still preserved. Perhaps the most popular of his papers was the one in which he brought together various observations regarding the meteor that exploded over Weston, Conn., in 1807. This was reprinted in full in England, and abstracts appeared in both Germany and France. Bowditch's paper on the motion of a pendulum suspended from two points is notable because he there discussed mathematically for the first time what were many years later to become famous, in connection with certain acoustical phenomena, as Lissajous curves (Loria, *Spezielle algebraische und transscendente ebene Kurven,* I, 1902, 482). Bowditch was not a genius or discoverer, but rather a singularly sagacious critic, of the Delambre type, with an exceptionally endowed mind. That he won such a prominent place among early American intellectuals, and accomplished so much of a scientific nature, while most of his time was devoted to other affairs, was mainly due to his methodical habits, mental alertness, and indefatigable energy. He was married first on Mar. 25, 1798, to Elizabeth, daughter of Francis Boardman, but she died about six months later. On Oct. 28, 1800, he married his cousin Mary, only daughter of Jonathan Ingersoll, by whom he had six sons (two of whom attained to positions of eminence) and two daughters. The union proved to be extraordinarily felicitous. Inflexible integrity, loftiness of purpose, warmth of heart, simplicity of bearing, and entire absence of selfish ambition, were personal characteristics of Bowditch to offset occasional lapses in good judgment and unwise impetuosity of speech. In appearance he was slight of stature, "with high forehead, bright and penetrating eye, open and intelligent countenance." The best portrait of him is the one by Gilbert Stuart, his last work (1828). It is unfinished, only the head being painted and that not entirely completed. The hair is gray and the eyes grayish brown (L. Park, *Gilbert Stuart*, 1926).

[Exact information regarding Bowditch's early American and English ancestry, back to the first part of the sixteenth century, has been only recently discovered: *New Eng. Hist. and Geneal. Reg.*, LXXII (1918), LVIII (1924). The most valuable printed source of general information concerning Bowditch is the *Memoir* by his eldest son, Nathaniel Ingersoll, which appeared in the posthumous fourth volume (1839) of the *Mécanique Céleste*. Since only 500 copies of this work were printed the biography was reprinted in 1840, with four pages of supplementary material which is still further developed in *Remarks concerning the Late Dr. Bowditch by the Rev. Dr. Palfrey with the Replies of Dr. Bowditch's Children* (1840). A third edition with further additions and illustrations by Bowditch's third son, Henry I., was published in 1884. There was a supplement entitled *Christmas Day, Dec. 25, 1886* issued with two broadsides entitled respectively Bowditch Ancestry and Ingersoll Ancestry. The bibliography of the writings of Nathaniel Bowditch in the *Memoir* was reprinted in Runkle's *Mathematical Mo.*, vol. II, 1860. Henry I. was also the author of an excellent anonymous *Memoir* of his father (1841, 1870), for the young, the first edition of which (practically the same as what appeared in Horace Mann's *Common School Jour.*, vol. II, 1840) was a little volume for the Warren Street Chapel; he published further: *Sketch of the Life and Character of Nathaniel Bowditch . . . made at the dedication of the Bowditch School* (1863). There is material of value in *Life and Correspondence of Henry Ingersoll Bowditch by his son V. Y. Bowditch* (1902). In the Boston Pub. Lib. are thirty-one volumes of Bowditch's manuscripts which include the journals of his five voyages 1795–1803; (the Essex Institute has Bowditch copies of the journals of the second and fifth voyages). There are also three volumes of correspondence, mainly connected with his translation, of which the four manuscript volumes were willed to Harvard College but by vote of the President and Fellows, in 1884, were deposited in the Boston Pub. Lib. There are also two volumes of valuable manuscript biographical material prepared by N. I. Bowditch. In the library of the American Academy of Arts and Sciences there is some Bowditch correspondence. Interesting facts are given in H. S. Tapley's *Salem Imprints 1768–1825* (1927).]

R. C. A.

BOWDOIN, JAMES (Aug. 7, 1726–Nov. 6, 1790), merchant, Revolutionary statesman, the son of James and Hannah (Pordage) Bowdoin, was born in Boston. The family was of French origin, his grandfather, Pierre Baudouin, a Huguenot refugee, having settled in New England in 1687, first in Maine, and three years later, during the Indian wars, at Boston. The first James Bowdoin became one of the leading merchants of America and at the time of his death in 1747 had accumulated what was probably the largest estate in New England. A final accounting to the Suffolk probate court in 1757 showed a total valuation of £82,875 sterling, a huge sum for that period. The second James Bowdoin graduated from Harvard in 1745 and became a merchant like his father. He married, Sept. 15, 1748, Elizabeth, daughter of John Erving, another prosperous Boston merchant. While not as active in business as his father had been, he was a successful man of affairs and made profitable use of his share of the estate. He met serious losses from time to time in the troublous years of revolutionary disturbance, but on Jan. 26, 1779, Samuel Dexter, writing him as to the havoc wrought to creditor interests by paper money, remarks, "The sum you had out on loan was vastly greater than mine; your loss, consequently, if your debtors have been as cruelly unjust as mine, is proportionally greater. But your real estates will, after all, leave you a gentleman of an ample fortune" (*Proceedings of the Massachusetts Historical Society*, ser. 1, vol. VI, p. 360). In addition to important properties in Boston, Bowdoin was a large holder of Maine lands. His familiarity with problems of commerce, industry, money, exchange, and related matters is apparent in his writings and public activities during the prolonged disputes with the mother country and in the domestic disturbances which followed the establishment of American independence. It was natural that British trade restriction should be opposed by merchants like Bowdoin, Hancock, Gerry, Quincy, and others, whose interests were adversely affected, but their property holdings also made their position especially dangerous should resistance prove unsuccessful.

Bowdoin's political career began in 1753 when he was elected to the General Court, and continued with brief intermissions, due in most cases to ill health, until Massachusetts had ratified the Federal Constitution thirty-five years later. He lacked a robust physique and contemporaries describe him as consumptive, facts which undoubtedly prevented him on several occasions from attaining greater distinction in public affairs. He served in the lower house for three terms, and in 1757 was chosen a member of the Council. His appearance in the latter body was of the utmost importance. The Council had, in general, been more inclined to support the imperial viewpoint than the popular branch, and with the rise of troublesome issues after the close of the French and Indian War, its attitude was likely to be decisive in developing Massachusetts policies. A divided Assembly would have been of great advantage to the British authorities. It was Bowdoin's influence that aligned the Council with the colonial interests (Thomas Hutchinson, *History of Massachusetts Bay,* III, 1828, p. 156). He was in close touch with Sam Adams, John Hancock, James Otis, and other popular leaders, and Hutchinson in one of his letters describes him as "talking their jargon, where government is the subject." Bowdoin was the author of many of the documents since published in the *Massachusetts State Papers,* protests, petitions, addresses to the British governors and similar statements on current issues. As might be expected from a man thoroughly conversant with colonial trade conditions, he continually stresses the economic aspects of the dispute, although some able constitutional arguments are offered as well. His letters to friends in England, especially those to former Gov. Thomas Pownall, with whom he was on cordial terms, show the same emphasis on the desirability of freer trade relations (*Massachusetts Historical Society Collections,* ser. 6, vol. IX, p. 142).

In 1774 Bowdoin's service under the Province Government was terminated when Gen. Gage negatived his election to the Council. He had served in that body for sixteen out of seventeen preceding years, covering the entire pre-Revolutionary agitation. A few days before the final disintegration of British authority the General Court elected him as delegate to the Continental Congress. At this point the failure of his own health and the serious illness of his wife led him to decline the new post and John Hancock was chosen to fill his place. Inability to accept this election was unfortunate. It deprived the Congress of a potential leader of temperate statesmanlike qualities and it later subjected Bowdoin himself to charges of luke-warmness in the cause of revolution. The letters of contemporaries and the fact that he retained the confidence and friendship of the other Massachusetts patriots are a sufficient refutation of charges of malingering or indifference. In August 1775 the Provincial Congress appointed him first member of the executive council of twenty-eight which handled much of the public business in the years preceding the establishment of regular government under the constitution of 1780. Still complaining of physical weakness, he felt obliged to resign in 1777. He was unable, in fact, to do much work between the outbreak of the war and the meeting of the constitutional convention, Sept. 1, 1779.

Bowdoin's election to the latter body marks the beginning of the great period in his career. In the next ten years Massachusetts was transformed from a loosely organized revolutionary community into a stable, well-governed commonwealth. It passed from the inflation and demoralization of war conditions through a slough of economic depression and bankruptcy to economic stability, restored credit, and commercial revival. In this period Bowdoin was an outstanding figure and his services at the most critical moment made him "the great governor" of that long interval between the departure of Gen. Gage and the inauguration of John A. Andrew. Bowdoin was elected president of the constitutional convention and chairman of the subcommittee which was charged with the actual drafting of the instrument. John Adams was the author of the greater part of the constitution which finally appeared, but John Lowell, himself a member, states that Bowdoin was frequently consulted and exercised considerable influence. Hancock was chosen governor at the first election, Bowdoin declining the lieutenant-governorship and also a place in the Senate. He served, however, with a committee of jurists which was engaged in the important task of revising and adjusting the old laws to meet the new conditions of statehood. With the restoration of peace a serious situation arose. Massachusetts like the rest of the country suffered from the stoppage of foreign trade, a staggering burden of public and private debt, and all the other social and economic evils which follow a protracted war. When Hancock announced his retirement from the governorship in January 1785, it was apparent that serious trouble impended. Party lines were not yet drawn, but Bowdoin was put forward as the candidate of the conservative mercantile interests and in this contest can be clearly traced the beginnings of the great division which eventually resulted in the Federalist and Republican alignments. The contest between Bowdoin and Thomas Cushing, the latter regarded as the "popular" candidate, was close and bitter. Bowdoin now had to face charges of luke-warmness in Revolutionary days and pro-British leanings, the second being rendered plausible by the fact that his only daughter had married John Temple, a former surveyor-general of customs who later inherited a baronetcy. Through lack of a popular majority the election was thrown into the legislature. Here the Senate, where commercial and property interests were disproportionately strong, insisted on the selection of Bowdoin and the lower chamber at length receded from its preference for his opponent. On May 26, 1785, his election as governor was formally announced.

Bowdoin's administration, and particularly his handling of the crisis of 1786–87, were long the theme of unqualified eulogy. That he performed great services for the state, and incidentally, for the country at large, is undeniable. Whether a higher quality of statesmanship could not have averted actual insurrection is another question. The legislature, as such bodies frequently do, wasted time on irrelevant matters and showed no disposition to attack the difficult problems demanding solution. The Governor can hardly be said to have shown the ablest type of leadership at this juncture. His formal address of May 31, 1785, was a clear and accurate summary of existing conditions. Time, he stated, was needed to remedy the situation. Retrenchment, strict economy, payment of interest when due, and a general adherence to "principles of honor and strict honesty" would bring eventual cure. As a diagnosis and statement of a wholesome regimen for the future it was admirable, but a patient suffering as acutely as Massachusetts was in 1785 needed immediate relief. In one matter, however, the Governor displayed the vision of a real statesman, in a plea for an enlargement of the powers of Congress which would permit adequate control of commerce, without which stable conditions were likely to prove impossible. Resolutions supporting this idea and recommending a convention of delegates from all the states to act on the problem were voted by the legislature and transmitted by the Governor to the delegates in Congress and the other state executives. Bowdoin therefore deserves an honorable place among those who took an early and influential part in the movement which eventually produced the Federal Constitution. At his suggestion the legislature passed an act intended to impose retaliatory restrictions on British shipping, the effects of which were promptly nullified by the selfish action of Connecticut in opening her ports, an action which at least confirmed Bowdoin's contentions as to the need of national control. His messages at subsequent sessions during the year show the same interest in and grasp of commercial principles displayed in the dispute with the mother country. His suggestions as to the need of developing American manufactures,

especially in woolens, are in line with those urged by the advocates of "the American system" several decades later. One manufacture, that of gunpowder, he declared might prove essential for the safety of the Commonwealth itself. He was reëlected without difficulty in 1786. Internal conditions were going from bad to worse and by the summer of 1786, the situation in Massachusetts was rapidly getting out of hand. County conventions were meeting and threatening to stop the operations of the courts. Foreclosure proceedings, inevitable under the existing depression, were stirring the debtor classes to actual resistance. In September several instances of armed interference with judicial processes actually occurred. The Governor met the situation with promptness and vigor. The legislature was summoned in special session, militia were ordered out to protect the courts and the Governor announced that the authority of the government would be exercised to maintain order and enforce the laws. Compared with the dilatory actions of the legislature at this period the Governor's conduct stood out in bold contrast. Funds were gathered from various voluntary subscribers, Bowdoin himself, it is said, contributing generously. Beginning in January 1787, Gen. Benjamin Lincoln's militiamen by a few vigorous blows dispersed the insurgents and ended the danger. "Vigour, decision, energy, will soon terminate this unnatural, this unprovoked insurrection, and prevent the effusion of blood," said Bowdoin to the February session of the legislature, "but the contrary may involve the Commonwealth in a civil war, & all its dreadful consequences; which may extend to the whole confederacy, & finally destroy the fair temple of American liberty, in the erecting of which, besides the vast expence of it, many thousands of valuable citizens have been sacrificed." There is abundant evidence that this view was shared in official circles throughout the confederation, that steps were being taken to meet possible developments, and that Bowdoin's Napoleonic methods were widely approved beyond New England and that their success greatly increased his prestige. In Massachusetts, however, his standing had suffered. There was an undercurrent of sympathy, not wholly unjustifiable, for the insurgents, and a feeling that needed reforms had been too slow in forthcoming. In a retrenchment movement the legislature had reduced the Governor's salary, an act which Bowdoin promptly vetoed on constitutional grounds, to his own political hurt. In the spring elections Hancock was again chosen governor by a decisive majority. Bowdoin retired Apr. 26, 1787, with a graceful acknowledgment of the fact that the public desires coincided with his own.

One more public service remained. The Massachusetts situation had furnished a powerful impetus to the movement toward effective union of the states. On Jan. 9, 1788, the Massachusetts convention met to pass on the adoption of the Federal Constitution. Bowdoin was a delegate from Boston and his son represented Dorchester. He spoke but twice in the course of debate, defending the principle of delegated powers under which he said, "the whole Constitution is a declaration of rights" and urging adoption as the only preventive of financial collapse and general anarchy. Ratification was voted by a narrow majority, and on Aug. 12 Bowdoin wrote to a relative in England his confident expectation that the states "from choice as well as necessity," and in view of past experiences would loyally support the new plan "and will be very happy under it" (*Proceedings of the Massachusetts Historical Society*, ser. 2, vol. XI, p. 178).

His death took place on Nov. 6, 1790. He had renewed in 1788 a long-standing correspondence on scientific matters with Benjamin Franklin, whose death preceded his own by a few months. Like Franklin, he had found time in the midst of public affairs and business activity to develop an interest in science and literature. He was especially interested in physics and astronomy and wrote a number of papers for the *Transactions of the American Academy of Arts and Sciences* (founded in 1780) of which he was the first president, and to which he bequeathed a valuable library. Amid the political disturbances of 1769 it is interesting to find him discussing with Gen. Gage the organization of an expedition to Lake Superior to observe the transit of Venus. He was a member of several learned societies, American and foreign, and the holder of honorary degrees from Harvard and Edinburgh. With such a combination of interests in life, it was eminently fitting that his chief memorial should have been the college chartered four years after his death and named in his honor, which in 1802 on the edge of the Maine wilderness began the work of developing in a new generation something of the same interest in letters, science, and public service.

Lacking the qualities which made Sam Adams a great popular leader, or the training and cast of thought which enabled John Adams, Thomas Jefferson, or Alexander Hamilton to exert such profound influence on the political theory of the day, and unlike Franklin or Robert Morris debarred from a wider field of service in diplomacy or administration, Bowdoin has, nevertheless, a

secure place among the founders of the republic. Massachusetts occupied a strategic position. A leader who contributed so largely to its conquest by the forces of independence and who rendered equally important service in consolidating that position amid the confusion and turmoil which followed the victory is entitled to national recognition.

[The chief sources of information regarding James Bowdoin are the Bowdoin and Temple Papers published in the *Mass. Hist. Soc. Colls.*, ser. 6, vol. IX and ser. 7, vol. VI. The preface in the former volume contains a list of scattered papers published from time to time in earlier volumes of the *Proceedings* of the same society. The collection of documents, *Speeches of the Governors of Mass. from 1765 to 1775; and the Answers of the House of Representatives to the Same* (1818), ed. by A. Bradford, includes many items drafted by committees of which Bowdoin was a member. His messages and other papers issued while governor are to be found in *Laws and Resolves of Mass. 1786–87* (1863, reprinted 1893). An account of Bowdoin's life and services is given by R. C. Winthrop in *Washington, Bowdoin and Franklin* (1876). Daniel Goodwin in *Provincial Pictures* (1886) has a brief sketch. Casual letters and references occur in the papers of the Adamses and other contemporaries, and Temple Prime in *Some Account of the Bowdoin Family* (1887) has genealogical data. There is a considerable monograph literature on Massachusetts history during the period of Bowdoin's public life, especially the later stages, among which the following will be found useful: A. E. Morse, *The Federalist Party in Mass. to the Year 1800* (1909); J. P. Warren, "The Confederation and the Shays Rebellion," *Am. Hist. Rev.*, XI, 42–67; H. A. Cushing, *Hist. of the Transition from Provincial to Commonwealth Government in Mass.* (1896); S. B. Harding, *The Contest over the Ratification of the Federal Constitution in the State of Mass.* (1896); and S. E. Morison, "The Struggle over the Adoption of the Constitution of Mass. (1780)," *Mass. Hist. Soc. Proc.*, L, 353–411.]   W. A. R.

BOWDOIN, JAMES (Sept. 22, 1752–Oct. 11, 1811), merchant, diplomat, was the only son of Gov. James Bowdoin [*q.v.*]. He was third in succession to bear the name, and the last of the Boston branch of the family in the male line. He was born in Boston, graduated at Harvard in 1771, studied at Christ Church, Oxford, traveled in Europe, and returned to Massachusetts shortly after the outbreak of the Revolution. Unable to enter military service because of bad health, which handicapped him throughout life, he engaged in mercantile business for several years. He married on May 18, 1781, his cousin Sarah, daughter of his father's half-brother, William Bowdoin. Like the other members of the family he seems to have been a successful business man but his property had now reached the stage where undoubtedly he could apply to his own affairs the rules he suggested "as a friend who had had a little experience upon this subject" to George W. Erving: "Avoid all speculations with a view to accumulation. You will find the legal interest of money upon good securities, or investments in the public stocks of the U. S. for your productive capital, and the lands of the U. S.

from their gradual increase in value will be the best plan of appropriating such sums as you may not require for your immediate support. . . . A man who is not and cannot be at the beginning and end of active commercial concerns ought never to be engaged in them . . ." (*Massachusetts Historical Society Collections,* ser. 7, vol. VI, p. 306). He was five times elected to the General Court as representative of Dorchester, 1786–90, was a member of the state Senate in 1794 and 1801, and of the Governor's Council in 1796. He was also a member of the convention of 1788, where he spoke and voted for the ratification of the Federal Constitution. In 1796 he moved from Dorchester to Boston. Since he was a Jeffersonian Republican, in spite of connections social and otherwise which might have been expected to draw him into the opposite party, strong Federalist predominance in the Boston district after 1801 ended any chance of political advancement in the region. In 1797 he published anonymously *Opinions Respecting the Commercial Intercourse Between the United States of America, and the Dominions of Great Britain, Including Observations upon the Necessity of an American Navigation Act,* which in its strictures on British trade regulations, its keen analysis of commercial principles, and its vigorous demand for a retaliatory policy, is reminiscent of some of his father's pronouncements thirty years before.

In November 1804 he was appointed minister to Spain by President Jefferson and sailed for his post the following spring, his health in the meantime having become so seriously impaired that he dared not risk a journey to Washington for a farewell interview with the President. The Administration was then engaged in devious negotiations with Spain regarding the possible acquisition of West Florida, the western boundaries of the Louisiana Purchase, and sundry spoliation claims. On reaching the Spanish coast in the summer of 1805 he learned that his predecessor had been successful in negotiating a treaty and that relations with Spain were so unsatisfactory that he deemed it inadvisable to proceed to Madrid, a decision which met the approval of the President and Secretary of State. He spent some time in England and then in Paris. On Mar. 17, 1806, negotiations were transferred to Paris, where he was empowered, together with Gen. Armstrong, minister to France, to conduct new negotiations respecting Florida. This, of course, meant that all transactions would be dominated by Napoleon whom Bowdoin described as "the wonder, the dread, the admiration of Europe." Spain, he had already discovered, was "so completely under control of this government that it has but the semblance of independence, and it may be considered as little more than a department of France with the Prince of Peace its prefect" (letter to President Jefferson, Mar. 1, 1806). His experience during the next two years was unfortunate. He failed to maintain working relations with his colleague, and his letters disclose frequent annoyances and rebuffs. Negotiations failed, Napoleon's ruthlessness, foresight, and deceit completely baffling the American diplomats who were as unsuited for such a contest as Massachusetts militia officers would have been for Austerlitz or Wagram. He returned to America in 1808, receiving, however, friendly assurances of confidence and esteem from the President.

The remainder of his life was given to study and the improvement of his agricultural property, especially the estate at Nashawn Island, Buzzard's Bay, where his death occurred three years later. One of his last activities was the translation of Louis Daubenton's *Instruction pour les bergers et pour les propriétaires de troupeaux* (1810), an edition of which he printed at his own expense in the interest of the growing woolen industry. He is reported to have been increasingly active in various philanthropic activities during his last years. He had already donated land and money to the college which had been named in honor of his father and he made additional bequests in his will, including a collection of paintings and drawings made while abroad, his library and scientific apparatus. Dying without issue, he made the college residuary legatee and following the death of his nephew, James Temple Bowdoin, a reversionary interest in the estate brought a further notable increase to its resources in 1844, although not without troublesome litigation.

[A brief biographical notice of the younger Bowdoin is prefixed to the "Bowdoin and Temple Papers," *Mass. Hist. Soc. Colls.,* ser. 6, vol. IV. A considerable body of correspondence, especially letters written from abroad, is found in *Ibid.,* ser. 7, vol. VI, pp. 199–456. An obituary notice of some merit appears in the *Independent Chronicle,* Boston, Oct. 21, 1811.]   W. A. R.

BOWEN, ABEL (Dec. 3, 1790–Mar. 11, 1850), wood engraver, publisher, one of twelve children of Abel Bowen and Delia Mason, was born in Sand Lake Village, Greenbush, N. Y. In 1811 he moved to Boston and soon established himself as a printer. He then began a varied activity, characteristic of a period when Americans apparently regarded themselves as capable jacks-of-all-trades. A wood engraver, he turned also to copper engraving. Stauffer lists portraits and views by him, some from his own drawings, somewhat dry and colorless. In 1821 he was associated with Alexander McKenzie, copperplate printer. He drew on stone the illustrations for an American edition of Sir Astley Paston Cooper's lectures. Of his work on wood, his copies of English cuts for an American edition of *The Young Ladies' Book* (1830) were "very remarkable for their fidelity to the original," writes W. J. Linton. The combination "engraver, publisher" describes his activity. Described by W. H. Whitmore as "one in the chain of local antiquaries," Bowen early began to publish or plan volumes illustrated with copperplates or wood engravings or both, many of them by himself. There were the *Naval Monument* (1816), Caleb H. Snow's *History of Boston* (1825), in which Abel's brother Henry appears as printer, and *Picture of Boston* (1828). In 1834 appeared the first number of the *American Magazine of Useful and Entertaining Knowledge*, in Boston, published by John L. Sibley and James B. Dow, and copyrighted by the Boston Bewick Company. This company was a group of wood engravers (Bowen, Alonzo Hartwell, John H. Hall, Wm. Croome, John C. Crosman, and others), associated "for the purpose of employing, improving, and extending the art of engraving. . . ." The Introduction to the magazine promises that "the engravings will be of the first order," and in volume one there is an article on Thomas Bewick, "our patron saint." At the end of the second volume the editor, in an adieu to his duties, states that the embellishments were selected chiefly by the engravers, and suggests that "the interests of the work might have been promoted by allowing the editor the privilege of a veto, at least." One is inclined to agree with him. The third volume was issued in 1837 without the name of the Bewick Company. Whitmore quotes "one of the artists of the last generation" thus : "Bowen was the real founder of the art of wood engraving here [*i. e.*, in Boston], not so much by his own productions as by the stimulus he gave to the subject." As to his influence, Linton names Croome, Devereux, Mallory, Kilburn, Childs, George Loring Brown, and Hammatt Billings among his pupils, for which list no confirmation has been found. Of Bowen's private life little has been recorded. We are told that he was married to Eliza Healy, had ten children, and struggled on, year after year, in the face of reverses, poverty, and long continued illness, and that he died after two years of illness, patiently borne.

[The principal source of information is W. H. Whitmore's "Abel Bowen : a Sketch," in *Bostonian Soc. Colls.*, vol. I (1887), containing impressions of a number of copperplates and woodblocks engraved by Bowen. D. M. Stauffer's *Am. Engravers upon Copper and Steel*

(1907), with Fielding's *Supplement* (1917), lists his work on copper. W. J. Linton's *Hist. of Wood-Engraving in America* (1882) deals with his engravings on wood.]   F.W.

BOWEN, FRANCIS (Sept. 8, 1811–Jan. 21, 1890), philosopher, was born in Charlestown, Mass., the son of Dijah and Elizabeth (Flint) Bowen. One of a large family, he was early obliged to support himself, at least in part, by clerking in a publishing house and by teaching. He was educated in the Mayhew School, Boston, in Phillips Exeter Academy (one term), and in Harvard College (three years), graduating from the latter with highest honors in 1833. His Bachelor's oration, we are assured, was "a sober, chaste performance" (*Proceedings of the Massachusetts Historical Society,* January 1890). He taught mathematics for two years at Exeter, after which he returned to Harvard as tutor in intellectual philosophy and political economy. In 1839 he went to Europe for a year of study and travel. In 1843 he succeeded Dr. Palfrey as proprietor and editor of the *North American Review,* a position which he held for a little over a decade. During the visit to America of Louis Kossuth, in 1851, the cause which the Hungarian revolutionist represented was sharply attacked by Bowen (*Hungary, The Rebellion of the Slavonic, Wallachian, and German Hungarians against the Magyars*). The imperialist paid for this temerity in offending popular American sentiment by losing an appointment to which he had been nominated as McLean professor of history in Harvard. In 1853, however, he was appointed Alvord professor of natural religion, moral philosophy, and civil polity in the same institution. This position he held for thirty-six years. He came into national prominence once again in November 1888. Long known as a protectionist in principle, he was then appealed to by the Republican national chairman for a public indorsement of the party's tariff platform, to which he replied by a stinging denunciation of the current tariff as a tyranny, crushing native industries and taxing the necessities of life (*Nation,* Nov. 8, 1888). At the age of seventy-four he resigned his position in Harvard, and died shortly thereafter. He was married to Arabella, daughter of Col. and Eliza (Austin) Stuart.

As a philosopher Bowen was chiefly interested in harmonizing philosophy with Christianity. His type of thought might be characterized as natural realism modified by Kantian elements. His most important work, *Modern Philosophy, from Descartes to Schopenhauer and Hartmann* (1877), is of value for its power of critical exposition and illustration and its terse, lucid, and animated style. Its analysis and discussion of

Kant's thought is particularly able and interesting. In his polemics Bowen was somewhat prone to bend logic to meet the demands of argument, as in his vigorous attack upon the theory of evolution. He too frequently confounded the appeal to reason with the appeal to the emotions. He also spread his energy over too many fields to attain supremacy in any of them. Besides numerous magazine articles, he was the author of: *Life of Sir William Phips* (1837); *Life of Baron Steuben* (1838); *Critical Essays on a Few Subjects Connected with the History and Present Condition of Speculative Philosophy* (1842); *Life of James Otis* (1844); *Life of Benjamin Lincoln* (1847); *Lowell Lectures on the Application of Metaphysical and Ethical Science to the Evidences of Religion* (1849); *Documents of the Constitution of England and America to 1789 compiled and edited* (1854); *Principles of Political Economy* (1856); *Virgil, with English Notes* (1860); *Treatise on Logic* (1864); *American Political Economy* (1870); *Modern Philosophy, from Descartes to Schopenhauer and Hartmann* (1877); *Gleanings from a Literary Life* (1880); *A Layman's Study of the English Bible* (1885).

[Sketch in *Old Charlestown* (1902), by Timothy T. Sawyer; Chas. W. Eliot, *Harvard Memories* (1923), p. 73; *Memorials of the Class of 1833 of Harvard Coll.* (1883); *Harv. Univ. Quinquennial Cat.*, 1915; *Boston Evening Transcript*, Jan. 22, 1890; *Boston Herald*, Jan. 22, 23, 1890; *Critic*, Feb. 1, 1890.]   E.S.B.

BOWEN, GEORGE (Apr. 30, 1816–Feb. 5, 1888), missionary, was born in Middlebury, Vt. His father, a New York merchant and man of means, spent his money in building up a library in his home, rather than in the education of his children. He took George from school at the age of twelve to train him to take over the business. George loathed the business and took refuge in the library, where he read omnivorously. At the age of sixteen he decided on a literary career combined with music. His love of operatic music set him to studying German, French, Italian, and Spanish. These he further mastered by four years of extensive travel in Europe (1836–40). A chapter in Gibbon's *Decline and Fall of the Roman Empire* had turned him in 1833 into a sceptic and bitter critic of all religion. During the years in Europe he built up his defenses against Christianity. The death of his fiancée in quiet Christian trust changed him. On returning home one evening he discovered that a librarian's error had placed in his hands Paley's *Natural Theology*. This work drove him to a rereading of the Bible and a fresh search. The result was a "conversion" that completely transformed his life (April 1844). Within four weeks he had offered himself to the American Board of Commissioners for Foreign Missions, and after three years at Union Theological Seminary, New York (1844–47), he sailed for India. He arrived in Bombay Jan. 19, 1848, and to this city he gave the remaining forty years of his life. He never married, he took no furlough, he went to no hills for his health. Slight of build and not robust, he remained at his post. Sensing keenly the social chasm between the native and the European he tried to bridge it by living in the simplicity of the poor, in a little room of an old pensioner's mud-walled house, on less than $200 a year. He withdrew from the American Board and earned his living by tutoring, and later, by editing and publishing the *Bombay Guardian* (associate editor, 1851–54; editor, 1854–88). His conduct pained his friends and stirred up the European community, which felt itself disgraced by this erratic missionary. Yet he was no ascetic, for he went wherever he was invited, and ate what was set before him. He later confessed that the chasm was more than social and the experiment not altogether successful, though he did not regret his step. He preached daily in the streets of the city in the Marathi and Hindustani languages, and served, without pay, as the editor of the Marathi publications of the Bombay Book and Tract Society, and agent of the Tract Depot, to which he transferred his living quarters. In 1871 he associated himself with the work begun by William Taylor, the traveling Methodist evangelist, for the Europeans and English-speaking Indians of Bombay. This relationship resulted in his joining the Methodists (1873). He became a charter member of the South India Conference, was three years presiding elder in Bombay, and twice, in the absence of the bishop, the president of the Conference. His editorials in the *Bombay Guardian*, "sharply pungent or sweetly fragrant," attracted attention and were published in Scotland (Edinburgh) and the United States (Presbyterian Board of Publications, Philadelphia) in three volumes: *Daily Meditations, The Amens of Christ,* and *Love Revealed.* They have been widely influential as books of devotion. His death, by pneumonia, revealed strikingly the hold he had gained upon the affections of the city of his life-service. He was known as "the white saint of India."

[The chief sources of information are the files of the *Bombay Guardian* (1851–88); the *Annual Reports* of the Missionary Soc. of the M. E. Ch.; the *Annual Reports* of the South India Conference of the M. E. Ch.; the introduction to Bowen's *Daily Meditations* (1865); Wm. Taylor, *Four Years' Campaign in India* (1876); and the many testimonials at the time of Bowen's death, particularly "In Memoriam, Geo. Bowen," *Christian Advocate* (N. Y.), 1888, pp. 120 ff.; see also E. M. Bliss, *Encyc. of Missions* (1891).]   O.M.B.

BOWEN, HENRY CHANDLER (Sept. 11, 1813–Feb. 24, 1896), merchant, publisher, editor, was descended from Lieut. Henry Bowen, one of the first settlers of Woodstock, Conn., who had come from Wales with his father, Griffith, in 1638. George Bowen, descendant in the fifth generation from Henry, kept the country store and tavern at Woodstock, and there Henry Chandler was born. His mother was Lydia Wolcott Eaton. He was educated at Woodstock and Dudley Academies. After four years as clerk in his father's store, he went to New York to work in a silk house. In 1838 he established the firm of Bowen & McNamee, which later became Bowen & Holmes. In 1850 Bowen & McNamee were attacked, especially by the *Journal of Commerce,* because of their refusal to sign a call, prepared by a large group of prominent merchants, for a meeting to indorse the fugitive slave law. They published a card in which they informed the public that while they were silk merchants, as individuals they entertained their own views "on the various religious, moral and political questions of the day." They then added, "We wish it distinctly understood that our goods, and not our principles, are on the market." In 1848 Bowen joined in founding the *Independent,* a weekly journal of Congregationalism with strong anti-slavery principles. Later he became its publisher and finally its sole proprietor. He promptly brought the paper from a losing to a paying condition. Henry Ward Beecher and Theodore Tilton became successive editors of the *Independent* and Bowen was drawn by his intimacy with them into the mazes of the famous legal action of Tilton *vs.* Beecher for alienation of affections. On Dec. 26, 1870, he carried from Tilton to Beecher a letter demanding that the latter, "for reasons which you explicitly understand," immediately resign his pastorship of Plymouth Church and leave Brooklyn. A few days later he abruptly terminated the contract which he had with Tilton as a special contributor to the *Independent* and as editor of the *Brooklyn Union,* which he also owned. In April 1872, as the result of an arbitration by friends of the three men, a tripartite agreement was signed by Bowen, Tilton, and Beecher in which Bowen declared that "having given credit . . . to tales and innuendoes affecting" Beecher and having repeated them, he now felt that he had done Beecher wrong. He expressly withdrew all "the charges, imputations and innuendoes" and promised that he would never by word or deed "recur to, repeat or allude" to them again. At the same time he paid Tilton $7,000 in satisfaction of the broken contracts and published in the *Independent* a card in which he recognized Tilton's

"honest purposes, and his chivalrous defense of what he believes to be true, as well as those qualities of heart which make him dear to those who know him best." Beecher reprinted with his cordial approval this "honorable testimony from Mr. Bowen" in the *Christian Union,* which he was then editing. In December 1873, charges were brought against Bowen before Plymouth Church of "uttering slanders affecting the good name" of its pastor, but the recommendation of the Examining Committee, that they be dismissed on the ground that he had agreed to keep to the letter and the spirit of the "tripartite agreement," was adopted. Shortly afterward he published a card protesting against the action because he had never seen a copy of the charges and because the committee had not put its recommendation "on the only pertinent basis that there was no evidence to sustain the charges." He expressed amazement that the "tripartite agreement" had been made public, "all the parties to which were solemnly pledged not to reveal it." Bowen was active in the development of Congregational interests in New York and Brooklyn, and was instrumental in the raising in 1852 of the Albany Fund for the erection of Congregational churches throughout the country, to which he made a substantial contribution. He participated in the organization of the Congregational Union, from which developed the Congregational Church Building Society. He was a generous benefactor of his native town, and subscribed liberally to rebuild and endow Woodstock Academy, to pay the town's Civil War debt, and to support the Woodstock Agricultural Society. He established a public park in Woodstock and held there for many years, on the Fourth of July, celebrations at which many eminent public men were speakers. He was married on June 6, 1844, to Lucy Maria, daughter of Lewis and Susanna (Aspinwall) Tappan of Brooklyn, and on Dec. 25, 1865, to Ellen, daughter of Dr. Hiram and Marian (Chandler) Holt of Woodstock. He had seven sons and three daughters by his first wife and one son by his second. He died in Brooklyn, Feb. 24, 1896.

[Obituaries of Bowen were published in the *Independent,* Feb. 27, Mar. 5, 1896, and in various New York and Brooklyn papers, Feb. 25, 1896. His ancestry is set forth in Edward Augustus Bowen, *The Lineage of the Bowens of Woodstock, Conn.* (1897) and in the *New Eng. Hist. and Geneal. Reg.,* L, 364–65. Frequent references to him will be found in Clarence Winthrop Bowen, *Hist. of Woodstock, Conn.* (1926). See also Paxton Hibben, *Henry Ward Beecher* (1927).] H.H.

BOWEN, HERBERT WOLCOTT (Feb. 29, 1856–May 29, 1927), writer, diplomat, was born in Brooklyn, N. Y., the second son of Henry Chandler Bowen [*q.v.*] and Lucy M. (Tappan) Bowen. The elder Bowen was long the editor and owner of the *Independent* and was prominent in the anti-slavery campaigns and in his support of Henry Ward Beecher in many of the controversies in which he was involved. The younger Bowen was educated at the Brooklyn Polytechnic and later abroad and graduated from Yale in the class of 1878. He and W. H. Taft, later United States president, were final contestants for the class championship in wrestling;—it has always been a matter of dispute as to which won the title. After studying law at Columbia University, Bowen was admitted to the bar and practised in New York until he was, in 1890, appointed consul in Barcelona. Here he served with distinction for nine years. In 1895 his post was made a consulate-generalship and he was promoted so that he might become the first occupant. Bowen's stay in Spain was ended by the outbreak of the Spanish-American War. During the period of hostilities he was frequently called to Washington and his familiarity with Spanish conditions was of service to the Departments of State and of War. In 1899 he was appointed minister-resident and consul general in Persia where he served acceptably for two years. Toward the end of 1901 he was sent to Venezuela as envoy extraordinary and minister plenipotentiary. When he arrived in Caracas, he found in the archives of the legation documents which he considered highly compromising to the good name of the United States and involving the personal integrity of one of his predecessors. These he forwarded to Washington with an explanatory letter, which was acknowledged in a perfunctory manner. A more insistent letter from Bowen drew from Secretary of State Hay a personal reply which in paternal language advised him not to add to the number of his enemies. Meantime, the seizure of the Venezuelan naval vessels and the blockade of Venezuelan ports by a combined German, British, and Italian squadron to enforce the claims of their nations long ignored, created a crisis. The Dictator, Castro, was at this time (December 1902) facing an internal revolt and believed the naval demonstration designed to aid the cause of his rival. He at once had hundreds of Germans, English, and Italian residents herded in the city jail. Bowen remonstrated with the Dictator and by his transparent frankness secured a complete ascendancy over him. On setting out to meet the revolutionists, Castro would have left complete powers in Bowen's hands. Bowen declined to accept unlimited powers, but he secured the liberation of all foreigners. When Castro returned in triumph after crushing the revolt, Bowen returned to the United States with a commission authorizing him

to effect a settlement of foreign claims or to provide for their submission to arbitration. Bowen found President Roosevelt desirous himself to act as arbitrator, but he insisted on carrying the matter to The Hague Tribunal. During the negotiations that followed, the relations between the President and the envoy were tense and led to mutual recriminations. While Bowen was still in Europe, articles appeared in newspapers alluding to the incriminating documents which he had found in Caracas and submitted to the Department of State. Though Bowen was in no way responsible for these articles, President Roosevelt preferred charges against him and selected Secretary of War W. H. Taft to pass upon them. As a result, Bowen was dismissed from the diplomatic service with a reprimand in June 1905. He retired to a farm near Woodstock, Conn., where he wrote his memoirs, published a few months before his death. He had published several books of verse and a brief digest of International Law (1896). He was twice married: on Feb. 26, 1895, to Augusta F. Vingert, and on Jan. 25, 1902, to Carolyn Mae Clegg.

[*Who's Who in America*, 1926–27; *Quarter-Centenary Record, Class of 1878, Yale Coll.* (1905); *In the Matter of the Charges of Mr. Herbert W. Bowen . . . against Mr. Francis B. Loomis . . . and the Counter Charges of Mr. Loomis against Mr. Bowen* (Govt. Printing Office, 1905); *Venezuelan Arbitrations of 1903 . . . with App. Containing . . . Bowen Pamphlet Entitled "Venezuelan Protocols"* (Govt. Printing Office, 1904); *Hartford Times*, May 30, 1927; personal information.]   S.B.

BOWEN, THOMAS MEADE (Oct. 26, 1835–Dec. 30, 1906), miner, lawyer, politician, was born near Burlington, Ia., was educated at an academy in the neighboring town of Mt. Pleasant, and was elected to the Iowa House of Representatives in 1856 from Wayne County. In 1858 he moved to Kansas where he engaged in the practise of law until the outbreak of the Civil War. During the war he was advanced from captain of the 1st Regiment of Nebraska Volunteers to colonel of the 13th Kansas Infantry and to the rank of brigadier-general by brevet. When the Confederacy collapsed he was stationed in Arkansas, and there he remained to take an active part in the reorganization of the state government; he was president of the constitutional convention held under the Reconstruction Act of 1867, and for four years served as a judge of the state supreme court. In 1871 he was appointed governor of Idaho Territory, but after about a week in Boise he resigned, the work and environment not being to his liking. Again he busied himself in Arkansas reconstruction politics, only to be defeated in 1873 by Stephen W. Dorsey in an attempt to win a seat in the United States Sen-

Bowen

ate. In 1875 Bowen moved to Colorado; after a few months in Denver he went to Del Norte, a new town in the San Luis Valley, where he established a law office and became interested in mining ventures. So poor was he at this time that he is said to have walked over half the distance between Denver and Del Norte. He made friends easily, and in 1876, shortly after the organization of the new state government, was elected judge of the fourth judicial district of Colorado. As judge he was fearless, but lacking in any sense of judicial dignity either on or off the bench. The most famous case that came before him was one that grew out of the rivalry between the Denver & Rio Grande and the Santa Fé railways for the control of the Royal Gorge. The struggle, legal and physical, had been in progress fully a year when attorneys for the Denver & Rio Grande appeared in Judge Bowen's court in the little Mexican village of San Luis and asked for an injunction restraining the Santa Fé from transacting business in Colorado on the ground that it was a foreign corporation. In spite of charges made in open court by the attorneys for the Santa Fé that the judge was biased, Bowen refused a change of venue and granted the injunction; a few days later his decision was set aside by Judge Moses Hallett in Denver (see files of *Denver Tribune,* June 1879), although the courts later, in effect, sustained Bowen's action. For several years he had been investing his money in mines; about 1880 his faith was abundantly rewarded by a rich strike in the Summittville (Colorado) district. He resigned his judgeship, was elected to the lower house of the Colorado legislature in 1882 and in the following year, after a prolonged fight in the Republican caucus, was elected to the United States Senate. He served the full term of six years (1883–89) without distinction. When he retired from the Senate he was practically penniless; again he engaged in mining, and again he found a fortune. His last years were spent in Pueblo, Colo.; at his death he was survived by his wife (Margaretta Thurston) to whom he was married while a resident of Arkansas. He was tall and slender, slovenly in dress, breezy in manner, open-handed, loyal to his friends, a boon companion. He had a ready tongue and a nimble wit. His knowledge of the law was not profound, but he was shrewd and clever if not always impartial. In the words of one of his successors in the Senate (Charles S. Thomas), "Bowen achieved some distinctions but ignored or despised their responsibilities."

[Frank Hall, *Hist. of Colo.* (1895), IV, 298; H. J. French, *Hist. of Idaho* (1914), I, 78; the files of the *Denver Tribune* and the *Rocky Mountain News* for

Bowers

1879 and the years following; obituaries in the *Pueblo Chieftain, Denver Republican,* and the *Rocky Mountain News,* Dec. 31, 1906.]

C. B. G.

BOWERS, ELIZABETH CROCKER (Mar. 12, 1830–Nov. 6, 1895), actress, was born at Ridgefield, Conn. Her father, the Rev. William Crocker, was a Methodist clergyman. She made her first appearance on the stage as Amanthis in the *Child of Nature,* Dec. 3, 1846. On Mar. 4, 1847, she married David P. Bowers, a well-known Philadelphia actor. Her first appearance on the stage as Mrs. D. P. Bowers was at the Walnut Street Theatre, Philadelphia, as Donna Victoria in *A Bold Stroke for a Husband,* Mar. 11, 1847. The following year she acted at the Arch Street Theatre and in 1853 became a member of the stock company at that house, remaining several seasons and becoming an immense favorite. On the death of her husband in 1857, she retired temporarily from the stage, but on Dec. 19, 1857, became lessee of the Walnut Street Theatre, opening it as the People's Theatre with *London Assurance* and remaining its manager until January 1859. A few months later she leased the Academy of Music, Philadelphia, for a short season and during this time married Dr. Brown, a chemist of Baltimore, who died in 1867. In 1861 she went to England, making her appearance at Sadler's Wells as Julia in *The Hunchback* and creating a very favorable impression. In 1863 she returned to this country and was seen at the Winter Garden, New York, playing the title rôle in *Lady Audley's Secret,* and Julia in *The Hunchback* to Lawrence Barrett's Sir Thomas Clifford. A starring tour followed, after which she reappeared at the Winter Garden, Oct. 15, 1866, in *Lady Audley's Secret.* On Nov. 23 of the same year, she acted Romeo to the Juliet of her sister, Mrs. F. B. Conway. On Dec. 16, 1867, she was seen at the Broadway Theatre (Wallack's) as Dora. After more starring tours she again appeared in New York, at Booth's Theatre as Lady Macbeth to Booth's Macbeth. During this engagement she also acted Beatrice in *Much Ado About Nothing,* Portia in *The Merchant of Venice* and Margaret in *Richard III.* On Jan. 20, 1883, she married James C. McCollum, and for the next few years retired from the stage, devoting her time to teaching elocution. Early in 1892 she took a benefit at Palmer's Theatre, New York, and on Feb. 3 was seen at that house as Mme. d'Arcay in the first performance of *The Broken Seal.* The following year, on Feb. 5, she played the Duchess of Berwick in the first New York performance of Oscar Wilde's comedy *Lady Windermere's Fan.* On Oct. 24 of the same year she appeared at the Em-

507

pire Theatre, New York, as Mrs. Kirkland in David Belasco's play *The Younger Son,* and on Dec. 11 played Lady Carolina in support of Rose Coghlan in Oscar Wilde's *A Woman of No Importance.* She was again seen at Palmer's on Oct. 8, 1894, as Mrs. Woodville in A. W. Gattie's drama *The Transgressor,* the occasion being the American début of Olga Nethersole. On Nov. 12 she played Lady Wargrave in the first American performance of Sidney Grundy's *The New Woman.* This was the last part she played in New York. "An actress of great distinction, she had beauty as well as talent," says a contemporary critic, "a voice of fascinating sweetness, a refined manner and a cultivated mind." She died in Washington Nov. 6, 1895.

[T. A. Brown, *Hist. of the Am. Stage* (1870) and *Hist. of the N. Y. Stage* (1903) ; Alan Dale (A. J. Cohen), *Familiar Chats with Queens of the Stage* (1890) ; *N. Y. Dram. Mirror,* XXXIV, 15 ; *Washington Post,* Nov. 7, 1895.]   A.H.

BOWERS, LLOYD WHEATON (Mar. 9, 1859–Sept. 9, 1910), lawyer, was born at Springfield, Mass., the son of Samuel Dwight and Martha Wheaton (Dowd) Bowers. On both sides his ancestors were Puritans who had settled in New England more than two centuries before his birth. His family removed in his infancy to Brooklyn, N. Y., and later to Elizabeth, N. J., and there he was prepared for college by a private tutor. Entering Yale in 1875, he was graduated as valedictorian of his class in 1879. His standing had been but once equalled. For one year he remained as a graduate student, then traveled in Europe, and, despite a tempting offer of a teaching position at Yale, turned to the profession of the law. He was graduated from the Columbia Law School, admitted to the New York bar, and received a clerkship in a leading firm of New York City in 1882. Such were his abilities that in one year he became managing clerk, and in January 1884 a member of the firm. Ill health, however, compelled him to rest, and as a result of a summer's travel in the Northwest he moved in October 1884 to Winona, Minn., where he formed a partnership with Thomas Wilson, former chief justice of the state supreme court. Here he practised until 1893. He then became the general counsel of the Chicago & North Western Railway Company, one of the great railway systems of the country, and in this office he served until 1909, when he was appointed by President Taft, an intimate friend since college days, solicitor-general of the United States. Little more than a year was given him to occupy this position of honor and responsibility.

The years of his work with the North West-

ern were a period of extraordinary industrial development. Incidentally to this development litigation arose—involving federal control of the railroads under the Interstate Commerce Act of 1887, the powers of the states to control intrastate commerce, and to tax corporations, and the application of the Sherman Anti-Trust Act of 1890—which involved social and political issues of vast importance. In this litigation Bowers played a conspicuous part. His success in winning cases for the government during his brief service as solicitor-general was phenomenal. He was regarded by his railroad associates, at least, as no mere partisan, but on the contrary as mindful of the railroads' duties as quasi-public corporations ; and according to an intimate associate he found especial happiness, as solicitor-general, in the fact that he could act solely as lawyer, rather than counsel, and for the whole country rather than for a special interest. Contrary criticism has been made, however, by men of other economic outlook, of the government's policy—for which he at least shared responsibility—in the cases decreeing the "dissolutions" of the Standard Oil and Tobacco trusts in 1910 (*221 United States Reports,* 1, 106). It is well known that only his death prevented his nomination by President Taft for appointment to the Supreme Court of the United States.

Although he published nothing, and was in that sense wholly absorbed in the law, he retained throughout life a catholicity of intellectual interests, particularly in literature. Art and music, in his later years, also shared his interest. Of sturdy frame, with dark seamed face and brilliant eyes under beetling brows, he was a striking figure. In forensic argument he was not of the calm and calculating type, though resourceful, but impetuous and masterful in manner. With juries he was far from successful ; but he was exceedingly strong in his grasp of the legal factors in a case and was effective with a court. Notwithstanding some reserve, his charm of manner, marked by kindly sympathy, easily won friends, whom he held by the attractions of a broad and generous nature. He married twice ; first (on Sept. 7, 1887) Louisa Bennett Wilson of Winona, Minn., who died on Dec. 20, 1897 ; and second (in 1906) Charlotte Josephine Lewis of Detroit, who survived him.

[*Memorials of the Chicago Bar Ass.,* 1910–11 ; *Hist. of the Class of '79, Yale Coll. 1875–1905,* pp. 111–12 ; *Who's Who in America,* 1910–11 ; *Chicago Daily Tribune,* Sept. 10, 1910.]   F.S.P.

BOWERS, THEODORE SHELTON (Oct. 10, 1832–Mar. 6, 1866), Union soldier, was born in Hummelstown, Dauphin County, Pa., the son of George and Ann Maria Bowers. His early life was spent in extreme poverty. As a boy he removed to Mt. Carmel, Ill., learned the printer's trade, and eventually became editor of the local newspaper, the *Register*. He entered the volunteer army in October 1861 as a private in the 48th Illinois Infantry. In January 1862, shortly before the advance against Forts Henry and Donelson, he was detailed as a clerk at Gen. Grant's headquarters, where he soon came to the favorable notice of the commanding general. He was appointed a first lieutenant in March, and soon after was regularly assigned as an aide to Gen. Grant. Faithful and efficient in the performance of his duties, and attached to his chief with a semi-feudal devotion, Bowers became one of that little official family which the great commander kept with him in all his campaigns, east or west. He was promoted to captain in November 1862, and major in February 1863. He was captured in Van Dorn's raid on Holly Springs, Miss., in December 1862, but made his escape in a few hours. Soon after the taking of Vicksburg, he succeeded Rawlins as Grant's adjutant-general, and was made a lieutenant-colonel (Aug. 30, 1863). In that capacity he served through the Virginia campaigns of 1864 and 1865, and was present at the surrender at Appomattox. After Grant's assignment to the command of all the armies, he obtained Bowers's appointment as a captain in the quartermaster department of the regular army (July 29, 1864). This insured that he would be retained in the service after the volunteer forces should be mustered out, but he never actually served under this commission, nor under a later regular-army appointment as major in the adjutant-general's department (Jan. 6, 1865), for he died before his discharge from his volunteer commission as lieutenant-colonel. His death occurred at Garrison, N. Y., as he was returning, with Gen. Grant, from a visit to West Point. Bowers left the train to attend to baggage, and in trying to board it again fell under the wheels. He was buried at West Point. "Gallant little Bowers," Charles King calls him, and a better description of him would be hard to find. His career was determined in the first place by the accident of his attracting Grant's attention, and later by his own merits and the mutual loyalty of his chief and himself. His services were recognized by the award of no less than four brevets, the last being as brigadier-general. The G. A. R. post at Mt. Carmel was named for him.

[F. B. Heitman, *Biog. Reg.* (1903), I, 234; article by Theodore G. Risley in *Jour. Ill. State Hist. Soc.*, XII, 407–11. The extensive correspondence indexed under Bowers's name in the *Official Records* consists of the letters received and sent by his office, and tells little

of his personal history. Obituary in the *United Service Mag.*, V (N. Y., 1866), pp. 360–63.]   T. M. S.

BOWIE, JAMES (1796–Mar. 6, 1836), Texas soldier, ~~was born in Burke County, Ga., the son of Rezin (probably James Rezin) Bowie. His mother's name is recorded in Spanish documents as Alvina (also Elvy) Jones, but the surname may be only a blundering attempt to write the word "Jane." The year of his birth has been variously given; some writers place it as late as 1805, but the date is inconsistent with the generally accepted statement that his parents moved to Catahoula Parish, La., in 1802.~~ He had four brothers—David, Rezin P., John J., and Stephen—all of whom appear in the early chronicles. Of his ~~youth~~ little is known. Tradition makes him a participant in a desperate encounter on the banks of the Mississippi, Sept. 19, 1827, in which, after being badly wounded by a bullet, he killed his opponent with a knife. It has been many times asserted (see Eugene C. Barker, *Quarterly of the Texas Historical Association*, VI, 148) that with two of his brothers, Rezin P. and John J., he made large sums of money through the sale of negro slaves smuggled into Louisiana and Texas by Lafitte the pirate. The story is, however, denied by the family of Rezin P. Bowie. About 1828 he came to Texas, making San Antonio his home and prospecting the San Saba region for a lost mine. On Oct. 5, 1830, he became a Mexican citizen and at once began to acquire extensive tracts of land, largely through the device of inducing Mexicans to apply for grants and then buying them, when obtained, at merely nominal prices (*Ibid.*, X, 77).

Bowie was married, Apr. 25, 1831, to Ursula, the daughter of Vice-Governor Juan Martin de Veramendi of San Antonio. The growing tension between the Americans and the Mexican Government found him usually with the element favoring resistance. As a captain he was in the fight at Nacogdoches in August 1832, and after the surrender of Piedras's command conveyed the prisoners to San Antonio. During the comparative quiet of the next twenty months he was busy with his own affairs, but on the revival of the movement against the central government he at once took a leading part. He was chosen a member of the first committee of safety, organized at Mina (now Bastrop), May 17, 1835. With the outbreak of hostilities shortly afterward his qualities of energy, daring, and resourcefulness came into full play. As a colonel of the revolutionary forces, though never in command of more than a handful of men, he was an important factor in the campaign which by Dec. 15 had cleared Texas of the Mexican army. When at the beginning of 1836 the army, with Santa Anna at its head, returned, Bowie was located with Col. William Barret Travis, and about 150 men (the number later increased to 188), at San Antonio. Retreating across the river and making their stand at the abandoned Alamo mission, they were overwhelmed after a desperate resistance, and all of them including Bowie, who was lying ill on a cot, were killed.

Bowie was six feet tall, well proportioned, with erect carriage, fair complexion, and small blue eyes. He was quiet and unobtrusive in demeanor. Of his courage, strength, and agility many stories are told; it has been said of him that he "was known to rope and ride alligators." One of his titles to fame is the reputed invention of the bowie knife. The accounts, however, are conflicting, some attributing it to his brother Rezin; but a correspondent, Gid L. Sowell, of Rosedale, Okla., in *Frontier,* August 1925, repeats a family tradition that James Bowie had injured himself in an Indian fight by letting his hand slip from the hilt to the blade of his butcher knife; that he thereupon suggested to John Sowell, the blacksmith of Gonzalez, the addition of a guard, and that Sowell, from a model cut in wood by Bowie, made the first weapon and gave it the name it has since borne. It is certain that the weapon became widely popular. As early as 1840, occasionally known as the "Arkansas toothpick," it was being made in large quantities by a firm in Sheffield, England, for the Texas trade.

[Louis J. Wortham, *Hist. of Texas* (1924); Dudley G. Wooten, *Comprehensive Hist. of Texas* (1898), founded upon H. Yoakum, *Hist. of Texas* (1855); Homer S. Thrall, *Pictorial Hist. of Texas* (1879); Evelyn Brogan, *Jas. Bowie, a Hero of the Alamo* (1922).]

W. J. G.

BOWIE, ODEN (Nov. 10, 1826–Dec. 4, 1894), governor of Maryland, the eldest son of William D. and Mary Eliza (Oden) Bowie, was born and spent most of his life on his father's estate "Fairview" in Prince Georges County, Md. His first instruction was received at home under a tutor, but upon his mother's death, when he was only nine, he was sent to the preparatory school attached to old St. John's College, Annapolis. After three years there he entered St. Mary's College, Baltimore, from which he graduated in 1845. Shortly after leaving college he enlisted as a private in the Baltimore and Washington Battalion and left for the Mexican border. At the battle of Monterey, Bowie's commander, Lieutenant-Colonel Watson, was mortally wounded. In imminent peril of his life, young Bowie stayed with the dying colonel until he received from him important messages and papers.

Almost surrounded by the enemy, he mounted his horse and made a desperate and successful dash for safety. For this gallant action he was promoted to a lieutenancy and later commissioned a captain in the Voltigeur Regiment. The Maryland legislature passed a set of complimentary resolutions expressing "The thanks of his native State for distinguished gallantry displayed during the three days' siege of Monterey" (Resolution 43, Act of 1847). Illness, due to the climate of Mexico, compelled him to return to Maryland before the close of the war.

From his father, who had served in both houses of the legislature, Bowie inherited a keen interest in politics. Almost immediately after his return from Mexico he became a candidate for the legislature. He was under age at the time, but would have arrived at his majority before the legislature convened, a fact, however, which was not generally known. His opponents, who talked much of his youth, succeeded in raising a doubt as to his elegibility and Bowie was defeated by ten votes. In 1849 he was again a candidate for the House of Delegates, and had the honor of being the only Democrat elected that year in his county. A few years later he was elected state senator, but in 1861, when a candidate for the same office, he was defeated by Federal military interference at the polls. In 1860 he was chosen president of the Baltimore & Potomac Railroad, then but recently organized, and filled that office until his death. It was largely due to his management and unflagging perseverance that the railroad finally achieved success. Bowie's sympathies were with the South, although he did not approve of the radical course of the secessionists. He used every effort to preserve the organization of the Democratic party and it was largely due to him that that party regained control of the state. He was chairman of the state central committee during the war, and in 1864 was sent as a delegate to the Chicago convention which nominated Gen. McClellan for the presidency. The Democratic nominee for lieutenant-governor in 1864, he was defeated by the Union candidate, Cox; but in 1867 he was elected governor of Maryland by the largest majority ever given by the state to any candidate. He did not become governor *de facto* until Jan. 13, 1869, and remained in office until Jan. 10, 1872. The settlement of the dispute with Virginia regarding oyster-beds, the collection of arrears from the Baltimore & Ohio Railroad due the state, and the collection from the United States government of money loaned by Maryland for war purposes were among the many questions settled during his able administration.

Bowie was active in the organization of the Maryland Jockey Club and was long its president. He owned many famous race horses, and it was a keen grief to him when in 1890, on account of failing health, he was compelled to part with them. Four years later he died at "Fairview" and was buried in the family graveyard a short distance from his home. He was married in 1851 to Alice, daughter of Charles H. and Rosalie Eugenia (Calvert) Carter.

[Heinrich E. Buchholz, *Governors of Md.* (1908); Walter Worthington Bowie, *The Bowies and their Kindred* (1899); *Baltimore Sun*, Dec. 5, 1894.] E. T. D.

BOWIE, RICHARD JOHNS (June 23, 1807–Mar. 12, 1881), politician, was born in Georgetown, D. C., the son of Col. Washington Bowie and Margaret (Johns) Bowie. He received a classical education under Dr. Carnahan and was a student at the university in Georgetown. He studied law under Clement Cox and was admitted to the bar of the District of Columbia when but nineteen. At the age of twenty-two he was admitted to practise before the United States Supreme Court. In the same year he moved to Rockville, Montgomery County, Md., where he immediately took an active interest in public affairs and rose to prominence in his profession. Politically he was a Whig. A man of brilliant intellect, combined with much legal learning, he soon became a leader in his party. In 1835–36–37 he was elected to the Maryland Senate. In 1845 he became prosecuting attorney for Montgomery County and held that office for four years. From 1849 to 1853 he was a representative in Congress. He was an ardent admirer of Henry Clay and it is claimed by his friends that he made the first public speech in the House of Representatives in favor of the compromise measures of 1850. He was an eloquent, forcible, and convincing speaker and always actively interested in any important measure brought before Congress during his four years in the House. In 1854 the Whigs nominated him for governor of Maryland. The Whig party had split asunder over the slavery question and that year was practically destroyed. The Democratic candidate was elected and Bowie suffered his first political defeat. He was a staunch Unionist, and with the unswerving honesty and moral courage that marked the man, he opposed secession and tried to avert the war which he feared was inevitable. At the election of 1861 he was chosen to succeed Judge LeGrand as chief justice of the court of appeals. During the four years of civil war, when citizens were illegally arrested, civil courts often disregarded, and martial law held sway,

the court over which he presided remained above suspicion or reproach. He remained on the bench of that court until his death, with the exception of a slight interval after the adoption of the constitution of 1867, when the judicial system of the state was again changed. In 1871 occurred the next general election and Judge Bowie was restored to the judicial seat by popular vote. In 1876, as he was approaching the age limit of seventy years, the legislature extended his term until the expiration of the period for which he had been elected. This great tribute was paid to a Republican judge by a Democratic legislature with only three dissenting votes. His private life was as irreproachable as his public career. He died at his residence "Glenview" after a few days of illness, and was buried in Rockville cemetery. He was married in 1833 to Catherine L. Williams, of Hagerstown, Md.

[*The Green Bag*, VI, 274; Walter Worthington Bowie, *The Bowies and Their Kindred* (1899); *Baltimore Sun*, Mar. 14, 1881.] E. T. D.

BOWIE, ROBERT (March 1750–Jan. 8, 1818), governor of Maryland, was born at "Mattaponi," near Nottingham, Prince Georges County, Md., the third son of Capt. William and Margaret (Sprigg) Bowie. He received his education at the schools of the Rev. John Eversfield, near Croom, and the Rev. Mr. Craddock, near Baltimore. In 1770 he eloped with Priscilla, the daughter of Gen. James John Mackall, of Calvert County. Though he was barely twenty, and the bride not yet fifteen, the marriage proved a happy one. His father gave him a house in Nottingham and a farm nearby. Upon the death of his father he inherited "Mattaponi," which thenceforth was his summer residence.

At a meeting of "Freeholders and citizens" held in Upper Marlborough in November 1774, young Bowie was appointed a member of a committee to see that the resolutions of the American Continental Congress were carried into effect. This was the beginning of his leadership in county and state affairs. In September 1775 a Committee of Observation was formed, and he, with several others, was instructed to enrol a company of "Minute Men." He was commissioned first lieutenant in a company of militia formed in Nottingham in 1776. In June of the same year, he was commissioned captain of the 2nd Battalion, Maryland Flying Artillery, and with this battalion he joined Washington in his campaign near New York. In the several important battles of the Revolution in which Bowie took part he showed courage and good judgment, though he won no special distinction.

After the close of the war he returned to his

native county, and became keenly interested in politics. From 1785 to 1790 he was a member of the House of Delegates, having been elected for six consecutive terms. While in the legislature he strongly advocated a measure for establishing St. John's College, Annapolis. Three years after retiring from the House of Delegates he was appointed a major of the militia and justice of the peace in Prince Georges County. In 1801–02–03 he was again a member of the legislature. At this time the people of Maryland were clamoring for a more radical democrat than Gov. Mercer to fill the executive chair. Bowie was the logical man, and on Nov. 17, 1803, the General Assembly cast the majority of votes in his favor. The following day he resigned from the House of Delegates to become governor of Maryland. He was reëlected in 1804 and again in 1805, which made his first administration cover the full three years for which he was eligible. After leaving the executive chair in 1807 he was again appointed a justice of the peace.

In 1811, when America was about to enter on her second war with England, Bowie came forward as a champion of the Republican party, which, almost to a man, advocated a declaration of war. In November 1811 the Republicans predominated in the legislature, and Bowie was again elected governor of Maryland. In June 1812, when war was finally declared, the delighted Governor "proceeded through the streets bare-headed to the State House, where he congratulated the leaders upon the welcome news" (*Annapolis Gazette*, June 12, 1812). Unfortunately, in August 1812 an article appeared in a Baltimore paper which maddened the Republicans against whom it was directed. An infuriated mob attacked a house where a number of Federalist leaders were being entertained, killing several and beating several more. Indignation meetings were held throughout the state and the Governor was urged to make an investigation and punish the instigators of the riot. Bowie, failing to apprehend the criminals, was accused of shielding them. Whether he was guilty or blameless, the unfortunate event terminated his public career, though he fought hard until his death to recover the gubernatorial seat. He was an implacable enemy, but a most loyal friend, and those who knew him in private life loved him well for his generosity and kindly spirit. He died at his home in Nottingham, and was buried in the family graveyard at "Mattaponi."

[Heinrich E. Buchholz, *Governors of Md.* (1908); Walter Worthington Bowie, *The Bowies and Their Kindred* (1899).]
             E. T. D.

BOWLER, METCALF (1726–Sept. 24, 1789), judge, was born in London. When about seventeen years of age he accompanied his father, Charles Bowler, to Boston, where the latter purchased land in the vicinity of the Common and Beacon Hill, later moving to Newport, R. I., and serving as collector of His Majesty's revenues. Business man, adventurer, genial host, and patriot, Metcalf Bowler lived prosperously through the days of Newport's commercial supremacy. His marriage to Anne, daughter of Bathsheba (Palmer) Fairchild and Maj. Fairchild, a business associate, founded a large family of eleven children. His commercial prosperity permitted him to maintain them in considerable state in what was later known as the Vernon House on Mary and Clarke Street. During the French and Indian War, both as an investment and an adventure, he fitted out four privateers, the *Prince Frederick,* the *New Concert,* the *Diana,* and the *Defence.* While these brought him large profits, lengthy litigation in prize suits, often with appeals to England, brought him equally great losses. Representative in the Rhode Island General Assembly, and speaker of the House of Representatives, 1767–76, he led the opposition to the Stamp Act, representing the colony, in 1765, at the New York Congress. Appreciation of his services resulted in his choice, the following year, as the one to present to the King a message of thanks for the act's repeal. The people's confidence in him was further evidenced by his election, in 1768, as assistant judge of the supreme court, and, in 1776, as chief justice. Service with the Committee of Correspondence in 1773, his signature upon the Rhode Island Declaration of Independence, and the marriage of his daughter, Bathsheba, to the Marquis Langfroi are but a few of the indications of his close association with the colonial cause. The accounts of the fame of his choice fruits and rare flowers and his *Treatise on Agriculture and Practical Husbandry* (1786) show him to have been a skilful horticulturist. Virtually ruined by the Revolution, he opened a small shop at Providence, and, in 1787, the "Queen's Head" tavern. Two golden eagles, devices derived from the Bowler coat of arms, which originally ornamented the gateposts of his Portsmouth farm, to-day face each other on Thames St., Newport. The wood-work and paneling of one of the rooms of his Portsmouth house may be seen in the American wing of the Metropolitan Museum.

[N. P. Bowler, *Record of the Descendants of Chas. Bowler* (1905); G. C. Mason's *Annals of Trinity Church, Newport* (1890–94); W. P. Sheffield, *Priva-*

teers and Privateersmen of Newport (1883); E. M. Stone, *Our French Allies* (1884).]   H. F. K.

BOWLES, SAMUEL (June 8, 1797–Sept. 8, 1851), newspaper editor, was born in Hartford, Conn. He was the son of a pewterer of Boston whose business had been ruined by the Revolution and who had removed to the former city in 1798, opening first a bakery and later a grocery. The father became a cripple and his means were slender; dying in 1813, he left Bowles as his only inheritance a watch and the family Bible. The boy, who had finished his common school education and gone into the grocery shop at fifteen, was now apprenticed to a printer. During this apprenticeship he joined with a dozen other youths in forming a literary and debating club, which gave him a taste for intellectual pursuits. This connection, he wrote later, "I consider an important era in my life— a sort of redeeming season, saving me from dangerous tendencies. It gave a good direction to my habits, strengthening my mind to resist temptation, and led me to prefer mental to sensual pleasure" (*Springfield Daily Republican,* Sept. 10, 1851). His first employment as printer was with the New Haven *Register,* where he rose to be foreman. In 1819 he formed a partnership with John Francis of Wethersfield in publishing the *Hartford Times,* an unsuccessful weekly sheet. His associate was intemperate and incompetent, he fell into debts which it took him many years to discharge, and constant overwork impaired his health. An attack of typhus which prostrated him for the greater part of a year also left him subject to recurrent attacks of dysentery throughout life. On Feb. 12, 1822, he married Huldah Deming of Wethersfield, a descendant of Miles Standish, who matched his hard sense, frugality, and industry with similar qualities of her own. More than two years later, in 1824, the *Hartford Times* having failed, he loaded his wife, his baby daughter, a hand printing press which he had hired, and some household goods upon a flatboat, and ascended the Connecticut River to establish a new weekly in Springfield, Mass.

Bowles took this step at the invitation of some Springfield Anti-Federalists, who helped him obtain loans aggregating $400 for the purchase of type and other equipment. The first issue of the *Springfield Republican* appeared on Sept. 8, 1824, with about 250 subscribers at $2 a year. Bowles was proprietor, publisher, reporter, editor, compositor, pressman, and business manager; and as his son's biographer says, "it must be owned by one who reads the first numbers that one man might have produced it all without any dangerous strain on his powers" (Merriam, I, 4). In

the next fifteen years the weekly *Republican* grew steadily but slowly. At one time it had as many as five rivals, while it also had to meet the competition of New York and Boston papers. But it crushed or absorbed the other local weeklies, while its thorough system of local intelligence gradually made it indispensable to readers of western Massachusetts. Bowles in 1824 supported William H. Crawford for the presidency and opposed John Quincy Adams. Four years later, however, distrusting Jackson for his autocratic temper, he stood behind Adams for reelection. Throughout Jackson's administration Bowles kept the *Republican* in the opposition, advocating the election of Clay in 1832 and being identified with the Whig party from the moment of its birth. His position upon slavery was that of most Massachusetts Whigs; he deplored the agitation of the question and assailed the Abolitionists, but opposed the spread of the institution and attacked the annexation of Texas and the Mexican War. But in these years the editorial vigor and the influence of the *Republican* were slight.

By the beginning of the forties the *Republican* had 1,200 subscribers, printed fourteen or fifteen columns of news weekly, and was ready for expansion. After the completion of the Boston & Albany Railroad in 1839 Springfield grew rapidly as a manufacturing and railway center. In 1842 Bowles publicly proposed the establishment of a daily edition, but was dissuaded by business friends from this risky undertaking as there was then no daily paper in Massachusetts outside Boston, and but one in Connecticut. But the elder of Bowles's surviving sons, Samuel Bowles, Jr., urged his father not to abandon the plan, and promised to assume the main responsibility. The first issue of the daily *Republican* appeared Mar. 27, 1844, an evening paper of four small pages. At the end of two years it had only two hundred subscribers, and not until after its transformation, in December 1845, into a morning paper, did it gain an air of permanency. The basis of its prosperity, and of the future power of the *Republican,* was the organization by the two Bowleses of a local correspondence which thoroughly covered every town and hamlet of the upper Connecticut valley.

Till his death from his dysenteric affection in 1851, Bowles remained identified with the weekly *Republican,* his son taking charge of the daily. He represented the best type of country editor of the period: slow, cautious, thrifty, measurably far-sighted though provincial in outlook, and shrewd though limited in education. He insisted upon complete editorial independence, and late in life boasted that he had rejected "with scorn" several alluring offers of financial aid if he would permit others to use his journal. Bowles's great service was in firmly establishing the organ which the energy and brilliance of his son made nationally famous.

[Samuel Bowles himself left one printed production, a pamphlet called *Geneal. and Hist. Notes of the Bowles Family* (Springfield, 1851), which sheds some light upon his early life. Thomas M. Farquhar's *Hist. of the Bowles Family* (1907) deals fully with his ancestry. The first chapters of George S. Merriam's *Life and Times of Samuel Bowles* (1885) furnish the best connected account of his career. This is supplemented by the history of the *Republican*, Richard Hooker's *Story of an Independent Newspaper* (1924). See also Willard G. Bleyer, *Main Currents in the Hist. of Am. Journalism* (1927), pp. 252 ff.]
A. N.

BOWLES, SAMUEL (Feb. 9, 1826–Jan. 16, 1878), editor, was the son of Samuel and Huldah Bowles. Born a year and a half after the founding of the *Springfield Republican,* the younger Bowles was reared in a frugal household, sharing his room with three of his father's apprentices. He attended the public schools, carried the weekly *Republican* to a round of subscribers, and early showed a preference for books over outdoor pursuits. When about thirteen he was sent to a private school and gained some knowledge of the Latin classics; but although he wished to go to college, his father, who desired him to be trained as a printer, disapproved. In later life he spoke of the want of a college education with deep regret, but in large measure he atoned for it by reading. The newspapers and magazines in his father's office engaged the boy so that "you might speak to him half a dozen times and he would never know it" (Merriam, I, 19). At seventeen he entered this office as a general helper—running errands, doing mechanical jobs, and writing local items. The youth's enterprising spirit was proved within a year by his insistence upon the establishment of a daily edition, and his agreement to assume most of the extra labor. Little capital was required, an associate contracting to print both the daily and weekly for one year for $1,450 (Hooker, p. 38). The issue began without a single subscriber or advertiser, and the prospectus announced that if the loss after a half-year or year proved too great, "we shall stop" (*Springfield Republican,* Mar. 27, 1844). To add to the difficulties, the younger Bowles's health broke down so seriously that in the winter of 1844–45 he went to Louisiana to recuperate, and could give no help beyond a series of fifteen news-letters. When he returned, however, he threw himself into the work with such energy that on Apr. 1, 1846, the owners could announce that "The *Republican* is now placed on a permanent basis." The staff was small and upon him fell the task of laboring till two or three o'clock in the morning to gather and write the late news, while he gave earnest attention to the editorial page.

In his early twenties Bowles's characteristic traits all asserted themselves—his impetuosity, his driving vigor, which sometimes kept him working forty hours at a stretch, his intensity, his nervousness, his exuberant over-activity, his erratic changes of mind, his combativeness. At the outset a newspaper war with the *Springfield Gazette* helped the *Republican* to strike its gait. "That aroused my ire and I determined that we would not be beaten," he wrote later. "After a year my opponents came to me and wanted a truce, but I said, 'No, you began the fight and now you shall have it.' And they did, till they were driven from the field." In 1848 the *Republican* absorbed the *Gazette,* and established its supremacy in western Massachusetts. The following year it was joined by the versatile and fluent Josiah Gilbert Holland. He and two other men already on the paper, William B. Calhoun, who as a leader-writer surpassed even his chief, and George Ashmun, known later as a Republican politician and a friend of Lincoln, made up an able editorial corps. Dr. Holland, after two years' service, bought a quarter interest in the *Republican* for $3,500. Bowles did much reporting: "News," he held, "is the distinctive object of the *Republican,* to which all other things must bend." He kept his ear constantly open; hearing local gossip, talking to politicians, pumping his wide acquaintance, and condensing the result for the paper. Telegraphic news was rapidly developed. A number of features were instituted: a daily column of "Local Items" maintained with distinctive enterprise, a weekly column of "Religious Intelligence," then new in secular journalism, a chapter of "Sunday Thoughts," by Dr. Holland, and agricultural advice. On the editorial page Bowles more and more displaced the long articles with pithy and pungent editorials. His father's death in 1851 found him able to take control of the paper in every department (Merriam, pp. 64 ff.).

Politically the course taken by Bowles showed as yet neither the independence nor the steadiness which later characterized it. During Polk's administration he supported the Wilmot Proviso and in 1848 declared emphatically: "Congress is the battleground of slavery and freedom ... Our motto is NO COMPROMISE, NO MORE SLAVE TERRITORY." But the paper wavered from this position in 1850, when it gave grudging support to Daniel Webster in his advocacy of Clay's compromise plan, and applauded the 7th of March speech as "broad, patriotic, and honest." At the beginning of 1851 Bowles announced that the *Republican* was still devotedly Whig, though the Whig party was clearly moribund. In the early fifties the *Republican* attacked the Abolitionists, urged citizens of Springfield to stay away from their meetings, and declared that the fugitive slave act must be sustained in the Northern courts. Bowles's attitude toward slavery, in brief, was still conservative. But the beginnings of the Kansas-Nebraska struggle gave him a new decision and aggressiveness. He declared of the Kansas-Nebraska bill that "it is a monstrous proposition," "a huge stride backward," a piece of legislation "against the spirit of republicanism" (*Republican,* Feb. 8, 1854). Thereafter the *Republican* was a leader in the struggle for the constitutional defeat of slavery. When Judge Loring issued a warrant for the arrest of the slave Anthony Burns, it demanded his removal from the bench; it vehemently supported the Emigrant Aid Society; and Bowles was one of the first men in the East to call for the organization of a new anti-slavery party.

By the beginning of 1854 the editor had definitely repudiated his old Whig allegiance. For the pretensions which the Native American Party briefly made in 1854–55 to be the real opposition to the Democrats he had nothing but scorn. The editor struck a telling blow at this party, whose anti-alien principles he cordially disliked, when he attended its national convention in Philadelphia in June 1855. Its sessions were supposedly secret and none but delegates were admitted to the floor. But Bowles's close contacts with Henry Wilson and other Massachusetts delegates enabled him to send daily letters to the *New York Tribune, Boston Atlas,* and *Springfield Republican,* packed with information, and slashing in their denunciation of the convention majority as "weak tools of political gamblers and slavery propagandists." He characteristically believed that the right of the public to obtain the facts rose superior to the oath of secrecy binding his friends. His exposure of the subserviency of the Know-Nothings to slavery did much to hasten the disintegration of the party the following year. Meanwhile Bowles was persistently urging the formation of a new party of freedom which should be "able to win in the great contest to be fought in '56 with the slave-power of the country." Both in the *Republican* and by personal efforts, using his tact and magnetism effectively, he labored with New England politicians for this end. In August 1855 he presided in Boston over a conference of influential men, the callers of which included Charles Francis Adams, R. H. Dana, Jr.,

George Boutwell, and H. L. Dawes, which was intended to bring about a fusion of Know-Nothings, Free-Soilers, and independent Whigs upon a Republican ticket; and though this effort proved a failure, he helped give the Republican party a strong state organization.

Perhaps partly because of his friendship with N. P. Banks, Bowles was one of the earliest editors to advocate the nomination of John C. Frémont by the Republican party (letter of Apr. 19, 1856; Merriam, I, 171). He was present at Cincinnati when the Democrats nominated Buchanan, and at Philadelphia when the Republicans chose Frémont; he had an exuberant confidence in Republican success, and labored with indefatigable energy, working two days and two nights without sleep in election week. With its espousal of the new party the *Springfield Republican* entered upon the flood-tide of its success. It rose rapidly to a circulation of more than 5,000 for the daily and more than 10,000 for the weekly, and the *New York Tribune* shortly hailed it as "the best and ablest country journal ever published on this continent." Its staff was small, numbering but three men beside Bowles, but all were accustomed to work twelve or more hours daily. Its Boston and Washington correspondence ranked with the best; its telegraphic news was painstakingly handled and condensed; and its editorial interpretation and leadership were unexcelled. At all times the local correspondence from Connecticut Valley towns and villages was admirably complete. The demand of the North and West for just such strong free-soil opinion as it furnished, and the desire of the flood of emigrant New Englanders for a weekly journal of home intelligence, gave the *Republican* a circulation and influence throughout all the free states and territories.

It is difficult to excuse Bowles for yielding at this moment of success to a step which came near proving irreparably disastrous. Already he had refused a position on the *New York Tribune* as editorial writer and head of its Washington bureau, while he had shown scant enthusiasm when Charles A. Dana at the close of 1856 undertook fruitless negotiations with a group of Philadelphians to establish a new daily, with a capital of $100,000, of which Bowles was to be editor. His place was as the master of provincial journalism. Yet early in 1857 he resigned the editorship of the *Republican* and assumed that of a new Boston newspaper, the *Traveller.* This represented an amalgamation of the old, weak, semi-religious journal of the same name; the *Atlas,* which had once been the leading Whig paper of New England but had lost ground, and the *Telegraph and*

Chronicle, a worthless anti-prohibition journal. Bowles, investing $10,000 in the enterprise, was given a salary of $3,000 a year and a bonus of one-tenth of the capital stock. The daily was to be Republican, independent, and progressive, to have a large staff, and to take the leadership among Boston journals; but it was unfortunately by no means so strong as it looked. The owners and officers were not united in any common policy; Bowles found his best efforts thwarted and misunderstood; while the capital was insufficient to ensure a vigorous start. After four months he resigned. The verdict of his friends was that "Sam Bowles and Boston did not suit each other" (Merriam, I, 183). Fortunately he had retained his controlling ownership of the *Republican,* and had kept his wife and family in Springfield. Following a short vacation in the West he returned to Springfield and Dr. Holland relinquished the editorship to him. Thereafter he was content to make his provincial environment yield, by hard work, the rewards of power which might have come more easily in one of the large cities.

In the heated years up till 1861 Bowles steadily increased the influence of the *Republican.* The basis of this influence was the vogue of the weekly newspaper, which dealt in national rather than local intelligence, and could be as well published from a small city as a metropolis. By 1860 the weekly *Republican* had a circulation of 11,-280 copies (as against 5,700 for the daily), and was read everywhere in the Mississippi Valley. Its power was far from reaching that of the weekly *New York Tribune,* but it equaled that of the weekly *Evening Post.* Bowles gave it intense and unwearying personal supervision. As a subordinate wrote, "he knew everything, saw everything, dictated everything, and his dictation dictated every time" (Merriam, I, 104). Electric, incisive, eager, a bundle of nerves, he drove himself and drove his small staff incessantly. News was rewritten with a thoroughness unknown elsewhere; everything that came over the telegraph was freshened and invigorated; the correspondents were held to a high standard; and the editorials were pungent, authoritative, and forcible. Two nights in the week Bowles snatched only a few hours' sleep in the office; other nights he brought a bottle of cold tea and labored till one or two o'clock. "The sparkle, the vivacity, the drive, the power of the *Republican,*" wrote Dr. Holland later, "cost life. We did not know when we tasted it and found it so charged with zest that we were tasting heart's blood, but that was the priceless element that commended it to our appetites. A pale man, weary and nervous, crept home at midnight, or at one, two, or three o'clock in the morning, and while all nature was fresh and the birds were singing and thousands of eyes were bending eagerly over the results of his night's labor, he was tossing and trying to sleep."

As one of the "Black Republican" leaders, Bowles denounced the execution of John Brown, supported Lincoln warmly, and when secession began declared sternly for "the defense of the Union and the enforcement of the laws" (*Republican,* Jan. 9, 1861). Unlike Greeley and Bryant, the editor after the beginning of the war did not join the ranks of the "radicals" who urged the President to hasten emancipation, prosecute the war without regard for the feelings of the border states, and adopt harsh measures with all rebels. When Lincoln modified Frémont's emancipation order, Bowles supported him; he defended the President against the Massachusetts Republican Convention of 1862; and he argued for his financial policy when he came into collision with Congress upon the further issue of legal-tender notes. At times he criticized Lincoln severely for his infringements upon civil rights and his interferences with military operations, while in 1863 he regarded his chances of reëlection as poor. But he loyally supported the President for renomination without any of the hesitancy which marked the radical editors just named, and declared that "his way of saving the country is recognized as the only way." Later the editor advocated the mild and magnanimous policies of reconstruction outlined by Lincoln, condemned the measures of Congress, and attacked the carpet-bag régime. In spite of this, he was in favor of the impeachment of Andrew Johnson.

The political and financial corruption of the seventies found in Bowles an assailant who did not hesitate at personal risk. His denunciation of James Fisk, and especially of his financial coup of 1868, of which the *Republican* said that "nothing so audacious, nothing more gigantic in the way of real swindling has ever been perpetrated in this country," provoked Fisk to institute a libel suit for $50,000. The suit was not pressed, but when Bowles next visited New York (December 1868) he was suddenly seized at his hotel upon a writ issued by the notorious Judge McCunn, and hurried off to Ludlow Street jail for the night. A little later Bowles's attacks upon the Erie Railroad looters brought him into collision with David Dudley Field, the counsel for Fisk, Gould, and Tweed. There ensued a sharp exchange of letters, later published in pamphlet form, in which Bowles showed how far

Field had overstepped the line proper to an honorable lawyer. In Massachusetts the editor marshalled his staff to an assault upon the corrupt railroad lobby at the State House which had battened upon the Hoosac Tunnel appropriations. But Bowles's zeal as a reformer was best manifested in the Liberal Republican movement of 1872. Shocked by the Crédit Mobilier and other scandals, he joined hands with Horace White, Murat Halstead, Carl Schurz, and other rebels in promoting the Cincinnati Convention, and when it met labored on the spot for the nomination of Charles Francis Adams. Keenly disappointed when Greeley was named instead, he wired the *Republican* to accept the ticket but "not to gush." He admitted that Greeley would give the country a "political hurly-burly and party interregnum," but till the end he argued for his election (*Republican,* July 26 *et seq.*). Greeley's indorsement by the South, he said, "means that *the war is really over.*"

The last twenty years of Bowles's life were marked by ill health caused by overwork and manifesting itself in insomnia, neuralgia, and dyspepsia. The prosperity of the *Republican* fortunately made possible the enlargement of its staff by men of ability, including Francis A. Walker, Frank B. Sanborn, and Charles G. Whiting, and enabled Bowles to take frequent vacations. He was in Europe for seven months in 1862, made a tour to California in company with Schuyler Colfax and A. D. Richardson in 1865, returned as far as Colorado in 1868, and was in Europe again in the summer of 1871. Newspaper letters written during his first western tour were reprinted in *Across the Continent: A Summer's Journey to the Rocky Mountains, the Mormons, and the Pacific States with Speaker Colfax* (1865), which reveals a keen observation and graphic, incisive style. His second Western trip gave him the material for *The Switzerland of America: A Summer Vacation in the Parks and Mountains of Colorado,* and the same year it appeared (1869) he combined the two under the title of *Our New West: Records of Travel Between the Mississippi River and the Pacific Ocean.* They have some permanent value as a study, descriptive but not analytic, of social conditions. When in the office Bowles continued to work, and to make his men work, at reckless speed. His look, said a friend, was never of repose; it "was always 'fire or tire.'" He himself wrote that "my will has carried me for years beyond my mental and physical power: that has been the offending rock" (Merriam, I, 398). His discipline was sharp, and he kept his force in a state of tension. His short, stinging

reproof, his irritable intolerance of shirking or blundering, his curt, generous praise of good work, his alternation of black and friendly moods, made him feared, obeyed, and admired.

Bowles had married Mary S. D. Schermerhorn of Geneva, N. Y., on Sept. 6, 1848, and the union was one of singular happiness and devotion; his letters reveal the constancy and depth of his feeling for his wife and their ten children. Mrs. Bowles made it her chief object to give him quiet and rest, and while tense and self-centered at his desk, at his home he was gracious, kindly, and delightful. His pleasure in domestic life did not interfere with social life outside, and even in ill health his acquaintance with politicians and others grew steadily larger and more intimate. His tall, slightly stooping figure, his keen eye and powerful personality, were well known in Washington and New York. At all gatherings his charm was marked. "I never knew a man who knew him," wrote Henry L. Dawes, "who wouldn't rather have him at his table than any other man in the world." He particularly liked association with women, "to chaff with and to rub your mind out of its morbidity." But his devotion to the *Republican* above all other interests and his irritable intensity made him enemies as well as friends. Even his laudatory biographer admits that he "overdid the part of censor," and he alienated many men by unreserved criticism (Merriam, II, 360–62). He was, as Wendell Phillips Garrison wrote, "a great gossip and by no means a safe confidant" (*Nation,* XLI, 553). Priding himself upon his independence of friends, local prejudices, and church or partisan allegiance, and declaring that "the *Republican* is one thing, Sam Bowles another," he was ruthlessly slashing at times. In 1874 he opposed the candidacy of his brother-in-law, Henry Alexander, Jr., for Congress, causing a permanent family estrangement. A year later came a rupture with his younger brother, Benjamin Franklin Bowles. The latter for many years had been in charge of the counting room, but his methods seemed to Bowles inadequate to meet new requirements, and Bowles dismissed him by letter. The younger brother, deeply wounded, went abroad and died (1876) in Paris. When Bowles decided in 1872 to dissolve his partnership with Clark W. Bryan and several associates who held minor shares in the *Republican,* giving them full control of the job-printing and book-binding business, he did so with a tactlessness which alienated Bryan, and caused him to purchase the *Springfield Union* and to make it a formidable rival of the *Republican.*

The editor's health, despite a trip to California

with Mrs. Bowles in 1873 and a tour to Europe the next year, steadily declined, and in 1876 he suffered an attack resembling paralysis. He supported Hayes for the presidency, but believed that Tilden had been legally elected, and was disgusted by the methods which were used to procure Republican victory. The new president's policies, however, filled him with exultation. Hayes's plans for reconciliation and reform were precisely those for which the *Republican* had striven for a decade. Bowles was also pleased that, following a financial slump in the first shock of the panic of 1873, the *Republican* had risen to an unprecedented prosperity (Merriam, II, 416). In December 1877, occurred another stroke of apoplexy, and six weeks later he died. A memorial service at the Springfield Unitarian Church, Jan. 23, 1878, was the occasion for an expression of admiration for the man from many of the most eminent national leaders.

The principal achievements of Bowles were two: he was a pioneer in the establishment of independent journalism, and he gave the country its first powerful demonstration of what might be done with a newspaper in a provincial city. Beginning with his declaration of complete independence in the year of the Kansas-Nebraska debate (*Republican*, May 31, 1854), he consistently placed public welfare above party success, and was able in 1872 to boast that in the emergence of the "Higher Journalism" which obeyed only its own elevated conscience, "the *Springfield Republican* may honorably claim to have been both a leader and a prophet" (*Weekly Republican*, Dec. 20, 1872). In asserting this independence he labored under the handicap of publishing in a small inland town, overwhelmingly and narrowly Republican in views. He succeeded because he made the *Republican* a model newspaper, which could find its patronage among intelligent readers all over the nation; it was model in the pithy condensation and the intelligence of its news, in its dignity, in its elevated moral tone, in its clarity, pungency, and sparkle, and in the force of its editorial opinions. As an editorial writer Bowles had marked limitations. Profound analysis was beyond him, he was incapable of elaborate or subtle thinking upon abstract topics, and his knowledge showed the deficiencies of a man who had never studied systematically and had read few books. He wrote for the crowd, not for the cultured few. Moreover, he was erratic and impulsive, and himself said that he had a "fine and vagrant head" (Bradford, p. 282). His judgment of men was poor. He wrote of Lincoln that he was "a simple Susan," and of John A. Andrew that he was

"conceited, dogmatic, and lacks breadth and tact for government," while he greatly overpraised Banks, Dawes, Colfax, and others. He scorned consistency, declaring that as a journalist he could not "live to be as old as Methuselah, and brood in silence over a thing till, just before I die, I think I have it right." But he was a master of the vivid, penetrating phrase, and he kindled all he wrote with the fire of his restless, emotional personality. As an administrator his nervousness, headlong energy, and imperious temper made him a hard master, but he had a faculty of extracting enormous quantities of high-grade work from his subordinates. He burned himself out too fast, but for a quarter-century he was one of the real leaders of American opinion. As Henry Watterson said, he became more than a journalist—he became one of the real statesmen of his time.

[The second Bowles was fortunate in his biographer. George S. Merriam's *Life and Times of Samuel Bowles* (2 vols., 1885), though at times somewhat unguarded in its laudation, gives a well-rounded impression of the editor and his work, and its full selection of letters affords an interesting insight into his personality. The review of this volume in the *Nation*, XLI, 553, probably by W. P. Garrison, offers a critical corrective of some of its judgments. Gamaliel Bradford, in *Union Portraits* (1916), pp. 263 ff., has ably analyzed Bowles's character. Richard Hooker gives a careful sketch of the *Republican* under his guidance in *The Story of an Independent Newspaper* (1924), and additional material is furnished by Willard G. Bleyer in *Main Currents in the Hist. of Am. Journalism* (1927), pp. 252 ff., and in George H. Payne's *Hist. of Journalism in the U. S.* (1920), pp. 323 ff. His place in the life of Springfield is somewhat inadequately indicated in M. A. Green, *Springfield 1636–1886* (1888), pp. 542 ff.]   A. N.

BOWLES, SAMUEL (Oct. 15, 1851–Mar. 14, 1915), editor, was the fourth of the name in direct succession and the third known as a journalist. As the eldest son, he was early trained by his father to take charge of the *Springfield Republican*. He attended the public schools of Springfield and entered Yale, but being of delicate health remained only two years and took special studies instead of the regular course. He traveled in Europe 1869–71, spending most of his time in Germany, and contributing some correspondence to the *Republican*. In 1873 he was placed upon the staff as editorial assistant under his father's exacting discipline, and after some experience in writing editorials and gathering news, undertook in 1875 the business management. The growth of the newspaper, the withdrawal of his uncle B. F. Bowles from the counting room, and the failing health of his father threw an increasing responsibility upon him, so that the death of the elder Bowles found him ready to assume full charge. Thereafter he performed for nearly four decades the duties of editor, publisher, and treasurer.

With the exception of his marriage on June 12, 1884, to Elizabeth Hoar of Concord, Mass., daughter of Rockwood Hoar, all the important events in the life of the third Bowles were connected with the *Republican*. He never became a public figure like his father; he traveled little, mingled little with political leaders, and wrote no books and few signed articles. But he held decisive control of the character of the *Republican*, and maintained it at the highest level of American journalism. He seldom contributed to its pages, saying that he could not write but could "tell others how and what they ought to write" (Hooker, p. 156). But while he placed his desk in the business department, he directed all the important editorial utterances, was in close touch with the news-gathering, and daily read and sternly criticized every column. Conservative in taste, he insisted upon a standard of old-fashioned dignity. Not until late in life did he remove from the front page the advertisements which gave the *Republican* an English look. His one important innovation was the founding (Sept. 15, 1878) of the *Sunday Republican*, which as a summary of the news of the week and a repository of special features largely took the place of the weekly *Republican*.

The third Bowles continued his father's policy of aggressive editorial independence. In 1884 he joined the mugwumps in attacking Blaine and supporting Cleveland, whose reëlection he advocated in 1888 and 1892. He opposed Bryan and free silver in 1896, but four years later accepted imperialism as "the paramount issue," and waged one of the greatest campaigns of the *Republican* in assailing the annexation of the Philippines. The same issue, raised by the seizure of Panama, helped Bowles decide in 1904 to stand with Parker against Roosevelt; but four years later he advocated the election of Taft. Two of his abiding editorial tenets were tariff reduction and international conciliation, and the *Republican* denounced all forms of jingoism—particularly what it called Henry Cabot Lodge's "aristocratic demagogism"—unsparingly. Both in the editorial and news departments Bowles was fortunate in the assistants he found and developed. The staff when he assumed charge included W. L. Warren as chief editorial writer, Charles G. Whiting, and Solomon B. Griffin, who for more than forty years was managing editor. With their aid Bowles made the *Republican* famous as a school for journalists, and among other pupils trained Talcott Williams, George Harvey, Robert H. Lyman, George Kibbe Turner, and Louis A. Coolidge. The talent which the *Republican* attracted gave it a high literary quality, and helped it overcome in its presentation of news the handicap of meager financial resources. By economy and conservative guidance Bowles kept it moderately prosperous, and was able to set conscience above revenue by excluding in 1914 all liquor advertisements.

The third Bowles, like his father, believed office holding incompatible with editorial independence, and repeatedly refused opportunities to enter public life. He was active in the Springfield Board of Trade, and was responsible for the leading position which Springfield took in the national movement for a safe and sane Fourth. He was always prominent at gatherings of journalists, was a member of the advisory board of the Pulitzer School of Journalism, and in 1913 became a director of the Associated Press. Despite his ill health, the finer side of social life appealed to him and he adorned it (Griffin, p. 36). Many of his subordinates found him, because of inherited dyspepsia and other ailments, irritable and sharp-tongued, but all admired his fine ability and sensitive conscience. He repeatedly said that "I realize I came after a great man; I have never expected personal fame," but his death was the occasion for many tributes to the devotion and skill with which he had maintained and enlarged the heritage from his father. Another recognition came in honorary degrees given him by Amherst College and Olivet College. He left two sons, of whom Sherman Hoar Bowles remained the controlling force in the *Republican* office.

[The fullest record of the career of the third Bowles is in the obituary notice of the *Springfield Republican*, Mar. 16, 1915. This is supplemented by the full and accurate obituary in the N. Y. *Evening Post*, Mar. 16, 1915, ~~probably prepared by his former colleague, E. P. Clark~~. *[written by O. G. Villard]* Richard Hooker, *The Story of an Independent Newspaper* (1924) outlines the history of the *Republican* under his control, and Solomon B. Griffin, *People and Politics as Observed by a Massachusetts Editor* (1923) adds many personal touches.]   A. N.

BOWLES, WILLIAM AUGUSTUS (Oct. 22, 1763–Dec. 23, 1805), adventurer, son of Thomas and Eleanor Bowles, was born in Frederick County, Md. At the age of thirteen he joined the British forces, and in 1778 was made an ensign in the Maryland Loyalist Corps. Shortly after the arrival of the corps at Pensacola (December 1778) he was cashiered. With this event began his life-long, though intermittent, connection with the Creek Indians, with whom he now took refuge. Reinstated in his commission in 1781, he was put on half-pay in 1783. After several years' wandering in the Southern states and the Bahamas he returned to the primitive life of the Creek country, partly, no doubt, because of his maladjustment to civilized society. While on the Island of Providence he had formed a connection with the governor, Lord Dunmore (formerly of Virginia) and a wealthy merchant, John Miller, which shaped his course for the rest of his life. Desiring to supplant Panton, Leslie & Company in the profitable trade with the Creek Indians, and nursing war-time grievances against Spain, these men made Bowles their instrument. With such backing he thrice attempted to drive Panton and the Spaniards out of the Floridas. According to his own statement, Bowles had a larger purpose, namely, to establish an independent Muscogean state trading with all nations. At other times he seems to have regarded himself as a second Robert Clive (*American Historical Review,* VII, 729), with Dunmore and Miller playing the part of the East India Company and the Creek warriors that of sepoys, and with the reincorporation of the Floridas in the British empire as his objective. Although he failed in every attempt, he alarmed the governments of Spain and the United States, caused Panton's company heavy losses, and destroyed Alexander McGillivray's ascendance over the Creek Indians.

Bowles first appeared in Florida in 1788, but soon retired, and in December 1790, at the end of the Nootka crisis, we find him in England with a party of Indians. In July 1791 he was again in Providence, and about Aug. 19 he appeared at St. Mark's, Fla., in his second and most formidable attempt to gain control of the Creek country. This time he made a determined effort to conciliate the Spanish officials, but one of his renegade followers later testified that, together with William Blount and John Sevier, Bowles was concerting a plan to drive Spain out of the Floridas and Louisiana. At any rate, after he had plundered Panton's store at St. Mark's, Gov. Carondelet procured his arrest through an unsavory stratagem (Feb. 26, 1792). Although much impressed by his striking personality, Carondelet sent him to Havana, whence, after a brief interval, he was taken to Spain. Kept in confinement at Madrid from September 1792 to January 1794, he was then sent to the Philippines. As he was being brought back to Spain he escaped from the ship and made his way to Sierra Leone, where the British governor showed him every courtesy (*Archivo de Indias, Papeles de Cuba, Leg. 2371,* Bowles to Grenville, June 5, 1798, draft, signed). Thence in 1798 he returned to England, where he prepared for his third filibustering expedition to Florida, obtaining for a time the backing of the Missionary Society. In September 1799, he was once more in Florida. Early the following year

he and his followers, who were mostly Lower Creeks, again plundered Panton's store and even captured the Spanish fort at St. Mark's. The fort was very shortly retaken by the Spaniards, but for nearly three years Bowles continued to live at Miccosukee with about sixty followers, who, said Benjamin Hawkins, were "more attentive to frolicking than fighting" (*Letters of Benjamin Hawkins,* 1916, p. 418). In 1802 Gov. Folch of Pensacola offered a reward of $4,500 for his capture, and in 1803 he was seized while at a feast at Tuskegee and was turned over to the Spanish officials (A. J. Pickett, *Alabama,* 1851, I, 191–92). Sent to Havana and imprisoned in the Morro Castle, he died on Dec. 23, 1805. He was married to a daughter of a Creek chieftain and left a number of descendants, among them Chief Bowles, the friend of Gen. Sam Houston.

[Most of the reliable information about Bowles is still buried in MSS. The chief printed sources are: *The Authentic Memoirs of Wm. Augustus Bowles* (1791), reprinted, with portrait, in the *Mag. of Hist.,* Extra 46 (Tarrytown, 1916); E. Alfred Jones, "The Real Author of the 'Authentic Memoirs of Wm. Augustus Bowles,'" *Md. Hist. Mag.,* XVIII, 300–308, showing that the *Memoirs* were written by Capt. Benjamin Baynton; Le Clerc Milfort, *Mémoire ou coup-d'œil rapide sur mes différents Voyages et mon Séjour dans la Nation Crëck* (Paris, 1802), pp. 116–28; *The Jour. of Andrew Ellicott* (1814), pp. 226–32; *Am. Hist. Rev.,* VII, 706–35; T. M. Farquhar, *Hist. of the Bowles Family* (1907).]
A. P. W.

BOWMAN, JOHN BRYAN (Oct. 16, 1824– Sept. 29, 1891), founder of Kentucky University, was of German stock that entered Kentucky by way of Virginia, his grandfather, Abram Bowman, having been colonel of the 8th Virginia German Regiment in the Revolutionary Army. John's father, also a John Bowman, married Mary Mitchum and settled in Mercer County. He was one of the incorporators and trustees of Bacon College, Harrodsburg (Robert Peter, *Transylvania University,* 1896, p. 20), so that his son had an early opportunity for observing the technique of academic organization and for developing an enthusiasm for higher education. At the age of fifteen the son united with the Christian church, an affiliation he retained until his death. After graduating from the newly-founded Bacon College in 1842 he studied law but did not practise; instead, having married Mary Dorcas Williams in 1845, he occupied himself with the management of "Old Forest Farm," his inherited estate in what was then called the Cane Run section of Mercer County. For ten years he lived there the life of a country gentleman and then, stirred by the collapse of his alma mater and concerned over the prospect of collegiate training in Kentucky, he attracted state-wide attention by a bold challenge to his church to erect a university on the ruins of the failing college. He was then only thirty, and he set to work with all the energy and hope of youth to achieve this ambition. For the projected university Mercer County contributed $30,000; then Bowman set out, driving and riding through the most favorable counties, exerting argument and personality, and astonishing even his friends by taking subscriptions to the amount of $150,000 in 150 days (*Report of Board of Curators of Kentucky University*, 1866). In 1858 the legislature granted the institution a charter naming it Kentucky University. Popular clamor forced it to open prematurely in Harrodsburg as Taylor Academy in that year; in 1859 the College of Arts and Sciences opened with nearly 200 students. During the Civil War, Bowman, a slaveholder, held to the Union, and as regent managed the affairs of the university so adroitly that, surrounded by armed forces as it often was, not a dollar was lost nor did classes suspend for more than a week. Accidental fire destroyed the buildings in 1864 and the university subsequently languished. A fortunate event, however, gave great encouragement to Bowman's plans. Accepting the provisions of the Morrill Act of 1862, the Kentucky Assembly had appointed a committee to receive bids for the location of an Agricultural and Mechanical College, and this committee suggested to Bowman the union of this new college with Kentucky University. Lexington having made the most favorable bid, it was decided to consolidate Transylvania University, Kentucky University, and the A. & M. College there, the whole being called Kentucky University. This institution opened in October 1865, with Bowman as regent. For nine years he directed the policies for the University, accepting no salary but having free residence in "Ashland," former home of Henry Clay, which the university had purchased and to which Bowman gave added fame by his hospitality. But dissensions presently arose, chiefly owing to the rival claims of church and state in regulating an institution under joint control. In June 1874 Bowman resigned his office and in 1878 the legislature provided for the separation of Kentucky University from the A. & M. College, thus preparing the way for the latter to become the present State University (A. F. Lewis, *History of Higher Education in Kentucky*, 1899, p. 91). Besides bringing the university to the point where in 1870 it was among the largest in the country, Bowman had busied himself with many other affairs: he had had a share in founding Hocker (now Hamilton) College, the Commercial College, and the College of the Bible,

all in Lexington; he had helped establish the street-railway system in the same city; he had argued in Washington for irrigation in New Mexico. President Grant offered him the appointment of minister to Ecuador, but he declined in order that he might devote himself to his educational programs. Pictures of Bowman reveal a face expressing considerable determination, and those who knew him agree that to much charm of bearing he added the force of an aggressive and tenacious character.

[W. H. English, *Conquest of the Country Northwest of the Ohio River 1778–83* (1896), containing genealogical material collected by Bowman himself, who contemplated writing a history of his family; Mabel H. Pollitt, *A Biography of J. K. Paterson* (1925), which gives a clear account of the union of the colleges; *Biog. Encyc. of Ky.* (1874), p. 627; personal information from Mrs. Nannie Bowman Moore of Harrodsburg and from Mrs. W. F. Lafferty of Lexington.]
G. C. K.

BOWMAN, THOMAS (July 15, 1817–Mar. 3, 1914), Methodist Episcopal bishop, educator, was born in Berwick, Pa., the son of John, a successful business man, and Sarah (Brittain) Bowman. He came of stock which had a decidedly religious strain, Scotch Presbyterian on his mother's side, but Methodist on the paternal ever since his grandfather, after whom he was named, was converted and later ordained by Francis Asbury, becoming a pioneer preacher of that denomination throughout eastern Pennsylvania. Thomas had sufficient mental ability to enter the junior class of Dickinson College at the age of eighteen, after one year's preparation at Wilbraham Academy, Mass., and three at Cazenovia Academy, N. Y. He graduated, valedictorian, in 1837. His first inclination was toward the law, which he studied for a year under Judge John Reed, noted Pennsylvania jurist, but turning to the ministry, he entered the Baltimore Conference in 1839. From 1840 to 1843, he taught in the Dickinson Grammar School. Owing to poor health and the circumstances of his aged parents, for five years he ran a farm and small flour mill in his native town. In 1842 he married Matilda Hartman, by whom he had eleven children. From 1848 to 1858 he was principal of Dickinson Seminary, Williamsport, Pa., from 1858 to 1872 president of Indiana Asbury (later DePauw) University; and in 1872 he was elected bishop.

Possessing a keen analytical mind and the gift of exposition he was an unusually successful teacher. Although much engaged in other labors, he preached continually, acquiring a wide popularity, and in 1864–65 serving as chaplain of the United States Senate. Through his executive talent, he contributed much to the educational and administrative activities of his church. When he took charge of Dickinson Seminary, it was practically without funds or prospects. He left it on a sound foundation with about four hundred students. He was an important factor in the development of Asbury University, not only serving as president for fourteen years, but also acting as trustee, 1875–95, president of the board, 1887–95, and chancellor, 1884–99. He is credited with having been the main agent in securing Washington DePauw's donations to the institution. As bishop he was indefatigable in superintending the work of the denomination in this country, and visited all the Conferences in Europe, China, Japan, India, and Mexico. A lecture by him "Romanism Enslaves, Degrades, Corrupts" was published in *Popular Lectures on the Errors of the Roman Catholic Church* (1878), but his activities left little time for authorship.

[The *Christian Advocate*, Mar. 12, 1914, contains portrait. See also the same paper for Mar. 26, Apr. 16, May 14, 1914; *First Fifty Years of Cazenovia Seminary* (1877); *Who's Who in America, 1912–13*.]

H. E. S.

BOWNE, BORDEN PARKER (Jan. 14, 1847–Apr. 1, 1910), philosopher, of Puritan descent, was the son of Margaret (Parker) Bowne and of Joseph Bowne, farmer, justice of the peace, and local preacher of his religious faith, well known as an opponent of slavery and of liquor. The boy grew up sensitive to his environment, shy in disposition, and attracted to books. His mind was alert and capable of deep impressions. He attended Pennington Seminary, and then by his own effort prepared himself to enter the sophomore class of the University of the City of New York. He made a brilliant reputation,—second to none in the history of the University, and was graduated valedictorian of his class in 1871. He taught school for a year, and then was pastor of a Methodist church in Whitestone, N. Y., in 1873. There followed a period of study in Europe at Halle and Göttingen, and he returned to America in 1875 to become for a year assistant professor of modern languages in the University of the City of New York. During the same time he was religious editor of the New York *Independent*. His interest in philosophy had developed strongly in college. He had written a discriminating criticism of the philosophy of Herbert Spencer, which was published in the *New Englander* without signature and was popularly ascribed to a much older man. In 1876 Boston University, of his own Methodist denomination, invited him to head its department of philosophy, and he accepted. His service for nearly thirty-five years as head of the department of philoso-

phy and as dean of the graduate school brought fame to the University. More than once he was invited to join other faculties, but he was loyal to the institution to which he had given himself. In 1905–06 he made a tour around the world, receiving a specially cordial reception in Japan. He gained a new respect for the Oriental peoples, especially China. At home he was always occupied with teaching or writing, so that he had little leisure for the enjoyment of nature or the cultivation of wide friendships, though he prized both. He took an interest in mechanical things, and found recreation in walking, but his favorite relaxation was gardening. He took special pride in his rose garden at Longwood. He was happy in his home life, simple in his tastes, but appreciative of artistic furnishings. To him personality was the secret of reality, life the expression of thought and the test of truth. He lectured in crisp, breezy fashion, with an original way of expression and with touches of humor. He clarified the subject by his lucid thought and language and by copious illustration, then left it to the student to think for himself. A written quiz was the usual test of attainment. A pupil could absent himself when he chose; when present he must be alert and responsive. The lecturer had little patience with laziness or uncertain grasp of intellect or faith.

His philosophical ideas were matured early in life, but he did not hesitate to change his terminology for the sake of clearness or emphasis. His early philosophy was an objective idealism, which resembled the thinking of Lotze, but Bowne was no man's understudy. Lotze was a monist in philosophy, but not so Bowne. Lotze cared for religion incidentally, Bowne made it central. His faith colored all his thought. As the years passed he stressed more and more the reality of the self back of all categories and laws, free from bondage to inanimate nature, learning empirically, and expressing itself in moral conduct. He called this doctrine transcendental empiricism, because man's experience is not limited to the senses. At a time when a mechanistic determinism was popular he rejected every argument against the freedom of personality. He insisted that no sound theory of knowledge was possible on any necessitarian basis. He never tired of maintaining the freedom of the self and its relation to the Unseen that was behind the universe. He anticipated the modern notion of relativity in insisting that time and space are only relative terms, not by any means to be thought of as controlling factors. He found values in the intuitional, the intellectual, the utilitarian, balancing them in the fashioning of his ethics. He brought all philosophy and religion to the pragmatic test of life. So insistent was he upon the central importance of personality that he came to believe that no other term so well defined his thought as Personalism, and by that name his philosophy has come to be known. After 1905, when he felt that he had established his philosophical position, he turned his attention to theology. He was of service to his fellow Methodists in clearing away obstructions to modern thinking. Rather conservative, as, for example, in his christology and in his attitude toward evolution, when so many men were captivated by the idea of that principle as an active agent in creation, he stood for the right of criticism and the duty of an open mind towards all investigation. His strength of conviction and outspoken opinions aroused the opposition of certain defenders of orthodoxy, and he was tried for heresy before his own New York East Conference, but he was in no danger of conviction. He took part in the defense of the accused in a similar trial of his colleague, Prof. Mitchell, an experience that embittered him against theological obscurantists. Religion was to him the sanction of ethics, as ethics was the expression of religion. His books covered the whole field of philosophy, and made valuable contributions to theology. They include: *The Philosophy of Herbert Spencer* (1874), *Studies in Theism* (1879), *Metaphysics* (1882), *The Theory of Thought and Knowledge* (1897), *Introduction to Psychological Theory* (1886), *Principles of Ethics* (1892), *The Christian Revelation* (1898), *The Immanence of God* (1905), *Personalism* (1908), *Studies in Christianity* (1909). After his death in 1910 Mrs. Bowne edited a series of sermons under the title *The Essence of Religion,* which revealed Bowne's religious experience. In 1912 his lectures were published on *Kant and Spencer: a Critical Exposition.*

[*The Meth. Rev.,* May–June, 1922, was a Bowne memorial number. Other valuable sources of information and estimate are the *Personalist,* I, 5–14; *Zion's Herald,* Dec. 18, 1912; *Am. Jour. of Theology,* July 1910; C. B. Pyle, *The Philosophy of B. P. Bowne* (1910).]   H. K. R.

BOWNE, JOHN (c. Mar. 1, 1627/28–Oct. 10, 1695), Quaker leader, was born at Matlock, Derbyshire, England, the son of Thomas, and grandson of Anthony Bowne, of the Lime Tree Farm, Matlock. He came to Boston in 1649, returned to England in 1650, and again came to Boston in 1651. He then removed to Flushing, L. I., purchasing a home lot in 1653, and marrying in 1656 Hannah Feake, daughter of Lieut. Robert Feake of New England. In 1662 he was arrested on a complaint that a meeting "of the

abominable sect called Quakers" was held every Sunday at his house. He was taken from his sick wife and child to New Amsterdam, where, refusing to pay a fine, he was imprisoned, first in the dungeon, then in the prison room of the Stadt Huys. After four months' imprisonment, during which his door was occasionally left open in hope that he would escape, he was banished. Being the most prominent leader of the Quakers, if he could be scared away or deported the disturbing sect might be scattered. The directors of the West India Company, on receipt of Stuyvesant's report of Bowne's banishment, issued on Apr. 16, 1663, N.S., their famous order establishing religious liberty in New Netherland, on the ground that "people's consciences should not be forced, but every one left free in his belief." Meanwhile Bowne landed in Ireland, crossed Ireland and England, visiting Quakers, and reached Amsterdam on May 9, 1663, N.S. The next day he appeared before the directors. They had lost the noble impulse of Apr. 16, and it took them a month to agree that Bowne should have his chest (left on board off Ireland), and a passport. He reached home a year and seven months after his arrest. He was thereafter a large land-holder and farmer. He married, second, Hannah Bickerstaff, and, third, Mary Cock. In 1683 he was county treasurer, and in 1691 was elected representative from Queens County to the General Assembly, but not seated, as he would not take the prescribed oaths, although willing to sign the Test and to engage to perform the tenor of the oaths under penalty of perjury. The Quaker record states that "John Bowne dyed the 20 day of the 10 month in the yeare 1695 And was buryed ye 23 day of the same being about 68 yeares of age. He did Freely Expose him selfe his house and Esteate to ye service of Truth And had a constant Meeting In his house neare About forty yeares. Hee allso suffered very much for ye truths seak."

[The manuscript of Bowne's *Journal,* giving a complete account of his imprisonment and banishment, is lost, but a copy is in the N. Y. Pub. Lib. Geo. Bishop's *New England Judged* (2nd ed. 1703) erroneously related the story of Bowne's banishment, and Jos. Besse's *Collection of the Sufferings of the people call'd Quakers* (1753) increased the errors. "John Bowne: Pioneer of Freedom," by John Cox, Jr. (not yet published) is the first careful study of the man, in relation to the background of time and conditions.]   J. C.

BOYCE, JAMES PETIGRU (Jan. 11, 1827– Dec. 28, 1888), Baptist minister, educator, of Scotch-Irish ancestry, the son of Ker and Amanda Jane Caroline (Johnston) Boyce, was born near tidewater at Charleston, S. C. His grandfather was a soldier in the Revolution, his father a wealthy cotton merchant in Charleston.

The boy early showed an inclination for books, was fitted for college before he was old enough to enter Charleston College, and later revealed his intellectual abilities there and at Brown University, where he graduated in 1847. A religious conversion turned his thoughts to the ministry as a profession, and he was licensed to preach. He spent two years at Princeton Theological Seminary, acquiring an enviable knowledge of theological literature, and specializing in the department of theology. In 1851 he settled as pastor of the Baptist Church in Columbia, S. C. In 1855 when only twenty-eight years old he was elected professor of theology in the theological department of the new Furman University at Greenville, S. C. On Dec. 20, 1858, he was married to Lizzie Llewellyn Ficklen.

Theological instruction in preparation for the Baptist ministry had hitherto been limited to personal guidance in the homes of leading ministers, and later to instruction in theological departments of academies and country colleges, such as Furman. Boyce was among the first to see that there was need of a theological seminary on an independent, well-endowed foundation, and he soon gave up the regular work of instruction at Furman, and became the spokesman for the new enterprise. The matter was agitated for several years before it took definite form. Boyce became a familiar figure on the plantations as he drove about soliciting support. He possessed an extensive tract of land near Greenville which brought him in large agricultural profits, and his father, also, assisted him financially so that he was able to live without salary. In 1859 the Southern Baptist Theological Seminary, with Boyce at its head, was organized at Greenville where it took over the theological department and library of Furman. The outbreak of the Civil War scattered its students, sent Boyce as a chaplain to a South Carolina regiment, and stopped any further receipt of funds. The recovery of educational institutions after the war was necessarily slow, and the Seminary had no buildings and little endowment. Out of his reduced fortune Boyce paid necessary bills to keep the school open, and it slowly recovered, ultimately moving to Louisville, Ky., where it became a credit to the denomination. Boyce shaped the curriculum on the elective principle, which he had learned from his president at Brown, Francis Wayland. As a theologian he maintained staunchly the conservative opinions that were characteristic of the Southern churches. He was highly regarded for his executive ability, for a number of years was president of the Southern Baptist Convention,

and once was vainly urged to become president of the South Carolina Railroad Company at a salary of $10,000. His last years brought him ill health, which sent him to California, Alaska, and Europe. He died at Pau, France.

[John A. Broadus, *Memoir of Jas. Petigru Boyce* (1893); John R. Sampey, *Southern Baptist Theol. Sem.* (1890); *Necrological Report Alumni Ass. Princeton Theol. Sem., May 7, 1889*; *News and Courier* (Charleston, S. C.), May 6, 8, 1875; *Courier-Jour.* (Louisville, Ky.), Dec. 27, 28, 29, 1888.]   H. K. R.

BOYD, BELLE (May 9, 1843–June 11, 1900), Confederate spy, was born in Martinsburg, Va., and from twelve to sixteen attended Mount Washington College. She was seventeen at the outbreak of the Civil War. The story of her achievements for the South rests mainly on her own none too trustworthy account in *Belle Boyd in Camp and Prison* (2 vols., London, 1865). It seems that during the early part of the war in conversation with Union officers quartered in Martinsburg, she picked up important military intelligence which she communicated to Southern officers, sometimes at the risk of her life. One of her notes was intercepted and she became a suspect. After the second capture of Martinsburg by the Union troops she went to Front Royal, where she found Gen. Shields occupying her aunt's house. While a council of war went on in the dining-room, Belle was lying in the closet above, her ear to a hole in the floor. The conference over, she saddled her horse, and with her passes, rode fifteen miles, returning undiscovered before dawn. But her most important service to the Confederate cause was a communication to Gen. Jackson's forces that by advancing rapidly they could save the bridges which the Federals were planning to destroy and keep open the road for an advance on Gen. Banks. Running over open fields, where her blue dress with its white apron was a target for picket shots and shells, she waved her bonnet at the first line of Confederates as a sign to advance, which they did. Jackson thanked her in the following terms: "I thank you, for myself and for the army, for the immense service that you have rendered your country today." After the retaking of Front Royal by the North, she was arrested in July 1862 and ordered to the Old Capitol prison in Washington, but was released a month later for lack of evidence against her. At this time, according to her own statement she received a commission as "captain and honorary aide-de-camp" to Gen. Jackson. In August 1863 she was arrested once more and kept in Carroll prison until Dec. 1. The following spring she sailed for England with letters from Jefferson Davis, was captured on her way but again released and continued on her trip. In August of the same year she married the man who had been her captor, Lieut. Sam Wylde Hardinge. Upon his death she went on the English stage, making her début as Pauline in the *Lady of Lyons* at the Theatre Royal, Manchester, in the latter part of 1866. A successful experience encouraged her to try the same career in America. Her first appearance was at Ben De Bar's Theatre, St. Louis. Then followed a starring tour of the South and Southwest. In January 1868 she appeared in New York in *The Honeymoon*. Later in the same year she joined the Miles and Bates stock company at Cincinnati but was soon engaged by the Greenwalls for their stock houses in Houston and Galveston. She married John Hammond, a former officer in the British army, in 1869, and Nathaniel High of Toledo in 1885. On Feb. 22, 1886, she presented a dramatic narrative of her own exploits as Confederate spy, at the People's Theatre, Toledo, Ohio. This type of lecture she continued until her sudden death from a heart attack, in Kilbourne, Wis., whither she had gone to speak. Dion Boucicault's play *Belle Lamar* is said to have been based on her experiences during the Civil War.

[Belle Boyd, *Belle Boyd in Camp and Prison* (1865); B. J. Lossing, *The Pictorial Field Book of the Civil War* (1874); T. A. Brown, *Hist. of the N. Y. Stage* (1903); *Milwaukee Jour.*, June 12, 1900; *N. Y. Times*, June 13, 1900.]　　　　　　　　M. A. K.

BOYD, DAVID FRENCH (Oct. 5, 1834– May 27, 1899), educator, the son of Thomas Jefferson and Minerva Anne (French) Boyd, was born at Wytheville, Va. His father's family had been established in America by John Boyd who emigrated from Ayrshire, Scotland, and settled in Maryland in the late seventeenth century. David Boyd was educated in the famous Pike Powers classical school at Staunton, Va., and at the University of Virginia, graduating in 1856. He taught school in his native town for one year and then in the fall of 1857 went to Sherman, Tex., to assist in the construction of a railroad in that part of the state. But on his arrival he found that the project had been abandoned and he turned back to school teaching. After three years at Homer, and Rocky Mount, both in Louisiana, he was elected professor of ancient languages and English literature in the Louisiana State Seminary of Learning which opened its doors on Jan. 2, 1860, at Pineville, near Alexandria, with William Tecumseh Sherman as superintendent. In June 1861 he resigned his position in the seminary and entered the service of the Confederacy as a private in Company B, 9th Louisiana Infantry, which was shortly sent to Virginia for duty. He quickly rose in the ranks until by May 1862 he was major and brigade commissary in Richard Taylor's brigade of Stonewall Jackson's corps, and took part in the famous Valley campaign of Jackson that terminated in the latter's death. When Taylor was transferred to the Trans-Mississippi department, he accompanied him as captain of engineers. In the latter part of 1863 he constructed Fort De Russy on the Red River below Alexandria. He was captured by the "Jayhawkers" in February 1864 near Black River, La., and was confined in Federal prisons at Natchez, Miss., and at New Orleans. Through the intercession of Gen. Sherman, he was exchanged in the following July for two Federal officers of the same rank. In December 1864 he became major and adjutant-general in Brent's cavalry brigade which guarded Kirby Smith's front from Arkansas to the Gulf of Mexico during the last stages of the war. He surrendered at New Orleans in June 1865.

Elected superintendent of the Louisiana State Seminary, Boyd reopened it in October 1865. He was immediately confronted with the difficult problems of how to obtain financial support from state legislatures that were controlled largely by the carpet-baggers and negroes, and how to preserve the institution for the exclusive use of the young white men of Louisiana. Coupled with these problems was the broader one concerning the public schools of the state. According to the Louisiana state constitution of 1868 there were to be no separate public schools for the white and the colored children of Louisiana. Boyd joined hands with other prominent men in the state in securing the passage of a law in 1869 and a supplementary law in 1870, providing that in every parish in the state there should be one or more public schools, with the understanding that one should be for white children and the other for negroes. Before these troublesome questions could be fully decided, the building in which the seminary had been housed from the beginning was burned to the ground on Oct. 15, 1869. For the moment the situation was very serious. Boyd secured accommodations for the seminary in a part of the building for the Louisiana State School for the Deaf and Dumb in the southern part of Baton Rouge, and in two weeks after the fire the students resumed their work. In 1870 the seminary was renamed by the state legislature the Louisiana State University and the title of its head was changed from superintendent to president. In 1876, largely through Boyd's efforts, the Louisiana Agricultural and Mechanical College, which had been chartered in 1870 and opened at Chalmette, near New Orleans, in 1874, was merged with the university. By that time Boyd had, by his aggressive policy, incurred the enmity of some of the leading politicians in Louisiana. Opposition to him grew with each succeeding session of the state legislature and even appeared in the state constitutional convention in 1879. As a result he was removed from the presidency of the university in 1880 by the new board of supervisors, appointed by Gov. Nicholls under the constitution of 1879, on the charge of mismanagement of funds. This charge was thoroughly investigated by a special committee appointed by the state legislature in 1882 and was found to be without the slightest foundation. In 1884 the board that had dismissed him recalled Boyd unanimously to the presidency of the university. During the first three of the four years intervening between his dismissal and recall, he was engaged in conducting private military academies in Virginia, one at Locust Dale and another at Greenwood, and in 1883–84 he served as president of the Polytechnic Institute at Auburn, Ala. His second administration in the Louisiana State University saw the removal of the university from the building of the State School for the Deaf and Dumb to the buildings and grounds of an abandoned United States army post in the northern part of Baton Rouge. He had since 1870 had this change of quarters in mind, as he realized that it would be quite impossible for the university to grow and develop without a home of its own. He acted, however, without waiting for the authorization of the board of supervisors of the university, was in consequence severely censured by the board, and shortly after resigned. He remained with the university, however, for two years as professor of mathematics (1886–88). In 1888–93 he served as superintendent of the Kentucky Military Institute at Farmdale, Ky.; in 1893–94 he was a professor in the Ohio Military Academy at Germantown, Ohio; and in 1894–97 he was a professor in the Michigan Military Academy at Orchard Lake, Mich. In January 1897 he returned to Baton Rouge as professor of philosophy and civics in the Louisiana State University, which position he retained until his death in Baton Rouge in 1899. He was married on Oct. 5, 1865, to Esther Gertrude Wright, daughter of Dr. Jesse D. Wright, formerly of Saybrook, Conn.; to them were born seven sons and one daughter. Boyd was a man of slight stature, and in his later years was somewhat stooped, which fact, together with his sloping shoulders, made him appear even smaller. He possessed, however, boundless energy and great physical endurance. He was quick to take ac-

tion and assume entire responsibility, when he thought something needed to be done. Had he been more cautious, he would have saved himself much trouble and embarrassment but his educational achievements in Louisiana would probably have been less.

[*W. T. Sherman as a Coll. President* (1912), ed. by W. E. Fleming, contains many letters that passed between Sherman and Boyd during 1859–61 while they were connected with the La. State Seminary of Learning. The same subject is covered by Boyd himself in the *Am. Coll.*, vol. II, no. 1, Apr. 1910, reprinted in the *Univ. Bull., La. State Univ.*, n. s., no. 10, Oct. 1910. "The Life and Services of D. F. Boyd" by A. A. Gunby in the *Univ. Bull., La. State Univ.*, ser. II, no. 2, June 1904, is an address delivered at the laying of the corner stone of the Alumni Memorial Hall at the La. State Univ., May 31, 1904. A sketch of Boyd by his son, Leroy S. Boyd, appears in T. M. Owens, *Hist. of Alabama* (1921), III, 187–89).]   E. M. V.

BOYD, JOHN PARKER (Dec. 21, 1764–Oct. 4, 1830), soldier of fortune, was born in Newburyport, Mass., the son of James and Susanna Boyd. The year following the end of the Revolution he obtained a commission as ensign, and rose to the rank of lieutenant. About 1789 he arrived in India, in quest of fortune. The conditions in that country favored a military adventurer. The British East India company and the French were in almost constant opposition, and the native Hindu and Mohammedan princes were frequently involved in warfare. Boyd, like the Italian condottieri, and other adventurers, sold his services, now to one prince, now to another. At one time the Nizam of Haidarabad, acting on British suggestions, engaged Boyd, who owned a body of troops, "a ready formed and experienced corps of 1800 men" (Compton, p. 340). Again, he entered the employ of the Peshwa of Poona at a salary of 3000 rupees a month, placed a new Peshwa on the throne, and commanded a brigade in the army of that native prince. "Riding into the very heart of Tippoo's dominions, he would strike a series of paralyzing blows, burn a dozen towns, exact a huge indemnity" (Powell, p. 10). "Military history presents no more fantastic picture than that of this Yankee adventurer spurring across an Indian countryside with a brigade of beturbaned lancers, and a score or so of lumbering elephants, the muzzles of field-guns frowning from their howdahs, tearing along behind him" (*Ibid.*, p. 14).

After nearly a score of years in India, Boyd returned to the United States, and in 1808 he reentered the army as colonel of the 4th Infantry. At the head of this regiment he fought under Harrison at the battle of Tippecanoe in 1811. At the opening of the War of 1812 he was commissioned brigadier-general, and served on the Canadian border. He led a brigade at the capture of Fort

George May 27, 1813, and at the battle of Chrystler's Farm on the following Nov. 11, he was in command. In this engagement, the climax of Wilkinson's disastrous campaign, about 2000 Americans were defeated by 800 of the enemy, and the battle—in the wor 's of the historian Adams—"was ill-fought both by the generals and the men," and "had no redeeming incident." Boyd was discharged from the army in 1815, and toward the end of his life was naval officer for the port of Boston. His character was thus described by a fellow officer in the War of 1812 : "A compound of ignorance, vanity, and petulance, with nothing to recommend him but that species of bravery in the field which is vaporing, boisterous, stifling reflection, blinding observation . . ." (Morgan Lewis, quoted in Adams, VII, p. 162). Adams adds that Boyd was competent only for the command of a regiment, and that he lacked the confidence of the army. "Brown was said to have threatened to resign rather than serve under him, and Winfield Scott . . . described Boyd as amiable and respectable in a subordinate position, but 'vacillating and imbecile beyond all endurance as a chief under high responsibilities'" (Adams, VII, 188).

[J. P. Boyd, *Documents and Facts Relative to Military Events* (1816), an attempted justification of his military conduct ; Herbert Compton, *Military Adventurers of Hindustan* (1893) ; E. A. Powell, *Gentlemen Rovers* (1913) ; Henry Adams, *Hist. of the U. S.* (1889), VI, VII, ; F. B. Heitman, *Hist. Reg.* (1890) ; *Vital Records of Newburyport, Mass.* (1911).]

E. K. A.

BOYD, LYNN (Nov. 22, 1800–Dec. 17, 1859), lawyer, congressman, was of Scotch descent, his ancestors settling early in Virginia. His grandfather, James Boyd, moved to South Carolina, served in the Revolution there and lost heavily at the hands of the British troops. His father, Abraham Boyd, who also fought in the Revolution, fell in early with the migration to Tennessee, crossing the mountains in company with Andrew Jackson, and settling at Nashville, where Lynn was born. In 1803 he removed to a farm in Christian County, Ky., where Lynn grew up as an ordinary laborer, working hard and getting little schooling. When only nineteen years old the youth was appointed to assist in securing from the Chickasaw Indians the Kentucky lands west of the Tennessee River, thereafter known as the Jackson Purchase on account of Andrew Jackson's connection with the mission. In 1826 he moved into the Purchase, settled on a farm in Calloway County, and the next year secured an election to the legislature to represent the four counties constituting the Purchase at that time. He always maintained a keen interest in this par-

ticular part of Kentucky and was looked upon by the people there as a special patron. In 1828 and 1829 he was returned from Calloway County as a representative at Frankfort at the same time that his father was representing Trigg County, and in 1831 Lynn, having returned to Trigg County, was elected as its representative.

Boyd had a degree of ambition which did not let him rest contented with merely state honors. In 1833 he ran for Congress from the first district and was defeated by his Whig opponent, but in 1835 he won, only to lose again in 1837. Determined to be in Congress he ran again in 1839, was elected, and continuously thereafter until 1855 he represented the first district at Washington, so strongly entrenching himself in the affections of the people that at times he was elected without opposition. He was a staunch supporter of Andrew Jackson and always remained a loyal Democrat. He stood squarely behind Jackson in opposition to the United States Bank. In return for this loyalty and out of sentiment for Boyd's father, Jackson steadily lent his influence to the advancement of the son. Boyd was much interested in the annexation of Texas and played a prominent part in the maneuvers leading up to the joint resolution of annexation. During the Mexican War he held the important chairmanship of the committee on military affairs, and later he became chairman of the committee on territories, where he was confronted with the task of trying to solve the difficult question of territorial organization necessitated by the Mexican conquest. He had a passion for the preservation of the Union, and when the compromise measures came before the House in 1850 he led the fight for their passage. Being now one of the most prominent figures in Washington he developed aspirations for the presidency, but his boom never went far. In 1856, however, he was Kentucky's favorite son for the vice-presidency. During the last four years of his congressional career (1851–55) he was speaker of the House. In 1855 he returned to Kentucky, but soon developed a desire to enter the United States Senate. As a step in this direction he sought the governorship in 1859. He received nothing better than the lieutenant-governorship, which he accepted but which he did not live to fill. He was the popular idol of western Kentucky; traditions of his manly vigor and handsome figure are still handed down. He was married twice, first in 1832 to Alice C. Bennett of Trigg County, and then in 1850 to Mrs. Anna L. Dixon of Pennsylvania, a relative of President Fillmore.

[G. W. Thompson, *Biog. Sketch of Hon. Lynn Boyd* (1852) ; *Ky. Statesman*, Dec. 20, 23, 1859 ; Richard H.

and Lewis Collins, *Hist. of Ky.*, vol. II (1874) ; H. Levin, ed., *Lawyers and Lawmakers of Ky.* (1897) ; R. F. Nichols, *The Democratic Machine, 1850–54* (1923).]

E. M. C.

BOYD, RICHARD HENRY (Mar. 15, 1843– Aug. 23, 1922), negro clergyman, was the son of Indiana Dixon, a slave of B. A. Gray, a planter in Noxubee County, Miss. Named Dick Gray by his master, he went by this name until 1867 or 1868 when he changed it himself to R. H. Boyd. When he was six years old, the Grays moved to Washington County, Tex., where they lived on a large plantation until the outbreak of the Civil War. Boyd accompanied his master as a servant in one of the Confederate armies fighting around Chattanooga. Upon the death of his master and three of his sons, the slave returned to take charge of the plantation. In the capacity of manager, he served efficiently, not only in the production of cotton but in selling it at points across the border in Mexico. Upon the break-up of this family a few years later, he became first a Texas cowboy and then a laborer at a sawmill in Montgomery County. In 1869 he was married to Hattie Moore. A turning point in his life came in 1870 or 1871 when he professed religion and entered the Baptist ministry. He was ordained in the latter part of the same year. Although inspired to preach, he was handicapped in that he had had no literary training. He had never attended a public school, and it was only after 1865 that he was even taught the alphabet. Having, however, a desire to learn, he secured the assistance of white people who taught him to read and to spell. After he was ordained to the ministry, he spent two years in what is now known as Bishop College at Marshall, Tex., a school founded and operated by the Home Missionary Society of New York. Entering seriously upon his task as a minister, Boyd not only served an influential church himself, but organized with six other churches the first negro Baptist Association in Texas about 1872. He built churches at Waverly, Old Danville, Navasota, Crockett, Palestine, and San Antonio. He was named secretary of the negro Baptist Convention of Texas and elected superintendent of missions in that state. Serving in these positions, he conceived the idea of publishing literature for negro Baptist Sunday Schools. He brought out his first religious pamphlets for the years of 1894 and 1895. He later published several useful works, among which should be mentioned the *Pastor's Guide,* the *Church Directory,* and *Jubilee and Plantation Songs.* An opportunity for the furtherance of his plans came in 1896, when, while attending the national Baptist convention at St. Louis, he was elected secretary of the home mission board to do mission work among the negroes of the United States. He soon gained sufficient impetus to organize, in January 1897, the National Baptist Publishing Board which issued the first series of negro Baptist literature ever published. His task was a difficult one, for neither he nor his denomination had any money. He had courage, however, and soon won the support of influential friends among the whites who were seriously impressed with the importance of this work. The publishing project rapidly developed into the source of supply of religious literature for the negro Baptists throughout the world. Unfortunately, however, in 1915, because of certain questions as to the management of its affairs, there came a split which resulted in two factions of the negro Baptists of the country, one adhering to the leadership of Boyd and the other to that of the president of the Baptist convention, Dr. E. C. Morris. The latter faction has since then established another large publishing house known as the Sunday School Publishing Board.

[*A Memorial Program,* published in pamphlet form by the National Baptist Publishing Board in March 1927, contains a brief sketch of Boyd. The *Nashville Tennesseean* and *Nashville Banner* contain long obituaries, Aug. 24, 1922. Additional information in detailed form may be obtained from *A Story of the National Baptist Publishing Board.*]

C. G. W.

BOYDEN, SETH (Nov. 17, 1788–Mar. 31, 1870), inventor, manufacturer, is called by Thomas A. Edison "one of America's greatest inventors." He was born in Foxborough, Mass., the son of Seth and Susanna (Atherton) Boyden and the brother of Uriah Atherton Boyden [*q.v.*]. His father was the inventor of a leather-splitting machine, the recipient of numerous awards for improvements in agriculture, and the proprietor of a small forge and machine shop. His grandfather, Uriah Atherton (who is said to have cast the first cannon made in America), was still operating his foundry at Foxborough during Seth Boyden's early life. With this background, a scanty education proved no serious handicap, and at the age of fifteen we find Seth enjoying a local reputation as a skilful mechanic and repairer of watches, clocks, and guns. At twenty-one he had constructed machines for manufacturing nails and cutting files, and at twenty-five he took an improved leather-splitting machine to Newark, N. J., to supply the trade with split sheepskins and leather for bookbinding. This seems to have been the most important move of his life, for the many industries of Newark afforded the opportunities that enabled him to maintain his continuous output of inventions. In 1819 he successfully duplicated the lacquer of a piece of European ornamental leather and established the first factory for the production of varnished or "patent" leather, founding an important American industry. With this enterprise barely established, he turned his attention to malleable cast-iron, the secret of which was also a jealously guarded European one. Here he applied himself to experiment for six years, succeeding in running off his first cast of malleable iron on July 4, 1826. In 1828 the Franklin Institute awarded him a premium for his malleable castings, and in 1831 he was granted the first patent issued for this material. That year he sold his "patent leather" factory to concentrate his efforts on the commercial production of malleable iron, and in 1837 sold the malleable iron business to engage in the construction of locomotives. He built three, and then turned to the manufacture of stationary steam engines, in which connection he made the first application of "cut-off" governing, a method effecting a more economical steam consumption. In connection with his engine works he was making a furnace grate bar in 1847 which he adapted to the manufacture of oxide of zinc, the same grate (the Wetherill) that is used in the "American Process" to-day. In 1849 he made an unsuccessful trip to the California gold fields. Returning the next year he then developed an inexpensive process for manufacturing "Russia" sheet-iron; achieved a reputation for his development of the famous Hilton strawberry; invented an important hat-forming machine; made a gold-like alloy "oroide"; and published a treatise on atmospheric electricity (1868). Incidentally, he is credited with having made the first daguerreotype in this country, and with extending important aid to Morse. He died in Hilton, N. J.

[Jos. Atkinson, *Hist. of Newark, N. J.* (1878); J. L. Bishop, *Hist. of Am. Manufacturers* (1861); Angus Sinclair, *Development of the Locomotive Engine* (1907); *Foxborough's Official Centennial Record* (1879); Records of the N. J. Zinc Co., N. Y.; E. C. Kreutzberg in *Iron Trade Rev.*, Feb. 11, 1926; *Brass World*, Mar. 1926; Patent Office records.]   F.A.T—r.

BOYDEN, URIAH ATHERTON (Feb. 17, 1804–Oct. 17, 1879), engineer, inventor. He was born at Foxborough, Norfolk County, Mass., son of Seth and Susanna (Atherton) Boyden. After attending country school, he assisted his father in farming and blacksmithing. At the age of twenty-one he went to Newark, N. J., to work for his oldest brother, Seth Boyden [*q.v.*], who was a manufacturer and inventor of note. He returned to New England and took part under James Hayward in the first survey for the Boston and Providence Railroad. Later he worked at the dry-dock in the Charlestown navy-yard under Col. L. Baldwin, and still later at Lowell

in the construction of the Suffolk, Tremont, and Lawrence mills, and the Boston and Lowell Railroad. This was an era of industrial expansion for New England and of pioneer experiment in engineering—particularly railroading and hydraulic development. Boyden had little formal education but his Yankee ingenuity and initiative enabled him to pick up quickly the main principles of applied science and technique. At the age of twenty-nine he opened an office in Boston as an engineer. From 1836 to 1838 he supervised the construction of the Nashua and Lowell Railroad. But it was not in railroading that he was to make his mark. He became engineer for the Amoskeag Manufacturing Company and designed hydraulic works at Manchester, N. H. In 1844, when he was forty, he devised a turbine water-wheel for the Appleton cotton-mills at Lowell. This was based on a design of Fourneyron, a Frenchman and the inventor of the outward-flow turbine, but Boyden's improvements made a more efficient design. Tests showed that his turbine, which was for seventy-five horse-power, delivered seventy-eight per cent of the power expended. Two years later he designed for the same company three turbines of 190 horse-power each. His compensation was to depend in a sliding scale upon the performance of the turbines. Tests, which Boyden also improved and systematized, showed an efficiency of eighty-two per cent, so that he was paid $5,500. Among the improvements was a well-designed scroll penstock, a suspended top bearing, and a diffuser showing the principles of the modern flaring draft-tube. He was the inventor of the hook-gauge, which with his other inventions he patented and which thereby contributed to his ample income. The principle with which his name is most commonly associated is the spiral approach, which has the advantage of admitting water to the turbine at a uniform velocity. The Boyden water-wheel soon became well known throughout the country and was adopted in many mills and power-plants; he has been called the father of American mixed-flow hydraulic turbine design but this title probably is not deserved —although Boyden might have liked to appropriate it. The science of hydraulics had not advanced much beyond the empirical stage, and as most of the formulas were known to Boyden, his work was along sound engineering lines. In his later years he retired from active practise and devoted his time to the study of pure science— an unusual procedure for a practical, "uneducated" engineer. In particular he investigated the velocity of light, the compressibility of water, and the subject of "caloric" or heat.

One elaborate experiment consisted of tests to determine the velocity of sounds traveling through the conduit pipes of the Charlestown and Chelsea water-works. It is interesting to note that as early as 1826, when he was twenty-two years old, the *New Jersey Eagle* published an article by him entitled "An Attempt to Explain the Cause of the Warmth at the Poles of the Earth." In 1874 he deposited $1,000 with the Franklin Institute, to be awarded to any resident of North America who should determine whether light and other physical rays travel at the same rate—a rather naïve proposal. He gave $1,000 to the town of Foxborough, which was later used to finance a small library called the Boyden Public Library. At his death most of his fortune, more than a quarter of a million dollars, was left to a Board of Trustees to be used for establishing observatories on mountain tops. Boyden never joined the American Society of Civil Engineers and never married, but lived frugally at a hotel in Boston—an old-fashioned figure of a man with fringe whiskers.

[*Lowell Hydraulic Experiments* by Jas. B. Francis (2d. ed., 1868); an article on "The American Mixed-Flow Turbine and its Setting" by Arthur T. Safford and Edward Pierce Hamilton in the *Trans. Am. Soc. Civil Engineers*, LXXXV (1922); *Thos. Boyden and his Descendants* by W. C. Boyden *et al.* (privately printed, Boston, 1901); *Boston Evening Transcript*, Oct. 17, 1879; *Boston Morning Jour.*, Oct. 18, 1879.]

P. B. M.

BOYÉ, MARTIN HANS (Dec. 6, 1812–Mar. 5, 1909), chemist, physicist, geologist, was born in Copenhagen, where his father, Mark Boyé, a chemist, superintended the Royal Porcelain Manufactory. Martin received his educational and scientific training in Copenhagen, graduating from the University of Copenhagen in 1832 and from the Polytechnic School in 1835. In 1836 he arrived in New York, "his object in coming to America being the desire to obtain an open field for research along his chosen line." In 1837 he became a student and assistant cf Robert Hare. The next year he was closely associated with Henry D. Rogers in the geological survey of the State of Pennsylvania—occupying himself chiefly with the chemical analysis of rocks and minerals, as well as in the study of certain interesting and new derivatives of platinum. Simultaneously, in the laboratory of Robert Hare he discovered and studied ethyl perchlorate, an exceedingly unstable ether, and also methyl perchlorate, which was not so treacherous. In 1844 he graduated as an M.D. from the Medical School of the University of Pennsylvania and was also accorded the A.M. degree *causa honoris* in recognition of numerous literary contributions of great merit. He was a member

of the American Philosophical Society; and was one of the twenty scientists who met in Philadelphia in 1840 and organized the American Association of Geologists which later passed into the American Association for the Advancement of Science; and was for seventy-two years a member of the Franklin Institute. He carried out many scientific studies of merit in association with James Curtis Booth [*q.v.*] (Booth & Boyé, Chemists, 27 N. 7th St.—as says an old City Directory), and was much occupied with the study of minerals and ores of Pennsylvania, in one of which—iron pyrites from Gap Mine, Lancaster County—he found four and one-half per cent of nickel (the mine being later worked for nickel, long used in our coins). In 1845 he became professor in the Central High School of Philadelphia, where he is said to have been an earnest, enthusiastic, and successful teacher. While thus engaged he wrote *A Treatise on Pneumatics: being the Physics of Gases, including Vapors* (1855) and *Chemistry, or the Physics of Atoms* (1857). Both books were vigorous presentations of their topics. He was also associated with James Curtis Booth in the preparation of the first part of the *Encyclopædia of Chemistry* (1850). The article on "Analysis" by Boyé was extended into an independent volume of exceptional merit. In 1845 he refined the oily product from cotton-seed, getting a bland, colorless oil, adapted for cooking and salad dressing, as well as for the making of a soap surpassing even the best Castile. A sample of the oil made in 1848 was preserved until 1876 when it gained the first premium at the Centennial Exposition in Philadelphia. In his later years he traveled extensively. He closed his career at Coopersburg, Pa., where he pursued "the most noble and useful avocation of man—agriculture."

[Edgar F. Smith, *Martin Hans Boyé—Chemist* (1924); sketch in C. R. Roberts, *Hist. of Lehigh County, Pa.* (1914), vol. II; *Who's Who in America*, 1908–09; *Science*, Mar. 19, 1909; *Press* (Phila.), Mar. 6, 1909.]

E. F. S.

BOYESEN, HJALMAR HJORTH (Sept. 23, 1848–Oct. 4, 1895), author, educator, was born at Frederiksvärn, a fishing village on the southern coast of Norway. His father was a teacher of mathematics at the naval academy there located. A considerable part of the son's childhood was passed in the home of a maternal grandfather who was a judge at Systrand on the Sogne-fjord, where the boy imbibed, with the wild beauty of the scene, a great deal of balladry and folk-lore from the servants of the house. He was educated in the Latin School at Drammen and the gymnasium at Christiania; later at the University of Leipsig and the University of

Christiania, where he received the degree of Ph.D. in 1868. From a residence in America his father had formed so great an admiration for the country that he exacted from each of his sons a promise to spend at least a year in the United States, and it was in fulfilment of this vow that Hjalmar and his brother sailed for this country early in 1869.

After several months of travel, Boyesen settled in Chicago as editor of a Norwegian weekly called the *Fremad,* in which he continuously opposed the denominational schools then flourishing among the Scandinavian settlers in the Middle West. His progress in English was unusually rapid, but he soon realized that in order to secure a mastery of the tongue sufficient for literary work he must associate chiefly with persons to whom it was native. He therefore left the *Fremad* and went as tutor in Greek and Latin to Urbana University, a Swedenborgian institution in Ohio. Acute homesickness during his residence there inspired what is probably his best novel, a story of Norwegian life called *Gunnar.* Through an accidental meeting between the author and Prof. Child of Harvard, the story came to the attention of William Dean Howells, then editor of the *Atlantic,* and was issued serially in that magazine in 1873. Its acceptance by Howells was a decisive incident in the life of Boyesen, persuading him to continue in America and in academic life, and the enduring friendship that ensued with Howells was of great influence in his career. To prepare himself more fully as a teacher, he spent the year 1873 in philosophical and linguistic studies at Leipsig and returned the next year to an appointment in the German department at Cornell. While there he married Elizabeth Keen of New York. In 1880 he came to New York as a literary free lance, but accepted a post in the German department of Columbia in the year following, and succeeded to the Gebhard Professorship of German there in 1882; eight years later he was given the chair of Germanic Languages and Literatures, which he continued to hold till death.

He was gifted with unusual versatility. An alert and stimulating teacher, he was more capable in communicating literary enthusiasm than in training pupils to rigorous scholarly method. Yet his scholarship, if relatively unoriginal, was fully competent, and his work on *Goethe and Schiller* (1879) embodied in its time the best treatment of *Faust* in the language. As a writer of criticism he sometimes missed the finer discriminations, owing to a warmth of temperament that occasionally betrayed him into controversial ardor or tempted him to paradox and overstatement; but his opinions were forceful and illuminative, and his *Essays on Scandinavian Literature* (1895) contain much sound and valuable matter. The *Essays on German Literature* (1892) and the *Commentary on the Writing of Henrik Ibsen* (1894) are somewhat less substantial; as is also the collection of *Literary and Social Silhouettes* (1894). He wrote the history of his native land in the *Story of Norway* (1886). His chief aspiration was to make a name in poetry, but he was not primarily a poet in temperament and he was more heavily handicapped in verse than in prose by the use of an adopted tongue; his *Idyls of Norway* (1882) are therefore somewhat mediocre in conception and rough in execution.

He was at his best in books for boys and in fiction. His juvenile books comprise *The Modern Vikings* (1887) and *Boyhood in Norway* (1892), both of them skilfully executed. The list of his novels demonstrates unusual industry and fertility. Themes from Norway furnished his best material, as in *Gunnar* (1874) and in many of the shorter stories that followed, but he has also admirable pictures of the Scandinavian settlements in the Middle West. *Falconberg* (1879) makes capital out of his experience in journalism, and *The Mammon of Unrighteousness* (1891) draws from the life at Urbana a good deal of satirical comment on the American faith in the power of education. His bent for satire is further illustrated in the *Social Strugglers* (1893) where he is especially interested in religious hypocrisy as a ladder for social ambition.

The main literary debt of his novels is to Tolstoy, Björnson, and Turgenev, though there is also a noticeable influence from Howells. The earlier romanticism of a work like *Gunnar* was discarded in favor of an ardent realism in the later novels. With this came an abundance of satire, sometimes a little heavy-fingered, and of humor that is always vigorous and occasionally even boisterous, rather than urbane. And though he gained a remarkable command of his adopted language, he occasionally betrayed his foreign birth, not only in negligible slips of idiom but also in missing certain of the nicer distinctions of social values in American life. But he was a sturdily convinced American; so much so that toward the close of his life he preferred not to speak his native tongue. And always a man of strong public spirit, he could be counted on for ardent defense of every cause that stirred his faith.

Among his other works of fiction are: *A Norseman's Pilgrimage* (1875), *Tales from Two*

Hemispheres (1876), *Queen Titania* (1881), *Ilka on the Hill-top* (1881), *A Daughter of the Philistines* (1883), *The Light of Her Countenance* (1889), *Vagabond Tales* (1889), *Against Heavy Odds* (1890), *A Fearless Trio* (1890), *A Golden Calf* (1892), and *Norseland Tales* (1894). These were accompanied by a very large number of stories and articles in the magazines; and *Ilka on the Hill-top* was successfully dramatized on the New York stage in 1884. His works were variously translated into German, Norwegian, Swedish, Russian, French, Italian, Spanish, and modern Greek.

[The best account is by B. W. Wells in the *Sewanee Review,* May 1896; there are articles by Theodore Stanton in the *Open Court,* Feb. 13, 1896, by G. M. Hyde in the *Dial,* Dec. 1, 1895, by W. H. Carpenter in the *Columbia Bulletin,* Dec. 1895, and anonymously in the *Critic,* Oct. 12, 1895. See also accounts of interviews with Boyesen in the *Sunday News-Tribune* (Detroit), Apr. 8, 1894, and in the *Book Buyer,* Oct. 1886.]

E. H. W.

BOYLE, JEREMIAH TILFORD (May 22, 1818–July 28, 1871), Union soldier, was the fourth son of Elizabeth (Tilford) and John Boyle, chief justice of the Kentucky court of appeals (1810–26) and one of the most noted of early western jurists. After the orthodox classical education at Centre and Princeton, Jeremiah studied law in the office of Gov. Owsley and at Transylvania and upon the completion of his work entered upon the practise of his profession at Danville, Ky. Here he remained in apparent content until the outbreak of the Civil War. He was a slaveholder and like most slave owners in Kentucky, a Whig. Not suspecting the coming of emancipation he determined his attitude toward secession more by his political affiliations than by his economic interests and became one of the most active of Union men during the short-lived effort for neutrality. In November 1861 his zeal in recruiting for the Union army gained for him a commission as brigadier-general of volunteers. His ensuing military career was distinguished more by activity than by success although he fought with "conspicuous gallantry" at Shiloh (*Official Records,* ser. 1, vol. X, pt. 1, p. 355). Shortly after this battle Secretary Stanton appointed him military commander of Kentucky, the appointment apparently being due to the pressing solicitations of the Kentucky delegation in Congress. Boyle remained military commander until Jan. 12, 1864, and his conduct during the period has been a subject of acrimonious controversy until this day. It cannot be said that he proved himself very efficient against his armed enemies. John Morgan raided the state almost at will, guerrillas ravaged the country, and Louis-

ville itself (Boyle's headquarters) was saved from Bragg only by the dilatoriness of Bragg himself. In fact, Boyle was finally removed from his position because of his military ineptitude (*Official Records,* ser. 1, vol. XXXII, pt. 2, p. 10). Against non-combatants, however, he displayed considerable ability although Kentucky historians are inclined to question the wisdom of his measures. His arrests of people suspected of sympathizing with the Confederacy, his use of troops to control elections, and his domination of the judiciary made open enemies of many people who had hitherto been neutral. His policy of assessing upon "disloyal" people of the neighborhood the damages caused by guerrillas alienated the more moderate of the Union men. Whatever the merits of these measures he succeeded in keeping the support of the active Union leaders of Kentucky (*Louisville Daily Journal,* Jan. 9, 1864). By his policy he forced the resignation of Gov. Magoffin and undoubtedly increased the bitterness between factions throughout the state. For the most part he acted on his own initiative and on occasion his zeal seemed to outrun that of Stanton himself. He retained, throughout, the respect of both friend and enemy for his personal integrity and after his removal whatever feeling existed against him was soon forgotten in the general execration of his successors. Upon retiring from the army, he helped organize the Louisville City Railway Company, of which he soon became president. In 1866 he became president of the moribund Evansville, Henderson & Nashville Railroad and made it a successful enterprise. He came to have large interests in railway and land properties in the West and amassed a large fortune before his death. From his marriage (1842) with Elizabeth Owsley Anderson were born twelve children, four of whom survived him.

[For the life of Boyle prior to the Civil War one must depend on brief sketches in encyclopedias and Kentucky history. For his military career an abundance of source material is scattered through the *Official Records* and through the files of contemporary newspapers, particularly the *Louisville Daily Jour.* and the *Louisville Daily Democrat.* E. M. Coulter, *Civil War and Readjustment in Ky.* (1926) has a good treatment of his conduct as military commander although the most detailed account is given by Manning in his (unpublished) "Reconstruction in Ky.," a thesis submitted to the Faculty of the University of Louisville in part fulfilment of the master's degree, 1926.]

R. S. C.

BOYLE, JOHN (Oct. 28, 1774–Jan. 28, 1835), judge, the son of John Boyle, was born on the Clinch River near Tazewell in Botetourt County, Va. His parents, inconspicuous in the history of their times, moved to Kentucky in 1779 and settled at Whitley's Station not far from Boonesborough. They later removed to Garrard County where they remained until death. Young Boyle had no educational advantages beyond the instruction he received in Latin, Greek, and in a few other subjects from Samuel Finley, a Presbyterian minister. Having a strong inclination for the law he began the study of that subject under Thomas Davis, who later represented Kentucky in Congress, and whom Boyle succeeded in that position in 1803. Boyle took little part in speech-making in the House of Representatives but by a close attention to his duties and by a strict adherence to the principles of Jefferson, won the admiration and good opinion of the President. He was elected for three successive terms, refusing further service in this capacity, due to his desire to return to his home life in Kentucky. In 1809, just before leaving Washington, he was offered by James Madison, the incoming President, the governorship of the Illinois Territory. After reaching Kentucky he rejected the honor and thereby made the vacancy which Ninian Edwards filled, who in turn by resigning his position on the bench of the Kentucky court of appeals left a justice-ship vacant which Boyle accepted. The next year (1810) Boyle was appointed chief justice to succeed George M. Bibb, who had resigned, and it was in this capacity that he did the work upon which his reputation chiefly rests. His decisions were logical, sound, and conservative, setting a great store on precedent.

He was a great power in the state in heading off the replevin laws, and other relief measures during the early twenties. When summoned before the legislature for his adherence to conservative principles, he ably defended the position of the court, and when the legislature sought to abolish the court after it had failed to unseat Boyle and the other justices, he continued the fight for the supremacy of the old court. In 1826 after the struggle was over and the old court had been reëstablished, he resigned and was immediately appointed by President Adams district judge for Kentucky. Twice he might have received an appointment to the United States Supreme Court had he desired it. Honored in his day as a great jurist, he died near Danville. He was married in 1797 to Elizabeth Tilford, who died in 1833, a victim of the cholera.

[Facts relating to the life and character of Boyle may be found in Richard H. and Lewis Collins, *Hist. of Ky.* (1874); *Biog. Encyc. of Ky.* (1877); H. Levin, ed., *Lawyers and Lawmakers of Ky.* (1897); Z. F. Smith, *Hist. of Ky.* (1886); Mrs. Chapman Coleman, *Life of John J. Crittenden* (1871), vol. I. His decisions in the Ky. court of appeals are published in Bibb's (4 vols.), Marshall's (3 vols.), Littell's (5 vols.), and Monroe's (7 vols.) *Reports.*]

E. M. C.

BOYLE, JOHN J. (Jan. 12, 1851–Feb. 10, 1917), sculptor, was the son of Samuel and Catherine (McAuley) Boyle, both of whom were of North of Ireland stock. On the father's side were generations of stone-cutters; the mother's father was a village blacksmith. J. J. Boyle was born in New York; but in 1851 his father moved to Philadelphia where two of his brothers lived. In early life he had little book-learning, save what he got from the public schools of his boyhood. On account of his father's early death, the need to earn came to him young. He worked first as iron-moulder, then as stone-cutter, next as stone-carver. Meanwhile he carried on studies with Eakins at the Pennsylvania Academy of Fine Arts. Then, having saved money enough, he went to Paris (1877) and entered the École des Beaux Arts where he remained three years.

During his course at the Beaux Arts, the summer of 1878 brought him decorative work on a London leather exchange building,—five panels and some caryatids. The next year he made two portraits, and exhibited a bronze bust at the Paris Salon. His true vein was to declare itself later. The opportunity came in 1880, when he received from Martin Ryerson the commission for "An Indian Family," a handsomely mounted bronze group now in Lincoln Park, Chicago. Before beginning this work, he spent two months among the Indians to be commemorated. In the treatment of the dominant male Indian, surrounded by squaw, papoose, and watchful dog, the composition prefigures the sturdy quality of Boyle's art. With a characteristic forthrightness far removed from complacency, the sculptor states that when "An Indian Family" was shown in Philadelphia, "its excellence impressed many." In fact, the Fairmount Park Art Association of that city promptly gave him a commission for an heroic group in similar vein, "The Stone Age," in which a vigilant aboriginal mother holding a stone hatchet clasps one papoose, while another crouches at her feet, not too near the slain bear cub with which the hatchet has just dealt. The work shows Boyle's characteristic massiveness of design, his deep emotion, untainted by sentimentality. It was executed in Paris,—clay, plaster, and bronze; the plaster model received honorable mention at the Salon of 1886; the bronze was set up in Fairmount Park in 1888.

In 1882, he was married, very happily, to a helpmeet with charm and understanding, Elizabeth Carroll of Philadelphia. After the completion of "The Stone Age," the couple enjoyed a period of travel and study, which included a tour in Switzerland, and eight months in Italy. In 1891–92 Boyle did "effective if ephemeral" work

Boyle

on the sculptural decorations for the Transportation Building at the Columbian Exposition. An intimate bronze group of mother and two children, "Tired Out," won applause and a medal at this exposition. At Buffalo in 1901 his two great groups, "The Savage Age," "East and West," were among the finest of the expositional decorations; their excellence entitled them to a permanency which circumstances denied them. Toward the close of 1893 he went to Philadelphia, where during the next two years he made for the Library of Congress in Washington the bronze statues of Plato and Lord Bacon, neither work remarkable except for entire competence from an architectural point of view. These indoor figures have not the vividness and color of his open-air sculptures. Perhaps the super-civilized subjects enticed him not. To this period belong also three heroic busts (in the University of Pennsylvania, Bryn Mawr College, First Unitarian Church, Philadelphia), as well as portraits for Hahnemann Hospital and for the Penn Charter School.

It has been noted that in general his genius is happiest in themes that are elemental rather than elegant. He is successful also in his delineations of vigorous, manly characters; himself an individualist, he delighted in strongly marked types. His heroic seated bronze statue of Franklin, presented by J. C. Strawbridge to the City of Philadelphia in 1900, gives the beholder a deep sense of the greatness of heart and brain in this our "first civilized American." The sculptor's enthusiasm has re-created "Poor Richard" in terms at once monumental and intimate.

In 1902, Boyle removed from the city of his boyhood to the city of his birth. His art was well known throughout the country; he had received many medals and honors. He was a charter member of the National Sculpture Society. From Jan. 1, 1906, to Dec. 31, 1908, he served as sculptor member of the Art Commission of the City of New York. In the midst of architectural decorations and portrait work, he turned with special zest to the statue of Commodore John Barry, for which Congress had appropriated $50,000 in 1906. This work, unveiled in Washington May 16, 1914, President Wilson making an address, consists of an heroic bronze figure of the Commodore, standing gallantly on a high, richly-wrought, widely-based stone pedestal. It remains the most important of the sculptor's later achievements. Within three years, after a long illness ending in pneumonia, he died in New York, his wife surviving him.

[C. H. Caffin, *Am. Masters of Sculpture* (1903); Lorado Taft, *Hist. of Am. Sculpture* (1903); *Fairmount Park Art Ass., an Account of its Origin and Activities* (1921); obituaries in *Public Ledger* (Phila.), *Phila.*

Inquirer, N. Y. Herald, Feb. 11, 1917. Numerous press notices detailed Boyle's activities from 1880 until the year preceding his death.] A. A—s.

BOYLE, THOMAS (June 29, 1776?–Oct. 12, 1825?), sea captain, was one of the outstanding privateersmen in the War of 1812. Aside from that, little is known of his life. It is said that he was born at Marblehead, Mass., was commanding a ship at sixteen, and was married in 1794 at Baltimore which was thereafter his home. In July 1812, he took command of the 14-gun privateer schooner *Comet.* The first cruise of four months netted prizes valued at about half a million dollars. In December 1812, he dodged the Chesapeake blockading squadron and made for Pernambuco, where he took three armed British merchantmen after fighting off their convoy, a Portuguese warship. Altogether, he captured twenty-seven prizes in the *Comet.* In 1814 he changed to an even faster vessel, the 16-gun brig *Chasseur,* known as "The Pride of Baltimore." A cruise in the English Channel and West Indies resulted in eighteen prizes. At one time, he was nearly surrounded by four British warships, but he outmaneuvered them all. His most unique exploit was his proclamation in 1814, declaring the British Isles in "a state of strict and rigorous blockade." He stated that he considered his force "adequate to maintain strictly, vigorously and effectually, the said blockade." This was a direct burlesque of the "paper blockades" of the American coast pompously proclaimed by Admirals Cochrane and Warren. Boyle dispatched it in a released cartel, requesting that it be posted in Lloyd's Coffee House. On his final cruise, he captured the British naval schooner *St. Lawrence* in a fifteen-minute fight off Cuba on Feb. 26, 1815. During the war, he captured some eighty prizes, valued at considerably more than a million. This compares favorably with the record of the *America* under Chever and others. Boyle was described as a quiet, unassuming man with a strong sense of humor and "superb audacity." Coggeshall, the contemporary privateersman-historian, said that Boyle combined "the impetuous bravery of a Murat with the prudence of a Wellington." Boyle took particular delight in tantalizing the stronger but slower British warships with his own fast craft. He returned to the merchant service after the war. In 1824, he beat off a pirate attack in the brig *Panopea* (*Niles' Weekly Register,* XXVI, p. 328). He is said to have died at sea a year later.

[Chapters are devoted to Boyle's exploits in E. S. Maclay, *Hist. of the Am. Privateers* (1889), pp. 279–99; and E. P. Statham, *Privateers and Privateering* (1910), pp. 307–16. There is a contemporary account in Geo. Coggeshall, *Hist. of the Am. Privateers* (2nd ed. 1856), pp. 132–39, 358–69. *Niles' Weekly Reg.,* IV,

71 (1813) quotes extracts from the *Comet's* log, and VII, 290 (1815) quotes the proclamation. Part of the *Chasseur's* log is quoted in the *Md. Hist. Mag.*, I, 168 ff., 218 ff. Dates of birth, marriage, and death are given in J. T. Sharf, *Hist. of Md.* (3 vols., 1879), III, 135n., but these could not be confirmed in local records.]

R. G. A.

BOYLSTON, ZABDIEL (Mar. 9, 1679–Mar. 1, 1766), physician, the first to introduce the practise of inoculation for smallpox into America, was the grandson of Thomas Boylston, Esq., who migrated from England to Watertown, Mass., in 1635, and the son of Mary Gardner and Dr. Thomas Boylston, the earliest physician of Muddy River (now Brookline, Mass.). Though he never obtained a medical degree, he received medical instruction from his father and from a Dr. Cutter of Boston. In a comparatively short time he acquired a good reputation and considerable wealth, and it has been said that "he was remarkable for his skill, his humanity, and close attention to his patients." However, one hears little of Boylston in the colony until June 1721. On Apr. 15, 1721, smallpox made its appearance in Boston, brought by a ship from the Tortugas (*Boston News-Letter*, Apr. 13–17, 17–24, 1721, nos. 893–94). By the middle of May the disease was rife in the colony. Boylston began to inoculate on June 26, and the circumstances which led him to employ this procedure demand consideration. Cotton Mather on Dec. 13, 1707, had been presented by his parishioners with a slave named Onesimus who later informed Mather that he had been inoculated in Africa, and that it was common among the Guramantese tribes so to protect themselves (Klebs, p. 70). On June 6, 1721, Mather circulated in manuscript an "Address to the Physicians of Boston" exhorting them to inoculate. The "Address" consisted chiefly of an abstract of the Timonius and Pylarinus papers (1714 and 1716) upon inoculation in Constantinople which had appeared in Volume XXIX of the *Philosophical Transactions of the Royal Society*. On June 24 Mather wrote a letter to Boylston in which he said, referring to inoculation, "If upon mature deliberation, you should think it advisiable [*sic*] to be proceeded in, it may save many lives that we set a great value on" (Fitz, p. 318). The result was decisive. Two days later Boylston inoculated his own son Thomas, and two negro slaves. He did not inoculate himself since he had had the disease in 1702. Later he inoculated his son John, and on July 21 seven patients received the pustule. There is no evidence to warrant the belief that Boylston yet knew of the inoculations carried out the preceding April in London at Lady Mary Wortley Montagu's instigation. The uproar created by the practise placed Boylston's and Mather's lives in danger. Their houses were attacked by enraged mobs and a hand grenade was thrown into Mather's study. Abusive attacks were launched against them in the *Boston News-Letter* and a war of pamphlets began in which Benjamin Colman [*q.v.*], William Douglass, William Cooper, Increase Mather [*q.v.*], Isaac Greenwood [*q.v.*], and many anonymous writers participated. Three times Boylston was called before the selectmen of Boston to account for his actions and the feeling finally became so intense that Boylston and Mather were forced to prepare a joint pamphlet in their own defense which appeared about Sept. 1, 1721 (*Some account of what is said of Inoculating or Transplanting the Small Pox By the Learned Dr. Emanuel Timonius, and Jacobus Pylarinus . . . Answer to the scruples of many about the Lawfulness of this Method*). Parts I and III of this work were by Mather, Part II chiefly by Boylston. There also appeared during these months a series of letters and pamphlets reporting the progress of Boylston's inoculations. Kittredge has pointed out that probably all were draughted by Mather, but they are to be looked upon as joint contributions since Boylston supplied the chief data. We may list them as follows: (1) "The Little Treatise on the Smallpox," June 29, 1721 (published in Mather's *The Angel of Bethesda*, 1722–23, pp. 112–41); (2) the so-called "Dummer Letter," *An Account of the Method and Success of Inoculating the Small-Pox, in Boston in New England*, dated Sept. 7, 1721 (published anonymously London, 1722); (3) "A Faithful Account of what has occur'd under the late Experiments of the Small-Pox . . . Published, partly to put a stop unto that unaccountable way of Lying . . . and partly for the Information & Satisfaction of our Friends in other Places," *Boston Gazette*, Oct. 30, 1721 (anonymous); (4) *Sentiments on the Small Pox Inoculated* (folio broad-sheet, Boston, Nov. 23, 1721); (5) "The way of Proceeding in the Small Pox inoculated in New England," *Philosophical Transactions*, no. 370, dated Nov. 30, 1721 (anonymous); (6) "Curiosa Variolarum," Mar. 10, 1721/22, an unpublished letter to J. Jurin of the Royal Society; (7) "The Case of the Small-Pox Inoculated; further Cleared," May 4, 1823 (unpublished, and also to Jurin, Original MS. in American Antiquarian Society Library). By the end of February 1721/22, Boylston had inoculated 241 persons of whom only six died after inoculation, and of these at least four had contracted the disease before inoculation. He did not publish his results under his own name until 1726, when he issued in London *An Historical*

Account of the Small-pox inoculated in New England dedicated to Princess Caroline. A second edition was brought out in Boston in 1730. Meanwhile, Boylston, at Sir Hans Sloane's invitation, had spent some two years in London in 1724–26 during which time he prepared his book and lectured to the Royal College of Physicians and to the Royal Society of which in July 1726 he was elected Fellow. However, he did not inoculate while in England. Boylston's *Historical Account* showed that he kept careful records of everything he did. The results are logically set forth and clearly tabulated, and the work is in every way a masterly clinical presentation,—the first of its kind from an American physician.

On returning to Boston, Boylston, having accomplished his great work, settled down quietly to a comfortable practise, inoculating from time to time when an epidemic threatened. He corresponded with his friends in London (see Sloane MSS. 4055) but his only published communication was the "Ambergris in Whales" which appeared in 1726 in the *Philosophical Transactions,* XXXIII, 193. He retired from practise in the forties and spent his declining years on his farm in Brookline raising highly-bred horses. At the age of eighty-four he was seen breaking a colt. He died on Mar. 1, 1766, after many years of pulmonary trouble (mentioned in his letter of Dec. 19, 1737, to Sir Hans Sloane), and was buried in the old cemetery at Brookline. Boylston was married on Jan. 18, 1705, to Jerusha Minot of Boston by whom he had eight children. The Boylston academic foundations in Harvard University were left by Ward Nicolas Boylston, grandnephew of Zabdiel Boylston. Those at the Medical School were left in honor of the inoculator.

[There is an excellent paper by Reginald H. Fitz, "Zabdiel Boylston, Inoculator, and the epidemic of smallpox in Boston in 1721," in *Bull. Johns Hopkins Hospital,* 1911, XXII, 315–27. The perplexing question of Boylston's relation to Cotton Mather in the authorship of the earlier anonymous inoculation pamphlets has been dealt with extensively by G. L. Kittredge in his "Lost Works of Cotton Mather," *Proc. Mass. Hist. Soc.,* Feb. 1912, pp. 418–79. For Boylston's relation to Douglass, Geo. H. Weaver's paper on Douglass (*Bull. Soc. Medical Hist. of Chicago,* 1921, XI, 229–59) may be consulted. The place of Boylston in the history of variolation is discussed by A. C. Klebs in his "Historic Evolution of Variolation," *Bull. Johns Hopkins Hospital,* 1913, XXIV, 69–83. The account of Boylston's life in Jas. Thacher's *Am. Medical Dict.* (1828) is the most extensive of the early accounts, but is inaccurate in many details. Photostats of Boylston letters and manuscripts were furnished the present writer by the authorities of the British Museum, the Royal Society, and the Mass. Hist. Soc.]
                                                    J.F.F.

BOYNTON, CHARLES BRANDON (June 12, 1806–Apr. 27, 1883), Presbyterian and Congregational clergyman, author, was born in West Stockbridge, Mass. The Boyntons were among the early settlers of the township. The names of his parents are not recorded, but they may have been Henry and Mary (Meacham) Boynton (J. F. and C. H. Boynton, pp. 234, 285; and H. Child, *Gazetteer of Berkshire County, Mass., 1725–1885,* 1885, p. 389). After attending the Stockbridge Academy he became a member of the class of 1827 at Williams College, but on account of ill health left in the senior year without taking his degree. Thereafter he engaged in business, was president of the first railroad in Berkshire County, studied and practised law, was a justice of the Berkshire County court and a member of the Massachusetts House of Representatives. On Nov. 5, 1834, he married Maria Van Buskirk of Troy, N. Y., by whom he had seven children. Having studied theology privately with the Rev. Mr. Woodbridge of Spencertown, N. Y., he was ordained by the Columbia Presbytery in October 1840. He held charges at Housatonic, Mass., 1840–45, and at Lansingburg, N. Y., 1845–46, and then went to Cincinnati to the Vine Street Church, at that time the Sixth Presbyterian, where he remained till March 1856. While in the West, Boynton became actively interested in the anti-slavery movement. In the autumn of 1854 he was one of a party sent to explore and report upon the climate, soil, productions, general resources, and promise of the territory of Kansas. His report, *A Journey Through Kansas* (1855), is an interesting account of the country before the trouble over slavery had grown acute. From 1856 to 1857 he was in his native Berkshires again as pastor of the South Church in Pittsfield. He then returned to the Vine Street Church in Cincinnati, only to leave it to be chaplain of the House of Representatives from 1865 to 1869. While in Washington he was pastor of several churches and a teacher in the United States Naval Academy. Meanwhile he was busy writing. In 1856 he had published anonymously *The Russian Empire: its Resources, Government, and Policy.* In 1864 appeared *English and French Neutrality and the Anglo-French Alliance, in their Relations to the United States and Russia.* Some chapters from this work were republished in 1865 as *The Navies of England, France, America, and Russia,* and the whole book, considerably revised, was reissued in 1866 as *The Four Great Powers: England, France, Russia, and America: their Policy, Resources, and Probable Future.* In these books Boynton advocated a strong navy and an alliance, formal or informal, with Russia to offset the encroachments of England and France, but his understanding of world politics was not equal to his earnestness and patriotism. In 1867–68 he brought out in two ponderous, stodgy volumes a *History of the Navy during the Rebellion,* a semi-official work, for which he had access to the archives of the Navy Department. He was pastor of the Vine Street Church in Cincinnati for the third time from 1873 to 1877, and died at the home of a daughter in Cincinnati on Apr. 27, 1883.

[*Congreg. Yearbook for 1884,* p. 20; *Cincinnati Enquirer,* Apr. 28, 1883; *Gen. Cat. of the Officers and Grads. of Williams Coll. 1795–1910* (1910); J. F. and C. H. Boynton, *The Boynton Family* (1897), p. 234. Several of Boynton's sermons have been published as pamphlets.]
G. H. G.

BOYNTON, EDWARD CARLISLE (Feb. 1, 1824–May 13, 1893), soldier, a descendant of John Boynton, who came from England to Salem, Mass., in 1638, was the son of Thomas Boynton, who served as an officer in the War of 1812, and of Sophia (Cabot) Boynton. He was born at Windsor, Vt., was appointed a cadet at the Military Academy in 1841, and graduated in 1846 in the class of McClellan and Stonewall Jackson. He was commissioned in the artillery, and served with Duncan's battery in the latter part of Gen. Taylor's campaign in Mexico. Joining the army of Gen. Scott, he was present at the siege of Vera Cruz, the battles of Cerro Gordo, Contreras, and Churubusco, and several minor actions, being severely wounded at Churubusco. After the Mexican War, he was assigned to duty at West Point, and remained there for seven and a half years, following this with a few months' service with the expedition against the Seminoles in Florida. While teaching at West Point he had acquired considerable reputation as a scientist, which led to the offer of professorships at the University of Mississippi and at the New York State Normal School. Accepting the former, he resigned his commission as first lieutenant (Feb. 16, 1856), and took up his duties as professor of chemistry, mineralogy, and geology. The outbreak of the Civil War created a situation intolerable for a Unionist professor in a seceding state. Although Boynton declined the colonelcy of a Vermont regiment, offered him in May 1861, relations continued strained, and finally (Sept. 6, 1861) he was dismissed from the institution for "evincing a want of attachment to the Government of the Confederate States." As an enemy of the existing order of things, his presence was not desired in Mississippi, nor could he wish to remain there, but with war flagrant the authorities were not inclined to put the services of an ex-officer of the army at the disposal of the United States. As a condition of

his being allowed to depart, they wisely exacted a pledge from him that he would not serve in the field against the Confederacy. For this reason he declined the colonelcy of another Vermont regiment, which was at once offered him. His abilities were utilized without breach of faith on his part, however, by his appointment as a captain in the 11th Infantry, and assignment to duty as adjutant and quartermaster of the Military Academy. His case may offer infinite opportunity for the casuist to exercise his ingenuity. At least once in 1864 the War Department grew restive, or perhaps forgetful, and considered ordering him to join his regiment in the field, but the idea was abandoned—fortunately, one must think. After all, the position he occupied was an important one, and had to be filled by some one, in war or peace. He continued on duty as adjutant at West Point until 1871, though he was relieved from the additional labor of the quartermaster's office as soon as the war ended. In 1872 he resigned from the army, and spent the remainder of his life at Newburgh, N. Y. For eight years he was superintendent of the water-works, and afterward was for some time secretary of the local board of trade. During his career as a teacher he had published several papers on chemical subjects. His long residence at West Point, with its revolutionary associations, turned his interest to historical matters, and led to the publication of a *History of West Point, and its Military Importance during the American Revolution; and the Origin and Progress of the United States Military Academy,* a large part of which is devoted to a minute study of the topography of the neighborhood, from a military viewpoint, to the system of defenses erected during the Revolution, and to the administration of the fortress during that period. Soon after his removal to Newburgh, he became a member of the board of trustees of Washington's headquarters there, and for several years was president of the Historical Society of Newburgh Bay and the Highlands. He compiled and published a collection of Washington's orders, issued at Newburgh. He also wrote some minor historical papers, and was part author of Webster's *Army and Navy Dictionary,* published in 1864. He married Mary J. Hubbard.

[Obituaries in the *Newburgh Daily Jour.,* May 13, 1893; *Bull. Ass. Grads. U. S. Mil. Acad.,* 1893, pp. 138–42; G. W. Cullum, *Biog. Reg.* (3rd ed., 1891), II, 265–66; unpublished War Department Records.]
T. M. S.

BOZEMAN, JOHN M. (1835–Apr. 20, 1867), trail-maker, was a native of Georgia, where he left a wife and two children, to try his luck at placer mining near Cripple Creek, Colo., in 1861.

Learning of rich gravels in Montana he set out with eleven companions, arriving in Virginia City in June 1862. The bonanzas of Idaho and of Alder Gulch, Bannack, and Virginia City were bringing thousands into Montana. The Mullan Road from Walla Walla to Fort Benton, opened in 1861, provided an approach from the west, but gold seekers from the east only reached the diggings by boat to the head of navigation of the Missouri and thence by road, or else by an equally circuitous route over the Oregon trail to Fort Hall and north to Virginia City. It was to discover a more direct route east that Bozeman and his partner, John M. Jacobs, left Bannack in the winter of 1862–63. Venturing along the old trail into the territory east of the Big Horn Mountains reserved by treaty to the Indians, and apparently quite insensible of danger, they were attacked by a party of marauding Sioux, robbed of horses, guns, and ammunition, and turned adrift on foot, finally reaching the Platte after severe hardships. Untaught by experience, Bozeman returned the following spring at the head of a party of freighters and emigrants, but, when about a hundred miles north of Fort Laramie, the party was induced by an Indian attack to follow the safer route west of the Big Horn Mountains via Bridger Pass into Virginia City. The determined Bozeman, however, again venturing across the Indian country, and traveling chiefly by night, finally crossed the divide (Bozeman Pass) between the Yellowstone and the Gallatin and reached Virginia City. In 1864 he conducted one of many caravans over his "road." The Indians had become increasingly menacing as their treaty lands were invaded, and in 1865–66 the government undertook to police the Bozeman road by successive Powder River expeditions and the erection of Forts Reno, Phil Kearny, and C. F. Smith. The Fetterman massacre of December 1866 reëstablished by force of arms the Indian claim, and led to the abandonment of the Bozeman road south and east of Fort C. F. Smith. Still blind to the Indian danger, Bozeman and a companion left Virginia City, on Apr. 16, 1867. Four days later, at the crossing of the Yellowstone, five Indians approached their noon camp. Assuming them to be friendly Crows, Bozeman welcomed them only to discover too late that they were Blackfeet. He was instantly shot, while his wounded companion escaped. He thus at last paid the penalty of ineptitude and lack of judgment in dealing with the hazards of the country.

[G. R. Hebard and E. A. Brininstool, *The Bozeman Trail* (1922); *Mont. Hist. Soc. Trans.*, vol. I, 1895; *Montana Post*, May 4, 1867.]   H. C. D.

BOZEMAN, NATHAN (Mar. 25, 1825–Dec. 16, 1905), physician, the son of Nathan and Harriet (Knotts) Bozeman, was of Dutch descent. He was born in Butler County, Ala., studied medicine at the University of Louisville, graduating in 1848, and began practise in Montgomery, Ala., where he became intimately acquainted with Marion Sims and his work. It was at that time that Sims first succeeded in curing vesico-vaginal fistula, a problem on which the gynecologists of Europe and America had worked for years without arriving at a solution. Bozeman took great interest in this question. He improved Sims's method by substituting the "button" or "shot" suture for Sims's clamp suture; this was a great advance as the new suture practically eliminated failures. In 1859 Bozeman for the first time performed kolpokleisis as a means of treating vesico-vaginal fistula. In the same year he made a trip to Europe demonstrating his methods. On his return he settled in New Orleans but soon the Civil War broke out and Bozeman served during the whole four years as a surgeon in the Confederate Army. After the war he settled in New York, where he established a private hospital for women. In 1868 he was attacked by Prof. Simon of Heidelberg on a question of priority concerning the operation of kolpokleisis. He at once crossed the Atlantic to defend his position by demonstrating his own method before the medical faculty of Heidelberg. In 1878 he was appointed surgeon to the New York State Women's Hospital. The work being too heavy, he resigned this position in 1888 and established a private sanitarium. He was a masterful surgeon, most skilful in adapting established methods to individual cases. He was remarkably successful in operations for vesical and fæcal fistulæ in women, particularly one complication of pyelitis, which he treated by catheterizing the ureter through a vesico-vaginal opening (1887–88). He invented a self-retaining vaginal speculum and an operating chair for the knee-chest position. His most important writings are: *Remarks on Vesico-Vaginal Fistula with an Account of a New Mode of Suture* (1856); *Application of the Button Suture to the Treatment of Varicose Dilatation of Veins* (1860); *The Gradual Preparatory Treatment of the Complications of Urinary and Fæcal Fistulæ in Women* (1887); *Chronic Pyelitis Successfully Treated by Kolpo-Uretero-Cystotomy* (1888). He was twice married: first, to Fannie Lamar of Macon, Ga., and, second, to Mrs. Amelia (Lamar) Ralston of the same city. He died of apoplexy, Dec. 16, 1905.

[Sketch of Bozeman by his son, Nathan Bozeman, in H. A. Kelly, *Cyc. of Am. Medic. Biog.* (1912), vol.

I; sketch in *Physicians and Surgeons of the U. S.* (1878), ed. by Wm. B. Atkinson; *Album, Am. Gynecol. Soc.,* 1918, p. 68. A complete list of Bozman's writings is contained in the *Cat. of the Surgeon-General's Lib.,* ser. 1, vol. II, and ser. 2, vol. II.]   A. A—n.

BOZMAN, JOHN LEEDS (Aug. 25, 1757–Apr. 20, 1823), lawyer, historian, the son of John and Lucretia (Leeds) Bozman, belonged to an old Maryland family and was born on an estate later named "Belleville" in Oxford Neck, Talbot County, Md. When he was ten years old, his father died, and his education was then guided by his grandfather, William Leeds. The youth attended Back Creek Academy, afterwards Washington Academy, Somerset County, and later entered Pennsylvania College (the University of Pennsylvania). After his graduation he became a lawyer's apprentice to Judge Robert Greensborough in 1777. His interest in law and his natural ambition caused him to go to England in 1784 for further study at the Middle Temple, London. On his return to Maryland he was admitted to the bar. He was a Federalist with perhaps Tory leanings imbibed from his grandfather. In 1794 he ran for a seat in the lower house of Maryland but was defeated, his record of public office-holding being limited to the appointive office of deputy attorney-general under Luther Martin, 1789–1807. When he abandoned the practise of law and retired to his farm is not known, but from that time he devoted himself to the accumulation of a library and literary pursuits (Bozman Papers, in the Library of Congress). He intended to write a series of "Law tracts or Essays on Several subjects arising under the Laws of Maryland," but prepared only one, under the title *Observations on the Statute of 21 Jac. I. Ch. 16 in application to Estates tail* (1794). He was also interested in the American Colonization Society. In support of the society's plan to transport the whole negro race to Africa he published an essay in 1820 entitled, *An Essay on the Late Institution of the American Society for Colonizing the Free People of Color of the United States.* His chief literary production was a history of Maryland on which he began working about 1805 but which he left uncompleted when he learned that another man had undertaken the same task. In 1811, however, he published what he had already written, under the title *A Sketch of the History of Maryland during the Three First Years after its Settlement.* Later, when the other author died, Bozman resumed his own work with the intention of writing a history of Maryland from its earliest settlement to the Confederation, but illness intervened, making him again discontinue his studies a few years before his death in 1823. The manuscript at the time of his death was complete to 1660 and practically ready for printing. His nephew, John Leeds Kerr, offered it to the Maryland legislature for publication. It was accepted and published in two volumes in 1837, under the title *The History of Maryland, from its First Settlement . . . to the Restoration.* The first volume is merely introductory, and the history itself is contained in the second. It is based on a study of the records at Annapolis and of printed works, but though accurate and detailed is not final, for much material has since been uncovered. The account is prejudiced against the Puritans, and this is in part responsible for the biased treatment of the Claiborne episode. It is not a finished history but is valuable as material for history (Justin Winsor, *Narrative and Critical History of the United States,* III, 560).

[The chief source is *A Memoir of John Leeds Bozman* by Samuel A. Harrison, Fund Pubs. No. 26 (1888). There is also a sketch of Bozman in a *Hist. of Talbot County, Md., 1661–1861* (1915) by Oswald Tilghman, but the account practically duplicates that of Harrison.]
                                                          H. B–C.

BRACE, CHARLES LORING (June 19, 1826–Aug. 11, 1890), philanthropist, born in Litchfield, Conn., came on both sides of old and distinguished New England stock. His father, John Brace [*q.v.*], was the grandson of Capt. Abel Brace, a Revolutionary officer, and was descended from Stephen Brace (or Bracy) who came from England to Hartford in 1660; his mother, Lucy Porter of Maine, was related to the Beechers and was a descendant of Rufus King. Charles, efficiently guided in his studies, and in trout-fishing, by his father, was ready for college at the age of fourteen but delayed two years, entering Yale in 1842 and graduating in 1846. He then taught country schools (Ellington and Winchendon, Conn.) for a year, returning to New Haven in 1847 to study theology in Yale Divinity School. The course there bred more doubts than convictions, and two ensuing years in New York turned his attention away from theology to thoughts of work among the delinquent classes of the metropolis. In the fall of 1850 he took brief walking trips in Ireland, England, and the Rhine country with two life-long Connecticut friends, John and Frederick Olmstead [*q.v.*], then lingered on through the winter in Berlin, and in the spring ventured into Hungary, where he was imprisoned for a month as a Kossuth sympathizer, being released through the efforts of the United States minister, only after thirteen trials by court martial. Upon his return to America he published *Hungary in 1851* (1852) and *Home Life in Germany* (1853). In 1854 he made a flying trip to the British Isles to bring back as his bride Letitia Neill whom he had met upon his previous visit. Meanwhile he had definitely entered upon his life-work. In 1853 he was influential in founding in New York City the Children's Aid Society, an organization which, under his direction, worked mainly among the foreign immigrants, establishing cheap lodging houses, industrial schools, night schools, summer camps, and sanitariums. It also, in the course of years, found homes and employment in the country for more than 100,000 city waifs. Brace was a pioneer in modern philanthropic methods, grounding all his efforts on the principle of self-help, and opposing every charitable enterprise which tended toward pauperization. During his years of work in the slum districts he showed himself brave, resourceful, and tolerant, inspired by a belief in the infinite worth of every human soul as having that within it "which shall live when the old world has passed by." His remarkable success brought him an international reputation, and he had a large circle of distinguished friends on both sides of the Atlantic, including Emerson, Theodore Parker, Asa Gray, Henry Ward Beecher, Darwin, John Morley, and John Stuart Mill. Of several later trips to Europe, the last, taken in quest of health, ended at Campfer in the Engadine, where he died on Aug. 11, 1890. In addition to his earlier books, Brace was the author of: *The Norse Folk; or, a Visit to the Homes of Norway and Sweden* (1857); *The Best Method of Disposing of our Pauper and Vagrant Children* (1859); *The Races of the Old World: a Manual of Ethnology* (1863); *Short Sermons to Newsboys* (1866); *The New West; or, California in 1867–68* (1869); *The Dangerous Classes of New York, And Twenty Years' Work Among Them* (1872); *Gesta Christi; or, a History of Humane Progress under Christianity* (1882); *The Unknown God; or, Inspiration Among Pre-Christian Races* (1890).

[The chief source is *The Life of Chas. Loring Brace,* largely told in his own letters (1894), edited by his daughter, Emma Brace. The N. Y. press contained obituaries at the time of his death.]   E. S. B.

BRACE, DEWITT BRISTOL (Jan. 5, 1859– Oct. 2, 1905), physicist, son of Lusk and Emily (Bristol) Brace, was born at Wilson, N. Y., received his preparatory education at Lockport, and graduated from Boston University in 1881. Then followed two years' graduate study at Johns Hopkins University, and two years more at the University of Berlin (Ph.D. 1885) to which he was attracted by the fame of Helmholtz and Kirchhoff. After a year as acting assistant professor of physics at the University of

Michigan, he became instructor in the department of chemistry and physics at the University of Nebraska. In 1888 he became head of the newly established department of physics, a position held until his death. In 1901 he married Elizabeth Russell Wing, a former graduate of the University of Nebraska.

His first decade at Nebraska was concerned with the cares incident to building up a department of physics and starting what later became the department of electrical engineering. Having very meager funds at his disposal, he converted a university carpenter into an instrument maker who constructed most of the institution's first real laboratory equipment. Later, he developed an electrician's helper into a most efficient lecture demonstrator and manipulator with whose help he eventually worked up an unexcelled series of lecture experiments. Little evidence exists, outside the memory of his students, of any research activity in that period. The university authorities, frowning for policy's sake upon such a misuse of public funds, cleared away, under trivial excuse, the key part of a set-up he had made, with borrowed apparatus, for remeasuring the velocity of light. He was by no means inactive, however, for during this time an interesting electric generator and also a rectifier were designed, constructed, and patented. Ill luck attended him here, too, for both became obsolete before they could be promoted. With scientific instruments he was more successful; among several, the Brace spectrophotometer (described in 1899) and the Brace Half Shade Elliptic Polarizer and Compensator (described in 1904) are of recognized merit.

The second decade was one of constantly accelerated scientific production. It was initiated in 1896 by a change occurring in his staff which led to the appointment of two young instructors actively interested in research and two teaching graduate students who formed the nucleus of a graduate organization. This called for research problems, research equipment, and graduate courses in theoretical physics. To create an atmosphere of research, he deemed it necessary that all should be busy with it. By shouldering the lion's share of both undergraduate and graduate instruction, he allowed his associates a generous part of their time for the purpose and at the same time impressed them with the importance of this phase of their duties.

His own chosen field was optics, and here he was primarily concerned with the fundamental principles affecting the velocity of propagation of light. In his doctor's thesis, he had described (G. M. Wiedermann, *Annalen der Physik und*

Chemie, Neue Folge, XXVI, 1885, p. 576) not
entirely conclusive attempts to prove that a
clockwise circular vibration travels along a magnetic field in a material medium with a velocity
different from that of a counter clockwise vibration. Sixteen years later, he proved by a very
ingenious device that the refractive index of
such a medium differed for the two vibrations to
an extent that permitted observable separation
of a plane polarized incident beam into two
beams circularly polarized in opposite directions.
Likewise, either he or his students were engaged for some years in studying the effects of
an electric field, static and kinetic mechanical
stresses, and "æther drift" on the velocity of
propagation of light through matter. These investigations were uniformly distinguished by the
sensitiveness of the methods used for detecting
or measuring the effects.

Although fifteen contributions under his own
name and about an equal number by his students
complete the list of publications for which he
was primarily responsible, these dealt largely
with the fundamental problems of the day and
were as crucial as the method of attack could
possibly be made. The more important of them
are to be found in the *London, Edinburgh, and
Dublin Philosophical Magazine,* October 1897,
November 1899, April 1901, February 1903,
April 1904, July 1905, September 1905, November 1905; and in the *Physical Review,* January
1904, November 1905. Brace also translated and
edited *The Laws of Radiation and Absorption*
(1901), consisting of memoirs by Prévost,
Kirchhoff, and others.

[*Who's Who in America,* 1903–05; Ellery W. Davis,
sketch in *Science,* Oct. 27, 1905; *Neb. State Jour.,* Oct.
3, 1905.]
                                                    C. A. S.

BRACE, JOHN PIERCE (Feb. 10, 1793–
Oct. 18, 1872), educator, author, editor, was born
in Litchfield, Conn., son of Susan (Pierce) and
James Brace, writing-master in Miss Sarah
Pierce's school. His aunt (Sarah) superintended his education, sending him to Williams College, where he was graduated in 1812. He made
some preparation for the ministry, sudied medicine, and spent two years in the Litchfield Law
School. But he was born for one profession,
and in 1814 became head teacher for Miss Pierce,
later becoming associate principal and gradually
taking the real leadership. He widened the
course of study, adding botany, astronomy, and
chemistry to the curriculum. When the school
was incorporated in 1827 he was also made secretary of the board of trustees. During these years
the school was a leader in the education of women. The establishment of other schools and

changed conditions lessening its prosperity,
Brace resigned in 1832 to become head of the
Hartford Female Seminary. The fifteen years
he was principal made this school equally notable. He later taught at the academy in New
Milford for two or three years. In 1849 he
entered upon a new work, the editorship of the
Hartford Courant, then a small paper which
could be prepared for publication by one person.
His office, a dingy little sanctum, was filled with
books, many of them valuable. Traces of his
earlier profession appear occasionally in his editorials, one entitled "Criticisms" attacking common mistakes in English. At the age of seventy
(1863), he retired to the old family home in
Litchfield. A relative bequeathed him a "handsome competence," and although he was confined by rheumatism to a wheeled chair, and
sometimes even bedridden, he spent his days not
unhappily, practically living in his library among
his books. He died in Litchfield, and was buried
in Hartford.

He was twice married: first, to Lucy Porter of
Portland, Me., descendant of Rufus King, and
sister of Mrs. Lyman Beecher; and, second, to
Louisa Moreau of Hartford. Contemporaries
emphasized his "vast and multifarious acquire-
ments," his "reputation as one of the most cultured men of his time," and his passion for imparting knowledge. His interests seemed all-
embracing, including subjects like heraldry and
astrology. He collected minerals, a valuable
herbarium, and, as the girls reported, "bugs
. . . and a plenty of butterflies and spiders." He
found time to correspond with foreign scientists,
and exchanged specimens. Besides his "exquisite feeling for nature," he was a famous fisherman and "gardened furiously." He left a few
poems—Indian ballads and descriptions of local
scenery—written for the school and for a literary
coterie in Litchfield; some scientific articles; and
two novels, *Tales of the Devils* (1847), and
*The Fawn of the Pale Faces or, Two Centuries
Ago* (1853), a story of early Connecticut, "ele-
gantly written" in the prevailing fashion.

[Emily Noyes Vanderpoel, *Chronicles of a Pioneer
School* (1903); Emma Brace (ed.), *Life of Chas. Loring Brace* (1894); Samuel Orcutt, *Hist. of the Towns
of New Milford and Bridgewater, Conn.* (1882); P. K.
Kilbourne, *Sketches and Chronicles of the Town of
Litchfield, Conn.* (1859); A. C. White (ed.), *Hist. of
the Town of Litchfield, Conn.* (1920).]   M. H. M.

BRACHVOGEL, UDO (Sept. 26, 1835–Jan.
30, 1913), author, the son of Ferdinand Brachvogel, was born at Herrengrebin near Danzig.
He received a classical education, and studied
law at the universities of Jena and Breslau.
After passing his first state examination in 1858,

he visited Vienna, where he counted among his friends the poet Friedrich Halm (Baron Münch-Bellinghausen), and the tragedienne Juli Rettich. There he published his first volume of poems, under the title *Jugendgedichte* (1860). He did not establish himself as a lawyer, but during the next six years, 1860–66, lived in Hungary as clerk or agent of a private company. When the latter dissolved Brachvogel emigrated to the United States. In 1867 he was in St. Louis on the editorial staff of the German newspaper *Die Westliche Post,* and in 1875 he removed to New York in answer to a call to the editorship of the *Belletristisches Journal,* for many years a leading German literary journal published weekly. He was married on Jan. 12, 1878, to Käthe Müller of Oldenburg, Germany, whom he met at the home of his friend, Carl Schurz. In 1886 he resided in Omaha, Neb., where at first he edited a German political daily, but soon became the agent of the Germania Life Insurance Company of New York. As general agent of the same company he was subsequently transferred to Chicago, but the last years of his life he spent in New York City as correspondent of various journals in America and abroad. A second volume of his poems appeared shortly before his death, in 1912, entitled *Gedichte* (Leipzig and New York), with a dedication to his wife, and a very good portrait of the author. Upon this volume of German verse, an excellent collection of the best of his many scattered ballads and metrical translations, Brachvogel's reputation as an author will mainly depend. His prose style, especially in his late period, does not satisfy high standards. In his poetical work the influence of Ferdinand Freiligrath is apparent both in form and spirit. We find the same devotion to the theme of personal and political freedom, and the fondness for the descriptive historical ballad. Noteworthy examples of the latter type are the poems: "Capua," "Römische Nacht," "Jacobus de Benedictis," "Persepolis," "Canossa," "Hängende-Gärten Mythe," "Commœdia divina und Tragœdia humana." In the group "Americana" there are two pieces which take rank with the best produced by German verse-writers in America, *viz.*: "Ne-ah-ga-rah (Donner der Wasser)," and "Indianer-Sommer"; there are also occasional poems above the level of daily journalistic effort, as: "La Cuba Libre," "Die Maine," "Titanic-Requiem." Some of the earlier poems as: "Pour la Gloire," "Die Spinnerin," "Eine Ungenannte" show flashes of poetic inspiration arising from deep human sympathy; the selections from American poets, Longfellow, Bret Harte, Joaquin Miller, Poe,

Whittier, and others, exhibit the author's artistic skill as a translator. The most ambitious among Brachvogel's prose translations was his rendering of Bret Harte's *Gabriel Conroy,* published in 1876 (Stuttgart), a year after the appearance of the original. An appreciative essay on Bret Harte appeared shortly after (in *Deutsche Bücherei XIV,* 1882). Brachvogel similarly introduced Bayard Taylor to German readers and translated Hawthorne's *Scarlet Letter* for Walter Damrosch's opera on that theme (1894). Others of his published essays were: "Die deutsche Presse in den Vereinigten Staaten" (in Armin Tenner's *Amerika,* Berlin and New York, 1884) and *Das Theissland und sein Dichter* (New York, 1881). The latter is reminiscent of Brachvogel's early residence in Hungary, and euolgizes Hungary's greatest lyrical poet Sandor Petöfy, a martyr to the cause of political freedom in the Hungarian revolution of 1849. The chief value of the essay consists in the author's artistic rendering into German of some of the choicest lyrics of the Hungarian poet-patriot.

Brachvogel was born into an age of old world culture when literature and journalism were not yet distinct callings, and when lyrical composition was the pastime of most persons of education and refinement. He was too young to take part in the revolutionary struggle of 1848–49, as did Hecker, Schurz, Sigel, Brentano, Ottendorfer and many others who became journalists in the United States and continued there the fight for liberty and union with pen and sword. Brachvogel arrived in the United States after the Civil War was over, nor was he of the aggressive disposition of his contemporary Joseph Pulitzer, associated with him in 1868 on the staff of the *Westliche Post* in St. Louis. At the latter's death Brachvogel corrected some of the legends that had grown up about the meteoric career of his much admired friend. (Cf. *Die Pulitzer Legende,* and *Aus Pulitzers Jugendjahren,* in *Rundschau zweier Welten,* ed. by G. S. Viereck, December 1911, and January 1912). Guided by a peaceful star, Udo Brachvogel was not a fighter, a leader, or man of action; he was an observer, a thinker, a contemplative poet.

[Alexander J. Schem, *Deutsch-amerikanisches Conversations-Lexicon* (New York, 1869–74) ; G. A. Zimmermann, *Deutsch in Amerika* (Chicago, 1892) ; G. A. Neef, *Vom Lande des Sternenbanners* (Heidelberg, 1905) ; *Jahrbuch des Verbands deutscher Schriftsteller in Amerika* (New York, 1911). G. S. Viereck in his article: "Udo Brachvogel, Deutsch-Amerikas grösster Balladendichter" (see *Das Buch der Deutschen in Amerika,* Philadelphia 1909, pp. 397–98), mentions a novel by Brachvogel, *King Corn* and several short stories, none of which have appeared in book form. It is probable that these and many other writings in prose and verse will be found among Udo Brachvogel's papers, which have been presented to the N. Y. Pub.

Lib. (see Descriptive Bulletin written by Mabel C. Weeks), by the surviving children of the author, Miss Claire Brachvogel and John K. Brachvogel (lawyer), both of New York City. The manuscript collection is unusually rich in letters of distinguished contemporaries in literary, artistic, and political careers.]   A. B. F.

BRACKENRIDGE, HENRY MARIE (May 11, 1786–Jan. 18, 1871), lawyer, author, son of Hugh Henry Brackenridge [*q.v.*] and his first wife, was born in the frontier village of Pittsburgh. His mother died in 1788 and the early years of his life were spent in the homes of various friends and relatives in and near Pittsburgh. The elder Brackenridge began his son's education by setting him to the horn-book at the age of two. From this time lessons were his daily regimen. At the age of seven he was sent by flatboat on a rough and dangerous voyage to the village of St. Genevieve in upper Louisiana to learn French. After returning to Pittsburgh three years later, he studied English and the classics chiefly under his father's guidance, although he spent a short time at the Pittsburgh Academy. He derived from his father a love of reading, a wide range of interests, and a liberal political philosophy. His wit, too, was an inheritance; he was known as "the comical son of a comical father" (*Niles' Register*, Oct. 6, 1832, p. 96). He studied law in Pittsburgh and was there admitted to the bar in 1806. Then, after a few months with his father in Carlisle, he went to Baltimore, where, for over a year, he studied admiralty law and found solace in the social life of the city, and particularly in its bookstores and libraries, while he waited for the practise which never developed. From Baltimore he went to Somerset, Pa., but the western territory soon lured him with its promise of greater opportunities. The years 1810–14 were spent in Missouri and Louisiana in the practise of law, and in the pursuit of various studies suggested by his new environment. The Spanish language, which he learned in St. Louis, was of great value in his later career, while his researches in natural history, geography, and Indian antiquities found expression in articles for the *Missouri Gazette* which attracted the notice of Thomas Jefferson. In 1811 he made a voyage up the Missouri with Manuel Lisa of the Missouri Fur Company, keeping a journal which was later used by Irving as a source for his *Astoria* (1836).

In November 1811 Brackenridge left St. Louis for New Orleans. There he studied Spanish law, thus laying the foundation for his later participation in Spanish American affairs, and continued his research on subjects of territorial interest. Chapters on Louisiana were added to his articles on Missouri and his journal of the Missouri River voyage to form his first book, *Views of Louisiana* (Pittsburgh, 1814. Reviewed in *Edinburgh Review,* July 1819. German translation, Weimar, 1818). Until the War of 1812 Brackenridge was also very busy with legal work. He assisted in framing the legislative act for the judiciary system of Louisiana, and served as deputy attorney-general and as district judge. During the war he sent information to the government regarding British preparations for invading Louisiana (*Recollections,* p. 280). This correspondence led President Madison to suggest the possibility of his appointment to the diplomatic service. Tempted by the hope of a diplomatic career, Brackenridge went to Washington, but his appointment was not secured until 1817, and he spent the interim practising law in Baltimore, and as a member of the Maryland legislature. Also, he wrote, in six weeks, a spirited but rather rhetorical *History of the Late War* (Baltimore, 1816; revised edition, 1817. French translations, 1820, 1822. Italian translation, 1824). His earlier studies in New Orleans were utilized in an article on the boundaries of Louisiana for Walsh's *American Register* (1817).

In 1817, when the question of recognizing the South American nations was the great political issue, Brackenridge published a pamphlet, *South America, A Letter on the Present State of that Country to James Monroe.* He urged recognition, recommending an American foreign policy such as was later defined in the Monroe Doctrine. In England the pamphlet was viewed as being "in some degree official" (*The Pamphleteer,* XIII, 37), and the Spanish minister employed an English writer to answer it (*Recollections,* p. 286). In France it was translated by the Abbé de Pradt, Bishop of Malines and diplomat, who commented on the brilliant talents of its author (*Ibid.,* p. 287). In connection with this issue Brackenridge found his opportunity for diplomatic service. He was made secretary of the commission sent to study the political situation in South America. The character of his views and their weight with the ranking commissioner are indicated by a note in Adams's Diary: "Rodney, the President hinted, is under the influence of Brackenridge, a mere enthusiast" (J. Q. Adams, *Memoirs,* IV, 155). The *Voyage to South America* (1819), a study of the political, social, economic, and intellectual status of the country, shows, however, that although Brackenridge was an enthusiast, he recognized the weaknesses of the Spanish American republics.

After his return from South America, Brackenridge continued his service in the Maryland legislature where he supported such liberal measures as the bill designed to admit Jews to public office (Speech of Jan. 20, 1819, in *Speeches on the Jew Bill,* Philadelphia, 1829). In 1821 his knowledge of Spanish affairs secured for him service under Andrew Jackson, then governor of Florida. First as secretary and translator, then as judge, he remained in Florida until 1832, when Jackson removed him from office. In presenting his case in *Letters to the Public* (1832), he attacked Jackson bitterly. After this time Brackenridge took little part in public affairs save for a brief reëntry into politics in 1840–41 as congressman (*Congressional Globe,* 26 Cong., 2 Sess., pp. 14, 141), and as a member of the commission provided for in the Mexican Treaty of Apr. 11, 1839. His later years, spent in the town of Tarentum which he established on the large estate near Pittsburgh acquired through his marriage to Caroline Marie (1827), were devoted to private business and to literature. In 1834 he published his *Recollections of Persons and Places in the West,* a valuable source for the early social history of the West, as well as for the personal history of his own early years. His "Biographical Notice of H. H. Brackenridge" (*Southern Literary Messenger,* January 1842), and his *History of the Western Insurrection in Western Pennsylvania* (1859) are largely concerned with a defense of his father's part in the Whiskey Rebellion. Most of his minor writings of this period deal with political and legal subjects. When he died in 1871, his career had spanned almost the whole of the nation's history. He had, without attaining positions of the highest eminence, been an intelligent and liberal participant in public affairs and an enlightened commentator on them.

[The sources for Brackenridge's biography are his own writings, particularly *Recollections of Persons and Places in the West* (1834; enlarged and revised edition, 1868); *Views of Louisiana; together with a Journal of a Voyage up the Missouri River, in 1811* (1814); *A Voyage to South America* (2 vols., 1819); and *Letters to the Public* (1832). The most complete list of his writings is in Joseph Sabin's *Dictionary of Books Relating to America,* vol. II (1869). An obituary appeared in the *Pittsburgh Daily Gazette,* Jan. 19, 1871.]

C. M. N.

BRACKENRIDGE, HUGH HENRY (1748–June 25, 1816), jurist, author, belonged to a family which came from near Campbeltown, Scotland, to a farm in York County, Pa., in 1753. Their economic status was such that they were able to complete the journey only by selling their surplus clothing. Hugh Henry, who was five years old at the time of the migration, early showed great zeal and capacity for learning. Encouraged by his mother, a woman of ability and intellectual ideals, he began the study of the classics with the help of a neighbouring clergyman,

and by the time he was thirteen years of age he had made notable progress, although his opportunities to secure reading matter were so limited that he often walked thirty miles to borrow books and newspapers. When he was fifteen years old he took charge of a school in Maryland in order to earn money for a higher education. About 1768 he entered Princeton, then under Dr. Witherspoon, where he served as master in the grammar school while he pursued his studies. He found congenial classmates in Philip Freneau and James Madison (Madison, *Writings,* 1900, I, 20, 22), who were, like himself, devoted to literature and attentive to political issues. In politics they were ardent Whigs. The Commencement poem, *The Rising Glory of America,* written by Brackenridge and Freneau in 1771 (published in 1772), is an expression of the growing national feeling. After his graduation Brackenridge, while head of an academy in Maryland, studied divinity. He took his master's degree at Princeton in 1774, writing *A Poem on Divine Revelation* for Commencement.

During the Revolution, Brackenridge contributed patriotic writings to the cause and served as chaplain. The first of his literary productions of this period were two plays, *The Battle of Bunker's Hill* (1776) and *The Death of General Montgomery* (1777). *The Battle of Bunker's Hill* was, according to Brackenridge's statement, written to be performed by the pupils in his academy. The theme of the drama, the superior fighting spirit of the American troops as compared with the British, was especially pointed by the device of putting praise of American valor into the mouths of the British officers, Howe and Gage. In the second play, *The Death of General Montgomery,* Brackenridge expressed bitter resentment against the instigation of Indian atrocities by the British. The Ghost of General Wolfe appears as a dramatic character to castigate the English government and to foretell the future greatness of the American Union. Both these dramas are written in dignified, if somewhat stilted, blank verse and are cast in the neo-classical mold, due attention being given to the dramatic unities. In style and structure they are superior to the other American plays of the time. Brackenridge, however, disavowed any ambitious dramatic intention in the compositions, insisting that they were designed only for academic and private performance. Evidence that they were used as the author intended is found in a list of plays performed by Harvard students at the time, which includes the titles of Brackenridge's pieces (Claude C. Robin, *New Travels through North America . . . in 1781,* English translation, Boston, 1784). His published sermons, *Six Political Discourses* (1788), were fiery exhortations to fight. During 1799 he edited the patriotic and literary *United States Magazine* in Philadelphia. Having given up the ministry on account of difficulties with the creed, he studied law with Samuel Chase in Annapolis, removing thence to the frontier village of Pittsburgh in 1781.

Pittsburgh was the scene of his most important work. He helped to stimulate the dawning cultural life of the community by assisting in the establishment of the first newspaper (*Pittsburgh Gazette,* 1786), the first bookstore (1789), and the Pittsburgh Academy (1787). He also had an active political career. In 1786–87 he was a member of the state assembly. In 1787–88 he was the foremost champion in the western country of the Federal Constitution, satirizing its opponents in contributions to the *Gazette;* and he was an unsuccessful candidate for the state constitutional convention. In the Whiskey Rebellion of 1793–94, Brackenridge, interested in the development of both the federal government and the western country, played a part which, though unsatisfactory to the insurrectionists, led federal officials to suspect him of disloyalty. He was, however, completely exonerated by Alexander Hamilton, who investigated his conduct (*Incidents of the Insurrection in the Western Parts of Pennsylvania,* 1795, II, 75–78).

His political experiences of this period found expression in many contributions to the local paper in ironical Hudibrastic verse and in prose. It was on the basis of these experiences, also, that he wrote his most important work, *Modern Chivalry,* a satirical picaresque novel which appeared in various parts from 1792 to 1815. *Modern Chivalry* was the first literary work of the West, and one of the most important American satires of its period. Written under the influence of Lucian, Swift, Samuel Butler, and Cervantes, it satirizes the various follies of the time, especially the social and political ambitions of the uneducated and the incapable. Although Brackenridge was a democrat, he did not accept the current romantic conception of "the people," having observed that the democratic fiat often made statesmen of illiterate persons.

Nevertheless, he was a leader of the Republican party in the West, and, as a reward for his exertions, he was appointed justice of the supreme court of Pennsylvania by Gov. McKean on Dec. 17, 1799. In 1801 he removed from Pittsburgh to Carlisle, where he resided until his death in 1816. His legal studies were the chief product of these years in Carlisle. He collaborated with the other members of the supreme court in a study of the English laws in force in Pennsylvania (1808). His chief contribution to legal literature was *Law Miscellanies* (1814). Brackenridge's political writings at this time included a campaign pamphlet for Gov. McKean (*The Standard of Liberty,* 1804) and informative newspaper articles on current affairs. His purely literary work of this later period showed deterioration. Additions to *Modern Chivalry* published in 1804–05 and 1815 are of interest chiefly for their criticism of new popular follies, such as the attack on the judiciary and the opposition to learning.

Brackenridge was married twice. The date of his first marriage and the name of his first wife, the mother of H. M. Brackenridge [*q.v.*], are unknown. In 1790, two years after her death, he married Sabina Wolfe, a farmer's daughter, for whose hand, in typically eccentric fashion, he proposed on their first meeting (John Pope, *A Tour through the Southern and Western Territories,* 1792, pp. 14–17). Although successful as a jurist, Brackenridge did his most important work as a writer of Revolutionary propaganda, and as a satirist of abuses in the new democracy. While his political activities, his eccentricity, and his caustic wit made for him many enemies, his ability and honesty won for him the respect of friends and enemies alike. He was, as portrayed by Gilbert Stuart, and as described by his own son, "a gentleman of the old school."

[H. M. Brackenridge's "Memoir of H. H. Brackenridge," *Southern Lit. Messenger,* Jan. 1842 (reprinted in *Modern Chivalry,* editions of 1846 and 1856), and *Recollections of Persons and Places in the West* (1834, revised edition 1868) are the chief sources. H. H. Brackenridge's *Incidents of the Insurrection in the Western Parts of Pa.* (1795) and *Gazette Publications* (1806) contain autobiographical material. Contemporary files of the *Pittsburgh Gazette* and *The Tree of Liberty* contain much material. C. F. Heartman's *Bibliography of the Writings of Hugh Henry Brackenridge* (1917) is indispensable. Brackenridge's professional career is surveyed in "Hugh Henry Brackenridge, Lawyer," by Myrl I. Eakin (*Western Pa. Hist. Mag.,* July 1927), and "Hugh Henry Brackenridge as a Judge of the State Supreme Court, 1799–1816," by Mildred Williams (*Ibid.,* Oct. 1927). C. M. Newlin's "The Writings of Hugh Henry Brackenridge" (*Ibid.,* Oct. 1927) is a study of his literary work. An article by D. P. Brown in the *Forum,* I, 396 ff., contains many colorful personal anecdotes.]   C. M. N.

BRACKENRIDGE, WILLIAM D. (June 10, 1810–Feb. 3, 1893), botanist, gained his position in science by the exceptional opportunities offered in the celebrated expedition under the command of Capt. Wilkes. Born in Ayr, Scotland, he began life as a gardener's boy and rose to be head gardener of Dr. Patrick Neill's grounds at Edinburgh. Several years were spent on the Continent, especially in Poland and as a student under Friedrich Otto, the garden director at Berlin. Brackenridge came to America about 1837 in the employ of Robert Buist, the Philadelphia nurseryman, and in the following year he seized the incomparable opportunity offered by the fitting out of the expedition that was to explore the Pacific for the United States Government. The places left open for botanists on this trip were naturally coveted. Nuttall, by his previous travels in the Pacific, was preëminently fitted for the position, Rafinesque hinted that he had desired it, and Asa Gray was actually slated to fill the chief berth. But Gray resigned in order to work with Torrey in the publication of a flora of North America, and Brackenridge, then comparatively obscure, was appointed assistant botanist to the eminent Dr. Pickering, chief naturalist of the party. The six sailing vessels left Hampton Roads, Va., on Aug. 19, 1838. Briefly, the itinerary was from Virginia to Madeira, thence to Rio de Janeiro, around the Horn to Chile and Peru, with inland trips, as to Lima in the Andean highlands, and thence among the islands of the Pacific to Tahiti, Samoa, the Fiji Islands, New Caledonia, and Sydney, Australia. Inland trips were made in New South Wales, and thence the party proceeded to New Zealand, the Fijis, the Hawaiian Islands, and back to the North American continent where Washington, Oregon, and the Mt. Shasta country of California were explored. The party continued past the Hawaiian Islands once more, through the Ladrones to Manila, where interior Philippine trips were made, and then through the Sulu Archipelago to Singapore, the Cape of Good Hope, and St. Helena, till New York was reached on June 9, 1842, after nearly four years of sailing and scientific collecting. Species of plants to the number of 10,000, representing about 40,000 specimens, had been collected, besides about a hundred living plants and many seeds. The botanical gleanings of the trip formed the nucleus of the National Herbarium.

In Washington Brackenridge was given a small greenhouse and was entrusted with the growing of the living plants, in addition to the preparation of the report on the ferns of the expedition. He remained in competent charge of the rare living plants even after their removal to the new Botanical Garden, in 1850, at the foot of the Capitol, where to this day many may be seen. But though a good field botanist, Brackenridge lacked training in systematic botany, and the difficulties of making a scientific report on the ferns, with descriptions in both Latin and English, were embarrassing. In this Asa Gray was of assistance, intimating, indeed, in his letter to Engelmann of Dec. 7, 1853, that most of the valuable work was his own, a claim which over-

stresses Latinity and nomenclature. Certainly the *Filices, Including Lycopodiaceæ and Hydropterides,* volume XVI (1854) was Brackenridge's, and his scientific masterpiece. Unhappily, the quarto volume of text and the magnificent folio of plates were practically all destroyed by fire in 1856, so that they are the scarcest of the reports of the expedition, and indeed among the rarest of all modern botanical monographs of value. In 1855 Brackenridge purchased thirty acres near Baltimore, Md., and there spent the rest of his life. For some years he was horticultural editor of the *American Farmer,* but he spent most of his energies as a nurseryman and landscape architect, so that his influence may be traced in many of the older estates around Baltimore, in which city he died.

[An excellent bit of historical reconstruction by Dr. J. H. Barnhart in *Jour. N. Y. Bot. Garden,* XX, 117–24 is the most extensive and valuable contribution to the meager knowledge about Brackenridge. There is also a brief notice of him in the *Gardener's Mo.,* XXVI, 375–76.]   D. C. P.

BRACKETT, ANNA CALLENDER (May 21, 1836–Mar. 9, 1911), educator, was the eldest of the five children of Samuel E. and Caroline S. Brackett. She received an education at both public and private schools in and about Boston, among others at Mr. Abbott's noted academy for girls. This training she capped with a course at the state normal school at Framingham, Mass., which she completed in 1856. She first exercised her teaching abilities in East Brookfield, Mass. From there she went as an assistant to the high school at Cambridge, Mass. So highly, however, did the Framingham State Normal School rate its own product that Miss Brackett was called back there for two years as assistant principal. In 1860 she went to Charleston, S. C., to become vice-principal of a normal school there, but was forced to retire from the city after the bombardment of Fort Sumter. She then became principal of the normal school at St. Louis—the first woman to head a normal school in the United States. Hearing that New York City was much in need of a private school for girls she came East again in 1870 and with Ida M. Eliot, her assistant in St. Louis, established a school on West Thirty-ninth St. It was in the education of American girls that she found her major interest for the next twenty-five years. Her books, *The Education of American Girls* and *Woman and the Higher Education,* published in 1874 and 1893 respectively, set forth a program based on a high respect for woman's mental vigor. Her own school maintained very high standards, so high, in fact, that some of her pupils were admitted to advanced standing at institutions such as Vassar. She was greatly influenced by the German philosopher Rosenkranz in his treatment of general educational philosophy. Her command of this author in his native tongue enabled her to contribute a translation of his philosophy of education as the first volume of the International Education Series, edited by William T. Harris. She was thus enabled to fill what seemed to her, during her normal school work, a regrettable lack of any such thoroughgoing exposition of the fundamental principles of education as was available abroad. This philosophical interest of Miss Brackett was also manifest in a deeply religious nature. She was a thorough student of the Bible and for many years, even after her retirement from active teaching in 1895, continued her Bible classes. She was a very popular editor of a page in *Harper's Bazar* on passing thoughts, where in 1892 appeared her informal essay on "The Technique of Rest." This proved so popular that more articles of a similar nature were called for which were finally collected into a volume by that name. For the use of her school she made a collection of poetry in collaboration with Miss Eliot. So well was this received that a later edition was undertaken for family use. Miss Brackett herself left about 150 poems of which some are quite charming. As her health failed, she came to spend more and more time at her home at Stowe in the Green Mountains of Vermont. There she kept open house, especially for those needing rest.

[The best source of biographical material on Anna Callender Brackett is Miss Edith Kendall's *In Memoriam*, undertaken to raise a scholarship fund in her honor. Her name also appears in *Who's Who in America* up to her death. Her activities in the National Education Association are reported in the bulletins of that association for 1871 and 1872.]   J. S. B.

BRACKETT, EDWARD AUGUSTUS (Oct. 1, 1818–Mar. 15, 1908), sculptor, was born in Vassalboro, Me., a descendant of Richard Brackett who settled in Braintree, Mass., in 1629, and a son of Reuben Brackett and Eliza (Starkey) Brackett. His parents were natives of Vassalboro, and members of the Society of Friends. His father was a farmer, clock-maker, and nurseryman. He was educated in the common schools of Vassalboro and at the Friends' School in Providence, R. I. His father moved to Lynn, Mass., and thence to Cincinnati in 1835. There Edward cut blocks for printing and began the study of art. In 1839, two years after his mother's death, he went to New York City, and a few months later to Washington, D. C., where he modeled a bust of Senator Tallmage. Returning to his Cincinnati home he was commissioned to make

a bust of William Henry Harrison. In 1841 he bought a tract of wooded land at Winchester, then part of South Woburn, Mass., and there built a house after his own plans. A studio in Boston was opened in the same year. In 1842 he married Amanda, daughter of Zaccheus Folger of Cincinnati, who died in 1871, leaving him two sons and two daughters. In the following year he married Elizabeth F., daughter of James B. Bellville, of Mount Washington, Ohio, by whom he had one daughter. He made his reputation and is best remembered by his portrait busts of Bryant, Longfellow, Allston, Sumner, Choate, Benjamin F. Butler, John Brown, Garrison, Wendell Phillips, and others. His bust of Brown, in private ownership, was highly praised by Jarvis. The Worcester Art Museum owns his most ambitious work, "The Ship-Wrecked Mother and Child." He is represented by portrait busts in the Metropolitian Museum of Art and the Boston Athenæum. As a sculptor he was entirely self-taught. He did not limit his activities, however, to this field, but is said to have always had some outside interest, such as the rearing of bees or the cultivation of winter grapes in hothouses. He served for one year in the Civil War as first lieutenant and battalion quartermaster of the 1st Massachusetts Cavalry. Shortly after the war he became interested in the habits of fish and their increase by artificial propagation, which interest brought him to the attention of the newly appointed Fish Commission of Massachusetts. In 1869 he was appointed one of the commissioners on Land Fisheries and in 1873 he abandoned his other activities to devote his attention to the science of pisciculture. He was chairman of the commission for twenty-seven years during which time he made annual reports. He was the inventor of the hatching trap that is now in universal use, and of a fish way which has been successful even over the highest dams. He also experimented in raising Mongolian pheasants, quail, and grouse for the purpose of stocking the state of Massachusetts. His interests further included spiritualism and poetry. He wrote: *Materialized Apparitions; if not Beings from Another Life What are They?* (1886), and three volumes of verse, *Twilight Hours: or Leisure Moments of an Artist* (1845); *The World We Live In* (1902); and *My House: Chips the Builder Threw Away* (1904).

[Herbert I. Brackett, *Brackett Genealogy* (1907); H. T. Tuckerman, *Book of the Artists* (1867); *Artists' Year Book* (1903); Lorado Taft, *Hist. of Am. Sculpture* (1903); *New Eng. Hist. and Geneal. Reg.*, LXII, 313; *Boston Daily Globe*, Mar. 16, 1908.]   L. M.

BRADBURY, JAMES WARE (June 10, 1802–Jan. 6, 1901), lawyer, senator, was born at

Parsonsfield, Me., the son of James Bradbury, a successful physician, and of Ann (Moulton) Bradbury. His great-grandfather was an active Whig of Revolutionary times, and among his ancestors was Robert Pike, the opponent of the persecution of the Quakers and of the witchcraft delusion. Bradbury fitted for college at Gorham Academy under Rev. Reuben Nasson and entered Bowdoin College as a sophomore in 1822. Among his classmates were Longfellow and Hawthorne and among other fellow students were William Pitt Fessenden and Franklin Pierce. On completing his course Bradbury ranked third in his class, standing just above Longfellow. After graduation he served as preceptor of Hallowell Academy for a year and studied law with two prominent Maine Democrats. After being admitted to the bar he took up his residence in Augusta. On Nov. 25, 1834, he was married to Eliza Ann Smith of that city. By unremitting industry, sound judgment as a counsellor, ability as an advocate, and strict integrity he won a high position at the bar. Among his clients were some of the principal railroads of the state and he appeared as counsel before courts and legislative committees. He drew many bills and was the author and champion of an important act protecting the rights of the smaller bondholders when a mortgage was foreclosed.

On coming to Augusta, in order to become acquainted with the people, he edited for a year the *Maine Patriot,* a Democratic paper. He usually avoided public office and stump speaking but he engaged actively in party management in the county and the state and was especially useful in maintaining harmony. In 1846 he was elected to the United States Senate as a compromise candidate. The Hamlin men and the conservatives had been deadlocked and rather than have the election fail Hamlin advised his friends to vote for Bradbury who though a conservative was a moderate one. Bradbury's action in the Senate justified the description. He strongly favored the compromise measures of 1850, and though these came to be regarded by many of New England's best men as a truckling to the South he never changed his opinion. Bradbury did not forget that his duty as a good Democrat was to smite the Whigs. His principal effort was the introduction of a resolution requesting information concerning President Taylor's removals from office and the delivery thereon of a very partisan speech. His most important individual constructive work was the preparing and championing a bill creating a Board of Accounts to pass on claims against the government. The bill

did not become a law but the act establishing the Court of Claims, passed a few years later, closely resembled his bill. Bradbury gave much attention to bills public and private in which his constituents were interested. One of his principal speeches was in behalf of the French Spoliation claimants, many of whom were Maine citizens. His chief opponent on this occasion was his college mate Senator Felch of Michigan. On the expiration of his term Bradbury declined being a candidate for reëlection and resumed the practise of law, which he continued with marked success until his retirement in 1876. He retained his interest in politics, however, was a delegate to the Democratic national convention of 1852, and is said to have taken an important part in securing the nomination of Franklin Pierce. When the Civil War broke out, Bradbury immediately took his stand in favor of maintaining the Union by force if need be, and in August 1861, when the Democratic state convention denounced the war, Bradbury instantly led a secession of nearly half the members. He regarded this as one of the most important acts of his life, believing that if the whole Democratic party in Maine had been represented as opposed to the war this evidence of division in the North would have encouraged England and France to recognize the Confederacy. The last years of his life, though uneventful, were characterized by quiet service to the community. He was president of the Maine Historical Society, 1873–89, overseer (elected 1850), and later trustee, of Bowdoin College, and chairman of the trustees' committee on finance for more than thirty years.

[Bradbury wrote two articles of an autobiographical nature, "Railroad Reminiscences" in the *Me. Hist. Soc. Colls.*, ser. 2, vol. VII, and "The First Democratic Convention in Me. during the Rebellion" in *Me. Hist. Soc. Colls.*, ser. 3, vol. II. The best account of his life is a sketch in the *Bradbury Memorial* (1890) by Wm. Barry Lapham. There is a good obituary in the *Daily Kennebec Jour.* (Augusta, Me.), Jan. 7, 1901. See also *Obit. Record Grads. Bowdoin Coll. for the Decade ending 1 June 1909.*]   L. C. H.

BRADBURY, THEOPHILUS (Nov. 13, 1739–Sept. 6, 1803), jurist, a descendant of Thomas Bradbury who settled at Salisbury, Mass., in 1638, and the son of Theophilus and Ann (Woodman) Bradbury, was born at Newbury, Mass. He attended the public schools there, proceeding in due course to Harvard College where he graduated in 1757. He then went to Falmouth (now Portland) and taught in the grammar school, at the same time studying law. On his admission to practise before the court of common pleas in May term 1762, he opened an office in Falmouth, being the first resident lawyer in that part of the country. In 1763 he was appointed collector of excise, and in 1765 was admitted to the bar of the superior court. For eleven years he and David Wyer, who had followed him a year later, were the only lawyers in the district, and between them monopolized all the legal business. A good lawyer, grave and dignified in manner and an excellent special pleader, Bradbury had great influence with both court and jury and enjoyed a lucrative practise. In 1777 he was appointed state attorney, but the destruction of Falmouth by the British in 1775 had prostrated all business, and in 1779 he resigned, went to Newburyport, Mass., and commenced practise anew in that town. Assisted by his family associations, he quickly acquired a prominent place in public life, representing his district in both branches of the General Court. In 1795 he was elected to the Fourth Congress as representative from Massachusetts, and was reëlected to the Fifth Congress in 1796. He was counsel for Newburyport in the suit which was brought against that town by the proprietors of the common land in the town of Newbury alleging that the respondents had in 1771 taken possession of certain of the common land, called "the middle ship yard," and had never made compensation. The case, which was of intense local interest, was heard at the April term of the court of general sessions at Salem 1797, and terminated in favor of Bradbury's clients. The same year he was appointed a justice of the supreme judicial court of Massachusetts. Upon the bench he displayed those qualities of courtesy and dignity combined with extensive knowledge of law and procedure which had distinguished his career as a practitioner. In February 1802 he had a paralytic stroke, which rendered him incapable of performing his judicial duties. It appearing that there was no reasonable ground to hope that he would ever be able to resume his seat on the bench, he was in July 1803 removed from office on address of the two branches of the General Court—the sole constitutional method available for meeting such a contingency. He only survived two months, dying at Newburyport, Sept. 6 following. He was married in 1762 to Sarah, daughter of Ephraim Jones of Falmouth.

[Wm. Willis, *Hist. of the Law, the Courts and the Lawyers of Me.* (1863), pp. 93, 123, and *The Hist. of Portland* (1831) ; W. T. Davis, *Hist. of the Judiciary of Mass.* (1900), p. 303 ; E. Vale Smith, *Hist. of Newburyport* (1854), p. 345 ; J. J. Currier, *Ould Newbury* (1896), p. 617.]   H. W. H. K.

BRADBURY, WILLIAM BATCHELDER (Oct. 6, 1816–Jan. 7, 1868), music teacher, piano manufacturer, was born in York, Me., and died in Montclair, N. J. He was the son of David and Sophia (Chase) Bradbury, and a descendant in the sixth generation from Thomas Bradbury who came from Derbyshire, England, to Agamenticus, now York, in 1634. The inheritance of a taste for music from his parents both of whom were "excellent singers," the father being the leader of a choir, and the fact that he readily mastered any musical instrument that came to his hand, though he never saw a piano or organ until he went to Boston at the age of seventeen, is about the extent of the record of Bradbury's boyhood. In Boston he entered the family of Sumner Hill, from whom he received his first lessons in harmony. Later, having come under the influence of Lowell Mason, he became his pupil in Boston and a close follower of his methods, so that in 1836 he was sent to Machias, Me., and later to St. John's, N. B., to conduct singing classes. In 1840 he went to a Brooklyn church as organist and the next year to the First Baptist Church in New York. There and in other churches he instituted free singing classes similar to those of Lowell Mason in Boston, which in both instances led to the introduction of music in the public schools. At annual festivals held in the Tabernacle the singers, all children, at times numbered 1,000. For use in these classes, festivals, and conventions he compiled many singing books adapted to the primitive needs of the time. In the first one, *The Young Choir* (1841), and in four later ones of more importance, *The Psalmodist* (1844), *Choralist* (1847), *Mendelssohn Collection* (1849), and *Psalmista* (1851), he was assisted by Thomas Hastings (1787–1872), pioneer in church choral singing and psalmody. *The Shawm* (1853), perhaps the most extensively used of any of the earlier books, included the sacred cantata "Daniel," music by George F. Root and Bradbury, words by C. M. Cady and Fannie J. Crosby. *The Jubilee* (1858) had a sale of over 200,000 copies; *Fresh Laurels* (1867), 1,200,000; *The Golden Chain*, about 2,000,000. *Esther* (cantata, 1856) was a favorite production of money-making choirs throughout the country for many years. Altogether over fifty different books were published. They all followed much the same pattern, consisting of the rudiments of notation and sight-reading, exercises in part singing, short easy glees, hymn-tunes, chants and anthems, aiming to afford adequate training to young aspirants for the church choir. In spite of the many critical sneers at "sugared American psalmody" and the belittling of its æsthetic value, it must be admitted that this music met the need of the time and fed the infantile musical life the country over as no other music could. While few of Bradbury's tunes are still in use, several have a strong hold on popular favor, *e.g.,* "Just as I am" and "He leadeth me," which are worthy examples of a sincere and simple musical expression of the sentiment of the text.

The years 1847–49 were spent abroad, mostly in study under Wenzel, Boehme, and Hauptmann at Leipsig, whence Bradbury sent letters to the *New York Observer* and other religious papers. In 1854, assisted by his brother, Edward G., and a German piano maker, he established the firm of Lighte, Newton & Bradbury, which soon became very successful as the Bradbury Piano Company, the instrument being endorsed by Theodore Thomas, William Mason, and many others. The business, later under the control of F. G. Smith, was finally absorbed by the Knabe Piano Company.

[The *N. Y. Musical Gazette* has a series of articles on Bradbury, running from Dec. 1867 to June 1868, the material for which was furnished by Bradbury himself. See also *Grove's Dict. of Music and Musicians, Am. Supp.* (1920), article "Tune-books"; Francis Oakley Jones, *Jones's Handbook of Music and Musicians* (1887); W. S. B. Mathews, *A Hundred Years of Music in America* (1889); articles by F. J. Metcalf and L. B. Starkweather, in the *Choir Herald* (Dayton, Ohio), vol. XIX, no. 7, Apr. 1916, pp. 122 ff., 145 ff.] S.S.

BRADDOCK, EDWARD (1695–July 13, 1755), British general, entered the army in 1710 as ensign in the Coldstream Guards, the regiment of his father, Major-General Edward Braddock. In that regiment he rose rapidly, becoming lieutenant of the grenadier company in 1716, captain-lieutenant with the army rank of lieutenant-colonel in 1734, captain in 1736, second major with the army rank of colonel in 1743, first major in 1745, and lieutenant-colonel of the regiment in 1745. He was probably not present either at Dettingen or Fontenoy, but accompanied the second battalion of the Coldstreams to Ostend in July 1745. Later in the year he served under Cumberland in the suppression of the Jacobite rebellion of 1745–46 (Daniel L. MacKinnon, *Origin and Services of the Coldstream Guards,* 1833, I, 381). In 1747 he commanded the second battalion in Lestock's and St. Clair's abortive attempt on Port l'Orient, was subsequently employed under the Prince of Orange at Bergen-op-Zoom, and was later quartered in Bois-le-Duc. Forty-three years' continuous service in one of the haughtiest regiments in the British army produced a man who was the sternest of disciplinarians, often brutal in dealing with civilians, and poor in purse, the butt of Fielding's satire and Walpole's wit. Appointed colonel of the 14th Regiment in 1753, he joined his men at Gibraltar, where he won their confidence and adoration (*Letters of Horace Walpole,* 1840, III, 145). Major-general in 1754,

he was selected by Cumberland to proceed to North America as commander-in-chief of all His Majesty's forces raised or to be raised there (T. W. Riker, "The Politics behind Braddock's Expedition," *American Historical Review,* XIII, 742–52). He sailed in December with two regiments of British foot and landed at Hampton, Va., in February 1755.

By the words of his instructions Braddock theoretically wielded greater military power than any man had ever enjoyed before in America, and his meeting in April with five colonial governors at Alexandria marked the nearest approach to the colonial unity which the Board of Trade had advocated for more than fifty years. But the British ministry had under-estimated the difficulties of campaigning in the wilderness of the new world. Braddock's own disdain of provincial troops complicated his task, and he found himself hampered by lack of money, provisions, transportation, and laborers. Dinwiddie, Washington, and Franklin contributed materially, and Braddock gratefully acknowledged their aid, but the inadequacy of preparations in England, and the prevailing jealousy of the colonies toward one another, constituted a problem not to be solved by a man of his training. In accordance with his orders to attack Fort Duquesne, he began the task of cutting a road westward from Fort Cumberland, with 1,400 British regulars, some 700 provincials from Virginia, Maryland, North Carolina, and South Carolina, and a detachment of sailors from the fleet. The first road across the Alleghanies, it became later a highway of western expansion and the foundation of the National Road. Its slow building through the thick and mysterious forests sapped the strength and spirits of the men.

At Little Meadows, for want of transportation (*English Historical Review,* January 1886, I, 150–52) the army divided, and Braddock, with 1,400 men, pushed on toward the fords of the Monongahela, throwing out flankers and advance pickets. But the absence of Indian allies, with whom he could not deal sympathetically, prevented adequate dispositions against surprise (*Correspondence of William Shirley,* 1912, II, 313), and on July 9, eight miles from Fort Duquesne, the advanced guard received a withering fire from some 900 French, Canadians, and Indians, stationed on either side of a heavily-wooded ravine. It fell back in confusion upon the van, under Lieutenant-Colonel Gage, marching too closely upon its heels, and out of the ensuing disorder it proved impossible to form the troops. Ten minutes later Braddock came up with the main body, but either because the order to form line-of-battle was not given or because the men were too confused to obey, the army preserved its column formation and was thus flanked on both sides by the enemy. Without knowledge of open fighting, Braddock refused to order his men to the shelter of the trees, as the provincials urged him to do. For three hours the redcoats presented the best of targets to their invisible foes. Sixty-three of the eighty-nine officers, and over half the army, were killed and wounded, and when Braddock, who had had four horses shot under him, was wounded in the arm and lungs, the remainder retreated in headlong rout to the camp of the second detachment. Braddock was borne back in a litter, and died four days later near Great Meadows, murmuring, according to tradition, "We shall better know how to deal with them another time."

[Winthrop Sargent, *The Hist. of an Expedition against Fort Duquesne* (1855) being vol. XV of the *Memoirs Pa. Hist. Soc.*, is the best and fullest account, and contains Orme's journal, the Morris journal, and Braddock's instructions. Braddock's orderly-book is printed as an appendix to W. H. Lowdermilk's *Hist. of Cumberland* (1878). Other documents are printed in *Pa. Arch.*; *The Official Records of Robert Dinwiddie* (2 vols., 1883–84), ed. by R. A. Brock; Sharpe Corres. in *Arch. of Md.*, vol. VI (1888); *Docs. Relative to the Col. Hist. of the State of N. Y.*, vol. VI (1855); and Jacob Nicolas Moreau, *The Conduct of the Late Ministry, or a Memorial Containing a Summary of Facts* (1757), a translation from the royally-authorized *Mémoire contenant le Précis des Faits* . . . (1756), and reprinted in N. B. Craig's *Olden Time*, vol. II (1847). The *Mo. Bull. of the Carnegie Lib. of Pittsburgh*, Nov. 1906, contains a list of references on Braddock's expedition. For a general account see H. Baker-Crothers, *Virginia and the French and Indian War* (1928).]   S.M.P.

BRADFORD, ALDEN (Nov. 19, 1765–Oct. 26, 1843), author, was a descendant of Gov. Bradford of Plymouth and also of John Alden and was the son of Col. Gamaliel and Sarah (Alden) Bradford of Duxbury, Mass. His father was a ship-owner, magistrate, and a person of considerable importance in an inconsiderable place. Young Alden was the first of the line to go to college, graduating from Harvard in 1786, after which he taught school for a year at Milton. After studying for the ministry under Samuel West, a leading liberal of his day, Bradford obtained a license to preach in 1790 but then accepted a tutorship in Greek at Harvard. He resigned this position three years later and became pastor of the Congregational Church at Wiscasset, Me. In 1795 he married Margaret Stevenson of Boston. Wiscasset was then a brisk little town but much given to tuberculosis, which Bradford attributed to the drinking of tea and spirits until he was himself attacked. He promptly gave up the ministry and was at once cured. He continued to reside at Wiscasset and was soon appointed clerk of the court for Lincoln County,

an office which he retained until with his fellow Federalists he was swept from office in 1811. He next established himself in a book-selling business in Boston but the firm was unsuccessful and it took him many years to clear off the debts. In 1812 he was appointed secretary of the Commonwealth of Massachusetts, which post he retained for twelve years. In 1824 he was again removed by the defeat of the Federalists, the excuse in Bradford's case being charges which were wholly unsubstantiated and which were later entirely refuted. He then became editor of the *Boston Gazette,* continuing a somewhat unprofitable interest in politics, although he obtained a minor appointment as justice of the peace at New Bedford. He seems to have taken up with several of the "isms" of the day, being known as a strong "anti-Masonry" man, a temperance advocate, and a Unitarian, or, as he called himself, a "Berean." Bradford was a prolific writer, the bibliography of his works containing over forty items. None of these have any living interest to-day except the few in which he printed original historical documents. His *History of Massachusetts to 1820* (1822–29) had a contemporaneous but not a permanent value, which may be said of other original historical works. His *Speeches of the Governors of Massachusetts 1763–75* (1815), usually cited as *Massachusetts State Papers,* is valuable for the original material printed in it. It is the printing of original letters and other papers which also gives value to his *Life of Jonathan Mayhew* (1838). He was a man of strong, upright character, of public spirit, of cultivated tastes,—of large use to his own generation and of some slight use to this.

[The only scholarly account of Bradford's life is the seven-page article, with bibliography, by S. E. Morison, in *Mass. Hist. Soc. Proc.*, LV, 153–64.]   J.T.A.

BRADFORD, ALEXANDER WARFIELD (Feb. 23, 1815–Nov. 5, 1867), lawyer, the son of Rev. John M. and Mary (Lush) Bradford, was born in Albany, N. Y. His primary education was received at the Albany Academy, whence he proceeded to Union College, Schenectady, where he graduated in 1832. On leaving Union he went to New York City, took up the study of law, and was admitted to the bar in 1837. Commencing practise, he also became active in political circles, being a staunch adherent of the old Whig party of that day. His progress in his profession was slow and he devoted a portion of his time to literary pursuits. In 1841 he published his *American Antiquities and Researches into the Origin and History of the Red Race,* a work which attracted much notice, as a pioneer venture in the ethnological field of the American Indian.

In 1843, he became corporation counsel to the City of New York, and in 1848 was elected surrogate for the city and county of New York, a position to which he was twice reëlected. As surrogate he was a conspicuous success. During his tenure of office he "contributed to build up almost a complete system of jurisprudence in the Surrogate Court," his thorough acquaintance with the law of wills and intestate property and the inter-relation of civil and canon law, giving his decisions a weight which extended beyond the confines of his own jurisdiction. He prepared *Reports of Cases Argued and Determined in the Surrogate's Court of the County of New York* (4 vols., 1851–57), covering the cases between 1849 and 1857. These reports have always been considered very valuable by the profession. He retired from the bench in 1858, being the same year elected a member of the state assembly, in which he served for one term. On his resumption of private practise he quickly acquired a lucrative legal connection, particularly in his special department of civil or ecclesiastical law. He was a member of the commission appointed in 1857 by the New York State legislature to reduce the law of the state to a systematic code. In 1865 they reported a civil code, "the first real code in good and correct sense of the term prepared in this country" (Charles Warren, *History of the American Bar*, 1911, p. 533). It failed, however, of adoption. His health gradually broke under the pressure of continuous application to professional duties, and he died in New York City Nov. 5, 1867.

He combined a singularly equable temperament with an unobtrusiveness which made him friends among all classes. His learning and general scholarship were universally recognized, and in his special sphere of law he had no peer in this country. He occasionally contributed to historical and other periodicals. For some years he was associated with Dr. Anthon in editing *The Protestant Churchman*. The *Catalogue of the Private Library of the Late A. W. Bradford, Esq.* (1868), prepared for the sale which took place after his death, discloses 920 items, covering a wide range of subjects, including a copy of John Eliot's Indian Bible, the first book printed in America.

[The *Testimonial of Respect of the Bar of N. Y. to the Memory of Alexander W. Bradford* (1868) contains an authoritative review of his life. An extended report of the meeting of the N. Y. bar on the occasion of his death appeared in the *N. Y. Times*, Nov. 8, 1867. A brief notice of his career occurs in *Hist. of the Bench and Bar of N. Y.*, ed. by D. McAdam *et al.* (1897), I, 266. The New York press of Nov. 7, 1867, contains obituaries, that in the *N. Y. Times* being contributed by an intimate acquaintance.]   H.W.H.K.

BRADFORD, AMORY HOWE (Apr. 14, 1846–Feb. 18, 1911), Congregational minister, the son of Rev. Benjamin Franklin Bradford and Mary A. Howe, was eighth in descent from Gov. William Bradford of the Plymouth Colony. He was born in Granby, N. Y., graduated from Hamilton College in 1867, and was married to Julia S. Stevens of Little Falls, N. Y., in 1870. In the latter year he entered on a life-long pastorate at Montclair, N. J. His church became, some years before his death, one of the strongest in the denomination. In 1884 he studied at Oxford University and his sermons were much appreciated in English pulpits. In 1888 he published his first book, *Spirit and Life*. It was followed by *Old Wine, New Bottles* (1892) ; *The Pilgrim in Old England* (1893) ; *Heredity and Christian Problems* (1895) ; *The Growing Revelation* (1897) ; *The Sistine Madonna* (1897) ; *The Holy Family* (1899) ; *The Return to Christ* (1900) ; *The Age of Faith* (1900) ; *Spiritual Lessons from the Brownings* (1900) ; *Messages of the Masters* (1902) ; *The Ascent of the Soul* (1902) ; *The Inward Light* (1905) ; *My Brother* (1910) ; and *Preludes and Interludes* (1911), edited by his son. These books were largely made up from his sermons and addresses, though considerable material was added. As may be inferred from their titles, their chief purpose was the promotion of progressive orthodoxy, that is the maintenance of all that was of value in the earlier orthodoxy, while restating it in terms that were in accord with the progress of historical and other scientific research. "Old Wine in New Bottles" was the name he gave to this procedure. From 1892 to 1899 he was an associate editor of the *Outlook*, then actively engaged in the same effort. Such studies inevitably lead to questions of philosophy, in which Bradford took an active interest, and in 1892 he was made president of the American Institute of Christian Philosophy. In the same year he delivered the Southworth Lectures at Andover Seminary. In 1895 he was sent to Japan, as one of a delegation to inspect the missions there ; and from 1901 to 1903 he was moderator of the National Council, the foremost position in the Congregational fellowship. In 1904 he was made president of the American Missionary Association.

[The chief source is an obituary by John R. Howard, formerly of Montclair, prepared for the family. Obituaries were also published in the *Outlook*, Mar. 4, 1911, the *Congregationalist*, Mar. 4, 1911, the *Newark Sun*, Feb. 20, 1911, and the *Sun* (N. Y.), Feb. 19, 1911.]
T.D.B.

BRADFORD, ANDREW (1686–Nov. 24, 1742), pioneer printer and magazine publisher, was the son of William Bradford [*q.v.*], the pioneer printer of the middle colonies, and of Elizabeth Sowle, daughter of Andrew Sowle, a London printer and publisher. When seven years of age he went with his father to New York City where the latter had been appointed "printer to the Crown." Most of his education he doubtless obtained as he learned the printing trade in his father's shop. Leaving New York City in 1712, he still continued for some time a sort of partnership with his father after he had taken up his residence in Philadelphia, where in 1714 he issued from his own press *The Laws of the Province of Pennsylvania*. Later appointed the official "printer to the Province," he became an importer of books published in England. Selling these in his shop, he exerted no mean influence upon the culture of Philadelphia. On Dec. 22, 1719, he began the *American Weekly Mercury*—the first newspaper in Pennsylvania and the third in the United States. In 1721 he was bold enough to express the hope that the General Assembly might find "some effectual remedy to revive the dying credit of this province" (*Weekly Mercury*, Jan. 2, 1721). For his criticism, brief as it was, he was summoned before the Provincial Council but suffered neither imprisonment nor fine, though he was warned not to publish in the future anything concerning the affairs of the government without the permission of the governor or secretary. He did not escape, however, so easily, a few years later when he published a series of essays about provincial matters—a series started by Benjamin Franklin but continued by other authors. For printing these contributions, especially the one on the tendency of power to perpetuate itself, he was again summoned before the Council (*Minutes of the Provincial Assembly,* III, 392), and later sent to prison. But he continued his newspaper without interruption. Whatever may have been the official decision in the case, he found so much favor with his fellow citizens that he was shortly afterward elected a councilman of the city. In supporting his case he set forth those principles that later enabled Andrew Hamilton, in New York City, to free John Peter Zenger in the most famous case for press freedom in colonial days. Benjamin Franklin has left a record of criticism of the *American Mercury* for its poor typographical appearance. But Isaiah Thomas (*History of Printing,* 1810, II, 326) asserts that the typography of the *American Mercury* was "equal to that of *Franklin's Gazette*." Franklin and Bradford were not only competing publishers for many years in the newspaper field, but for a short time were competitors in the magazine field. In January 1741 Bradford issued the first copy of the *American Magazine*. Three days later

Franklin followed with a rival, the *General Magazine* (A. H. Smyth, *The Philadelphia Magazines,* 1892, p. 26). Neither magazine lasted longer than six months. Bradford was twice married, first to a woman named Dorcas and next to Cornelia Smith of New York City, a relative of his father's second wife. He adopted William 3rd, a son of his brother, William 2nd. His adopted son became the famous "patriot-printer" of the Revolution and his widow, Cornelia, was one of the first women to edit a newspaper in America. While Andrew Bradford led a less spectacular life than that of his father or that of his adopted son, he held official positions from both city and church. He was postmaster at Philadelphia during the decade 1728–38. Elected a vestryman of Christ's Church in 1726, he was reëlected for eleven years and in all probability for other terms, though official confirmation is lacking. He derived considerable wealth from successful real estate investments in Philadelphia.

[The most detailed biographical sketch of Bradford may be found in the *Address,* delivered in 1869 by Horatio G. Jones before the Hist. Soc. of Phila. See also "Bradford Family of Printers," by Henry Lewis Bullen, in the *Am. Bull.,* Apr., July, 1913; and Henry Darrach, *Bradford Family* (1906). Bradford's connection with the *Am. Mercury* is told in detail by Jas. Melvin Lee in *Hist. of Am. Journalism* (1917), pp. 31 ff.] J. M. L.

BRADFORD, AUGUSTUS WILLIAMSON (Jan. 9, 1806–Mar. 1, 1881), governor of Maryland, was born at Bel Air, Harford County, Md., in the year 1806, the son of Samuel and Jane (Bond) Bradford. He was of British descent, both his paternal and maternal ancestors having come to this country before the Revolution. He received his elementary education at Bel Air Academy under the Rev. Reuben H. Davis, who was a noted teacher in his day. In 1822 he entered St. Mary's College, Baltimore, from which institution he graduated at the head of his class in 1824, when in his eighteenth year. He returned to Bel Air to take up the study of law in the office of the then well-known lawyer, Otho Scott. In 1827 he was admitted to the bar and practised law in his native town until 1831. In that year he decided to make his home in Baltimore, feeling that in that city there would be a wider field for him in his profession than in the village of Bel Air. During the outbreak of the cholera epidemic in 1832 he returned to Bel Air, where he lived for the following six years. In 1838 he again took up his residence in Baltimore to stay for the remainder of his life. He soon became a prominent member of the Whig party, and for a number of years devoted much of his time to its political organization. He was an ardent admirer and supporter of Henry Clay, and in 1844 was an elector on the Clay ticket. The defeat of Clay was such a bitter blow to him that for some years thereafter he would neither go upon the stump nor attend any political meetings. During this period of political inactivity he devoted himself to law, and acquired a good practise, although he never rose to any great distinction in his chosen profession. In 1835 he was happily married to Elizabeth Kell, the youngest daughter of Judge Kell of Baltimore. There were twelve children by this union, seven of whom were living at the time of his death. In 1845 he was appointed by Gov. Pratt clerk of the Baltimore county court and filled that office faithfully and efficiently until the close of the year 1851. For the next ten years he took very little part in public affairs.

In 1861 the people of America were much concerned lest the differences between the North and the South should lead to civil war. Peace conferences were held in various parts of the country and in the spring of 1861 Gov. Hicks sent Bradford as a representative of Maryland to the conference held in Washington. He there made a strong speech in favor of the Union, and in the following summer, when the Union party was formed in Maryland, Bradford was named its candidate for governor. Gen. Benjamin C. Howard was nominated by the Democrats. On Sept. 11 President Lincoln's secretary of war, Simon Cameron, wrote that "the passage of any act of secession by the legislature of Maryland must be prevented." The members of the legislature not strongly in favor of the Republican administration were arrested, and Maryland consequently, so far at least as her government was concerned, was definitely on the side of the Union. Bradford was elected by a majority of 31,000, but it is beyond question that this great majority was due in part to intimidation and unlawful use of the soldiery. The federal administration and its Maryland representatives seemed to feel that they were justified in using rather questionable methods to prevent the people of Maryland from voting for any one who was not a candidate on the Union ticket. The military officers were given authority to suspend the habeas corpus and to arrest any suspicious persons and keep them confined until after the election. No one knowing Bradford's high sense of duty and honor could believe that he had any direct share in the way in which his gubernatorial campaign was managed, but it is to be regretted that that military interference with the voters against which he fought so courageously during his administration should have helped to carry him into office. In his inaugural address (January 1862) Bradford stood strongly in favor of the Union. From the beginning of his administration he endeavored un-

ceasingly to have Maryland support the federal government, but at the same time he opposed any unlawful use of the soldiery. When Gen. Lee's army invaded Maryland in 1862 Bradford issued a proclamation calling upon the citizens to enrol themselves in military organizations, promising them they would not be required to join the federal army without their full consent. Organizations and volunteers immediately responded to the proclamation. Again in 1863, upon the second invasion of the state, Bradford called for 10,000 volunteers, and in June of that year he decided to equip them and organize them into companies without waiting for regimental organization. Many men too old to be drafted offered their services for home defense, and were accepted by the governor. On June 21, 1863, he issued his third appeal for volunteers, and this was answered by the formation of three other regiments. In November 1863 he came into serious conflict with the federal authorities. Major-General Schenck had issued an order for military officers to be present at the polls on the day of election to carry out certain restrictions upon the voters and to arrest any suspicious persons. Bradford wrote to President Lincoln assuring him of the state's loyalty and begging him to prevent any such interference by the soldiery. The President's reply was not satisfactory, and in November 1863 Bradford issued a proclamation declaring that whatever power the state possessed was to be used to support the proper officials in the discharge of their duties. Schenck immediately issued an order forbidding the newspapers to publish the proclamation, which did not appear in the Baltimore papers until the morning of the election, too late for circulation in the rural parts of the state. As a result there was the same military interference at the polls as in 1861.

Bradford was opposed to slavery both on moral and economic grounds, but he also opposed federal interference with the slaves in Maryland and exerted his efforts to have the practise of carrying off the slaves at night discontinued. The question of negro emancipation was discussed at the legislative session of 1864, and Bradford called a state convention to meet in Annapolis that year with a view to abolishing slavery. At that convention was adopted the constitution which abolished slavery in Maryland and disfranchised all who fought for or aided the Confederacy. In the summer of 1864 the Confederate forces invaded Maryland, camping near Reisterstown. A squad of them, detailed for the purpose, visited Bradford's residence, about four miles from Baltimore, and burned it to the ground, destroying his furniture, private papers, and entire library. The Governor was absent from home at the time, but the Confederates left a note telling him that the house had been burned in retaliation for the burning of the home of Gov. Leitcher of Virginia by Gen. Hunter. Under the constitution of 1864 Thomas Swann was elected governor of Maryland and on Jan. 10, 1866, Bradford retired. His speech at the induction of Gov. Swann into office was exceptionally eloquent. In 1867 he was appointed by President Johnson surveyor of the port of Baltimore, and held that office until Gen. Grant removed him in April 1869. In 1874, without his knowledge or consent, he was nominated by Grant to the office of appraiser-general in the Baltimore custom house, but immediately declined the position on the ground that he was not fitted by training for an office which required an experienced and judicious merchant. After his retirement as surveyor of the port of Baltimore he held no public office, but devoted the remainder of his life to his legal practise and his well-loved family. His last appearance in public life was as presidential elector on the Greeley ticket in 1872. The following story aptly illustrates his high sense of duty. His eldest son, a youth of twenty, had entered the Confederate army and been made an officer on the staff of a distinguished general. In 1864 he was found entering Washington in a wagon, was arrested as a spy and placed in the Capitol Prison. To the adjutant-general of the state fell the difficult task of telling Bradford of his son's arrest. After many minutes of silently pacing the floor the chief executive said, "Berry, I have made up my mind; if William has come within our lines as a spy he must take the consequences. My duty to my official position will not permit me to take any action." Happily it was proved that the young officer was not a spy, but an ill man trying to get to his home. "After a life full of years and of honor" Bradford died at his home in Baltimore, in his seventy-sixth year.

[H. E. Buchholz, *Governors of Md.* (1908); J. T. Scharf, *Hist. of Md.* (1879); *Sun* (Baltimore), Mar. 2, 1881; *Baltimore American and Commercial Advertiser,* Mar. 2, 1881; papers loaned by Bradford's son, Samuel Bradford.]   E. T. D.

BRADFORD, EDWARD GREEN (July 17, 1819–Jan. 16, 1884), jurist, born at Bohemia Manor, Cecil County, Md., a descendant of William Bradford, governor of Plymouth Colony, was the son of Moses and Phœbe (George) Bradford. His father was editor for several years of the *Delaware Gazette,* a Federalist paper; his mother was of a wealthy Irish family. They moved to Wilmington, Del., soon after his birth. He was educated in the Wilmington schools, Bristol College, Philadelphia, and at Delaware College. He graduated in 1839 and studied law under Chief Justice Gilpin, then attorney-general. He was admitted to the bar in 1842 and appointed deputy attorney-general immediately. He held this position for eight years. He had shown an interest in politics while still a law student and took an active part in the Harrison-Tyler campaign of 1840. In 1849 he represented New Castle County in the state legislature and was offered the Whig nomination for Congress but did not accept it. President Lincoln, in 1861, appointed him United States district attorney for Delaware and President Johnson reappointed him in July 1865. A man of courageous opinions, he resigned his office the following year because of disapproval of Johnson's policies. For some years he practised law successfully and in 1871 was appointed by President Grant as United States district court judge for Delaware. At various times in his life he took a decided stand in politics. He was active in the organization of the Republican party in Delaware, at the outbreak of the Civil War he was a declared Union man and during the reconstruction period took an advanced position on suffrage. His career as judge was rather uneventful, although many important cases came before him. Other offices held by him were city solicitor of Wilmington, director for thirty years of the Wilmington Farmers' Bank, and vestryman of Trinity Church for a long period. At the time of his death the Wilmington *Daily Republican,* in an editorial which spoke highly of his abilities, stated that he would have been a worthy successor of John Middleton Clayton as United States senator, an office which he had all his life greatly desired. The weakness of the Republican party in the state was given as the only reason for his non-election.

[J. T. Scharf, *Hist. of Del.* (1888), I, 560; *Daily Republican* (Wilmington), Jan. 17, 1884.]   M. A. K.

BRADFORD, EDWARD HICKLING (June 9, 1848–May 7, 1926), orthopædic surgeon, educator, and public servant, descendant of William Bradford, governor of Plymouth Colony, was the son of Charles F. Bradford, a Boston merchant, by his wife Eliza E. Hickling. He was born in Roxbury, Mass., and prepared for college at the Roxbury Latin School. Entering Harvard, he received his A.B. in 1869, and after a brief trial of business, matriculated at the Harvard Medical School, won an M.A. in 1872, and was graduated as M.D. in 1873, while serving as a surgical house pupil (1872–73) at the Massachusetts General Hospital. In 1873–75 he pursued his medical studies overseas in the clinics of Vienna, Paris, Berlin, Strassburg, and London. In 1875 he began general practise in Boston and was made a member of the staff of the Boston Dispensary in 1876, and of the Boston Children's Hospital in 1878. He also served as surgeon to out-patients at the Boston City Hospital and was appointed to the visiting staff in 1885. As the years went by, his broad view of medicine focused more and more sharply upon the cripple. He finally resigned from all his important hospital positions except that at the Children's Hospital, and eventually was appointed chief of its orthopædic staff. He became a member of the teaching force in the department of surgery in the Harvard Medical School in 1881, and as a result of brilliant work in his chosen field, was made assistant professor of orthopædic surgery in 1889. A new chair was created for him in 1903. He was the first full professor of orthopædic surgery. This chair he occupied until 1912. During these years he was an alert, resourceful, constructive, persuasive member of the Faculty of Medicine. In 1887, conscious of the need of some national association to foster the growth and raise the standards of this fast developing specialty, he was influential in founding the American Orthopædic Association and was elected its president in 1888. Bradford and Lovett's text-book on *Orthopædic Surgery,* published in 1890, was the standard for many years and ran through numerous editions. Bradford founded in 1893 the Boston Industrial School for Crippled and Deformed Children, the first of its kind in America. This school still remains a model. It was Bradford who persuaded the State of Massachusetts, in 1904, to establish its unique Hospital School at Canton. Until his death, as chairman of the trustees, he guided the academic and vocational training of the physically handicapped minor wards of the state. In 1912 when he gave up his active hospital duties and was made emeritus professor, he accepted the appointment of dean of the Harvard Medical School. Through the trying war years he increased the usefulness of the institution and did important work on the supervising committee of the selective service commission of the State of Massachusetts. In 1918, he relinquished the duties of deanship and in 1919 was made a member of the board of overseers of Harvard College and chairman of its medical committee. He was married to Edith Fiske of Boston on June 20, 1900. In his personality were combined humor, generosity, urbanity, patience, and humility. His open mind sought and found truth which he shared with others. He was a man of deep religious faith. To serve his fellow men with intelligence and kindness was the activating motive of his life.

[Robt. B. Osgood, "Edward Hickling Bradford," *Jour. of Bone and Joint Surgery,* July 1926; *Boston Medic. and Surgic. Jour.,* May 27, 1926; *Eleventh Report of the Class of 1869, Harvard Coll.* (1919); *Boston Evening Transcript,* May 8, 1926; Records of the Harvard Medical School, Boston City Hospital, Boston Dispensary, Boston Children's Hospital; information from Mrs. E. H. Bradford.] R.B.O.

BRADFORD, GAMALIEL (Jan. 15, 1831– Aug. 20, 1911), banker, publicist, was born in Boston, the son of Gamaliel and Sophia Blake (Rice) Bradford, and the seventh in descent from Gov. William Bradford of Plymouth Colony. His father, who was superintendent of the Massachusetts General Hospital, died Oct. 22, 1839, leaving his family comparatively poor. In 1849 Bradford graduated sixth in his class at Harvard and for the next year or two was in the employ of the *Nautical Almanac* at Cambridge. During this period he made two trips to Europe and acquired an abiding enthusiasm for music, riding, and German. At the invitation of his cousin, George Baty Blake, he became a clerk in the banking house of Blake, Howe & Company, displayed great aptitude for the business, was made a partner in 1858, and retired with an ample competence in 1868. After spending a year in Washington he returned to Boston and devoted the rest of his long life to the study of government and to the advocacy of certain reforms. In April 1878 he was elected to the Massachusetts Historical Society, and until increasing deafness cut him off from general conversation he did his full share to enliven the Society's meetings. On a good many topics he held strong convictions, and all who knew him became acquainted with them. Early in life he had been, like his father, an abolitionist; during the Civil War he was a mordant critic of Secretary Chase's currency measures; later he advocated civil service reform and city charters, waged and won almost single-handed a campaign to retain the yearly election in Masachusetts, joined the Mugwumps when Blaine was nominated by the Republicans in 1884, and thereafter opposed the Republican policies of centralization, high tariffs, and imperialism. His pet theory was that the executive—mayor, governor, or president— should normally have the power to initiate legislation, and to that end he urged that members of the cabinet have seats in the legislature. This is the principal theme of his one book, a substantial two-volume treatise on *The Lesson of Popular Government* (1899). [See the review in the *Nation,* LXVIII, 335–36, 359–61.] The purely theoretical character of his studies is brought out in the fact that he failed to recognize the extent to which a strong executive can influence legislation unofficially. The only office that he ever held was member of the Wellesley School Committee, although three times he offered himself as a candidate for governor and once polled some three thousand votes. Such influence as he had was exerted largely through his letters to the papers; he contributed several thousand, over a period of forty years, to the Boston *Advertiser* and *Transcript,* the Springfield *Republican,* the New York *Times, Tribune, Evening Post,* and *Nation,* and the *Bankers' Magazine.* Into these casual communications he poured an amazing wealth of information, shrewdness, and literary power. He lived during the winter in apartments overlooking the Charles River at Harvard Bridge; his summer home was at Wellesley Hills. When returning one Sunday evening from a call on his son he was knocked down by a trolley car and died a few hours afterward. He was buried in Mount Auburn Cemetery.

On Oct. 30, 1861, Bradford married Clara Crowninshield Kinsman of Newburyport, Mass., who died June 9, 1866. Of their three children the only one to reach maturity was Gamaliel Bradford, the biographical essayist.

[*Proc. Mass. Hist. Soc.,* vols. XLV (1912), XLVII (1914); *Who's Who in America,* 1910–11; *Harvard Quinquennial Cat. 1636–1915* (1915); H. S. Bradford, *One Branch of the Bradford Family* (privately printed, 1898); *Nation,* XCIII, 156 (Aug. 24, 1911); obituary and editorial in *Boston Evening Transcript,* Aug. 21, 1911. The Mass. Hist. Soc. has six folio scrapbooks containing his letters and miscellaneous writings, with editorials and cartoons against him.]   G. H. G.

BRADFORD, JOHN (June 6, 1749–Mar. 20, 1830), pioneer printer of Kentucky, was born in Prince William (later Fauquier) County, Va., the son of Daniel and Alice Bradford. His father was the eldest son of John Bradford and his wife Mary. His grandfather of the same name is said to have been born about the year 1680 and to have married in 1710. Beyond this his lineage is uncertain. It may be added, however, that he was not related to the Bradfords of Massachusetts unless very remotely. After his marriage in 1771 to Eliza James, a daughter of Capt. Benjamin James of Fauquier County, he evidently went to Kentucky in 1779, but the rest of his family did not join him there until six years later. Before the arrival of his wife, there is evidence that he served in Bowman's campaign against the Indians and as a deputy surveyor under George May, the chief surveyor of what was then Kentucky County, Va. He first settled on Cane Run, but in or about the year 1787 he moved with his family to Lexington where he thereafter made his home. At the third —sometimes called the fourth—convention which

assembled at Danville on Sept. 4, 1786, to discuss the separation from the State of Virginia and the establishment of a new state, a committee appointed to induce a printer to settle in the territory finally selected Bradford, even though he was without practical experience. The first number of his paper, the *Kentucke Gazette* (spelling changed to "Kentucky" in March 1789), came from his log cabin print shop on Aug. 11, 1787. Associated with him in the enterprise was his brother Fielding—a partnership which lasted until June 7, 1788. Greatly handicapped in getting paper, ink, etc., Bradford produced a newspaper that compared very favorably with the precursors of the press in other territories. From his shop in 1788, he sent forth the *Kentucke Almanac,* the pioneer pamphlet of the West. In connection with his duties as Printer of the Territory he published in 1792, the acts of the first session of the Kentucky legislature, the first book printed in Kentucky. In addition to his printing, he continued at times his work as a civil engineer and served as a deputy under Col. Thomas Marshall, first chief surveyor of Fayette County and father of Chief Justice John Marshall. The epithet, "the Kentucky Franklin," was sometimes applied to Bradford, for he was both a printer and a philosopher, and was also interested in mathematics and astronomy. Like Franklin he did much to promote education. He was in turn clerk of the board of Transylvania Seminary, a member of the board, and then chairman. Resigning the chairmanship in 1795, he became, with the founding of Transylvania University in 1799, the first chairman of the board. Resigning again in 1811, he became chairman again in September 1823 and held that office until November 1828. He was instrumental in founding the Lexington Library which he often served as one of its trustees. He held numerous offices connected with the county of Fayette and represented that county in the House of Representatives of Kentucky in 1797 and again in 1802. In his early newspaper days he was somewhat litigious, as were most pioneer printers, but in later years he became more charitable in his views, and in his respect for the rights of others. In politics he was a Jeffersonian Republican and was a member of the Democratic Society of Lexington which was modeled after the Jacobin Society of Philadelphia. He was never so partisan, however, but that he was willing to admit to the columns of his paper the contributions of those who were opposed to him in political matters. Through the pamphlets which came from his press he did much to promote public discussion of political affairs. On Aug.

25, 1826, he began the publication of his "Notes of Kentucky" in the *Kentucky Gazette* which in 1802 he had transferred to his son Daniel, but which in 1809 had been sold to Thomas Smith who in turn in 1814 had returned the paper to Fielding Bradford, Jr. In this series John Bradford contributed sixty-two papers, the last of which appeared in January 1829. Because he had been so closely associated with the Kentucky pioneers, he knew intimately about the struggling days of Kentucky and could therefore write with authority. At the time of his death he was high sheriff of Fayette County.

[Clarence S. Brigham in the *Proc. Am. Antiquarian Soc.*, vol. XXIV, pt. 2 (1914), pp. 380 ff., in tracing the history of the *Ky. Gazette,* shows the connection of Bradford and his descendants with that newspaper. Jas. Melvin Lee in *Hist. of Am. Journalism* (1917), ch. XI, outlines the conditions under which Bradford started his paper. Valuable material will be found in *Biog. Encyc. of Ky.* (1878), p. 415; Lewis and R. H. Collins, *Hist. of Ky.* (1874), II, 170 ff.; W. H. Perrin, *Pioneer Press of Ky.* (1888), pp. 14 ff.; *Ky. State Hist. Soc. Reg.*, XVII; *Mag. of Am. Hist.*, XVIII, 125; *Niles' Weekly Reg.*, XXXVIII, 174.]   J.M.L.

BRADFORD, JOSEPH (Oct. 24, 1843–Apr. 13, 1886), actor, journalist, poet, and playwright, born near Nashville, Tenn., was christened William Randolph Hunter. His father, being one of the wealthiest slave owners in the South, was able to rear the son in luxury and to surround him with books which furnished a background for his later literary career. At sixteen young Hunter matriculated on Sept. 29, 1860, in the United States Naval Academy at Annapolis. His standing in his class at the end of the first year was high, but the official record also recorded 120 demerits. He was dismissed on Apr. 14, 1862. On July 9 he enlisted as an acting master's mate and served successfully in the North Atlantic Blockading Squadron on the U. S. S. *Minnesota* and on the U. S. S. *Putnam.* His service in the navy, under his real name, caused a break in the family ties. Under the assumed name of Joseph Bradford he then went on the stage in Baltimore. (His father's wealth went to the next of kin, but the memory of his mother was recalled in the adoption of her maiden name.) Later he played in light comedies with several stock companies in various cities along the Atlantic Coast. A road tour took him to Boston, where he decided to write plays rather than to act in them. Here he also wrote numerous poems often based on topics of the day. Of these the most extensively quoted in the press was the one on the death of Gen. Grant. In addition to his work as a playwright, he wrote for Boston newspapers. His best journalistic work was possibly done for the *Boston*

Courier over the signature of "Jay Bee." Of his more important plays, mention may be made of the following: *New German* (1872), a play in five acts, written in collaboration with F. Stinson; *Law in New York* (1873), with Stinson; *20,000 Leagues Under the Sea* (1874), libretto by Bradford; music by G. Operti; *The Conditional Pardon* (1875), a play in five acts, with Stinson; *Fritz's Brother* (1875), with J. K. Emmet; *Out of Bondage* (1876), a play in four acts; *In and Out of Bondage* (1877), a musical drama; *Our Bachelors* (1877), a comedy in four acts; *A. A. 1900* (1879), a comedy in four acts; *John Mishler* (1882), a play in three acts and a prologue; *One of the Finest* (1883); *A Wonderful Woman* (1883); *Cherubs* (1885); *Rose and Coe* (1886), a comedy in three acts.

[Biographical material about Jos. Bradford is scant and jejune. The most important source of information is the *Naval Acad. Reg.*, 1860, p. 15. His work as a playwright is recorded in various items preserved in the Theatre Collection of the Harvard Coll. Lib. Obituaries published in Boston and New York papers paid a fine tribute to his contributions to lighter drama and comedy, but were incomplete as to details of his life.]
                                        J.M.L.

BRADFORD, THOMAS (May 4, 1745–May 7, 1838), printer and publisher, was the eldest son of William Bradford [*q.v.*], the "patriot-printer." His mother, Rachel, was the daughter of Thomas Budd who with George Keith opposed in 1692 Lieutenant-Governor Lloyd in the Quaker wrangle that resulted in the withdrawal of William Bradford [*q.v.*], the first printer of that name, from Philadelphia to New York. For several years Thomas Bradford attended what is now the University of Pennsylvania, but in 1762 he went to work for his father on the *Pennsylvania Journal and Weekly Advertiser,* a paper that first bore the joint imprint of father and son on Sept. 4, 1766. He took an active part in resisting the Stamp Act and was one of the principal promoters of the movement among the merchants of Pennsylvania and its sister state of Delaware to have no commercial transactions with England until the obnoxious act was repealed. The partnership with his father lasted until the occupation of Philadelphia by the British troops in 1777, when publication was temporarily suspended. After the evacuation of that city by the British, the *Journal* resumed publication with the name of only the son in its imprint. During the Revolutionary War Bradford also served as captain of a militia company and later as deputy commissary-general of prisoners in the American army where he had the rank of lieutenant-colonel. The business rather than the editorial side of newspaper publishing was always the more interesting to him and doubtless had much to do with his decision to start a daily paper that specialized in the news of the business world. This paper, started by him in 1797, was called the *Merchants' Daily Advertiser*. After the death of his younger brother, the Hon. William Bradford [*q.v.*], attorney-general of the United States, he came into possession of the larger part of the estate. The pressure of outside business interests practically forced him to turn over the management of the *Merchants' Daily Advertiser* to his son Samuel. The latter, being more interested in politics, changed the name of the paper in 1798 to the *True American* which was the pioneer paper to have a literary supplement. The son, however, lacked the executive ability of his father who had to resume active management of the paper in 1801. In spite of the fact that Bradford had cherished since the days of the Stamp Act a hatred of England, he was perfectly willing to publish the political pamphlets of William Cobbett who was attacking everything that was French and was stoutly defending England. Fearful of the windows of his print shop, Bradford insisted that the pamphlets should appear anonymously. In fact, he insisted upon such high rates of payment that he practically forced Cobbett to become a publisher—something that Bradford later regretted because of the extensive sale of Cobbett's pamphlets. After the death in 1805 of his wife, Mary Fisher, whom he had married in 1768, Bradford took even a more energetic interest in civic affairs. He was especially active in the American Philosophical Society of which he was a charter member. In spite of close application to business, he retained remarkable health. When seventy-five years old he made a trip from Philadelphia to Pittsburgh on horseback in order to inspect several tracts of land scattered over several counties in western Pennsylvania. He seems to have suffered no physical inconvenience from the trip, since immediately upon his return to Philadelphia he resumed active control of his affairs which in his absence had been managed by his second son, William Bradford, who later became a bookseller in Philadelphia. Meanwhile his elder son, Samuel, had become a publisher in New York. One other son, Thomas, became a member of the Philadelphia bar. In addition to these three sons, he had three daughters. He did not leave as direct an imprint upon the journalism of his day as did the other editorial members of the Bradford family, because he was chiefly interested in the commercial side, yet the financial page and the book page of the modern metropolitan journal go back in their evolution to innovations

made by him. His remarkable health continued until about six months before his death when he suddenly lost the use of his eyes. Accustomed to activity, he chafed under this affliction until his death in his ninety-fourth year.

[Brief biographies of Bradford's children may be found in *Bradford Family—1660–1906* (1906) by Henry Darrach. His newspaper activities are recorded in a bibliographical way by Clarence S. Brigham in the *Proc. Am. Antiquarian Soc.*, vol. XXXII (1922). His business relations with Cobbett are taken up in *The Life and Letters of William Cobbett in England and America* (1912) by Lewis Melville. An appreciation of his life appears in *Hist. of Phila.* (1884) by J. T. Sharf and T. Westcott. There is an editorial tribute to his services in the *Public Ledger* (Phila.), May 9, 1838.]

J. M. L.

BRADFORD, WILLIAM (1589/90–May 9/19, 1657), Pilgrim Father, was born at Austerfield, Yorkshire, into a family of substantial yeomen. His father, William Bradford (d. 1591), married Alice Hanson, daughter of the village shopkeeper, June 21/31, 1584. Their third child and only son, the future governor, was baptized at the parish church in Austerfield March 19/29, 1589/90 (*Mayflower Descendant*, VII, 65, IX, 115–17). His mother married again in 1593, after which he was brought up by his grandfather and uncles to follow the plow. The people of that region were "ignorant and licentious," but William, a puny boy, began to read the Bible at the age of twelve, and to attend the sermons of a noted non-conformist, the Rev. Richard Clyfton, at Babworth. Braving the wrath of his uncles, William joined, while still a lad, the small group which met at the house of William Brewster [*q.v.*] in Scrooby, and which became a separatist church in 1606. The attitude of their neighbors, and of the authorities, determined the Scrooby congregation "to goe into the Low-Countries, where they heard was freedome of Religion for all men." In the spring of 1609 Bradford joined the company in a stormy passage from Hull to Amsterdam, of whose hardships he gives a vivid picture. In 1609 he removed with the congregation, then under the Rev. John Robinson, to Leyden. On coming of age in 1611, Bradford converted "a comfortable inheritance left him of his honest parents" into money, which was consumed in certain "designs, by the Providence of God frowned upon" (C. Mather, *Magnalia*). He became a citizen of Leyden, is described in contemporary documents as a fustian weaver (1613) and say worker (1620), and owned a house on the Achtergracht, which he sold on a mortgage in 1619. At this period of his life Bradford must have acquired that wide knowledge of theological and general literature to which his writings bear witness. The influence of the liberal and catholic spirit of his pastor, John Robinson, and of Elder Brewster, lasted throughout his life. Bradford defines his theological position (Calvinist in theology, Congregational in polity) in his Dialogues, but like Robinson he disowned sectarian labels, and wished to retain fellowship with all reformed churches. For, as he wrote, "it is too great arrogancie for any man or church to thinke that he or they have so sounded the word of God to the bottome." His liberalism much impressed the Jesuit, Father Druillette, who was entertained by him with a fish dinner at Plymouth, one Friday in 1650. Of Bradford's personal appearance or peculiarities not the slightest hint has come down to us, except that in the inventory of his estate, beside various "sad-colored" clothes, we find a red waistcoat, silver buttons, a colored hat, a violet cloak, and a Turkey grogram suit.

Bradford took a responsible part in the preparations for removal to the new world. He was probably one of those chosen to dispose "the commone stock . . . for the making of general provision." He signed a letter to Carver and Cushman, the agents at London, ordering them not to deviate from the original terms, in dealing with the merchant adventurers; this attitude he stoutly maintained amid the embarrassments of the final embarkation at Southampton.

From the sailing of the *Speedwell* from Delfshaven (*c.* Aug. 1, 1620), Bradford's life is inseparable from the history of the Pilgrim colony. He signed the Mayflower Compact on Nov. 11/21. Later in the same day the *Mayflower* anchored in Cape Cod (Provincetown) harbor. Bradford was "adjoined for council and advice" to the first exploring expedition which started out on Nov. 15/25, under Miles Standish. He was of the company of twenty who left Cape Cod harbor in the shallop, had the first encounter with the Indians, scudded into Plymouth harbor before a snow storm, rested the Sabbath on Clark's Island, landed at Plymouth (traditionally on the rock) on Dec. 11/21, and decided to settle there. He was taken ill during the first winter, but recovered; and in April 1621, on the death of John Carver, William Bradford was elected governor of the colony.

The situation of the Pilgrims when they arrived at Cape Cod, so eloquently described by Bradford in his ninth chapter, was much worse when the young governor took office. The great sickness had taken thirteen out of the twenty-four heads of families, all but four of their wives, and all but six of the unattached bachelors. The *Mayflower* had returned to England, provisions were running low, and there would be no harvest for

four months. There were only twenty-one men and six big boys to do the planting; and they had no cattle until 1624. They knew nothing about deep-sea fishing and fur-trading, and had no means to do either. In like circumstances, many other colonies had perished. In Bradford's opinion, only the guiding hand of God kept Plymouth Colony alive. The presence of Samoset and Squanto [*qq.v.*], the windfalls of corn from unexpected quarters, the mysterious voice that warned them of the store-house fire, the messenger losing his way and thereby delivering his warning, the "sweet and gentle showers" that came out of a clear sky just in time to save the crop, the turning back of the ship which was sent out to foreclose the colony for the creditors; of such interventions Bradford is so certain of the source that he simply remarks, "Behold now another providence of God." Yet other events, no less necessary than these to save the colony, were due primarily to the inspired leadership of the Governor, and of men like Brewster, Winslow, and Standish, on whom he leaned. By sheltering both Hobbomock and Squanto, and playing them off against one another, Bradford obtained the best intelligence as to movements of the Indian tribes; and his Indian policy, a nice balance of kindness and firmness, obtained their friendship and secured his people.

Bradford urged rotation in office in 1624, but the freemen would not let him off; and he was re-elected governor of the colony thirty times: every year from 1622 to 1656 with the exception of 1633, 1634, 1636, 1638, and 1644; when he "by importunity gat off" (Winthrop, *Journal,* Jan. 1, 1633); and on those occasions he was elected an assistant. Until 1639, when he was voted £20, he received no salary; and until 1651 had the privilege of dining the court of assistants at his own expense during their monthly sessions. In 1645 he was granted "a guard of two halbertes" to attend him at the General Court. The Pilgrims had slight opportunity to show political genius in their little colony; but their experience in church affairs had given them training for self-government, and they had the English instinct for majority rule. Their institutions were simple, and adapted to immediate needs rather than precedent, principles, or the terms of a charter. Bradford owned Jean Bodin's *Republic,* whose gibes at the communistic "conceits" of Plato he repeats in describing the failure of the "common course" at Plymouth; but that is the only instance in all his writings of interest in political science. He regarded the colony as an overseas Congregational church, and conducted it as such, whenever possible. Writing to the London merchants in

1623, he wished "our friends at Leyden . . . and we be considered as one body." "And indeed if they should not come to us, we would not stay here, if we might gain ever so much wealth" (*American Historical Review,* VIII, 300). Most of them were brought over by 1630, at great expense to the poor colony. Yet the franchise was never restricted to church members, as in Massachusetts-Bay.

Bradford's difficulties during the early years of the colony were greatly augmented by "untowarde persons mixt amongst them from the first," people from various parts of England who were engaged as servants or attached to the colony by the merchants. Some of them, such as Miles Standish, John Alden, and Richard Warren, became "useful Instruments"; others failed to pull their weight, and several were lazy and seditious. Two of the merchants' protégés, Lyford the lewd parson, and Oldham the mad trader, started a dangerous faction. Weston, not content with cheating the Pilgrims in England, came to plague them at Plymouth. Thomas Morton established a disorderly house at their back door, and armed the Indians. Bradford dealt with such people as a genuine Christian and a consummate politician. After much forbearance the greedy and the factious would show themselves up, decamp or be expelled, come to grief, straggle back to Plymouth, beg forgiveness and fresh assistance, receive both, betray their benefactors again, and again come to grief. The Pilgrims always forgave the injury, and recovered from the wound. When, in 1627, Bradford and seven leading Pilgrims bought out the merchant adventurers, and so acquired title to the land, houses, cattle, and implements at Plymouth, they decided, in order to preserve peace and union, to share and share alike with the "mixt multitude"; and distributed land and cattle by a method that "gave all good contente." This stroke of statesmanship placed the colony on a sound economic basis, and assimilated the outsiders to Pilgrim ideals. It created a quasi-corporation known as the "Old Comers" or "Purchasers," which became the governing class of the colony. In religious matters, although Bradford never professed toleration as a principle, his temper was distinctly liberal, for the period. Plymouth Colony passed no law against dissenters until 1650 and was little troubled by them; but Bradford lived to take part in the first legislation against Quakers (*Publications of the Colonial Society of Massachusetts,* XVII, 383).

During his first fifteen years of office, Bradford exercised a more plenary authority than any other English colonial governor between 1619

and 1685. The freemen (signers of the compact and those admitted subsequently to their number) met as a general court, elected the governor and assistants, and passed, sparingly at first, laws and regulations; but in practise they vested almost complete discretionary authority in their governor. Democracy has been read into the Pilgrim government by later historians; it cannot be found in the records, or in Bradford's *History*. In 1623 he declared that the generality were allowed to share in the government "only in some weighty maters, when we thinke good." Twenty years later, there were only 232 freemen in the jurisdiction, out of 634 men bearing arms (*Plymouth Colony Records,* VIII, 173–177; 187–196). The Governor was principal judge, and treasurer until 1637. The right of strangers to sojourn depended largely on his personal consent. As responsible for the business management, first to the merchants and then to the "Old Comers," he superintended agriculture and trade, apportioned the proceeds, and made the annual allotments of land. No distinction was made between executive, legislative, and judicial authority. Whether the Governor should do as he thought best in a given instance, or take the advice of his assistants or other leading freemen, or submit it for discussion or decision to church meeting or general court, depended on his own tact, and on circumstances. "Surely his energy must have been vast, his discretion remarkable, his ability commanding, or those stern and uncompromising men and women would scarcely have permitted him to regulate their affairs so long" (Usher, *The Pilgrims,* 1918, p. 205).

If Bradford had had any love of power or of gain, his opportunity came in 1630, when the "Warwick patent" from the Council for New England made him, and whomsoever he chose to associate with him, proprietors both of jurisdiction and soil. Bradford at once shared his right to the soil with the "Old Comers," and allowed the government to go on as before. In 1636, he was one of a committee which drafted a body of laws, defining the duties of Governor, Assistant, and General Court, requiring trial by jury in all but petty cases, and defining seven capital offenses. These laws of 1636 placed the governorship on a quasi-constitutional basis; yet even after that his position was much more independent than that of Winthrop or Haynes. In 1639 the grand jury of Plymouth evinced some jealousy as to the Old Comers' power to allot land, the Undertakers' monopoly of trade (see below), and the want of a colony treasurer. After considerable debate in the General Court it was decided by mutual consent that Bradford and his associates surrender the Warwick patent to the freemen of the colony, reserving certain tracts of land for themselves. Apart from the Lyford faction, this is the only evidence of discontent with Bradford's rule that can be discovered.

In his business management, Bradford had the common sense to see that the colony would never prosper until its members were given a stake in its prosperity. He recognized that the merchant adventurers had a right to a return on their investment, and strove as best he could to repay them; but, in warm contact as he was with the struggle for existence, he could not altogether avoid the typical pioneer attitude toward financial backers. "At great charges in this adventure, I confess you have beene, and many losses may sustain," he writes the merchants; "but the loss of his (Carver's) and many other honest and industrious mens' lives, cannot be vallewed at any prise." In 1627 the colony's debt of £1,800 to the original merchant adventurers was assumed by Bradford, with seven Pilgrims and four London merchants. These twelve "Undertakers," in return for that burden, were assigned by the Old Comers a monopoly of fishing and trading. Under Bradford's direction the Undertakers pushed these enterprises with great vigor, but indifferent success. Isaac Allerton, their agent in London, and the London partners, corruptly converted most of the profits to their own uses; so that in 1631, after sending over hundreds of pounds' worth of beaver, the Undertakers were £5,771 in debt; and after another ten years' labor, when the Undertakers resigned their monopoly, the Plymouth group still owed £1,200 to the London men. "Thus they were abused in their simplicitie, and . . . sould," writes Bradford. The colony helped them out; but in 1648 Winslow and Prence had to sell their homes; Alden and Standish, 300 acres of land; and Bradford, a farm he owned at Rehoboth, in order to discharge the balance of £400. Bradford must have continued trading on his own account, since the principal items in the inventory of his estate (1657) are debts worth £153 upon the "Dutch account att the Westward" (the Manomet trading post), and goods and debts to the value of £256 in the trading stock at the Kennebec. His house, orchard, and sundry parcels of land at Plymouth, were valued at £45. The rest of the inventory shows that he was far from being the wealthiest man in a colony of slender estates; but had accumulated property comparable to that of the better sort of English yeomen. He left a great silver "beer bowle," two silver wine cups and thirteen spoons, four Venice glasses, sundry pewter pots and flagons, and forty-nine pewter dishes, weighing ninety-seven pounds. His library was the largest at Plymouth except Elder Brewster's. Besides theology it included "divers Duch books," and works by Peter Martyr, Guicciardini, La Primaudaye, John Speed, and Jean Bodin.

Toward new colonies such as Massachusetts-Bay, Bradford held out the hand of fellowship; and the harsh insolence which the Plymouth Colony sometimes received from the Bay authorities, was disarmed by his mild answers, and firm insistence on the rights of Plymouth. He brought the colony into all common enterprises, such as the Pequot war and the New England Confederation; and attended the synod of 1647 at Cambridge, as messenger of the Plymouth Church. He welcomed the great Puritan migration to New England; although, believing as he did in maintaining his colony as a compact community, he regretted the dispersal of population occasioned by the increase of cattle-raising (Bradford, *History*, 1912, II, 151). Probably his influence prevented the recognition as a township of Duxbury, the first offshoot of Plymouth, until 1637. He endeavored, without much success, to induce his people to give proper support to the ministry, and to establish free schools. When the Plymouth church called a distinguished non-conformist, the Rev. Charles Chauncy, to its teaching eldership, Bradford encouraged his abortive project of founding a Plymouth rival to Harvard College. The study of Hebrew, "that most ancient language, and holy tongue, in which the Law and Oracles of God were write; and in which God, and angels, spake to the holy patriarks, of old time," consoled the Governor in his old age, and thinking and writing about the heroic first decade afforded him great satisfaction. He died on May 9/19, 1657, believing that the glory was departed from Plymouth Colony.

Bradford married at Amsterdam, Dec. 10, 1613, Dorothy May, daughter of a member of the English Church there (*Mayflower Descendant*, IX, 115–17). She was drowned in Cape Cod harbor, Dec. 7/17, 1620. Their only son, John, afterward came to Plymouth, married, and died without issue. Alice (Carpenter), widow of Edward Southworth, a former member of the Leyden church, arrived at Plymouth in the *Anne* with her two small boys, in July 1623; Bradford married her on August 14. By this marriage, he had a daughter and two sons, William (1624–1704) and Joseph (1630–1715) whose descendants are now numbered by the thousand.

Bradford began to write his *History of Plimmoth Plantation* (sometimes idiotically called the "Log of the *Mayflower*"), about 1630, and probably completed Book I, down to the landing at

Plymouth, within a year or two. Book II, which carries the story through 1646, was written between that year and 1650; the list of *Mayflower* passengers at the end, in 1651. He drew chiefly upon his own memory, but used a letter-book of correspondence, and his own rough notes and journal of the first year of settlement. Bradford was not writing for publication, and included matters which even in his day could not have been printed. He probably intended the book to be handed down in his family, as a perpetual monument to a high enterprise. His English is that of an educated, though not a learned man, deeply versed in the Geneva (not the King James) version of the Bible. It is not without conscious art, for he freely employs alliteration, and other conscious devices of contemporary English literature (E. F. Bradford, in *New England Quarterly*, I, 133–56). Touches of humor and irony enliven a plain story. Certain passages are worthy of Clarendon or Milton. But the peculiar quality of the work is imparted by the beauty, simplicity, and sincerity of the author's character. Although the *History* was not printed in full until 1856, the manuscript was used by colonial historians such as Morton, Hubbard, Prince, and Hutchinson, and Book I was printed in 1841, from a manuscript copy in the Plymouth church records. Directly and indirectly, it has been responsible for giving the Pilgrims and their colony the prominent place they occupy in American history, and popular tradition. There is no authority in Bradford for the sentimental and excessive claims that have been made for the Pilgrims; but there is ample ground for his own faith in their high mission.

[Bradford's *Hist. of Plimmoth Plantation* is the principal source for his life. The cheapest complete edition is the one issued by the Commonwealth of Massachusetts in 1897 and still (1927) in print (Secretary of State's office, State House, Boston). The best is the one published by the Mass. Hist. Soc. (2 vols., 1912), with valuable notes by Worthington C. Ford. The interesting history of the MS. which now reposes in the State Lib. at Boston is told in every edition. A complete facsimile of it, edited by J. H. Doyle, was published in London, 1896. A surviving fragment of Bradford's letterbook, covering the years 1624–30, is printed in *Colls. Mass. Hist. Soc.*, ser. 1, vol. III, pp. 27–84 and as a pamphlet by the Mass. Soc. of Mayflower Descendants (1906). "Mourt's Relation" (*A Relation . . . of the English Plantation Settled at Plymouth*, London, 1622), including parts of Bradford's journal; and Winslow's *Good News from New England* (1624) are reprinted with other source material in E. Arber, *The Story of the Pilgrim Fathers* (1897), and A. Young, *Chronicles of the Pilgrim Fathers* (1841); *Good News* is also in *Mayflower Descendant*, XXV–XXVI; Bradford's letters to Governor Winthrop are printed in *Colls. Mass. Hist. Soc.*, ser. 4, vol. VI, pp. 156–61; an important letter of 1623 in *Am. Hist. Rev.*, VIII, 294–301. His first "Dialogue between some young men born in New England and sundry ancient men that came out of Holland" is printed in the Plymouth Church Records (*Pubs. Colonial Soc., Mass.*, XXII, 115–41), in Young's *Chroni-*

cles, and in *Old South Leaflets*, II, no. 49. The second Dialogue has disappeared; the third Dialogue, together with Bradford's long descriptive poem of 1654 and "A Word to New Plymouth," is in *Proc. Mass. Hist. Soc.*, XI, 396–482. "A Word to New England" and "Of Boston in New-England" are in the *Colls. Mass. Hist. Soc.*, ser. 3, vol. VII, pp. 27–8. His will and inventory are in *Mayfl. Desc.*, II, 228–34; his marriage records *Ibid.*, IX, 115–17. The *Plymouth Colony Records* (12 vols., Boston, 1855–61) are an important source. There is no good biography of Bradford. A fresh and enlightening study of the Plymouth Colony is that of R. G. Usher, *The Pilgrims and Their History* (1918); the principal older works are listed in Channing, Hart, and Turner's Guide, §§128–31.]   S. E. M.

BRADFORD, WILLIAM (May 20, 1663– May 23, 1752), pioneer printer of the English middle colonies, was the son of William and Anne Bradford, humble folk of the Established Church in the parish of Barnwell, Leicestershire, England, where he was born. He was apprenticed to Andrew Sowle, chief London Quaker printer, and united with his master's sect. On Apr. 28, 1685, in London, he married his master's daughter, Elizabeth, who died in New York, July 8, 1731, aged sixty-eight years. Bradford afterward married the widow Cornelia Smith, through whose relatives he suffered pecuniary losses. The assumption that he accompanied Penn to America in 1682 seems untenable, notwithstanding claim on his tombstone. Hildeburn (James G. Wilson, *Memorial History of New York*, I, 572) declares that another of the name then came, who attained some local importance in Sussex (now part of Delaware) County. Our Bradford, on leaving London with Penn's consent, in 1685, brought over a letter recommendatory from George Fox. It appears that Bradford and his wife resided temporarily at Philadelphia on their arrival late that year, but that soon residence and printery were removed to Oxford township, where the domicile continued until removal to New York, whilst the press was reëstablished at Philadelphia in 1688, where Bradford added a bookstore. The first issue of his press, in 1685, was an almanac by Samuel Atkins, in which Penn was dubbed "Lord Penn," an offense for which Bradford was reprimanded and ordered to print no more without license by the council (*Pennsylvania Colonial Records*, I, 165). In 1687 he was warned not to print anything about the Quakers without their official consent. He was reprehended by Gov. John Blackwell and his council, in 1689, for printing Penn's charter. So, harassed by both civil and religious leaders and disappointed in the unproductiveness of his press and the lack of encouragement in his pet scheme to print an English Bible in 1688, he transferred his press to his "assignes" and, on receiving a certificate of removal in July 1689, returned to England. Better encouragement from the Yearly

Meeting induced him to return and resume his press. In 1690 he was associated in founding the first paper-mill in English America. In 1692 he was released from his official printing contract, and became involved in the turbulence that had arisen from the schism led by George Keith, whose propaganda he forwarded by the press. Bradford was arrested; his types, paper, and other things were seized by the sheriff. The case is enmeshed in conflicting partisan statements. A summation seems to show that he refused to furnish security for his recognizance, so was committed in a dwelling, but allowed considerable freedom. At his trial he pleaded his own cause with great skill, maintaining the right of peremptory challenge of biased jurors in a libel action, and that the burden of proof was upon his prosecutors, whilst the jurors were judges of law as well as of fact. At a subsequent term he pleaded not guilty; and the jury,—out forty-eight hours,—not agreeing, he was discharged. On Apr. 28, 1693, Gov. Fletcher ordered the restoration of his seized property. Meanwhile, on Mar. 23, 1693, the New York council, under Fletcher's direction, offered inducements for a printer to come to New York, to print the acts of assembly and other official papers, and have the benefit of serving the public. Bradford accepted the offer and was established as "Printer to King William and Queen Mary." His first warrant for salary was retroactive to Apr. 10, 1693. From 1693 to 1724 he printed more than 250 pieces, and from 1725 to 1743 about 150 more. In the beginning, his issues were mainly public documents and religious controversial pamphlets, but after 1710 they were more varied. Bradford was admitted a freeman of New York in 1695, and the same year began to print the "Votes" of the assembly, which were the earliest legislative proceedings to be printed in America. In 1694, 1710, 1713, 1716, and 1726, he printed collections of New York laws. He printed the first New York paper currency (May 31, 1709), the first American Book of Common Prayer (1710), the first drama written in English America (1714), the first history of New York (1727), and the first copperplate plan of New York (Lyne's survey, undated, but 1730). He was a vestryman of Trinity Church, 1703–10; official printer to New Jersey, 1703–33, with slight interruption, and clerk of New Jersey, 1711. In his sixty-third year, he began New York's first newspaper, the *New-York Gazette,* Nov. 8, 1725 (earliest issue extant No. 18), which apparently expired on Nov. 19, 1744. Until 1733 it was the only newspaper in New York. It was never a well-edited product. Foreign news copy predomi-

nated and advertising was sparse. Journalism was for Bradford a losing venture. Having been printer to the Crown under four reigns, he retired in 1742, in his eightieth year, succeeded by his former apprentice, James Parker. He lived in retirement with his son, William, at New York, until his sudden death on the evening of May 23, 1752. Parker (*Post-Boy,* May 25, 1752) paid high tribute to Bradford as "a Man of great Sobriety and Industry;—a real Friend to the Poor and Needy; and kind and affable to all . . . his Temperance was exceedingly conspicuous, and he was almost a Stranger to sickness all his Life." No portrait of Bradford exists. His first tombstone was damaged and removed to the New York Historical Society, whilst a new one of Italian marble was dedicated in Trinity churchyard, May 20, 1863, and that night an august celebration took place in Cooper Institute. The Bradford Club was named for him in 1859. The Grolier Club, in April 1893, paid him tribute in a "Bradford Exhibition." On Nov. 8, 1925, journalists and printers celebrated the founding of his newspaper, and in 1926 there was formed the William Bradford Memorial Fellowship in Journalism. There are historical markers on the sites of his printing shops, at 81 Pearl St., and in Hanover Square.

[A collation of a great variety of conflicting statements in the following books and articles is imperative for the elimination of error: *Antiquarian Researches,* by Nathan Kite (Manchester, 1844), reprinted from the *Friend,* vols. XVI and XVII (Phila., 1843); Memoir of Bradford in the *Home Jour.,* Feb. 14, 1852, anonymous; "Wm. Bradford," by W. B., in *Hist. Mag.,* III (1859), 171 ff.; *Address at Celebration, May 20, 1863,* by John Wm. Wallace (1863), the fullest biography, in which real facts are hidden in a mass of pedantry and irrelevancy; chapter headed "Of Persecution and Prosecution" in *News of a Trumpet sounding in the Wilderness,* by Daniel Leeds (N. Y., 1697), and for Bradford's birth date *Am. Almanack,* 1739, of Titan Leeds, under May 20. The following works of Chas. R. Hildeburn are indispensable: *A Century of Printing: the Issues of the Press in Pa.,* vol. I (1885); *List of the Issues of the Press in N. Y.* (1889); chap. XV in Wilson's *Memorial Hist. of N. Y.,* vol. I (1891), containing facts not found elsewhere; *Cat. of Books Printed by Wm. Bradford* (1893); *Sketches of Printers and Printing in Colonial N. Y.* (1895); see also I. N. P. Stokes, *The Iconography of Manhattan Island,* chronology and appendix, vol. IV (1922).] V. H. P.

BRADFORD, WILLIAM (Jan. 19, 1721/22–Sept. 25, 1791), "patriot-printer of 1776," was born in Hanover Square, New York City, the son of William Bradford and his wife Sytje, daughter of Abraham Santvoort, and the grandson of William Bradford [*q.v.*], the pioneer printer of the English middle colonies. He was also a nephew of Andrew Bradford [*q.v.*] of Philadelphia, founder of the first newspaper in the middle colonies, by whom he was taught the art of typography and then taken into a partnership (1739–40). In 1741 our Bradford went to London to visit relatives and improve his opportunities as a printer and bookseller. Upon his return to Philadelphia in 1742, having imported the furnishings for a printery as well as the stock for a bookstore he set up in business, calling it "The Sign of the Bible." On Aug. 15 of this year he married Rachel Budd, daughter of Thomas Budd, of Northampton Township, Burlington County, N. J., and thereby gained much prestige. On Dec. 2, 1742, he issued the first number of a newspaper, under the title of the *Weekly Advertiser, or Pennsylvania Journal,* which in time became one of the best printed as well as most widely circulated of newspapers in America and, save for two suspensions during the American Revolution, continued to be printed by Bradford or his son Thomas [*q.v.*], or in partnership, until Sept. 18, 1793 (last known issue, according to Brigham). In establishing this paper Bradford became a rival of Benjamin Franklin, who for some years had been publishing the *Pennsylvania Gazette,* then a rather poor affair. From 1748 to 1753 Bradford printed a number of treatises or sermons of Gilbert Tennent and Hervey's *Meditations* (1750) in two volumes. In 1754 he established at the corner of Front and Market Streets a London Coffee-House for Merchants and Traders, which for years was a noted resort and the Merchants Exchange of his city. Not deterred by an intercolonial war, Bradford established in October 1757 the *American Magazine and Monthly Chronicle,* a literary periodical representing loyalty to the British Crown and "the Church of England and the Proprietary side of things," which lasted through October 1758. Under a similar title he and his son Thomas, from January to September 1769, printed *The American Magazine, or General Repository,* edited by Lewis Nichola. Although busy as a printer, journalist, bookseller, keeper of a coffee-house, and otherwise, Bradford found time to be a social leader. In 1762, in partnership with John Kidd, he established the Philadelphia Insurance Company, a successful venture of which he was principal manager. His bookstore went to better quarters in 1764, adjoining his coffee-house, so that he then controlled a group of businesses in a number of adjoining buildings. From 1760 to 1765 some two dozen publications issued from his press, comprising politics, religion, and literature, in fairly good proportions. In 1742 to 1823, the printery he established continued under him or his family as one of the principal publishing houses of the country.

When in 1747–48 Philadelphia was threatened by war and her shipping was in danger, Bradford became a lieutenant in a volunteer company of "Associators." It was his first military connection. In 1756, the country being at war, he was again in arms and was promoted to a captaincy. He was an uncompromising opponent of the Stamp Act of 1765. The day before the act took effect he issued his newspaper (Oct. 31) in mourning, with skull and crossbones, and denounced the measure in print as "the detestable Stamp Act, which no American can mention without abhorrence." As a member of the Sons of Liberty he demanded its repeal. He was a signer of the Non-Importation Resolutions of 1765. He was an early advocate for a continental congress, and in his newspaper, July 27, 1774, expressed the need by a dissected snake device and the words "Unite or Die," which device his paper carried till October 1775. When the first Congress met at Philadelphia in September, Bradford and his son were made its printers. In January 1775 he was active in the Convention of Pennsylvania, which defended "the rights and liberties of America." Bradford realized war was inevitable. He became captain of a company of the "Associators" of 1775, advancing money for military needs. After Bunker Hill he was more defiant. In June 1776 he was despatched by the Continental Congress with wagons and money for the army in Canada. After the Declaration of Independence he joined the patriot army at Amboy. Although fifty-six years of age and really exempt, and notwithstanding he had a wife and family and large business interests of benefit to his country, he became major of the second battalion of the Pennsylvania militia (July 1776), in the brigade of Gen. John Cadwalader, and reached the rank of colonel. He was in the campaign of Trenton and was severely wounded at the battle of Princeton. In 1777 he was named chairman of the Pennsylvania State Navy Board and from January 1778 he alone conducted its affairs until the board was abolished. He retired from active service after the British evacuation of Philadelphia in June 1778. His health was shattered and his personal affairs were greatly injured by the war. It is said that "full seven-eights of his credits were worthless." On May 12, 1779, he was appointed president of the court of inquiry respecting military officers, his last army connection. By his wife Rachel (b. Jan. 7, 1720/1; d. June 25 or 26, 1780), he had six children, three sons and three daughters. Although Bradford had suffered severely in body and fortune, he frequently said to his children, "Though I bequeath you no estate I leave you in the enjoyment of liberty" (Isaiah Thomas, *History of Printing in America,* 1810, II, 50). In his latter days he was afflicted by three apoplectic strokes, affecting his mind, and on Sept. 25, 1791, "he died as a child falls asleep, and the springs of nature quite worn out, the machine stopped."

[The principal source is a good volume biography, *An Old Philadelphian,* by John W. Wallace (1884), of which only 100 copies were printed. Of secondary account are: *Bradford Family* (1873), by S. S. Purple, pp. 5–6; *Bradford Family* (1906), by Henry Darrach, p. 6; "The Bradford Family of Printers," by H. L. Bullen, in the *Am. Collector,* I (1926), pp. 166–68. Details on his newspaper are in Clarence S. Brigham's "Bibliography of Am. Newspapers," pt. XIII, *Proc. Am. Antiquarian Soc.,* 1922, pp. 168–75. C. R. Hildeburn's *A Century of Printing; the Issues of the Press in Pa.* (1885) has the fullest record of Bradford's productive press.]   V. H. P.

BRADFORD, WILLIAM (Sept. 14, 1755– Aug. 23, 1795), jurist, was the great-grandson of William Bradford [*q.v.*], who introduced printing into the American middle colonies and the son of William Bradford [*q.v.*] the so-called "patriot-printer of 1776," and his wife Rachel Budd. Born in Philadelphia he was educated at Princeton, N. J., 1769–72 (A.B.)— 1775 (A.M.). The following year he spent in reading and in attending the lectures of Dr. Witherspoon on theology to profit by his logical method. He studied law under Edward Shippen, afterward chief justice of Pennsylvania, writing prose and verse with Addison and Shenstone as his models, while he read his Coke. His tastes were for civil rather than for military life, but like his father he patriotically answered the call of America in the Revolution. Volunteering as a private in 1776, he soon became major of brigade to Gen. Roberdeau and later a captain in Col. Hampton's continental regiment. He was elected by Congress, Apr. 10, 1777, deputy muster-master general with the rank of colonel in the Continental Army. After serving during the critical years 1777–79 at Valley Forge, White Plains, Fredericksborough, and Raritan, his broken health forced him to resign Apr. 1, 1779. Returning to his legal studies he was admitted to the bar of the supreme court of Pennsylvania and made his home at Yorktown, Pa., in 1779. At the early age of twenty-five, and but a year after he began to practise law, he was appointed through the influence of the president of the state, Joseph Reed, to succeed Jonathan D. Sergeant as attorney-general of Pennsylvania. For eleven consecutive years and under different administrations he retained this office. His contemporaries considered him a lawyer of high tone, eloquent, and of great

purity of life and purpose. With Joseph Reed, James Wilson, and J. D. Sergeant, he pleaded and won the case of Pennsylvania against Connecticut before the Congressional Commission in the Wyoming land titles contention in 1782. Promoted, Aug. 22, 1791, by Gov. Mifflin, to be justice of the supreme bench of Pennsylvania, he attracted the notice of Washington, who, on Jan. 28, 1794, made him the second attorney-general of the United States in the place of Edmund Randolph promoted to the secretaryship of state. Washington valued Bradford as a personal friend and as a lawyer, and it was upon his report as one of the commissioners appointed by the President to attempt an amicable settlement of the "Whisky Insurrection" by conferences at Pittsburgh that Washington issued his proclamation of force "to secure the execution of the laws" when these peaceful efforts failed. Bradford and his wife, Susan Vergereau Boudinot, only daughter of Elias Boudinot [*q.v.*] of New Jersey, were intimates in the Washington circle, the so-called "Republican Court," and Bradford had formed in his student days a warm friendship with James Madison. Secretaries Pickering and Wolcott sought Bradford, ill at his country home, to aid them in formulating the letter which brought Washington from Mount Vernon to consider the indiscretions of Edmund Randolph as secretary of state in his dealings with the French minister Fauchet. It was from the exhaustion of dealing with this controversy and from the arduous trips at night to "Rose Hill," the country seat of his father-in-law, that Bradford contracted the fatal fever that led to his unexpected and untimely end. He influenced the revision of the criminal jurisprudence of Pennsylvania by his report of Dec. 3, 1792, which, spread upon the journals of the Pennsylvania Senate (Feb. 22, 1793), led to the statute of Apr. 22, 1794, which substituted "imprisonment at hard labor" for the death penalty for all capital crimes "except murder of the first degree." The Report was subsequently published in book form and was widely read. Bradford was buried in St. Mary's Churchyard at Burlington, N. J.

[Horace Binney Wallace, sketch in the *Am. Law Jour.,* Apr. 1852 (reprinted in J. W. Wallace's *An Old Philadelphian,* 1884, pp. 482–87); R. W. Griswold, *The Republican Court* (1856), pp. 298n., 300, 303, 310n., 335, 338 and note, 339.]   J. C. B.

BRADFORD, WILLIAM (Apr. 30, 1823– Apr. 25, 1892), marine painter, was born in Fairhaven, Mass., which is only about one mile distant from New Bedford. He was the son of Melvin and Hannah (Kempton) Bradford. The Bradfords were a Quaker family and in this faith William was brought up. All of his biographers refer to his mother as being of excellent character and strong religious convictions, and he himself is said to have attributed one of his most effective traits as an artist—patience—to the self-control and calmness which are required by the Society of Friends. In 1846 he was married to Mary Breed, an estimable and accomplished woman, the daughter of Nathan Breed of Lynn, Mass., who was also of old New England Quaker stock. From early youth Bradford had had an inclination toward art but it was not until eight years after his marriage that his career as an artist was begun. At that time he and his father, who were in business together, failed, and to make a livelihood he turned to painting pictures of ships in Lynn and other harbors. The correctness of his work and the carefulness with which it was rendered won him reputation and secured purchasers. From this he passed to studies of the coast, the rocks, and sea on the New England and Canadian shore, going as far north as Labrador. For two years he shared his studio at Fairhaven with Albert Van Beest, a Dutch painter and ex-officer of the Dutch navy—a man of education and training but of no great talent. Bradford made an Arctic expedition with Dr. Hayes and at one time he himself chartered a vessel and went to Labrador where, clad in the sealskin coat of the Eskimo, he made studies of icebergs and ice-floes. These paintings were done with great fidelity to detail, were realistic, accurate, and most carefully rendered. To-day they would be described as photographic and hard, but they brought to those who saw them then a truthful impression of what the artist himself had seen.

Exhibitions of Bradford's paintings were held in Providence and other cities in the United States and also in England. One of his paintings, "Steamer *Panther* among Icebergs and Field-Ice in Melville Bay, under the light of the Midnight Sun," was purchased by Queen Victoria and exhibited, with her permission, at the Royal Academy in 1875. Among his other patrons in England were the Marchioness of Lorne and the Baroness Burdett Coutts. One of his paintings entitled "Arctic Whaler Homeward Bound" is in the permanent collection of the Art Institute of Chicago. Another, "Tracking a Whaler through Icebergs in Baffin's Bay," is in the permanent collection of the New Bedford Free Public Library. Among his other recorded works are "Fishing Boats in the Bay of Fundy," "Ship-wreck off Nantucket," "Lighthouse in St. John's Harbor," "Fishing Boats

getting Under Way," "Island of Grand Manan," "Fishing Boats at Anchor," "A Sudden Squall in the Bay of Fundy," "Swift Breeze in the Harbor of Eastport," "The Coast of Labrador," "Crushed by Icebergs," "Scenes in the North" and "Arctic Scene," the last exhibited at the National Academy of Design, New York, in 1896.

[H. T. Tuckerman, *Book of the Artists* (1867); Samuel Isham, *Hist. of Am. Painting* (1905); *Art Jour.*, XXV, 255; Austin Jones, article on Bradford in the *Am. Friend*, Dec. 20, 1900; Geneal. Records in the Free Pub. Lib., New Bedford, Mass.; *N. Y. Times*, Apr. 26, 1892.]   L. M.

BRADISH, LUTHER (Sept. 15, 1783–Aug. 30, 1863), diplomat and statesman, was born in Cummington, Hampshire County, Mass., son of Col. John and Hannah (Warner) Bradish. He was descended from Robert Bradish, who settled in Cambridge, Mass., in 1635. Graduating from Williams College in 1804, he went to New York and combined teaching with the study of law until his admission to the bar. Soon after this the collection of a large claim necessitated a trip to South America, the West Indies, and the British Isles. He returned to the United States in time to serve as a volunteer in the War of 1812. In 1814 he married Helen Elizabeth, daughter of George Gibbs of Newport, R. I., but two years later both she and their only child died. In 1820 John Quincy Adams, then secretary of state, requested him to sound the disposition of the Turkish Government regarding a treaty with the United States which would open the Black Sea to American trade. Provided with no authority beyond a special passport, he crossed the Atlantic on the *Columbus,* flagship of Commodore Bainbridge, and made the circuit of the western Mediterranean with the United States squadron. Supposedly engaged on a secret mission, he was dismayed by rumors current in every port that he was authorized to negotiate a treaty with the Porte. A dispatch vessel took him from Gibraltar to Smyrna, whence he went by land to Constantinople. There he was well received in diplomatic circles and held conversations with high Turkish officials. The latter, however, were unwilling to commit themselves on the prospect of an American negotiation, and temporized until the first mutterings of the Greek Revolution destroyed all hope of a definite answer. Convinced that that indecision of the Porte was due to a desire to curry favor with European powers hostile to the entry of a new rival into the Levant trade, Bradish advised that any attempt on the part of the United States to negotiate a treaty should be made without the customary intervention of a nation already represented at Constantinople. This procedure was successfully followed by Charles Rhind in 1830. After spending several months in Constantinople, Bradish visited Egypt and became personally acquainted with Mehemet Ali, the Pasha. Crossing the desert to Palestine, he traveled through Syria, returned to Constantinople by sea, and continued to Vienna on horseback. Until 1826 he remained in Europe, extending his travels to Scandinavia and Russia, while he spent considerable time in the great capitals and studied assiduously their languages, manners, and antiquities. On his return to America he resided in Franklin County, New York, where he owned extensive properties. After playing a prominent part in Philhellene activities, he was elected to the state Assembly as a Whig. This position he held from 1827 to 1830, and again from 1835 to 1838. Chosen speaker of the Assembly in 1838, he was in the same year elected lieutenant-governor. During the two terms that he held this office he established a remarkable reputation as a parliamentarian while presiding over the Senate, and as member of the court for correction of errors came off victorious in a dispute with the supreme court of the state. In 1842 he was the unsuccessful Whig nominee for governor, but was immediately appointed assistant United States treasurer for New York by his intimate friend, President Fillmore. After two years he retired from politics and devoted himself to educational and philanthropic interests in New York City, where he made his home after 1842. In 1849 he succeeded Albert Gallatin as president of the New York Historical Society and held the office until his death. He was also for many years president of the American Bible Society. By a second marriage in 1839 to Mary Eliza Hart of New York he had one daughter. His broad culture, urbane disposition, and eminent public services gained universal respect. He died suddenly at Newport, R. I.

[Sketches in the *Eclectic Mag.*, Sept. 1863, and in *Memorial Biogs. of the New Eng. Hist. and Geneal. Soc.*, V, 268–76; Bradish's report to Adams in *House Exec. Doc. No. 250*, 22 Cong., 1 Sess.; his papers (eleven boxes) in the Lib. of the N. Y. Hist. Soc.]
W. L. W—t.

BRADLEY, CHARLES HENRY (Feb. 13, 1860–Jan. 30, 1922), educator, was born in Johnson, Vt., the son of Harmon Howe and Sarah Grout (Ferguson) Bradley, and a descendant of Stephen Bradley, of Guilford, Conn. He was educated in the local public schools and at the State Normal School in his native village. At the age of twenty, he moved to Massachusetts as instructor in the State Primary School,

at Palmer, of which, in 1885, he was made assistant superintendent. In March 1888 he was made head of the Farm and Trades School, an institution established in 1814 on Thompson's Island in Boston Harbor for the purpose of providing homes and education for worthy boys in destitute circumstances. In this position he remained for thirty-four years.

The Farm and Trades School, with its 157 acres of land, was the first institution of its kind in this country to make agriculture the basis of its educational policy. It was already successful when Bradley took charge of it, but he soon, through the improvements which he initiated, gave it a national reputation. He held there the first sloyd classes in the United States. He enlarged the curriculum to include such practical subjects as iron and metal work, shoe repairing, stationary engineering, and typewriting, so that each boy was equipped to earn his living by a trade. Nearly ten years before the George Junior Republic, Bradley started a boys' government plan, called "Cottage Row City," which was in successful operation for many years. He set up, in 1905, a meteorological observatory, which was later connected with the United States Weather Bureau. In the same year he visited Europe on a tour of inspection of similar schools, only to find that he was usually the teacher instead of the listener.

Bradley's innovations drew many visitors to Thompson's Island. He was offered positions as head of the New York State Reformatory in Elmira, N. Y., and as head of the House of Refuge in New York City, but preferred to remain in Boston. He was a founder and the first president of the Vermont Association of Boston. Norwich University gave him the honorary degree of Master of Arts in 1911, and he was later one of its trustees. He was a member of many patriotic organizations, including the Society of Colonial Wars, the Sons of the American Revolution, the Bostonian Society, and the New England Historical and Genealogical Society; and active in the Masonic Order. He was married on June 7, 1883, to Mary Chilton Brewster, of Duxbury, Mass., eighth in direct descent from Elder William Brewster.

[Excellent memoir in the *New Eng. Hist. and Geneal. Reg.*, LXXVII (1923), lx; also good obituary in the *Boston Evening Transcript*, Jan. 30, 1922.] C. M. F.

BRADLEY, CHARLES WILLIAM (June 27, 1807–Mar. 8, 1865), diplomat, Sinologist, was a descendant of a family which had lived in New England at least since 1640. He was the son of Luther and Mary (Atwater) Bradley, and was born at New Haven, Conn. As a youth he began to learn printing, but abandoned this to enter Washington (now Trinity) College, Hartford, Conn., in 1825. He withdrew before graduation, however, and continued his studies at the General Theological Seminary, New York City, completing his course in 1830, and later receiving an honorary M.A. both from Trinity and from Yale, as well as an LL.D. from Hobart College in 1846. Shortly before leaving the Seminary, a fall gave a shock to his nervous system which permanently affected his health, making him a victim of restlessness, excitability, and repeated morbid depressions. Nevertheless, he was for ten years rector of Episcopal parishes in North Haven, East Haddam, Sharon, and Derby, Conn., but the work proved to be too hard for him, and he passed the next few years in enforced idleness. In 1846–47 he was secretary of state for Connecticut, and in this capacity he collated, indexed, and arranged the state records in a manner which rendered them more generally accessible, besides preparing *The Connecticut Register: being an Official State Calendar of Public Officers and Institutions in Connecticut for 1847* (1848). After two years of foreign travel (1847–49), Bradley began his real career, which centered in China and lasted fourteen years (1849–63). His first brief position with a mercantile firm was severed because of his opposition to any connection with the opium traffic, and he then entered the United States Government service, being consul at Amoy (1849–54), Singapore (1854–57), and Ningpo (1857–60), respectively. In 1857 he brought back to the United States a treaty with Siam, returning with its ratification; in 1858 he accompanied the Pei-ho expedition at the request of Mr. Reed, the United States minister to China; and in 1859 he was the senior member of the Commission on American Claims against the Chinese Government. Feeling, however, that his services had not been duly recognized by his Government, he resigned from the service in 1860 and paid a brief visit to the United States, but soon returned to China, where he was an assistant in the Imperial Chinese Customs at Hankow until 1863. In this latter year, his health utterly broken, he retired to his native city, where he died.

As his career shows, Bradley's interests and activities were rather wide. In his diplomatic career he manifested all due firmness regarding the interests of his government, while opposing whatever he regarded as infringing on Chinese rights. He collected a fairly large library, of which the Oriental section was, naturally, the more valuable; but his nervous afflic-

tion forbade any extensive literary activity, though he gave his knowledge freely to other scholars. Besides the work already mentioned, he seems to have published only two brief studies: *Patronomatology*, a portion of a treatise on the philosophy of surnames, read before the Connecticut State Lyceum, and arising from his interest in the history of proper names (Baltimore, 1842), and an "Outline of the System adopted for Romanizing the [Chinese] Dialect of Amoy" (*Journal of the American Oriental Society*, IV, 1854, pp. 335–40); and he also presented to the same society a paper on "The Kings and Kingdom of Siam" (*Ibid.*, VI, 1859, p. 583), which was never printed in full. He bequeathed his Oriental library to the American Oriental Society, to which he had already given more than 850 books and manuscripts, and for the same society he collected over $1,000, primarily for the purchase of Chinese type, which still forms the nucleus of its "Charles W. Bradley Type Fund."

[*Proc. Am. Oriental Soc.*, May 1865, pp. 60–62, Oct. 1871, p. 28; *New Eng. Hist. and Geneal. Reg.*, XXII (1868), 360–61.]   L. H. G.

BRADLEY, DENIS MARY (Feb. 25, 1846– Dec. 13, 1903), Roman Catholic bishop, was born in County Kerry, Ireland, of sturdy, laboring parentage. On the death of his father, his mother in 1854 brought her young brood to Manchester, N. H., where she maintained a humble home by taking in boarders and working as a seamstress. The boy's schooling, aside from the religious training of the home, was left to New Hampshire's pioneer Catholic master, Thomas Cochran. In 1864, Bradley matriculated at Holy Cross College in Worcester, receiving his bachelor's degree three years later from Georgetown College, as Holy Cross was not chartered to give degrees. He was no "poor scholar," for his mother by scrimping had hoarded three hundred golden dollars, then at high premium, to pay his modest expenses. Inspired with a religious calling, the young man entered St. Joseph's Seminary at Troy, N. Y., where after four years in cloistered study of theology, he was ordained on July 3, 1871, by Bishop Bernard McQuade of Rochester. Bradley's superior, Rt. Rev. David W. Bacon, first bishop of Portland, named the young neophyte a curate at the cathedral; for him a pleasant location because his sister was prioress of the neighboring Mercy Convent. Interested in Father Mathew's temperance movement, Bradley won the friendship of Neal Dow, who fathered the Maine prohibition law. In 1879, Bradley said the first Mass in the State Reform School, which evidenced his popularity with the non-Catholics of Portland even more than did their generosity in subscribing a share of the purse to give the priest his first vacation. After his return from abroad, he was appointed pastor of St. Joseph's Church in Manchester by Bishop James A. Healy. During the French-Canadian influx into New England, Manchester was separated from the Portland diocese, in 1884, and was given its own episcopal see. Nominated by the New England bishops, Bradley was appointed to the new diocese and consecrated by the saintly Archbishop John J. Williams of Boston. The youngest bishop in America, Bradley was well fitted for the appointment. He knew and loved the state. Of medium height and slender build, he was of a rigorous constitution. This was well, for journeyings to and ministrations in every scattered hamlet tested his metal and vitality. He was gracious and dignified, meeting the world with a sweet smile and a bright eye. Though of deep voice, he was no orator, nor was he a scholar. His sermons, however, simple and sincere, touched his hearers. When nativist opposition or factory strife demanded attention, he met the situation with a firm moderation which satisfied his priests and co-religionists and won the approval of fair-minded men. It was as the architect of his diocese, as an administrator and builder, as a supporter of Catholic schools, as a friend of labor, and as a competent business man, that the bishop did his real service.

[M. H. Dowd, *Life of Denis M. Bradley* (n.d.) ; John E. Finen *et al.*, *Hist. of the Cath. Ch. in New Eng.* (1899) ; G. C. Delany, *Life and Writings of John B. Delany* (1911) ; G. F. Willey, *Book of Manchester* (1896) ; Henry Gabriels, *Hist. Sketch of St. Joseph's Provincial Seminary, Troy, N. Y.* (1905) ; *Cath. Encyc.* under "New Hampshire"; *Daily Patriot* (Concord, N. H.), Dec. 14, 1903.]   R.J.P.

BRADLEY, FRANK HOWE (Sept. 20, 1838–Mar. 27, 1879), geologist, was born in New Haven, Conn., graduated at Yale in 1863, and later took special courses in natural history in the Sheffield Scientific School. His tastes early took a geological trend and in 1857, while not yet nineteen years of age, he had discovered a new species of trilobite in the Potsdam sandstone of New York and proved the existence of crinoids in beds of the same horizon. After graduation he spent more than a year at Panama and vicinity where he made large collections of coral and other zoölogical materials. During 1867 he was assistant geologist on the survey of Illinois under J. G. Norwood and in 1869 served likewise on the survey of Indiana under Edward Travers Cox. A paper prepared by him on the Carboniferous rocks of Vermillion County was

commented upon by Dana as a "valuable chapter" in the report of that year. In 1872 he became a member of the National Survey under F. V. Hayden and was assigned to the Snake River division in Idaho. "Among his important results, as set forth in his excellent report, there is the identification of fossils of the Quebec group in Idaho, and also at the base of the Teton range" (J. D. Dana). From 1869 to 1875 he held the chair of geology and mineralogy in the University of Tennessee, and while there made a detailed section of the unaltered Lower Silurian formations and the beds of crystalline rocks to the east, publishing his results under the caption "On the Silurian Age of the Southern Appalachians" in the *American Journal of Science* for 1876. The same year he also published a small geological map of the United States. He eventually gave up his position at Knoxville to undertake private mining ventures in the hope of securing a competence sufficient to allow him to follow his scientific calling untrammelled by financial difficulties. It was while thus engaged that he met his tragic fate, being killed by the caving in of a gold mine near Nacoochee, Ga., in which he was at work.

He is described as "a man of profound zeal for science, of exactness in observation, of great energy, and of independent judgment and purpose." He was tall, of erect figure, neat in dress, but after a fashion dictated by his work and not by prevalent modes, in this indicating his independence of character. "His lines of action were laid down by his sense of what was just and once fixed there was no swerving." He was often accused of obstinacy, and in his work met with more opposition or friction than would otherwise have been the case. He was married in 1867 to Sarah M. Bolles of New Haven by whom he had two children, a daughter and an infant son that died on the day of his own death.

[J. D. Dana, "Frank Howe Bradley," *Am. Jour. Sci.*, May 1879, pp. 415–19.]   G.P.M.

BRADLEY, JOHN EDWIN (Aug. 8, 1839–Oct. 7, 1912), college president, the son of Stephen and Hannah (Austin) Bradley, was born in Lee, Mass., and was graduated from Williams College in 1865. After three years as principal of the high school at Pittsfield, Mass., he was called in 1868 to be the first principal of the Albany Free Academy, N. Y. Here he performed what was probably his most distinctive and constructive work in the educational field. He was among the pioneeers who labored in the difficult period that marked the transition from the private academy to the free public high school. To him fell not only the lot of organizing the first public high school of the city of Albany but also the still more difficult task of winning public support for the enterprise. He remained in charge of the school for eighteen years and made it one of the leading high schools in the state. In 1876 he accepted the position of superintendent of schools in Minneapolis. In this growing city of the Northwest, also, there was much pioneer work to be done. He introduced manual training into the high schools, and promoted a movement for the better training of the younger teachers of the city school system. During his six years of service in Minneapolis, the number of public schools increased from 28 to 49; the number of teachers from 296 to 572 and the pupils from 14,194 to 23,797, the school enrolment during these years growing about twice as rapidly as the population. Having established a solid reputation as an administrator in the public school systems of both the East and the Middle West, Bradley became in 1892 the president of Illinois College, an old institution of fine traditions at Jacksonville, Ill. It was for him a new field, involving many serious difficulties. He had succeeded a very popular former president; the curriculum of the old college had to be modernized to meet the demands of a new age and the increasing competition of near-by universities. The new president went about his task with keen intelligence and firm resolution but funds could not be found to ward off annual deficits. He became discouraged over the outlook and in 1900 resigned. Subsequently he served for six years as superintendent of schools at Randolph, Mass., where he died at the age of seventy-three.

Bradley was a man of dignified bearing whose kindly disposition won the affectionate regard of students in both high school and college. His wife, Martha J. Gould, whom he married in 1870, helped to make their home an attractive social center for students. His degrees included the A.M. and LL.D. conferred by Williams and the Ph.D. awarded by the Regents of the University of New York. He represented the State of New York at the Paris Exposition of 1878; was for several years a member of the National Council of Education and was several times elected to the National Council of Congregational Churches. He published many articles on educational topics and a small volume of addresses, *Work and Play* (1900).

[For career in Albany, see Jas. M. Ruso, "Hist. of Albany H. S.," in *Albany Express*, Nov. 16, 1893; *Argus*, Aug. 10, 1886; *Hist. of the Albany H. S.*, pamphlet published in 1876; for career in Minneapolis, *Reports of Minneapolis Board of Ed.*, 1887–92, especially the last one; also, *Illustrated Minneapolis, A Souvenir of the Minneapolis Jour.*, 1891; for career

at Illinois College, manuscript records of trustees and faculty.]   C.H.R.

BRADLEY, JOSEPH P. (Mar. 14, 1813–Jan. 22, 1892), justice of the Supreme Court, was born at Berne, Albany County, N. Y. (The "P" does not represent the initial letter of a name. His father's name was Philo and Joseph adopted the "P" probably as a patronymic. See Stern, *post*.) The first Bradley came to this country from England in 1645. Joseph's great-grandfather was a soldier in the War of Independence, and his grandfather served in the War of 1812. His mother was Mercy Gardner, of Rhode Island stock. The Bradleys were a race of farmers, and Joseph, the eldest of eleven children, passed a laborious youth amid straitened circumstances on a small farm in his native county. He early displayed pronounced intellectual traits and a determination to get forward. Attending school four months each year, he became at the age of sixteen a country school-teacher. Later a Lutheran parson, becoming attracted to him, gave him lessons in Greek and Latin. At the age of twenty he entered Rutgers College, from which he graduated three years later, an outstanding member of a famous class. The same year, 1836, he entered upon the study of law in the office of Archer Gifford, at that time collector of the Port of Newark. He was admitted to the New Jersey bar in November 1839. In 1844 he was married to Mary, daughter of Chief Justice Hornblower of New Jersey. At the height of his professional career he devoted himself especially to patent, commercial, and corporation cases. Having a talent for mathematics he became an actuary of the Prudential Insurance Company. He was also counsel for various railroads. His first appearance before the Supreme Court of the United States occurred in December 1860, in connection with the case of Milnor *vs.* the New Jersey R. R. and Transportation Company (see appendix to 24 *Howard* in 16 *Lawyers' Edition Extra Annotated*, pp. 799–810), Bradley's argument in which anticipated the later decision of the court in Gilman *vs.* Philadelphia (3 *Wallace*, 713).

Politically Bradley was originally a Whig; and in the winter of 1860–61 he passed several weeks in Washington for the purpose of urging upon Congress a compromise between North and South along the lines of the Corwin Amendment. The firing upon Fort Sumter, however, caused him to take up immediately a strong Unionist position. He denounced secession as treason, and urged that in crushing the rebellion the National Government was restrained only by "the laws of God and the Law of Nations." Later in championing the Thirteenth Amendment he espoused the "state suicide" doctrine of Sumner—states which had attempted secession were not entitled to be counted in amending the Constitution; and if they were to be subsequently restored to their former status in the Union, it could be only through the grace of Congress. In 1862 he ran a hopeless race for Congress in support of the Lincoln administration, and in 1868 he headed the New Jersey electoral ticket for Grant. He was nominated for the Supreme Court by President Grant, along with Judge William Strong of the Pennsylvania supreme court, on the morning of the day, Feb. 7, 1870, in the afternoon of which the Court handed down its decision in Hepburn *vs.* Griswold (8 *Wallace,* 603). This coincidence has provoked the charge that the Supreme Court was "packed" in order to bring about the later decision in Knox *vs.* Lee (12 *Wallace,* 457), when the new majority of the Court, speaking through Strong and Bradley, overturned Hepburn *vs.* Griswold. The available evidence leaves the question in some obscurity. The way for the two nominations had been paved by an Act of Congress passed in April 1869, to take effect the ensuing December, whereas the decision in Hepburn *vs.* Griswold was not settled in conference till November 1869. It cannot be seriously questioned, however, that the views of both Bradley and Strong on the legal-tender question were known to those in authority when their nominations were sent in. Strong had participated in a decision of the Pennsylvania supreme court which sustained the act set aside in Hepburn *vs.* Griswold; while Bradley's leanings both as a railroad lawyer (the general attitude of the railroad interests being strongly favorable toward the legal-tender act) and as a strong nationalist during the war were scarcely open to serious doubt. We also have the testimony of Boutwell, then secretary of the treasury, that he knew in advance what the decision in Hepburn *vs.* Griswold was to be. The order of the reconstructed Court granting a reargument of the constitutional question raised by the legal-tender act was entered Apr. 11, 1870, and precipitated an acrimonious dispute among the justices, the facts concerning which were first made known in 1902 (Charles Bradley, pp. 61–74). The charge made in a paper first filed and then withdrawn by Chief Justice Chase, that the Court had acted in the matter in derogation of a previous understanding, was apparently without foundation; while in view of the fact that the original decision was by a virtual minority of the Court, the rehearing was obviously proper even if not positively required.

In 1877 Bradley was appointed a member of the famous Electoral Commission created by Congress to pass upon the electoral votes of Florida, Louisiana, South Carolina, and Oregon. Because he was the last member chosen to the Commission and took the place in it originally proffered Justice David Davis, whose political leanings were ambiguous, it came to be assumed that he would pursue a non-partisan course in what had become a bitterly partisan contest. In point of fact his vote on all critical issues before the Commission was uniformly cast in the Republican interest, with the result that Hayes was elected. His position, however, which was that developed by William M. Evarts as counsel for Hayes, was not only quite consistent throughout, but was also strongly defensible in itself. It was in brief that, in the absence at least of legislation by Congress, the two Houses, in counting the electoral vote, were performing a purely ministerial function and had therefore no power to revise the canvass by state authorities of an election of Electors, either on the suggestion of fraud or for any other cause (Charles Bradley, pp. 165–215). A charge by Justice Field that Bradley had originally vacillated in this opinion was disavowed by the former so far as derogatory to Bradley's "honor or integrity."

In his twenty-two years on the bench Bradley was the author of many notable opinions. His concurring opinion in Knox *vs.* Lee (12 *Wallace,* 554) contains the first obvious invocation in a Supreme Court opinion of the doctrine that the national government possesses certain inherent powers—a doctrine which has been utilized by the Court since then more than once. His dissenting opinion in the Slaughter House Cases (16 *Wallace,* 36, 111) anticipates remarkably present-day concepts of "due process of law" and "liberty and property" in interpretation of the Fourteenth Amendment, and was unquestionably influential in projecting these concepts into our constitutional law. In a series of opinions he contributed more than any of his contemporaries to the elaboration of the principles which still guide the Court in drawing the line between the "exclusive" power of Congress over interstate commerce and the taxing powers of the states (see Transportation Company *vs.* Parkersburg, 107 *United States Reports,* 691; Brown *vs.* Houston, 114 *U. S. R.,* 622; Coe *vs.* Errol, 116 *U. S. R.,* 517; Robbins *vs.* Shelby Taxing Dist., 120 *U. S. R.,* 498; Philadelphia, etc., S. S. Company *vs.* Pennsylvania, 122 *U. S. R.,* 326; Leloup *vs.* Mobile, 127 *U. S. R.,* 640). In the Mormon Church Case (136 *U. S. R.* 1), in sustaining the right of Congress to revoke the charter of this organization, he foreshadowed in a measure the doctrine, later brought to fruition in the Insular Cases (182 *U. S. R.*), of the plenary power of Congress in territories; while in Boyd *vs.* United States (116 *U. S. R.,* 616) he laid down the guiding lines of the Court's present interpretation of the Fourth and Fifth Amendments on the subject of self-incrimination by the forced production of documents.

Bradley's most notable exposition of national power is to be found in his opinion in *ex parte* Siebold (100 *U. S. R.,* 371), in which, in sustaining the right of Congress to cast penally enforceable duties upon state election officials in connection with the election of members of the House of Representatives, he asserts the territorial sovereignty of the national government, acting within the sphere of its powers "on every foot of American soil," strongly deprecates state jealousy of national power, and preaches the gospel of national and state coöperation for common purposes. At the same time, Bradley was far from wishing to see the states crowded to the wall in consequence of the outcome of the Civil War. In the Civil Rights Cases (109 *U. S. R.,* 3) he asserted the necessity of construing the War Amendments in the light of the Tenth Amendment, and on that basis arrived at the conclusion that Congress has no power under the Fourteenth Amendment to anticipate state action hostile to equality under the law or to supply the deficiencies of state laws—a view which has rendered legislative powers of Congress under the Amendment practically nugatory. His opinion in Hans *vs.* Louisiana (134 *U. S. R.,* 1), extending the immunity which is conferred upon the states by the Eleventh Amendment to suits commenced or prosecuted by their own citizens also manifests his conservative tendency as respects the traditional position of the states in the Union.

Bradley was master of a vigorous and incisive, if somewhat prolix, judicial style, in which, as well as in many of his ideas, the influence of Chief Justice Marshall can be readily detected. His last opinion from the bench was his dissent in Maine *vs.* Grand Trunk Railway Company (142 *U. S. R.,* 217, 231). The views which he therein expressed have since been substantially adopted by the court (see Galveston, etc., Railroad Company *vs.* Texas, 210 *U. S. R.,* 217).

Bradley's diversions were intellectual. While history and belles-lettres claimed his attention to some extent, his chief interest was given to mathematical and genealogical studies. In addition to the immense labor of compiling a history of his own family, which was privately published shortly following his death, he also compiled the history of his wife's family and connections, besides collecting the records of many collateral branches. A further reminder of his characteristic interests is a "Perpetual Calendar for finding the day of the week on which any day of the month falls in any year before or after Christ, old style or new" (see Charles Bradley, p. 333). His general library comprised some six thousand volumes, his law library some ten thousand volumes. The latter upon his death was secured by the Prudential Insurance Company of Newark, N. J., and is maintained in that city "complete and entire even to the pictures on the walls." He was also a man who keenly relished the intellectual exchanges of social life and cultivated many distinguished friendships.

[*Miscellaneous Writings of the Late Hon. Jos. P. Bradley . . . and a Review of His "Judicial Record" by Wm. Draper Lewis . . . and An Account of His "Dissenting Opinions" by the Late A. Q. Keasbey . . .* edited and compiled by his son Chas. Bradley (1902); sketch by Horace Stern, in Wm. D. Lewis (ed.), *Gt. Am. Lawyers,* VI (1909), 345 ff.; U. S. Supreme Court Reports from 12 *Wallace* to 142 *U. S.;* citation should also be made of pertinent pages in Chas. Warren's *Supreme Court in U. S. Hist.* (1922).]   E.S.C.

BRADLEY, LYDIA MOSS (July 31, 1816–Jan. 16, 1908), philanthropist, was the daughter of Capt. Zealy Moss of Loudoun County, Va., who served in the Revolutionary army. After the war, Zealy and his wife, Jeanette (Glasscock) of Fauquier County, Va., moved to Vevay, Ind., where Lydia was born. Her father entered the Baptist ministry, but was also owner of a farm on which every one worked. It was not very long before Lydia demonstrated that she had her share of sturdy heritage. Still in her teens and slight for her age, she one day traded her saddle-horse for a tract of timber land, which she set out to clear. With some help from her father, this was accomplished, and the girl sold her land at a profit. She was married to Tobias S. Bradley of Vevay on May 11, 1837, and moved with him to Peoria, Ill., where her brother, William S. Moss, lived. Tobias was soon engaged in a number of enterprises including a steamboat line to St. Louis, a ferry boat, a saw-mill and a pottery works, and, in partnership with his brother-in-law, a distillery. He purchased a farm, constantly added to it, and bought a considerable interest in the First National Bank of Peoria, later becoming its president. Their six children all died in early youth, and the Bradleys determined to commemorate them by founding an educational institution. But Mr. Bradley died in 1867, leaving an estate of $500,000. Mrs. Bradley, still slight, almost fragile, in appearance, proceeded at once to increase her fortune to the proportions necessary for her philanthropy. She became a business woman, though without giving up her practise of making her own butter and salting down her own meat. By economy and good investments but mainly by the development of real estate, at the time of her death she had multiplied her estate fourfold. Her interest in Peoria was expressed in frequent gifts to its institutions. She relieved one church of a $30,000 mortgage and contributed handsomely to all the others; she donated a hospital site, built a Home for Aged Women, and presented the city with a park named for her daughter, Laura Bradley. Meanwhile plans for her school went forward. A representative was sent to investigate other institutions and advice was sought of such men as President Harper of Chicago University and Prof. John Dewey. In 1897 the two buildings of the Bradley Polytechnic Institute were erected on a twenty-acre campus in Peoria at a cost of $250,000 and with an endowment of $2,000,000. Horology Hall contained a school of watchmaking and allied trades which had been started on a small scale in Indiana and brought to Peoria by Mrs. Bradley in 1893. In the general department, housed in Bradley Hall, four years of academic work and two of college, embracing the usual courses in literature, science, and the arts, were taught. But special emphasis was laid on practical study, and the domestic science course for girls was among the first in the Middle West. According to its charter, the aim of the general department was "to furnish students with the means of living independent, industrious, and useful lives." Evening classes in vocational subjects, and a summer school in domestic science and manual training, were later added.

[*Bradley Polytechnic Institute, The First Decade, 1897–1907* (Peoria, 1908); *Who's Who in America,* 1908–09.]   M.A.K.

BRADLEY, MILTON (Nov. 8, 1836–May 30, 1911), manufacturer, was born in Vienna, Me., the son of Lewis and Fannie (Lyford) Bradley. His father operated, at Mercer, the first starch mill in Maine, an enterprise which helped to inaugurate the potato industry in that state. In 1847 the family moved to Lowell, Mass., where Milton Bradley graduated from the high school in 1854. He then entered the office of Oliver E. Cushing, a draftsman and patent agent, making good use of his spare time by peddling stationery among the girl operatives of the Lowell mills. Having earned and saved two or three hundred dollars he entered the Lawrence Scientific School at Cambridge, commuting from Lowell and teaching at night. In 1856 the family moved to Hartford, and Milton, after completing one and a half years of a two-year course, decided to accompany them. In search of employment he found himself in Springfield, Mass., in June of 1856 and secured work as a draftsman in the locomotive works of Blanchard & Kimball (later Bemis & Company). When Bemis & Company went out of business in 1858, Bradley set up for himself as a mechanical draftsman and patent securer. His most interesting job at this time was making the drawings and superintending the construction of a private car, in the shops of T. W. Wason & Company, for the Khedive of Egypt. He became interested in lithographing in 1859, went to Providence, learned the process, brought a press to Springfield in 1860, and inaugurated the lithographing business in western Massachusetts. His first important lithographing job was a portrait of Lincoln made from an original photograph brought home from the Chicago nominating convention by Samuel Bowles of the *Springfield Republican*. Business during the war, however, was so poor that Bradley took up the idea of printing games. A parlor game, known as "The Checkered Game of Life," he peddled personally throughout New York state, and the sale was so rapid that success seemed to point in the direction of the manufacture of games. Accordingly in 1864 Milton Bradley & Company was formed by the admission of J. F. Tapley and Clark W. Bryan, and in 1870 a separate building for the enterprise was secured. Tapley and Bryan retired in 1878 and the firm was reorganized as the Milton Bradley Company. Bradley was a pioneer in America in the game business. Although the Puritan mind was averse to the idea, success was instantaneous and sustained. The "Checkered Game of Life" marked a new era in parlor pastimes. "The Wheel of Life," a scientific toy which made simple pictures printed on strips of paper become animated, has been described as the original moving picture machine. The company prospered greatly from the rise of croquet and their manuals became standard for the rules of the game. Simultaneously with the development of the manufacture of games came that of kindergarten materials. It was in 1869 that Milton Bradley fell under the spell of the Froebelian philosophy chiefly through the influence of Elizabeth Peabody, and a neighbor, Edward Wiebe. Wiebe was a Springfield music teacher and a friend of Froebel's widow, and had brought from Germany the manuscript of a book on kindergartening called the *Paradise of Childhood* (1869) which Bradley published. This book, the first manual on kindergartens published in the United States, did much to promote the interest in kindergartens in America and was followed by the manufacture of kindergarten materials and the publication of children's books. In 1893 the Milton Bradley Company purchased the *Kindergarten News* and published it as the *Kindergarten Review* with Henry W. Blake as editor, a publication which became the organ of the International Kindergarten Union. Earlier Bradley had published a children's magazine, *Work and Play*. He was particularly interested in color instruction and himself wrote and published *Color in the School Room* (1890), *Color in the Kindergarten* (1893), *Elementary Color* (1895), and *Water Colors in the Schoolroom* (1900). He was twice married: in 1860 to Villona Eaton; and in 1864 to Ellen Thayer.

[*Milton Bradley, A Successful Man; A Brief Sketch of His Career and the Growth of the Institution Which He Founded, Published by Milton Bradley Company in Commemoration of Their Fiftieth Anniversary* (Springfield, 1910); *Springfield Present and Prospective*, ed. by Jas. E. Tower (1905), p. 192; *Who's Who in America*, 1910–11; *Springfield Daily Republican*, May 31, 1911.] H.U.F.

BRADLEY, STEPHEN ROW (Feb. 20, 1754–Dec. 9, 1830), jurist, senator, was descended from Stephen Bradley, one of Cromwell's Ironsides who emigrated, about the year 1650, from England to Connecticut. S. R. Bradley was born in the town of Wallingford (later known as Cheshire), the son of Moses and Mary (Row) Bradley. He graduated from Yale College in 1775, and early in 1776 was commissioned a captain of volunteers in the American army. He served in various capacities as commissary, quartermaster, aide to Gen. Wooster, and at the end of the war retired with the rank of colonel. He studied law in the famous school of Judge Tapping Reeve, at Litchfield, Conn., and in 1779 like many other active and ambitious young men, he emigrated from Connecticut to the district known as the New Hampshire Grants, where the Green Mountain Boys sought to establish a new Commonwealth of Vermont, in opposition to the claims of New York. Bradley was one of two lawyers who were the first to be admitted to the Vermont bar. He opened a law office in Westminster. His rapid rise in influence is shown by the fact that before the end of his first year in Vermont he had been chosen as one of the agents to present Vermont's cause to the Continental Congress, and had written a pamphlet entitled *Vermont's Appeal to the Candid and Impartial World* (1780), an eloquent and militant argument for Vermont's right to statehood. By direction of Gov. Chit-

tenden the appeal was "published to the world," and circulated throughout several states. Bradley served as a member of the legislature and as speaker, and was the second judge of the supreme court who was a lawyer, most of the early judges being laymen. He was an active member of the commission that negotiated a settlement with New York, which made possible Vermont's admission as the first state to come into the Union after the original thirteen. In the convention called to consider ratification of the United States Constitution, Bradley was one of the leaders in the debate, favoring approval, which was carried by a large majority. He was elected one of Vermont's first United States senators, drawing the four-year term. He was defeated in 1794 for a reëlection, but was chosen in 1801 to fill a vacancy and was reëlected for a full term, this period continuing from October 1801 to March 1813. He served as president *pro tempore*, 1802–03 and in 1808.

Bradley introduced the bill which established a national flag of fifteen stripes and fifteen stars and this flag, sometimes known as the Bradley flag, was used from 1795 to 1814. His leadership is indicated by the fact that he issued the call for the caucus of Republican members of Congress which nominated James Madison as a candidate for president. Bradley was not an active partisan and his independence of party ties was shown on various occasions. In the controversy between the schools of political thought represented by Chief Justice Marshall and President Thomas Jefferson, which culminated in the establishment of a powerful and independent judiciary, Bradley, although a Republican, did not support the attempt to impeach certain judges. In a speech delivered in the Senate on Apr. 25, 1812, he protested against a declaration of war before an army was organized, and S. G. Goodrich, better known by his pen name, "Peter Parley," a son-in-law of Bradley, in his *Recollections of a Lifetime* (1856), says that the senator retired from public life because of his dissatisfaction with the war policy of the Madison administration. Jeremiah Mason, one of the famous lawyers of the time, was a student in Bradley's office and in his *Memoir and Correspondence* (1873), he tells of Bradley's sagacity, his wit, and his great store of anecdotes. Other contemporaries mention his urbanity and social charm. He was thrice married: to Merab Atwater, to Thankful Taylor, and to Belinda Willard.

[A. J. Beveridge, *Life of John Marshall* (1916–19); Chas. Francis Adams, ed., *Memoirs of J. Q. Adams* (1874–77); F. B. Dexter, *Biog. Sketches Grads. Yale Coll.*, vol. III (1903); B. H. Hall, *Hist. of Eastern*

Vermont (1858) ; W. H. Crockett, Vermont (1921), vols. II, III ; Records of the Governors and Council of the State of Vermont (1874), II, 200–22 ; P. C. Dodge, ed., Encyc. of Vermont Biog. (1912).]   W. H. C.

BRADLEY, WILLIAM CZAR (Mar. 23, 1782–Mar. 3, 1867), congressman, was born in Westminster, Vt., the son of Stephen Rowe Bradley [q.v.] and Merab (Atwater) Bradley. His mother died during his infancy. Scarlet fever, when he was two, was probably responsible for impairing his hearing. His early youth was spent with his grandparents in Cheshire, Conn., but he fitted for college at Charlestown, N. H. During his freshman year at Yale he was expelled for a prank for which he was not responsible though he later said he was guilty of other similar acts. Upon his return home his disgusted father gave him a dung fork and set him to work at a manure heap. But he retrieved himself by deciding to become a lawyer, studying with Judge Simeon Strong of Amherst, then with a Mr. Ashmun of Blandford, Mass., and later returning to his father's office to complete his studies. At seventeen he delivered the Fourth of July oration at Westminster, the program including an ode he had written. At eighteen he was secretary of the commissioner of bankruptcy of Westminster and at twenty married Sarah Richards, daughter of Hon. Mark Richards of Westminster who was lieutenant-governor of Vermont. Admitted to the bar when but twenty (1802), because of his youth he was refused permission to practise before the supreme court of the state, but the legislature made him attorney for Windham County, thus giving him access to the supreme court. In 1806–07 he represented Westminster in the Vermont legislature. In 1812 he was a member of the Governor's Council which preceded the present state Senate. He was twice a representative in Congress,—in 1813–15, when he was an ardent supporter of Madison's war policy, and again in 1823–27. A quarrel with John Quincy Adams, which turned him to the support of Jackson, caused his retirement from public life at Washington, when but forty-five. What he himself considered his greatest public service was the surveying, as agent of the treasury department, under the Treaty of Ghent, of the northeastern boundary between the United States and Canada. In this work he spent five years (1817–22), and though Great Britain at first rejected this line it was finally adopted by the Ashburton Treaty. After his retirement from national affairs and his return to the practise of law he continued within the state of Vermont to be the actual leader of Jacksonian democracy and al-

most its perpetual candidate for governor. In 1848 he joined the Free-Soil party and in 1850 was a member of the state legislature. Later he was a member of the young Republican party, heading the Frémont electoral ticket in 1856. In 1857 he was a member of the state constitutional convention. In 1858 he took formal leave of the bar after fifty-six years of practise.

He seems to have more enjoyed leading the uphill fight of Vermont democracy than the actual holding of public office, and his relish of the contest was said to be in inverse proportion to his chance of being elected. Though called a "free thinker" in his day, he would now be looked upon simply as a man of independent and investigating mind. He had some reputation as a poet, especially as a writer of occasional verse, and specimens of his poetry are given by Frederick Frothingham (In Memoriam, 1867). Of these "A Ballad of Judgment and Mercy" is considered the best.

[In addition to Frothingham, see A Tribute of Affection to the Memory of Hon. Wm. C. Bradley (1869), by Bradley's grand-daughter Mrs. S. B. Willard, which is largely dependent upon Frothingham but contains some new material in the form of letters ; see also obituary in the Rutland Herald, Mar. 7, 1867.]

C. R. W—s.

BRADLEY, WILLIAM O'CONNELL (Mar. 18, 1847–May 23, 1914), governor of Kentucky, senator, was born near Lancaster in Garrard County, Ky., and was in part descended from Irish ancestry. He was the only son and the youngest child of Robert McAfee Bradley, a noted criminal lawyer and expert in land litigation, and his wife Nancy Ellen (Totten) Bradley, who was a grand-niece of George Robertson, chief justice of the Kentucky court of appeals. When he was yet young his family moved to Somerset and there he received what schooling the town afforded. He never attended college, and often in later life mentioned the fact with pride. In 1861 he was appointed a page in the legislature at Frankfort. But coming from a family that strongly supported the Union, he wanted a more active career. Therefore, he soon joined the Federal Army as recruiting agent in Pulaski County and later volunteered for active service in Louisville. On account of his age his father both times secured his release. He now studied law under the direction of his father, and in 1865 by special enactment of the legislature he was given the right to take the examination for license to practise law, being only eighteen years of age. He entered his father's office at Lancaster, where the family had now settled. Having a liking for political advancement, he ran for prosecuting attorney for Garrard County in 1870 on the Republican ticket and won. He then began a political career in Kentucky which for almost thirty years was characterized by successive defeats on account of his having the misfortune to live in a state normally Democratic. But his party stood loyally behind him, and in time he became the preëminent Republican leader in Kentucky and ultimately won political success. Four times he was nominated by his party for United States senator and four times defeated; an equal number of times he was nominated for the United States House of Representatives, making hard but losing fights the first three times, and refusing to accept the nomination the fourth time; and twice he unsuccessfully ran for governor, in 1887 and 1891. He took an important part in the national councils of the Republican party, serving as elector in 1872 and 1876, as delegate to six national conventions and as national committeeman for twelve years. In 1888 he received 106 votes in the national convention for vice-presidential nominee and in 1896 the Kentucky Republicans endorsed him for the presidential nomination. His first important political victory and the first of any consequence for the Republican party in Kentucky came in 1895, when he was elected governor of the state by a majority of almost 10,000, due largely to the disorganization of the Democrats on the money question. In 1908 a badly torn Democratic legislature elected him to the United States Senate over J. C. W. Beckham, the Democratic candidate. He died in office in Washington in 1914. He was married on July 11, 1867, to Margaret R. Duncan.

[*Lexington Leader*, May 24, 1914; *Who's Who in America*, 1912–13; *Biog. Cyc. of the Commonwealth of Ky.* (1896); M. H. Thatcher, *Stories and Speeches of Wm. O. Bradley; with Biog. Sketch* (Lexington, 1916).]   E. M. C.

BRADSTREET, ANNE (*c.* 1612–Sept. 16, 1672), colonial poet, wife of Simon Bradstreet, came to Massachusetts Bay in 1630 with the party under Winthrop, which also included her husband and her father and mother (Deputy Governor Thomas Dudley and Dorothy Dudley). The future poet was eighteen years of age and two years a wife when the voyage was undertaken, and in America she found "new manners, at which my heart rose. But after I was convinced it was the way of God, I submitted to it." The rebellion of heart was not unnatural. Her life in England had been pleasant. She was born probably at Northampton, where her father, home from Protestant wars, was as steward retrieving the fortunes of his employer, the Puritan Earl of Lincoln. She

knew a culture once compared to that of Lucy Hutchinson, who "had at one time eight tutors in . . . languages, music, dancing. . . ." Her husband, the son of a non-conformist minister, had been taken into the Earl's household as a youth of fourteen years, had received the M.A. degree at Cambridge in 1624, and had returned to the estate as steward. In Massachusetts the Bradstreets settled at Ipswich, but removed to North Andover about 1644. During these years, while Anne was writing the first book of poems by an English woman in America, she moved in the highest circles, as her father, and later her husband, both held leading administrative offices. Eight children were born to her, and among her descendants were Richard Henry Dana, Wendell Phillips, and Oliver Wendell Holmes.

In the light of her century, technique and capacity rather than content were at fault in her earlier poetry, published at London in 1650 under the title, *The Tenth Muse*. Her inspiration was chiefly literary. She was apart from the Cavalier tradition, but close to another considerable body of material, didactic and religious. She enjoyed the poetry of Francis Quarles, and imitated *La Semaine* of Du Bartas, which, translated by Joshua Sylvester and published in *Bartas His Deuine Weekes and Works* (1605), greatly influenced English men of letters. In a poem she expressed herself as enamoured of Du Bartas's learning, natural philosophy, grave divinity, physic, and astronomy. Quite natural were her own attempts to sing of physics in the "Elements," of vital forces and human characteristics in the "Humours" and "Ages" of man, and natural philosophy in the "Seasons." In a long rimed history, "The Four Monarchyes" she selectively paraphrased many pages of Raleigh's *History of the World* (1614), using the Bible, Plutarch, and Usher as contributory sources. Through the "Dialogue between Old England and New" she gave voice to her anti-ritualistic beliefs, but did not incline greatly to democracy. On the whole, these works are tedious, unleavened by imaginative power, and cramped in diction. She never mastered the pentameter couplet. "Contemplations," written later, enjoys modern appreciation. In the more intricate rime scheme of seven-line stanzas, closing with an Alexandrine, she expressed herself with a grace and beauty which brightened her time and environment. Herein, she was perhaps quickened into action by the "Spectacles" in the Sylvester volume. At least she linked herself more closely to the influence of Sidney and Spenser, and in sustained verse wrote of a spiritual passion amidst elements of nature authentic to poetic tradition, if not to New England landscape. In her own period Nathaniel Ward wrote commendatory verses for the first volume, and John Rogers and John Norton, in the second, saw poetic beauties theretofore unpenned in New England. Cotton Mather became unduly fulsome in his comment on her life in his *Magnalia Christi Americana* (1702).

[Anne Bradstreet's work has been published in five editions. The first was entitled, *The Tenth Muse Lately Sprung up in America. Or Severall Poems, Compiled with Great Variety of Wit and Learning . . . By a Gentlewoman in those Parts* (London, 1650). The second and posthumous edition, *Several Poems . . .* (Boston, 1678), included later poetry, especially "Contemplations." The third (Boston, 1758) was a reprint of the second. The fourth, *The Works of Anne Bradstreet in Prose and Verse* (Charlestown, Mass., 1867), ed. by John Harvard Ellis, is based on the second, collated with the first, and contains hitherto unpublished material and scholarly biographical and critical comment. It remains without an equal. In 1897 the Duodecimos published *The Poems of Mrs. Anne Bradstreet . . .* with spelling modernized and an introduction by Chas. Eliot Norton. Helen Campbell has written a biography, *Anne Bradstreet and Her Time* (1890). See also the *Bradstreet Geneal. Table*, and a short account by Metta Bradstreet in *Colls. Topsfield Hist. Soc.*, I, 3–9. The *Pubs. Ipswich Hist. Soc.*, XII, contain "Thos. Dudley and Simon and Ann Bradstreet: a Study of House-Lots."]

L. N. R.

BRADSTREET, JOHN (c. 1711–Sept. 25, 1774), British and colonial officer, either was born in Nova Scotia, or immigrated at an early age. Close connection with two generations of military Bradstreets influenced him to purchase an ensign's commission in Philipps's regiment of British foot in 1735. Visits to Louisburg in 1736 and 1738, and his relationship with the famous La Tour family of Nova Scotia, gave him knowledge of French methods, while garrison duty on the frontiers of a sparsely-settled province taught him the value of irregular troops, and peculiarly fitted him for his later career. When England entered the War of the Austrian Succession, he was serving as lieutenant at Canso. Captured by Du Vivier in 1744, he was imprisoned in Louisburg, and later exchanged at Boston, where he met Gov. Shirley. His arguments as to the vulnerability of Louisburg were so forcible that Pepperell described him as the "first projector of the expedition" that resulted in the capture of the stronghold in 1745 (*Documentary History of the State of Maine*, 1908, XI, 300, 301). Bradstreet maintained that he would have had the chief command had he been a native New Englander, but he was commissioned only as second colonel of the first regiment of Massachusetts troops, Pepperell's "York Provincials" (*6 Massachusetts Historical Society Collections*, X, 497). He served during the siege with distinction, and was recommended by both Shirley and Pep-

perell for the lieutenant-colonelcy of Pepperell's regiment, raised in 1745 on the British establishment. The selection, however, was dictated in England, and Bradstreet obtained only a captain's commission, and the newly-created post of lieutenant-governor of St. John's, Newfoundland, which he held until his death. After commanding the provincial garrison at Louisburg, not without arousing criticism, he went to St. John's, where he remained until 1754. A driving personal ambition, which was his dominating characteristic, led him in 1747 to attempt to purchase from Pepperell the colonelcy of the regiment, wholly for the sake of rank (Usher Parsons, *The Life of Sir William Pepperell*, 1855, p. 150), and undoubtedly to inspire the unsuccessful petition of Lord Baltimore in 1753 for the reëstablishment of a seventeenth century proprietary claim to Newfoundland. The petition requested that "J. Bradstreet, Esq., a gentleman of great honour and ability," be appointed governor (Public Records Office, *Colonial Office*, 194: 13, July 26, 1753). In 1755 Braddock ordered him as captain in Pepperell's newly raised regiment, the 51st, to Oswego with two companies to reinforce the weakened garrison, and to oversee the building of boats on the lake. His extraordinary abilities with that class of irregulars known as "battoe-men" were recognized when Shirley, in 1756, gave him the command of all matters relating to transportation of supplies and provisions on the New York frontier, without, however, additional pay or rank (*Correspondence of William Shirley*, 1912, II, 419). Bradstreet performed this important work with zeal, and won contemporary renown by beating off several French attacks as he was returning, in the spring of 1756, from carrying supplies to the Oswego garrison. Commissioned in 1757 as captain in the second battalion of the Royal Americans, he was chosen by Loudoun as one of his aides-de-camp, a post in which he performed quartermaster duties. In December 1757 he offered to bear part of the expense of an expedition against Fort Frontenac, to be reimbursed and recommended for promotion if successful. When Loudoun accepted the offer, Bradstreet carried forward preparations with such energy that he completed nearly 1,500 batteaux by the end of May. Wolfe, always a severe critic of Americans, marked him out at this time for especial praise (*Historical Manuscripts Commission, Report on the Manuscripts of Mrs. Stopford-Sackville*, 1910, II, 261). Pitt's sweeping changes of December 1757, which gave Bradstreet his coveted rank of lieutenant-colonel and made him deputy quartermaster-general in America, deferred the Frontenac plan until after Abercromby's defeat at Ticonderoga, when it was adopted at a council of war. The Frontenac expedition was singularly adapted to Bradstreet's abilities, for it involved, not the strategy of a siege, but the swift transport of an army over a long and difficult wilderness water-way. Though Bradstreet quarrelled with his provincial leaders, his 3,000 men, of whom but 150 were of the regular army, easily captured Fort Frontenac (Kingston, Ontario), August 1758, destroyed the fortifications, stores, and boats, and thus broke the line of French communication between the St. Lawrence and the Ohio.

For the remainder of the war Bradstreet acted as deputy quartermaster-general, and in 1762 was promoted to be colonel in America. In the suppression of Pontiac's rebellion, in 1764, he commanded the northern of the two armies that penetrated into Indian territory. He transported his small force to Detroit, re-garrisoned posts to the westward that had been captured by Indians, but gave little evidence of understanding Indian character, and allowed himself to be duped into signing a premature peace without sufficiently drastic terms. In 1772 the rules of seniority made him major-general; two years later he died of the dropsy "at his house in Broad Street," and was buried in Trinity Church with full honors of war (*Rivington's New York Gazetteer*, Sept. 29, 1774). He left two daughters, by his wife Mary.

[Information regarding the family of Nova Scotia Bradstreets is in R. H. R. Smythies, *Hist. Records of the 40th Reg.* (1894), and more particularly in Bradstreet's will, printed in the *New Eng. Hist. and Gen. Reg.*, XVI, 315, and in 12 *Wendell's N. Y. S. C. Reports*, 602, and 5 *Peters Reports*, 402. The Pepperell Papers, partly printed in 6 *Mass. Hist. Soc. Colls.*, vol. X, contain material on Bradstreet's first important command. The calendar of Bradstreet papers in *Am. Antiq. Soc. Proc.*, n.s., XIX (1908), 105–81, begins with 1755, and additional material is in the *N. Y. Col. Docs.*, *Corres. of Wm. Shirley* (1912); *Corres. of Wm. Pitt* (ed. by G. S. Kimball, 1906); the unprinted collections of Loudoun and Abercromby papers in the possession of the Henry E. Huntington Lib., San Marino, Cal.; and *An Impartial Account of Lt. Col. Bradstreet's Expedition to Fort Frontenac, . . . by a Volunteer on the Expedition* (London, 1759). Bradstreet's letters during the Pontiac rebellion are in Hough's ed. of the *Diary of the Siege of Detroit* (1860), and in *Western Reserve Hist. Soc. Tracts*, 13, 14 (1873). For a general account see H. Baker-Crothers, *Virginia and the French and Indian War* (1928).]   S.M.P.

BRADSTREET, SIMON (March 1603–March 1697), early colonial statesman, was the grandson of a Suffolk gentleman of estate and the son of a non-conformist minister living in Lincolnshire. He was educated at Emmanuel College, Cambridge, where he took the A.B. degree in 1620 and the A.M. in 1624. His connec-

tion with the New England colony began in 1629 when he was made assistant of the Company of Massachusetts Bay just as its emphasis of interest in colonizing was passing from trade to religion. He sailed to New England in 1630 with Winthrop's fleet, from which time down to 1692, with the exception of the three years of the Dominion, 1686–89, he was continuously in public employ. His two marriages brought him into close connection with the small governing group in the colony, his first wife being the well-known Puritan poet, Anne Bradstreet [*q.v.*], and his second wife Mrs. Ann (Downing) Gardner, niece of John Winthrop [*q.v.*]. He served as assistant of Massachusetts for forty-nine years, during which time he had many other public responsibilities. He was secretary of the colony from 1630 to 1636 and frequently received appointment to important committees of the General Court. His diplomatic qualities became manifest early in his public career, and marked him as one of the colony's most suitable envoys in its dealings with the outside world. He was chosen in 1643 one of five to treat with Connecticut, New Haven, and Plymouth concerning the establishment of a confederacy. As a result of their negotiations the New England Confederation was formed and he and William Hathorne were chosen commissioners the following year. Bradstreet acted in that capacity for thirty-three years, during which time his ideas were most influential in molding the development of that first colonial union ("Acts of the Commissioners of the United Colonies" in *Plymouth Colony Records*, X, 108, 187–88).

Massachusetts found it hard to accept colonial status upon the restoration of Charles II, and in 1661 appointed a commission of which Bradstreet was a member, to consider the relations of the colony to the mother country. Finally the General Court decided to send agents to England to negotiate with Charles for favor and selected Bradstreet and John Norton. Both accepted appointment reluctantly. As a result of their successful mission Charles confirmed the charter, but sent a letter making such demands on the colony that the agents were charged, upon their return to New England, with having been too mild. After the death of Leverett, Bradstreet was elected governor in 1679, in which post he served until the establishment of the Dominion under Dudley's commission in 1686. While governor, as well as earlier, he won the reputation of being "moderate" toward England, even Edward Randolph reporting him as one of the three "most popular and well principled men" in the magistracy (*Calendar of State Papers, Colonial, 1675–*

76, §§849, 1067; 1681–85, §1445). As the charter struggle drew on, this conciliatory attitude brought him increasingly into ill favor with the supporters of the old theocracy, resulting in his being declared an enemy of his country in 1684 (*Ibid.*, 1681–85, §1589). He held office however until 1686, when the Dominion of New England was established under the temporary rule of Joseph Dudley. Because of his moderate proclivities Bradstreet received appointment as councillor of the new Dominion, but refused to serve on the grounds that a government without a representative assembly was contrary to Magna Charta. Upon the revolt against the Dominion in April 1689, he and many others formed a council of safety which called a convention of representatives from the towns to settle the government until orders should come from England. The convention voted for restoration of charter government with the officials in office in 1686. Somewhat reluctantly Bradstreet, at this time an old man of eighty-six, assumed the office of governor, continuing therein until the arrival of Sir William Phips, the new royal governor, in May 1692.

Bradstreet was one of the colony's large landowners, several tracts having been given him from time to time as a reward for his public services. He, like many of the moderate party, was interested in land speculation and colonization, and with such men as the Winthrops, Richard Wharton and others, was a member of the Atherton Company for developing a large territory in the Narragansett country. He was also interested in mercantile affairs, and belonged to a company incorporated for trading on the frontier (*Massachusetts Colony Records*, II, 138; III, 53; *Calendar of State Papers, Colonial,* 1661–68, §§493, 967; 1677–80, §837–I). He lived at various times in Cambridge, Ipswich, Andover, and Boston, but spent his last years in Salem, where he died.

[*The Records of the Gov. and Co. of the Mass. Bay in New Eng.* (1850), ed. by Nathaniel Shurtleff; and "Acts of the Commissioners of the United Colonies" (volumes IX and X of *Records of the Colony of New Plymouth in New Eng.,* 1855), also ed. by Nathaniel Shurtleff, are the best sources for a study of the life of Bradstreet. There is also material in Samuel Sewall's "Diary" (5 *Mass. Hist. Soc. Colls.,* vol. V), in the "Winthrop Papers," (5 *Mass. Hist. Soc. Colls.,* vol. VIII and 6 *Mass. Hist. Soc. Colls.,* vol. II).]

V.F.B.

BRADWELL, JAMES BOLESWORTH (Apr. 16, 1828–Nov. 29, 1907), lawyer, was born at Loughborough, England, where his parents, Thomas and Elizabeth (Gutteridge) Bradwell, then resided. In 1829 when he was sixteen months old the family emigrated to the United States, first settling in Utica, N. Y. Five years later they went west to Jacksonville, Ill., and thence to Wheeling, Ill., where in May 1834 his father took up land. James spent his youth on the farm, obtained some knowledge at the local school, and, by manual labor, defrayed his expenses while attending Wilson's Academy, Chicago, and Knox College, Galesburg, Ill. He then determined to study law. This he was enabled to do by working at various trades as a journeyman in Illinois and Tennessee, reading law in his spare time. He was admitted to the Tennessee bar at Memphis in 1852. For two years he was principal of a private school in Memphis, but he returned to Chicago in 1854 and was admitted to the Chicago bar on June 3, 1855. Opening an office in that city, in a short time he acquired a substantial practise, his acquaintance with the laboring classes and their problems materially assisting him. He also took an active interest in public affairs and became favorably known through his natural gifts as an eloquent and forceful speaker. In 1861 he was elected judge of the Cook County court, and being reëlected in 1865 occupied the position for eight years. At that time the court possessed probate jurisdiction, and he made a special study of this branch of law, assembling an extensive library of works on the subject, and by his opinions establishing a reputation, which, after his retirement from office, caused him to be regarded as an expert in all matters concerning wills and administration. In 1873 he was elected to the lower house of the state legislature, and by reëlection served till 1877. There he came to the front as a zealous advocate of reforms particularly in the direction of equalizing the legal status of men and women, and procured the passage of a bill making women eligible for school offices. In 1878 he prepared and issued the first volume of a series of *Reports of the Decisions of the Appellate Courts of the State of Illinois,* which extended to twenty volumes, covering the period 1877–87 (originally known as "Bradwell's Reports," now cited as *Illinois Appellate Court Reports,* I–XX). He had in 1868 assisted his wife, Myra (Colby) Bradwell [*q.v.*], in establishing the *Chicago Legal News* of which she was the editor and publisher, and, after her death in 1894, he assumed active control and undertook the editorial work. In 1903 he was compelled to retire from practise through ill health, and died in Chicago.

Possessed of much ability and indomitable perseverance, his interests covered a wide field. He was an expert in photography and in addition invented a process for making half-tones by which he produced the first half-tone cut made in Chicago. Associating himself closely with his wife's efforts on behalf of woman suffrage and other movements having for their object the complete emancipation of women, he promoted much legislation on that subject, and presided at the organization of the American Woman Suffrage Association at Cleveland. In his later years he was of patriarchal appearance, being more than six feet tall, with a long white beard and whiskers.

[F. B. Wilkie, *Sketches and Notices of the Chicago Bar* (1871), p. 66; I. M. Palmer, ed., *The Bench and Bar of Illinois* (1899), II, 831; J. W. Leonard, ed., *The Book of Chicagoans* (1905); *Proc. Ill. State Bar Ass.,* 1909, p. 410; *Chicago Daily Tribune, Chicago Daily News,* and *Inter-Ocean* (Chicago), Nov. 29, 1907.]

H. W. H. K.

BRADWELL, MYRA (Feb. 12, 1831–Feb. 14, 1894), lawyer and editor, was descended on both sides from pioneer Puritan stock. Her father, Eben Colby, was a member of a well-known New Hampshire family, related by marriage to the Chases, and her mother, Abigail (Willey), was descended from Isaac Willey who came to Boston in 1640. She herself was born at Manchester, Vt. While she was still quite young her father moved to Portage in western New York, where her early education was obtained. In 1843 the family went to Chicago, and she attended school at Kenosha and the Ladies Seminary at Elgin. Unable to obtain a college education since all the western institutions of higher learning were closed to women at that time, she became a school teacher. In 1852 she married James B. Bradwell [*q.v.*], an Englishman of good family and attainments who had come to the United States when young and studied law at Memphis, Tenn. Settling in Memphis, they established a select private school, but two years later went back to Chicago, where Bradwell, having been admitted to the Illinois bar in 1855, opened a law office, subsequently becoming judge of the Cook County court. Mrs. Bradwell took up the study of law, in the first place merely with the idea of assisting her husband in his work, but later determined to qualify herself for practise. In 1868, in the face of much discouragement, she established the *Chicago Legal News,* the pioneer weekly legal newspaper of the West. Assuming the dual position of editor and business manager (being the first woman in the world to occupy such a post) she quickly made a success of the venture, procuring a charter from the legislature and a special act making copies of the *News* containing the laws of the state and the opinions of the supreme court judges evidence of such laws and opinions. The plant of the *News* was totally destroyed in the Chicago fire of 1871, but

she promptly had the paper printed and published in Milwaukee on the regular date. In 1869 she passed the necessary examination and applied to the supreme court of Illinois for admission to the bar. This was refused, the assigned reason being that she was as a married woman under disability. The case was re-argued and again she was refused, this time on the ground that she was a woman (Bradwell *vs.* The State, 55 *Illinois,* 535). The case was carried to the Supreme Court of the United States where the decision of the Illinois court was sustained, May 1873, on the ground that it was within the power of a state to prescribe the qualifications for admission to the bar of its own courts and that with the exercise of this power the United States Supreme Court could not interfere. S. P. Chase dissented (Bradwell *vs.* The State, 16 *Wallace,* 130). In 1882 she procured the passage of an act by the Illinois legislature granting to all persons, irrespective of sex, freedom in selecting a profession. She never renewed her application, but in 1885 the Illinois supreme court *proprio motu* directed a license to practise to be issued to her on her original application. She was admitted to practise before the Supreme Court of the United States, Mar. 28, 1892. She also became a member of the Illinois State Bar Association and the Illinois Press Association— being in each case the first woman to do so.

She devoted much of her time to the promotion of legislation enlarging the sphere of women's activities. She summoned the first Woman Suffrage Convention at Chicago in 1869 and for a number of years was an active member of the executive of the Illinois Woman Suffrage Association, assisting also in the formation of the American Woman Suffrage Association at Cleveland. In 1876 she was one of the Illinois representatives at the Centennial exhibition. She took a leading part in procuring the location of the World's Fair at Chicago in 1893, was one of the lady managers and acted as chairman of the committee on law reform at the auxiliary congress. She died in Chicago, Feb. 14, 1894.

[An excellent review of her life and activities appeared in the *Am. Law Rev.,* XXVIII, 278. See also *Ill. State Bar Ass. Report,* 1894, p. 86; *Mich. Law Jour.,* III, 77, and articles in the *Chicago Legal News,* XXVII, XXVIII. An article "Women Lawyers in the United States," in the *Green Bag,* II, 14, should be consulted.]

H. W. H. K.

BRADY, ANTHONY NICHOLAS (Aug. 22, 1843–July 22, 1913), business man, promoter, of Irish parentage, the son of Nicholas and Ellen (Malone) Brady, was born at Lille, France, and was brought from that country to the United States when a child. He received an elementary education in the schools of Troy, N. Y., but was little drawn toward academic training or education even if the circumstances of his parents would have permitted it. After employment at the Delavan House in Albany during his fifteenth year he determined upon an independent venture. Business of all kinds attracted him from the outset, and various early experiments led to his first effort of a considerable sort which occurred at the age of nineteen, when he opened a tea store at Albany. The enterprise was successful and led to the establishment of other similar stores in Troy and elsewhere and then in New York. During this early period he married Marcia A. Myers, daughter of a Vermont lawyer. His tea stores furnished one of the earliest examples on a small scale of the chain store plan in American retailing. The profits, however, were not sufficiently large to retain the interest of the young promoter. He was attracted by the extensive building movement then in progress in the state of New York, and directed his attention toward operations in building materials. From this it was a natural and easy step to the taking on of contracts for public improvements, including sewers, pavements, and the like. He obtained control of large granite quarries in New York and elsewhere, and furnished material with which to carry out the contracts he had undertaken largely from his own sources of supply. From this, his attention shifted to public utility services, his earliest undertakings being in gas. By this time he had perceived the fact that the field of most immediate profit in public utility construction would undoubtedly be found in tractions. He began to direct his investment of funds, now very considerable in amount, toward the purchase of traction lines in Providence and the neighboring places. New York naturally attracted him as the most promising field of effort, and after 1880, he more and more shifted his interests to that city. He was one of the organizers of the Metropolitan Traction Company, and in 1887 participated in the reorganization of the Brooklyn Rapid Transit Company, continuing as chairman of the board of directors of that enterprise up to his death. More than any other "traction magnate" he influenced plans for the subway development of New York. Although his immediate personal activities had thus been shifted to New York, he did not surrender his general participation and direction of other traction enterprises and in his later years he was engaged in extending his ownership in the street railways of Washington and Philadelphia. Moreover, during his later life he began to expand his field of operations largely in electrical public utilities, becoming concerned in the New York Edison Company as well as in other kindred enterprises.

Public utility reorganization, however, was by no means the measure or limit of his financial ambitions. He had become interested comparatively early in his career in the field of speculation and development of oil, and was one of the first and most vigorous competitors of the Standard Oil Company. Working in conjunction with his traction associates, he succeeded in giving to the Manhattan Oil Company at Lima, Ohio, valuable contracts for the supply of a large part of the oil used by the more considerable businesses of Chicago. Later on, a fairly close junction of interest between Brady and the so called Standard Oil group was formed, and he became associated with the latter in a large number of enterprises that had only a more or less indirect connection with the oil industry. The idea of consolidation, which he had found so effective and profitable in connection with tractions and public utilities, constituted the basis of his operations in these other fields, and he attempted to carry out promotion and combination schemes, not only in oil but also in tobacco and rubber, meeting with unusual success, not merely in a financial way but also in the actual development and improvement of operating conditions. During his final years, he tended more and more to devote his attention to traction interests, and only a year before his death was instrumental in extending the control of the Brooklyn Rapid Transit so as to take in the Coney Island and Brooklyn lines, the only remaining independent mileage in that portion of New York. A list of his directorships would be a long one but the number of enterprises in which he was a real though unseen power was probably much greater than the number of those in which he appeared as an active figure. At the time of his death his interests were very diversified and estimates of his real worth varied widely, conservative figures placing it at $50,000,000. Florid in complexion and of thick-set figure he was the exemplification of the "self-made man."

[*Who's Who in America*, 1912–13; *Albany Evening Jour.*, July 23, 24, 1913; *N. Y. Tribune*, July 24, 1913; *N. Y. Times*, July 24, 1913; *Sun* (N. Y.), July 23, 24, 1913.]

H. P. W.

BRADY, CYRUS TOWNSEND (Dec. 20, 1861–Jan. 24, 1920), Episcopal clergyman, novelist, was born at Allegheny, Pa., the son of Jasper Ewing Brady, Jr., a banker and expert accountant, and of Harriet Cora Townsend. The Bradys were a Scotch-Irish family that had been settled in Pennsylvania since about 1744 and from generation to generation had displayed a genius for frontier fighting and for begetting numerous sons as bellicose as their fathers. Cyrus graduated from the United States Naval Academy in 1883 and after three years in the navy went west and found employment with the Missouri Pacific and Union Pacific Railroads. Though of Presbyterian antecedents, he was confirmed, while living in Omaha, in the Episcopal Church and proceeded to study for holy orders under Bishop Worthington of Nebraska. Since he was already married to Clarissa Sidney Guthrie and had several children to support, giving up his work was out of the question. He therefore read theology on trolley cars, during noon hours, and late at night, was ordained deacon in 1889 and priest in 1890, served several small charges in Missouri and Colorado, and was archdeacon of Kansas until 1895. His duties carried him over five states and, stalwart, two-fisted descendant of Indian fighters though he was, Brady found his work strenuous. "In three years, by actual count," he wrote later, "I travelled over 91,000 miles by railroad, wagon, and on horseback, preaching or delivering addresses upward of 11,000 times, besides writing letters, papers, making calls, marrying, baptizing, and doing all the other endless work of an itinerant missionary."

He returned east to be archdeacon of Pennsylvania, 1895–99, and rector of St. Paul's, Overbrook, Philadelphia, 1899 to 1902, meanwhile acting as chaplain of the 1st Pennsylvania Volunteer Infantry in the Spanish-American War and contracting camp and typhoid fever while in the service. His first novel, a story of the American Revolution entitled *For Love of Country,* appeared in 1898 and is said to have been dictated into a phonograph. He followed it the next year with a romance of the War of 1812, *For the Freedom of the Sea,* and thereafter the overflowing energies that had gone into his archidiaconal activities were poured into authorship. During the next twenty years he published more than seventy volumes. From 1902 to 1905 he made his home in Brooklyn, giving all his time to literary work, but he was rector of Trinity, Toledo, Ohio, 1905–09, of St. George's, Kansas City, Mo., 1909–13, and of the Church of the Ascension, Mt. Vernon, N. Y., 1913–14, resigning from the last because he considered the salary too low. Thereafter he was connected with St. Stephen's in New York City, where he preached from time to time. He died of pneumonia at his home in Yonkers, N. Y., Jan. 24, 1920, after an illness of two days. He was survived by his sec-

ond wife, who was a Mary Barrett, and by his three sons and three daughters.

By experience and temperament Brady was ideally fitted to be a purveyor of cheap fiction. Although he was far from being a good observer, his life at sea, in the west, and in the east had given him an abundance of raw material, while in thought and feeling he was completely in harmony with the vast public that devoured his books as they were published and later applauded them when they were translated into moving pictures. His novels have no literary merit, but they are interesting to the historian of literature as an indication of popular taste over a period of twenty years. Besides his novels, Brady wrote juvenile stories, popular biographies of Stephen Decatur (1900), John Paul Jones (1900), and Andrew Jackson (1906), an historical work, *The Conquest of the Southwest* (1905), and some miscellaneous matter. His sentimentality and lack of invention are least in evidence and his good qualities—a gift for brisk, exciting narrative and a genuine love of "red-blooded" men—are displayed to best advantage in the series of volumes called *American Fights and Fighters.*

[B. McK. H. Swope, *Hist. of the Families of Mckinney—Brady—Quigley* (1905); W. G. Murdock, *Brady Family Reunion and Fragments of Brady Hist. and Biog.* (1909); *Who's Who in America,* 1918–19; *N. Y. Times,* Jan. 25, 27, 1920; *N. Y. Tribune,* Jan. 25, 1920 (a friendly and apparently well-informed obituary). There are a few biographical details in Brady's anecdotal *Recollections of a Missionary in the Great West* (1900).]　　　　　　　　　　　　　G.H.G.

BRADY, JAMES TOPHAM (Apr. 9, 1815– Feb. 9, 1869), lawyer, politician, was of pure Irish ancestry. His parents had emigrated from Ireland in 1812, settling at first in Newark, N. J., and moving in 1814 to New York City, where he was born Apr. 9, 1815. His father, Thomas J. Brady, a man of much intellectual attainment, had opened a private preparatory school, being subsequently admitted to the New York bar, and the son was given a thorough classical education. He entered his father's law office in 1831, and while yet a student gave evidence of the possession of unusual forensic ability, assisting his father in all his court cases. He was admitted to the New York bar in 1836, and his first case brought him prominently before the public. It related to the status of a slave, Coppen, and though he was unsuccessful his handling of the matter was masterly. From that day he was in constant demand in all classes of cases. He possessed from the start a valuable asset in an innate courtesy and urbanity of manner which was charming. His briefs were always carefully prepared, nothing being left to chance, and he was tireless in his study of all conceivable contingencies. As a student he had acquired a thorough knowledge of the underlying principles of law, and in his practise he did not concern himself much with precedent. Technicalities had no attraction for him and he always strove to bring himself within some broad principle. He was endowed by nature with a facility of speech, which, assiduously cultivated and molded by long study, and embellished with felicitous classical quotations, became well-nigh irresistible with a jury, whilst his arguments, clear, logical, never verbose, were put with a force and sincerity which always impressed the court.

Shortly after the Coppen case, he appeared as junior counsel to Daniel Webster in Goodyear *vs.* Day—"the India Rubber Case"—his opening speech drawing forth unstinted praise from his celebrated colleague. Henceforth he was recognized as a leader of the New York bar, and for the next twenty years appeared on one side or the other in almost all the important law-suits of the time. In 1843 he was appointed district attorney for New York, and in 1845 became for a short period corporation counsel, but these were the only public offices he ever filled. Later in his career he was offered the position of attorney-general of the United States, but declined.

His ability was displayed over the whole field of law, civil and criminal, and his services were requisitioned in every class of litigation and before all courts, both trial and appellate. He was intensely interested in the subject of insanity, of which he made a special study in all its phases. The Parrish and Allaire will cases, and the trial of Cole for murder, in the latter of which he invoked the defense of moral insanity, are outstanding instances of his facile handling of extremely difficult problems of medical jurisprudence. In purely civil cases he was equally effective. In one case he obtained $300,000 damages, the largest verdict up to that time given in a civil court. On the criminal side his influence over juries was phenomenal. He was counsel in fifty-two murder trials, and only failed in one. In one week he defended in four homicide cases and secured acquittals in all. In 1865, toward the end of his career, he was appointed a member of the commission which sat at New Orleans to investigate the charges of maladministration against Generals Banks and Butler and the Gulf Military Department but the ensuing report was never published.

He was equally prominent in politics, but never a leader, his independent habits of thought not being those of the professional politician. Prior to the war he was an ardent Democrat and ultra state's man, and in 1860 permitted himself to be nominated as candidate for governor of New York as a supporter of Breckinridge, actuated solely by a desire to uphold the principles he believed in, and knowing well that there was not the slightest chance of his election. He was a strong supporter of the administrative measures of the Government during the war, appearing on the public platform, and making speeches, which, by their brilliance of thought and patriotic spirit, attracted national attention. He was "absolutely indifferent to the prizes of political life" (*In Memoriam,* post.). In 1861 he refused the Tammany nomination for mayor of New York City, declining also repeated invitations to enter the state legislature and Congress. Every important position in the control of the Democratic party of New York was in turn proffered him in vain. He died in New York City, Feb. 9, 1869. He never married. His brother, John R. Brady, was a judge of the supreme court of New York, 1869-91.

Of medium height, and good physique, he always attracted attention by his piercing eye and monumental head, which was larger, it is said, than that of Webster. His manner was courtly, his conversation sparkling, and he was insensibly the center of attraction in the social circles where he loved to relax. He possessed cultured tastes, particularly in literature, and contributed many fugitive pieces to the *Knickerbocker Magazine* and other current periodicals. His best known work, "A Christmas Dream," written for the *New World* in 1846 and republished in book form, was extremely popular.

[The sources of information respecting the public and professional career of Brady are extensive and easily accessible. The files of the New York press covering the period 1835-69 do ample justice to his manifold activities. *In Memoriam, James T. Brady,* being a Report of a meeting of the Bar of the City of New York, Feb. 13, 1869, testifies to the high regard entertained for him by the legal profession. An excellent summary of his life appeared in the *Am. Law Rev.,* III, 779, and *The Bench and Bar of New York* by L. B. Proctor (1870), p. 238; see also *Central Law Jour.,* I, 544, and the *Green Bag,* III, 305.]   H. W. H. K.

BRADY, MATHEW B. (*c.* 1823–Jan. 15, 1896), pioneer photographer, was born, according to his statement to George Alfred Townsend, in Warren County, N. Y. His father was an Irishman; of his mother nothing is recorded. In spite of his meager schooling he managed to pick up some sort of an education. He had his own way of spelling the first part of his given name, and he appears not to have known what the initial "B." represented. At Saratoga he met William Page, the portrait painter, who encouraged him to draw and who later, in New York, introduced him to S. F. B. Morse. Brady became deeply interested in Daguerre's discovery (made known in 1839) as well as in the photographic experiments of Morse and Prof. J. W. Draper, in the fall of that year, and soon began experimenting on his own account. Improvements rapidly brought the daguerreotype to the stage of a commercial success, and in either 1842 or 1843 Brady established a portrait studio at the corner of Broadway and Fulton St. in New York. His work soon attracted attention, and his studio was patronized by thousands. At each of the annual exhibitions of the American Institute in the years 1844–48 his exhibit received the first premium award of a silver medal and in 1849 the first gold medal ever awarded to daguerreotypes. About this time he began to make tinted daguerreotypes on ivory, an innovation that brought him increased patronage. He published, in 1850, his *Gallery of Illustrious Americans,* which had a considerable circulation. In 1851 he took a collection of forty-eight portraits to the World's Fair, in London, receiving the prize medal "for American daguerreotypes," with a commendation for their "beauty of execution," and in 1853 he received the prize medal at the World's Fair in New York. About 1855 he brought over from England Alexander Gardner, an expert in the wet-plate process invented by Scott-Archer, and thereupon discarded the daguerreotype for the photograph. He established a branch studio at Washington in 1858, and in 1859 a second studio, farther uptown, in New York, subsequently abandoning the one at Fulton St. The most eminent Americans in all walks of life sat for him, and he became famous as well as prosperous.

At the beginning of the Civil War he interested President Lincoln and others, including Allan Pinkerton, the head of the secret service, in his proposal to photograph battle and camp scenes, and received permission for himself and his assistants to accompany the armies. Zealous in their work, often regardless of danger, and at all times handicapped by the vexing difficulties of the photographing process of that day, these men carried their cameras to every scene that promised an interesting picture. More than 3,500 photographs are said to have been taken—many of them scenes of actual conflict, others of places devastated by gunfire, of troops on the march or in bivouac, and of individual officers and men. After the war he sought to recover copies of those that had passed from his hands, and in a booklet published by him in 1870, *Brady's National Photographic Collection of War Views and Portraits of Representative Men,* proposed the purchase of the collection by the Government for a permanent exhibit. In 1875 the Govern-

ment purchased, for $25,000, a set of 2,000 of these photographs, at present stored in the War College. Another and less complete set had gone to Anthony & Company of New York, in payment of money due for photographic supplies; and this collection, with additions from a number of private collections, has been the basis for the various photographic histories of the Civil War that have appeared. Brady lost heavily by the war; the panic of 1873 completed his financial ruin, and the money obtained from the Government soon disappeared. He continued as a photographer in Washington until he was advanced in age, but never regained the prestige of his earlier days. He spent his declining years, afflicted with rheumatism and failing eyesight, in comparative poverty. In 1895, in Washington, he was run over by a vehicle, and for months thereafter was confined to his bed. Partly recovering, he went to New York, where he was tenderly cared for by a few friends, and some money was raised for him. Taken ill, he was carried to the Presbyterian Hospital, where he died.

Brady was married, about 1860, to Julia Handy, of the Eastern Shore of Maryland, who died on May 23, 1887. He was of slight but trim and square-shouldered figure, about five feet six in height, with a face expressive of refinement and intelligence. All pictures of him present him with a mustache and pointed beard, and those of Civil War times show him wearing a broad-brimmed flat hat, "like that of a Paris art student," and a linen duster. His work as a photographer was marked by initiative, enterprise, and artistry. He was usually the first to avail himself of every improvement in technique, many of the innovations being his own; and he succeeded in a rare degree in picturing his subjects in natural and unconstrained attitudes, with their individual characters strongly revealed. His nature was improvident; he could make money, but he could not retain it. He was a genial, friendly, modest man, deferential in manner, and he bore with uncomplaining cheerfulness the pathetic poverty of his last days.

[G. A. Townsend, interview with Brady in the N. Y. *World,* Apr. 12, 1891; material furnished by Brady's nephew, L. C. Handy, of Washington; obituaries in the *Evening Star* and the *Post,* of Washington, Jan. 18, 1896.]   W. J. G.

BRAGG, BRAXTON (Mar. 22, 1817–Sept. 27, 1876), Confederate soldier, was born at Warrenton, N. C., the son of Thomas Bragg, a contractor and builder, and of Margaret Crossland, an energetic and intelligent woman. He received his early education at his home town, was appointed a cadet at West Point in 1833, and graduated four years later as a second lieutenant, 3rd Artillery. He participated in the Seminole War, and in 1845 he joined Taylor's army in Texas. In 1846 he took part in the battles at Fort Brown and Monterey, for both of which actions he was brevetted. At about the same time he was promoted to captain, of Battery C, 3rd Artillery. Bragg's most distinguished service in this war was at Buena Vista, Feb. 23, 1847, where his battery, by its extraordinary activity, filled gaps in the American lines, and broke the attack of a vastly superior Mexican force. For this Bragg was brevetted lieutenant-colonel. In 1849 he married Elisa Brooks Ellis of Louisiana, and in 1856 resigned from the army and purchased a plantation in Louisiana. He became a commissioner of public works, and designed the drainage and levee system of his adopted state.

Early in 1861 Bragg was appointed a colonel, and soon after a major-general in the Louisiana militia. On Feb. 23, he was commissioned a brigadier-general, Confederate States Army, and assigned to command the coast between Pensacola and Mobile. In January 1862 he became a major-general. On Feb. 15, 1862, he proposed to the Secretary of War that his command be in part sent to Kentucky, where he foresaw that important events would take place. His advice was accepted, and he was ordered north. At Corinth, Miss., he assisted Gen. Johnston to organize his army. Bragg was given command of the 2nd Corps, and in addition was chief of staff. He went with the army to Shiloh. On Apr. 6, at the first attack at Shiloh, the 2nd Corps was in second line, but it soon became merged into the front line, Bragg supervising the Confederate right. With great energy he assaulted the Federal lines, and captured thousands of prisoners and many guns. A considerable part of the success of this day was due to the energy and vigor of Bragg. On Apr. 7, the Federals, reënforced by Buell's fresh army, had only exhausted Confederates in front of them. Fighting bravely, the latter slowly retreated until the order was given to withdraw to Corinth whither they were not followed. On Apr. 12 Bragg was promoted to general, and on June 27 relieved Beauregard of the command of the Army of Tennessee. On July 20, Gen. Kirby Smith at Knoxville advised Bragg that the Federals were about to seize Chattanooga. Kirby Smith suggested that Bragg strike into middle Tennessee to relieve the situation. Bragg at once adopted this idea. He promptly started his command for Chattanooga where he arrived with most of his army by the end of the month, ahead

of the Federals. On July 30 it was agreed that Kirby Smith, with about 18,000 men, should turn the Union forces at Cumberland Gap and advance into Kentucky. Bragg at the same time, with 30,000, was to march on and seize Munfordville, Ky., and then join Kirby Smith. This plan of action was political. It was hoped that a Confederate army in Kentucky would induce that state to join the South. The plan was defective from a military point of view, in that it failed to provide for defeating the Federal army under Buell, then in front of Chattanooga.

Due to lack of transportation, a month's delay occurred, and Bragg did not start until Aug. 27. He then moved rapidly, and captured Munfordville on Sept. 17. He was now between Buell's army and its base at Louisville, and could either have attacked the one or taken the other. But he did not feel strong enough to attack Buell, and the political nature of his expedition led him to Frankfort to install a Confederate state governor. This was fatal to the success of his campaign. Buell reached Louisville, united his forces, and set out to fight Bragg. On Oct. 8, Buell fought a part of Bragg's army at Perryville. Tactically the battle was drawn, but Bragg being unwilling to fight to a decision withdrew that night into Tennessee. Kentucky had shown no desire to join the South, and the campaign was a failure. It led to great dissatisfaction with Bragg, but he retained his command.

At the end of December a new Federal army under Rosecrans advanced on Bragg, then near Stone River, Tenn. Bragg, always energetic, attacked on Dec. 31, although he had only about 38,000 men against 47,000. The Confederate attack made great gains, but Bragg failed to force the fighting on the next day or otherwise exploit his victory. After minor fighting he judged his men were exhausted and faced by superior numbers, and on Jan. 3, 1863, withdrew to Tullahoma. This was a repetition of Shiloh and Perryville. Although full of energy, Bragg was not persistent. After Stone River he invited his subordinates to express their opinion of him, and received frank statements that his presence was not wanted. President Davis however decided to keep him in command.

In June 1863, Rosecrans maneuvered Bragg out of Tullahoma, and by Sept. 9, out of Chattanooga. Forced into the mountains, Bragg sought to destroy fractions of the Federal forces while they were separated one from another. Several combinations failed, due to lack of support by subordinate generals. This was the result of quarrels, and resentment. But on Sept.

19 and 20, Bragg attacked Rosecrans at Chickamauga. He won a notable victory, and forced
the Federals with severe losses back into Chattanooga where he laid siege to them. In this he
made a serious error. Had he continued his offensive he might have captured large forces, but
siege operations brought him nothing. Grant,
assigned to the command of the Federals con-
fronting him, opened a line of supply, and then
attacked Bragg at Chattanooga on Nov. 23 to
25. The Confederate center broke, and Bragg
retreated to Dalton, Ga., where on Dec. 2, 1863,
he surrendered command of his army to Johnston. This ended Bragg's important services.
During 1864, he was at Richmond, nominally as
commander-in-chief. Practically he was military adviser to President Davis. He had several
minor commands. His last battle was on Mar.
8, 1865, at Kingston, N. C., against a part of
Sherman's forces. He accompanied President
Davis in his flight to Georgia, was captured on
May 9, and was paroled.

After the war Bragg practised as a civil engineer at Mobile and later in Texas, was a commissioner of public works of Alabama for four
years, and supervised the harbor improvements
of Mobile. He died at Galveston, suddenly.

Tall, bearded, and ungainly, he was intelligent and energetic and had a stern sense of
duty. Irritable and quarrelsome, he made many
enemies. This prevented him from securing that
loyalty from subordinates which military commanders need. He was a strict disciplinarian,
and the Confederates had in the west no organizer to equal him. Bragg's greatest military
fault was in not following up his successes.
His victories were fruitless.

[The chief source of information for Bragg's campaigns is the *Official Records. Battles and Leaders of
the Civil War* (1887–88) contains notable articles; secondary works are *Braxton Bragg,* by D. C. Seitz (1924),
a complete story of his life; and the *Story of the Civil
War* by John C. Ropes (1904), the latter excellent as
to the 1862 campaigns.]   C. H. L—a.

BRAGG, EDWARD STUYVESANT (Feb.
20, 1827–June 20, 1912), Union soldier, congressman, was descended from one of the Vermont settlers who had been ousted from his
lands in the dispute between New Hampshire
and New York during the Revolutionary period
and who pushed out into the Chenango Valley of
New York. His son, Joel Bragg (1784–1870),
grew up in what was then a frontier environment, married a German woman, Margaretha
Kohl of Lancaster, Pa., and became the owner
of a sawmill, a grist-mill, and a tavern at Unadilla, Otsego County, N. Y. In the country
made known to the world by James Fenimore
Cooper, Edward Stuyvesant was born and grew
to manhood. The youth attended not less than
four of the neighboring academies, which in
those days held the place later occupied by high
schools, and then spent several years at Geneva
(later Hobart) College, but from the early age
of twelve he had fixed on the law as his calling
and at twenty he was "reading" in the office of
Judge Charles C. Noble at Unadilla. In 1848
he was admitted to the bar on court examination.
He had been in practise only two years when the
pioneering instinct that had moved his father
and grandfather impelled him to seek his fortune in the tide of westward migration and he
chose the new state of Wisconsin as the scene of
his future activities. He settled at Fond du Lac,
on the southern end of Lake Winnebago, and
that was his home for more than six decades.
Within four years he had married, on Jan. 2,
1854, Cornelia Colman, a grand-daughter of one
of the founders of Rochester, N. Y., and had
been elected district attorney of the county. A
Douglas Democrat, he was a delegate to the
Charleston Convention of 1860. The opening
of the Civil War found him a "War Democrat,"
intensely devoted to the Union cause and eager
to take the field. In June 1861 he raised a company and was commissioned captain in the 6th
Wisconsin Volunteer Infantry. This regiment
was destined to see as much active service in
the war as any other Wisconsin organization.
In its period of training it was one of the regiments whose "watch-fires of a hundred circling
camps" helped to inspire Julia Ward Howe's
"Battle Hymn of the Republic." Bragg's promotions to major, lieutenant-colonel, and colonel
quickly followed the reports of his superiors on
the battles in which the Sixth was engaged,
following one another in rapid succession—
Gainesville, South Mountain, Antietam (where
he was severely wounded), Fredericksburg,
Chancellorsville, the Wilderness (where he temporarily commanded a Pennsylvania regiment),
Spotsylvania, Laurel Hill, North Anna, and
Cold Harbor. On June 8, 1864, he commanded
the Iron Brigade, leading in the assault on
Petersburg. In this long series of engagements,
his conduct and bravery had been extolled by
the commanding officers and his exploit at Fitz-
Hugh's Crossing, when he crossed the Rappahannock with his troops in boats under the
enemy's fire and captured their works, made him
a brigadier-general of volunteers. He had taken
part in every one of the Iron Brigade's major
battles except Gettysburg, from which he was
kept by illness.

Bragg was in no sense one of the "political

generals" so numerous in the war (he did not belong to the national party that was dominant in the North); but he was always keenly interested in politics. While serving in the field he was nominated for Congress in his district and defeated. After the war he was a delegate to the Union national convention of 1866, was elected state senator in 1867, and was a delegate to the national Democratic convention that nominated Greeley for president in 1872. His district sent him to Congress for four terms (1877–83 and 1885–87). Twice (1884 and 1896) he was chairman of the Wisconsin delegation to national Democratic conventions. In seconding the nomination of Cleveland for president in 1884, "the little General" hurled at the New York delegation, controlled by Tammany, a piercing epigram that was to be remembered and repeated in three campaigns: "We love him for the enemies he has made!" In a canvass when every Democratic vote was needed it was audacity to the verge of recklessness, but it went to the heart of a situation that in Bragg's opinion required blood-letting. At such a time no consideration of political expediency had weight with him. He was a politician—and a clever one—up to the point where his convictions asserted themselves. Beyond that point politics might go to the winds. Twelve years later, when the Democrats nominated Bryan for president on a Free-Silver platform he was among the outstanding "Gold Democrats" of the country who refused Bryan their support. In 1900, again, similar reasons led Bragg, a life-long Democrat, to support McKinley and the Republican ticket. After the expiration of his last term in Congress, Bragg had been named by President Cleveland as minister to Mexico, but this appointment expired with the Cleveland Administration in 1889. In 1902 President Roosevelt appointed him consul general at Hong Kong, China. Bragg remained there four years, returned to America in 1906, supported Taft for the presidency in 1908, and died at Fond du Lac on June 20, 1912.

[F. W. Halsey, *The Pioneers of Unadilla Village* (1902); Maurice McKenna, ed., *Fond du Lac County, Wis., Past and Present* (1912); *Official Records*, ser. 1; Rufus R. Dawes, *Service with the Sixth Wisconsin Volunteers* (1890).]   W. B. S.

BRAGG, THOMAS (Nov. 9, 1810–Jan. 21, 1872), lawyer, Confederate statesman, born in Warrenton, N. C., was the brother of Braxton Bragg [*q.v.*], and the son of Thomas Bragg, carpenter and contractor, and his intelligent and handsome wife, Margaret Crossland. After studying in the local academy and for three years in Capt. Partridge's military school at Middletown, Conn., young Thomas read law under a

supreme court judge in Warrenton and then, at twenty-three, began practise in the neighboring county of Northampton. Assiduous devotion to his profession for the next twenty-two years brought him a comfortable living and a fine reputation as a lawyer who prepared his cases thoroughly, and directed his appeals to intelligence and character. Reading in his home at night in the company of his wife, Isabella Cuthbert (married on Oct. 4, 1837), was his chief recreation, pipe-smoking his constant dissipation. But party prominence came slowly. Whiggish Northampton, liking neither his sternness and aloofness nor his Democracy, sent him but once (1842) to the legislature though he then acquitted himself well as a hard-working and level-headed chairman of the judiciary committee of the House and as a candidate for attorney-general (*House Journal*, 1842–43, pp. 513 and *passim*). But ability and energy at last triumphed. Having thrice stumped his district as candidate for elector, in 1854 he voluntarily went out to meet the able and popular Whig candidate for governor. Pleased at his showing, Democratic leaders gave him their nomination. He won then narrowly, but handsomely two years later. Voluminous "official papers" and neatly indexed letter-books speak eloquently of Bragg's attention to the state's business. True to his party's recently assumed position, he urged the immediate liberalization of the senatorial franchise and the development of the state's resources through improved banking, geological surveys, and rapid extension of the state railway system. But, constitutionally conservative, he mildly defended the past and he left unmodified the inequitable tax system. Solemnly warning against federal encroachment on the state's domain he counseled no hostile counteraction (*Legislative Documents*, 1854–55, 1856–57). "A sound and reliable statesman" was the Raleigh *Standard's* verdict (Dec. 1, 1858), and a seat in the federal Senate was his reward. Thoroughly Jeffersonian, Bragg in Washington set himself against public extravagance. Free homesteads and distribution of federal funds to the states he deemed corrupting and intended to corrupt. To the old and complicated issue of the Florida Land Claims he endeavored to apply the principles of private justice, made a speech on it in opposition to Mallory and the redoubtable Toombs, and lost no laurels in the contest (*Congressional Globe*, 36 Cong., 1 Sess., pp. 1249, 2040, 2630). Then came the Civil War. In 1856 he had counseled conservatism and in 1860 delay. In 1861 he believed secession impracticable (though justifiable), but because of popular feeling he "kept his opinions within his own breast" (Cowper). Soon he was busy, as an aid to the governor, in preparing military defense. As attorney-general of the Confederacy, Nov. 21, 1861–Mar. 18, 1862, he apparently drafted a plan of organization for the department; and he worked out the nominations submitted by the President on Mar. 19, 1862 (*Journal of the Congress of the Confederate States*, V, 26; II, 108). Then he returned to Raleigh and in the dual capacity of representative of President Davis and chairman of a strong citizens' committee sought to keep the state in line. Although in 1864 Davis rejected his proposal for deferring conscription pending the elections (Dunbar Rowland, *Jefferson Davis, Constitutionalist*, 1923, VI, 201), he was credited by Holden with chief responsibility for Gov. Vance's loyalty. After the war Bragg resumed, from financial necessity, the practise of law. Ere long, too, he was deep in the fight for decent government, his judgment ripened, his once black full beard now grizzled, his fine eyes looking out from beneath heavy brows calmly and directly as of old, but unsmilingly. His death was deemed to have been hastened by his exertions as counsel for the impeachment of Gov. Holden, once his political friend and patron, whose trial he closed with a masterly plea for a verdict free from considerations of political purposes or consequences.

[The sketch by Pulaski Cowper, Bragg's private secretary, in the *N. C. Univ. Mag.*, Jan. 1891, informing, and reasonably accurate. Ashe and Boyd in their volumes on North Carolina and J. G. de R. Hamilton, *Reconstruction in N. C.* (1914) supply background and important details. Bragg's speech against Holden is in *The Trial of Wm. W. Holden* (1871); his own report of his debate with Gilmer in 1856 is in W. J. Peele's *Lives of Distinguished North Carolinians* (1898), which also reproduces his portrait. An obituary appeared in the *Daily Sentinel* (Raleigh), Jan. 23, 1872.]

C.C.P.

BRAINARD, DANIEL (May 15, 1812–Oct. 10, 1866), surgeon and pioneer in medical education, was the fifth child of a family of nine born to Jeptha, Jr., and Catherine (Comstock) Brainard. His father, a descendant in the fifth generation from that Daniel Brainard who as a boy of eight arrived in America from England in 1649, was a farmer in Oneida County, N. Y., first at Western and later at Whitesboro (Lucy Abigail Brainard, *The Genealogy of the Brainerd-Brainard Family in America, 1649–1908*). Though accounts differ as to which of these was the birthplace of the young Daniel, evidence favors the former place. In Whitesboro, he attended the common schools and the Oneida Institute, and here, in 1829, he began the study of medicine with Dr. R. S. Sykes. Shortly after-

ward he moved to the near-by town of Rome, continuing his medical studies with Dr. Harold H. Pope. His medical course was taken at Fairfield Medical College, Fairfield, N. Y., followed by two courses at Jefferson Medical College in Philadelphia, where he was graduated in 1834. He early specialized in anatomy and physiology, and even before taking his medical degree, he lectured upon these subjects at Fairfield and at Whitesboro. He returned after graduation to the latter place, where though nominally in practise, he devoted two years to the study of languages and science. Early in 1836, he started for the then far west and the spring of that year found him in Chicago, a town of between two and three thousand inhabitants. Here he established himself for practise. His early bent toward medical teaching is shown by his application to the state authorities in 1837 for a charter for a medical college to be named in honor of Dr. Benjamin Rush. The time for launching the medical school was not then ripe, so Brainard contented himself temporarily with a private school of anatomy conducted in his office. In the meantime, after a somewhat discouraging start, he had won a firm footing in the medical practise of the fast-growing town.

Not yet satisfied with his preparation for teaching he went, in 1839, to Paris where he remained nearly two years. His later work and his writings show how deeply he was influenced by his contact with the French school of surgery. Returning to Chicago, he was appointed, in 1842, to the chair of anatomy in St. Louis University, where he delivered two courses of lectures. His early dreams materialized with the opening of Rush Medical College on Dec. 4, 1843, on which occasion he delivered the introductory address. He was given the chair of anatomy and surgery in the new faculty, and he remained professor of surgery until his death, always the dominating figure in the affairs of the school. In April 1844 appeared the first number of the *Illinois Medical and Surgical Journal*, which after various changes of name became the *Chicago Medical Journal*. Brainard aided in its foundation and for years contributed clinical reports and editorials to its pages. He also took part in the establishment of the first general hospital in Chicago in 1847, being one of three physicians who constituted its medical staff. In 1853 he again went to Paris where before the Academy of Science he read a paper on "The Venom of Rattlesnakes; the Effects of the Venom, and the Means of Neutralizing its Absorption." This was followed by a paper before the same society by himself and Dr. Greene on "Iodine as an Antidote for Curare." Later before the Société de Chirurgie of Paris, he read a paper entitled "On the Injection of Iodine in Tissues and Cavities of the Body for the Cure of Spina Bifida, Chronic Hydrocephalus, Edema, Fibrinous Effusions, Edematous Erysipelas, etc." At this time, he was made a corresponding member of the Société de Chirurgie. In 1854, he was elected president of the Illinois State Medical Society. In the same year he was awarded a prize by the American Medical Association for his essay entitled "An Essay on a New Method of Treating Ununited Fractures and Certain Deformities of the Osseous System" (published in the *Transactions of the American Medical Association*, 1854). This essay is one of the American medical classics. In a somewhat less complete form, it was published in Paris in French shortly before its American appearance. These essays and numerous articles on clinical surgery make up his contributions to medical literature. At the time of his death he was engaged upon an extensive surgical work which remained unfinished. It was in the fall of 1866, while cholera was epidemic in Chicago, that Brainard returned from a short visit in Paris where he had left his family. On the afternoon of Oct. 9, while lecturing to his class at the college, he devoted a portion of the hour to a discussion of the local cholera situation and of the precautions to be taken against it. That evening at his home he began an article on the same subject. Retiring in apparently good health, he was stricken with cholera early the next morning and died on the evening of that day.

Brainard was tall, well proportioned, and strongly built. His portraits show a large head with long wavy hair and a strong face with a large straight nose, clear piercing eyes, and a heavy drooping mustache. He was a man of great dignity, very reserved, and taciturn to a degree. These characteristics gave him a reputation of being short-tempered and ill-natured. As a lecturer, his command of terse English enabled him to give a maximum of instruction with a minimum of words. He was a forceful public speaker and took an active interest not only in medical society work, but also in matters relating to his city and state. For twenty years he dominated surgical thought in his city while his reputation was extended into international surgical circles. He was married to Evelyn Sleight of Naperville, Ill., on Feb. 6, 1845.

[Jas. Nevins Hyde, "Early Medical Chicago" in the *Chicago Medic. Jour. and Examiner*, 1876; E. Fletcher Ingalls, in the *Ill. Medic. Jour.*, XXII, 1912; Kelly and Burrage, *Am. Medic. Biogs.* (1920).] J. M. P.

BRAINARD, JOHN GARDINER CALKINS (Oct. 21, 1796–Sept. 26, 1828), poet, whose reputation evoked a eulogy from Whittier and a sneer from Poe, was the youngest son of Sarah (Gardiner) Brainard and Jeremiah G. Brainard, a graduate of Yale College in the class of 1779, and a judge of the superior court of Connecticut. His taste for poetry appeared early in boyhood, and at Yale, where he was graduated in the class of 1815. The traditions of his family (the Brainards or Brainerds, of Flemish origin, had come to Hartford about 1649) led into the practise of the law, a profession for which he was temperamentally unsuited. His lovable nature which had made him a favorite at college shrank from the rough professional business of the day. He studied faithfully in the office of his brother, William F. Brainard; he was admitted to the bar (1819) with honor; he developed a small clientele in Middletown, Conn.; but he was, throughout this unlucky episode, thoroughly unhappy. In his own words he could not endure the "personal altercation, contradiction and . . . hard collision" of his contemporaries. To understand this, one needs only to look at his portrait which mirrors clearly his gentle and introspective spirit. He retired from the law, and returned to his birthplace, New London, where, had he possessed energy, he might have matured his gift for verse. Yet, though his mild nature recoiled from the world, he needed its stimulus, and in the winter of 1822 he became associated with P. B. Goodsell, the Hartford publisher, as editor of the *Connecticut Mirror*. This was a compromise, for Brainard was ruffled by the severe tasks of journalism. The militant politics of the age aroused in him no enthusiasm for editorial or controversy. Yet the necessity of regular writing overcame his timidity, and he had now in the periodical a medium for his delicate poetic talent. Thus he found, in spite of recurrent indolence and excessive sensibility, his vocation: to write was, if we consider his life as a whole, his one passion. It was so in college that he had interested his classmates; even as a lawyer he had written "The Memoirs of Gabriel Gap" for a New Haven paper, the *Microscope;* and he now composed steadily for the *Connecticut Mirror*. He had all the ambition of the sensitive man, and in this period was to be the crisis of his career. It occurred in 1825, in the publication of his *Occasional Pieces of Poetry*, an attractive volume made up of some fifty pieces culled from the *Mirror*. The book made a stir, and might have stimulated any one save Brainard to further effort. He was now well-known, a clumsy little man with paddling walk, pale sensitive face, abstracted air, careless dress, and great personal charm. If not too frightened, he could display, says a contemporary, repartee of the first order. It was now that Brainard's friends rightly urged a second volume to solidify his reputation. He tried to respond to this sensible advice, but as usual procrastinated, and the only other volume brought out in his lifetime was the unimportant *Fort Braddock Letters* (1827). He had that curious temperament, often found in literary men, of extravagant ambition inhibited by the profound and disheartening conviction of failure. He could not, he told S. G. Goodrich despairingly, sustain the necessary continuity of thought to hold to his purpose. "There was," says an intimate friend, "a sad prophecy in this presentiment—a prophecy which he at once made and fulfilled." The fulfilment came in the spring of 1827 when Brainard resigned from the *Connecticut Mirror* because of ill health, and again settled in New London. Never endowed with robust animal spirits, he now fell into moods of deep dejection. These coupled with his piety lent a religious gloom to his later poetry, such as, "The Invalid on the East End of Long Island." The story of the last months before his death reads, with pathetic but rather sentimental death-bed scenes, like a page from the religious annuals during America's epoch of the mezzotint and weeping willow to which epoch Brainard, along with his admirer, Lydia Huntley Sigourney, indubitably belonged. At his father's home in New London he studied the doctrines of Christian grace; he became a communicant in the First Congregational Church; and he died of consumption, venerated for his moral verse. For the weakness of Brainard's life there is confirmation in the revised edition of his poetry (1832), in *Fugitive Tales* (1830), and in the new gleanings from his verse in the *Mirror* (1842). All that he wrote reveals his carelessness, and lack of self-control. His poetry imitated sentimental models. He wrote with the same gentle elegance of Niagara Falls which he had not seen and the Connecticut River which he beheld daily. Yet in his vein of natural pathos, as in "The dead leaves strew the forest walk," he is superior to most of his school, and in other passages on Connecticut scenery his nature, so sensitive to sorrow, shows a corresponding exaltation in the presence of beauty.

[There is no life of Brainard, and extremely little manuscript material has survived (Yale Univ. Lib.). The best biographical sketches are J. G. Whittier, *The Literary Remains of John G. C. Brainard* (1832) and Royal Robbins, *The Poems of John G. C. Brainard* (1842). Other references may be found in F. B. Dexter, *Biog. Sketches Grads. Yale Coll.*, VI (1915), 734–36; E. A. and G. L. Duyckinck, *Cyc. of Am. Lit.*

(1855), II, 226–30; S. G. Goodrich, *Recollections of a Lifetime* (1856), II, 143–60; S. T. Williams, "The Lit. of Conn.," in *Hist. of Conn.* (1925), ed. by N. G. Osborn, II, 518–20.]
S.T.W.
J.A.P.

BRAINERD, DAVID (Apr. 20, 1718–Oct. 9, 1747), missionary to the Indians, though but twenty-nine at the time of his death, became widely known and influential through the autobiography of his intensely pietistic life, left in the form of a diary. He was a native of Haddam in the colony of Connecticut, the son of Hezekiah Brainerd, one of His Majesty's Council. His mother, Dorothy Hobart, was the daughter of Rev. Jeremiah Hobart, and grand-daughter of Rev. Peter Hobart who, driven out of Hingham, England, by the Puritan persecutions, settled in Hingham, Mass. Probably many of the emotional experiences which Brainerd attributed to a Divine agency were pathological in origin. Certainly by the time he entered college, and very likely earlier, he was a victim of tuberculosis. From childhood he was highly emotional, unhealthily introspective, over-conscientious, and subject to periods of dark depression. Although concerned for his soul, terrified by the thought of death, and driven to the performance of religious duties at the age of seven, it was only after many terrible struggles with their grim background of Calvinistic theology, that on July 12, 1739, he felt himself converted. In the fall of that year he entered Yale to prepare for the ministry. Here in 1742 an event occurred which long preyed upon his mind. He was sympathetic toward the Whitefield revival to which the college authorities were opposed, and in the company of two or three students of like mind remarked that a tutor, Mr. Whittelsey, had "no more grace than this chair." His utterance was reported to Rector Clap, who ordered him to apologize before faculty and students. Because he refused, and on the ground that he had attended a Separatist meeting, and made a derogatory remark regarding the Rector himself, though any memory of this he denied, he was expelled; and in spite of the fact that in 1743 he offered to make abject apology if he might receive his degree, it was denied him. This act was strongly disapproved by some of the clergy, and there is a tradition that it hastened the founding of Princeton College, the first three presidents of which had been among Brainerd's strongest supporters (D. D. Field, *Genealogy of the Brainerd Family*, 1857, p. 265, and John Maclean, *History of the College of New Jersey*, 1877, I, 55–56).

After studying with Rev. Jedediah Mills of Ripton, Conn., he was licensed to preach by the

Association of Ministers at Danbury, Conn., July 29, 1742, and the same year was appointed missionary to the Indians by the Correspondents of the Society in Scotland for the Propagation of Christian Knowledge. Beginning Apr. 1, 1743, he labored for a year at Kaunaumeek, a settlement in the woods between Stockbridge and Albany, and then persuaded the Indians to move to Stockbridge, where they could be under Rev. John Sergeant [q.v.]. On June 12, 1744, he was ordained by the Presbytery of New York at Newark, N. J., and took up work at the Forks of the Delaware, near what is now Easton, Pa. From here he went to Crossweeksung, not far from the present town of Freehold, N. J., where his work was notably successful. In May 1746 he removed from that place with all the Indians to Cranberry, about fifteen miles distant. Early the following year, however, the condition of his health forced him to relinquish his work, and in October he died at the home of Jonathan Edwards, to whose daughter, Jerusha, he was engaged to be married.

Brainerd was a mystic of saintly character, controlled absolutely by a sense of God and duty, indifferent to any labor or risk his devotion to these entailed, yet eminently practical in his missionary program. His religious experiences, elevations and depressions of spirit, physical weakness, travels and labors, doctrinal teachings, and methods of work, are all set forth in his diary. For years this was to many a manual of religious guidance, and down to the middle of the nineteenth century, probably no person except Henry Martyn of England and India, who himself was made a missionary by reading Brainerd's life, did more to stimulate and direct missionaries in their form of work. The Society in Scotland for Propagating Christian Knowledge published portions of the diary during Brainerd's lifetime, the first in 1746 under the title, *Mirabilia Dei inter Indicos,* and the second later in the same year under the title, *Divine Grace Displayed.* These were commonly known as *Brainerd's Journal.* In 1749 Jonathan Edwards published *An Account of the Life of the Late Reverend Mr. David Brainerd,* which contains the diary with the parts already published omitted. An abridgment of this was published in England by John Wesley in 1768. A second edition with the diary in full was published by Sereno E. Dwight in 1822, and a third with an essay on Brainerd's life and character by J. M. Sherwood in 1884.

[In addition to the above mentioned works see Wm. B. Sprague, *Annals Am. Pulpit,* vol. III (1858).]

H.E.S.

BRAINERD, ERASTUS (Feb. 25, 1855–Dec. 25, 1922), editor, was a descendant of a very old Connecticut family and the son of Norman Leslie and Leora (Campbell) Brainerd. His childhood days were spent in Middletown, Conn., his birthplace. He fitted himself for Trinity College, at Hartford, but changed his plans and entered Harvard in 1870. He received the degree of B.A. in 1874. The following year was spent in graduate study. During his college days he developed a rather fine appreciation of the arts and their masters. From October 1874 to April 1878 he worked with James R. Osgood & Company, Boston publishers, and prepared for them a series of five volumes, namely: the *Life of Titian,* the *Life of Sir John E. Millais, Great Artists, Gems of the Dresden Gallery,* and the *Gray Collection of Engravings,* the latter being the most admirable. He also was curator of engravings at the Boston Museum of Fine Arts in 1876–77. In 1878 he went to Europe, there encountering several unique experiences. In the Island of Malta he was made a member of the famous knighthood which was originally established there. In Scotland he was initiated into the Scottish Rite of Masonry by the Duke of Buccleuch. When he returned to America in 1879 he began a varied newspaper career. He was successively associated with the editorial staffs of the New York *World,* the Philadelphia *Press,* the *Atlanta Constitution* and the *Atlanta Star* and somewhat later the *Press* and *Daily News* of Philadelphia. Of the latter, he was editor-in-chief and proprietor. He was married on May 30, 1882, to Mary Bella Beale of Richmond, Va. They moved to Seattle, Wash., in 1890, and Brainerd edited the *Press* and the *Press Times* of Seattle for the three years following. In 1893 he was appointed land commissioner of Washington, serving a four-year term. When the rush to the Yukon region began in 1897 Brainerd directed a most extensive and successful advertising campaign for Seattle as the starting and outfitting point for Alaska. A complete file of fourteen volumes of correspondence including letters to and from the Seattle Chamber of Commerce and newspaper clippings was compiled by Brainerd and entitled *Alaska and the Klondyke.* Shortly after, Brainerd made a visit to Alaska and spent almost five years there. After his return he edited the *Seattle Post-Intelligencer* from 1904 to 1911, and the *San Francisco Call* from March to September 1913. He was a man of many interests and exceptionally well informed on most varied subjects. His document called *Seattle and Ship Subsidy* (1902) shows his interest in economics and politics. In 1919 he served as consul for Paraguay, his jurisdiction covering Washington, Oregon, Idaho and Alaska. His death occurred at his home in Seattle.

[*Who's Who in America*, 1922–23; *Report of the Class Sec. of the Class of 1874 of Harvard Coll.* (1894, 1899, 1924); J. P. Nichols, "Advertising and the Klondike," *Wash. Hist. Quart.*, XIII, 20–26.]   M.S.

BRAINERD, EZRA (Dec. 17, 1844–Dec. 8, 1924), botanist, geologist, educator, was the son of Lawrence Robbins Brainerd and Catherine (Wood) Brainerd, and was born at St. Albans, Vt. His education was in the public schools of his native town; in 1860 he entered Middlebury College, graduating four years later with the degree of A.B. For the next two years he was a tutor there, and then for two years attended Andover Theological Seminary, duly graduating though never ordained. For the next two years he was professor of rhetoric at Middlebury College; subsequently he taught physics and applied mathematics and from 1885 to 1906 was president of the college. His first scientific inclinations showed themselves in physics and surveying. Early in his career he began the study of geology, where his ability as a surveyor stood him in good stead. His work on the geology of the Champlain valley and the origin of certain Vermont formations won the admiration of Le Conte. In 1900 he published the *Blackberries of New England,* the first of his botanical papers to attract wide notice, and in the same year he was among the trio of editors who issued the *Flora of Vermont,* considered the model of a state floral catalogue. By 1904 he had published his first paper on violets, and from then until the close of his life he was constantly at work upon the study of hybridism in the genus *Viola.* The genus contains an enormous number of natural hybrids, and their pure species parents he endeavored to discover by growing the plants under controlled conditions and by studying the unit characters as they emerged in subsequent generations, according to Mendelian laws. He traveled all over the country in the study of violets, sustained an immense correspondence, and published innumerable titles on the subject, those of most philosophical interest being the series *Hybridism in the Genus Viola.* The result was an international reputation. In conjunction with Dr. A. K. Pietersen, studies in the hybridism of the genus *Rubus* were carried on at the Vermont Experiment Station; the results were published in 1920 as *Bulletin 217* of the Vermont Experiment Station. The methods that had been employed in the study were along approved genetic principles, and the publication was warmly received by the geneticists; as an avowed study in systematic classification the work was considered a failure by some specialists in systematic botany. Brainerd's last publications were his "Violets of North America," and "Some Natural Violet Hybrids of North America," constituting *Bulletin 224* and *Bulletin 239,* respectively, of the Vermont Experiment Station. These were incomplete, largely popular expositions of the subject, as Brainerd stated in private correspondence, being essentially illustrations (by Schuyler Mathews) with some textual notes by Brainerd.

His tenancy of the president's chair marked an era of expansion from poverty and obscurity to thriving prosperity for Middlebury College. Executive detail was, however, never congenial to his temperament which was distinctly that of the scholastic. He was, from its incipiency on a field expedition, the perpetual president of the Vermont Botanical Society; throughout life a fresh and enthusiastic love of nature, such as the old-style naturalists displayed, marked his botanical interests; the subjects that he chose for monographic study were largely selected on the basis of their metaphysical significance. To the end of his life he retained a great memory and a facility with the classic tongues. He was twice married, in 1868 to Frances Viola Rockwell, and, after her death, to Mary Wright in 1897.

[The only important biographical material in print is that entitled *A Memorial of Ezra Brainerd* (privately printed at Middlebury, Vt., 1927), which includes a personal eulogy by Prof. Chas. B. Wright, and a record of Brainerd's scientific achievements compiled from material supplied by Edward Foyles, of the Am. Mus. of Nat. Hist., Dr. G. P. Burns of the Univ. of Vermont and Mr. W. W. Eggleston of the Dept. of Agriculture, Washington, D. C. To this is appended a bibliography of his publications. For further personal and academic detail the writer is indebted to the private correspondence of Prof. Chas. B. Wright, to the records of Middlebury College, and to members of Brainerd's family.]
D.C.P.

BRAINERD, JOHN (Feb. 28, 1720–Mar. 18, 1781), missionary to the Indians, was born in Haddam, Conn., the son of Hezekiah and Mrs. Dorothy (Hobart) Mason Brainerd, and brother of David Brainerd [*q.v.*], whose work he continued. He graduated from Yale in 1746. The following year when failing health compelled David to leave the Indian settlement, known as Bethel, at Cranberry, N. J., the Correspondents of the Society in Scotland for the Propagation of Christian Knowledge asked the younger Brainerd to take his place. He was licensed by the New York Presbytery, Apr. 11, 1747, and in his diary under date of Apr. 14, David wrote: "This day my brother went to my people." The following October David died, and John was ordained in February 1748, and soon received his missionary commission from Edinburgh.

Although he labored with devotion and apparently with good judgment for years, the Bethel enterprise ultimately failed. A pestilence carried off a considerable number of the Indian converts; their title to the land they occupied was questioned, and it was taken from them; and Brainerd's health sometimes interfered with his activities, for like his brother he seems to have suffered from tuberculosis. Dissatisfied with conditions, the Correspondents dismissed him May 7, 1755, and he took charge of the church at Newark, N. J., lately served by President Aaron Burr [q.v.] of the College of New Jersey. Plans were made to buy land for the Indians near New Brunswick, N. J., and in June 1756 Brainerd was again put in charge of the undertaking, but the plan failed and in September 1757 he returned to the church in Newark. In 1754 he had been made a trustee of the College of New Jersey, and in January 1758 he journeyed to Stockbridge, Mass., with Rev. Caleb Smith to secure sanction for the removal of Jonathan Edwards [q.v.] from the pastorate there to the presidency of the college. In May, the government having provided land for the Indians in Burlington County, he again took charge of the mission. That summer he served as chaplain of the expedition to Crown Point, and on his return settled at the Indian town, Brotherton, N. J., with supervision over several Indian and white settlements. In 1768 he removed to Bridgetown (Mount Holly), where he built up a congregation and erected a church. His activities were now chiefly among the whites. The Revolutionary War broke up his work at Bridgetown, and he took charge of the Presbyterian church at Deerfield, N. J. Here he died, and was buried under the church.

He was twice married, first, in November 1752, to Experience Lyon, who died in 1757; and second, to Mrs. Experience Price.

[Thos. Brainerd, *The Life of John Brainerd* (1865) contains much documentary material and Brainerd's journal, Oct. 15, 1749–Nov. 21, 1759; the Jour. of John Brainerd, 1761–1762 (MS.) is in the library of Princeton University. T. Brainerd reprints *A Genuine Letter from John Brainerd to His Friend in England*, London, 1753. See also W. B. Sprague, *Annals Am. Pulpit*, III (1858); Lucy A. Brainard, *The Genealogy of the Brainerd-Brainard Family in America 1649–1908* (1908).]
H.E.S.

BRAINERD, LAWRENCE (Mar. 16, 1794–May 9, 1870), capitalist, senator, one of twelve children born to Ezra and Mabel (Porter) Brainerd, was a native of East Hartford, Conn. At the age of nine years he went to Troy, N. Y., to live with Joseph S. Brainerd, an uncle. Five years later, he removed with this uncle to St. Albans, Vt. He attended the St. Albans Academy for two years and entered the store of a local merchant as clerk. At the age of twenty-two he established a mercantile business of his own in which he was very successful. He bought a large tract of swamp land near Lake Champlain, drained and improved it, and developed it into a 1,200-acre farm, one of the best in Vermont. When the Bank of St. Albans was established in 1826, he became a heavy stockholder, a director, and later its president. He was active in steamboat enterprises in the early days of that method of transportation, in 1847 superintending the building at Shelburne Harbor of the *United States,* then considered one of the finest steamboats ever built. He became interested early in railroad development and the construction of the Vermont & Canada line was due largely to his energy and aid, in coöperation with John Smith and Joseph Clark. He pledged practically his entire fortune to make possible the building of the railroad. From the construction of the road until his death he was a director and in later years was associated with his son-in-law, Gov. John Gregory Smith, in the management of the corporation. He was also engaged in railroad building in Canada and was a promoter of the Missisquoi Railroad. He took an active interest in public affairs, being particularly interested in the anti-slavery cause and in temperance reform. Originally a Democrat, he was affiliated with the Free-Soil wing of the party. In 1834 he was a member of the legislature and in 1846, 1847, 1848, 1852, and 1854, he was a candidate of the Free-Soil Democratic party for governor. He was elected United States senator in 1854 to fill the vacancy caused by the death of Senator Upham, was president of the convention called to organize the Republican party in Vermont, was a delegate to a preliminary national Republican convention at Pittsburgh in February 1856, and called to order the first Republican national convention, held at Philadelphia in June 1856. Much interested in agricultural development, he was a president of the Vermont Agricultural Society. In 1819 he married Fidelia B. Gadcomb and twelve children were born to them. He was a man of large frame and great physical strength.

[*St. Albans Daily Messenger,* May 9, 1870; W. H. Crockett, *Vermont*, vol. III (1921); H. C. Williams, ed., *Biog. Encyc. of Vermont* (1885).]
W.H.C.

BRAINERD, THOMAS (June 17, 1804–Aug. 21, 1866), Presbyterian minister, editor, son of Jesse and Mary (Thomas) Brainerd, was born at Leyden, Lewis County, N. Y., but spent his childhood and early youth at Rome, N. Y. He graduated from the Academy at Louisville,

N. Y., taught school at the age of seventeen, and developed tendencies toward a professional career. His first inclination in this direction was the law, toward which he began preparatory studies; but at the age of twenty-one coming under the influence of Charles G. Finney the evangelist, and being pressed further by a distressful experience, he resolved to enter the ministry. He took his theological course at Andover Theological Seminary, graduating in 1831. He then placed himself for a brief season under the guidance of Dr. James Patterson of Philadelphia with a view to connecting himself with the Presbyterian Church. On Oct. 7, 1831, he was ordained by the Third Presbytery of New York and accepted a commission under the Home Missionary Society, going to Cincinnati to take charge of the new and struggling Fourth Church in the outskirts of the city. In this field he labored for two years. In 1833 Lyman Beecher, who was pastor of the Second Church as well as president of Lane Theological Seminary, invited him to the position of an associate in the Second Church. This he accepted. At the same time he became an associate editor of the *Cincinnati Journal* and, later, editor of the *Youth's Magazine,* and assisted in editing the *Presbyterian Quarterly Review.* During the controversy involving the trial of Lyman Beecher for heresy he stood faithfully by his chief and became a firm advocate of what were known as the "New School" views, joining in 1837 the New School Presbyterian Church when it was organized. From Cincinnati he was called to the pastorate of the Third ("Old Pine Street") Church of Philadelphia and spent the remainder of his life (1837–66) in this field. During the Civil War he loyally supported the Union, and by his earnest support of the government influenced 130 young men to enlist in the Northern army. In 1864 the New School General Assembly elected him to the position of moderator. He died at Scranton, Pa., suddenly, of apoplexy, Aug. 21, 1866. In appearance he was large and dignified; in manner gentle and amiable. He was rather popular than scholarly in his tastes; full of zeal and energy, quick and impulsive, but broad in his interests. He was twice married: on Oct. 20, 1831, to Sarah J. Langstroth, and on Oct. 29, 1836, to Mrs. Mary Whiting.

His extant literary productions are not extensive. Though he was a prolific writer, most of what he wrote was designed for use in the newspapers and periodicals for which he was responsible as editor and contributor. It concerned matters under discussion at the time and was therefore naturally of an ephemeral nature.

His outstanding work is *The Life of John Brainerd* (1865), a volume of permanent value as a source of information concerning a remarkable personality.

[Mary Brainerd, *Life of Rev. Thos. Brainerd* (1870); files of the *Presbyt. Quart. Rev.*]   A.C.Z.

BRAMLETTE, THOMAS E. (Jan. 3, 1817–Jan. 12, 1875), governor of Kentucky, was born in Cumberland County, Ky., a part of the state favored by nature much less than the Blue Grass section, and here he grew up with what meager schooling this section afforded. Believing the legal profession would be the easiest road to distinction, he studied law and was admitted to the bar when twenty years of age. Four years later he was elected to represent Clinton County in the legislature, and having identified himself prominently with the Whig party he secured in 1848 the appointment of commonwealth's attorney from John J. Crittenden, the incoming governor. In this position he attracted attention by his strict adherence to duty and his fearless prosecution of criminals. After two years he resigned to resume his legal practise and in 1852 he removed to Columbia, Adair County. In 1856 he was elected judge for the 6th circuit and for the next five years served with distinction, his decisions being so clear and logical as rarely to be reversed by the court of appeals. With the approach of the Civil War he assumed a strong attitude in favor of the preservation of the Union, exhibiting little sympathy or patience for the strange neutrality doctrine the state had set forth in 1861. In July of this year while Kentucky was attempting to maintain her neutral position, he accepted a commission in the Federal Army and boldly set about raising the 3rd Kentucky Infantry, which he commanded as colonel—all of which was in violation of the state's tacit agreement with the Federal Government. On account of a disagreement in 1862 as to the unit he should command, he resigned from the army, and, on being offered by President Lincoln the position of United States district attorney, accepted. Using the same vigor and energy which characterized his work as commonwealth's attorney, he sought to enforce the wartime laws passed by Kentucky against Confederates and Southern sympathizers. He succeeded in convicting of treason Thomas C. Shacklett and saw him sentenced to ten years in jail, fined $10,000, and deprived of his slaves.

But it was as governor during the last two years of the war and the two years following that Bramlette made his most lasting reputation. In 1863 he was designated as the Union Democratic candidate for governor on the rejection of the honor by Joshua F. Bell, the candidate named by the convention. On account of army supervision of the election he won by an overwhelming majority over Charles A. Wickliffe, the Peace Democrat. He began his administration with as pronounced and as loud support of the war as could be heard in the state, yet within less than a year he was one of Lincoln's most bitter critics and opponents, undergoing much the same transformation as that which characterized the vast majority of Kentuckians. In the early part of 1864 when Lincoln ordered the enlistment of negro troops, he threatened to array the state against the Federal Government, and was long and persistently charged with having written but later having amended the proclamation "to bloodily baptize the state into the Confederacy." In the national Democratic convention of 1864 he was the choice of the Kentucky Democrats for vice-president, but he refused to countenance the move. He opposed Lincoln's election and wrote him menacing letters. He bitterly quarreled with Gen. Stephen G. Burbridge, the commander of Federal troops in Kentucky, and succeeded in February 1865 in having him removed. On Lincoln's death he repented of all the harsh things he had said about the President and appointed officially a day of prayer and mourning. Never sympathizing with the Federal military régime in Kentucky, he welcomed back the returning Confederate soldiers in 1865 and 1866 and recommended the repeal of all laws against them. He favored the thirteenth amendment and, without success, urged upon the legislature its adoption. In 1867 on leaving the governorship he aspired to the United States Senate but failed of election. He thereupon settled in Louisville and practised law until his death in 1875. He was married twice, first to Sallie Travis, in 1837, and after her death to Mrs. Mary E. Adams, in 1874.

[*Ky. Yeoman*, Sept. 26, 1868; *Official Records*, ser. 1, vol. IV; *Ky. Senate Jour.*, 1865; Thos. Speed, R. M. Kelly, and A. Pirtle, *The Union Regiments of Ky.* (1897); Richard H. and Lewis Collins, *Hist. of Ky.* (1874), II; H. Levin, ed., *The Lawyers and Lawmakers of Ky.* (1897); E. M. Coulter, *The Civil War and Readjustment in Ky.* (1926).]   E. M. C.

BRANCH, JOHN (Nov. 4, 1782–Jan. 4, 1863), governor of North Carolina, senator, secretary of the navy, was born at Halifax, N. C., the third child in a wealthy and prominent family. His parents were Col. John and Mary (Bradford) Branch. He was educated at the University of North Carolina, graduating in 1801; he studied law, but never actively engaged in practise, preferring the life of a wealthy planter and politician. Parton's characteriza-

tion of him may be accepted: "Inheriting an ample estate, he lived for many years upon his plantations and employed himself in superintending their culture. He was a man of respectable talents, good presence, and high social position." A leader in society, he was famous for his dinners and entertainments. His long public career was uneven in that it did not show an orderly progression from offices of lesser to those of higher importance, as the following analysis will demonstrate: state senator, 1811, 1813–17, 1822, 1834; speaker of the state Senate, 1815–17; governor, 1817–20; United States senator, 1823–29; secretary of the navy, 1829–31; representative in Congress, 1831–33; member of the North Carolina constitutional convention, 1835; governor of Florida Territory, 1834–45. He was a faithful member of the Democratic party, abandoning it only once in order to oppose Van Buren in 1836. He seemed to have the confidence of the party and the people, for he suffered only one defeat—that in his candidacy against Dudley, a Whig, for governor in 1838. The evidence is convincing that he was a man of firmness and integrity, although a biographer of Jackson alluded to him as "weakwilled" (J. S. Bassett, *Life of Andrew Jackson*, II, 414), McLane referred to him in a letter to Van Buren as a "miserable old woman" (*Ibid.*), and Archibald D. Murphey wrote slightingly of him as one of three in control of the Assembly in 1814 (W. H. Hoyt, ed., *The Papers of Archibald D. Murphey*, 1914, I, 75). In the last case, Murphey changed his opinion and dedicated his important "Memoir on Internal Improvements" to Branch. As governor Branch favored state aid to education, internal improvements, reorganization of the supreme court, abolition of imprisonment for debt, and elimination and punishment of impostors in the medical profession. His messages on education were notable pronouncements as to the "imperious duty" to republican institutions and civilization that rested upon the state. In 1819 he acted as president of the North Carolina branch of the American Colonization Society. In the United States Senate, to which he was elected after a long contest, Branch was allied with the "Jackson men," signalizing his union with this group by opposing the nomination of Henry Clay as secretary of state. In debate he made speeches in advocacy of the abolition of imprisonment for debt, in favor of pensions for privates as well as for officers, and in opposition to internal improvements financed by the general government. Perhaps due to the friendship of Eaton, or it may have been in order to give social tone to the cabinet, he was, when Jackson became President, made secretary of the navy,—the first of five North Carolinians to hold this place. His service in this office, although described by Jackson as satisfactory, was unimportant. His reports urged a naval school, revision of the law respecting the Marine Corps, and equalization of pay. An investigation was made, on order of Congress, of the use of liquor by officers. The chief interest in connection with Branch's membership in Jackson's first cabinet was the manner of his retirement. Like Berrien and Ingham, he was involved in the complications and embarrassments incident to the Eaton affair. With the "reorganization" of the cabinet, he was forced to resign. He declined appointment to a foreign mission and to the territorial governorship of Florida and severed relations with Jackson, becoming a supporter of Calhoun. The details in the chain of events leading to his resignation were revealed in a letter to Edward B. Freeman, published in *Niles' Register* (Sept. 3, 1831) and elsewhere. One important statement in it was that Jackson, shortly before the purging of the cabinet, had stated that he "did not claim the right to dictate" to his official household as to "social relations." Branch characterized Jackson's decision to dismiss as "arbitrary and unjust." In the bitter feelings and controversies provoked by the dismissals, Branch came near being involved in a duel with Senator Forsyth of Georgia. As a mark of public confidence and as a popular justification, he was unanimously elected to the House of Representatives in 1831. During his one term, he spoke on such topics as the bank, Indian affairs, the tariff, and the navy. Retiring voluntarily from Congress, his last public service to North Carolina was rendered as a member of the state constitutional convention of 1835, wherein he advocated annual sessions of the legislature and removal of all religious qualifications for office-holding. On several occasions he chose to uphold the rights of the states, endangered in his opinion by the Jackson administration. In 1836, he acquired large estates in Florida, to which territory his family moved and in which he spent most of his time until the death of his first wife in 1851, when he returned to North Carolina. During this period, by appointment of President Tyler, he was governor of the territory, 1843–45, in which term Florida became a state. He was married twice: first, to Elizabeth Foort, by whom he had nine children, and second, to Mrs. Eliza (Jordan) Bond. He died at Enfield.

[For documentary sources there are Gov. Branch's Letter-Book (N. C. Hist. Commission); *Reports of*

the Sec. Navy, 1830–31; and the *Annals of Congress*, 1823–29. Letters concerning the disruption of the cabinet were published in the *Raleigh Register* (Sept. 1, 1831). A monograph by Marshall DeLancey Haywood "John Branch, 1782–1863" (*N. C. Booklet*, Oct. 1915), may be read with profit. See also study of John Branch by R. D. W. Connor in *N. C. Rev.*, Apr. 1913. There is a review of Branch's administration as governor of North Carolina in S. A. Ashe, *Hist. of N. C.*, II (1925), 255–77.]
W. W. P.

BRANCH, LAWRENCE O'BRYAN (Nov. 28, 1820–Sept. 17, 1862), lawyer, congressman, Confederate soldier, born at Enfield, N. C., of a prominent and wealthy family, was at an early age left an orphan when his parents (Joseph and Susan Simpson O'Bryan Branch) died. Brought back from Tennessee, where his father had been living, he became a member of the household of his uncle and guardian, John Branch [*q.v.*]. After being tutored by William J. Bingham and Salmon P. Chase, he studied for a part of one year at the University of North Carolina. He then entered Princeton, from which institution he graduated with distinction in 1838. While editing a newspaper in Tennessee, he studied law, and when he soon moved to Florida, under special act of the territorial legislature he was admitted to practise, though not then of age. The Seminole war breaking out shortly thereafter, he volunteered, serving throughout as aide-de-camp to Gen. Reid. In 1844 he was married to Nancy Haywood Blount, daughter of Gen. William Augustus Blount. Despite his success as a lawyer in Florida, he returned to North Carolina in 1848 and there supplemented his professional activities by management of his estates and by engaging in industrial undertakings, especially in railroads. In the last connection, he became (1852–55) president of the Raleigh and Gaston Railroad Company. His participation in politics began in 1852, when he was chosen presidential elector on the Pierce ticket. Effectively active in the Democratic party, he was, in 1854, elected—although an unwilling candidate—to the House of Representatives, in which body he was a member continuously from 1855 to 1861. A partisan, Southern Democrat, he was not an extremist. While speaking frankly for his district, state, and section, he repeatedly cautioned the South against immoderation. Not one of the foremost leaders, he was a forceful speaker and won sufficient distinction to be placed upon the then important Committee on Territories. He made speeches on finance, party politics, the Brooks-Sumner affair, the acquisition of Cuba, and various phases of the slavery dispute. Favoring low tariffs and the "depositing" among the states of the proceeds of the sale of public land, he opposed the "distribution" of these funds and the proposed Homestead Act. His speeches on the Kansas-Nebraska Act and its operation are valuable sources of information for those seeking the views and attitude of moderate Southerners. An admirer and consistent supporter of President Buchanan and an exponent of party policy in public finance, he was offered, on the resignation of Howell Cobb, the place of secretary of the treasury. Earlier he had declined Buchanan's offer of the position of postmaster general. Feeling that the secession of North Carolina was imminent, he again refused. His good sense and practical comprehension of politics were at no time better demonstrated than in the campaign of 1860. In a letter to his constituents of May 15, 1860, he opposed the plan of the "fire-eaters" and the inclusion in the party platform of the new doctrine of "Congressional protection to slavery in the Territories." The disruption of the party, its defeat for the sake of an abstraction, and the surrender of "all the fruits of twenty years of successful struggle with Freesoilism and Abolitionism"—*i.e.*, the principle of non-intervention by Congress—were results he saw and stated. When it was clear that seceded states were to be "coerced," he withdrew from Congress to advocate the secession of North Carolina. When that state called for troops, he volunteered as a private, but was, upon the governor's appointment, promptly given the joint office of quartermaster and paymaster-general. Wishing active service, he resigned to become colonel of the 33rd North Carolina Regiment. Later, on Jan. 17, 1862, he was commissioned brigadier-general by President Davis and was placed in command of the Confederate forces around New Bern. Operating against the greatly superior army of Gen. Burnside, he was forced to retreat, skilfully withdrawing his troops from the peninsula—a feat highly praised. He was then ordered to join Stonewall Jackson. Between January and September of 1862, he took part creditably in the battles of Hanover Court House, the Seven Days battles around Richmond, Cedar Run, Second Manassas, Fairfax Court House, Ox Hill, Harper's Ferry, and Antietam. At the last battle, after leading his brigade successfully, he was shot through the head and killed. He had been complimented by Gen. Lee and his death occurred, it is thought, on the eve of a career of higher military responsibility.

[For Branch's speeches in Congress, see *Cong. Globe*, 1855–61. The important *Letter to his Constituents*, May 15, 1860, is preserved in the Weeks Collection at the Univ. of N. C. Sketches are printed in S. A. Ashe, *Biog. Hist. of N. C.*, VII, 55 ff., and in *Confed. Mil. Hist.*, ed. by C. A. Evans (1899), IV, 298–300. An excellent short biography is that of John Hughes—*Laurence O'Bryan Branch, An Oration* (1884). For his military service, see W. Clark, *Histories of the Several Regiments and Battalions from N. C.* (1901), IV, 465–79, and D. H. Hill, *Bethel to Sharpsburg* (in press, 1927).]
W. W. P.

BRANDEGEE, FRANK BOSWORTH (July 8, 1864–Oct. 14, 1924), politician, was born in New London, son of Augustus and Nancy Christian (Bosworth) Brandegee. Having been graduated from Yale in 1885, he spent a year of travel in Great Britain and on the Continent. Upon his return he studied law, was admitted to the New London County bar, and commenced practise in New London as a member of the firm of Brandegee, Noyes & Brandegee. In 1888, the year of his admission to the bar, he also entered politics, going as a delegate to the Republican national convention at Chicago in June; and in November following he was elected to the state House of Representatives. To three other national conventions—those of 1892, 1900, and 1904—he was a delegate. With the exception of two years, he was corporation counsel of New London from 1889 to 1902, when he resigned; and for a time he also served as United States attorney in his district. In 1898 he was again elected to the Connecticut House of Representatives, of which he was speaker during the session of 1899. Chosen in 1902 as representative from the third Connecticut district in the Fifty-seventh Congress, for the unexpired term of Charles A. Russell (to Mar. 4, 1903), he was twice reëlected (Fifty-eighth and Fifty-ninth Congresses). In 1905 he resigned from the House of Representatives on being elected (May 9) United States senator for the unexpired term (1905–09) of Orville H. Platt, who had been a Connecticut senator since 1879. Brandegee was three times reëlected—in 1909, 1915, and 1921—and was a member of the committees on Foreign Relations, Judiciary, Library, and Patents. He was found dead on Oct. 14, 1924, in his house in Washington, where he had ended his life by inhaling gas. Financial difficulties, caused by unfortunate investments in real estate, were assigned as the probable cause of his suicide. For some months previous, he had been living in comparative seclusion.

An indifferent speaker, Brandegee made no particular impression by his utterances in the Senate, and outside of it he was rarely heard in public address. It was through his service on committees and through his private counsels that for a time he exerted a considerable influence—an influence largely negative, if not reactionary, in effect. He delighted in obstructive tactics, and he opposed and voted against all of the following measures alike: direct election of senators; extension of the parcel post; federal regulation of child labor; the Federal Reserve system; the income tax; prohibition; woman suffrage. He objected to any inquiry regarding William Lorimer of Illinois, whose election to the Senate was finally (1912) declared invalid; or regarding Truman H. Newberry of Michigan, whose seat was retained by a vote of 46 to 41 (1922). "In what many of us might consider a sort of consistent wrong-headedness," commented the *New York Times* (editorial of Oct. 15, 1924), "kinder observers might find a consistent disregard of political consequences." During the controversy over the League of Nations, in the Senate discussion of the peace treaty with Germany, Brandegee was a bitter irreconcilable. "I shall never vote for it," he was quoted as saying, "until hell freezes over, and I think that event is probably somewhat remote. I am not to be buncoed by any oleaginous lingo about 'humanity' or 'men everywhere'" (*New York Times,* Oct. 15, 1924). One bill to which he lent his support was that for the soldiers' bonus (adjusted compensation). He was accounted a lawyer of ability and in many respects a cultivated man.

[*Geneal. and Biog. Record of New London County, Conn.* (1905); Dwight Loomis and J. G. Calhoun, *The Judicial and Civil Hist. of Conn.* (1895); *N. Y. Times,* Oct. 15, 18, 23, and 26, 1924; N. G. Osborn, *Men of Mark in Conn.* (1906); *Who's Who in America,* 1924–25.]   G. S. B.

BRANDEGEE, TOWNSHEND STITH (Feb. 16, 1843–Apr. 7, 1925), botanist, the son of Elishama and Florence (Stith) Brandegee, was born in Berlin, Conn., where his father was a physician with a taste for natural history. His early education was inculcated, he wrote, in a "little red schoolhouse where they hired a new teacher every term, who always made the pupils begin at the first lesson. Consequently in geography we never reached Asia or Oceania. . . . My father owned a small farm, of which I have ploughed the field with oxen, cut the grass with a scythe, etc. . . . At the age of 19 I enlisted in First Regiment Conn., Artillery, Co. G, and served two years until discharged as private in the rear rank. Gen. Grant and I took Richmond." In 1866 he entered the Sheffield Scientific School of Yale, graduating in 1870. Primarily he was preparing to be an engineer, but he pursued botanical studies under Prof. A. A. Eaton, having as a boy devoted especial attention to ferns. He is mentioned in reports on the flora of Connecticut as "having made rare finds" in the vicinity of Yale. In 1871 he was made county surveyor and city engineer of Cañon

City, Colo., where he spent spare time in collecting ferns for the well known Connecticut botanist, John Redfield. His specimens at length reached Asa Gray who in 1875 recommended him as botanical collector and assistant topographer to Hayden's exploring expedition of southwestern Colorado and adjacent Utah. He was successively attached as engineer to the survey of the Royal Gorge, the Santa Fé surveys in New Mexico and Arizona, and the Northern Transcontinental survey through Wyoming to Washington and Oregon. In spare hours he discovered many new western species, and assembled for Prof. C. S. Sargent several splendid collections of western timbers, first in connection with the United States Census work and later for the Jesup collection of the American Museum of Natural History.

Carrying out a commission, in 1886, to obtain certain rare timbers, he visited Santa Cruz Island off Santa Barbara, Cal., which turned his attention to the peculiar fascination of the biology of islands. This determined him definitely to devote his life to botany, and so he relinquished his engineering work, although on subsequent occasions he prepared forest maps of various western regions, combining his engineering training with his botanical knowledge. In 1889 he made a memorable trip to Magdalena Bay, Baja California, Mexico, as a volunteer in the California Academy of Sciences expedition. From that time until the close of his life he was intermittently active as a botanist of Baja California and was indeed the leading authority upon its flora, as upon that of the islands of the Gulf of California. His explorations extended into Sonora, Sinaloa, Puebla, and Vera Cruz. At the same time he pursued assiduously his explorations of California itself, especially its southern half. At first he sent his specimens to Eastern authorities, for identification, but as he gained confidence he began publishing his own species and many notes (some ninety in all), contributory to the habits, habitats, and life histories of the plants of the western states and Mexico. From 1909 to 1924 he was engaged upon his most important undertaking, *Plantæ Mexicanæ Purpusianæ,* of which twelve fascicles appeared (1909–24) through the *University of California Publications.* These were descriptions of new species collected by Dr. C. A. Purpus in Mexico.

On May 29, 1889, he married Dr. Mary Katherine (Layne) Curran (Oct. 28, 1844–Apr. 3, 1920), best known to science as Katherine Brandegee, curator of the herbarium of the California Academy of Sciences. Their wedding trip took the form of a botanical collecting journey afoot from San Diego to San Francisco. Brandegee was a man of retiring manner, reticent of his opinions but holding them staunchly. He was among the last of the old, self-trained botanists, as he was among the first of the pioneer collectors of the West. Throughout most of his life he retained the bodily vigor of his early days as a plowboy and as a mountain surveyor, and his love of sports was unquenchable; his death at Berkeley, Cal., from pneumonia released him from the rather pitiful last years of his life, when deafness, blindness, and partial paralysis had put a stop to his long activity.

[The sole authority on the lives of the two Brandegees is W. A. Setchell's "Townshend Stith Brandegee and Mary Katherine (Layne) (Curran) Brandegee," in *Univ. of Cal. Pubs. in Botany,* XIII (1926), pp. 155–78, with bibliographies. Fragments of autobiographic notes left by the subjects of the memoir are printed therein.]   D. C. P.

BRANDON, GERARD CHITTOCQUE (Sept. 15, 1788–Mar. 28, 1850), lawyer, planter, governor of Mississippi, was born at Selma Plantation, near Natchez, when the Natchez District was under the dominion of Spain, the eldest son of Gerard Brandon and his wife, Dorothy Nugent. Gerard Brandon was a native of County Donegal, Ireland. He was a follower of Robert Emmet and escaped to America on the failure of his cause, settling in Charleston, S. C. He served in the War of the Revolution under Marion and in Col. Washington's cavalry and took part in the battles of Cowpens and King's Mountain. He migrated to West Florida about 1782.

Gerard C. Brandon was educated at Princeton and William and Mary and was graduated at the latter institution, dividing honors with William Cabell Rivers. He began the practise of law at Washington, the capital of Mississippi Territory, in 1812, and was also a soldier in the War of 1812. He was elected to the legislature of Mississippi Territory in 1815. In 1816 he married Margaret Chambers of Bardstown, Ky., and abandoned the law for the life of a planter, living near Fort Adams in Wilkinson County, Miss. A member of the constitutional convention of 1817 and speaker of the House of Representatives in 1822, he was lieutenant-governor under Governors Holmes and Leake in 1825–26 and was elected governor in 1827, being the first native Mississippian to hold the office. He served for two terms of two years each and his administrations were successful from a political, as well as from an economic, point of view. He was solicited to accept the United States senatorship on the expiration of his last term as

governor, but declined the honor. Elected to the constitutional convention of 1832, he was the only member who had served in the convention of 1817. He was opposed to the further introduction of slaves into Mississippi, and was opposed to the election of the judiciary by the people,—which was the main issue in the election of delegates to the convention. After the adoption of an elective judiciary system, which was the first departure from the appointive system, he resigned, and returned to Wilkinson County. Thereafter he would never allow himself to be elected to public office. He was a typical Southern planter, cultured, genial, and hospitable, and though he filled with credit and ability every official position that he ever occupied, and enjoyed the distinction that a life in the public service gave, he did not undervalue the blessings of private life, and in no occupation took a keener interest than in that of a planter. He was twice married. By his first marriage he had two children, Gerard and John C. Brandon. In 1824 he married Elizabeth Stanton of Natchez and they had six sons and two daughters. He died at his Columbia Springs plantation, near Fort Adams, Mar. 28, 1850.

[The best sources of information are: Brandon's letter-book as governor, the Mississippi archives; *Mississippi Official and Statistical Register of 1908,* pp. 131–32; letters to Gov. Brandon (1825–32), Mississippi archives; sketch in Dunbar Rowland's *Mississippi,* I (1907), 287–93.]   D. R.

BRANNAN, JOHN MILTON (July 1, 1819–Dec. 16, 1892), Union soldier, was born in the District of Columbia, near the city of Washington. He early took an interest in military affairs, and in 1837 secured appointment to the United States Military Academy from the state of Indiana, graduating with the class of 1841, number twenty-three in a class of fifty-two members. On July 1, following graduation, he was commissioned a brevet second lieutenant of artillery, and went for his first station to Plattsburg, N. Y., where he had considerable field service during the border disturbances of 1841–42. He received his full second lieutenancy, May 16, 1842. The outbreak of war with Mexico found Brannan a first lieutenant of artillery, and on Apr. 17, 1847, he was appointed adjutant of his regiment, the historic 1st Artillery. It is interesting to note that at this time the commissioned roster of Brannan's regiment included such names as Joseph Hooker, Irvin McDowell, John B. Magruder, Ambrose P. Hill, and Thomas J. ("Stonewall") Jackson, all of whom distinguished themselves during the Civil War. Brannan took part with his regiment in the siege and occupation of Vera Cruz, and in the subsequent battles of Cerro Gordo, La Hoya, Contreras, and Churubusco, the regiment suffering severe losses in both officers and men. At Churubusco especially, the 1st Artillery was subjected to Mexican artillery fire of round-shot and grape, and to rifle fire from hostile infantry, stationed on the roof and in the windows of the Convent of San Pablo. The Mexican position was gallantly assaulted and taken, and official records show that Lieutenants Brannan and Seymour were the first officers of their regiment to enter the enemy's works (C. M. Wilcox, *History of the Mexican War, 1892*, pp. 384–89). For this and for similar gallantry in the previous battle of Contreras, Brannan was brevetted captain, Aug. 20, 1847. In the final operations against the Mexican capital, he also took part in the historic assault on the Belen Gate, which led to the capture of the castle of Chapultepec. Here he was severely wounded. After the surrender of the city, the 1st Artillery formed, for a time, part of the American army of occupation; and Brannan's name is found in the list of the original members of the Aztec Society, organized in the City of Mexico by American officers, to commemorate the successful termination of their country's first great war on foreign soil. Returning to the United States, Brannan was promoted captain, Nov. 4, 1854; served at various frontier stations with organizations of his regiment; and in 1856–58 engaged in military operations against the hostile Seminole Indians in Florida.

With the outbreak of the Civil War, Brannan was appointed brigadier-general of volunteers, and as commander of the difficult Department of Key West, Fla., directed operations on the St. John's River, involving the enemy's evacuation of Jacksonville and the action of Pocotaligo, S. C., Oct. 24, 1862. For his services at Jacksonville, Brannan was brevetted lieutenant-colonel in the regular army, Sept. 25, 1862. Promoted a major in the regular service, Aug. 1, 1863, he was actually commanding a division in the action of Hoover's Gap, the advance of the Army of the Cumberland on Tullahoma, the action at Elk River, and the battle of Chickamauga. For services in this battle, he was brevetted a colonel, Sept. 20, 1863. He was chief of artillery, Army of the Cumberland, and commanded the Artillery Reserve with supervision of the defenses of Chattanooga until the summer of 1864. Meanwhile, he was present at the battle of Missionary Ridge, Nov. 25, 1863, and accompanied Gen. Sherman on his Georgia campaign, with engagements at Resaca, Dallas, and Kenesaw Mountain. In the siege and sur-

render of the city of Atlanta, he commanded the Union artillery with distinction. On Jan. 23, 1865, he was brevetted a major-general of volunteers, and on Mar. 13 of the same year brigadier-general, United States Army, for gallant and meritorious services in the Atlanta campaign. On the latter date, too, he received the brevet of major-general in the regular army, for gallant and meritorious services in the field during the war. Brannan was honorably mustered out of the volunteer service, May 31, 1866, and like many distinguished officers holding important commands during the war between the states, went back to duty as a regimental field officer, in the comparatively monotonous routine of peace-time army posts. He commanded the garrison at Ogdensburg, N. Y., at the time of the threatened Fenian Raids; was promoted lieutenant-colonel, 4th Artillery, Jan. 10, 1877; was transferred back to the 1st Artillery, Mar. 16, 1877; and was in command of the troops during the Philadelphia railroad riots of the latter year. He received his long delayed promotion to colonel, 4th Artillery, Mar. 15, 1881 and was retired from active service, Apr. 19, 1882. Until his death, he resided in New York City.

Brannan's life was characterized by marked devotion to duty. His sympathetic interest in the welfare of his soldiers was particularly shown during the serious yellow fever epidemics of 1847, 1873, and 1874. During the wavering tide in the battle of Chickamauga, his buoyant optimism and inspiring words did much to snatch victory from defeat. He was a gallant, resourceful soldier, whose name is closely identified with distinguished service in two of his country's greatest wars.

[*Bull. Ass. Grads. Mil. Acad.*, 1893; J. H. Smith, *The War with Mexico* (1919); *Battles and Leaders of the Civil War* (1887–88); G. W. Cullum, *Biog. Reg.* (3rd ed., 1891); *Soc. Army of the Cumberland, Twenty-fourth Reunion* (1894), pp. 223–27.]   C. D. R.

BRANNAN, SAMUEL (Mar. 2, 1819–May 5, 1889), California pioneer, was born in Saco, York County, Me., where he was educated and spent the early years of his life. When he was fourteen years old he removed with his sister to Lake County, Ohio, where he learned the trade of a printer. Completing his apprenticeship in 1836, he visited most of the states of the Union during the next five years as a journeyman printer. His conversion to the Mormon faith in 1842 proved to be the turning point in his career. In that year he moved to New York City, where he published the *New York Messenger* and later the *New York Prophet* for the Mormon church. He soon became a leading spirit in the church and was made an elder, and his ability was shortly given even larger recognition; for in November 1845, when a conference of Mormons in New York City decided to move some of their number to a new home in Mexican California, Brannan was chosen to conduct the expedition. He chartered the ship *Brooklyn,* and sailed from New York City on Feb. 4, 1846, with two hundred and thirty-eight emigrants, including seventy men, sixty-eight women, and one hundred children. After sailing around South America and making a brief stop at the Sandwich (Hawaiian) Islands, the *Brooklyn* passed through the Golden Gate and anchored before the village of Yerba Buena (San Francisco) on the last day of July 1846. By this time the Mexican War was in progress, and California had been occupied by American troops.

Though somewhat disappointed at seeing the stars and stripes floating above the adobe custom house, Brannan and his followers went ashore and made themselves at home in their new environment. They were the first Anglo-American settlers to arrive in California after its capture by the United States,—an advance contingent of the hundreds of thousands that were soon to follow. At this time Brannan is described as "deep-chested, broad-shouldered, shaggy-headed," with "flashing black eyes." "His dress was dandified, his speech bombastic, his manners coarse, his courage and generosity boundless." Shortly after his arrival, Sam, as his contemporaries called him, became a leader in the village. He performed the first non-Catholic wedding ceremony, preached the first sermon in the English language, advocated the first public school, was defendant in the first jury trial, and set up and operated the first California flour mills. On Jan. 9, 1847, he began the publication of the *California Star,* which was the first newspaper in San Francisco. In the same year he moved to Sutter's Fort, where he conducted a store until 1849. Early in 1848 gold was found at the fort; and it is claimed that Brannan was the first to carry the news of this important discovery to San Francisco. On this occasion it is said that he "bolted into San Francisco from the diggings, travel-stained with his long journey, and rushed through the old Plaza hatless, crying out with his bull-throated bellow: '*Gold! Gold! Gold* from the American River!'"

In 1849 he closed his store at Sutter's Fort and returned to San Francisco, which had grown into a thriving city. To him this offered greater opportunities for leadership. He was elected a member of the first city council, played a major part in the great fire companies, and helped to organize the Society of California Pioneers.

The San Francisco Committee of Vigilance of 1851 was organized in his office. He was its second member, its first president, and its first spokesman before the public. Much of its immediate success was due to his fearless initiative; but his impetuous nature and his frequent demands for summary punishment finally led to his resignation. Meanwhile, he had made extensive investments in real estate in San Francisco and Sacramento, and became one of the wealthiest men in California. In the fifties and early sixties he used this wealth in promoting agriculture, establishing banks, organizing railway, telegraph, and express companies, and contributing large sums for philanthropic purposes. The later years of his life were marred by a too frequent indulgence in strong drink. Then his brilliant personality became "clouded by dissipation, his wealth melted away, his position was lost, and he died in poverty and obscurity, in Escondido, San Diego County." In an attempt to evaluate his services to California, H. H. Bancroft, who did not have a favorable impression of him, nevertheless wrote: "He probably did more for San Francisco and for other places than was effected by the combined efforts of scores" of other men.

[J. A. B. Scherer, *The First Forty-Niner* (1925); M. F. Williams, *Hist. of the San Francisco Committee of Vigilance of 1851* (1921); Z. S. Eldredge, *The Beginnings of San Francisco* (1912), vol. II; F. Soule, J. H. Gihon and J. Nisbet (editors), *The Annals of San Francisco* (1855); Hubert H. Bancroft, *Hist. of Cal.* (1885–86), vols. II, V, and *Popular Tribunals* (1887), vol. I; J. S. Hittell, *Hist. of the City of San Francisco* (1878); T. H. Hittell, *Hist. of Cal.* (1885–97), vols. II, III; W. A. Linn, *The Story of the Mormons* (1902); the *Cal. Star,* 1847–48.] R. P. Bi—r.

BRANNER, JOHN CASPER (July 4, 1850– Mar. 1, 1922), geologist, was born at New Market in Jefferson County, Tenn., the son of Michael T. Branner and his wife Elsie (Baker) Branner. The family was among the early settlers in the Shenandoah Valley of Virginia, where Casper Branner received a grant of land in 1760 from Lord Fairfax. About 1799, Michael Branner moved to Jefferson County, Tenn., where his great-grandson, John Casper Branner, passed his youth. The latter's education was acquired in the local schools which were not of a high grade, but of which he made the most, being of an active, energetic, and inquiring disposition. In 1866 he entered Maryville College, near Knoxville, where he remained two years, and in 1870 he entered Cornell University at Ithaca, N. Y. Here his natural scientific tendency developed rapidly and he early attracted the attention of Prof. C. F. Hartt, who invited him, though as yet an undergraduate, to accompany him on a trip to Brazil. Such an opportunity could not be overlooked and he sailed in 1874 for Rio de Janeiro, where he remained for six years. Brazil was at this time a country little known geologically and the expedition was of importance in being the first serious attempt at systematic work. A result was the establishment on the part of the Brazilian government of a *Commissão Geologico do Imperio do Brazil* of which Dr. Hartt was director and Branner assistant. This organization was discontinued in 1877 when Branner became associated with J. E. Mills in operating gold mines in the state of Minas Geraes. He returned to New York in 1880, but a few months later was again in Brazil, in the employ of Thomas Edison, searching for a vegetable fiber of a quality suitable for incandescent lights. He returned in 1881, and a year later was commissioned by the United States Department of Agriculture to study the question of cotton culture in Brazil, a duty with which he was occupied until the spring of 1884, when he returned again to the States and shortly after received an appointment as topographer on the Geological Survey of Pennsylvania under J. P. Lesley. In the spring of 1885 he was elected professor of geology in Indiana University of which David Starr Jordan was then president. In 1887 he was appointed state geologist of Arkansas, and in 1891 he followed Dr. Jordan to the newly established Stanford University in California, where he remained as professor of geology through the rest of his active career, though elected vice-president of the university in 1898 and president in 1913. He retired with the title of president emeritus in 1916 and died at Stanford, Cal., in 1922. Notwithstanding his many official duties in connection with the university, he had three times visited Brazil: in 1899 to study the ocean reefs lying off the coast of Pernambuco; in 1907 to study the black diamond areas of Bahia and the geology of the states of Alagôas and Sergipe, and in 1911 for a further study of the Brazilian coast.

Branner's reports of the Survey were monographic in character and are in themselves sufficiently indicative of the administrative ability and industry of the man. His work in Brazil was largely in the nature of reconnaissance but sufficiently stimulating to cause the Brazilian government to follow it up, and it made a place for another American, Dr. O. A. Derby, who for many years, or until 1915, was employed as government geologist in the state of São Paulo. The final work of geological importance of Branner's life was consummated after his retirement from the presidency of Stanford University and consisted in the compilation of a geological map,

with explanatory text, of Brazil, which was published in both English and Portuguese by the Geological Society of America. A good linguist, he translated from the Portuguese Herculano's *History of the Origin and Establishment of the Inquisition in Portugal*. Tall and robust and of imposing appearance, he had sufficient independence of thought to regard self-respect as of more importance than the respect of one's neighbors, but he was without egotism. He combined the faculty of investigator with that of teacher, in the latter calling being highly successful, rarely failing to arouse an enthusiastic interest among his pupils. He was married in 1883 to Susan D. Kennedy of Oneida, N. Y., by whom he had three children.

[R. A. F. Penrose, "Memorial to John Casper Branner," *Bull. Geol. Soc. of America*, XXXVI, 15–44, containing bibliography; C. R. Keyes, "John Casper Branner," *Pan American Geologist*, XXXVII, 261; R. A. F. Penrose, "John Casper Branner," *Memoirs Nat. Acad. Sci.*, vol. XXI (1927), containing bibliography.]

G. P. M.

BRANNON, HENRY (Nov. 26, 1837–Nov. 24, 1914), jurist, was a younger son of Robert and Catherine (Copenhaver) Brannon. Of Irish descent, his father was a native of Winchester, Va., where he himself was born. His youth was spent on his father's farm in the Shenandoah Valley, and his early education was obtained at private schools and the Winchester Academy. Entering the University of Virginia in 1854, he graduated in 1858 and then moved to Weston, Lewis County, in the western part of the state, where his elder brother, John, was practising law. He read law in his brother's office, was admitted to the Virginia bar in 1859, and commenced practise at Weston. In 1860 he was elected prosecuting attorney for Lewis County, occupying that position for four years. An efficient official, he acquired a wide practise, and took an active part in local politics, being a strong Republican. Though too young to be prominent in the movement which resulted in the formation of the State of West Virginia, he was elected in 1870 as representative of Lewis County in the House of Delegates, and served two terms, acting as chairman of the legislative committee on education. In 1880 he was nominated and elected judge of the 11th judicial circuit, succeeding his brother in that office. His practical acquaintance with rural conditions combined with a thorough knowledge of *nisi prius* law made him an excellent circuit judge, and at the end of his term in 1888 he was nominated and elected an associate justice of the supreme court of appeals. This office he filled for twenty-four years, being reelected in 1900 on the expiration of his first term. He retired from the bench Dec. 31, 1912, declining a renomination. During his long occupancy of the appellate court bench, he had a preponderant share in shaping the law of West Virginia in its initial stages, and by his strong common sense and freedom from tradition made an admirable interpreter of the law of a new state. New problems had to be faced, particularly those arising in regard to oil-bearing properties, and his decisions on questions of leaseholds commanded the respect and approval of other jurisdictions wherein oil development occurred at periods subsequent to its appearance in West Virginia. Though not erudite, and having no pretense to scientific legal training, his mental equipment was such that he instinctively grasped the vital points of the cases before him, his capacity for exhaustive analysis was keen, and his opinions were invariably expressed with singular clarity and force. He wrote a treatise, *Rights and Privileges Guaranteed by the Fourteenth Amendment to the Constitution of the United States* (1901), which, by its depth of thought and scholarly style, is a distinct contribution to political science. He was a great lover of literature, having an intimate knowledge of French and Spanish, and possessing an extensive library of the best authors in those languages. He was married to Hetta J. Arnold of Weston.

[His career and characteristics are well summarized in *Proc. of the W. Va. Bar Ass.*, 1914, p. 133. See also *Hist. of Lewis Co., W. Va.*, by E. C. Smith (1920); *Prominent Men of W. Va.*, by G. W. Atkinson and A. F. Gibbens (1890), p. 995; *Contemporary Biography of W. Va.* (1894), p. 204; *W. Va. Reports,* vols. LXXI and LXXIII.]   H.W.H.K.

BRANT, JOSEPH (1742–Nov. 24, 1807), Mohawk chief, whose Indian name was Thayendanegea, was the son of a Mohawk chief, probably the one known as "Nickus Brant." Apparently his mother was not a Mohawk and certainly was not of sachem stock, hence (Iroquois rank descending through the females) Joseph never became a sachem though he won the lesser rank of chief. His rise was facilitated by his sister Molly's relations with Sir William Johnson [*q.v.*]. At the age of thirteen Brant accompanied Johnson in the campaign of 1755. Six years later he and two other Mohawks entered Moor's Charity School in Lebanon, Conn. He left school in 1763 to act as interpreter for a missionary, but soon entered the Iroquois contingent aiding the whites against Pontiac. A convert to the Anglican church, Brant aided the Rev. John Stewart in translating various religious works into the Mohawk tongue. Guy Johnson, son-in-law of Sir William, became superintendent of Indian Affairs in 1774, and made Brant his secretary. The latter strove hard to bring the Iroquois to

the aid of the British in the Revolution, trying to discredit Samuel Kirkland, missionary to the Oneidas, who succeeded in winning the Oneidas and Tuscaroras to the American side. Now a war chief, Brant appeared at Montreal as Mohawk spokesman in a conference with Sir Guy Carleton. He was given a captain's commission and sent to England. Here he was presented at court, was entertained by Boswell and other notables, and was painted in Mohawk regalia by Romney. Back in America, he plunged into the conflict. Soon his name awoke terror throughout New York, especially in the Mohawk Valley. Commanding with skill the Indians of St. Leger's expedition, Brant displayed desperate courage at the battle of Oriskany (Aug. 6, 1777). Thereafter his Indians, sometimes alone, sometimes in conjunction with Tories under the Butlers and Johnsons, harried the Mohawk Valley, southern New York, and northern Pennsylvania. Though he certainly directed the Cherry Valley Massacre of 1778 and numerous others, his biographers assert that he did not participate in that of Wyoming (1779). Denying that he was "a monster of cruelty," he and his defenders claimed that he sought to protect women, children, prisoners, and wounded. If so, he did not always succeed. He frustrated the efforts of Red Jacket to induce the Iroquois to make a separate peace with the Americans. At the close of the struggle the Mohawks retired west of the Niagara River, whence Brant sought to procure a settlement with the United States. Failing, he induced Gov. Haldimand of Canada to assign them land. Visiting England again in 1785, he procured funds to indemnify the Iroquois for their losses in war and to purchase new lands. Following further efforts to arrange matters with the United States, including a vain trip to Philadelphia, Brant devoted most of his energies to the domestic welfare of his fellows in the Grand River settlement. He had helped establish "the Old Mohawk Church" and now translated religious works into that dialect. He opposed successfully the attempts of land speculators to preempt the lands of the Mohawks. But his old age was saddened by the dissoluteness of his eldest son and the intrigues of his old enemy, Red Jacket.

[The chief manuscript sources are the Haldimand Papers and the Kirkland MSS. The most essential printed sources are B. F. Stevens' *Fac-Similes of Manuscripts in European Archives Relating to America, 1773–83* (1889–95); Jas. Sullivan and A. C. Flick, *The Papers of Sir Wm. Johnson* (1921–27); Adam Shortt and A. G. Doughty, *Docs. Relating to the Constitutional Hist. of Canada, 1759–91* (1907); *Jours. of the Provincial Congress, Provincial Convention, Committee of Safety and Council of Safety of the State of New*

York (1842); Eleazar Wheelock, *Narrative of the Original Design, Rise, Progress and Present State of the Indian Charity-School at Lebanon in Conn.* (1763), and *A Brief Narrative of the Indian Charity School* (1766). W. L. Stone's *Life of Joseph Brant* (1838), the chief secondary authority, should be supplemented by L. A. Wood's *War Chief of the Six Nations* (1914); L. H. Morgan, *League of the Ho-de-no-sau-nee or Iroquois* (1904); S. G. Drake, *The Aboriginal Races of America* (1860); Nelson Greene, *Hist. of the Mohawk Valley* (1925); and the biographies of Johnson, Burgoyne, St. Leger, and Red Jacket.]   M.L.B.

BRANTLEY, THEODORE (Feb. 12, 1851–Sept. 16, 1922), judge, born in Wilson County, Tenn., was the son of Eliza (Brown) Brantley and Edwin T. Brantley, a Presbyterian minister. In 1870 he entered Stewart College (now Southwestern-Presbyterian University) at Clarksville, Tenn., where he graduated in 1874. He then began the study of law while teaching, and from time to time attended sessions of Cumberland University at Lebanon, Tenn., which awarded him the degree of bachelor of laws in 1880. For the next three years he practised law and then became professor of ancient languages in Lincoln University, Lincoln, Ill. In 1887 he accepted a similar position at the College of Montana, Deer Lodge, Mont., which he relinquished after two years to resume the practise of law. On June 9, 1891, he was married to Lois Reat. In 1893 the Republican party drafted him as candidate for judge in a district overwhelmingly Democratic, and he was elected. In 1898 he was elected chief justice of the state supreme court, and was reëlected in 1904, 1910, and 1916. He came into office when the Constitution was new, and most of its provisions had not yet been interpreted. The mining interest which dominated the politics of the state had written it, and they held that the legislature had only delegated powers. A farmer and labor movement directed against this control was arising. The whole of Brantley's tenure was one of political agitation, and out of his court decisions came a reformed constitution and a new system of law. In 1909 the court held: "No Act of the legislature will be declared invalid as repugnant to the fundamental law except in the clearest cases" (39 *Montana Reports*, 200). While the constitution definitely restricted the taxation of mines as such, Brantley's opinion left the way open for heavy taxes upon their proceeds. It also paved the way to approval of a long line of social legislation.

When Brantley came to the supreme bench water and irrigation rights were vaguely defined. Common law practise was generally acknowledged in principle, but there were laws reflecting the California and Colorado codes. In a country of little rainfall the right to use the water in streams creates the value of real estate.

It was the work of the courts to define these rights and the important decisions numbered more than a hundred. Brantley's early decisions prepared the way for the great decision in 1921 that the common law doctrine of riparian rights does not prevail, but that water rights depend upon prior appropriation for beneficial use (61 *Montana*, 152). This decision was essential to the agricultural development of the state. When an attack was made on the primary law in 1900, Brantley supported the law on the ground that the constitution stated that "all political power is vested in and derived from the people" (24 *Montana*, 3911). In 1914 the constitutionality of the initiative and referendum amendment was attacked on technical grounds. The court held that in view of the overwhelming majority in favor of the amendment the irregularities if corrected would not change the decision of the people, and brushed them all aside (49 *Montana*, 419). In spite of his philosophical view of the law and his interpretations influenced by ideals of economic and social development, Brantley preserved throughout his career the admiration of both liberals and conservatives. All had confidence in his fairness and ability, and his most startling opinions were received with respect. At his death all were willing to acknowledge the new order in Montana which had been so largely the result of his work.

[*Who's Who in America*, 1922–23; "In Memoriam," 64 *Montana Reports*, pp. viii–xxxiii; *Helena Independent*, Sept. 17, 1922; Brantley's judicial opinions are found in *Montana Reports*, XXII–LXIV.]   P.C.P.

BRASHEAR, JOHN ALFRED (Nov. 24, 1840–Apr. 8, 1920), scientist, maker of astronomical lenses, belonged to a family of French Huguenots named Brasseuir who emigrated to America and settled in Calvert County, Md., in 1658. In 1775 a descendant of this family, Otho Brashear (the original Brasseuir had undergone several changes in spelling), emigrated from Maryland to the present site of Brownsville, Pa. Here his grandson, Basil Brown Brashear, a saddler by trade, married a school-teacher, the daughter of one Nathaniel Smith, who had emigrated to Brownsville probably from Massachusetts. John Alfred Brashear was the first of their seven children. His maternal grandfather, who had a passion for astronomy, taught the boy the constellations by the time he was eight, presented him with his own prized volumes of Dr. Dick's *Works* (1850), and paid for John's first view of the heavens through a telescope. "Young as I was," Brashear wrote in later years, "the scenery of the moon and the rings of Saturn impressed me deeply.... The entrancing beauty of that first sight has never been forgotten." All of young Brashear's formal education was obtained in the common schools of Brownsville and in a four-months' course in bookkeeping at Duff's Mercantile College, Pittsburgh. During 1856–59 he served his apprenticeship in the pattern-making trade at the engine works of John Snowden & Sons in Brownsville. After working at his trade for two years in Kentucky he came to Pittsburgh in 1861 where he resided until his death. On Sept. 24, 1862, he married Phœbe Stewart. Until he suffered a physical breakdown in 1881, Brashear endured the rigors of life in the mills in conjunction with long hours of night work devoted to study. The memory of the beauty of his first vision of the heavens persisted with such compelling force throughout these difficult years that he decided, since he could not afford to buy a good object glass, that he would make a telescope for himself. He knew nothing about the polishing of lenses, but he bought a glass for a five-inch lens and some books to tell him how to go about the work. He was arising at 5:30 to go to work in the mills and not returning until 6:00 o'clock or even later. But, with the constant and invaluable aid of his wife, he labored over the polishing of the glass far into the nights. It was three years before the lens was mounted, temporarily, and stuck through an open window for its first revelation of the heavens. From this modest beginning, Brashear rose to become the peer of any maker of astronomical lenses and instruments of precision of his day. Through his first lens he made the acquaintance of Prof. Samuel Pierpont Langley who was then at the old Allegheny Observatory, and through Langley he met William Thaw who gave him the financial aid necessary in going into business for himself in 1881. It was the perfection of his work that caused the demand for his lenses by astronomers everywhere, and it is impossible to estimate accurately the progress in the science of astronomy due to his mechanical genius. To-day his glasses are still in use not only in America but in Europe, the Orient, and the Islands of the Pacific.

Brashear's great contribution to science lay in his mastery of the art of making a plane surface. Through this, he rendered invaluable aid in the work of the distinguished physicist, Henry A. Rowland of Johns Hopkins University. The speculum-metal plates from which the famous Rowland Diffraction Gratings were made required a very accurate surface, no error of even one-fifth of a light wave, or one two-hundred-thousandth of an inch. The surfaces were polished and prepared for Rowland's Ruling Engine

by Brashear and his son-in-law James B. McDowell. Another great contribution to science was the Brashear Method for silvering mirrors. "Perhaps his most important achievement was in connection with the design and development of the spectroscope for astronomical uses" (*Mechanical Engineering,* XLII, 311). The mechanical genius of Brashear, though great, was overshadowed by the personality of the man. The force that dominated him was a sincere desire to share the beauty of the universe with all mankind. It made of him a unique figure, of broad sympathy and rare understanding. To literally thousands of people he was known familiarly as "Uncle John," and it was Brashear the man, rather than Brashear the scientist, who was the recipient of uncounted honors in the later years of his life. Only the genius of his personality can explain the positions of trust he held during his last twenty-five years. He was a man without formal education, and one whose entire life had demonstrated an inability to grapple successfully with business and financial problems. Yet, as chairman of the Allegheny Observatory Committee he was entrusted with the raising of the $300,000 necessary for the new observatory. It was characteristic of him that he did not stop until he had a room in the new building where anybody who wanted to could see and hear about his "starry heavens" free. For twenty-five years he served as a trustee of the Western University of Pennsylvania (University of Pittsburgh), and though he thrice refused its chancellorship he served as acting chancellor for three years. He was one of three men selected by Andrew Carnegie to draw up plans for the Carnegie Institute of Technology. And when Henry C. Frick decided to make his gift of a half million dollars to establish the Frick Educational Commission, he did it on condition that Brashear undertake the work of getting the activities of the Commission under way. On his death in 1920, Brashear was mourned not only as Pittsburgh's, but as Pennsylvania's "best loved citizen."

[The chief source is *John A. Brashear, The Autobiography of a Man Who Loved the Stars* (1925). In her work in editing this Autobiography, the author of the above sketch has had intimate contact with the published papers and countless letters left by Dr. Brashear (now in the custody of his secretary, Martha C. Hoyt, Secretary of the Frick Educational Commission) as well as the help of a committee of scientific men appointed by the American Society of Mechanical Engineers to help her obtain an accurate estimate of Brashear's life-work.]
                           E.Y.

BRATTLE, THOMAS (June 20, 1658–May 18, 1713), merchant, was born in Boston, the son of Thomas and Elizabeth (Tyng) Brattle. His father, a trader and landowner, held various political offices in the colony, commanded several expeditions against the Indians, and on his death in 1683 was rated the wealthiest man in New England. His son Thomas graduated from Harvard College in 1676 in a class of three students, was executor and chief beneficiary of his father's will, returned in November 1689 from travel and study abroad, and spent the rest of his life in Boston, where his public spirit, his intellectual attainments, and his liberalism in politics and in religion were of marked service to the community. He never married. Nothing is known of his business affairs except that he evidently managed them as well as he did the finances of Harvard College, of which he was treasurer from 1693 until his death. Under his intelligent, conscientious administration the resources of the College were almost tripled in value. His relations with the Harvard Corporation, however, were not entirely peaceful. His inclinations toward the forms of the Church of England led him to become the chief organizer in 1698 of the Brattle Street Church, whose members dispensed with the "relation of experiences" as a qualification for membership, used the Lord's Prayer, had the Bible read without comment as a part of the services, and deviated in other particulars from the principles of the Cambridge Platform. Thomas Brattle thus brought down on himself the enmity of Increase and Cotton Mather. Much controversy ensued. By amending the new charter of Harvard College Increase Mather succeeded in having Brattle, his brother William, and John Leverett excluded from the Harvard Corporation, but the Brattles were reinstated in 1703 when the Mather power was failing, and the long, rancorous warfare ended with the election of Leverett to the presidency in 1707. Highly honorable to Brattle was his letter dated Oct. 8, 1692, addressed to an unnamed clergyman, in which he examined the Salem witchcraft proceedings in detail and condemned them as "ignorance and folly." He took great interest in mathematics and astronomy and sent to the Royal Society of London accounts of several eclipses that he had observed. He is said to have been an F. R. S., but his name does not appear in the lists of the Society's members in T. Thomson, *History of the Royal Society* (1812) or in the *Records of the Royal Society* (2nd ed., 1901). That fact, however, is not decisive, for Brattle's status may have been similar to Cotton Mather's [G. L. Kittredge, "Cotton Mather's Election into the Royal Society" in *Publications of the Colonial Society of Massachusetts*, XIV]. Brattle owned the first organ ever brought to New England and willed it to the Brattle Street Church, which on theological grounds felt obliged re-

spectfully to decline it. According to the provisions of the will it was thereupon offered to King's Chapel, the Episcopalian society, which accepted it. In the Boston that was witnessing the old age of Increase Mather and the childhood of Benjamin Franklin, Thomas Brattle was an admirable, and a significant, personality.

[E. D. Harris, *An Account of Some of the Descendants of Capt. Thos. Brattle* (1867); Josiah Quincy, *Hist. of Harvard Univ.* (1840); J. L. Sibley, *Biog. Sketches of Grads. of Harvard Univ.*, II (1881)—with full refs. to sources; *Diary of Samuel Sewall 1674–1729* in *Colls. Mass. Hist. Soc.*, ser. 5, vols. V–VII; Ebenezer Turell, *Life and Character of the Rev. Benj. Colman* (1749); Justin Winsor, ed., *Memorial Hist. of Boston* (1881–83); Brattle's contributions to the Royal Society are in the *Philosophical Transactions* for July and Aug. 1704, pp. 1630–38 and for Oct., Nov., and Dec., 1707, pp. 2471–72; his letter on the Salem witchcraft trials was reprinted in *Colls. Mass. Hist. Soc.*, V, 61–80, and in G. L. Burr, *Narratives of the Witchcraft Cases 1648–1706* (1914). For interpretation of Brattle's career see Brooks Adams, *The Emancipation of Mass.* (1887) and K. B. Murdock, *Increase Mather, the Foremost Am. Puritan* (1925).]   G. H. G.

BRATTLE, WILLIAM (Nov. 22, 1662–Feb. 15, 1716/17), Congregational minister, educator, was the son of the wealthy and prominent Thomas and Elizabeth (Tyng) Brattle of Boston. After graduating from Harvard College in 1680 he became a tutor, and from 1696 to 1700 was a Fellow in the Corporation. During the four years while President Increase Mather was in Europe, Brattle and John Leverett, as the principle directors and teachers in the College, followed a policy which "inclined to the order of things which was coming" (Josiah Quincy, *The History of Harvard University*, 1840, I, 66). Even Cotton Mather noted that the College flourished under their "prudent government" (Cotton Mather, *Magnalia Christi Americana*, 1702, Bk. IV, p. 131). As a tutor, Brattle was described by a student as "able, faithful, and tender," and his heroism during the smallpox epidemic, together with his "fatherly goodness" and continued benefactions, won him the title of "Father of the College." As late as 1765 his *Compendium Logicae Secundum Principia D. Renati Cartesii*, the first American text-book on logic, was used at Harvard.

In 1696, the year of his election to the Harvard Corporation, Brattle was also ordained pastor of the church in Cambridge. On this occasion he evidenced his independence regarding established ecclesiastical usages, and as the result of his unceasing exertion, his church discontinued the formal and public relation of religious experience required of candidates for church membership. This liberalism, as well as his championship of other innovations, was probably an important factor in his exclusion from the Har-

He was never elected a member of the society, however, though that honor was conferred on his brother William [q.v.], largely that the society might not possess in Thomas' sci-

vard Corporation in 1700, to which position, however, he returned three years later when the influence of his group replaced that of the Mathers. Although it has been held that Brattle's doctrinal opinions were of the strict Puritan school (William B. Sprague, *Annals of the American Pulpit*, 1856, I, 236 ff.) manuscript notes taken on his sermons by John Hancock (1671–1752) indicate as strong an interest in ethical questions as in Calvinistic theology. God's delight in mercy and Christ's mission to save sinners were doctrines which apparently found an important place in his sermons. "Follow peace with all men," and "let us excite within us compassions" were mellow sentiments. His preaching, which enjoyed a high reputation, was described as "calm, and soft, and melting" (Abiel Holmes, "The History of Cambridge," *Massachusetts Historical Society Collections*, 1800, VII). Indeed, though Brattle was sympathetic with the organization of the liberal Brattle Street Church, initiated by his brother Thomas, he seems to have mingled very little in theological controversies, and "being of a catholic and pacific spirit" to have sought harmony (Dr. Benjamin Colman, quoted by Alexander McKenzie, *Lectures on the History of the Church in Cambridge*, p. 142).

From his marriage with Elizabeth Hayman one son, William, who achieved distinction in the provincial militia, survived him. Toward the end of his life Brattle married Elizabeth Gerrish. Skilful in business, he was a generous but quiet philanthropist. Urbane, scholarly, serenely tolerant, William Brattle, by his character and influence, contributed to the mellowing of orthodox Puritanism.

[Manuscript notes taken on Brattle's sermons by John Hancock (Harvard Univ. Lib.) and by John Leverett (Mass. Hist. Soc. Lib.) are indexes to Brattle's doctrinal position. Samuel Sewall's *Diary* makes frequent references to him. The best secondary accounts are those in Edward Harris, *An Account of Some of the Descendants of Capt. Thos. Brattle* (1867); Alexander McKenzie, *Lectures on the Hist. of the First Church in Cambridge* (1873); and John Langdon Sibley, *Biog. Sketches Grads. Harvard Univ.* (1885).]   M. E. C.

BRATTON, JOHN (Mar. 7, 1831–Jan. 12, 1898), Confederate soldier, the son of Dr. William Bratton, Jr., and his second wife, Isabella Means, was born at Winnsboro, S. C. After preparation at Mount Zion Academy he entered the South Carolina College from which he was graduated in 1850. Three years later he received a "medical diploma" from the South Carolina Medical College and shortly afterward began the practise of medicine in Fairfield County. In 1859 he married Elizabeth, daughter of Theodore S. Du Bose. He continued in his profession with

moderate success until the beginning of the Civil War when he entered the military service of South Carolina as a private in the 6th Regiment of Volunteers. He was almost immediately promoted captain. Twice subsequently, however, he reënlisted as a private at the expiration of periods of enlistment when his regiment was reorganized. In 1862 he was elected colonel of the 6th Regiment which had become a part of Micah Jenkins's Brigade, Longstreet's Corps. After the death of Jenkins, during the Battle of the Wilderness, May 6, 1864, "Old Reliable," as Bratton was now known to his men, was appointed brigadier-general (June 27, 1864). He was several times cited for gallantry and was twice wounded. On one occasion (Battle of Seven Pines, May 31, 1862) being wounded, he was taken prisoner and was held in Fortress Monroe until exchanged several months later. Of the brigades which composed the Army of Northern Virginia at Appomattox, his was the most completely manned and was the only one which left the field as an organized unit (*Official Records*, ser. I, *passim*).

After the war Bratton did not resume the practise of medicine but became a farmer and was soon drawn into active public life. He did not seek political office but was from time to time pressed into service as a member of the constitutional convention in 1865, as state senator (1865–66), and as congressman (1884–85). He was a delegate to all the Taxpayers' Conventions, was chairman of the delegates from South Carolina to the national Democratic convention of 1876, was chairman of the state Democratic committee in 1880, and was elected by the legislature to fill the vacant office of state comptroller in 1881. In politics he adhered to the conservative party which under Wade Hampton [*q.v.*] delivered the state from Republican rule in 1876. Though a farmer he did not support the Farmer's Movement in South Carolina. His feeling against this "class movement," as he characterized it, was such that he was led to become a candidate for the governorship in 1890 in opposition to B. R. Tillman [*q.v.*], the Farmers' leader. His dignified campaign, conducted amidst all manner of political excess and extravagance, won the admiration of all classes but was at no time formidable. Like many conservatives, he retired from politics after the victory of the Tillmanites. He died at Winnsboro, Jan. 12, 1898.

[Brief but accurate sketches of Bratton's life appear in the *Confed. Mil. Hist.* (1899), V, 378–80; the *Cyc. of Eminent and Representative Men of the Carolinas* (1892), I, 433–36; *News and Courier* (Charleston, S. C.), Jan. 13, 1898. A few of Bratton's letters in manuscript are contained in the W. G. Hinson Collection owned by the Charleston (S. C.) Lib. Soc. This also includes a scrapbook of clippings from leading newspapers of the state relating to the gubernatorial campaign of 1890.]   J. H. E—y.

BRAWLEY, WILLIAM HIRAM (May 13, 1841–Nov. 15, 1916), congressman and federal judge, son of Hiram Brawley and Harriet Foote, was born in Chester, S. C., and was educated in the preparatory schools of his native town and in the South Carolina College. He was a college graduate and a Confederate soldier before he was twenty years of age, was with the 6th South Carolina Volunteers in the attack on Fort Sumter, fought with his regiment in the battles in Virginia, and was wounded at the battle of Seven Pines, May 31, 1862. This wound necessitated the amputation of his left arm. After a short time spent in managing his father's plantation in April 1864, he successfully ran the blockade to England, where he completed his studies in law and literature. He returned home in November 1865, was admitted to the bar in 1866, elected solicitor of the sixth circuit in 1868, and in 1874 resigned that office to move to Charleston, where he practised law in association with Hon. W. D. Porter, and later with Hon. Joseph Barnwell. He was elected to the state legislature in 1882 and served continuously till 1890. In this year he was elected to the Fifty-first Congress where he served till February 1894 when he was appointed by President Cleveland district judge for South Carolina. He was married twice: in 1868 to Marion E. Porter, daughter of his law partner, and July 11, 1907, to Mildred Frost. He died in Charleston, Nov. 15, 1916.

Brawley's early and continued success in law practise was due to his high power of clearly stating and analyzing current issues as well as legal principles. His personal influence and his position as chairman of the judiciary committee made him the acknowledged leader in the South Carolina legislature. Added to this was oratorical ability marked even in a state much given to oratory. His appeal to the legislature in 1886 in behalf of the sufferers from the Charleston earthquake of that year was one of the bursts of impassioned eloquence heard only from gifted speakers on rare occasions. His address on the causes of the Civil War, delivered at Chester, S. C., May 10, 1905, on the occasion of the laying of the cornerstone of a monument to the Confederate dead, awakened interest in the whole country and formed the subject of an editorial in *Harper's Weekly*. Probably his greatest service as a speaker was in opposition to the Free Silver movement. His speech against the Bland Silver Bill was one of three opposition speeches from Southern members, and he was the only Southern member to vote against the bill. He spoke with equal ability on the bill to repeal the Sherman Silver Purchase Act, and it was doubtless in recognition of this service that President Cleveland offered him without solicitation the post of federal judge. Polished in manners, widely read, courteous but forceful in address, striking in appearance, and courageously honest in his convictions, he won to his support even those who differed from his financial views.

[*Who's Who in America*, 1912–13; W. R. Brooks, *S. C. Bench and Bar*, I (1908), 351–65; J. C. Hemphill, sketch in *Men of Mark in S. C.* (1906); *News and Courier* (Charleston, S. C.), Nov. 16, 1916.]

         J. E. W—y.

BRAXTON, CARTER (Sept. 10, 1736–Oct. 10, 1797), Revolutionary statesman, born at Newington, King and Queen County, Va., inherited wealth and gentle blood. His father, George Braxton, a planter, was sometime member of the House of Burgesses and president of the Colonial Council. His mother, Mary, was the daughter of Councilor Robert Carter (called, because of his wealth and power, King Carter). Braxton was educated at the College of William and Mary, and was later a member of its board of visitors (*William and Mary Quarterly Historical Magazine*, II, 37, XXVII, 239). When nineteen, he married Judith Robinson of a prominent Middlesex County family. Upon the death of his wife in December 1757, he went to England where he remained until the fall of 1760. In May 1761 he married Elizabeth, daughter of Richard Corbin, colonial receiver-general. When only twenty-five years of age, Braxton was sent to the House of Burgesses from King William County to which he had moved. He served actively from 1761 to 1775, with the exception of a brief period in the early seventies when he was county sheriff. In the dispute with Great Britain he was loyal to Virginia, but held the more conservative views of the Tidewater leaders. His name appears, however, with those of Washington, Jefferson, Henry, Peyton Randolph, and others of the House who signed the *Resolutions* of May 1769 that the Virginia House of Burgesses had the sole right to tax the inhabitants of the colony. He also signed the non-importation agreement at that time (*Journals of the House of Burgesses of Virginia, 1766–69*, 1906, pp. xxxviii ff.). He represented his county in the Revolutionary conventions of 1774, 1775, and 1776. It was Braxton who doubtless prevented bloodshed by adjusting a dispute between Patrick Henry and Gov. Dunmore over the gunpowder taken to the latter from the Williamsburg magazine in April 1775 (John Daly Burk, *History of Virginia,* 1804–16, IV, 13 ff.). The convention of July 1775 appointed him a member of the Committee of Safety, the governing body of the colony until the state government was inaugurated (W. W. Hening, *The Statutes at Large,* 1819–23, IX, 49, 328). Upon the death of Peyton Randolph, the convention appointed Braxton as his successor in Congress. He took his seat on Feb. 23, 1776, and was one of the signers of the Declaration of Independence (for his views regarding independence see letter to his uncle, Landon Carter, in *Letters of Members of the Continental Congress,* 1921, I, 420). He was not reappointed to his seat in Congress. This was probably due in part to his address to the Virginia convention, in which he advocated a conservative form of government for Virginia, and showed little faith in democracy (Burk, *History of Virginia,* IV, 13 ff.; Charles Campbell, *History of Virginia,* 1860, pp. 641–47; text of address in Peter Force, *American Archives,* 4th ser., VI, 748–754). In any event, he was returned that year to the Virginia Assembly, where he continued to serve, in the House and in the Council, until about the time of his death (E. G. Swem and John W. Williams, *Register of the General Assembly of Virginia, 1776–1918,* 1918. *Calendar of Virginia State Papers,* IV, 1884, p. 68; *Ibid.,* VII, 1888, p. 151). He supported the act of 1785 to establish religious freedom in Virginia, and was lay delegate from his parish to the convention which reorganized the former established church. In 1786 he removed to Richmond where he died. Losses during the Revolution, his long public service, and his unfortunate commercial ventures during his last years had wrecked his fortune.

[The best early biographical account of Braxton is in John Sanderson, *Biography of the Signers of the Declaration of Independence* (1828), V. The author of the articles dealing with the Virginia signers seems to have known his ground well. He was a contemporary of many people who knew Braxton, and doubtless of Braxton himself. His article on Braxton is well written, accurate, and unbiased. There are a few references to Braxton in the *Jours. of the Continental Congress, 1774–89,* IV (1906). Frederick Horner, *Hist. of the Blair, Banister, and Braxton Families* (1898), makes some additions to the account in Sanderson.]

R. L. M.

BRAY, THOMAS (1656–Feb. 15, 1729/30), Anglican clergyman, was born at Marton, Shropshire, England, and graduated from All Souls College, Oxford, in 1678. A country rector and author of popular catechetical lectures, in 1696 he was chosen by Henry Compton, Bishop of London, to serve as his commissary in Maryland. Largely by Bray's zeal was effected the establishment of the Church of England in that colony, where the Revolution and royal government had recently strengthened the hands of the Anglican minority. Between 1696 and 1699 he unsuccessfully solicited royal assent to the provincial church act of 1692 reënacted in 1696. He then went over to Maryland to secure the passage of a revised measure. Meanwhile he had recruited missionaries for Maryland and other colonies, and had inaugurated his notable scheme for furnishing the colonial clergy —later also the English parochial clergy—with libraries, chiefly of religious books. By 1699 he had formed some thirty such collections, sixteen in Maryland; several became also lending libraries for the laity as well as the clergy. To support these activities, with episcopal aid Bray organized a voluntary society, the Society for Promoting Christian Knowledge (1699). Moreover, in 1701 he actively promoted the chartering of the Society for the Propagation of the Gospel, whose missionary enterprises were so important in colonial history.

Bray resided in Maryland only from March 1700 to the following summer. He procured a new church act, conducted a general visitation, undertook the discipline of the baser clergy, and planned the extension of Anglicanism in Pennsylvania and other colonies. Returning to England he met powerful Quaker opposition to the establishment. His pamphlets in the cause were assailed by Joseph Wyeth (Wyeth's *An Answer to a Letter from Dr. Bray,* 1700, and *Remarks on Dr. Bray's Memorial,* 1701); the Board of Trade, moreover, rejected the Act of 1700. But though the Quakers, Bray asserted, spent large sums to defeat him, he won royal approval for the Revised Act of 1702, based upon his suggestions. Previously Bray had resigned his office, but not his interest in Maryland and in the colonies generally.

In 1706 he became rector of St. Botolph's Without, Aldgate. Already distinguished for his "ecclesiastical imperialism," in his city parish he became the aggressive leader of the religious-philanthropic movement of the pre-Wesleyan era: the founder or an active member of numerous societies, for suppressing vice, founding libraries, charity schools, and hospitals, relieving proselytes, etc. In part these organizations represented merely the resurgence of the old negative Puritan morality; in other respects they gave evidence of a new social earnestness, not without its effect on the colonies. Two of Bray's societies, merged under his will, furnished the institutional basis for the Georgia

Trust. One was the Trustees of Parochial Libraries (1710–30), the other the Associates of Dr. Bray, a trust created in 1723 to assist him in administering the D'Allone legacy for converting negroes and Indians. In his *Missionalia* (1727) Bray ridiculed Berkeley's Bermuda college scheme, and presented a rival project for artisan-missions on the American frontiers. The same year he interested himself in the lot of the poor prisoners in London, anticipating Oglethorpe's prison investigations. In 1734 his parishioner, Thomas Coram [*q.v.*], wrote that in 1729 Bray had said he hoped before he died to find a way to settle English unemployed and foreign Protestants in America, but regarded Coram's projected colony between Maine and Nova Scotia as too far north. There is evidence that Bray suggested to Oglethorpe, or discussed with him, the debtor-colony scheme. In 1730 his Associates were enlarged to embrace this third charity, and petitioned for the charter of Georgia.

"He was a Great Small man," declared Coram, "and had done Great good things in his life Time."

[For further details of Bray's career and for a partial list of his writings, see *Dict. of Nat. Biog.*, VI, 239–41. The primary source for his life is [Samuel Smith], *Publick Spirit illustrated in the Life and Designs of Dr. Bray* (London, 1746; 2nd ed., ed. by H. J. Todd, London, 1808). A manuscript version in the Bodleian Lib. was printed by B. C. Steiner in *Md. Hist. Soc. Fund Pub. No. 37* (1901) but was incorrectly ascribed to Richard Rawlinson. See this volume for reprints of several of Bray's writings, as also *Thos. Bray Club Pubs.*, Nos. 1–7. Consult further: B. C. Steiner, "Rev. Thos. Bray and his American Libraries," *Am. Hist. Rev.*, II, 59–75; and "Two Missionary Schemes," *Sewanee Rev.*, XI, 289–305; A. B. Keep, *Hist. of the N. Y. Soc. Lib.* (1908); V. W. Crane, *The Southern Frontier to the Founding of Ga.* (1928), ch. XIII.]

V. W. C.

BRAYMAN, MASON (May 23, 1813–Feb. 27, 1895), editor, lawyer, Union soldier, was born in Buffalo, the son of Daniel Brayman, a young pioneer from Connecticut, and his wife, Anna English, a native of Nova Scotia, who had lived in Otsego County, N. Y., before her marriage. He early showed a bent for journalism and the year after he reached his majority, in the latter part of the Jackson administration, he became editor of the Buffalo *Bulletin*. In later years he edited several newspapers— among them the Louisville *Advertiser* and the *Illinois State Journal*. He chose the law as his profession, however, was admitted to the New York bar and, after removing to Michigan, served for a time as city attorney of Monroe in that state. In 1842 he settled in Illinois and practised law there. His introduction to the *Illinois Revised Statutes* (1845) is a survey of the

conditions under which Illinois legal machinery operated during the first quarter-century of the state's existence. Brayman held a special commission from Gov. Ford to compose the difficulties between the Mormons at Nauvoo and their hostile neighbors, and censured the anti-Mormons for attempting to take vengeance on non-Mormon residents for defending Nauvoo from attack. In 1847 during the session of the state constitutional convention, his journalistic aptitude was turned to good account in reporting the proceedings for the St. Louis *Union*. His daily letters, if preserved, would have made a unique record of the work of that important body, written from the standpoint of a trained observer, thoroughly informed as to the state's institutions. Early in the construction of the Illinois Central Railroad, Brayman acted as general solicitor of that corporation (1851–55) and secured its right of way. Judge Elliott Anthony, president of the state bar association, described Brayman in those years as "a most careful, painstaking lawyer, who understood real-estate law and our statutes relating to the same as well as any man I ever knew." In the first year of the Civil War, Brayman, although nearing his fiftieth year, volunteered, was at first commissioned major in the 29th Illinois, and was under fire at Belmont, Fort Donelson, and Shiloh. Gallantry in the field won him promotion. After advancing to colonel and brigadier-general, he finally reached the rank of major-general of volunteers by brevet. He was put in command of troops at Bolivar, Tenn., in the late fall of 1862 and remained there until the following June. While at that post he repulsed a Confederate attack led by Van Dorn, the last fighting in which he was engaged during the war. To him was assigned the task of reorganizing the Ohio regiments at Camp Dennison and he presided over a military court of inquiry in the case of Gen. Sturgis. From July 1864 to the spring of 1865 he was in command at Natchez. Later he served as president of a commission on claims at New Orleans. After the close of hostilities he tried unsuccessfully to revive several railroad projects in Missouri and Arkansas in which he had been interested before the war and then returned to journalism as editor of the *Illinois State Journal*, but in 1873 he removed to Wisconsin, where he continued newspaper work until 1876. In that year he was appointed governor of Idaho Territory by President Grant. During his term of office the Nez Percé and Bannock Indian wars occurred, in which Brayman's methods of providing for the armed defense of the Territory made him locally unpopular. After the expiration of his term he moved to Wisconsin, where he had built a home on the shore of Green Lake, but after a few years he went to Kansas City where he remained for the rest of his life. He had long been a prominent layman in the Baptist denomination, was always interested in education, had been one of the regents of the University of Illinois in its early years, and a charter member of the Chicago Historical Society. He was married to Mary Williams of Chautauqua County, N. Y.

[Article in the Buffalo *Express,* Mar. 10, 1895; statement by Daniel Brayman, Feb. 24, 1864, given in *Pubs. Buffalo Hist. Soc.,* vol. IX; "The Periodical Press of Buffalo," *Ibid.,* vol. XIX; Thos. Ford, *Hist. of Ill.* (1854); Elder Brigham H. Roberts, *The Rise and Fall of Nauvoo* (1900); *Bench and Bar of Ill.* (1899), ed. by John M. Palmer, II, 628–30; H. T. French, *Hist. of Idaho,* I (1914), 80–82.] W.B.S.

BRAYTON, CHARLES RAY (Aug. 16, 1840–Sept. 23, 1910), Republican boss of Rhode Island, was born at Apponaug, a part of the town of Warwick, R. I. He was the son of William Daniel and Anna Ward (Clarke) Brayton. His father was a Republican representative in Congress from 1857 to 1861, and subsequently (1862–71) collector of internal revenue for Rhode Island. Charles entered Brown University in 1859, but left in 1861 to organize a volunteer company later merged in the 3rd Rhode Island Volunteers. Enlisting Aug. 27 as a first lieutenant, he became captain Nov. 28, 1862, lieutenant-colonel Nov. 17, 1863, and colonel Apr. 1, 1864. On Mar. 13, 1865, he was made a brigadier-general of volunteers by brevet "for faithful and meritorious services." On Mar. 7, 1867, he was made a captain in the 17th United States Infantry, but resigned on July 6. From 1870 to 1874 he held the office of United States pension agent for Rhode Island; then, until 1880, he was postmaster at Providence. In 1886 he became chief of the state police under a state prohibitory law of that year, but before long resigned and aided in the repeal of the law. In 1891, at the age of fifty-one, he was admitted to the bar. His career as a manipulator of politics began soon after the Civil War, when he allied himself with Henry B. Anthony [*q.v.*], United States senator from Rhode Island from 1859 until his death in 1884. Upon Anthony's death Brayton transferred his political allegiance to Senator Nelson W. Aldrich [*q.v.*]. The precise nature of his relations with Anthony and Aldrich is obscure, but with their coöperation and in their interest he presently became, and for more than thirty years remained, the unquestioned boss of the Republican party in the state. His task was facilitated

by the lack of a veto power in the governor, and by the provision of the state constitution which gives to each town or city one senator and at least one representative in the General Assembly. As most of the towns are small, it was possible for the representatives of less than one-tenth of the population of the state to control legislation. It was an open secret that under Brayton's administration votes were regularly bought, while he himself frankly admitted the receipt of annual retainers from railway and other corporations. In 1900 he became blind, but his political activities continued. The first serious attack upon his power was made in 1902–03, when a state Lincoln party organization attempted unsuccessfully to obtain a constitutional convention. The election of a Democratic governor, James H. Higgins, in 1906, was followed by a demand by the Governor for the ousting of Brayton from his headquarters in the sheriff's office at the state capitol, and although the demand was refused, he presently withdrew. In 1896, at the earnest insistence of his supporters, he consented to become a member of the Republican national committee. He died suddenly at Providence as a result of an accident. He was married, Mar. 13, 1865, to Antoinette Percival Belden.

[The main facts of Brayton's life are given in obituaries, Sept. 24, 1910, in the *N. Y. Times, N. Y. Tribune, Sun* (N. Y.), *Providence Jour.,* and other papers. His military record is in F. B. Heitman, *Hist. Reg.* (1903). For a vivid description of the Brayton regime, including his own account of his principles and methods, see a series of articles by E. G. Lowry in the *N. Y. Evening Post,* Mar.–May 1903 (reprinted in part in a contemporary pamphlet with an introduction by Bishop W. M. McVickar); also Lincoln Steffens, "Rhode Island: A State for Sale," in *McClure's Mag.,* XXIV, 337–53 (Feb. 1905).] W.M.

BRAZER, JOHN (Sept. 21, 1789–Feb. 25, 1846), Unitarian clergyman, was born in Worcester, Mass., the son of Samuel and Betsey Brazer. Poverty forced him to postpone entering college until he was twenty-one. His academic success at Harvard was so brilliant that he led his class in scholarship. After taking his degree in 1813 and serving an apprenticeship as a tutor he was appointed in 1817 professor of Latin. According to a colleague he became one of the chief agents in "effecting a transition from the severe and ceremonial academical government of the olden time to an intercourse with the pupils more courteous and winning." His study of theology did not narrow his unusually broad intellectual interests nor warp his sound and thorough scholarship. In 1820 he resigned his professorship and was ordained pastor of the important North Church in Salem, serving this charge until his death. On Apr. 19, 1821, he was married to Anne Warren Sever. His wide and critical acquaintance with contemporary literature and thought, his classical elegance of style and chaste delivery, together with an unusual devotion to the poor of the community, explain in part his enviable success as a clergyman. Harvard gave him the degree of D.D. in 1836 and he served as a member of the Board of Overseers. His influence was broadened by contributions to the *North American Review* and the *Christian Examiner*. These covered a wide range of subjects, varying from "Ancient Modes of Burial of the Dead" to a review of Mill's *Treatise on Logic*. After a long illness he died at Charleston, S. C. (*New England Historical and Genealogical Register,* XXVI, 316). Amiable and sensitive, he was small in person, "finely turned and moulded," with a natural grace and fluency and with epicurean tastes.

Brazer's point of view was symptomatic of the forces which crystallized in Transcendentalism. His Dudleian Lecture (May 13, 1835) anticipates Emerson's *Nature* and *Divinity School Address* in denying that the great truths of religion can be ascertained through *a priori* reasonings or metaphysical assumptions. The truths of natural theology, he urged, can be attained solely in the manner by which other facts are determined, the inductive mode of reasoning. Thus he insisted that theology must be brought down to earth, and, like Emerson, found ample proof for the existence of God in "order, beauty, harmony, and the concurrence of means to ends."

For Brazer it was an inevitable conclusion that God must sit enthroned "within every heart" (*Review of the Argument in Support of Natural Religion,* 1835, p. 28). This theory of man's transcendental intuitions of the perfect and absolute, essential states of human thought, was closely related to his pantheism. God's perfections, he remarked, are "recognized in every upspringing blade of grass, in every opening flower, in every passing cloud, in every beam of light" (*Sermons,* 1849, p. 46). Brazer contended that there could be no necessary opposition between "earth and heaven, things seen and things unseen, things temporal and things spiritual" (*Introductory Essay to a Good Life,* 1836). Divine influence was not, therefore, supernaturally imparted to the human soul, and the proofs for the supernatural illumination of the human mind by the spirit of God were all to be accounted for on "principles strictly natural." His individualism and egalitarianism led him to declare that the presence of God's spirit was "equally offered to all persons, in all places, and in all times" (*Essay on the Doctrine of Divine Influence,* 1835, p. 125). Brazer's lucid exposition of doctrines that have been considered Emersonian, before Emerson's own formulation of them, gives him a definite though minor place in the history of American thought.

[The best sketch of Brazer's life is that by his friend, the Rev. Samuel Gilman, in Wm. B. Sprague's *Annals of the Am. Unitarian Pulpit* (1865), pp. 504–10. Woodbridge Riley briefly discusses his significance in *Am. Philosophy, the Early Schools* (1907), p. 207.]

M.E.C.